씨뮬이 제안하는 가장 효율적인 학습법!

온·오프 블렌디드 러닝 (on/off Blended Learning)

STEP ONE
OFF-LINE

기출은 수능 대비의 기본!
기본에 가장 충실한 씨뮬로 실전연습하자

- 다양한 구성의 기출문제집으로 목표에 맞는 학습 가능
- 씨뮬 교재를 풀면 온라인에서 자동채점 & 성적분석 가능

STEP TWO
ON-LINE

스터디센스 STUDY SENSE

QR 찍고 회원가입 → 씨뮬 문제 풀기→ 자동채점 → 성적분석

- 내 등급컷과 취약 유형까지 완벽 분석
- AI 문제 추천으로 취약 유형을 한 번 더 학습
- 오답노트로 복습 또 복습해서 틀린 문제 정복하기

STEP THREE
OFF-LINE

모의고사 맞춤제작 OneUP

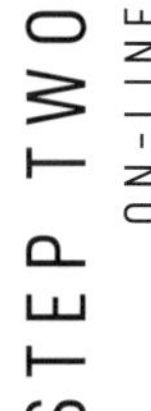

'원하는 문제만 골라서 맞춤 교재'를 만들고 싶다면? OneUP

- 원하는 제본 형태로 제작 가능
- 학평, 모평, 수능, 종로 사설 모의고사 맞춤 제작

CONTENTS

고 1 ▸ 영어 — 독해

유형+ 씨뮬

구성 + 특징

01

내신 대비 서브 노트

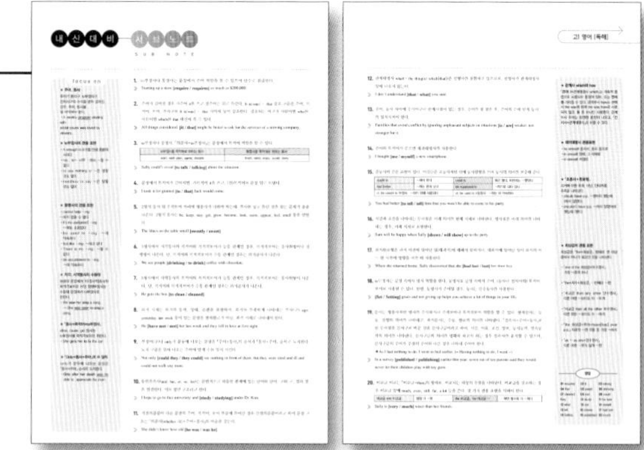

고1 영어 독해 시험에 자주 나오는 문법 사항 내신 요약입니다.

내신 영어 독해 시험에 자주 나오는 문법 사항을 정리한 학습 자료입니다. 서브 노트를 활용하여 중간 · 기말고사 직전에 빠르게 영어 문법을 익혀 봅시다.

02

가장 효율적인 24일의 학습 체계

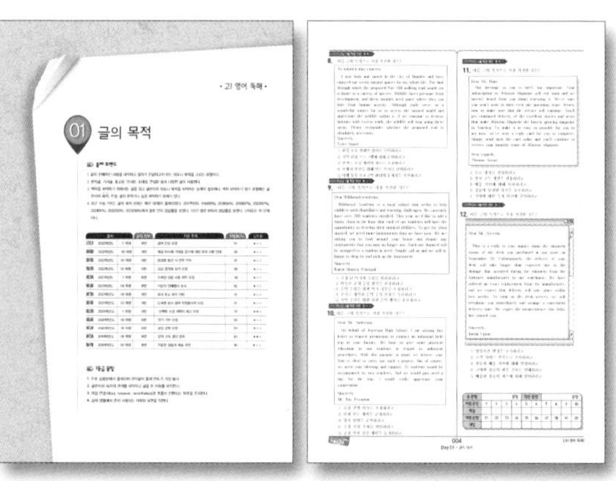

유형 학습이 처음이라 불안하다면? 수능 체계를 잘 모른다면?
더욱더 학습 효과가 큰 교재입니다.

❶ 최신 기출 순서로 엄선된 학평 기출 문제를 24일 동안 학습합니다.

❷ 매일매일 12개 지문 이내 분량으로 압축적, 효율적 학습이 가능하며 채점을 간단히 매일 할 수 있게 체크 박스를 붙였습니다.

❸ 각 지문마다 난이도, 소요 시간, 출처를 안내하였습니다. 난이도는 정답률 85% 이상이면 별 1개(★), 정답률 60~84%이면 별 2개(★★), 정답률 59% 이하는 별 3개(★★★)를 주었습니다.

03

출제 트렌드와 대표 기출

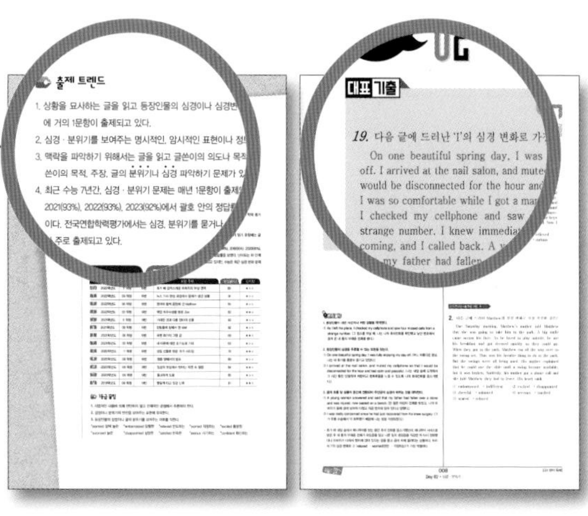

기출 문제 분석을 통해 공부의 올바른 '방향'을 설정합니다.

❶ 최신 출제 트렌드와 1등급 꿀팁을 제공합니다. 수능 영어를 대비해 무엇이 중요한지, 어떻게 공부해야 할지 최신 7년간의 수능 출제 경향과 꿀팁을 정리했습니다.

❷ 각 유형의 대표 기출 문제를 통해 출제 핵심을 파악할 수 있습니다.

유형+ 씨물

STRUCTURE & FEATURES

04

문법 플러스 / 어휘 플러스

문법과 어휘를 알면 영어 독해에 자신감이 생깁니다.

❶ 독해의 뼈대를 이루는 기본 문법 20개를 학습합니다.

❷ 독해 실력을 높이기 위해 수능에 필수적인 철자가 혼동되는 어휘, 유의어, 반의어, 파생어, 접두사, 접미사, 다의어를 학습합니다.

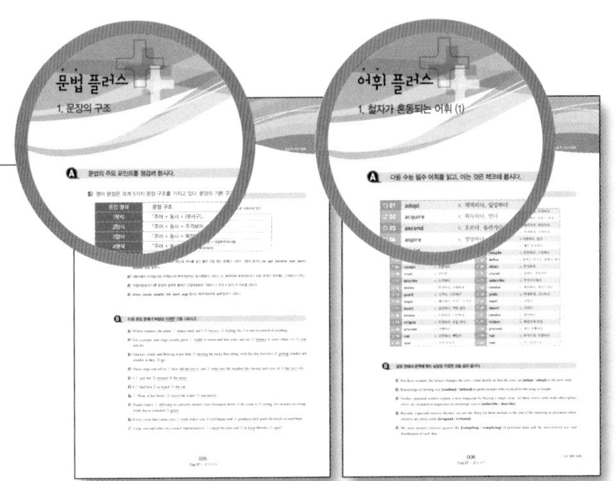

05

미니 고난도 Test

21~24일은 간단하게 미니 테스트를 할 수 있습니다.

❶ 영어 절대 평가의 변별력을 좌우할 수 있는 고난도 문제로 자신의 실력을 점검할 수 있도록 하였습니다.

❷ 빈칸 문제, 전체 흐름, 글의 순서, 주어진 문장의 위치 파악, 문단 요약, 장문의 이해(1), 장문의 이해(2) 위주로 문제를 수록하였습니다.

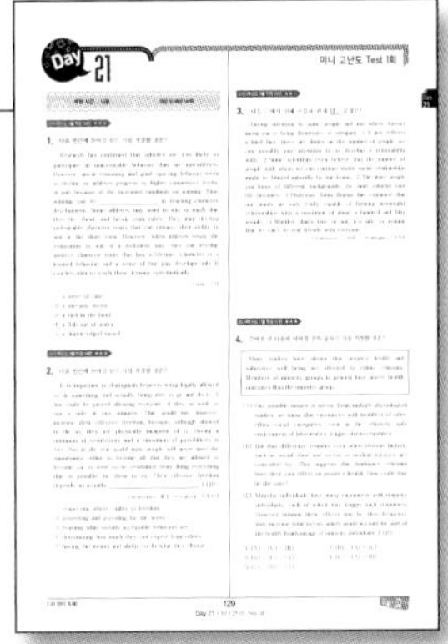

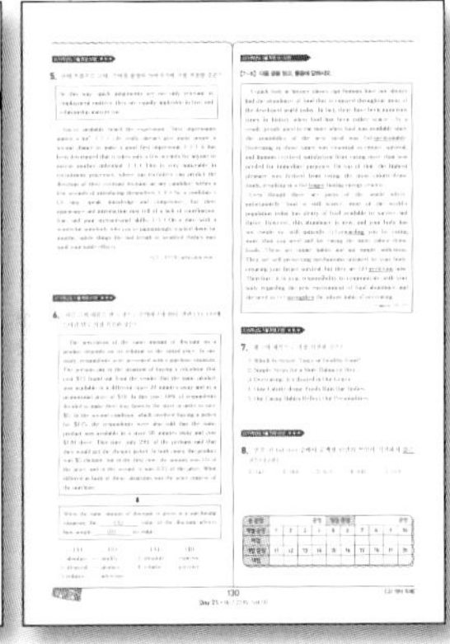

06

체계적이고 효율적인 해설

어려운 문항은 상세하게, 쉬운 문항은 명료하게~ 효율적인 똑똑한 해설입니다.

❶ 각 지문의 어려운 내용을 이해하기 쉽게 풀이하며 많이 틀린 문항에 대해서는 상세하게 풀이를 제시합니다.

❷ 직독직해를 통해 영문의 기본 구조를 마스터하도록 하였습니다.

❸ 골드교육 홈피 학습지원 자료 코너에서 지문에 나온 어휘를 한글 파일 형태로 다운받을 수 있습니다.

내 신 대 비 서 브 노 트

SUB NOTE

focus on

★ 주어, 동사

주어가 분사구, to부정사구, 전치사구의 수식을 받아 길어진 경우, 주어, 동사를 잘 파악해야 한다.

• A weekly program dealing with social issues was loved by viewers.

★ to부정사의 관용 표현

• A enough to B B할 만큼 충분히 A하다
• too... to~ 너무 …해서 ~할 수 없다
• to say nothing of ~은 말할 것도 없이
• needless to say ~은 말할 것도 없이

★ 동명사의 관용 표현

• cannot help -ing ~하지 않을 수 없다
• It's no use[good] -ing ~해도 소용없다
• be used to -ing ~에 익숙하다
• feel like -ing ~하고 싶다
• There is no -ing ~할 수 없다
• be accustomed to -ing ~에 익숙하다

★ 지각, 사역동사의 수동태

능동태 문장에서 지각[사역]동사의 목적격보어로 쓰인 원형부정사는 수동태 문장에서 to부정사로 변한다.

• We saw her sing a song.
→ She was seen to sing a song.

★ 「Only+동사+주어」의 수 일치

only가 문두에 나오는 문장은 「동사+주어」 순서로 도치된다.

• Only after her death was he able to appreciate his mom.

1. to부정사나 동명사는 문장에서 주어 역할을 할 수 있으며 단수로 취급한다.

≫ Starting up a store **[require / requires]** as much as $200,000

2. 주어가 길어진 경우 가주어 it을 쓰고 진주어는 뒤로 돌린다. It is[was] ~ that 강조 구문은 주어, 목적어, 보어, 부사구를 It is[was] ~ that 사이에 넣어 강조한다. 강조되는 어구가 사람이면 who를, 사물이면 which를 that 대신에 쓸 수 있다.

≫ All things considered, **[it / that]** might be better to ask for the services of a moving company.

3. to부정사나 동명사, 「의문사+to부정사」는 문장에서 목적어 역할을 할 수 있다.

to부정사를 목적어로 취하는 동사	동명사를 목적어로 취하는 동사
want, wish plan, agree, decide	finish, mind, enjoy, avoid, deny

≫ Sally could't avoid **[to talk / talking]** about the situation.

4. 문장에서 목적어가 길어지면, 가목적어 it을 쓰고, (진)목적어를 문장 뒤로 보낸다.

≫ I took it for granted **[to / that]** Jack would come.

5. 2형식 동사 뒤 주격보어 자리에 형용사가 나와야 하는데, 부사를 넣고 틀린 것을 찾는 문제가 종종 나온다. 2형식 동사는 be, keep, stay, get, grow, become, look, seem, appear, feel, smell 등을 말한다.

≫ The lilacs on the table smell **[sweetly / sweet]**.

6. 5형식에서 지각동사의 목적어와 목적격보어가 능동 관계인 경우, 목적격보어는 동사원형이나 진행형이 나온다. 단, 목적어와 목적격보어가 수동 관계인 경우는 과거분사가 나온다.

≫ We see people **[drinking / to drink]** coffee with chocolate.

7. 5형식에서 사역동사의 목적어와 목적격보어가 능동 관계인 경우, 목적격보어는 동사원형이 나온다. 단, 목적어와 목적격보어가 수동 관계인 경우는 과거분사가 나온다.

≫ He gets the box **[to clean / cleaned]**.

8. 과거 시제는 과거의 동작, 상태, 습관을 표현하며, 과거를 뚜렷하게 나타내는 부사(구) ago, yesterday,last week 등이 있는 문장은 현재완료가 아닌, 과거 시제로 나타내야 한다.

≫ He **[have met / met]** her last week and they fell in love at first sight.

9. 부정어(구)나 only가 문두에 나오는 문장은 「주어+동사」의 순서가 「동사+주어」 순서로 도치된다. 도치 구문은 뒤에 나오는 주어에 맞게 수를 일치 시킨다.

≫ Not only **[could they / they could]** see nothing in front of them, but they were tired and ill and could not walk any more.

10. 등위접속사(and, but, or, so, for)는 문법적으로 대등한 관계에 있는 단어와 단어, 구와 구, 절과 절을 연결한다. 이를 병렬 구조라고 한다.

≫ I hope to go to that university and **[study / studying]** under Dr. Kim.

11. 직접의문문이 다른 문장의 주어, 목적어, 보어 부분에 들어간 경우 간접의문문이라고 하며 문장 구조는 「의문사[whether /if]+주어+동사」의 어순을 갖는다.

≫ She didn't know how old **[he was / was he]**.

12. 관계대명사 what(= the thing(s) which[that])은 선행사를 포함하고 있으므로, 선행사가 관계대명사 앞에 나오지 않는다.

≫ I don't understand **[that / what]** you said.

13. 주어, 동사 사이에 수식어구나 관계사절이 있는 경우, 주어를 잘 찾은 후, 주어의 수에 맞게 동사를 일치시켜야 한다.

≫ Families that avoid conflict by ignoring unpleasant subjects or situations **[is / are]** weaker, not stronger for it.

14. 주어와 목적어가 같으면 재귀대명사를 사용한다.

≫ I bought **[me / myself]** a new smartphone.

15. 준동사와 같은 표현이 있다. 이것들은 조동사처럼 뒤에 동사원형을 쓰며 동사의 의미를 보충해 준다.

ought to	~해야 한다	used to	하곤 했다, 이전에는 ~했었다
had better	~하는 편이 낫다	be supposed to	~하기로 되어 있다
cf. be used+ to 부정사 : ~하기 위해 사용되다		cf. be used to +동명사 : ~하는 데 익숙하다	

≫ You had better **[to tell / tell]** him that you won't be able to come to his party.

16. 시간과 조건을 나타내는 부사절은 미래 의미를 현재 시제로 나타낸다. 명사절은 미래 의미를 나타내는 경우, 미래 시제로 표현한다.

≫ Sam will be happy when Sally **[shows / will show]** up to the party.

17. 과거완료형은 과거 이전에 일어난 일(대과거)에 대해서 말하거나, 대과거에 일어난 일이 과거의 어느 한 시점에 영향을 미칠 때 사용된다.

≫ When she returned home, Sally discovered that she **[had lost / lost]** her door key.

18. to부정사는 문장 속에서 명사 역할을 한다. 동명사도 문장 속에서 주어, (동사나 전치사의) 목적어, 보어로 사용될 수 있다. 한편, 동명사가 주어일 경우, 동사는 단수동사를 사용한다.

≫ **[Set / Setting]** goals and not giving up helps you achieve a lot of things in your life.

19. 분사는 형용사처럼 명사를 수식하거나 주격보어나 목적격보어 역할을 할 수 있다. 현재분사는 능동, 진행의 의미를 나타내고, 과거분사는 수동, 완료의 의미를 나타낸다. 「접속사+주어+동사」로 된 부사절을 분사구로 바꾼 것을 분사구문이라고 하며, 시간, 이유, 조건, 양보, 동시동작, 연속동작의 의미를 나타낸다. 분사구문의 의미를 명확히 하고자 하는 경우 접속사를 유지할 수 있으며, 분사구문의 주어가 주절의 주어와 다른 경우 나타내 주어야 한다.

■ As I had nothing to do, I went to bed earlier. (= Having nothing to do, I went ~)

≫ In a survey **[published / publishing]** earlier this year, seven out of ten parents said they would never let their children play with toy guns.

20. 비교급 비교는 「비교급+than」의 형태로, 비교되는 대상의 우열을 나타낸다. 비교급을 강조하는 경우 비교급 앞에 much, even, still, far, a lot 등을 쓴다. 몇 가지 관용 표현을 익혀야 한다.

비교급 and 비교급	점점 더 ~한	the 비교급... the 비교급 ~	…하면 할수록 더 ~하다

≫ Sally is **[very / much]** wiser than her friends.

★ 관계사 which와 how

「콤마(,)+관계대명사 which」는 계속적 용법으로 사용되어 문장의 일부, 또는 전체를 가리킬 수 있다. 관계부사 how는 선행사 the way와 함께 the way how로 사용되지 않고, 둘 중 하나만 사용한다. 관계부사 뒤에는 완전한 문장이 나오고, 「전치사+관계대명사」로 바꿀 수 있다.

★ 재귀대명사 관용표현

- by oneself 혼자서, 혼자 힘으로
- in oneself 원래, 그 자체로
- of oneself 저절로

★「조동사+완료형」

과거에 대한 후회, 비난, 안타까움, 추측을 나타낸다.

- should have p.p. ~했어야 했는데 (하지 않았다)
- shouldn't have p.p. ~하지 말았어야 했는데 (했다)

★ 최상급의 관용 표현

최상급은 「the+최상급」 형태로 셋 이상 중에서 하나가 최고인 것을 나타낸다.

- 「one of the 최상급+복수명사」 가장 ~중의 하나
- 「the+서수+최상급」 …번째로 ~한
- 「비교급 than any other 단수명사」 다른 어떤 ~보다도 더 …하게
- 「비교급 than all the other 복수명사」 다른 모든 ~보다도 더 …하게
- 「the 최상급+주어+have[has] ever p.p.」 지금껏 ~한 것들 중 가장 ~하게
- 「as ~ as any+단수명사」 다른 어떤 …못지 않게 ~한

정답

01 requires	02 it	03 talking
04 that	05 sweet	06 drinking
07 cleaned	08 met	09 could
they	10 study	11 he was
12 what	13 are	14 myself
15 tell	16 shows	17 had lost
18 Setting	19 published	20 much

고1 영어 [독해]

※문법 / 어휘 플러스는 정답 및 해설 참조

DAY 01 글의 목적

1 ⑤ 2 ② 3 ② 4 ⑤ 5 ②
6 ① 7 ④ 8 ③ 9 ③ 10 ①
11 ② 12 ③

DAY 02 심경 • 분위기

1 ② 2 ② 3 ③ 4 ⑤ 5 ⑤
6 ③ 7 ① 8 ① 9 ① 10 ①
11 ⑤ 12 ①

DAY 03 필자의 주장

1 ④ 2 ⑤ 3 ⑤ 4 ③ 5 ③
6 ① 7 ③ 8 ② 9 ② 10 ⑤
11 ④ 12 ⑤

DAY 04 함축 • 지칭 추론

1 ③ 2 ③ 3 ⑤ 4 ④ 5 ⑤
6 ③ 7 ② 8 ④ 9 ④ 10 ③

DAY 05 글의 요지

1 ① 2 ① 3 ① 4 ③ 5 ⑤
6 ⑤ 7 ⑤ 8 ④ 9 ② 10 ①

DAY 06 글의 주제

1 ② 2 ② 3 ④ 4 ① 5 ①
6 ② 7 ① 8 ① 9 ② 10 ②

DAY 07 글의 제목

1 ① 2 ① 3 ② 4 ② 5 ④
6 ① 7 ⑤ 8 ③ 9 ⑤ 10 ②

DAY 08 도표 정보 파악

1 ③ 2 ⑤ 3 ⑤ 4 ④ 5 ④
6 ⑤ 7 ③ 8 ⑤ 9 ④ 10 ⑤

DAY 09 내용 일치 • 불일치

1 ④ 2 ③ 3 ③ 4 ④ 5 ⑤
6 ③ 7 ⑤ 8 ④ 9 ③ 10 ⑤

DAY 10 안내문

1 ③ 2 ④ 3 ④ 4 ④ 5 ②
6 ④ 7 ⑤ 8 ② 9 ④ 10 ②

DAY 11 어법 정확성 파악

1 ③ 2 ④ 3 ③ 4 ④ 5 ②
6 ⑤ 7 ③ 8 ② 9 ④ 10 ④
11 ④ 12 ③

DAY 12 어휘 적절성 파악

1 ⑤ 2 ② 3 ⑤ 4 ⑤ 5 ④
6 ③ 7 ③ 8 ③ 9 ② 10 ③

DAY 13 빈칸 추론 (1) 어휘, 짧은 어구

1 ② 2 ② 3 ⑤ 4 ① 5 ②
6 ② 7 ③ 8 ② 9 ① 10 ①
11 ⑤

DAY 14 빈칸 추론 (2) 긴 어구, 문장

1 ③ 2 ① 3 ⑤ 4 ③ 5 ②
6 ① 7 ① 8 ② 9 ④ 10 ①

DAY 15 흐름에 무관한 문장 찾기

1 ④ 2 ④ 3 ④ 4 ③ 5 ④
6 ④ 7 ③ 8 ④ 9 ④ 10 ④

DAY 16 문단 내 글의 순서 파악

1 ⑤ 2 ② 3 ⑤ 4 ③ 5 ⑤
6 ③ 7 ② 8 ③ 9 ⑤ 10 ④
11 ③ 12 ④

DAY 17 주어진 문장의 위치 파악

1 ⑤ 2 ③ 3 ④ 4 ⑤ 5 ④
6 ⑤ 7 ④ 8 ② 9 ④ 10 ⑤
11 ③ 12 ②

DAY 18 문단 요약

1 ② 2 ① 3 ③ 4 ① 5 ②
6 ① 7 ② 8 ① 9 ① 10 ③
11 ①

DAY 19 장문의 이해 (1)

1 ① 2 ⑤ 3 ② 4 ④ 5 ①
6 ④ 7 ⑤ 8 ⑤ 9 ① 10 ④
11 ② 12 ④

DAY 20 장문의 이해 (2)

1 ④ 2 ③ 3 ③ 4 ④ 5 ②
6 ④ 7 ② 8 ④ 9 ⑤ 10 ③
11 ② 12 ⑤

DAY 21 미니 고난도 Test 1회

1 ⑤ 2 ⑤ 3 ③ 4 ② 5 ⑤
6 ④ 7 ③ 8 ⑤

DAY 22 미니 고난도 Test 2회

1 ③ 2 ③ 3 ③ 4 ② 5 ②
6 ④ 7 ④ 8 ③

DAY 23 미니 고난도 Test 3회

1 ② 2 ① 3 ④ 4 ③ 5 ③
6 ① 7 ② 8 ④

DAY 24 미니 고난도 Test 4회

1 ② 2 ③ 3 ③ 4 ⑤ 5 ③
6 ② 7 ② 8 ⑤

01 글의 목적

출제 트렌드

1. 글의 전체적인 내용을 파악하고 필자가 전달하고자 하는 의도나 목적을 고르는 유형이다.
2. 편지글, 기사글, 광고문, 안내문, 초대장, 연설문 등의 다양한 글이 사용된다.
3. 맥락을 파악하기 위해서는 글을 읽고 글쓴이의 의도나 목적을 파악하는 능력이 필요하다. 맥락 파악하기 읽기 유형에는 글쓴이의 목적, 주장, 글의 분위기나 심경 파악하기 문제가 있다.
4. 최근 수능 7년간, 글의 목적 문제는 매년 1문항이 출제되었다. 2017학년도 수능(95%), 2018(94%), 2019(97%), 2020(97%), 2021(91%), 2022(93%), 2023(98%)에서 괄호 안의 정답률을 보였다. 7년간 평균 95%의 정답률을 보였다. 난이도는 하 단계이다.

	출처		문항 번호	지문 주제	정답률(%)	난이도
대표	2022학년도	11 학평	18번	급여 인상 요청	87	★☆☆
1	2022학년도	09 학평	18번	학급 파티에 가져올 음식에 대한 유의 사항 안내	94	★☆☆
2	2022학년도	06 학평	18번	분실물 발견 시 연락 부탁	97	★☆☆
3	2022학년도	03 학평	18번	모금 음악회 참석 요청	88	★☆☆
4	2021학년도	11 학평	18번	오래된 신문 사용 허락 요청	94	★☆☆
5	2021학년도	09 학평	18번	식당의 연례행사 초대	92	★☆☆
6	2021학년도	06 학평	18번	회사 로고 제작 의뢰	91	★☆☆
7	2021학년도	03 학평	18번	도서관 공사 참여 자원봉사자 모집	91	★☆☆
8	2020학년도	11 학평	18번	산책로 조성 계획의 재고 요청	70	★★☆
9	2020학년도	09 학평	18번	악기 기부 요청	90	★☆☆
10	2020학년도	06 학평	18번	공장 견학 요청	93	★☆☆
11	2019학년도	06 학평	18번	잡지 구독 갱신 권유	83	★★☆
12	2018학년도	09 학평	18번	주문한 상품의 배송 지연	90	★☆☆

1등급 꿀팁

1. 주로 실용문에서 출제되며 편지글이 출제 빈도가 가장 높다.
2. 글쓴이와 독자의 관계를 파악하고 글을 쓴 이유를 파악한다.
3. 역접 연결사(but, however, nevertheless)로 흐름이 전환되는 부분을 주의한다.
4. 실제 생활에서 흔히 사용되는 어휘와 표현을 익힌다.

제한 시간 : 20분 | 정답 및 해설 002쪽

대표 기출

2022학년도 11월 학평 18번

18. 다음 글의 목적으로 가장 적절한 것은?

Dear Mr. Krull,

I have greatly enjoyed working at Trincom Enterprises as a sales manager. Since I joined in 2015, I have been a loyal and essential member of this company, and have developed innovative ways to contribute to the company. Moreover, in the last year alone, I have brought in two new major clients to the company, increasing the company's total sales by 5%. Also, I have voluntarily trained 5 new members of staff, totaling 35 hours. I would therefore request your consideration in raising my salary, which I believe reflects my performance as well as the industry average. I look forward to speaking with you soon.

Kimberly Morss

① 부서 이동을 신청하려고
② 급여 인상을 요청하려고
③ 근무 시간 조정을 요구하려고
④ 기업 혁신 방안을 제안하려고
⑤ 신입 사원 연수에 대해 문의하려고

문제 풀이

1. 수신자와 발신자 간의 관계를 파악하고 글의 주제를 추론해 본다.

수신자	Mr. Krull
발신자	Kimberly Morss
글의 주제	급여 인상 요청

2. 글의 세부 내용을 파악한다.

① I have been a loyal and essential member of this company, and have developed innovative ways to contribute to the company. (저는 이 회사의 충성스럽고 필수 구성원이었고, 회사에 기여할 수 있는 혁신적인 방법들을 개발해 왔습니다.)
② I have brought in two new major clients to the company, increasing the company's total sales by 5%. (저는 작년 한 해만 두 개의 주요 고객사를 회사에 새로 유치하여 회사의 총매출을 5% 증가시켰습니다.)
③ Also, I have voluntarily trained 5 new members of staff, totaling 35 hours. (게다가 저는 신규 직원 5명을 자발적으로 교육해 왔고, 그 합계가 35시간입니다.)
④ ~which I believe reflects my performance as well as the industry average. (저는 이것이 업계 평균뿐만 아니라 제 성과도 반영한다고 믿습니다.)

3. 글의 주제와 세부 내용을 종합하여 글의 목적을 파악한다.

• 이 글의 목적을 보여주는 핵심 표현은 'request your consideration in raising my salary,'이다. 회사에 기여한 주요 내용을 바탕으로 급여 인상을 고려해 달라는 내용이다. 글의 목적은 ② '급여 인상을 요청하려고'이다.

2022학년도 9월 학평 18번 ★☆☆

1. 다음 글의 목적으로 가장 적절한 것은?

Dear Parents/Guardians,

Class parties will be held on the afternoon of Friday, December 16th, 2022. Children may bring in sweets, crisps, biscuits, cakes, and drinks. We are requesting that children do not bring in home-cooked or prepared food. All food should arrive in a sealed packet with the ingredients clearly listed. Fruit and vegetables are welcomed if they are pre-packed in a sealed packet from the shop. Please DO NOT send any food into school containing nuts as we have many children with severe nut allergies. Please check the ingredients of all food your children bring carefully. Thank you for your continued support and cooperation.

Yours sincerely,
Lisa Brown, Headteacher

① 학급 파티 일정 변경을 공지하려고
② 학교 식당의 새로운 메뉴를 소개하려고
③ 학생의 특정 음식 알레르기 여부를 조사하려고
④ 학부모의 적극적인 학급 파티 참여를 독려하려고
⑤ 학급 파티에 가져올 음식에 대한 유의 사항을 안내하려고

2022학년도 6월 학평 18번 ★☆☆

2. 다음 글의 목적으로 가장 적절한 것은?

Dear Boat Tour Manager,

On March 15, my family was on one of your Glass Bottom Boat Tours. When we returned to our hotel, I discovered that I left behind my cell phone case. The case must have fallen off my lap and onto the floor when I took it off my phone to clean it. I would like to ask you to check if it is on your boat. Its color is black and it has my name on the inside. If you find the case, I would appreciate it if you would let me know.

Sincerely,
Sam Roberts

① 제품의 고장 원인을 문의하려고
② 분실물 발견 시 연락을 부탁하려고
③ 시설물의 철저한 관리를 당부하려고
④ 여행자 보험 가입 절차를 확인하려고
⑤ 분실물 센터 확장의 필요성을 건의하려고

2022학년도 3월 학평 18번 ★☆☆

3. 다음 글의 목적으로 가장 적절한 것은?

Dear Ms. Robinson,

The Warblers Choir is happy to announce that we are invited to compete in the International Young Choir Competition. The competition takes place in London on May 20. Though we wish to participate in the event, we do not have the necessary funds to travel to London. So we are kindly asking you to support us by coming to our fundraising concert. It will be held on March 26. In this concert, we shall be able to show you how big our passion for music is. Thank you in advance for your kind support and help.

Sincerely,
Arnold Reynolds

① 합창 대회 결과를 공지하려고
② 모금 음악회 참석을 요청하려고
③ 음악회 개최 장소를 예약하려고
④ 합창곡 선정에 조언을 구하려고
⑤ 기부금 사용 내역을 보고하려고

2021학년도 11월 학평 18번 ★☆☆

4. 다음 글의 목적으로 가장 적절한 것은?

To the school librarian,

I am Kyle Thomas, the president of the school's English writing club. I have planned activities that will increase the writing skills of our club members. One of the aims of these activities is to make us aware of various types of news media and the language used in printed newspaper articles. However, some old newspapers are not easy to access online. It is, therefore, my humble request to you to allow us to use old newspapers that have been stored in the school library. I would really appreciate it if you grant us permission.

Yours truly,
Kyle Thomas

① 도서관 이용 시간 연장을 건의하려고
② 신청한 도서의 대출 가능 여부를 문의하려고
③ 도서관에 보관 중인 자료 현황을 조사하려고
④ 글쓰기 동아리 신문의 도서관 비치를 부탁하려고
⑤ 도서관에 있는 오래된 신문의 사용 허락을 요청하려고

2021학년도 9월 학평 18번 ★☆☆

5. 다음 글의 목적으로 가장 적절한 것은?

Dear Mr. Dennis Brown,

We at G&D Restaurant are honored and delighted to invite you to our annual Fall Dinner. The annual event will be held on October 1st, 2021 at our restaurant. At the event, we will be introducing new wonderful dishes that our restaurant will be offering soon. These delicious dishes will showcase the amazing talents of our gifted chefs. Also, our chefs will be providing cooking tips, ideas on what to buy for your kitchen, and special recipes. We at G&D Restaurant would be more than grateful if you can make it to this special occasion and be part of our celebration. We look forward to seeing you. Thank you so much.

Regards,
Marcus Lee, Owner - G&D Restaurant

① 식당 개업을 홍보하려고
② 식당의 연례행사에 초대하려고
③ 신입 요리사 채용을 공고하려고
④ 매장 직원의 실수를 사과하려고
⑤ 식당 만족도 조사 참여를 부탁하려고

2021학년도 6월 학평 18번 ★☆☆

6. 다음 글의 목적으로 가장 적절한 것은?

Dear Mr. Jones,

I am James Arkady, PR Director of KHJ Corporation. We are planning to redesign our brand identity and launch a new logo to celebrate our 10th anniversary. We request you to create a logo that best suits our company's core vision, 'To inspire humanity.' I hope the new logo will convey our brand message and capture the values of KHJ. Please send us your logo design proposal once you are done with it. Thank you.

Best regards,
James Arkady

① 회사 로고 제작을 의뢰하려고
② 변경된 회사 로고를 홍보하려고
③ 회사 비전에 대한 컨설팅을 요청하려고
④ 회사 창립 10주년 기념품을 주문하려고
⑤ 회사 로고 제작 일정 변경을 공지하려고

2021학년도 3월 학평 18번 ★☆☆

7. 다음 글의 목적으로 가장 적절한 것은?

Dear members of Eastwood Library,

Thanks to the Friends of Literature group, we've successfully raised enough money to remodel the library building. John Baker, our local builder, has volunteered to help us with the remodelling but he needs assistance. By grabbing a hammer or a paint brush and donating your time, you can help with the construction. Join Mr. Baker in his volunteering team and become a part of making Eastwood Library a better place! Please call 541-567-1234 for more information.

Sincerely,
Mark Anderson

① 도서관 임시 휴관의 이유를 설명하려고
② 도서관 자원봉사자 교육 일정을 안내하려고
③ 도서관 보수를 위한 모금 행사를 제안하려고
④ 도서관 공사에 참여할 자원봉사자를 모집하려고
⑤ 도서관에서 개최하는 글쓰기 대회를 홍보하려고

2020학년도 11월 학평 18번 ★★☆

8. 다음 글의 목적으로 가장 적절한 것은?

> To whom it may concern:
>
> I was born and raised in the city of Boulder and have enjoyed our scenic natural spaces for my whole life. The land through which the proposed Pine Hill walking trail would cut is home to a variety of species. Wildlife faces pressure from development, and these animals need space where they can hide from human activity. Although trails serve as a wonderful source for us to access the natural world and appreciate the wildlife within it, if we continue to destroy habitats with excess trails, the wildlife will stop using these areas. Please reconsider whether the proposed trail is absolutely necessary.
>
> Sincerely,
> Tyler Stuart

① 환경 보호 캠페인 참여를 부탁하려고
② 지역 관광 프로그램에 대해 문의하려고
③ 산책로 조성 계획의 재고를 요청하려고
④ 보행자 안전을 위해 인도 설치를 건의하려고
⑤ 야생 동물 보호구역 관리의 문제점을 지적하려고

2020학년도 9월 학평 18번 ★☆☆

9. 다음 글의 목적으로 가장 적절한 것은?

> Dear Wildwood residents,
>
> Wildwood Academy is a local school that seeks to help children with disabilities and learning challenges. We currently have over 200 students enrolled. This year we'd like to add a music class in the hope that each of our students will have the opportunity to develop their musical abilities. To get the class started, we need more instruments than we have now. We are asking you to look around your house and donate any instruments that you may no longer use. Each one donated will be assigned to a student in need. Simply call us and we will be happy to drop by and pick up the instrument.
>
> Sincerely,
> Karen Hansen, Principal

① 고장 난 악기의 수리를 의뢰하려고
② 학부모 공개 수업 참석을 권장하려고
③ 음악 수업을 위한 악기 기부를 요청하려고
④ 추가로 개설된 음악 수업 신청을 독려하려고
⑤ 지역 주민을 위한 자선 음악 행사를 홍보하려고

2020학년도 6월 학평 18번 ★☆☆

10. 다음 글의 목적으로 가장 적절한 것은?

> Dear Mr. Anderson
>
> On behalf of Jeperson High School, I am writing this letter to request permission to conduct an industrial field trip in your factory. We hope to give some practical education to our students in regard to industrial procedures. With this purpose in mind, we believe your firm is ideal to carry out such a project. But of course, we need your blessing and support. 35 students would be accompanied by two teachers. And we would just need a day for the trip. I would really appreciate your cooperation.
>
> Sincerely,
> Mr. Ray Feynman

① 공장 견학 허가를 요청하려고 ② 단체 연수 계획을 공지하려고
③ 입사 방법을 문의하려고 ④ 출장 신청 절차를 확인하려고
⑤ 공장 안전 점검 계획을 통지하려고

2019학년도 6월 학평 18번 ★★☆

11. 다음 글의 목적으로 가장 적절한 것은?

> Dear Mr. Hane,
>
> Our message to you is brief, but important: Your subscription to *Winston Magazine* will end soon and we haven't heard from you about renewing it. We're sure you won't want to miss even one upcoming issue. Renew now to make sure that the service will continue. You'll get continued delivery of the excellent stories and news that make *Winston Magazine* the fastest growing magazine in America. To make it as easy as possible for you to act now, we've sent a reply card for you to complete. Simply send back the card today and you'll continue to receive your monthly issue of *Winston Magazine*.
>
> Best regards,
> Thomas Strout

① 무료 잡지를 신청하려고
② 잡지 구독 갱신을 권유하려고
③ 배송 지연에 대해 사과하려고
④ 경품에 당첨된 사실을 통보하려고
⑤ 기사에 대한 독자 의견에 감사하려고

2018학년도 9월 학평 18번 ★☆☆

12. 다음 글의 목적으로 가장 적절한 것은?

> Dear Mr. Stevens,
>
> This is a reply to your inquiry about the shipment status of the desk you purchased at our store on September 26. Unfortunately, the delivery of your desk will take longer than expected due to the damage that occurred during the shipment from the furniture manufacturer to our warehouse. We have ordered an exact replacement from the manufacturer, and we expect that delivery will take place within two weeks. As soon as the desk arrives, we will telephone you immediately and arrange a convenient delivery time. We regret the inconvenience this delay has caused you.
>
> Sincerely,
> Justin Upton

① 영업시간 변경을 공지하려고
② 고객 서비스 만족도를 조사하려고
③ 상품의 배송 지연에 대해 설명하려고
④ 구매한 상품의 환불 절차를 안내하려고
⑤ 배송된 상품의 파손에 대해 항의하려고

총 문항				문항	맞은 문항					문항
개별 문항	1	2	3	4	5	6	7	8	9	10
채점										
개별 문항	11	12	13	14	15	16	17	18	19	20
채점										

문법 플러스

1. 문장의 구조

정답 및 해설 006쪽

A 문법의 주요 포인트를 점검해 봅시다.

1 영어 문장은 크게 5가지 문장 구조를 가지고 있다. 문장의 기본 구조는 「주어+동사」로 이루어져 있다.

문장 형식	문장 구조
1형식	「주어 + 동사 + (부사구)」
2형식	「주어 + 동사 + 주격보어」
3형식	「주어 + 동사 + 목적어」
4형식	「주어 + 동사 + 간접목적어(사람) + 직접목적어(사물)」
5형식	「주어 + 동사 + 목적어+목적격보어」

2 2형식 동사 뒤에 형용사가 와야 하는데, 부사를 넣고 틀린 것을 찾는 문제가 나온다. 2형식 동사는 be, get, become, look, seem, appear 등을 말한다.

3 5형식에서 지각동사와 사역동사의 목적격보어는 동사원형이 나온다. 단, 목적어와 목적격보어가 수동 관계인 경우에는 과거분사가 온다.

4 직접의문문이 다른 문장의 일부로 들어간 간접의문문은 「의문사 + 주어 + 동사」의 어순을 갖는다.

5 allow, cause, enable, tell, want, urge 동사는 목적격보어로 to부정사가 나온다.

B 다음 문장 중에서 어법상 어색한 것을 고르시오.

1 Within minutes, the plane ① shakes hard, and I ② freezes, ③ feeling like I'm not in control of anything.

2 For example, tree rings usually grow ① width in warm and wet years and are ② thinner in years when it is ③ cold and dry.

3 Glaciers, wind, and flowing water help ① moving the rocky bits along, with the tiny travelers ② getting smaller and smaller as they ③ go.

4 These rings can tell us ① how old the tree is, and ② what was the weather like during each year of ③ the tree's life.

5 I ① saw her ② crossed ③ the street.

6 I ① had him ② to repair ③ the car.

7 ① None of her books ② leaves the reader ③ unconcern.

8 People find it ① difficulty to correctly identify fruit-flavoured drinks if the color is ② wrong, for instance an orange drink that is coloured ③ green.

9 Every event that causes you ① smile makes you ② feel happy and ③ produces feel-good chemicals in your brain.

10 I urge you and other city council representatives ① cancel the plan and ② to keep libraries ③ open!

어휘 플러스

1. 철자가 혼동되는 어휘 (1)

정답 및 해설 006쪽

A 다음 수능 필수 어휘를 읽고, 아는 것은 체크해 봅시다.

□ 01	adopt	v. 채택하다, 입양하다	□ 21	adapt	v. 적응하다, 각색하다
□ 02	acquire	v. 획득하다, 얻다	□ 22	require	v. 요구하다, 필요로 하다
□ 03	ascend	v. 오르다, 올라가다	□ 23	descend	v. 내려가다, 내려오다
□ 04	aspire	v. 열망하다, 포부를 가지다	□ 24	inspire	v. 격려하다, 고취하다
□ 05	assist	v. 도와주다	□ 25	resist	v 저항하다, 참다
□ 06	attain	v. 획득하다	□ 26	retain	v. 계속 유지하다
□ 07	comply	v. 따르다, 응하다	□ 27	compile	v. 편집하다, 수집하다
□ 08	confine	v. 한정하다, 감금하다	□ 28	define	v.정의를 내리다, 명확히 하다
□ 09	contain	v. 포함하다	□ 29	obtain	v. 획득하다
□ 10	cruel	a. 잔인한	□ 30	crucial	a. 중대한, 결정적인
□ 11	describe	v. 묘사하다	□ 31	subscribe	v. 정기구독하다
□ 12	evolve	v. 발전하다, 진화하다	□ 32	revolve	v. 회전하다, 회전시키다
□ 13	guard	v. 지키다, 수호하다	□ 33	guide	v. 안내하다, 지도하다
□ 14	impel	v. 재촉하다, 억지로 시키다	□ 34	expel	v. 내쫓다
□ 15	insert	v. 삽입하다, 끼워 넣다	□ 35	desert	v. 버리다
□ 16	involve	v. 포함하다, 수반하다	□ 36	revolve	v. 회전하다
□ 17	irrigate	v. 관개하다, 물을 대다	□ 37	irritate	v. 짜증나게 하다
□ 18	precede	v. 선행하다	□ 38	proceed	v. 계속 진행되다
□ 19	rob	v. 강탈하다, 빼앗다	□ 39	rub	v. 문지르다, 마찰하다
□ 20	soar	v. 높이 치솟다	□ 40	roar	v. 으르렁거리다

B 괄호 안에서 문맥에 맞는 낱말로 적절한 것을 골라 봅시다.

1 For these reasons, the farmer changes the cow's food slowly so that the cow can **[adapt / adopt]** to the new food.

2 Knowledge of writing was **[confined / defined]** to professionals who worked for the king or temple.

3 Further, potential readers explore a new magazine by buying a single issue; all those insert cards with subscription offers are included in magazines to encourage you to **[subscribe / describe]**.

4 Records, especially nursery rhymes, are just the thing for those periods at the end of the morning or afternoon when children are often easily **[irrigated / irritated]**.

5 We must protect citizens against the **[compiling / complying]** of personal data and the unrestricted use and distribution of such data.

심경·분위기

출제 트렌드

1. 상황을 묘사하는 글을 읽고 등장인물의 심경이나 심경변화를 추론하거나 글의 분위기를 추론하는 유형으로 고1 학력 평가에 거의 1문항이 출제되고 있다.
2. 심경 · 분위기를 보여주는 명시적인, 암시적인 표현이나 정보를 제공한다.
3. 맥락을 파악하기 위해서는 글을 읽고 글쓴이의 의도나 목적을 파악하는 능력이 필요하다. 맥락 파악하기 읽기 유형에는 글쓴이의 목적, 주장, 글의 분위기나 심경 파악하기 문제가 있다.
4. 최근 수능 7년간, 심경 · 분위기 문제는 매년 1문항이 출제되었다. 2017학년도 수능(94%), 2018(94%), 2019(95%), 2020(95%), 2021(93%), 2022(93%), 2023(92%)에서 괄호 안의 정답률을 보였다. 7년간 평균 93.7%의 정답률을 보였다. 난이도는 하 단계이다. 전국연합학력평가에서는 심경, 분위기를 묻거나, 심경 변화를 묻는 문제로 출제되고 있지만, 수능은 최근 심경 변화 문제가 주로 출제되고 있다.

	출처		문항 번호	지문 주제	정답률(%)	난이도
대표	2022학년도	11 학평	19번	휴가 때 갑작스러운 아버지의 부상 연락	89	★☆☆
1	2022학년도	09 학평	19번	뉴스 기사 완성 과정에서 문제가 생긴 상황	91	★☆☆
2	2022학년도	06 학평	19번	엄마와 함께 공원에 간 Matthew	95	★☆☆
3	2022학년도	03 학평	19번	학업 최우수상을 받은 Zoe	82	★★☆
4	2021학년도	11 학평	19번	기대한 것과 다른 엄마의 선물	92	★☆☆
5	2021학년도	09 학평	19번	한밤중에 잠에서 깬 Matt	92	★☆☆
6	2021학년도	06 학평	19번	유명 화가의 그림 값	80	★★☆
7	2021학년도	03 학평	19번	새 이웃에 대한 호기심과 기대	93	★☆☆
8	2020학년도	11 학평	19번	생일 선물로 받은 개가 사라짐	78	★★☆
9	2020학년도	09 학평	19번	청중 앞에서의 발표	89	★☆☆
10	2020학년도	06 학평	19번	일상의 부담에서 벗어난 자연 속 힐링	84	★★☆
11	2020학년도	03 학평	19번	돌고래의 도움	85	★☆☆
12	2019학년도	11 학평	19번	빨갛게 타고 있던 난로	81	★★☆

1등급 꿀팁

1. 지엽적인 내용에 의해 판단하지 말고 전체적인 관점에서 추론해야 한다.
2. 감정이나 분위기의 반전을 보여주는 표현에 유의한다.
3. 등장인물의 감정이나 글의 분위기를 보여주는 어휘를 익힌다.

*alarmed 깜짝 놀란 *embarrassed 당황한 *relieved 안도하는 *worried 걱정하는 *excited 흥분된
*surprised 놀란 *disappointed 실망한 *satisfied 만족한 *jealous 시기하는 *confident 확신하는

심경·분위기

 제한 시간 : 20분 | 정답 및 해설 007쪽

대표 기출

2022학년도 11월 학평 19번

19. 다음 글에 드러난 'I'의 심경 변화로 가장 적절한 것은?

On one beautiful spring day, I was fully enjoying my day off. I arrived at the nail salon, and muted my cellphone so that I would be disconnected for the hour and feel calm and peaceful. I was so comfortable while I got a manicure. As I left the place, I checked my cellphone and saw four missed calls from a strange number. I knew immediately that something bad was coming, and I called back. A young woman answered and said that my father had fallen over a stone and was injured, now seated on a bench. I was really concerned since he had just recovered from his knee surgery. I rushed getting into my car to go see him.

① nervous → confident
② relaxed → worried
③ excited → indifferent
④ pleased → jealous
⑤ annoyed → grateful

문제 풀이

1. 등장인물이 겪은 사건이나 처한 상황을 파악한다.

① As I left the place, I checked my cellphone and saw four missed calls from a strange number. (그 장소를 떠날 때, 나는 나의 휴대전화를 확인했고 낯선 번호에서 걸려 온 네 통의 부재중 전화를 봤다.)

2. 등장인물의 심경을 추론할 수 있는 표현을 찾는다.

① On one beautiful spring day, I was fully enjoying my day off. (어느 아름다운 봄날, 나는 내 휴가를 충분히 즐기고 있었다.)

② I arrived at the nail salon, and muted my cellphone so that I would be disconnected for the hour and feel calm and peaceful. (나는 네일 숍에 도착해서 그 시간 동안 단절되어 차분하고 평화로움을 느낄 수 있도록 나의 휴대전화를 음소거했다.)

3. 글의 흐름 및 상황이 중간에 전환되어 주인공의 심경이 바뀌는 것을 파악한다.

① A young woman answered and said that my father had fallen over a stone and was injured, now seated on a bench. (한 젊은 여성이 전화를 받았고, 나의 아버지가 돌에 걸려 넘어져 다쳤고 지금 벤치에 앉아 있다고 말했다.)

② I was really concerned since he had just recovered from his knee surgery. (그가 무릎 수술에서 막 회복했기 때문에 나는 정말 걱정되었다.)

• 휴가 때 네일 숍에서 매니큐어를 받는 동안 휴대 전화를 음소거했는데, 매니큐어 서비스를 받은 후 네 통의 부재중 전화가 와있음을 알고 나쁜 일이 생겼음을 직감한 뒤 다시 전화했더니 아버지가 다쳐서 벤치에 앉아 있다는 말을 듣고 급히 차에 올라타는 상황이다. 따라서 'I'의 심경 변화로 ② 'relaxed → worried(편한 → 걱정되는)'가 가장 적절하다.

2022학년도 9월 학평 19번 ★☆☆

1. 다음 글에 나타난 'I'의 심경 변화로 가장 적절한 것은?

It was two hours before the submission deadline and I still hadn't finished my news article. I sat at the desk, but suddenly, the typewriter didn't work. No matter how hard I tapped the keys, the levers wouldn't move to strike the paper. I started to realize that I would not be able to finish the article on time. Desperately, I rested the typewriter on my lap and started hitting each key with as much force as I could manage. Nothing happened. Thinking something might have happened inside of it, I opened the cover, lifted up the keys, and found the problem — a paper clip. The keys had no room to move. After picking it out, I pressed and pulled some parts. The keys moved smoothly again. I breathed deeply and smiled. Now I knew that I could finish my article on time.

① confident → nervous
② frustrated → relieved
③ bored → amazed
④ indifferent → curious
⑤ excited → disappointed

2022학년도 6월 학평 19번 ★☆☆

2. 다음 글에 드러난 Matthew의 심경 변화로 가장 적절한 것은?

One Saturday morning, Matthew's mother told Matthew that she was going to take him to the park. A big smile came across his face. As he loved to play outside, he ate his breakfast and got dressed quickly so they could go. When they got to the park, Matthew ran all the way over to the swing set. That was his favorite thing to do at the park. But the swings were all being used. His mother explained that he could use the slide until a swing became available, but it was broken. Suddenly, his mother got a phone call and she told Matthew they had to leave. His heart sank.

① embarrassed → indifferent
② excited → disappointed
③ cheerful → ashamed
④ nervous → touched
⑤ scared → relaxed

2022학년도 3월 학평 19번 ★★☆

3. 다음 글에 드러난 Zoe의 심경 변화로 가장 적절한 것은?

The principal stepped on stage. "Now, I present this year's top academic award to the student who has achieved the highest placing." He smiled at the row of seats where twelve finalists had gathered. Zoe wiped a sweaty hand on her handkerchief and glanced at the other finalists. They all looked as pale and uneasy as herself. Zoe and one of the other finalists had won first placing in four subjects so it came down to how teachers ranked their hard work and confidence. "The Trophy for General Excellence is awarded to Miss Zoe Perry," the principal declared. "Could Zoe step this way, please?" Zoe felt as if she were in heaven. She walked into the thunder of applause with a big smile.

① hopeful → disappointed ② guilty → confident
③ nervous → delighted ④ angry → calm
⑤ relaxed → proud

2021학년도 11월 학평 19번 ★☆☆

4. 다음 글에 드러난 "I"의 심경 변화로 가장 적절한 것은?

When my mom came home from the mall with a special present for me I was pretty sure I knew what it was. I was absolutely thrilled because I would soon communicate with a new cell phone! I was daydreaming about all of the cool apps and games I was going to download. But my mom smiled really big and handed me a book. I flipped through the pages, figuring that maybe she had hidden my new phone inside. But I slowly realized that my mom had not got me a phone and my present was just a little book, which was so different from what I had wanted.

① worried → furious ② surprised → relieved
③ ashamed → confident ④ anticipating → satisfied
⑤ excited → disappointed

2021학년도 9월 학평 19번 ★☆☆

5. 다음 글의 상황에 나타난 분위기로 가장 적절한 것은?

In the middle of the night, Matt suddenly awakened. He glanced at his clock. It was 3:23. For just an instant he wondered what had wakened him. Then he remembered. He had heard someone come into his room. Matt sat up in bed, rubbed his eyes, and looked around the small room. "Mom?" he said quietly, hoping he would hear his mother's voice assuring him that everything was all right. But there was no answer. Matt tried to tell himself that he was just hearing things. But he knew he wasn't. There was someone in his room. He could hear rhythmic, scratchy breathing and it wasn't his own. He lay awake for the rest of the night.

① humorous and fun ② boring and dull
③ calm and peaceful ④ noisy and exciting
⑤ mysterious and frightening

2021학년도 6월 학평 19번 ★★☆

6. 다음 글에 드러난 Cindy의 심경 변화로 가장 적절한 것은?

One day, Cindy happened to sit next to a famous artist in a café, and she was thrilled to see him in person. He was drawing on a used napkin over coffee. She was looking on in awe. After a few moments, the man finished his coffee and was about to throw away the napkin as he left. Cindy stopped him. "Can I have that napkin you drew on?", she asked. "Sure," he replied. "Twenty thousand dollars." She said, with her eyes wide-open, "What? It took you like two minutes to draw that." "No," he said. "It took me over sixty years to draw this." Being at a loss, she stood still rooted to the ground.

① relieved → worried ② indifferent → embarrassed
③ excited → surprised ④ disappointed → satisfied
⑤ jealous → confident

2021학년도 3월 학평 19번 ★☆☆

7. 다음 글에 드러난 Shirley의 심경으로 가장 적절한 것은?

On the way home, Shirley noticed a truck parked in front of the house across the street. New neighbors! Shirley was dying to know about them. "Do you know anything about the new neighbors?" she asked Pa at dinner. He said, "Yes, and there's one thing that may be interesting to you." Shirley had a billion more questions. Pa said joyfully, "They have a girl just your age. Maybe she wants to be your playmate." Shirley nearly dropped her fork on the floor. How many times had she prayed for a friend? Finally, her prayers were answered! She and the new girl could go to school together, play together, and become best friends.

① curious and excited ② sorry and upset
③ jealous and annoyed ④ calm and relaxed
⑤ disappointed and unhappy

2021학년도 11월 학평 19번 ★★☆

8. 다음 글에 드러난 'I'의 심경 변화로 가장 적절한 것은?

On my seventh birthday, my mom surprised me with a puppy waiting on a leash. It had beautiful golden fur and an adorable tail. It was exactly what I had always dreamed of. I took the dog everywhere and slept with it every night. A few months later, the dog got out of the backyard and was lost. I sat on my bed and cried for hours while my mother watched me silently from the doorway of my room. I finally fell asleep, exhausted from my grief. My mother never said a word to me about my loss, but I knew she felt the same as I did.

① delighted → sorrowful ② relaxed → annoyed
③ embarrassed → worried ④ excited → horrified
⑤ disappointed → satisfied

2020학년도 9월 학평 19번 ★☆☆

9. 다음 글에 드러난 Salva의 심경 변화로 가장 적절한 것은?

Salva had to raise money for a project to help southern Sudan. It was the first time that Salva spoke in front of an audience. There were more than a hundred people. Salva's knees were shaking as he walked to the microphone. "H-h-hello," he said. His hands trembling, he looked out at the audience. Everyone was looking at him. At that moment, he noticed that every face looked interested in what he had to say. People were smiling and seemed friendly. That made him feel a little better, so he spoke into the microphone again. "Hello," he repeated. He smiled, feeling at ease, and went on. "I am here to talk to you about a project for southern Sudan."

① nervous → relieved ② indifferent → excited
③ worried → disappointed ④ satisfied → frustrated
⑤ confident → embarrassed

2020학년도 6월 학평 19번 ★★☆

10. 다음 글에 드러난 Erda의 심경으로 가장 적절한 것은?

Erda lay on her back in a clearing, watching drops of sunlight slide through the mosaic of leaves above her. She joined them for a little, moving with the gentle breeze, feeling the warm sun feed her. A slight smile was spreading over her face. She slowly turned over and pushed her face into the grass, smelling the green pleasant scent from the fresh wild flowers. Free from her daily burden, she got to her feet and went on. Erda walked between the warm trunks of the trees. She felt all her concerns had gone away.

① relaxed ② puzzled ③ envious ④ startled ⑤ indifferent

2020학년도 3월 학평 19번 ★☆☆

11. 다음 글에 드러난 'I'의 심경 변화로 가장 적절한 것은?

I was diving alone in about 40 feet of water when I got a terrible stomachache. I was sinking and hardly able to move. I could see my watch and knew there was only a little more time on the tank before I would be out of air. It was hard for me to remove my weight belt. Suddenly I felt a prodding from behind me under the armpit. My arm was being lifted forcibly. Around into my field of vision came an eye. It seemed to be smiling. It was the eye of a big dolphin. Looking into that eye, I knew I was safe. I felt that the animal was protecting me, lifting me toward the surface.

* prodding: 쿡 찌르기

① excited → bored ② pleased → angry
③ jealous → thankful ④ proud → embarrassed
⑤ frightened → relieved

2019학년도 11월 학평 19번 ★★☆

12. 다음 글에 드러난 Norm의 심경으로 가장 적절한 것은?

Norm and his friend Jason went on a winter camping trip. In the middle of the night, Norm suddenly woke up sensing something was terribly wrong. To his surprise, the stove was glowing red! Norm shook Jason awake and told him to look at the stove. Jason said he had filled it with every piece of wood he could fit into it. Norm thought the cabin was going to catch fire. He started swearing at Jason. He pulled Jason out of his bed, opened the front door and threw him out into the snow. Norm yelled out in anger, "Don't come back in until I get this stove cooled off!"

① alarmed and upset ② thrilled and joyful
③ touched and grateful ④ ashamed and guilty
⑤ encouraged and satisfied

총 문항				문항	맞은 문항					문항
개별 문항	1	2	3	4	5	6	7	8	9	10
채점										
개별 문항	11	12	13	14	15	16	17	18	19	20
채점										

문법 플러스

2. 주어의 이해

정답 및 해설 011쪽

A 문법의 주요 포인트를 점검해 봅시다.

1. 명사뿐만 아니라 여러 단어로 이루어진 명사구는 문장의 주어로 쓰인다. 주어로 쓰인 명사구는 단수 취급한다. 일반적으로 주어 뒤에 동사가 나오지만, 부정어나 강조어가 나오면 「주어+동사」가 도치되어 주어가 동사 뒤로 가게 된다.
2. 동명사, 부정사는 명사의 성격을 가지고 있기 때문에 문장의 주어의 역할을 할 수 있으며 단수 취급한다.
3. 접속사 that절, 관계대명사 what절, 간접의문문과 같은 명사절은 명사 역할을 하므로 문장의 주어로 쓰일 수 있다. 명사절 주어는 단수 취급한다.
4. 문장에서 주어가 길어지면 가주어 it을 쓰고, (진)주어를 문장 뒤로 보낸다.
5. 진주어가 부정사일 때 to부정사 앞에 의미상의 주어를 쓸 수 있다. 사람의 성질을 나타내는 형용사가 올 때는 「of+목적격」을 쓰고, 그 외의 경우는 「for+목적격」을 쓴다.

B 다음 괄호 안에서 어법상 올바른 것을 고르시오.

1. **[To keep / Keep]** your word is very important in business.
2. Hiring much more employees than now **[is / are]** waste of money.
3. **[That / Which]** the universe is expanding is one of the fundamental ideas of modern cosmology.
4. **[That / Whether]** you win or lose depends on your own gaming skills.
5. **[What / if]** he gave me was his website and e-mail address.
6. **[It / That]** is no use crying over spilt milk.
7. It is honest **[of her / for her]** to say that.
8. Only after we lose our health **[we realize / do we realize]** the value of it.
9. Not only **[does TV take up / TV takes up]** more of Jack's time but also it tempts him to eat more junk food.
10. No sooner **[had Charlie / Charlie had]** seen me than he ran away.

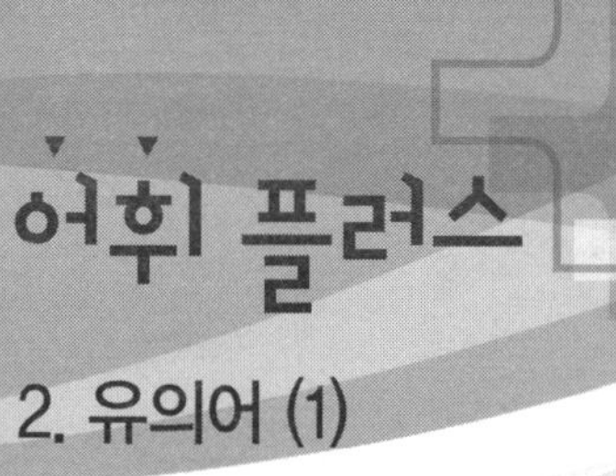

어휘 플러스

2. 유의어 (1)

정답 및 해설 011쪽

A 다음 수능 필수 어휘를 읽고, 아는 것은 체크해 봅시다.

□ 01	abundant	a. 풍부한(= plentiful)	□ 21	arise	v. 발생하다(= occur)
□ 02	accomplish	v. 실현하다(= realize)	□ 22	assessment	n. 평가(= evaluation)
□ 03	accumulate	v. 축적하다(= collect)	□ 23	assist	v. 원조하다(= aid)
□ 04	accurate	a. 정확한(= precise)	□ 24	associate	v. 연관 짓다(= relate)
□ 05	achieve	v. 성취하다(= perform)	□ 25	attribute	v. ~의 탓으로 돌리다(= ascribe)
□ 06	acknowledge	v. 인정하다(= admit)	□ 26	aware	a. 의식하고 있는(= conscious)
□ 07	acquire	v. 획득하다(= obtain)	□ 27	bare	a. 벌거벗은(= naked)
□ 08	adjust	v. 적응하다(= adapt)	□ 28	behave	v. 행동하다(= act, conduct)
□ 09	admire	v. 존경하다(= respect)	□ 29	bias	n. 편견(= prejudice)
□ 10	advance	v. 진보하다(= progress)	□ 30	blame	v. 비난하다(= accuse)
□ 11	allow	v. 허용하다(= permit)	□ 31	broad	a. 광범위한(= wide)
□ 12	alter	v. 변경하다(= change)	□ 32	calculate	v. 추산하다(= estimate)
□ 13	amaze	v. 놀라게 하다(= astonish)	□ 33	capacity	n. 용량, 능력(= ability)
□ 14	announce	v. 알리다(= declare)	□ 34	circumstance	n. 상황(= situation)
□ 15	anticipate	v. 기대하다(= expect)	□ 35	colleague	n. 동료(= coworker)
□ 16	anxiety	n. 걱정, 불안(= concern)	□ 36	combine	v. 결합하다(= unite)
□ 17	apparent	a. 명백한(= evident)	□ 37	comment	n. 논평(= remark)
□ 18	approach	v. 다가가다(= access)	□ 38	commerce	n. 무역(= trade)
□ 19	appropriate	a. 적절한(= suitable)	□ 39	complex	a. 복잡한(= complicated)
□ 20	argue	v. 논쟁하다(= dispute)	□ 40	compose	v. 구성하다(= constitute)

B 괄호 안에서 문맥에 맞는 낱말로 적절한 것을 골라 봅시다.

1 Renaissance artists **[achieved / blamed]** perspective using geometry, which resulted in a naturalistic, precise, three-dimensional representation of the real world.

2 Some prominent journalists say that archaeologists should work with treasure hunters because treasure hunters have **[accumulated / dispersed]** valuable historical artifacts that can reveal much about the past.

3 We **[allow /anticipate]** the future as if we found it too slow in coming and we were trying to hurry it up.

4 The storyline is **[complicated / apparent]**. In my case, reading the novel first helped me fully understand and better enjoy the musical.

5 As far as I know, he'll introduce us to all kinds of experimental music that he's **[blamed / composed]** with his computer.

필자의 주장

출제 트렌드

1. 글에서 제시된 근거를 바탕으로 필자의 주장을 찾는 유형이다. 고1 학력 평가에 1문제가 출제된다.
2. 필자의 주장을 명시적으로 제시하거나 암시적으로 제시하는 경우가 있다.
3. 맥락을 파악하기 위해서는 글을 읽고 글쓴이의 의도나 목적을 파악하는 능력이 필요하다. 맥락 파악하기 읽기 유형에는 글쓴이의 목적, 필자의 주장, 글의 분위기나 심경 파악하기 문제가 있다.
4. 최근 수능 7년간, 필자의 주장 문제는 2017학년도 수능을 제외하고 2018학년도부터 매년 1문항이 출제되었다. 2018학년도 수능(91%), 2019(88%), 2020(89%), 2021(83%), 2022(83%), 2023(80%)에서 괄호 안의 정답률을 보였다. 6년간 평균 85.6%의 정답률을 보였다. 난이도는 하 단계이다.
5. 맥락 파악하기 유형의 문제들 –글의 목적(95%), 심경 · 분위기(93.7%), 필자의 주장(85.6%) – 중에서 정답률을 비교해 보니, 학생들은 필자의 주장 문제를 더 어렵게 느끼는 것으로 보인다.

출처			문항 번호	지문 주제	정답률(%)	난이도
대표	2022학년도	11 학평	20번	상업용 블로그는 사람들이 흥미 있어 할 정보를 제공해야 한다	93	★☆☆
1	2022학년도	09 학평	20번	글을 쓸 때보다 말할 때 더 많은 단어를 사용해야 한다	71	★★☆
2	2022학년도	06 학평	20번	회의에서 다룰 사항은 미리 작성해서 공유하라	90	★☆☆
3	2022학년도	03 학평	20번	큰일을 잘 이루려면 작은 일부터 제대로 하라	88	★☆☆
4	2021학년도	11 학평	20번	학생과의 관계에서 교사의 비언어적인 메시지의 중요성	89	★☆☆
5	2021학년도	09 학평	20번	독자가 능동적으로 사고할 수 있게 글을 써라	84	★★☆
6	2021학년도	06 학평	20번	불편해도 성공을 위해 새로운 것을 시도하라	91	★☆☆
7	2021학년도	03 학평	20번	이메일 전송 검토 필요	92	★☆☆
8	2020학년도	11 학평	20번	집중을 방해하는 요인에 대처할 줄 알아야 한다	86	★☆☆
9	2020학년도	09 학평	20번	목표 설정	78	★★☆
10	2020학년도	06 학평	20번	건강에 좋은 음식으로 식사를 시작할 것	90	★☆☆
11	2019학년도	06 학평	20번	지속된 인간 관계를 위해 일관된 노력이 필요하다	62	★★☆
12	2018학년도	09 학평	20번	과정에 초점을 둔 대화	78	★★☆

1등급 꿀팁

1. 앞부분만 보고 바로 정답을 체크하지 말고, 글의 중간이나 결론에서 강조되고 있는 내용에 유의해야 한다.
2. 필자가 다른 사람과 다른 주장을 펼치며 반박하는 경우가 있으니 내용에 유의한다.
3. 의무, 당위성, 주장을 보여주는 표현에 유의한다.

제한 시간 : 20분 | 정답 및 해설 012쪽

대표 기출

2022학년도 11월 학평 20번

20. 다음 글에서 필자가 주장하는 바로 가장 적절한 것은?

You already have a business and you're about to launch your blog so that you can sell your product. Unfortunately, here is where a 'business mind' can be a bad thing. Most people believe that to have a successful business blog promoting a product, they have to stay strictly 'on the topic.' If all you're doing is shamelessly promoting your product, then who is going to want to read the latest thing you're writing about? Instead, you need to give some useful or entertaining information away for free so that people have a reason to keep coming back. Only by doing this can you create an interested audience that you will then be able to sell to. So, the best way to be successful with a business blog is to write about things that your audience will be interested in.

① 인터넷 게시물에 대한 윤리적 기준을 세워야 한다.
② 블로그를 전문적으로 관리할 인력을 마련해야 한다.
③ 신제품 개발을 위해 상업용 블로그를 적극 활용해야 한다.
④ 상품에 대한 고객들의 반응을 정기적으로 분석할 필요가 있다.
⑤ 상업용 블로그는 사람들이 흥미 있어 할 정보를 제공해야 한다.

문제 풀이

1. 특정 개념과 관련된 어구 또는 반복되는 어구를 통해 필자의 주장을 파악한다

① Most people believe that to have a successful business blog promoting a product, they have to stay strictly 'on the topic.' (대부분의 사람은 제품을 홍보하는 성공적인 상업용 블로그를 갖기 위해서 그들이 엄격하게 '그 주제에' 머물러야 한다고 믿는다.)

2. 필자가 말하고자 하는 바를 확인하면서 필자의 주장을 추론한다.

① Instead, you need to give some useful or entertaining information away for free so that people have a reason to keep coming back. (대신에, 여러분은 사람들이 계속해서 다시 방문할 이유를 갖도록 유용하거나 재미있는 정보를 무료로 제공해야 한다.)

② Only by doing this can you create an interested audience that you will then be able to sell to. (오직 이렇게 함으로써 여러분은 여러분이 그다음에 판매를 할 수 있게 될 관심 있는 독자를 만들 수 있다.)

③ So, the best way to be successful with a business blog is to write about things that your audience will be interested in. (따라서, 상업용 블로그로 성공할 가장 좋은 방법은 여러분의 독자들이 관심 가질 것들에 대해 쓰는 것이다.)

• 성공적인 상업용 블로그를 갖기 위해서는 사람들이 계속해서 다시 방문할 수 있도록 유용하거나 재미있는 정보를 무료로 제공해야 한다는 내용이다. 글의 마지막 문장인 'So, the best way to be successful with a business blog is to write about things that your audience will be interested in.'에서 필자의 주장이 잘 드러나 있다. 정답은 ⑤ '상업용 블로그는 사람들이 흥미 있어 할 정보를 제공해야 한다.'가 가장 적절하다.

2022학년도 9월 학평 20번 ★★☆

1. 다음 글에서 필자가 주장하는 바로 가장 적절한 것은?

Experts on writing say, "Get rid of as many words as possible." Each word must do something important. If it doesn't, get rid of it. Well, this doesn't work for speaking. It takes more words to introduce, express, and adequately elaborate an idea in speech than it takes in writing. Why is this so? While the reader can reread, the listener cannot rehear. Speakers do not come equipped with a replay button. Because listeners are easily distracted, they will miss many pieces of what a speaker says. If they miss the crucial sentence, they may never catch up. This makes it necessary for speakers to talk *longer* about their points, using more words on them than would be used to express the same idea in writing.

① 연설 시 중요한 정보는 천천히 말해야 한다.
② 좋은 글을 쓰려면 간결한 문장을 사용해야 한다.
③ 말하기 전에 신중히 생각하는 습관을 길러야 한다.
④ 글을 쓸 때보다 말할 때 더 많은 단어를 사용해야 한다.
⑤ 청중의 이해를 돕기 위해 미리 연설문을 제공해야 한다.

2022학년도 6월 학평 20번 ★☆☆

2. 다음 글에서 필자가 주장하는 바로 가장 적절한 것은?

Meetings encourage creative thinking and can give you ideas that you may never have thought of on your own. However, on average, meeting participants consider about one third of meeting time to be unproductive. But you can make your meetings more productive and more useful by preparing well in advance. You should create a list of items to be discussed and share your list with other participants before a meeting. It allows them to know what to expect in your meeting and prepare to participate.

① 회의 결과는 빠짐없이 작성해서 공개해야 한다.
② 중요한 정보는 공식 회의를 통해 전달해야 한다.
③ 생산성 향상을 위해 정기적인 평가회가 필요하다.
④ 모든 참석자의 동의를 받아서 회의를 열어야 한다.
⑤ 회의에서 다룰 사항은 미리 작성해서 공유해야 한다.

2022학년도 3월 학평 20번 ★☆☆

3. 다음 글에서 필자가 주장하는 바로 가장 적절한 것은?

When I was in the army, my instructors would show up in my barracks room, and the first thing they would inspect was our bed. It was a simple task, but every morning we were required to make our bed to perfection. It seemed a little ridiculous at the time, but the wisdom of this simple act has been proven to me many times over. If you make your bed every morning, you will have accomplished the first task of the day. It will give you a small sense of pride and it will encourage you to do another task and another. By the end of the day, that one task completed will have turned into many tasks completed. If you can't do little things right, you will never do the big things right.

* barracks room: (병영의) 생활관 ** accomplish: 성취하다

① 숙면을 위해서는 침대를 깔끔하게 관리해야 한다.
② 일의 효율성을 높이려면 협동심을 발휘해야 한다.
③ 올바른 습관을 기르려면 정해진 규칙을 따라야 한다.
④ 건강을 유지하기 위해서는 기상 시간이 일정해야 한다.
⑤ 큰일을 잘 이루려면 작은 일부터 제대로 수행해야 한다.

2021학년도 11월 학평 20번 ★☆☆

4. 다음 글에서 필자가 주장하는 바로 가장 적절한 것은?

Some experts estimate that as much as half of what we communicate is done through the way we move our bodies. Paying attention to the nonverbal messages you send can make a significant difference in your relationship with students. In general, most students are often closely tuned in to their teacher's body language. For example, when your students first enter the classroom, their initial action is to look for their teacher. Think about how encouraging and empowering it is for a student when that teacher has a friendly greeting and a welcoming smile. Smiling at students — to let them know that you are glad to see them — does not require a great deal of time or effort, but it can make a significant difference in the classroom climate right from the start of class.

① 교사는 학생 간의 상호 작용을 주의 깊게 관찰해야 한다.
② 수업 시 교사는 학생의 수준에 맞는 언어를 사용해야 한다.
③ 학생과의 관계에서 교사는 비언어적 표현에 유의해야 한다.
④ 학교는 학생에게 다양한 역할 경험의 기회를 제공해야 한다.
⑤ 교사는 학생 안전을 위해 교실의 물리적 환경을 개선해야 한다.

2021학년도 9월 학평 20번 ★★☆

5. 다음 글에서 필자가 주장하는 바로 가장 적절한 것은?

As you set about to write, it is worth reminding yourself that while you ought to have a point of view, you should avoid telling your readers what to think. Try to hang a question mark over it all. This way you allow your readers to think for themselves about the points and arguments you're making. As a result, they will feel more involved, finding themselves just as committed to the arguments you've made and the insights you've exposed as you are. You will have written an essay that not only avoids passivity in the reader, but is interesting and gets people to think.

① 저자의 독창적인 견해를 드러내야 한다.
② 다양한 표현으로 독자에게 감동을 주어야 한다.
③ 독자가 능동적으로 사고할 수 있도록 글을 써야 한다.
④ 독자에게 가치판단의 기준점을 명확히 제시해야 한다.
⑤ 주관적 관점을 배제하고 사실을 바탕으로 글을 써야 한다.

2021학년도 6월 학평 20번 ★☆☆

6. 다음 글에서 필자가 주장하는 바로 가장 적절한 것은?

Sometimes, you feel the need to avoid something that will lead to success out of discomfort. Maybe you are avoiding extra work because you are tired. You are actively shutting out success because you want to avoid being uncomfortable. Therefore, overcoming your instinct to avoid uncomfortable things at first is essential. Try doing new things outside of your comfort zone. Change is always uncomfortable, but it is key to doing things differently in order to find that magical formula for success.

① 불편할지라도 성공하기 위해서는 새로운 것을 시도해야 한다.
② 일과 생활의 균형을 맞추는 성공적인 삶을 추구해야 한다.
③ 갈등 해소를 위해 불편함의 원인을 찾아 개선해야 한다.
④ 단계별 목표를 설정하여 익숙한 것부터 도전해야 한다.
⑤ 변화에 적응하기 위해 직관적으로 문제를 해결해야 한다.

Day 03

2021학년도 3월 학평 20번 ★☆☆

7. 다음 글에서 필자가 주장하는 바로 가장 적절한 것은?

At a publishing house and at a newspaper you learn the following: *It's not a mistake if it doesn't end up in print.* It's the same for email. Nothing bad can happen if you haven't hit the Send key. What you've written can have misspellings, errors of fact, rude comments, obvious lies, but it doesn't matter. If you haven't sent it, you still have time to fix it. You can correct any mistake and nobody will ever know the difference. This is easier said than done, of course. Send is your computer's most attractive command. But before you hit the Send key, make sure that you read your document carefully one last time.

① 중요한 이메일은 출력하여 보관해야 한다.
② 글을 쓸 때에는 개요 작성부터 시작해야 한다.
③ 이메일을 전송하기 전에 반드시 검토해야 한다.
④ 업무와 관련된 컴퓨터 기능을 우선 익혀야 한다.
⑤ 업무상 중요한 내용은 이메일보다는 직접 전달해야 한다.

2020학년도 11월 학평 20번 ★☆☆

8. 다음 글에서 필자가 주장하는 바로 가장 적절한 것은?

When I was in high school, we had students who could study in the coffee shop and not get distracted by the noise or everything happening around them. We also had students who could not study if the library was not super quiet. The latter students suffered because even in the library, it was impossible to get the type of complete silence they sought. These students were victims of distractions who found it very difficult to study anywhere except in their private bedrooms. In today's world, it is impossible to run away from distractions. Distractions are everywhere, but if you want to achieve your goals, you must learn how to tackle distractions. You cannot eliminate distractions, but you can learn to live with them in a way that ensures they do not limit you.

① 자신에게 적합한 시간 관리법을 찾아야 한다.
② 집중을 방해하는 요인에 대처할 줄 알아야 한다.
③ 학습 공간과 휴식 공간을 명확하게 분리해야 한다.
④ 집중력 향상을 위해 정돈된 학습환경을 유지해야 한다.
⑤ 공공장소에서 타인에게 피해를 주는 행동을 삼가야 한다.

2020학년도 9월 학평 20번 ★★☆

9. 다음 글에서 필자가 주장하는 바로 가장 적절한 것은?

Any goal you set is going to be difficult to achieve, and you will certainly be disappointed at some points along the way. So why not set your goals much higher than you consider worthy from the beginning? If they are going to require work, effort, and energy, then why not exert 10 times as much of each? What if you are underestimating your capabilities? You might be protesting, saying, "What of the disappointment that comes from setting unrealistic goals?" However, take just a few moments to look back over your life. Chances are that you have more often been disappointed by setting targets that are too low and achieving them — only to be shocked that you still didn't get what you wanted.

* exert: 발휘하다

① 매사에 최선을 다하는 태도를 가져야 한다.
② 목표는 자신의 생각보다 높게 설정해야 한다.
③ 변화하는 상황에 따라 목표를 수정해야 한다.
④ 과거의 실패를 되돌아보는 습관을 길러야 한다.
⑤ 목표 달성을 위해 계획을 구체적으로 세워야 한다.

2020학년도 6월 학평 20번 ★☆☆

10. 다음 글에서 필자가 주장하는 바로 가장 적절한 것은?

The dish you start with serves as an anchor food for your entire meal. Experiments show that people eat nearly 50 percent greater quantity of the food they eat first. If you start with a dinner roll, you will eat more starches, less protein, and fewer vegetables. Eat the healthiest food on your plate first. As age-old wisdom suggests, this usually means starting with your vegetables or salad. If you are going to eat something unhealthy, at least save it for last. This will give your body the opportunity to fill up on better options before you move on to starches or sugary desserts.

* anchor: 닻 ** starch: 녹말

① 피해야 할 음식 목록을 만들어라.
② 다양한 음식들로 식단을 구성하라.
③ 음식을 조리하는 방식을 바꾸어라.
④ 자신의 입맛에 맞는 음식을 찾아라.
⑤ 건강에 좋은 음식으로 식사를 시작하라.

2019학년도 11월 학평 20번 ★★☆

11. 다음 글에서 필자가 주장하는 바로 가장 적절한 것은?

We tend to go long periods of time without reaching out to the people we know. Then, we suddenly take notice of the distance that has formed and we scramble to make repairs. We call people we haven't spoken to in ages, hoping that one small effort will erase the months and years of distance we've created. However, this rarely works: relationships aren't kept up with big one-time fixes. They're kept up with regular maintenance, like a car. In our relationships, we have to make sure that not too much time goes by between oil changes, so to speak. This isn't to say that you shouldn't bother calling someone just because it's been a while since you've spoken; just that it's more ideal not to let yourself fall out of touch in the first place. Consistency always brings better results.

① 가까운 사이일수록 적당한 거리를 유지해야 한다.
② 사교성을 기르려면 개방적인 태도를 가져야 한다.
③ 대화를 할 때 상대방의 의견을 먼저 경청해야 한다.
④ 인간관계를 지속하려면 일관된 노력을 기울여야 한다.
⑤ 원활한 의사소통을 위해 솔직하게 감정을 표현해야 한다.

2018학년도 9월 학평 20번 ★★☆

12. 다음 글에서 필자가 주장하는 바로 가장 적절한 것은?

How do you encourage other people when they are changing their behavior? Suppose you see a friend who is on a diet and has been losing a lot of weight. It's tempting to tell her that she looks great and she must feel wonderful. It feels good for someone to hear positive comments, and this feedback will often be encouraging. However, if you end the discussion there, then the only feedback your friend is getting is about her progress toward an outcome. Instead, continue the discussion. Ask about what she is doing that has allowed her to be successful. What is she eating? Where is she working out? What are the lifestyle changes she has made? When the conversation focuses on the process of change rather than the outcome, it reinforces the value of creating a sustainable process.

① 상대방의 감정을 고려하여 조언해야 한다.
② 토론 중에는 지나치게 공격적인 질문을 삼가야 한다.
③ 효과적인 다이어트를 위해 구체적인 계획을 세워야 한다.
④ 지속적인 성장을 위해서는 단점보다 장점에 집중해야 한다.
⑤ 행동을 바꾸려는 사람과는 과정에 초점을 두어 대화해야 한다.

총 문항				문항	맞은 문항					문항
개별 문항	1	2	3	4	5	6	7	8	9	10
채점										
개별 문항	11	12	13	14	15	16	17	18	19	20
채점										

3. 목적어와 보어의 이해

정답 및 해설 016쪽

A 문법의 주요 포인트를 점검해 봅시다.

1 to부정사와 동명사는 문장에서 목적어의 역할을 할 수 있다.
- to부정사만을 목적어로 취하는 동사 : want, wish, plan, agree, decide, promise
- 동명사를 목적어로 취하는 동사 : finish, mind, enjoy, avoid, deny
- to부정사와, 동명사 모두를 목적어로 취하는 동사 : start, begin, continue, like, hate

2 간접의문문(의문사+주어+동사), what, that, if[whether]가 이끄는 명사절은 타동사의 목적어 역할을 할 수 있다.

3 문장에서 목적어가 길어지면, 가목적어 it을 쓰고, (진)목적어를 문장 뒤로 보낸다.

4 주격보어는 주어를 설명해 주는 말로, 명사(구), 형용사(구) 뿐만 아니라, to부정사(구), 동명사(구), 현재분사, 과거분사, 명사절이 주격보어가 될 수 있다.

5 목적격보어는 목적어의 상태나 성질을 설명해 주는 말로, 명사(구), 형용사, to부정사, 원형부정사, 현재분사, 과거분사가 목적격보어가 될 수 있다. 지각동사와 사역동사의 목적어와 목적격보어가 능동 관계인 경우 목적격보어를 동사원형으로 쓰고, 수동 관계인 경우 목적격보어를 과거분사로 쓴다. 지각동사와 일부 사역동사(have, get)는 능동 관계인 경우 현재분사를 쓸 수 있다.

B 다음 괄호 안에서 어법상 올바른 것을 고르시오.

1 Sam promised not **[being / to be]** late again.

2 He narrowly avoided **[getting / to get]** into a fight on Chuseok holiday.

3 His wish is **[to visit / to be visited]** a lot of countries.

4 She thinks that the key to happiness is **[having / being had]** a lot of friends.

5 He encouraged her **[applying / to apply]** for the job.

6 She saw him **[leave / to leave]** a few minutes ago.

7 Sally had her purse **[steal / stolen]** on the bus.

8 I wonder **[that / whether]** we should tell her or not.

9 I find **[it /that]** difficult to talk to you about anything serious.

10 I used to consider it necessary **[that / to]** children watch TV at least for an hour.

어휘 플러스

3. 반의어 (1)

정답 및 해설 017쪽

A 다음 수능 필수 어휘를 읽고, 아는 것은 체크해 봅시다.

□ 01	ability	n. 능력	□ 21	inability	n. 무능력
□ 02	abnormal	a. 이상한, 비정상적인	□ 22	normal	a. 정상적인
□ 03	absence	n. 결석	□ 23	presence	n. 출석
□ 04	absorb	v. 흡수하다	□ 24	release	v. 방출하다
□ 05	accelerate	v. 가속하다	□ 25	decelerate	v. 감속하다
□ 06	accept	v. 수락하다	□ 26	refuse	v. 거절하다(= reject)
□ 07	accurate	a. 정확한	□ 27	inaccurate	a. 정확하지 않은
□ 08	active	a. 활동적인	□ 28	passive	a. 소극적인(= inactive)
□ 09	adequate	a. 충분한	□ 29	inadequate	a. 불충분한
□ 10	aggressive	a. 공격적인	□ 30	defensive	a. 방어적인
□ 11	allow	v. 허용하다	□ 31	prohibit	v. 금지하다
□ 12	ally	n. 동맹국, 협력자	□ 32	opponent	n. 적, 반대자
□ 13	altruism	n. 이타주의, 이타심	□ 33	egoism	n. 이기주의
□ 14	animate	a. 살아있는	□ 34	inanimate	a. 죽은, 생기 없는
□ 15	appropriate	a.적절한	□ 35	inappropriate	a. 부적당한
□ 16	approve	v. 허가하다, 승인하다	□ 36	disapprove	v. 불허하다
□ 17	assemble	v. 조립하다	□ 37	disassemble	v. 해체하다
□ 18	attach	v. 붙이다	□ 38	detach	v. 떼다
□ 19	backward	ad. 뒤로, 거꾸로	□ 39	forward	ad. 앞으로
□ 20	capable	a. ~할 수 있는, 유능한	□ 40	incapable	a. ~할 수 없는

B 괄호 안에서 문맥에 맞는 낱말로 적절한 것을 골라 봅시다.

1 In the **[absence / presence]** of other information, you probably conclude that the shorter one is a woman while the taller one is a man.

2 They say the survey is **[accurate / inaccurate]** because it is based on incorrect figures.

3 My grandmother is over 80, but is still very **[active / passive]**.

4 He was **[allowed / prohibited]** to stay up long enough to finish the book.

5 The typical scenario in the less developed world is one in which a very few commercial agriculturalists are technologically advanced while the vast majority are **[capable / incapable]** of competing.

04 함축·지칭 추론

출제 트렌드

1. 함축적 의미 추론 문제는 글의 흐름상 중요한 개념을 담고 있는 어구를 밑줄로 제시한 후 내포된 의미를 찾는 유형이다. 변별력을 가릴 수 있는 고난도 독해 문제이다. 고1 학력 평가에에서 1문제가 출제된다.
2. 지칭 추론은 글에서 대명사가 가리키는 대상이 나머지와 다른 하나를 찾는 유형이다. 수능과 고1 학력 평가에서는 단 문항으로 출제되지 않고, 복합문에서 1문제가 출제되고 있다.
3. 최근 수능 7년간, 함축 · 지칭 추론 문제는 2017-2018학년까지 지칭 문제가 매년 1문제씩 출제되다가, 2019학년도 이후 함축 문제가 매년 1문제씩 출제되고 있다. 2017학년도 수능(86%), 2018(86%), 2019(54%), 2020(72%), 2021(63%), 2022(35%), 2023(68%)에서 괄호 안의 정답률을 보였다. 평균적으로 지칭 문제는 2년간 86%, 함축 문제는 5년간 58.4%의 정답률을 보였다. 지칭과 함축 난이도는 각각 하, 상 단계에 해당한다. 지칭 문제를 함축 문제로 교체함으로써 시험의 난이도가 체감적으로 더 올라갔으며, 함축 문제가 지속적으로 출제될 전망이다.

출처			문항 번호	지문 주제	정답률(%)	난이도
대표	2022학년도	11 학평	21번	노력만이 가치 있다는 확고한 신념에 대한 의심	54	★★★
1	2022학년도	09 학평	21번	고객의 부당한 요구를 거절해야 할 때가 있다	74	★★☆
2	2022학년도	06 학평	21번	스트레스 관리 원칙	83	★★☆
3	2022학년도	03 학평	21번	진취적이며 적극적으로 구직 활동을 하라	62	★★☆
4	2021학년도	11 학평	21번	기후 변화에 대한 우리의 책임	60	★★☆
5	2021학년도	09 학평	21번	제자리에 있지 않는 물건	46	★★★
6	2021학년도	06 학평	21번	선택적 지각	53	★★★
7	2021학년도	03 학평	21번	후회를 극복하고 다음 기회를 계획하라	76	★★☆
8	2020학년도	09 학평	21번	빈번한 핸드폰 교체	72	★★☆
9	2018학년도	06 학평	30번	전학생 Amy에게 말을 걸어준 친구	59	★★★
10	2018학년도	03 학평	20번	Serene과 그녀의 어머니	71	★★☆

1등급 꿀팁

1. 함축적 의미 추론은 먼저 밑줄 친 어구를 읽고 파악할 점을 예상해 본다.
2. 함축적 의미 추론은 글의 중심 개념을 파악하고, 이를 풀이한 선택지를 찾는다.
3. 지칭 추론은 일화에 나오는 인물들의 관계 파악이 중요하다.
4. 지칭 추론은 대명사는 앞에서 언급한 명사를 가리키므로, 밑줄 친 부분 바로 앞 문장을 주의 깊게 읽는다.

제한 시간 : 15분 | 정답 및 해설 017쪽

대표 기출

2022학년도 11월 학평 21번

21. 밑줄 친 <u>challenge this sacred cow</u>가 다음 글에서 의미하는 바로 가장 적절한 것은? [3점]

Our language helps to reveal our deeper assumptions. Think of these revealing phrases: When we accomplish something important, we say it took "blood, sweat, and tears." We say important achievements are "hard-earned." We recommend a "hard day's work" when "day's work" would be enough. When we talk of "easy money," we are implying it was obtained through illegal or questionable means. We use the phrase "That's easy for you to say" as a criticism, usually when we are seeking to invalidate someone's opinion. It's like we all automatically accept that the "right" way is, inevitably, the harder one. In my experience this is hardly ever questioned. What would happen if you do <u>challenge this sacred cow</u>? We don't even pause to consider that something important and valuable could be made easy. What if the biggest thing keeping us from doing what matters is the false assumption that it has to take huge effort?

* invalidate: 틀렸음을 입증하다

① resist the tendency to avoid any hardship
② escape from the pressure of using formal language
③ doubt the solid belief that only hard work is worthy
④ abandon the old notion that money always comes first
⑤ break the superstition that holy animals bring good luck

문제 풀이

1. 주제문을 통해 글의 주제를 파악한다.
① 주제문: Our language helps to reveal our deeper assumptions. (우리의 언어는 우리의 더 깊은 전제를 드러내는 것을 돕는다.)

2. 글의 흐름을 따라가며 글의 주제를 뒷받침하는 세부 사항을 파악한다.
① When we accomplish something important, we say it took "blood, sweat, and tears." We say important achievements are "hard-earned." (우리가 중요한 무언가를 성취할 때, 우리는 그것이 '피, 땀, 그리고 눈물'을 필요로 했다고 말한다. 우리는 중요한 성과는 '힘들게 얻은' 것이라고 말한다.)
② We recommend a "hard day's work" when "day's work" would be enough. (우리는 '하루 동안의 일'이라는 말로도 충분할 때 '힘든 하루 동안의 일'이라는 말을 권한다.)
③ When we talk of "easy money," we are implying it was obtained through illegal or questionable means. (우리가 '쉬운 돈'이라고 말할 때, 우리는 그것이 불법적이거나 의심스러운 수단을 통해 얻어졌다는 것을 넌지시 드러내고 있다.)
④ "That's easy for you to say" as a criticism, usually when we are seeking to invalidate someone's opinion. (우리는 보통 누군가의 의견이 틀렸음을 입증하려고 할 때, '말은 쉽지'라는 문구를 비판으로 사용한다.)
⑤ It's like we all automatically accept that the "right" way is, inevitably, the harder one. (이는 마치 우리 모두가 '올바른' 방법은 반드시 더 어려운 방법이라는 것을 자동적으로 받아들이는 것과 같다.)

3. 글의 주제와 관련해서 밑줄 친 부분의 함축적 의미를 추론한다.
• 우리의 언어는 우리의 더 깊은 전제를 드러내는 것을 돕는데, 예를 들어 우리는 중요한 성과를 말할 때 '힘들게 얻은' 것이라고 말하는 경향이 있고, 중요하고 가치 있는 무언가를 쉬운 것으로 만들 수 있다는 사실을 생각조차 하지 않는다는 내용이다. 밑줄 친 부분이 의미하는 바로 ③ 'doubt the solid belief that only hard work is worthy(오직 노력만이 가치 있다는 확고한 신념 의심하기)'가 가장 적절하다.

2022학년도 9월 학평 21번 ★★☆

1. 밑줄 친 <u>fire a customer</u>가 다음 글에서 의미하는 바로 가장 적절한 것은?

Is the customer *always* right? When customers return a broken product to a famous company, which makes kitchen and bathroom fixtures, the company nearly always offers a replacement to maintain good customer relations. Still, "there are times you've got to say 'no,'" explains the warranty expert of the company, such as when a product is undamaged or has been abused. Entrepreneur Lauren Thorp, who owns an e-commerce company, says, "While the customer is 'always' right, sometimes you just have to <u>fire a customer</u>." When Thorp has tried everything to resolve a complaint and realizes that the customer will be dissatisfied no matter what, she returns her attention to the rest of her customers, who she says are "the reason for my success."

① deal with a customer's emergency
② delete a customer's purchasing record
③ reject a customer's unreasonable demand
④ uncover the hidden intention of a customer
⑤ rely on the power of an influential customer

2022학년도 6월 학평 21번 ★★☆

2. 밑줄 친 <u>put the glass down</u>이 다음 글에서 의미하는 바로 가장 적절한 것은? [3점]

A psychology professor raised a glass of water while teaching stress management principles to her students, and asked them, "How heavy is this glass of water I'm holding?" Students shouted out various answers. The professor replied, "The absolute weight of this glass doesn't matter. It depends on how long I hold it. If I hold it for a minute, it's quite light. But, if I hold it for a day straight, it will cause severe pain in my arm, forcing me to drop the glass to the floor. In each case, the weight of the glass is the same, but the longer I hold it, the heavier it feels to me." As the class nodded their heads in agreement, she continued, "Your stresses in life are like this glass of water. If you still feel the weight of yesterday's stress, it's a strong sign that it's time to <u>put the glass down</u>."

① pour more water into the glass
② set a plan not to make mistakes
③ let go of the stress in your mind
④ think about the cause of your stress
⑤ learn to accept the opinions of others

2022학년도 3월 학평 21번 ★★☆

3. 밑줄 친 Leave those activities to the rest of the sheep이 다음 글에서 의미하는 바로 가장 적절한 것은? [3점]

A job search is not a passive task. When you are searching, you are not browsing, nor are you "just looking". Browsing is not an effective way to reach a goal you claim to want to reach. If you are acting with purpose, if you are serious about anything you chose to do, then you need to be direct, focused and whenever possible, clever. Everyone else searching for a job has the same goal, competing for the same jobs. You must do more than the rest of the herd. Regardless of how long it may take you to find and get the job you want, being proactive will logically get you results faster than if you rely only on browsing online job boards and emailing an occasional resume. Leave those activities to the rest of the sheep.

① Try to understand other job-seekers' feelings.
② Keep calm and stick to your present position.
③ Don't be scared of the job-seeking competition.
④ Send occasional emails to your future employers.
⑤ Be more active to stand out from other job-seekers.

2021학년도 11월 학평 21번 ★★☆

4. 밑줄 친 a slap in our own face가 다음 글에서 의미하는 바로 가장 적절한 것은? [3점]

When it comes to climate change, many blame the fossil fuel industry for pumping greenhouse gases, the agricultural sector for burning rainforests, or the fashion industry for producing excessive clothes. But wait, what drives these industrial activities? Our consumption. Climate change is a summed product of each person's behavior. For example, the fossil fuel industry is a popular scapegoat in the climate crisis. But why do they drill and burn fossil fuels? We provide them strong financial incentives: some people regularly travel on airplanes and cars that burn fossil fuels. Some people waste electricity generated by burning fuel in power plants. Some people use and throw away plastic products derived from crude oil every day. Blaming the fossil fuel industry while engaging in these behaviors is a slap in our own face.

* scapegoat: 희생양

① giving the future generation room for change
② warning ourselves about the lack of natural resources
③ refusing to admit the benefits of fossil fuel production
④ failing to recognize our responsibility for climate change
⑤ starting to deal with environmental problems individually

2021학년도 9월 학평 21번 ★★★

5. 밑줄 친 "matter out of place"가 다음 글에서 의미하는 바로 가장 적절한 것은?

Nothing is trash by nature. Anthropologist Mary Douglas brings back and analyzes the common saying that dirt is "matter out of place." Dirt is relative, she emphasizes. "Shoes are not dirty in themselves, but it is dirty to place them on the dining-table; food is not dirty in itself, but it is dirty to leave pots and pans in the bedroom, or food all over clothing; similarly, bathroom items in the living room; clothing lying on chairs; outdoor things placed indoors; upstairs things downstairs, and so on." Sorting the dirty from the clean—removing the shoes from the table, putting the dirty clothing in the washing machine—involves systematic ordering and classifying. Eliminating dirt is thus a positive process.

① something that is completely broken
② a tiny dust that nobody notices
③ a dirty but renewable material
④ what can be easily replaced
⑤ a thing that is not in order

2021학년도 6월 학평 21번 ★★★

6. 밑줄 친 want to use a hammer가 다음 글에서 의미하는 바로 가장 적절한 것은? [3점]

We have a tendency to interpret events selectively. If we want things to be "this way" or "that way" we can most certainly select, stack, or arrange evidence in a way that supports such a viewpoint. Selective perception is based on what seems to us to stand out. However, what seems to us to be standing out may very well be related to our goals, interests, expectations, past experiences, or current demands of the situation—"with a hammer in hand, everything looks like a nail." This quote highlights the phenomenon of selective perception. If we want to use a hammer, then the world around us may begin to look as though it is full of nails!

① are unwilling to stand out
② make our effort meaningless
③ intend to do something in a certain way
④ hope others have a viewpoint similar to ours
⑤ have a way of thinking that is accepted by others

2021학년도 3월 학평 21번 ★★☆

7. 밑줄 친 translate it from the past tense to the future tense가 다음 글에서 의미하는 바로 가장 적절한 것은? [3점]

Get past the 'I wish I hadn't done that!' reaction. If the disappointment you're feeling is linked to an exam you didn't pass because you didn't study for it, or a job you didn't get because you said silly things at the interview, or a person you didn't impress because you took entirely the wrong approach, accept that it's *happened* now. The only value of 'I wish I hadn't done that!' is that you'll know better what to do next time. The learning pay-off is useful and significant. This 'if only I ...' agenda is virtual. Once you have worked that out, it's time to translate it from the past tense to the future tense: 'Next time I'm in this situation, I'm going to try to ...'.

* agenda: 의제 ** tense: 시제

① look for a job linked to your interest
② get over regrets and plan for next time
③ surround yourself with supportive people
④ study grammar and write clear sentences
⑤ examine your way of speaking and apologize

2020학년도 9월 학평 21번 ★★☆

8. 밑줄 친 have that same scenario가 다음 글에서 의미하는 바로 가장 적절한 것은? [3점]

There are more than 700 million cell phones used in the US today and at least 140 million of those cell phone users will abandon their current phone for a new phone every 14-18 months. I'm not one of those people who just "must" have the latest phone. Actually, I use my cell phone until the battery no longer holds a good charge. At that point, it's time. So I figure I'll just get a replacement battery. But I'm told that battery is no longer made and the phone is no longer manufactured because there's newer technology and better features in the latest phones. That's a typical justification. The phone wasn't even that old; maybe a little over one year? I'm just one example. Can you imagine how many countless other people have that same scenario? No wonder cell phones take the lead when it comes to "e-waste."

① have frequent trouble updating programs
② cannot afford new technology due to costs
③ spend a lot of money repairing their cell phones
④ are driven to change their still usable cell phones
⑤ are disappointed with newly launched phone models

2018학년도 6월 학평 30번 ★★★

9. 밑줄 친 she[her]가 가리키는 대상이 나머지 넷과 다른 것은?

"Wanna work together?" a cheerful voice spoke on Amy's first day at a new school. It was Wilhemina. Amy was too surprised to do anything but nod. The big black girl put ① her notebook down beside Amy's. After dropping the notebook, ② she lifted herself up onto the stool beside Amy. "I'm Wilhemina Smiths, Smiths with an *s* at both ends," ③ she said with a friendly smile. "My friends call me Mina. You're Amy Tillerman." Amy nodded and stared. As the only new kid in the school, ④ she was pleased to have a lab partner. But Amy wondered if Mina chose her because ⑤ she had felt sorry for the new kid.

2018학년도 3월 학평 20번 ★★☆

10. 밑줄 친 부분이 가리키는 대상이 나머지 넷과 다른 것은?

Serene tried to do a pirouette in front of her mother but fell to the floor. Serene's mother helped ① her off the floor. She told her that she had to keep trying if she wanted to succeed. However, Serene was almost in tears. ② She had been practicing very hard the past week but she did not seem to improve. Serene's mother said that ③ she herself had tried many times before succeeding at Serene's age. She had fallen so often that she sprained her ankle and had to rest for three months before she was allowed to dance again. Serene was surprised. Her mother was a famous ballerina and to Serene, ④ her mother had never fallen or made a mistake in any of her performances. Listening to her mother made ⑤ her realize that she had to put in more effort than what she had been doing so far.

* pirouette: 피루엣(한쪽 발로 서서 빠르게 도는 발레 동작)

총 문항				문항	맞은 문항					문항
개별 문항	1	2	3	4	5	6	7	8	9	10
채점										
개별 문항	11	12	13	14	15	16	17	18	19	20
채점										

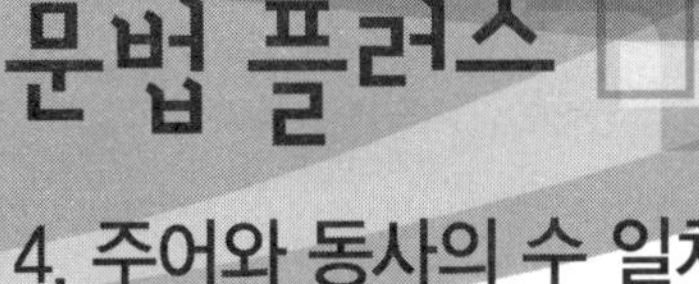

문법 플러스

정답 및 해설 022쪽

4. 주어와 동사의 수 일치

A 문법의 주요 포인트를 점검해 봅시다.

1 문장을 보고 주어와 동사를 정확히 구분할 수 있어야 한다. 주어 자리에 주어가 제대로 왔는지, 동사 자리에 동사가 제대로 왔는지 구분할 수 있어야 한다. 수 일치의 기본 원칙은 단수주어는 단수동사를, 복수주어는 복수동사를 사용한다는 것이다. 수 일치 문제는 수능에서 출제 빈도가 높으므로 평소에 독해 연습을 할 때, 주어, 동사를 찾는 연습을 하는 것이 좋다.

2 주어와 동사 사이에 수식어구나 관계사절이 들어갈 때가 많은데, 동사의 단수, 복수는 주어가 결정하므로 수식어구 때문에 헷갈리지 않도록 유의해야 한다.

- Families that avoid conflict by ignoring unpleasant subjects or situations **are** weaker, not stronger for it.

3 관계대명사절 안의 동사는 선행사의 수에 일치시킨다. 선행사가 단수주어면 동사는 단수동사, 선행사가 복수주어이면 복수동사를 사용한다.

- Kids shouldn't watch TV programs which **contain** violence.

4 도치 구문은 뒤에 나오는 주어에 맞게 수를 일치시킨다.

- Only after her death **was** I able to appreciate her.

5 most of ~, some of ~, all of ~, a lot of ~, 「분수 + of ~」 등이 주어로 쓰인 경우, 동사는 of 뒤에 나오는 명사(구)의 수에 일치시킨다. 「the number of+복수명사」는 뒤에 단수동사를 쓰고, 「A number of+복수명사」는 뒤에 복수동사를 쓴다.

- Some of his friends **think** he is silly to work and save for a smartwatch.

B 다음 괄호 안에서 어법상 올바른 것을 고르시오.

1 The main purpose of food labels **[is / are]** to inform you what is inside the food you are purchasing.

2 In warm environments, clothes that have a wicking capacity **[is / are]** helpful in dissipating heat from the body.

3 As a result, the pressure to conform to the standards and expectations of friends and other social groups **[is / are]** likely to be intense.

4 Judith Rich Harris, who is a developmental psychologists, **[arguing / argues]** that three main forces shape our development; personal temperament, our parents, and our peers.

5 Artificial light, which typically contains only a few wavelengths of light, **[do / does]** not seem to have the same effect on mood that sunlight has.

6 Because most of the plastic particles in the ocean **[is / are]** so small, there is no practical way to clean up the ocean.

7 Perhaps even more striking **[is / are]** the experience of wine tasters.

8 Memories of how we interacted **[seems / seem]** funny to me today.

9 The historical tendency, framed in the outdated dualism of us versus them, **[is / are]** strong enough to make a lot of people cling to the status quo.

10 Henry Fried, one of the foremost clock makers in the United States, **[give / gives]** a simple explanation for this question.

어휘 플러스

4. 파생어 (1)

정답 및 해설 022쪽

A 다음 수능 필수 어휘를 읽고, 아는 것은 체크해 봅시다.

□ 01	adherent	n. 지지자; a. 달라붙는	□ 21	adherence	n. 고수, 집착
□ 02	beneficial	a. 유익한, 이로운	□ 22	beneficient	a. 도움을 주는
□ 03	childish	a. 유치한, 어른답지 못한	□ 23	childlike	a. 어린애 같은, 귀여운
□ 04	comparable	a. 비교될 만한, 필적하는	□ 24	comparative	a. 비교의, 상대적인
□ 05	comprehensible	a. 이해하기 쉬운	□ 25	comprehensive	a. 종합적인
□ 06	confident	a. 확신하는, 자신감이 있는	□ 26	confidential	a. 기밀의, 은밀한
□ 07	considerable	a. 상당한	□ 27	considerate	a. 사려 깊은
□ 08	credible	a. 믿을 수 있는	□ 28	credulous	a. 쉽게 속는
□ 09	continual	a. 반복되는	□ 29	continuous	a. 계속되는, 지속적인
□ 10	different	a. 다른	□ 30	indifferent	a. 무관심한
□ 11	distinguishable	a. 구별할 수 있는	□ 31	distinguished	a. 두드러진
□ 12	economic	a. 경제의, 경제학의	□ 32	economical	a. 절약하는, 실속 있는
□ 13	famous	a. 유명한	□ 33	infamous	a. 악명 높은
□ 14	favorable	a. 호의적인, 유리한	□ 34	favorite	a. 가장 좋아하는
□ 15	forgetful	a. 잘 잊어버리는	□ 35	forgettable	a. 쉽게 잊혀질
□ 16	healthy	a. 건강한	□ 36	healthful	a. 건강에 좋은
□ 17	imaginable	a. 상상할 수 있는	□ 37	imaginative	a. 상상력이 풍부한
□ 18	industrious	a. 근면한	□ 38	industrial	a. 산업의
□ 19	ingenious	a. 독창적인	□ 39	ingenuous	a. 솔직한, 정직한
□ 20	literal	a. 문자 그대로의	□ 40	literate	a. 읽고 쓸 수 있는, 교양이 있는

B 괄호 안에서 문맥에 맞는 낱말로 적절한 것을 골라 봅시다.

1 Some empires were big, but the rigid social control required to hold an empire together was not **[beneficial / beneficient]** to science, just as it was not beneficial to reason.

2 For instance, we may even look at a failure in a bright light if we are **[confidential / confident]** of ourselves.

3 In other words, higher-status individuals can be **[different / indifferent]** while lower-status persons are required to be attentive with their gaze.

4 Control over direct discharge of mercury from **[industrious / industrial]** operations is clearly needed for prevention.

5 You may also need an on-off switch. One with individual switches for each socket will be more **[economic / economical]**.

05 글의 요지

출제 트렌드

1. 글을 읽고 중심 내용을 찾는 유형으로 선택지는 우리말로 제시하고 있다. 고1 학력 평가에서 1문제가 출제된다.
2. 글의 중반부 이후에 중심 내용이 제시되는 경우가 많다.
3. 중심 내용을 파악하기 위해서는 글을 읽고 전체적인 내용을 이해하고, 추론하는 능력이 필요하다. 중심 내용 파악하기 읽기 유형에는 요지, 주제, 제목 파악하기 문제가 있다.
4. 최근 수능 7년간, 글의 요지 문제는 매년 1문제가 출제되었다. 2017학년도 수능(92%), 2018(87%), 2019(82%), 2020(78%), 2021(89%), 2022(89%), 2023(78%)에서 괄호 안의 정답률을 보였다. 7년간 평균 85% 정도 정답률이 나왔으며 난이도는 하 단계이다.

출처			문항 번호	지문 주제	정답률(%)	난이도
대표	2022학년도	11 학평	22번	두려움을 주는 뉴스는 사람들이 문제에 덜 대처하게 할 수 있다	79	★★☆
1	2022학년도	09 학평	22번	아이들의 집중을 위해 과도한 교실 장식을 지양해야 함	85	★☆☆
2	2022학년도	06 학평	22번	자신의 감정 때문에 상황을 오해할 수 있다	85	★☆☆
3	2022학년도	03 학평	22번	수면은 건강 유지와 기능 발휘에 도움이 된다	92	★☆☆
4	2021학년도	11 학평	22번	고객 정보는 활용해야 함	78	★★☆
5	2021학년도	09 학평	22번	자신의 의견이 최선이 아닐 수 있다는 것을 인정하는 것이 필요하다	65	★★☆
6	2021학년도	06 학평	22번	과제가 일정 수준에 도달하게 개선 기회를 주면 동기 부여에 도움이 된다	75	★★☆
7	2021학년도	03 학평	22번	자기 의심은 스트레스를 유발하고, 객관적 판단을 흐린다	69	★★☆
8	2020학년도	11 학평	22번	더 나은 선택에 대한 두려움	65	★★☆
9	2020학년도	09 학평	22번	학습에 끼치는 문화의 영향	78	★★☆
10	2020학년도	06 학평	22번	목표보다는 과정에 전념하라	70	★★☆

1등급 꿀팁

1. 핵심 어구가 반복적으로 제시되는 경우가 많다. 핵심 어구를 요약한 것이 요지가 된다.
2. 글의 흐름이 반전되는 부분을 유의해야 한다.
3. 주로 설명문이나 논설문에서 출제되지만, 시사 글이 나오기도 한다.

제한 시간 : 15분 | 정답 및 해설 022쪽

대표 기출

2022학년도 11월 학평 22번

22. 다음 글의 요지로 가장 적절한 것은?

The old saying is that "knowledge is power," but when it comes to scary, threatening news, research suggests the exact opposite. Frightening news can actually rob people of their inner sense of control, making them less likely to take care of themselves and other people. Public health research shows that when the news presents health-related information in a pessimistic way, people are actually less likely to take steps to protect themselves from illness as a result. A news article that's intended to warn people about increasing cancer rates, for example, can result in fewer people choosing to get screened for the disease because they're so terrified of what they might find. This is also true for issues such as climate change. When a news story is all doom and gloom, people feel depressed and become less interested in taking small, personal steps to fight ecological collapse.

① 두려움을 주는 뉴스는 사람들이 문제에 덜 대처하게 할 수 있다.
② 정보를 전달하는 시기에 따라 뉴스의 영향력이 달라질 수 있다.
③ 지속적인 환경 문제 보도가 사람들의 인식 변화를 가져온다.
④ 정보 제공의 지연은 정확한 문제 인식에 방해가 될 수 있다.
⑤ 출처가 불분명한 건강 정보는 사람들에게 유익하지 않다.

문제 풀이

1. 특정 개념과 관련된 어구 또는 반복되는 어구를 찾는다.

① 글의 핵심어구는 threatening news, frightening news이다.

2. 반론을 주의하며, 글의 요지를 추론한다.

① The old saying is that "knowledge is power," but when it comes to scary, threatening news, research suggests the exact opposite. (속담은 '아는 것이 힘이다'라고 말하지만, 무섭고 위협적인 뉴스에 관한 한, 연구는 정반대를 시사한다.)

② ~ when the news presents health-related information in a pessimistic way, people are actually less likely to take steps to protect themselves from illness as a result. (건강과 관련된 정보를 비관적인 방식으로 제시할 때, 결과적으로 사람들이 질병으로부터 스스로를 보호하기 위한 조치를 취할 가능성이 실제로 더 낮다.)

③ When a news story is all doom and gloom, people feel depressed and become less interested in taking small, personal steps to fight ecological collapse. (뉴스가 완전히 암울할 때, 사람들은 우울하고 생태학적 붕괴와 싸우기 위한 작고 개인적인 조치를 취하는 것에 흥미를 덜 느끼게 된다.)

3. 주제문을 통해 글의 요지를 확인하고 요지를 드러내는 선택지를 고른다.

Frightening news can actually rob people of their inner sense of control, making them less likely to take care of themselves and other people.
(두려움을 주는 뉴스는 실제로 사람들에게서 내면의 통제력을 빼앗을 수 있어서, 그들이 스스로와 다른 사람들을 돌볼 가능성을 더 낮게 만든다.)

• 아는 것이 힘이라는 속담과는 달리, 무섭고 위협적인 뉴스를 접하는 경우에는 사람들이 스스로를 돌볼 가능성이 더 낮다는 내용이다. 따라서 글의 요지로 ① '두려움을 주는 뉴스는 사람들이 문제에 덜 대처하게 할 수 있다.'가 가장 적절하다.

2022학년도 9월 학평 22번 ★☆☆

1. 다음 글의 요지로 가장 적절한 것은?

A recent study from Carnegie Mellon University in Pittsburgh, called "When Too Much of a Good Thing May Be Bad," indicates that classrooms with too much decoration are a source of distraction for young children and directly affect their cognitive performance. Being visually overstimulated, the children have a great deal of difficulty concentrating and end up with worse academic results. On the other hand, if there is not much decoration on the classroom walls, the children are less distracted, spend more time on their activities, and learn more. So it's our job, in order to support their attention, to find the right balance between excessive decoration and the complete absence of it.

① 아이들의 집중을 돕기 위해 과도한 교실 장식을 지양할 필요가 있다.
② 아이들의 인성과 인지 능력을 균형 있게 발달시키는 것이 중요하다.
③ 아이들이 직접 교실을 장식하는 것은 창의력 발달에 도움이 된다.
④ 다양한 교실 활동은 아이들의 수업 참여도를 증진시킨다.
⑤ 풍부한 시각 자료는 아이들의 학습 동기를 높인다.

2022학년도 6월 학평 22번 ★☆☆

2. 다음 글의 요지로 가장 적절한 것은?

Your emotions deserve attention and give you important pieces of information. However, they can also sometimes be an unreliable, inaccurate source of information. You may feel a certain way, but that does not mean those feelings are reflections of the truth. You may feel sad and conclude that your friend is angry with you when her behavior simply reflects that she's having a bad day. You may feel depressed and decide that you did poorly in an interview when you did just fine. Your feelings can mislead you into thinking things that are not supported by facts.

① 자신의 감정으로 인해 상황을 오해할 수 있다.
② 자신의 생각을 타인에게 강요해서는 안 된다.
③ 인간관계가 우리의 감정에 영향을 미친다.
④ 타인의 감정에 공감하는 자세가 필요하다.
⑤ 공동체를 위한 선택에는 보상이 따른다.

2022학년도 3월 학평 22번 ★☆☆

3. 다음 글의 요지로 가장 적절한 것은?

Many people view sleep as merely a "down time" when their brain shuts off and their body rests. In a rush to meet work, school, family, or household responsibilities, people cut back on their sleep, thinking it won't be a problem, because all of these other activities seem much more important. But research reveals that a number of vital tasks carried out during sleep help to maintain good health and enable people to function at their best. While you sleep, your brain is hard at work forming the pathways necessary for learning and creating memories and new insights. Without enough sleep, you can't focus and pay attention or respond quickly. A lack of sleep may even cause mood problems. In addition, growing evidence shows that a continuous lack of sleep increases the risk for developing serious diseases.

* vital: 매우 중요한

① 수면은 건강 유지와 최상의 기능 발휘에 도움이 된다.
② 업무량이 증가하면 필요한 수면 시간도 증가한다.
③ 균형 잡힌 식단을 유지하면 뇌 기능이 향상된다.
④ 불면증은 주위 사람들에게 부정적인 영향을 미친다.
⑤ 꿈의 내용은 깨어 있는 시간 동안의 경험을 반영한다.

2021학년도 11월 학평 22번 ★★☆

4. 다음 글의 요지로 가장 적절한 것은?

Information is worthless if you never actually use it. Far too often, companies collect valuable customer information that ends up buried and never used. They must ensure their data is accessible for use at the appropriate times. For a hotel, one appropriate time for data usage is check-in at the front desk. I often check in at a hotel I've visited frequently, only for the people at the front desk to give no indication that they recognize me as a customer. The hotel must have stored a record of my visits, but they don't make that information accessible to the front desk clerks. They are missing a prime opportunity to utilize data to create a better experience focused on customer loyalty. Whether they have ten customers, ten thousand, or even ten million, the goal is the same: create a delightful customer experience that encourages loyalty.

① 기업 정보의 투명한 공개는 고객 만족도를 향상시킨다.
② 목표 고객층에 대한 분석은 기업의 이익 창출로 이어진다.
③ 고객 충성도를 높이기 위해 고객 정보가 활용될 필요가 있다.
④ 일관성 있는 호텔 서비스 제공을 통해 단골 고객을 확보할 수 있다.
⑤ 사생활 침해에 대한 우려로 고객 정보를 보관하는 데 어려움이 있다.

2021학년도 9월 학평 22번 ★★☆

5. 다음 글의 요지로 가장 적절한 것은?

It's important that you think independently and fight for what you believe in, but there comes a time when it's wiser to stop fighting for your view and move on to accepting what a trustworthy group of people think is best. This can be extremely difficult. But it's smarter, and ultimately better for you to be open-minded and have faith that the conclusions of a trustworthy group of people are better than whatever you think. If you can't understand their view, you're probably just blind to their way of thinking. If you continue doing what you think is best when all the evidence and trustworthy people are against you, you're being dangerously confident. The truth is that while most people can become incredibly open-minded, some can't, even after they have repeatedly encountered lots of pain from betting that they were right when they were not.

① 대부분의 사람들은 진리에 도달하지 못하고 고통을 받는다.
② 맹목적으로 다른 사람의 의견을 받아들이는 것은 위험하다.
③ 남을 설득하기 위해서는 타당한 증거로 주장을 뒷받침해야 한다.
④ 믿을만한 사람이 누구인지 판단하려면 열린 마음을 가져야 한다.
⑤ 자신의 의견이 최선이 아닐 수 있다는 것을 인정하는 것이 필요하다.

Day 05

2021학년도 6월 학평 22번 ★★☆

6. 다음 글의 요지로 가장 적절한 것은?

Rather than attempting to punish students with a low grade or mark in the hope it will encourage them to give greater effort in the future, teachers can better motivate students by considering their work as incomplete and then requiring additional effort. Teachers at Beachwood Middle School in Beachwood, Ohio, record students' grades as *A*, *B*, *C*, or *I*(Incomplete). Students who receive an *I* grade are required to do additional work in order to bring their performance up to an acceptable level. This policy is based on the belief that students perform at a failure level or submit failing work in large part because teachers accept it. The Beachwood teachers reason that if they no longer accept substandard work, students will not submit it. And with appropriate support, they believe students will continue to work until their performance is satisfactory.

① 학생에게 평가 결과를 공개하는 것은 학습 동기를 떨어뜨린다.
② 학생에게 추가 과제를 부여하는 것은 학업 부담을 가중시킨다.
③ 지속적인 보상은 학업 성취도에 장기적으로 부정적인 영향을 준다.
④ 학생의 자기주도적 학습 능력은 정서적으로 안정된 학습 환경에서 향상된다.
⑤ 학생의 과제가 일정 수준에 도달하도록 개선 기회를 주면 동기 부여에 도움이 된다.

2021학년도 3월 학평 22번 ★★☆

7. 다음 글의 요지로 가장 적절한 것은?

If you care deeply about something, you may place greater value on your ability to succeed in that area of concern. The internal pressure you place on yourself to achieve or do well socially is normal and useful, but when you doubt your ability to succeed in areas that are important to you, your self-worth suffers. Situations are uniquely stressful for each of us based on whether or not they activate our doubt. It's not the pressure to perform that creates your stress. Rather, it's the self-doubt that bothers you. Doubt causes you to see positive, neutral, and even genuinely negative experiences more negatively and as a reflection of your own shortcomings. When you see situations and your strengths more objectively, you are less likely to have doubt as the source of your distress.

* distress: 괴로움

① 비판적인 시각은 객관적인 문제 분석에 도움이 된다.
② 성취 욕구는 스트레스를 이겨 낼 원동력이 될 수 있다.
③ 적절한 수준의 스트레스는 과제 수행의 효율을 높인다.
④ 실패의 경험은 자존감을 낮추고, 타인에 의존하게 한다.
⑤ 자기 의심은 스트레스를 유발하고, 객관적 판단을 흐린다.

2020학년도 11월 학평 22번 ★★☆

8. 다음 글의 요지로 가장 적절한 것은?

FOBO, or Fear of a Better Option, is the anxiety that something better will come along, which makes it undesirable to commit to existing choices when making a decision. It's an affliction of abundance that drives you to keep all of your options open and to avoid risks. Rather than assessing your options, choosing one, and moving on with your day, you delay the inevitable. It's not unlike hitting the snooze button on your alarm clock only to pull the covers over your head and fall back asleep. As you probably found out the hard way, if you hit snooze enough times, you'll end up being late and racing for the office, your day and mood ruined. While pressing snooze feels so good at the moment, it ultimately demands a price.

* affliction: 고통

① 적당한 수준의 불안감은 업무 수행에 도움이 된다.
② 성급한 의사 결정은 의도하지 않은 결과를 초래한다.
③ 반복되는 실수를 줄이기 위해서는 신중함이 요구된다.
④ 더 나은 선택을 위해 결정을 미루는 것은 결국 해가 된다.
⑤ 규칙적인 생활 습관은 직장에서의 성공 가능성을 높인다.

2020학년도 9월 학평 22번 ★★☆

9. 다음 글의 요지로 가장 적절한 것은?

Learners function within complex developmental, cognitive, physical, social, and cultural systems. Research and theory from diverse fields have contributed to an evolving understanding that all learners grow and learn in culturally defined ways in culturally defined contexts. While humans share basic brain structures and processes, as well as fundamental experiences such as relationships with family, age-related stages, and many more, each of these phenomena is shaped by an individual's precise experiences. Learning does not happen in the same way for all people because cultural influences are influential from the beginning of life. These ideas about the intertwining of learning and culture have been supported by research on many aspects of learning and development.

* intertwine: 뒤얽히다

① 문화 다양성에 대한 체계적 연구가 필요하다.
② 개인의 문화적 경험이 학습에 영향을 끼친다.
③ 인간의 뇌 구조는 학습을 통해 복잡하게 진화했다.
④ 원만한 대인관계 형성은 건강한 성장의 토대가 된다.
⑤ 학습 발달 단계에 적합한 자극을 제공하는 것이 좋다.

2020학년도 6월 학평 22번 ★★☆

10. 다음 글의 요지로 가장 적절한 것은?

A goal-oriented mind-set can create a "yo-yo" effect. Many runners work hard for months, but as soon as they cross the finish line, they stop training. The race is no longer there to motivate them. When all of your hard work is focused on a particular goal, what is left to push you forward after you achieve it? This is why many people find themselves returning to their old habits after accomplishing a goal. The purpose of setting goals is to win the game. The purpose of building systems is to continue playing the game. True long-term thinking is goal-less thinking. It's not about any single accomplishment. It is about the cycle of endless refinement and continuous improvement. Ultimately, it is your commitment to the process that will determine your progress.

① 발전은 한 번의 목표 성취가 아닌 지속적인 개선 과정에 의해 결정된다.
② 결승선을 통과하기 위해 장시간 노력해야 원하는 바를 얻을 수 있다.
③ 성공을 위해서는 구체적인 목표를 설정하는 것이 중요하다.
④ 지난 과정을 끊임없이 반복하는 것이 성공의 지름길이다.
⑤ 목표 지향적 성향이 강할수록 발전이 빠르게 이루어진다.

총 문항				문항	맞은 문항					문항
개별 문항	1	2	3	4	5	6	7	8	9	10
채점										
개별 문항	11	12	13	14	15	16	17	18	19	20
채점										

문법 플러스

5. 동사의 시제

정답 및 해설 027쪽

A 문법의 주요 포인트를 점검해 봅시다.

1 시제란 동사가 나타내는 시간을 말한다. 기본 시제는 현재, 과거, 미래 시제이다.

2 현재의 습관, 사실, 불변의 진리는 현재 시제를 쓴다. 과거의 습관, 역사적 사실은 과거 시제를 쓴다. 미래의 일을 나타낼 때는 미래 시제를 쓴다. 단순현재형은 장기간 지속되는 동작을, 현재진행형은 잠시 지속되는 동작을 나타낸다. 진행형은 원칙적으로 동작을 표시하는 동사이므로 지각동사(see, hear 등), 소유동사(have, belong), 인식동사(know, remember 등)와 같은 동사에는 진행형을 쓸 수 없다. think 동사가 '믿다' 또는 '의견을 가지다'라는 의미일 때는 진행형을 쓰지 않지만 '고려하다'라는 의미일 때는 진행형이 가능하다.
■ Sarah **is thinking** about quitting her job.

3 시간이나 조건을 나타내는 부사절에서는 미래를 나타내는 경우 미래 시제 대신에 현재 시제를 쓴다.

4 어떤 문장에서 과거 시점을 보여주는 부사구가 있는 경우, 현재완료 시제를 쓰지 않고 과거 시제를 쓴다.

5 과거 이전의 사실은 과거완료 시제를 쓴다. 시제일치는 예외가 있다. 원칙상, 주절의 시제가 과거이면 시제일치의 원칙에 따라 종속절은 과거나 과거완료로만 쓸 수 있다. 그러나 시제일치에 상관없이 불변의 진리나 현재 습관, 상태는 현재 시제로 나타내며, 역사적 사실은 과거 시제로 나타낸다. 또한 주절에 주장, 제안, 요구, 명령 등의 동사가 나오면 that 이하 종속절은 「should+동사원형」으로 표현한다. 단, 의향이 아니라 객관적 사실을 나타내는 경우에는 that절에 직설법을 사용할 수 있다.

B 다음 괄호 안에서 어법상 올바른 것을 고르시오.

1 A bar code **[consists / consisted]** of a pattern of lines and bars that a computer can translate into information.

2 In 1903, the Curies **[win / won]** the nobel prize in physics for their discoveries.

3 By the time you **[will receive / receive]** this letter, everything will be settled.

4 A president needs people who **[tell / will tell]** him frankly.

5 In the summer 2001, he **[has visited / visited]** Asan, Korea, to participate in a house-building project.

6 Yesterday, we **[have had / had]** the heaviest snowfall we have had in ten years.

7 When Sally entered the classroom, the lecture **[have / had]** already begun.

8 Tom told her that he **[will / would]** try anything to help her.

9 I **[am thinking / thinks]** where to go next.

10 He wanted to know how long her mother **[has / had]** been dead.

어휘 플러스

정답 및 해설 027쪽

5. 철자가 혼동되는 어휘 (2)

A 다음 수능 필수 어휘를 읽고, 아는 것은 체크해 봅시다.

□ 01	abroad	ad. 해외로, 해외에	□ 21	aboard	ad. 승선하여, ~에 타고
□ 02	coverage	n. 보상 범위, 보도	□ 22	courage	n. 용기
□ 03	carrier	n. 운반인, 운반기	□ 23	career	n. 직업, 경력
□ 04	commodity	a. 상품, 일용품	□ 24	community	n. 지역사회, 공동체
□ 05	conception	n. 개념	□ 25	exception	n. 제외, 예외
□ 06	confidence	n. 자신감	□ 26	conference	n. 협의, 회의
□ 07	contract	n. 계약; v. 계약하다	□ 27	contrast	n. 대조, 차이; v. 대조하다
□ 08	cooperation	n. 협동, 협력	□ 28	corporation	n. 주식회사, 법인
□ 09	corruption	n. 타락, 부패	□ 29	eruption	n. 폭발, 분화
□ 10	command	v. 명령하다	□ 30	comment	n. 논평; 견해를 밝히다
□ 11	considerable	a. 상당히, 많은, 중요한	□ 31	considerate	a. 이해심이 있는, 사려 깊은
□ 12	employer	n. 고용주	□ 32	employee	n. 종업원
□ 13	emergence	n. 출현, 발생	□ 33	emergency	n. 비상사태
□ 14	fit	a. 적당한, 컨디션이 좋은	□ 34	feat	n. 위업, 공적, 묘기
□ 15	generous	a. 관대한, 너그러운	□ 35	general	a. 일반적인; n. 장군
□ 16	inventive	a. 창의적인, 발명의	□ 36	incentive	a. 고무하는, 격려하는
□ 17	level	a. 수평의, 같은 수준의	□ 37	label	n. 라벨; v. 라벨을 붙이다
□ 18	morality	n. 도덕, 덕행	□ 38	mortality	n. 사망률, 사망자 수
□ 19	particle	n. (아주 작은) 입자, 조각	□ 39	principle	n. 원리, 원칙
□ 20	thirsty	a. 목마른, 갈망하는	□ 40	thrifty	a. 절약하는, 아끼는

B 괄호 안에서 문맥에 맞는 낱말로 적절한 것을 골라 봅시다.

1 Therefore, instead of seeking security through means of mass destruction, we should achieve it through global understanding and **[corporation / cooperation]** before it is too late.

2 The **[contrast /contract]** between Western Europe and America is particularly sharp.

3 While detailed knowledge of a single area once guaranteed success, today the top rewards go to those who can operate with equal **[conference / confidence]** in different realms.

4 But I will say that you were so **[general / generous]** that you took our breath away, even accustomed as we are to your thoughtfulness.

5 The shapes of Korean kites are based on scientific **[particles / principles]** which enable them to make good use of the wind.

글의 주제

출제 트렌드

1. 글을 읽고 필자가 전달하고자 하는 중심 내용을 파악할 수 있는지 글에 대한 종합적 이해 능력을 측정하는 문제이다. 고1 학력 평가에서 1문항이 출제된다. 글의 핵심 내용과 방향이 뚜렷하고 문장 간의 연결이 긴밀한 지문이 제시된다.
2. 중심 내용을 파악하기 위해서는 글을 읽고 전체적인 내용을 이해하고, 추론하는 능력이 필요하다. 중심 내용 파악하기 읽기 유형에는 요지, 주제, 제목 파악하기 문제가 있다.
3. 최근 수능 7년간, 글의 주제 문제는 매년 1문제가 출제되었다. 2017학년도 수능(73%), 2018(84%), 2019(51%), 2020(65%), 2021(62%), 2022(77%), 2023(68%)에서 괄호 안의 정답률을 보였다. 최근 수능에서 3점 문제로 자주 출제되었고, 7년간 평균 68.6% 정도 정답률을 보이고 있다. 난이도는 중 단계이다. 이 문제 유형은 2019학년도 수능부터 더 어렵게 출제되고 있다.

출처			문항 번호	지문 주제	정답률(%)	난이도
대표	2022학년도	11 학평	23번	녹는 얼음과 상승하는 바다가 하루의 길이에 미치는 영향	80	★★☆
1	2022학년도	09 학평	23번	인간 진화를 위한 소속감의 유용성	62	★★☆
2	2022학년도	06 학평	23번	아이들이 수학적인 이해를 구축하는 방법	82	★★☆
3	2022학년도	03 학평	23번	삶에 광범위하게 영향을 미치는 기후에 대한 지식	67	★★☆
4	2021학년도	11 학평	23번	훈련을 통해 두뇌를 행복하게 할 수 있음	78	★★☆
5	2021학년도	09 학평	23번	젊은이들이 채식을 선호하는 이유	79	★★☆
6	2021학년도	06 학평	23번	호기심의 장점	64	★★☆
7	2021학년도	03 학평	23번	대화 중 거짓말을 하는 사람은 시간의 지연을 보임	70	★★☆
8	2020학년도	11 학평	23번	재생 가능한 에너지원의 부작용	78	★★☆
9	2020학년도	09 학평	23번	아이들 발달에서 놀이의 역할	64	★★☆
10	2020학년도	03 학평	23번	소비자에게 촉감의 중요성	84	★★☆

1등급 꿀팁

1. 글의 일부만을 보여주는 선택지보다는 글 전체의 중심 내용을 포괄하는 선택지를 고른다.
2. 주로 주제문은 지문의 처음이나 끝 부분에 제시되지만, 글 전체에 대한 추론적 이해 여부를 묻기 위해 명시적으로 드러나지 않을 수도 있다.
3. 역접 연결어가 나오는 문장에 중심 내용이 담겨 있는 경우가 많다.
4. 지문을 읽을 때 글쓴이가 전달하고자 하는 내용을 영어로 한 문장으로 써 본다.

제한 시간 : 15분 | 정답 및 해설 028쪽

대표 기출

2022학년도 11월 학평 23번

23. 다음 글의 주제로 가장 적절한 것은?

The most remarkable and unbelievable consequence of melting ice and rising seas is that together they are a kind of time machine, so real that they are altering the duration of our day. It works like this: As the glaciers melt and the seas rise, gravity forces more water toward the equator. This changes the shape of the Earth ever so slightly, making it fatter around the middle, which in turns slows the rotation of the planet similarly to the way a ballet dancer slows her spin by spreading out her arms. The slowdown isn't much, just a few thousandths of a second each year, but like the barely noticeable jump of rising seas every year, it adds up. When dinosaurs lived on the Earth, a day lasted only about twenty-three hours.

① cause of rising temperatures on the Earth
② principles of planets maintaining their shapes
③ implications of melting ice on marine biodiversity
④ way to keep track of time without using any device
⑤ impact of melting ice and rising seas on the length of a day

1. 글에서 반복적으로 제시된 핵심 개념을 파악한다.

- consequence of melting ice and rising seas(녹는 얼음과 상승하는 바다의 결과), altering the duration of our day(하루의 기간을 바꿈)

2. 핵심 개념에 대해 필자가 제시하는 견해를 찾는다.

① As the glaciers melt and the seas rise, gravity forces more water toward the equator. (빙하가 녹고 바다가 높아지면서 중력이 적도를 향해 더 많은 물을 밀어 넣는다.)
② This changes the shape of the Earth ever so slightly, making it fatter around the middle, which in turns slows the rotation of the planet~. (이것은 지구의 모양을 아주 약간 변화시켜 가운데 주변으로 그것을 더 불룩하게 만들고, 이는 결과적으로 행성의 회전을 늦춘다.)
③ The slowdown isn't much, just a few thousandths of a second each year, but like the barely noticeable jump of rising seas every year, it adds up. (이 감속이 매년 단지 몇천 분의 1초로 크지 않지만, 해마다 상승하는 바다의 알아차리기 힘든 증가처럼, 그것은 쌓인다.)
④ When dinosaurs lived on the Earth, a day lasted only about twenty-three hours. (공룡들이 지구에 살았을 때, 하루는 약 23시간만 지속되었다.)

3. 핵심 개념과 필자의 견해를 고려하여 글의 주제를 추론한다.

- 녹는 얼음과 상승하는 바다가 합쳐져서 우리 하루의 기간을 바꾸고 있다는 내용의 글이므로, 글의 주제로 ⑤ 'impact of melting ice and rising seas on the length of a day(녹는 얼음과 상승하는 바다가 하루의 길이에 미치는 영향)'가 가장 적절하다.

2022학년도 9월 학평 23번 ★★☆

1. 다음 글의 주제로 가장 적절한 것은?

For creatures like us, evolution smiled upon those with a strong need to belong. Survival and reproduction are the criteria of success by natural selection, and forming relationships with other people can be useful for both survival and reproduction. Groups can share resources, care for sick members, scare off predators, fight together against enemies, divide tasks so as to improve efficiency, and contribute to survival in many other ways. In particular, if an individual and a group want the same resource, the group will generally prevail, so competition for resources would especially favor a need to belong. Belongingness will likewise promote reproduction, such as by bringing potential mates into contact with each other, and in particular by keeping parents together to care for their children, who are much more likely to survive if they have more than one caregiver.

① skills for the weak to survive modern life
② usefulness of belonging for human evolution
③ ways to avoid competition among social groups
④ roles of social relationships in children's education
⑤ differences between two major evolutionary theories

2022학년도 6월 학평 23번 ★★☆

2. 다음 글의 주제로 가장 적절한 것은?

Every day, children explore and construct relationships among objects. Frequently, these relationships focus on how much or how many of something exists. Thus, children count — "One cookie, two shoes, three candles on the birthday cake, four children in the sandbox." Children compare — "Which has more? Which has fewer? Will there be enough?" Children calculate — "How many will fit? Now, I have five. I need one more." In all of these instances, children are developing a notion of quantity. Children reveal and investigate mathematical concepts through their own activities or experiences, such as figuring out how many crackers to take at snack time or sorting shells into piles.

① difficulties of children in learning how to count
② how children build mathematical understanding
③ why fingers are used in counting objects
④ importance of early childhood education
⑤ advantages of singing number songs

2022학년도 3월 학평 23번 ★★☆

3. 다음 글의 주제로 가장 적절한 것은? [3점]

The whole of human society operates on knowing the future weather. For example, farmers in India know when the monsoon rains will come next year and so they know when to plant the crops. Farmers in Indonesia know there are two monsoon rains each year, so next year they can have two harvests. This is based on their knowledge of the past, as the monsoons have always come at about the same time each year in living memory. But the need to predict goes deeper than this; it influences every part of our lives. Our houses, roads, railways, airports, offices, and so on are all designed for the local climate. For example, in England all the houses have central heating, as the outside temperature is usually below 20°C, but no air-conditioning, as temperatures rarely go beyond 26°C, while in Australia the opposite is true: most houses have air-conditioning but rarely central heating.

① new technologies dealing with climate change
② difficulties in predicting the weather correctly
③ weather patterns influenced by rising temperatures
④ knowledge of the climate widely affecting our lives
⑤ traditional wisdom helping our survival in harsh climates

2021학년도 11월 학평 23번 ★★☆

4. 다음 글의 주제로 가장 적절한 것은?

We used to think that the brain never changed, but according to the neuroscientist Richard Davidson, we now know that this is not true — specific brain circuits grow stronger through regular practice. He explains, "Well-being is fundamentally no different than learning to play the cello. If one practices the skills of well-being, one will get better at it." What this means is that you can actually train your brain to become more grateful, relaxed, or confident, by repeating experiences that evoke gratitude, relaxation, or confidence. Your brain is shaped by the thoughts you repeat. The more neurons fire as they are activated by repeated thoughts and activities, the faster they develop into neural pathways, which cause lasting changes in the brain. Or in the words of Donald Hebb, "Neurons that fire together wire together." This is such an encouraging premise: bottom line — we can intentionally create the habits for the brain to be happier.

* evoke: (감정을) 불러일으키다 ** premise: 전제

① possibility of forming brain habits for well-being
② role of brain circuits in improving body movements
③ importance of practice in playing musical instruments
④ effect of taking a break on enhancing memory capacity
⑤ difficulty of discovering how neurons in the brain work

2021학년도 9월 학평 23번 ★★☆

5. 다음 글의 주제로 가장 적절한 것은?

Vegetarian eating is moving into the mainstream as more and more young adults say no to meat, poultry, and fish. According to the American Dietetic Association, "approximately planned vegetarian diets are healthful, are nutritionally adequate, and provide health benefits in the prevention and treatment of certain diseases." But health concerns are not the only reason that young adults give for changing their diets. Some make the choice out of concern for animal rights. When faced with the statistics that show the majority of animals raised as food live in confinement, many teens give up meat to protest those conditions. Others turn to vegetarianism to support the environment. Meat production uses vast amounts of water, land, grain, and energy and creates problems with animal waste and resulting pollution.

* poultry: 가금류(닭·오리·거위 등)

① reasons why young people go for vegetarian diets
② ways to build healthy eating habits for teenagers
③ vegetables that help lower your risk of cancer
④ importance of maintaining a balanced diet
⑤ disadvantages of plant-based diets

2021학년도 6월 학평 23번 ★★☆

6. 다음 글의 주제로 가장 적절한 것은?

Curiosity makes us much more likely to view a tough problem as an interesting challenge to take on. A stressful meeting with our boss becomes an opportunity to learn. A nervous first date becomes an exciting night out with a new person. A colander becomes a hat. In general, curiosity motivates us to view stressful situations as challenges rather than threats, to talk about difficulties more openly, and to try new approaches to solving problems. In fact, curiosity is associated with a less defensive reaction to stress and, as a result, less aggression when we respond to irritation.

* colander: (음식 재료의 물을 빼는 데 쓰는) 체

① importance of defensive reactions in a tough situation
② curiosity as the hidden force of positive reframes
③ difficulties of coping with stress at work
④ potential threats caused by curiosity
⑤ factors that reduce human curiosity

Day 06

2021학년도 3월 학평 23번 ★★☆

7. 다음 글의 주제로 가장 적절한 것은?

When two people are involved in an honest and open conversation, there is a back and forth flow of information. It is a smooth exchange. Since each one is drawing on their past personal experiences, the pace of the exchange is as fast as memory. When one person lies, their responses will come more slowly because the brain needs more time to process the details of a new invention than to recall stored facts. As they say, "Timing is everything." You will notice the time lag when you are having a conversation with someone who is making things up as they go. Don't forget that the other person may be reading your body language as well, and if you seem to be disbelieving their story, they will have to pause to process that information, too.

* lag: 지연

① delayed responses as a sign of lying
② ways listeners encourage the speaker
③ difficulties in finding useful information
④ necessity of white lies in social settings
⑤ shared experiences as conversation topics

2020학년도 11월 학평 23번 ★★☆

8. 다음 글의 주제로 가장 적절한 것은?

The use of renewable sources of energy to produce electricity has increasingly been encouraged as a way to harmonize the need to secure electricity supply with environmental protection objectives. But the use of renewable sources also comes with its own consequences, which require consideration. Renewable sources of energy include a variety of sources such as hydropower and ocean-based technologies. Additionally, solar, wind, geothermal and biomass renewable sources also have their own impact on the environment. Hydropower dams, for example, have an impact on aquatic ecosystems and, more recently, have been identified as significant sources of greenhouse emissions. Wind, solar, and biomass also cause negative environmental impacts, such as visual pollution, intensive land occupation and negative effects on bird populations.

* geothermal: 지열의 ** biomass: 에너지로 사용 가능한 생물체

① environmental side effects of using renewable energy sources
② practical methods to meet increasing demand for electricity
③ negative impacts of the use of traditional energy sources
④ numerous ways to obtain renewable sources of energy
⑤ effective procedures to reduce greenhouse emissions

2020학년도 9월 학평 23번 ★★☆

9. 다음 글의 주제로 가장 적절한 것은?

Animals as well as humans engage in play activities. In animals, play has long been seen as a way of learning and practicing skills and behaviors that are necessary for future survival. In children, too, play has important functions during development. From its earliest beginnings in infancy, play is a way in which children learn about the world and their place in it. Children's play serves as a training ground for developing physical abilities — skills like walking, running, and jumping that are necessary for everyday living. Play also allows children to try out and learn social behaviors and to acquire values and personality traits that will be important in adulthood. For example, they learn how to compete and cooperate with others, how to lead and follow, how to make decisions, and so on.

① necessity of trying out creative ideas
② roles of play in children's development
③ contrasts between human and animal play
④ effects of children's physical abilities on play
⑤ children's needs at various developmental stages

2020학년도 3월 학평 23번 ★★☆

10. 다음 글의 주제로 가장 적절한 것은?

Although individual preferences vary, touch (both what we touch with our fingers and the way things feel as they come in contact with our skin) is an important aspect of many products. Consumers like some products because of their feel. Some consumers buy skin creams and baby products for their soothing effect on the skin. In fact, consumers who have a high need for touch tend to like products that provide this opportunity. When considering products with material properties, such as clothing or carpeting, consumers like goods they can touch in stores more than products they only see and read about online or in catalogs.

* property: 속성

① benefits of using online shopping malls
② touch as an important factor for consumers
③ importance of sharing information among consumers
④ necessity of getting feedback from consumers
⑤ popularity of products in the latest styles

총 문항				문항	맞은 문항					문항
개별 문항	1	2	3	4	5	6	7	8	9	10
채점										
개별 문항	11	12	13	14	15	16	17	18	19	20
채점										

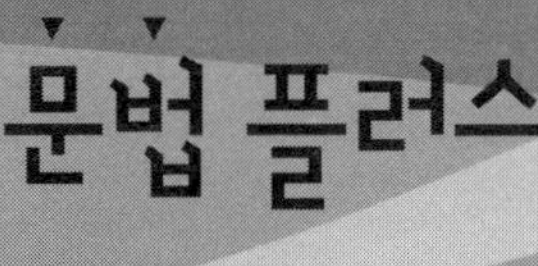

6. 조동사

정답 및 해설 033쪽

A 문법의 주요 포인트를 점검해 봅시다.

조동사는 본동사와 함께 쓰여 본동사의 의미를 보충해 주는 동사를 말한다. 조동사의 기본 원칙은 조동사 뒤에 본동사는 동사원형을 쓴다. 「조동사+have+p.p.」는 '과거에 대한 확신, 강한 부정, 유감, 추측' 등의 의미를 나타낸다. use to 구문과 「should have+p.p.」 구문이 시험에 자주 나오므로 특히 유의해야 한다.

■ 「be used to+동사원형」	~하는 데 사용되다	■ 「be[get] used to+-ing」	~하는 데 익숙하다
■ must have p.p.	~했음에 틀림없다	■ cannot have p.p.	~했을 리가 없다
■ should[ought to] have p.p.	~했어야 했는데 (하지 않았다)	■ shouldn't have p.p.	~하지 않았어야 했는데 (했다)
■ may[might] have p.p.	~했을지도 모른다	■ need not have p.p.	~할 필요가 없었는데
■ 「had better+동사원형」	~하는 편이 좋다	■ 「had better not+동사원형」	~하지 않는 편이 좋다
■ 「cannot (help) but+동사원형」	~하지 않을 수 없다	■ cannot help ~ing	~하지 않을 수 없다
■ would rather A than B	B 하느니 차라리 A하겠다	■ cannot ... too ~	아무리 ~해도 지나치지 않다
■ 「used to+동사원형」	과거의 규칙적 동작(~하곤 했다. 지금은 그렇지 않다) / 과거의 상태 (~이 있었다)		

B 밑줄 친 부분에 유의하여 다음 문장을 해석해 보시오.

1 We often hear stories of ordinary people who, if education had focused on creativity, could have become great artists or scientists.

2 Those victims of education should have received training to develop creative talents while in school.

3 We might have heard that many people suffer from dry skin as the weather gets colder.

4 Imagine the loss of self-esteem that manager must have felt.

5 I shouldn't have accepted his proposal.

C 다음 괄호 안에서 어법상 올바른 것을 고르시오.

6 You don't look very well. You'd better not **[go / goes]** to work today.

7 Anybody will **[can / be able to]** create a delicious pie at home.

8 When I was a kid, there used to **[be / being]** a school over there.

9 I cannot help but **[like / liking]** him.

10 I would rather stay home than **[hang / hanging]** out with my friends.

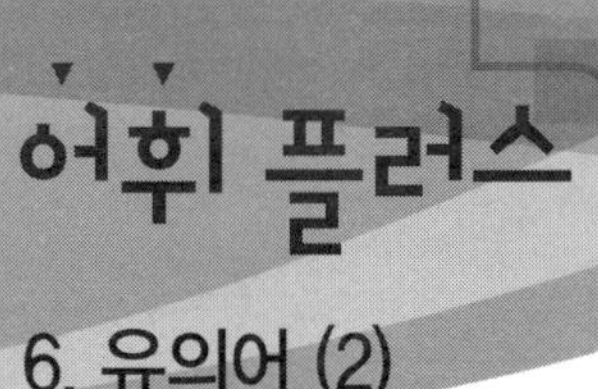

어휘 플러스

6. 유의어 (2)

정답 및 해설 033쪽

A 다음 수능 필수 어휘를 읽고, 아는 것은 체크해 봅시다.

□ 01	comprehend	v. 이해하다(= understand)	□ 21	differ	v. 일치하지 않다(= disagree)
□ 02	confirm	v. 검증하다(= prove)	□ 22	diminish	v. 축소하다(= reduce)
□ 03	conflict	v. 충돌하다(= collide); n. 갈등	□ 23	disappoint	v. 실망시키다(= dismay)
□ 04	consequence	n. 결과(= result)	□ 24	disaster	n. 재해(= catastrophe)
□ 05	considerable	a. 상당한(= substantial)	□ 25	discover	v. 발견하다(= detect)
□ 06	contain	v. 포함하다(= include)	□ 26	discuss	v. 논의하다(= debate)
□ 07	contrary	a. 반대의(= opposite)	□ 27	distinguish	v. 구별하다(= differentiate)
□ 08	contribute	v. 기부하다(= donate)	□ 28	disturb	v. 방해하다(= interrupt)
□ 09	cooperate	v. 협동하다(= collaborate)	□ 29	diverse	a. 다양한(= various)
□ 10	correct	a. 정확한(= accurate)	□ 30	donate	v. 기증하다(= contribute)
□ 11	crop	n. 수확(량)(= yield)	□ 31	ease	v. 편하게 하다(= comfort)
□ 12	decide	v. 결심하다(= determine)	□ 32	effect	n. 영향(= impact, influence)
□ 13	decrease	v. 줄이다(= reduce)	□ 33	effort	n. 수고(= endeavor)
□ 14	defend	v. 방어하다(= protect)	□ 34	eliminate	v. 제거하다(= remove)
□ 15	deficient	a. 결핍한(= lacking)	□ 35	emit	v. 내뿜다(= release)
□ 16	deliberate	a. 의도적인(= intentional)	□ 36	emphasize	v. 강조하다(= stress)
□ 17	demand	v. 요구하다(= request, claim)	□ 37	endure	v. 견디다(= withstand)
□ 18	deny	v. 거절하다(= refuse)	□ 38	enhance	v. 증진시키다(= improve)
□ 19	describe	v. 기술하다(= depict)	□ 39	enormous	a. 거대한(= tremendous)
□ 20	desire	v. 바라다(= aspire)	□ 40	ensure	v. 보장하다(= guarantee)

B 괄호 안에서 문맥에 맞는 낱말로 적절한 것을 골라 봅시다.

1 Many of you may not know how to smooth things over with your family members after **[effort / conflict]**.

2 The crucial factor in the success of the suffragette movement was that its supporters were consistent in their views, and this created a **[considerable / deficient]** degree of social influence.

3 Sperm whales travel in social groups that **[cooperate / disturb]** to defend and protect each other, and may even share suckling of calves.

4 She plans on finding volunteer work to **[contribute / disappoint]** to the community while getting teaching experience.

5 Identifying what we can do in the workplace serves to **[eliminate / enhance]** the quality of our professional career.

글의 제목

출제 트렌드

1. 제목 찾기는 글을 읽고 필자가 전달하고자 하는 중심 내용을 파악할 수 있는지 글에 대한 종합적 이해 능력을 측정하는 문제이다. 고1 학력 평가에서 1문항이 출제된다. 다양한 글감에서 출제되며, 선택지가 영어로 제시된다.
2. 중심 내용을 파악하기 위해서는 글을 읽고 전체적인 내용을 이해하고, 추론하는 능력이 필요하다. 중심 내용 파악하기 읽기 유형에는 요지, 주제, 제목 파악하기 문제가 있다.
3. 최근 수능 7년간, 글의 제목 문제는 2017학년도 2문제, 2018학년도 이후 매년 1문제가 출제되었다. 2017학년도 수능 22번(80%), 23번(75%), 2018(71%), 2019(68%), 2020(69%), 2021(54%), 2022(52%), 2023(78%)에서 괄호 안의 정답률을 보였다. 7년간 평균 68.3% 정도 정답률을 보였다. 난이도는 중 단계이다. 이 문제 유형은 2022학년도 수능이 다른 해에 비해 상대적으로 어렵게 출제되었다. 제목 문제도 계속 어렵게 출제될 수 있어, 주의가 필요하다.
4. 글의 중심 내용을 물어보는 -글의 요지, 주제, 제목 문제의 정답률을 비교하면 요지(85%) 〉 주제(68.6%) 〉 제목(68.3%) 순서였다. 요지 문제보다 제목, 주제 문제가 상대적으로 어려운 것을 알 수 있다.

	출처		문항 번호	지문 주제	정답률(%)	난이도
대표	2022학년도	11 학평	24번	옳은 것이 새로운 가능성을 막을 수 있다	57	★★★
1	2022학년도	09 학평	24번	더 많은 용기가 더 많은 기회를 가져온다	69	★★☆
2	2022학년도	06 학평	24번	알고리즘 세대	80	★★☆
3	2022학년도	03 학평	24번	감정에 자세한 이름을 붙이는 것은 이롭다	66	★★☆
4	2021학년도	11 학평	24번	현대 사회와 정체성 확립	61	★★☆
5	2021학년도	09 학평	24번	시련과 갈등에서 창의성이 나온다	56	★★★
6	2021학년도	06 학평	24번	엘리베이터는 고층 빌딩을 가능하게 한다	76	★★☆
7	2021학년도	03 학평	24번	구매 후 사용하지 않는 물건은 낭비이다	79	★★☆
8	2020학년도	11 학평	24번	씹기는 포유류가 생존하는 것을 돕는다	78	★★☆
9	2020학년도	09 학평	24번	억지 미소도 스트레스 해소에 도움이 됨	66	★★☆
10	2020학년도	06 학평	24번	지나침이 없는 교육의 양	75	★★☆

1등급 꿀팁

1. 주제 추론 유형보다 내용을 좀 더 종합적으로 파악한다.
2. 보통 제목은 주제를 압축해 표현하거나 비유적, 상징적인 어구로 나타낸다.
3. 반복되는 어구, 역접이나 결과, 요약 연결어 다음에 나오는 내용에 유의한다.
4. 선택지로 제시된 제목이 너무 지엽적이거나 너무 포괄적인 경우 답안에서 배제한다.

글의 제목

제한 시간 : 15분 | 정답 및 해설 034쪽

대표기출

2022학년도 11월 학평 24번

24. 다음 글의 제목으로 가장 적절한 것은?

Have you ever brought up an idea or suggestion to someone and heard them immediately say "No, that won't work."? You may have thought, "He/she didn't even give it a chance. How do they know it won't work?" When you are right about something, you close off the possibility of another viewpoint or opportunity. Being right about something means that "it is the way it is, period." You may be correct. Your particular way of seeing it may be true with the facts. However, considering the other option or the other person's point of view can be beneficial. If you see their side, you will see something new or, at worse, learn something about how the other person looks at life. Why would you think everyone sees and experiences life the way you do? Besides how boring that would be, it would eliminate all new opportunities, ideas, invention, and creativity.

① The Value of Being Honest
② Filter Out Negative Points of View
③ Keeping Your Word: A Road to Success
④ Being Right Can Block New Possibilities
⑤ Look Back When Everyone Looks Forward

문제 풀이

1. 글에서 반복적으로 나오는 어구 또는 특정 개념과 관련된 어구를 통해 글의 내용을 추측한다.

• 반복적인 어구: Being right about something(무언가에 대해 옳다는 것), Your particular way of seeing(자신의 특별한 보는 방식) possibility of another viewpoint or opportunity(다른 관점이나 기회의 가능성), the other person's point of view(다른 사람의 관점), their side(그들의 관점)

2. 특정 개념에 대해 필자가 제시하는 견해를 찾는다.

① When you are right about something, you close off the possibility of another viewpoint or opportunity. (여러분이 무언가에 대해 옳다면, 여러분은 다른 관점이나 기회의 가능성을 닫아 버린다.)
② Your particular way of seeing it may be true with the facts. (여러분이 그것을 보는 특정한 방법이 사실에 부합할 수도 있다.)
③ However, considering the other option or the other person's point of view can be beneficial. (하지만 다른 선택지나 다른 사람의 관점을 고려하는 것은 도움이 될 수 있다.)
④ Why would you think everyone sees and experinces life the way you do? Besides how boring that would be, it would eliminate all new opportunities, ideas, invention, and creativity. (왜 모두가 여러분이 하는 방식대로 삶을 보거나 경험할 것이라고 생각하는가? 그것이 얼마나 지루할지는 제외하더라도, 그것은 모든 새로운 기회, 아이디어, 발명, 그리고 창의성을 없앨 것이다.)

3. 선택지를 살펴보고 글의 요지를 정확하게 담고 있는 제목을 선택한다.

• 무언가에 대해 옳다고 여기는 것은 다른 관점이나 기회의 가능성을 닫을 수 있고 다른 사람의 관점을 고려하는 것이 오히려 도움이 될 수 있다는 내용이므로, 글의 제목으로 ④ 'Being Right Can Block New Possibilities(옳은 것이 새로운 가능성을 막을 수 있다)'가 가장 적절하다.

2022학년도 11월 학평 24번 ★★★

1. 다음 글의 제목으로 가장 적절한 것은?

Many people make a mistake of only operating along the safe zones, and in the process they miss the opportunity to achieve greater things. They do so because of a fear of the unknown and a fear of treading the unknown paths of life. Those that are brave enough to take those roads less travelled are able to get great returns and derive major satisfaction out of their courageous moves. Being overcautious will mean that you will miss attaining the greatest levels of your potential. You must learn to take those chances that many people around you will not take, because your success will flow from those bold decisions that you will take along the way.

* tread: 밟다

① More Courage Brings More Opportunities
② Travel: The Best Way to Make Friends
③ How to Turn Mistakes into Success
④ Satisfying Life? Share with Others
⑤ Why Is Overcoming Fear So Hard?

2022학년도 9월 학평 24번 ★★☆

2. 다음 글의 제목으로 가장 적절한 것은?

Only a generation or two ago, mentioning the word *algorithms* would have drawn a blank from most people. Today, algorithms appear in every part of civilization. They are connected to everyday life. They're not just in your cell phone or your laptop but in your car, your house, your appliances, and your toys. Your bank is a huge web of algorithms, with humans turning the switches here and there. Algorithms schedule flights and then fly the airplanes. Algorithms run factories, trade goods, and keep records. If every algorithm suddenly stopped working, it would be the end of the world as we know it.

① We Live in an Age of Algorithms
② Mysteries of Ancient Civilizations
③ Dangers of Online Banking Algorithms
④ How Algorithms Decrease Human Creativity
⑤ Transportation: A Driving Force of Industry

2022학년도 3월 학평 24번 ★★☆

3. 다음 글의 제목으로 가장 적절한 것은?

Our ability to accurately recognize and label emotions is often referred to as *emotional granularity*. In the words of Harvard psychologist Susan David, "Learning to label emotions with a more nuanced vocabulary can be absolutely transformative." David explains that if we don't have a rich emotional vocabulary, it is difficult to communicate our needs and to get the support that we need from others. But those who are able to distinguish between a range of various emotions "do much, much better at managing the ups and downs of ordinary existence than those who see everything in black and white." In fact, research shows that the process of labeling emotional experience is related to greater emotion regulation and psychosocial well-being.

* nuanced: 미묘한 차이가 있는

① True Friendship Endures Emotional Arguments
② Detailed Labeling of Emotions Is Beneficial
③ Labeling Emotions: Easier Said Than Done
④ Categorize and Label Tasks for Efficiency
⑤ Be Brave and Communicate Your Needs

2021학년도 11월 학평 24번 ★★☆

4. 다음 글의 제목으로 가장 적절한 것은?

In modern times, society became more dynamic. Social mobility increased, and people began to exercise a higher degree of choice regarding, for instance, their profession, their marriage, or their religion. This posed a challenge to traditional roles in society. It was less evident that one needed to commit to the roles one was born into when alternatives could be realized. Increasing control over one's life choices became not only possible but desired. Identity then became a problem. It was no longer almost ready-made at birth but something to be discovered. Traditional role identities prescribed by society began to appear as masks imposed on people whose real self was to be found somewhere underneath.

* impose: 부여하다

① What Makes Our Modern Society So Competitive?
② How Modern Society Drives Us to Discover Our Identities
③ Social Masks: A Means to Build Trustworthy Relationships
④ The More Social Roles We Have, the Less Choice We Have
⑤ Increasing Social Mobility Leads Us to a More Equal Society

2021학년도 9월 학평 24번 ★★★

5. 다음 글의 제목으로 가장 적절한 것은?

Diversity, challenge, and conflict help us maintain our imagination. Most people assume that conflict is bad and that being in one's "comfort zone" is good. That is not exactly true. Of course, we don't want to find ourselves without a job or medical insurance or in a fight with our partner, family, boss, or coworkers. One bad experience can be sufficient to last us a lifetime. But small disagreements with family and friends, trouble with technology or finances, or challenges at work and at home can help us think through our own capabilities. Problems that need solutions force us to use our brains in order to develop creative answers. Navigating landscapes that are varied, that offer trials and occasional conflicts, is more helpful to creativity than hanging out in landscapes that pose no challenge to our senses and our minds. Our two million-year history is packed with challenges and conflicts.

① Technology: A Lens to the Future
② Diversity: A Key to Social Unification
③ Simple Ways to Avoid Conflicts with Others
④ Creativity Doesn't Come from Playing It Safe
⑤ There Are No Challenges That Can't Be Overcome

2021학년도 6월 학평 24번 ★★☆

6. 다음 글의 제목으로 가장 적절한 것은?

When people think about the development of cities, rarely do they consider the critical role of vertical transportation. In fact, each day, more than 7 billion elevator journeys are taken in tall buildings all over the world. Efficient vertical transportation can expand our ability to build taller and taller skyscrapers. Antony Wood, a Professor of Architecture at the Illinois Institute of Technology, explains that advances in elevators over the past 20 years are probably the greatest advances we have seen in tall buildings. For example, elevators in the Jeddah Tower in Jeddah, Saudi Arabia, under construction, will reach a height record of 660m.

① Elevators Bring Buildings Closer to the Sky
② The Higher You Climb, the Better the View
③ How to Construct an Elevator Cheap and Fast
④ The Function of the Ancient and the Modern City
⑤ The Evolution of Architecture: Solutions for Overpopulation

2021학년도 3월 학평 24번 ★★☆

7. 다음 글의 제목으로 가장 적절한 것은?

Think, for a moment, about something you bought that you never ended up using. An item of clothing you never ended up wearing? A book you never read? Some piece of electronic equipment that never even made it out of the box? It is estimated that Australians alone spend on average $10.8 billion AUD (approximately $9.99 billion USD) every year on goods they do not use — more than the total government spending on universities and roads. That is an average of $1,250 AUD (approximately $1,156 USD) for each household. All the things we buy that then just sit there gathering dust are waste — a waste of money, a waste of time, and waste in the sense of pure rubbish. As the author Clive Hamilton observes, 'The difference between the stuff we buy and what we use is waste.'

① Spending Enables the Economy
② Money Management: Dos and Don'ts
③ Too Much Shopping: A Sign of Loneliness
④ 3R's of Waste: Reduce, Reuse, and Recycle
⑤ What You Buy Is Waste Unless You Use It

2020학년도 11월 학평 24번 ★★☆

8. 다음 글의 제목으로 가장 적절한 것은?

Chewing leads to smaller particles for swallowing, and more exposed surface area for digestive enzymes to act on. In other words, it means the extraction of more fuel and raw materials from a mouthful of food. This is especially important for mammals because they heat their bodies from within. Chewing gives mammals the energy needed to be active not only during the day but also the cool night, and to live in colder climates or places with changing temperatures. It allows them to sustain higher levels of activity and travel speeds to cover larger distances, avoid predators, capture prey, and make and care for their young. Mammals are able to live in an incredible variety of habitats, from Arctic tundra to Antarctic pack ice, deep open waters to high-altitude mountaintops, and rainforests to deserts, in no small measure because of their teeth.

* enzyme: 효소

① Chewing: A Way to Ease Indigestion
② Boost Your Energy by Chewing More!
③ How Chewing Helps Mammals Survive
④ Different Types and Functions of Teeth
⑤ A Harsh Climate Makes Mammals Stronger

2020학년도 6월 학평 24번 ★★☆

9. 다음 글의 제목으로 가장 적절한 것은?

Every event that causes you to smile makes you feel happy and produces feel-good chemicals in your brain. Force your face to smile even when you are stressed or feel unhappy. The facial muscular pattern produced by the smile is linked to all the "happy networks" in your brain and will in turn naturally calm you down and change your brain chemistry by releasing the same feel-good chemicals. Researchers studied the effects of a genuine and forced smile on individuals during a stressful event. The researchers had participants perform stressful tasks while not smiling, smiling, or holding chopsticks crossways in their mouths (to force the face to form a smile). The results of the study showed that smiling, forced or genuine, during stressful events reduced the intensity of the stress response in the body and lowered heart rate levels after recovering from the stress.

① Causes and Effects of Stressful Events
② Personal Signs and Patterns of Stress
③ How Body and Brain React to Stress
④ Stress: Necessary Evil for Happiness
⑤ Do Faked Smiles Also Help Reduce Stress?

2020학년도 3월 학평 24번 ★★☆

10. 다음 글의 제목으로 가장 적절한 것은?

In life, they say that too much of anything is not good for you. In fact, too much of certain things in life can kill you. For example, they say that water has no enemy, because water is essential to all life. But if you take in too much water, like one who is drowning, it could kill you. Education is the exception to this rule. You can never have too much education or knowledge. The reality is that most people will never have enough education in their lifetime. I am yet to find that one person who has been hurt in life by too much education. Rather, we see lots of casualties every day, worldwide, resulting from the lack of education. You must keep in mind that education is a long-term investment of time, money, and effort into humans.

* casualty: 피해자

① All Play and No Work Makes Jack a Smart Boy
② Too Much Education Won't Hurt You
③ Too Heads Are Worse than One
④ Don't Think Twice Before You Act
⑤ Learn from the Future, Not from the Past

총 문항				문항	맞은 문항					문항
개별 문항	1	2	3	4	5	6	7	8	9	10
채점										
개별 문항	11	12	13	14	15	16	17	18	19	20
채점										

문법 플러스

7. 수동태

정답 및 해설 039쪽

A 문법의 주요 포인트를 점검해 봅시다.

1. 능동태는 주어가 동작의 주체임을 나타내며 수동태는 주어가 동작의 영향을 받는 대상임을 나타낸다. 수동태를 만드는 기본 원칙은 능동태의 '목적어'를 찾아 수동태의 주어로 보내야 한다. 동사는 「be동사+과거분사」 형태로 바꿔야 한다. 이때 능동태의 시제가 현재이면, 수동태도 현재로 변형하며, 능동태의 시제가 과거이면, 수동태도 과거로 변형한다.

2. 수동태는 다양한 형태를 가지고 있다. 조동사의 수동태는 「조동사+be+p.p.」, 진행형의 수동태는 「be+being+p.p.」, 완료형의 수동태는 「have+been+p.p.」, 부정사의 수동태는 「to+be+p.p」, 동명사의 수동태는 「being+p.p.」 형태를 갖는다.

3. 지각동사나 사역동사가 들어 있는 문장을 수동태로 바꿀 경우, 목적격보어인 원형부정사는 to부정사로 바뀌진다.

4. 특히, 시험에 유의할 점은 자동사(appear, disappear)는 목적어가 없으므로 수동태로 쓸 수 없다는 점이다. 또한 타동사의 일부 동사(have, resemble)는 수동태로 쓸 수 없으니 유의해야 한다.

5. 한편, by 이외의 전치사를 쓰는 수동태를 유의한다.

▪ be surprised at	~에 깜짝 놀라다	▪ be interested in	~에 관심이 있다
▪ be covered with	~로 덮여 있다	▪ be composed of	~로 구성되다

B 다음 괄호 안에서 어법상 올바른 것을 고르시오.

1. A vague shape **[appeared / was appeared]** through the mist.

2. When we read a number, we **[are more influenced / influence more]** by the leftmost digit than by the rightmost, since that is the order in which we read, and process them.

3. One study revealed that students chose tasting notes appropriate for red wines, such as 'prune and chocolate', when they **[gave / were given]** white wine coloured with a red dye.

4. A great depth—it is dark and cold there—photography is the principal way of exploring a mysterious deep-sea world, 95 percent of which **[has never seen / has never been seen]** before.

5. Never before had these subjects **[considered / been considered]** appropriate for artists.

6. The owner will be center stage, with a group of others around him or her, soon **[to follow / to be followed]** by newly formed groups around those who obtained a sizable share, until all food has been distributed.

7. The door must not **[leave / be left]** open

8. The man was seen **[enter / to enter]** the room.

9. She **[said / is said]** to be rich.

10. I was surprised **[at / of]** the news of his death.

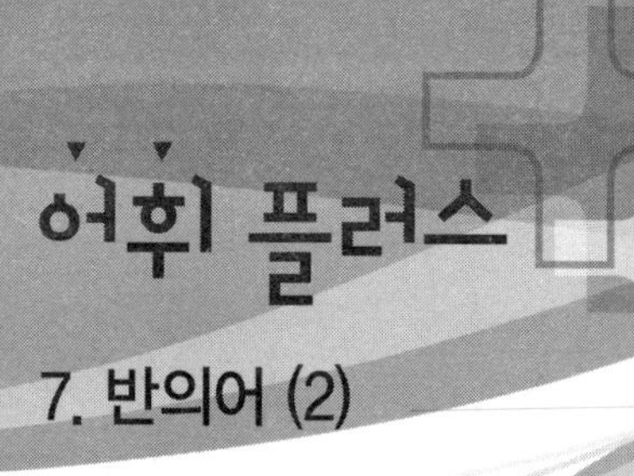

어휘 플러스

7. 반의어 (2)

정답 및 해설 039쪽

A 다음 수능 필수 어휘를 읽고, 아는 것은 체크해 봅시다.

□ 01	cause	v. ~의 원인이 되다	□ 21	result	v. 결과를 낳다
□ 02	compatible	a. 양립할 수 있는	□ 22	incompatible	a. 양립할 수 없는
□ 03	competent	a. 유능한, 능숙한	□ 23	incompetent	a. 무능한
□ 04	complete	a. 완전한, 완료된	□ 24	incomplete	a. 불완전한, 미완성의
□ 05	compulsory	a. 강제적인	□ 25	voluntary	a. 자발적인
□ 06	conceal	v. 감추다, 숨기다	□ 26	reveal	v. 드러내다 (= disclose)
□ 07	concrete	a. 구체적인	□ 27	abstract	a. 추상적인
□ 08	deficient	a. 결핍된	□ 28	sufficient	a. 충분한
□ 09	demand	n. 수요; v. 요구하다	□ 29	supply	n. 공급; v. 공급하다
□ 10	deny	v. 부정하다	□ 30	admit	v. 인정하다
□ 11	descend	v. 하강하다	□ 31	ascend	v. 상승하다
□ 12	desirable	a. 바람직한, 호감 가는	□ 32	undesirable	a. 바람직하지 않은
□ 13	diminish	v. 줄어들다, 축소하다	□ 33	increase	v. 증가하다
□ 14	direct	a. 직접적인	□ 34	indirect	a. 간접적인
□ 15	discourage	v. 낙담시키다	□ 35	encourage	v. 용기를 북돋다
□ 16	disprove	v. 틀렸음을 입증하다	□ 36	prove	v. 입증하다
□ 17	domestic	a. 국내의	□ 37	international	a. 국제적인
□ 18	drought	n. 가뭄	□ 38	flood	n. 홍수
□ 19	encourage	v. 격려하다	□ 39	discourage	v. 용기를 꺾다
□ 20	exclude	v. 제외하다, 배제하다	□ 40	include	v. 포함하다, ~을 포함시키다

B 괄호 안에서 문맥에 맞는 낱말로 적절한 것을 골라 봅시다.

1 Each year, only a few people are attacked by tigers or bears, and most of these incidents are **[discouraged / caused]** by the people themselves.

2 The most normal and **[competent / incompetent]** child encounters what seem like insurmountable problems in living.

3 In recent years, Colombia has not received much money from its exports. Its major export crop is coffee but the **[supply / demand]** for coffee in the world has dropped.

4 Naturally, people should be driven to "forget" **[desirable / undesirable]** events.

5 Feeling exhausted and **[encouraged / discouraged]**, she asked Grandma, "Why don't we just get rid of all the butterflies, so that there will be no more eggs or caterpillars?"

08 도표 정보 파악

출제 트렌드

1. 도표 정보 파악 문제는 제시된 정보와 선택지의 내용이 일치하는지 판단하는 능력을 측정한다. 고1 학력 평가에서 1문항이 출제된다.
2. 최근에는 도표가 복잡해지고 도표를 서술하는 정보도 어려워지고 있다. 도표 외에 표가 나오기도 한다.
3. 세부 내용을 파악하기 위해서는 글에 제시된 특정 정보를 사실적이고 정확하게 이해하는 능력이 필요하다. 세부 내용 파악하기 읽기 유형에는 도표 정보 파악, 내용 일치 · 불일치, 안내문 파악하기 문제가 있다.
4. 최근 수능 7년간, 도표 정보 파악 문제는 2017학년도 이후 매년 1문제가 출제되고 있다. 2017학년도 수능(94%), 2018(94%), 2019(91%), 2020(95%), 2021(93%), 2022(93%), 2023(94%)에서 괄호 안의 정답률을 보였다. 7년간 평균 93.4% 정도 정답률을 보였다. 난이도는 하 단계이다. 쉬운 문제이라고 방심하지 말고 실수하지 않도록 주의해야 한다.

	출처		문항 번호	지문 주제	정답률(%)	난이도
대표	2022학년도	11 학평	25번	고기를 덜먹거나 먹지 않는 이유에 관한 조사	83	★★☆
1	2022학년도	09 학평	25번	대륙별 도시 인구 점유율	87	★☆☆
2	2022학년도	06 학평	25번	반려동물을 보유한 미국 가정의 비율	90	★☆☆
3	2022학년도	03 학평	25번	온라인 강의와 온라인 학습 자료 이용 비율	72	★★☆
4	2021학년도	11 학평	25번	문화 활동에 참여하는 비율	78	★★☆
5	2021학년도	09 학평	25번	정보 출처들에 대한 소비자의 신뢰도	80	★★☆
6	2021학년도	06 학평	25번	건강 관련 지출 GDP 점유율	84	★★☆
7	2021학년도	03 학평	25번	교육용 디지털 콘텐츠 사용을 위한 기기 비율	83	★★☆
8	2020학년도	11 학평	25번	아이들의 스포츠 참여 평균 연령과 참여 기간	86	★☆☆
9	2020학년도	09 학평	25번	실내 냉방을 위한 에너지 사용	90	★☆☆
10	2020학년도	06 학평	25번	인터넷 접속 장치들의 중요도 조사	68	★★☆

1등급 꿀팁

1. 도표 상단의 제목과 가로축과 세로축의 정보를 보고 무엇에 관한 도표인지 파악한다.

2. 증감이나 비교를 나타내는 표현을 익혀 두어야 한다.

증가	rise, increase, go up, grow, soar
감소	fall, decrease, go down, drop, decline
비교	「배수사 + as + 원급 + as~」, 「배수사 + 비교급 + than ~」 (~보다 몇 배 …한)
비율	a rate of A to B (A와 B의 비율), more than A out of B (B중에서 A 이상)

3. 지문의 선택지에서 언급되는 것을 도표에서 찾아 맞는지 체크한다.

4. 다양한 도표(막대 그래프, 꺾은선 그래프, 파이 그래프)를 접해 보고 그 내용을 분석하는 연습을 해 본다.

Day 08

대표 기출

2022학년도 11월 학평 25번

25. 다음 도표의 내용과 일치하지 않는 것은?

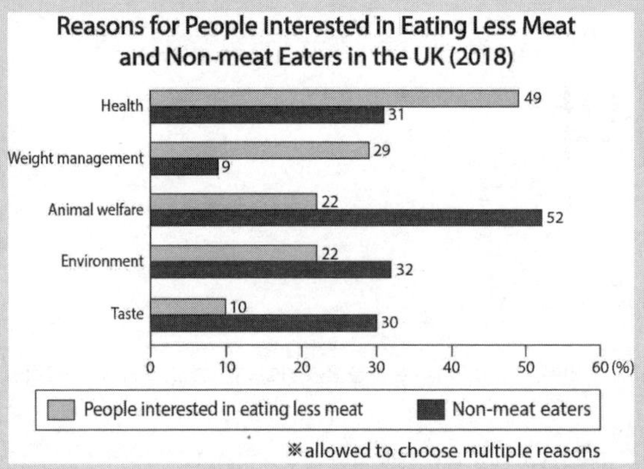

The graph above shows the survey results on reasons for people interested in eating less meat and those eating no meat in the UK in 2018. ① For the group of people who are interested in eating less meat, health is the strongest motivator for doing so. ② For the group of non-meat eaters, animal welfare accounts for the largest percentage among all reasons, followed by environment, health, and taste. ③ The largest percentage point difference between the two groups is in animal welfare, whereas the smallest difference is in environment. ④ The percentage of non-meat eaters citing taste is four times higher than that of people interested in reducing their meat consumption citing taste. ⑤ Weight management ranks the lowest for people who don't eat meat, with less than 10 percent.

문제 풀이

1. 도표 제목 및 가로축과 세로축 정보를 파악한다.

① 제목: Reasons for People Interested in Eateing Less Meat and Non-meat Eaters in the UK (2018) (2018년 영국의 고기를 덜먹거나 먹지 않는 데 관심이 있는 사람들에 대한 이유에 관한 조사)

② 가로축: 비율(%) / 세로축: 이유 (Heath 건강, Weight management 체중 관리, Animal welfare 동물 복지, Environment 환경, Taste 맛)

2. 글의 도입부를 통해 표 이해를 위한 개요를 파악한다.

① The graph above shows the survey results on reasons for people interested in eating less meat and those eating no meat in the UK in 2018. (위의 그래프는 고기를 덜 먹는 것에 관심 있는 사람들과 고기를 먹지 않는 사람들의 이유에 대한 2018년 영국에서의 조사 결과를 보여 준다.)

3. 도표와 선택지의 내용이 서로 일치하는지 확인한다.

④ The percentage of non-meat eaters citing taste is four times higher than that of people interested in reducing their meat consumption citing taste. (맛을 언급하는 고기를 먹지 않는 사람들의 비율은 맛을 언급하는 고기 섭취를 줄이는 데 관심이 있는 사람들의 비율보다 4배 높다. 체중 관리는 고기를 먹지 않는 사람들에게 10퍼센트 미만으로 가장 낮은 순위를 차지한다.)가 일치하지 않는다.

• 맛을 언급하는 고기를 먹지 않는 사람들의 비율은 10%이고, 맛을 언급하는 고기 섭취를 줄이는 데 관심 있는 사람들의 비율은 30%이므로 이는 세 배가 더 높은 비율이다. 따라서 정답은 ④번이다.

도표 정보 파악

제한 시간 : 15분 | 정답 및 해설 039쪽

2022학년도 9월 학평 25번 ★☆☆

1. 다음 도표의 내용과 일치하지 않는 것은?

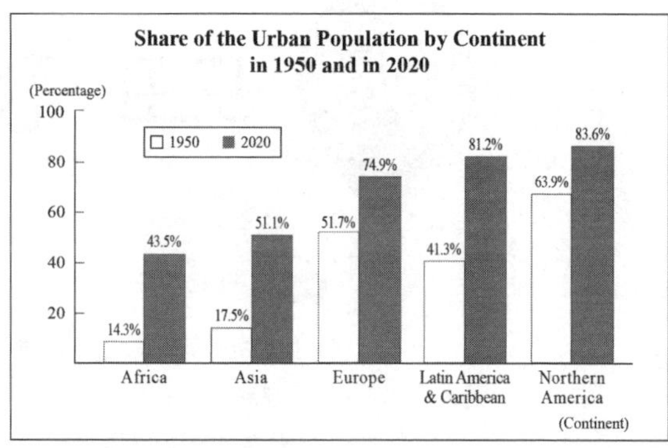

The graph above shows the share of the urban population by continent in 1950 and in 2020. ① For each continent, the share of the urban population in 2020 was larger than that in 1950. ② From 1950 to 2020, the share of the urban population in Africa increased from 14.3% to 43.5%. ③ The share of the urban population in Asia was the second lowest in 1950 but not in 2020. ④ In 1950, the share of the urban population in Europe was larger than that in Latin America and the Caribbean, whereas the reverse was true in 2020. ⑤ Among the five continents, Northern America was ranked in the first position for the share of the urban population in both 1950 and 2020.

2022학년도 6월 학평 25번 ★☆☆

2. 다음 도표의 내용과 일치하지 않는 것은?

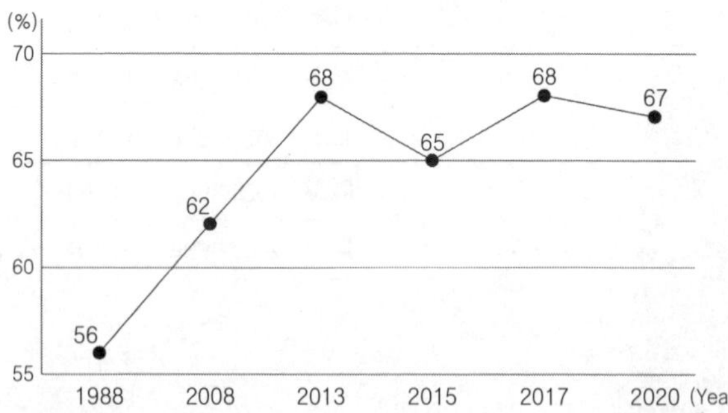

The graph above shows the percent of households with pets in the United States (U.S.) from 1988 to 2020. ① In 1988, more than half of U.S. households owned pets, and more than 6 out of 10 U.S. households owned pets from 2008 to 2020. ② In the period between 1988 and 2008, pet ownership increased among U.S. households by 6 percentage points. ③ From 2008 to 2013, pet ownership rose an additional 6 percentage points. ④ The percent of U.S. households with pets in 2013 was the same as that in 2017, which was 68 percent. ⑤ In 2015, the rate of U.S. households with pets was 3 percentage points lower than in 2020.

2022학년도 3월 학평 25번 ★★☆

3. 다음 도표의 내용과 일치하지 않는 것은?

Percentage of UK People
Who Used Online Course and Online Learning Material
(in 2020, by age group)

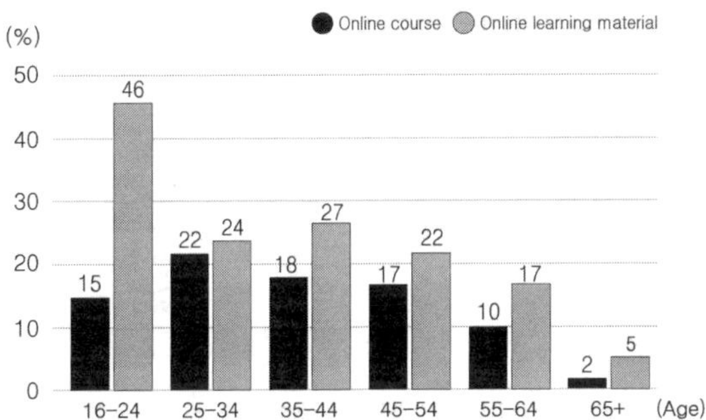

The above graph shows the percentage of people in the UK who used online courses and online learning materials, by age group in 2020. ① In each age group, the percentage of people who used online learning materials was higher than that of people who used online courses. ② The 25-34 age group had the highest percentage of people who used online courses in all the age groups. ③ Those aged 65 and older were the least likely to use online courses among the six age groups. ④ Among the six age groups, the gap between the percentage of people who used online courses and that of people who used online learning materials was the greatest in the 16-24 age group. ⑤ In each of the 35-44, 45-54, and 55-64 age groups, more than one in five people used online learning materials.

2021학년도 11월 학평 25번 ★★☆

4. 다음 도표의 내용과 일치하지 않는 것은?

Percentage of U.S. Students Participating in Cultural Activities (2016)

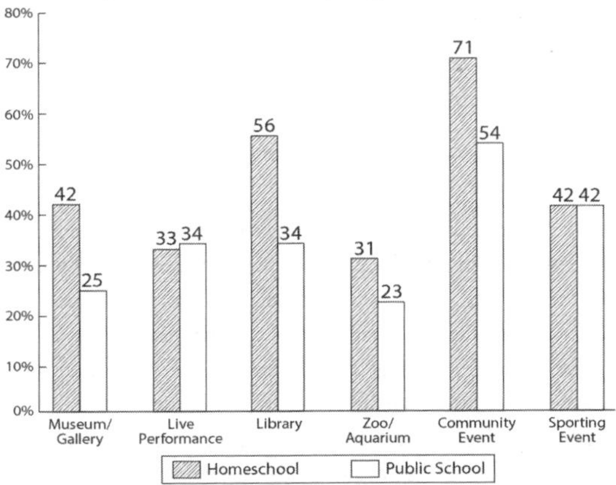

The graph above shows the percentage of U.S. homeschooled and public school students participating in cultural activities in 2016. ① With the exception of live performances and sporting events, the percentage of homeschooled students participating in cultural activities was higher than that of public school students. ② For each group of students, community events accounted for the largest percentage among all cultural activities. ③ The percentage point difference between homeschooled students and their public school peers was largest in visiting libraries. ④ The percentage of homeschooled students visiting museums or galleries was more than twice that of public school students. ⑤ Going to zoos or aquariums ranked the lowest for both groups of students, with 31 and 23 percent respectively.

2021학년도 9월 학평 25번 ★★☆

5. 다음 도표의 내용과 일치하지 않는 것은?

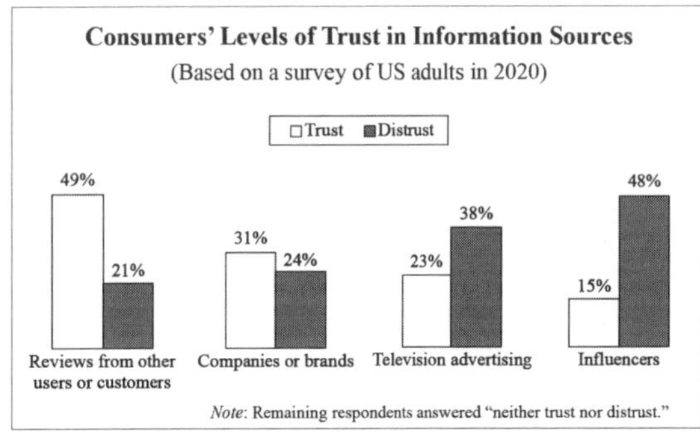

The graph above shows the consumers' levels of trust in four different types of information sources, based on a survey of US adults in 2020. ① About half of US adults say they trust the information they receive from reviews from other users or customers. ② This is more than double those who say they hold distrust for reviews from other users or customers. ③ The smallest gap between the levels of trust and distrust among the four different types of information sources is shown in the companies or brands' graph. ④ Fewer than one-fifth of adults say they trust information from television advertising, outweighed by the share who distrust such information. ⑤ Only 15% of adults say they trust the information provided by influencers, while more than three times as many adults say they distrust the same source of information.

2021학년도 6월 학평 25번 ★★☆

6. 다음 도표의 내용과 일치하지 않는 것은?

Health Spending as a Share of GDP for Selected OECD Countries (2018)

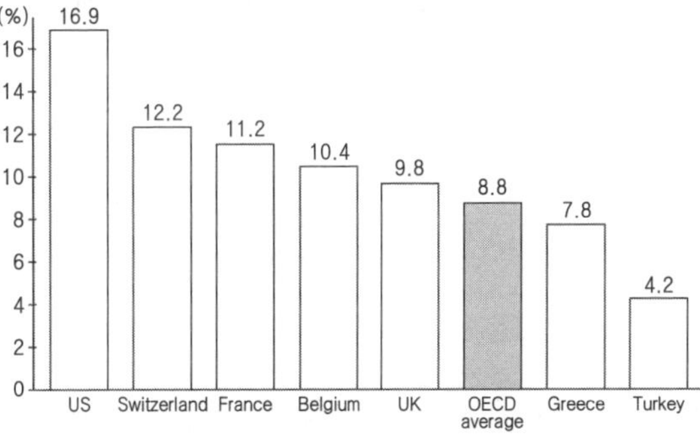

The above graph shows health spending as a share of GDP for selected OECD countries in 2018. ① On average, OECD countries were estimated to have spent 8.8 percent of their GDP on health care. ② Among the given countries above, the US had the highest share, with 16.9 percent, followed by Switzerland at 12.2 percent. ③ France spent more than 11 percent of its GDP, while Turkey spent less than 5 percent of its GDP on health care. ④ Belgium's health spending as a share of GDP sat between that of France and the UK. ⑤ There was a 3 percentage point difference in the share of GDP spent on health care between the UK and Greece.

2021학년도 3월 학평 25번 ★★☆

7. 다음 도표의 내용과 일치하지 않는 것은?

Devices Students Used to Access Digital Content

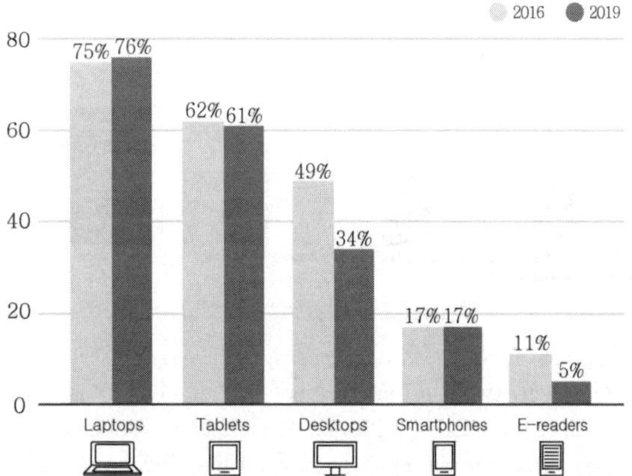

The above graph shows the percentage of students from kindergarten to 12th grade who used devices to access digital educational content in 2016 and in 2019. ① Laptops were the most used device for students to access digital content in both years. ② Both in 2016 and in 2019, more than 6 out of 10 students used tablets. ③ More than half the students used desktops to access digital content in 2016, and more than a third used desktops in 2019. ④ The percentage of smartphones in 2016 was the same as that in 2019. ⑤ E-readers ranked the lowest in both years, with 11 percent in 2016 and 5 percent in 2019.

2020학년도 11월 학평 25번 ★☆☆

8. 다음 표의 내용과 일치하지 않는 것은?

Age Children Quit Regularly Playing a Sport

Sport	Average Age of Last Regular Participation	Average Length in Years of Participation
Soccer	9.1	3.0
Ice Hockey	10.9	3.1
Tennis	10.9	1.9
Basketball	11.2	3.2
Field Hockey	11.4	5.1
Golf	11.8	2.8
Skateboarding	12.0	2.8
Track and Field	13.0	2.0

The above table shows the average age of last regular participation of children in a sport and the average length of participation based on a 2019 survey. ① Among the eight sports above, soccer was the only sport that children quit at an average age of younger than 10. ② Children quit playing ice hockey and tennis at the same age on average, but the average length of participation in tennis was shorter than that in ice hockey. ③ Basketball, field hockey, and golf were sports which children quit playing on average before they turned 12, but golf had the shortest average participation length among the three sports. ④ Skateboarding was a sport children quit at the average age of 12, and the average length of participation was the same as golf. ⑤ Meanwhile, children quit participating in track and field at the average age of 13, but the average length of participation was the shortest among the eight sports.

2020학년도 9월 학평 25번 ★☆☆

9. 다음 도표의 내용과 일치하지 않는 것은?

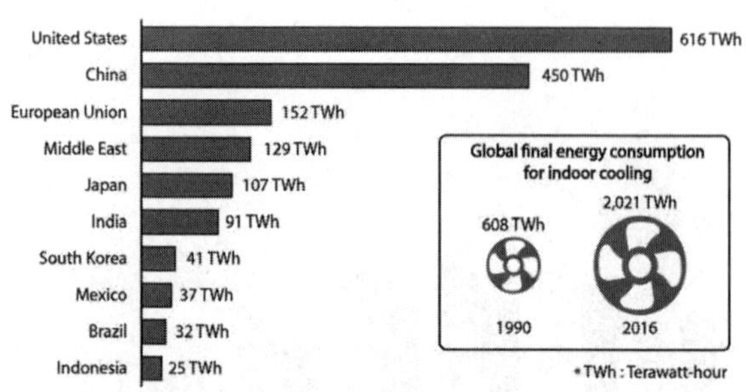

The graph above shows the final energy consumption for indoor cooling by country/region in 2016. ① The global final energy consumption for indoor cooling was over three times larger in 2016 than in 1990. ② It was the United States that had the largest final energy consumption, which amounted to 616 TWh. ③ The combined amount of the final energy consumption of the European Union, the Middle East, and Japan was less than the amount of China's final energy consumption. ④ The difference in amount between India's and South Korea's final energy consumption was more than 60 TWh. ⑤ Indonesia's final energy consumption was the smallest among the countries/regions above, totaling 25 TWh.

2020학년도 6월 학평 25번 ★★☆

10. 다음 도표의 내용과 일치하지 않는 것은?

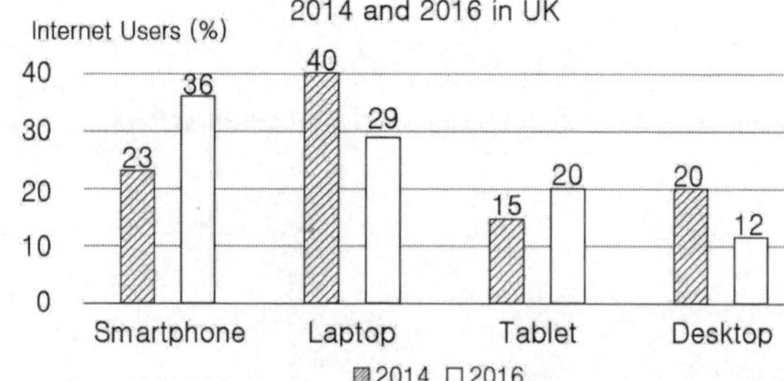

The above graph shows what devices British people considered the most important when connecting to the Internet in 2014 and 2016. ① More than a third of UK Internet users considered smartphones to be their most important device for accessing the Internet in 2016. ② In the same year, the smartphone overtook the laptop as the most important device for Internet access. ③ In 2014, UK Internet users were the least likely to select a tablet as their most important device for Internet access. ④ In contrast, they were the least likely to consider a desktop as their most important device for Internet access in 2016. ⑤ The proportion of UK Internet users who selected a desktop as their most important device for Internet access increased by half from 2014 to 2016.

* proportion: 비율

총 문항			문항	맞은 문항					문항
개별 문항	1	2	3	4	5	6	7	8	9	10
채점										
개별 문항	11	12	13	14	15	16	17	18	19	20
채점										

8. 가정법

정답 및 해설 043쪽

A 문법의 주요 포인트를 점검해 봅시다.

1 가정법의 기본 형태와 의미를 알아야 한다. 가정법 과거는 현재 사실과 반대되는 것을 가정한다. 가정법 과거완료는 과거의 사실과 반대되는 것을 가정한다. 혼합가정법은 과거의 일이 현재에 영향을 미칠 때 사용한다. 가정법 미래는 가능성이 희박하거나 불가능한 미래를 나타낼 때 사용한다.

종류	형태	의미
*가정법 과거	「If+주어+과거동사 ~ 주어+조동사 과거형+동사원형~」	만일 ~하면 ~할 것이다
*가정법 과거완료	「If+주어+had+과거분사 ~ 주어+조동사 과거형+have+과거분사~」	만일 ~했다면 ~했을 것이다
*혼합 가정법	「If+주어+had+과거분사 ~ 주어+조동사 과거형+동사원형~」	(과거에) 만일 ~했다면, (지금) ~할 것이다
*가정법 미래	「If+주어+should[were to]+동사원형, 주어+조동사+동사원형」	혹시라도 ~한다면; (그럴리가 없겠지만) 만약 ~한다면 …할 것이다

2 I wish~는 다음에 동사의 과거형이 오면 가정법 과거 (~하면 좋을 텐데)의 의미를 나타내고 「had+p.p.」가 오면 가정법 과거완료(~했으면 좋을 텐데)의 의미를 나타낸다. 또한 It's time that 뒤에는 가정법 과거 표현이 사용된다. '~할 때이다'는 의미이다. 「as if+가정법 과거」는 '마치 ~인 것처럼'의 의미를 나타내고, 「as if+가정법 과거완료」는 '마치 ~였던 것처럼'의 의미를 나타낸다.

3 가정법에서 「If+주어+동사」에서 If가 생략되면, 「동사+주어」로 도치된 문장이 된다.

4 전치사구, 명사구가 if절을 대신하여 가정의 의미를 지니는 경우도 있다.

5 주장(insist), 제안(suggest), 요구(demand), 명령(order)을 나타내는 동사에 이어지는 that절에서는 「주어+(should)+동사원형」을 쓴다. 단순한 사실을 전달할 때는 문장의 수와 시제에 맞추어 써야 한다. 수능에 출제된 적이 있으므로 유의해야 한다.

B 다음 괄호 안에서 어법상 올바른 것을 고르시오.

1 If you **[take / took]** the train, you would save time.

2 If you were at a social gathering in a large building and you overheard someone say that "the roof is on fire," what **[would be / would have been]** your reaction?

3 If he **[took / had taken]** actions in advance, he could have avoided the misfortune.

4 The clock hands were built to mimic the natural movements of the sun. If clocks **[were invented / had been invented]** in the southern hemisphere, Fried thinks, "clockwise" would be the opposite direction.

5 **[Without / With]** the formation and maintenance of social bonds, early human beings probably would not have been able to cope with or adapt to their physical environments.

6 Too many companies advertise their new products as if their competitors **[did not exist /had not existed]**.

7 **[It were / Were it]** not for music, our life you be as dry as a desert.

8 The growing number of foreigners is damaging the economy of the country. It is time that the government **[takes / took]** some measures.

9 She insisted that she **[saw / see]** the famous movie star last week.

10 If you **[turned / had turned]** a light toward Mars that day, it would have reached Mars in 186 seconds.

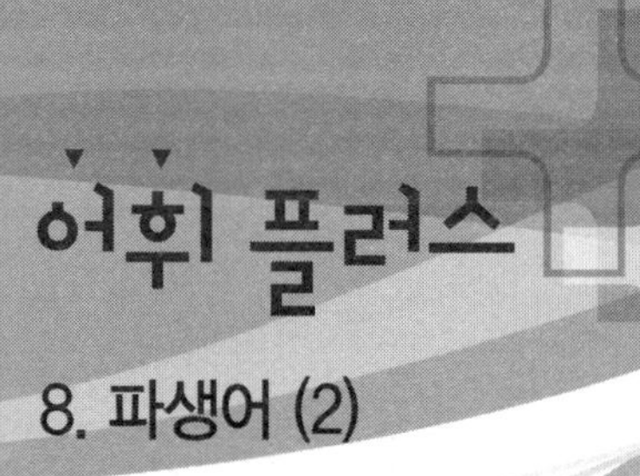

어휘 플러스

8. 파생어 (2)

정답 및 해설 043쪽

A 다음 수능 필수 어휘를 읽고, 아는 것은 체크해 봅시다.

□ 01	medical	a. 의학의, 의술의	□ 21	medicinal	a. 약용의, 약효 있는
□ 02	memorable	a. 기억할 만한	□ 22	memorial	a. 기념의, 추도의; n. 기념비
□ 03	momentary	a. 순간적인	□ 23	momentous	a. 중요한
□ 04	nomination	n. 지명, 추천, 임명	□ 24	nominee	n. 지명된 사람, 후보
□ 05	nutritious	a. 영양분이 많은	□ 25	nutritional	a. 영양(상)의
□ 06	object	n. 목표, 물체	□ 26	objection	n. 반대
□ 07	observation	n. 관찰	□ 27	observance	n. 준수
□ 08	organic	a. 유기체의	□ 28	organized	a. 조직적인
□ 09	practical	a. 실질적인, 실용적인	□ 29	practicable	a. 실천할 수 있는
□ 10	precedence	n. 우선함	□ 30	precedent	n. 선례 a. 앞서는
□ 11	produce	v. 생산하다; n. 농산물	□ 31	product	n. 제품
□ 12	respectful	a. 예의바른	□ 32	respective	a. 각각의
□ 13	sensational	a. 선풍적인	□ 33	sensationally	adv. 세상이 떠들썩하게
□ 14	sensitive	a. 민감한	□ 34	sensible	a. 지각 있는, 분별력 있는
□ 15	sensuous	a. 감각적인, 관능적인	□ 35	sensuously	adv. 감각적으로
□ 16	successful	a. 성공적인	□ 36	successive	a. 잇따른, 연속적인
□ 17	tolerant	a. 관대한, 잘 견디는	□ 37	tolerable	a. 참을 수 있는
□ 18	variable	a. 변하기 쉬운, 가변성의	□ 38	various	a. 다양한
□ 19	valuable	a. 소중한, 값비싼	□ 39	valueless	a. 무가치한
□ 20	visible	a. 알아볼 수 있는	□ 40	visual	a. 시각의, 눈으로 보는

B 괄호 안에서 문맥에 맞는 낱말로 적절한 것을 골라 봅시다.

1 An Egyptian sculpture no bigger than a person's hand is more monumental than that gigantic pile of stones that constitutes the war **[memorial / memorable]** in Leipzig, for instance.

2 A professor lectured for an hour on the dishonesty of certain dictionary editors who omitted a word from the dictionary because of moral **[objections / objects]**.

3 To solve a problem, you must look beyond how you feel and combine information that you already know with new **[observations / observance]**.

4 With his edible **[produce / product]** sculptures, Elffers hopes to share that joy.

5 Rarely is a computer more **[sensuous / sensitive]** and accurate than a human in managing the same geographical or environmental factors.

내용 일치·불일치

출제 트렌드

1. 글의 내용을 토대로 선택지가 글의 내용과 일치하는지 여부를 판단하는 능력을 측정하는 문제이다. 수능은 2문항씩 출제되다가 2014년 이후에는 매년 1문항이 출제되고 있다. 고1 학력 평가에서도 최근에는 1문항이 출제되고 있다.
2. 동 · 식물, 사물에 대한 설명문, 개인의 전기나 일화를 소재로 문제가 나온다.
3. 세부 내용을 파악하기 위해서는 글에 제시된 특정 정보를 사실적이고 정확하게 이해하는 능력이 필요하다. 세부 내용 파악하기 읽기 유형에는 도표 정보 파악, 내용 일치 · 불일치, 안내문(실용 자료 파악) 파악하기 문제가 있다.
4. 최근 수능 7년간, 내용 일치 · 불일치 문제는 2017학년도 이후 매년 1문제가 출제되고 있다. 2017학년도 수능(93%), 2018(95%), 2019(96%), 2020(94%), 2021(96%), 2022(97%), 2023(96%)에서 괄호 안의 정답률을 보였다. 7년간 평균 95.2% 정도 정답률을 보였다. 난이도는 하 단계이다.

	출처		문항 번호	지문 주제	정답률(%)	난이도
대표	2022학년도	11 학평	26번	Margaret Knight	90	★☆☆
1	2022학년도	09 학평	26번	Wilbur Smith	85	★☆☆
2	2022학년도	06 학평	26번	Claude Bolling	94	★☆☆
3	2022학년도	03 학평	26번	Antonie van Leeuwenhoek	92	★☆☆
4	2021학년도	11 학평	26번	Bessie Coleman	88	★☆☆
5	2021학년도	09 학평	26번	Paul Laurence Dunbar	70	★★☆
6	2021학년도	06 학평	26번	Lithops	65	★★☆
7	2021학년도	03 학평	26번	Elizabeth Catlett	91	★☆☆
8	2020학년도	11 학평	26번	Sarah Breedlove	83	★★☆
9	2020학년도	09 학평	26번	Jessie Redmon Fauset	84	★★☆
10	2020학년도	06 학평	26번	Sigrid Undset의 삶	87	★☆☆

1등급 꿀팁

1. 선택지를 미리 읽어보면 지문의 내용을 빨리 이해하는 데 도움이 된다.
2. 선택지 순서대로 관련된 내용을 지문에서 찾아 일치 여부를 판단한다.
3. 일반적인 상식이 아니라 글에서 언급된 정보를 토대로 일치 여부를 판단해야 한다.
4. 긍정과 부정의 표현을 바꿔 놓은 선택지에 주의해야 한다.

내용 일치·불일치

제한 시간 : 15분 | 정답 및 해설 044쪽

대표 기출

2022학년도 11월 학평 26번

26. Margaret Knight에 관한 다음 글의 내용과 일치하지 않는 것은?

Margaret Knight was an exceptionally prolific inventor in the late 19th century; journalists occasionally compared her to Thomas Edison by nicknaming her "a woman Edison." From a young age, she built toys for her older brothers. After her father died, Knight's family moved to Manchester. Knight left school in 1850, at age 12, to earn money for her family at a nearby textile factory, where she witnessed a fellow worker injured by faulty equipment. That led her to create her first invention, a safety device for textile equipment, but she never earned money from the invention. She also invented a machine that cut, folded and glued flat-bottomed paper bags and was awarded her first patent in 1871 for it. It eliminated the need for workers to assemble them slowly by hand. Knight received 27 patents in her lifetime and entered the National Inventors Hall of Fame in 2006.

* prolific: 다작(多作)의 ** patent: 특허

① 기자들이 '여자 Edison'이라는 별명을 지어 주었다.
② 가족을 위해 돈을 벌려고 학교를 그만두었다.
③ 직물 장비에 쓰이는 안전장치를 발명하여 많은 돈을 벌었다.
④ 밑이 평평한 종이 가방을 자르고 접고 붙이는 기계를 발명했다.
⑤ 2006년에 국립 발명가 명예의 전당에 입성했다.

문제 풀이

1. 글의 전반부에서 소재를 파악하고 무엇에 관한 정보인지 파악한다.

- Margaret Knight was an exceptionally prolific inventor in the late 19th century~ (Margaret Knight는 19세기 후반에 특출나게 다작한 발명가였다.)

2. 선택지의 핵심 정보를 확인하고 글의 내용을 예측한다.

① 기자들이 '여자 Edison'이라는 별명을 지어 주었다.
→ journalists occasionally compared her to Thomas Edison by nicknaming her "a woman Edison."

② 가족을 위해 돈을 벌려고 학교를 그만두었다.
→ Knight left school in 1850, at age 12, to earn money for her family ~.

④ 밑이 평평한 종이 가방을 자르고 접고 붙이는 기계를 발명했다.
→ She also invented a machine that cut, folded and glued flat-bottomed paper bags

⑤ 2006년에 국립 발명가 명예의 전당에 입성했다.
→ Knight received 27 patents in her lifetime and entered the National Inventors Hall of Fame in 2006.

3. 지문과 일치하지 않는 선택지를 찾는다.

- 'That led her to create her first invention, a safety device for textile equipment, but shenever earned money from the invention.'에서 직물 장비에 쓰이는 안전장치를 만들도록 이끌었지만 결코 그 발명품으로 돈을 벌지는 못했다고 했으므로, ③은 글의 내용과 일치하지 않는다

2022학년도 9월 학평 26번 ★☆☆

1. Wilbur Smith에 관한 다음 글의 내용과 일치하지 않는 것은?

Wilbur Smith was a South African novelist specialising in historical fiction. Smith wanted to become a journalist, writing about social conditions in South Africa, but his father was never supportive of his writing and forced him to get a real job. Smith studied further and became a tax accountant, but he finally turned back to his love of writing. He wrote his first novel, *The Gods First Make Mad*, and had received 20 rejections by 1962. In 1964, Smith published another novel, *When the Lion Feeds*, and it went on to be successful, selling around the world. A famous actor and film producer bought the film rights for *When the Lion Feeds*, although no movie resulted. By the time of his death in 2021 he had published 49 novels, selling more than 140 million copies worldwide.

① 역사 소설을 전문으로 하는 소설가였다.
② 아버지는 그가 글 쓰는 것을 지지하지 않았다.
③ 첫 번째 소설은 1962년까지 20번 거절당했다.
④ 소설 *When the Lion Feeds*는 영화화되었다.
⑤ 죽기 전까지 49편의 소설을 출간했다.

2022학년도 6월 학평 26번 ★☆☆

2. Claude Bolling에 관한 다음 글의 내용과 일치하지 않는 것은?

Pianist, composer, and big band leader, Claude Bolling, was born on April 10, 1930, in Cannes, France, but spent most of his life in Paris. He began studying classical music as a youth. He was introduced to the world of jazz by a schoolmate. Later, Bolling became interested in the music of Fats Waller, one of the most excellent jazz musicians. Bolling became famous as a teenager by winning the Best Piano Player prize at an amateur contest in France. He was also a successful film music composer, writing the music for more than one hundred films. In 1975, he collaborated with flutist Rampal and published *Suite for Flute and Jazz Piano Trio*, which he became most well-known for. He died in 2020, leaving two sons, David and Alexandre.

① 1930년에 프랑스에서 태어났다.
② 학교 친구를 통해 재즈를 소개받았다.
③ 20대에 Best Piano Player 상을 받았다.
④ 성공적인 영화 음악 작곡가였다.
⑤ 1975년에 플루트 연주자와 협업했다.

2022학년도 3월 학평 26번 ★☆☆

3. Antonie van Leeuwenhoek에 관한 다음 글의 내용과 일치하지 않는 것은?

Antonie van Leeuwenhoek was a scientist well known for his cell research. He was born in Delft, the Netherlands, on October 24, 1632. At the age of 16, he began to learn job skills in Amsterdam. At the age of 22, Leeuwenhoek returned to Delft. It wasn't easy for Leeuwenhoek to become a scientist. He knew only one language — Dutch — which was quite unusual for scientists of his time. But his curiosity was endless, and he worked hard. He had an important skill. He knew how to make things out of glass. This skill came in handy when he made lenses for his simple microscope. He saw tiny veins with blood flowing through them. He also saw living bacteria in pond water. He paid close attention to the things he saw and wrote down his observations. Since he couldn't draw well, he hired an artist to draw pictures of what he described.

* cell: 세포 ** vein: 혈관

① 세포 연구로 잘 알려진 과학자였다.
② 22살에 Delft로 돌아왔다.
③ 여러 개의 언어를 알았다.
④ 유리로 물건을 만드는 방법을 알고 있었다.
⑤ 화가를 고용하여 설명하는 것을 그리게 했다.

2021학년도 11월 학평 26번 ★☆☆

4. Bessie Coleman에 관한 다음 글의 내용과 일치하지 않는 것은?

Bessie Coleman was born in Texas in 1892. When she was eleven, she was told that the Wright brothers had flown their first plane. Since that moment, she dreamed about the day she would soar through the sky. At the age of 23, Coleman moved to Chicago, where she worked at a restaurant to save money for flying lessons. However, she had to travel to Paris to take flying lessons because American flight schools at the time admitted neither women nor Black people. In 1921, she finally became the first Black woman to earn an international pilot's license. She also studied flying acrobatics in Europe and made her first appearance in an airshow in New York in 1922. As a female pioneer of flight, she inspired the next generation to pursue their dreams of flying.

* flying acrobatics: 곡예 비행

① 11살 때 Wright 형제의 첫 비행 소식을 들었다.
② 비행 수업을 듣기 위해 파리로 가야 했다.
③ 국제 조종사 면허를 딴 최초의 흑인 여성이 되었다.
④ 유럽에서 에어쇼에 첫 출현을 했다.
⑤ 다음 세대가 비행의 꿈을 추구하도록 영감을 주었다.

2021학년도 9월 학평 26번 ★★☆

5. Paul Laurence Dunbar에 관한 다음 글의 내용과 일치하지 않는 것은?

Paul Laurence Dunbar, an African-American poet, was born on June 27, 1872. By the age of fourteen, Dunbar had poems published in the *Dayton Herald*. While in high school he edited his high school newspaper. Despite being a fine student, Dunbar was financially unable to attend college and took a job as an elevator operator. In 1893, Dunbar published his first book, *Oak and Ivy*, at his own expense. In 1895, he published the second book, *Majors and Minors*, which brought him national and international recognition. The poems written in standard English were called "majors," and those in dialect were termed "minors." Although the "major" poems in standard English outnumber those written in dialect, it was the dialect poems that brought Dunbar the most attention.

① 14세쯤에 *Dayton Herald*에 시를 발표했다.
② 고등학교 재학 시 학교 신문을 편집했다.
③ 재정상의 이유로 대학에 진학하지 못했다.
④ 두 번째 출판한 책으로 국내외에서 인정받게 되었다.
⑤ 표준 영어로 쓴 시들로 가장 큰 주목을 받았다.

2021학년도 6월 학평 26번 ★★☆

6. Lithops에 관한 다음 글의 내용과 일치하지 않는 것은?

Lithops are plants that are often called 'living stones' on account of their unique rock-like appearance. They are native to the deserts of South Africa but commonly sold in garden centers and nurseries. Lithops grow well in compacted, sandy soil with little water and extreme hot temperatures. Lithops are small plants, rarely getting more than an inch above the soil surface and usually with only two leaves. The thick leaves resemble the cleft in an animal's foot or just a pair of grayish brown stones gathered together. The plants have no true stem and much of the plant is underground. Their appearance has the effect of conserving moisture.

* cleft: 갈라진 틈

① 살아있는 돌로 불리는 식물이다.
② 원산지는 남아프리카 사막 지역이다.
③ 토양의 표면 위로 대개 1인치 이상 자란다.
④ 줄기가 없으며 땅속에 대부분 묻혀 있다.
⑤ 겉모양은 수분 보존 효과를 갖고 있다.

2021학년도 3월 학평 26번 ★★☆

7. Elizabeth Catlett에 관한 다음 글의 내용과 일치하지 않는 것은?

Elizabeth Catlett was born in Washington, D.C. in 1915. As a granddaughter of slaves, Catlett heard the stories of slaves from her grandmother. After being disallowed entrance from the Carnegie Institute of Technology because she was black, Catlett studied design and drawing at Howard University. She became one of the first three students to earn a master's degree in fine arts at the University of Iowa. Throughout her life, she created art representing the voices of people suffering from social injustice. She was recognized with many prizes and honors both in the United States and in Mexico. She spent over fifty years in Mexico, and she took Mexican citizenship in 1962. Catlett died in 2012 at her home in Mexico.

① 할머니로부터 노예 이야기를 들었다.
② Carnegie Institute of Technology로부터 입학을 거절당했다.
③ University of Iowa에서 석사 학위를 취득했다.
④ 미국과 멕시코에서 많은 상을 받았다.
⑤ 멕시코 시민권을 결국 받지 못했다.

2020학년도 11월 학평 26번 ★★☆

8. Sarah Breedlove에 관한 다음 글의 내용과 일치하지 않는 것은?

Born in 1867, Sarah Breedlove was an American businesswoman and social activist. Orphaned at the age of seven, her early life was marked by hardship. In 1888, she moved to St. Louis, where she worked as a washerwoman for more than a decade, earning barely more than a dollar a day. During this time, long hours of backbreaking labor and a poor diet caused her hair to fall out. She tried everything that was available but had no success. After working as a maid for a chemist, she invented a successful hair care product and sold it across the country. Not only did she sell, she also recruited and trained lots of women as sales agents for a share of the profits. In the process she became America's first self-made female millionaire and she gave Black women everywhere an opportunity for financial independence.

① 미국인 사업가이자 사회 운동가였다.
② St. Louis에서 10년 넘게 세탁부로 일했다.
③ 장시간의 노동과 열악한 식사로 머리카락이 빠졌다.
④ 모발 관리 제품을 수입하여 전국에 판매했다.
⑤ 흑인 여성들에게 재정적 독립의 기회를 주었다.

2020학년도 9월 학평 26번 ★★☆

9. Jessie Redmon Fauset에 관한 다음 글의 내용과 일치하지 않는 것은?

Jessie Redmon Fauset was born in Snow Hill, New Jersey, in 1884. She was the first black woman to graduate from Cornell University. In addition to writing novels, poetry, short stories, and essays, Fauset taught French in public schools in Washington, D.C. and worked as a journal editor. While working as an editor, she encouraged many well-known writers of the Harlem Renaissance. Though she is more famous for being an editor than for being a fiction writer, many critics consider her novel *Plum Bun* Fauset's strongest work. In it, she tells the story of a black girl who could pass for white but ultimately claims her racial identity and pride. Fauset died of heart disease April 30, 1961, in Philadelphia.

* pass for: ~으로 여겨지다

① Cornell University를 졸업한 최초의 흑인 여성이었다.
② Washington, D.C.의 공립학교에서 프랑스어를 가르쳤다.
③ 편집자보다는 소설가로서 더 유명하다.
④ 흑인 소녀의 이야기를 다룬 소설을 썼다.
⑤ Philadelphia에서 심장병으로 사망했다.

2020학년도 6월 학평 26번 ★☆☆

10. Sigrid Undset에 관한 다음 글의 내용과 일치하지 않는 것은?

Sigrid Undset was born on May 20, 1882, in Kalundborg, Denmark. She was the eldest of three daughters. She moved to Norway at the age of two. Her early life was strongly influenced by her father's historical knowledge. At the age of sixteen, she got a job at an engineering company to support her family. She read a lot, acquiring a good knowledge of Nordic as well as foreign literature, English in particular. She wrote thirty six books. None of her books leaves the reader unconcerned. She received the Nobel Prize for Literature in 1928. One of her novels has been translated into more than eighty languages. She escaped Norway during the German occupation, but she returned after the end of World War Ⅱ.

* Nordic: 북유럽 사람(의)

① 세 자매 중 첫째 딸로 태어났다.
② 어린 시절의 삶은 아버지의 역사적 지식에 큰 영향을 받았다.
③ 16세에 가족을 부양하기 위해 취업하였다.
④ 1928년에 노벨 문학상을 수상하였다.
⑤ 독일 점령 기간 중 노르웨이를 탈출한 후, 다시 돌아오지 않았다.

총 문항				문항	맞은 문항					문항
개별 문항	1	2	3	4	5	6	7	8	9	10
채점										
개별 문항	11	12	13	14	15	16	17	18	19	20
채점										

문법 플러스

9. 부정사

정답 및 해설 048쪽

A 문법의 주요 포인트를 점검해 봅시다.

1 부정사는 문장 안에서 명사, 형용사, 부사로서의 역할을 한다.

2 plan, agree, decide, want, wish, hope 등의 동사는 목적어로 to부정사를 가져 온다.

3 동사의 목적어로 동명사와 부정사 둘 다 오는 경우, 의미상 차이에 유의해야 한다.

▪ 「stop+동명사」	~하는 것을 멈추다	▪ 「stop+to부정사」	~하기 위해 멈추다
▪ 「remember+동명사」	(과거) ~했던 것을 기억하다	▪ 「remember+to부정사」	(미래) ~할 것을 기억하다
▪ 「forget+동명사」	(과거) ~했던 것을 잊다	▪ 「forget+to부정사」	(미래) ~할 것을 잊다
▪ 「regret+동명사」	~한 것을 후회하다	▪ 「regret+to부정사」	~해야 해서 유감이다
▪ 「try+동명사」	시험 삼아 ~해보다	▪ 「try+to부정사」	~하려고 노력하다

4 ▪ too... to부정사 = 「so... that+주어+cannot ~」 (너무 …해서 ~할 수 없다)

The cat is **too** fat **to** climb up the tree. = The cat is **so** fat **that** it **can't** climb up the tree.

▪ ~ enough to부정사 = 「so... that+주어+can ~」 (매우 …해서 ~할 수 있다)

The case is light **enough** for me **to** carry. = The case is **so** light **that** I **can** carry it.

5 지각동사의 목적어와 목적격보어가 능동 관계인 경우, 목적격보어는 동사원형이나 진행형을 쓴다. 사역동사의 목적어와 목적격보어가 능동 관계인 경우, 목적격보어는 동사원형을 쓴다. 지각[사역]동사의 목적어와 목적격보어가 수동 관계인 경우, 목적격보어는 과거분사를 쓴다.

B 다음 괄호 안에서 어법상 올바른 것을 고르시오.

1 Several minutes later the conductor turned around from the front of the traincar to see Einstein **[to continue / continuing]** to search under his seat for the missing ticket.

2 It is often believed that the function of school is **[to produce / to be produced]** knowledgeable people.

3 To make it as easy as possible for you to act now, we've sent a reply card for you **[completing / to complete]**.

4 "You are what you eat." That phrases is often used **[to showing / to show]** the relationship between the foods you eat and your physical health.

5 You can lead a horse to water, but you can't make him **[to drink / drink]**.

6 She encouraged me **[apply / to apply]** for the job.

7 The belief that humans have morality and animals don't is such a longstanding assumption that it could well be called a habit of mind, and bad habits, as well all know, are extremely hard **[breaking / to break]**.

8 Chances are that you have more often been disappointed by setting targets that are too low and achieving them—only **[shocked / to be shocked]** that you still didn't get what you wanted.

9 The doctor said, with tears in his eyes, "I regret to tell you that Simba is dead." Finally, Simba stopped **[to breathe / breathing]**.

10 "I feel like I've lost an old friend. I can remember **[reporting / to report]** Samba's birth." said a doctor.

어휘 플러스

9. 철자가 혼동되는 어휘 (3)

정답 및 해설 048쪽

A 다음 수능 필수 어휘를 읽고, 아는 것은 체크해 봅시다.

□ 01	abject	a. 비참한, 비열한	□ 21	object	n. 사물, 목표
□ 02	abuse	v. 남용하다	□ 22	amuse	v. 기쁘게 하다
□ 03	accept	v. 허가하다	□ 23	except	pre. ~을 제외하고
□ 04	access	v. 접근하다, 이용하다	□ 24	excess	n. 과다, 초과
□ 05	accessible	a. 접근하기 쉬운	□ 25	acceptable	a. 받아들일 수 있는
□ 06	accompany	v. 동참하다	□ 26	company	n. 회사, 일행
□ 07	acquire	v. 획득하다	□ 27	inquire	v. 묻다, 문의하다
□ 08	active	a. 활동적인	□ 28	actual	a. 현실의, 사실상의
□ 09	addictive	a. 중독성의	□ 29	additive	a. 부가적인; n. 첨가물
□ 10	affect	v. 영향을 미치다	□ 30	effect	n. 결과, 효과
□ 11	affluent	a. 부유한, 풍족한	□ 31	fluent	a. 유창한
□ 12	altar	n. 제단	□ 32	alter	v. 변경하다, 바꾸다
□ 13	altitude	n. 고도, 높이	□ 33	attitude	n. 태도
□ 14	amuse	v. 즐겁게 하다	□ 34	amaze	v. 놀라게 하다
□ 15	angle	n. 각도	□ 35	angel	n. 천사
□ 16	anticipating	a. 기대하는	□ 36	participating	a. 참여하는
□ 17	appeal	v. 간청하다, 항의하다	□ 37	appear	v. 나타나다
□ 18	approve	v. 승인하다	□ 38	improve	v. 개선하다
□ 19	archive	v. 공문서, 기록	□ 39	achieve	v. 성취하다
□ 20	aspect	n. 외관, 모양, 관점	□ 40	aspire	v. 열망하다

B 괄호 안에서 문맥에 맞는 낱말로 적절한 것을 골라 봅시다.

1 He has everything he needs for the trip **[accept / except]** one thing.

2 All of us use the cultural knowledge we **[acquire / inquire]** as members of our own society to organize our perception and behavior.

3 Newton, for example, imagined that masses **[effect / affect]** each other by exerting a force, while in Einstein's theory the effects occur through a bending of space and time and there is no concept of gravity as a force.

4 Their knowledge of the deadly effects of extreme **[attitude / altitude]** was limited and their equipment was poor.

5 When there is no immediate danger, it is usually best to **[approve / improve]** of the child's play without interfering.

10 안내문

출제 트렌드

1. 실생활에서 접할 수 있는 안내문이나 포스터를 보고 제시된 정보와 선택지의 내용이 서로 일치하는지 판단하는 능력을 측정한다. 고1 학력 평가에서 2문항이 출제되고 있다. 관광, 공연, 행사, 전시회, 강좌, 관람 등과 관련된 실용문이 제시된다.
2. 세부 내용을 파악하기 위해서는 글에 제시된 특정 정보를 사실적이고 정확하게 이해하는 능력이 필요하다. 세부 내용 파악하기 읽기 유형에는 도표 정보 파악, 내용 일치 · 불일치, 안내문 파악하기 문제가 있다.
3. 최근 수능 7년간, 안내문(실용 자료 내용) 파악하기 문제는 2017학년도 이후 매년 2문제가 출제되고 있다. 2017학년도 수능 26번(96%), 27번(94%), 2018년도 수능 26번(95%), 27번(93%), 2019학년도 수능 27번(97%), 28번(95%), 2020학년도 수능 27번(97%), 28번(95%), 2021학년도 수능 27번(96%), 28번(95%), 2022학년도 수능 27번(97%), 28번(96%), 2023학년도 수능 27번(97%), 28번(96%)에서 괄호 안의 정답률을 보였다. 7년간 평균 95.6%의 정답률을 보였다. 난이도는 하 단계이다.
4. 글의 세부 내용 유형의 도표 정보 파악, 일치 · 불일치, 안내문 문제의 정답률을 비교하면 안내문(96.3%) 〉 일치 · 불일치(96.2%) 〉 도표 정보 파악(92.5%) 순서였다. 도표 정보 파악이 약간 더 어렵다는 것을 알 수 있다.

	출처		문항 번호	지문 주제	정답률(%)	난이도
대표	2022학년도	11 학평	27번	E-Waste Recycling Day	93	★☆☆
1	2022학년도	11 학평	28번	Undersea Walking Activity	87	★☆☆
2	2022학년도	09 학평	27번	2022 Springfield Park Yoga Class	96	★☆☆
3	2022학년도	09 학평	28번	Kenner High School's Water Challenge	87	★☆☆
4	2022학년도	06 학평	27번	Kids Taekwondo Program	95	★☆☆
5	2022학년도	06 학평	28번	Moonlight Chocolate Factory Tour	94	★☆☆
6	2022학년도	03 학평	27번	Rachel의 꽃 교실	94	★☆☆
7	2022학년도	03 학평	28번	야간 궁궐 투어	90	★☆☆
8	2021학년도	11 학평	27번	자연 사진 콘테스트 안내문	83	★★☆
9	2021학년도	11 학평	28번	Willow Valley Hot Air Balloon Ride에 관한 안내문	92	★☆☆
10	2021학년도	09 학평	27번	Premier Reading Challenge	92	★☆☆

1등급 꿀팁

1. 일치하는 문제인지, 일치하지 않는 문제인지 지시문을 잘 읽는다.
2. 선택지 순서대로 관련된 내용을 지문에서 찾아 일치 여부를 빨리 판단한다. 주로 본문에 언급된 순서대로 선택지가 나열된다.

제한 시간 : 15분 | 정답 및 해설 049쪽

대표 기출

2022학년도 11월 학평 27번

27. E-Waste Recycling Day에 관한 다음 안내문의 내용과 일치하지 않는 것은?

> **E-Waste Recycling Day**
>
> E-Waste Recycling Day is an annual event in our city. Bring your used electronics such as cell phones, tablets, and laptops to recycle. Go green!
>
> **When**
> Saturday, December 17, 2022
> 8:00 a.m. – 11:00 a.m.
>
> **Where**
> Lincoln Sports Center
>
> **Notes**
> • Items NOT accepted: light bulbs, batteries, and microwaves
> • All personal data on the devices must be wiped out in advance.
> • This event is free but open only to local residents.
>
> Please contact us at 986-571-0204 for more information.

① 3시간 동안 진행된다.
② Lincoln 스포츠 센터에서 열린다.
③ 전자레인지는 허용되지 않는 품목이다.
④ 기기 속 모든 개인 정보는 미리 삭제되어야 한다.
⑤ 거주 지역에 상관없이 참가할 수 있다.

문제 풀이

1. 글의 전반부에서 소재를 파악하고 무엇에 관한 정보인지 파악한다.
E-Waste Recycling Day(전자 폐기물 재활용의 날)

2. 선택지의 핵심 정보를 확인하고 글의 내용을 예측한다.
① 3시간 동안 진행된다.
→ **When** ~ 8:00 a.m. – 11:00 a.m.
② Lincoln 스포츠 센터에서 열린다.
→ **Where** Lincoln Sports Center
③ 전자레인지는 허용되지 않는 품목이다.
→ Items NOT accepted: light bulbs, batteries, and microwaves
④ 기기 속 모든 개인 정보는 미리 삭제되어야 한다.
→ All personal data on the devices must be wiped out in advance.

3. 지문과 일치하지 않는 선택지를 찾는다.
• This event is free but open only to local residents.'에서 이 행사는 무료지만 지역 주민에게만 개방된다고 했으므로 ⑤ '주 지역에 상관없이 참가할 수 있다.'는 안내문의 내용과 일치하지 않는다.

2022학년도 11월 학평 28번 ★☆☆

1. Undersea Walking Activity에 관한 다음 안내문의 내용과 일치하는 것은?

> **Undersea Walking Activity**
>
> Enjoy a fascinating underwater walk on the ocean floor. Witness wonderful marine life on foot!
>
> **Age Requirement**
> 10 years or older
>
> **Operating Hours**
> from Tuesday to Sunday
> 9:00 a.m. – 4:00 p.m.
>
> **Price**
> $30 (insurance fee included)
>
> **What to Bring**
> swim suit and towel
>
> **Notes**
> • Experienced lifeguards accompany you throughout the activity.
> • With a special underwater helmet, you can wear glasses during the activity.
> • Reservations can be made on-site or online at www.seawalkwonder.com.

① 연중무휴로 운영된다.
② 가격에 보험료는 포함되어 있지 않다.
③ 숙련된 안전 요원이 활동 내내 동행한다.
④ 특수 수중 헬멧 착용 시 안경을 쓸 수 없다.
⑤ 현장 예약은 불가능하다.

2022학년도 11월 학평 27번 ★☆☆

2. 2022 Springfield Park Yoga Class에 관한 다음 안내문의 내용과 일치하지 않는 것은?

> Internet
>
> **2022 Springfield Park Yoga Class**
>
> The popular yoga class in Springfield Park returns! Enjoy yoga hosted on the park lawn. If you can't make it to the park, join us online on our social media platforms!
>
> ◈ When: Saturdays, 2 p.m. to 3 p.m., September
>
> ◈ Registration: At least TWO hours before each class starts, sign up here.
>
> ◈ Notes
> • For online classes: find a quiet space with enough room for you to stretch out.
> • For classes in the park: mats are not provided, so bring your own!
>
> ※ The class will be canceled if the weather is unfavorable.
>
> For more information, click here.

① 온라인으로도 참여할 수 있다.
② 9월 중 토요일마다 진행된다.
③ 수업 시작 2시간 전까지 등록해야 한다.
④ 매트가 제공된다.
⑤ 날씨가 좋지 않으면 취소될 것이다.

2022학년도 9월 학평 28번 ★☆☆

3. Kenner High School's Water Challenge에 관한 다음 안내문의 내용과 일치하는 것은?

Kenner High School's Water Challenge

Kenner High School's Water Challenge is a new contest to propose measures against water pollution. Please share your ideas for dealing with water pollution!

Submission
- How: Submit your proposal by email to admin@khswater.edu.
- When: September 5, 2022 to September 23, 2022

Details
- Participants must enter in teams of four and can only join one team.
- Submission is limited to one proposal per team.
- Participants must use the proposal form provided on the website.

Prizes
- 1st: $50 gift certificate
- 2nd: $30 gift certificate
- 3rd: $10 gift certificate

Please visit www.khswater.edu to learn more about the challenge.

① 제안서는 직접 방문하여 제출해야 한다.
② 9월 23일부터 제안서를 제출할 수 있다.
③ 제안서는 한 팀당 4개까지 제출할 수 있다.
④ 제공된 제안서 양식을 사용해야 한다.
⑤ 2등은 10달러의 상품권을 받는다.

2022학년도 6월 학평 27번 ★☆☆

4. Kids Taekwondo Program에 관한 다음 안내문의 내용과 일치하지 <u>않는</u> 것은?

Kids Taekwondo Program

Enjoy our taekwondo program this summer vacation.

□ Schedule
- Dates: August 8th – August 10th
- Time: 9:00 a.m. – 11:00 a.m.

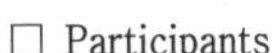

□ Participants
- Any child aged 5 and up

□ Activities
- Self-defense training
- Team building games to develop social skills

□ Participation Fee
- $50 per child (includes snacks)

□ Notice
- What to bring: water bottle, towel
- What not to bring: chewing gum, expensive items

① 8월 8일부터 3일간 운영한다.
② 5세 이상의 어린이가 참가할 수 있다.
③ 자기 방어 훈련 활동을 한다.
④ 참가비에 간식비는 포함되지 않는다.
⑤ 물병과 수건을 가져와야 한다.

2022학년도 6월 학평 28번 ★☆☆

5. Moonlight Chocolate Factory Tour에 관한 다음 안내문의 내용과 일치하는 것은?

Moonlight Chocolate Factory Tour

Take this special tour and have a chance to enjoy our most popular chocolate bars.

□ Operating Hours
- Monday – Friday, 2:00 p.m. – 5:00 p.m.

□ Activities
- Watching our chocolate-making process
- Tasting 3 types of chocolate (dark, milk, and mint chocolate)

□ Notice
- Ticket price: $30
- Wearing a face mask is required.
- Taking pictures is not allowed inside the factory.

① 주말 오후 시간에 운영한다.
② 초콜릿 제조 과정을 볼 수 있다.
③ 네 가지 종류의 초콜릿을 시식한다.
④ 마스크 착용은 참여자의 선택 사항이다.
⑤ 공장 내부에서 사진 촬영이 가능하다.

2022학년도 3월 학평 27번 ★☆☆

6. Rachel's Flower Class에 관한 다음 안내문의 내용과 일치하지 <u>않는</u> 것은?

Rachel's Flower Class

Make Your Life More Beautiful!

Class Schedule (Every Monday to Friday)

Flower Arrangement	11 a.m. – 12 p.m.
Flower Box Making	1 p.m. – 2 p.m.

Price
- $50 for each class
  (flowers and other materials included)
- Bring your own scissors and a bag.

Other Info.
- You can sign up for classes either online or by phone.
- No refund for cancellations on the day of your class

To contact, visit www.rfclass.com or call 03-221-2131.

① 플라워 박스 만들기 수업은 오후 1시에 시작된다.
② 수강료에 꽃값과 다른 재료비가 포함된다.
③ 수강생은 가위와 가방을 가져와야 한다.
④ 수업 등록은 전화로만 할 수 있다.
⑤ 수업 당일 취소 시 환불을 받을 수 없다.

Day 10

2022학년도 3월 학평 28번 ★☆☆

7. Nighttime Palace Tour에 관한 다음 안내문의 내용과 일치하는 것은?

> **Nighttime Palace Tour**
>
> 
>
> Date: Friday, April 29 – Sunday, May 15
>
> Time
>
> | | |
> |---|---|
> | Friday | 7 p.m. – 8:30 p.m. |
> | Saturday & Sunday | 6 p.m. – 7:30 p.m. |
> | | 8 p.m. – 9:30 p.m. |
>
> Tickets & Booking
> - $15 per person (free for kids under 8)
> - Bookings will be accepted up to 2 hours before the tour starts.
>
> Program Activities
> - Group tour with a tour guide (1 hour)
> - Trying traditional foods and drinks (30 minutes)
>
> ※ You can try on traditional clothes with no extra charge.
> ※ For more information, please visit our website, www.palacenighttour.com.

① 금요일에는 하루에 두 번 투어가 운영된다.
② 8세 미만 어린이의 티켓은 5달러이다.
③ 예약은 투어 하루 전까지만 가능하다.
④ 투어 가이드의 안내 없이 궁궐을 둘러본다.
⑤ 추가 비용 없이 전통 의상을 입어 볼 수 있다.

2021학년도 11월 학평 27번 ★★☆

8. 2021 Camptonville Nature Photo Contest에 관한 다음 안내문의 내용과 일치하지 않는 것은?

> **2021 Camptonville Nature Photo Contest**
>
> This is the fourth year of the annual Camptonville Nature Photo Contest. You can show the beauty of nature in Camptonville by sharing your most amazing photos!
>
> Submission
> – Upload a maximum of 20 photos onto our website www.camptonvillephotocontest.org.
> – Deadline is December 1.
>
> Prizes
> • 1st Place: $500 • 2nd Place: $200 • 3rd Place: $100
> (Winners will be posted on our website on December 31.)
>
> Details
> – All winning photos will be exhibited at City Hall.
> – Please contact us at 122-861-3971 for further information.

① 매년 열리는 대회이며 올해가 네 번째이다.
② 최대 20장의 사진을 이메일로 제출해야 한다.
③ 제출 마감 기한은 12월 1일이다.
④ 수상자는 웹 사이트에 게시될 것이다.
⑤ 모든 수상작은 시청에 전시될 것이다.

2021학년도 11월 학평 28번 ★☆☆

9. Willow Valley Hot Air Balloon Ride에 관한 다음 안내문의 내용과 일치하는 것은?

> **Willow Valley Hot Air Balloon Ride**
>
> Enjoy the best views of Willow Valley from the sky with our hot air balloon ride!
>
> • Capacity: up to 8 people including a pilot
>
> • Time Schedule
>
> | | |
> |---|---|
> | Spring & Summer (from April to September) | 5:00 a.m. – 7:00 a.m. |
> | Autumn & Winter (from October to March) | 6:00 a.m. – 8:00 a.m. |
>
> ※ Duration of Flight: about 1 hour
>
> • Fee: $150 per person (insurance not included)
>
> • Note
> – Reservations are required and must be made online.
> – You can get a full refund up to 24 hours in advance.
> – Visit www.willowvalleyballoon.com for more information.

① 조종사를 제외하고 8인까지 탈 수 있다.
② 여름에는 오전 6시에 시작한다.
③ 요금에 보험이 포함되어 있다.
④ 예약은 온라인으로 해야 한다.
⑤ 환불은 예외 없이 불가능하다.

2021학년도 9월 학평 27번 ★☆☆

10. Premier Reading Challenge에 관한 다음 안내문의 내용과 일치하지 않는 것은?

> **Premier Reading Challenge**
>
> This is not a competition, but rather a challenge to inspire students with the love of reading.
>
> • Participants
> - Students from 6th grade to 9th grade
>
> • Dates
> - From June 1st to December 31st
>
> 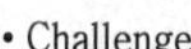
>
> • Challenge
> - Each student in 6th and 7th grade must read 15 books.
> - Each student in 8th and 9th grade must read 20 books.
>
> • Prize
> - A bookmark for every participant
> - A Certificate of Achievement for students who complete the challenge
>
> • Registration
> - Online only — www.edu.prc.com
>
> ※ For more information, see the school librarian or visit the website above.

① 6학년부터 9학년까지의 학생들을 대상으로 한다.
② 6월부터 5개월간 진행되는 행사이다.
③ 7학년의 도전과제는 15권의 책을 읽는 것이다.
④ 모든 참가자는 책갈피를 받는다.
⑤ 온라인으로만 등록할 수 있다.

총 문항				문항	맞은 문항					문항
개별 문항	1	2	3	4	5	6	7	8	9	10
채점										
개별 문항	11	12	13	14	15	16	17	18	19	20
채점										

문법 플러스

10. 동명사

정답 및 해설 051쪽

문법의 주요 포인트를 점검해 봅시다.

1 동명사는 명사 역할을 하며 문장에서 주어, 목적어, 보어의 역할을 한다. 또한 동명사는 동사의 성격도 있어 문장 속에서 목적어, 보어, 수식어구를 가져올 수 있다.

2 동명사가 주어일 경우, 동사는 단수동사를 사용한다.

3 finish, mind, enjoy, avoid 동사는 동명사를 목적어로 가져 온다. 동사의 목적어로 동명사와 부정사 중 어느 하나만이 올 수 있는 경우와 둘 다 오더라도 그 의미상 차이가 있는 경우에 유의해야 한다.

4 동명사의 의미상의 주어는 동명사 앞에 배치한다. 의미상 주어가 사람일 때는 소유격, 목적격을 모두 사용할 수 있으며, 사물일 때는 그대로 쓴다. 또한 동명사를 부정할 때는 부정어를 동명사 바로 앞에 둔다.
▪ Sam insists on **her** being innocent.

5 동명사의 관용 표현은 시험에 자주 나온다.

▪ be used to-ing	~에 익숙하다	▪ be accustomed to	~에 익숙하다
▪ be devoted to -ing	~에 전념하다	▪ object to -ing	~에 반대하다
▪ look forward to	~을 고대하다	▪ can't help -ing	~하지 않을 수 없다
▪ spend (시간/돈) -ing	~하는 데 시간(돈)을 쓰다	▪ have a hard time -ing	~하는 데 어려움을 겪다
▪ have difficulty (in) -ing	~하는 데 어려움을 겪다		

B 다음 괄호 안에서 어법상 올바른 것을 고르시오.

1 **[Introducing / Introduce]** a new product category is difficult, especially if the new category is not contrasted against the old one.

2 He saw that flies seemed to avoid **[to land / landing]** on the stripes.

3 When the conversation focuses on the process of change rather than the outcome, it reinforces the value of **[create / creating]** a sustainable process.

4 Once somebody makes a discovery, others review it carefully before **[to use / using]** the information in their own research.

5 Chances are, that person will have a hard time **[to know / knowing]** exactly which star you're looking at.

6 If this view is correct, we should have difficulty **[to understand / understanding]** the emotion expressed in culturally unfamiliar music.

7 To try to solve this mystery, wildlife biologist Tim Cargo spent more than a decade **[to study / studying]** zebras in Tanzania.

8 The animal doctor came and tried **[to give / giving]** the lion some red meat full of medicine.

9 She cannot help **[to have / having]** a cup of coffee when she's tired.

10 I looked forward to **[meet / meeting]** her.

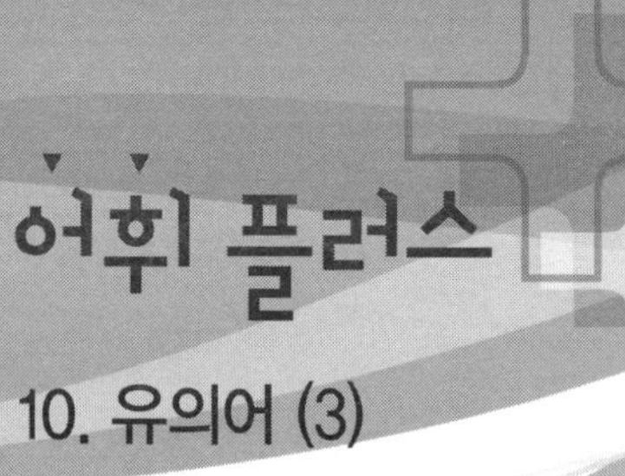

어휘 플러스

10. 유의어 (3)

정답 및 해설 051쪽

A 다음 수능 필수 어휘를 읽고, 아는 것은 체크해 봅시다.

□ 01	entrance	n. 입장, 입학(= admission)	□ 21	gather	v. 모으다(= assemble)
□ 02	enroll	v. 등록하다(= register)	□ 22	generate	v. 생성하다(= produce)
□ 03	establish	v. 설립하다(= found)	□ 23	genuine	a. 진짜의(= authentic)
□ 04	ethical	a. 도덕상의(= moral)	□ 24	ignore	v. 무시하다(= disregard)
□ 05	evaluate	v. 평가하다(= assess)	□ 25	immediate	a. 즉각적인(= prompt)
□ 06	evident	a. 명백한(= obvious)	□ 26	imitate	v. 모방하다(= mimic)
□ 07	evolve	v. 발전하다(= progress)	□ 27	impress	v. 감동시키다(= move, touch)
□ 08	exceed	v. 초과하다(= surpass)	□ 28	incredible	a. 믿어지지 않는(= unbelievable)
□ 09	excel	v. 탁월하다(= outstrip)	□ 29	indifferent	a. 무관심한(= unconcerned)
□ 10	exchange	v. 교환하다(= trade)	□ 30	induce	v. 야기하다(= cause)
□ 11	exhibit	v. 진열하다(= display)	□ 31	inevitable	a. 불가피한(= unavoidable)
□ 12	expect	v. 기대하다(= anticipate)	□ 32	influence	v. 영향을 미치다(= affect)
□ 13	expert	n. 전문가(= professional)	□ 33	inherent	a. 타고난(= innate)
□ 14	face	v. 직면하다(= confront)	□ 34	integrate	v. 통합하다(= combine)
□ 15	fascinate	v. 매혹하다(= attract)	□ 35	interpret	v. 통역하다(= translate)
□ 16	firm	n. 회사(= company)	□ 36	invent	v. 고안하다(= devise)
□ 17	focus	v. 집중하다(= concentrate)	□ 37	investigate	v. 조사하다(= exam)
□ 18	follow	v. 따르다(= observe)	□ 38	isolate	v. 고립시키다(= separate)
□ 19	frighten	v. 겁먹게 만들다(= terrify)	□ 39	jealous	a. 시기하는(= envious)
□ 20	fundamental	a. 필수적인(= essential)	□ 40	measure	v. 측정하다(= gauge)

B 괄호 안에서 문맥에 맞는 낱말로 적절한 것을 골라 봅시다.

1 After graduating from university, Rawlings worked as a journalist while simultaneously trying to **[establish / isolate]** herself as a fiction writer.

2 In the modern world, almost every country uses coins and paper money to **[exceed / exchange]** for other objects of value.

3 These essays were then **[evaluated / ignored]** according to the criteria of purity, truthfulness, elegance, and propriety. These criteria were, however, so vague that candidates had little choice but to detect the literary preferences of the examiner.

4 We must show every young person, no matter how deprived his background may be, that he has a **[genuine / indifferent]** opportunity to fulfill himself and play a constructive role in our society.

5 Our **[incredible / lagging]** growth rate leads to a continuous recruitment of ambitious programmer analysts who have the desire to make a significant contribution to an expanding company.

11 어법 정확성 파악

출제 트렌드

1. 어법 정확성 문제는 지문의 문장 구조를 이해하는지 유무를 판단하는 유형이다. 어법 정확성 문제는 지문 속에 밑줄을 그어 놓고 '밑줄 친 부분 중, 어법상 틀린 것을 고르는' 문제와 '각 네모 안에서 어법에 맞는 유형'을 고르는 문제가 출제되었다.
2. 2014년 이후 수능에서는 두 문항 중 한 문항이 출제되고, 2019학년도 이후 최근 수능에서는 '밑줄 친 부분 중, 어법상 틀린 것을 고르는' 문제 유형이 출제되고 있다. 고1 학력 평가에서도 '밑줄 친 부분 중, 어법상 틀린 것을 고르는' 문제가 1문제 출제되고 있다. 3점 고난이도 문제로 출제될 때가 많다. 선택지 중 1~2개가 어려워 오답률이 높은 유형이다.
3. 최근 수능 7년간, 어법 정확성 파악 문제는 2017학년도 이후 매년 1문제가 출제되고 있다. 2020학년도를 제외하고, 3점 문항으로 출제되었다. 2017학년도 수능(48%), 2018(51%), 2019(35%), 2020(54%), 2021(61%), 2022(54%), 2023(40%)에서 괄호 안의 정답률을 보였다. 7년간 평균 49%의 정답률을 보였다. 난이도는 상 단계이다. 수능에서 가장 어려운 문제 유형 중 하나라고 할 수 있다.

출처			문항 번호	지문 주제	정답률(%)	난이도
대표	2022학년도	11 학평	29번	인공 지능의 핵심적인 특징	51	★★★
1	2022학년도	09 학평	29번	인간의 뇌 크기가 줄어든 이유	71	★★☆
2	2022학년도	06 학평	29번	첨단 생활방식으로 인한 천연 자원 사용의 증가	62	★★☆
3	2022학년도	03 학평	29번	인간은 유유상종의 경향이 있다	65	★★☆
4	2021학년도	11 학평	29번	식품 속 미네랄의 감소 원인	51	★★★
5	2021학년도	09 학평	29번	Say의 법칙	50	★★★
6	2021학년도	06 학평	29번	진짜 미소와 가짜 미소의 구별법	66	★★☆
7	2021학년도	03 학평	29번	악기를 탐구하는 시간의 필요성	64	★★☆
8	2020학년도	11 학평	29번	동물의 냄새 인식은 그들의 생태에 달려있다	57	★★★
9	2020학년도	09 학평	29번	음식 평가와 시각 정보	44	★★★
10	2020학년도	03 학평	29번	발달 과정에 미치는 또래 집단의 강력한 영향	54	★★★
11	2019학년도	06 학평	29번	빛의 질의 중요성	51	★★★
12	2018학년도	06 학평	28번	미세 플라스틱	35	★★★

1등급 꿀팁

1. 평소 글을 읽으면서 주어와 동사가 무엇인지 살펴보는 습관이 필요하다.
2. 어법 사항 중에서 특히 출제가 빈번히 되었던 어법 항목은 특히 유의해야 한다.
(주어와 동사의 수 일치, 병렬 구조, 분사, 동명사, to부정사, 관계사, 접속사)

어법 정확성 파악

제한 시간 : 20분 | 정답 및 해설 052쪽

대표 기출

2022학년도 11월 학평 29번

29. 다음 글의 밑줄 친 부분 중, 어법상 <u>틀린</u> 것은? [3점]

You may have seen headlines in the news about some of the things machines powered by artificial intelligence can do. However, if you were to consider all the tasks ① <u>that</u> AI-powered machines could actually perform, it would be quite mind-blowing! One of the key features of artificial intelligence ② <u>is</u> that it enables machines to learn new things, rather than requiring programming specific to new tasks. Therefore, the core difference between computers of the future and ③ <u>those</u> of the past is that future computers will be able to learn and self-improve. In the near future, smart virtual assistants will know more about you than your closest friends and family members ④ <u>are</u>. Can you imagine how that might change our lives? These kinds of changes are exactly why it is so important ⑤ <u>to recognize</u> the implications that new technologies will have for our world.

문제 풀이

1. 글의 내용을 파악하면서 읽는다.

- Therefore, the core difference between computers of the future and those of the past is that future computers will be able to learn and self-improve. (미래의 컴퓨터들과 과거의 그것들 사이의 핵심적인 차이점은 미래의 컴퓨터가 학습하고 스스로 개선할 수 있을 것이라는 점이다.)

2. 밑줄 친 부분이 포함된 문장의 구조를 파악하여 문법성을 판단한다.

① that 뒤에 목적어가 없는 불완전한 문장이 왔고, 앞에 있는 선행사 all the tasks를 수식하는 관계대명사 절이므로 목적격 관계대명사 that은 적절하게 쓰였다.
② 문장의 주어인 One of the key features of artificial intelligence의 동사로 단수동사 is는 적절하게 쓰였다.
③ 지시대명사 those는 의미상 computers라는 복수명사를 대신 받아야 하므로 적절하게 쓰였다.
⑤ why가 이끄는 절의 주어 자리에 가주어 it이 왔고, to recognize 이하가 진주어로 왔으므로 적절하게 쓰였다.

3. 어법상 틀린 것으로 생각되는 선택지를 숙고해 분석하고 답을 확정한다.

④ 문장의 동사인 know를 대신하는 대동사가 와야 하므로 are를 do로 고쳐야 한다.

2022학년도 9월 학평 29번 ★★☆

1. 다음 글의 밑줄 친 부분 중, 어법상 <u>틀린</u> 것은? [3점]

The human brain, it turns out, has shrunk in mass by about 10 percent since it ① <u>peaked</u> in size 15,000–30,000 years ago. One possible reason is that many thousands of years ago humans lived in a world of dangerous predators ② <u>where</u> they had to have their wits about them at all times to avoid being killed. Today, we have effectively domesticated ourselves and many of the tasks of survival — from avoiding immediate death to building shelters to obtaining food — ③ <u>has</u> been outsourced to the wider society. We are smaller than our ancestors too, and it is a characteristic of domestic animals ④ <u>that</u> they are generally smaller than their wild cousins. None of this may mean we are dumber — brain size is not necessarily an indicator of human intelligence — but it may mean that our brains today are wired up differently, and perhaps more efficiently, than ⑤ <u>those</u> of our ancestors.

2022학년도 6월 학평 29번 ★★☆

2. 다음 글의 밑줄 친 부분 중, 어법상 <u>틀린</u> 것은?

Despite all the high-tech devices that seem to deny the need for paper, paper use in the United States ① <u>has</u> nearly doubled recently. We now consume more paper than ever: 400 million tons globally and growing. Paper is not the only resource ② <u>that</u> we are using more of. Technological advances often come with the promise of ③ <u>using</u> fewer materials. However, the reality is that they have historically caused more materials use, making us ④ <u>dependently</u> on more natural resources. The world now consumes far more "stuff" than it ever has. We use twenty-seven times more industrial minerals, such as gold, copper, and rare metals, than we ⑤ <u>did</u> just over a century ago. We also each individually use more resources. Much of that is due to our high-tech lifestyle.

* copper: 구리

2022학년도 3월 학평 29번 ★★☆

3. 다음 글의 밑줄 친 부분 중, 어법상 틀린 것은?

We usually get along best with people who we think are like us. In fact, we seek them out. It's why places like Little Italy, Chinatown, and Koreatown ① exist. But I'm not just talking about race, skin color, or religion. I'm talking about people who share our values and look at the world the same way we ② do. As the saying goes, birds of a feather flock together. This is a very common human tendency ③ what is rooted in how our species developed. Imagine you are walking out in a forest. You would be conditioned to avoid something unfamiliar or foreign because there is a high likelihood that ④ it would be interested in killing you. Similarities make us ⑤ relate better to other people because we think they'll understand us on a deeper level than other people.

* species: 종(생물 분류의 기초 단위)

2021학년도 11월 학평 29번 ★★★

4. 다음 글의 밑줄 친 부분 중, 어법상 틀린 것은? [3점]

The reduction of minerals in our food is the result of using pesticides and fertilizers ① that kill off beneficial bacteria, earthworms, and bugs in the soil that create many of the essential nutrients in the first place and prevent the uptake of nutrients into the plant. Fertilizing crops with nitrogen and potassium ② has led to declines in magnesium, zinc, iron and iodine. For example, there has been on average about a 30% decline in the magnesium content of wheat. This is partly due to potassium ③ being a blocker against magnesium absorption by plants. Lower magnesium levels in soil also ④ occurring with acidic soils and around 70% of the farmland on earth is now acidic. Thus, the overall characteristics of soil determine the accumulation of minerals in plants. Indeed, nowadays our soil is less healthy and so are the plants ⑤ grown on it.

* pesticide: 살충제

2021학년도 9월 학평 29번 ★★★

5. 다음 글의 밑줄 친 부분 중, 어법상 틀린 것은? [3점]

An economic theory of Say's Law holds that everything that's made will get sold. The money from anything that's produced is used to ① buy something else. There can never be a situation ② which a firm finds that it can't sell its goods and so has to dismiss workers and close its factories. Therefore, recessions and unemployment are impossible. Picture the level of spending like the level of water in a bath. Say's Law applies ③ because people use all their earnings to buy things. But what happens if people don't spend all their money, saving some of ④ it instead? Savings are a 'leakage' of spending from the economy. You're probably imagining the water level now falling, so there's less spending in the economy. That would mean firms producing less and ⑤ dismissing some of their workers.

* recession: 경기 후퇴

2021학년도 6월 학평 29번 ★★☆

6. 다음 글의 밑줄 친 부분 중, 어법상 틀린 것은? [3점]

There have been occasions ① in which you have observed a smile and you could sense it was not genuine. The most obvious way of identifying a genuine smile from an insincere ② one is that a fake smile primarily only affects the lower half of the face, mainly with the mouth alone. The eyes don't really get involved. Take the opportunity to look in the mirror and manufacture a smile ③ using the lower half your face only. When you do this, judge ④ how happy your face really looks — is it genuine? A genuine smile will impact on the muscles and wrinkles around the eyes and less noticeably, the skin between the eyebrow and upper eyelid ⑤ are lowered slightly with true enjoyment. The genuine smile can impact on the entire face.

2021학년도 3월 학평 29번 ★★☆

7. 다음 글의 밑줄 친 부분 중, 어법상 틀린 것은? [3점]

Although there is usually a correct way of holding and playing musical instruments, the most important instruction to begin with is ① that they are not toys and that they must be looked after. ② Allow children time to explore ways of handling and playing the instruments for themselves before showing them. Finding different ways to produce sounds ③ are an important stage of musical exploration. Correct playing comes from the desire ④ to find the most appropriate sound quality and find the most comfortable playing position so that one can play with control over time. As instruments and music become more complex, learning appropriate playing techniques becomes ⑤ increasingly relevant.

2020학년도 11월 학평 29번 ★★★

8. 다음 글의 밑줄 친 부분 중, 어법상 <u>틀린</u> 것은? [3점]

Each species of animals can detect a different range of odours. No species can detect all the molecules that are present in the environment ① <u>in which</u> it lives — there are some things that we cannot smell but which some other animals can, and vice versa. There are also differences between individuals, relating to the ability to smell an odour, or how ② <u>pleasantly</u> it seems. For example, some people like the taste of coriander — known as cilantro in the USA — while others find ③ <u>it</u> soapy and unpleasant. This effect has an underlying genetic component due to differences in the genes ④ <u>controlling</u> our sense of smell. Ultimately, the selection of scents detected by a given species, and how that odour is perceived, will depend upon the animal's ecology. The response profile of each species will enable it ⑤ <u>to locate</u> sources of smell that are relevant to it and to respond accordingly.

* coriander: 고수

2020학년도 9월 학평 29번 ★★★

9. 다음 글의 밑줄 친 부분 중, 어법상 <u>틀린</u> 것은? [3점]

Although it is obvious that part of our assessment of food is its visual appearance, it is perhaps surprising ① <u>how</u> visual input can override taste and smell. People find it very ② <u>difficult</u> to correctly identify fruit-flavoured drinks if the colour is wrong, for instance an orange drink that is coloured green. Perhaps even more striking ③ <u>is</u> the experience of wine tasters. One study of Bordeaux University students of wine and wine making revealed that they chose tasting notes appropriate for red wines, such as 'prune and chocolate', when they ④ <u>gave</u> white wine coloured with a red dye. Experienced New Zealand wine experts were similarly tricked into thinking ⑤ <u>that</u> the white wine Chardonnay was in fact a red wine, when it had been coloured with a red dye.

* override: ~에 우선하다 ** prune: 자두

2020학년도 6월 학평 29번 ★★★

10. 다음 글의 밑줄 친 부분 중, 어법상 <u>틀린</u> 것은? [3점]

Positively or negatively, our parents and families are powerful influences on us. But even ① <u>stronger</u>, especially when we're young, are our friends. We often choose friends as a way of ② <u>expanding</u> our sense of identity beyond our families. As a result, the pressure to conform to the standards and expectations of friends and other social groups ③ <u>is</u> likely to be intense. Judith Rich Harris, who is a developmental psychologist, ④ <u>arguing</u> that three main forces shape our development: personal temperament, our parents, and our peers. The influence of peers, she argues, is much stronger than that of parents. "The world ⑤ <u>that</u> children share with their peers," she says, "is what shapes their behavior and modifies the characteristics they were born with, and hence determines the sort of people they will be when they grow up."

* temperament: 기질

2019학년도 6월 학평 29번 ★★★

11. 다음 글의 밑줄 친 부분 중, 어법상 <u>틀린</u> 것은?

Bad lighting can increase stress on your eyes, as can light that is too bright, or light that shines ① <u>directly</u> into your eyes. Fluorescent lighting can also be ② <u>tiring</u>. What you may not appreciate is that the quality of light may also be important. Most people are happiest in bright sunshine — this may cause a release of chemicals in the body ③ <u>that</u> bring a feeling of emotional well-being. Artificial light, which typically contains only a few wavelengths of light, ④ <u>do</u> not seem to have the same effect on mood that sunlight has. Try experimenting with working by a window or ⑤ <u>using</u> full spectrum bulbs in your desk lamp. You will probably find that this improves the quality of your working environment.

* fluorescent lighting: 형광등

2018학년도 6월 학평 28번 ★★★

12. 다음 글의 밑줄 친 부분 중, 어법상 <u>틀린</u> 것은? [3점]

Plastic is extremely slow to degrade and tends to float, ① <u>which</u> allows it to travel in ocean currents for thousands of miles. Most plastics break down into smaller and smaller pieces when exposed to ultraviolet (UV) light, ② <u>forming</u> microplastics. These microplastics are very difficult to measure once they are small enough to pass through the nets typically used to collect ③ <u>themselves</u>. Their impacts on the marine environment and food webs are still poorly understood. These tiny particles are known to be eaten by various animals and to get into the food chain. Because most of the plastic particles in the ocean ④ <u>are</u> so small, there is no practical way to clean up the ocean. One would have to filter enormous amounts of water to collect a ⑤ <u>relatively</u> small amount of plastic.

* degrade: 분해되다

총 문항				문항	맞은 문항					문항
개별 문항	1	2	3	4	5	6	7	8	9	10
채점										
개별 문항	11	12	13	14	15	16	17	18	19	20
채점										

문법 플러스

11. 분사, 분사구문

정답 및 해설 058쪽

A 문법의 주요 포인트를 점검해 봅시다.

1 분사는 명사를 수식하거나 보어 역할을 한다. 현재분사는 능동의 의미, 과거분사는 수동의 의미를 갖는다.

2 주어와 동사 없이 분사가 이끄는 분사구문은 '때, 이유, 조건, 양보, 부대상황(동시 동작, 연속 동작)을 나타낸다.

a. 시간 (때) **Walking** along the street, I ran into Jack. (= When I walked along the street,~

b. 이유 **Having** no money, he can't go to the concert. (= Because he has no money, ~)

c. 조건 **Turning** to the right, you'll find the museum. (= If you turn to the right, you'll find~)

d. 양보 **Feeling** tired, she kept running. (= Though she felt tired, she kept ~)

e. 동시 동작 **Walking** on his tiptoes, he tried not to wake her. (= He walked on his tiptoes, and he tried not to ~)

f. 연속 동작 **Opening** the bottle, Mike poured the drink. (= Mike opened the bottle and poured the drink.)

3 「with+목적어+분사」 표현은 목적어와 분사의 관계가 능동이면 현재분사를, 수동이면 과거분사를 사용한다.

- **With the night falling**, the boys went back home.
- I can do that **with my eyes closed**.

4 분사구문의 주어와 주절의 주어가 다를 때 분사구문의 주어를 분사 앞에 써 준다.

- As the dog barked at him, he ran away. → **The dog** barking at him, he ran away.

5 완료분사구문은 주절의 시제보다 앞선 시제를 나타낸다. 또한 수동형 분사구문에서 being이나 having been은 생략 가능하다.

- After they had found(= **Having found** a hotel), they looked for somewhere to have dinner.
- As the bottle is made of glass(= **Being** made of glass), it can be easily broken.

B 다음 괄호 안에서 어법상 올바른 것을 고르시오.

1 He was a responsible man **[dealt / dealing]** with an irresponsible kid.

2 Instead of making guesses, scientists follow a system **[designed / designing]** to prove if their ideas are true or false.

3 Fluorescent lighting can also be **[tired / tiring]**. What you may not appreciate is that the quality of light may also be important.

4 If you're an early human, perhaps Homo Eretus, walking around the jungles, you may see an animal **[to approach / approaching]**.

5 Teachers take an active role in developing and deeping students' comprehension by asking questions that cause them to read the text again, **[resulting / resulted]** in multiple readings of the same text.

6 **[Asking / Being asked]** to leave by the Chinese restaurant manager, she was embarrassed.

7 After **[dropped / dropping]** the notebook, she lifted herself up onto the stool beside Amy.

8 His hands **[trembling / trembled]**, he looked out at the audience.

9 She sat on the chair with her legs **[crossing / crossed]**.

10 Rather, non-verbal communication should function as a supplement, **[served / serving]** to enhance the richness of the content of the message that is being passed across.

11. 반의어 (3)

정답 및 해설 058쪽

A 다음 수능 필수 어휘를 읽고, 아는 것은 체크해 봅시다.

□ 01	explicit	a. 명백한, 명시적인	□ 21	implicit	a. 암묵적인, 묵시적인
□ 02	extraordinary	a. 비범한	□ 22	ordinary	a. 보통의, 평범한
□ 03	fertile	a. 비옥한, 생식력이 있는	□ 23	barren	a. 불모지의
□ 04	flexible	a. 융통성 있는, 유연한	□ 24	inflexible	a. 융통성없는(= rigid)
□ 05	float	v. (물위, 공중에) 뜨다	□ 25	sink	v. 가라앉다
□ 06	fold	v. 접다, 포개다	□ 26	unfold	v. 펼치다
□ 07	formal	a. 공식적인, 격식을 차린	□ 27	informal	a. 비공식적인, 비정규적인
□ 08	gradual	a. 점진적인	□ 28	sudden	a. 갑작스러운
□ 09	guilty	a. 유죄의	□ 29	innocent	a. 순결한, 무죄의
□ 10	hire	v. 고용하다	□ 30	fire	v. 해고하다
□ 11	horizontal	a. 수평의	□ 31	vertical	a. 수직의
□ 12	immigration	n. (타국에서 오는) 이민	□ 32	emigration	n. (타국으로가는) 이민
□ 13	immoral	a. 부도덕한	□ 33	moral	a. 도적적인
□ 14	import	v. 수입하다; n. 수입	□ 34	export	v. 수출하다; n. 수출
□ 15	increase	v. 증가시키다	□ 35	decrease	v. 감소시키다
□ 16	inferior	a. 열등한, 하위의	□ 36	superior	a. 보다 위의, 상위의
□ 17	innate	a. 타고난, 선천적인	□ 37	acquired	a. 습득한, 후천적인
□ 18	interior	a. 내부의, 실내의	□ 38	exterior	a. 외부의
□ 19	intolerable	a. 참을 수 없는	□ 39	tolerable	a. 참을 수 있는
□ 20	intrinsic	a. 내재된, 본질적인	□ 40	extrinsic	a. 외적인, 외부의

B 괄호 안에서 문맥에 맞는 낱말로 적절한 것을 골라 봅시다.

1 To start with, you need well drained, not necessarily over **[barren / fertile]** soil in order to make the vine's roots dig deep into the soil.

2 The branches then go through a complex process to become strong and **[flexible / inflexible]** paper.

3 For example, according to American law, if someone is accused of a crime, he is considered **[guilty / innocent]** until the court proves that the person is guilty.

4 Those who are hurt tend to see the act as one with severe consequences and as part of an ongoing pattern that is inexcusable and **[moral / immoral]**.

5 They were all washed and dressed to an **[tolerable / intolerable]** state of discomfort.

12 어휘 적절성 파악

출제 트렌드

1. 글의 흐름에 맞지 않는 어휘를 찾는 유형과 글의 흐름에 적절한 어휘를 찾는 유형이 출제되고 있다.
2. 어휘 적절성 문제는 구체적으로 '밑줄 친 부분 중 문맥상 낱말의 쓰임이 적절하지 않는' 것을 고르는 문제와 '(A), (B), (C)의 각 네모 안에서 문맥에 맞는 낱말로 적절한' 것을 고르는 문제가 출제되고 있다. 수능에서는 2문항이 출제되다가, 2014학년도부터 한 문항이 출제되고 있다. 고1 학력 평가에서도 1문항이 출제된다.
3. 주제가 분명하고 글의 흐름이 뚜렷한 글을 사용해 문제가 출제되고 있다.
4. 최근 수능 7년간, 어휘 적절성 파악 문제는 2017학년도 수능(57%), 2018(49%), 2019(57%), 2020(55%), 2021(73%), 2022(55%), 2023(58%)에서 괄호 안의 정답률을 보였다. 7년간 평균 57.7%의 정답률을 보였다. 난이도는 상 단계이다.

출처			문항 번호	지문 주제	정답률(%)	난이도
대표	2022학년도	11 학평	30번	식물의 성장은 옥신에 의해 조절됨	53	★★★
1	2022학년도	09 학평	30번	허브의 위약 효과	61	★★☆
2	2022학년도	06 학평	30번	자신의 삶에 대한 통제력을 가져라	64	★★☆
3	2022학년도	03 학평	30번	거절당하는 상황을 연습하라	45	★★★
4	2021학년도	11 학평	30번	동물 종의 멸종을 막기 위한 동물원의 회복 프로그램	25	★★★
5	2021학년도	09 학평	30번	인간의 사회적 교류를 발전시키는 사냥	54	★★★
6	2021학년도	06 학평	30번	자연계의 복잡한 형태는 그것의 기능에 필수적이다	36	★★★
7	2021학년도	03 학평	30번	인공조명의 비용 하락	61	★★☆
8	2020학년도	11 학평	30번	사육으로 인한 뇌 크기 감소	54	★★★
9	2020학년도	09 학평	30번	유대를 위한 경쟁과 협력	60	★★☆
10	2020학년도	06 학평	30번	에너지를 많이 소모하지만 효율적인 두뇌	71	★★☆

1등급 꿀팁

1. '밑줄 친 부분 중 문맥상 낱말의 쓰임이 적절하지 않는' 문제는 적절하지 않는 어휘 대신에 어떤 단어를 써야 할지 숙고해 본다.
2. '(A), (B), (C)의 각 네모 안에서 문맥에 맞는 낱말로 적절한' 것을 고르는 문제는 네모 안에 반의어, 유의어가 쌍으로 제시되는 경우가 많으므로 단어 공부를 할 때, 반의어, 유의어 학습을 부지런히 하도록 한다.

제한 시간 : 15분 | 정답 및 해설 058쪽

대표 기출

2022학년도 11월 학평 30번

30. 다음 글의 밑줄 친 부분 중, 문맥상 낱말의 쓰임이 적절하지 않은 것은? [3점]

Plant growth is controlled by a group of hormones called auxins found at the tips of stems and roots of plants. Auxins produced at the tips of stems tend to accumulate on the side of the stem that is in the shade. Accordingly, the auxins ① stimulate growth on the shaded side of the plant. Therefore, the shaded side grows faster than the side facing the sunlight. This phenomenon causes the stem to bend and appear to be growing ② towards the light. Auxins have the ③ opposite effect on the roots of plants. Auxins in the tips of roots tend to limit growth. If a root is horizontal in the soil, the auxins will accumulate on the lower side and interfere with its development. Therefore, the lower side of the root will grow ④ faster than the upper side. This will, in turn, cause the root to bend ⑤ downwards, with the tip of the root growing in that direction.

문제 풀이

1. 글의 앞부분을 읽으며 글의 소재나 요지를 파악한다.

• Plant growth is controlled by a group of hormones called auxins found at the tips of stems and roots of plants. (식물의 성장은 식물의 줄기와 뿌리 끝에서 발견되는 옥신이라고 불리는 호르몬 그룹에 의해 조절된다.)

2. 글의 문맥을 바탕으로 문장 간 또는 문장 내 논리적인 흐름을 통해 밑줄 친 낱말의 적절성을 파악한다.

① Accordingly, the auxins stimulate growth on the shaded side of the plant. (따라서, 옥신은 식물의 그늘진 면에서의 성장을 자극한다.)

② This phenomenon causes the stem to bend and appear to be growing towards the light. (이 현상은 줄기가 휘어지게 하고 빛을 향하여 성장하는 것처럼 보이게 한다.)

③ Auxins have the opposite effect on the roots of plants. (옥신은 식물의 뿌리에서는 반대의 효과를 가진다.)

⑤ This will, in turn, cause the root to bend downwards, with the tip of the root growing in that direction. (이는 결과적으로 뿌리의 끝부분이 그 방향으로 자란 채 뿌리가 아래로 휘어지게 한다.)

3. 문맥상 적절해 보이지 않는 ④ faster의 대안을 생각해 보고 문맥을 점검하여 답을 정한다.

• 식물의 뿌리 끝에 있는 옥신은 성장을 억제하는 경향이 있다고 했으므로 뿌리의 아래쪽은 위쪽보다 성장이 느려야 한다는 흐름이 되어야 문맥상 자연스럽다. 따라서 ④ 'faster(더 빠르게)'를 'slower(더 느리게)'로 고쳐야 한다.

2022학년도 9월 학평 30번 ★★☆

1. 다음 글의 밑줄 친 부분 중, 문맥상 낱말의 쓰임이 적절하지 않은 것은? [3점]

It is widely believed that certain herbs somehow magically improve the work of certain organs, and "cure" specific diseases as a result. Such statements are unscientific and groundless. Sometimes herbs appear to work, since they tend to ① increase your blood circulation in an aggressive attempt by your body to eliminate them from your system. That can create a ② temporary feeling of a high, which makes it seem as if your health condition has improved. Also, herbs can have a placebo effect, just like any other method, thus helping you feel better. Whatever the case, it is your body that has the intelligence to ③ regain health, and not the herbs. How can herbs have the intelligence needed to direct your body into getting healthier? That is impossible. Try to imagine how herbs might come into your body and intelligently ④ fix your problems. If you try to do that, you will see how impossible it seems. Otherwise, it would mean that herbs are ⑤ less intelligent than the human body, which is truly hard to believe.

* placebo effect: 위약 효과

2022학년도 6월 학평 30번 ★★☆

2. 다음 글의 밑줄 친 부분 중, 문맥상 낱말의 쓰임이 적절하지 않은 것은? [3점]

Do you sometimes feel like you don't love your life? Like, deep inside, something is missing? That's because we are living someone else's life. We allow other people to ① influence our choices. We are trying to meet their expectations. Social pressure is deceiving — we are all impacted without noticing it. Before we realize we are losing ownership of our lives, we end up ② ignoring how other people live. Then, we can only see the greener grass — ours is never good enough. To regain that passion for the life you want, you must ③ recover control of your choices. No one but yourself can choose how you live. But, how? The first step to getting rid of expectations is to treat yourself ④ kindly. You can't truly love other people if you don't love yourself first. When we accept who we are, there's no room for other's ⑤ expectations.

2022학년도 3월 학평 30번 ★★★

3. 다음 글의 밑줄 친 부분 중, 문맥상 낱말의 쓰임이 적절하지 않은 것은? [3점]

Rejection is an everyday part of our lives, yet most people can't handle it well. For many, it's so painful that they'd rather not ask for something at all than ask and ① risk rejection. Yet, as the old saying goes, if you don't ask, the answer is always no. Avoiding rejection ② negatively affects many aspects of your life. All of that happens only because you're not ③ tough enough to handle it. For this reason, consider rejection therapy. Come up with a ④ request or an activity that usually results in a rejection. Working in sales is one such example. Asking for discounts at the stores will also work. By deliberately getting yourself ⑤ welcomed you'll grow a thicker skin that will allow you to take on much more in life, thus making you more successful at dealing with unfavorable circumstances.

* deliberately: 의도적으로

2021학년도 9월 학평 30번 ★★★

5. 다음 글의 밑줄 친 부분 중, 문맥상 낱말의 쓰임이 적절하지 않은 것은? [3점]

Hunting can explain how humans developed *reciprocal altruism* and *social exchange*. Humans seem to be unique among primates in showing extensive reciprocal relationships that can last years, decades, or a lifetime. Meat from a large game animal comes in quantities that ① exceed what a single hunter and his immediate family could possibly consume. Furthermore, hunting success is highly ② variable; a hunter who is successful one week might fail the next. These conditions ③ encourage food sharing from hunting. The costs to a hunter of giving away meat he cannot eat immediately are ④ high because he cannot consume all the meat himself and leftovers will soon spoil. The benefits can be large, however, when those who are given his food return the generous favor later on when he has failed to get food for himself. In essence, hunters can ⑤ store extra meat in the bodies of their friends and neighbors.

* reciprocal altruism: 상호 이타주의 ** primates: 영장류

Day 12

2021학년도 11월 학평 30번 ★★★

4. 다음 글의 밑줄 친 부분 중, 문맥상 낱말의 쓰임이 적절하지 않은 것은?

For species approaching extinction, zoos can act as a last chance for survival. ① Recovery programs are established to coordinate the efforts of field conservationists and wildlife authorities. As populations of those species ② diminish it is not unusual for zoos to start captive breeding programs. Captive breeding acts to protect against extinction. In some cases captive-bred individuals may be released back into the wild, supplementing wild populations. This is most successful in situations where individuals are at greatest threat during a ③ particular life stage. For example, turtle eggs may be removed from high-risk locations until after they hatch. This may ④ increase the number of turtles that survive to adulthood. Crocodile programs have also been successful in protecting eggs and hatchlings, ⑤ capturing hatchlings once they are better equipped to protect themselves.

* captive breeding: 포획 사육 ** hatch: 부화하다

2021학년도 6월 학평 30번 ★★★

6. 다음 글의 밑줄 친 부분 중, 문맥상 낱말의 쓰임이 적절하지 않은 것은? [3점]

Detailed study over the past two or three decades is showing that the complex forms of natural systems are essential to their functioning. The attempt to ① straighten rivers and give them regular cross-sections is perhaps the most disastrous example of this form-and-function relationship. The natural river has a very ② irregular form: it curves a lot, spills across floodplains, and leaks into wetlands, giving it an ever-changing and incredibly complex shoreline. This allows the river to ③ prevent variations in water level and speed. Pushing the river into tidy geometry ④ destroys functional capacity and results in disasters like the Mississippi floods of 1927 and 1993 and, more recently, the unnatural disaster of Hurricane Katrina. A $50 billion plan to "let the river loose" in Louisiana recognizes that the ⑤ controlled Mississippi is washing away twenty-four square miles of that state annually.

* geometry: 기하학 ** capacity: 수용능력

2021학년도 3월 학평 30번 ★★☆

7. 다음 글의 밑줄 친 부분 중, 문맥상 낱말의 쓰임이 적절하지 않은 것은? [3점]

When the price of something fundamental drops greatly, the whole world can change. Consider light. Chances are you are reading this sentence under some kind of artificial light. Moreover, you probably never thought about whether using artificial light for reading was worth it. Light is so ① cheap that you use it without thinking. But in the early 1800s, it would have cost you four hundred times what you are paying now for the same amount of light. At that price, you would ② notice the cost and would think twice before using artificial light to read a book. The ③ increase in the price of light lit up the world. Not only did it turn night into day, but it allowed us to live and work in big buildings that ④ natural light could not enter. Nearly nothing we have today would be ⑤ possible if the cost of artificial light had not dropped to almost nothing.

* artificial: 인공의

2020학년도 11월 학평 30번 ★★★

8. (A), (B), (C)의 각 네모 안에서 문맥에 맞는 낱말로 가장 적절한 것은? [3점]

Recent research suggests that evolving humans' relationship with dogs changed the structure of both species' brains. One of the various (A) [physical / psychological] changes caused by domestication is a reduction in the size of the brain: 16 percent for horses, 34 percent for pigs, and 10 to 30 percent for dogs. This is because once humans started to take care of these animals, they no longer needed various brain functions in order to survive. Animals who were fed and protected by humans did not need many of the skills required by their wild ancestors and (B) [developed / lost] the parts of the brain related to those capacities. A similar process occurred for humans, who seem to have been domesticated by wolves. About 10,000 years ago, when the role of dogs was firmly established in most human societies, the human brain also (C) [expanded / shrank] by about 10 percent.

	(A)		(B)		(C)
①	physical	……	developed	……	expanded
②	physical	……	lost	……	expanded
③	physical	……	lost	……	shrank
④	psychological	……	developed	……	shrank
⑤	psychological	……	lost	……	shrank

2020학년도 9월 학평 30번 ★★☆

9. (A), (B), (C)의 각 네모 안에서 문맥에 맞는 낱말로 가장 적절한 것은? [3점]

Social connections are so essential for our survival and well-being that we not only cooperate with others to build relationships, we also compete with others for friends. And often we do both at the same time. Take gossip. Through gossip, we bond with our friends, sharing interesting details. But at the same time, we are (A) [creating / forgiving] potential enemies in the targets of our gossip. Or consider rival holiday parties where people compete to see who will attend *their* party. We can even see this (B) [harmony / tension] in social media as people compete for the most friends and followers. At the same time, competitive exclusion can also (C) [generate / prevent] cooperation. High school social clubs and country clubs use this formula to great effect: It is through selective inclusion *and exclusion* that they produce loyalty and lasting social bonds.

	(A)		(B)		(C)
①	creating	……	harmony	……	prevent
②	creating	……	tension	……	generate
③	creating	……	tension	……	prevent
④	forgiving	……	tension	……	prevent
⑤	forgiving	……	harmony	……	generate

2020학년도 6월 학평 30번 ★★☆

10. (A), (B), (C)의 각 네모 안에서 문맥에 맞는 낱말로 가장 적절한 것은?

The brain makes up just two percent of our body weight but uses 20 percent of our energy. In newborns, it's no less than 65 percent. That's partly why babies sleep all the time — their growing brains (A) [warn / exhaust] them — and have a lot of body fat, to use as an energy reserve when needed. Our muscles use even more of our energy, about a quarter of the total, but we have a lot of muscle. Actually, per unit of matter, the brain uses by far (B) [more / less] energy than our other organs. That means that the brain is the most expensive of our organs. But it is also marvelously (C) [creative / efficient]. Our brains require only about four hundred calories of energy a day — about the same as we get from a blueberry muffin. Try running your laptop for twenty-four hours on a muffin and see how far you get.

	(A)		(B)		(C)
①	warn	……	less	……	efficient
②	warn	……	more	……	efficient
③	exhaust	……	more	……	efficient
④	exhaust	……	more	……	creative
⑤	exhaust	……	less	……	creative

총 문항				문항	맞은 문항					문항
개별 문항	1	2	3	4	5	6	7	8	9	10
채점										
개별 문항	11	12	13	14	15	16	17	18	19	20
채점										

12. 접속사

정답 및 해설 063쪽

A 문법의 주요 포인트를 점검해 봅시다.

1 두 단어 이상이 모여 주어와 동사의 기능을 갖추고 있는 것을 절이라고 하며, 절과 절을 연결하기 위해 사용하는 것을 접속사라고 한다. 접속사 종류에는 등위, 종속, 상관접속사가 있다.

2 등위접속사(and, but, or, so, for)는 대등한 관계에 있는 단어나 구와 절을 연결한다. 등위접속사로 연결된 대상은 항상 같은 형태(병렬구조)를 지닌다.

3 종속접속사는 종속절(명사절, 부사절, 형용사절)을 주절에 연결한다.

명사절을 이끄는 접속사	that, if, whether		
부사절을 이끄는 시간 접속사	when, while, as, before, after, as soon as	부사절을 이끄는 양보 접속사	although, even though, even if
부사절을 이끄는 이유 접속사	because, as, since, now that	부사절을 이끄는 목적 접속사	so that... may(will), in case
부사절을 이끄는 조건 접속사	if, once, as long as	부사절을 이끄는 결과 접속사	so... that ~

* in that(~라는 점에서)은 판단 근거를 나타내는 종속접속사로 사용된다.

4 상관접속사는 두 개 이상의 단어로 이루어진 등위접속사를 말한다.

5 접속사와 의미가 비슷한 전치사(구)를 유의해야 한다. 접속사 뒤에는 「주어+동사」가 나오지만, 전치사 뒤에는 「명사(구)」가 나온다.

B 다음 괄호 안에서 어법상 올바른 것을 고르시오.

1 The wine experts were similarly tricked into thinking **[that /although]** the white wine Chardonnay was in fact a red wine, when it had been coloured with a red dye.

2 Since the nineteenth century, shopkeepers have taken advantage of this trick by choosing prices ending 9, to give the impression **[whether / that]** a product is cheeper than it is.

3 **[Once / In case]** I realized something strange was happening, my heart started beating fast.

4 **[Though / Because]** she is more famous for being an editor than for fiction writer, many critics consider her novel *Plum Bun* Fauset's strongest work.

5 It is so important for us to identify context related to Information **[because / though]** if we fail to do so, we may judge and react too quickly.

6 Many of the manufactured products made today contain so many chemicals and artificial ingredients **[which / that]** it is sometimes difficult to know exactly what is inside them.

7 Labels on food are **[as / like]** the table of contents found in books.

8 Icy hockey is unusual among the major sports in **[such / that]** teams frequently play with different numbers of players.

9 We study philosophy **[because / because of]** the mental skill it helps us develop.

10 **[In spite of / Although]** his efforts, he failed to win the prize

어휘 플러스

12. 접두사

정답 및 해설 063쪽

A 다음 수능 필수 어휘를 읽고, 아는 것은 체크해 봅시다.

□ 01	ad-	~을 향하여, 첨가	ad(~을 향하여)+apt(맞추다) = adapt(적응시키다)
□ 02	ante- / anti-	앞에, 전에	anti(미리)+cip(잡다)+ate(접사) = anticipate(예상하다)
□ 03	pre-	미리, 먼저	pre(미리)+dict(말하다) = predict(예언하다)
□ 04	pro-	앞으로, 찬성하여	pro(앞으로)+ceed(가다) = proceed(전진하다)
□ 05	post-	이후에, 뒤에	post(이후에)+pone(놓다) = postpone(미루다)
□ 06	re-	다시, 뒤로	re(다시)+spect(보다) = respect(존경하다)
□ 07	sub-	~의 아래에	sub(~의 아래에)+conscious(의식하는) = subconscious(잠재의식의)
□ 08	super-/sur-	~위에, 초월해서	super(~위에)+vise(보다) = supervise(감독하다)
□ 09	com/con/cor-	함께	com(함께)+pose(두다) = compose(구성하다, 작곡하다)
□ 10	sym/syn-	함께, 동시에, 강조	sym(함께)+pathy(감정) = sympathy(공감, 동정)
□ 11	mis-	잘못된, 나쁜	mis(잘못된)+take(취하다) = mistake(실수)
□ 12	en/em-	~하게 하다	en(~하게 하다)+able(가능한) = enable(가능케 하다)
□ 13	in-	안으로, 반대, 부정	in(안으로)+come(오다) = income(수입)
□ 14	inter-	~사이의, 상호간에	inter(~사이의)+national(국가의) = international(국제적인)
□ 15	out-	밖으로, 능가하는	out(밖으로)+look(보다) = outlook(전망, 예측)
□ 16	per-	완전히, 두루	per(완전히)+severe(엄격한) = persever(인내하다)
□ 17	ex-	밖으로, ~을 넘어서	ex(밖으로)+pose(두다) = expose(노출하다, 드러내다)
□ 18	dis-	분리, 부정	dis(반대)+agree(동의하다) = disagree(반대하다)
□ 19	de/di-	아래, 분리, 강조	de(아래)+spise(보다) = despise(경멸하다)
□ 20	anti-	대항하여, 반대하여	anti(대항하여)+biotic(생물의) = antibiotic(항생 물질)

B 괄호 안에서 문맥에 맞는 낱말로 적절한 것을 골라 봅시다.

1 They found that they could understand and **[predict / postpone]** events better if they reduced passion and prejudice, replacing these with observation and inference.

2 Our collection letters **[proceed / compose]** automatically in a series, and occasionally a payment crosses a letter in the mails.

3 Steve had **[supervised / exposed]** one of his company's warehouses for four years.

4 In laboratory experiments, people **[enabled / exposed]** to 110-decibel bursts of noise experienced a decrease in their ability to solve problems.

5 I walked the dog four times a day just because you said it was very important that she be out that many times — I **[composed / disagreed]**, as you'll recall, but nonetheless I walked her.

13 빈칸 추론 (1) 어휘, 짧은 어구

출제 트렌드

1. 빈칸에 들어갈 어휘나 짧은 어구를 추론하는 유형은 고1 학력 평가에서 거의 2문항이 출제된다. 빈칸 문제는 논리적이고 종합적인 이해력을 요구하는 문제로 난이도와 변별력이 높게 출제된다.
2. 논리적 관계를 파악하기 위해서는 글을 읽고 내용의 논리적 관계(예를 들어, 원인과 결과 관계)를 파악하는 능력이 필요하다. 논리적 관계 파악하기에는 단어나, 구, 절, 문장 또는 연결어가 들어갈 빈칸의 내용을 추론하는 문제 유형이 있다.
3. 최근 수능 7년간, 빈칸 추론 (1) 어휘, 짧은 어구 문제는 주로 31번, 32번 문항으로 출제되었다. 2017학년도 수능에서 (45/43%), 2018(64/60%), 2019(57/63%), 2020(43/65%), 2021(54/57%)), 2022(67/47%), 2023(47/68%)에서 괄호 안의 정답률을 보였다. 평균 55.7%의 정답률을 보였으며, 난이도는 상 단계이다.

출처			문항 번호	지문 주제	정답률(%)	난이도
대표	2022학년도	11 학평	31번	자유를 제한하는 것이 자기 통제와 성과를 향상시킨다	66	★★☆
1	2022학년도	11 학평	32번	서로를 위해 일하게 함으로써 우리의 삶을 바꾸는 혁신	45	★★★
2	2022학년도	09 학평	31번	인간의 판단력을 빼앗는 로봇	50	★★★
3	2022학년도	09 학평	32번	사람은 자신의 발달에 능동적인 기여자이다	56	★★★
4	2022학년도	06 학평	31번	한계가 창의력을 증진시킬 수 있다	54	★★★
5	2022학년도	06 학평	32번	수요 법칙이 적용되지 않는 기펜재	57	★★★
6	2022학년도	03 학평	31번	실감나는 글을 쓰기 위해 세밀하게 표현하라	47	★★★
7	2022학년도	03 학평	32번	대화는 지식을 공유하는 강력한 방법이다	53	★★★
8	2021학년도	11 학평	31번	사전 통보의 중요성	65	★★☆
9	2021학년도	11 학평	32번	우리가 누구인지를 규정하는 기억	67	★★☆
10	2021학년도	09 학평	31번	단순함이 기업에 비교우위를 준다	58	★★★
11	2021학년도	09 학평	32번	경제와 언어의 상관관계	67	★★☆

1등급 꿀팁

1. 글의 주제나 요지가 빈칸으로 제시되는 경우가 많으므로 지문의 주제나 요지를 확인하다.
2. 글의 소재 및 중심 요지를 파악하고 핵심 어구에 줄을 그으며 읽어 간다.
3. 글을 읽을 때 특히 빈칸 전후 부분을 살펴보면서 빈칸에 들어갈 단서를 찾아본다.
4. 평소에 다양한 주제와 소재의 지문을 꾸준히 접한다.

빈칸추론 (1) 어휘, 짧은 어구

제한 시간 : 17분 | 정답 및 해설 064쪽

대표 기출

2022학년도 11월 학평 31번

31. 다음 빈칸에 들어갈 말로 가장 적절한 것을 고르시오.

To demonstrate how best to defeat the habit of delaying, Dan Ariely, a professor of psychology and behavioral economics, performed an experiment on students in three of his classes at MIT. He assigned all classes three reports over the course of the semester. The first class had to choose three due dates for themselves, up to and including the last day of class. The second had no deadlines — all three papers just had to be submitted by the last day of class. In his third class, he gave students three set deadlines over the course of the semester. At the end of the semester, he found that students with set deadlines received the best grades, the students with no deadlines had the worst, and those who could choose their own deadlines fell somewhere in the middle. Ariely concludes that ____________ — whether by the professor or by students who recognize their own tendencies to delay things — improves self-control and performance.

① offering rewards
② removing obstacles
③ restricting freedom
④ increasing assignments
⑤ encouraging competition

문제 풀이

1. 등장인물이 겪은 사건이나 처한 상황을 파악한다.
- Cindy happened to sit next to a famous artist in a café. He was drawing on a used napkin over coffee. (까페에서 한 유명한 화가를 만났는데, 그는 커피를 마시면서 사용하던 냅킨에 그림을 그리고 있었음.)

2. 등장인물의 심경을 추론할 수 있는 표현을 찾는다.
① she was thrilled to see him in person. (유명한 화가를 카페에서 직접 만나게 되어 흥분됨)
② She was looking on in awe. (경외심을 갖고 그를 바라봄.)
③ Being at a loss, she stood still rooted to the ground. (그녀는 어쩔 줄 몰라 꼼짝 못한 채 서 있었음.)

3. 글의 흐름 및 상황이 중간에 전환되어 주인공의 심경이 바뀌는 것을 파악한다.
① "Can I have that napkin you drew on?", she asked. "Sure," he replied. "Twenty thousand dollars." (Cindy가 그가 찬 냅킨을 가질 수 없냐고 물었더니, 그가 2만 달러를 요구함)

- 까페에서 유명한 예술가를 들떠 있던 Cindy가 그가 냅킨에 그림을 그리자 그것을 가지고 싶어 했다. 그래서 가져도 되냐고 했더니 예술가가 2만 달러를 요구하자 Cindy가 매우 놀라고 당황했다. 정답은 ③ excited → surprised가 가장 적절하다.

2022학년도 11월 학평 32번 ★★★

1. 다음 빈칸에 들어갈 말로 가장 적절한 것은?

The best way in which innovation changes our lives is by ____________________. The main theme of human history is that we become steadily more specialized in what we produce, and steadily more diversified in what we consume: we move away from unstable self-sufficiency to safer mutual interdependence. By concentrating on serving other people's needs for forty hours a week — which we call a job — you can spend the other seventy-two hours (not counting fifty-six hours in bed) relying on the services provided to you by other people. Innovation has made it possible to work for a fraction of a second in order to be able to afford to turn on an electric lamp for an hour, providing the quantity of light that would have required a whole day's work if you had to make it yourself by collecting and refining sesame oil or lamb fat to burn in a simple lamp, as much of humanity did in the not so distant past. [3점]

* a fraction of a second: 아주 짧은 시간 ** refine: 정제하다

① respecting the values of the old days
② enabling people to work for each other
③ providing opportunities to think creatively
④ satisfying customers with personalized services
⑤ introducing and commercializing unusual products

2022학년도 9월 학평 31번 ★★★

2. 다음 빈칸에 들어갈 말로 가장 적절한 것은?

We worry that the robots are taking our jobs, but just as common a problem is that the robots are taking our __________. In the large warehouses so common behind the scenes of today's economy, human 'pickers' hurry around grabbing products off shelves and moving them to where they can be packed and dispatched. In their ears are headpieces: the voice of 'Jennifer', a piece of software, tells them where to go and what to do, controlling the smallest details of their movements. Jennifer breaks down instructions into tiny chunks, to minimise error and maximise productivity — for example, rather than picking eighteen copies of a book off a shelf, the human worker would be politely instructed to pick five. Then another five. Then yet another five. Then another three. Working in such conditions reduces people to machines made of flesh. Rather than asking us to think or adapt, the Jennifer unit takes over the thought process and treats workers as an inexpensive source of some visual processing and a pair of opposable thumbs. [3점]

* dispatch: 발송하다 ** chunk: 덩어리

① reliability　② judgment
③ endurance　④ sociability
⑤ cooperation

2022학년도 9월 학평 32번 ★★★

3. 다음 빈칸에 들어갈 말로 가장 적절한 것은?

The prevailing view among developmental scientists is that people are active contributors to their own development. People are influenced by the physical and social contexts in which they live, but they also play a role in influencing their development by interacting with, and changing, those contexts. Even infants influence the world around them and construct their own development through their interactions. Consider an infant who smiles at each adult he sees; he influences his world because adults are likely to smile, use "baby talk," and play with him in response. The infant brings adults into close contact, making one-on-one interactions and creating opportunities for learning. By engaging the world around them, thinking, being curious, and interacting with people, objects, and the world around them, individuals of all ages are "______________________________________."

① mirrors of their generation
② shields against social conflicts
③ explorers in their own career path
④ followers of their childhood dreams
⑤ manufacturers of their own development

2022학년도 6월 학평 31번 ★★★

4. 다음 빈칸에 들어갈 말로 가장 적절한 것은?

One of the big questions faced this past year was how to keep innovation rolling when people were working entirely virtually. But experts say that digital work didn't have a negative effect on innovation and creativity. Working within limits pushes us to solve problems. Overall, virtual meeting platforms put more constraints on communication and collaboration than face-to-face settings. For instance, with the press of a button, virtual meeting hosts can control the size of breakout groups and enforce time constraints; only one person can speak at a time; nonverbal signals, particularly those below the shoulders, are diminished; "seating arrangements" are assigned by the platform, not by individuals; and visual access to others may be limited by the size of each participant's screen. Such ____________________ are likely to stretch participants beyond their usual ways of thinking, boosting creativity.

① restrictions ② responsibilities
③ memories ④ coincidences
⑤ traditions

2022학년도 6월 학평 32번 ★★★

5. 다음 빈칸에 들어갈 말로 가장 적절한 것은?

The law of demand is that the demand for goods and services increases as prices fall, and the demand falls as prices increase. *Giffen goods* are special types of products for which the traditional law of demand does not apply. Instead of switching to cheaper replacements, consumers demand more of giffen goods when the price increases and less of them when the price decreases. Taking an example, rice in China is a giffen good because people tend to purchase less of it when the price falls. The reason for this is, when the price of rice falls, people have more money to spend on other types of products such as meat and dairy and, therefore, change their spending pattern. On the other hand, as rice prices increase, people ______________________________. [3점]

① order more meat ② consume more rice
③ try to get new jobs ④ increase their savings
⑤ start to invest overseas

2022학년도 3월 학평 31번 ★★★

6. 다음 빈칸에 들어갈 말로 가장 적절한 것은?

Generalization without specific examples that humanize writing is boring to the listener and to the reader. Who wants to read platitudes all day? Who wants to hear the words great, greater, best, smartest, finest, humanitarian, on and on and on without specific examples? Instead of using these 'nothing words,' leave them out completely and just describe the ________________. There is nothing worse than reading a scene in a novel in which a main character is described up front as heroic or brave or tragic or funny, while thereafter, the writer quickly moves on to something else. That's no good, no good at all. You have to use less one word descriptions and more detailed, engaging descriptions if you want to make something real.

* platitude: 상투적인 말

① similarities ② particulars
③ fantasies ④ boredom
⑤ wisdom

2022학년도 3월 학평 32번 ★★★

7. 다음 빈칸에 들어갈 말로 가장 적절한 것은?

Face-to-face interaction is a uniquely powerful — and sometimes the only — way to share many kinds of knowledge, from the simplest to the most complex. It is one of the best ways to stimulate new thinking and ideas, too. Most of us would have had difficulty learning how to tie a shoelace only from pictures, or how to do arithmetic from a book. Psychologist Mihàly Csikszentmihàlyi found, while studying high achievers, that a large number of Nobel Prize winners were the students of previous winners: they had access to the same literature as everyone else, but ____________________ made a crucial difference to their creativity. Within organisations this makes conversation both a crucial factor for high-level professional skills and the most important way of sharing everyday information.

* arithmetic: 계산 ** literature: (연구) 문헌

① natural talent ② regular practice
③ personal contact ④ complex knowledge
⑤ powerful motivation

2021학년도 11월 학평 31번 ★★☆

8. 다음 빈칸에 들어갈 말로 가장 적절한 것은?

We don't send telegraphs to communicate anymore, but it's a great metaphor for giving advance notice. Sometimes, you must inform those close to you of upcoming change by conveying important information well in advance. There's a huge difference between saying, "From now on, we will do things differently," which doesn't give people enough time to understand and accept the change, and saying something like, "Starting next month, we're going to approach things differently." Telegraphing empowers people to __________. Telegraphing involves the art of seeing an upcoming event or circumstance and giving others enough time to process and accept the change. Telegraph anything that will take people out of what is familiar and comfortable to them. This will allow processing time for them to accept the circumstances and make the most of what's happening.

① unite ② adapt ③ object
④ compete ⑤ recover

2021학년도 11월 학평 32번 ★★☆

9. 다음 빈칸에 들어갈 말로 가장 적절한 것은?

Not only does memory underlie our ability to think at all, it defines the content of our experiences and how we preserve them for years to come. Memory ______________________. If I were to suffer from heart failure and depend upon an artificial heart, I would be no less myself. If I lost an arm in an accident and had it replaced with an artificial arm, I would still be essentially *me*. As long as my mind and memories remain intact, I will continue to be the same person, no matter which part of my body (other than the brain) is replaced. On the other hand, when someone suffers from advanced Alzheimer's disease and his memories fade, people often say that he "is not himself anymore," or that it is as if the person "is no longer there," though his body remains unchanged.

* intact: 손상되지 않은

① makes us who we are
② has to do with our body
③ reflects what we expect
④ lets us understand others
⑤ helps us learn from the past

2021학년도 9월 학평 31번 ★★★

10. 다음 빈칸에 들어갈 말로 가장 적절한 것은?

Sometimes it is the ______________________ that gives a business a competitive advantage. Until recently, bicycles had to have many gears, often 15 or 20, for them to be considered high-end. But fixed-gear bikes with minimal features have become more popular, as those who buy them are happy to pay more for much less. The overall profitability of these bikes is much higher than the more complex ones because they do a single thing really well without the cost of added complexity. Companies should be careful of getting into a war over adding more features with their competitors, as this will increase cost and almost certainly reduce profitability because of competitive pressure on price.

* high-end: 최고급의

① simpler product
② affordable price
③ consumer loyalty
④ customized design
⑤ eco-friendly technology

2021학년도 9월 학평 32번 ★★☆

11. 다음 빈칸에 들어갈 말로 가장 적절한 것은?

Many evolutionary biologists argue that humans ______________________________. We needed to trade, and we needed to establish trust in order to trade. Language is very handy when you are trying to conduct business with someone. Two early humans could not only agree to trade three wooden bowls for six bunches of bananas but establish rules as well. What wood was used for the bowls? Where did you get the bananas? That business deal would have been nearly impossible using only gestures and confusing noises, and carrying it out according to terms agreed upon creates a bond of trust. Language allows us to be specific, and this is where conversation plays a key role.

① used body language to communicate
② instinctively knew who to depend on
③ often changed rules for their own needs
④ lived independently for their own survival
⑤ developed language for economic reasons

총 문항				문항	맞은 문항					문항
개별 문항	1	2	3	4	5	6	7	8	9	10
채점										
개별 문항	11	12	13	14	15	16	17	18	19	20
채점										

문법 플러스

13. 관계대명사

정답 및 해설 069쪽

A 문법의 주요 포인트를 점검해 봅시다.

1 관계대명사는 문장 내에서 「접속사+대명사」의 역할을 하며, 선행사를 수식하는 형용사절의 역할을 한다. 관계대명사의 주격, 소유격, 목적격의 결정은 선행사가 관계대명사절에서 어떤 역할을 하느냐에 따라 결정된다. 관계사 what(= the thing(s) which[that])은 선행사를 포함하고 있으므로, 따로 선행사가 관계사 앞에 나와 있지 않다.

▫ 관계대명사

선행사	주격	목적격	소유격
사람	who	who(m)	whose
사물/동물	which	which	of which 또는 whose
사람/사물/동물	that	that	–

2 목적격 관계대명사와 「주격관계대명사+be동사」는 생략할 수 있다.

3 관계대명사 who, which는 계속적 용법이 있지만, that은 계속적 용법이 없다.

4 관계대명사에 -ever를 붙이면 복합관계대명사가 된다. 복합관계대명사는 선행사를 포함하고 있으며, 명사절이나 양보의 부사절로 사용할 수 있다. 명사절로 사용된 경우에는 복합관계사가 문장 속에서 주어, 목적어, 보어의 역할을 한다. 부사절로 사용된 경우에는 복합관계사 뒤에 완전한 문장이 나온다.

▫ 복합관계대명사

	whoever	whatever	whichever
명사절 (부정)	anyone who (~하는 사람은 누구든지)	anything that (~하는 것은 무엇이든지)	any one that (~하는 어느 쪽이든지)
부사절 (양보)	no matter who (누가 ~하더라도)	no matter what (무엇이[을] ~하더라도)	no matter which (어느 쪽이[을] ~하더라도)

B 다음 괄호 안에서 어법상 올바른 것을 고르시오.

1 Most people are happiest in bright sunshine—this may cause a release of chemicals in the body **[who / that]** bring a feeling of emotional well-being.

2 "The world **[that / where]** children share with their peers," she says, "is what shapes their behavior and modifies the characteristic they were born with."

3 Plastic is extremely slow to degrade and tends to float, **[which / where]** allows it to travel in ocean currents for thousands of miles.

4 Old ideas are replaced when scientists find new information **[that / what]** they cannot explain.

5 It is important to remember, however, that this new way of painting was challenging to its public not only in the way that it was made but also in **[that, what]** was shown.

6 In the northern hemisphere, the shadows rotate in the direction **[which / where]** we now call "clockwise."

7 Directors can simply point the camera at **[whatever / whenever]** they want the audience to look at.

8 He is the author about **[which / whom]** we've been talking.

9 Sally slid on the ice, **[that / which]** made everyone laugh.

10 He just produced **[which / what]** was in him, and brought us a rich treasure of music.

어휘 플러스

13. 철자가 혼동되는 어휘 (4)

정답 및 해설 070쪽

A 다음 수능 필수 어휘를 읽고, 아는 것은 체크해 봅시다.

□ 01	asset	n. 자산	□ 21	assert	v. 단언하다
□ 02	assume	v. 추정하다, ~인체하다	□ 22	consume	v. 소비하다
□ 03	attention	n. 배려, 관심, 주의	□ 23	intention	n. 의도, 의향
□ 04	attribute	v. ~의 탓으로 돌리다	□ 24	contribute	v. 공헌하다, 기부하다
□ 05	bald	n. 대머리	□ 25	bold	a. 대범한
□ 06	banish	v. 추방하다, 내쫓다	□ 26	vanish	v. 사라지다
□ 07	blow	v. 바람에 날리다	□ 27	glow	n. 백열, 달아오름
□ 08	concentrate	v. 집중하다, 모으다	□ 28	contaminate	v. 오염시키다
□ 09	consistent	a. 일관된	□ 29	conscious	a. 의식하고 있는, 지각 있는
□ 10	convenience	n. 편의, 편리	□ 30	consequences	n. 결과, 중요성
□ 11	counsel	n. 상담, 조언	□ 31	council	n. 위원회
□ 12	deliberate	a. 신중한	□ 32	delicate	a. 섬세한
□ 13	economic	a. 경제의	□ 33	economics	n. 경제학
□ 14	eliminate	v. 제거하다, 삭제하다	□ 34	illuminate	v. (~에 불을) 비추다, 밝히다
□ 15	emerging	a. 최근 생겨난	□ 35	encouraging	a. 힘을 북돋워 주는
□ 16	enclose	v. 에워싸다, 둘러싸다	□ 36	enhance	v. 높이다, 강화하다
□ 17	evolved	v. 진화시키다	□ 37	involved	a. 복잡한, 뒤얽힌
□ 18	fraction	n. 조각, 파편	□ 38	friction	n. 마찰
□ 19	gem	n. 보석	□ 39	germ	n. 세균
□ 20	high	a. 높은; ad. 높이	□ 40	highly	ad. 매우, 대단히

B 괄호 안에서 문맥에 맞는 낱말로 적절한 것을 골라 봅시다.

1 Nine-tenths of the wood **[assumed / consumed]** in the Third World is used for cooking and heating.

2 The painter, the writer, the musician — all artists **[attribute / contribute]** to a better life for everyone.

3 Another **[conscious / consistent]** research finding is that when a learning activity is undertaken explicitly to attain some extrinsic reward, people respond by seeking the least demanding way of ensuring the reward.

4 This hole helps the kite fly fast regardless of the wind speed by **[concentrating / contaminating]** the wind on days when the wind is light, and letting it pass through when the wind is blowing hard.

5 Ordinary consumers can own a copy of the **[high / highly]** valued originals.

빈칸 추론 (2) 긴 어구, 문장

출제 트렌드

1. 빈칸에 들어갈 긴 어구나 절을 추론하는 유형은 고1 학력 평가에서 거의 2문항이 출제된다. 종합적 사고력을 요구하는 문제로 난이도와 변별력이 매우 높게 출제된다.
2. 빈칸 앞뒤에 제시되는 내용을 논리적으로 이해하고 있는지 글의 흐름을 종합적으로 파악할 수 있는지를 측정하는 문제가 출제된다. 3점 배점이 집중되는 유형이다.
3. 논리적 관계를 파악하기 위해서는 글을 읽고 내용의 논리적 관계(예를 들어, 원인과 결과 관계)를 파악하는 능력이 필요하다. 논리적 관계 파악하기에는 단어나, 구, 절, 문장 또는 연결어가 들어갈 빈칸의 내용을 추론하는 문제 유형이 있다.
4. 최근 수능 7년간, 빈칸 추론(2) 긴 어구, 문장 문제는 주로 33, 34번 문항으로 출제되었다. 2017학년도 수능(33/52%), 2018(52/53%), 2019(32/32%), 2020(48/45%), 2021(55/43%), 2022(50/31%)), 2023(47/21%)에서 괄호 안의 정답률을 보였다. 평균 42.6%의 정답률을 보였으며, 난이도는 상 단계에 속한다. 수능에서 가장 어려운 고난이도 문제 그룹에 속한다.

출처			문항 번호	지문 주제	정답률(%)	난이도
대표	2022학년도	11 학평	33번	유혹으로부터 스스로를 차단함으로써 습관을 깰 수 있다	61	★★☆
1	2022학년도	11 학평	34번	집은 실내 환경에 적응된 종들을 수용하고 새로운 방향으로 진화를 유도함	55	★★★
2	2022학년도	09 학평	33번	신선함의 요구는 환경적인 대가를 치르게 한다	52	★★★
3	2022학년도	09 학평	34번	사람은 두 개의 정보를 동시에 처리할 수 없다	55	★★★
4	2022학년도	06 학평	33번	선천적 성질보다는 후천적 환경의 영향이 크다	47	★★★
5	2022학년도	06 학평	34번	기후 변화에 대응하는 데 실패한 이유	48	★★★
6	2022학년도	03 학평	33번	자막의 부재가 등장인물의 감정을 잘 느끼게 한다	63	★★☆
7	2022학년도	03 학평	34번	홈 이점은 실제로 부담이 된다	21	★★★
8	2021학년도	11 학평	33번	언어를 익히게 만드는 아기들의 소리 패턴 기억	44	★★★
9	2021학년도	11 학평	34번	심해 생물이 생물 발광을 활용하는 이유	59	★★★
10	2021학년도	09 학평	33번	인간은 실수로부터 얻은 이익을 공유해서 영리하다	42	★★★

1등급 꿀팁

1. 빈칸이 첫 문장이나 마지막 문장에 있는 경우, 글의 주제나 요지가 될 가능성이 높다.
2. 빈칸은 주로 중요 문장이 들어가므로 중심 내용을 먼저 찾는다.
3. 전체적인 내용을 종합하여 빈칸에 들어갈 말을 논리적으로 추론한다.
4. 선택지를 선택한 후에는 빈칸에 넣고 문맥상 적절한지 확인해 본다.

빈칸 추론 (2) 긴 어구, 문장

제한 시간 : 15분 | 정답 및 해설 071쪽

대표 기출

2022학년도 11월 학평 33번

33. 다음 빈칸에 들어갈 말로 가장 적절한 것을 고르시오.

If you've ever made a poor choice, you might be interested in learning how to break that habit. One great way to trick your brain into doing so is to sign a "Ulysses Contract." The name of this life tip comes from the Greek myth about Ulysses, a captain whose ship sailed past the island of the Sirens, a tribe of dangerous women who lured victims to their death with their irresistible songs. Knowing that he would otherwise be unable to resist, Ulysses instructed his crew to stuff their ears with cotton and tie him to the ship's mast to prevent him from turning their ship towards the Sirens. It worked for him and you can do the same thing by ______________________. For example, if you want to stay off your cellphone and concentrate on your work, delete the apps that distract you or ask a friend to change your password!

* lure: 유혹하다 ** mast: 돛대

① letting go of all-or-nothing mindset
② finding reasons why you want to change
③ locking yourself out of your temptations
④ building a plan and tracking your progress
⑤ focusing on breaking one bad habit at a time

문제 풀이

1. 글의 도입부에 제시된 글의 소재를 파악하고 글의 내용을 예측한다.

- 글의 소재: poor choice(좋지 못한 습관)와 how to break that habit(그 습관을 깨는 방법)

2. 전개 부분을 읽고 글의 주제를 추론해 본다.

① One great way to trick your brain into doing so is to sign a "Ulysses Contract." (그렇게 하도록 여러분의 뇌를 속이는 한 가지 좋은 방법은 'Ulysses 계약'에 서명하는 것이다.)

② ~lured victims to their death with their irresistible songs.(저항할 수 없는 노래들로 희생자들을 죽음으로 유혹했다) crew to stuff their ears with cotton and tie him to the ship's mast to prevent him from turning their ship towards the Sirens.(그는 그렇게 하지 않으면 저항할 수 없다는 것을 알고 Ulysses는 자신이 배를 사이렌으로 돌리는 것을 막기 위해 자신의 선원들에게 그들의 귀를 솜으로 막고 그를 배의 돛대에 묶으라고 지시했다.)

3. 도입과 전개 부분을 통해 파악한 글의 주제를 염두하고 빈칸 내용을 추론한다. 특히 빈칸과 인접한 문장에서 단서를 찾는다.

- 안 좋은 습관을 깨는 방법으로 Ulysses 계약에 서명하는 것을 제시하고 있는데, 선장 Ulysses가 저항할 수 없는 유혹에서 벗어나기 위해 선원들에게 자신을 배의 돛대에 묶으라고 지시했다는 내용이다. 따라서 빈칸에 ③ 'locking yourself out of your temptations'가 들어가서 빈칸이 포함되는 문장이 '그것은 그에게 효과가 있었고 여러분은 여러분의 유혹으로부터 스스로를 차단함으로써 같은 일을 할 수 있다.'가 되는 것이 가장 적절하다. 특히 글의 마지막 부분에 제시된 사례인 휴대 전화를 멀리하고 일에 집중하고 싶으면 주의를 산만하게 하는 앱들을 삭제하거나 친구에게 비밀번호를 바꿔달라고 요청하라는 내용을 통해 빈칸에 들어갈 말을 추론할 수 있다.

2022학년도 11월 학평 34번 ★★★

1. 다음 빈칸에 들어갈 말로 가장 적절한 것은?

Our homes aren't just ecosystems, they're unique ones, hosting species that are adapted to indoor environments and pushing evolution in new directions. Indoor microbes, insects, and rats have all evolved the ability to survive our chemical attacks, developing resistance to antibacterials, insecticides, and poisons. German cockroaches are known to have developed a distaste for glucose, which is commonly used as bait in roach traps. Some indoor insects, which have fewer opportunities to feed than their outdoor counterparts, seem to have developed the ability to survive when food is limited. Dunn and other ecologists have suggested that as the planet becomes more developed and more urban, more species will ______________________. Over a long enough time period, indoor living could drive our evolution, too. Perhaps my indoorsy self represents the future of humanity. [3점]

* glucose: 포도당 ** bait: 미끼

① produce chemicals to protect themselves
② become extinct with the destroyed habitats
③ evolve the traits they need to thrive indoors
④ compete with outside organisms to find their prey
⑤ break the boundaries between wildlife and humans

2022학년도 9월 학평 33번 ★★★

2. 다음 빈칸에 들어갈 말로 가장 적절한 것은?

The demand for freshness can ______________________. While freshness is now being used as a term in food marketing as part of a return to nature, the demand for year-round supplies of fresh produce such as soft fruit and exotic vegetables has led to the widespread use of hot houses in cold climates and increasing reliance on total quality control — management by temperature control, use of pesticides and computer/satellite-based logistics. The demand for freshness has also contributed to concerns about food wastage. Use of 'best before', 'sell by' and 'eat by' labels has legally allowed institutional waste. Campaigners have exposed the scandal of over-production and waste. Tristram Stuart, one of the global band of anti-waste campaigners, argues that, with freshly made sandwiches, over-ordering is standard practice across the retail sector to avoid the appearance of empty shelf space, leading to high volumes of waste when supply regularly exceeds demand. [3점]

* pesticide: 살충제 ** logistics: 물류, 유통

① have hidden environmental costs
② worsen the global hunger problem
③ bring about technological advances
④ improve nutrition and quality of food
⑤ diversify the diet of a local community

2022학년도 9월 학평 34번 ★★★

3. 다음 빈칸에 들어갈 말로 가장 적절한 것은?

In the studies of Colin Cherry at the Massachusetts Institute for Technology back in the 1950s, his participants listened to voices in one ear at a time and then through both ears in an effort to determine whether we can listen to two people talk at the same time. One ear always contained a message that the listener had to repeat back (called "shadowing") while the other ear included people speaking. The trick was to see if you could totally focus on the main message and also hear someone talking in your other ear. Cleverly, Cherry found it was impossible for his participants to know whether the message in the other ear was spoken by a man or woman, in English or another language, or was even comprised of real words at all! In other words, people could not ________________________. [3점]

① decide what they should do in the moment
② remember a message with too many words
③ analyze which information was more accurate
④ speak their own ideas while listening to others
⑤ process two pieces of information at the same time

2022학년도 6월 학평 33번 ★★★

4. 다음 빈칸에 들어갈 말로 가장 적절한 것은?

In a study at Princeton University in 1992, research scientists looked at two different groups of mice. One group was made intellectually superior by modifying the gene for the glutamate receptor. Glutamate is a brain chemical that is necessary in learning. The other group was genetically manipulated to be intellectually inferior, also done by modifying the gene for the glutamate receptor. The smart mice were then raised in standard cages, while the inferior mice were raised in large cages with toys and exercise wheels and with lots of social interaction. At the end of the study, although the intellectually inferior mice were genetically handicapped, they were able to perform just as well as their genetic superiors. This was a real triumph for nurture over nature. Genes are turned on or off ________________________. [3점]

* glutamate: 글루타민산염 ** manipulate: 조작하다

① by themselves for survival
② free from social interaction
③ based on what is around you
④ depending on genetic superiority
⑤ so as to keep ourselves entertained

2022학년도 6월 학평 34번 ★★★

5. 다음 빈칸에 들어갈 말로 가장 적절한 것은?

Researchers are working on a project that asks coastal towns how they are preparing for rising sea levels. Some towns have risk assessments; some towns even have a plan. But it's a rare town that is actually carrying out a plan. One reason we've failed to act on climate change is the common belief that ________________________. For decades, climate change was a prediction about the future, so scientists talked about it in the future tense. This became a habit — so that even today many scientists still use the future tense, even though we know that a climate crisis is ongoing. Scientists also often focus on regions most affected by the crisis, such as Bangladesh or the West Antarctic Ice Sheet, which for most Americans are physically remote. [3점]

① it is not related to science
② it is far away in time and space
③ energy efficiency matters the most
④ careful planning can fix the problem
⑤ it is too late to prevent it from happening

2022학년도 3월 학평 33번 ★★☆

6. 다음 빈칸에 들어갈 말로 가장 적절한 것은?

Most times a foreign language is spoken in film, subtitles are used to translate the dialogue for the viewer. However, there are occasions when foreign dialogue is left unsubtitled (and thus incomprehensible to most of the target audience). This is often done if the movie is seen mainly from the viewpoint of a particular character who does not speak the language. Such absence of subtitles allows the audience to feel a similar sense of incomprehension and alienation that the character feels. An example of this is seen in *Not Without My Daughter*. The Persian language dialogue spoken by the Iranian characters is not subtitled because the main character Betty Mahmoody does not speak Persian and the audience is ________________________. [3점]

* subtitle: 자막(을 넣다) ** incomprehensible: 이해할 수 없는
*** alienation: 소외

① seeing the film from her viewpoint
② impressed by her language skills
③ attracted to her beautiful voice
④ participating in a heated debate
⑤ learning the language used in the film

Day 14

2022학년도 3월 학평 34번 ★★★

7. 다음 빈칸에 들어갈 말로 가장 적절한 것은?

One dynamic that can change dramatically in sport is the concept of the home-field advantage, in which perceived demands and resources seem to play a role. Under normal circumstances, the home ground would appear to provide greater perceived resources (fans, home field, and so on). However, researchers Roy Baumeister and Andrew Steinhilber were among the first to point out that these competitive factors can change; for example, the success percentage for home teams in the final games of a playoff or World Series seems to drop. Fans can become part of the perceived demands rather than resources under those circumstances. This change in perception can also explain why a team that's struggling at the start of the year will ____________________ to reduce perceived demands and pressures. [3점]

* perceive: 인식하다 ** playoff: 우승 결정전

① often welcome a road trip
② avoid international matches
③ focus on increasing ticket sales
④ want to have an eco-friendly stadium
⑤ try to advertise their upcoming games

2021학년도 11월 학평 33번 ★★★

8. 다음 빈칸에 들어갈 말로 가장 적절한 것은?

Over time, babies construct expectations about what sounds they will hear when. They hold in memory the sound patterns that occur on a regular basis. They make hypotheses like, "If I hear *this* sound first, it probably will be followed by *that* sound." Scientists conclude that much of babies' skill in learning language is due to their ____________________. For babies, this means that they appear to pay close attention to the patterns that repeat in language. They remember, in a systematic way, how often sounds occur, in what order, with what intervals, and with what changes of pitch. This memory store allows them to track, within the neural circuits of their brains, the frequency of sound patterns and to use this knowledge to make predictions about the meaning in patterns of sounds. [3점]

① lack of social pressures
② ability to calculate statistics
③ desire to interact with others
④ preference for simpler sounds
⑤ tendency to imitate caregivers

2021학년도 11월 학평 34번 ★★★

9. 다음 빈칸에 들어갈 말로 가장 적절한 것은?

Some deep-sea organisms are known to use bioluminescence as a lure, to attract prey with a little glow imitating the movements of their favorite fish, or like fireflies, as a sexual attractant to find mates. While there are many possible evolutionary theories for the survival value of bioluminescence, one of the most fascinating is to ____________________. The color of almost all bioluminescent molecules is blue-green, the same color as the ocean above. By self-glowing blue-green, the creatures no longer cast a shadow or create a silhouette, especially when viewed from below against the brighter waters above. Rather, by glowing themselves, they can blend into the sparkles, reflections, and scattered blue-green glow of sunlight or moonlight. Thus, they are most likely making their own light not to see, but to be un-seen. [3점]

* bioluminescence: 생물 발광 ** lure: 가짜 미끼

① send a signal for help
② threaten enemies nearby
③ lift the veil of hidden prey
④ create a cloak of invisibility
⑤ serve as a navigation system

2021학년도 9월 학평 33번 ★★★

10. 다음 빈칸에 들어갈 말로 가장 적절한 것은?

One big difference between science and stage magic is that while magicians hide their mistakes from the audience, in science you make your mistakes in public. You show them off so that everybody can learn from them. This way, you get the advantage of everybody else's experience, and not just your own idiosyncratic path through the space of mistakes. This, by the way, is another reason why we humans are so much smarter than every other species. It is not that our brains are bigger or more powerful, or even that we have the ability to reflect on our own past errors, but that we ____________________ that our individual brains have earned from their individual histories of trial and error.

* idiosyncratic: (개인에게) 특유한

① share the benefits
② overlook the insights
③ develop creative skills
④ exaggerate the achievements
⑤ underestimate the knowledge

총 문항				문항	맞은 문항					문항
개별 문항	1	2	3	4	5	6	7	8	9	10
채점										
개별 문항	11	12	13	14	15	16	17	18	19	20
채점										

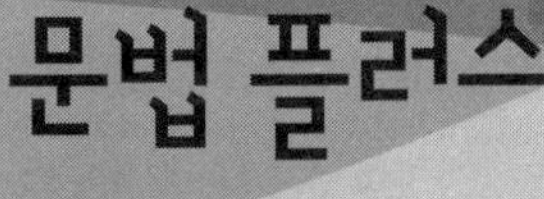

문법 플러스

14. 관계부사

정답 및 해설 076쪽

A 문법의 주요 포인트를 점검해 봅시다.

1 관계부사는 선행사가 시간이면 when, 장소이면 where, 이유이면 why, 방법이면 how를 사용한다. 관계부사 이하는 완전한 문장이 나오며 관계부사는 문장 속에서 부사(구)의 역할을 한다. 관계부사 how는 선행사 the way와 함께 쓰지 않는다. 관계부사는 「전치사+관계대명사」로 바꿀 수 있다

ㅁ관계부사

때	장소	이유, 원인	방법
when / that	where / that	why / that	how / that
=in[at/on] which	=in[at/on] which	=for which	=in which

2 선행사로 place, time, reason과 같은 일반적인 명사가 오면, 관계부사나 선행사 중 하나가 생략될 수 있다.

3 관계부사는 when과 where만 계속적 용법이 있다.

4 복합관계부사는 관계부사에 -ever가 붙은 형태로, 선행사를 포함하고 있어서 선행사와 관계사의 역할을 동시에 하고 있다.

ㅁ복합관계부사

복합관계부사	시간, 장소의 부사절	양보의 부사절
whenever	at any time when (~할 때마다)	no matter when (언제 ~할지라도)
wherever	at any place where (~하는 곳은 어디나)	no matter where (어디에서 ~할지라도)
however	-	no matter how (아무리 ~할지라도)

B 다음 괄호 안에서 어법상 올바른 것을 고르시오.

1 Near the surface, **[where / which]** the water is clear and there is enough light, it is quite possible for an amateur photographer to take great shots with an inexpensive underwater camera.

2 The day **[where / when]** she is least busy is Tuesday.

3 Tell me the reason **[when / why]** you didn't attend the meeting.

4 Culture and gender may affect **[the way / the way how]** people perceive, interpret, and respond to conflict.

5 Select clothing appropriate for the temperature and environmental conditions **[in which / which]** you will be doing exercise.

6 She went to the zoo, **[which / where]** she lost her smart phone.

7 She always blames me **[wherever / whenever]** anything goes wrong.

8 **[Wherever / However]** humble it may be, there is no place like a home.

9 This is the place **[wherever / where]** she loves to go camping.

10 The president has to be escorted **[wherever / however]** he goes.

어휘 플러스

14. 유의어 (4)

정답 및 해설 076쪽

A 다음 수능 필수 어휘를 읽고, 아는 것은 체크해 봅시다.

□ 01	necessity	n. 필요성(= requirement)	□ 21	prey	n. 희생자(= victim)
□ 02	observe	v. 관찰하다(= watch)	□ 22	proceed	v. 진행하다(= continue)
□ 03	obtain	v. 획득하다(= acquire)	□ 23	produce	v. 제조하다(= manufacture)
□ 04	occur	v. 일어나다(= happen)	□ 24	progress	v. 발전하다(= advance)
□ 05	opportunity	n. 기회(= chance)	□ 25	promote	v. 촉진하다(= encourage)
□ 06	outcome	n. 성과(= consequence)	□ 26	property	n. 소유물(= possessions)
□ 07	overall	a. 전체의(= general)	□ 27	propose	v. 제안하다(= suggest)
□ 08	overcome	v. 압도[극복]하다(= overwhelm)	□ 28	protect	v. 지키다(= preserve, conserve)
□ 09	particular	a. 특정한(= specific)	□ 29	prove	v. 입증하다(= verify)
□ 10	passion	n. 열정(= enthusiasm)	□ 30	provide	v. 공급하다(= supply)
□ 11	patient	a. 참을성이 있는(= tolerant)	□ 31	purpose	n. 의도(= intention)
□ 12	peer	n. 동료; v. 응시하다(= gaze)	□ 32	pursue	v. 추적하다(= chase)
□ 13	perceive	v. 알아차리다(= notice)	□ 33	rapid	a. 신속한(= swift)
□ 14	permanent	a. 불변의(= eternal)	□ 34	rational	a. 합리적인(= reasonable)
□ 15	persuade	v. 설득시키다(= convince)	□ 35	realize	v. 알아차리다(= recognize)
□ 16	pollute	v. 오염시키다(= contaminate) cf. decontaminate 정화하다	□ 36	receive	v. 받아들이다(= accept)
□ 17	populate	v. 거주시키다(= reside)	□ 37	recognize	v. 인정하다(= admit)
□ 18	portray	v. 표현하다(= describe)	□ 38	refuse	v. 거절하다(= reject)
□ 19	potential	n. 가능성(= possibility)	□ 39	regard	v. 간주하다(= consider)
□ 20	predict	v. 예견하다(= foretell)	□ 40	region	n. 지방(= district)

B 괄호 안에서 문맥에 맞는 낱말로 적절한 것을 골라 봅시다.

1 Many people went outside around August 27 this year to **[observe / promote]** the close encounter between Earth and Mars.

2 The only way to **[overcome / promote]** this problem is to be more connected to others, and this connection will reduce fear and isolation.

3 If technology produced automobiles that **[pollute / decontaminate]** the air, it is because pollution was not recognized as a problem which engineers had to consider in their designs.

4 Researchers in psychology follow the scientific method to perform studies that help explain and may **[predict / refuse]** human behavior.

5 Recently, however, there has been a lot of research that **[proves / pollutes]** our mind affects illness and healing.

15 흐름에 무관한 문장 찾기

출제 트렌드

1. 글의 일관성 측면에서 글의 내용과 맞지 않거나 주제가 다른 문장을 찾아내는 유형이다 고1 학력 평가에서 1문제가 출제된다. 일관된 글의 흐름이 뚜렷하게 나타난 지문을 사용해 주로 출제된다.
2. 간접 쓰기를 위해서는 글의 전체적인 맥락과 문장 간의 흐름을 파악하여 가상의 글쓰기에 적용할 수 있는 능력이 필요하다. 간접 쓰기 문항 유형에는 흐름에 무관한 문장 찾기, 글의 순서 파악하기, 주어진 문장의 적합한 위치, 문단 요약하기 문제가 있다.
3. 최근 수능 7년간, 흐름에 무관한 문장 찾기 문제는 매년 1문항이 출제되었다, 2017학년도 수능(69%), 2018(86%), 2019(72%), 2020(68%), 2021(81%), 2022(74%), 2023(80%)에서 괄호 안의 정답률을 보였다. 7년간 평균 76%의 정답률을 보였다. 난이도는 중 단계이다.

출처			문항 번호	지문 주제	정답률(%)	난이도
대표	2022학년도	11 학평	35번	시 쓰기의 신체적 이점과 정신적 이점	71	★★☆
1	2022학년도	09 학평	35번	ICTs의 빠른 진화의 장점	52	★★★
2	2022학년도	06 학평	35번	패션이 우리의 삶에서 하는 역할	70	★★☆
3	2022학년도	03 학평	35번	음료에 있는 가벼운 자극제는 섭취에 주의해야 한다	62	★★☆
4	2021학년도	11 학평	35번	세상을 왜곡되게 믿게 만드는 검색 알고리즘	66	★★☆
5	2021학년도	09 학평	35번	Zeigarnik 효과	70	★★☆
6	2021학년도	06 학평	35번	도시의 회복력	62	★★☆
7	2021학년도	03 학평	35번	변화된 뮤지션들의 입지	68	★★☆
8	2020학년도	11 학평	35번	바넘 효과	66	★★☆
9	2020학년도	09 학평	35번	훨씬 더 큰 에너지의 원천	63	★★☆
10	2020학년도	06 학평	35번	정보 공개에 대한 문화 차이	61	★★☆

1등급 꿀팁

1. 동일한 소재를 다루고 있으나 관점이 다른 문장을 무관한 문장으로 출제하는 경우가 많다.
2. 글의 흐름과 무관한 문장 찾기는 글의 초반부에 주목해야 한다. 첫 문장을 통해 글의 기본 흐름을 파악하고 뒤에 나오는 문장들이 같은 흐름으로 이어지고 있는지 확인한다.
3. 비교하는 표현이나, 연결어, 지시어 등의 흐름이 자연스러운지 확인한다.
4. 다양한 지문에서 글의 흐름, 요지, 주제 등을 파악하는 연습을 한다.

흐름에 무관한 문장 찾기

제한 시간 : 15분 | 정답 및 해설 077쪽

대표 기출

2022학년도 11월 학평 35번

35. 다음 글에서 전체 흐름과 관계 없는 문장은?

Developing a personal engagement with poetry brings a number of benefits to you as an individual, in both a personal and a professional capacity. ① Writing poetry has been shown to have physical and mental benefits, with expressive writing found to improve immune system and lung function, diminish psychological distress, and enhance relationships. ② Poetry has long been used to aid different mental health needs, develop empathy, and reconsider our relationship with both natural and built environments. ③ Poetry is also an incredibly effective way of actively targeting the cognitive development period, improving your productivity and scientific creativity in the process. ④ Poetry is considered to be an easy and useful means of expressing emotions, but you fall into frustration when you realize its complexity. ⑤ In short, poetry has a lot to offer, if you give it the opportunity to do so.

* cognitive: 인지적인

문제 풀이

1. 첫 문장이 글의 전체적인 흐름을 지배하므로, 첫 문장을 유의하며 반복적인 어구 또는 특정 개념과 관련된 어구를 통해 글의 요지를 추측한다.

- 반복적인 어구: poetry(시), benefits(이익)
- 글의 요지: Developing a personal engagement with poetry brings a number of benefits to you as an individual, in both a personal and a professional capacity. (시와의 개인적 관계를 발전시키는 것은 개인적인 능력과 전문적인 능력 모두에서 한 개인으로서의 여러분에게 많은 이점을 가져다준다.)

2. 글의 요지를 고려하면서 흐름에서 벗어난 문장을 찾는다.

① 표현적 글쓰기가 면역 체계와 폐 기능을 향상시키고, 심리적 고통을 줄이며 관계를 증진시키는 것으로 밝혀지면서, 시를 쓰는 것은 신체적 이점과 정신적 이점을 지닌 것으로 보여 왔음
② 시는 여러 정신 건강에 필요한 것들을 지원하고, 공감 능력을 개발하고, 자연적인 환경과 만들어진 환경 둘 다와의 관계를 재고하기 위해 오랫동안 사용되어 왔음
③ 시는 또한 인지 발달 시기를 적극적으로 겨냥하는 믿을 수 없을 정도로 효과적인 방법이고, 그 과정에서 여러분의 생산성과 과학적인 창의력을 향상시킴
④ (시는 감정을 표현하는 쉽고 유용한 수단으로 여겨지지만, 그것의 복잡성을 깨달았을 때 여러분은 좌절감에 빠짐)
⑤ 간단히 말해서, 여러분이 시에게 그렇게 할 기회를 준다면, 시는 제공할 많은 것을 가지고 있음

3. 글의 전개 방식을 확인하면서 ④가 부적절함을 확인한다.

- 시 쓰기의 신체적 이점과 정신적 이점에 대해 설명한 글이다. 하지만 ④는 시를 쓸 때 그것의 복잡성을 깨닫게 되면 좌절감에 빠지게 된다는 부정적인 측면에 대한 내용이므로 글의 전체 흐름에서 벗어난다.

2022학년도 9월 학평 35번 ★★★

1. 다음 글에서 전체 흐름과 관계 없는 문장은?

The fast-paced evolution of Information and Communication Technologies (ICTs) has radically transformed the dynamics and business models of the tourism and hospitality industry. ① This leads to new levels/forms of competitiveness among service providers and transforms the customer experience through new services. ② Creating unique experiences and providing convenient services to customers leads to satisfaction and, eventually, customer loyalty to the service provider or brand (i.e., hotels). ③ In particular, the most recent *technological* boost received by the tourism sector is represented by mobile applications. ④ Increasing competitiveness among service providers does not necessarily mean promoting quality of customer services. ⑤ Indeed, empowering tourists with mobile access to services such as hotel reservations, airline ticketing, and recommendations for local attractions generates strong interest and considerable profits.

* hospitality industry: 서비스업(호텔·식당업 등)

2022학년도 6월 학평 35번 ★★☆

2. 다음 글에서 전체 흐름과 관계 없는 문장은?

According to Marguerite La Caze, fashion contributes to our lives and provides a medium for us to develop and exhibit important social virtues. ① Fashion may be beautiful, innovative, and useful; we can display creativity and good taste in our fashion choices. ② And in dressing with taste and care, we represent both self-respect and a concern for the pleasure of others. ③ There is no doubt that fashion can be a source of interest and pleasure which links us to each other. ④ Although the fashion industry developed first in Europe and America, today it is an international and highly globalized industry. ⑤ That is, fashion provides a sociable aspect along with opportunities to imagine oneself differently — to try on different identities.

* virtue: 가치

2022학년도 3월 학평 35번 ★★☆

3. 다음 글에서 전체 흐름과 관계 없는 문장은?

Who hasn't used a cup of coffee to help themselves stay awake while studying? Mild stimulants commonly found in tea, coffee, or sodas possibly make you more attentive and, thus, better able to remember. ① However, you should know that stimulants are as likely to have negative effects on memory as they are to be beneficial. ② Even if they could improve performance at some level, the ideal doses are currently unknown. ③ If you are wide awake and well-rested, mild stimulation from caffeine can do little to further improve your memory performance. ④ In contrast, many studies have shown that drinking tea is healthier than drinking coffee. ⑤ Indeed, if you have too much of a stimulant, you will become nervous, find it difficult to sleep, and your memory performance will suffer.

* stimulant: 자극제 ** dose: 복용량

2021학년도 9월 학평 35번 ★★☆

5. 다음 글에서 전체 흐름과 관계 없는 문장은?

The Zeigarnik effect is commonly referred to as the tendency of the subconscious mind to remind you of a task that is incomplete until that task is complete. Bluma Zeigarnik was a Lithuanian psychologist who wrote in the 1920s about the effects of leaving tasks incomplete. ① She noticed the effect while watching waiters serve in a restaurant. ② The waiters would remember an order, however complicated, until the order was complete, but they would later find it difficult to remember the order. ③ Zeigarnik did further studies giving both adults and children puzzles to complete then interrupting them during some of the tasks. ④ They developed cooperation skills after finishing tasks by putting the puzzles together. ⑤ The results showed that both adults and children remembered the tasks that hadn't been completed because of the interruptions better than the ones that had been completed.

2021학년도 11월 학평 35번 ★★☆

4. 다음 글에서 전체 흐름과 관계 없는 문장은?

Internet activist Eli Pariser noticed how online search algorithms encourage our human tendency to grab hold of everything that confirms the beliefs we already hold, while quietly ignoring information that doesn't match those beliefs. ① We set up a so-called "filter-bubble" around ourselves, where we are constantly exposed only to that material that we agree with. ② We are never challenged, never giving ourselves the opportunity to acknowledge the existence of diversity and difference. ③ Creating a difference that others don't have is a way to succeed in your field, leading to the creation of innovations. ④ In the best case, we become naive and sheltered, and in the worst, we become radicalized with extreme views, unable to imagine life outside our particular bubble. ⑤ The results are disastrous: intellectual isolation and the real distortion that comes with believing that the little world we create for ourselves is *the* world.

* naive: 세상을 모르는 ** radicalize: 과격하게 만들다 *** distortion: 왜곡

2021학년도 6월 학평 35번 ★★☆

6. 다음 글에서 전체 흐름과 관계 없는 문장은? [3점]

Health and the spread of disease are very closely linked to how we live and how our cities operate. The good news is that cities are incredibly resilient. Many cities have experienced epidemics in the past and have not only survived, but advanced. ① The nineteenth and early-twentieth centuries saw destructive outbreaks of cholera, typhoid, and influenza in European cities. ② Doctors such as Jon Snow, from England, and Rudolf Virchow, of Germany, saw the connection between poor living conditions, overcrowding, sanitation, and disease. ③ A recognition of this connection led to the replanning and rebuilding of cities to stop the spread of epidemics. ④ In spite of reconstruction efforts, cities declined in many areas and many people started to leave. ⑤ In the mid-nineteenth century, London's pioneering sewer system, which still serves it today, was built as a result of understanding the importance of clean water in stopping the spread of cholera.

* resilient: 회복력이 있는 ** sewer system: 하수 처리 시스템

2021학년도 3월 학평 35번 ★★☆

7. 다음 글에서 전체 흐름과 관계 없는 문장은?

Today's music business has allowed musicians to take matters into their own hands. ① Gone are the days of musicians waiting for a gatekeeper (someone who holds power and prevents you from being let in) at a label or TV show to say they are worthy of the spotlight. ② In today's music business, you don't need to ask for permission to build a fanbase and you no longer need to pay thousands of dollars to a company to do it. ③ There are rising concerns over the marketing of child musicians using TV auditions. ④ Every day, musicians are getting their music out to thousands of listeners without any outside help. ⑤ They simply deliver it to the fans directly, without asking for permission or outside help to receive exposure or connect with thousands of listeners.

2020학년도 11월 학평 35번 ★★☆

8. 다음 글에서 전체 흐름과 관계 없는 문장은?

The Barnum Effect is the phenomenon where someone reads or hears something very general but believes that it applies to them. ① These statements appear to be very personal on the surface but in fact, they are true for many. ② Human psychology allows us to want to believe things that we can identify with on a personal level and even seek information where it doesn't necessarily exist, filling in the blanks with our imagination for the rest. ③ This is the principle that horoscopes rely on, offering data that appears to be personal but probably makes sense to countless people. ④ Reading daily horoscopes in the morning is beneficial as they provide predictions about the rest of the day. ⑤ Since the people reading them want to believe the information so badly, they will search for meaning in their lives that make it true.

* horoscope: 별자리 운세

2020학년도 9월 학평 35번 ★★☆

9. 다음 글에서 전체 흐름과 관계 없는 문장은?

In a single week, the sun delivers more energy to our planet than humanity has used through the burning of coal, oil, and natural gas through *all of human history*. And the sun will keep shining on our planet for billions of years. ① Our challenge isn't that we're running out of energy. ② It's that we have been focused on the wrong source — the small, finite one that we're using up. ③ Indeed, all the coal, natural gas, and oil we use today is just solar energy from millions of years ago, a very tiny part of which was preserved deep underground. ④ Our efforts to develop technologies that use fossil fuels have shown meaningful results. ⑤ Our challenge, and our opportunity, is to learn to efficiently and cheaply use the *much more abundant* source that is the new energy striking our planet each day from the sun.

2020학년도 6월 학평 35번 ★★☆

10. 다음 글에서 전체 흐름과 관계 없는 문장은?

Given the widespread use of emoticons in electronic communication, an important question is whether they help Internet users to understand emotions in online communication. ① Emoticons, particularly character-based ones, are much more ambiguous relative to face-to-face cues and may end up being interpreted very differently by different users. ② Nonetheless, research indicates that they are useful tools in online text-based communication. ③ One study of 137 instant messaging users revealed that emoticons allowed users to correctly understand the level and direction of emotion, attitude, and attention expression and that emoticons were a definite advantage in non-verbal communication. ④ In fact, there have been few studies on the relationships between verbal and nonverbal communication. ⑤ Similarly, another study showed that emoticons were useful in strengthening the intensity of a verbal message, as well as in the expression of sarcasm.

* ambiguous: 모호한 ** verbal: 언어적인 *** sarcasm: 풍자

총 문항				문항	맞은 문항					문항
개별 문항	1	2	3	4	5	6	7	8	9	10
채점										
개별 문항	11	12	13	14	15	16	17	18	19	20
채점										

문법 플러스

15. 병렬 구조

정답 및 해설 081쪽

A 문법의 주요 포인트를 점검해 봅시다.

1 문장에서 여러 단어, 어구, 절이 열거될 때 같은 모양을 유지하는 현상을 병렬 구조라고 한다. 단어가 나열되는 경우 품사가 같은지 확인한다.

2 부정사, 동명사, 분사와 같은 준동사도 병렬 구조의 원리를 따른다.

3 비교 구문에서도 병렬 구조를 지켜야 한다.

4 비교 구문이 병렬 구조를 이루는 경우, 명사의 반복을 피하기 위해 「the+명사」 대신에 that을 쓴다. 명사가 복수일 때는 those를 써야 한다.

- **The population** of Tokyo is larger than **that** of Seoul.

5 상관접속사에 의해 연결되는 내용도 비슷한 구조로 병렬되어야 한다.

not A but B	A가 아니라 B	either A or B	A 또는 B
not only A but also B	A뿐만 아니라 B도	neither A nor B	A도 B도 아닌
B as well as A	A뿐만 아니라 B도	both A and B	A, B 둘 다

상관접속사 not A but B, not only A but also B, B as well as A, either A or B, neither A nor B에서 동사의 시제 일치는 B에 일치시킨다. both A and B는 복수 취급한다.

B 다음 괄호 안에서 어법상 올바른 것을 고르시오.

1 The old man is extremely kind and **[generous / generously]**.

2 He spoke angrily and **[bitter / bitterly]** about the war.

3 Sally raised her hand and **[snapped / to snap]** her fingers.

4 Try experiments with working by a window or **[use / using]** full spectrum bulbs in your desk lamp.

5 Each day, as school closes, dozens of students come to the library to do homework, use the library's computers, or **[socializing / socialize]** in a safe place.

6 But now the tools of digital age give us a way to easily get, share, and **[acting / act]** on information in new ways.

7 Suddenly, I saw a hand reach out from between the steps and **[grab / grabbed]** my ankle.

8 Although energy can be changed in form, it can be neither created nor **[to destroy / destroyed]**.

9 To do properly is more important than **[finishing / to finish]** quickly.

10 The population of Tokyo is larger than **[that / those]** of Seoul.

어휘 플러스

15. 반의어 (4)

정답 및 해설 082쪽

A 다음 수능 필수 어휘를 읽고, 아는 것은 체크해 봅시다.

□ 01	introvert	n. 내향적인 사람	□ 21	extrovert	n. 외향적인 사람
□ 02	justice	n. 정의, 공정함	□ 22	injustice	n. 불의
□ 03	latter	a. 나중의, 후자의	□ 23	former	a. 전자의
□ 04	legal	a. 법률의, 합법적인	□ 24	illegal	a. 불법적인; adv. illegally
□ 05	literacy	n. 읽고 쓸 줄 아는 능력	□ 25	illiteracy	n. 문맹, 무식
□ 06	major	a. 주요한, 대다수의	□ 26	minor	a. 소수의
□ 07	maximize	v. 극대화하다	□ 27	minimize	v. 최소화하다
□ 08	meaningful	a. 의미 있는	□ 28	meaningless	a. 의미 없는
□ 09	mental	a. 정신의, 마음의	□ 29	physical	a. 신체의
□ 10	merge	v. 합치다	□ 30	separate	v. 분리하다
□ 11	merit	n. 장점	□ 31	demerit	n. 단점
□ 12	odd	a. 홀수의, 특이한	□ 32	even	a. 짝수의, 빈번한
□ 13	optimistic	a. 낙관적인	□ 33	pessimistic	a. 비관적인
□ 14	overestimate	v. 과대평가하다	□ 34	underestimate	v. 과소평가하다
□ 15	patient	a. 참을성이 있는	□ 35	impatient	a. 참을성이 없는
□ 16	permanent	a. 영구적인, 불변의	□ 36	temporary	a. 임시의, 일시적인
□ 17	permit	v. 허락하다	□ 37	forbid	v. 금하다
□ 18	pessimism	n. 비관주의	□ 38	optimism	n. 낙관주의
□ 19	positive	a. 긍정적인	□ 39	negative	a. 부정적인
□ 20	poverty	n. 가난	□ 40	wealth	n. 부, 재산

B 괄호 안에서 문맥에 맞는 낱말로 적절한 것을 골라 봅시다.

1 We shouldn't download games **[legally / illegally]**.

2 When they enter the eye of an observer, they set off a chain of neurochemical events, the end product of which is an internal **[physical / mental]** image that we call color.

3 This **[merges / separates]** men from other animals, but this also reduces them to the level of animals.

4 As the students' attitudes became more **[pessimistic / optimistic]**, their confidence with math grew too.

5 In much of social science, evidence is used only to affirm a particular theory — to search for the **[negative / positive]** instances that uphold it.

16 문단 내 글의 순서 파악

출제 트렌드

1. 주어진 글을 포함한 네 부분의 글을 논리적 흐름 또는 시간적 흐름에 맞게 바른 순서로 배열할 수 있는지 측정한다. 최근 수능에서 2문항이 출제되고 있으며 난이도가 높은 편이다. 출제되는 2문항 중에서 1문항은 연결어로 힌트를 제시하는 평이한 문항이 출제되고, 다른 1문항은 3점 문항으로 지문도 길고 고난이도 문항이다. 고1 학력 평가에서도 2문항이 출제되고 있다.
2. 글의 응집성과 논리적인 흐름을 파악하는 능력을 평가한다.
3. 간접 쓰기를 위해서는 글의 전체적인 맥락과 문장 간의 흐름을 파악하여 가상의 글쓰기에 적용할 수 있는 능력이 필요하다. 간접 쓰기 문항 유형에는 흐름에 무관한 문장 찾기, 글의 순서 파악하기, 주어진 문장의 적합한 위치, 문단 요약하기 문제가 있다.
4. 최근 수능 7년간, 문단 내 글의 순서 파악 문제는 매년 2문항이 출제되었다. 36, 37번 문항으로 출제되었는데, 37번 문항이 난이도가 더 높다. 36번과 37번 문항 비교 시 36번이 67%, 37번이 46.4% 정답률을 보였다. 2017학년도 수능(72/54%), 2018(75/41%), 2019(59/36%), 2020(62/52%), 2021(76/49%), 2022(71/67%), 2023(60/33%)에서 괄호 안의 정답률을 보였다. 7년간 평균 57.6%의 정답률을 보였다. 난이도는 상 단계이다.

	출처		문항 번호	지문 주제	정답률(%)	난이도
대표	2022학년도	11 학평	36번	로봇에 의해 위협받고 있는 일자리들	67	★★☆
1	2022학년도	11 학평	37번	너도 밤나무 뿌리의 역할	60	★★☆
2	2022학년도	09 학평	36번	굶주림에 대한 원인	66	★★☆
3	2022학년도	09 학평	37번	일 처리에 적합한 시간대가 있다	46	★★★
4	2022학년도	06 학평	36번	선생님의 손에 감사하는 Douglas	82	★★☆
5	2022학년도	06 학평	37번	흡혈귀가 존재할 수 없다는 증거	66	★★☆
6	2022학년도	03 학평	36번	사람들의 필요를 충족시킨 시골 건축업자들의 단순한 방식	61	★★☆
7	2022학년도	03 학평	37번	좋은 음악과 연주 그리고 나쁜 음악과 연주가 있다	61	★★☆
8	2021학년도	11 학평	36번	전자 상거래의 팽창	44	★★★
9	2021학년도	11 학평	37번	문학 작품의 표현 방식과 이해	45	★★★
10	2021학년도	09 학평	37번	간단한 요청에 응한 사람이 더 큰 요청에 호의적이다	39	★★★
11	2021학년도	03 학평	37번	화학방정식	63	★★☆
12	2020학년도	11 학평	37번	독립 변인과 종속 변인 간의 인과 관계	59	★★★

1등급 꿀팁

1. 주어진 글 바로 다음에 이어질 첫 문장을 것이 매우 중요하다.
2. 연결사는 문장 간의 논리적 관계를 나타내므로 연결사를 단서로 문장의 순서를 정한다.
3. 대명사와 지시어는 앞에서 언급된 대상을 지칭하므로, 대명사와 지시어가 가리키는 말을 찾는다.

문단 내 글의 순서 파악

제한 시간 : 20분 | 정답 및 해설 082쪽

대표 기출

2022학년도 11월 학평 36번

주어진 글 다음에 이어질 글의 순서로 가장 적절한 것은?

36.

> Things are changing. It has been reported that 42 percent of jobs in Canada are at risk, and 62 percent of jobs in America will be in danger due to advances in automation.

(A) However, what's difficult to automate is the ability to creatively solve problems. Whereas workers in "doing" roles can be replaced by robots, the role of creatively solving problems is more dependent on an irreplaceable individual.

(B) You might say that the numbers seem a bit unrealistic, but the threat is real. One fast food franchise has a robot that can flip a burger in ten seconds. It is just a simple task but the robot could replace an entire crew.

(C) Highly skilled jobs are also at risk. A supercomputer, for instance, can suggest available treatments for specific illnesses in an automated way, drawing on the body of medical research and data on diseases.

① (A) - (C) - (B)　② (B) - (A) - (C)
③ (B) - (C) - (A)　④ (C) - (A) - (B)
⑤ (C) - (B) - (A)

문제 풀이

1. **주어진 문장을 통해 글의 소재 및 핵심 어구와 전개 방향을 파악한다.**
- 주어진 문장: Things are changing. It has been reported that 42 percent of jobs in Canada are at risk, and 62 percent of jobs in America will be in danger due to advances in automation. (상황이 변화하고 있다. 캐나다의 일자리 중 42%가 위기에 처해 있고, 미국의 일자리 중 62%가 자동화의 발전으로 인해 위기에 처할 것이라고 보도되어 왔다.)
- 핵심 어구: jobs, in danger, automation
- 전개 방식: 자동화의 발전으로 인한 일자리의 위기 → 로봇을 사용하는 패스트 푸드 체인점 → 슈퍼컴퓨터의 등장으로 위협을 받고 있는 고도로 숙련된 직업들 → 창의적으로 문제를 해결하는 역할은 자동화가 어려움

2. **주어진 문장으로부터 논리적 전개를 파악한다. 파악할 때 연결어구와 지시어를 활용한다.**

(B) You might say that the numbers seem a bit unrealistic, but the threat is real. ~ : 'the numbers'는 주어진 문장에서 언급된 42%와 62%를 가리키므로 주어진 문장 다음에 (B)가 온다.

(C) Highly skilled jobs are also at risk. A supercomputer, for instance, can suggest available treatments for specific illnesses in an automated way, ~ : 첫 문장 'Highly skilled jobs are also at risk.'의 'also'로 보아 앞에도 위기 상황을 설명한 내용이 나와야 하므로 (C)는 (B) 다음에 와야 한다.

(A) However, what's difficult to automate is the ability to creatively solve problems. ~: 'However'로 보아 앞에 제시된 내용과 상반된 내용이 서술됨을 알 수 있으므로 (C) 다음에 (A)가 와야 한다.

- 그러므로 이 글의 문단 순서는 (B) - (C) - (A) 이며, 정답은 ③번이다.

2022학년도 11월 학평 37번 ★★☆

1. 주어진 글 다음에 이어질 글의 순서로 가장 적절한 것은?

> Each beech tree grows in a particular location and soil conditions can vary greatly in just a few yards. The soil can have a great deal of water or almost no water. It can be full of nutrients or not.

(A) This is taking place underground through the roots. Whoever has an abundance of sugar hands some over; whoever is running short gets help. Their network acts as a system to make sure that no trees fall too far behind.

(B) However, the rate is the same. Whether they are thick or thin, all the trees of the same species are using light to produce the same amount of sugar per leaf. Some trees have plenty of sugar and some have less, but the trees equalize this difference between them by transferring sugar.

(C) Accordingly, each tree grows more quickly or more slowly and produces more or less sugar, and thus you would expect every tree to be photosynthesizing at a different rate. [3점]

* photosynthesize: 광합성하다

① (A) - (C) - (B)　② (B) - (A) - (C)
③ (B) - (C) - (A)　④ (C) - (A) - (B)
⑤ (C) - (B) - (A)

2022학년도 9월 학평 36번 ★★☆

2. 주어진 글 다음에 이어질 글의 순서로 가장 적절한 것은?

With nearly a billion hungry people in the world, there is obviously no single cause.

(A) The reason people are hungry in those countries is that the products produced there can be sold on the world market for more than the local citizens can afford to pay for them. In the modern age you do not starve because you have no food, you starve because you have no money.

(B) However, far and away the biggest cause is poverty. Seventy-nine percent of the world's hungry live in nations that are net exporters of food. How can this be?

(C) So the problem really is that food is, in the grand scheme of things, too expensive and many people are too poor to buy it. The answer will be in continuing the trend of lowering the cost of food.

* net exporter: 순 수출국 ** scheme: 체계, 조직

① (A) − (C) − (B)
② (B) − (A) − (C)
③ (B) − (C) − (A)
④ (C) − (A) − (B)
⑤ (C) − (B) − (A)

2022학년도 9월 학평 37번 ★★★

3. 주어진 글 다음에 이어질 글의 순서로 가장 적절한 것은?

Most people have a perfect time of day when they feel they are at their best, whether in the morning, evening, or afternoon.

(A) When your mind and body are less alert than at your "peak" hours, the muse of creativity awakens and is allowed to roam more freely. In other words, when your mental machinery is loose rather than standing at attention, the creativity flows.

(B) However, if the task you face demands creativity and novel ideas, it's best to tackle it at your "worst" time of day! So if you are an early bird, make sure to attack your creative task in the evening, and vice versa for night owls.

(C) Some of us are night owls, some early birds, and others in between may feel most active during the afternoon hours. If you are able to organize your day and divide your work, make it a point to deal with tasks that demand attention at your best time of the day. [3점]

* roam: (어슬렁어슬렁) 거닐다

① (A) − (C) − (B)
② (B) − (A) − (C)
③ (B) − (C) − (A)
④ (C) − (A) − (B)
⑤ (C) − (B) − (A)

2022학년도 6월 학평 36번 ★★☆

4. 주어진 글 다음에 이어질 글의 순서로 가장 적절한 것은?

Mrs. Klein told her first graders to draw a picture of something to be thankful for. She thought that most of the class would draw turkeys or Thanksgiving tables. But Douglas drew something different.

(A) The class was so responsive that Mrs. Klein had almost forgotten about Douglas. After she had the others at work on another project, she asked Douglas whose hand it was. He answered softly, "It's yours. Thank you, Mrs. Klein."

(B) Douglas was a boy who usually spent time alone and stayed around her while his classmates went outside together during break time. What the boy drew was a hand. But whose hand? His image immediately attracted the other students' interest.

(C) So, everyone rushed to talk about whose hand it was. "It must be the hand of God that brings us food," said one student. "A farmer's," said a second student, "because they raise the turkeys." "It looks more like a police officer's," added another, "they protect us."

① (A) − (C) − (B)
② (B) − (A) − (C)
③ (B) − (C) − (A)
④ (C) − (A) − (B)
⑤ (C) − (B) − (A)

2022학년도 6월 학평 37번 ★★☆

5. 주어진 글 다음에 이어질 글의 순서로 가장 적절한 것은?

> According to legend, once a vampire bites a person, that person turns into a vampire who seeks the blood of others. A researcher came up with some simple math, which proves that these highly popular creatures can't exist.

(A) In just two-and-a-half years, the original human population would all have become vampires with no humans left. But look around you. Have vampires taken over the world? No, because there's no such thing.

(B) If the first vampire came into existence that day and bit one person a month, there would have been two vampires by February 1st, 1600. A month later there would have been four, the next month eight, then sixteen, and so on.

(C) University of Central Florida physics professor Costas Efthimiou's work breaks down the myth. Suppose that on January 1st, 1600, the human population was just over five hundred million. [3점]

① (A) – (C) – (B)　② (B) – (A) – (C)
③ (B) – (C) – (A)　④ (C) – (A) – (B)
⑤ (C) – (B) – (A)

2022학년도 3월 학평 36번 ★★☆

6. 주어진 글 다음에 이어질 글의 순서로 가장 적절한 것은?

> Toward the end of the 19th century, a new architectural attitude emerged. Industrial architecture, the argument went, was ugly and inhuman; past styles had more to do with pretension than what people needed in their homes.

(A) But they supplied people's needs perfectly and, at their best, had a beauty that came from the craftsman's skill and the rootedness of the house in its locality.

(B) Instead of these approaches, why not look at the way ordinary country builders worked in the past? They developed their craft skills over generations, demonstrating mastery of both tools and materials.

(C) Those materials were local, and used with simplicity — houses built this way had plain wooden floors and whitewashed walls inside.

* pretension: 허세, 가식

① (A) – (C) – (B)　② (B) – (A) – (C)
③ (B) – (C) – (A)　④ (C) – (A) – (B)
⑤ (C) – (B) – (A)

2022학년도 3월 학평 37번 ★★☆

7. 주어진 글 다음에 이어질 글의 순서로 가장 적절한 것은?

> Robert Schumann once said, "The laws of morals are those of art." What the great man is saying here is that there is good music and bad music.

(A) It's the same with performances: a bad performance isn't necessarily the result of incompetence. Some of the worst performances occur when the performers, no matter how accomplished, are thinking more of themselves than of the music they're playing.

(B) The greatest music, even if it's tragic in nature, takes us to a world higher than ours; somehow the beauty uplifts us. Bad music, on the other hand, degrades us.

(C) These doubtful characters aren't really listening to what the composer is saying — they're just showing off, hoping that they'll have a great 'success' with the public. The performer's basic task is to try to understand the meaning of the music, and then to communicate it honestly to others. [3점]

* incompetence: 무능 ** degrade: 격하시키다

① (A) – (C) – (B)　② (B) – (A) – (C)
③ (B) – (C) – (A)　④ (C) – (A) – (B)
⑤ (C) – (B) – (A)

2021학년도 11월 학평 36번 ★★★

8. 주어진 글 다음에 이어질 글의 순서로 가장 적절한 것은?

> Roughly twenty years ago, brick-and-mortar stores began to give way to electronic commerce. For good or bad, the shift fundamentally changed consumers' perception of the shopping experience.

(A) Before long, the e-commerce book market naturally expanded to include additional categories, like CDs and DVDs. E-commerce soon snowballed into the enormous industry it is today, where you can buy everything from toilet paper to cars online.

(B) Nowhere was the shift more obvious than with book sales, which is how online bookstores got their start. Physical bookstores simply could not stock as many titles as a virtual bookstore could. There is only so much space available on a shelf.

(C) In addition to greater variety, online bookstores were also able to offer aggressive discounts thanks to their lower operating costs. The combination of lower prices and greater selection led to the slow, steady rise of online bookstores.

* brick-and-mortar: 오프라인 거래의

① (A) - (C) - (B)
② (B) - (A) - (C)
③ (B) - (C) - (A)
④ (C) - (A) - (B)
⑤ (C) - (B) - (A)

2021학년도 11월 학평 37번 ★★★

9. 주어진 글 다음에 이어질 글의 순서로 가장 적절한 것은?

> Literary works, by their nature, suggest rather than explain; they imply rather than state their claims boldly and directly.

(A) What a text implies is often of great interest to us. And our work of figuring out a text's implications tests our analytical powers. In considering what a text suggests, we gain practice in making sense of texts.

(B) But whatever the proportion of a work's showing to telling, there is always something for readers to interpret. Thus we ask the question "What does the text suggest?" as a way to approach literary interpretation, as a way to begin thinking about a text's implications.

(C) This broad generalization, however, does not mean that works of literature do not include direct statements. Depending on when they were written and by whom, literary works may contain large amounts of direct telling and lesser amounts of suggestion and implication. [3점]

① (A) - (C) - (B)
② (B) - (A) - (C)
③ (B) - (C) - (A)
④ (C) - (A) - (B)
⑤ (C) - (B) - (A)

2021학년도 9월 학평 37번 ★★★

10. 주어진 글 다음에 이어질 글의 순서로 가장 적절한 것은?

> In a study, a researcher pretending to be a volunteer surveyed a California neighborhood, asking residents if they would allow a large sign reading "Drive Carefully" to be displayed on their front lawns.

(A) The reason that they agreed was this: two weeks earlier, these residents had been asked by another volunteer to make a small commitment to display a tiny sign that read "Be a Safe Driver" in their windows.

(B) Since it was such a small and simple request, nearly all of them agreed. The astonishing result was that the initial small commitment deeply influenced their willingness to accept the much larger request two weeks later.

(C) To help them understand what it would look like, the volunteer showed his participants a picture of the large sign blocking the view of a beautiful house. Naturally, most people refused, but in one particular group, an incredible 76 percent actually approved. [3점]

① (A) - (C) - (B)
② (B) - (A) - (C)
③ (B) - (C) - (A)
④ (C) - (A) - (B)
⑤ (C) - (B) - (A)

2021학년도 3월 학평 37번 ★★☆

11. 주어진 글 다음에 이어질 글의 순서로 가장 적절한 것은?

> If you had to write a math equation, you probably wouldn't write, "Twenty-eight plus fourteen equals forty-two." It would take too long to write and it would be hard to read quickly.

(A) For example, the chemical formula for water is H_2O. That tells us that a water molecule is made up of two hydrogen ("H" and "2") atoms and one oxygen ("O") atom.

(B) You would write, "28 + 14 = 42." Chemistry is the same way. Chemists have to write chemical equations all the time, and it would take too long to write and read if they had to spell everything out.

(C) So chemists use symbols, just like we do in math. A chemical formula lists all the elements that form each molecule and uses a small number to the bottom right of an element's symbol to stand for the number of atoms of that element. [3점]

* chemical formula: 화학식 ** molecule: 분자

① (A) – (C) – (B)
② (B) – (A) – (C)
③ (B) – (C) – (A)
④ (C) – (A) – (B)
⑤ (C) – (B) – (A)

2020학년도 11월 학평 37번 ★★★

12. 주어진 글 다음에 이어질 글의 순서로 가장 적절한 것은?

> Even though two variables seem to be related, there may not be a causal relationship.

(A) Does this mean that the size of one's feet (independent variable) causes an improvement in reading skills (dependent variable)? Certainly not. This false relationship is caused by a third factor, age, that is related to shoe size as well as reading ability.

(B) Hence, when researchers attempt to make causal claims about the relationship between an independent and a dependent variable, they must control for — or rule out — other variables that may be creating a spurious relationship.

(C) In fact, the two variables may merely seem to be associated with each other due to the effect of some third variable. Sociologists call such misleading relationships spurious. A classic example is the apparent association between children's shoe size and reading ability. It seems that as shoe size increases, reading ability improves.

* variable: 변인 ** spurious: 허위의, 가짜의

① (A) – (C) – (B)
② (B) – (A) – (C)
③ (B) – (C) – (A)
④ (C) – (A) – (B)
⑤ (C) – (B) – (A)

총 문항				문항	맞은 문항					문항
개별 문항	1	2	3	4	5	6	7	8	9	10
채점										
개별 문항	11	12	13	14	15	16	17	18	19	20
채점										

문법 플러스

정답 및 해설 088쪽

16. 명사, 대명사

A 문법의 주요 포인트를 점검해 봅시다.

1 명사는 셀 수 있는 명사와 셀 수 없는 명사로 나눈다. 대명사의 수는 명사의 수와 일치한다.

many, (a) few, a large number of	+셀 수 있는 명사
much, (a) little, a large amount of	+셀 수 없는 명사
lots of / a lot of / plenty of / some / any / no	+셀 수 있는 명사, 셀 수 없는 명사 모두 가능

2 지시대명사 this / that은 앞에 언급된 어구나 내용을 받는다. this[these]는 가까운 것, that[those]은 먼 것을 가리킨다. 한편, 지시대명사 that / those는 앞 명사의 반복을 피하기 위해 사용하기도 한다.

3 부정대명사 either, neither, someone, anyone, no one, everyone 등은 단수로 취급한다. both는 복수로 취급한다. 막연한 것을 지칭할 때는 부정대명사 one[some], 구체적인 것을 지칭할 때는 it을 쓴다.

one..., the other ~	(둘 중에서) 하나는 …, 다른 하나는 ~
one..., another ~, the other~	(셋 중에서) 하나는 …, 다른 하나는 ~, 또 다른 하나는 ~
some... others~	(막연한 다수 중) 일부는 …, 다른 일부는 ~
some... the others~	(한정된 다수 중) 일부는 …, 나머지 일부는 ~

4 절 안에서 목적어가 주어와 동일한 대상을 가리키는 경우 재귀대명사를 사용한다.

5 「소유격+명사」는 소유대명사로 나타낼 수 있다. 한정어가 명사 앞에 올 때는 소유격이 명사 앞에 오지 못하고, 「한정어(a / an / this / that / some / any / no)+명사+of+소유대명사」의 형태로 쓴다.
ㅁ한 명의 내 친구 : a my friend (x), a friend of mine (o)

B 다음 괄호 안에서 어법상 올바른 것을 고르시오.

1 Many lottery players are convinced that the numbers they have picked are "better" numbers because **[it / they]** were selected by the players.

2 A powerful flashlight will easily light your way and the creatures around you, revealing marine life in **[its / their]** true colors.

3 He drank some cold milk, and **[this / which]** satisfied his thirst.

4 The climate of Vietnam is warmer than **[that / those]** of Korea.

5 Both of my elder sisters **[is / are]** in New York.

6 There are two apples on the table. One is yours, and **[the other / another]** is mine.

7 When you attempt to do something and fail, you have to ask **[you / yourself]** why you have failed to do what you intended.

8 These microplastics are very difficult to measure once they are small enough to pass through the nets typically used to collect **[them / themselves]**.

9 The two players blamed **[each other / themselves]** for the mistake; one blamed the other.

10 She gave me **[some books of hers / some her books]**.

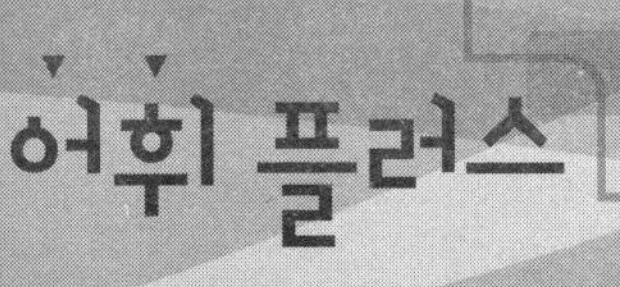

16. 접미사

정답 및 해설 088쪽

A 다음 접미사가 붙은 어휘를 읽어 보고 아는 것은 체크해 봅시다.

□ 01	-ice	n. 성질, 상태	justice(정의), service(서비스), notice(주목, 통지)
□ 02	-ance, -ence	n. 성질, 상태, 행위	disturbance(교란), presence(출석)
□ 03	-tion, -sion -	n. 성질, 상태, 행위	corruption(부패), consideration(고려)
□ 04	-(e)ty, ity	n. 성질, 상태, 행위	poverty(가난), safety(안전), vanity(허영, 무익)
□ 05	-ics	n. 학문	economics(경제학), politics(정치학)
□ 06	-er, -or, ee	n. 행위자	employer(고용주), inventor(발명가), employee(피고용인)
□ 07	-able, ible-	a. ~할 수 있는	acceptable(받아들일 수 있는), reliable(믿을 수 있는)
□ 08	-al	a. ~의, ~적인	commercial(상업의), habitual(습관적인)
□ 09	-ate ~	a. ~한,~적인	considerate(사려 깊은), passionate(열렬한)
□ 10	-ent, -ant	a. ~하는, 성질, 성향	present(참석한), pleasant(기쁜)
□ 11	-ful	a. 가득 찬	careful(주의 깊은), sorrowful(슬픈)
□ 12	-y	a. ~이 많은	rainy(비가 많이 내리는), snowy(눈이 내리는)
□ 13	-ish	a. ~스러운 v. ~하다	childish(유치한), selfish(이기적인), accomplish(성취하다)
□ 14	-ive, -sive, -ative	a. ~적인	active(활동적인), attractive(매혹적인)
□ 15	-less	a ~이 없는	faultless(흠 없는), countless(셀 수 없는, 무수한)
□ 16	-ous	a ~한,~스러운	dangerous(위험한), humorous(유머러스한)
□ 17	-ly -	ad. ~하게	carefully(주의 깊게), comfortably(편안하게)
□ 18	-ate	v. ~하게 하다	motivate(동기를 부여하다), originate(유래하다)
□ 19	-en	v. ~하게 만들다	deepen(깊게하다), encourge(용기를 북돋다)
□ 20	-ize	v. ~하게 만들다	globalize(세계화하다), industrialize(산업화하다)

B 괄호 안에서 문맥에 맞는 낱말로 적절한 것을 골라 봅시다.

1 Due to serious smog caused by the recent forest fires, the Ministry of Education has announced that all schools will be closed until further **[disturbance / notice]**.

2 To keep a pleasant working environment, **[employees / employers]** cannot allow certain kinds of behaviors such as arriving late or bothering others.

3 When it was over, she applauded his **[passionate / habitual]** performance and clapped for a long time.

4 Art designers must picture the dress on the model – in the mood and setting that will make it seem most **[dangerous / attractive]**.

5 They are **[industrialized / fascinated]** by the beauty of these plants and have been motivated to conserve them after discovering the tragic realities these plants face.

17 주어진 문장의 위치 파악

출제 트렌드

1. 지문에서 분리한 문장이 본래 위치했던 곳을 찾아내는 능력을 묻는 문제이다.
2. 수능에서 2문항이 출제되고 있다. 2문항 중 1문항은 비연계 고난이도 문항으로 출제되며 높은 수준의 논리적 판단 능력을 요구하고 있다. 고1 학력 평가에서도 2문항이 출제되고 있다.
3. 간접 쓰기를 위해서는 글의 전체적인 맥락과 문장 간의 흐름을 파악하여 가상의 글쓰기에 적용할 수 있는 능력이 필요하다. 간접 쓰기 문항 유형에는 흐름에 무관한 문장 찾기, 글의 순서 파악하기, 주어진 문장의 적합한 위치, 문단 요약하기 문제가 있다.
4. 최근 수능 7년간, 주어진 문장의 적합한 위치 파악 문제는 매년 2문항이 출제되었다. 38, 39번 문항으로 출제되었는데, 39번 문항이 난이도 더 높다. 38번과 39번 문항 비교 시 38번이 55.9%, 39번이 53% 정답률을 보였다. 2017학년도 수능(57/68%), 2018(66/55%), 2019(65/37%), 2020(69/40%), 2021(54/69%)), 2022(31/47%), 2023(54/56%)에서 괄호 안의 정답률을 보였다. 7년간 평균 54.9%의 정답률을 보였다. 난이도는 상 단계에 속한다.

	출처		문항 번호	지문 주제	정답률(%)	난이도
대표	2021학년도	06 학평	38번	파장으로 이동하는 소리	60	★★☆
1	2022학년도	11 학평	38번	언어는 서로 협력하는 우리의 능력에 기여한다	50	★★★
2	2022학년도	11 학평	39번	다른 화학적 성질과 온도를 가진 물의 특징	55	★★★
3	2022학년도	09 학평	38번	텔레비전 시청은 사회적 관계에 부정적인 영향을 끼칠 수 있다	51	★★★
4	2022학년도	09 학평	39번	정량적인 측정을 하는 온도계가 필요하다	46	★★★
5	2022학년도	06 학평	38번	마찰(력)의 특징과 역할	77	★★☆
6	2022학년도	06 학평	39번	다른 감각을 통해 세상을 이해하는 시각 장애인	50	★★★
7	2022학년도	03 학평	38번	생태계에서 생물종이 다양할 경우의 이점	56	★★★
8	2022학년도	03 학평	39번	우리는 많은 방식으로 밤하늘과 연결되어 있다	38	★★★
9	2021학년도	11 학평	38번	영양 보충제의 한계	62	★★☆
10	2021학년도	11 학평	39번	운동 에너지와 위치 에너지	36	★★★
11	2021학년도	09 학평	38번	카페인의 각성 효과에 관한 연구	69	★★☆
12	2021학년도	09 학평	39번	성공을 보상하는 방법	57	★★★

1등급 꿀팁

1. 주어진 문장을 먼저 읽고 전후에 올 수 있는 내용을 추정해 보는 연습을 한다.
2. 글을 읽다가 흐름이 끊기거나 논리적으로 자연스럽지 못한 부분을 찾아낸다.
3. 대명사의 지칭 대상이 있는지, 연결사의 전후 내용이 논리적인지 확인한다.
4. 주어진 문장을 선택한 위치에 넣은 후 글의 연결성이 자연스러운지 재검토한다.

주어진 문장의 위치 파악

제한 시간 : 20분 | 정답 및 해설 089쪽

대표 기출

2021학년도 6월 학평 38번

글의 흐름으로 보아, 주어진 문장이 들어가기에 가장 적절한 곳을 고르시오.

38.

> As the sticks approach each other, the air immediately in front of them is compressed and energy builds up.

Sound and light travel in waves. An analogy often given for sound is that of throwing a small stone onto the surface of a still pond. Waves radiate outwards from the point of impact, just as sound waves radiate from the sound source. (①) This is due to a disturbance in the air around us. (②) If you bang two sticks together, you will get a sound. (③) When the point of impact occurs, this energy is released as sound waves. (④) If you try the same experiment with two heavy stones, exactly the same thing occurs, but you get a different sound due to the density and surface of the stones, and as they have likely displaced more air, a louder sound. (⑤) And so, a physical disturbance in the atmosphere around us will produce a sound.

* analogy: 비유 ** radiate: 사방으로 퍼지다

문제 풀이

1. 글의 주제와 요지를 포함한 전반적인 내용을 개략적으로 파악한다.
 • 글의 주제: 물리적 교란 작용과 소리 생성

2. 글의 주제와 요지를 염두에 두고 읽으면서 문장과 문장 사이의 흐름이 부자연스럽거나 단절된 곳을 파악한다.
 • 소리 파장: 고요한 연못 표면의 돌멩이를 던지면, 음파가 음원으로부터 사방으로 퍼지는 것처럼 파장이 충격 지점으로부터 바깥으로 퍼져나간다.
 (①) This is due to a disturbance in the air around us.
 (이것은 우리 주변의 공기 중의 교란 작용 때문이다.)
 (②) If you bang two sticks together, you will get a sound.
 (만약에 당신이 막대기 두 개를 함께 쾅 친다면, 소리를 듣게 될 것이다.)
 (③) When the point of impact occurs, this energy is released as sound waves. (충돌점이 발생하면 이 에너지는 음파로 퍼져나간다.)
 (④) If you try the same experiment with two heavy stones, exactly the same thing occurs, but you get a different sound due to the density and surface of the stones, and as they have likely displaced more air, a louder sound. (두 개의 무거운 돌을 가지고 같은 실험을 해보면 똑같은 일이 일어나지만, 돌의 밀도와 표면 때문에 당신은 다른 소리를 듣게 되고, 그 돌이 아마 더 많은 공기를 바꿔 놓았기 때문에 당신은 더 큰 소리를 듣게 된다.)
 (⑤) And so, a physical disturbance in the atmosphere around us will produce a sound. (따라서 우리 주변의 대기 중에서 일어나는 물리적 교란 작용이 소리를 만든다.)

3. 주어진 문장의 내용을 숙지하고 글이 전개되는 흐름을 파악하여 주어진 문장이 들어가기에 가장 적절한 곳을 고른다.
 • '막대기들이 서로 가까워질 때, 그것들 바로 앞에 있는 공기가 압축되고 에너지는 축적된다'에서 주어진 문장의 '에너지'가 (③) 이하에 언급된 음파로 퍼져가는 '이 에너지'를 의미하므로, 주어진 문장은 ③이 적절하다.

2022학년도 11월 학평 38번 ★★★

1. 글의 흐름으로 보아, 주어진 문장이 들어가기에 가장 적절한 곳은?

> Nevertheless, language is enormously important in human life and contributes largely to our ability to cooperate with each other in dealing with the world.

Should we use language to understand mind or mind to understand language? (①) Analytic philosophy historically assumes that language is basic and that mind would make sense if proper use of language was appreciated. (②) Modern cognitive science, however, rightly judges that language is just one aspect of mind of great importance in human beings but not fundamental to all kinds of thinking. (③) Countless species of animals manage to navigate the world, solve problems, and learn without using language, through brain mechanisms that are largely preserved in the minds of humans. (④) There is no reason to assume that language is fundamental to mental operations. (⑤) Our species *homo sapiens* has been astonishingly successful, which depended in part on language, first as an effective contributor to collaborative problem solving and much later, as collective memory through written records. [3점]

* appreciate: (제대로) 인식하다

2022학년도 11월 학평 39번 ★★★

2. 글의 흐름으로 보아, 주어진 문장이 들어가기에 가장 적절한 곳은?

> If we could magically remove the glasses, we would find the two water bodies would not mix well.

Take two glasses of water. Put a little bit of orange juice into one and a little bit of lemon juice into the other. (①) What you have are essentially two glasses of water but with a completely different chemical makeup. (②) If we take the glass containing orange juice and heat it, we will still have two different glasses of water with different chemical makeups, but now they will also have different temperatures. (③) Perhaps they would mix a little where they met; however, they would remain separate because of their different chemical makeups and temperatures. (④) The warmer water would float on the surface of the cold water because of its lighter weight. (⑤) In the ocean we have bodies of water that differ in temperature and salt content; for this reason, they do not mix.

2022학년도 9월 학평 38번 ★★★

3. 글의 흐름으로 보아, 주어진 문장이 들어가기에 가장 적절한 곳은?

> Unfortunately, it is also likely to "crowd out" other activities that produce more sustainable social contributions to our social well-being.

Television is the number one leisure activity in the United States and Europe, consuming more than half of our free time. (①) We generally think of television as a way to relax, tune out, and escape from our troubles for a bit each day. (②) While this is true, there is increasing evidence that we are more motivated to tune in to our favorite shows and characters when we are feeling lonely or have a greater need for social connection. (③) Television watching does satisfy these social needs to some extent, at least in the short run. (④) The more television we watch, the less likely we are to volunteer our time or to spend time with people in our social networks. (⑤) In other words, the more time we make for *Friends*, the less time we have for friends in real life.

* *Friends*: 프렌즈(미국의 한 방송국에서 방영된 시트콤)

2022학년도 9월 학평 39번 ★★★

4. 글의 흐름으로 보아, 주어진 문장이 들어가기에 가장 적절한 곳은?

> What we need is a reliable and reproducible method for measuring the relative hotness or coldness of objects rather than the rate of energy transfer.

We often associate the concept of temperature with how hot or cold an object feels when we touch it. In this way, our senses provide us with a qualitative indication of temperature. (①) Our senses, however, are unreliable and often mislead us. (②) For example, if you stand in bare feet with one foot on carpet and the other on a tile floor, the tile feels colder than the carpet *even though both are at the same temperature*. (③) The two objects feel different because tile transfers energy by heat at a higher rate than carpet does. (④) Your skin "measures" the rate of energy transfer by heat rather than the actual temperature. (⑤) Scientists have developed a variety of thermometers for making such quantitative measurements. [3점]

* thermometer: 온도계

2022학년도 6월 학평 38번 ★★☆

5. 글의 흐름으로 보아, 주어진 문장이 들어가기에 가장 적절한 곳은?

> For example, if you rub your hands together quickly, they will get warmer.

Friction is a force between two surfaces that are sliding, or trying to slide, across each other. For example, when you try to push a book along the floor, friction makes this difficult. Friction always works in the direction opposite to the direction in which the object is moving, or trying to move. So, friction always slows a moving object down. (①) The amount of friction depends on the surface materials. (②) The rougher the surface is, the more friction is produced. (③) Friction also produces heat. (④) Friction can be a useful force because it prevents our shoes slipping on the floor when we walk and stops car tires skidding on the road. (⑤) When you walk, friction is caused between the tread on your shoes and the ground, acting to grip the ground and prevent sliding.

* skid: 미끄러지다 ** tread: 접지면, 바닥

2022학년도 6월 학평 39번 ★★★

6. 글의 흐름으로 보아, 주어진 문장이 들어가기에 가장 적절한 곳은?

> But, a blind person will associate the same friend with a unique combination of experiences from their non-visual senses that act to represent that friend.

Humans born without sight are not able to collect visual experiences, so they understand the world entirely through their other senses. (①) As a result, people with blindness at birth develop an amazing ability to understand the world through the collection of experiences and memories that come from these non-visual senses. (②) The dreams of a person who has been without sight since birth can be just as vivid and imaginative as those of someone with normal vision. (③) They are unique, however, because their dreams are constructed from the non-visual experiences and memories they have collected. (④) A person with normal vision will dream about a familiar friend using visual memories of shape, lighting, and colour. (⑤) In other words, people blind at birth have similar overall dreaming experiences even though they do not dream in pictures.

Day 17

2022학년도 3월 학평 38번 ★★★

7. 글의 흐름으로 보아, 주어진 문장이 들어가기에 가장 적절한 곳은?

> But, when there is biodiversity, the effects of a sudden change are not so dramatic.

When an ecosystem is biodiverse, wildlife have more opportunities to obtain food and shelter. Different species react and respond to changes in their environment differently. (①) For example, imagine a forest with only one type of plant in it, which is the only source of food and habitat for the entire forest food web. (②) Now, there is a sudden dry season and this plant dies. (③) Plant-eating animals completely lose their food source and die out, and so do the animals that prey upon them. (④) Different species of plants respond to the drought differently, and many can survive a dry season. (⑤) Many animals have a variety of food sources and don't just rely on one plant; now our forest ecosystem is no longer at the death! [3점]

* biodiversity: (생물학적) 종 다양성 ** habitat: 서식지

2022학년도 3월 학평 39번 ★★★

8. 글의 흐름으로 보아, 주어진 문장이 들어가기에 가장 적절한 곳은?

> Since the dawn of civilization, our ancestors created myths and told legendary stories about the night sky.

We are connected to the night sky in many ways. (①) It has always inspired people to wonder and to imagine. (②) Elements of those narratives became embedded in the social and cultural identities of many generations. (③) On a practical level, the night sky helped past generations to keep track of time and create calendars — essential to developing societies as aids to farming and seasonal gathering. (④) For many centuries, it also provided a useful navigation tool, vital for commerce and for exploring new worlds. (⑤) Even in modern times, many people in remote areas of the planet observe the night sky for such practical purposes.

* embed: 깊이 새겨 두다 ** commerce: 무역

2021학년도 11월 학평 38번 ★★☆

9. 글의 흐름으로 보아, 주어진 문장이 들어가기에 가장 적절한 곳은?

> Worse, some are contaminated with other substances and contain ingredients not listed on the label.

According to top nutrition experts, most nutrients are better absorbed and used by the body when consumed from a whole food instead of a supplement. (①) However, many people feel the need to take pills, powders, and supplements in an attempt to obtain nutrients and fill the gaps in their diets. (②) We hope these will give us more energy, prevent us from catching a cold in the winter, or improve our skin and hair. (③) But in reality, the large majority of supplements are artificial and may not even be completely absorbed by your body. (④) For example, a recent investigative report found heavy metals in 40 percent of 134 brands of protein powders on the market. (⑤) With little control and regulation, taking supplements is a gamble and often costly.

* contaminate: 오염시키다 ** supplement: 보충제

2021학년도 11월 학평 39번 ★★★

10. 글의 흐름으로 보아, 주어진 문장이 들어가기에 가장 적절한 곳은?

> But after this brief moment of rest, the pendulum swings back again and therefore part of the total energy is then given in the form of kinetic energy.

In general, kinetic energy is the energy associated with motion, while potential energy represents the energy which is "stored" in a physical system. Moreover, the total energy is always conserved. (①) But while the total energy remains unchanged, the kinetic and potential parts of the total energy can change all the time. (②) Imagine, for example, a pendulum which swings back and forth. (③) When it swings, it sweeps out an arc and then slows down as it comes closer to its highest point, where the pendulum does not move at all. (④) So at this point, the energy is completely given in terms of potential energy. (⑤) So as the pendulum swings, kinetic and potential energy constantly change into each other. [3점]

* pendulum: 추(錘) ** arc: 호(弧)

2021학년도 9월 학평 38번 ★★☆

11. 글의 흐름으로 보아, 주어진 문장이 들어가기에 가장 적절한 곳은?

> However, using caffeine to improve alertness and mental performance doesn't replace getting a good night's sleep.

Studies have consistently shown caffeine to be effective when used together with a pain reliever to treat headaches. (①) The positive correlation between caffeine intake and staying alert throughout the day has also been well established. (②) As little as 60 mg (the amount typically in one cup of tea) can lead to a faster reaction time. (③) One study from 2018 showed that coffee improved reaction times in those with or without poor sleep, but caffeine seemed to increase errors in the group with little sleep. (④) Additionally, this study showed that even with caffeine, the group with little sleep did not score as well as those with adequate sleep. (⑤) It suggests that caffeine does not fully make up for inadequate sleep.

2021학년도 9월 학평 39번 ★★★

12. 글의 흐름으로 보아, 주어진 문장이 들어가기에 가장 적절한 곳은?

> The sales director kept an air horn outside his office and would come out and blow the horn every time a salesperson settled a deal.

Rewarding business success doesn't always have to be done in a material way. (①) A software company I once worked for had a great way of recognizing sales success. (②) The noise, of course, interrupted anything and everything happening in the office because it was unbelievably loud. (③) However, it had an amazingly positive impact on everyone. (④) Sometimes rewarding success can be as easy as that, especially when peer recognition is important. (⑤) You should have seen the way the rest of the sales team wanted the air horn blown for them.

* air horn: (압축 공기로 작동하는) 경적

총 문항				문항	맞은 문항					문항
개별 문항	1	2	3	4	5	6	7	8	9	10
채점										
개별 문항	11	12	13	14	15	16	17	18	19	20
채점										

17. 형용사, 부사

정답 및 해설 094쪽

A 문법의 주요 포인트를 점검해 봅시다.

1 형용사는 명사를 수식하거나 주어나 목적어의 보어로 사용된다. alive, alike, awake, ashamed, afraid 등은 서술적 형용사로 사용된다. 부사는 형용사, 동사, 다른 부사를 수식한다.

2 보통 「형용사+ly」인 경우 부사가 되나, -ly로 끝나는 형용사(friendly, lovely, lonely)도 있으므로 유의해야 한다.

3 부사에 -ly를 붙임으로써 의미가 달라지는 부사에 유의한다.

high (높이)	highly (매우)	late (늦게)	lately (최근에)
deep (깊게)	deeply (매우)	free (공짜로)	freely (자유롭게)
dear (비싸게)	dearly (마음으로부터)	near (가까이)	nearly (거의)
hard (열심히)	hardly (거의 ~아니다)	pretty (대단히)	prettily (예쁘게)

4 most(대부분의)가 형용사일 때는 '대부분의' 의미이다. most가 대명사로 쓰일 때는 「most of+한정어(the, these, those, 소유격)+단 · 복수명사」의 형태로 쓴다. '~의 대부분'의 의미이다. of 이하가 단수명사가 오면 단수동사를 쓰고 복수명사가 오면 복수동사를 쓴다. almost(거의)는 부사로 쓰인다. almost 뒤에는 종종 all, every, any 등이 온다.

5 동사와 부사가 결합된 동사구에서 목적어가 대명사일 경우에는 「동사+대명사+부사」의 어순이 되어야 한다.

B 다음 괄호 안에서 어법상 올바른 것을 고르시오.

1 I caught a bird **[alive / live]**.

2 Bad lighting can increase stress on your eyes, as can light that is too bright, or light that shines **[direct / directly]** into your eyes.

3 One would have to filter enormous amounts of water to collect a **[relative / relatively]** small amount of plastic.

4 As we grew older, Mom made sure we did our part by keeping our rooms **[neat / neatly]**.

5 The kite rose **[high / highly]** in the sky.

6 She was **[high / highly]** pleased and full of expectations about being in a new place.

7 **[Almost / Most]** people began to worry about him.

8 Many people think the secret is kimchi, a traditional Korean dish served with **[most / almost]** every meal.

9 Sam got up **[late / lately]** this morning, so he was late for school.

10 She promised to **[bring it back / bring back it]** next time.

어휘 플러스

정답 및 해설 095쪽

17. 철자가 혼동되는 어휘 (5)

다음 수능 필수 어휘를 읽고, 아는 것을 체크해 봅시다.

□ 01	alternation	n. 교체, 교대	□ 21	alternative	n. 양자택일, 대안
□ 02	enclose	v. 에워싸다, 둘러싸다	□ 22	enhance	v. 높이다, 강화하다
□ 03	infinite	a. 무한한, 끝없는	□ 23	definite	a. 뚜렷한
□ 04	inhibit	v. 억제, 제어하다	□ 24	inhabit	v. 거주하다
□ 05	jealous	a. 질투가 많은	□ 25	zealous	a. 열심인, 열광적인
□ 06	medication	n. 약물	□ 26	meditation	n. 명상
□ 07	momentary	a. 순간적인	□ 27	momentous	a. 중요한
□ 08	natural	a. 자연의	□ 28	neutral	a. 중립의
□ 09	objective	n. 목표, 목적	□ 29	objection	n. 반대
□ 10	preferred	a. 선취권이 있는	□ 30	prepared	a. 준비되어 있는
□ 11	principal	a. 주요한; n. 교장, 원금	□ 31	principle	n.원리, 원칙
□ 12	quite	ad. 아주, 완전히	□ 32	quiet	a. 고요한
□ 13	shortage	n. 부족, 결핍	□ 33	strength	n. 강점, 힘
□ 14	sit	v. 앉다	□ 34	seat	v. 앉히다
□ 15	stain	n. 얼룩, 때, 반점	□ 35	strain	n. 긴장
□ 16	statue	n. 조상, 상	□ 36	status	n. 지위
□ 17	stale	a.신선하지 않은	□ 37	stable	a 안정된, 견실한
□ 18	support	v. 유지하다, 받치다	□ 38	manipulate	v. 교묘하게 다루다
□ 19	thorough	a. 철저한, 완전한	□ 39	through	prep. ~을 통하여
□ 20	valuable	a. 귀중한, 가치 있는	□ 40	invaluable	a. 매우 귀중한(= priceless)

B 괄호 안에서 문맥에 맞는 낱말로 적절한 것을 골라 봅시다.

1 Solar energy can be a practical **[alternation / alternative]** energy source for us in the foreseeable future.

2 Their physical layout encourages some uses and **[inhabits / inhibits]** others; we do not go backstage in a theater unless especially invited.

3 Some universities remain silent on the important issues of the day, justifying their silence on the grounds that universities are **[natural / neutral]** and should not become involved.

4 Uniform helps to conceal the personal taste and financial **[statue / status]** of children's parents.

5 But such mental rehearsal is disastrous cognitive static when it becomes trapped in a **[stable / stale]** routine that captures attention, intruding on all other attempts to focus elsewhere.

문단 요약

출제 트렌드

1. 글을 읽고 글 전체의 내용을 이해한 후 이것을 하나의 문장으로 완성하도록 요구하는 유형이다. 쓰기 능력을 간접적으로 평가하는 유형이다. 고1 학력 평가에서 1문항이 출제되고 있다. 글의 내용을 요약하는 요약문에서 빈칸 두 개를 제시한다. 빈칸에는 본문에 나오는 핵심어를 그대로 사용하거나, 핵심어의 동의어가 정답이 되기도 한다.
2. 간접 쓰기를 위해서는 글의 전체적인 맥락과 문장 간의 흐름을 파악하여 가상의 글쓰기에 적용할 수 있는 능력이 필요하다. 간접 쓰기 문항 유형에는 흐름에 무관한 문장 찾기, 글의 순서 파악하기, 주어진 문장의 적합한 위치, 문단 요약하기 문제가 있다
3. 최근 수능 7년간, 문단 요약하기 문제는 2017학년도 이후 매년 1문제가 출제되고 있다. 2017학년도 수능(64%), 2018(67%), 2019(74%), 2020(69%), 2021(57%), 2022(69%), 2023(75%)에서 괄호 안의 정답률을 보였다. 7년간 평균 67.9% 정도 정답률을 보였다. 난이도는 중 단계이다.
4. 간접 쓰기 유형 35–40번 문제 중 가장 어려운 문제는 문단 내 글의 순서 파악 37번 문항이다. 문제를 풀 때 시간이 부족한 경우, 빈칸 33, 34번과 37번 문항은 전략적으로 나중에 푸는 것이 좋다.

출처			문항 번호	지문 주제	정답률(%)	난이도
대표	2021학년도	06 학평	40번	작은 노트가 사람들의 행동을 변화 시킴	67	★★☆
1	2022학년도	11 학평	40번	삶의 의미를 찾는 강력한 도구인 성찰적 일기 쓰기	63	★★☆
2	2022학년도	09 학평	40번	기부할 이유를 단독으로 제시하는 것이 효과적이다	46	★★★
3	2022학년도	06 학평	40번	청소년들의 학문적 성공의 요인	68	★★☆
4	2022학년도	03 학평	40번	망가니즈를 이용하는 common blackberry의 능력	57	★★★
5	2021학년도	11 학평	40번	과학적 불확실성에 대한 미디어의 지나친 단순화	53	★★★
6	2021학년도	09 학평	40번	의견 불일치가 학습의 흥미를 높인다	41	★★★
7	2021학년도	03 학평	40번	휴대 전화의 존재 여부에 따른 공감 수준의 차이	54	★★★
8	2020학년도	11 학평	40번	내집단과 동일시하려는 경향	53	★★★
9	2020학년도	09 학평	40번	음악과 감정의 연관성	67	★★☆
10	2020학년도	06 학평	40번	긍정적 이미지를 만들어 주는 좋은 코치	73	★★☆
11	2020학년도	03 학평	40번	운전 중에 비협조적인 이유	73	★★☆

1등급 꿀팁

1. 요약문의 빈칸은 글의 주제나 요지를 담고 있다는 점을 유의해야 한다.
2. 제시된 요약문을 먼저 읽은 후에 본문의 내용을 읽고 판단한다.
3. 요약문을 완성한 후 다시 읽어 보면서 요지와 일치하는지 판단한다.

Day 18

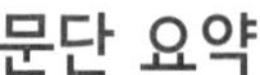

문단 요약

제한 시간 : 17분 | 정답 및 해설 095쪽

대표 기출

2021학년도 6월 학평 40번

40. 다음 글의 내용을 한 문장으로 요약하고자 한다. 빈칸 (A), (B)에 들어갈 말로 가장 적절한 것은?

A woman named Rhonda who attended the University of California at Berkeley had a problem. She was living near campus with several other people — none of whom knew one another. When the cleaning people came each weekend, they left several rolls of toilet paper in each of the two bathrooms. However, by Monday all the toilet paper would be gone. It was a classic tragedy-of-the-commons situation: because some people took more toilet paper than their fair share, the public resource was destroyed for everyone else. After reading a research paper about behavior change, Rhonda put a note in one of the bathrooms asking people not to remove the toilet paper, as it was a shared item. To her great satisfaction, one roll reappeared in a few hours, and another the next day. In the other note-free bathroom, however, there was no toilet paper until the following weekend, when the cleaning people returned.

⬇

A small ___(A)___ brought about a change in the behavior of the people who had taken more of the ___(B)___ goods than they needed.

	(A)		(B)
①	reminder	······	shared
②	reminder	······	recycled
③	mistake	······	stored
④	mistake	······	borrowed
⑤	fortune	······	limited

문제 풀이

1. 요약문과 선택지를 먼저 훑어봄으로써 글의 요지를 추론해 보고 빈칸에 들어갈 내용에 대한 단서를 확보한다.

- 이 글은 모두가 사용하는 공용 화장실의 화장지가 빨리 사라지자 Rhonda가 화장지를 가져가지 말라는 쪽지를 남기자 화장지가 다시 나타났다는 내용의 글이다.

2. 요약문을 통해 얻은 단서를 바탕으로 글을 읽고 요지를 파악한다.

(1) 글의 요지: 공공재의 경우, 사람들은 자기 몫보다 더 많이 그것을 사용하기 쉽지만 행동의 제재를 받으면 행동의 변화를 가져온다.

(2) 요지를 뒷받침하는 예

① 청소부가 주말마다 화장실에 화장지를 두고 갔다.

② 월요일 즈음 모든 화장지가 없어지곤 했다.

③ Rhonda가 공공재 회복을 위해 화장실 화장지는 공유재이므로 가져가지 말라고 쪽지를 남겼다.

④ 두 개의 화장지가 다시 나타났다.

3. 글을 읽으면서 파악한 요지를 바탕으로 요약문의 빈칸에 들어갈 말로 가장 적절한 단어를 선택지에서 고른다.

- 자그마한 (A) 상기 시키는 메모(reminder)는 그들이 필요한 것보다 더 많은 (B) 공유재를 가져갔던 사람의 행동에 변화를 가져왔다. 가장 적절한 답은 ①번이다.

2022학년도 11월 학평 40번 ★★☆

1. 다음 글의 내용을 한 문장으로 요약하고자 한다. 빈칸 (A), (B)에 들어갈 말로 가장 적절한 것은?

One of the most powerful tools to find meaning in our lives is reflective journaling — thinking back on and writing about what has happened to us. In the 1990s, Stanford University researchers asked undergraduate students on spring break to journal about their most important personal values and their daily activities; others were asked to write about only the good things that happened to them in the day. Three weeks later, the students who had written about their values were happier, healthier, and more confident about their ability to handle stress than the ones who had only focused on the good stuff. By reflecting on how their daily activities supported their values, students had gained a new perspective on those activities and choices. Little stresses and hassles were now demonstrations of their values in action. Suddenly, their lives were full of meaningful activities. And all they had to do was reflect and write about it — positively reframing their experiences with their personal values.

* hassle: 귀찮은 일

⬇

Journaling about daily activities based on what we believe to be ___(A)___ can make us feel that our life is meaningful by ___(B)___ our experiences in a new way.

	(A)		(B)
①	factual	···	rethinking
②	worthwhile	···	rethinking
③	outdated	···	generalizing
④	objective	···	generalizing
⑤	demanding	···	describing

2022학년도 9월 학평 40번 ★★★

2. 다음 글의 내용을 한 문장으로 요약하고자 한다. 빈칸 (A), (B)에 들어갈 말로 가장 적절한 것은?

My colleagues and I ran an experiment testing two different messages meant to convince thousands of resistant alumni to make a donation. One message emphasized the opportunity to do good: donating would benefit students, faculty, and staff. The other emphasized the opportunity to feel good: donors would enjoy the warm glow of giving. The two messages were equally effective: in both cases, 6.5 percent of the unwilling alumni ended up donating. Then we combined them, because two reasons are better than one. Except they weren't. When we put the two reasons together, the giving rate dropped below 3 percent. Each reason alone was more than twice as effective as the two combined. The audience was already skeptical. When we gave them different kinds of reasons to donate, we triggered their awareness that someone was trying to persuade them — and they shielded themselves against it.

* alumni: 졸업생 ** skeptical: 회의적인

⬇

In the experiment mentioned above, when the two different reasons to donate were given ___(A)___, the audience was less likely to be ___(B)___ because they could recognize the intention to persuade them.

	(A)		(B)
①	simultaneously	……	convinced
②	separately	……	confused
③	frequently	……	annoyed
④	separately	……	satisfied
⑤	simultaneously	……	offended

2022학년도 6월 학평 40번 ★★☆

3. 다음 글의 내용을 한 문장으로 요약하고자 한다. 빈칸 (A), (B)에 들어갈 말로 가장 적절한 것은? [3점]

According to a study of Swedish adolescents, an important factor of adolescents' academic success is how they respond to challenges. The study reports that when facing difficulties, adolescents exposed to an authoritative parenting style are less likely to be passive, helpless, and afraid to fail. Another study of nine high schools in Wisconsin and northern California indicates that children of authoritative parents do well in school, because these parents put a lot of effort into getting involved in their children's school activities. That is, authoritative parents are significantly more likely to help their children with homework, to attend school programs, to watch their children in sports, and to help students select courses. Moreover, these parents are more aware of what their children do and how they perform in school. Finally, authoritative parents praise academic excellence and the importance of working hard more than other parents do.

⬇

The studies above show that the children of authoritative parents often succeed academically, since they are more ___(A)___ to deal with their difficulties and are affected by their parents' ___(B)___ involvement.

	(A)		(B)
①	likely	……	random
②	willing	……	minimal
③	willing	……	active
④	hesitant	……	unwanted
⑤	hesitant	……	constant

Day 18

2022학년도 3월 학평 40번 ★★★

4. 다음 글의 내용을 한 문장으로 요약하고자 한다. 빈칸 (A), (B)에 들어갈 말로 가장 적절한 것은?

The common blackberry *(Rubus allegheniensis)* has an amazing ability to move manganese from one layer of soil to another using its roots. This may seem like a funny talent for a plant to have, but it all becomes clear when you realize the effect it has on nearby plants. Manganese can be very harmful to plants, especially at high concentrations. Common blackberry is unaffected by damaging effects of this metal and has evolved two different ways of using manganese to its advantage. First, it redistributes manganese from deeper soil layers to shallow soil layers using its roots as a small pipe. Second, it absorbs manganese as it grows, concentrating the metal in its leaves. When the leaves drop and decay, their concentrated manganese deposits further poison the soil around the plant. For plants that are not immune to the toxic effects of manganese, this is very bad news. Essentially, the common blackberry eliminates competition by poisoning its neighbors with heavy metals.

* manganese: 망가니즈(금속 원소) ** deposit: 축적물

⬇

The common blackberry has an ability to ___(A)___ the amount of manganese in the surrounding upper soil, which makes the nearby soil quite ___(B)___ for other plants.

	(A)		(B)
①	increase	·······	deadly
②	increase	·······	advantageous
③	indicate	·······	nutritious
④	reduce	·······	dry
⑤	reduce	·······	warm

2021학년도 11월 학평 40번 ★★★

5. 다음 글의 내용을 한 문장으로 요약하고자 한다. 빈칸 (A), (B)에 들어갈 말로 가장 적절한 것은?

There is often a lot of uncertainty in the realm of science, which the general public finds uncomfortable. They don't want "informed guesses," they want certainties that make their lives easier, and science is often unequipped to meet these demands. In particular, the human body is fantastically complex, and some scientific answers can never be provided in black-or-white terms. All this is why the media tends to oversimplify scientific research when presenting it to the public. In their eyes, they're just "giving people what they want" as opposed to offering more accurate but complex information that very few people will read or understand. A perfect example of this is how people want definitive answers as to which foods are "good" and "bad." Scientifically speaking, there are no "good" and "bad" foods; rather, food quality exists on a continuum, meaning that some foods are *better* than others when it comes to general health and well-being.

* continuum: 연속(체)

⬇

With regard to general health, science, by its nature, does not ___(A)___ the public's demands for certainty, which leads to the media giving less ___(B)___ answers to the public.

	(A)		(B)
①	satisfy	······	simple
②	satisfy	······	complicated
③	ignore	······	difficult
④	ignore	······	simple
⑤	reject	······	complicated

2021학년도 9월 학평 40번 ★★★

6. 다음 글의 내용을 한 문장으로 요약하고자 한다. 빈칸 (A), (B)에 들어갈 말로 가장 적절한 것은? [3점]

> Nancy Lowry and David Johnson conducted an experiment to study a teaching environment where fifth and sixth graders were assigned to interact on a topic. With one group, the discussion was led in a way that built an agreement. With the second group, the discussion was designed to produce disagreements about the right answer. Students who easily reached an agreement were less interested in the topic, studied less, and were less likely to visit the library to get additional information. The most noticeable difference, though, was revealed when teachers showed a special film about the discussion topic—during lunch time! Only 18 percent of the agreement group missed lunch time to see the film, but 45 percent of the students from the disagreement group stayed for the film. The thirst to fill a knowledge gap—to find out who was right within the group—can be more powerful than the thirst for slides and jungle gyms.

⬇

> According to the experiment above, students' interest in a topic ___(A)___ when they are encouraged to ___(B)___.

	(A)		(B)
①	increases	……	differ
②	increases	……	approve
③	increases	……	cooperate
④	decreases	……	participate
⑤	decreases	……	argue

2021학년도 3월 학평 40번 ★★★

7. 다음 글의 내용을 한 문장으로 요약하고자 한다. 빈칸 (A), (B)에 들어갈 말로 가장 적절한 것은?

> In one study, researchers asked pairs of strangers to sit down in a room and chat. In half of the rooms, a cell phone was placed on a nearby table; in the other half, no phone was present. After the conversations had ended, the researchers asked the participants what they thought of each other. Here's what they learned: when a cell phone was present in the room, the participants reported the quality of their relationship was worse than those who'd talked in a cell phone-free room. The pairs who talked in the rooms with cell phones thought their partners showed less empathy. Think of all the times you've sat down to have lunch with a friend and set your phone on the table. You might have felt good about yourself because you didn't pick it up to check your messages, but your unchecked messages were still hurting your connection with the person sitting across from you.
>
> * empathy: 공감

⬇

> The presence of a cell phone ___(A)___ the connection between people involved in conversations, even when the phone is being ___(B)___.

	(A)		(B)
①	weakens	……	answered
②	weakens	……	ignored
③	renews	……	answered
④	maintains	……	ignored
⑤	maintains	……	updated

2020학년도 11월 학평 40번 ★★★

8. 다음 글의 내용을 한 문장으로 요약하고자 한다. 빈칸 (A), (B)에 들어갈 말로 가장 적절한 것은?

> In their study in 2007 Katherine Kinzler and her colleagues at Harvard showed that our tendency to identify with an in-group to a large degree begins in infancy and may be innate. Kinzler and her team took a bunch of five-month-olds whose families only spoke English and showed the babies two videos. In one video, a woman was speaking English. In the other, a woman was speaking Spanish. Then they were shown a screen with both women side by side, not speaking. In infant psychology research, the standard measure for affinity or interest is attention—babies will apparently stare longer at the things they like more. In Kinzler's study, the babies stared at the English speakers longer. In other studies, researchers have found that infants are more likely to take a toy offered by someone who speaks the same language as them. Psychologists routinely cite these and other experiments as evidence of our built-in evolutionary preference for "our own kind."
>
> * affinity: 애착

⬇

> Infants' more favorable responses to those who use a ___(A)___ language show that there can be a(n) ___(B)___ tendency to prefer in-group members.

	(A)		(B)
①	familiar	……	inborn
②	familiar	……	acquired
③	foreign	……	cultural
④	foreign	……	learned
⑤	formal	……	innate

Day 18

2020학년도 9월 학평 40번 ★★☆

9. 다음 글의 내용을 한 문장으로 요약하고자 한다. 빈칸 (A), (B)에 들어갈 말로 가장 적절한 것은?

One way that music could express emotion is simply through a learned association. Perhaps there is nothing naturally sad about a piece of music in a minor key, or played slowly with low notes. Maybe we have just come to hear certain kinds of music as sad because we have learned to associate them in our culture with sad events like funerals. If this view is correct, we should have difficulty interpreting the emotions expressed in culturally unfamiliar music. Totally opposed to this view is the position that the link between music and emotion is one of resemblance. For example, when we feel sad we move slowly and speak slowly and in a low-pitched voice. Thus when we hear slow, low music, we hear it as sad. If this view is correct, we should have little difficulty understanding the emotion expressed in culturally unfamiliar music.

⬇

It is believed that emotion expressed in music can be understood through a(n) ____(A)____ learned association or it can be understood due to the ____(B)____ between music and emotion.

(A) ······ (B)
① culturally ······ similarity
② culturally ······ balance
③ socially ······ difference
④ incorrectly ······ connection
⑤ incorrectly ······ contrast

2020학년도 6월 학평 40번 ★★☆

10. 다음 글의 내용을 한 문장으로 요약하고자 한다. 빈칸 (A), (B)에 들어갈 말로 가장 적절한 것은? [3점]

Have you noticed that some coaches get the most out of their athletes while others don't? A poor coach will tell you what you did wrong and then tell you not to do it again: "Don't drop the ball!" What happens next? The images you see in your head are images of you dropping the ball! Naturally, your mind recreates what it just "saw" based on what it's been told. Not surprisingly, you walk on the court and drop the ball. What does the good coach do? He or she points out what could be improved, but will then tell you how you could or should perform: "I know you'll catch the ball perfectly this time." Sure enough, the next image in your mind is you *catching* the ball and *scoring* a goal. Once again, your mind makes your last thoughts part of reality—but this time, that "reality" is positive, not negative.

⬇

Unlike ineffective coaches, who focus on players' ____(A)____, effective coaches help players improve by encouraging them to ____(B)____ successful plays.

(A) ······ (B)
① scores ······ complete
② scores ······ remember
③ mistakes ······ picture
④ mistakes ······ ignore
⑤ strengths ······ achieve

2020학년도 3월 학평 40번 ★★☆

11. 다음 글의 내용을 한 문장으로 요약하고자 한다. 빈칸 (A), (B)에 들어갈 말로 가장 적절한 것은?

While there are many evolutionary or cultural reasons for cooperation, the eyes are one of the most important means of cooperation, and eye contact may be the most powerful human force we lose in traffic. It is, arguably, the reason why humans, normally a quite cooperative species, can become so noncooperative on the road. Most of the time we are moving too fast—we begin to lose the ability to keep eye contact around 20 miles per hour—or it is not safe to look. Maybe our view is blocked. Often other drivers are wearing sunglasses, or their car may have tinted windows. (And do you really want to make eye contact with those drivers?) Sometimes we make eye contact through the rearview mirror, but it feels weak, not quite believable at first, as it is not "face-to-face."

* tinted: 색이 옅게 들어간

⬇

While driving, people become ____(A)____, because they make ____(B)____ eye contact.

(A) ······ (B)
① uncooperative ······ little
② careful ······ direct
③ confident ······ regular
④ uncooperative ······ direct
⑤ careful ······ little

총 문항				문항	맞은 문항				문항
개별 문항	1	2	3	4	5	6	7	8	9	10
채점										
개별 문항	11	12	13	14	15	16	17	18	19	20
채점										

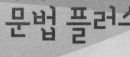

문법 플러스

18. 비교 구문

정답 및 해설 101쪽

A 문법의 주요 포인트를 점검해 봅시다.

1 비교 구문은 크게 원급 비교, 비교급 비교, 최상급 비교가 있다. 원급 비교는 「as+형용사/부사의 원급+as」, 비교급 비교의 형태는 「형용사/부사의 비교급+than」, 최상급 비교는 「the+형용사/부사의 최상급」 형태를 취한다.

2 원급 비교

■ as 원급 as ~	~만큼 …하게	■ 배수+as 원급 as ~	~보다 …배 …하게
■ not as[so] 원급 as ~	~만큼 …하지 못하게(= less ~than)	■ not so much as A as B	A라기 보다는 B(= B rather than A)

3 비교급 비교

■ 비교급+than ~	~보다 더 …하게	■ 비교급 and 비교급	점점 더 ~한[하게]
■ not 비교급 than ~	~보다 더 …하지 않게	■ no more than ~	단지 (= only), ~도 채 안 되는
■ no 비교급 than ~	~처럼 …하지 않게	■ no less than ~	~만큼이나 (= as much as)
■ the+비교급..., the+비교급~	…하면 할수록, 더 ~하다		

*비교급 앞에는 the를 붙이지 않지만, of the two(둘 중에서 더 ~한)와 이유 표현이 뒤에 나올 때는 the를 쓰기도 한다.

4 최상급 비교

■ the 최상급+in 장소[of]~	~중에서 가장 …한	■ 비교급 than any other 단수명사	다른 어떤 ~보다도 더 …하게
■ the 최상급+주어+have[has] ever p.p.	지금껏 ~한 것들 중 가장 ~하게	■ 비교급 than all the other 복수명사	다른 모든 ~보다도 더 …하게
■ no A is as[so] ~ as B	어떤 A도 B만큼 ~하지 않다	■ as 원급 as ever 동사	~중에서 가장 …한
■ no A is 비교급 than B	어떤 A도 B보다 ~하지 않다		

*형용사의 최상급은 the를 써야 쓰지만 부사의 최상급은 the를 생략할 수 있다.

5 또한 비교급을 강조하려면 부사 much, even, still, far, a lot 등을 쓴다.

B 다음 괄호 안에서 어법상 올바른 것을 고르시오.

1 This cell phone is not as **[expensive / more expensive]** as yours.

2 We believe that we are always better off gathering as much information as possible and spending as **[much / more]** time as possible in careful consideration.

3 The study indicates that the material presented by the storytellers has much more interest and personal impact **[as / than]** that gained via the traditional method.

4 This room is nearly two times as **[large / larger]** as that one.

5 Old shoes are usually **[less / more]** comfortable than new shoes.

6 He is cleverer than all the other **[boys / boy]** in his class.

7 She is not so much a scholar **[than / as]** a journalist.

8 Admiral Lee was as **[brave / more brave]** a man as ever breathed.

9 However, the **[higher / high]** the expectations, the more difficult it is to be satisfied.

10 Armed with scientific knowledge, people build tools and machines that transform the way we live, making our lives **[very / much]** easier and better.

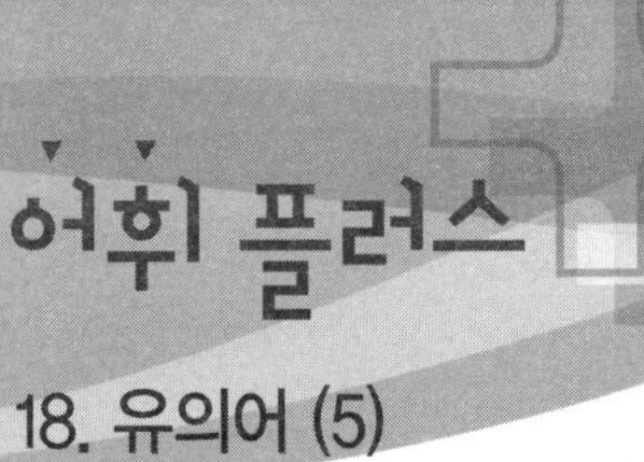

18. 유의어 (5)

정답 및 해설 101쪽

A 다음 수능 필수 어휘를 읽고, 아는 것을 체크해 봅시다.

□ 01	register	v. 기재하다(= enroll)	□ 21	stimulate	v. 고무하다(= encourage)
□ 02	regulate	v. 조절하다(= control)	□ 22	stress	n. 긴장, 강조(= emphasis)
□ 03	reject	v. 거절하다(= refuse)	□ 23	struggle	v. 분투하다(= strive)
□ 04	reliable	a. 믿을 수 있는(= dependable)	□ 24	submit	v. 굴복하다(= surrender)
□ 05	relieve	v. 완화하다(= lessen)	□ 25	sufficient	a. 충분한(= enough)
□ 06	remove	v. 제거하다(= eliminate)	□ 26	suggest	v. 암시하다(= imply)
□ 07	replace	v. 교체하다(= substitute)	□ 27	support	v. 받치다(= uphold)
□ 08	request	v. 요청하다(= require)	□ 28	suppose	v. 가정하다(= assume)
□ 09	require	v. 요구하다(= demand)	□ 29	surround	v. 둘러싸다(= enclose)
□ 10	reserve	v. 예약하다(= book)	□ 30	suspect	v. 의심하다(= doubt)
□ 11	resolve	v. 해결하다(= solve)	□ 31	synthetic	a. 인공의(= artificial)
□ 12	restrict	v. 한정하다(= confine)	□ 32	tendency	n. 추세(= trend)
□ 13	reveal	v. 드러내다(= disclose)	□ 33	terrific	a. 굉장한(= great)
□ 14	reward	v. 보상하다(= compensate)	□ 34	thorough	a. 철저한(= complete)
□ 15	risk	v. 위험을 무릅쓰다(= venture)	□ 35	transform	v. 변형시키다(= convert)
□ 16	rule	v. 통치하다(= govern)	□ 36	transport	v. 수송하다(= convey)
□ 17	shelter	n. 피난처(= refuge)	□ 37	trigger	v. 촉발시키다(= cause)
□ 18	slight	a. 사소한(= trivial)	□ 38	ultimate	a. 최후의(= final)
□ 19	slip	v. 미끄러지다(= slide)	□ 39	unique	a. 독특한(= unusual)
□ 20	spot	n. 얼룩(= stain)	□ 40	vast	a. 방대한(= immense)

B 괄호 안에서 문맥에 맞는 낱말로 적절한 것을 골라 봅시다.

1 Laughing reduces hormones associated with stress response. Thus, it helps **[relieve / trigger]** stress, depression, anxiety, and anger.

2 Unfortunately, our jobs now have us both traveling most weeks, and we simply cannot keep up with a daily paper. So we would like to **[request / remove]** that you stop delivery to our home.

3 They are steamed, boiled, and then washed many times to **[remove / reserve]** any impure materials.

4 But when you're making a decision, following your instincts is necessary but not **[sufficient / unique]**. Learning how to use your instincts as a guide in decision making requires effort.

5 My grandmother wanted to go to school, but the harsh immigrant life pushed her to **[support / rule]** her family.

19 장문의 이해 (1)

출제 트렌드

1. 하나의 긴 문단이나 두 개 이상의 문단으로 구성된 1지문을 읽고 2개 문제를 푸는 유형이다. 1문제는 제목, 주제, 요지와 글의 중심 내용 이해력을 측정하는 문제가 출제되고 다른 1문제는 어휘 추론, 빈칸 추론과 같은 세부적인 내용을 묻는 문제가 출제된다. 수능에서 매년 1세트씩 출제되었다. 한 문항은 제목을 묻는 문항으로, 다른 한 문항은 어휘 추론 문제로 출제되고 있다. 고1 학력 평가에서도 수능 흐름에 맞게 2문항이 출제되고 있다.
2. 수필, 문학 작품과 같은 평이한 글이 제시될 수도 있고 철학, 사회 현상, 인간관계와 같은 추상적인 글이 제시되기도 한다. 비교적 난이도가 높은 유형이다.
3. 최근 수능 7년간, 장문의 이해 (1) 41–42번 문항은 매년 2문제가 출제되고 있다. 41번 문항은 고정적으로 제목 문제가 출제되었는데, 42번 문항은 2017–2018학년도 수능은 빈칸 문제로 출제되었고 2019년 이후 수능은 문맥상 낱말의 쓰임이 적절하지 않는 문제로 출제되었다. 2017학년도 수능(71/51%), 2018(67/76%), 2019(72/54%), 2020(52/53%), 2021(66/73%), 2022(64/61%), 2023(57/62%)에서 괄호 안의 정답률을 보였다. 7년간 평균 62.8% 정도 정답률을 보였다. 난이도는 중 단계이다. 7년간 평균 41번 문항은 64.1%, 42번 문항은 61.4%의 정답률을 보였다.

출처			문항 번호	지문 주제	정답률(%)	난이도
대표	2021학년도	06 학평	41~42번	점진적 노력으로 사회적 불안감을 극복하라	44 / 58	★★★
1 ~ 2	2022학년도	11 학평	41~42번	시각을 위해 함께 작동하는 눈과 두뇌	74 / 64	★★☆
3 ~ 4	2022학년도	09 학평	41~42번	곤충에 대한 당신의 인식을 바꿔라	61 / 59	★★☆
5 ~ 6	2022학년도	06 학평	41~42번	심장을 위한 최고의 취침 시간	85 / 73	★★☆
7 ~ 8	2022학년도	03 학평	41~42번	불행으로부터 자신을 구하기 위해 타인을 이해하라	55 / 59	★★★
9 ~ 10	2021학년도	011 학평	41~42번	유전자가 아니라 우리 손에 달려있는 건강	55 / 61	★★★
11 ~ 12	2021학년도	09 학평	41~42번	회사는 고객의 불만을 받아들여야 한다	61 / 44	★★★

1등급 꿀팁

1. 문제를 먼저 살펴본 후 지문을 읽는 것이 효율적이다.
2. 글의 제목 문제는 글의 주제를 파악하고 주제를 담고 있는 제목을 선택한다.
3. 어휘 추론 문제는 그의 요지나 흐름에 적절하지 않는 어휘를 찾아낸다.

대표 기출

2021학년도 6월 학평 41~42번

【41~42】 다음 글을 읽고 물음에 답하시오.

If you were afraid of standing on balconies, you would start on some lower floors and slowly work your way up to higher ones. It would be easy to face a fear of standing on high balconies in a way that's totally controlled. Socializing is (a) trickier. People aren't like inanimate features of a building that you just have to be around to get used to. You have to interact with them, and their responses can be unpredictable. Your feelings toward them are more complex too. Most people's self-esteem isn't going to be affected that much if they don't like balconies, but your confidence can (b) suffer if you can't socialize effectively.

It's also harder to design a tidy way to gradually face many social fears. The social situations you need to expose yourself to may not be (c) available when you want them, or they may not go well enough for you to sense that things are under control. The progression from one step to the next may not be clear, creating unavoidable large (d) decreases in difficulty from one to the next. People around you aren't robots that you can endlessly experiment with for your own purposes. This is not to say that facing your fears is pointless when socializing. The principles of gradual exposure are still very (e) useful. The process of applying them is just messier, and knowing that before you start is helpful.

41. 윗글의 제목으로 가장 적절한 것은?

① How to Improve Your Self-Esteem
② Socializing with Someone You Fear: Good or Bad?
③ Relaxation May Lead to Getting Over Social Fears
④ Are Social Exposures Related with Fear of Heights?
⑤ Overcoming Social Anxiety Is Difficult; Try Gradually!

42. 밑줄 친 (a)~(e) 중에서 문맥상 낱말의 쓰임이 적절하지 않은 것은?

① (a) ② (b) ③ (c) ④ (d) ⑤ (e)

제한 시간 : 20분	정답 및 해설 102쪽

문제 풀이

1. 글의 전반적인 흐름을 파악한다.

① 도입: If you were afraid of standing on balconies, you would start on some lower floors and slowly work your way up to higher ones. It would be easy to face a fear of standing on high balconies in a way that's totally controlled. Socializing is trickier. (발코니에 서 있는 것을 두려워한다면, 당신은 더 낮은 층에서 시작해서 서서히 더 높은 층으로 올라가면 된다. 완전히 통제된 방식으로 높은 발코니에 서 있는 두려움을 직면하기는 쉬울 것이다. 사람을 사귄다는 것은 더 까다롭다.)

② 요지: 두렵다고 사람 사귀는 것을 꺼리지 말고, 사교적 두려움을 직면하고 사귐의 과정 중에 전진적인 노출을 하도록 해라.

③ 부연: 건물과 로봇과 달리 사람을 사귀는 것은 쉽지 않다.
You have to interact with them, and their responses can be unpredictable. Your feelings toward them are more complex too. (사람을 사귀려면 상호 작용을 해야 하고 그들의 반응도 예측하기 어렵고, 그들을 향한 당신의 감정도 복잡하다.
It's also harder to design a tidy way to gradually face many social fears. (사교적 두려움을 점차적으로 마주하게 할 깔끔한 방법을 설계하는 것 또한 더 어렵다.)

④ 결론: 사람을 사귈 때 두려움을 직면하는 것이 의미가 없는 일이 아니며, 점진적인 노출의 원칙은 유용하다.
This is not to say that facing your fears is pointless when socializing. The principles of gradual exposure are still very useful. (이것은 사람을 사귈 때 당신의 두려움을 직면하는 것은 의미가 없다고 말하는 것은 아니다. 점진적인 노출의 원칙은 여전히 매우 유용하다.)

• 41. 글의 내용을 종합적으로 파악하여 제목으로 적절한 선택지를 고른다. 사교적인 두려움을 극복하는 것은 어렵지만 점진적으로 하라는 내용이므로, 정답은 ⑤ Overcoming Social Anxiety Is Difficult; Try Gradually!이다.
① 자기 존중감을 증진하는 법
② 당신이 두려워하는 사람을 사귀는 것: 좋은 것일까? 나쁜 것일까?
③ 휴식이 사교적인 두려움을 극복하게 이끌수 있다.
④ 사회적인 노출이 고소 공포증과 관련이 있을까?
⑤ 사교적인 두려움을 극복하는 것은 어렵다. (하지만) 점차로 노력해 봐라!

2. 글의 맥락에 맞게 어휘의 적절성을 파악하여 문맥에 맞지 않는 말을 고른다.

• 42. 사람들은 사교적 두려움을 점차적으로 마주하고자 나름 깔끔한 방법을 설계하고자 하지만 뜻대로 되지 않는다는 내용이 와야 하므로 ④번의 단계에서 단계로 진행할 때 피할 수 없는 큰 어려움이 줄어든 것이 아니라 늘어나게 된다고 해야 문맥에 맞다.

2022학년도 11월 학평 41~42번 ★★☆

【1~2】 다음 글을 읽고, 물음에 답하시오.

Mike May lost his sight at the age of three. Because he had spent the majority of his life adapting to being blind — and even cultivating a skiing career in this state — his other senses compensated by growing (a) stronger. However, when his sight was restored through a surgery in his forties, his entire perception of reality was (b) disrupted. Instead of being thrilled that he could see now, as he'd expected, his brain was so overloaded with new visual stimuli that the world became a frightening and overwhelming place. After he'd learned to know his family through touch and smell, he found that he couldn't recognize his children with his eyes, and this left him puzzled. Skiing also became a lot harder as he struggled to adapt to the visual stimulation.

This (c) confusion occurred because his brain hadn't yet learned to see. Though we often tend to assume our eyes function as video cameras which relay information to our brain, advances in neuroscientific research have proven that this is actually not the case. Instead, sight is a collaborative effort between our eyes and our brains, and the way we process (d) visual reality depends on the way these two communicate. If communication between our eyes and our brains is disturbed, our perception of reality is altered accordingly. And because other areas of May's brain had adapted to process information primarily through his other senses, the process of learning how to see was (e) easier than he'd anticipated.

1. 윗글의 제목으로 가장 적절한 것은?

① Eyes and Brain Working Together for Sight
② Visualization: A Useful Tool for Learning
③ Collaboration Between Vision and Sound
④ How to Ignore New Visual Stimuli
⑤ You See What You Believe

2. 밑줄 친 (a)~(e) 중에서 문맥상 낱말의 쓰임이 적절하지 않은 것은?

① (a) ② (b) ③ (c) ④ (d) ⑤ (e)

2022학년도 9월 학평 41~42번 ★★☆

【3~4】 다음 글을 읽고, 물음에 답하시오.

In a society that rejects the consumption of insects there are some individuals who overcome this rejection, but most will continue with this attitude. It may be very (a) difficult to convince an entire society that insects are totally suitable for consumption. However, there are examples in which this (b) reversal of attitudes about certain foods has happened to an entire society. Several examples in the past 120 years from European-American society are: considering lobster a luxury food instead of a food for servants and prisoners; considering sushi a safe and delicious food; and considering pizza not just a food for the rural poor of Sicily. In Latin American countries, where insects are already consumed, a portion of the population hates their consumption and (c) associates it with poverty. There are also examples of people who have had the habit of consuming them and (d) encouraged that habit due to shame, and because they do not want to be categorized as poor or uncivilized. According to Esther Katz, an anthropologist, if the consumption of insects as a food luxury is to be promoted, there would be more chances that some individuals who do not present this habit overcome ideas under which they were educated. And this could also help to (e) revalue the consumption of insects by those people who already eat them.

3. 윗글의 제목으로 가장 적절한 것은?

① The More Variety on the Table, The Healthier You Become
② Edible or Not? Change Your Perspectives on Insects
③ Insects: A Key to Solve the World Food Shortage
④ Don't Let Uniqueness in Food Culture Disappear
⑤ Experiencing Various Cultures by Food

4. 밑줄 친 (a)~(e) 중에서 문맥상 낱말의 쓰임이 적절하지 않은 것은?

① (a) ② (b) ③ (c) ④ (d) ⑤ (e)

2022학년도 6월 학평 41~42번 ★★☆

【5~6】 다음 글을 읽고, 물음에 답하시오.

U.K. researchers say a bedtime of between 10 p.m. and 11 p.m. is best. They say people who go to sleep between these times have a (a) lower risk of heart disease. Six years ago, the researchers collected data on the sleep patterns of 80,000 volunteers. The volunteers had to wear a special watch for seven days so the researchers could collect data on their sleeping and waking times. The scientists then monitored the health of the volunteers. Around 3,000 volunteers later showed heart problems. They went to bed earlier or later than the (b) ideal 10 p.m. to 11 p.m. timeframe.

One of the authors of the study, Dr. David Plans, commented on his research and the (c) effects of bedtimes on the health of our heart. He said the study could not give a certain cause for their results, but it suggests that early or late bedtimes may be more likely to disrupt the body clock, with (d) positive consequences for cardiovascular health. He said that it was important for our body to wake up to the morning light, and that the worst time to go to bed was after midnight because it may (e) reduce the likelihood of seeing morning light which resets the body clock. He added that we risk cardiovascular disease if our body clock is not reset properly.

* disrupt: 혼란케 하다 ** cardiovascular: 심장 혈관의

5. 윗글의 제목으로 가장 적절한 것은?

① The Best Bedtime for Your Heart
② Late Bedtimes Are a Matter of Age
③ For Sound Sleep: Turn Off the Light
④ Sleeping Patterns Reflect Personalities
⑤ Regular Exercise: A Miracle for Good Sleep

6. 밑줄 친 (a)~(e) 중에서 문맥상 낱말의 쓰임이 적절하지 않은 것은?

① (a) ② (b) ③ (c) ④ (d) ⑤ (e)

2022학년도 3월 학평 41~42번 ★★★

【7~8】 다음 글을 읽고, 물음에 답하시오.

The longest journey we will make is the eighteen inches between our head and heart. If we take this journey, it can shorten our (a) misery in the world. Impatience, judgment, frustration, and anger reside in our heads. When we live in that place too long, it makes us (b) unhappy. But when we take the journey from our heads to our hearts, something shifts (c) inside. What if we were able to love everything that gets in our way? What if we tried loving the shopper who unknowingly steps in front of us in line, the driver who cuts us off in traffic, the swimmer who splashes us with water during a belly dive, or the reader who pens a bad online review of our writing?

Every person who makes us miserable is (d) like us — a human being, most likely doing the best they can, deeply loved by their parents, a child, or a friend. And how many times have we unknowingly stepped in front of someone in line? Cut someone off in traffic? Splashed someone in a pool? Or made a negative statement about something we've read? It helps to (e) deny that a piece of us resides in every person we meet.

* reside: (어떤 장소에) 있다

7. 윗글의 제목으로 가장 적절한 것은?

① Why It Is So Difficult to Forgive Others
② Even Acts of Kindness Can Hurt Somebody
③ Time Is the Best Healer for a Broken Heart
④ Celebrate the Happy Moments in Your Everyday Life
⑤ Understand Others to Save Yourself from Unhappiness

8. 밑줄 친 (a)~(e) 중에서 문맥상 낱말의 쓰임이 적절하지 않은 것은?

① (a) ② (b) ③ (c) ④ (d) ⑤ (e)

2021학년도 11월 학평 41~42번 ★★★

【9~10】 다음 글을 읽고, 물음에 답하시오.

Since the turn of the twentieth century we've believed in genetic causes of diagnoses — a theory called genetic determinism. Under this model, our genes (and subsequent health) are determined at birth. We are "destined" to inherit certain diseases based on the misfortune of our DNA. Genetic determinism doesn't (a) consider the role of family backgrounds, traumas, habits, or anything else within the environment. In this dynamic we are not (b) active participants in our own health and wellness. Why would we be? If something is predetermined, it's not (c) necessary to look at anything beyond our DNA. But the more science has learned about the body and its interaction with the environment around it (in its various forms, from our nutrition to our relationships to our racially oppressive systems), the more (d) simplistic the story becomes. We are not merely expressions of coding but products of a remarkable variety of interactions that are both within and outside of our control. Once we see beyond the narrative that genetics are (e) destiny, we can take ownership of our health. This allows us to see how "choiceless" we once were and empowers us with the ability to create real and lasting change.

* oppressive: 억압적인

9. 윗글의 제목으로 가장 적절한 것은?

① Health Is in Our Hands, Not Only in Our Genes
② Genetics: A Solution to Enhance Human Wellness
③ How Did DNA Dominate Over Environment in Biology?
④ Never Be Confident in Your Health, but Keep Checking!
⑤ Why Scientific Innovation Affects Our Social Interactions

10. 밑줄 친 (a)~(e) 중에서 문맥상 낱말의 쓰임이 적절하지 않은 것은? [3점]

① (a) ② (b) ③ (c) ④ (d) ⑤ (e)

2021학년도 9월 학평 41~42번 ★★★

【11~12】 다음 글을 읽고, 물음에 답하시오.

The market's way of telling a firm about its failures is harsh and brief. Not only are complaints less expensive to handle but they also can cause the seller to (a) improve. The seller may learn something as well. I remember a cosmetics company that received complaints about sticky sunblock lotion. At the time, all such lotions were more or less sticky, so the risk of having customers buy products from a rival company was not (b) great. But this was also an opportunity. The company managed to develop a product that was not sticky and captured 20 percent of the market in its first year. Another company had the (c) opposite problem. Its products were not sticky enough. The company was a Royal Post Office in Europe and the product was a stamp. The problem was that the stamp didn't stick to the envelope. Management contacted the stamp producer who made it clear that if people just moistened the stamps properly, they would stick to any piece of paper. What to do? Management didn't take long to come to the conclusion that it would be (d) less costly to try to educate its customers to wet each stamp rather than to add more glue. The stamp producer was told to add more glue and the problem didn't occur again.

Since it is better for the firm to have buyers complain rather than go elsewhere, it is important to make it (e) easier for dissatisfied customers to complain.

* stamp: 우표

11. 윗글의 제목으로 가장 적절한 것은?

① Designs That Matter the Most to Customers
② Complaints: Why Firms Should Welcome Them
③ Cheap Prices Don't Necessarily Mean Low Quality
④ More Sticky or Less Sticky: An Unsolved Problem
⑤ Treat Your Competitors Like Friends, Not Enemies

12. 밑줄 친 (a)~(e) 중에서 문맥상 낱말의 쓰임이 적절하지 않은 것은? [3점]

① (a) ② (b) ③ (c) ④ (d) ⑤ (e)

총 문항				문항	맞은 문항					문항
개별 문항	1	2	3	4	5	6	7	8	9	10
채점										
개별 문항	11	12	13	14	15	16	17	18	19	20
채점										

Day 19

문법 플러스

19. 어순에 주의해야 할 구문

정답 및 해설 107쪽

A 문법의 주요 포인트를 점검해 봅시다.

1 간접의문문이란 직접의문문이 다른 문장의 일부가 되어 문장 안에 포함되는 것을 말한다. 직접의문문과 달리 「의문사[whether/if]+주어+동사」의 어순이 됨에 주의해야 한다. think, believe, guess suppose, imagine 등의 동사가 쓰인 간접의문문은 의문사가 문장 앞으로 나간다.

- (직접의문문) Where **does he live**?
- (간접의문문) I don't know **where he lives**.
- (간접의문문) **Where** do you **think he lives**?

2 감탄문은 What a/an 형용사+명사+주어+동사! 또는 How 형용사/부사+주어+동사!의 어순을 취한다.

3 「what, such, quite+관사+형용사+명사」의 어순을 가지고, 「how, so, as, too+형용사+관사+명사」 어순을 취한다.

4 「enough+명사」 또는 「명사+enough」 어순이 가능하지만 enough가 형용사나 부사를 수식할 때는 뒤에서 꾸민다. 즉 「형용사/부사+enough」 어순을 취한다.

5 동사와 부사가 결합된 동사구에서 목적어가 대명사일 경우에는 「동사+대명사+부사」의 어순이 되어야 한다.

B 다음 괄호 안에서 어법상 올바른 것을 고르시오.

1 I asked a clerk where **[did they have / they had]** books about computers.

2 I wonder **[that / if]** you've ever regretted becoming a baseball player.

3 You'll notice **[how much the interactions/ how the interactions much]** with the people in your life will improve as a direct result of this simple act.

4 They made **[so / such]** a fuss over a little accident.

5 The rope is **[strong enough / enough strong]** to hold your weight.

C 다음 직접화법의 의문문을 간접화법으로 바꿔 쓰시오.

6 Peter asked me, "Can you help me with my science project?"
→ Peter asked me ______________________________.

7 Sally asked me, "What do you want?"
→ Sally asked me ______________________________.

8 Ben said to me, "Did you enjoy your trip?"
→ Ben asked me ______________________________.

9 My son often asks me, "Why is the sky blue?
→ My son often asks me ______________________________.

10 Sarah asked him, "What major are you going into?"
→ Sarah asked him ______________________________.

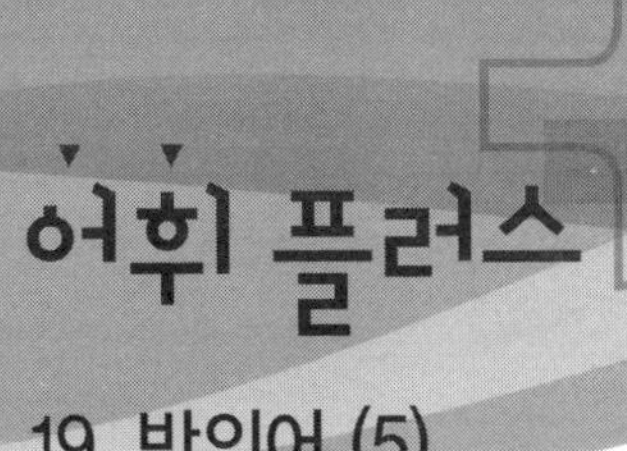

19. 반의어 (5)

정답 및 해설 107쪽

A 다음 수능 필수 어휘를 읽고, 아는 것은 체크해 봅시다.

□ 01	pure	a. 순수한, 깨끗한	□ 21	impure	a. 순수하지 못한, 불결한
□ 02	qualify	v. 자격을 얻다	□ 22	disqualify	v. 자격을 잃게 하다
□ 03	receive	v. 받아들이다	□ 23	reject	v. 거절하다
□ 04	refuse	v. 거절하다, 거부하다	□ 24	accept	v. 받아들이다, 수락하다
□ 05	retail	a. 소매의	□ 25	wholesale	a. 도매의
□ 06	rigid	a. 뻣뻣한	□ 26	flexible	a. 유연성이 있는
□ 07	significant	a. 중요한	□ 27	insignificant	a. 중요하지 않은
□ 08	specific	a. 구체적인	□ 28	vague	a. 애매모호한, 추상적인
□ 09	static	a. 정적인, 고정된	□ 29	dynamic	a. 동적인
□ 10	subjective	a. 주관적인	□ 30	objective	a. 객관적인
□ 11	suitable	a. 적합한	□ 31	unsuitable	a. 적합하지 않은
□ 12	surplus	n. 흑자, 나머지	□ 32	deficit	n. 적자, 부족분
□ 13	tangible	a. 유형의, 만질 수 있는	□ 33	intangible	a. 무형의, 만질 수 없는
□ 14	tragic	a. 비극의	□ 34	comic	a. 희극의
□ 15	understand	v. 이해하다	□ 35	misunderstand	v. 오해하다
□ 16	unpredictable	a. 예측할 수 없는	□ 36	predictable	a. 예측할 수 있는
□ 17	usual	a. 보통의, 평소의	□ 37	unusual	a. 평소 같지 않은, 이상한
□ 18	verbal	a. 언어의, 구두의	□ 38	nonverbal	a. 비언어의
□ 19	visible	a. 눈에 보이는	□ 39	invisible	a. 눈에 보이지 않는
□ 20	vulnerable	a. 취약한, 연약한	□ 40	invulnerable	a. 해칠 수 없는, 안전한

B 괄호 안에서 문맥에 맞는 낱말로 적절한 것을 골라 봅시다.

1 Sam **[received / rejected]** the idea as “absurd.”

2 Argument is often considered disrespectful in **[rigid / flexible]** families.

3 Wilkinson showed that the blood donors are typically sharing their **[deficits / surpluses]** and, in so doing, are saving unsuccessful foragers that are close to starvation.

4 A person calls you on the telephone. Apparently assuming you will recognize her voice, she does not provide any **[nonverbal / verbal]** content which would help you identify her.

5 The principal effect of seat belt legislation has been a shift in the burden of risk from those already best protected in cars, to the most **[vulnerable / invulnerable]**, pedestrians and cyclists, outside cars.

C 다음 수능 필수 어휘를 읽고, 아는 것은 체크해 봅시다.

□ 01	absolute	a. 절대적인	□ 21	relative	a. 상대적인
□ 02	abundant	a. 풍부한	□ 22	scarce	a. 결핍된
□ 03	admire	v. 칭송하다	□ 23	condemn	v. 경멸하다
□ 04	appreciate	v. 높이 평가하다	□ 24	depreciate	v. 가치를 폄하하다
□ 05	conservative	a. 보수적인	□ 25	progressive	a. 진보적인
□ 06	consume	v. 소비하다	□ 26	produce	v. 생산하다
□ 07	contract	v. 수축하다	□ 27	expand	v. 팽창하다
□ 08	decline	v. 거절하다	□ 28	accept	v. 수락하다
□ 09	employ	v. 고용하다	□ 29	dismiss	v. 해고하다
□ 10	favorable	a. 우호적인	□ 30	hostile	a. 적대적인
□ 11	inferior	a. 열등한	□ 31	superior	a. 우수한
□ 12	internal	a. 내적인	□ 32	external	a. 외적인
□ 13	junior	a. 연하의	□ 33	senior	a. 연상의
□ 14	lengthen	v. 늘이다	□ 34	shorten	v. 줄이다
□ 15	natural	a. 자연의	□ 35	artificial	a. 인공의
□ 16	surrender	v. 항복하다	□ 36	conquer	v. 정복하다
□ 17	tighten	v. 팽팽하게 하다	□ 37	loosen	v. 느슨하게 하다
□ 18	urban	a. 도시의	□ 38	rural	a. 시골의
□ 19	valueless	a. 무가치한	□ 39	invaluable	a. 더 없이 귀한
□ 20	weaken	v. 약화시키다	□ 40	strengthen	v. 강화시키다

D 괄호 안에서 문맥에 맞는 낱말로 적절한 것을 골라 봅시다.

1 America being a cultural melting pot, all Americans need to learn about each other and **[depreciate /appreciate]** the contributions made by the various racial groups.

2 Since you started in the mail room in 1979, your contributions to this firm have been **[valueless / invaluable]**.

3 Research has shown that we automatically assign to good-looking individuals such **[favorable / hostile]** traits as talent, kindness, honesty, and intelligence.

4 The RPC, founded in 1996, describes itself as a **[conservative / progressive]** organization fighting for social change.

5 Excessive dependence on foreign imports may **[strengthen / weaken]** a nation's capability to defend itself in a crisis.

장문의 이해 (2)

출제 트렌드

1. 네 개의 문단으로 이루어진 복합문을 읽고 이에 따른 3개의 질문을 푸는 유형이다. 수능 흐름에 맞게 고1 학력 평가에서도 3문항이 출제되고 있다.
2. 빠른 독해력과 종합적인 사고력이 요구된다. 소설이나 수필에서 발췌한 글감을 토대로 비교적 쉬운 글이 제시되며 감동적이고 교훈적인 글이 출제된다.
3. 최근 수능 7년간, 장문의 이해 (2) 43–45번 문항은 매년 3문제가 출제되고 있다. 43번은 문단의 순서, 44번은 지칭 추론, 45번은 내용 일치 파악 문제로 출제되었다. 2017학년도 수능(71/79/86%), 2018(91/86/90%), 2019(91/90/88%), 2020(93/93/92%), 2021(91/87/92%), 2022(95/93/94%), 2023(91/85/86%)에서 괄호 안의 정답률을 보였다. 7년간 평균 88.8% 정도 정답률을 보였다. 7년간 평균 43번 문항은 89%, 44번 문항은 87.6%, 45번 문항은 89.7%의 정답률을 보였다. 난이도는 하 단계이다.
4. 난이도가 높지 않으므로, 난이도가 높은 빈칸 4문제를 먼저 풀지 말고 전략적으로 장문의 이해(1), (2) 문제를 먼저 푸는 것이 유리하다.

출처			문항 번호	지문 주제	정답률(%)	난이도
대표	2022학년도	11 학평	43~45번	Marie의 공감과 따뜻함	82/71/77	★★☆
1 ~ 3	2022학년도	09 학평	43~45번	손자를 위해 최고의 학교를 찾은 할아버지	72/71/74	★★☆
4 ~ 6	2022학년도	06 학평	43~45번	농부의 소중한 시계를 찾아준 어린 소년	81/77/80	★★☆
7 ~ 9	2022학년도	03 학평	43~45번	긍정적인 마음가짐	69/66/74	★★☆
10 ~ 12	2021학년도	11 학평	43~45번	사려 깊은 왕자	76/76/83	★★☆

1등급 꿀팁

1. 글을 읽기 전에 제시된 문제가 무엇인지 먼저 파악한다.
2. 제시된 사건의 순서를 파악한 후 글의 순서를 정해야 한다.
3. 등장인물들의 말과 행동을 이해한 후, 지칭 대상이 다른 것을 파악한다.
4. 사건의 세부 사항을 파악한 후 내용 일치 문제를 해결한다.

장문의 이해 (2)

제한 시간 : 20분 | 정답 및 해설 107쪽

대표 기출 2022학년도 11월 학평 43~45번

[43 ~ 45] 다음 글을 읽고, 물음에 답하시오.

(A)

On my daughter Marie's 8th birthday, she received a bunch of presents from her friends at school. That evening, with her favorite present, a teddy bear, in her arms, we went to a restaurant to celebrate her birthday. Our server, a friendly woman, noticed my daughter holding the teddy bear and said, "My daughter loves teddy bears, too." Then, we started chatting about (a) her family.

(B)

When Marie came back out, I asked her what she had been doing. She said that she gave her teddy bear to our server so that she could give it to (b) her daughter. I was surprised at her sudden action because I could see how much she loved that bear already. (c) She must have seen the look on my face, because she said, "I can't imagine being stuck in a hospital bed. I just want her to get better soon."

(C)

I felt moved by Marie's words as we walked toward the car. Then, our server ran out to our car and thanked Marie for her generosity. The server said that (d) she had never had anyone doing anything like that for her family before. Later, Marie said it was her best birthday ever. I was so proud of her empathy and warmth, and this was an unforgettable experience for our family.

(D)

The server mentioned during the conversation that her daughter was in the hospital with a broken leg. (e) She also said that Marie looked about the same age as her daughter. She was so kind and attentive all evening, and even gave Marie cookies for free. After we finished our meal, we paid the bill and began to walk to our car when unexpectedly Marie asked me to wait and ran back into the restaurant.

43. 주어진 글 (A)에 이어질 내용을 순서에 맞게 배열한 것으로 가장 적절한 것은?

① (B) – (D) – (C)　② (C) – (B) – (D)
③ (C) – (D) – (B)　④ (D) – (B) – (C)
⑤ (D) – (C) – (B)

44. 밑줄 친 (a)~(e) 중에서 가리키는 대상이 나머지 넷과 다른 것은?

① (a)　② (b)　③ (c)　④ (d)　⑤ (e)

45. 윗글에 관한 내용으로 적절하지 않은 것은?

① Marie는 테디 베어를 팔에 안고 식당에 갔다.
② 'I'는 Marie의 갑작스러운 행동에 놀랐다.
③ 종업원은 Marie의 관대함에 고마워했다.
④ 종업원은 자신의 딸이 팔이 부러져서 병원에 있다고 말했다.
⑤ 종업원은 Marie에게 쿠키를 무료로 주었다.

문제 풀이

1. 주어진 글 (A)를 읽고, 글 (B), (C), (D)의 첫 문장이나 마지막 문장을 통해 글의 순서를 추측해 본다.

(1) 글 (A): 딸(Marie)의 생일을 축하하기 위해 식당에 갔는데, 딸이 안고 있는 테디 베어를 보고, 여자 종업원이 자신의 딸도 테디 베어를 좋아한다고 말했다.

(2) 글 (D): 그 여자 종업원은 자신의 딸이 다리가 부러져 병원에 있다고 말하며 Marie가 자신의 딸과 또래처럼 보인다고 말하며 만족스러운 서비스를 제공해 주었다. 필자는 식사를 마치고 요금을 지불하고 차로 걸어가고 있는데 Marie가 기다려 달라고 부탁하고 식당으로 다시 뛰어 들어갔다.
- (D) 문장 처음의 the server는 (A)의 our server를 가리킨다.

(3) 글 (B): Marie는 돌아왔을 때, 필자는 그녀가 무엇을 하고 있었냐는 물었는데, Marie는 자신의 테디 베어를 종업원에게 주고서 그녀의 딸에게 전달해 주라고 말했다고 답했다.
- 필자가 (D)의 끝부분 ~Marie asked me to wait and ran back into restaurant을 통해 Marie가 식당 안으로 들어갔는데, (B)의 앞부분 When Marie came back out~에서 다시 돌아왔다고 했으므로 (D) 다음에 (B)가 옴을 알 수 있다.

(4) 글 (C): 딸의 말에 감동을 하고 있었는데, 종업원이 우리 차로 달려 나와 Marie의 관대함에 고마워했다.
- (C)의 앞부분에서 Marie's words 때문에 필자가 감동을 받았는데, (B)의 끝부분에 Marie의 감동스런 말이 언급되고 있으므로 (B) 다음에 (C)가 와야 한다.

• 주어진 단서를 종합하여 글의 순서를 정한다. 글은 (A) -) (D) -) (B) -) (C) 순서로 진행하는 것이 흐름상 자연스럽다. 그러므로 정답은 ④번이다.

2. 글의 흐름에 맞추어 글의 내용을 이해하고 글의 세부 사항을 확인한다.

• ③ 병원 침대에 갇혀 있는 것을 상상할 수 없다고 하면서 그녀가 빨리 낫기를 바란다는 내용으로 보아 (c)는 Marie를 가리키고, 나머지는 모두 종업원을 가리킨다.

3. 글의 세부 사항은 본문과 선택지 순서가 일치하게 전개된다.

• ④ (D)의 'The server mentioned during the conversation that her daughter was in the hospital with a broken leg.'에서 종업원은 자신의 딸이 다리가 부러져서 병원에 있다고 했으므로, ④가 윗글에 관한 내용으로 적절하지 않다.

2022학년도 9월 학평 43~45번 ★★☆

【1~3】 다음 글을 읽고, 물음에 답하시오.

(A)

A boy had a place at the best school in town. In the morning, his granddad took him to the school. When (a) <u>he</u> went onto the playground with his grandson, the children surrounded them. "What a funny old man," one boy smirked. A girl with brown hair pointed at the pair and jumped up and down. Suddenly, the bell rang and the children ran off to their first lesson.

* smirk: 히죽히죽 웃다

(B)

In some schools the children completely ignored the old man and in others, they made fun of (b) <u>him</u>. When this happened, he would turn sadly and go home. Finally, he went onto the tiny playground of a very small school, and leant against the fence, exhausted. The bell rang, and the crowd of children ran out onto the playground. "Sir, are you all right? Shall I bring you a glass of water?" a voice said. "We've got a bench in the playground — come and sit down," another voice said. Soon a young teacher came out onto the playground.

(C)

The old man greeted (c) <u>him</u> and said: "Finally, I've found my grandson the best school in town." "You're mistaken, sir. Our school is not the best — it's small and cramped." The old man didn't argue with the teacher. Instead, he made arrangements for his grandson to join the school, and then the old man left. That evening, the boy's mom said to (d) <u>him</u>: "Dad, you can't even read. How do you know you've found the best teacher of all?" "Judge a teacher by his pupils," the old man replied.

* cramped: 비좁은

(D)

The old man took his grandson firmly by the hand, and led him out of the school gate. "Brilliant, I don't have to go to school!" the boy exclaimed. "You do, but not this one," his granddad replied. "I'll find you a school myself." Granddad took his grandson back to his own house, asked grandma to look after him, and went off to look for a teacher (e) <u>himself</u>. Every time he spotted a school, the old man went onto the playground, and waited for the children to come out at break time.

1. 주어진 글 (A)에 이어질 내용을 순서에 맞게 배열한 것으로 가장 적절한 것은?

① (B) - (D) - (C)　② (C) - (B) - (D)
③ (C) - (D) - (B)　④ (D) - (B) - (C)
⑤ (D) - (C) - (B)

2. 밑줄 친 (a)~(e) 중에서 가리키는 대상이 나머지 넷과 <u>다른</u> 것은?

① (a)　② (b)　③ (c)　④ (d)　⑤ (e)

3. 윗글에 관한 내용으로 적절하지 <u>않은</u> 것은?

① 갈색 머리 소녀가 노인과 소년을 향해 손가락질했다.
② 노인은 지쳐서 울타리에 기댔다.
③ 노인은 선생님과 논쟁을 벌였다.
④ 노인은 글을 읽을 줄 몰랐다.
⑤ 소년은 학교에 가지 않아도 된다고 소리쳤다.

2022학년도 6월 학평 43~45번 ★★☆

【4~6】 다음 글을 읽고, 물음에 답하시오.

(A)

Once, a farmer lost his precious watch while working in his barn. It may have appeared to be an ordinary watch to others, but it brought a lot of happy childhood memories to him. It was one of the most important things to (a) <u>him</u>. After searching for it for a long time, the old farmer became exhausted.

* barn: 헛간(곡물·건초 따위를 두는 곳)

(B)

The number of children looking for the watch slowly decreased and only a few tired children were left. The farmer gave up all hope of finding it and called off the search. Just when the farmer was closing the barn door, a little boy came up to him and asked the farmer to give him another chance. The farmer did not want to lose out on any chance of finding the watch so let (b) <u>him</u> in the barn.

(C)

After a little while the boy came out with the farmer's watch in his hand. (c) <u>He</u> was happily surprised and asked how he had succeeded to find the watch while everyone else had failed. He replied "I just sat there and tried listening for the sound of the watch. In silence, it was much easier to hear it and follow the direction of the sound." (d) <u>He</u> was delighted to get his watch back and rewarded the little boy as promised.

(D)

However, the tired farmer did not want to give up on the search for his watch and asked a group of children playing outside to help him. (e) <u>He</u> promised an attractive reward for the person who could find it. After hearing about the reward, the children hurried inside the barn and went through and round the entire pile of hay looking for the watch. After a long time searching for it, some of the children got tired and gave up.

4. 주어진 글 (A)에 이어질 내용을 순서에 맞게 배열한 것으로 가장 적절한 것은?

① (B) – (D) – (C)
② (C) – (B) – (D)
③ (C) – (D) – (B)
④ (D) – (B) – (C)
⑤ (D) – (C) – (B)

5. 밑줄 친 (a)~(e) 중에서 가리키는 대상이 나머지 넷과 <u>다른</u> 것은?

① (a) ② (b) ③ (c) ④ (d) ⑤ (e)

6. 윗글에 관한 내용으로 적절하지 <u>않은</u> 것은?

① 농부의 시계는 어린 시절의 행복한 기억을 불러일으켰다.
② 한 어린 소년이 농부에게 또 한 번의 기회를 달라고 요청했다.
③ 소년이 한 손에 농부의 시계를 들고 나왔다.
④ 아이들은 시계를 찾기 위해 헛간을 뒤져나왔다.
⑤ 아이들 중 일부는 지쳐서 시계 찾기를 포기했다.

2022학년도 3월 학평 43~45번 ★★☆

[7~9] 다음 글을 읽고, 물음에 답하시오.

(A)

One day a young man was walking along a road on his journey from one village to another. As he walked he noticed a monk working in the fields. The young man turned to the monk and said, "Excuse me. Do you mind if I ask (a) <u>you</u> a question?" "Not at all," replied the monk.

* monk: 수도승

(B)

A while later a middle-aged man journeyed down the same road and came upon the monk. "I am going to the village in the valley," said the man. "Do you know what it is like?" "I do," replied the monk, "but first tell (b) <u>me</u> about the village where you came from." "I've come from the village in the mountains," said the man. "It was a wonderful experience. I felt as though I was a member of the family in the village."

(C)

"I am traveling from the village in the mountains to the village in the valley and I was wondering if (c) <u>you</u> knew what it is like in the village in the valley." "Tell me," said the monk, "what was your experience of the village in the mountains?" "Terrible," replied the young man. "I am glad to be away from there. I found the people most unwelcoming. So tell (d) <u>me</u>, what can I expect in the village in the valley?" "I am sorry to tell you," said the monk, "but I think your experience will be much the same there." The young man lowered his head helplessly and walked on.

(D)

"Why did you feel like that?" asked the monk. "The elders gave me much advice, and people were kind and generous. I am sad to have left there. And what is the village in the valley like?" he asked again. "(e) <u>I</u> think you will find it much the same," replied the monk. "I'm glad to hear that," the middle-aged man said smiling and journeyed on.

7. 주어진 글 (A)에 이어질 내용을 순서에 맞게 배열한 것으로 가장 적절한 것은?

① (B) – (D) – (C)
② (C) – (B) – (D)
③ (C) – (D) – (B)
④ (D) – (B) – (C)
⑤ (D) – (C) – (B)

8. 밑줄 친 (a)~(e) 중에서 가리키는 대상이 나머지 넷과 <u>다른</u> 것은?

① (a) ② (b) ③ (c) ④ (d) ⑤ (e)

9. 윗글에 관한 내용으로 적절하지 <u>않은</u> 것은?

① 한 수도승이 들판에서 일하고 있었다.
② 중년 남자는 골짜기에 있는 마을로 가는 중이었다.
③ 수도승은 골짜기에 있는 마을에 대해 질문받았다.
④ 수도승의 말을 듣고 젊은이는 고개를 숙였다.
⑤ 중년 남자는 산속에 있는 마을을 떠나서 기쁘다고 말했다.

2021학년도 11월 학평 43~45번 ★★☆

【10~12】 다음 글을 읽고, 물음에 답하시오.

(A)

One day a poor man brought a bunch of grapes to a prince as a gift. He was very excited to be able to bring a gift for (a) <u>him</u> because he was too poor to afford more. He placed the grapes beside the prince and said, "Oh, Prince, please accept this small gift from me." His face beamed with happiness as he offered his small gift.

(B)

If the prince had offered the grapes to them, they might have made funny faces and shown their distaste for the grapes. That would have hurt the feelings of that poor man. He thought to himself that it would be better to eat all of them cheerfully and please (b) <u>him</u>. He did not want to hurt the feelings of that poor man. Everyone around him was moved by his thoughtfulness.

(C)

The prince thanked him politely. As the man looked at him expectantly, the prince ate one grape. Then (c) <u>he</u> ate another one. Slowly the prince finished the whole bunch of grapes by himself. He did not offer grapes to anyone near him. The man who brought those grapes to (d) <u>him</u> was very pleased and left. The close friends of the prince who were around him were very surprised.

(D)

Usually the prince shared whatever he had with others. He would offer them whatever he was given and they would eat it together. This time was different. Without offering it to anyone, (e) <u>he</u> finished the bunch of grapes by himself. One of the friends asked, "Prince! How come you ate all the grapes by yourself and did not offer them to any one of us?" He smiled and said that he ate all the grapes by himself because the grapes were too sour.

10. 주어진 글 (A)에 이어질 내용을 순서에 맞게 배열한 것으로 가장 적절한 것은?

① (B) – (C) – (D)
② (C) – (B) – (D)
③ (C) – (D) – (B)
④ (D) – (B) – (C)
⑤ (D) – (C) – (B)

11. 밑줄 친 (a)~(e) 중에서 가리키는 대상이 나머지 넷과 <u>다른</u> 것은?

① (a) ② (b) ③ (c) ④ (d) ⑤ (e)

12. 윗글의 왕자에 관한 내용으로 적절하지 <u>않은</u> 것은?

① 가난한 남자에게 포도 한 송이를 선물로 받았다.
② 가난한 남자의 감정을 상하게 하고 싶지 않았다.
③ 곁에 있던 어떤 이에게도 포도를 권하지 않았다.
④ 가지고 있는 어떤 것이든 평소에 다른 사람들과 나눴다.
⑤ 포도가 너무 시어서 혼자 다 먹지 못했다.

총 문항				문항	맞은 문항					문항
개별 문항	1	2	3	4	5	6	7	8	9	10
채점										
개별 문항	11	12	13	14	15	16	17	18	19	20
채점										

문법 플러스

20. 강조와 도치

정답 및 해설 111쪽

A 문법의 주요 포인트를 점검해 봅시다.

1 It is[was] ~ that 강조 구문(…하는 것은 바로 ~이다)은 It is와 that 사이에 강조하고자 하는 어구를 둔다. 동사는 사이에 두지 않는다. It is와 that을 제외할 때 완전한 문장이면 강조 구문이고, 완전하지 않으면 It-that 가주어, 진주어 구문이다.

2 동사 앞에 do[does/did]를 써서 동사의 의미를 강조할 수 있다. 해석은 '정말 ~하다'라고 한다.
cf. 대동사 do: 대동사는 앞에 나온 동사나 동사구를 대신하는 동사를 말한다. 동사의 반복을 피하기 위해서 사용한다. 일반동사의 대동사로 do가 사용되며 인칭, 시제에 따라서 do가 does, did로 변한다. be동사는 대동사로 be를 사용한다.
▪ She speaks English better than he **does**. (does = speaks English)

3 부정어, 부사(구), 보어, only가 문두로 나가면 「주어+동사」가 도치되어 「동사+주어」의 어순이 된다.

4 here, there가 문두에 오는 경우, 「동사+주어」 어순이 된다. 단, 주어가 인칭대명사일 때는 도치되지 않는다.

5 「so+동사+주어」는 앞 문장에 대해 긍정 동의 표현이며 「neither+동사+주어」는 앞 문장에 대해 부정 동의 표현이다.

B 다음 괄호 안에서 어법상 올바른 것을 고르시오.

1 It was exactly at nine **[that / where]** the earthquake occurred.

2 You **[do / does]** look pale.

3 Here **[comes the last train / the last train comes]**!

4 So great **[her astonishment was / was her astonishment]** that she was speechless.

5 Only after understanding the situation **[does the teacher / the teacher does]** make a comment.

6 He can't speak English and **[either / neither]** can I.

7 When Sally signed up for Microbiology, so **[did I / I did]**.

8 Little **[did she / she did]** understand the situation.

9 Not until then **[I realized / did I realize]** the horror of an accident at sea.

10 Not only **[this flower does / does this flower]** look pretty but it is also used to tell how much smog is in the air over the city.

20. 다의어

정답 및 해설 112쪽

A 다음 수능 필수 어휘를 읽고, 아는 것은 체크해 봅시다.

□ 01	account	(은행) 계좌, (인터넷) 계정, 이유, 설명; 설명하다, 비율을 차지하다
□ 02	appreciate	감사하다, 감상하다, 이해하다
□ 03	charge	요금, 고발, 책임; 요금을 청구하다, 고발하다, 책임을 지우다, 충전하다
□ 04	content	내용(물), 목차, 함유량; 만족하는
□ 05	current	흐름, 추세; 현재의, 현행의
□ 06	deal	취급, 대우, 거래, 많음; 다루다, 대우하다, 거래하다
□ 07	fashion	패션, 의류업, 유행, 방식; 만들어내다
□ 08	feature	얼굴 생김새, 특징, 지형, 특집 기사; 특징으로 하다, 특집으로 다루다
□ 09	figure	수치, (중요한) 인물, 형체; 계산하다, 이해하다
□ 10	issue	쟁점, 발행(물); 발행하다, 발표하다
□ 11	leave	휴가; 두고 가다, 떠나다
□ 12	mean	평균, 수단; 비열한; 의미하다, 의도하다
□ 13	object	목표, 물체, 대상; 반대하다
□ 14	odd	이상한, 짝이 맞지 않는, 비정기적인, 홀수의, 남짓한(a little more than)
□ 15	present	선물, 현재; 현재의, 출석한; 제출하다, 보여 주다
□ 16	scale	저울, (어류) 비늘, 규모, 등급
□ 17	subject	주제, 과목, 대상; 영향 받기 쉬운, 지배를 받는; 지배하다, 복종시키다
□ 18	term	용어, 기간, 임기, 관계
□ 19	tip	끝, 첨단(point), 사례금, 정보; 뒤집어엎다
□ 20	treat	다루다, 치료하다, 대접하다

B 괄호 안에서 문맥에 맞는 낱말로 적절한 것을 골라 봅시다.

1 A light mist lay along the earth, partly veiling the lower **[accounts/ features]** of the landscape, but above it the taller trees showed in well-defined masses against a clear sky.

2 The RPC also works on **[issues / scales]** such as fair housing, gender equality, and environmental justice.

3 The past and the **[present / leave]** are our means; only the future is our end.

4 The **[figure / term]** euphemism derives from a Greek word meaning "to speak with good words" and involves substituting a more pleasant, less objectionable way of saying something for a blunt or more direct way.

5 Besides coal and peat, hydro was the only source that **[treated / accounted]** for more than 20% of the total electricity generation in both 1971 and 2007.

Day 21

미니 고난도 Test 1회

제한 시간 : 12분 | 정답 및 해설 112쪽

2021학년도 3월 학평 32번 ★★★

1. 다음 빈칸에 들어갈 말로 가장 적절한 것은?

Research has confirmed that athletes are less likely to participate in unacceptable behavior than are non-athletes. However, moral reasoning and good sporting behavior seem to decline as athletes progress to higher competitive levels, in part because of the increased emphasis on winning. Thus winning can be ________________ in teaching character development. Some athletes may want to win so much that they lie, cheat, and break team rules. They may develop undesirable character traits that can enhance their ability to win in the short term. However, when athletes resist the temptation to win in a dishonest way, they can develop positive character traits that last a lifetime. Character is a learned behavior, and a sense of fair play develops only if coaches plan to teach those lessons systematically.

* trait: 특성

① a piece of cake
② a one-way street
③ a bird in the hand
④ a fish out of water
⑤ a double-edged sword

2021학년도 3월 학평 34번 ★★★

2. 다음 빈칸에 들어갈 말로 가장 적절한 것은?

It is important to distinguish between being legally allowed to do something, and actually being able to go and do it. A law could be passed allowing everyone, if they so wish, to run a mile in two minutes. That would not, however, increase their *effective* freedom, because, although allowed to do so, they are physically incapable of it. Having a minimum of restrictions and a maximum of possibilities is fine. But in the real world most people will never have the opportunity either to become all that they are allowed to become, or to need to be restrained from doing everything that is possible for them to do. Their effective freedom depends on actually ________________________. [3점]

* restriction: 제약 ** restrain: 저지하다

① respecting others' rights to freedom
② protecting and providing for the needy
③ learning what socially acceptable behaviors are
④ determining how much they can expect from others
⑤ having the means and ability to do what they choose

2020학년도 3월 학평 39번 ★★☆

3. 다음 글에서 전체 흐름과 관계 없는 문장은?

Paying attention to some people and not others doesn't mean you're being dismissive or arrogant. ① It just reflects a hard fact: there are limits on the number of people we can possibly pay attention to or develop a relationship with. ② Some scientists even believe that the number of people with whom we can continue stable social relationships might be limited naturally by our brains. ③ The more people you know of different backgrounds, the more colorful your life becomes. ④ Professor Robin Dunbar has explained that our minds are only really capable of forming meaningful relationships with a maximum of about a hundred and fifty people. ⑤ Whether that's true or not, it's safe to assume that we can't be real friends with everyone.

* dismissive: 무시하는 ** arrogant: 거만한

2019학년도 11월 학평 37번 ★★★

4. 주어진 글 다음에 이어질 글의 순서로 가장 적절한 것은?

Many studies have shown that people's health and subjective well-being are affected by ethnic relations. Members of minority groups in general have poorer health outcomes than the majority group.

(A) One possible answer is stress. From multiple physiological studies, we know that encounters with members of other ethnic-racial categories, even in the relatively safe environment of laboratories, trigger stress responses.

(B) But that difference remains even when obvious factors, such as social class and access to medical services are controlled for. This suggests that dominance relations have their own effect on people's health. How could that be the case?

(C) Minority individuals have many encounters with majority individuals, each of which may trigger such responses. However minimal these effects may be, their frequency may increase total stress, which would account for part of the health disadvantage of minority individuals. [3점]

① (A) − (C) − (B)
② (B) − (A) − (C)
③ (B) − (C) − (A)
④ (C) − (A) − (B)
⑤ (C) − (B) − (A)

2019학년도 11월 학평 39번 ★★★

5. 글의 흐름으로 보아, 주어진 문장이 들어가기에 가장 적절한 곳은?

> In this way, quick judgements are not only relevant in employment matters; they are equally applicable in love and relationship matters too.

You've probably heard the expression, "first impressions matter a lot". (①) Life really doesn't give many people a second chance to make a good first impression. (②) It has been determined that it takes only a few seconds for anyone to assess another individual. (③) This is very noticeable in recruitment processes, where top recruiters can predict the direction of their eventual decision on any candidate within a few seconds of introducing themselves. (④) So, a candidate's CV may 'speak' knowledge and competence, but their appearance and introduction may tell of a lack of coordination, fear, and poor interpersonal skills. (⑤) On a date with a wonderful somebody who you've painstakingly tracked down for months, subtle things like bad breath or wrinkled clothes may spoil your noble efforts.

* CV: 이력서(curriculum vitae)

2019학년도 11월 학평 40번 ★★★

6. 다음 글의 내용을 한 문장으로 요약하고자 한다. 빈칸 (A), (B)에 들어갈 말로 가장 적절한 것은?

> The perception of the same amount of discount on a product depends on its relation to the initial price. In one study, respondents were presented with a purchase situation. The persons put in the situation of buying a calculator that cost $15 found out from the vendor that the same product was available in a different store 20 minutes away and at a promotional price of $10. In this case, 68% of respondents decided to make their way down to the store in order to save $5. In the second condition, which involved buying a jacket for $125, the respondents were also told that the same product was available in a store 20 minutes away and cost $120 there. This time, only 29% of the persons said that they would get the cheaper jacket. In both cases, the product was $5 cheaper, but in the first case, the amount was 1/3 of the price, and in the second, it was 1/25 of the price. What differed in both of these situations was the price context of the purchase.

⬇

> When the same amount of discount is given in a purchasing situation, the ____(A)____ value of the discount affects how people ____(B)____ its value.

	(A)		(B)
①	absolute	……	modify
②	absolute	……	express
③	identical	……	produce
④	relative	……	perceive
⑤	relative	……	advertise

2019학년도 9월 학평 41~42번

[7~8] 다음 글을 읽고, 물음에 답하시오.

> A quick look at history shows that humans have not always had the abundance of food that is enjoyed throughout most of the developed world today. In fact, there have been numerous times in history when food has been rather scarce. As a result, people used to eat more when food was available since the availability of the next meal was (a) <u>questionable</u>. Overeating in those times was essential to ensure survival, and humans received satisfaction from eating more than was needed for immediate purposes. On top of that, the highest pleasure was derived from eating the most calorie-dense foods, resulting in a (b) <u>longer</u> lasting energy reserve.
>
> Even though there are parts of the world where, unfortunately, food is still scarce, most of the world's population today has plenty of food available to survive and thrive. However, this abundance is new, and your body has not caught up, still naturally (c) <u>rewarding</u> you for eating more than you need and for eating the most calorie-dense foods. These are innate habits and not simple addictions. They are self-preserving mechanisms initiated by your body, ensuring your future survival, but they are (d) <u>irrelevant</u> now. Therefore, it is your responsibility to communicate with your body regarding the new environment of food abundance and the need to (e) <u>strengthen</u> the inborn habit of overeating.
>
> * innate: 타고난

2019학년도 9월 학평 41번 ★★★

7. 윗글의 제목으로 가장 적절한 것은?

① Which Is Better, Tasty or Healthy Food?
② Simple Steps for a More Balanced Diet
③ Overeating: It's Rooted in Our Genes
④ How Calorie-dense Foods Ruin Our Bodies
⑤ Our Eating Habits Reflect Our Personalities

2019학년도 9월 학평 42번 ★★★

8. 밑줄 친 (a)~(e) 중에서 문맥상 낱말의 쓰임이 적절하지 <u>않은</u> 것은? [3점]

① (a) ② (b) ③ (c) ④ (d) ⑤ (e)

총 문항				문항	맞은 문항					문항
개별 문항	1	2	3	4	5	6	7	8	9	10
채점										
개별 문항	11	12	13	14	15	16	17	18	19	20
채점										

제한 시간 : 12분 | 정답 및 해설 115쪽

2020학년도 9월 학평 31번 ★★★

1. 다음 빈칸에 들어갈 말로 가장 적절한 것은?

As the tenth anniversary of the terrorist attacks of September 11, 2001, approached, 9/11-related media stories peaked in the days immediately surrounding the anniversary date and then dropped off rapidly in the weeks thereafter. Surveys conducted during those times asked citizens to choose two "especially important" events from the past seventy years. Two weeks prior to the anniversary, before the media blitz began, about 30 percent of respondents named 9/11. But as the anniversary drew closer, and the media treatment intensified, survey respondents started identifying 9/11 in increasing numbers — to a high of 65 percent. Two weeks later, though, after reportage had decreased to earlier levels, once again only about 30 percent of the participants placed it among their two especially important events of the past seventy years. Clearly, the __________ of news coverage can make a big difference in the *perceived* significance of an issue among observers as they are exposed to the coverage.

* blitz: 대선전, 집중 공세

① accuracy ② tone ③ amount
④ source ⑤ type

2020학년도 11월 학평 34번 ★★★

2. 다음 빈칸에 들어갈 말로 가장 적절한 것은?

Back in 1996, an American airline was faced with an interesting problem. At a time when most other airlines were losing money or going under, over 100 cities were begging the company to service their locations. However, that's not the interesting part. What's interesting is that the company turned down over 95 percent of those offers and began serving only four new locations. It turned down tremendous growth because ______________________________. Sure, its executives wanted to grow each year, but they didn't want to grow too much. Unlike other famous companies, they wanted to set their own pace, one that could be sustained in the long term. By doing this, they established a safety margin for growth that helped them continue to thrive at a time when the other airlines were flailing. [3점]

* flail: 마구 흔들리다

① it was being faced with serious financial crises
② there was no specific long-term plan on marketing
③ company leadership had set an upper limit for growth
④ its executives worried about the competing airlines' future
⑤ the company had emphasized moral duties more than profits

2019학년도 11월 학평 35번 ★★☆

3. 다음 글에서 전체 흐름과 관계 없는 문장은?

Training and conditioning for baseball focuses on developing strength, power, speed, quickness and flexibility. ① Before the 1980s, strength training was not an important part of conditioning for a baseball player. ② People viewed baseball as a game of skill and technique rather than strength, and most managers and coaches saw strength training as something for bodybuilders, not baseball players. ③ Unlike more isolated bodybuilding exercises, athletic exercises train as many muscle groups and functions as possible at the same time. ④ They feared that weight lifting and building large muscles would cause players to lose flexibility and interfere with quickness and proper technique. ⑤ Today, though, experts understand the importance of strength training and have made it part of the game.

2019학년도 9월 학평 36번 ★★★

4. 주어진 글 다음에 이어질 글의 순서로 가장 적절한 것은?

Almost all major sporting activities are played with a ball.

(A) A ball might have the correct size and weight but if it is made as a hollow ball of steel it will be too stiff and if it is made from light foam rubber with a heavy center it will be too soft.

(B) The rules of the game always include rules about the type of ball that is allowed, starting with the size and weight of the ball. The ball must also have a certain stiffness.

(C) Similarly, along with stiffness, a ball needs to bounce properly. A solid rubber ball would be too bouncy for most sports, and a solid ball made of clay would not bounce at all.

* stiffness: 단단함

① (A) − (C) − (B) ② (B) − (A) − (C)
③ (B) − (C) − (A) ④ (C) − (A) − (B)
⑤ (C) − (B) − (A)

2021학년도 3월 학평 38번 ★★★

5. 글의 흐름으로 보아, 주어진 문장이 들어가기에 가장 적절한 곳은?

> Meanwhile, improving by 1 percent isn't particularly notable, but it can be far more meaningful in the long run.

It is so easy to overestimate the importance of one defining moment and underestimate the value of making small improvements on a daily basis. Too often, we convince ourselves that massive success requires massive action. (①) Whether it is losing weight, winning a championship, or achieving any other goal, we put pressure on ourselves to make some earthshaking improvement that everyone will talk about. (②) The difference this tiny improvement can make over time is surprising. (③) Here's how the math works out: if you can get 1 percent better each day for one year, you'll end up thirty-seven times better by the time you're done. (④) Conversely, if you get 1 percent worse each day for one year, you'll decline nearly down to zero. (⑤) What starts as a small win or a minor failure adds up to something much more.

2019학년도 9월 학평 43~45번

[6~8] 다음 글을 읽고, 물음에 답하시오.

(A)

> Two students met their teacher at the start of a track through a forest. He gave them instructions to follow the path to its end, in preparation for a test later in the week. The path split into two: one was clear and smooth, the other had fallen logs and other obstacles in the way. One student chose to avoid the obstacles, taking the easier path to the end. (a) He felt clever as he ran without stopping.

(B)

> He requested that they join him at a specific location in three days. When they arrived, they could see a ravine that was a few meters wide. The students looked at their teacher and he said just one word. "Jump!" The first student looked at the distance and his heart sank. The teacher looked at (b) him. "What's wrong? This is the leap to greatness. Everything that you've done until now should have prepared you for this moment."
>
> * ravine: 계곡, 협곡

(C)

> The student shrugged (c) his shoulders and walked away, knowing he hadn't prepared adequately for greatness. The second student looked at the teacher and smiled. He knew now that the obstacles that had been placed in his path were part of his preparation. By choosing to overcome challenges, not avoid them, he was ready to make the leap. (d) He ran as fast as he could and launched himself into the air. He made it across!

(D)

> The second student chose to tackle the obstacles, battling through every challenge in his path. The student who chose the easy path finished first and felt proud of himself. "I'm glad I chose to avoid the rocks and logs. They were only there to slow me down," (e) he thought to himself. The second student arrived at the finish feeling tired and regretting the path he had chosen. The teacher smiled at them both.

2019학년도 9월 학평 43번 ★★★

6. 주어진 글 (A)에 이어질 내용을 순서에 맞게 배열한 것으로 가장 적절한 것은?

① (B) − (D) − (C)　　② (C) − (B) − (D)
③ (C) − (D) − (B)　　④ (D) − (B) − (C)
⑤ (D) − (C) − (B)

2019학년도 9월 학평 44번 ★★★

7. 밑줄 친 (a)~(e) 중에서 가리키는 대상이 나머지 넷과 다른 것은?

① (a)　② (b)　③ (c)　④ (d)　⑤ (e)

2019학년도 9월 학평 45번 ★★☆

8. 윗글에 관한 내용으로 적절하지 않은 것은?

① 스승이 두 제자에게 길을 끝까지 따라가라고 지시했다.
② 길이 두 갈래로 갈라져 있었다.
③ 첫 번째 제자는 계곡의 너비를 보고 자신감을 보였다.
④ 두 번째 제자는 스승을 보고 미소를 지었다.
⑤ 두 번째 제자는 자신의 선택을 후회하며 길의 끝에 도착했다.

총 문항				문항	맞은 문항					문항
개별 문항	1	2	3	4	5	6	7	8	9	10
채점										
개별 문항	11	12	13	14	15	16	17	18	19	20
채점										

제한 시간 : 12분 | 정답 및 해설 118쪽

2020학년도 6월 학평 31번 ★★★

1. 다음 빈칸에 들어갈 말로 가장 적절한 것은?

When reading another scientist's findings, think critically about the experiment. Ask yourself: Were observations recorded during or after the experiment? Do the conclusions make sense? Can the results be repeated? Are the sources of information reliable? You should also ask if the scientist or group conducting the experiment was unbiased. Being unbiased means that you have no special interest in the outcome of the experiment. For example, if a drug company pays for an experiment to test how well one of its new products works, there is a special interest involved: The drug company profits if the experiment shows that its product is effective. Therefore, the experimenters aren't __________. They might ensure the conclusion is positive and benefits the drug company. When assessing results, think about any biases that may be present!

① inventive
② objective
③ untrustworthy
④ unreliable
⑤ decisive

2020학년도 9월 학평 34번 ★★★

2. 다음 빈칸에 들어갈 말로 가장 적절한 것은?

We're often told that newborns and infants are comforted by rocking because this motion is similar to what they experienced in the womb, and that they must take comfort in this familiar feeling. This may be true; however, to date there are no convincing data that demonstrate a significant relationship between the amount of time a mother moves during pregnancy and her newborn's response to rocking. Just as likely is the idea that newborns come to associate gentle rocking with being fed. Parents understand that rocking quiets a newborn, and they very often provide gentle, repetitive movement during feeding. Since the appearance of food is a primary reinforcer, newborns may ____________________ because they have been conditioned through a process of associative learning. [3점]

* womb: 자궁 ** reinforcer: 강화물

① acquire a fondness for motion
② want consistent feeding
③ dislike severe rocking
④ remember the tastes of food
⑤ form a bond with their mothers

2018학년도 11월 학평 35번 ★★☆

3. 다음 글에서 전체 흐름과 관계 없는 문장은?

Wouldn't it be nice if you could take your customers by the hand and guide each one through your store while pointing out all the great products you would like them to consider buying? ① Most people, however, would not particularly enjoy having a stranger grab their hand and drag them through a store. ② Rather, let the store do it for you. ③ Have a central path that leads shoppers through the store and lets them look at many different departments or product areas. ④ You can use this effect of music on shopping behavior by playing it in the store. ⑤ This path leads your customers from the entrance through the store on the route you want them to take all the way to the checkout.

Day 23

2019학년도 9월 학평 37번 ★★★

4. 주어진 글 다음에 이어질 글의 순서로 가장 적절한 것은?

To be successful, you need to understand the vital difference between believing you will succeed, and believing you will succeed easily.

(A) Unrealistic optimists, on the other hand, believe that success will happen to them — that the universe will reward them for all their positive thinking, or that somehow they will be transformed overnight into the kind of person for whom obstacles don't exist anymore.

(B) Put another way, it's the difference between being a realistic optimist, and an unrealistic optimist. Realistic optimists believe they will succeed, but also believe they have to make success happen — through things like careful planning and choosing the right strategies.

(C) They recognize the need for giving serious thought to how they will deal with obstacles. This preparation only increases their confidence in their own ability to get things done.

① (A) – (C) – (B)
② (B) – (A) – (C)
③ (B) – (C) – (A)
④ (C) – (A) – (B)
⑤ (C) – (B) – (A)

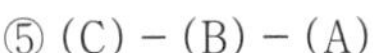

2020학년도 11월 학평 38번 ★★★

5. 주어진 글 다음에 이어질 글의 순서로 가장 적절한 것은?

> It is the reason that individuals with certain forms of blindness do not entirely lose their circadian rhythm.

Daylight isn't the only signal that the brain can use for the purpose of biological clock resetting, though it is the principal and preferential signal, when present. (①) So long as they are reliably repeating, the brain can also use other external cues, such as food, exercise, and even regularly timed social interaction. (②) All of these events have the ability to reset the biological clock, allowing it to strike a precise twenty-four-hour note. (③) Despite not receiving light cues due to their blindness, other phenomena act as their resetting triggers. (④) Any signal that the brain uses for the purpose of clock resetting is termed a zeitgeber, from the German "time giver" or "synchronizer." (⑤) Thus, while light is the most reliable and thus the primary zeitgeber, there are many factors that can be used in addition to, or in the absence of, daylight.

* circadian rhythm: 24시간 주기 리듬

2019학년도 9월 학평 40번 ★★☆

6. 다음 글의 내용을 한 문장으로 요약하고자 한다. 빈칸 (A), (B)에 들어갈 말로 가장 적절한 것은? [3점]

> In a study, psychologist Laurence Steinberg of Temple University and his co-author, psychologist Margo Gardner divided 306 people into three age groups: young adolescents, with a mean age of 14; older adolescents, with a mean age of 19; and adults, aged 24 and older. Subjects played a computerized driving game in which the player must avoid crashing into a wall that appears, without warning, on the roadway. Steinberg and Gardner randomly assigned some participants to play alone or with two same-age peers looking on. Older adolescents scored about 50 percent higher on an index of risky driving when their peers were in the room—and the driving of early adolescents was fully twice as reckless when other young teens were around. In contrast, adults behaved in similar ways regardless of whether they were on their own or observed by others.
>
> * reckless: 무모한

⬇

> The ___(A)___ of peers makes adolescents, but not adults, more likely to ___(B)___.

	(A)		(B)
①	presence	……	take risks
②	presence	……	behave cautiously
③	indifference	……	perform poorly
④	absence	……	enjoy adventures
⑤	absence	……	act independently

2019학년도 6월 학평 41~42번

【7~8】 다음 글을 읽고, 물음에 답하시오.

> Many advertisements cite statistical surveys. But we should be (a) <u>cautious</u> because we usually do not know how these surveys are conducted. For example, a toothpaste manufacturer once had a poster that said, "More than 80% of dentists recommend *Smiley Toothpaste*." This seems to say that most dentists (b) <u>prefer</u> *Smiley Toothpaste* to other brands. But it turns out that the survey questions allowed the dentists to recommend more than one brand, and in fact another competitor's brand was recommended just as often as *Smiley Toothpaste*! No wonder the UK Advertising Standards Authority ruled in 2007 that the poster was (c) <u>misleading</u> and it could no longer be displayed.
>
> A similar case concerns a well-known cosmetics firm marketing a cream that is supposed to rapidly reduce wrinkles. But the only evidence provided is that "76% of 50 women agreed." But what this means is that the evidence is based on just the personal opinions from a small sample with no objective measurement of their skin's condition. Furthermore, we are not told how these women were selected. Without such information, the "evidence" provided is pretty much (d) <u>useful</u>. Unfortunately, such advertisements are quite typical, and as consumers we just have to use our own judgment and (e) <u>avoid</u> taking advertising claims too seriously.

2019학년도 6월 학평 41번 ★★☆

7. 윗글의 제목으로 가장 적절한 것은?

① The Link between Advertisements and the Economy
② Are Statistical Data in Advertisements Reliable?
③ Statistics in Advertisements Are Objective!
④ The Bright Side of Public Advertisements
⑤ Quality or Price, Which Matters More?

2019학년도 6월 학평 42번 ★★★

8. 밑줄 친 (a)~(e) 중에서 문맥상 낱말의 쓰임이 적절하지 <u>않은</u> 것은? [3점]

① (a) ② (b) ③ (c) ④ (d) ⑤ (e)

총 문항				문항	맞은 문항					문항
개별 문항	1	2	3	4	5	6	7	8	9	10
채점										
개별 문항	11	12	13	14	15	16	17	18	19	20
채점										

Day 24

제한 시간 : 12분 | 정답 및 해설 122쪽

2019학년도 11월 학평 31번 ★★★

1. 다음 빈칸에 들어갈 말로 가장 적절한 것은?

People engage in typical patterns of interaction based on the relationship between their roles and the roles of others. Employers are expected to interact with employees in a certain way, as are doctors with patients. In each case, actions are restricted by the role responsibilities and obligations associated with individuals' positions within society. For instance, parents and children are linked by certain rights, privileges, and obligations. Parents are responsible for providing their children with the basic necessities of life — food, clothing, shelter, and so forth. These expectations are so powerful that not meeting them may make the parents vulnerable to charges of negligence or abuse. Children, in turn, are expected to do as their parents say. Thus, interactions within a relationship are functions not only of the individual personalities of the people involved but also of the role requirements associated with the __________ they have.

* vulnerable: 비난받기 쉬운 ** negligence: 태만

① careers
② statuses
③ abilities
④ motivations
⑤ perspectives

2019학년도 11월 학평 34번 ★★★

2. 다음 빈칸에 들어갈 말로 가장 적절한 것은?

Focusing on the differences among societies conceals a deeper reality: their similarities are greater and more profound than their dissimilarities. Imagine studying two hills while standing on a ten-thousand-foot-high plateau. Seen from your perspective, one hill appears to be three hundred feet high, and the other appears to be nine hundred feet. This difference may seem large, and you might focus your attention on what local forces, such as erosion, account for the difference in size. But this narrow perspective misses the opportunity to study the other, more significant geological forces that created what are actually two very similar mountains, one 10,300 feet high and the other 10,900 feet. And when it comes to human societies, people have been standing on a ten-thousand-foot plateau, letting the differences among societies ________________________________. [3점]

* erosion: 침식

① prove the uniqueness of each society
② prevent cross-cultural understanding
③ mask the more overwhelming similarities
④ change their perspective on what diversity is
⑤ encourage them to step out of their mental frame

2018학년도 9월 학평 35번 ★★★

3. 다음 글에서 전체 흐름과 관계 없는 문장은?

Water is the ultimate commons. Once, watercourses seemed boundless and the idea of protecting water was considered silly. But rules change. Time and again, communities have studied water systems and redefined wise use. ① Now Ecuador has become the first nation on Earth to put the rights of nature in its constitution. ② This move has proclaimed that rivers and forests are not simply property but maintain their own right to flourish. ③ Developing a water-based transportation system will modernize Ecuador's transportation infrastructure. ④ According to the constitution, a citizen might file suit on behalf of an injured watershed, recognizing that its health is crucial to the common good. ⑤ More countries are acknowledging nature's rights and are expected to follow Ecuador's lead.

* commons: 공유 자원
** watershed: (강) 유역

2019학년도 6월 학평 36번 ★★★

4. 주어진 글 다음에 이어질 글의 순서로 가장 적절한 것은?

> Mirrors and other smooth, shiny surfaces reflect light. We see reflections from such surfaces because the rays of light form an image on the retina of our eyes.

(A) Keep your eyes on the reflected image while you are writing and not on your paper. After a little practice, it will be easier to write "backwards." When your friend receives such a message he will be able to read it by holding the paper up to a mirror.

(B) Stand a mirror upright on the table, so that a piece of paper on the table can be clearly seen in the mirror. Now write a message that looks right when you look in the mirror.

(C) Such images are always reversed. Look at yourself in a mirror, wink your right eye and your left eye seems to wink back at you. You can use a mirror to send a coded message to a friend.

* retina: (눈의) 망막

① (A) − (C) − (B)
② (B) − (A) − (C)
③ (B) − (C) − (A)
④ (C) − (A) − (B)
⑤ (C) − (B) − (A)

2020학년도 9월 학평 38번 ★★★

5. 글의 흐름으로 보아, 주어진 문장이 들어가기에 가장 적절한 곳은?

The few times that they do occur, it is the possessor who tries to make someone leave the circle.

Reciprocity can be explored in captivity by handing one chimpanzee a large amount of food, such as a watermelon or leafy branch, and then observing what follows. (①) The owner will be center stage, with a group of others around him or her, soon to be followed by newly formed groups around those who obtained a sizable share, until all food has been distributed. (②) Beggars may complain and cry, but aggressive conflicts are rare. (③) She will hit them over their head with her branch or bark at them in a high-pitched voice until they leave her alone. (④) Whatever their rank, possessors control the food flow. (⑤) Once chimpanzees enter reciprocity mode, their social rank no longer matters. [3점]

* reciprocity: 호혜주의, 상호의 이익

2021학년도 6월 학평 43~45번

[6~8] 다음 글을 읽고, 물음에 답하시오.

(A)

When I was 17, I discovered a wonderful thing. My father and I were sitting on the floor of his study. We were organizing his old papers. Across the carpet I saw a fat paper clip. Its rust dusted the cover sheet of a report of some kind. I picked it up. I started to read. Then I started to cry.

(B)

"Daddy," I said, handing him the pages, "this speech — how did you ever get permission to give it? And weren't you scared?" "Well, honey," he said, "I didn't ask for permission. I just asked myself, 'What is the most important challenge facing my generation?' I knew immediately. Then (a) <u>I</u> asked myself, 'And if I weren't afraid, what would I say about it in this speech?'"

(C)

It was a speech he had written in 1920, in Tennessee. Then only 17 himself and graduating from high school, he had called for equality for African Americans. (b) <u>I</u> marvelled, proud of him, and wondered how, in 1920, so young, so white, and in the deep South, where the law still separated black from white, (c) <u>he</u> had had the courage to deliver it. I asked him about it.

(D)

"I wrote it. And I delivered it. About half way through I looked out to see the entire audience of teachers, students, and parents stand up — and walk out. Left alone on the stage, (d) <u>I</u> thought to myself, 'Well, I guess I need to be sure to do only two things with my life: keep thinking for myself, and not get killed.'" He handed the speech back to me, and smiled. "(e) <u>You</u> seem to have done both," I said.

2021학년도 6월 학평 43번 ★★☆

6. 주어진 글 (A)에 이어질 내용을 순서에 맞게 배열한 것으로 가장 적절한 것은?

① (B) − (D) − (C)　　② (C) − (B) − (D)
③ (C) − (D) − (B)　　④ (D) − (B) − (C)
⑤ (D) − (C) − (B)

2021학년도 6월 학평 44번 ★★★

7. 밑줄 친 (a) ~ (e) 중에서 가리키는 대상이 나머지 넷과 <u>다른</u> 것은?

① (a)　② (b)　③ (c)　④ (d)　⑤ (e)

2021학년도 6월 학평 45번 ★★☆

8. 윗글에 관한 내용으로 적절하지 <u>않은</u> 것은?

① 아버지와 나는 서류를 정리하고 있었다.
② 나는 서재에서 발견한 것을 읽고 나서 울기 시작했다.
③ 아버지는 연설을 하기 위한 허락을 구하지 않았다.
④ 아버지가 연설문을 썼을 당시 17세였다.
⑤ 교사, 학생, 학부모 모두 아버지의 연설을 끝까지 들었다.

총 문항				문항	맞은 문항					문항
개별 문항	1	2	3	4	5	6	7	8	9	10
채점										
개별 문항	11	12	13	14	15	16	17	18	19	20
채점										

단기 특강, 24일의 기적!

씨뮬 유형+

고1

전국연합 학력평가

기출문제집

영어 - 독해

정답 및 해설

씨뮬과 함께하는 기출 완전정복 커리큘럼

씨뮬 = 실전 연습

내신, 학평, 수능까지 실전 대비 최고의 연습, 씨뮬

씨뮬과 함께 1등급, SKY, 의치한까지

01
예비 고1
예비 고1 3월 전국연합 3년간 모의고사
고등학교 첫 시험을 발 빠르게 준비하여 단 한 권으로 학습 주도권을 잡는 교재
※ 국어, 수학, 영어, 한국사, 사회, 과학 수록
02
고1~3
유형⁺ 씨뮬
학평, 수능의 문제 유형을 연습하고 출제 경향을 파악할 수 있는 교재
※ 고1~3 국어 독서/문학
※ 고1~3 영어 독해, 고3 영어 어법 · 어휘
03
고1~3
전국연합 3년간
최근 3년간 시행된 학평, 모평, 수능 문제들로 완벽한 수능 대비를 할 수 있는 기본 중의 기본서
※ 고1 통합사회, 통합과학
※ 고1~3 국어, 수학, 영어
04
고1~3
사설 3년간
종로, 이투스에서 출제된 고난도 모의고사 문제들을 연습할 수 있는 교재
※ 고1~3 국어, 영어
05
고3
6 · 9 · 수능 평가원 3/4년간
평가원에서 최근 3/4년간 출제한 6월, 9월 모평 및 수능 문제들이 수록된 수능 출제 경향 파악에 가장 적합한 교재
※ 고3 국어, 수학, 영어
06
고3
최신 1년간
최근 1년간 시행된 학평, 모평, 수능 문제 뿐 아니라 종로 모의고사까지 수록되어 최신 출제 경향을 한 권으로 파악할 수 있는 교재
※ 고3 국어, 수학, 영어

독자 여러분의 애정 어린 충고로

씨뮬은 해마다 새롭게 완성되어 갑니다!

실제 크기의 시험지와 OMR 카드를 제공해 주어서 실제 시험을 보는 것 같아 실제 시험에서 떨리지 않았고 문제에 대한 해설이 친절히 서술되어 있어 어려운 문제도 혼자만의 노력으로 이해할 수 있었어요. 역시 씨뮬!
—》 **황*현**

모의고사가 모아져 있는 책 중 씨뮬이 정말 최고예요. 특히 영어는 듣기 연습용 받아쓰기도 있어서 많은 도움이 되었습니다. 감사합니다.
—》 **조*빈**

회차별 영단어 핸드북뿐 아니라 책 마지막 부분에 있는 수능 필수 영숙어 파트가 도움이 많이 되었다. 수능에서뿐만 아니라 내신 시험에도 나오는 표현들이 많아 유용했다.
—》 **김*희**

모의고사를 대비하기 위해 구매하였습니다. 다른 문제집들은 실제 모의고사 시험지처럼 되어 있지 않아서 긴장감이 많이 떨어지는데, 씨뮬은 실제 시험지처럼 되어 있고 OMR 카드도 있어서 모의고사 대비하기 아주 좋아요!
—》 **김*연**

씨뮬 교재가 실제 모의고사 종이 크기이다 보니 실제 시험을 치는 듯한 느낌이 들어 더 집중이 잘 되는 것 같다. 해설도 꼼꼼하게 되어 있어 내가 어디서 해석이 안 되는지 바로 찾을 수 있어서 좋았다.
—》 **김*진**

국어에 자신감이 없어서 시작했는데 해설이 꼼꼼하고 추가적인 작품이나 문법이 수록돼 있어서 더 깊이 있게 공부할 수 있었어요.
—》 **배*진**

이 책을 구매했던 이유들 중 하나인, 실전과 비슷한 종이 재질 덕분에 더욱 실감나게 학습할 수 있었습니다. 그리고 맨 뒤에 부착되어 있는 OMR 카드로 체킹 실수를 줄이는 연습도 되었습니다. 꼼꼼한 해설지와 문제 풀이로 공부하면서 그 외에 실전 감각 또한 함양할 수 있는 씨뮬 모의고사입니다!
—》 **권*희**

백분위 95~96을 왔다갔다했어요. 수학 실력을 늘리기 위해 책을 구매해 풀어 본 후 높은 점수를 받게 되었습니다.
—》 **정*현**

모의고사 볼 때처럼 큰 종이로 되어 있어 더 몰입감 있게 집중할 수 있었던 것 같습니다. 또 해설도 자세하고 고난도 문제와 등급컷도 알려 주어 좋았습니다!
—》 **서*준**

어느 정도 실력이 쌓이고 나면 모의고사로 실전 대비 훈련을 하며 실력을 굳혀 나가야 되죠. 그리고 그 연습 방법으로는 '씨뮬'이라는 교재가 정말 완벽한 것 같아요. 여러분들에게 '씨뮬' 적극 추천합니다.
—》 **백*민**

내신에서 학평까지 실전 연습은 씨뮬 기출 하나로 충분하다

전국연합학력평가 3년간 모의고사 | 11th 국영수 고1~3

01 실제 시험 그대로 실전 감각 익히기
02 핵심을 짚어주는 명쾌한 해설
03 오답 노트 & OMR 카드
04 같은 작가 다른 작품(국어), 기출문법[구문] 모아보기(영어), 준 킬러 문항 연습(수학)
05 [12th] 전국연합 3년간 수학 교재의 중요 문항에 동영상 강의 제공 예정

※문법 / 어휘 플러스는 정답 및 해설 참조

DAY 01 글의 목적

1 ⑤ 2 ② 3 ② 4 ⑤ 5 ②
6 ① 7 ④ 8 ③ 9 ③ 10 ①
11 ② 12 ③

DAY 02 심경 • 분위기

1 ② 2 ② 3 ③ 4 ⑤ 5 ⑤
6 ③ 7 ① 8 ① 9 ① 10 ①
11 ⑤ 12 ①

DAY 03 필자의 주장

1 ④ 2 ⑤ 3 ⑤ 4 ③ 5 ③
6 ① 7 ③ 8 ② 9 ② 10 ⑤
11 ④ 12 ⑤

DAY 04 함축 • 지칭 추론

1 ③ 2 ③ 3 ⑤ 4 ④ 5 ⑤
6 ③ 7 ② 8 ④ 9 ④ 10 ③

DAY 05 글의 요지

1 ① 2 ① 3 ① 4 ③ 5 ⑤
6 ⑤ 7 ⑤ 8 ④ 9 ② 10 ①

DAY 06 글의 주제

1 ② 2 ② 3 ④ 4 ① 5 ①
6 ② 7 ① 8 ① 9 ② 10 ②

DAY 07 글의 제목

1 ① 2 ① 3 ② 4 ② 5 ④
6 ① 7 ⑤ 8 ③ 9 ⑤ 10 ②

DAY 08 도표 정보 파악

1 ③ 2 ⑤ 3 ⑤ 4 ④ 5 ④
6 ⑤ 7 ③ 8 ⑤ 9 ④ 10 ⑤

DAY 09 내용 일치 • 불일치

1 ④ 2 ③ 3 ③ 4 ④ 5 ⑤
6 ③ 7 ⑤ 8 ④ 9 ③ 10 ⑤

DAY 10 안내문

1 ③ 2 ④ 3 ④ 4 ④ 5 ②
6 ④ 7 ⑤ 8 ② 9 ④ 10 ②

DAY 11 어법 정확성 파악

1 ③ 2 ④ 3 ③ 4 ④ 5 ②
6 ⑤ 7 ③ 8 ② 9 ④ 10 ④
11 ④ 12 ③

DAY 12 어휘 적절성 파악

1 ⑤ 2 ② 3 ⑤ 4 ⑤ 5 ④
6 ③ 7 ③ 8 ③ 9 ② 10 ③

DAY 13 빈칸 추론 (1) 어휘, 짧은 어구

1 ② 2 ② 3 ⑤ 4 ① 5 ②
6 ② 7 ③ 8 ② 9 ① 10 ①
11 ⑤

DAY 14 빈칸 추론 (2) 긴 어구, 문장

1 ③ 2 ① 3 ⑤ 4 ③ 5 ②
6 ① 7 ① 8 ② 9 ④ 10 ①

DAY 15 흐름에 무관한 문장 찾기

1 ④ 2 ④ 3 ④ 4 ③ 5 ④
6 ④ 7 ③ 8 ④ 9 ④ 10 ④

DAY 16 문단 내 글의 순서 파악

1 ⑤ 2 ② 3 ⑤ 4 ③ 5 ⑤
6 ③ 7 ② 8 ③ 9 ⑤ 10 ④
11 ③ 12 ④

DAY 17 주어진 문장의 위치 파악

1 ⑤ 2 ③ 3 ④ 4 ⑤ 5 ④
6 ⑤ 7 ④ 8 ② 9 ④ 10 ⑤
11 ③ 12 ②

DAY 18 문단 요약

1 ② 2 ① 3 ③ 4 ① 5 ②
6 ① 7 ② 8 ① 9 ① 10 ③
11 ①

DAY 19 장문의 이해 (1)

1 ① 2 ⑤ 3 ② 4 ④ 5 ①
6 ④ 7 ⑤ 8 ⑤ 9 ① 10 ④
11 ② 12 ④

DAY 20 장문의 이해 (2)

1 ④ 2 ③ 3 ③ 4 ④ 5 ②
6 ④ 7 ② 8 ④ 9 ⑤ 10 ③
11 ② 12 ⑤

DAY 21 미니 고난도 Test 1회

1 ⑤ 2 ⑤ 3 ③ 4 ② 5 ⑤
6 ④ 7 ③ 8 ⑤

DAY 22 미니 고난도 Test 2회

1 ③ 2 ③ 3 ③ 4 ② 5 ②
6 ④ 7 ④ 8 ③

DAY 23 미니 고난도 Test 3회

1 ② 2 ① 3 ④ 4 ③ 5 ③
6 ① 7 ② 8 ④

DAY 24 미니 고난도 Test 4회

1 ② 2 ③ 3 ③ 4 ⑤ 5 ③
6 ② 7 ② 8 ⑤

단기 특강, 24일의 기적!

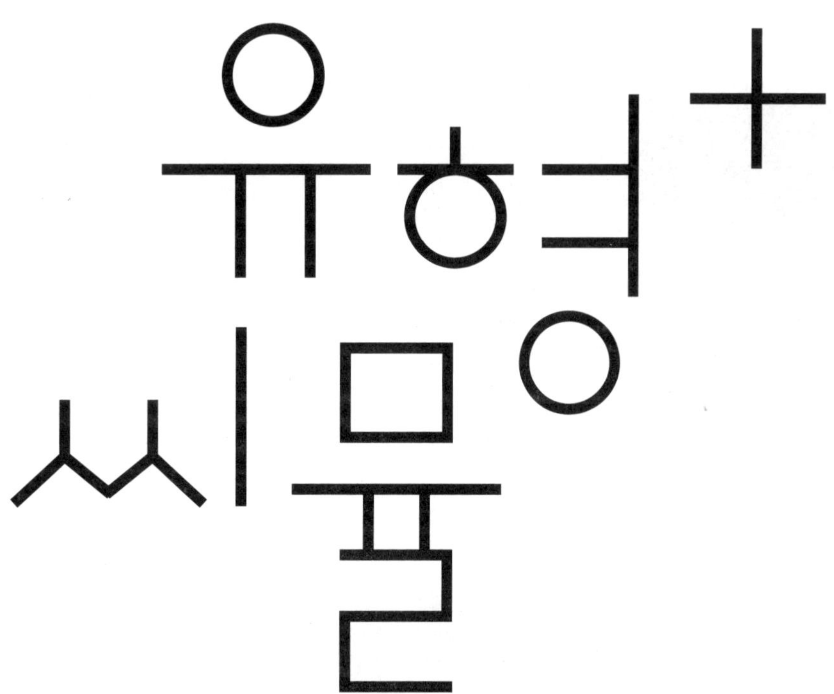

정답 및 해설

고1 영어 독해

CONTENTS

01. 글의 목적

Day 01

본문 002쪽

1. ⑤ 2. ② 3. ② 4. ⑤ 5. ②
6. ① 7. ④ 8. ③ 9. ③ 10. ①
11. ② 12. ③

정답률 87%

대표 기출 ② 급여 인상 요청

직독/직해

Dear Mr. Krull, 친애하는 Krull 씨께
I have greatly enjoyed working / 저는 일하는 것을 매우 즐겨 왔습니다 /
at Trincom Enterprises / as a sales manager. Trincom Enterprises에서 / 영업 부장으로
Since I joined in 2015, / 2015년에 입사한 이후 /
I have been a loyal and essential member of this company, / 저는 이 회사의 충성스럽고 필수 구성원이었습니다 /
and have developed innovative ways / 그리고 혁신적인 방법들을 개발해 왔습니다 /
to contribute to the company. 회사에 기여할 수 있는
Moreover, / in the last year alone, / I have brought in two new major clients to the company, / 게다가 / 작년 한 해만 / 저는 회사에 두 개의 새로운 주요 고객사를 유치했습니다 /
increasing the company's total sales by 5%. (그래서) 5%까지 회사의 총매출을 증가시켰습니다
Also, / I have voluntarily trained 5 new members of staff, / totaling 35 hours. 게다가 / 저는 신규 직원 5명을 자발적으로 교육해 왔습니다 / 그 합계가 35시간입니다
I would therefore request / 따라서 저는 요청합니다 /
your consideration in raising my salary, / 제 급여를 인상하는 것에 대한 당신의 고려를 /
which I believe reflects my performance / 저는 이것이 제 성과도 반영한다고 믿습니다 /
as well as the industry average. 업계 평균뿐만 아니라
I look forward to speaking with you soon. 저는 당신과 곧 이야기하기를 기대합니다
Kimberly Morss Kimberly Morss

친애하는 Krull 씨께
저는 Trincom Enterprises에서 영업 부장으로 일하는 것을 매우 즐겨 왔습니다. 2015년에 입사한 이후, 저는 이 회사의 충성스럽고 필수 구성원이었고, 회사에 기여할 수 있는 혁신적인 방법들을 개발해 왔습니다. 게다가, 저는 작년 한 해만 두 개의 주요 고객사를 회사에 새로 유치하여 회사의 총매출을 5% 증가시켰습니다. 게다가 저는 신규 직원 5명을 자발적으로 교육해 왔고, 그 합계가 35시간입니다. 따라서 저는 제 급여를 인상하는 것에 대한 당신의 고려를 요청하고, 저는 이것이 업계 평균뿐만 아니라 제 성과도 반영한다고 믿습니다. 저는 당신과 곧 이야기하기를 기대합니다.
Kimberly Morss

문제풀이

입사 이후 자신이 한 성과에 대해 열거하면서 급여 인상을 고려해달라고 요청하고 있으므로, 글의 목적으로 ② '급여 인상을 요청하려고'가 가장 적절하다.

어휘·어구

enterprise 기업
sales manager 영업 부장
loyal 충성스러운
essential 필수의
develop 개발하다
innovative 혁신적인
contribute 기여하다
moreover 게다가
major 주요한
client 고객
increase 향상시키다
voluntarily 자발적으로
train 훈련시키다
request 요청하다
consideration 고려
salary 급여
reflect 반영하다
performance 성과
as well as ~뿐만 아니라
industry 업계, 산업
average 평균
look forward to ~하기를 고대하다

정답률 94%

1. ⑤ 학급 파티에 가져올 음식에 대한 유의 사항 안내

직독/직해

Dear Parents / Guardians, 부모님들 / 보호자들께
Class parties will be held / 학급 파티가 열립니다 /
on the afternoon of Friday, / December 16th, 2022. 금요일 오후에 / 2022년 12월 16일
Children may bring in / 아이들은 가지고 올 수 있습니다 /
sweets, crisps, biscuits, cakes, and drinks. 사탕류, 포테이토 칩, 비스킷, 케이크, 그리고 음료를
We are requesting / that children do not bring in / 우리는 요청합니다 / 아이들이 가져오지 않기를 /
home-cooked or prepared food. 집에서 만들거나 준비한 음식을
All food should arrive / in a sealed packet / 모든 음식은 가져와야 합니다 / 밀봉된 꾸러미로 /
with the ingredients clearly listed. 성분이 명확하게 명기된 채
Fruit and vegetables are welcomed / 과일과 채소는 환영합니다 /
if they are pre-packed / 사전 포장된 것이라면 /
in a sealed packet from the shop. 가게에서 밀봉된 꾸러미로
Please DO NOT send any food into school / 어떤 음식도 학교에 보내지 마십시오 /
containing nuts / as we have many children / 견과류가 포함된 / 학생들이 많기 때문에 /
with severe nut allergies. 심한 견과류 알레르기가 있는
Please check the ingredients of all food / 모든 음식의 성분을 확인해 주십시오 /
your children bring / carefully. 아이들이 가져오는 / 주의 깊게
Thank you for your continued support and cooperation. 여러분의 지속적인 지원과 협조에 감사드립니다
Yours sincerely,
Lisa Brown, Head teacher
교장 Lisa Brown 드림

부모님들/보호자들께,
학급 파티가 2022년 12월 16일 금요일 오후에 열립니다. 아이들은 사탕류, 포테이토 칩, 비스킷, 케이크, 그리고 음료를 가지고 올 수 있습니다. 우리는 아이들이 집에서 만들거나 준비한 음식을 가져오지 않기를 요청합니다. 모든 음식은 성분이 명확하게 명기된 채 밀봉된 꾸러미로 가져와야 합니다. 과일과 채소는 가게에서 밀봉된 꾸러미로 사전 포장된 것이라면 환영합니다. 심한 견과류 알레르기가 있는 학생들이 많기 때문에 견과류가 포함된 어떤 음식도 학교에 보내지 마십시오. 아이들이 가져오는 모든 음식의 성분을 주의 깊게 확인해 주십시오. 여러분의 지속적인 지원과 협조에 감사드립니다.
교장 Lisa Brown 드림

문제풀이

예정된 학급 파티에 가져올 수 있는 음식과 가져올 수 없는 음식에 대해 안내하고 있으므로, 글의 목적으로 ⑤ '학급 파티에 가져올 음식에 대한 유의 사항을 안내하려고'가 가장 적절하다.

어휘·어구

guardian 보호자
crisp 포테이토 칩
request 요청하다
sealed 포장된
packet 꾸러미
ingredient 성분
contain ~이 들어있다
severe 심각한
allergy 알레르기
support 지원
cooperation 협조, 협동

정답률 97%

2. ② 분실물 발견 시 연락 부탁

직독/직해

Dear Boat Tour Manager, 보트 투어 담당자께,
On March 15, / my family was on one of your Glass Bottom Boat Tours. 3월 15일에 / 저희 가족은 귀사의 Glass Bottom Boat Tours 중 하나에 참여했습니다
When we returned to our hotel, / I discovered / 저희가 호텔에 돌아왔을 때 / 저는 알게 되었습니다 /
that I left behind my cell phone case. 휴대 전화 케이스를 두고 왔다는 것을
The case must have fallen off my lap / 케이스가 제 무릎에서 떨어졌던 것이 분명합니다 /
and onto the floor / 그리고 바닥으로 /
when I took it off my phone / to clean it. 제가 그것을 휴대 전화에서 분리했을 때 / 그것을 닦기 위해
I would like to ask you to check / if it is on your boat. 확인해 주시길 부탁드립니다 / 그것이 보트에 있는지
Its color is black / and it has my name / 그것의 색깔은 검은색입니다 / 그리고 제 이름이 있습니다 /
on the inside. 안쪽에
If you find the case, / I would appreciate it / 케이스를 찾으신다면 / 감사하겠습니다 /
if you would let me know. 저에게 알려주시면
Sincerely, 진심으로
Sam Roberts Sam Roberts 드림

보트 투어 담당자께,
3월 15일에 저희 가족은 귀사의 Glass Bottom Boat Tours 중 하나에 참여했습니다. 저희가 호텔에 돌아왔을 때, 저는 휴대 전화 케이스를 두고 왔다는 것을 알게 되었습니다. 케이스를 닦기 위해 휴대 전화에서 분리했을 때 케이스가 제 무릎에서 바닥으로 떨어졌던 것이 분명합니다. 그것이 보트에 있는지 확인해 주시길 부탁드립니다. 그것의 색깔은 검은색이고 안쪽에 제 이름이 있습니다. 케이스를 찾으신다면, 저에게 알려주시면 감사하겠습니다.
진심으로,
Sam Roberts 드림

문제풀이

샘은 보트 투어 후 휴대 전화 케이스를 보트에 온 것 같다고 투어 담당자에게 그것이 보트에 있는지 확인을 부탁하고 있으므로, 글의 목적으로 ②

'분실물 발견 시 연락을 부탁하려고'가 가장 적절하다.

어휘·어구

discover ~을 알다
leave behind ~을 놓아 둔 채 잊고 오다
appreciate 감사히 여기다

정답률 88%

3. ② 모금 음악회 참석 요청

직독/직해

Dear Ms. Robinson,
Robinson 씨께
The Warblers Choir is happy to announce /
Warblers 합창단이 알려드리게 되어 기쁩니다 /
that we are invited to compete /
실력을 겨루도록 초청받은 사실을 /
in the International Young Choir Competition.
국제 청년 합창 대회에서
The competition takes place / in London on May 20.
대회는 열립니다 / 5월 20일 런던에서
Though we wish to participate / in the event, /
비록 참가하고 싶지만 / 그 대회에 /
we do not have the necessary funds /
저희에게는 필요한 자금이 없습니다 /
to travel to London. 런던에 가는 데
So we are kindly asking you to support us /
그래서 귀하께서 저희를 후원해 주시기를 정중하게 부탁드립니다 /
by coming to our fundraising concert.
저희 모금 음악회에 참석하셔서
It will be held / on March 26.
그것은 개최될 것입니다 / 3월 26일에
In this concert, / we shall be able to show you /
이 음악회에서 / 저희는 귀하께 보여드릴 수 있을 것입니다 /
how big our passion for music is.
음악에 대한 저희의 열정이 얼마나 큰지
Thank you in advance / for your kind support and help.
미리 감사드립니다 / 귀하의 친절한 후원과 도움에 대해
Sincerely,
Arnold Reynolds
Arnold Reynolds 드림

Robinson 씨께,
Warblers 합창단이 국제 청년 합창 대회에서 실력을 겨루도록 초청받은 사실을 알려드리게 되어 기쁩니다. 대회는 5월 20일 런던에서 열립니다. 비록 그 대회에 참가하고 싶지만, 저희에게는 런던에 가는 데 필요한 자금이 없습니다. 그래서 귀하께서 저희 모금 음악회에 참석하셔서 저희를 후원해 주시기를 정중하게 부탁드립니다. 음악회는 3월 26일에 개최될 것입니다. 이 음악회에서 저희는 음악에 대한 저희의 열정이 얼마나 큰지 귀하께 보여드릴 수 있을 것입니다. 귀하의 친절한 후원과 도움에 대해 미리 감사드립니다.
Arnold Reynolds 드림

문제풀이

국제 대회 참가를 위한 자금 모금을 위해 모금 음악회를 연다는 것을 알리며 참석과 후원을 부탁하고 있으므로, 글의 목적으로 ② '모금 음악회 참석을 요청하려고'가 가장 적절하다.

어휘·어구

choir 합창단
announce 알리다, 공고하다
compete 겨루다, 경쟁하다
international 국제적인
participate in ~에 참가하다
necessary 필요한
support 후원(하다)
fundraising 모금
passion 열정
in advance 미리, 앞서

정답률 94%

4. ⑤ 오래된 신문 사용 허락 요청

직독/직해

To the school librarian, 학교 사서 선생님께
I am Kyle Thomas, / 저는 Kyle Thomas입니다 /
the president of the school's English writing club.
학교 영어 글쓰기 동아리 회장인
I have planned activities /
저는 활동들을 계획해 왔습니다 /
that will increase the writing skills of our club members.
저희 동아리 회원들의 글쓰기 실력을 증진시킬
One of the aims of these activities /
이러한 활동들의 목표 중 하나는 /
is to make us aware of various types of news media
저희가 뉴스 미디어의 다양한 유형을 인식하게 만드는 것입니다 /
and the language used in printed newspaper articles.
그리고 인쇄된 신문 기사에 사용된 언어를
However, / 그러나 /
some old newspapers are not easy to access online.
일부 오래된 신문은 온라인으로 접근하는 것이 쉽지 않습니다
It is, therefore, my humble request to you /
그러므로 선생님께 드리는 저의 겸허한 요청입니다 /
to allow us to use old newspapers /
오래된 신문을 저희가 사용할 수 있도록 허락해 달라는 것이 /
that have been stored in the school library.
학교 도서관에 보관되어 온
I would really appreciate it /
저는 그것을 정말 감사히 여기겠습니다 /
if you grant us permission.
만약 선생님께서 저희에게 허락해 주시면
Yours truly, Kyle Thomas
Kyle Thomas 드림

학교 사서 선생님께,
저는 학교 영어 글쓰기 동아리 회장인 Kyle Thomas입니다. 저는 저희 동아리 회원들의 글쓰기 실력을 증진시킬 활동들을 계획해 왔습니다. 이러한 활동들의 목표 중 하나는 저희가 뉴스 미디어의 다양한 유형과 인쇄된 신문 기사에 사용된 언어를 인식하게 만드는 것입니다. 그러나 일부 오래된 신문은 온라인으로 접근하는 것이 쉽지 않습니다. 그러므로 학교 도서관에 보관되어 온 오래된 신문을 저희가 사용할 수 있도록 허락해 달라는 것이 선생님께 드리는 저의 겸허한 요청입니다. 만약 선생님께서 저희에게 허락해 주시면 저는 그것을 정말 감사히 여기겠습니다.
Kyle Thomas 드림

문제풀이

영어 글쓰기 동아리 활동을 위해 도서관에 보관되어 온 오래된 신문을 사용할 수 있도록 허락해 달라는 내용이므로 글의 목적으로 가장 적절한 것은 ⑤ '도서관에 있는 오래된 신문의 사용 허락을 요청하려고'이다.

어휘·어구

aim 목표
various 다양한
article (신문 등의) 기사
access 접근하다; 접근
humble 겸손한
appreciate 감사하다
grant 승인
permission 허락

정답률 92%

5. ② 식당의 연례행사 초대

직독/직해

Dear Mr. Dennis Brown, Dennis Brown씨께
We at G&D Restaurant / 우리 G&D 식당은 /
are honored and delighted to invite you /
당신을 초대하게 되어 영광이고 기쁩니다 /
to our annual Fall Dinner. 우리의 연례행사인 Fall Dinner에
The annual event will be held / on October 1st, 2021 /
그 연례행사는 열릴 것입니다 / 2021년 10월 1일에 /
at our restaurant. 우리 식당에서
At the event, / 그 행사에서 /
we will be introducing new wonderful dishes /
우리는 새로운 멋진 음식들을 소개할 것입니다 /
that our restaurant will be offering soon.
우리 식당이 곧 제공할
These delicious dishes will showcase /
이 맛있는 음식들은 보여줄 것입니다 /
the amazing talents of our gifted chefs.
우리의 뛰어난 요리사들의 멋진 재능을
Also, / our chefs will be providing cooking tips, /
또한 / 우리 요리사들은 요리 비법들을 제공할 것입니다 /
ideas on what to buy for your kitchen, /
당신의 주방을 위해 무엇을 사야 할지에 대한 생각들 /
and special recipes. 그리고 특별한 요리법들을
We at G&D Restaurant would be more than grateful /
우리 G&D 식당은 매우 감사할 것입니다 /
if you can make it to this special occasion /
만약 당신이 이 특별 행사에 오신다면 /
and be part of our celebration.
그리고 우리의 축하 일부가 되어준다면
We look forward to seeing you.
우리는 당신을 곧 뵙기를 고대합니다
Thank you so much. 대단히 감사합니다
Regards, 존경을 담아
Marcus Lee, Owner - G&D Restaurant
G&D 식당 주인, Marcus Lee 드림

Dennis Brown씨께,
우리 G&D 식당은 당신을 우리의 연례행사인 Fall Dinner에 초대하게 되어 영광이고 기쁩니다. 그 연례행사는 2021년 10월 1일에 우리 식당에서 열릴 것입니다. 그 행사에서, 우리는 우리 식당이 곧 제공할 새로운 멋진 음식들을 소개할 것입니다. 이 맛있는 음식들은 우리의 뛰어난 요리사들의 멋진 재능을 보여줄 것입니다. 또한, 우리 요리사들은 요리 비법들과 당신의 주방을 위해 무엇을 사야 할지에 대한 생각들, 그리고 특별한 요리법들을 제공할 것입니다. 우리 G&D 식당은 만약 당신이 이 특별 행사에 와서 우리의 축하 일부가 되어준다면 매우 감사할 것입니다. 우리는 당신을 곧 뵙기를 고대합니다. 대단히 감사합니다.
존경을 담아, G&D 식당 주인, Marcus Lee 드림

문제풀이

식당의 연례행사인 Fall Dinner에 대한 세부 사항들을 소개하면서 행사에 와서 축하를 해달라고 부탁하고 있으므로, 글의 목적으로 ② '식당의 연례행사에 초대하려고'가 가장 적절하다.

어휘·어구

be honored 영광스럽다
delighted 아주 기쁜
annual 연례의
showcase 전시하다, 소개하다
gifted 타고난 재능이 있는, 유능한
grateful 감사하고 있는
occasion 행사
celebration 축하
look forward to ~을 학수고대하다

정답률 91%

6. ① 회사 로고 제작 의뢰

직독/직해

Dear Mr. Jones, Jones 씨에게
I am James Arkady, / 저는 James Arkady입니다 /
PR Director of KHJ Corporation.
KHJ Corporation의 홍보부 이사
We are planning to redesign our brand identity /
저희는 회사 브랜드 정체성을 다시 설계할 계획입니다 /

and launch a new logo /
그리고 새로운 로고를 출시할 (계획입니다) /

to celebrate our 10th anniversary.
회사의 창립 10주년을 기념하기 위해

We request you to create a logo /
로고를 제작해 주시기를 요청합니다 /

that best suits our company's core vision, /
저희 회사의 핵심 비전을 가장 잘 반영한 /

'To inspire humanity.' '인류애를 고양하자'

I hope / the new logo will convey our brand message /
저는 바랍니다 / 새로운 로고가 저희 회사 브랜드 메시지를 전달하기를 /

and capture the values of KHJ.
그리고 KHJ의 가치를 담기를

Please send us your logo design proposal /
로고 디자인 제안서를 저희에게 보내 주십시오 /

once you are done with it.
그것을 완성하는 대로

Thank you. 감사합니다

Best regards,

James Arkady James Arkady 드림

Jones 씨에게
저는 KHJ Corporation의 홍보부 이사 James Arkady입니다. 저희는 회사의 창립 10주년을 기념하기 위해 회사 브랜드 정체성을 다시 설계하고 새로운 로고를 출시할 계획입니다. 저희 회사의 핵심 비전 '인류애를 고양하자'를 가장 잘 반영한 로고를 제작해 주시기를 요청합니다. 새로운 로고가 저희 회사 브랜드 메시지를 전달하고 KHJ의 가치를 담기를 바랍니다. 로고 디자인 제안서를 완성하는 대로 저희에게 보내 주십시오. 감사합니다.
James Arkady 드림

문제풀이

회사 창립 10주년을 기념하기 위해 회사의 핵심 비전을 잘 반영한 로고 제작을 요청하고 있으므로, 글의 목적으로 ① '회사 로고 제작을 의뢰하려고'가 가장 적절하다.

어휘·어구

PR director 홍보부 이사
corporation 기업, 법인
identity 정체성
launch (상품 등을) 시장에 내놓다
celebrate 기념하다
anniversary 기념일
core 가장 중요한, 핵심의
inspire 고무하다
convey 전달하다
capture 포착하다
proposal 제안

정답률 91%

7. ④ 도서관 공사 참여 자원봉사자 모집

직독/직해

Dear members of Eastwood Library, /
Eastwood 도서관 회원들께 /

Thanks to the Friends of Literature group, /
Friends of Literature 모임 덕분에 /

we've successfully raised /
우리는 성공적으로 모았습니다 /

enough money to remodel the library building.
도서관 건물을 리모델링하기에 충분한 돈을

John Baker, our local builder, /
우리 지역의 건축업자인 John Baker 씨가 /

has volunteered to help us with the remodelling /
우리의 리모델링을 돕기로 자원했습니다 /

but he needs assistance.
하지만 그분은 도움이 필요합니다

By grabbing a hammer or a paint brush /
망치나 페인트 붓을 쥠으로써 /

and donating your time, /
그리고 여러분의 시간을 기부함으로써 /

you can help with the construction.
여러분은 공사를 도울 수 있습니다

Join Mr. Baker in his volunteering team /
Baker 씨의 자원봉사 팀에 동참하십시오 /

and become a part /
그리고 일원이 되십시오 /

of making Eastwood Library a better place!
Eastwood 도서관을 더 좋은 곳으로 만드는 데

Please call 541-567-1234 / for more information.
541-567-1234로 전화해 주십시오 / 더 많은 정보를 위해

Sincerely, Mark Anderson
Mark Anderson 드림

Eastwood 도서관 회원들께
Friends of Literature 모임 덕분에, 우리는 도서관 건물을 리모델링하기에 충분한 돈을 성공적으로 모았습니다. 우리 지역의 건축업자인 John Baker 씨가 우리의 리모델링을 돕기로 자원했지만, 그분은 도움이 필요합니다. 망치나 페인트 붓을 쥐고 여러분의 시간을 기부함으로써, 여러분은 공사를 도울 수 있습니다. Baker 씨의 자원봉사 팀에 동참하여 Eastwood 도서관을 더 좋은 곳으로 만드는 데 일원이 되십시오! 더 많은 정보를 위해 541-567-1234로 전화해 주십시오.
Mark Anderson 드림

문제풀이

도서관 건물을 리모델링하는 작업에 동참하기를 제안하고 있으므로, 글의 목적으로 ④ '도서관 공사에 참여할 자원봉사자를 모집하려고'가 가장 적절하다.

어휘·어구

successfully 성공적으로
raise (자금 등을) 모으다
remodel 리모델링하다, 개축하다
local 지역의
builder 건축업자
volunteer 자원하다
assistance 도움
grab 쥐다
hammer 망치
donate 기부하다
construction 공사
information 정보

정답률 70%

8. ③ 산책로 조성 계획의 재고 요청

직독/직해

To whom it may concern: 관계자 귀하

I was born and raised / in the city of Boulder /
저는 태어나고 자랐습니다 / Boulder 시에서 /

and have enjoyed our scenic natural spaces /
그리고 우리의 경치 좋은 자연 공간들을 누려왔습니다 /

for my whole life. 평생 동안

The land through which the proposed Pine Hill walking trail would cut /
제안된 Pine Hill 산책로가 지나가게 될 그 땅은 /

is home to a variety of species.
다양한 종들의 서식지입니다

Wildlife faces pressure from development, /
야생 동물은 개발로 인한 압력에 직면해 있습니다 /

and these animals need space /
그리고 이 동물들은 공간이 필요합니다 /

where they can hide from human activity.
인간 활동으로부터 숨을 수 있는

Although trails serve as a wonderful source /
비록 산책로들은 훌륭한 원천으로서의 역할을 하지만 /

for us to access the natural world /
우리가 자연 세계에 접근할 수 있는 /

and appreciate the wildlife within it, /
그리고 그 안에 있는 야생 동물을 감상할 수 있는 /

if we continue to destroy habitats /
만약 우리가 계속해서 서식지를 파괴한다면 /

with excess trails, / 과도한 산책로들로 /

the wildlife will stop using these areas.
야생 동물은 이 지역들을 이용하는 것을 중단할 것입니다

Please reconsider / 재고해 주시기 바랍니다 /

whether the proposed trail is absolutely necessary.
제안된 산책로가 정말로 필요한지

Sincerely, Tyler Stuart Tyler Stuart 드림

관계자 귀하,
저는 Boulder 시에서 태어나고 자랐으며 평생 동안 우리의 경치 좋은 자연 공간들을 누려왔습니다. 제안된 Pine Hill 산책로가 지나가게 될 그 땅은 다양한 종들의 서식지입니다. 야생 동물은 개발로 인한 압력에 직면해 있고, 이 동물들은 인간 활동으로부터 숨을 수 있는 공간이 필요합니다. 비록 산책로들은 우리가 자연 세계에 접근하고 그 안에 있는 야생 동물을 감상할 수 있는 훌륭한 원천으로서의 역할을 하지만, 만약 계속해서 우리가 과도한 산책로들로 서식지를 파괴한다면 야생 동물은 이 지역들을 이용하는 것을 중단할 것입니다. 제안된 산책로가 정말로 필요한지 재고해 주시기 바랍니다.
Tyler Stuart 드림

문제풀이

과도한 산책로들로 인해 야생 동물의 서식지가 파괴되는 것을 우려하는 글로, 글의 마지막 문장인 'Please reconsider whether the proposed trail is absolutely necessary.(제안된 산책로가 정말로 필요한지 재고해 주시기 바랍니다.)'에 글의 목적이 드러나 있다. 따라서 글의 목적으로 ③ '산책로 조성 계획의 재고를 요청하려고'가 가장 적절하다.

어휘·어구

scenic 경치가 좋은
walking trail 산책로
cut through ~사이로 길을 내다
face 직면하다
pressure 압력
development 개발
access 접근하다
appreciate 감상하다
destroy 파괴하다
habitat 서식지
excess 과도한
reconsider 재고하다
absolutely 정말로, 절대적으로
necessary 필요한

정답률 90%

9. ③ 악기 기부 요청

직독/직해

Dear Wildwood residents, Wildwood 지역 주민들께

Wildwood Academy is a local school /
Wildwood Academy는 지역 학교입니다 /

that seeks to help children /
아이들을 돕고자 하는 /

with disabilities and learning challenges.
장애와 학습의 어려움을 가진

We currently have over 200 students enrolled.
현재 200명이 넘는 학생들이 등록되어 있습니다

This year we'd like to add a music class /
올해 저희는 음악 수업을 추가 개설하고자 합니다 /

in the hope that each of our students will have the opportunity /
학생들 각각이 그들의 기회를 갖기를 바라며 /

to develop their musical abilities.
음악적 능력을 발전시킬

To get the class started, /
이 수업을 시작하기 위해 /

we need more instruments than we have now.
저희는 지금 가지고 있는 것보다 더 많은 악기가 필요합니다

We are asking you to look around your house and donate any instruments /
저희는 여러분이 집을 둘러보고 악기를 기부하기를 요청합니다 /

that you may no longer use.
더 이상 사용하지 않을지도 모르는

Each one donated will be assigned to a student in need.
기부된 각 악기는 필요로 하는 학생에게 배정될 것입니다

Simply call us and we will be happy to drop by /
전화만 주시면 기꺼이 저희가 방문하여 /

and pick up the instrument.
악기를 가져가겠습니다

Sincerely,
Karen Hansen, Principal
교장 Karen Hansen 드림

Wildwood 지역 주민들께,
Wildwood Academy는 장애와 학습의 어려움을 가진 아이들을 돕고자 하는 지역 학교입니다. 현재 200명이 넘는 학생들이 등록되어 있습니다. 올해 저희는 학생들 각각이 그들의 음악적 능력을 발전시킬 기회를 갖기를 바라며 음악 수업을 추가 개설하고자 합니다. 이 수업을 시작하기 위해, 저희는 지금 저희가 가지고 있는 것보다 더 많은 악기가 필요합니다. 저희는 여러분이 집을 둘러보고 더 이상 사용하지 않을지도 모르는 악기를 기부하기를 요청합니다. 기부된 각 악기는 필요로 하는 학생에게 배정될 것입니다. 전화만 주시면 기꺼이 저희가 방문하여 악기를 가져가겠습니다.
교장 Karen Hansen 드림

문제풀이

'This year we'd like to add a music class in the hope that each of our students will have the opportunity to develop their musical abilities.(올해 저희는 학생들 각각이 그들의 음악적 능력을 발전시킬 기회를 갖기를 바라며 음악 수업을 추가 개설하고자 합니다.)' 그리고 'We are asking you to look around your house and donate any instruments that you may no longer use.(저희는 여러분이 집을 둘러보고 더 이상 사용하지 않을지도 모르는 악기를 기부하기를 요청합니다.)'에서 음악 수업 개설을 위해 악기 기부를 요청하고 있으므로 글의 목적이 ③ '음악 수업을 위한 악기 기부를 요청하려고'임을 알 수 있다.

《 어휘·어구 》

seek 찾다, 추구하다
disability 장애
enroll 등록하다
instrument 악기, 도구
donate 기부하다
no longer 더 이상 ~않는
assign 배정하다, 할당하다

정답률 93%

10. ① 공장 견학 요청

직독/직해

Dear Mr. Anderson Anderson 씨에게
On behalf of Jeperson High School, /
Jeperson 고등학교를 대표해서 /
I am writing this letter / to request permission /
저는 이 편지를 쓰고 있습니다 / 허가를 요청하기 위해 /
to conduct an industrial field trip / in your factory.
산업 현장견학을 할 수 있도록 / 당신의 공장에서
We hope to give some practical education /
저희는 몇 가지 실제적인 교육을 하기를 희망합니다 /
to our students / in regard to industrial procedures.
우리 학생들에게 / 산업 절차와 관련해
With this purpose in mind, / we believe /
이러한 목적을 생각할 때 / 우리는 믿습니다 /
your firm is ideal / to carry out such a project.
귀사가 이상적이라고 / 그러한 프로젝트를 진행하기 위해
But of course, / we need your blessing and support.
그러나 물론 / 저희는 귀사의 승인과 협조가 필요합니다
35 students would be accompanied /
35명의 학생들이 동행할 것입니다 /
by two teachers. 두 명의 선생님과
And we would just need a day / for the trip.
저희는 단 하루를 예정하고 있습니다 / 이 현장 견학을 위해
I would really appreciate your cooperation.
협조해 주시면 정말 감사하겠습니다
Sincerely, Mr. Ray Feynman
Ray Feynman 드림

Anderson 씨에게
Jeperson 고등학교를 대표해서, 저는 당신의 공장에서 산업 현장견학을 할 수 있도록 허가를 요청하기 위해, 이 편지를 쓰고 있습니다. 저희는 학생들에게 산업 절차와 관련해 몇 가지 실제적인 교육을 하기를 희망합니다. 이러한 목적을 생각할 때, 저희는 그러한 프로젝트를 진행하기 위해 귀사가 이상적이라고 믿습니다. 물론, 저희는 귀사의 승인과 협조가 필요합니다. 두 명의 선생님이 35명의 학생들과 동행할 것입니다. 저희는 이 현장 견학을 위해 단 하루를 예정하고 있습니다. 협조해 주시면 정말 감사하겠습니다.
Ray Feynman 드림

문제풀이

'I am writing this letter to request permission to conduct an industrial field trip in your factory.(저는 당신의 공장에서 산업 현장견학을 할 수 있도록 허가를 요청하기 위해, 이 편지를 쓰고 있습니다.)'로 보아 글의 목적으로 가장 적절한 것은 ①이다.

《 어휘·어구 》

on behalf of ~를 대표해서
request 요청하다, 신청하다
permission 허가, 허락
industrial 산업의, 공업의
field trip 현장 견학
practical 실제적인, 현실적인
in regard to ~와 관련하여
procedure 절차
firm 회사
carry out ~을 수행하다
blessing 승인, 축복
accompany 동반하다
appreciate 감사하다
cooperation 협조, 협동

정답률 83%

11. ② 잡지 구독 갱신 권유

직독/직해

Dear Mr. Hane, / Hane 씨께 /
Our message to you is brief, / but important: /
귀하에게 보내는 우리의 메시지는 간단합니다 / 하지만 중요합니다 /
Your subscription to *Winston Magazine* /
귀하의 'Winston Magazine' 구독 기간이 /
will end soon / 곧 끝납니다 /
and we haven't heard from you / about renewing it. /
그리고 우리는 귀하로부터 듣지 못했습니다 / 그것을 갱신하는 것에 대해 /
We're sure / you won't want to miss /
우리는 확신합니다 / 귀하가 놓치고 싶지 않을 거라는 것을 /
even one upcoming issue. 다음의 단 한 호라도
Renew now / 지금 갱신하십시오 /
to make sure that the service will continue.
서비스를 지속하는 것을 확실히 하기 위해서는
You'll get continued delivery / of the excellent stories
귀하는 계속 받게 될 것입니다 / 훌륭한 이야기와 뉴스를
and news / that make *Winston Magazine* /
/ 'Winston Magazine'을 만들어 주는 /
the fastest growing magazine in America.
미국에서 가장 빠르게 성장하는 잡지로
To make it as easy as possible for you to act now, /
지금 귀하가 가능한 한 쉽게 할 수 있도록 /
we've sent a reply card for you / to complete.
우리는 귀하에게 회신용 카드를 보냈습니다 / 작성할
Simply send back the card today / and you'll continue
카드를 오늘 보내 주기만 하십시오 / 그러면 귀하는 계속 받게 될 것입니다
to receive / your monthly issue of *Winston Magazine*.
/ 귀하의 월간지 'Winston Magazine'을
Best regards,
Thomas Strout Thomas Strout 올림

Hane 씨께,
귀하에게 보내는 우리의 메시지는 간단하지만, 중요합니다. 귀하의 'Winston Magazine' 구독 기간이 곧 끝나는데 귀하로부터 그것을 갱신하는 것에 대해 듣지 못했습니다. 우리는 귀하가 다음의 단 한 호라도 놓치고 싶지 않을 거라는 것을 확신합니다. 서비스를 지속하는 것을 확실히 하기 위해서는 지금 갱신하십시오. 귀하는 'Winston Magazine'을 미국에서 가장 빠르게 성장하는 잡지로 만들어 주는 훌륭한 이야기와 뉴스를 계속 받게 될 것입니다. 지금 가능한 한 쉽게 구독 신청을 할 수 있도록, 우리는 귀하가 작성할 회신용 카드를 보냈습니다. 카드를 오늘 보내 주기만 하면 귀하는 월간지 'Winston Magazine'을 계속 받게 될 것입니다.
Thomas Strout 올림

문제풀이

'Renew now to make sure that the service will continue.(서비스를 지속하는 것을 확실히 하기 위해서는 지금 갱신하십시오.)'와 'Simply send back the card today and you'll continue to receive your monthly issue of *Winston Magazine*.(오늘 보내 주기만 하면 귀하는 월간지 'Winston Magazine'을 계속 받게 될 것입니다.)'을 통해 'Winston Magazine'을 계속 받아 보기 위해 구독을 갱신할 것을 권유하면서 갱신 방법을 안내하고 있다는 것을 알 수 있다. 따라서 글의 목적으로 가장 적절한 것은 ② '잡지 구독 갱신을 권유하려고'이다.

《 어휘·어구 》

brief 간단한
subscription 구독
renew 갱신하다
upcoming 다가오는, 곧 있을
issue (정기 간행물의) 호
delivery 배달

정답률 90%

12. ③ 주문한 상품의 배송 지연

직독/직해

Dear Mr. Stevens, Stevens 씨께,
This is a reply / to your inquiry /
회신 드립니다 / 문의하신 것에 대해 /
about the shipment status of the desk /
책상의 배송 상황에 관해 /
you purchased / at our store / on September 26.
고객님께서 구매하신 / 저희 상점에서 / 9월 26일에
Unfortunately, / 불행히도 /
the delivery of your desk / will take longer /
고객님의 책상 배송이 / 더 오래 걸릴 것입니다 /
than expected / due to the damage /
예상된 것보다 / 파손 때문에 /
that occurred / during the shipment /
발생한 / 배송되는 동안 /
from the furniture manufacturer / to our warehouse.
가구 제조업체에서 / 저희 창고로
We have ordered an exact replacement /
저희는 똑같은 대체품을 주문했으며 /
from the manufacturer, / 제조업체로부터 /
and we expect / 예상합니다 /
that delivery will take place / within two weeks.
그 배송이 이루어질 것으로 / 2주 안에
As soon as the desk arrives, /
저희는 그 책상이 도착하자마자 /
we will telephone you immediately /
고객님께 즉시 전화 드려 /

and arrange a convenient delivery time.
편리한 배송 시간을 정할 것입니다

We regret the inconvenience /
불편을 끼쳐 드려 죄송합니다 /

this delay has caused you. 이 지연으로 인해

Sincerely, Justin Upton Justin Upton 드림

Stevens 씨께,
고객님께서 9월 26일에 저희 상점에서 구매하신 책상의 배송 상황에 관해 문의하신 것에 대해 회신 드립니다. 불행히도, 고객님의 책상 배송이 가구 제조업체에서 저희 창고로 배송되는 동안 발생한 파손 때문에 예상된 것보다 더 오래 걸릴 것입니다. 저희는 제조업체로부터 똑같은 대체품을 주문했으며, 그 배송이 2주 안에 이루어질 것으로 예상합니다. 저희는 그 책상이 도착하자마자 고객님께 즉시 전화 드려 편리한 배송 시간을 정할 것입니다. 이 지연으로 인해 불편을 끼쳐 드려 죄송합니다.

문제풀이

상점에서 구매한 책상의 배송 상황 문의에 대한 회신으로 배송 도중 파손되어 똑같은 대체품을 다시 주문한 관계로 배송이 예상보다 더 오래 걸릴 것이라고 설명하고 있다. 따라서 글의 목적으로 가장 적절한 것은 ③ '상품의 배송 지연에 대해 설명하려고'이다.

이렇게 풀자_ 글의 목적을 묻는 유형은 필자의 의도가 무엇인지 파악하면 비교적 쉽게 풀 수 있는 유형으로, 여기서는 'the delivery of your desk will take longer than expected'나 'the inconvenience this delay has caused you'에 필자의 의도가 잘 나타나 있다.

어휘·어구

inquiry 문의, 질문
shipment 배송, 수송
status (진행 과정상의) 상황
unfortunately 불행하게도, 유감스럽게도
delivery 배달, 배송
due to ~ 때문에
damage 파손, 손상, 피해
manufacturer 제조업체, 생산 회사
warehouse 창고
order 주문하다
replacement 대체(품), 교체(품)
take place 일어나다, 발생하다
immediately 즉시, 즉각
convenient 편리한
regret 유감스럽게[안타깝게] 생각하다
inconvenience 불편
delay 지연

본문 005쪽

문법 플러스 1. 문장의 구조

1. ②	2. ①	3. ①	4. ②	5. ②
6. ②	7. ③	8. ①	9. ①	10. ①

1 [해석]▶ 곧 비행기가 심하게 흔들리고 나는 아무 것도 통제할 수 없다는 것을 느껴며 몸이 굳는다.
[해설]▶ shakes와 freeze는 1형식 동사로 쓰였다. 접속사 and가 앞 문장과 뒷 문장을 연결하고 있다. 주어 I에 해당하는 동사가 필요하다.

2 [해석]▶ 예를 들면, 나이테는 온화하고 습한 해에는 더 넓어지고 춥고 건조한 해에는 더 좁아진다.
[해설]▶ grow는 2형식 동사로 쓰였다. 보어는 형용사가 와야 한다. 그런데 접속사 and의 앞뒤 문장이 병렬 구조를 이루고 있으므로 형용사 wide의 비교급인 wider로 고쳐야 한다.

3 [해석]▶ 빙하, 바람과 흐르는 물은 이 암석 조각들을 운반하는 것을 도와주고, 작은 여행자(암석 조각)들은 이동하면서 점점 작아진다.
[해설]▶ help는 목적어로 동사원형 또는 to부정사를 취한다.

4 [해석]▶ 이 나이테는 그 나무의 나이가 몇 살인지, 그 나무가 매해 살아오는 동안 날씨가 어떠했는지를 우리에게 알려줄 수 있다.
[해설]▶ tell은 4형식 동사로 쓰였다. tell의 직접목적어로 의문사절이 병렬적으로 연결되어 있다. 의문사절이 다른 문장의 일부로 들어가는 경우 「의문사+주어+동사」의 어순을 갖기 때문에 ② what the weather was like로 고쳐야 한다.

5 [해석]▶ 나는 그녀가 거리를 가로지르는 것을 보았다.
[해설]▶ 지각동사(saw)의 목적어와 목적격보어가 능동 관계인 경우 목적격보어는 동사원형(cross) 또는 현재분사(crossing)를 사용한다.

6 [해석]▶나는 그가 차를 수리하도록 했다.
[해설]▶ 사역동사의 목적어와 목적격보어의 관계가 능동관계인 경우 동사원형(repair)을 사용한다.

7 [해석]▶ 독자의 관심을 끌지 못한 그녀의 책은 없다.
[해설]▶ 「none of+복수명사」가 주어로 오면 격식체에서는 단수동사로 받는다. 일상체에서는 복수동사와 함께 쓴다. leave는 '~한 상태로 남겨두다'는 뜻을 갖는 5형식 동사로 쓰였다. 목적어의 상태를 알려주고 싶은 경우, 목적격보어는 형용사를 사용한다. 'unconcern'을 'unconcerned'로 고쳐 써야 한다.

8 [해석]▶ 만약 예를 들어 초록색 빛깔의 오렌지 음료와 같이 색깔이 잘못되어 있다면, 사람들은 과일 맛이 나는 음료를 정확하게 식별하는 것이 매우 어렵다는 것을 알게 된다.
[해설]▶ 불완전 타동사 find의 목적격보어로서 형용사 difficult가 와야 한다.

9 [해석]▶ 여러분을 미소 짓게 만드는 온갖 사건들은 여러분이 행복감을 느끼게 하고, 여러분의 뇌에서 기분을 좋게 만들어주는 화학 물질을 생산해 내도록 한다.
[해설]▶ cause는 5형식 동사로 쓰면 to부정사를 목적격보어로 취한다.

10 해석▶ 저는 귀하와 다른 시의회 의원들이 그 계획을 취소하고 도서관을 계속해서 열 것을 강력히 촉구합니다.
[해설]▶ urge는 5형식 동사로 쓰면, to부정사를 목적어로 취한다. and는 to cancel과 to keep을 병렬적으로 연결하고 있다.

본문 006쪽

어휘 플러스 1. 철자가 혼동되는 어휘 (1)

1. adapt	2. confined
3. subscribe	4. irritated
5. compiling	

1 [해석]▶ 이런 이유들로 인해, 농부는 젖소가 새로운 먹이에 적응할 수 있도록 먹이를 천천히 바꾼다.

2 [해석]▶ 쓰는 것을 아는 것은 왕이나 사원에서 일하는 전문가에게 한정되었다.

3 [해석]▶ 게다가, 잠재적 독자들은 낱권의 잡지를 구매함으로써 새로운 잡지를 탐색한다. 구독 안내가 있는 그 모든 삽입 광고 카드는 여러분의 구독을 독려하기 위해 잡지에 들어가 있다.

4 [해석]▶ 레코드, 특히 자장가는 아이들이 종종 쉽게 짜증내는 아침의 끝이나 오후의 기간 동안 안성맞춤의 것이 된다.

5 [해석]▶ 우리는 사적 자료의 수집과 그러한 자료의 무제한적 사용과 배포에 반대하여 시민들을 보호해야 한다.

02. 심경 · 분위기

본문 008쪽

Day 02

1. ② 2. ② 3. ③ 4. ⑤ 5. ⑤
6. ③ 7. ① 8. ① 9. ① 10. ①
11. ⑤ 12. ①

정답률 89%

대표 기출 ② 휴가 때 갑작스러운 아버지의 부상 연락

직독/직해

On one beautiful spring day, /
어느 아름다운 봄날 /
I was fully enjoying my day off.
나는 내 휴가를 충분히 즐기고 있었다
I arrived at the nail salon, /
나는 네일 숍에 도착했다 /
and muted my cellphone /
그리고 나의 휴대전화를 음소거했다 /
so that I would be disconnected for the hour /
그 시간 동안 단절되기 위해 /
and feel calm and peaceful.
그리고 차분하고 평화로움을 느낄 수 있도록
I was so comfortable / while I got a manicure.
나는 아주 편안했다 / 매니큐어를 받는 동안
As I left the place, / I checked my cellphone /
그 장소를 떠날 때 / 나는 나의 휴대전화를 확인했다 /
and saw four missed calls from a strange number.
그리고 낯선 번호에서 걸려 온 네 통의 부재중 전화를 봤다
I knew immediately / 나는 즉시 알았다 /
that something bad was coming, / and I called back.
나쁜 어떤 일이 생겼다는 것을 / 그래서 회신 전화를 했다
A young woman answered and said /
한 젊은 여성이 전화를 받고 말했다 /
that my father had fallen over a stone /
나의 아버지가 돌에 걸려 넘어졌고 /
and was injured, / now seated on a bench.
그래서 다쳤고 / 지금 벤치에 앉아 있다고 (말했다)
I was really concerned /
나는 정말 걱정되었다 /
since he had just recovered from his knee surgery.
그가 막 무릎 수술에서 회복했기 때문에
I rushed getting into my car / to go see him.
나는 급히 차에 올랐다 / 그를 보러 가기 위해

어느 아름다운 봄날, 나는 내 휴가를 충분히 즐기고 있었다. 나는 네일 숍에 도착해서 그 시간 동안 단절되어 차분하고 평화로움을 느낄 수 있도록 나의 휴대전화를 음소거했다. 나는 매니큐어를 받는 동안 아주 편안했다. 그 장소를 떠날 때, 나는 나의 휴대전화를 확인했고 낯선 번호에서 걸려 온 네 통의 부재중 전화를 봤다. 나는 즉시 나쁜 어떤 일이 생겼다는 것을 알고 다시 전화했다. 한 젊은 여성이 전화를 받았고, 나의 아버지가 돌에 걸려 넘어져 다쳤고 지금 벤치에 앉아 있다고 말했다. 그가 무릎 수술에서 막 회복했기 때문에 나는 정말 걱정되었다. 나는 그를 보러 가기 위해 급히 차에 올랐다.

① 긴장한 → 자신감 있는
② 편한 → 걱정되는
③ 신이 나는 → 무관심한
④ 기쁜 → 질투하는
⑤ 짜증이 난 → 감사하는

문제풀이

휴가 때 네일 숍에서 매니큐어를 받는 동안 휴대전화를 음소거했는데, 매니큐어 서비스를 받은 후 네 통의 부재중 전화가 와있음을 알고 나쁜 일이 생겼음을 직감한 뒤 다시 전화했더니 아버지가 다쳐서 벤치에 앉아 있다는 말을 듣고 급히 차에 올라타는 상황이다. 따라서 'I'의 심경 변화로 ② 'relaxed → worried(편한 → 걱정되는)'가 가장 적절하다.

어휘·어구

nail salon 네일 숍
mute 소리를 음소거하다
disconnect 연락을 끊다
peaceful 평화로운
comfortable 편안한
manicure 매니큐어
missed calls 부재중 전화
immediately 즉시
injure 상처를 입히다
concern 걱정하다
recover 회복하다
knee 무릎
surgery 수술
rush 돌진하다
nervous 긴장한
relaxed 편한
indifferent 무관심한
pleased 기쁜
jealous 질투하는
annoyed 짜증이 난
grateful 감사하는

정답률 91%

1. ② 뉴스 기사 완성 과정에서 문제가 생긴 상황

직독/직해

It was two hours before the submission deadline /
제출 마감 시간 두 시간 전이었다 /
and I still hadn't finished my news article.
그리고 나는 여전히 뉴스 기사를 완성하지 못했다
I sat at the desk, / but suddenly, /
나는 책상에 앉았다 / 그러나 갑자기 /
the typewriter didn't work.
타자기가 작동하지 않았다
No matter how hard I tapped the keys, /
내가 키를 아무리 세게 두드려도 /
the levers wouldn't move / to strike the paper.
레버는 움직이지 않았다 / 종이를 두드리려
I started to realize / that I would not be able to finish /
나는 깨닫기 시작했다 / 내가 끝낼 수 없으리라는 것을 /
the article on time. 제시간에 그 기사를
Desperately, / I rested the typewriter / on my lap /
필사적으로 / 나는 타자기를 올려놓았다 / 내 무릎 위에 /
and started hitting each key /
그리고 각각의 키를 누르기 시작했다 /
with as much force as I could manage.
내가 할 수 있을 만큼 힘껏
Nothing happened. 아무 일도 일어나지 않았다
Thinking something might have happened /
무슨 일이 일어났을지도 모르겠다고 생각하면서 /
inside of it, / I opened the cover, /
그것의 내부에 / 나는 그 덮개를 열었다 /
lifted up the keys, / and found the problem /
키들을 들어 올렸다 / 그리고 문제를 발견했다 /
— a paper clip. 종이 집게(가 문제였다)
The keys had no room to move.
키들이 움직일 공간이 없었다
After picking it out, / I pressed and pulled /
그것을 집어서 꺼낸 후에 / 나는 누르고 당겼다 /
some parts. 몇 개의 부품들을
The keys moved smoothly again.
키들이 매끄럽게 다시 움직였다
I breathed deeply / and smiled.
나는 깊게 숨을 내쉬었다 / 그리고 미소 지었다
Now I knew / that I could finish my article / on time.
이제는 나는 알았다 / 내가 기사를 끝낼 수 있음을 / 제시간에

제출 마감 시간 두 시간 전이었고 나는 여전히 뉴스 기사를 완성하지 못했다. 나는 책상에 앉았는데, 갑자기, 타자기가 작동하지 않았다. 내가 키를 아무리 세게 두드려도, 레버는 종이를 두드리려 움직이지 않았다. 나는 내가 제시간에 그 기사를 끝낼 수 없으리라는 것을 깨닫기 시작했다. 필사적으로, 나는 타자기를 내 무릎 위에 올려놓고 각각의 키를 내가 할 수 있을 만큼 힘껏 누르기 시작했다. 아무 일도 일어나지 않았다. 그것의 내부에 무슨 일이 일어났을지도 모르겠다고 생각하면서, 나는 그 덮개를 열고, 키들을 들어 올리고, 문제를 발견했다 — 종이 집게. 키들이 움직일 공간이 없었다. 그것을 집어서 꺼낸 후에, 나는 몇 개의 부품들을 누르고 당겼다. 키들이 매끄럽게 다시 움직였다. 나는 깊게 숨을 내쉬고 미소 지었다. 이제는 내가 제시간에 기사를 끝낼 수 있음을 알았다.

① 자신감 있는 → 긴장한
② 좌절한 → 안도한
③ 지루한 → 놀란
④ 무관심한 → 호기심있는
⑤ 신이 난 → 실망한

문제풀이

제출 마감 시간 두 시간 전임에도 불구하고 뉴스 기사를 완성하지 못한 상황에서 타자기가 갑자기 작동하지 않았고, 타자기 내부를 살펴보고 나서 문제를 해결하고 제시간에 기사를 끝낸 상황이다. 따라서 'I'의 심경 변화로 ② 'frustrated → relieved(좌절한 → 안도한)'가 가장 적절하다.

어휘·어구

submission 제출
article 기사
typewriter 타자기
tap 가볍게 두드리다, 치다
lever 레버
strike 치다
realize 깨닫다
desperately 필사적으로
rest ~을 놓다
force 힘
manage (어떻게든) 해내다
confident 자신감 있는
nervous 긴장한
frustrated 좌절한
relieved 안도한
indifferent 무관심한
curious 호기심 있는
disappointed 실망한

정답률 95%

2. ② 엄마와 함께 공원에 간 Matthew

직독/직해

One Saturday morning, / 어느 토요일 아침 /
Matthew's mother told Matthew /
Matthew의 어머니는 Matthew에게 말했다 /
that she was going to take him to the park.
그녀가 그를 공원으로 데리고 갈 것이라고
A big smile came across his face.
그의 얼굴에 환한 미소가 그려졌다
As he loved to play outside, / he ate his breakfast /
그는 밖에 나가서 노는 것을 좋아했기 때문에 / 그는 아침을 먹었다 /
and got dressed quickly / so they could go.
그리고 서둘러 옷을 입었다 / 그들이 나가기 위해
When they got to the park, / Matthew ran all the way /
그들이 공원에 도착했을 때 / Matthew는 바로 뛰어갔다 /
over to the swing set. 그네를 향해
That was his favorite thing to do / at the park.
그것은 그가 가장 하기 좋아하는 것이었다 / 공원에서
But the swings were all being used.
하지만 그네는 이미 모두 사용되고 있었다
His mother explained / that he could use the slide /
그의 어머니는 설명했다 / 그가 미끄럼틀을 탈 수 있다고 /

until a swing became available, / but it was broken.
그네를 이용할 수 있을 때까지 / 하지만 그것은 부서져 있었다

Suddenly, / his mother got a phone call /
갑자기 / 그의 어머니가 전화를 받았다 /

and she told Matthew / they had to leave.
그리고 그녀는 Matthew에게 말했다 / 그들이 떠나야 한다고

His heart sank. 그는 가슴이 내려앉았다

어느 토요일 아침, Matthew의 어머니는 Matthew에게 공원으로 데리고 갈 것이라고 말했다. 그의 얼굴에 환한 미소가 그려졌다. 그는 밖에 나가서 노는 것을 좋아했기 때문에, 나가기 위해 서둘러 아침을 먹고 옷을 입었다. 그들이 공원에 도착했을 때, Matthew는 그네를 향해 바로 뛰어갔다. 그것은 그가 공원에서 가장 하기 좋아하는 것이었다. 하지만 그네는 이미 모두 사용되고 있었다. 그의 어머니는 그네를 이용할 수 있을 때까지 미끄럼틀을 탈 수 있다고 설명했지만, 그것은 부서져 있었다. 갑자기 그의 어머니가 전화를 받고 Matthew에게 그들이 떠나야 한다고 말했다. 그는 가슴이 내려앉았다.

① 당황한 → 무관심한
② 신이 난 → 실망한
③ 즐거운 → 부끄러운
④ 긴장한 → 감동한
⑤ 무서운 → 편안한

문제풀이

엄마와 함께 공원을 갈 거라는 말을 듣고 신이 난 Matthew는 공원에 도착하자마자 가장 좋아하던 그네를 타려 했지만 그네가 이미 다 사용 중이었고, 대신 미끄럼틀을 타려 했지만 부서져있는 상태이며, 설상가상으로 어머니가 전화를 받은 뒤 떠나야 한다고 말씀하셔서 가슴이 내려앉은 상황이다. 따라서 Matthew의 심경 변화로 ② 'excited → disappointed(신이 난 → 실망한)'가 가장 적절하다.

어휘·어구

get dressed 옷을 입다
available 이용할 수 있는
broken 부서진, 고장 난
embarrassed 당황한
indifferent 무관심한
disappointed 실망한
cheerful 즐거운
ashamed 부끄러운
nervous 긴장한
touched 감동한
relaxed 편안한, 긴장을 푼

3. ③ 학업 최우수상을 받은 Zoe

직독/직해

The principal stepped on stage.
교장 선생님이 무대 위로 올라갔다

"Now, / I present this year's top academic award /
이제 / 올해의 학업 최우수상을 수여하겠습니다 /

to the student / 학생에게 /

who has achieved the highest placing."
최고 등수를 차지한

He smiled at the row of seats /
그는 좌석 열을 향해 미소를 지었다 /

where twelve finalists had gathered.
열두 명의 최종 입상 후보자가 모여 있는

Zoe wiped a sweaty hand / on her handkerchief /
Zoe는 땀에 젖은 손을 문질러 닦았다 / 손수건에 /

and glanced at the other finalists.
그리고 나머지 다른 최종 입상 후보자들을 힐끗 보았다

They all looked as pale and uneasy / as herself.
그들은 모두 창백하고 불안해 보였다 / 그녀만큼

Zoe and one of the other finalists /
Zoe와 다른 최종 입상 후보자 중 한 명이 /

had won first placing / in four subjects /
1등을 차지했다 / 네 개 과목에서 /

so it came down to / how teachers ranked /
그래서 좁혀졌다 / 선생님들이 어떻게 평가 하느냐로 /

their hard work and confidence.
그들의 노력과 자신감을

"The Trophy for General Excellence /
전체 최우수상을 위한 트로피는 /

is awarded to Miss Zoe Perry," /
Zoe Perry 양에게 수여됩니다 /

the principal declared. 교장 선생님이 공표했다

"Could Zoe step this way, please?"
Zoe는 이리로 나와 주시겠습니까

Zoe felt / as if she were in heaven.
Zoe는 느꼈다 / 마치 천국에 있는 것처럼

She walked into the thunder of applause /
그녀는 우레와 같은 박수갈채를 받으며 걸어갔다 /

with a big smile. 환하게 웃으며

교장 선생님이 무대 위로 올라갔다. "이제, 최고 등수를 차지한 학생에게 올해의 학업 최우수상을 수여하겠습니다." 그는 열두 명의 최종 입상 후보자가 모여 있는 좌석 열을 향해 미소를 지었다. Zoe는 땀에 젖은 손을 손수건에 문질러 닦고 나머지 다른 최종 입상 후보자들을 힐끗 보았다. 그들은 모두 그녀만큼 창백하고 불안해 보였다. Zoe와 다른 최종 입상 후보자 중 한 명이 네 개 과목에서 1등을 차지했으므로, 그들의 노력과 자신감을 선생님들이 어떻게 평가 하느냐로 좁혀졌다. "전체 최우수상을 위한 트로피는 Zoe Perry 양에게 수여됩니다."라고 교장 선생님이 공표했다. "Zoe는 이리로 나와 주시겠습니까?" Zoe는 마치 천국에 있는 기분이었다. 그녀는 환하게 웃으며 우레와 같은 박수갈채를 받으며 걸어갔다.

① 희망에 찬 → 실망한
② 죄책감이 있는 → 자신 있는
③ 긴장한 → 기쁜
④ 화난 → 침착한
⑤ 느긋한 → 자랑스러운

문제풀이

교장 선생님의 학업 최우수상 발표를 앞두고 손에 땀이 날 정도로 긴장한 Zoe가 결국 최우수상 대상자로 호명되어 상을 받으러 나가는 상황이므로, Zoe의 심경 변화로 ③ 'nervous → delighted(긴장한 → 기쁜)'가 가장 적절하다.

어휘·어구

principal (학)교장
present 수여하다
academic 학업의
award 상
row 열, 횡렬
finalist 최종 입상 후보자
gather 모이다
sweaty 땀에 젖은
handkerchief 손수건
glance 힐끗 보다
pale 창백한
uneasy 불안한
subject 과목
rank 평가하다, 순위를 매기다
confidence 자신감
declare 선언하다, 분명히 말하다
applause 박수갈채
guilty 죄책감이 있는
relaxed 느긋한

정답률 92%

4. ⑤ 기대한 것과 다른 엄마의 선물

직독/직해

When my mom came home from the mall /
엄마가 상점에서 집에 왔을 때 /

with a special present for me /
나를 위한 특별한 선물을 가지고 /

I was pretty sure / I knew what it was.
나는 꽤 확신했다 / 내가 그것이 무엇인지 알고 있다고

I was absolutely thrilled / 나는 완전히 들떴다 /

because I would soon communicate with a new cell phone!
왜냐하면 곧 새로운 휴대폰으로 소통할 것이기 때문이었다

I was daydreaming / 나는 상상에 잠겨 있었다 /

about all of the cool apps and games /
모든 멋진 앱과 게임에 대해 /

I was going to download. 내가 다운로드할

But my mom smiled really big /
하지만 엄마는 매우 크게 미소지었다 /

and handed me a book. 그리고 나에게 책 한 권을 건네주었다

I flipped through the pages, /
나는 책장을 넘겨보았다 /

figuring that maybe she had hidden my new phone inside.
아마도 그녀가 나의 새로운 휴대폰을 안에 숨겨 두었을 것이라 생각하며

But I slowly realized / 그러나 나는 서서히 깨달았다 /

that my mom had not got me a phone /
나는 엄마가 나에게 휴대폰을 사 주지 않았다는 것을 /

and my present was just a little book, /
그리고 나의 선물이 겨우 작은 책이라는 것을 /

which was so different from what I had wanted.
그것은 내가 원했던 것과는 너무 달랐다

엄마가 나를 위한 특별한 선물을 가지고 상점에서 집에 왔을 때 나는 그것이 무엇인지 알고 있다고 꽤 확신했다. 나는 완전히 들떴는데 왜냐하면 곧 새로운 휴대폰으로 소통할 것이기 때문이었다! 나는 내가 다운로드할 모든 멋진 앱과 게임에 대해 상상에 잠겨 있었다. 하지만 엄마는 매우 크게 미소지으며 나에게 책 한 권을 건네주었다. 나는 아마도 그녀가 나의 새로운 휴대폰을 안에 숨겨 두었을 것이라 생각하며 책장을 넘겨보았다. 그러나 나는 엄마가 나에게 휴대폰을 사 주지 않았고 나의 선물이 겨우 작은 책이라는 것을 서서히 깨달았으며, 그것은 내가 원했던 것과는 너무 달랐다.

① 걱정하는 → 분노하는
② 놀란 → 안도한
③ 부끄러운 → 확신하는
④ 기대하는 → 만족한
⑤ 흥분한 → 실망한

문제풀이

엄마가 상점에서 사온 선물이 새 휴대폰일 것이라고 들떠있다가 막상 엄마가 주신 선물이 겨우 작은 책 한권이라는 것을 알고 매우 실망한 상황이므로 'I'의 심경 변화로 ⑤ 'excited(흥분한) → disappointed(실망한)'가 가장 적절하다.

어휘·어구

thrilled 신이 난
daydream 공상에 빠지다
figure 생각하다

5. ⑤ 한밤중에 잠에서 깬 Matt

직독/직해

In the middle of the night, / Matt suddenly awakened.
한밤중에 / Matt는 갑자기 잠에서 깼다

He glanced at his clock.
그는 그의 시계를 흘긋 보았다

It was 3:23. 3시 23분이었다

For just an instant / he wondered /
잠시 동안 / 그는 궁금했다 /

what had wakened him. 무엇이 그를 깨웠는지

Then he remembered. 그때 그는 기억했다

He had heard someone come into his room.
그는 누군가 그의 방에 들어온 것을 들었다

Matt sat up in bed, / rubbed his eyes, /
Matt는 침대에 꼿꼿이 앉았다 / 눈을 비볐다 /

and looked around the small room.
그리고 작은 방을 둘러보았다

"Mom?" he said quietly, /
그는 "엄마?"라고 조용히 말했다 /

hoping he would hear his mother's voice /
엄마의 목소리를 듣기를 바라면서 /

assuring him / that everything was all right.

그를 안심시키는 / 모든 것이 괜찮다고

But there was no answer.
그런데 답이 없었다

Matt tried to tell himself /
Matt는 스스로에게 말하려고 애썼다 /

that he was just hearing things.
그가 막 물건들의 소리를 들었다고

But he knew / he wasn't.
하지만 그는 알았다 / 그가 그렇지 않았다는 것을

There was someone / in his room.
누군가가 있었다 / 그의 방에

He could hear rhythmic, scratchy breathing /
그는 규칙적으로 긁는 듯한 숨소리를 들을 수 있었다 /

and it wasn't his own.
그리고 그것은 그의 것이 아니었다

He lay awake / for the rest of the night.
그는 깬 상태로 누워있었다 / 남은 밤 동안

한밤중에, Matt는 갑자기 잠에서 깼다. 그는 그의 시계를 흘긋 보았다. 3시 23분이었다. 잠시 동안 그는 무엇이 그를 깨웠는지 궁금했다. 그때 그는 기억했다. 그는 누군가 그의 방에 들어온 것을 들었다. Matt는 침대에 꼿꼿이 앉아서 눈을 비비고 작은 방을 둘러보았다. 모든 것이 괜찮다고 그를 안심시키는 엄마의 목소리를 듣기를 바라면서 그는 "엄마?"라고 조용히 말했다. 그런데 답이 없었다. Matt는 그가 막 물건들의 소리를 들었다고 스스로에게 말하려고 애썼다. 하지만 그는 그렇지 않았다는 것을 알았다. 누군가가 그의 방에 있었다. 그는 규칙적으로 긁는 듯한 숨소리를 들을 수 있었고, 그것은 그의 것이 아니었다. 그는 남은 밤 동안 깬 상태로 누워있었다.

① 익살스럽고 재미있는 ② 지루하고 따분한
③ 차분하고 평화로운 ④ 시끄럽고 신 나는
⑤ 기이하고 무서운

문제풀이

한밤중에 자신의 방에 누군가 들어온 소리를 듣고 잠에서 깬 후 무서워하면서 남은 밤 동안 깬 상태로 누워있었다고 한 것으로 보아, 글의 분위기로 ⑤ 'mysterious and frightening(기이하고 무서운)'이 가장 적절하다.

어휘·어구

awaken 깨다
glance at ~을 흘끗 보다
assure 안심시키다
rhythmic 리드미컬한, 규칙적으로 순환하는
scratchy 긁는 듯한
humorous 익살스러운
dull 따분한
mysterious 기이한
frightening 무서운

정답률 80%

6. ③ 유명 화가의 그림 값

직독/직해

One day, / 어느 날 /
Cindy happened to sit next to a famous artist /
Cindy는 우연히 유명한 화가 옆에 앉게 되었다 /

in a café, / and she was thrilled to see him / in person.
한 카페에서 / 그리고 그녀는 그를 만나게 되어 감격했다 / 직접

He was drawing / on a used napkin / over coffee.
그는 그림을 그리고 있었다 / 사용한 냅킨에 / 커피를 마시면서

She was looking on / in awe.
그녀는 지켜보고 있었다 / 경외심을 가지고

After a few moments, / the man finished his coffee /
잠시 후 / 그 남자는 커피를 다 마셨다 /

and was about to throw away the napkin / as he left.
그리고 그 냅킨을 버리려고 했다 / 자리를 뜨면서

Cindy stopped him. Cindy는 그를 멈춰 세웠다

"Can I have that napkin / you drew on?", / she asked.
냅킨을 제가 가져도 될까요 / 당신이 그림을 그렸던 / 그녀가 물었다

"Sure," / he replied.

그럼요 / 그가 대답했다

"Twenty thousand dollars."
2만 달러입니다

She said, / with her eyes wide-open, /
그녀는 말했다 / 눈을 동그랗게 뜨고 /

"What? / It took you like two minutes / to draw that."
뭐라고요 / 당신은 2분밖에 안 걸렸잖아요 / 그것을 그리는 데

"No," / he said.
아니요 / 그가 말했다

"It took me over sixty years / to draw this."
나는 60년 넘게 걸렸어요 / 이것을 그리는 데

Being at a loss, / she stood still rooted to the ground.
어쩔 줄 몰라 / 그녀는 꼼짝 못한 채 서 있었다

어느 날, Cindy는 우연히 한 카페에서 유명한 화가 옆에 앉게 되었고, 그녀는 그를 직접 만나게 되어 감격했다. 그는 커피를 마시면서 사용한 냅킨에 그림을 그리고 있었다. 그녀는 경외심을 가지고 지켜보고 있었다. 잠시 후, 그 남자는 커피를 다 마시고 나서 자리를 뜨면서 그 냅킨을 버리려고 했다. Cindy는 그를 멈춰 세웠다. "당신이 그림을 그렸던 냅킨을 제가 가져도 될까요?"라고 그녀가 물었다. "그럼요."라고 그가 대답했다. "2만 달러입니다." 그녀는 눈을 동그랗게 뜨고 말했다. "뭐라고요? 당신은 그것을 그리는 데 2분밖에 안 걸렸잖아요." "아니요." 라고 그가 말했다. "나는 이것을 그리는 데 60년 넘게 걸렸어요." 그녀는 어쩔 줄 몰라 꼼짝 못한 채 서 있었다.

① 안심한 → 걱정하는 ② 무관심한 → 당황한
③ 신나는 → 놀란 ④ 실망한 → 만족한
⑤ 질투 나는 → 자신감 있는

문제풀이

커피숍에서 우연히 만난 유명 화가가 냅킨에 그린 그림을 버리려고 하는 것을 보고 냅킨을 가져도 되는지를 물었는데, 화가가 흔쾌히 수락하면서 무려 2만 달러를 요구해서 당황한 상황이므로, Cindy의 심경 변화로 ③ 'excited(신나는) → surprised(놀란)'가 가장 적절하다.

어휘·어구

over ~하면서
awe 경외심
at a loss 어찌 할 줄 몰라 하는
relieved 안심한
indifferent 무관심한
embarrassed 당황한
satisfied 만족한
jealous 질투 나는
confident 자신감 있는

7. ① 새 이웃에 대한 호기심과 기대

직독/직해

On the way home, / Shirley noticed a truck parked /
집에 오는 길에 / Shirley는 트럭 한 대를 알아차렸다 /

in front of the house across the street.
길 건너편 집 앞에 주차된

New neighbors! 새 이웃이었다

Shirley was dying to know about them.
Shirley는 그들에 대해 알고 싶어 죽을 지경이었다

"Do you know anything about the new neighbors?" /
새 이웃에 대해 뭔가 알고 계세요 /

she asked Pa at dinner.
그녀는 저녁 식사 시간에 아빠에게 물었다.

He said, / "Yes, / and there's one thing /
그는 말했다 / 그럼 / 그리고 한 가지 있지 /

that may be interesting to you."
네 흥미를 끌 만한 것이

Shirley had a billion more questions.
Shirley는 더 묻고 싶은 게 엄청나게 많았다.

Pa said joyfully, / "They have a girl just your age.
아빠는 기쁘게 말했다 / 그들에게는 딱 네 나이의 여자아이가 한 명 있어

Maybe she wants to be your playmate."
아마도 그 애는 네 놀이 친구가 되고 싶을지도 몰라

Shirley nearly dropped her fork / on the floor.
Shirley는 거의 포크를 떨어뜨릴 뻔했다 / 바닥에

How many times had she prayed for a friend?
그녀가 얼마나 많이 친구를 달라고 기도했던가

Finally, / her prayers were answered!
마침내 / 그녀의 기도가 응답받았다

She and the new girl could go to school together, /
그녀와 새로 온 여자아이는 함께 학교에 갈 수 있을지도 모른다 /

play together, / and become best friends.
함께 놀 (수 있을지도 모른다) / 그리고 제일 친한 친구가 될 (수 있을지도 모른다)

집에 오는 길에, Shirley는 트럭 한 대가 길 건너편 집 앞에 주차된 것을 알아차렸다. 새 이웃이었다! Shirley는 그들에 대해 알고 싶어 죽을 지경이었다. 저녁 식사 시간에 그녀는 "새 이웃에 대해 뭔가 알고 계세요?"라고 아빠에게 물었다. 그는 "그럼. 그리고 네 흥미를 끌 만한 것이 한 가지 있지."라고 말했다. Shirley는 더 묻고 싶은 게 엄청나게 많았다. 아빠는 "그들에게는 딱 네 나이의 여자아이가 한 명 있어. 아마도 그 애는 네 놀이 친구가 되고 싶을지도 몰라."라고 기쁘게 말했다. Shirley는 거의 포크를 바닥에 떨어뜨릴 뻔했다. 그녀가 얼마나 많이 친구를 달라고 기도했던가? 마침내 그녀의 기도가 응답받았다! 그녀와 새로 온 여자아이는 함께 학교에 가고, 함께 놀고, 그리고 제일 친한 친구가 될 수 있을지도 모른다.

① 호기심 있고 신나는
② 미안하고 속상한
③ 질투가 나고 짜증나는
④ 차분하고 느긋한
⑤ 실망스럽고 불행한

문제풀이

새로 생긴 이웃에게 같은 또래의 친구가 있음을 알고 그동안 친구를 달라고 열심히 기도했었던 Shirley가 기뻐하고 기대하고 있는 상황이므로, Shirley의 심경으로 ① 'curious and excited(호기심 있고 신나는)'가 가장 적절하다.

어휘·어구

notice 알아차리다
park 주차하다
neighbor 이웃
be dying to do ~하고 싶은 생각이 간절하다
interesting 흥미를 끄는
joyfully 기쁘게
playmate 놀이 친구
pray 기도하다
curious 호기심 있는
jealous 질투심이 많은
annoyed 짜증이 난
relaxed 느긋한
disappointed 실망한

정답률 78%

8. ① 생일 선물로 받은 개가 사라짐

직독/직해

On my seventh birthday, / my mom surprised me /
나의 일곱 번째 생일에 / 우리 엄마는 나를 놀라게 했다 /

with a puppy waiting on a leash.
목줄을 매고 기다리고 있는 개로

It had beautiful golden fur and an adorable tail.
그것은 아름다운 황금빛 털과 사랑스러운 꼬리를 가지고 있었다

It was exactly what I had always dreamed of.
그것은 바로 내가 항상 꿈꿨던 것이었다

I took the dog everywhere /
나는 그 개를 어디든지 데리고 다녔다 /

and slept with it every night.
그리고 매일 밤 같이 잤다

A few months later, / 몇 달 후에 /
the dog got out of the backyard / and was lost.
그 개는 뒷마당에서 빠져나갔다 / 그리고 사라졌다

I sat on my bed / and cried for hours /
나는 나는 침대에 앉았다 / 그리고 몇 시간 동안 울었다 /
while my mother watched me silently /
엄마가 조용히 나를 바라보는 동안 /
from the doorway of my room.
내 방 문간에서
I finally fell asleep, / exhausted from my grief.
나는 마침내 잠이 들었다 / 슬픔에 지쳐
My mother never said a word to me /
엄마는 절대 나에게 한마디도 하지 않았다 /
about my loss, /
나의 상실에 관해 /
but I knew / she felt the same as I did.
하지만 나는 알았다 / 엄마도 나와 똑같이 느꼈다는 것을

나의 일곱 번째 생일에, 우리 엄마는 목줄을 매고 기다리고 있는 개로 나를 놀라게 했다. 그것은 아름다운 황금빛 털과 사랑스러운 꼬리를 가지고 있었다. 그것은 바로 내가 항상 꿈꿨던 것이었다. 나는 그 개를 어디든지 데리고 다녔고 매일 밤 같이 잤다. 몇 달 후에, 그 개는 뒷마당에서 빠져나가 사라졌다. 엄마가 내 방 문간에서 조용히 나를 바라보는 동안 나는 침대에 앉아 몇 시간 동안 울었다. 나는 마침내 슬픔에 지쳐 잠이 들었다. 엄마는 절대 나의 상실에 관해 나에게 한마디도 하지 않았지만, 나는 엄마도 나와 똑같이 느꼈다는 것을 알았다.

① 기쁜 → 슬픈 ② 느긋한 → 짜증이 난
③ 당황한 → 걱정하는 ④ 신이 난 → 겁에 질린
⑤ 실망한 → 만족한

문제풀이

항상 꿈꿔왔던 개를 생일 선물로 받아 기뻤지만 몇 달 후 개가 사라져서 슬퍼했던 상황이므로, 'I'의 심경 변화로 ① 'delighted(기쁜) → sorrowful(슬픈)'이 가장 적절하다.

어휘·어구

leash 개 목줄, 사슬
adorable 사랑스러운
doorway 문간
exhaust 기진맥진하게 만들다
grief 슬픔, 비탄
delighted 기쁜
sorrowful 슬픈
relaxed 편안한, 느긋한
annoyed 짜증이 난
embarrassed 당황한
horrified 겁에 질린
disappointed 실망한
satisfied 만족한

9. ① 청중 앞에서의 발표

직독/직해

Salva had to raise money / Salva는 모금을 해야 했다 /
for a project to help southern Sudan.
남부 수단을 돕기 위한 프로젝트를 위해서
It was the first time that Salva spoke in front of an audience.
Salva가 관중 앞에서 말하는 것은 처음이었다
There were more than a hundred people.
백 명이 넘는 사람들이 있었다
Salva's knees were shaking /
Salva의 다리가 후들거리고 있었다 /
as he walked to the microphone.
그가 마이크로 걸어갈 때
"H-h-hello," he said.
"아-아-안녕하세요," 그가 말했다
His hands trembling, / 그의 손이 떨리면서 /
he looked out at the audience.
그는 관중을 바라보았다
Everyone was looking at him.
모든 사람들이 그를 보고 있었다
At that moment, / 그때 /
he noticed that every face looked interested /
그는 모든 얼굴이 관심을 보이는 것을 알아챘다 /
in what he had to say. 그가 할 말에
People were smiling and seemed friendly.
사람들은 미소 짓고 있었고 우호적으로 보였다
That made him feel a little better, /
그것이 그의 기분을 좀 더 나아지게 했다 /
so he spoke into the microphone again.
그래서 그는 다시 마이크에 대고 말했다
"Hello," he repeated. "안녕하세요," 그는 반복했다
He smiled, feeling at ease, / and went on.
그는 안심하여 미소를 지었다 / 그리고 말을 이어갔다
"I am here / 저는 이 자리에 섰습니다 /
to talk to you about a project for southern Sudan."
남부 수단을 위한 프로젝트에 관해 여러분께 말씀드리고자

Salva는 남부 수단을 돕기 위한 프로젝트를 위해서 모금을 해야 했다. Salva가 관중 앞에서 말하는 것은 처음이었다. 백 명이 넘는 사람들이 있었다. 그가 마이크로 걸어갈 때 Salva의 다리가 후들거리고 있었다. "아-아-안녕하세요," 그가 말했다. 그의 손이 떨리면서, 그는 관중을 바라보았다. 모든 사람들이 그를 보고 있었다. 그때, 그는 모든 얼굴이 그가 할 말에 관심이 있어보임을 알아차렸다. 사람들은 미소 짓고 있었고 우호적으로 보였다. 그것이 그의 기분을 좀 더 나아지게 해서 그는 다시 마이크에 대고 말했다. "안녕하세요," 그는 반복했다. 그는 안심하여 미소를 지었고 말을 이어갔다. "저는 남부 수단을 위한 프로젝트에 관해 여러분께 말씀드리려고 이 자리에 섰습니다."

① 긴장한 → 안도한
② 무관심한 → 신이 난
③ 걱정스러운 → 실망한
④ 만족한 → 좌절한
⑤ 자신 있는 → 당황한

문제풀이

Salva가 백 명이 넘는 사람들 앞에서 처음으로 말을 하게 되어 다리가 후들거리고 손이 떨렸는데 미소 짓는 사람들의 우호적인 모습을 보고서 안심하고 말을 이어갔다고 했다. 따라서 Salva의 심경 변화로 가장 적절한 것은 ① 'nervous(긴장한) → 안도한(relieved)'이다.

어휘·어구

raise money 모금하다
audience 청중, 관중
tremble 떨다, 진동하다
notice 알아채다
feel at ease 편안하게 느끼다
go on 이야기를 계속하다

10. ① 일상의 부담에서 벗어난 자연 속 힐링

직독/직해

Erda lay on her back in a clearing, /
Erda는 숲속의 빈터에 드러누웠다 /
watching drops of sunlight slide /
햇살 가닥들이 스며드는 것을 보면서 /
through the mosaic of leaves / above her.
모자이크 모양의 나뭇잎 사이로 / 그녀 위쪽의
She joined them for a little, /
그녀는 잠시 그들과 함께 했다 /
moving with the gentle breeze, /
부드러운 미풍과 함께 움직이면서 /
feeling the warm sun feed her.
따뜻한 태양이 그녀에게 자양분을 주는 것을 느끼며
A slight smile was spreading / over her face.
옅은 미소가 번지고 있었다 / 그녀의 얼굴에
She slowly turned over / 그녀는 천천히 몸을 뒤집었다 /
and pushed her face into the grass, /
그리고 그녀의 얼굴을 풀밭으로 내밀었다 /
smelling the green pleasant scent /
푸르고 쾌적한 향기를 맡으면서 /
from the fresh wild flowers.
신선한 야생화로부터 풍겨오는
Free from her daily burden, / she got to her feet /
그녀의 일상의 부담으로부터 벗어나 / 그녀는 일어섰다 /
and went on. 그리고 계속 갔다
Erda walked / between the warm trunks of the trees.
Erda 걸었다 / 나무들의 따뜻한 기둥 사이를
She felt / all her concerns had gone away.
그녀는 느꼈다 / 그녀의 모든 걱정들이 사라져 버렸다는 것을

Erda는 숲속의 빈터에 드러누워 그녀 위쪽의 모자이크 모양의 나뭇잎 사이로 부서진 햇살이 스며드는 것을 지켜보았다. 그녀는 따뜻한 태양이 자신에게 자양분을 주는 것을 느끼며, 미풍을 따라 움직이면서 그것들과 잠시 함께했다. 그녀의 얼굴에 옅은 미소가 번지고 있었다. 그녀는 몸을 천천히 돌려 신선한 야생화로부터 풍겨오는 푸르고 쾌적한 향기를 맡으며 풀밭으로 얼굴을 내밀었다. 일상의 부담에서 벗어나 그녀는 일어서서 걸었다. Erda는 나무들의 따뜻한 기둥 사이를 걸었다. 그녀는 모든 걱정이 사라졌음을 느꼈다.

① 편안한 ② 당혹스러운 ③ 부러워하는 ④ 놀란 ⑤ 무관심한

문제풀이

Erda가 숲속의 빈터에서 누워서 따스한 햇살을 느끼고, 야생화의 쾌적한 향기를 맡으면서 옅은 미소를 짓고 있는 모습을 묘사하는 내용이다. 'Free from her daily burden(일상의 부담으로부터 벗어나)'와 'She felt all her concerns had gone away.(그녀는 모든 걱정이 사라졌음을 느꼈다.)'로 보아 Erda의 심경으로 가장 적절한 것은 ① 'relaxed(편안한)'이다.

어휘·어구

lie on one's back 반듯이(바로) 눕다
clearing (숲속의) 빈터
mosaic 모자이크
breeze 미풍
scent 향기, 냄새
burden 부담
trunk (나무의) 기둥
concern 걱정, 근심
relaxed 편안한
puzzled 당혹스러운
envious 부러워하는
startled 놀란
indifferent 무관심한

11. ⑤ 돌고래의 도움

직독/직해

I was diving alone in about 40 feet of water /
40피트 정도의 물속에서 혼자 잠수하고 있었다 /
when I got a terrible stomachache.
그때 나는 배가 심하게 아팠다
I was sinking and hardly able to move.
나는 가라앉고 있었고 거의 움직일 수가 없었다
I could see my watch / 나는 시계를 볼 수 있었다 /
and knew there was only a little more time on the tank / before I would be out of air.
그리고 탱크 잔여 시간이 조금 밖에 없다는 것을 알았다 / 공기가 다 써서 없어지기 전까지
It was hard / for me to remove my weight belt.
힘들었다 / 내가 중량 벨트를 벗기가
Suddenly I felt a prodding / from behind me under the armpit.
갑자기 나는 쿡 찌르는 것을 느꼈다 / 뒤에서 겨드랑이 밑으로
My arm was being lifted forcibly.
내 팔이 강제로 들어 올려지고 있었다

Around into my field of vision / came an eye.
내 시야의 언저리로 / 눈이 하나 들어왔다

It seemed to be smiling.
그것은 웃고 있는 것 같았다

It was the eye of a big dolphin.
그것은 큰 돌고래의 눈이었다

Looking into that eye, / I knew I was safe.
그 눈을 들여다보니 / 나는 안전하다는 것을 알았다

I felt that the animal was protecting me, /
나는 그 동물이 나를 보호해 주고 있다고 느꼈다 /

lifting me toward the surface.
수면으로 나를 밀어 올리며

40피트 정도의 물속에서 혼자 잠수하고 있었을 때, 나는 배가 심하게 아팠다. 나는 가라앉고 있었고 거의 움직일 수가 없었다. 나는 시계를 볼 수 있었고 공기가 다 써서 없어지기 전까지 (산소) 탱크 잔여 시간이 조금 밖에 없다는 것을 알았다. 중량 벨트를 벗기가 힘들었다. 갑자기 나는 뒤에서 겨드랑이 밑으로 쿡 찌르는 것을 느꼈다. 내 팔이 강제로 들어 올려지고 있었다. 내 시야에 눈이 하나 들어왔다. 그것은 웃고 있는 것 같았다. 그것은 큰 돌고래의 눈이었다. 그 눈을 들여다보니, 나는 안전하다는 것을 알았다. 나는 그 동물이 수면으로 나를 밀어 올려 보호해 주고 있다고 느꼈다.

① 신이 난 → 지루한
② 기쁜 → 화가 난
③ 질투하는 → 감사하는
④ 자랑스러운 → 당황하는
⑤ 겁이 난 → 안도한

문제풀이

나는 홀로 다이빙을 하다가 심한 복통을 느꼈고 탱크에 산소가 얼마 남지 않았는데 스스로 중량 벨트를 벗기 힘들어하고 있다. 이때 갑자기 돌고래가 뒤에서 나를 수면 위로 밀어 올려주고 있는 상황이다. 따라서 나의 심경변화로 가장 적절한 것은 ⑤ 'frightened(겁이 난) → relieved(안도한)'이다.

어휘·어구

stomachache 복통
sink 가라앉다
hardly 거의 ~않다
remove 벗다, 제거하다
weight belt 중량 벨트 (잠수·운동 때 무게를 더하기 위해 착용하는 벨트·재킷)
armpit 겨드랑이
lift 들어 올리다, 올리다
forcibly 강제적으로, 강력하게
field of vision 시야
surface 표면

12. ① 빨갛게 타고 있던 난로

직독/직해

Norm and his friend Jason / went on a winter
Norm과 그의 친구 Jason은 / 겨울 캠프 여행을 갔다

camping trip.

In the middle of the night, / Norm suddenly woke
한밤중에 / Norm은 갑자기 감지하고 잠에서 깼다

up sensing / something was terribly wrong.
/ 무언가가 대단히 잘못된 것을

To his surprise, / the stove was glowing red!
놀랍게도 / 난로가 빨갛게 타고 있었다

Norm shook Jason awake / and told him to look at
Norm은 Jason을 흔들어 깨웠고 / 그에게 난로를 보라고 말했다

the stove.

Jason said / he had filled it with every piece of wood /
Jason은 말했다 / 자신이 모든 나뭇조각을 난로에 채웠다고 /

he could fit into it. 거기에 끼워 넣을 수 있는

Norm thought / the cabin was going to catch fire.
Norm은 생각했다 / 오두막에 불이 날 것이라고

He started swearing at Jason.
그는 Jason에게 욕을 하기 시작했다

He pulled Jason out of his bed, / opened the front
그는 Jason을 그의 침대 밖으로 끌어내려 / 앞문을 열고

door / and threw him out into the snow.
/ 그를 눈 속으로 내쫓았다

Norm yelled out in anger, / "Don't come back in /
Norm은 화가 나서 소리쳤다 / 들어오지 마 /

until I get this stove cooled off!"
내가 이 난로를 식힐 때까지

Norm과 그의 친구 Jason은 겨울 캠프 여행을 갔다. 한밤중에 Norm은 갑자기 무언가가 대단히 잘못된 것을 감지하고 잠에서 깼다. 놀랍게도 난로가 빨갛게 타고 있었다! Norm은 Jason을 흔들어 깨웠고 그에게 난로를 보라고 말했다. Jason은 자신이 거기에 끼워 넣을 수 있는 모든 나뭇조각을 난로에 채웠다고 말했다. Norm은 오두막에 불이 날 것이라고 생각했다. 그는 Jason에게 욕을 하기 시작했다. 그는 Jason을 그의 침대 밖으로 끌어내려 앞문을 열고 그를 눈 속으로 내쫓았다. Norm은 화가 나서 "내가 이 난로를 식힐 때까지 들어오지 마!"라고 소리쳤다.

① 놀라고 화가 난
② 흥분하고 기쁜
③ 감동받고 고마워하는
④ 부끄럽고 죄책감이 드는
⑤ 고무되고 만족하는

문제풀이

Norm은 한밤중에 난로가 빨갛게 타고 있는 것을 보고 놀라 Jason에게 난로를 살펴보라고 했지만, Jason이 모든 나뭇조각을 난로에 채운 것 때문에 불이 날 것처럼 난로가 타고 있었다는 사실을 알고 화를 내며 Jason을 쫓아낸 상황이므로, Norm의 심경으로 ① 'alarmed and upset(놀라고 화가 난)'이 가장 적절하다.

어휘·어구

catch fire 불붙다
swear 욕을 하다
cool off 식히다

본문 011쪽

문법 플러스 2. 주어의 이해

1. To keep 2. is 3. That 4. Whether
5. What 6. It 7. of her 8. do we realize
9. does TV take up 10. had Charlie

1 [해석]▶ 사업할 때 약속을 지키는 것은 매우 중요하다.
[해설]▶ 부정사(구)는 문장 속에서 주어 역할을 할 수 있다. 동사 Keep을 선택하면, 문장 속에서 동사가 2개가 되어 틀린 문장이 된다.

2 [해석]▶ 지금보다 더 많은 직원을 고용한다는 것은 비용 낭비다.
[해설]▶ 동명사가 이끄는 구는 문장의 주어 역할을 할 수 있다. 동명사구는 단수 동사를 취한다.

3 [해석]▶ 우주가 팽창하고 있다는 것은 현대 우주론의 기본 개념들 중의 하나이다.
[해설]▶ 접속사 that은 주어 역할을 할 수 있다. That ~ expanding이 문장의 주어에 해당한다.

4 [해석]▶ 이기느냐 지느냐의 여부는 게임 기술에 달려 있다.
[해설]▶ that과 whether는 문장 속에서 주어의 역할을 할 수 있는데, A냐 B냐, A일지, B일지와 같은 선택을 나타내는 의미가 나올 경우에는 whether가 적절하다.

5 [해석]▶ 그가 나에게 준 것은 그의 웹 사이트와 이메일 주소였다.
[해설]▶ 관계사 what은 문장 속에서 주어 역할을 하는 절을 이끌 수 있다. '그가 내게 준 모든 것'이므로 what(= The things that)을 쓰는 것이 적절하다.

6 [해석]▶ 엎질러진 우유를 보고 울어 봤자 소용없다.
[해설]▶ it은 가주어, crying ~ milk는 진주어이다. 주어가 길 경우 가주어를 문장 앞에 두고, 진주어를 뒤로 보낸다.

7 [해석]▶ 그녀가 그렇게 말하는 것을 보니 그녀는 정직하다.
[해설]▶ 사람의 성질을 나타내는 형용사가 올 때는 「of+목적격」을 쓰고, 그 외의 경우는 「for+목적격」을 쓴다. honest는 성질을 나타내는 형용사이다.

8 [해석]▶ 건강을 잃고 나서야 우리는 그 소중함을 깨닫는다.
[해설]▶ 부사구 only가 문두에 나오면, 「주어+동사」 어순이 「동사+주어」, 또는 「조동사+주어+동사」 어순으로 바뀐다.

9 [해석]▶ TV는 Jack의 시간을 더 많이 차지할 뿐만 아니라 그로 하여금 더 많은 인스턴트 음식을 먹도록 유혹한다.
[해설]▶ 부정어(Not only)가 문두에 나오면 「동사+주어」 또는 「조동사+주어+동사」 순서로 도치된다.

10 [해석]▶ 찰리가 나를 보자마자 도망갔다.
[해설]▶ 부정어(No sooner)가 문두에 나오면 「조동사+주어+동사」 순서로 도치된다. no sooner A than B는 'A 하자마자 B'하다는 의미이다.

본문 012쪽

어휘 플러스 2. 유의어 (1)

1. achieved 2. accumulated
3. anticipate 4. complicated
5. composed

1 [해석]▶ 르네상스 시대의 예술가들은 기하학을 사용하여 원근법을 성취했는데 그것은 실제 세계를 사실적이고 정확하고 3차원적으로 묘사하게 했다.

2 [해석]▶ 일부 저명한 언론인은 보물 사냥꾼이 과거에 대해 많은 것을 드러낼 수 있는 가치 있는 역사적 유물을 축적해 왔기 때문에 고고학자는 보물 사냥꾼과 협업해야 한다고 말한다.

3 [해석]▶ 우리는 마치 미래가 너무 느리게 오고 있다고 생각해서 그것을 서둘러 오게 하려고 하는 것처럼 미래를 고대한다.

4 [해석]▶ 줄거리가 복잡하거든. 나의 경우에, 소설을 먼저 읽은 것이 그 뮤지컬을 완전하게 이해하고 더 잘 즐기는 데 도움이 되었어.

5 [해석]▶ 내가 알기로는, 그가 컴퓨터로 작곡한 모든 종류의 실험 음악을 우리에게 소개할 것 같아.

03. 필자의 주장

Day 03

본문 014쪽

1. ④ 2. ⑤ 3. ⑤ 4. ③ 5. ③
6. ① 7. ③ 8. ② 9. ② 10. ⑤
11. ④ 12. ⑤

대표 기출 ⑤ 상업용 블로그는 사람들이 흥미 있어 할 정보를 제공해야 한다

직독/직해

You already have a business /
여러분은 이미 사업체를 가지고 있다 /
and you're about to launch your blog /
그리고 여러분의 블로그를 막 시작하려는 참이다 /
so that you can sell your product.
여러분의 제품을 팔 수 있도록
Unfortunately, / here is where /
유감스럽게도 / 여기가 지점이다 /
a 'business mind' can be a bad thing.
'비즈니스 정신'이 나쁜 것이 될 수 있는
Most people believe / that to have a successful business blog promoting a product, /
대부분의 사람은 믿는다 / 제품을 홍보하는 성공적인 상업용 블로그를 갖기 위해서 /
they have to stay strictly / 'on the topic.'
그들이 엄격하게 머물러야 한다고 / '그 주제에'
If all you're doing / 만일 여러분이 하는 일의 전부가 /
is shamelessly promoting your product, /
뻔뻔스럽게 여러분의 제품을 홍보하는 것이라면 /
then who is going to want to read /
그렇다면 누가 읽고 싶어 하겠는가 /
the latest thing / you're writing about?
최신의 것을 / 여러분이 쓰고 있는
Instead, / you need to give /
대신에 / 여러분은 제공해야 한다 /
some useful or entertaining information away /
유용하거나 재미있는 정보를 /
for free / so that people have a reason /
무료로 / 사람들이 이유를 갖도록 /
to keep coming back. 계속해서 다시 방문할
Only by doing this / can you create /
오직 이렇게 함으로써 / 여러분은 만들 수 있다 /
an interested audience / 관심 있는 독자를 /
that you will then be able to sell to.
여러분이 그다음에 판매를 할 수 있게 될
So, / the best way to be successful /
따라서 / 성공할 가장 좋은 방법은 /
with a business blog / is to write about things /
상업용 블로그로 / 것들에 대해 쓰는 것이다 /
that your audience will be interested in.
여러분의 독자들이 관심 가질

여러분은 이미 사업체를 가지고 있고 여러분의 제품을 팔 수 있도록 여러분의 블로그를 막 시작하려는 참이다. 유감스럽게도, 여기가 '비즈니스 정신'이 나쁜 것이 될 수 있는 지점이다. 대부분의 사람은 제품을 홍보하는 성공적인 상업용 블로그를 갖기 위해서 그들이 엄격하게 '그 주제에' 머물러야 한다고 믿는다. 만일 여러분이 하는 일의 전부가 뻔뻔스럽게 여러분의 제품을 홍보하는 것이라면, 그렇다면 누가 여러분이 쓰고 있는 최신의 것을 읽고 싶어 하겠는가? 대신에, 여러분은 사람들이 계속해서 다시 방문할 이유를 갖도록 유용하거나 재미있는 정보를 무료로 제공해야 한다. 오직 이렇게 함으로써 여러분은 여러분이 그다음에 판매를 할 수 있게 될 관심 있는 독자를 만들 수 있다. 따라서, 상업용 블로그로 성공할 가장 좋은 방법은 여러분의 독자들이 관심 가질 것들에 대해 쓰는 것이다.

문제풀이

성공적인 상업용 블로그를 갖기 위해서는 사람들이 계속해서 다시 방문할 수 있도록 유용하거나 재미있는 정보를 무료로 제공해야 한다는 내용이므로, 필자가 주장하는 바로 ⑤ '상업용 블로그는 사람들이 흥미 있어 할 정보를 제공해야 한다.'가 가장 적절하다.

이렇게 풀자 글의 마지막 문장인 'So, the best way to be successful with a business blog is to write about things that your audience will be interested in.'에서 필자의 주장이 드러나 있다.

어휘·어구

business 사업체
be about to-v 막 ~하려고 하다
launch 시작하다
product 제품
successful 성공적인
promote 홍보하다
strictly 엄격하게
shamelessly 뻔뻔스럽게
useful 유용한
entertaining 재미있는
reason 이유
create 만들어내다
interested 관심 있는
audience 독자, 청중
be interested in ~에 관심이 있다

1. ④ 글을 쓸 때보다 말할 때 더 많은 단어를 사용해야 한다

직독/직해

Experts on writing say, / 글쓰기 전문가들은 말한다 /
"Get rid of as many words as possible."
"가능한 한 많은 단어를 삭제하라"
Each word must do / something important.
각 단어는 해야 한다 / 무언가 중요한 일을
If it doesn't, / get rid of it.
만일 그것이 그렇지 않다면 / 그것을 삭제하라
Well, / this doesn't work for speaking.
자 / 이것은 말하기에서는 통하지 않는다
It takes more words / 더 많은 단어가 필요하다 /
to introduce, express, and adequately elaborate an idea /
아이디어를 소개하고, 표현하며, 적절히 부연 설명하는 데 /
in speech / than it takes in writing.
말할 때는 / 글을 쓸 때 필요한 것보다
Why is this so? 이것은 왜 그러한가
While the reader can reread, /
독자는 글을 다시 읽을 수 있는 반면 /
the listener cannot rehear.
청자는 다시 들을 수 없다
Speakers do not come equipped with /
화자는 갖추고 있지 않다 /
a replay button. 반복 재생 버튼을
Because listeners are easily distracted, /
청자들은 쉽게 주의력이 흐려지기 때문에 /
they will miss / many pieces of what a speaker says.
그들은 놓칠 것이다 / 화자가 말하는 것 중 많은 부분을
If they miss the crucial sentence, /
그들이 중요한 문장을 놓친다면 /
they may never catch up.
그들은 절대로 따라잡을 수 없을 것이다
This makes it necessary / for speakers to talk *longer* /
이것은 필요가 있게 한다 / 화자들이 더 길게 말할 (필요가) /
about their points, / using more words on them /
그들의 요점에 대해 / 그것들에 더 많은 단어를 사용하여 /
than would be used to express /
표현하기 위해 사용될 단어 수보다 /
the same idea / in writing.
같은 아이디어를 / 글을 쓸 때

글쓰기 전문가들은 "가능한 한 많은 단어를 삭제하라"고 말한다. 각 단어는 무언가 중요한 일을 해야 한다. 만일 그렇지 않다면 그것을 삭제하라. 자, 이것은 말하기에서는 통하지 않는다. 말할 때는 아이디어를 소개하고, 표현하며, 적절히 부연 설명하는 데 글을 쓸 때 필요한 것보다 더 많은 단어가 필요하다. 이것은 왜 그러한가? 독자는 글을 다시 읽을 수 있는 반면 청자는 다시 들을 수 없다. 화자는 반복 재생 버튼을 갖추고 있지 않다. 청자들은 쉽게 주의력이 흐려지기 때문에, 그들은 화자가 말하는 것 중 많은 부분을 놓칠 것이다. 그들이 중요한 문장을 놓친다면, 절대로 따라잡을 수 없을 것이다. 이것은 화자들이 글을 쓸 때 같은 아이디어를 표현하기 위해 사용될 단어 수보다 그것들(요점)에 대해 더 많은 단어를 사용하여 그들의 요점에 대해 더 길게 말할 필요가 있게 한다.

문제풀이

독자는 글은 다시 읽을 수 있는 반면에 청자는 다시 들을 수 없고, 쉽게 주의력이 흐려지기 때문에 말할 때는 글을 쓸 때보다 더 많은 단어를 사용해서 요점에 대해 더 길게 말해야 한다는 내용의 글이다. 따라서 필자가 주장하는 바로 ④ '글을 쓸 때보다 말할 때 더 많은 단어를 사용해야 한다.'가 가장 적절하다.

이렇게 풀자 'It takes more words to introduce, express, and adequately elaborate an idea in speech than it takes in writing.'과 'This makes it necessary for speakers to talk *longer* about their points, using more words on them than would be used to express the same idea in writing.'에서 필자의 주장이 드러나 있다.

어휘·어구

get rid of 제거하다
express 표현하다
adequately 적절히
elaborate 자세히 말하다
equipped with ~을 갖춘
distracted 주의가 산만한
crucial 중요한
sentence 문장
catch up 따라잡다
necessary 필요한

2. ⑤ 회의에서 다룰 사항은 미리 작성해서 공유하라

직독/직해

Meetings encourage creative thinking /
회의는 창의적인 사고를 촉진한다 /
and can give you ideas /
그리고 여러분에게 아이디어들을 제공할 수 있다 /
that you may never have thought of / on your own.
여러분이 절대 떠올리지 못할 / 혼자서는
However, on average, / 하지만 평균적으로 /
meeting participants consider /
회의 참석자들은 여긴다 /
about one third of meeting time / to be unproductive.
회의 시간의 약 1/3을 / 비생산적이라고
But you can make your meetings /
그러나 여러분은 회의를 만들 수 있다 /
more productive and more useful /
더 생산적이고 더 유용하게 /
by preparing well / in advance.
준비를 잘함으로써 / 사전에
You should create / a list of items to be discussed /
여러분은 만들어야 한다 / 논의하게 될 사항들의 목록을 /
and share your list with other participants /

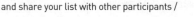

그리고 다른 회의 참석자들과 여러분의 목록을 공유해야 한다 /
before a meeting. 회의 전에
It allows them to know / what to expect /
그것은 그들이 알 수 있게 해준다 / 무엇을 기대하는지를 /
in your meeting / and prepare to participate.
여러분의 회의에서 / 그리고 회의 참석을 준비할 수 있게 (해준다)

회의는 창의적인 사고를 촉진하고 여러분이 혼자서는 절대 떠올리지 못할 아이디어들을 여러분에게 제공할 수 있다. 하지만 평균적으로, 회의 참석자들은 회의 시간의 약 1/3을 비생산적이라고 여긴다. 그러나 여러분은 사전에 준비를 잘함으로써 회의를 더 생산적이고 더 유용하게 만들 수 있다. 여러분은 논의하게 될 사항들의 목록을 만들고 회의 전에 다른 회의 참석자들과 여러분의 목록을 공유해야 한다. 그것은 참석자들이 회의에서 무엇을 기대하는지를 알고 회의 참석을 준비할 수 있게 해준다.

문제풀이

회의 전에 논의해야 할 사항의 목록을 만들어서 다른 회의 참석자들과 공유하면 회의를 더 생산적이고 유용하게 할 수 있다는 내용의 글이다. 따라서 필자가 주장하는 바로 ⑤ '회의에서 다룰 사항은 미리 작성해서 공유해야 한다.'가 가장 적절하다.

이렇게 풀자 글의 후반부에 제시된 'You should create a list of items to be discussed and share your list with other participants before a meeting.'에서 필자의 주장이 드러나 있다. 필자의 주장은 'should', 'need to'와 같은 당위적 표현이 사용된 부분을 유의해야 한다.

어휘·어구

encourage 부추기다, 권장하다
creative 창의적인
on average 평균적으로
participant 참석자
consider 여기다, 고려하다
unproductive 비생산적인
useful 유용한
in advance 사전에, 미리
discuss 논의하다

3. ⑤ 큰일을 잘 이루려면 작은 일부터 제대로 하라

직독/직해

When I was in the army, / 내가 군대에 있을 때 /
my instructors would show up /
교관들이 모습을 드러내곤 했었다 /
in my barracks room, / 나의 병영 생활관에 /
and the first thing they would inspect /
그리고 그들이 가장 먼저 검사하곤 했던 것은 /
was our bed. 우리의 침대였다
It was a simple task, / 단순한 일이었다 /
but every morning we were required /
하지만 매일 아침 우리는 요구받았다 /
to make our bed to perfection.
침대를 완벽하게 정돈하도록
It seemed a little ridiculous / at the time, /
그것은 약간 우스꽝스럽게 보였다 / 그 당시에 /
but the wisdom of this simple act /
하지만 이 단순한 행위의 지혜는 /
has been proven to me / many times over.
나에게 증명되었다 / 여러 차례 거듭하여
If you make your bed every morning, /
만일 여러분이 매일 아침 침대를 정돈한다면 /
you will have accomplished / the first task of the day.
여러분은 성취하게 될 것이다 / 하루의 첫 번째 과업을
It will give you a small sense of pride /
그것은 여러분에게 작은 자존감을 준다 /
and it will encourage you to do /
그리고 그것은 (~을) 하도록 용기를 줄 것이다 /
another task and another. 다른 과업을 잇따라
By the end of the day, / that one task completed /
하루가 끝날 때쯤에는 / 완수된 그 하나의 과업이 /
will have turned into / many tasks completed.
변하게 될 것이다 / 완수된 많은 과업으로
If you can't do little things right, /
만일 여러분이 작은 일들을 제대로 할 수 없으면 /
you will never do the big things right.
결코 큰일들을 제대로 할 수 없을 것이다

내가 군대에 있을 때, 교관들이 나의 병영 생활관에 모습을 드러내곤 했었는데, 그들이 가장 먼저 검사하곤 했던 것은 우리의 침대였다. 단순한 일이었지만, 매일 아침 우리는 침대를 완벽하게 정돈하도록 요구받았다. 그 당시에 그것은 약간 우스꽝스럽게 보였지만, 이 단순한 행위의 지혜는 여러 차례 거듭하여 나에게 증명되었다. 만일 여러분이 매일 아침 침대를 정돈한다면, 여러분은 하루의 첫 번째 과업을 성취하게 될 것이다. 그것은 여러분에게 작은 자존감을 주고, 또 다른 과업을 잇따라 하도록 용기를 줄 것이다. 하루가 끝날 때쯤에는, 완수된 그 하나의 과업이 완수된 많은 과업으로 변하게 될 것이다. 만일 여러분이 작은 일들을 제대로 할 수 없으면, 결코 큰일들을 제대로 할 수 없을 것이다.

문제풀이

하루의 첫 번째 과업을 제대로 성취하면 하루가 끝날 때쯤에 많은 과업들을 완수할 것이고, 작은 일들을 제대로 하지 못한다면 결코 큰일을 제대로 할 수 없을 것이라는 내용의 글이다. 따라서 필자가 주장하는 바로 ⑤ '큰일을 잘 이루려면 작은 일부터 제대로 수행해야 한다.'가 가장 적절하다.

이렇게 풀자 글의 마지막 문장인 'If you can't do little things right, you will never do the big things right.'에서 필자의 주장이 드러나 있다.

어휘·어구

army 군대
instructor 교관
inspect 검사하다, 검열하다
task 일, 과업
require 요구하다
make one's bed 침대를 정돈하다
perfection 완벽
ridiculous 우스꽝스러운
wisdom 지혜
prove 증명하다
pride 자존감
encourage 용기를 주다
complete 완수하다
turn into 변하다

정답률 89%

4. ③ 학생과의 관계에서 교사의 비언어적인 메시지의 중요성

직독/직해

Some experts estimate / 일부 전문가들은 추정한다 /
that as much as half of what we communicate /
우리가 전달하는 것의 절반 정도가 /
is done / through the way we move our bodies.
행해진다고 / 우리가 우리의 몸을 움직이는 방식을 통해
Paying attention to the nonverbal messages /
비언어적인 메시지에 주의를 기울이는 것은 /
you send / can make a significant difference /
여러분이 보내는 / 중요한 차이를 만들 수 있다 /
in your relationship with students.
학생들과 여러분의 관계에
In general, / 일반적으로 /
most students are often closely tuned in to their teacher's body language.
대부분의 학생들은 자신의 선생님의 몸짓 언어에 종종 관심이 면밀하게 맞춰져 있다
For example, / 예를 들어 /
when your students first enter the classroom, /
여러분의 학생들이 처음 교실에 들어갈 때 /
their initial action is to look for their teacher.
그들의 첫 행동은 자신의 선생님을 찾는 것이다
Think about how encouraging and empowering it is /
그것이 얼마나 격려가 되고 힘을 주는지 생각해 보자 /
for a student / 학생에게 /
when that teacher has a friendly greeting and a welcoming smile.
그 선생님이 친근한 인사를 하고 환영하는 미소를 짓는다면
Smiling at students / — to let them know /
학생들에게 미소 짓는 것 / 그들에게 알려 주는 것이 /
that you are glad to see them /
여러분이 그들을 알게 돼서 기쁘다는 것을
— does not require a great deal of time or effort, /
많은 시간이나 노력을 요구하는 것은 아니다 /
but it can make a significant difference /
그러나 그것은 중요한 차이를 만들 수 있다 /
in the classroom climate / 교실 분위기에 /
right from the start of class. 수업의 바로 그 시작부터

일부 전문가들은 우리가 전달하는 것의 절반 정도가 우리가 우리의 몸을 움직이는 방식을 통해 행해진다고 추정한다. 여러분이 보내는 비언어적인 메시지에 주의를 기울이는 것은 학생들과 여러분의 관계에 중요한 차이를 만들 수 있다. 일반적으로 대부분의 학생들은 자신의 선생님의 몸짓 언어에 종종 관심이 면밀하게 맞춰져 있다. 예를 들어 여러분의 학생들이 처음 교실에 들어갈 때 그들의 첫 행동은 자신의 선생님을 찾는 것이다. 그 선생님이 친근한 인사를 하고 환영하는 미소를 짓는다면 그것이 학생에게 얼마나 격려가 되고 힘을 주는지 생각해 보자. 학생들에게 미소 짓는 것, 즉 그들에게 여러분이 그들을 알게 돼서 기쁘다는 것을 알려 주는 것이 많은 시간이나 노력을 요구하는 것은 아니지만, 그것은 수업의 바로 그 시작부터 교실 분위기에 중요한 차이를 만들 수 있다.

문제풀이

학생들을 처음 맞이했을 때 선생님이 친근한 인사를 하고 환영하는 미소를 짓는 것이 학생에게 힘이 되고 교실 분위기에 중요한 차이를 만들 수 있듯이 교사의 비언어적인 표현이 학생과의 관계에서 중요하다는 내용의 글이므로 필자가 주장하는 바로 가장 적절한 것은 ③ '학생과의 관계에서 교사는 비언어적 표현에 유의해야 한다.'이다.

어휘·어구

expert 전문가
estimate 추정하다
pay attention to ~에 주목하다
nonverbal 비언어적인
significant 중요한
in general 일반적으로
tune in 맞추다
initial 처음의
encouraging 환영하는

5. ③ 독자가 능동적으로 사고할 수 있게 글을 써라

직독/직해

As you set about to write, / 글을 쓰려고 할 때 /
it is worth reminding yourself /
자신에게 상기시키는 것은 가치가 있다 /
that while you ought to have a point of view, /
당신은 당신의 관점을 가져야 하는 한편 /
you should avoid telling your readers / what to think.
당신은 독자에게 말하는 것을 피해야 한다고 / 무엇을 생각할지
Try to hang a question mark over it all.
그것 전체에 물음표를 달기 위해 노력해라
This way you allow your readers to think for themselves /
이런 방식으로 당신은 독자들이 스스로 생각할 수 있게 한다 /
about the points / and arguments you're making.
요점에 대해 / 그리고 당신이 하는 주장들에 대해

As a result, / they will feel more involved, /
결과적으로 / 그들은 좀 더 열중하는 느낌을 받을 것이다 /
finding themselves / 자신을 발견하면서 /
just as committed to the arguments you've made /
당신이 한 주장에 몰입되는 /
and the insights you've exposed / as you are.
그리고 당신이 드러내는 통찰력에 (몰입되는) / 당신만큼이나
You will have written an essay / 당신은 글을 쓰게 될 것이다 /
that not only avoids passivity in the reader, /
독자들의 수동성을 피할 뿐만 아니라 /
but is interesting / and gets people to think.
흥미로운 / 그리고 사람들을 생각하게 만드는

글을 쓰려고 할 때, 당신은 당신의 관점을 가져야 하는 한편, 독자에게 무엇을 생각할지 말하는 것을 피해야 한다고 상기시키는 것은 가치가 있다. 그것(논점) 전체에 물음표를 달기 위해 노력해라. 이런 방식으로 당신은 독자들이 요점과 당신이 하는 주장들에 대해 스스로 생각할 수 있게 한다. 결과적으로 독자들은 당신만큼이나 당신이 한 주장과 당신이 드러내는 통찰력에 몰입되는 자신을 발견하면서, 좀 더 열중하는 느낌을 받을 것이다. 당신은 독자들의 수동성을 피할 뿐만 아니라 흥미롭고 사람들을 생각하게 만드는 글을 쓰게 될 것이다.

문제풀이

글을 쓸 때, 자신의 관점은 가지되 독자에게 생각해야 할 것을 강요하지 말고 독자들이 적극적으로 몰입하고 스스로 생각하게 만드는 글을 써야 한다는 내용으로 보아, 필자가 주장하는 바로 ③ '독자가 능동적으로 사고할 수 있도록 글을 써야 한다.'가 가장 적절하다.

어휘·어구

set about to do ~하려고 하다
argument 주장, 논점
committed 몰입된
insight 통찰력
expose 노출하다
passivity 수동성

6. ① 불편해도 성공을 위해 새로운 것을 시도하라

직독/직해

Sometimes, / you feel the need to avoid something /
가끔 / 당신은 무언가를 피할 필요가 있다고 느낀다 /
that will lead to success / out of discomfort.
성공으로 이끌어 줄 / 불편하기 때문에
Maybe you are avoiding extra work /
아마도 당신은 추가적인 일을 피하고 있다 /
because you are tired. 피곤하기 때문에
You are actively shutting out success /
당신은 적극적으로 성공을 차단하고 있다 /
because you want to avoid being uncomfortable.
불편한 것을 피하고 싶기 때문에
Therefore, / overcoming your instinct /
따라서 / 당신의 본능을 극복하는 것이 /
to avoid uncomfortable things / at first /
불편한 것을 피하고자 하는 / 처음에는 /
is essential. 필요하다
Try doing new things / outside of your comfort zone.
새로운 일을 시도해봐라 / 편안함을 주는 곳을 벗어나서
Change is always uncomfortable, /
변화는 항상 불편하다 /
but it is key / 하지만 그것은 핵심이다 /
to doing things differently / in order to find /
일을 색다르게 하는 데 있어 / 찾기 위해 /
that magical formula for success.
성공을 위한 마법 공식을

가끔 당신은 불편하기 때문에 성공으로 이끌어 줄 무언가를 피할 필요가 있다고 느낀다. 아마도 당신은 피곤하기 때문에 추가적인 일을 피하고 있다. 당신은 불편한 것을 피하고 싶기 때문에 적극적으로 성공을 차단하고 있다. 따라서 처음에는 불편한 것을 피하고자 하는 당신의 본능을 극복하는 것이 필요하다. 편안함을 주는 곳을 벗어나서 새로운 일을 시도해봐라. 변화는 항상 불편하지만, 성공을 위한 마법 공식을 찾기 위해 그것(변화)은 일을 색다르게 하는 데 있어 핵심이다.

문제풀이

불편한 것이 싫어서 성공을 차단하는 경향이 있지만 편안함을 주는 곳을 벗어나 새로운 일을 시도해봐야 성공할 수 있다는 내용이므로, 필자가 주장하는 바로 ① '불편할지라도 성공하기 위해서는 새로운 것을 시도해야 한다.'가 가장 적절하다.

이렇게 풀자 글의 중반에 언급된 'Therefore' 이후의 문장에서 필자의 주장이 잘 드러나 있다.

어휘·어구

discomfort 불편
actively 적극적으로
shut out ~을 막다, 차단하다
uncomfortable 불편한
overcome 극복하다
instinct 본능
essential 필수적인
comfort zone 편안한 곳
formula 공식

7. ③ 이메일 전송 전 검토 필요

직독/직해

At a publishing house and at a newspaper /
출판사와 신문사에서 /
you learn the following: /
여러분은 다음에 나오는 것을 알게 된다 /
It's not a mistake / if it dosen't end up print.
그것은 실수가 아니다 / 결국 인쇄물로 나오지 않으면
It's the same for email.
그것은 이메일에서도 마찬가지다
Nothing bad can happen /
어떤 나쁜 일도 일어날 수 없다 /
if you haven't hit the Send key.
여러분이 전송 버튼을 눌러 버리기 전까지는
What you've written /
여러분이 쓴 것은 /
can have misspellings, errors of fact, rude comments, obvious lies, /
잘못 쓴 철자, 사실의 오류, 무례한 말, 명백한 거짓말들이 있을 수도 있다 /
but it doesn't matter.
하지만 그것은 문제가 되지 않는다
If you haven't sent it, / you still have time to fix it.
만약 그것을 전송하지 않았다면 / 여러분에게는 아직 그것을 고칠 시간이 있다
You can correct any mistake /
여러분은 어떤 실수라도 수정할 수 있다 /
and nobody will ever know the difference.
그리고 누구도 결코 그 변화를 모를 것이다
This is easier said than done, / of course.
이것은 말은 쉽지만, 행동은 어렵다 / 물론,
Send is your computer's most attractive command.
전송은 여러분 컴퓨터의 가장 매력적인 명령어이다
But before you hit the Send key, /
하지만 여러분이 그 전송 버튼을 누르기 전에 /
make sure that you read your document carefully one last time.
반드시 문서를 마지막으로 한번 주의 깊게 읽어 보라

출판사와 신문사에서 여러분은 다음에 나오는 것을 알게 된다. '결국 인쇄물로 나오지 않으면 그것은 실수가 아니다.' 그것은 이메일에서도 마찬가지다. 여러분이 전송 버튼을 눌러 버리기 전까지는 어떤 나쁜 일도 일어날 수 없다. 여러분이 쓴 것에는 잘못 쓴 철자, 사실의 오류, 무례한 말, 명백한 거짓말들이 있을 수도 있지만, 그것은 문제가 되지 않는다. 만약 그것을 전송하지 않았다면, 여러분에게는 아직 그것을 고칠 시간이 있다. 여러분은 어떤 실수라도 수정할 수 있고 누구도 결코 그 변화를 모를 것이다. 물론, 이것은 말은 쉽지만, 행동은 어렵다. 전송은 여러분 컴퓨터의 가장 매력적인 명령어이다. 하지만 여러분이 그 전송 버튼을 누르기 전에, 반드시 문서를 마지막으로 한번 주의 깊게 읽어 보라.

문제풀이

이메일을 전송하기 전에는 얼마든지 오류를 수정할 시간이 있기 때문에 전송 전에 반드시 문서를 주의 깊게 읽으라는 내용이므로, 필자가 주장하는 바로 ③ '이메일을 전송하기 전에 반드시 검토해야 한다.'가 가장 적절하다.

이렇게 풀자 글의 마지막 문장인 'But before you hit the Send key, make sure that you read your document carefully one last time.'에 필자의 주장이 드러나 있다.

어휘·어구

publishing house 출판사
end up 결국 ~이 되다
happen 일어나다
misspelling 잘못 쓴 철자
rude 무례한
comment 말
obvious 명백한
matter 문제가 되다
correct 수정하다
attractive 매력적인
command 명령(어)
make sure 반드시 ~을 하다
document 문서, 서류

8. ② 집중을 방해하는 요인에 대처할 줄 알아야 한다

직독/직해

When I was in high school, /
내가 고등학교에 다닐 때 /
we had students who could study in the coffee shop /
커피숍에서 공부할 수 있는 학생들이 있었다 /
and not get distracted by the noise /
그리고 소음에 의해 방해를 받지 않을 수 있는 /
or everything happening around them.
혹은 그들 주변에서 일어나는 모든 것에
We also had students who could not study /
또한 공부를 할 수 없는 학생들도 있었다 /
if the library was not super quiet.
도서관이 아주 조용하지 않으면
The latter students suffered /
후자의 학생들은 고통을 받았다 /
because even in the library, /
심지어 도서관에서조차 /
it was impossible /
불가능했기 때문에 /
to get the type of complete silence they sought.
그들이 추구했던 완전한 침묵 유형을 얻는 것이
These students were victims of distractions /
이 학생들은 집중에 방해가 되는 것들의 희생자였다 /
who found it very difficult to study anywhere /
어디에서도 공부하는 것이 매우 어렵다는 것을 알게 된 /
except in their private bedrooms.
개인 침실을 제외하고는
In today's world, / it is impossible /
요즘 세상에서는 / 불가능하다 /
to run away from distractions.
집중에 방해가 되는 것들로부터 도망치는 것은
Distractions are everywhere, /
집중에 방해가 되는 것들은 어디에나 있다 /
but if you want to achieve your goals, /

하지만 만일 여러분의 목표를 달성하고 싶다면 /
you must learn how to tackle distractions.
여러분은 집중에 방해가 되는 것들에 대처하는 법을 배워야 한다
You cannot eliminate distractions, /
집중에 방해가 되는 것들을 제거할 수는 없다 /
but you can learn to live with them /
하지만 여러분은 그것들과 함께 살아가는 것을 배울 수 있다
in a way / that ensures they do not limit you.
방식으로 / 그것들이 여러분을 제한하지 않도록 하는

내가 고등학교에 다닐 때, 커피숍에서 공부하면서 소음이나 그들 주변에서 일어나는 모든 것에 의해 방해를 받지 않을 수 있는 학생들이 있었다. 또한 도서관이 아주 조용하지 않으면 공부를 할 수 없는 학생들도 있었다. 후자의 학생들은 심지어 도서관에서조차 그들이 추구하는 유형의 완전한 침묵을 얻는 것이 불가능했기 때문에 고통을 받았다. 이 학생들은 개인 침실을 제외하고는 어디에서도 공부하는 것이 매우 어렵다는 것을 알게 된 집중에 방해가 되는 것들의 희생자였다. 요즘 세상에서는 집중에 방해가 되는 것들로부터 도망치는 것은 불가능하다. 집중에 방해가 되는 것들은 어디에나 있지만, 만일 여러분의 목표를 달성하고 싶다면 여러분은 집중에 방해가 되는 것들에 대처하는 법을 배워야 한다. 집중에 방해가 되는 것들을 제거할 수는 없지만, 그것들이 여러분을 제한하지 않도록 하는 방식으로 그것들과 함께 살아가는 것을 배울 수 있다.

문제풀이

요즘 세상에서는 집중에 방해되는 것들이 어디에나 있어서 피할 수 없기 때문에, 목표를 달성하고 싶다면 집중에 방해가 되는 것들에 대처하는 법을 배워야 한다는 내용이다. 따라서 필자가 주장하는 바로 가장 적절한 것은 ② '집중을 방해하는 요인에 대처할 줄 알아야 한다.'가 가장 적절하다.

이렇게 풀자 글의 뒷부분에 제시된 문장 'you must learn how to tackle distractions.(여러분은 집중에 방해가 되는 것들에 대처하는 법을 배워야 한다)'에 필자의 주장이 드러나 있다.

어휘·어구

- **get distracted** 정신이 산만해지다
- **suffer** 고통을 받다
- **complete** 완전한
- **seek** 추구하다
- **victim** 희생자
- **distraction** 주의 산만
- **private** 개인의
- **achieve** 달성하다, 이루다
- **tackle** 다루다, 해결하다
- **eliminate** 없애다, 제거하다
- **ensure** 보장하다
- **limit** 제한하다

9. ② 목표 설정

직독/직해

Any goal you set is going to be difficult to achieve, /
여러분이 세우는 어떤 목표든 달성하기 어려울 것이다 /
and you will certainly be disappointed at some points along the way.
그리고 여러분은 분명히 도중에 어느 시점에서 실망하게 될 것이다
So why not set your goals much higher /
그렇다면 여러분의 목표들을 훨씬 더 높게 세우는 건 어떤가? /
than you consider worthy from the beginning?
시작부터 여러분이 가치 있다고 여기는 것보다
If they are going to require work, effort, and energy, /
만약에 그것들이 일, 노력, 그리고 에너지를 요구한다면 /
then why not exert 10 times as much of each?
각각을 10배 더 많이 발휘하는 것은 어떤가?
What if you are underestimating your capabilities?
만약 여러분이 자신의 능력을 과소평가하고 있다면 어떻게 되겠는가?
You might be protesting, saying, /
여러분은 이렇게 말하며 이의를 제기할지도 모른다 /
"What of the disappointment that comes from setting unrealistic goals?"
비현실적 목표를 세우는 것으로부터 오는 실망은 어찌할 것인가?
However, take just a few moments /
그러나 그저 잠깐의 시간을 가져봐라 /
to look back over your life.
여러분의 삶을 되돌아보기 위해
Chances are that /
가능성은 다음과 같다 /
you have more often been disappointed /
여러분은 보다 자주 실망해왔다 /
by setting targets that are too low and achieving them /
너무 낮은 목표를 세우고 그것을 성취함으로써 /
— only to be shocked / 충격을 받게 되고 /
that you still didn't get what you wanted.
아직 자신이 원했던 것을 얻지 못한 것에

여러분이 세우는 어떤 목표든 달성하기 어려울 것이고, 여러분은 분명히 도중에 어느 시점에서 실망하게 될 것이다. 그러니 여러분의 목표들을 시작부터 여러분이 가치 있다고 여기는 것보다 훨씬 더 높게 세우는 것은 어떤가? 만약에 그것들이 일, 노력, 그리고 에너지를 요구한다면, 각각을 10배 더 많이 발휘하는 것은 어떤가? 만약 여러분이 자신의 능력을 과소평가하고 있는 것이라면 어떻게 되겠는가? "비현실적 목표를 세우는 것으로부터 오는 실망은 어찌할 것인가?"라고 말하며, 여러분은 이의를 제기할지도 모른다. 그러나 여러분의 삶을 되돌아보기 위해 그저 잠깐의 시간을 가져봐라. 아마 여러분은 너무 낮은 목표들을 세우고 그것들을 달성은 했으나, 결국 자신이 원했던 것을 여전히 얻지 못한 것에 깜짝 놀라며 더욱 자주 실망했을 것이다.

문제풀이

첫 문장에서 문제 제기를 한 다음, 그 해결안으로서 목표를 훨씬 더 높게 세우는 것을 제안하고 있다. 따라서 필자의 주장으로 가장 적절한 것은 ② '목표는 자신의 생각보다 높게 설정해야 한다.'이다.

이렇게 풀자 주장 찾기 유형에서는 보통 명령문 또는 '~해야 한다'라는 의미를 갖는 must, have to, should 등이 포함된 문장에 필자의 주장이 직접적으로 드러난다. 이 문제에서는 Why not ~?(~하는 게 어떤가?)에 필자의 주장을 담았다. 'Why not set your goals much higher than you consider worthy from the beginning?(그렇다면 여러분의 목표들을 시작부터 여러분이 가치 있다고 여기는 것보다 훨씬 더 높게 세우는 것은 어떤가?)'에 필자의 주장이 잘 드러나 있다.

어휘·어구

- **worthy** 가치 있는
- **what if** ~라면 어떻게 될까?
- **underestimate** 과소평가하다
- **capability** 능력, 역량, 재능
- **protest** 항의하다, 이의를 제기하다
- **unrealistic** 비현실적인
- **look back** 돌이켜보다

10. ⑤ 건강에 좋은 음식으로 식사를 시작할 것

직독/직해

The dish you start with / serves as an anchor food /
당신이 먼저 먹는 요리가 / 닻을 내리는 음식의 역할을 한다 /
for your entire meal. 당신의 전체 식사에
Experiments show / 실험이 보여준다 /
that people eat nearly 50 percent greater quantity of the food /
사람들이 음식을 거의 50% 더 많이 먹는다는 것을 /
they eat first. 그들이 처음 먹는
If you start with a dinner roll, /
만약 당신이 디너롤로 시작하면 /
you will eat more starches, less protein, and fewer vegetables.
당신은 더 많은 녹말과 더 적은 단백질, 그리고 더 적은 채소를 먹을 것이다
Eat the healthiest food / on your plate / first.
가장 건강에 좋은 음식을 먹어라 / 접시에 있는 / 먼저
As age-old wisdom suggests, / this usually means /
오래된 지혜가 제시하듯이 / 이것은 보통 의미한다 /
starting with your vegetables or salad.
채소나 샐러드를 먼저 먹는 것을
If you are going to eat something unhealthy, /
만약 당신이 건강에 좋지 않은 음식을 먹을 것이라면 /
at least save it for last.
적어도 그것을 마지막 순서로 남겨둬라
This will give your body the opportunity /
이것은 당신의 몸에 기회를 줄 것이다 /
to fill up on better options / 더 나은 선택 사항들로 채울
before you move on to starches or sugary desserts.
당신이 녹말이나 설탕이 든 디저트로 이동하기 전에

당신이 먼저 먹는 요리가 당신의 전체 식사에 닻을 내리는 음식의 역할을 한다. 실험은 사람들이 먼저 먹는 음식을 거의 50% 더 많이 먹는다는 것을 보여준다. 만약 당신이 디너롤로 시작하면, 당신은 더 많은 녹말과 더 적은 단백질, 그리고 더 적은 채소를 먹을 것이다. 접시에 있는 가장 건강에 좋은 음식을 먼저 먹어라. 오래된 지혜에서 알 수 있듯이, 이것은 보통 야채나 샐러드를 먼저 먹는 것을 의미한다. 만약 당신이 건강에 좋지 않은 음식을 먹을 것이라면, 적어도 그것을 마지막 순서로 남겨둬라. 이것은 당신이 녹말이나 설탕이 든 디저트로 이동하기 전에 당신의 몸을 더 나은 선택 사항들로 채울 기회를 줄 것이다.

문제풀이

식사할 때 처음 먹는 음식을 다른 음식보다 거의 50% 더 많이 먹는다고 하였고, 따라서 식탁에 있는 건강에 좋은 음식, 즉 채소나 샐러드와 같은 음식으로 식사를 시작하는 것이 좋다는 내용의 글이다. 그러므로 필자가 주장하는 바로 가장 적절한 것은 ⑤ '건강에 좋은 음식으로 식사를 시작하라.'이다.

어휘·어구

- **serve as** ~의 역할을 하다
- **entire** 전체의
- **quantity** 양
- **protein** 단백질
- **vegetable** 야채, 채소
- **plate** 접시
- **opportunity** 기회
- **fill up** ~을 채우다

11. ④ 지속된 인간관계를 위해 일관된 노력이 필요하다

직독/직해

We tend to go long periods of time /
우리는 오랜 시간을 보내는 경향이 있다 /
without reaching out / to the people we know.
연락 없이 / 우리가 아는 사람들에게
Then, we suddenly take notice / of the distance
그러다가 우리는 갑자기 알아차린다 / 생겨 버린 거리감을
that has formed / and we scramble to make repairs.
/ 그리고 허둥지둥 수리를 한다
We call people / we haven't spoken to in ages, /
우리는 사람들에게 전화를 한다 / 오랫동안 이야기하지 못했던 /
hoping that one small effort will erase /
작은 노력 하나가 지우기를 바라면서 /
the months and years of distance we've created.
우리가 만들어 낸 몇 달과 몇 년의 거리감을
However, this rarely works: / 하지만 이것은 거의 효과가 없다 /
relationships aren't kept up with big one-time fixes.
관계들은 커다란 일회성의 해결책들로는 지속되지 않는다
They're kept up with regular maintenance, /
그것들은 정기적인 정비로 유지된다 /

like a car. 자동차처럼
In our relationships, / we have to make sure /
우리의 관계들에서 / 우리는 확실히 해야 한다 /
that not too much time goes by between oil changes, /
오일 교환 사이에 너무 많은 시간이 흐르지 않도록 /
so to speak. 말하자면
This isn't to say / 이것은 말하는 것이 아니다 /
that you shouldn't bother calling someone /
여러분이 누군가에게 애써 전화해서는 안 된다고 /
just because it's been a while since you've spoken; /
단지 이야기한 지 오래되었기 때문에 /
just that it's more ideal / not to let yourself fall out
더 이상적이라는 것이다 / 스스로를 연락이 끊기지 않게 하는 것이
of touch / in the first place.
/ 애당초
Consistency always brings better results.
일관성은 항상 더 나은 결과들을 가져온다

우리는 우리가 아는 사람들에게 연락 없이 오랜 시간을 보내는 경향이 있다. 그러다가 우리는 생겨 버린 거리감을 갑자기 알아차리고 허둥지둥 수리를 한다. 우리는 오랫동안 이야기하지 못했던 사람들에게 전화를 하면서, 작은 노력 하나가 우리가 만들어 낸 몇 달과 몇 년의 거리감을 지우기를 바란다. 하지만 이것은 거의 효과가 없다. 왜냐하면 관계들은 커다란 일회성의 해결책들로는 지속되지 않기 때문이다. 그것들은 자동차처럼 정기적인 정비로 유지된다. 말하자면, 우리의 관계들에서 우리는 (엔진) 오일 교환 사이에 너무 많은 시간이 흐르지 않도록 확실히 해야 한다. 이것은 여러분이 단지 이야기한 지 오래되었기 때문에 누군가에게 애써 전화해서는 안 된다고 말하는 것이 아니라, 애당초 스스로를 연락이 끊기지 않게 하는 것이 더 이상적이라고 말하는 것이다. 일관성은 항상 더 나은 결과들을 가져온다.

문제풀이

인간관계는 자동차처럼 정기적인 정비로 유지된다고 하면서, 일관성을 가지고 연락이 끊기지 않게 하는 것이 이상적이라는 내용이다. 따라서 필자가 주장하는 바로 가장 적절한 것은 ④ '인간관계를 지속하려면 일관된 노력을 기울여야 한다.'이다.

이렇게 풀자_ 글의 마지막 부분에 언급된 'just that it's more ideal not to let yourself fall out of touch in the first place.'와 'Consistency always brings better results.'에서 필자의 주장을 추론할 수 있다.

어휘·어구

scramble 허둥지둥 해내다
rarely 드물게, 좀처럼 ~하지 않는
relationship 관계
keep up with ~와 계속 연락하고 지내다
maintenance 유지, 정비
so to speak 말하자면
bother 신경 쓰다, 애를 쓰다, 괴롭히다
in the first place 애당초
consistency 일관성

정답률 78%

12. ⑤ 과정에 초점을 둔 대화

직독/직해

How do you encourage other people /
여러분은 다른 사람들을 어떻게 격려하는가 /
when they are changing their behavior?
그들이 자신의 행동을 바꾸려고 할 때
Suppose / you see a friend /
가정해 보자 / 여러분이 한 친구를 만난다고 /
who is on a diet /
다이어트 중이며 /
and has been losing a lot of weight.
몸무게가 많이 줄고 있는
It's tempting / to tell her /
~하고 싶을 것이다 / 그녀에게 말하고 /
that she looks great /
그녀가 멋져 보이고 /
and she must feel wonderful.
기분이 정말 좋겠다고
It feels good / 기분이 좋고 /
for someone / to hear positive comments, /
누구든 / 긍정적인 말을 들으면 /
and this feedback will often be encouraging.
이런 피드백은 종종 고무적일 것이다
However, / 그러나 /
if you end the discussion there, /
만약 여러분이 거기서 대화를 끝낸다면 /
then the only feedback / your friend is getting /
유일한 피드백은 / 여러분의 친구가 받게 되는 /
is about her progress / toward an outcome.
그녀의 진전에 대한 것뿐이다 / 결과를 향한
Instead, / continue the discussion.
그 대신 / 그 대화를 계속해라
Ask about what she is doing /
어떤 것을 하고 있는지 물어라 /
that has allowed her to be successful.
그녀의 성공을 가능하게 한
What is she eating?
그녀는 무엇을 먹고 있는가
Where is she working out?
그녀는 어디에서 운동을 하고 있는가
What are the lifestyle changes / she has made?
생활방식의 변화는 무엇인가 / 그녀가 만들어 낸
When the conversation focuses /
그 대화가 초점을 둘 때 /
on the process of change /
변화의 과정에 /
rather than the outcome, /
결과보다 /
it reinforces the value / of creating a sustainable
그것은 가치를 강화시킨다 / 지속 가능한 과정을 만들어 내는
process.

여러분은 다른 사람들이 자신의 행동을 바꾸려고 할 때 그들을 어떻게 격려하는가? 여러분이 다이어트 중이며 몸무게가 많이 줄고 있는 한 친구를 만난다고 가정해 보자. 그녀가 멋져 보이고 기분이 정말 좋겠다고 그녀에게 말하고 싶을 것이다. 누구든 긍정적인 말을 들으면 기분이 좋고 이런 피드백은 종종 고무적일 것이다. 그러나 만약 여러분이 거기서 대화를 끝낸다면, 여러분의 친구가 받게 되는 유일한 피드백은 결과를 향한 그녀의 진전에 대한 것뿐이다. 그 대신, 그 대화를 계속해라. 그녀의 성공을 가능하게 한 어떤 것을 하고 있는지 물어라. 그녀는 무엇을 먹고 있는가? 그녀는 어디에서 운동을 하고 있는가? 그녀가 만들어 낸 생활방식의 변화는 무엇인가? 그 대화가 결과보다 변화의 과정에 초점을 둘 때, 그것은 지속 가능한 과정을 만들어 내는 가치를 강화시킨다.

문제풀이

자신의 행동을 바꾸려고 하는 사람들을 격려할 때는 긍정적인 피드백을 주는 것에만 그치지 말고 변화의 과정에 초점을 두어 계속 대화하라고 이야기하고 있다. 따라서 필자가 주장하는 바로 가장 적절한 것은 ⑤ '행동을 바꾸려는 사람과는 과정에 초점을 두어 대화해야 한다.'이다.

이렇게 풀자_ 글에 전반적으로 언급된 소재나 논제를 이해한 후, 이에 대해 필자가 말하는 의견이나 주장을 파악하는 것이 중요하다. 여기서는 마지막 문장 'When the conversation focuses on the process of change rather than the outcome, it reinforces the value of creating a sustainable process.'에 행동을 바꾸려는 사람과 대화할 때는 결과보다 변화의 과정에 초점을 두어 대화해야 한다는 필자의 주장이 직접적으로 잘 드러나 있다.

어휘·어구

on a diet 다이어트 중인, 식이요법 중인
tempting 솔깃한
positive 긍정적인
feedback 피드백, 의견
encouraging 격려하는, 용기를 북돋워 주는
progress 진전, 진척
outcome 결과, 성과
work out 운동하다
focus on ~에 초점을 맞추다, ~에 주력하다
process 과정
reinforce 강화하다, 보강하다
sustainable (환경 파괴 없이) 지속 가능한

본문 017쪽

문법 플러스 3. 목적어와 보어의 이해

1. to be 2. getting 3. to visit
4. having 5. to apply 6. leave
7. stolen 8. whether 9. it 10. that

1 [해석]▶ 샘은 다시는 늦지 않겠노라고 약속했다.
[해설]▶ 동사 promise는 뒤에 to부정사를 목적어로 가져온다.

2 [해석]▶ 그는 추석 명절에 싸우려는 것을 가까스로 피했다.
[해설]▶ 동사 avoid 뒤에 동명사를 목적어로 가져온다.

3 [해석]▶ 그의 소원은 많은 나라를 방문하는 것이다.
[해설]▶ to부정사는 문장 속에서 보어 역할을 할 수 있다. 이 문장은 to visit가 be동사의 주격보어로 사용되었다. 괄호 뒤에 목적어 (a lot of countries)가 있으므로 to부정사의 수동태가 아닌 to부정사의 능동태가 필요하다.

4 [해석]▶ 그녀는 행복의 열쇠는 많은 친구를 두는 거라고 생각한다.
[해설]▶ 동명사의 문장 속에서 보어 역할을 할 수 있다. having은 that절 안에서 be동사의 주격보어 역할을 하고 있다.

5 [해석]▶ 그는 그녀가 그 직업에 지원해 보도록 격려했다.
[해설]▶ 「encourage+목적어+to부정사」 구문이다. encourage는 목적격보어로 to부정사를 가져온다.

6 [해석]▶ 그녀는 그가 몇 분 전에 떠난 것을 보았다.
[해설]▶ 「지각동사(saw)+목적어+목적격보어」 구문이다. 지각동사의 목적어와 목적격보어가 능동 관계인 경우 원형부정사나 현재분사를 목적격보어로 가져온다.

7 [해석]▶ Sally는 버스에서 지갑을 도난당했다.
[해설]▶ 「사역동사(had)+목적어+목적격보어」 구문이다. 사역동사의 목적어와 목적격보어가 능동 관계인 경우 목적격보어를 원형부정사를 쓰고, 수동 관계인 경우 과거분사를 쓴다. 여기서는 목적어 her purse와 목적격보어 stolen이 수동관계이므로 목적격보어를 과거분사로 써야 한다.

8 [해석]▶ 나는 우리가 그녀에게 말해야 하는 건지 아닌지 모르겠다.
[해설]▶ 동사 wonder(…할까[…이 어떨까] 생각하다)와 목적절 끝에 whether와 어울리는 or not이 있으므로 괄호에는 whether가 오는 것이 맞다.

9 [해석]▶ 나는 너와 심각한 문제에 대해 이야기하는 것이 어렵다.
[해설]▶ find, think make 등의 목적어가 to부정사나 that절이고 목적격보어가 뒤따를 때는, 목적어 자리에 가목적어 it을 쓰고, to부정사나 that절은 목적격보어 뒤에 쓴다.

10 해석▶ 나는 아이들이 적어도 한 시간 TV를 시청하는 것이 필요하다고 생각하곤 했다.
[해설]▶ consider의 목적어로 to부정사나 that절이 나오고 뒤에 목적격보어가 따라올 경우, 목적어 자리에 to부정사 또는 that절 대신에 가목적어 it을 사용한다. 괄호 이하 부분이 완전한 문장이 왔으므로, 접속사 that이 필요하다. 「consider+it(가목적어)+목적격보어+that절~」 구조이다.

본문 018쪽

어휘 플러스 3. 반의어 (1)

1. absence
2. inaccurate
3. active
4. allowed
5. incapable

1 [해석]▶ 다른 정보가 없다면, 당신은 아마도 키가 작은 친구가 여자이고 키가 큰 친구가 남자라고 결론을 내릴 것이다.

2 [해석]▶ 그들은 그 조사가 틀린 수치에 기반을 두었기 때문에 부정확하다고 말했다.

3 [해석]▶ 나의 할머니는 80세가 넘는데, 여전히 활동적이시다.

4 [해석]▶ 그는 그 책을 다 읽을 때까지 (밤늦게까지) 깨어도 된다는 허락을 받았다.

5 [해석]▶ 저개발국에서 쓰이는 전형적인 시나리오는 아주 소수의 상업적 농업 경영인들이 기술적으로 발전해 있는 반면에 대다수는 경쟁할 수 없다는 것이다.

04. 함축 · 지칭 추론

Day 04

본문 020쪽

1. ③ 2. ③ 3. ⑤ 4. ④ 5. ⑤
6. ③ 7. ② 8. ④ 9. ④ 10. ③

정답률 54%

대표 기출 ③ 노력만이 가치 있다는 확고한 신념에 대한 의심

직독/직해

Our language helps / 우리의 언어는 돕는다 /
to reveal our deeper assumptions.
우리의 더 깊은 전제를 드러내는 것을
Think of these revealing phrases: /
이것을 잘 드러내는 문구들을 생각해 보라 /
When we accomplish something important, /
우리가 중요한 무언가를 성취할 때 /
we say / it took "blood, sweat, and tears."
우리는 말한다 / 그것이 '피, 땀, 그리고 눈물'을 필요로 했다고 말한다
We say / important achievements are "hard-earned."
우리는 말한다 / 중요한 성과는 '힘들게 얻은' 것이라고
We recommend a "hard day's work" /
우리는 '힘든 하루 동안의 일'이라는 말을 권한다 /
when "day's work" would be enough.
'하루 동안의 일'이라는 말로도 충분할 때
When we talk of "easy money," /
우리가 '쉬운 돈'이라고 말할 때 /
we are implying / it was obtained through illegal or questionable means.
우리는 넌지시 드러내고 있다 / 그것이 불법적이거나 의심스러운 수단을 통해 얻어졌다는 것을
We use the phrase / "That's easy for you to say" /
우리는 문구를 사용한다 / '말은 쉽지'라는 /
as a criticism, / 비판으로 /
usually when we are seeking to invalidate /
보통 우리가 틀렸음을 입증하려고 할 때 /
someone's opinion. 누군가의 의견이
It's like we all automatically accept /
이는 마치 우리 모두가 자동적으로 받아들이는 것과 같다 /
that the "right" way is, / inevitably, the harder one.
'올바른' 방법은 ~이라는 것을 / 반드시 더 어려운 방법(이라는 것을)
In my experience / this is hardly ever questioned.
나의 경험상 / 이것은 거의 한 번도 의문이 제기되지 않는다
What would happen / 무슨 일이 일어날까 /
if you do challenge this sacred cow?
만약 여러분이 정말로 이 신성한 소에 맞선다면
We don't even pause to consider /
우리는 잠시 멈춰서 생각해 보지도 않는다 /
that something important and valuable /
중요하고 가치 있는 무언가를 /
could be made easy.
쉬운 것으로 만들 수 있다는 사실을
What if / the biggest thing /
만약 ~라면 어떨까? / 가장 큰 것이
keeping us from doing what matters
우리가 중요한 일을 하지 못하게 하는
is the false assumption / 잘못된 전제이다 /
that it has to take huge effort?
그것은 엄청난 노력을 필요로 한다는

우리의 언어는 우리의 더 깊은 전제를 드러내는 것을 돕는다. 이것을 잘 드러내는 문구들을 생각해 보라. 우리가 중요한 무언가를 성취할 때, 우리는 그것이 '피, 땀, 그리고 눈물'을 필요로 했다고 말한다. 우리는 중요한 성과는 '힘들게 얻은' 것이라고 말한다. 우리는 '하루 동안의 일'이라는 말로도 충분할 때 '힘든 하루 동안의 일'이라는 말을 권한다. 우리가 '쉬운 돈'이라고 말할 때, 우리는 그것이 불법적이거나 의심스러운 수단을 통해 얻어졌다는 것을 넌지시 드러내고 있다. 우리는 보통 누군가의 의견이 틀렸음을 입증하려고 할 때, '말은 쉽지'라는 문구를 비판으로 사용한다. 이는 마치 우리 모두가 '올바른' 방법은 반드시 더 어려운 방법이라는 것을 자동적으로 받아들이는 것과 같다. 나의 경험상 이것은 거의 한 번도 의문이 제기되지 않는다. 만약 여러분이 정말로 이 신성한 소에 맞선다면 무슨 일이 일어날까? 우리는 중요하고 가치 있는 무언가를 쉬운 것으로 만들 수 있다는 사실을 잠시 멈춰서 생각해 보지도 않는다. 만약 우리가 중요한 일을 하지 못하게 하는 가장 큰 것이 중요한 일은 엄청난 노력을 필요로 한다는 잘못된 전제라면 어떨까?

① 고난을 피하려는 충동을 억제한다
② 격식 차린 언어 사용에 대한 압박에서 벗어난다
③ 오직 노력만이 가치 있다는 확고한 신념을 의심한다
④ 돈이 항상 우선이라는 낡은 관념 버린다
⑤ 신성한 동물이 행운을 가져온다는 미신을 깬다

문제풀이

우리의 언어는 우리의 더 깊은 전제를 드러내는 것을 돕는데, 예를 들어 우리는 중요한 성과를 말할 때 '힘들게 얻은' 것이라고 말하는 경향이 있고, 중요하고 가치 있는 무언가를 쉬운 것으로 만들 수 있다는 사실을 생각조차 하지 않는다는 내용이다. 밑줄 친 부분이 의미하는 바로 ③ 'doubt the solid belief that only hard work is worthy(오직 노력만이 가치 있다는 확고한 신념 의심하기)'가 가장 적절하다.

이렇게 풀자 중요한 성과는 '힘들게 얻은' 것, '힘든 하루 동안의 일'로 표현하거나 '쉬운 돈'은 불법적이거나 의심스러운 수단을 통해 얻어졌다는 것을 암시한다거나 '올바른' 방법은 반드시 더 어려운 방법이라고 자동적으로 받아들이며, 중요하고 가치 있는 무언가를 쉬운 것으로 만들 수 있다는 사실을 잠시 멈춰서 생각해 보지도 않는다는 내용들을 통해 밑줄 친 부분이 의미하는 바를 추론할 수 있다.

어휘 · 어구

reveal 드러내다
assumption 전제
phrase 문구
accomplish 성취하다, 이루다(*n.* accomplishment)
hard-earned 힘들게 얻은, 애써서 번
recommend 추천하다
imply 넌지시 비추다
obtain 얻다, 획득하다
illegal 불법적인
questionable 의심스러운, 수상한
criticism 비평
seek to-v ~하도록 시도하다
opinion 의견
automatically 자동적으로
accept 받아들이다
inevitably 반드시, 불가피하게
experience 경험
happen 일어나다
challenge 도전하다, 이의를 제기하다
sacred 신성한
pause 멈추다
consider 생각하다, 고려하다
valuable 가치 있는
keep ~ from v-ing ~가 … 하는 것을 막다
take effort 노력을 필요로 하다
resist 참다, 저항하다
tendency 경향
hardship 고난
escape 벗어나다, 달아나다
pressure 압박
formal 격식 차린

language 언어
doubt 의심하다
solid 탄탄한
worthy 가치 있는
abandon 버리다
notion 관념, 개념
come first 최우선 고려사항이다
superstition 미신
holy 신성한

정답률 74%

1. ③ 고객의 부당한 요구를 거절해야 할 때가 있다

직독/직해

Is the customer *always* right?
고객은 항상 옳은가

When customers return a broken product /
고객들이 고장 난 제품을 반품할 때 /

to a famous company, / 한 유명한 회사에 /

which makes kitchen and bathroom fixtures, /
그 회사는 주방과 욕실 설비를 만드는데 /

the company nearly always offers a replacement /
그 회사는 거의 항상 대체품을 제공한다 /

to maintain good customer relations.
좋은 고객 관계를 유지하기 위해

Still, / "there are times you've got to say 'no,'" /
그럼에도 / "'안 돼요.'라고 말을 해야 할 때가 있다." /

explains the warranty expert of the company, /
그 회사의 상품 보증 전문가는 설명한다 /

such as when a product is undamaged /
상품이 멀쩡할 때와 같이 /

or has been abused. 혹은 남용되었을 때와 같이

Entrepreneur Lauren Thorp, /
기업가 Lauren Thorp는 /

who owns an e-commerce company, / says, /
전자 상거래 회사를 소유하고 있는데 / 말한다 /

"While the customer is 'always' right, /
"고객이 '항상' 옳지만 /

sometimes you just have to fire a customer."
때로는 당신이 고객을 해고해야만 한다."

When Thorp has tried everything /
Thorp가 모든 것을 해봤을 때 /

to resolve a complaint / and realizes /
불만을 해결하기 위해 / 그리고 깨달을 때 /

that the customer will be dissatisfied no matter what, /
그 고객이 어떤 경우에도 만족하지 않을 것이란 사실을 /

she returns her attention /
그녀는 자신의 주의를 돌리는데 /

to the rest of her customers, /
나머지 다른 고객들에게 /

who she says are "the reason for my success."
그 고객들은 "내 성공의 이유"라고 그녀는 말한다

고객은 항상 옳은가? 주방과 욕실 설비를 만드는 한 유명한 회사에 고객들이 고장 난 제품을 반품할 때, 그 회사는 좋은 고객 관계를 유지하기 위해 거의 항상 대체품을 제공한다. 그럼에도, 그 회사의 상품 보증 전문가는 상품이 멀쩡하거나 남용되었을 때와 같이, "'안 돼요.'라고 말을 해야 할 때가 있다."라고 설명한다. 전자 상거래 회사를 소유한 기업가 Lauren Thorp는 "고객이 '항상' 옳지만, 때로는 당신이 고객을 해고해야만 한다."라고 말한다. Thorp가 (고객의) 불만을 해결하기 위해 모든 것을 해봤는데 그 고객이 어떤 경우에도 만족하지 않을 것이란 사실을 깨달을 때, 그녀는 자신의 주의를 나머지 다른 고객들에게 돌리는데, 그 고객들은 "내 성공의 이유"라고 그녀는 말한다.

① 고객의 긴급 상황을 해결해야
② 고객의 구매 기록을 제거해야
③ 고객의 부당한 요구를 거절해야
④ 고객의 숨은 의도를 밝혀야
⑤ 영향력 있는 고객의 힘에 의존해야

문제풀이

고객이 고장 난 제품을 반품할 때 기업은 항상 좋은 고객 관계를 유지하기 위해 대체품을 제공하지만, 상품에 문제가 없는 경우와 상품이 남용되는 때에는 반품을 거절할 필요가 있으며, 불만 해결을 위해 최선을 다해도 고객이 만족하지 않는다면 그 고객 대신 다른 고객들에게 주의를 돌리는 것이 필요하다는 내용이다. 따라서 밑줄 친 부분이 의미하는 바로 ③ 'reject a customer's unreasonable demand(고객의 부당한 요구를 거절해야)'가 가장 적절하다.

어휘·어구

fixture 설비
replacement 대체품
relation 관계
warranty (상품 등의) 보증
undamaged 손상되지 않은
abuse 남용하다
entrepreneur 기업가
e-commerce 전자 상거래
fire 해고하다
resolve 해결하다
complaint 불만
dissatisfied 불만스런
attention 주의, 관심
reason 이유
success 성공
deal with ~을 다루다
emergency 긴급 상황
delete 삭제하다
purchasing 구매
reject 거절하다
unreasonable 부당한, 불합리한
demand 요구
uncover 밝히다, 폭로하다
hidden 숨은
intention 의도
rely on ~에 의존하다
influential 영향을 미치는

정답률 83%

2. ③ 스트레스 관리 원칙

직독/직해

A psychology professor raised a glass of water /
한 심리학 교수가 물 잔을 들어 올렸다 /

while teaching stress management principles /
스트레스 관리 원칙을 가르치던 중 /

to her students, / and asked them, /
자신의 학생들에게 / 그리고 그들에게 물었다 /

"How heavy is this glass of water / I'm holding?"
이 물 잔은 얼마나 무거울까요 / 제가 들고 있는

Students shouted out various answers.
학생들은 다양한 대답을 외쳤다

The professor replied, / 교수가 대답했다 /

"The absolute weight of this glass / doesn't matter.
이 잔의 절대 무게는 / 중요하지 않습니다.

It depends on / how long I hold it.
이는 달려 있죠 / 제가 그것을 얼마나 오랫동안 들고 있느냐에

If I hold it for a minute, / it's quite light.
만약 제가 이것을 1분 동안 들고 있다면 / 그건 꽤 가볍죠

But, / if I hold it for a day straight, /
하지만 / 제가 이것을 하루 종일 들고 있다면 /

it will cause severe pain in my arm, /
이것은 제 팔에 심각한 고통을 야기하게 됩니다 /

forcing me to drop the glass to the floor.
그리고 제가 잔을 바닥에 떨어뜨리게 할 것입니다

In each case, / the weight of the glass is the same, /
각 사례에서 / 잔의 무게는 같습니다 /

but the longer I hold it, / the heavier it feels to me."
하지만 제가 오래 들고 있을수록 / 그것은 저에게 더 무겁게 느껴지죠

As the class nodded their heads in agreement, /
학생들은 동의하며 고개를 끄덕였을 때 /

she continued, / 교수는 계속해서 말했다 /

"Your stresses in life / are like this glass of water.
여러분이 인생에서 느끼는 스트레스들은 / 이 물 잔과 같습니다.

If you still feel / the weight of yesterday's stress, /
만약 여러분이 아직도 느낀다면 / 어제 받은 스트레스의 무게를 /

it's a strong sign / that it's time to put the glass down."
그것은 강한 신호입니다 / 잔을 내려놓아야 할 때라는

한 심리학 교수가 자신의 학생들에게 스트레스 관리 원칙을 가르치던 중 물이 든 유리잔(물 잔)을 들어 올리고 "제가 들고 있는 이 물 잔은 얼마나 무거울까요?"라고 물었다. 학생들은 다양한 대답을 외쳤다. 교수가 대답했다. "이 잔의 절대 무게는 중요하지 않습니다. 이는 제가 이 잔을 얼마나 오랫동안 들고 있느냐에 달려 있죠. 만약 제가 이것을 1분 동안 들고 있다면, 그건 꽤 가볍죠. 하지만, 제가 이것을 하루 종일 들고 있다면 이것은 제 팔에 심각한 고통을 야기하게 되고, 제가 잔을 바닥에 떨어뜨리게 할 것입니다. 각 사례에서 잔의 무게는 같지만, 제가 오래 들고 있을수록 그것은 저에게 더 무겁게 느껴지죠." 학생들은 동의하며 고개를 끄덕였고, 교수는 계속해서 말했다. "여러분이 인생에서 느끼는 스트레스들은 이 물 잔과 같습니다. 만약 여러분이 아직도 어제 받은 스트레스의 무게를 느낀다면, 그것은 잔을 내려놓아야 할 때라는 강한 신호입니다."

① 잔에 물을 더 부어야
② 실수를 하지 않기 위해 계획을 세워야
③ 마음속에 있는 스트레스를 풀어야
④ 스트레스의 원인에 대해 생각해야
⑤ 다른 사람들의 의견을 받아들이는 것을 배울

문제풀이

물이 든 물 잔의 무게는 그것을 들고 있는 시간에 따라 비례하는 데, 인생에서 느끼는 스트레스가 바로 물 잔과 같다는 내용이다. 따라서 밑줄 친 부분이 의미하는 바로 ③ 'let go of the stress in your mind(마음속에 있는 스트레스를 풀어야)'가 가장 적절하다.

어휘·어구

psychology 심리학
professor 교수
management 관리
principle 원칙
various 다양한
reply 대답하다
absolute 절대적인
weight 무게
matter 중요하다
depend on ~에 달려 있다
severe 심각한
agreement 동의
accept 받아들이다
opinion 의견

정답률 62%

3. ⑤ 진취적이며 적극적으로 구직 활동을 하라

직독/직해

A job search is not a passive task.
구직 활동은 수동적인 일이 아니다

When you are searching, / you are not browsing, /
여러분은 구직 활동을 할 때 / 이것저것 훑어보고 다니지 않으며 /

nor are you "just looking".
'그냥 구경만 하지'도 않는다

Browsing is not an effective way /
훑어보고 다니는 것은 효과적인 방법이 아니다 /

to reach a goal / you claim to want to reach.
(~하는) 목표에 도달할 수 있는 / 여러분이 도달하기 원한다고 주장하는
If you are acting with purpose, / if you are serious /
만약 여러분이 목적을 가지고 행동한다면 / 만약 여러분이 진지하다면 /
about anything you chose to do, /
하고자 선택한 어떤 것에 대해 /
then you need to be direct, focused /
그렇다면 여러분은 직접적이고, 집중해야 한다 /
and whenever possible, clever.
그리고 가능한 한 영리해야 한다
Everyone else searching for a job /
일자리를 찾는 다른 모든 사람이 /
has the same goal, / competing for the same jobs.
같은 목표를 가지고 있다 / 같은 일자리를 얻기 위해 경쟁하면서
You must do more / than the rest of the herd.
여러분은 더 많은 것을 해야 한다 / 그 무리의 나머지 사람들보다
Regardless of how long it may take /
얼마나 오랜 시간이 걸리든지 간에 상관없이 /
you to find and get / the job you want, /
여러분이 찾아서 얻는 데 / 여러분이 원하는 직업을 /
being proactive / 진취적인 것이 /
will logically get you results faster /
논리적으로 여러분이 더 빨리 결과를 얻게 해줄 것이다
than if you rely only on /
~에만 의존하는 것보다 /
browsing online job boards /
온라인 취업 게시판을 검색하는 데(에만) /
and emailing an occasional resume.
그리고 가끔 이력서를 이메일로 보내는 것(에만)
Leave those activities / to the rest of the sheep.
그런 활동들은 남겨 두라 / 나머지 양들에게

구직 활동은 수동적인 일이 아니다. 여러분은 구직 활동을 할 때, 이것저것 훑어보고 다니지 않으며 '그냥 구경만 하지'도 않는다. 훑어보고 다니는 것은 여러분이 도달하기 원한다고 주장하는 목표에 도달할 수 있는 효과적인 방법이 아니다. 만약 여러분이 목적을 가지고 행동한다면, 하고자 선택한 어떤 것에 대해 여러분이 진지하다면, 그렇다면 여러분은 직접적이고, 집중해야 하며, 가능한 한 영리해야 한다. 일자리를 찾는 다른 모든 사람이 같은 목표를 가지고 있고, 같은 일자리를 얻기 위해 경쟁한다. 여러분은 그 무리의 나머지 사람들보다 더 많은 것을 해야 한다. 여러분이 원하는 직업을 찾아서 얻는 데 얼마나 오랜 시간이 걸리든지 간에, 온라인 취업 게시판을 검색하고 가끔 이력서를 이메일로 보내는 것에만 의존하는 것보다는 진취적인 것이 논리적으로 여러분이 더 빨리 결과를 얻게 해줄 것이다. 그런 활동들은 나머지 양들에게 남겨 두라.

① 다른 구직자들의 감정을 이해하려고 애써라.
② 평정심을 유지하고 여러분의 현재 위치를 굳게 지켜라.
③ 구직 경쟁을 두려워하지 마라.
④ 여러분의 미래 고용주에게 가끔 이메일을 보내라.
⑤ 다른 구직자들 중에 두드러지기 위해 더 적극적이 되어라.

문제풀이

구직 활동을 하는 다른 모든 사람이 같은 목표를 가지고 같은 일자리를 얻기 위해 경쟁하기 때문에 다른 사람들보다 더 많은 것을 진취적으로 하라는 내용이다. 따라서 밑줄 친 부분이 의미하는 바로 ⑤ 'Be more active to stand out from other job-seekers.(다른 구직자들 중에 두드러지기 위해 더 적극적이 되어라.)'가 가장 적절하다.

어휘·어구

job search 구직 활동
passive 수동적인
browse 훑어보다
effective 효과적인
reach 도달하다
claim 주장하다, 공언하다
direct 직접적인
focused 집중하는
rest 나머지
herd 무리
regardless of ~에 상관없이
proactive 진취적인
logically 논리적으로
occasional 가끔의
resume 이력서
sheep 양, 어리석은 사람
stick to ~을 굳게 지키다, 고수하다
stand out 두드러지다

정답률 60%

4. ④ 기후 변화에 대한 우리의 책임

직독/직해

When it comes to climate change, /
기후 변화에 관해 /
many blame the fossil fuel industry /
많은 사람들은 화석 연료 산업을 탓한다
for pumping greenhouse gases, /
온실가스를 배출하는 것에 대해 /
the agricultural sector for burning rainforests, /
열대 우림을 태우는 것에 대해 농업 분야를 /
or the fashion industry for producing excessive clothes.
혹은 과다한 의복을 생산하는 것에 대해 패션 산업을
But wait, / what drives these industrial activities?
하지만 잠깐 / 무엇이 이러한 산업 활동들을 가동시키는가
Our consumption. 우리의 소비이다
Climate change is a summed product /
기후 변화는 합쳐진 산물이다 /
of each person's behavior. 각 개인 행위의
For example, / 예를 들어 /
the fossil fuel industry is a popular scapegoat /
화석 연료 산업은 일반적인 희생양이다 /
in the climate crisis.
기후 위기에 있어서
But why do they drill and burn fossil fuels?
하지만 왜 그들은 화석 연료를 시추하고 태울까
We provide them strong financial incentives: /
우리가 그들에게 강력한 금전적인 동기를 제공한다 /
some people regularly travel /
어떤 사람들은 정기적으로 여행한다 /
on airplanes and cars / that burn fossil fuels.
비행기와 차로 / 화석 연료를 태우는
Some people waste electricity /
어떤 사람들은 전기를 낭비한다 /
generated by burning fuel in power plants.
발전소에서 연료를 태움으로써 생산된 (전기를)
Some people use and throw away plastic products /
어떤 사람들은 플라스틱 제품을 사용하고 버린다 /
derived from crude oil / every day.
원유로부터 얻어진 / 매일
Blaming the fossil fuel industry /
화석 연료 산업을 탓하는 것은 /
while engaging in these behaviors /
이러한 행위들에 참여하면서 /
is a slap in our own face.
스스로의 얼굴 때리기이다

기후 변화에 관해 많은 사람들은 온실가스를 배출하는 것에 대해 화석 연료 산업을, 열대 우림을 태우는 것에 대해 농업 분야를, 혹은 과다한 의복을 생산하는 것에 대해 패션 산업을 탓한다. 하지만 자, 무엇이 이러한 산업 활동들을 가동시키는가? 우리의 소비이다. 기후 변화는 각 개인 행위의 합쳐진 산물이다. 예를 들어 화석 연료 산업은 기후 위기에 있어서 일반적인 희생양이다. 하지만 왜 그들은 화석 연료를 시추하고 태울까? 우리가 그들에게 강력한 금전적인 동기를 제공한다. 예를 들어, 어떤 사람들은 화석 연료를 태우는 비행기와 차로 정기적으로 여행한다. 어떤 사람들은 발전소에서 연료를 태움으로써 생산된 전기를 낭비한다. 어떤 사람들은 원유로부터 얻어진 플라스틱 제품을 매일 사용하고 버린다. 이러한 행위들에 참여하면서 화석 연료 산업을 탓하는 것은 스스로의 얼굴 때리기이다.

① 미래 세대에게 변화의 여지를 주는 것
② 천연 자원의 부족에 대해 우리 자신에게 경고하는 것
③ 화석연료 생산의 이점을 인정하지 않는 것
④ 기후 변화에 대한 우리의 책임을 인식하지 못하는 것
⑤ 환경 문제를 개별적으로 다루기 시작하는 것

문제풀이

기후 변화와 관련해 다양한 분야의 행동들을 비난하지만 결국 산업 활동을 촉진하는 것은 우리의 소비이고, 결국 기후 변화는 각 개인 행위의 합쳐진 산물이라는 내용의 글이다. 따라서 기후 변화에 대해 화석 연료 산업을 탓하는 것은 우리 스스로를 탓하는 것이라고 할 수 있으므로 밑줄 친 부분이 의미하는 바로는 ④ 'failing to recognize our responsibility for climate change(기후 변화에 대한 우리의 책임을 인식하지 못하는 것)'가 가장 적절하다.

이렇게 풀자 밑줄 친 부분이 의미하는 바를 추론하는 유형은 밑줄 친 부분의 사전적 의미보다는 마치 빈칸 유형을 푸는 마음가짐으로 접근해야 한다. 'Climate change is a summed product of each person's behavior.(기후 변화는 각 개인 행위의 합쳐진 산물이다.)'와 'But why do they drill and burn fossil fuels? We provide them strong financial incentives.(하지만 왜 그들은 화석 연료를 시추하고 태울까? 우리가 그들에게 강력한 금전적인 동기를 제공한다.)'에서 기후 변화에 대해 화석 연료를 탓하는 것은 결국 우리 자신의 책임을 인식하지 못하는 것을 의미하는 것으로 유추할 수 있다.

어휘·어구

when it comes to ~에 관해
fossil fuel 화석 연료
pump 퍼내다
greenhouse gases 온실가스
agricultural 농업의
excessive 과도한
industrial 산업의
summed 합쳐진
financial 금전적인
incentive 동기
regularly 정기적으로
generate 발생시키다
power plant 발전소
throw away 버리다
derive 유래하다
engage in ~에 참여하다

정답률 46%

5. ⑤ 제자리에 있지 않는 물건

직독/직해

Nothing is trash by nature.
어떤 것도 본래부터 쓰레기인 것은 없다
Anthropologist Mary Douglas / 인류학자인 Mary Douglas는 /
brings back and analyzes the common saying /
흔히 하는 말을 소환하여 해석한다 /
that dirt is "matter out of place."
더러운 것은 "제자리에 있지 않은 물체"라는
Dirt is relative, / she emphasizes.
더러운 것은 상대적인 것이다 / 그녀는 강조한다
"Shoes are not dirty in themselves, / but it is dirty /
신발은 그 자체로는 더럽지 않다 / 하지만 더러운 것이다 /
to place them on the dining-table; /
그것들이 식탁 위에 놓여 있을 때 /
food is not dirty in itself, /
음식은 그 자체로는 더럽지 않다 /
but it is dirty / to leave pots and pans / in the bedroom, /
하지만 더럽다 / 냄비와 팬을 놓아두는 것은 / 침실에 /
or food all over clothing; / similarly, /
혹은 음식이 옷에 다 묻어 있을 때 / 유사하게 /
bathroom items in the living room; /
거실에 있는 욕실용품 /

clothing lying on chairs; / 의자 위에 놓여 있는 옷 /
outdoor things placed indoors; / 실내에 놓인 실외 물품들 /
upstairs things downstairs, / and so on."
아래층에 있는 위층 물건들 / 등등이 (더러운 것이다)
Sorting the dirty from the clean /
깨끗한 것과 더러운 것을 분류하는 것은 /
— removing the shoes from the table, /
식탁에서 신발을 치우는 것 /
putting the dirty clothing / in the washing machine /
더러운 옷을 넣는 것 / 세탁기에 /
— involves systematic ordering and classifying.
체계적인 정리와 분류를 포함하는 것이다
Eliminating dirt / is thus a positive process.
더러운 것을 제거하는 것은 / 그러므로 긍정적인 과정이다

어떤 것도 본래부터 쓰레기인 것은 없다. 인류학자인 Mary Douglas는 더러운 것은 "제자리에 있지 않은 물체"라는 흔히 하는 말을 소환하여 해석한다. 더러운 것은 상대적인 것이라고 그녀는 강조한다. "신발은 그 자체로는 더럽지 않지만, 식탁 위에 놓여 있을 때 더러운 것이며, 음식은 그 자체로는 더럽지 않지만, 침실에 냄비와 팬을 놓아둔다면, 혹은 음식이 옷에 다 묻어 있을 때, 유사하게, 거실에 있는 욕실용품, 의자 위에 놓여 있는 옷, 실내에 놓인 실외 물품들, 아래층에 있는 위층 물건들, 등등이 더러운 것이다." 깨끗한 것과 더러운 것을 분류하는 것 — 식탁에서 신발을 치우는 것, 세탁기에 더러운 옷을 넣는 것 — 은 체계적인 정리와 분류를 포함하는 것이다. 그러므로 더러운 것을 제거하는 것은 긍정적인 과정이다.

① 완전히 망가진 무언가
② 아무도 알아보지 못하는 작은 먼지
③ 더럽지만 재생 가능한 물질
④ 쉽게 대체될 수 있는 것
⑤ 적절하지 않은 물건

문제풀이

본래부터 쓰레기인 물건은 없고, 더러운 것은 상대적인 것으로 물건이 있어야 할 곳에 제대로 있지 않은 경우에 더러운 것으로 여겨진다는 내용이므로, 밑줄 친 부분이 의미하는 바로 ⑤ 'a thing that is not in order(적절하지 않은 물건)'가 가장 적절하다.

이렇게 풀자 식탁 위에 놓인 신발, 침실에 있는 냄비와 팬, 거실에 있는 욕실용품, 실내에 놓인 실외 물품들의 사례를 통해 밑줄 친 부분의 의미를 추론할 수 있다.

어휘·어구

anthropologist 인류학자
analyze 분석하다
out of place 제자리에 있지 않은
relative 상대적인
emphasize 강조하다
sort 분류하다
remove 제거하다
systematic 체계적인
classify 분류하다
eliminate 제거하다
completely 완전히
notice 알아차리다
renewable 재생 가능한
material 물질
replace 대체하다
in order 적절한

정답률 53%

6. ③ 선택적 지각

직독/직해

We have a tendency / to interpret events selectively.
우리는 경향이 있다 / 사건을 선택적으로 해석하는
If we want things to be / "this way" or "that way" /
만약 우리가 일이 되기를 원한다면 / "이렇게" 혹은 "그렇게" /
we can most certainly select, stack, or arrange evidence /
우리는 분명 증거를 선택하거나 쌓거나 배열할 수 있다 /
in a way that supports such a viewpoint.
그런 관점을 뒷받침하는 방식으로
Selective perception is based /
선택적인 지각은 기초한다 /
on what seems to us to stand out.
우리에게 두드러져 보이는 것에
However, / what seems to us to be standing out /
하지만 / 우리에게 두드러져 보이는 것은 /
may very well be related to our goals, interests, expectations, past experiences, /
우리의 목표, 관심사, 기대, 과거의 경험과 매우 관련이 있을지도 모른다 /
or current demands of the situation /
혹은 상황에 대한 현재의 요구와 /
— "with a hammer in hand, /
— "망치를 손에 들고 있으면 /
everything looks like a nail."
모든 것은 못처럼 보인다
This quote highlights / 이 인용문은 강조한다 /
the phenomenon of selective perception.
선택적 지각의 현상을
If we want to use a hammer, /
만약 우리가 망치를 사용하기를 원한다면 /
then the world around us /
우리 주변 세상은 /
may begin to look / as though it is full of nails!
보이기 시작할지도 모른다 / 못으로 가득 찬 것처럼

우리는 사건을 선택적으로 해석하는 경향이 있다. 만약 우리가 일이 "이렇게" 혹은 "그렇게" 되기를 원한다면, 우리는 분명 그런 관점을 뒷받침하는 방식으로 증거를 선택하거나 쌓거나 배열할 수 있다. 선택적인 지각은 우리에게 두드러져 보이는 것에 기초한다. 하지만 우리에게 두드러져 보이는 것은 우리의 목표, 관심사, 기대, 과거의 경험 혹은 상황에 대한 현재의 요구와 매우 관련이 있을지도 모른다 — "망치를 손에 들고 있으면, 모든 것은 못처럼 보인다." 이 인용문은 선택적 지각의 현상을 강조한다. 만약 우리가 망치를 사용하기를 원한다면, 우리 주변 세상은 못으로 가득 찬 것처럼 보이기 시작할지도 모른다!

① 두드러지고 싶어 하지 않는다
② 우리의 노력을 무의미하게 만든다
③ 특정한 방식으로 뭔가를 하려고 한다
④ 다른 사람들이 우리의 관점과 비슷한 관점을 갖길 바란다
⑤ 다른 사람들에 의해 받아들여지는 사고방식을 갖는다

문제풀이

선택적 지각에 관한 글로, 우리는 사건을 선택적으로 해석하는 경향이 있는데, 우리의 목표나 관심사 등 현재의 요구와 관련이 있는 것을 기초로 선택적 지각을 한다는 내용이다. 따라서 밑줄 친 부분이 의미하는 바로 ③ 'intend to do something in a certain way(특정한 방식으로 뭔가를 하려고 한다)'가 가장 적절하다.

어휘·어구

tendency 경향
interpret 해석하다
selectively 선택적으로
stack 쌓다
arrange 배열하다
evidence 증거
viewpoint 관점, 견해
perception 지각, 인식
stand out 두드러지다, 눈에 띄다
be related to ~와 관계가 있다
expectation 기대
current 현재의
quote 인용문
highlight 강조하다
phenomenon 현상
be unwilling to do ~하는 데 마음이 내키지 않다
meaningless 무의미한

정답률 76%

7. ② 후회를 극복하고 다음 기회를 계획하라

직독/직해

Get past the 'I wish I hadn't done that!' reaction.
'내가 그것을 하지 말았어야 했는데!'라는 반응을 넘어서라
If the disappointment you're feeling /
만약 여러분이 느끼는 실망이 /
is linked to an exam you didn't pass /
통과하지 못한 시험과 관련된다면 /
because you didn't study for it, /
네가 시험공부를 하지 않았기 때문에 /
or a job you didn't get /
혹은 얻지 못한 일자리(와 관련된다면) /
because you said silly things at the interview, /
면접에서 바보 같은 말을 해서 /
or a person you didn't impress /
혹은 좋은 인상을 주지 못한 사람(과 관련된다면) /
because you took entirely the wrong approach, /
완전히 잘못된 접근 방법을 택해서 /
accept that it's *happened* now.
이제는 그 일이 '일어나 버렸다'는 것을 받아들여라
The only value of 'I wish I hadn't done that!' /
'내가 그것을 하지 말았어야 했는데!'의 유일한 가치는 /
is that you'll know better / what to do next time.
여러분이 더 잘 알게 되리라는 것이다 / 다음에 무엇을 할지
The learning pay-off / is useful and significant.
배움으로 얻게 되는 이득은 / 유용하고 의미가 있다
This 'if only I ...' agenda / is virtual.
이러한 '내가 …하기만 했다면'이라는 의제는 / 가상이다
Once you have worked that out, /
일단 여러분이 그것을 파악했다면 /
it's time to translate it /
그것을 바꿀 때이다 /
from the past tense to the future tense: /
과거 시제에서 미래 시제로 /
'Next time I'm in this situation, /
다음에 내가 이 상황일 때 /
I'm going to try to ...'.
나는 …하려고 할 것이다

'내가 그것을 하지 말았어야 했는데!'라는 반응을 넘어서라. 만약 여러분이 느끼는 실망이 시험공부를 하지 않았기 때문에 통과하지 못한 시험, 면접에서 바보 같은 말을 해서 얻지 못한 일자리, 혹은 완전히 잘못된 접근 방법을 택해서 좋은 인상을 주지 못한 사람과 관련된다면, 이제는 그 일이 '일어나 버렸다'는 것을 받아들여라. '내가 그것을 하지 말았어야 했는데!'의 유일한 가치는 여러분이 다음에 무엇을 할지 더 잘 알게 되리라는 것이다. 배움으로 얻게 되는 이득은 유용하고 의미가 있다. 이러한 '내가 …하기만 했다면'이라는 의제는 가상이다. 일단 여러분이 그것을 파악했다면, 그것을 과거 시제에서 미래 시제로 바꿀 때이다: '다음에 내가 이 상황일 때 나는 …하려고 할 것이다.'

① 여러분의 흥미와 관련된 일을 찾아라
② 후회를 잊고 다음번 계획을 세워라
③ 도와주는 사람들을 네 주변에 두어라
④ 문법을 공부하고 간결한 문장을 써라
⑤ 너의 말하는 방식을 검토하고 사과하라

문제풀이

이미 벌어진 일에 대해 후회하지 말고, 일단 벌어진 일을 파악했다면 다음번에 같은 상황이 벌어질 경우 할 일에 대해 생각하라는 내용이므로, 밑줄 친 부분이 의미하는 바로 가장 적절한 것은 ② 'get over regrets and plan for next time(후회를 잊고 다음번 계획을 세워라)'이다.

이렇게 풀자 마지막 문장인 'Next time I'm in this situation, I'm going to try to ...'가 밑줄 친 말의 의미를 추론하는 단서이다.

어휘·어구

reaction 반응
disappointment 실망
be linked to ~과 연관되다
silly 바보 같은

interview 면접, 인터뷰
impress 좋은 인상을 주다
entirely 완전히, 전적으로
approach 접근 방법
accept 받아들이다
value 가치
pay-off 이득
useful 유용한
significant 의미가 있는, 중요한
virtual 가상의
work ~ out ~을 파악하다, 알아내다
translate 바꾸다, 번역하다, 고치다
situation 상황
get over ~에서 회복하다, ~을 이겨내다
surround 둘러싸다
supportive 지지가 되는, 도와주는
sentence 문장
examine 조사하다, 검토하다
apologize 사과하다

정답률 72%

8. ④ 빈번한 핸드폰 교체

직독/직해

There are more than 700 million cell phones /
휴대전화가 7억 개가 넘는다 /
used in the US today / 오늘날 미국에서 사용되는 /
and at least 140 million of those cell phone users /
그리고 이 휴대전화 사용자들 중 적어도 1억 4천만 명은 /
will abandon their current phone for a new phone /
새 휴대전화를 위해 그들의 현재 휴대전화를 버릴 것이다 /
every 14-18 months. 14~18개월마다
I'm not one of those people /
나는 그런 사람들 중 한 명은 아니다 /
who just "must" have the latest phone.
최신 휴대전화를 '반드시' 가져야 하는
Actually, I use my cell phone /
사실 나는 내 휴대전화를 사용한다 /
until the battery no longer holds a good charge.
배터리가 더 이상 충전이 잘 되지 않을 때까지
At that point, it's time.
그때라면 때가 된 것이다
So I figure I'll just get a replacement battery.
그래서 나는 그저 교체용 배터리를 사야겠나고 생각한다
But I'm told that battery is no longer made /
그러나 나는 그 배터리가 더 이상 만들어지지 않는다고 듣게 된다 /
and the phone is no longer manufactured /
그리고 그 휴대전화는 더 이상 제조되지 않는다고 /
because there's newer technology and better features in the latest phones.
최신 휴대전화에 더 새로운 기술과 더 나은 기능들이 있기 때문에
That's a typical justification.
그것이 전형적인 정당화이다
The phone wasn't even that old; /
그 휴대전화는 그렇게 오래되지도 않았다 /
maybe a little over one year?
아마도 1년 좀 넘게?
I'm just one example.
나는 단지 한 사례일 뿐이다
Can you imagine / how many countless other people have that same scenario?
당신은 상상할 수 있는가 / 얼마나 수많은 다른 사람들이 이와 똑같은 시나리오를 갖는지?
No wonder cell phones take the lead /
휴대전화가 선두에 있다는 것은 놀랍지 않다 /
when it comes to "e-waste."
전자 쓰레기에 관한 한

오늘날 미국에서 사용되는 휴대전화가 7억 개가 넘고 이 휴대전화 사용자들 중 적어도 1억 4천만 명은 새 휴대전화를 위해 14~18개월마다 그들의 현재 휴대전화를 버릴 것이다. 나는 최신 휴대전화를 '반드시' 가져야 하는 그런 사람들 중 한 명은 아니다. 사실 나는 배터리가 더 이상 충전이 잘 되지 않을 때까지 내 휴대전화를 사용한다. 그때라면 때가 된 것이다. 그래서 나는 그저 교체용 배터리를 사야겠다고 생각한다. 그러나 나는 그 배터리가 더 이상 만들어지지 않고, 최신 휴대전화에 더 새로운 기술과 더 나은 기능들이 있기 때문에 그 휴대전화는 더 이상 제조되지 않는다고 듣게된다. 그것이 전형적인 정당화이다. 그 휴대전화는 심지어 그렇게 오래되지 않았다. 아마도 1년 좀 넘게? 나는 단지 한 사례일 뿐이다. 얼마나 수많은 다른 사람들이 이와 똑같은 시나리오를 갖는지 당신은 상상할 수 있는가? '전자 쓰레기'에 대해서는, 휴대전화가 선두에 있다는 것은 놀랍지 않다.

① 프로그램을 업데이트하는 데 자주 곤란을 겪다
② 비용으로 인해 신기술을 도입하지 못하다
③ 자신들의 핸드폰 수리에 많은 돈을 쓰다
④ 아직 사용할 만한 자신의 핸드폰을 바꾸게 되다
⑤ 새로 출시한 전화기 모델에 실망하다

문제풀이

7억 개가 넘는 휴대전화가 사용되고 있으며 14-18개월마다 사용자들은 새로운 것으로 교체한다고 하면서 그 구체적인 한 예로서 자신도 스스로 정당화를 통해 휴대전화를 교체하게 된다고 했다. 따라서 밑줄 친 'have that same scenario (그와 똑같은 시나리오를 갖다)'라는 말의 의미로 가장 적절한 것은 ④ 'are driven to change their still usable cell phones(아직 사용할 만한 자신의 핸드폰을 바꾸게 되다)'이다.

구조 다시보기

도입	오늘날 미국에서 많은 수의 휴대전화가 버려짐
예시	정당화를 통해 그리 오래 되지도 않은 휴대전화를 교체함 • 정당화 1: 교체하려는 배터리가 더 이상 제조되지 않음 • 정당화 2: 새 휴대전화의 기술과 기능이 더 나음
시사	전자쓰레기에 있어 휴대전화가 선두에 있음

어휘·어구

abandon 버리다
current 지금의, 현재의
charge 충전
figure (~이라고) 판단하다, 생각하다
replacement 교체
feature 기능
justification 정당화
take the lead 선두에 있다

정답률 59%

9. ④ 전학생 Amy에게 말을 걸어준 친구

직독/직해

"Wanna work together?" a cheerful voice spoke /
"같이 공부할래?"라고 명랑한 목소리로 말했다 /
on Amy's first day at a new school. Amy의 새 학교에서 첫날
It was Wilhemina. Wilhemina였다
Amy was too surprised / to do anything but nod.
Amy는 너무 놀랐다 / 고개를 끄덕이기만 했다
The big black girl put her notebook down /
그 덩치 큰 흑인 소녀는 그녀의 공책을 내려놓았다 /
beside Amy's. Amy의 공책 옆에
After dropping the notebook, / 공책을 놓은 후에 /
she lifted herself up onto the stool beside Amy.
그녀는 Amy 옆 의자에 올라갔다
"I'm Wilhemina Smiths, / Smiths with an s at both ends," / she said with a friendly smile.
나는 Wilhemina Smiths야 / 이름 양 끝에 s가 있는 Smiths야 / 그녀는 다정한 미소를 지으며 말했다
"My friends call me Mina. 내 친구들은 나를 Mina라고 불러
You're Amy Tillerman." 네가 Amy Tillerman이지
Amy nodded and stared.
Amy는 고개를 끄덕이며 빤히 쳐다보았다
As the only new kid in the school, /
학교에서 유일한 새로 온 학생인 /
she was pleased / to have a lab partner.
그녀는 기뻤다 / 실험실 파트너가 생겨서
But Amy wondered / if Mina chose her /
하지만 Amy는 궁금했다 / Mina가 자신을 선택한 것이 아닌지 /
because she had felt sorry for the new kid.
그녀가 전학생이 안 됐다고 느껴서

"같이 공부할래?"라고 Amy의 새 학교에서 첫날 명랑한 목소리로 말했다. Wilhemina였다. Amy는 너무 놀라 고개를 끄덕이기만 했다. 그 덩치 큰 흑인 소녀는 Amy의 공책 옆에 ① 그녀의 공책을 내려놓았다. 공책을 놓은 후에 ② 그녀는 Amy 옆 의자에 올라갔다. "나는 Wilhemina Smiths야, 이름 양 끝에 s가 있는 Smiths야."라고 ③ 그녀는 다정한 미소를 지으며 말했다. "내 친구들은 나를 Mina라고 불러. 네가 Amy Tillerman이지." Amy는 고개를 끄덕이며 빤히 쳐다보았다. 학교에서 유일한 새로 온 학생인 ④ 그녀는 실험실 파트너가 생겨서 기뻤다. 하지만 Amy는 ⑤ 그녀가 전학생이 안 됐다고 느껴서 자신을 선택한 것이 아닌지 궁금했다.

문제풀이

①, ②, ③, ⑤는 Wilhemina Smiths를, ④는 Amy Tillerman을 가리킨다.

이렇게 풀자_ 글 속의 등장인물은 'Amy Tillerman'와 'Wilhemina Smiths'로, 학교 첫 날 전학생인 Amy에게 Wilhemina가 함께 실험을 하자고 말을 건 상황을 묘사하는 글이다. 각 지시대명사가 가리키는 대상을 파악하며 글을 읽어야 한다.

어휘·어구

cheerful 발랄한, 쾌활한
nod 끄덕이다
stool 등받이 없는 의자
friendly 다정한
stare 빤히 쳐다보다, 응시하다
lab 실험실

정답률 71%

10. ③ Serene과 그녀의 어머니

직독/직해

Serene tried to do a pirouette / in front of her mother /
Serene은 피루엣을 하려고 했다 / 그녀의 어머니 앞에서 /
but fell to the floor. 하지만 바닥으로 넘어졌다
Serene's mother / helped her off the floor.
Serene의 어머니는 / 그녀가 일어나는 것을 도왔다
She told her / that she had to keep trying /
그녀는 그녀에게 말했다 / 그녀가 계속 노력해야 한다는 것을 /
if she wanted to succeed.
그녀가 성공하고 싶으면
However, / Serene was almost in tears.
하지만 / Serene은 눈물이 날 지경이었다
She had been practicing very hard / the past week /
그녀는 정말 열심히 연습해 오고 있었다 / 지난주에 /
but she did not seem to improve.
하지만 그녀는 나아지지 않은 듯 보였다
Serene's mother said / Serene의 어머니는 말했다 /
that she herself had tried many times /
그녀 자신이 여러 번 시도했다는 것을 /
before succeeding at Serene's age.
Serene의 나이였을 때 성공해 내기 전에
She had fallen so often that she sprained her ankle /
그녀는 너무 자주 넘어져 그녀의 발목을 삐었다 /
and had to rest for three months /
그리고 3개월 동안 쉬어야 했다 /
before she was allowed to dance again.
그녀가 다시 춤을 출 수 있게 되기까지

Serene was surprised.
Serene은 놀랐다

Her mother was a famous ballerina /
그녀의 어머니는 유명한 발레리나였다 /

and to Serene, / her mother had never fallen /
그리고 Serene에게 / 그녀의 어머니는 결코 넘어진 적이 없었다 /

or made a mistake / in any of her performances.
또는 실수를 한 적이 없었다 / 그녀의 어떠한 공연에서도

Listening to her mother made her realize /
어머니의 말을 듣고 그녀는 깨달았다 /

that she had to put in more effort /
그녀가 더 많은 노력을 기울여야 했다는 것을 /

than what she had been doing so far.
그녀가 지금까지 했던 것보다

Serene은 그녀의 어머니 앞에서 피루엣을 하려고 했지만 바닥으로 넘어졌다. Serene의 어머니는 ① 그녀가 일어나는 것을 도왔다. 그녀는 성공하고 싶으면 계속 노력해야 한다고 Serene에게 말했다. 하지만 Serene은 눈물이 날 지경이었다. 지난주 ② 그녀는 정말 열심히 연습했지만 나아지지 않은 듯 보였다. Serene의 어머니는 ③ 그녀 자신이 Serene의 나이였을 때 성공해 내기 전에 여러 번 시도했다고 말했다. 그녀는 너무 자주 넘어져 발목을 삐어서 다시 춤을 출 수 있게 되기까지 3개월 동안 쉬어야 했다. Sereno은 놀랐다. 그녀의 어머니는 유명한 발레리나였고, Serene에게 ④ 그녀의 어머니는 어떠한 공연에서도 결코 넘어지거나 실수를 한 적이 없었다. 어머니의 말을 듣고 ⑤ 그녀는 자신이 지금까지 했던 것보다 더 많은 노력을 기울여야 했다는 것을 깨달았다.

문제풀이

Serene의 나이였을 때 피루엣을 성공하기 위해 여러 번 시도했던 사람은 Serene의 어머니이므로 ③ she는 문장 맨 앞에 오는 Serene's mother를 가리킨다. 나머지는 모두 Serene을 가리킨다.

어휘·어구

in front of ~의 앞에
succeed 성공하다
in tears 눈물을 흘리며
practice 연습하다
improve 나아지다
sprain (손목 · 발목 등을) 삐다
ankle 발목
famous 유명한
make a mistake 실수하다
performance 공연
realize 깨닫다
put in effort 노력을 기울이다
so far 지금까지

본문 023쪽

문법 플러스 4. 주어와 동사의 수 일치

1. is 2. are 3. is 4. argues 5. does
6. are 7. is 8. seem 9. is 10. gives

1 [해석]▶ 식품 라벨의 주된 목적은 여러분이 구입하고 있는 식품 안에 무엇이 들어 있는지 알려주는 것이다.
[해설]▶ 문장의 주어부가 The main purpose of food labels인데 핵심 주어는 단수명사 purpose이므로 단수동사 is가 맞다.

2 [해석]▶ 따뜻한 환경에서는 수분을 흡수하거나 배출할 수 있는 기능이 있는 옷이 몸에서 열을 발산하는 데 도움이 된다.
[해설]▶ 주어가 clothes이고 that have a wicking capacity는 주어를 수식하는 관계대명사절이므로, 복수주어에 맞춰 are가 오는 것이 적절하다.

3 [해석]▶ 그 결과, 친구와 다른 사회 집단의 기준과 기대에 부합해야 한다는 압박감이 거세질 가능성이 있다.
[해설]▶ 주어가 the pressure로 단수이므로 단수동사 is는 올바른 표현이다.

4 [해석]▶ 발달심리학자 Judith Rich Harris는 우리의 발달을 형성하는 세 가지 주요한 힘은 개인적인 기질, 우리의 부모, 우리의 또래들이라고 주장한다.
[해설]▶ 문장의 주어가 Judith Rich Harris이고 그 뒤에 관계절이 연결되어 주어와 동사가 멀어진 구조로, 정동사 argues가 맞다.

5 [해석]▶ 전형적으로 단지 몇 개의 빛 파장만 들어있는 인공조명이 분위기에 미치는 효과는 햇빛이 미치는 효과와 똑같지 않을 수 있다.
[해설]▶ Artificial light가 주어이고, which typically contains only a few wavelengths of lights는 Artificial light에 대해 부연 설명해 주는 계속적 용법의 관계대명사절이다. 따라서 단수주어인 Artificial light에 맞춰 동사는 does를 써야 한다.

6 [해석]▶ 바닷속에 있는 대부분의 플라스틱 조각들은 너무 작아서 바다를 청소할 실질적인 방법은 없다.
[해설]▶ 「most of+복수명사」는 복수동사를 가져온다. most of the plastic particles가 주어이고 in the ocean은 주어를 수식하는 전치사구이므로 복수동사 are를 사용해야 한다.

7 [해석]▶ 포도주 맛을 감정하는 사람들의 경험은 훨씬 더 놀라울 것이다.
[해설]▶ 보어가 문두로 나가면서 주어와 동사가 도치된 문장이다 주어 the experience of wine tasters가 단수주어이므로 단수동사 is가 와야 한다.

8 [해석]▶ 우리가 소통했던 방식에 대한 기억들이 현재 나에게는 우스워 보인다.
[해설]▶ 문장의 주어는 복수명사 Memories이므로 복수동사 seem이 와야 한다.

9 [해석]▶ '우리' 대 '그들'이라는 시대에 뒤떨어진 이원론의 틀에 갇힌 역사적 경향은 많은 사람이 현재 상태를 충분히 고수하게 만들기에 충분히 강하다.
[해설]▶ 문장의 주어는 The historical tendency이고, 문장의 동사로 단수동사 is가 쓰였다. framed in the outdated dualism of us versus them은 문장의 주어인 The historical tendency를 수식하는 과거분사구이다.

10 해석▶ 미국의 가장 유명한 시계 제작자 중 한 명인 Henry Fried는 이 질문에 대한 간단한 설명을 제공한다.
[해설] 주어가 Henry Fried이고 콤마 이하의 one ~ States는 동격인 삽입구이므로 단수동사 gives가 와야 한다.

본문 024쪽

어휘 플러스 4. 파생어 (1)

1. beneficial 2. confident
3. indifferent 4 industrial
5. economical

1 [해석]▶ 일부 제국들은 컸지만, 제국을 하나로 뭉치게 하는 데 필요한 엄격한 사회적 통제는 그것이 이성에 이롭지 못했던 것처럼 과학에도 이롭지 못했다.
2 [해석]▶ 예를 들면, 우리가 자신에 대해 자신감을 가지면 실패조차도 긍정적으로 바라볼 수 있다.

3 [해석]▶ 다시 말해서, 더 낮은 직급의 사람들은 그들의 시선에 신경을 쓰도록 요구받는 반면, 더 높은 직급의 사람들은 무관심할 수 있다.

4 [해석]▶ 예방을 위해서 산업 활동으로부터 나오는 수은을 직접적으로 방출하는 것에 대한 통제가 절실하게 필요하다.

5 [해석]▶ 켜고 끄는 스위치도 필요할 거예요. 각각의 소켓에 개별적인 스위치가 있으면 더 경제적일 거예요.

05. 글의 요지

본문 026쪽

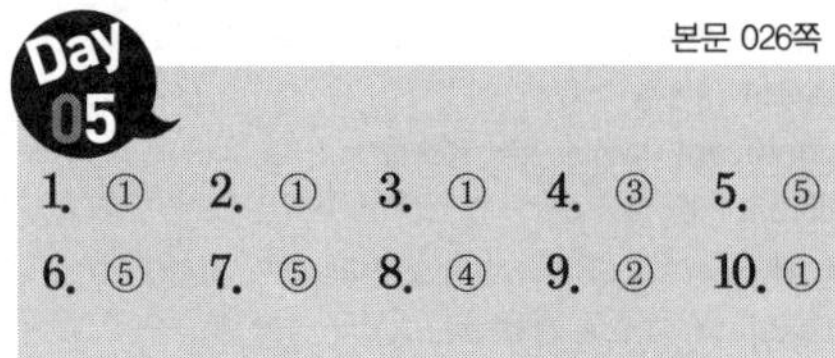
Day 05

1. ① 2. ① 3. ① 4. ③ 5. ⑤
6. ⑤ 7. ⑤ 8. ④ 9. ② 10. ①

정답률 79%

대표 기출 ① 두려움을 주는 뉴스는 사람들이 문제에 덜 대처하게 할 수 있다

직독/직해

The old saying is that "knowledge is power," /
속담은 '아는 것이 힘이다'라고 말한다 /

but when it comes to scary, threatening news, /
하지만 무섭고 위협적인 뉴스에 관한 한 /

research suggests the exact opposite.
연구는 정반대를 시사한다

Frightening news can actually rob /
두려움을 주는 뉴스는 실제로 빼앗을 수 있다 /

people of their inner sense of control, /
사람들에게서 내면의 통제력을 /

making them less likely to take care of /
그들이 돌볼 가능성을 더 낮게 만든다 /

themselves and other people.
스스로와 다른 사람들을

Public health research shows /
공중 보건 연구는 보여준다 /

that when the news presents health-related information / in a pessimistic way, /
뉴스가 건강과 관련된 정보를 제시할 때 / 비관적인 방식으로 /

people are actually less likely to take steps /
사람들이 조치를 취할 가능성이 실제로 더 낮다는 것을 /

to protect themselves / from illness / as a result.
스스로를 보호하기 위한 / 질병으로부터 / 결과적으로

A news article that's intended to warn people /
사람들에게 경고하려는 의도가 있는 뉴스 기사는 /

about increasing cancer rates, /
증가하는 암 발생률에 대해 /

for example, / can result in fewer people choosing /
예를 들어 / 더 적은 사람들이 선택하는 결과를 가져올 수 있다 /

to get screened for the disease /
그 병에 대해 검사받는 것을 /

because they're so terrified of /
그들이 ~대해 너무 두려워하기 때문에 /

what they might find. 발견될지도 모를 것에

This is also true / for issues such as climate change.
이것은 또한 해당이 된다 / 기후 변화와 같은 문제에도

When a news story is all doom and gloom, /
뉴스가 완전히 암울할 때 /

people feel depressed /
사람들은 우울하다 /

and become less interested in /
그리고 흥미를 덜 느끼게 된다 /

taking small, personal steps /
작고 개인적인 조치를 취하는 것에 /

to fight ecological collapse.
생태학적 붕괴와 싸우기 위한

속담은 '아는 것이 힘이다'라고 말하지만, 무섭고 위협적인 뉴스에 관한 한, 연구는 정반대를 시사한다. 두려움을 주는 뉴스는 실제로 사람들에게서 내면의 통제력을 빼앗을 수 있어서, 그들이 스스로와 다른 사람들을 돌볼 가능성을 더 낮게 만든다. 공중 보건 연구는 뉴스가 건강과 관련된 정보를 비관적인 방식으로 제시할 때, 결과적으로 사람들이 질병으로부터 스스로를 보호하기 위한 조치를 취할 가능성이 실제로 더 낮다는 것

을 보여준다. 예를 들어, 증가하는 암 발생률에 대해 사람들에게 경고하려는 의도가 있는 뉴스 기사는 그들이 발견할지도 모를 것에 대해 너무 두려워하기 때문에 더 적은 사람들이 그 병에 대해 검사받는 것을 선택하는 결과를 가져올 수 있다. 이것은 또한 기후 변화와 같은 문제에도 해당이 된다. 뉴스가 완전히 암울할 때, 사람들은 우울하고 생태학적 붕괴와 싸우기 위한 작고 개인적인 조치를 취하는 것에 흥미를 덜 느끼게 된다.

문제풀이

아는 것이 힘이라는 속담과는 달리, 무섭고 위협적인 뉴스를 접하는 경우에는 사람들이 스스로를 돌볼 가능성이 더 낮다는 내용이다. 따라서 글의 요지로 ① '두려움을 주는 뉴스는 사람들이 문제에 덜 대처하게 할 수 있다.'가 가장 적절하다.

이렇게 풀자 글의 앞부분에 제시된 문장 'Frightening news can actually rob people of their inner sense of control, making them less likely to take care of themselves and other people.'에 요지가 드러나 있다.

구조 다시보기

도입	아는 것이 힘이라는 속담이 있음
반박	무섭고 위협적인 뉴스는 사람들이 스스로를 돌볼 가능성을 낮춤
예시 1	건강 관련 정보가 비관적인 방식으로 제시될 때 사람들은 스스로를 보호할 조치를 취할 가능성이 낮음
예시 2	기후 변화 관련 뉴스가 암울할 경우 사람들은 우울해서 생태학적 붕괴와 싸울 조치를 덜 취하게 됨

어휘·어구

old saying 속담, 옛말
knowledge 지식
when it comes to ~에 관한 한
scary 무서운
threatening 위협하는
suggest 시사하다
exact 정확한
opposite 반대
frightening 무서운
actually 실제로
rob A of B A에게서 B를 빼앗다
inner 내면의
sense of control 통제력
take care of 돌보다
public health 공중 보건
present 제시하다
related 관련된
pessimistic 비관적인
protect 보호하다
illness 질병
as a result 결과적으로
article 기사
intend 의도하다
rate 비율
result in 결과가 ~가 되다
screen 검진하다
disease 질병
terrified 겁이 난, 두려운
issue 문제, 이슈
doom and gloom 완전히 암울함
depressed 우울한
personal 개인적인
ecological 생태학적인
collapse 붕괴

정답률 85%

1. ① 아이들의 집중을 위해 과도한 교실 장식을 지양해야 함

직독 직해

A recent study from Carnegie Mellon University in Pittsburgh, /
피츠버그시 Carnegie Mellon University의 최근 한 연구는 /
called "When Too Much of a Good Thing May Be Bad," /
"너무 많은 좋은 것이 나쁠 수도 있을 때"라고 불리는 /
indicates / that classrooms with too much decoration /
보여준다 / 너무 많은 장식이 있는 교실이 /
are a source of distraction for young children /
어린이들의 주의 산만의 원인이다 /
and directly affect their cognitive performance.
그리고 직접적으로 그들의 인지 수행에 영향을 미친다는 것을
Being visually overstimulated, /
시각적으로 지나치게 자극되었을 때 /
the children have a great deal of difficulty concentrating /
아이들은 집중하는 데 많이 어려워한다 /
and end up with worse academic results.
그리고 결국 더 안 좋은 학습 결과로 끝이 난다
On the other hand, / if there is not much decoration /
반면에 / 장식이 많지 않으면 /
on the classroom walls, /
교실 벽에 /
the children are less distracted, /
아이들은 덜 산만해진다 /
spend more time on their activities, /
그리고 그들의 활동에 더 많은 시간을 사용한다 /
and learn more. 그리고 더 많이 배운다
So it's our job, / in order to support their attention, /
그래서 우리가 할 일이다 / 그들의 집중을 돕기 위해 /
to find the right balance / between excessive decoration and the complete absence of it.
적절한 균형을 찾는 것이 / 지나친 장식과 장식이 전혀 없는 것 사이의

"너무 많은 좋은 것이 나쁠 수도 있을 때"라고 불리는 피츠버그시 Carnegie Mellon University의 최근 한 연구는, 너무 많은 장식이 있는 교실이 어린이들의 주의 산만의 원인이고 직접적으로 그들의 인지 수행에 영향을 미친다는 것을 보여준다. 시각적으로 지나치게 자극되었을 때, 아이들은 집중하는 데 많이 어려워하고 결국 더 안 좋은 학습 결과로 끝이 난다. 반면에, 교실 벽에 장식이 많지 않으면, 아이들은 덜 산만해지고, 그들의 활동에 더 많은 시간을 사용하고, 더 많이 배운다. 그래서 그들의 집중을 돕기 위해, 지나친 장식과 장식이 전혀 없는 것 사이의 적절한 균형을 찾는 것이 우리가 할 일이다.

문제풀이

장식이 지나치게 많은 교실은 아이들의 주의 산만의 원인이 되어 집중하는 데 어려움을 겪게 해서 안 좋은 학습 결과를 가져올 수 있다는 내용이다. 따라서 글의 요지로 ① '아이들의 집중을 돕기 위해 과도한 교실 장식을 지양할 필요가 있다.'가 가장 적절하다.

구조 다시보기

도입	장식이 많은 교실은 아이들의 인지 수행에 좋지 않은 영향을 미침
부연	지나친 시각적 자극은 아이들의 집중을 방해함
대조	장식이 많지 않은 교실은 아이들이 덜 산만해져서 더 많이 배우게 됨
결론	교실 벽의 지나친 장식과 장식이 없는 것 사이의 적절한 균형을 찾아야 함

어휘·어구

indicate 나타내다
decoration 장식
distraction 주의 산만
directly 직접적으로
affect 영향을 미치다
cognitive 인지적인
performance 수행
visually 시각적으로
overstimulated 지나치게 자극된
have a difficulty v-ing ~하는 데 어려움을 겪다
concentrate 집중하다
end up with 결국 ~하게 되다
academic 학업의
balance 균형
excessive 과도한
complete 완전한
absence 부재

2. ① 자신의 감정 때문에 상황을 오해할 수 있다

직독 직해

Your emotions deserve attention /
당신의 감정은 주목할 만하다 /
and give you important pieces of information.
그리고 당신에게 중요한 정보를 준다
However, / they can also sometimes be /
하지만 / 그것들은 또한 가끔 될 수 있다 /
an unreliable, inaccurate source of information.
신뢰할 수 없고, 부정확한 정보의 원천이
You may feel a certain way, / but that does not mean /
당신이 분명하게 느낄지는 모른다 / 하지만 그것은 의미하지 않는다 /
those feelings are reflections of the truth.
그런 감정들이 사실의 반영임을
You may feel sad and conclude /
당신은 슬퍼서 결론을 내릴지도 모른다 /
that your friend is angry with you /
당신의 친구가 당신에게 화가 났다고 /
when her behavior simply reflects /
그녀의 행동이 단지 나타낼 때에도 /
that she's having a bad day.
그녀가 안 좋은 날을 보내고 있음을
You may feel depressed and decide /
당신은 기분이 우울해서 결정을 내릴지도 모른다 /
that you did poorly in an interview /
당신이 면접에서 못했다고 /
when you did just fine.
잘했을 때도
Your feelings can mislead you into thinking /
당신의 감정은 당신을 속여 생각하게 할 수 있다 /
things that are not supported by facts.
사실에 의해 뒷받침되지 않는 것들을

당신의 감정은 주목할 만하고 당신에게 중요한 정보를 준다. 하지만 감정은 또한 가끔 신뢰할 수 없고, 부정확한 정보의 원천이 될 수 있다. 당신이 분명하게 느낄지는 모르지만, 그것은 그런 감정들이 사실의 반영임을 의미하지 않는다. 친구의 행동이 단지 그녀가 안 좋은 날을 보내고 있음을 나타낼 때에도, 당신은 슬프기 때문에 그녀가 당신에게 화가 났다고 결론을 내릴지도 모른다. 당신은 기분이 우울해서 면접에서 잘했을 때도 못했다고 결정을 내릴지도 모른다. 당신의 감정은 당신을 속여 사실에 의해 뒷받침되지 않는 것들을 생각하게 할 수 있다.

문제풀이

감정은 중요한 정보를 제공하지만 가끔은 부정확한 정보의 원천이 될 수 있고, 감정은 사실에 의해 뒷받침되지 않는 것들을 생각하게 할 수 있다는 내용이다. 따라서 글의 요지로 ① '자신의 감정으로 인해 상황을 오해할 수 있다.'가 가장 적절하다.

이렇게 풀자 자신이 슬프기 때문에 친구의 행동이 단지 친구가 자신에게 화가 났다고 결론 내리는 것과 면접을 잘했음에도 불구하고 자신의 기분이 우울해서 면접을 잘하지 못했다고 결정을 내리는 사례를 통해 글의 요지를 추론할 수 있다.

구조 다시보기

도입	감정은 중요한 정보를 제시함
주제	감정은 부정확한 정보의 원천이 될 수 있음

예시1	자신의 슬픈 감정으로 인해 친구의 상태를 오해함
예시2	자신의 우울한 감정으로 인해 면접을 못 봤다고 결정 내림
결론	감정은 자신을 속여 사실에 의해 뒷받침되지 않는 것들을 생각하게 함

어휘·어구

deserve ~을 받을 만하다
attention 주목
unreliable 신뢰할 수 없는
inaccurate 부정확한
reflection 반영
conclude 결론을 내리다
behavior 행동
mislead 오해하게 하다
support 뒷받침하다

정답률 92%

3. ① 수면은 건강 유지와 기능 발휘에 도움이 된다

직독 직해

Many people view sleep / as merely a "down time" /
많은 사람이 수면을 ~로 본다 / 그저 '가동되지 않는 시간'으로 /
when their brain shuts off / and their body rests.
뇌가 멈추고 / 신체가 휴식을 취하는
In a rush to meet work, school, family, or household responsibilities, /
일, 학교, 가족, 혹은 가정의 책임을 다하기 위해 서두르는 와중에 /
people cut back on their sleep, /
사람들은 그들의 수면 시간을 줄인다 /
thinking it won't be a problem, /
그리고 그것이 문제가 되지 않을 것이라 생각한다 /
because all of these other activities /
왜냐하면 이런 모든 다른 활동들이 /
seem much more important.
훨씬 더 중요해 보이기 때문이다
But research reveals / 하지만 연구는 보여준다 /
that a number of vital tasks carried out /
수행되는 많은 매우 중요한 과업이 /
during sleep / help to maintain good health /
수면 중에 / 건강을 유지하는 데 도움이 된다는 것을 /
and enable people to function / at their best.
그리고 사람들이 기능할 수 있게 해 준다는 것을 / 최상의 수준으로
While you sleep, / your brain is hard at work /
잠을 자는 동안 / 여러분의 뇌는 열심히 일한다 /
forming the pathways / 경로를 형성하느라 /
necessary for learning and creating memories and new insights.
학습하고 기억과 새로운 통찰을 만드는 데 필요한
Without enough sleep, /
충분한 수면이 없다면 /
you can't focus and pay attention /
여러분은 집중하고 주의를 기울일 수 없다 /
or respond quickly.
또는 빠르게 반응을 (할 수 없다.)
A lack of sleep / may even cause mood problems.
수면 부족은 / 심지어 감정 문제를 일으킬 수도 있다
In addition, / growing evidence shows /
게다가 / 점점 더 많은 증거가 보여준다 /
that a continuous lack of sleep /
계속되는 수면 부족이 /
increases the risk for developing serious diseases.
심각한 질병 발생 위험을 증가시킨다는 것을

많은 사람이 수면을 그저 뇌가 멈추고 신체가 휴식을 취하는 '가동되지 않는 시간'으로 본다. 일, 학교, 가족, 혹은 가정의 책임을 다하기 위해 서두르는 와중에, 사람들은 그들의 수면 시간을 줄이고, 그것이 문제가 되지 않을 것이라 생각하는데, 왜냐하면 이런 모든 다른 활동들이 훨씬 더 중요해 보이기 때문이다. 하지만 연구는 수면 중에 수행되는 많은 매우 중요한 과업이 건강을 유지하는 데 도움이 되고 사람들이 최상의 수준으로 기능할 수 있게 해 준다는 것을 보여준다. 잠을 자는 동안, 여러분의 뇌는 학습하고 기억과 새로운 통찰을 만드는 데 필요한 경로를 형성하느라 열심히 일한다. 충분한 수면이 없다면, 여러분은 집중하고 주의를 기울이거나 빠르게 반응할 수 없다. 수면 부족은 심지어 감정 (조절) 문제를 일으킬 수도 있다. 게다가, 계속되는 수면 부족이 심각한 질병 발생 위험을 증가시킨다는 것을 점점 더 많은 증거가 보여준다.

문제풀이

수면 중에 수행되는 많은 것들이 사람들의 건강을 유지하는 데 도움이 되고 최상의 수준으로 기능할 수 있게 해주기 때문에 수면이 부족하면 신체적인 문제뿐만 아니라 감정 조절 문제까지 일으킬 수 있다는 내용이다. 따라서 글의 요지로 ① '수면은 건강 유지와 최상의 기능 발휘에 도움이 된다.'가 가장 적절하다.

이렇게 풀자 글의 중반에 제시된 문장인 'But research reveals that a number of vital tasks carried out during sleep help to maintain good health and enable people to function at their best.'에서 글의 요지를 추론할 수 있다.

어휘·어구

merely 그저
down time 가동되지 않는 시간
shut off 멈추다
in a rush 서둘러
household 가정의
responsibility 책임
cut back on ~을 줄이다
reveal 밝히다
carry out ~을 수행하다
maintain 유지하다
function 기능하다
at one's best 최상의 수준으로
form 형성하다
pathway 경로
insight 통찰
pay attention 주의를 기울이다
respond 반응하다
cause 일으키다
in addition 게다가
evidence 증거
continuous 계속적인
increase 증가시키다
disease 질병

정답률 78%

4. ③ 고객 정보는 활용해야 함

직독 직해

Information is worthless / 정보는 가치가 없다 /
if you never actually use it.
만약 여러분이 결코 그것을 실제로 사용하지 않는다면
Far too often, / 너무나 자주 /
companies collect valuable customer information /
기업들은 귀중한 고객 정보를 수집한다 /
that ends up buried and never used.
결국에는 묻히고 절대로 사용되지 않는
They must ensure / their data is accessible for use /
그들은 보장해야 한다 / 그들의 정보가 사용을 위해 접근 가능하도록 /
at the appropriate times.
적절한 때에
For a hotel, / 호텔의 경우 /
one appropriate time for data usage is check-in /
정보 사용을 위한 하나의 적절한 때는 체크인이다 /
at the front desk. 프런트 데스크에서의
I often check in at a hotel / I've visited frequently, /
나는 호텔에 종종 체크인한다 / 내가 자주 방문했던 /
only for the people at the front desk /
결국 프런트 데스크에 있는 사람들이 /
to give no indication /
표시를 보여 주지 않는다 /
that they recognize me as a customer.
나를 고객으로 알아차린다는
The hotel must have stored a record of my visits, /
그 호텔은 내 방문 기록을 저장하고 있음이 분명하다 /
but they don't make that information accessible to the front desk clerks.
그러나 그들은 그 정보가 프런트 데스크 직원들에게 접근 가능하도록 해 주지 않는다
They are missing a prime opportunity to utilize data /
그들은 정보를 활용할 최적의 기회를 놓치고 있다 /
to create a better experience /
더 나은 경험을 만들 수 있도록 /
focused on customer loyalty.
고객 충성도에 초점을 맞춘
Whether they have ten customers, ten thousand, or even ten million, /
그들이 열 명, 만 명 혹은 심지어 천만 명의 고객을 가지고 있든 /
the goal is the same: /
목표는 동일하다 /
create a delightful customer experience /
즐거운 고객 경험을 만드는 것이다 /
that encourages loyalty.
충성도를 높이는

만약 여러분이 결코 정보를 실제로 사용하지 않는다면 그것은 가치가 없다. 너무나 자주 기업들은 결국에는 묻히고 절대로 사용되지 않는 귀중한 고객 정보를 수집한다. 그들은 그들의 정보가 적절한 때의 사용을 위해 접근 가능하도록 보장해야 한다. 호텔의 경우 정보 사용을 위한 하나의 적절한 때는 프런트 데스크의 체크인이다. 나는 내가 자주 방문했던 호텔에 종종 체크인하는데 결국 프런트 데스크에 있는 사람들이 그들이 나를 고객으로 알아차린다는 표시를 보여 주지 않는다. 그 호텔은 내 방문 기록을 저장하고 있음이 분명하지만 그들은 그 정보가 프런트 데스크 직원들에게 접근 가능하도록 해 주지 않는다. 그들은 고객 충성도에 초점을 맞춘 더 나은 경험을 만들 수 있도록 정보를 활용할 최적의 기회를 놓치고 있다. 그들이 열 명, 만 명 혹은 심지어 천만 명의 고객을 가지고 있든 목표는 동일하다. 즉, 그것은 충성도를 높이는 즐거운 고객 경험을 만드는 것이다.

문제풀이

호텔을 방문했던 고객의 정보를 프런트 데스크 직원이 활용할 수 없다면, 고객 충성도에 초점을 맞춘 더 나은 경험을 만들 수 있도록 정보를 활용할 최적의 기회를 놓치고 있는 것과 마찬가지로 정보는 실제로 사용하지 않는다면 가치가 없으므로, 기업은 적절한 때에 정보에 접근할 수 있도록 해야 한다는 내용의 글이다. 따라서 글의 요지로 가장 적절한 것은 ③ '고객 충성도를 높이기 위해 고객 정보가 활용될 필요가 있다.'이다.

구조 다시보기

도입	정보는 사용하지 않으면 가치가 없음
문제 제기	기업은 수집한 고객 정보를 잘 사용하지 않음
주제	고객 정보가 적절한 때에 사용되도록 보장해야 함
예시	고객에게 기쁨을 주고 충성도를 높일 수 있는 방법인데도, 호텔 방문객들에 대한 과거 정보를 프런트 데스크 직원이 접근할 수 없음

어휘·어구

worthless 가치 없는
bury 묻다, 매장하다
ensure 보장하다
accessible 접근하기 쉬운
appropriate 적절한
usage 사용

frequently 자주
indication 표시, 암시
recognize 인식하다
accessible 이용 가능한
miss 놓치다
prime 최고의
opportunity 기회
utilize 활용하다, 이용하다
loyalty 충성도
encourage 촉구하다

정답률 65%

5. ⑤ 자신의 의견이 최선이 아닐 수 있다는 것을 인정하는 것이 필요하다

직독/직해

It's important / that you think independently /
중요하다 / 독자적으로 생각하는 것이 /
and fight for what you believe in, /
그리고 자신이 믿는 것을 위해 싸우는 것은 /
but there comes a time / when it's wiser /
하지만 때가 온다 / 더 현명한 /
to stop fighting for your view /
자신의 생각을 위해 싸우는 것을 중단하고 /
and move on to accepting / 받아들이는 쪽으로 나아가는 것이 /
what a trustworthy group of people think is best.
신뢰할 수 있는 사람들의 집단이 가장 좋다고 생각하는 것을
This can be extremely difficult.
이것은 매우 어려울 수 있다
But it's smarter, and ultimately better /
하지만 더 영리하고 궁극적으로 더 좋다 /
for you to be open-minded / and have faith /
여러분이 마음을 열고 / 믿음을 갖는 것이 /
that the conclusions of a trustworthy group of people / 신뢰할 수 있는 사람들 집단의 결론이 /
are better than / 더 낫다는 /
whatever you think. 여러분이 생각하는 어떤 것보다
If you can't understand their view, /
여러분이 그들의 생각을 이해할 수 없다면 /
you're probably just blind / to their way of thinking.
여러분은 아마도 단지 보지 못하는 것이다 / 그들이 생각하는 방식을
If you continue doing / what you think is best /
계속한다면 / 여러분이 가장 좋다고 생각하는 것을 /
when all the evidence and trustworthy people are against you, /
모든 증거와 신뢰할 수 있는 사람들이 여러분에게 반대할 때 /
you're being dangerously confident.
여러분은 위험할 정도로 자신감에 차 있는 것이다
The truth is / 사실은 ~이다 /
that while most people can become incredibly open-minded, /
대부분의 사람은 믿을 수 없을 정도로 마음을 열게 되는 반면에 /
some can't, / 어떤 사람들은 그럴 수 없다는 (것이다) /
even after they have repeatedly encountered /
반복해서 겪고 난 후에도 /
lots of pain from betting / that they were right /
확신하는 것으로부터 많은 고통을 / 자신이 옳았다고 /
when they were not. 옳지 않았을 때

독자적으로 생각하고 자신이 믿는 것을 위해 싸우는 것은 중요하지만, 자신의 생각을 위해 싸우는 것을 중단하고 신뢰할 수 있는 사람들의 집단이 가장 좋다고 생각하는 것을 받아들이는 쪽으로 나아가는 것이 더 현명한 때가 온다. 이것은 매우 어려울 수 있다. 하지만 여러분이 마음을 열고 신뢰할 수 있는 사람들 집단의 결론이 여러분이 생각하는 어떤 것보다 더 낫다는 믿음을 갖는 것이 더 영리하고 궁극적으로 더 좋다. 여러분이 그들의 생각을 이해할 수 없다면, 여러분은 아마도 단지 그들이 생각하는 방식을 보지 못하는 것이다. 모든 증거와 신뢰할 수 있는 사람들이 여러분에게 반대할 때 여러분이 가장 좋다고 생각하는 것을 계속한다면, 여러분은 위험할 정도로 자신감에 차 있는 것이다. 사실 대부분의 사람은 믿을 수 없을 정도로 마음을 열게 되는 반면에, 어떤 사람들은 자신이 옳지 않았을 때 옳았다고 확신하는 것으로부터 많은 고통을 반복해서 겪고 난 후에도 그럴 수 없다는 것이다.

문제풀이

자신이 믿는 것을 위해 싸우는 것을 중단하고 신뢰할 수 있는 집단이 최선이라고 생각하는 것을 받아들이는 것은 어려울 수 있지만 마음을 열고 그들의 의견을 받아들이는 것이 더 영리하고 궁극적으로 더 좋다는 내용이다. 따라서 글의 요지로 ⑤ '자신의 의견이 최선이 아닐 수 있다는 것을 인정하는 것이 필요하다.'가 가장 적절하다.

어휘·어구

independently 독자적으로, 독립적으로
accept 받아들이다
trustworthy 신뢰할 만한
extremely 매우, 극도로
ultimately 궁극적으로
conclusion 결론
evidence 증거
confident 자신만만한
incredibly 믿을 수 없을 정도로
encounter 만나다, 마주치다
bet 단언하다

정답률 75%

6. ⑤ 과제가 일정 수준에 도달하게 개선 기회를 주면 동기 부여에 도움이 된다

직독/직해

Rather than attempting to punish students /
학생을 벌주려 하기보다 /
with a low grade or mark /
낮은 등급이나 점수로 /
in the hope / 바람에서 /
it will encourage them to give greater effort /
그것이 학생들이 더 많은 노력을 기울이게 장려할 것이라는 /
in the future, / 미래에 /
teachers can better motivate students /
교사들은 학생들에게 동기 부여를 더 잘할 수 있다 /
by considering their work as incomplete /
그들의 과제가 미완성이라고 생각함으로써 /
and then requiring additional effort.
그리고 나서 추가적인 노력을 요구함으로써
Teachers at Beachwood Middle School in Beachwood, Ohio, /
Ohio주 Beachwood의 Beachwood 중학교 교사들은 /
record students' grades / as A, B, C, or I (Incomplete).
학생들의 등급을 기록한다 / 'A', 'B', 'C' 혹은 'I' (미완성)로
Students who receive an I grade /
'I' 등급을 받은 학생들은 /
are required to do additional work /
추가 과제를 하도록 요구받는다 /
in order to bring their performance up /
자신의 과제 수행을 끌어올리기 위해 /
to an acceptable level.
수용 가능한 수준까지
This policy is based on the belief /
이런 방침은 믿음에 근거한다 /
that students perform at a failure level /
학생들이 낙제 수준으로 수행한다는 /
or submit failing work / 혹은 낙제 과제를 제출한다는 /
in large part because teachers accept it.
대체로 교사가 그것을 받아들이기 때문에
The Beachwood teachers reason /
Beachwood의 교사들은 생각한다 /
that if they no longer accept substandard work, /
그들이 더 이상 기준 이하의 과제를 받아들이지 않는다면 /
students will not submit it.
학생들이 그것을 제출하지 않을 것이라고
And with appropriate support, / they believe /
그리고 적절한 도움을 받아 / 그들은 믿는다 /
students will continue to work /
학생들은 계속해서 노력할 것이라고 /
until their performance is satisfactory.
자신의 과제 수행이 만족스러울 때까지

학생들이 미래에 더 많은 노력을 기울이도록 장려하고 싶은 바람에서 낮은 등급이나 점수로 학생을 벌주려 하기보다, 교사들은 그들의 과제가 미완성이라고 생각하고 추가적인 노력을 요구함으로써 학생들에게 동기 부여를 더 잘할 수 있다. Ohio주 Beachwood의 Beachwood 중학교 교사들은 학생들의 등급을 'A', 'B', 'C' 혹은 'I' (미완성)로 기록한다. 'I' 등급을 받은 학생들은 자신의 과제 수행을 수용 가능한(기준에 맞는) 수준까지 끌어올리기 위해 추가 과제를 하도록 요구받는다. 이런 방침은 학생들이 낙제 수준으로 수행하거나 대체로 교사가 낙제 과제를 받아들이기 때문에 그것을 제출한다는 믿음에 근거한다. Beachwood의 교사들은 그들이 더 이상 기준 이하의 과제를 받아들이지 않는다면, 학생들이 그것을 제출하지 않을 것이라고 생각한다. 그리고 학생들은 적절한 도움을 받아 자신의 과제 수행이 만족스러울 때까지 계속해서 노력할 것이라고 그들은 믿는다.

문제풀이

교사들은 낮은 등급이나 점수로 학생들 벌주려 하기 보다는 그들의 과제에 대한 추가적인 노력을 요구함으로써 학생들에게 동기 부여를 더 잘할 수 있다는 내용이다. 따라서 글의 요지로 ⑤ '학생의 과제가 일정 수준에 도달하도록 개선 기회를 주면 동기 부여에 도움이 된다.'가 가장 적절하다.

이렇게 풀자 글의 첫 번째 문장의 'teachers can better motivate students by considering their work as incomplete and then requiring additional effort'에서 글의 요지를 추론할 수 있다.

구조 다시보기

주제	과제에 대한 추가적인 노력 요구가 학생들에게 동기 부여가 될 수 있음
사례	Beachwood 중학교 교사들의 성적 기록 방식 A, B, C, I(미완성)
부연	I(미완성) 등급 학생들은 과제 수행을 기준에 맞는 수준까지 끌어올리기 위해 추가 과제를 하도록 요구받게 됨

어휘·어구

attempt 시도하다
punish 벌하다
encourage 격려하다
motivate 동기를 부여하다
consider 고려하다, 생각하다
incomplete 미완성의
additional 추가의
performance 수행
acceptable 받아들일 수 있는
submit 제출하다
reason 추론하다, 생각하다
substandard 표준 이하의

정답률 69%

7. ⑤ 자기 의심은 스트레스를 유발하고 객관적인 판단을 흐린다

직독/직해

If you care deeply about something, /
만약 여러분이 무언가에 깊이 관심을 둔다면 /
you may place greater value /
여러분은 더 큰 가치를 둘지도 모른다 /
on your ability to succeed / in that area of concern.
성공하기 위한 여러분의 능력에 / 그 관심 영역에서
The internal pressure you place on yourself /
여러분 스스로에게 가하는 내적 압박은 /
to achieve or do well socially /
성취하거나 사회적으로 성공하기 위해서 /

is normal and useful, /
정상적이고 유용하다 /
but when you doubt your ability /
하지만 여러분의 능력을 의심하면 /
to succeed in areas that are important to you, /
자신에게 중요한 영역에서 성공하기 위한 /
your self-worth suffers.
여러분의 자아 존중감은 상처를 입는다
Situations are uniquely stressful / for each of us /
상황은 다른 방식으로 스트레스를 준다 / 우리 각자에게 저마다 /
based on whether or not they activate our doubt.
우리의 의심을 활성화하는지 여부에 따라
It's not the pressure to perform /
결코 수행에 대한 압박이 아니다 /
that creates your stress.
여러분의 스트레스를 유발하는 것은
Rather, / it's the self-doubt / that bothers you.
오히려 / 바로 자기 의심이다 / 여러분을 괴롭히는 것은
Doubt causes you to see /
의심은 여러분이 보게 한다 /
positive, neutral, and even genuinely negative experiences /
긍정적인, 중립적인 그리고 심지어 진짜로 부정적인 경험을 /
more negatively / 더 부정적으로 /
and as a reflection of your own shortcomings.
그리고 여러분 자신의 단점을 반영한 것으로
When you see situations and your strengths /
상황과 여러분의 강점을 볼 때 /
more objectively, / 더 객관적으로 /
you are less likely to have doubt /
여러분은 의심을 덜 가질 것이다 /
as the source of your distress.
괴로움의 원천인

만약 여러분이 무언가에 깊이 관심을 둔다면, 그 관심 영역에서 성공하기 위한 여러분의 능력에 더 큰 가치를 둘지도 모른다. 성취하거나 사회적으로 성공하기 위해서 여러분 스스로에게 가하는 내적 압박은 정상적이고 유용하지만, 자신에게 중요한 영역에서 성공하기 위한 여러분의 능력을 의심하면, 여러분의 자아 존중감은 상처를 입는다. 상황은 우리의 의심을 활성화하는지 여부에 따라 우리 각자에게 저마다 다른 방식으로 스트레스를 준다. 여러분의 스트레스를 유발하는 것은 결코 수행에 대한 압박이 아니다. 오히려, 여러분을 괴롭히는 것은 바로 자기 의심이다. 의심은 긍정적인, 중립적인 그리고 심지어 진짜로 부정적인 경험을 더 부정적으로 보게 하고, 여러분 자신의 단점을 반영한 것으로 (그것들을) 보게 한다. 상황과 여러분의 강점을 더 객관적으로 볼 때, 여러분은 괴로움의 원천인 의심을 덜 가질 것이다.

문제풀이

스트레스를 유발하는 것은 수행에 대한 압박이 아닌 자기 의심으로, 상황과 강점을 객관적으로 볼 때 의심을 덜 가지게 될 것이라는 내용이므로, 글의 요지로 ⑤ '자기 의심은 스트레스를 유발하고, 객관적 판단을 흐린다.'가 가장 적절하다.

구조 다시보기

문제점	자기 능력에 대한 의심이 자아 존중감에 상처를 줌
근본 원인	수행에 대한 압박이 아닌 자기 의심이 스트레스를 유발함
해결 방안	상황과 강점을 더 객관적으로 보는 것이 의심을 덜 갖게 함

어휘·어구

care about ~에 관심을 두다, ~을 걱정하다
place value on ~에 가치를 두다
ability 능력
concern 관심, 염려
internal 내적인
pressure 압박, 압력
achieve 성취하다
do well 성공하다
socially 사회적으로
normal 정상적인, 일반적인
doubt 의심하다; 의심
self-worth 자아 존중감
suffer 상처를 입다, 괴로워하다
activate 활성화하다
perform 수행하다, 실행하다
self-doubt 자기 의심
bother 괴롭히다
positive 긍정적인
neutral 중립적인
genuinely 진짜로, 정말로
negative 부정적인
reflection 반영
shortcoming 단점
strength 강점
objectively 객관적으로
source 원천, 근원

정답률 

8. ④ 더 나은 선택에 대한 두려움

직독/직해

FOBO, or Fear of a Better Option, /
FOBO 혹은 더 나은 선택에 대한 두려움은 /
is the anxiety that something better will come along, /
더 나은 무언가가 생길 것이라는 불안감인데 /
which makes it undesirable to commit to existing choices /
기존의 선택지들에 전념하는 것을 탐탁지 않게 한다 /
when making a decision. 이것은 결정을 내릴 때
It's an affliction of abundance / 그것은 풍족함의 고통이다 /
that drives you to keep all of your options open /
여러분이 모든 선택지를 열어 두게 만드는 /
and to avoid risks. 그리고 위험을 피하게 만드는
Rather than assessing your options, / choosing one, /
여러분의 선택지들을 평가하기 보다는 / 하나를 선택하기 (보다는) /
and moving on with your day, /
그리고 여러분의 하루를 살아가기보다는 /
you delay the inevitable.
여러분은 반드시 해야 할 것을 미룬다
It's not unlike / 그것은 다르지 않다 /
hitting the snooze button on your alarm clock /
알람시계의 스누즈 버튼을 누르는 것과 /
only to pull the covers over your head /
결국 이불을 머리 위로 뒤집어쓰고 /
and fall back asleep. 다시 잠들어 버리는 것과
As you probably found out the hard way, /
아마도 여러분이 고생하면서 알게 되었듯이 /
if you hit snooze enough times, /
스누즈 버튼을 많이 누르게 되면 /
you'll end up being late / 여러분은 결국 늦게 될 것이다 /
and racing for the office, /
그리고 사무실로 달리게 (될 것이다) /
your day and mood ruined.
여러분의 하루와 기분을 망치게 된다
While pressing snooze / 스누즈 버튼을 누르는 것이 /
feels so good at the moment, /
그때는 기분이 아주 좋겠지만 /
it ultimately demands a price.
그것은 결국 대가를 요구한다

FOBO 혹은 더 나은 선택에 대한 두려움은 더 나은 무언가가 생길 것이라는 불안감인데, 이것은 결정을 내릴 때 기존의 선택지들에 전념하는 것을 탐탁지 않게 한다. 그것은 여러분이 모든 선택지를 열어 두고 위험을 피하게 만드는 풍족함의 고통이다. 여러분의 선택지들을 평가하고, 하나를 선택하고 여러분의 하루를 살아가기보다는, 여러분은 반드시 해야 할 것을 미룬다. 그것은 알람시계의 스누즈 버튼을 누르고 결국 이불을 머리 위로 뒤집어쓰고 다시 잠들어 버리는 것과 다르지 않다. 아마도 여러분이 고생하면서 알게 되었듯이 스누즈 버튼을 많이 누르게 되면, 여러분은 결국 늦게 되어 사무실로 달리게 되고, 여러분의 하루와 기분을 망치게 된다. 스누즈 버튼을 누르는 것이 그때는 기분이 아주 좋겠지만, 그것은 결국 대가를 요구한다.

문제풀이

우리는 결정을 내릴 때 기존의 선택지들에 전념하는 것을 탐탁지 않아 하고, 더 나은 무언가가 생길 것이라는 불안감을 가지고 있어서 선택하기 보다는 반드시 해야 할 것을 미루는 경향이 있다는 내용이다. 알람시계의 스누즈 버튼을 누르는 것은 당시에는 기분을 좋게 하지만 결국 하루와 기분을 망치는 대가를 요구하게 된다는 것으로 보아, 글의 요지로 ④ '더 나은 선택을 위해 결정을 미루는 것은 결국 해가 된다.'가 가장 적절하다.

이렇게 풀자 알람시계의 스누즈 버튼을 누르는 행위가 결국에 초래하는 결과를 통해 글의 요지를 추론할 수 있다.

어휘·어구

anxiety 불안, 근심
come along 생기다, 나타나다
undesirable 바람직하지 않은
commit 전념하다
existing 존재하는
abundance 풍부함
assess 평가하다
delay 미루다
inevitable 피할 수 없는 것, 필연적인 것
snooze button 스누즈 버튼(알람을 지연시키는 버튼)
the hard way 고생하면서
end up -ing 결국 ~하게 되다
ruin 망치다
ultimately 결국, 궁극적으로
demand 요구하다

정답률 

9. ② 학습에 끼치는 문화의 영향

직독/직해

Learners function within complex developmental, cognitive, physical, social, and cultural systems.
학습자들은 복잡한 발달적, 인지적, 신체적, 사회적, 그리고 문화적 체계 안에서 기능한다
Research and theory from diverse fields /
다양한 분야에서의 연구와 이론은 /
have contributed to an evolving understanding /
이해를 점차 발전시키는 데 기여해 왔다 /
that all learners grow and learn /
모든 학습자들이 성장하고 배운다는
in culturally defined ways in culturally defined contexts.
문화적으로 한정된 맥락 안에서 문화적으로 한정된 방식으로
While humans share basic brain structures and processes, /
인간은 기본적인 뇌 구조와 처리과정을 공유하지만 /
as well as fundamental experiences /
기본적인 경험뿐만 아니라 /
such as relationships with family, age-related stages, and many more, /
가족과의 관계, 나이와 관련된 단계, 그리고 더 많은 것들과 같은 /
each of these phenomena is shaped /
각각의 이러한 현상은 형성된다 /
by an individual's precise experiences.
개인의 정확한 경험에 의해
Learning does not happen in the same way for all people /
학습은 모든 사람들에게 똑같은 방식으로 일어나지는 않는다 /
because cultural influences are influential from the beginning of life.
문화적 영향이 인생의 시작부터 영향력이 있기 때문에

These ideas about the intertwining of learning and culture /
학습과 문화의 뒤얽힘에 관한 이러한 생각은 /
have been supported by research on many aspects of learning and development.
학습과 발달의 많은 측면에 대한 연구에 의해 지지되어 왔다

학습자들은 복잡한 발달적, 인지적, 신체적, 사회적, 그리고 문화적 체계 안에서 기능한다. 다양한 분야에서의 연구와 이론은 모든 학습자들이 문화적으로 한정된 맥락 안에서 문화적으로 한정된 방식으로 성장하고 배운다는 점에 대한 이해를 점차 발전시키는 데 기여해 왔다. 인간은 가족과의 관계, 나이와 관련된 단계, 그리고 더 많은 것들과 같은 기본적인 경험뿐만 아니라 기본적인 뇌 구조와 처리과정을 공유하지만, 각각의 이러한 현상은 개인의 정확한 경험에 의해 형성된다. 학습은 문화적 영향이 인생의 시작부터 영향력이 있기 때문에 모든 사람들에게 똑같은 방식으로 일어나지는 않는다. 학습과 문화의 뒤얽힘에 관한 이러한 생각은 학습과 발달의 많은 측면에 대한 연구에 의해 지지되어 왔다.

문제풀이

인간은 기본적인 뇌구조와 처리과정 그리고 가족과의 관계 등 근본적인 경험을 공유하지만 각각의 현상은 개인의 경험에 의하며 학습은 문화적 영향으로 인해 모든 사람들에게 똑같은 방식으로 일어나지 않는다는 것이 글의 중심 내용이다. 따라서 글의 요지로 가장 적절한 것은 ② '개인의 문화적 경험이 학습에 영향을 끼친다.'이다.

이렇게 풀자 글의 두 번째 문장 'Research and theory from diverse fields have contributed to an evolving understanding that all learners grow and learn in culturally defined ways in culturally defined contexts.(다양한 분야에서의 연구와 이론은 모든 학습자들이 문화적으로 한정된 맥락 안에서 문화적으로 한정된 방식으로 성장하고 배운다는 점에 대한 이해를 점차 발전시키는 데 기여해 왔다.)'에 글의 요지가 잘 드러나 있다.

어휘·어구

function 기능하다
complex 복잡한
cognitive 인식의
contribute to ~에 기여하다
evolve 서서히 발전시키다
context 맥락, 전후 사정
fundamental 기본의, 근본적인
phenomenon 현상, 사건 (pl. phenomena)
precise 정확한
aspect 측면, 양상

10. ① 목표보다는 과정에 전념하라

직독/직해

A goal-oriented mind-set / 목표 지향적인 사고방식은 /
can create a "yo-yo" effect. "요요" 효과를 낼 수 있다
Many runners work hard for months, /
많은 달리기 선수들이 몇 달 동안 열심히 연습한다 /
but as soon as they cross the finish line, /
그러나 결승선을 통과하자마자 /
they stop training. 그들은 훈련을 중단한다
The race is no longer there / to motivate them.
그 경기는 더 이상 그곳에 없다 / 그들에게 동기를 주기 위해서
When all of your hard work is focused /
당신이 애쓰는 모든 일이 집중될 때 /
on a particular goal, / what is left /
특정한 목표에 / 무엇이 남아있는가 /
to push you forward / after you achieve it?
당신을 앞으로 밀고 나가기 위해 / 당신이 그것을 성취한 후에
This is / why many people find themselves /
이것이다 / 많은 사람들이 자신을 발견하는 이유는 /
returning to their old habits /
그들의 옛 습관으로 되돌아가는 /
after accomplishing a goal.
목표를 성취한 후에
The purpose of setting goals / is to win the game.
목표를 설정하는 목적은 / 경기에서 이기는 것이다
The purpose of building systems /
시스템을 구축하는 목적은 /
is to continue playing the game.
게임을 계속하기 위한 것이다
True long-term thinking / is goal-less thinking.
진정한 장기적 사고는 / 목표 지향적이지 않은 사고이다
It's not about any single accomplishment.
그것은 어떤 하나의 성취에 관한 것이 아니다
It is about the cycle of endless refinement and continuous improvement.
그것은 끝없는 정제와 지속적인 개선의 순환에 관한 것이다
Ultimately, / it is your commitment to the process /
궁극적으로 / 그 과정에 당신이 전념하는 것이다 /
that will determine your progress.
당신의 발전을 결정짓는 것은

목표 지향적인 사고방식은 "요요" 효과를 낼 수 있다. 많은 달리기 선수들이 몇 달 동안 열심히 연습하지만, 결승선을 통과하는 순간 훈련을 중단한다. 그 경기는 더 이상 그들에게 동기를 주지 않는다. 당신이 애쓰는 모든 일이 특정한 목표에 집중될 때, 당신이 그것을 성취한 후에 당신을 앞으로 밀고 나갈 수 있는 것은 무엇인가? 이것이 많은 사람들이 목표를 성취한 후 옛 습관으로 되돌아가는 자신을 발견하는 이유이다. 목표를 설정하는 목적은 경기에서 이기는 것이다. 시스템을 구축하는 목적은 게임을 계속하기 위한 것이다. 진정한 장기적 사고는 목표 지향적이지 않은 사고이다. 그것은 어떤 하나의 성취에 관한 것이 아니다. 그것은 끝없는 정제와 지속적인 개선의 순환에 관한 것이다. 궁극적으로, 당신의 발전을 결정짓는 것은 그 과정에 당신이 전념하는 것이다.

문제풀이

목표 지향적인 사고방식은 "요요"효과를 낼수 있으므로 진정한 장기적 사고는 목표 지향적이지 않은 사고이고, 끝없는 정제와 지속적인 개선의 순환에 관한 것이어서 당신의 발전을 결정짓는 것은 그 과정에 전념하는 것이라는 내용의 글이다. 따라서 이 글의 요지로 가장 적절한 것은 ① '발전은 한 번의 목표 성취가 아닌 지속적인 개선 과정에 의해 결정된다.'이다.

이렇게 풀자 글의 요지는 글의 핵심 내용으로, 글의 주제문과 밀접한 관련이 있다. 'True long-term thinking is goal-less thinking.(진정한 장기적 사고는 목표 지향적이지 않은 사고이다.)'와 'It is about the cycle of endless refinement and continuous improvement.(그것은 끝없는 정제와 지속적인 개선의 순환에 관한 것이다.)'에 이 글의 주제가 가장 잘 나타나 있다.

어휘·어구

goal-oriented 목표 지향적인
effect 효과
no longer 더 이상 ~하지 않는
motivate 동기를 부여하다
particular 특정한
achieve 성취하다
purpose 목표, 목적
long-term 장기적인
refinement 정제, 개선
improvement 개선
commitment 전념
determine 결정하다, 결심하다
progress 진보, 발전

본문 029쪽

문법 플러스 5. 동사의 시제

1. consists 2. won 3. receive
4. will tell 5. visited 6. had 7. had
8. would 9. am thinking 10. had

1 [해석]▶ 바코드는 컴퓨터가 정보로 번역할 수 있는 선과 막대 패턴으로 이루어져 있다.
[해설]▶ 과학적 사실이나 불변의 진리를 나타낼 때는 현재 시제를 사용한다.
2 [해석]▶ 퀴리 부부는 1903년 그들의 발견으로 노벨 물리학상을 받았다.
[해설]▶ 과거의 역사적 사실은 현재 시제를 쓰지 않고 과거 시제를 써야 한다.
3 [해석]▶ 당신이 이 편지를 받을 때면, 모든 일이 해결되었을 것이다.
[해설]▶ 때나 조건 부사절은 미래를 나타내는 경우에도 미래 시제를 쓰지 않고 현재 시제를 쓴다.
4 [해석]▶ 대통령은 자신에게 솔직하게 말해 줄 수 있는 사람들이 필요하다.
[해설]▶ 형용사절이나 명사절은 미래를 나태는 경우 미래 시제를 쓰면 된다.
5 [해석]▶ 2001년 여름에, 그는 한국 아산에 집짓기 프로젝트에 참가했다.
[해설]▶ 명백한 과거를 나타내는 부사(in the summer 2001)가 있는 경우, 현재완료 시제를 쓰지 않고 과거 시제를 써야한다.
6 [해석]▶ 어제 10년만에 가장 심한 폭설이 내렸다.
[해설]▶ 명백한 과거를 나타내는 부사(yesterday)가 있는 경우, 과거 시제를 써야 한다.
7 [해석]▶ 샐리가 강의실에 들어갔을 때, 강의가 이미 시작했었다.
[해설]▶ 과거의 특정 시점 이전에 일어난 일은 과거완료를 써야 한다.
8 [해석]▶톰은 그녀에게 그녀를 도울 수 있는 일은 뭐든지 하겠다고 말했다.
[해설]▶ 주절의 동사가 과거라면 종속절의 동사는 과거나 과거완료가 와야 한다.
9 [해석]▶ 나는 다음에 어디로 가야 할지 고민하고 있다.
[해설]▶ 일반적으로 상태동사(be동사), 인지동사(think), 지각동사(see, hear, feel), 소유동사(have)는 진행형을 쓰지 않는다. think 동사가 '믿다' 또는 '의견을 가지다'라는 의미로 쓰일 때는 진행형을 쓰지 않는다. 하지만 think 동사가 '사려(고려)하다'라는 의미를 나타낼 경우 진행형을 쓸 수 있다.
10 해석▶ 그는 그녀의 어머니가 돌아가신 지 얼마나 되었는지 알고 싶어 했다.
[해설]▶ 그녀의 어머니가 돌아간 것은 그가 알고 싶어한 시점보다 먼저 일어난 일이이므로 과거완료 시제가 와야 한다.

본문 030쪽

어휘 플러스 5. 철자가 혼동되는 어휘 (2)

1. cooperation 2. contrast
3. confidence 4. generous
5. principles

1 [해석]▶ 그러므로 대량 파괴라는 수단을 통해서 안보를 추구하는 대신에 너무 늦기 전에 전 세계의 상호 이해와 협동을 통해서 그것을 달성해야 한다.
2 [해석]▶ 서유럽과 미국의 차이는 특히 확실하다.
3 [해석]▶ 한 분야의 세세한 지식이 한 때 성공을 보장해 준 반면, 오늘 날 최고의 포상은 다양한 영역에서 동일한 자신감을 가지고 일하는 사람들에게 돌아간다.
4 [해석]▶ (대신에) 저는 당신이 너무 사려 깊어서, 비록 당신의 사려 깊음에 익숙함에도, 당신이 우리를 놀라게 했다고 말하겠어요.
5 [해석]▶ 한국 연들의 형태는 그것들이 바람을 잘 이용하게 해주는 과학적인 원리에 기초를 두고 있다.

06. 글의 주제

Day 06

본문 032쪽

1. ② 2. ② 3. ④ 4. ① 5. ①
6. ② 7. ① 8. ① 9. ② 10. ②

대표 기출 ⑤ 녹는 얼음과 상승하는 바다가 하루의 길이에 미치는 영향

직독/직해

The most remarkable and unbelievable consequence / of melting ice and rising seas /
가장 놀랍고 믿을 수 없는 결과는 / 녹는 얼음과 상승하는 바다의 /

is that together they are a kind of time machine, /
그것들이 합쳐서 일종의 타임머신이라는 것이다 /

so real that they are altering / the duration of our day.
이는 너무나 현실적이어서 그것들이 바꾸고 있다 / 우리 하루의 기간을

It works like this: / As the glaciers melt /
그것은 이와 같이 작동한다 / 즉, 빙하가 녹으면서 /

and the seas rise, / gravity forces more water /
그리고 바다가 높아지면서 / 중력이 더 많은 물을 밀어 넣는다 /

toward the equator. 적도를 향해

This changes the shape of the Earth ever so slightly, /
이것은 지구의 모양을 아주 약간 변화시켜 /

making it fatter around the middle, /
가운데 주변으로 그것을 더 불룩하게 만들고 /

which in turns slows / the rotation of the planet /
이는 결과적으로 늦춘다 / 행성의 회전을 /

similarly to the way / a ballet dancer slows her spin /
유사한 방식으로 / 발레 무용수가 그녀의 회전을 늦추는 (방식과) /

by spreading out her arms.
발레 무용수가 양팔을 뻗어

The slowdown isn't much, / 이 감속이 크지는 않다 /

just a few thousandths of a second each year, /
매년 단지 몇천 분의 1초로 /

but like the barely noticeable jump /
하지만 알아차리기 힘든 증가처럼 /

of rising seas every year, / it adds up.
해마다 상승하는 바다의 / 그것은 쌓인다

When dinosaurs lived on the Earth, /
공룡들이 지구에 살았을 때 /

a day lasted only about twenty-three hours.
하루는 약 23시간만 지속되었다

녹는 얼음과 상승하는 바다의 가장 놀랍고 믿을 수 없는 결과는 그것들이 합쳐서 일종의 타임머신이라는 것이고, 이는 너무나 현실적이어서 그것들이 우리 하루의 기간을 바꾸고 있다. 그것은 이와 같이 작동한다. 즉, 빙하가 녹고 바다가 높아지면서 중력이 적도를 향해 더 많은 물을 밀어 넣는다. 이것은 지구의 모양을 아주 약간 변화시켜 가운데 주변으로 그것을 더 불룩하게 만들고, 이는 결과적으로 발레 무용수가 양팔을 뻗어 그녀의 회전을 늦추는 방식과 유사한 방식으로 행성의 회전을 늦춘다. 이 감속이 매년 단지 몇천 분의 1초로 크지는 않지만, 해마다 상승하는 바다의 알아차리기 힘든 증가처럼, 그것은 쌓인다. 공룡들이 지구에 살았을 때, 하루는 약 23시간만 지속되었다.

① 지구에서 기온 상승의 원인
② 모양을 유지하는 행성들의 원리
③ 녹는 얼음이 해양 생물다양성에 미치는 영향
④ 어떤 장치도 사용하지 않고 시간을 기록하는 방법
⑤ 녹는 얼음과 상승하는 바다가 하루의 길이에 미치는 영향

문제풀이

녹는 얼음과 상승하는 바다가 합쳐져서 우리 하루의 기간을 바꾸고 있다는 내용의 글이므로, 글의 주제로 ⑤ 'impact of melting ice and rising seas on the length of a day(녹는 얼음과 상승하는 바다가 하루의 길이에 미치는 영향)'가 가장 적절하다.

어휘·어구

remarkable 놀라운
unbelievable 믿을 수 없는
consequence 결과
melting 녹는
alter 바꾸다
duration 기간
glacier 빙하
gravity 중력
equator 적도
slightly 약간
rotation 회전
similarly 비슷하게
spin 회전
spread out 몸을 뻗다
slowdown 감속
barely 거의 ~않다
noticeable 눈에 띄는
cause 원인
temperature 기온
principle 원리
maintain 유지하다
implication 영향, 함축
marine 해양의
biodiversity 생물다양성
keep track of ~을 기록하다
device 장치
impact 영향
length 길이

1. ② 인간 진화를 위한 소속감의 유용성

직독/직해

For creatures like us, / evolution smiled upon /
우리와 같은 창조물에게 있어 / 진화는 ~에게 미소 지었다 /

those with a strong need to belong.
소속하려는 강한 욕구를 가진 것들(에게)

Survival and reproduction are the criteria of success / by natural selection, /
생존과 번식은 성공의 기준이다 / 자연 선택에 의한 /

and forming relationships with other people /
그리고 다른 사람들과 관계를 형성하는 것은 /

can be useful / for both survival and reproduction.
유용할 수 있다 / 생존과 번식 모두에

Groups can share resources, /
집단은 자원을 공유할 수 있다 /

care for sick members, / scare off predators, /
아픈 구성원을 돌볼 (수 있다) / 포식자를 쫓아버릴 (수 있다) /

fight together against enemies, /
적에 맞서서 함께 싸울 (수 있다) /

divide tasks / so as to improve efficiency, /
일을 나눌 (수 있다) / 효율성을 향상시키기 위해 /

and contribute to survival / in many other ways.
그리고 생존에 기여할 (수 있다) / 많은 다른 방식으로

In particular, / if an individual and a group want /
특히 / 한 개인과 한 집단이 원한다면 /

the same resource, / 같은 자원을 /

the group will generally prevail, /
집단이 일반적으로 이길 것이다 /

so competition for resources /
그래서 자원에 대한 경쟁은 /

would especially favor / a need to belong.
특별히 좋아할 것이다 / 소속하려는 욕구를

Belongingness will likewise promote reproduction, /
마찬가지로 소속되어 있다는 것은 번식을 촉진시킬 것이다 /

such as by bringing potential mates into contact with each other, /
이를테면 잠재적인 짝을 서로 만나게 해줌으로써 /

and in particular / by keeping parents together /
그리고 특히 / 부모가 함께 있도록 함으로써인데 /

to care for their children, /
자녀를 돌보기 위해

who are much more likely to survive /
자녀들은 훨씬 더 생존하기 쉬울 것이다 /

if they have more than one caregiver.
한 명보다 많은 돌보는 이가 있으면

우리와 같은 창조물에게 있어 진화는 소속하려는 강한 욕구를 가진 것들에 미소 지었다. 생존과 번식은 자연 선택에 의한 성공의 기준이고, 다른 사람들과 관계를 형성하는 것은 생존과 번식 모두에 유용할 수 있다. 집단은 자원을 공유할 수 있고, 아픈 구성원을 돌보고, 포식자를 쫓아버리고, 적에 맞서서 함께 싸우고, 효율성을 향상시키기 위해 일을 나누고, 많은 다른 방식으로 생존에 기여할 수 있다. 특히, 한 개인과 한 집단이 같은 자원을 원한다면, 집단이 일반적으로 이기고, 그래서 자원에 대한 경쟁은 소속하려는 욕구를 특별히 좋아할 것이다. 마찬가지로 소속되어 있다는 것은 번식을 촉진시키는데, 이를테면 잠재적인 짝을 서로 만나게 해주거나, 특히 부모가 자녀를 돌보기 위해 함께 있도록 함으로써인데, 자녀들은 한 명보다 많은 돌보는 이가 있으면 훨씬 더 생존하기 쉬울 것이다.

① 약자가 현대 생활에서 살아남기 위한 기술
② 인간 진화를 위한 소속감의 유용성
③ 사회 집단에서 경쟁을 피하는 방법
④ 아이들의 교육에 있어 사회적 관계의 역할
⑤ 두 주요 진화 이론 간의 차이점

문제풀이

다른 사람들과 관계를 형성하는 것이 생존과 번식 모두에 유용할 수 있고 소속된다는 것이 결국 진화에 유리하다는 내용이므로, 글의 주제로 ② 'usefulness of belonging for human evolution(인간 진화를 위한 소속감의 유용성)'이 가장 적절하다.

어휘·어구

creature 창조물, 생명체
evolution 진화
survival 생존
reproduction 번식
criteria 기준
natural selection 자연 선택
relationship 관계
resource 자원
scare off 겁주어 떼어내다
predator 포식자
enemy 적
divide 나누다
improve 향상하다
efficiency 효율성
contribute to ~에 기여하다
in particular 특히
individual 개인
prevail 이기다, 우세하다
competition 경쟁
favor 선호하다
belongingness 소속성
likewise 마찬가지로
promote 촉진하다
potential 잠재적인
bringing ~ into contact with ~을 접촉시키다
caregiver 돌보는 사람
usefulness 유용성
social 사회의
education 교육
difference 차이점
major 주요한

evolutionary 진화의
theory 이론

2. ② 아이들이 수학적인 이해를 구축하는 방법

직독/직해

Every day, / children explore and construct /
매일 / 아이들은 탐구하고 구성한다 /
relationships among objects.
사물 사이의 관계들을
Frequently, / these relationships focus on /
빈번히 / 이런 관계들은 초점을 맞춘다 /
how much or how many of something exists.
무언가가 얼마만큼 혹은 얼마나 많이 존재하는지에
Thus, children count / 따라서 아이들은 센다
— "One cookie, / two shoes, /
쿠키 하나 / 신발 두 개 /
three candles on the birthday cake, /
생일 케이크 위에 초 세 개 /
four children in the sandbox."
모래 놀이통에 아이 네 명
Children compare / — "Which has more? / Which has fewer? /
아이들은 비교한다 / 어떤 게 더 많지 / 어떤 게 더 적지 /
Will there be enough?" 충분할까
Children calculate / — "How many will fit? /
아이들은 계산한다 / 몇 개가 알맞을까 /
Now, I have five. / I need one more."
나는 지금 다섯 개를 가지고 있어 / 나는 하나 더 필요하네
In all of these instances, / children are developing /
이 모든 예시에서 / 아이들은 발달시키는 중이다 /
a notion of quantity. 양의 개념을
Children reveal and investigate /
아이들은 밝히고 연구한다 /
mathematical concepts / 수학적 개념을 /
through their own activities or experiences, /
그들만의 활동이나 경험을 통해 /
such as figuring out / how many crackers to take /
알아내는 것과 같은 / 몇 개의 크래커를 가져갈지 /
at snack time / or sorting shells into piles.
간식 시간에 / 혹은 조개껍질들을 더미로 분류하는 것(과 같은)

매일, 아이들은 사물 사이의 관계들을 탐구하고 구성한다. 빈번히, 이런 관계들은 무언가가 얼마만큼 혹은 얼마나 많이 존재하는지에 초점을 맞춘다. 따라서 아이들은 센다. "쿠키 하나, 신발 두 개, 생일 케이크 위에 초 세 개, 모래 놀이통에 아이 네 명." 아이들은 비교한다. "어떤 게 더 많지? 어떤 게 더 적지? 충분할까?" 아이들은 계산한다. "몇 개가 알맞을까? 나는 지금 다섯 개를 가지고 있어. 나는 하나 더 필요하네." 이 모든 예시에서, 아이들은 양의 개념을 발달시키는 중이다. 아이들은 간식 시간에 몇 개의 크래커를 가져갈지 알아내는 것이나 조개껍질들을 더미로 분류하는 것과 같은, 그들만의 활동이나 경험을 통해 수학적 개념을 밝히고 연구한다.

① 세는 법을 배우는 데 있어 아이들의 어려움
② 아이들이 수학적인 이해를 구축하는 방법
③ 사물을 세는 데 손가락이 사용되는 이유
④ 초기 유아 교육의 중요성
⑤ 숫자 노래 부르기의 장점

문제풀이

아이들은 사물 사이의 관계를 탐구할 때 수를 셈으로써 양의 개념을 발달시킨다는 내용이므로, 글의 주제로 ② 'how children build mathematical understanding(아이들이 수학적인 이해를 구축하는 방법)'이 가장 적절하다.

어휘·어구

construct 구성하다
relationship 관계
frequently 빈번히, 자주
exist 존재하다
compare 비교하다
calculate 계산하다
fit 적합하다, 알맞다
instance 예시, 사례
notion 개념
quantity 양
reveal 밝히다, 드러내다
investigate 조사하다, 연구하다
mathematical 수학적인
figure out 알아내다
sort 분류하다
difficulty 어려움
childhood education 유아 교육
advantage 장점

3. ④ 삶에 광범위하게 영향을 미치는 기후에 대한 지식

직독/직해

The whole of human society / 전체 인간 사회는 /
operates on knowing the future weather.
미래 날씨를 아는 것을 기반으로 운영된다
For example, / farmers in India know /
예를 들어 / 인도의 농부들은 안다 /
when the monsoon rains will come next year /
내년에 몬순 장마가 올 시기를 /
and so they know / when to plant the crops.
그래서 그들은 안다 / 작물을 심을 시기를
Farmers in Indonesia know /
인도네시아의 농부들은 안다 /
there are two monsoon rains each year, /
매년 몬순 장마가 두 번 있다는 것을 /
so next year / they can have two harvests.
그래서 이듬해에 / 그들은 수확을 두 번 할 수 있다
This is based on their knowledge of the past, /
이것은 과거에 대한 그들의 지식에 기반한 것이다 /
as the monsoons have always come /
왜냐하면 몬순은 항상 왔기 때문이다 /
at about the same time each year /
매년 거의 같은 시기에 /
in living memory. 살아 있는 기억 속에서
But the need to predict / goes deeper than this; /
하지만 예측할 필요는 / 이것보다 더 깊어진다 /
it influences every part of our lives.
그것은 우리 생활의 모든 부분에 영향을 미친다
Our houses, roads, railways, airports, offices, and so on /
우리의 집, 도로, 철도, 공항, 사무실 등은 /
are all designed / for the local climate.
모두 설계된다 / 지역의 기후에 맞추어
For example, / in England all the houses /
예를 들어 / 영국에서는 모든 집은 /
have central heating, / 중앙난방을 갖추고 있다 /
as the outside temperature is usually below 20°C, /
외부 기온이 대체로 섭씨 20도 미만이기 때문에 /
but no air-conditioning, / 하지만 냉방기는 없다 /
as temperatures rarely go beyond 26°C, /
기온이 섭씨 26도 위로 올라가는 일은 거의 없어서 /
while in Australia / the opposite is true: /
반면 호주에서는 / 그 반대가 사실이다 /
most houses have air-conditioning /
대부분의 집에 냉방기는 있다 /
but rarely central heating.
하지만 중앙난방은 거의 없다

전체 인간 사회는 미래 날씨를 아는 것을 기반으로 운영된다. 예를 들어, 인도의 농부들은 내년에 몬순 장마가 올 시기를 알고, 그래서 그들은 작물을 심을 시기를 안다. 인도네시아의 농부들은 매년 몬순 장마가 두 번 있다는 것을 알고, 그래서 이듬해에 그들은 수확을 두 번 할 수 있다. 이것은 과거에 대한 그들의 지식에 기반한 것인데, 살아 있는 기억 속에서 몬순은 매년 항상 거의 같은 시기에 왔기 때문이다. 하지만 예측할 필요는 이것보다 더 깊어지며, 그것은 우리 생활의 모든 부분에 영향을 미친다. 우리의 집, 도로, 철도, 공항, 사무실 등은 모두 지역의 기후에 맞추어 설계된다. 예를 들어, 영국에서는 외부 기온이 대체로 섭씨 20도 미만이기 때문에 모든 집은 중앙난방을 갖추고 있지만, 기온이 섭씨 26도 위로 올라가는 일은 거의 없어서 냉방기는 없는 반면, 호주에서는 그 반대가 사실이어서, 대부분의 집에 냉방기는 있지만 중앙난방은 거의 없다.

① 기후 변화를 다루는 새로운 기술
② 날씨를 정확하게 예측하는 것에 있어서 어려움
③ 기온 상승에 의해 영향을 받는 기후 패턴
④ 우리의 삶에 광범위하게 영향을 미치는 기후에 대한 지식
⑤ 열악한 기후에서 우리의 생존을 돕는 전통 지혜

문제풀이

인간 사회는 미래의 날씨를 아는 것을 기반으로 운영된다는 내용으로, 농부들이 작물을 심을 시기를 아는 것과 건물들이 지역의 기후에 맞게 설계된다는 사례들을 통해, 글의 주제로 ④ 'knowledge of the climate widely affecting our lives(우리의 삶에 광범위하게 영향을 미치는 기후에 대한 지식)'가 가장 적절하다.

구조 다시보기

주제	인간 사회는 미래 날씨를 아는 것을 기반으로 운영됨
사례	농부들은 미래 날씨를 예측해 작물 심을 시기를 알게 됨
주제 재진술	날씨 예측이 생활 전반에 영향을 미침
사례	도로 및 건물들은 지역 기후에 맞추어 설계됨

어휘·어구

society 사회
operate 운영되다, 돌아가다
monsoon 몬순(특히 인도양에서 여름은 남서, 겨울은 북동에서 부는 계절풍)
crop 작물
harvest 수확
predict 예측하다
influence 영향을 미치다
railway 철도
local 지역의
climate 기후
central heating 중앙난방
temperature 기온
air-conditioning 냉방(기)
rarely 거의 없게
opposite 정반대(의)
technology 기술
deal with ~을 다루다
correctly 정확하게
knowledge 지식
affect 영향을 미치다
traditional 전통의
survival 생존
harsh 모진, 가혹한

4. ① 훈련을 통해 두뇌를 행복하게 할 수 있음

직독/직해

We used to think / that the brain never changed, /
우리는 생각했었다 / 뇌가 절대 변하지 않는다고 /
but according to the neuroscientist Richard Davidson, /
그러나 신경과학자 Richard Davidson에 따르면 /
we now know / that this is not true /

이제 우리는 안다 / 이것이 사실이 아님을 /
— specific brain circuits grow stronger /
즉, 특정한 뇌 회로가 더 강해진다는 것을 안다 /
through regular practice.
규칙적인 연습을 통해
He explains, / 그는 설명한다 /
"Well-being is fundamentally no different /
행복은 기본적으로 다르지 않다
than learning to play the cello.
첼로를 연주하는 것을 배우는 것과
If one practices the skills of well-being, /
만약 어떤 이가 행복의 기술을 연습한다면 /
one will get better at it."
그 사람은 그것을 더 잘하게 될 것이다
What this means / 이것이 의미하는 것은 /
is that you can actually train your brain /
여러분이 뇌를 실제로 훈련시킬 수 있다는 것이다 /
to become more grateful, relaxed, or confident, /
더 감사하고, 편안하고 또는 자신감을 갖도록 /
by repeating experiences / 경험을 반복함으로써 /
that evoke gratitude, relaxation, or confidence.
감사, 휴식 또는 자신감을 불러일으키는
Your brain is shaped / by the thoughts you repeat.
여러분의 뇌는 형성된다 / 여러분이 반복하는 생각에 의해
The more neurons fire / as they are activated /
뉴런은 더 많이 점화할수록 / 그것이 활성화되면서 /
by repeated thoughts and activities, /
반복된 생각과 활동에 의해 /
the faster they develop into neural pathways, /
그것은 신경 경로로 더 빠르게 발달하게 된다 /
which cause lasting changes in the brain.
이는 뇌에 지속적인 변화를 야기한다
Or in the words of Donald Hebb, /
혹은 Donald Hebb의 말을 빌리면 /
"Neurons that fire together wire together."
함께 점화하는 뉴런은 함께 연결된다
This is such an encouraging premise: / bottom line /
이는 대단히 고무적인 전제이다 / 결론은 /
— we can intentionally create the habits /
우리가 습관을 의도적으로 만들 수 있다는 것이다 /
for the brain to be happier.
뇌가 더 행복해지도록

우리는 뇌가 절대 변하지 않는다고 생각했었지만 신경과학자 Richard Davidson에 따르면 우리는 이제 이것이 사실이 아님을 즉, 특정한 뇌 회로가 규칙적인 연습을 통해 더 강해진다는 것을 안다. 그는 "행복은 첼로를 연주하는 것을 배우는 것과 기본적으로 다르지 않다. 만약 어떤 이가 행복의 기술을 연습한다면 그 사람은 그것을 더 잘하게 될 것이다."라고 설명한다. 이것이 의미하는 것은 여러분이 감사, 휴식 또는 자신감을 불러일으키는 경험을 반복함으로써 더 감사하고, 편안하고 또는 자신감을 갖도록 여러분의 뇌를 실제로 훈련시킬 수 있다는 것이다. 여러분의 뇌는 여러분이 반복하는 생각에 의해 형성된다. 뉴런은 그것이 반복된 생각과 활동에 의해 활성화되면서 더 많이 점화할수록, 그것은 신경 경로로 더 빠르게 발달하게 되고 이는 뇌에 지속적인 변화를 야기한다. 혹은 Donald Hebb의 말을 빌리면 "함께 점화하는 뉴런은 함께 연결된다." 이는 대단히 고무적인 전제이다. 즉, 결론은 뇌가 더 행복해지도록 우리가 습관을 의도적으로 만들 수 있다는 것이다.

① 행복을 위한 두뇌 습관을 형성할 수 있는 가능성
② 신체 움직임을 개선하는데 있어서 뇌 회로의 역할
③ 악기를 연주할 때 연습의 중요성
④ 휴식이 메모리 용량 향상에 미치는 영향
⑤ 뇌의 뉴런이 어떻게 작용하는지를 발견하는 어려움

문제풀이

특정한 뇌 회로는 규칙적인 연습을 통해 더 강해지고, 행복은 첼로를 배우는 것과 같아서, 감사나 휴식, 자신감의 경험을 반복함으로써 뇌를 훈련할 수 있으므로 우리는 뇌가 행복해지도록 의도적으로 습관을 만들 수 있다는 내용의 글이다. 따라서 글의 주제로 가장 적절한 것은 ① 'possibility of forming brain habits for well-being(행복을 위한 두뇌 습관을 형성할 가능성)'이다.

어휘·어구

neuroscientist 신경과학자
specific 특정한
circuit 회로
grateful 감사하는
confident 자신에 찬
gratitude 감사
neuron 신경 단위, 뉴런
activate 활성화시키다
neural 신경(계)의

정답률 79%

5. ① 젊은이들이 채식을 선호하는 이유

직독/직해

Vegetarian eating is moving into the mainstream /
채식은 주류가 되어가고 있다 /
as more and more young adults /
점점 더 많은 젊은이가 /
say no to meat, poultry, and fish.
고기, 가금류, 그리고 생선에 반대함에 따라
According to the American Dietetic Association, /
American Dietetic Association에 따르면 /
"approximately planned vegetarian diets /
대략적으로 계획된 채식 식단은 /
are healthful, / 건강에 좋다 /
are nutritionally adequate, /
영양학적으로 적당하다 /
and provide health benefits /
그리고 건강상의 이점을 제공한다 /
in the prevention and treatment of certain diseases."
특정 질병들을 예방하고 치료하는 데
But health concerns are not the only reason /
하지만 건강에 대한 염려들이 유일한 이유는 아니다 /
that young adults give for changing their diets.
젊은이들로 하여금 그들의 식단을 바꾸게 하는
Some make the choice / 몇몇은 선택한다 /
out of concern for animal rights.
동물의 권리에 대한 관심 때문에
When faced with the statistics / that show /
통계자료에 직면할 때 / 보여주는 /
the majority of animals raised as food /
음식으로 길러지는 동물들의 대다수가 /
live in confinement, / 갇혀 산다는 것을 /
many teens give up meat /
많은 십대는 고기를 포기한다 /
to protest those conditions. 그런 상황에 저항하기 위해
Others turn to vegetarianism /
다른 사람들은 채식주의자가 된다 /
to support the environment.
환경을 지지하기 위해
Meat production uses /
고기 생산은 사용한다 /
vast amounts of water, land, grain, and energy /
거대한 양의 물, 땅, 곡식, 그리고 에너지를 /
and creates problems /
그리고 문제들을 발생시킨다 /
with animal waste and resulting pollution.
가축에서 나오는 쓰레기와 그에 따른 오염과 같은

채식은 점점 더 많은 젊은이가 고기, 가금류, 그리고 생선에 반대함에 따라 주류가 되어가고 있다. American Dietetic Association에 따르면, 대략적으로 계획된 채식 식단은 건강에 좋고, 영양학적으로 적당하며, 특정 질병들을 예방하고 치료하는 데 건강상의 이점을 제공한다. 하지만 건강에 대한 염려들이 젊은이들로 하여금 그들의 식단을 바꾸게 하는 유일한 이유는 아니다. 몇몇은 동물의 권리에 대한 관심 때문에 선택한다. 음식으로 길러지는 동물들의 대다수가 갇혀 산다는 것을 보여주는 통계자료에 직면할 때, 많은 십대는 그런 상황에 저항하기 위해 고기를 포기한다. 다른 사람들은 환경을 지지하기 위해 채식주의자가 된다. 고기 생산은 거대한 양의 물, 땅, 곡식, 그리고 에너지를 사용하고 가축에서 나오는 쓰레기와 그에 따른 오염과 같은 문제들을 발생시킨다.

① 젊은이들이 채식을 선호하는 이유
② 십 대들을 위한 건강한 식습관을 기르는 방법
③ 당신의 암 위험을 낮추는 것을 돕는 채소
④ 균형 잡힌 식단 유지의 중요성
⑤ 식물 위주 식단의 단점

문제풀이

더 많은 젊은이들이 건강과 동물의 권리, 환경의 지지를 위해 채식주의자가 된다는 내용이므로, 글의 주제로 ① 'reasons why young people go for vegetarian diets(젊은이들이 채식을 선호하는 이유)'가 가장 적절하다.

어휘·어구

vegetarian eating 채식
mainstream 주류
approximately 대략
nutritionally 영양학적으로
adequate 적당한
prevention 예방
treatment 치료
concern 관심, 염려
statistics 통계
majority 대다수
confinement 감금
production 생산
pollution 오염
go for ~을 좋아하다, 찬성하다
eating habit 식습관
maintain 유지하다
balanced diet 균형 잡힌 식단
disadvantage 단점

구조 다시보기

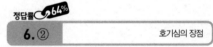

주제	채식은 젊은이들에게 주류가 되어감
근거	- 채식은 건강에 좋음 - 동물의 권리를 보호할 수 있음 - 환경을 보호할 수 있음

6. ② 호기심의 장점

직독/직해

Curiosity makes us much more likely to view /
호기심은 우리가 훨씬 더 여기게 한다 /
a tough problem / 어려운 문제를 /
as an interesting challenge to take on.
맡아야 할 흥미로운 도전으로
A stressful meeting with our boss /
스트레스를 받는 상사와의 회의는 /
becomes an opportunity to learn.
배울 기회가 된다
A nervous first date / 긴장되는 첫 데이트는 /
becomes an exciting night out with a new person.
새로운 사람과의 멋진 밤이 된다
A colander becomes a hat.
주방용 체는 모자가 된다
In general, / curiosity motivates us /
일반적으로 / 호기심은 우리가 ~하게 동기를 부여한다 /
to view stressful situations as challenges /
스트레스받는 상황을 도전으로 여기게 /
rather than threats, / 위협보다는 /
to talk about difficulties more openly, /
어려움을 더욱 터놓고 말하게 /
and to try new approaches /
그리고 새로운 접근을 시도하게 /
to solving problems. 문제 해결에 있어서
In fact, / curiosity is associated /
실제로 / 호기심은 관련이 있다 /
with a less defensive reaction to stress /
스트레스에 대한 방어적인 반응이 덜한 것과 /

and, as a result, / less aggression /
그리고 그 결과 / 공격성이 줄어드는 것과 (관련이 있다) /
when we respond to irritation.
우리가 짜증에 반응할 때

호기심은 우리가 어려운 문제를 맡아야 할 흥미로운 도전으로 훨씬 더 여기게 한다. 스트레스를 받는 상사와의 회의는 배울 기회가 된다. 긴장되는 첫 데이트는 새로운 사람과의 멋진 밤이 된다. 주방용 체는 모자가 된다. 일반적으로, 호기심은 우리가 스트레스 받는 상황을 위협보다는 도전으로 여기게 하고, 어려움을 더욱 터놓고 말하게 하고, 문제 해결에 있어서 새로운 접근을 시도하게 동기를 부여한다. 실제로 호기심은 스트레스에 대한 방어적인 반응이 덜하고, 그 결과 우리가 짜증에 반응할 때 공격성이 줄어드는 것과 관련이 있다.

① 힘든 상황에서 방어적인 반응의 중요성
② 긍정적인 재구성의 숨겨진 힘으로서의 호기심
③ 직장에서 스트레스에 대처하는 것의 어려움
④ 호기심에 의해 야기되는 잠재적인 위험
⑤ 인간의 호기심을 줄이는 요소

문제풀이

호기심은 우리로 하여금 어려운 문제를 해결해야 할 흥미로운 도전으로 여기게 하고, 문제 해결에 있어 새로운 접근을 시도하게 동기를 부여한다는 내용이다. 따라서 글의 주제로 ② 'curiosity as the hidden force of positive reframes(긍정적인 재구성의 숨겨진 힘으로서의 호기심)'가 가장 적절하다.

구조 다시보기

주제	호기심은 문제를 흥미로운 도전으로 여기게 함
예시	스트레스 받는 상사와의 회의와 긴장되는 첫 데이트 등
부연	호기심은 스트레스 받는 상황을 도전으로 여기게 하고 문제 해결에 있어 새로운 접근법은 시도하도록 동기를 부여함

《 어휘·어구 》

curiosity 호기심
challenge 도전
take on ~을 맡다
opportunity 기회
threat 위협
approach 접근
be associated with ~와 관련되다
defensive 방어의
reaction 반응
aggression 공격(성)
respond to ~에 대응하다
irritation 짜증
cope with ~에 대처하다
potential 잠재적인
reduce 줄이다

정답률 70%

7. ① 대화 중 거짓말을 하는 사람은 시간의 지연을 보임

직독/직해

When two people are involved /
두 사람이 참여하면 /
in an honest and open conversation, /
솔직하고 진솔한 대화에 /
there is a back and forth flow of information.
정보가 왔다 갔다 하며 흘러간다
It is a smooth exchange.
그것은 순조로운 주고받기이다
Since each one is drawing on their past personal experiences, /
각자 자신의 개인적인 과거 경험에 의존하고 있기 때문에 /
the pace of the exchange / is as fast as memory.
주고받는 속도는 / 기억만큼 빠르다
When one person lies, /
한 사람이 거짓말하면 /
their responses will come more slowly /
그 사람의 반응이 더 느리게 나올 것이다 /
because the brain needs more time /
뇌는 더 많은 시간이 필요하기 때문이다 /
to process the details of a new invention /
새로 꾸며 낸 이야기의 세부 사항을 처리하는 데 /
than to recall stored facts.
저장된 사실을 기억해 내는 데 비해
As they say, / "Timing is everything."
사람들이 말하는 것처럼 / 타이밍이 가장 중요하다
You will notice the time lag /
여러분은 시간의 지연을 알아차릴 것이다 /
when you are having a conversation with someone /
누군가와 대화를 하고 있으면 /
who is making things up / as they go.
이야기를 꾸며 내고 있는 / 말을 하면서
Don't forget / 잊지 말아라 /
that the other person may be reading your body language as well, /
상대방이 여러분의 몸짓 언어 역시 읽고 있을지도 모른다는 것을 /
and if you seem to be disbelieving their story, /
그리고 여러분이 그 사람의 이야기를 믿지 않고 있는 것처럼 보이면 /
they will have to pause /
그 사람은 잠시 멈춰야 할 것이라는 점을 /
to process that information, too.
그 정보를 처리하기 위해 또한

두 사람이 솔직하고 진솔한 대화에 참여하면 정보가 왔다 갔다 하며 흘러간다. 그것은 순조로운 주고받기이다. 각자 자신의 개인적인 과거 경험에 의존하고 있기 때문에, 주고받는 속도는 기억만큼 빠르다. 한 사람이 거짓말하면, 그 사람의 반응이 더 느리게 나올 텐데, 뇌는 저장된 사실을 기억해 내는 데 비해 새로 꾸며 낸 이야기의 세부 사항을 처리하는 데 더 많은 시간이 필요하기 때문이다. 사람들이 말하는 것처럼 "타이밍이 가장 중요하다." 여러분은 말을 하면서 이야기를 꾸며 내고 있는 누군가와 대화를 하고 있으면, 시간의 지연을 알아차릴 것이다. 상대방이 여러분의 몸짓 언어 역시 읽고 있을지도 모른다는 것과 여러분이 그 사람의 이야기를 믿지 않고 있는 것처럼 보이면, 그 사람은 그 정보를 처리하기 위해 또한 잠시 멈춰야 할 것이라는 점을 잊지 말아라.

① 거짓말의 신호로서 지연된 반응
② 청자가 화자를 격려하는 법
③ 유용한 정보를 찾는 데 있어 어려움
④ 사회적인 환경에서 선의의 거짓말의 필요성
⑤ 대화 주제로 공유된 경험

문제풀이

대화 중 거짓말을 하게 되면 우리의 뇌는 꾸며낸 이야기의 세부 사항을 처리하는 데 더 많은 시간이 필요해서 반응이 더 느리게 되고, 결국 대화 중에 시간의 지연이 생긴다는 내용이므로, 글의 주제로 ① 'delayed responses as a sign of lying(거짓말의 신호로서의 지연된 반응)'이 가장 적절하다.

이렇게 풀자 'their responses will come more slowly(그 사람의 반응이 더 느리게 나올 것이다)', 'You will notice the time lag(여러분은 시간의 지연을 알아차릴 것이다)', 'they will have to pause to process that information(그 사람은 그 정보를 처리하기 위해 잠시 멈춰야 할 것이다)'를 통해 글의 주제를 추론할 수 있다.

구조 다시보기

도입	진솔한 대화는 순조로운 주고받기임
주제	거짓말을 하면 대화에서 시간 지연이 생김
근거	새로 꾸며낸 이야기의 세부 사항을 처리하는 데 뇌는 더 많은 시간이 필요함

《 어휘·어구 》

be involved in ~에 참여하다, ~과 관련되다
conversation 대화
back and forth 왔다 갔다 하는
smooth 순조로운, 원활히 진행되는
exchange 주고받기, 교환
draw on ~에 의존하다
personal 개인적인
experience 경험
pace 속도
response 반응
process 처리하다
detail 세부 사항
invention 꾸며 낸 이야기, 창작
recall 기억해 내다
make ~ up ~을 꾸며 내다, ~을 지어 내다
disbelieve 믿지 않다, 의심하다
pause 잠시 멈추다
delayed 지연된
encourage 격려하다
necessity 필요성
white lie 악의 없는 거짓말
setting 환경

정답률 78%

8. ① 재생 가능한 에너지원의 부작용

직독/직해

The use of renewable sources of energy to produce electricity /
전력을 생산하기 위한 재생 가능한 에너지원의 사용은 /
has increasingly been encouraged /
점점 장려되어 왔다 /
as a way to harmonize / 조화시키기 위한 방법으로 /
the need to secure electricity supply /
전력 공급 확보의 필요성과 /
with environmental protection objectives.
환경 보호 목적을
But the use of renewable sources /
하지만 재생 가능한 자원의 이용은 /
also comes with its own consequences, /
또한 그 자체의 결과를 수반하는데 /
which require consideration. 이는 고려할 필요가 있다
Renewable sources of energy /
재생 가능한 에너지원은 /
include a variety of sources / 다양한 자원을 포함한다 /
such as hydropower and ocean-based technologies.
수력 발전과 해양 기반 기술처럼
Additionally, / 게다가 /
solar, wind, geothermal and biomass renewable sources /
태양열, 풍력, 지열과 바이오매스 재생 에너지원은 /
also have their own impact on the environment.
또한 환경에 저마다의 영향을 미친다
Hydropower dams, for example, /
예를 들어, 수력 발전 댐은 /
have an impact on aquatic ecosystems /
수생 생태계에 영향을 미쳐왔다 /
and, more recently, / 그리고 더 최근에는 /
have been identified as significant sources of greenhouse emissions.
온실가스 배출의 중요한 원인으로 확인되었다
Wind, solar, and biomass /
풍력, 태양열 그리고 바이오매스는 /
also cause negative environmental impacts, /
또한 부정적인 환경적 영향을 초래한다 /
such as visual pollution, intensive land occupation /
시각 공해, 집약적인 토지 점유 같은 /
and negative effects on bird populations.
그리고 조류 개체 수에 미치는 부정적인 영향과 같은

전력을 생산하기 위한 재생 가능한 에너지원의 사용은 전력 공급 확보의 필요성과 환경 보호 목적을 조화시키기 위한 방법으로 점점 장려되어 왔다. 하지만 재생 가능한 자원의 이용 또한 그 자체의 결과를 수반하는데,

이는 고려할 필요가 있다. 재생 가능한 에너지원은 수력 발전과 해양 기반 기술처럼 다양한 자원을 포함한다. 게다가, 태양열, 풍력, 지열과 바이오매스(에너지로 사용 가능한 생물체) 재생 에너지원 또한 환경에 저마다의 영향을 미친다. 예를 들어, 수력 발전 댐은 수생 생태계에 영향을 미치고, 더 최근에는 온실가스 배출의 중요한 원인으로 확인되었다. 풍력, 태양열 그리고 바이오매스 또한 시각 공해, 집약적인 토지 점유 그리고 조류 개체 수에 미치는 부정적인 영향과 같은 부정적인 환경적 영향을 초래한다.

① 재생 가능한 에너지원 사용으로 인한 환경적인 부작용
② 증가하는 전력 수요를 충족시킬 수 있는 실용적인 방법
③ 전통적인 에너지원 사용으로 인한 부정적인 영향
④ 재생 가능한 에너지원을 확보하기 위한 수많은 방법
⑤ 온실가스 배출을 줄일 효과적인 절차

문제풀이

재생 가능한 에너지원의 사용은 전력 공급 확보와 환경 보호 목적을 조화시키기 위한 방법으로 장려되어 왔지만 실제로는 환경에 부정적인 영향을 미치고, 최근에는 온실가스 배출의 중요 원인으로 확인되었다는 내용으로 보아, 글의 주제로 ① 'environmental side effects of using renewable energy sources(재생 가능한 에너지원 사용으로 인한 환경적인 부작용)'가 가장 적절하다.

이렇게 풀자 수력 발전 댐이 수생 생태계에 영향을 미치고 온실가스 배출의 중요 원인으로 확인되었다는 내용과, 풍력 등의 재생 가능한 에너지원이 환경에 부정적인 영향을 미친다는 내용을 통해 글의 주제를 추론할 수 있다.

어휘·어구

renewable 재생 가능한
electricity 전기, 전력
encourage 장려하다
harmonize 조화시키다
secure 확보하다, 획득하다
supply 공급
environmental 환경의
protection 보호
objective 목적
come with ~이 딸려 있다
consequence 결과
consideration 고려, 심사숙고
hydropower 수력
aquatic 수생의
ecosystem 생태계
identify 확인하다
significant 중요한
greenhouse emission 온실가스 배출
negative 부정적인
visual 시각의, 시각적인
pollution 오염
intensive 집약적인
occupation 점유, 점령
population 개체 수
side effect 부작용
practical 실용적인
method 방법
traditional 전통적인
numerous 수많은
obtain 얻다, 획득하다
procedure 절차
reduce 줄이다

정답률 64%

9. ② 아이들 발달에서 놀이의 역할

직독/직해

Animals as well as humans engage in play activities.
인간뿐만 아니라 동물도 놀이 활동에 참여한다
In animals, 동물에게 있어
play has long been seen /
놀이는 오랫동안 여겨져 왔다 /
as a way of learning and practicing skills and behaviors /
기술과 행동을 학습하고 연마하는 방식으로 /
that are necessary for future survival.
미래 생존에 필요한
In children, too, /
아이들에게 있어서도 /
play has important functions during development.
놀이는 발달하는 동안 중요한 기능을 한다
From its earliest beginnings in infancy, /
유아기의 가장 초기부터 /
play is a way in which children learn about the world and their place in it.
놀이는 아이들이 세상과 그 안에서의 그들의 위치에 대해 배우는 방식이다
Children's play serves as a training ground /
아이들의 놀이는 훈련의 토대로서 역할을 한다 /
for developing physical abilities — /
신체능력을 발달시키기 위한 /
skills like walking, running, and jumping /
걷기, 달리기, 그리고 점프하기와 같은 기술 /
that are necessary for everyday living.
매일의 삶에 필요한
Play also allows children to try out and learn social behaviors /
놀이는 또한 아이들이 사회적 행동을 시도하고 배우도록 해준다 /
and to acquire values and personality traits /
그리고 가치와 성격적 특성을 습득하도록 한다 /
that will be important in adulthood.
성인기에 중요할
For example, they learn /
예를 들어, 그들은 배운다 /
how to compete and cooperate with others, /
다른 사람들과 경쟁하고 협력하는 방식 /
how to lead and follow, / 이끌고 따르는 방식 /
how to make decisions, and so on.
결정하는 방식 등

인간뿐만 아니라 동물도 놀이 활동에 참여한다. 동물에게 있어 놀이는 오랫동안 미래 생존에 필요한 기술과 행동을 학습하고 연마하는 방식으로 여겨져 왔다. 아이들에게 있어서도 놀이는 발달하는 동안 중요한 기능을 한다. 유아기의 가장 초기부터, 놀이는 아이들이 세상과 그 안에서의 그들의 위치에 대해 배우는 방식이다. 아이들의 놀이는 신체능력 — 매일의 삶에 필요한 걷기, 달리기, 그리고 점프하기와 같은 기술을 발달시키기 위한 훈련의 토대로서 역할을 한다. 놀이는 또한 아이들이 사회적 행동을 시도하고 배우며, 성인기에 중요할 가치와 성격적 특성을 습득하도록 한다. 예를 들어, 그들은 다른 사람들과 경쟁하고 협력하는 방식, 이끌고 따르는 방식, 결정하는 방식 등을 배운다.

① 창의적인 아이디어를 시도해보는 것의 필요성
② 아이들의 발달에 있어 놀이의 역할
③ 인간과 동물의 놀이 사이의 대조
④ 아이들의 신체적 능력이 놀이에 끼치는 효과
⑤ 다양한 발달 단계에서 아이들의 요구

문제풀이

아이들의 발달 동안 놀이가 중요한 기능을 한다고 하면서 어떤 기능들인지 구체적으로 설명하고 있다. 따라서 글의 주제로 가장 적절한 것은 ② 'roles of play in children's development(아이들의 발달에 있어 놀이의 역할)'이다.

구조 다시보기

도입	인간도 동물도 놀이 활동에 참여함
요지	아이들의 발달에 있어 놀이는 중요한 기능을 함
상술	• 세상과 자신의 위치에 대해 배움 • 매일의 삶에 필요한 신체능력을 발달시킴 • 사회적 행동을 배우며 가치와 성격적 특성을 습득함

어휘·어구

engage in ~에 참여하다
infancy 유아기
serve as ~의 역할을 하다
ground 토대
try out 시험해보다
acquire 배우다, 습득하다
personality trait 개성
compete 경쟁하다
cooperate 협력하다

정답률 84%

10. ② 소비자에게 촉감의 중요성

직독/직해

Although individual preferences vary, /
개인의 선호는 다양하지만 /
touch (both what we touch with our fingers /
촉감은(우리가 손가락으로 만지는 것 /
and the way things feel / 그리고 느껴지는 방식 둘 다 /
as they come in contact with our skin) /
물건이 우리의 피부에 접촉될 때) /
is an important aspect of many products.
많은 제품의 중요한 측면이다
Consumers like some products /
소비자들은 어떤 제품을 좋아한다 /
because of their feel. 그것의 감촉 때문에
Some consumers buy skin creams and baby
일부 소비자들은 피부용 크림과 유아용품을 구입한다
products / for their soothing effect / on the skin.
/ 그것들의 진정 효과 때문에 / 피부에 대한
In fact, / consumers who have a high need for touch /
실제로 / 촉감에 대한 욕구가 많은 소비자들은 /
tend to like products that provide this opportunity.
이런 기회를 제공하는 제품들을 좋아하는 경향이 있다
When considering products / 제품들을 고려할 때 /
with material properties, / 물질적 속성이 있는 /
such as clothing or carpeting, / 의류나 카펫과 같은 /
consumers like goods they can touch in stores /
소비자들은 상점에서 만져볼 수 있는 제품들을 좋아한다 /
more than products they only see and read about /
보고 읽기만 하는 제품들보다 /
online or in catalogs. 온라인이나 카탈로그에서

개인의 선호는 다양하지만, 촉감(우리가 손가락으로 만지는 것과 물건이 우리의 피부에 접촉될 때 느껴지는 방식 둘 다)은 많은 제품의 중요한 측면이다. 소비자들은 어떤 제품을 그것의 감촉 때문에 좋아한다. 일부 소비자들은 피부에 대한 진정 효과 때문에 피부용 크림과 유아용품을 구입한다. 실제로, 촉감에 대한 욕구가 많은 소비자는 이런 기회를 제공하는 제품들을 좋아하는 경향이 있다. 의류나 카펫과 같은 물질적 속성이 있는 제품들을 고려할 때, 소비자들은 온라인이나 카탈로그에서 보고 읽기만 하는 제품보다 상점에서 만져볼 수 있는 제품을 더 좋아한다.

① 온라인 쇼핑몰 이용의 이점
② 소비자에게 중요한 요소로서의 촉감
③ 소비자 간의 정보 공유의 중요성
④ 소비자의 피드백을 받는 것의 필요성
⑤ 최신 스타일 제품의 인기

문제풀이

촉감은 제품의 중요한 측면이라고 하면서, 감촉 때문에 어떤 제품을 좋아하고 구입하는 소비자의 예를 들고 있다. 따라서 글의 주제로 가장 적절한 것은 ② 'touch as an important factor for consumers(소비자에게 중요한 요소로서의 촉감)'이다.

구조 다시보기

주제	촉감은 많은 제품의 중요한 측면임

부연	제품의 감촉 때문에 그것을 좋아하는 소비자들이 있음
예시	• 크림, 유아용품: 피부 진정효과 때문에 구입 • 의류, 카펫: 상점에서 만져볼 수 있는 제품을 선호

《 어휘·어구 》

individual 개인의
preference 선호
vary 다양하다
both A and B A와 B 둘 다
come in contact with ~와 접촉하다
aspect 측면, 양상
consumer 소비자
feel 감촉, 느끼다
soothing 진정시키는, 통증을 완화하는
effect 효과, 영향
tend to do ~하는 경향이 있다
opportunity 기회
clothing 의복, 의류
benefit 이로움, 혜택
factor 요소, 요인
share 나누다, 공유하다
necessity 필요성, 필수품
popularity 인기
latest 최신의

본문 035쪽

문법 플러스+ 6. 조동사

1 ~ 5. (하단 해석 참조)
6. go 7. be able to 8. be 9. like
10. hang

1 [해석]▶ 만약 교육이 창의성에 집중했다면 보통 사람이 위대한 예술가나 과학자가 될 수 있었을 거라는 이야기를 우리는 종종 듣는다.

2 [해석]▶ 교육의 희생자들은 학교를 다니는 동안 창의력을 개발하도록 훈련을 받았어야 했는데 그렇지 못했다.

3 [해석]▶ 여러분은 날씨가 추워지면서 많은 사람이 건조한 피부로 인해 고민하고 있다는 것을 들어봤을 것입니다.

4 [해석]▶ 그 관리자가 분명히 느꼈을 자존감의 상실감을 상상해 보라.

5 [해석]▶ 그의 제안을 받아들이지 않았어야 했는데 나는 받아들였다.

6 [해석]▶ 너는 몸 상태가 좋아 보이지 않아 보여. 오늘은 일하러 가지 않는 것이 좋겠어.
[해설]▶ 「had better not+동사원형」은 '~하지 않는 편이 좋다'는 의미로 동사원형을 써야 한다.

7 [해석]▶ 누구든지 집에서 맛있는 파이를 만들 수 있다.
[해설]▶ can의 미래 표현은 will can으로 쓰지 않고 will be able to로 바꿔 쓴다.

8 [해석]▶ 내가 어렸을 때, 저기에는 학교가 있었다.
[해설]▶ 「used to+동사원형」은 과거의 상태를 나타낼 때 '~이 있었는데 (지금은 그렇지 않다)'라는 의미를 가지고 있다.

9 [해석]▶ 나는 그를 좋아하는 것을 멈출 수가 없어.
[해설]▶ 「cannot (help) but+동사원형」은 '~하지 않을 수 없다'는 의미로서 cannot help but 다음에 동사원형이 와야 한다.

10 해석▶ 친구들과 밖으로 나가지 않고 집에 있고 싶어.
[해설]▶ would rather A than B는 'B 하느니 차라리 A하겠다'는 의미로서 A, B 자리에는 동사원형이 와야 한다.

본문 036쪽

어휘 플러스+ 6. 유의어 (2)

1. conflict 2. considerable
3. cooperate 4. contribute
5. enhance

1 [해석]▶ 여러분 중 많은 분들이 갈등을 겪은 이후에 가족 구성원들과의 상황을 진정시키는 방법을 알지 못할 수도 있습니다.

2 [해석]▶ 여성 참정권 운동이 성공을 거둔 중대한 요인은 지지자들이 자신들의 관점에서 '일관적'이었다는 것이었는데, 이것이 상당한 정도의 사회적 영향력을 행사하였다.

3 [해석]▶ 향유고래는 서로를 방어하고 보호하기 위해서 협동하는 사회적 집단을 이루어 이동하고, 심지어는 새끼 젖을 먹이는 것을 공유할 수도 있다.

4 [해석]▶ 그녀는 가르치는 경험을 하면서 동시에 지역 사회에 이바지할 수 있는 자원봉사를 찾을 예정입니다.

5 [해석]▶ 직장에서 우리가 할 수 있는 것을 확인하는 것은 우리가 하는 전문적 일의 질을 높이는 데 도움이 된다.

07. 글의 제목

Day 07 본문 038쪽

1. ① 2. ① 3. ② 4. ② 5. ④
6. ① 7. ⑤ 8. ③ 9. ⑤ 10. ②

정답률 57%

대표 기출 ④ 옳은 것이 새로운 가능성을 막을 수 있다

직독/직해

Have you ever brought up /
해놓았던 적이 있는가 /
an idea or suggestion to someone /
누군가에게 아이디어나 제안을 /
and heard them immediately say /
그리고 그들이 즉시 ~라고 말한 것을 들은 적이 있는가 /
"No, that won't work."?
"아니, 그건 안 될 거야."라고
You may have thought, /
여러분은 아마도 생각했을 것이다 /
"He/she didn't even give it a chance.
"그 사람은 기회조차 주지 않았어 /
How do they know / it won't work?"
어떻게 그들은 알지(라고) / 그것이 안 될 것이라는 것을
When you are right about something, /
여러분이 무언가에 대해 옳다면 /
you close off the possibility /
여러분은 가능성을 닫아 버린다 /
of another viewpoint or opportunity.
다른 관점이나 기회의
Being right about something means /
무언가에 대해 옳다는 것은 의미한다 /
that "it is the way it is, period."
"그것은 원래 그런 거야, 끝."을
You may be correct. 여러분이 옳을 수도 있다
Your particular way of seeing it /
여러분이 그것을 보는 특정한 방법이 /
may be true with the facts.
사실에 부합할 수도 있다
However, / considering the other option /
하지만 / 다른 선택지를 고려하는 것은 /
or the other person's point of view /
혹은 다른 사람의 관점을 (고려하는 것은) /
can be beneficial. 도움이 될 수 있다.
If you see their side, / you will see something new /
만약 여러분이 그들의 관점을 안다면 / 여러분이 새로운 것을 볼 것이다 /
or, at worse, / learn something /
혹은 그것보다는 나쁘더라도 / 무언가를 배울 것이다 /
about how the other person looks at life.
다른 사람이 삶을 바라보는 방식에 관한
Why would you think / 왜 여러분은 생각하는가 /
everyone sees and experiences life /
모두가 삶을 보거나 경험할 것이라고 /
the way you do? 여러분이 하는 방식대로
Besides how boring that would be, /
그것이 얼마나 지루할지는 제외하고라도 /
it would eliminate / 그것은 없앨 것이다 /
all new opportunities, ideas, invention, and creativity.
모든 새로운 기회, 아이디어, 발명 그리고 창의성을

누군가에게 아이디어나 제안을 해놓았는데 그들이 즉시 "아니, 그건 안 될 거야."라고 말한 것을 들은 적이 있는가? 여러분은 아마도 "그 사람은 기회조차 주지 않았어. 어떻게 그들은 그것이 안 될 것이라는 것을 알지?"라고 생각했을 것이다. 여러분이 무언가에 대해 옳다면, 여러분은 다른 관점이나 기회의 가능성을 닫아 버린다. 무언가에 대해 옳다는 것은 "그것은 원래 그런 거야, 끝."을 의미한다. 여러분이 옳을 수도 있다. 여러분이 그것을 보는 특정한 방법이 사실에 부합할 수도 있다. 하지만 다른 선택지나 다른 사람의 관점을 고려하는 것은 도움이 될 수 있다. 만약 여러분이 그들의 관점을 안다면, 여러분이 새로운 것을 보거나 그것보다는 나쁘더라도 다른 사람이 삶을 바라보는 방식에 관한 무언가를 배울 것이다. 왜 모두가 여러분이 하는 방식대로 삶을 보거나 경험할 것이라고 생각하는가? 그것이 얼마나 지루할지는 제외하고라도, 그것은 모든 새로운 기회, 아이디어, 발명, 그리고 창의성을 없앨 것이다.

① 정직함의 가치
② 부정적인 관점을 걸러내라
③ 약속 지키기: 성공으로 가는 길
④ 옳은 것이 새로운 가능성을 막을 수 있다
⑤ 모두가 앞을 볼 때 뒤를 봐라

문제풀이

무언가에 대해 옳다고 여기는 것은 다른 관점이나 기회의 가능성을 닫을 수 있고 다른 사람의 관점을 고려하는 것이 오히려 도움이 될 수 있다는 내용이므로, 글의 제목으로 ④ 'Being Right Can Block New Possibilities(옳은 것이 새로운 가능성을 막을 수 있다)'가 가장 적절하다.

이렇게 풀자 글의 중간에 제시된 문장 'When you are right about something, you close off the possibility of another viewpoint or opportunity.'와 마지막 문장인 'it would eliminate all new opportunities, ideas, invention, and creativity.'를 통해 글의 제목을 추론할 수 있다.

어휘·어구

bring out ~을 꺼내다, ~을 끌어내다
suggestion 제안
immediately 즉시
close off ~을 차단시키다
possibility 가능성
viewpoint 관점
opportunity 기회
period 끝, 이상
correct 옳은, 정확한
particular 특정한
consider 고려하다
option 선택지
point of view 관점
beneficial 유익한
experience 경험하다
besides ~외에
eliminate 제거하다
invention 발명
creativity 창의성
value 가치
honest 정직한
filter out 걸러내다
negative 부정적인
success 성공
block 막다
forward 앞으로

정답률 69%

1. ① 더 많은 용기가 더 많은 기회를 가져온다

직독/직해

Many people make a mistake /
많은 사람들이 실수를 저지른다 /
of only operating along the safe zones, /
안전 구역에서만 움직이는 /
and in the process / they miss the opportunity /
그리고 그 과정에서 / 그들은 기회를 놓친다 /
to achieve greater things.
더 위대한 일들을 달성할
They do so / because of a fear of the unknown /
그들은 그렇게 한다 / 미지의 세계에 대한 두려움 때문에 /
and a fear of treading the unknown paths of life.
그리고 알려지지 않은 삶의 경로를 밟는 것에 대한 두려움 (때문에)
Those that are brave enough to take /
택할 만큼 충분히 용감한 사람들은 /
those roads less travelled /
사람들이 덜 다니는 이런 길들을 /
are able to get great returns /
엄청난 보상을 받을 수 있다 /
and derive major satisfaction /
그리고 큰 만족감을 끌어낼 수 있다 /
out of their courageous moves.
그들의 용감한 행동으로부터
Being overcautious will mean / that you will miss /
지나치게 조심하는 것은 의미할 것이다 / 여러분이 놓칠 것이라는 사실을
attaining the greatest levels of your potential.
여러분의 잠재력의 최고 수준을 달성하는 것을
You must learn to take those chances /
여러분은 그러한 기회를 택하는 것을 배워야 한다 /
that many people around you will not take, /
여러분 주변에 있는 많은 사람들이 선택하지 않을 /
because your success will flow /
왜냐하면 여러분의 성공은 나올 것이기 때문이다 /
from those bold decisions /
용감한 결정으로부터 /
that you will take / along the way.
여러분이 내릴 / 삶의 과정에서

많은 사람들이 안전 구역에서만 움직이는 실수를 저지르고, 그 과정에서 그들은 더 위대한 일들을 달성할 기회를 놓친다. 그들은 미지의 세계에 대한 두려움과 알려지지 않은 삶의 경로를 밟는 것에 대한 두려움 때문에 그렇게 한다. 사람들이 덜 다니는 이런 길들을 택할 만큼 충분히 용감한 사람들은 엄청난 보상을 받을 수 있고 그들의 용감한 행동으로부터 큰 만족감을 끌어낼 수 있다. 지나치게 조심하는 것은 여러분의 잠재력의 최고 수준을 달성하는 것을 놓칠 것이라는 사실을 의미할 것이다. 여러분은 주변에 있는 많은 사람들이 선택하지 않을 그러한 기회를 택하는 것을 배워야 하는데, 왜냐하면 여러분의 성공은 삶의 과정에서 여러분이 내릴 용감한 결정으로부터 나올 것이기 때문이다.

① 더 많은 용기가 더 많은 기회를 가져온다
② 여행: 친구를 사귀는 가장 좋은 방법
③ 실수를 성공으로 바꾸는 방법
④ 만족스러운 삶? 다른 사람들과 공유하라
⑤ 공포를 극복하는 게 왜 그렇게 어려운가?

문제풀이

미지의 세계에 대한 두려움을 극복하고 많이 사람들이 선택하지 않은 기회를 택하는 것을 배워야 인생에서 성공을 할 수 있다는 내용이므로, 글의 제목으로 ① 'More Courage Brings More Opportunities(더 많은 용기가 더 많은 기회를 가져온다)'가 가장 적절하다.

어휘·어구

operate 작동하다
process 과정
achieve 달성하다
return 수익, 이익
derive 끌어내다
satisfaction 만족감
courageous 용감한
overcautious 지나치게 조심하는
attain 달성하다, 이루다
potential 잠재력
bold 용감한, 대담한
turn A into B A를 B로 바꾸다
satisfying 만족시키는
overcome 극복하다

정답률 80%

2. ① 알고리즘 세대

직독/직해

Only a generation or two ago, /
한 세대나 두 세대 전만 해도 /

mentioning the word *algorithms* /
'알고리즘'이라는 단어를 언급하는 것은 /

would have drawn a blank / from most people.
아무런 반응을 얻지 못했다 / 대부분의 사람들로부터

Today, / algorithms appear /
오늘날 / 알고리즘은 나타난다 /

in every part of civilization. 문명의 모든 부분에서

They are connected to everyday life.
그것들은 일상에 연결되어 있다

They're not just / in your cell phone or your laptop /
그것들은 단지 있을 뿐 아니라 / 여러분의 휴대 전화나 노트북 내부에 /

but in your car, your house, your appliances, and your toys.
또한 여러분의 자동차, 집, 전자 제품과 장난감 안에도 있다

Your bank is a huge web of algorithms, /
여러분의 은행은 알고리즘의 거대한 망이다 /

with humans turning the switches / here and there.
인간들이 스위치를 돌리고 있는 / 여기저기서

Algorithms schedule flights /
알고리즘은 비행 일정을 잡는다 /

and then fly the airplanes.
그리고 비행기를 운항한다

Algorithms run factories, / trade goods, /
알고리즘은 공장을 운영한다 / 상품을 거래한다 /

and keep records. 그리고 기록 문서를 보관한다

If every algorithm suddenly stopped working, /
만약 모든 알고리즘이 갑자기 작동을 멈춘다면 /

it would be the end of the world / as we know it.
이는 세상의 끝이 될 것이다 / 우리가 알고 있듯이

한 세대나 두 세대 전만 해도, '알고리즘'이라는 단어를 언급하는 것은 대부분의 사람들로부터 아무런 반응을 얻지 못했다. 오늘날, 알고리즘은 문명의 모든 부분에서 나타난다. 그것들은 일상에 연결되어 있다. 그것들은 여러분의 휴대 전화나 노트북 내부뿐만 아니라 여러분의 자동차, 집, 전자 제품과 장난감 안에도 있다. 여러분의 은행은 인간들이 여기저기서 스위치를 돌리고 있는, 알고리즘의 거대한 망이다. 알고리즘은 비행 일정을 잡고 비행기를 운항한다. 알고리즘은 공장을 운영하고, 상품을 거래하며, 기록 문서를 보관한다. 만약 모든 알고리즘이 갑자기 작동을 멈춘다면, 이는 우리가 알고 있듯이 세상의 끝이 될 것이다.

① 우리는 알고리즘의 세대에 산다
② 고대 문명의 신비
③ 온라인 뱅킹 알고리즘의 위험
④ 알고리즘이 인간의 창의성을 줄이는 방법
⑤ 운송: 산업의 원동력

문제풀이

오늘날 문명의 모든 부분에서 알고리즘이 나타나는데 그것들은 일상과 연결되어 있어서 알고리즘이 멈추면 우리의 세상도 끝이 날 것이라는 내용이므로, 글의 제목으로 ① 'We Live in an Age of Algorithms(우리는 알고리즘의 세대에 산다)'가 가장 적절하다.

《 어휘·어구 》

generation 세대
mention 언급하다
algorithm 알고리즘
draw a blank 아무 반응을 얻지 못하다
appear 나타나다
civilization 문명
connect 연결하다
laptop 노트북
appliances 가전제품
schedule 일정을 잡다
run 운영하다
factory 공장
trade 거래하다
keep records 기록 문서를 보관하다
mystery 신비
ancient 고대의
danger 위험(성)
decrease 줄이다
creativity 창의성
transportation 운송
driving force 원동력
industry 산업

정답률 66%

3. ② 감정에 자세한 이름을 붙이는 것은 이롭다

직독/직해

Our ability to accurately recognize and label emotions /
감정을 정확하게 인식하고 그것에 이름을 붙일 수 있는 우리의 능력은 /

is often referred to as *emotional granularity*.
흔히 '감정 입자도'라고 일컬어진다

In the words of Harvard psychologist Susan David, /
Harvard 대학의 심리학자인 Susan David의 말에 의하면 /

"Learning to label emotions /
감정에 이름을 붙이는 법을 배우는 것은 /

with a more nuanced vocabulary /
더 미묘한 차이가 있는 어휘로 /

can be absolutely transformative."
절대적으로 (사람을) 변화시킬 수 있다

David explains / David는 설명한다 /

that if we don't have a rich emotional vocabulary, /
우리가 풍부한 감정적인 어휘를 갖고 있지 않으면 /

it is difficult to communicate our needs /
우리의 욕구를 전달하는 것은 어렵다 /

and to get the support that we need /
그리고 우리가 필요한 지지를 얻는 것이 (어렵다) /

from others. 다른 사람들로부터

But those who are able to distinguish /
하지만 구별할 수 있는 사람들은 /

between a range of various emotions /
광범위한 다양한 감정을 /

"do much, much better at managing /
관리하는 것을 훨씬, 훨씬 더 잘한다 /

the ups and downs of ordinary existence /
평범한 존재로 사는 중에 겪는 좋은 일들과 궂은일들을 /

than those who see everything / in black and white."
모든 것을 보는 사람들보다 / 흑백 논리로

In fact, / research shows /
실제로 / 연구는 보여 준다 /

that the process of labeling emotional experience /
감정적인 경험에 이름을 붙이는 과정은 /

is related to greater emotion regulation and psychosocial well-being.
더 큰 감정 통제와 심리 사회적인 행복과 관련 있다는 것을

감정을 정확하게 인식하고 그것에 이름을 붙일 수 있는 우리의 능력은 흔히 '감정 입자도'라고 일컬어진다. Harvard 대학의 심리학자인 Susan David의 말에 의하면, "감정에 더 미묘한 차이가 있는 어휘로 이름을 붙이는 법을 배우는 것은 절대적으로 (사람을) 변화시킬 수 있다." David는 우리가 풍부한 감정적인 어휘를 갖고 있지 않으면, 우리의 욕구를 전달하고 우리가 필요한 지지를 다른 사람들로부터 얻는 것이 어렵다고 설명한다. 하지만 광범위한 다양한 감정을 구별할 수 있는 사람들은 "모든 것을 흑백 논리로 보는 사람들보다 평범한 존재로 사는 중에 겪는 좋은 일들과 궂은일들을 관리하는 것을 훨씬, 훨씬 더 잘한다." 실제로, 연구는 감정적인 경험에 이름을 붙이는 과정은 더 큰 감정 통제와 심리 사회적인 행복과 관련 있다는 것을 보여 준다.

① 진정한 우정은 감정적인 논쟁을 견디게 한다
② 감정에 자세한 이름을 붙이는 것은 이롭다
③ 감정에 이름 붙이기: 행동보다 말이 쉽다
④ 효율성을 위해 업무를 분류하고 이름을 붙여라
⑤ 용기를 내서 여러분의 욕구를 전달하라

문제풀이

감정을 정확하게 인식하고 어휘로 이름을 붙이는 능력을 가진 사람들, 즉, 풍부한 감정적 어휘를 갖고 있으면서 광범위한 다양한 감정을 구별할 수 있는 사람들이 일 관리를 훨씬 더 잘한다는 내용을 통해, 글의 제목으로 ② 'Detailed Labeling of Emotions Is Beneficial(감정에 자세한 이름을 붙이는 것은 이롭다)'이 가장 적절하다.

《 어휘·어구 》

accurately 정확하게
recognize 인식하다
label 이름을 붙이다
emotion 감정
refer to A as B A를 B라 부르다
granularity 입자도
psychologist 심리학자
vocabulary 어휘
absolutely 절대적으로
transformative (사람을) 변화시키는
explain 설명하다
communicate 전달하다
distinguish 구별하다
a range of 다양한
various 다양한
manage 관리하다
ordinary 평범한
existence 존재
process 과정
related to ~에 관련된
regulation 통제
psychosocial 심리 사회적인
well-being 행복
friendship 우정
endure 인내하다
argument 논쟁
detailed 자세한, 상세한
beneficial 이로운
categorize 분류하다
efficiency 효율성

정답률 61%

4. ② 현대 사회와 정체성 확립

직독/직해

In modern times, / society became more dynamic.
현대에는 / 사회가 더욱 역동적이게 되었다

Social mobility increased, /
사회적 유동성이 증가하였다 /

and people began to exercise a higher degree of choice /
그리고 사람들은 더 높은 정도의 선택권을 행사하기 시작했다 /

regarding, for instance, their profession, their marriage, or their religion.
예를 들어 자신의 직업, 결혼 혹은 종교와 관련하여

This posed a challenge / 이것은 이의를 제기했다 /

to traditional roles in society.
사회의 전통적인 역할에

It was less evident / 덜 분명해졌다 /

that one needed to commit to the roles /
개인이 역할에 전념할 필요가 있다는 것은 /

one was born into / 자신이 타고난 /

when alternatives could be realized.
대안이 실현될 수 있을 때

Increasing control over one's life choices became not only possible but desired.
개인의 삶의 선택에 대한 통제력을 늘리는 것이 가능해졌을 뿐만 아니라 바람직하게 되었다

Identity then became a problem.
그러자 정체성이 문제가 되었다

It was no longer almost ready-made at birth but something to be discovered.
그것은 더 이상 태어날 때 대체로 주어진 것이 아닌 발견되어져야 할 것이었다

Traditional role identities / prescribed by society /
전통적인 역할 정체성은 / 사회에 의해 규정되어진 /

began to appear as masks / imposed on people /
가면처럼 보이기 시작했다 / 사람들에게 부여된 /

whose real self was to be found somewhere underneath.
아래 어딘가에서 자신의 진정한 자아가 발견되어져야 할

현대에는 사회가 더욱 역동적이게 되었다. 사회적 유동성이 증가하였고 사람들은 예를 들어 자신의 직업, 결혼 혹은 종교와 관련하여 더 높은 정도의 선택권을 행사하기 시작했다. 이것은 사회의 전통적인 역할에 이의를 제기했다. 대안이 실현될 수 있을 때 개인이 자신이 타고난 역할에 전념할 필요가 있다는 것은 덜 분명해졌다. 개인의 삶의 선택에 대한 통제력을 늘리는 것이 가능해졌을 뿐만 아니라 바람직하게 되었다. 그러자 정체성이 문제가 되었다. 그것은 더 이상 태어날 때 대체로 주어진 것이 아닌 발견되어져야 할 것이었다. 사회에 의해 규정되어진 전통적인 역할 정체성은 아래 어딘가에서 자신의 진정한 자아가 발견되어져야 할 사람들에게 부여된 가면처럼 보이기 시작했다.

① 무엇이 우리 현대 사회를 그렇게 경쟁적으로 만드는가?
② 현대 사회가 우리의 정체성을 발견하도록 이끄는 방법
③ 소셜 마스크: 신뢰할 수 있는 관계를 형성하는 수단
④ 사회적 역할을 많이 가질수록 선택의 폭은 줄어든다
⑤ 증가하는 사회적 이동성은 더 평등한 사회로 이끈다

문제풀이

현대 사회는 역동적이어서 사람들은 더 높은 선택권을 행사하기 시작했고, 따라서 개인의 삶의 선택에 대한 통제력을 늘리는 것이 가능해졌을 뿐만 아니라 바람직하게 되었으며, 따라서 전통적인 역할 정체성은 가면에 불과할 뿐 정체성은 직접 발견되어야 할 것이라는 내용의 글이다. 따라서 글의 제목으로 가장 적절한 것은 ② 'How Modern Society Drives Us to Discover Our Identities (현대 사회가 우리의 정체성을 발견하도록 이끄는 방법)'이다.

어휘 · 어구

dynamic 역동적인
degree 정도
regarding ~에 관하여
profession 직업
traditional 전통적인
commit to ~전념하다
alternative 대안
identity 정체성
prescribe 규정하다
underneath ~아래에

5. ④ 시련과 갈등에서 창의성이 나온다

직독/직해

Diversity, challenge, and conflict /
다양성, 어려움, 그리고 갈등은 /

help us maintain our imagination.
우리의 상상력을 유지하는 것을 돕는다

Most people assume / that conflict is bad /
대부분의 사람은 단정한다 / 갈등은 나쁘다 /

and that being in one's "comfort zone" / is good.
그리고 "안전지대"에 있는 것이 / 좋다고

That is not exactly true.
그것은 정확히 사실은 아니다

Of course, / we don't want to find ourselves /
물론 / 우리는 자신의 모습을 보고 싶어 하지 않는다 /

without a job or medical insurance / or in a fight /
직장이나 의료보험이 없는 / 혹은 다툼에 빠진 /

with our partner, family, boss, or coworkers.
배우자, 가족, 직장 상사 혹은 직장 동료들과의

One bad experience / 하나의 나쁜 경험이 /

can be sufficient to last us a lifetime.
우리에게 평생 지속되는 데 충분할 수 있다

But small disagreements with family and friends, /
하지만 가족과 친구들과의 작은 의견 충돌 /

trouble with technology or finances, /
기술적이거나 재정적인 문제 /

or challenges at work and at home /
혹은 직장과 가정에서의 어려움은 /

can help us think through / our own capabilities.
우리가 진지하게 고민하게 도와줄 수 있다 / 우리의 능력에 대해

Problems that need solutions / 해결책이 필요한 문제들은 /

force us to use our brains / 우리의 뇌를 사용하도록 강요한다 /

in order to develop creative answers.
창의적인 해답들을 개발하기 위해

Navigating landscapes that are varied, /
변화무쌍한 지형을 운전하는 것은 /

that offer trials and occasional conflicts, /
시련과 때때로 갈등을 주는 /

is more helpful to creativity / 창의성에 더 도움이 된다 /

than hanging out in landscapes / 지형을 다니는 것보다 /

that pose no challenge / to our senses and our minds.
아무런 어려움을 주지 않는 / 우리 감각과 마음에

Our two million-year history / 우리의 2백 만 년 역사는 /

is packed with challenges and conflicts.
어려움과 갈등들로 가득 차 있다

다양성, 어려움, 그리고 갈등은 우리의 상상력을 유지하는 것을 돕는다. 대부분의 사람은 갈등은 나쁘고 "안전지대"에 있는 것이 좋다고 단정한다. 그것은 정확히 사실은 아니다. 물론, 우리는 직장이나 의료보험이 없거나, 배우자, 가족, 직장 상사 혹은 직장 동료들과의 다툼에 빠진 자신의 모습을 보고 싶어 하지 않는다. 하나의 나쁜 경험이 우리에게 평생 지속되는 데 충분할 수 있다. 하지만 가족과 친구들과의 작은 의견 충돌, 기술적이거나 재정적인 문제, 직장과 가정에서의 어려움이 우리의 능력에 대해 진지하게 고민하게 도와줄 수 있다. 해결책이 필요한 문제들은 창의적인 해답들을 개발하기 위해 우리의 뇌를 사용하도록 강요한다. 시련과 때때로 갈등을 주는, 변화무쌍한 지형을 운전하는 것은 우리 감각과 마음에 아무런 어려움을 주지 않는 지형을 다니는 것보다 창의성에 더 도움이 된다. 우리의 2백 만 년 역사는 어려움과 갈등들로 가득 차 있다.

① 기술: 미래를 내다보는 렌즈
② 다양성: 사회 통합의 비결
③ 다른 사람들과의 갈등을 피하는 간단한 방법
④ 창의성은 그것을 안전하게 두는 것으로부터 오지 않는다
⑤ 극복될 수 없는 어려움은 없다

문제풀이

어려움과 갈등은 상상력을 유지하는 것을 돕는다는 내용으로, 안전지대에 있는 것보다는 충돌과 어려움을 해결하면서 뇌를 사용하는 것이 창의성에 도움이 된다는 것으로 보아 글의 제목으로 ④ 'Creativity Doesn't Come from Playing It Safe(창의성은 그것을 안전하게 두는 것으로부터 오지 않는다)'가 가장 적절하다.

어휘 · 어구

diversity 다양성
challenge 어려움, 도전
conflict 갈등, 충돌
imagination 상상력
assume 당연한 것으로 여기다
comfort 안전
insurance 보험
sufficient 충분한
disagreement 불일치
finance 재정
capability 능력
solution 해결책
navigate 운전하다, 조종하다
occasional 때때로의
landscape 지역, 풍경
unification 통합
overcome 극복하다

6. ① 엘리베이터는 고층빌딩을 가능하게 한다

직독/직해

When people think about the development of cities, /
사람들은 도시의 발전에 관해 생각할 때 /

rarely do they consider / 그들은 거의 고려하지 않는다 /

the critical role of vertical transportation.
수직 운송 수단의 중요한 역할을

In fact, each day, / 실제로 매일 /

more than 7 billion elevator journeys /
70억 회 이상의 엘리베이터 이동이 /

are taken in tall buildings / all over the world.
높은 빌딩에서 이루어진다 / 전 세계에서

Efficient vertical transportation /
효율적인 수직 운송 수단은 /

can expand our ability to build /
우리의 능력을 확장할 수 있다 /

taller and taller skyscrapers.
점점 더 높은 고층 건물들을 만들 수 있는

Antony Wood, / Antony Wood는 /

a Professor of Architecture at the Illinois Institute of Technology, /
Illinois 공과대학 건축학과 교수인 /

explains / 설명한다 /

that advances in elevators over the past 20 years /
지난 20년간의 엘리베이터의 발전이 /

are probably the greatest advances /
아마도 가장 큰 발전이라고 /

we have seen in tall buildings.
우리가 높은 건물들에서 봐 왔던

For example, / 예를 들어 /

elevators in the Jeddah Tower in Jeddah, Saudi Arabia, /
사우디 아라비아 Jeddah의 Jeddah Tower에 있는 엘리베이터는 /

under construction, / 건설 중인 /

will reach a height record of 660m.
660m라는 기록적인 높이에 이를 것이다

사람들은 도시의 발전에 관해 생각할 때, 수직 운송 수단의 중요한 역할을 거의 고려하지 않는다. 실제로 매일 70억 회 이상의 엘리베이터 이동이 전 세계 높은 빌딩에서 이루어진다. 효율적인 수직 운송 수단은 점점 더 높은 고층 건물들을 만들 수 있는 우리의 능력을 확장할 수 있다. Illinois 공과대학 건축학과 교수인 Antony Wood는 지난 20년간의 엘리베이터의 발전은 아마도 우리가 높은 건물들에서 봐 왔던 가장 큰 발전이라고 설명한다. 예를 들어, 건설 중인 사우디 아라비아 Jeddah의 Jeddah Tower에 있는 엘리베이터는 660m라는 기록적인 높이에 이를 것이다.

① 엘리베이터는 건물이 하늘에 더 가깝게 한다
② 더 높이 올라갈수록, 전망이 더 좋다
③ 엘리베이터를 저렴하고 빠르게 건축하는 방법
④ 고대 도시와 현대 도시의 기능
⑤ 건축의 진화: 인구 과잉의 해결책

문제풀이

효율적인 운송 수단인 엘리베이터가 점점 더 높은 고층 건물을 만들 수 있는 우리의 능력을 확장할 수 있었다는 내용이므로, 글의 제목으로 ① 'Elevators Bring Buildings Closer to the Sky (엘리베이터는 건물이 하늘에 더 가깝게 한다)'가 가장 적절하다.

어휘 · 어구

development 발전
critical 대단히 중요한
vertical 수직의
transportation 운송[교통] 수단
efficient 효율적인
expand 확장하다
skyscraper 고층 건물, 마천루
architecture 건축
advance 발전
under construction 공사 중인
function 기능
ancient 고대의
modern 현대의

evolution 진화
solution 해결책
overpopulation 인구 과잉

정답률 79%

7. ⑤ 구매 후 사용하지 않는 물건은 낭비이다

직독/직해

Think, for a moment, about something /
물건에 대해 잠시 생각해 봐라 /
you bought / that you never ended up using.
여러분이 사 놓은 / 결국 한 번도 사용하지 않았던
An item of clothing / you never ended up wearing?
옷 한 벌 / 결국 한 번도 입지 않은
A book / you never read?
책 한 권 / 한 번도 읽지 않은
Some piece of electronic equipment /
어떤 전자 기기 /
that never even made it out of the box?
심지어 상자에서 꺼내 보지조차 않은
It is estimated that Australians alone spend /
단독으로 호주인들은 쓰는 것으로 추산된다 /
on average $10.8 billion AUD /
평균적으로 108억 호주 달러 /
(approximately $9.99 billion USD) / every year /
약 99억 9천 미국 달러 / 매년 /
on goods they do not use /
사용하지 않는 물건에 /
— more than the total government spending /
이는 정부 지출 총액을 넘는 금액이다 /
on universities and roads. 대학과 도로에 사용하는
That is an average of $1,250 AUD /
그 금액은 평균 1,250 호주 달러이다 /
(approximately $1,156 USD) /
약 1,156 미국 달러 /
for each household. 각 가구당
All the things we buy / 우리가 사는 모든 물건은 /
that then just sit there gathering dust /
그러고 나서 제자리에서 먼지를 끌어모으기만 /
are waste— / a waste of money, a waste of time, /
낭비이다 / 돈 낭비, 시간 낭비 /
and waste / in the sense of pure rubbish.
그리고 낭비이다 / 순전히 쓸모없는 물건이라는 의미에서
As the author Clive Hamilton observes, /
작가 Clive Hamilton이 말하는 것처럼 /
'The difference / between the stuff we buy /
차이는 / "우리가 사는 물건과 /
and what we use / is waste.'
우리가 사용하는 것 사이에서의 / 낭비이다

여러분이 사 놓고 결국 한 번도 사용하지 않았던 물건에 대해 잠시 생각해 봐라. 결국 한 번도 입지 않은 옷 한 벌? 한 번도 읽지 않은 책 한 권? 심지어 상자에서 꺼내 보지조차 않은 어떤 전자 기기? 단독으로 호주인들은 사용하지 않는 물건에 매년 평균적으로 108억 호주 달러(약 99억 9천 미국 달러)를 쓰는 것으로 추산되는데, 이는 대학과 도로에 사용하는 정부 지출 총액을 넘는 금액이다. 그 금액은 각 가구당 평균 1,250 호주 달러(약 1,156 미국 달러)이다. 우리가 사고 나서 제자리에서 먼지를 끌어모으기만 하는 모든 물건은 낭비인데, 돈 낭비, 시간 낭비, 그리고 순전히 쓸모없는 물건이라는 의미에서 낭비이다. 작가 Clive Hamilton이 말하는 것처럼 "우리가 사는 물건에서 우리가 사용하는 것을 뺀 것은 낭비이다".

① 소비는 경제를 활성화한다
② 돈 관리: 지켜야 할 사항
③ 너무 많은 쇼핑: 외로움의 표시
④ 쓰레기의 3R: 줄이기, 재사용하기, 그리고 재활용하기
⑤ 사용하지 않는다면, 당신이 사는 것은 낭비이다

문제풀이

구매 후 한 번도 사용하지 않은 물건은 돈, 시간, 그리고 쓸모없는 물건이라는 의미에서 모두 낭비라는 내용이므로, 글의 제목으로 ⑤ 'What You Buy Is Waste Unless You Use It(사용하지 않는다면, 당신이 사는 것은 낭비이다)'이 가장 적절하다.

《 어휘·어구 》

end up ~ing 결국 ~하다
an item of clothing 옷 한 벌
electronic equipment 전자 기기
estimate 추산하다
average 평균
billion 십 억
approximately 약, 대략
goods 물건, 제품, 상품
government 정부
household 가구, 세대
gather 모으다
in the sense of ~이라는 의미에서
pure 순전한, 순수한
rubbish 쓸모없는 물건, 쓰레기
observe (발언, 의견을) 말하다
stuff 물건
enable 가능하게 하다, 용이하게 하다
economy 경제
management 관리
dos and don'ts 지켜야 할 사항
loneliness 외로움

8. ③ 씹기는 포유류가 생존하는 것을 돕는다

직독/직해

Chewing leads to smaller particles for swallowing, /
씹기는 삼킴을 위한 더 작은 조각들로 이어진다 /
and more exposed surface area /
그리고 더 노출된 표면으로 (이어진다) /
for digestive enzymes to act on.
소화 효소가 작용하는
In other words, / 다시 말해 /
it means the extraction of more fuel and raw materials /
그것은 더 많은 연료와 원료를 추출하는 것을 의미한다 /
from a mouthful of food. 한입의 음식으로부터
This is especially important for mammals /
이것은 포유류에게는 특히 중요하다 /
because they heat their bodies from within.
그들이 체내에서 자신의 몸을 따뜻하게 하기 때문에
Chewing gives mammals the energy /
씹기는 포유류에게 에너지를 준다 /
needed to be active / 활동하는 데 필요한 /
not only during the day but also the cool night, /
낮 동안은 물론 서늘한 밤 동안에도 /
and to live in colder climates /
그리고 더 추운 기후에서 사는 데 (필요한) /
or places with changing temperatures.
혹은 기온이 변하는 장소에서 (사는 데 필요한)
It allows them / 그것은 그들이 ~하게 한다 /
to sustain higher levels of activity and travel speeds /
더 높은 수준의 활동과 이동 속도를 유지하도록 /
to cover larger distances, avoid predators, capture prey, /
더 먼 거리를 가고, 천적을 피하고, 먹이를 포획하게 하도록 /
and make and care for their young.
그리고 새끼를 낳고 돌보게 하도록
Mammals are able to live / 포유류는 살 수 있다 /
in an incredible variety of habitats, /
매우 다양한 서식지에서 /
from Arctic tundra to Antarctic pack ice, /
북극 툰드라부터 남극의 유빙까지 /
deep open waters to high-altitude mountaintops, /
심해부터 고도가 높은 산꼭대기까지 /
and rainforests to deserts, /
그리고 열대 우림부터 사막까지 /
in no small measure because of their teeth.
어느 정도는 그들의 이빨로 인해

씹기는 삼킴을 위한 더 작은 조각들과 소화 효소가 작용하는 더 노출된 표면으로 이어진다. 다시 말해, 그것은 한입의 음식으로부터 더 많은 연료와 원료를 추출하는 것을 의미한다. 이것은 그들이 체내에서 자신의 몸을 따뜻하게 하기 때문에 포유류에게는 특히 중요하다. 씹기는 포유류에게 낮 동안은 물론 서늘한 밤 동안에도 활동하고, 더 추운 기후나 기온이 변하는 장소에서 사는 데 필요한 에너지를 준다. 그것은 그들에게 더 먼 거리를 가고, 천적을 피하고, 먹이를 포획하고 새끼를 낳고 돌보게 하는 더 높은 수준의 활동과 이동 속도를 유지하게 한다. 포유류는 어느 정도는 그들의 이빨로 인해 북극 툰드라부터 남극의 유빙까지, 심해부터 고도가 높은 산꼭대기까지 그리고 열대 우림부터 사막까지 매우 다양한 서식지에서 살 수 있다.

① 씹기: 소화 불량을 완화하는 방법
② 더 씹음으로써 여러분의 에너지를 증가시켜라
③ 씹는 것이 포유류가 생존하는 것을 돕는 방법
④ 이빨의 다양한 형태와 기능
⑤ 열악한 기후가 포유류를 더욱더 강하게 만든다

문제풀이

씹는 것은 포유류가 체내에서 자신의 몸을 따뜻하게 하기 때문에 중요하며 열악한 기후나 장소에서도 살 수 있는 에너지를 준다는 내용으로 보아, 글의 제목으로 ③ 'How Chewing Helps Mammals Survive(씹는 것이 포유류가 생존하는 것을 돕는 방법)'가 가장 적절하다.

《 어휘·어구 》

chewing 저작, 씹기
particle 작은 조각
swallow 삼키다
surface 표면
digestive 소화의
act on ~에 작용하다
extraction 추출
raw material 원료
mammal 포유류
active 활동적인
climate 기후
temperature 기온, 온도
sustain 유지하다
predator 천적
capture 포획하다
incredible 믿을 수 없는, 엄청난
habitat 서식지
arctic 북극의
antarctic 남극의
altitude 고도
in no small measure 어느 정도
ease 덜해지다
indigestion 소화 불량
boost 북돋우다
survive 생존하다
function 기능
harsh 혹독한, 모진

9. ⑤ 억지 미소도 스트레스 해소에 도움이 됨

직독/직해

Every event / that causes you to smile /
모든 사건들은 / 여러분을 미소짓게 만드는 /
makes you feel happy /
여러분이 행복감을 느끼게 한다 /
and produces feel-good chemicals / in your brain.
그리고 기분을 좋게 만들어 주는 화학물질을 생산하다 / 여러분의 뇌에서
Force your face to smile /

당신의 얼굴이 미소짓게 하라 /

even when you are stressed or feel unhappy.
심지어 스트레스를 받거나 불행하다고 느낄 때조차도

The facial muscular pattern produced by the smile /
미소에 의해 만들어지는 안면 근육의 형태는

is linked to all the "happy networks" / in your brain /
모든 "행복 연결망"과 연결되어 있다 / 당신의 두뇌에 있는 /

and will in turn naturally calm you down /
그리고 결국 자연스럽게 여러분을 안정시킨다 /

and change your brain chemistry /
그리고 여러분 뇌의 화학작용을 변화시킨다/

by releasing the same feel-good chemicals.
기분을 좋게 만들어주는 동일한 화학물질들을 배출함으로써

Researchers studied / 연구자들이 연구했다 /

the effects of a genuine and forced smile on individuals /
진정한 미소와 억지 미소가 개개인들에게 미치는 영향을 /

during a stressful event.
스트레스가 상당한 상황에서

The researchers had participants perform stressful tasks /
연구자들은 참가자들에게 스트레스를 수반한 과업을 수행하게 했다 /

while not smiling, smiling, or holding chopsticks crossways /
미소짓지 않거나, 미소짓거나 또는 젓가락을 옆으로 물고서 /

in their mouths / 그들의 입에 /

(to force the face to form a smile).
얼굴이 미소를 짓도록 하기 위해

The results of the study showed /
연구의 결과가 보여주었다 /

that smiling, forced or genuine, /
미소는 강요된 것이든, 진정한 것이든 /

during stressful events /
스트레스가 상당한 상황동안 /

reduced the intensity of the stress response /
스트레스 반응의 강도를 줄였다 /

in the body / and lowered heart rate levels /
신체에서 / 그리고 심장 박동률의 수준을 낮추었다 /

after recovering from the stress.
스트레스로부터 회복한 후의

여러분을 미소 짓게 만드는 온갖 사건들은 여러분이 행복감을 느끼게 하고, 여러분의 뇌에서 기분을 좋게 만들어주는 화학물질을 생산해내도록 한다. 심지어 스트레스를 받거나 불행하다고 느낄 때조차 미소를 지어보자. 미소에 의해 만들어지는 안면 근육의 형태는 뇌의 모든 "행복 연결망"과 연결되어 있고, 따라서 자연스럽게 여러분을 안정시키고 기분을 좋게 만들어주는 동일한 화학물질들을 배출함으로써 뇌의 화학작용을 변화시킬 것이다. 연구자들은 스트레스가 상당한 상황에서 진정한 미소와 억지 미소가 개개인들에게 미치는 영향을 연구하였다. 연구자들은 참가자들이 미소 짓지 않거나, 미소 짓거나, (억지 미소를 짓게 하기 위해) 입에 젓가락을 옆으로 물고서 스트레스를 수반한 과업을 수행하도록 했다. 연구의 결과는 미소가, 억지이든 진정한 것이든, 스트레스가 상당한 상황에서 인체의 스트레스 반응의 강도를 줄였고, 스트레스로부터 회복한 후의 심장 박동률의 수준도 낮추었다는 것을 보여주었다.

① 스트레스 상황의 원인과 결과
② 스트레스의 개인적인 징후와 양상
③ 신체와 정신이 스트레스에 반응하는 방식
④ 스트레스: 행복의 필요악
⑤ 억지 미소도 스트레스를 줄이는데 도움이 되는가?

문제풀이

미소에 의해 만들어지는 안면 근육의 형태가 뇌의 모든 행복 연결망과 연결되어 있으므로, 진정한 미소뿐만 아니라 억지 미소도 스트레스 상황을 극복하는데 도움을 주었다는 내용의 글이다. 따라서 글의 제목으로 가장 적절한 것은 ⑤ 'Do Faked Smiles Also Help Reduce Stress?(억지 미소도 스트레스를 줄이는데 도움이 되는가?)'이다.

이렇게 풀자 글의 제목을 찾는 문제에서는 우선 반복적인 어구나 특정 개념과 관련된 어구를 통해 글의 주제를 추측할 수 있다. 이 글에서는 '미소', '스트레스' '뇌' 등이 반복적으로 등장한다. 글의 흐름을 따라가면서 필자의 의견을 파악해야 하는데, 이 글과 같이 연구를 통해서 필자의 의견을 드러내는 경우에는 연구의 결과에 해당하는 부분이 글의 주제가 될 수 있다. 'smiling, forced or genuine, during stressful events reduced the intensity of the stress response in the body and lowered heart rate levels after recovering from the stress.(미소는, 억지이든 진정한 것이든, 스트레스가 상당한 상황에서 인체의 스트레스 반응의 강도를 줄였고, 스트레스로부터 회복한 후의 심장 박동률의 수준도 낮추었다)'가 연구의 결론이다. 마지막으로 선택지 중에 글의 요지를 정확하게 담고 있는 제목을 선택하면 된다.

구조 다시보기

도입	미소는 뇌에서 기분을 좋게 하는 화학물질을 생산하게 함
부연	억지 미소도 기분을 좋게 하는 화학물질을 배출함
연구 과제	진정한 미소와 억지 미소가 개개인에게 미치는 영향 조사
연구 과정	미소짓거나, 미소짓지 않거나, 억지 미소를 짓게 함
연구 결과	진정한 미소든 억지 미소든 스트레스를 줄임

어휘·어구

chemicals 화학물질
muscular 근육의
in turn 결국
chemistry 화학작용
release 방출하다
genuine 진정한
participant 참가자
intensity 강도
recover 복구하다
necessary evil 필요악

정답률 75%

10. ② 지나침이 없는 교육의 양

직독/직해

In life, / they say that too much of anything is not
삶에서 / 어떤 것이든 과도하면 이롭지 않다고들 한다

good for you.

In fact, / 실제로 /

too much of certain things in life can kill you.
삶에서 어떤 것이 과도하면 치명적일 수 있다

For example, / they say that water has no enemy, /
예를 들어 / 물은 적이 없다고들 한다 /

because water is essential / to all life.
필수적이기 때문에 / 모든 생물에게

But if you take in too much water, /
그러나 만일 너무 많은 물을 들이마시면 /

like one who is drowning, / it could kill you.
물에 빠진 사람처럼 / 그것은 목숨을 앗아갈 수 있다

Education is the exception / to this rule.
교육은 예외다 / 이 규칙에서

You can never have too much education or knowledge.
교육이나 지식은 아무리 많이 있어도 지나치지 않다

The reality / 실상은 /

is that most people will never have enough education / in their lifetime.
대부분의 사람은 아무리 많은 교육을 받아도 지나치지 않을 거라는 것이다 / 평생동안

I am yet to find / 나는 아직 본 적이 없다 /

that one person who has been hurt in life /
삶에서 피해를 본 사람을 /

by too much education.
교육을 너무 받아서

Rather, we see lots of casualties every day, worldwide, /
오히려 우리는 매일, 전 세계에서 수많은 피해자들을 본다 /

resulting from the lack of education.
교육의 부족으로 인해 생긴

You must keep in mind / 여러분은 명심해야 한다 /

that education is a longterm investment of time, money, and effort / into humans.
교육이 시간, 돈, 그리고 노력을 장기 투자하는 것임을 / 인간에게

삶에서, 어떤 것이든 과도하면 이롭지 않다고들 한다. 실제로, 삶에서 어떤 것이 과도하면 위험할 수 있다. 예를 들어, 물은 모든 생물에게 필수적이기 때문에 적이 없다고 한다. 그러나 만일 물에 빠진 사람처럼 너무 많은 물을 들이마시면, 위험할 수 있다. 교육은 이 규칙에서 예외다. 교육이나 지식은 아무리 많이 있어도 지나치지 않다. 실상은 대부분의 사람은 평생 아무리 많은 교육을 받아도 지나치지 않을 거라는 것이다. 나는 교육을 너무 받아서 삶에서 피해를 본 사람을 아직 본 적이 없다. 오히려 우리는 매일, 전 세계에서 교육의 부족으로 인해 생긴 수많은 피해자들을 본다. 교육이 인간에게 시간, 돈, 그리고 노력을 장기 투자하는 것임을 명심해야 한다.

① 놀기만 하고 공부하지 않으면 똑똑해진다
② 아무리 교육을 많이 받아도 해롭지 않을 것이다
③ 너무 많은 머리를 맞대는 것은 하나의 머리보다 더 좋지 않다
④ 행동하기 전에 두 번 생각하지 마라
⑤ 과거가 아닌, 미래로부터 배워라

문제풀이

삶에서 무엇이든 과도하면 이롭지 않지만 교육은 예외라고 하면서 필자는 교육을 너무 많이 받아서 피해를 입은 사람은 본 적이 없고, 오히려 세계적으로 교육의 부족으로 인한 수많은 피해자들을 본다고 했다. 이러한 내용을 가장 잘 나타낸 제목은 ② 'Too Much Education Won't Hurt You(아무리 교육을 많이 받아도 해롭지 않을 것이다)'이다.

어휘·어구

essential 필수적인
take in ~을 들이마시다, 섭취하다
drown 물에 빠지다
exception 예외
knowledge 지식
result from ~로 인해 생기다, ~의 원인이다.
keep in mind ~을 명심하다
long-term investment 장기 투자
effort 노력, 수고
twice 두 번, 2회

본문 041쪽

문법 플러스 7. 수동태

1. appeared	2. are more influenced
3. was given	4. has never been seen
5. been considered	6. to be followed
7. be left	8. to enter
9. is said	10. at

1 [해석]▶ 희미한 모습이 안개 사이로 나타났다.
[해설]▶ appear는 자동사이므로 수동태 형태를 쓰지 않는다.

2 [해석]▶ 우리는 숫자를 읽을 때, 가장 오른쪽보다는 가장 왼쪽 숫자에 의해 영향을 더 받는데, 왜냐하면 그것이 우리가 그것들을 읽고 처리하는 순서이기 때문이다.
[해설]▶ we는 가장 왼쪽 숫자에 의해 영향을 받는 대상이므로 동사는 수동태 형태인 are influenced를 써야 한다.

3 [해석]▶ 한 연구는 학생들이 붉은색 색소를 물들인 백포도주를 받았을 때, '자두와 초콜릿'과 같은 적포도주에 적합한 시음표를 선택했다는 것을 보여주었다.
[해설]▶ 주어 students가 white wine을 주는 것이 아니라 받는 대상이므로, 수동태 were given이 와야 맞다

4 [해석]▶ 더 깊은 곳에서는—그곳은 어둡고 차갑다—사진술(photography)이 신비로운 심해의 세계를 탐험하는 주요한 방법이며, 그곳의 95%는 예전에는 전혀 볼 수 없었다.
[해설]▶ 관계대명사 which가 가리키는 a mysterious deep-sea world가 행위의 주체가 아니라 대상이므로, 수동의 의미를 나타내는 현재완료 수동태가 와야 한다.

5 [해석]▶ 이전에는 이런 대상들이 결코 화가들에게 적절하다고 여겨지지 않았다.
[해설]▶ 「consider+목적어(these subjects)+목적격보어(appropriate)」의 5형식 능동태 문장을 수동태 문장으로 바꾸면 능동태의 목적어(these subjects)가 수동태의 주어가 되고, 과거완료 시제(had considered)는 과거완료 수동태 시제(had been considered)가 된다. 그런데 부정어(never)가 문두로 나와서 주어와 동사가 도치되었다.

6 [해석]▶ 먹이 소유자가 다른 침팬지들에 둘러싸여 중심에 있게 되고, 모든 먹이가 다 분배될 때까지 꽤 큰 몫을 얻은 침팬지들 주변으로 새로이 형성된 무리들이 곧 뒤따르게 된다.
[해설]▶ 꽤 큰 몫을 얻은 침팬지가 새로이 형성된 무리들에 의해 뒤따름을 받는 것이므로 to부정사의 수동태로 써야 한다.

7 [해석]▶ 문을 열린 채로 두지 마라.
[해설]▶ You must not leave the door open을 수동태로 만든 문장이다. 조동사의 수동태는 조동사 뒤에 be+p.p. 형태를 쓴다.

8 [해석]▶ 그 남자가 그 방에 들어가는 것이 목격되었다.
[해설]▶ 지각동사가 들어 있는 문장을 수동태로 바꾸면 목적격보어인 원형부정사는 to부정사로 바뀐다.

9 [해석]▶ 사람들이 그녀는 부자라고 말한다.
[해설]▶ They say that she is rich.와 같이 say, believe, think 동사가 that절을 목적어로 취할 때 가주어 it을 사용하거나 that절의 주어를 수동태의 주어로 사용할 수 있다. 이 문장을 수동태로 바꾸면 (1) It is said that she is rich. (2) She is said to be rich.로 바꿀 수 있다.

10 해석▶ 나는 그의 죽음 소식을 듣고 놀랐다.
[해설]▶The news of his death surprised me.라는 능동태 문장을 수동태로 바꾼 문장이다. 수동태는 「by+행위자」를 표시하는 경우, by 이외의 전치사를 사용할 수 있다.

본문 042쪽

어휘 플러스 7. 반의어 (2)

1. caused	2. competent
3. demand	4. undesirable
5. discouraged	

1 [해석]▶ 매년, 소수의 사람들만이 호랑이나 곰의 공격을 받는데, 이러한 사건의 대부분은 사람들 자신에 의해 야기된다.

2 [해석]▶ 가장 정상적이고 유능한 아이라 하더라도 살면서 극복할 수 없는 문제들처럼 보이는 것을 만난다.

3 [해석]▶ 최근에 콜롬비아는 수출로 많은 돈을 벌지 못했다. 콜롬비아의 주요 수출 작물은 커피지만 세계의 커피 수요가 하락했다.

4 [해석]▶ 자연스럽게 사람들은 바람직하지 않은 사건을 '잊도록' 이끌릴 것이다.

5 [해석]▶ 지치고 낙담한 채, 그녀는 할머니에게 "나비를 모두 없애서 더 이상의 알이나 애벌레가 생기지 않게 하면 어때요?"라고 물었다.

08. 도표 정보 파악

본문 044쪽

Day 08

1. ③	2. ⑤	3. ⑤	4. ④	5. ④
6. ⑤	7. ③	8. ⑤	9. ④	10. ⑤

정답률 83%

대표 기출 ④ 고기를 덜먹거나 먹지 않는 이유에 관한 조사

직독/직해

The graph above shows / 위 그래프는 보여 준다 /
the survey results on reasons / 이유에 대한 조사 결과를 /
for people interested in eating less meat / 고기를 덜먹는 것에 관심 있는 사람들의 /
and those eating no meat / in the UK in 2018. 그리고 고기를 먹지 않는 사람들의 / 2018년 영국에서
For the group of people / 사람들의 집단에서 /
who are interested in eating less meat, / 고기를 덜먹는 것에 관심 있는 /
health is the strongest motivator / for doing so. 건강은 가장 강력한 동기이다 / 그렇게 하는
For the group of non-meat eaters, / 고기를 먹지 않는 사람들의 집단에서 /
animal welfare accounts for the largest percentage / 동물 복지가 가장 큰 비율을 차지하고 있다 /
among all reasons, / followed by environment, health, and taste. 모든 이유 중에서 / 환경, 건강, 그리고 맛이 그 뒤를 따른다
The largest percentage point difference / 가장 큰 퍼센트 포인트 차이는 /
between the two groups / is in animal welfare, / 두 집단 사이의 / 동물 복지에 있다 /
whereas the smallest difference / is in environment. 반면에 가장 작은 차이는 / 환경에 있다
The percentage of non-meat eaters / citing taste / 고기를 먹지 않는 사람들의 비율은 / 맛을 언급하는 /
is four times higher / than that of people interested / 4배 더 높다 / 관심 있는 사람들의 비율보다 /
in reducing their meat consumption / citing taste. 고기 섭취를 줄이는 데 / 맛을 언급하는
Weight management ranks the lowest / 체중 관리는 가장 낮은 순위를 차지한다 /
for people who don't eat meat, / 고기를 먹지 않는 사람들에게 /
with less than 10 percent. 10% 미만으로

위 그래프는 2018년 영국에서 고기를 덜먹는 것에 관심 있는 사람들과 고기를 먹지 않는 사람들의 이유에 대한 조사 결과를 보여 준다. ① 고기를 덜먹는 것에 관심 있는 사람들의 집단에서, 건강은 그렇게 하는 가장 강력한 동기이다. ② 고기를 먹지 않는 사람들의 집단에서, 모든 이유 중에서 동물 복지가 가장 큰 비율을 차지하고 있고, 환경, 건강, 그리고 맛이 그 뒤를 따른다. ③ 두 집단 사이의 가장 큰 퍼센트포인트 차이는 동물 복지에 있는 반면, 가장 작은 차이는 환경에 있다. ④ 맛을 언급하는 고기를 먹지 않는 사람들의 비율은 맛을 언급하는 고기 섭취를 줄이는 데 관심 있는 사람들의 비율보다 4배 더 높다. ⑤ 체중 관리는 고기를 먹지 않는 사람들에게 10% 미만으로 가장 낮은 순위를 차지한다.

문제풀이

맛을 언급하는 고기를 먹지 않는 사람들의 비율은 10%이고, 맛을 언급하는 고기 섭취를 줄이는 데 관

심 있는 사람들의 비율은 30%이므로 이는 세 배가 더 높은 비율이다. 따라서 ④ 'The percentage of non-meat eaters citing taste is four times higher than that of people interested in reducing their meat consumption citing taste.'가 도표의 내용과 일치하지 않는다.

《어휘·어구》

survey 설문 조사
result 결과
interested in ~에 관심 있는
motivator 동기요인
welfare 복지
account for 차지하다
difference 차이
whereas ~임에 반하여
environment 환경
cite 말하다, 인용하다
taste 맛
reduce 줄이다
consumption 소비
management 관리
rank (순위를) 차지하다

정답률 87%

1. ③ 대륙별 도시 인구 점유율

직독/직해

The graph above shows / 위 그래프는 보여준다 /
the share of the urban population by continent / 대륙별 도시 인구 점유율을
in 1950 and in 2020. 1950년과 2020년의
For each continent, / 각 대륙에서 /
the share of the urban population / in 2020 / 도시 인구 점유율이 / 2020년의 /
was larger than that / in 1950. 그것보다 더 컸다 / 1950년의
From 1950 to 2020, / 1950년부터 2020년까지 /
the share of the urban population / 도시 인구 점유율은 /
in Africa / increased from 14.3% to 43.5%. 아프리카의 / 14.3%에서 43.5%로 증가했다
The share of the urban population / in Asia / 도시 인구 점유율은 / 아시아의 /
was the second lowest / in 1950 / 두 번째로 낮았다 / 1950년에는 /
but not in 2020. 하지만 2020년에는 그렇지 않았다
In 1950, / the share of the urban population / 1950년에는 / 도시 인구 점유율이 /
in Europe / was larger than that / 유럽의 / 그것보다 더 컸다 /
in Latin America and the Caribbean, / 라틴 아메리카와 카리브해 지역의 /
whereas the reverse was true / in 2020. 반면 역전이 일어났다 / 2020년에는
Among the five continents, / 다섯 개 대륙 중에서 /
Northern America was ranked / in the first position / 북아메리카는 차지했다 / 1위를 /
for the share of the urban population / 도시 인구 점유율에서 /
in both 1950 and 2020. 1950년과 2020년 모두

위 그래프는 1950년과 2020년의 대륙별 도시 인구 점유율을 보여준다. ① 각 대륙에서, 2020년의 도시 인구 점유율이 1950년의 그것보다 더 컸다. ② 1950년부터 2020년까지 아프리카의 도시 인구 점유율은 14.3%에서 43.5%로 증가했다. ③ 아시아의 도시 인구 점유율은 1950년에는 두 번째로 낮았지만, 2020년에는 그렇지 않았다. ④ 1950년에는 유럽의 도시 인구 점유율이 라틴 아메리카와 카리브해 지역의 그것보다 더 컸지만, 2020년에는 역전이 일어났다. ⑤ 다섯 개 대륙 중에서, 북아메리카는 도시 인구 점유율에서 1950년과 2020년 모두 1위를 차지했다.

문제풀이

아시아의 도시 인구 점유율은 1950년과 2020년 모두 두 번째로 낮았으므로, ③ 'The share of the urban population in Asia was the second lowest in 1950 but not in 2020.'가 도표의 내용과 일치하지 않는다.

《어휘·어구》

share 점유율
urban 도시의
population 인구
continent 대륙
increase 증가하다
whereas 반면
reverse 역전

정답률 90%

2. ⑤ 반려동물을 보유한 미국 가정의 비율

직독/직해

The graph above shows / 위 그래프는 보여준다 /
the percent of households with pets / 반려동물을 보유한 가정의 비율을 /
in the United States (U.S.) / from 1988 to 2020. 미국에서 / 1988년부터 2020년까지
In 1988, / more than half of U.S. households / owned pets, / 1988년에는 / 절반 이상의 미국 가정이 반려동물을 보유했다 /
and more than 6 out of 10 U.S. households / 그리고 10개 중 6개 이상의 미국 가정이 /
owned pets / from 2008 to 2020. 반려동물을 보유했다 / 2008년에서 2020년까지
In the period between 1988 and 2008, / 1988년과 2008년 사이 기간에 /
pet ownership increased / 반려동물 보유는 증가했다 /
among U.S. households / by 6 percentage points. 미국 가정들에서 / 6% 포인트
From 2008 to 2013, / pet ownership rose / 2008년에서 2013년까지 / 반려동물 보유는 올랐다 /
an additional 6 percentage points. 6% 포인트가 추가로
The percent of U.S. households with pets / in 2013 / 반려동물을 보유한 미국 가정의 비율은 / 2013년에 /
was the same as that in 2017, / 2017년의 비율과 같았다 /
which was 68 percent. 이는 68%였다
In 2015, / the rate of U.S. households with pets / 2015년에는 / 반려동물을 보유한 미국 가정의 비율이 /
was 3 percentage points lower / than in 2020. 3% 포인트 더 낮았다 / 2020년보다

위 그래프는 1988년부터 2020년까지 반려동물을 보유한 미국 가정의 비율을 보여준다. ① 1988년에는 절반 이상의 미국 가정이 반려동물을 보유했고, 2008년에서 2020년까지 10개 중 6개 이상의 미국 가정이 반려동물을 보유했다. ② 1988년과 2008년 사이 기간에, 반려동물 보유는 미국 가정들에서 6% 포인트 증가했다. ③ 2008년에서 2013년까지, 반려동물 보유는 6% 포인트가 추가로 올랐다. ④ 2013년의 반려동물을 보유한 미국 가정의 비율은 2017년의 비율과 같고, 68%였다. ⑤ 2015년에는, 반려동물을 보유한 미국 가정의 비율이 2020년보다 3% 포인트 더 낮았다.

문제풀이

반려동물을 보유한 미국 가정의 비율은 2015년에는 65%였고, 2020년에는 67%였으므로, 2015년의 수치가 2020년보다 2% 포인트 낮았다는 것을 알 수 있다. 따라서 ⑤ 'In 2015, the rate of U.S. households with pets was 3 percentage points lower than in 2020.'가 도표의 내용과 일치하지 않는다.

《어휘·어구》

household 가정
ownership 소유
additional 추가의
rate 비율

정답률 72%

3. ⑤ 온라인 강의와 온라인 학습 자료 이용 비율

직독/직해

The above graph shows / 위 도표는 보여 준다 /
the percentage of people in the UK / 영국 사람들의 비율을
who used online courses and online learning materials, / 온라인 강의와 온라인 학습 자료를 이용한 /
by age group / in 2020. 연령 집단별로 / 2020년에
In each age group, / the percentage of people / 각 연령 집단에서 / 사람들의 비율이 /
who used online learning materials / was higher / 온라인 학습 자료를 이용한 / 더 높았다 /
than that of people who used online courses. 온라인 강의를 이용한 사람들의 비율보다
The 25–34 age group / 25세~34세 연령 집단에서 /
had the highest percentage of people / 사람들의 비율이 가장 높았다 /
who used online courses / in all the age groups. 온라인 강의를 이용한 / 모든 연령 집단 중에서
Those aged 65 and older / 65세 이상인 사람들이 /
were the least likely to use online courses / 온라인 강의를 이용할 가능성이 가장 낮았다 /
among the six age groups. 여섯 개의 연령 집단 중
Among the six age groups, / 여섯 개의 연령 집단 중에서 /
the gap / between the percentage of people / who used online courses / 차이는 / 사람들의 비율과 / 온라인 강의를 이용한 /
and that of people / who used online learning materials / 사람들의 비율 / 온라인 학습 자료를 이용한 /
was the greatest in the 16–24 age group. 16세~24세 연령 집단에서 가장 컸다
In each of the 35–44, 45–54, and 55–64 age groups, / 35세~44세, 45세~54세, 55세~64세의 각 연령 집단 중에서 /
more than one in five people / 다섯 명 중 한 명 이상의 사람들이 /
used online learning materials. 온라인 학습 자료를 이용했다

위 도표는 2020년에 온라인 강의와 온라인 학습 자료를 이용한 영국 사람들의 비율을 연령 집단별로 보여 준다. ① 각 연령 집단에서, 온라인 학습 자료를 이용한 사람들의 비율이 온라인 강의를 이용한 사람들의 비율보다 더 높았다. ② 모든 연령 집단 중에서, 25세~34세 연령 집단에서 온라인 강의를 이용한 사람들의 비율이 가장 높았다. ③ 여섯 개의 연령 집단 중, 65세 이상인 사람들이 온라인 강의를 이용할 가능성이 가장 낮았다. ④ 여섯 개의 연령 집단 중에서, 온라인 강의를 이용한 사람들의 비율과 온라인 학습 자료를 이용한 사람들의 비율 차이는 16세~24세 연령 집단에서 가장 컸다. ⑤ 35세~44세, 45세~54세, 55세~64세의 각 연령 집단 중에서, 다섯 명 중 한 명 이상의 사람들이 온라인 학습 자료를 이용했다.

문제풀이

55세~64세 집단에서는 17%의 사람들이 온라인 학습 자료를 이용했다고 했으므로, 이는 다섯 명

중 한 명 이하의 사람들이 이용했다는 것을 알 수 있다. 따라서 ⑤ 'In each of the 35-44, 45-54, and 55-64 age groups, more than one in five people used online learning materials.'가 도표의 내용과 일치하지 않는다.

어휘•어구

course 강의
learning material 학습 자료
age group 연령 집단

정답률 78%

4. ④ 문화 활동에 참여하는 비율

직독/직해

The graph above shows the percentage /
위 도표는 비율을 보여 준다 /
of U.S. homeschooled and public school students /
미국의 홈스쿨링을 받는 학생과 공립 학교 학생의 /
participating in cultural activities in 2016.
2016년에 문화 활동에 참여하는
With the exception of live performances and sporting events, /
라이브 공연과 스포츠 행사를 제외하고 /
the percentage of homeschooled students /
홈스쿨링을 받는 학생의 비율이 /
participating in cultural activities /
문화 활동에 참여하는 /
was higher / than that of public school students.
더 높았다 / 공립 학교 학생의 그것보다
For each group of students, /
각 집단의 학생에 있어 /
community events accounted for the largest percentage /
지역 사회 행사는 가장 큰 비율을 차지했다 /
among all cultural activities.
모든 문화 활동 중에서
The percentage point difference /
퍼센트 포인트 차이는 /
between homeschooled students and their public school peers /
홈스쿨링을 받는 학생과 그들의 공립 학교 또래 간의 /
was largest / in visiting libraries.
가장 컸다 / 도서관 방문에서
The percentage of homeschooled students /
홈스쿨링을 받는 학생의 비율은 /
visiting museums or galleries /
박물관이나 미술관에 방문하는 /
was more than twice that of public school students.
공립 학교 학생의 그것의 두 배 이상이었다
Going to zoos or aquariums ranked the lowest /
동물원이나 수족관에 가는 것이 가장 낮은 순위를 차지했다 /
for both groups of students, /
두 집단의 학생에 있어 /
with 31 and 23 percent respectively.
각각 31퍼센트와 23퍼센트였다

위 도표는 2016년에 문화 활동에 참여하는 미국의 홈스쿨링을 받는 학생과 공립 학교 학생의 비율을 보여 준다. ① 라이브 공연과 스포츠 행사를 제외하고 문화 활동에 참여하는 홈스쿨링을 받는 학생의 비율이 공립 학교 학생의 그것보다 높았다. ② 각 집단의 학생에 있어 지역 사회 행사는 모든 문화 활동 중에서 가장 큰 비율을 차지했다. ③ 홈스쿨링을 받는 학생과 그들의 공립 학교 또래 간의 퍼센트포인트 차이는 도서관 방문에서 가장 컸다. ④ 박물관이나 미술관에 방문하는 홈스쿨링을 받는 학생의 비율은 공립학교 학생의 그것의 두 배 이상이었다. ⑤ 동물원이나 수족관에 가는 것이 두 집단의 학생에 있어 가장 낮은 순위를 차지했는데 각각 31퍼센트와 23퍼센트였다.

문제풀이

박물관이나 미술관에 방문하는 홈스쿨링을 받는 학생의 비율은 42%이고, 공립학교 학생의 비율은 25%로 두 배보다 작았으므로 ④ 'The percentage of homeschooled students visiting museums or galleries was more than twice that of public school students.(박물관이나 미술관에 방문하는 홈스쿨링을 받는 학생의 비율은 공립학교 학생의 그것의 두 배 이상이었다.)'는 도표의 내용과 일치하지 않는다.

어휘•어구

with the exception of ~은 제외하고
account for (부분, 비율을) 차지하다
gallery 미술관
aquarium 수족관
respectively 각각

정답률 80%

5. ④ 정보 출처들에 대한 소비자의 신뢰도

직독/직해

The graph above shows / 위 그래프는 보여준다 /
the consumers' levels of trust / 소비자들의 신뢰 정도를 /
in four different types of information sources, /
네 가지 다른 종류의 정보 출처들에 대한 /
based on a survey of US adults / in 2020.
미국 성인들을 대상으로 한 설문조사에 기초하여 / 2020년
About half of US adults say /
미국 성인의 대략 절반이 말한다 /
they trust the information / they receive from reviews /
그들이 정보를 신뢰한다고 / 그들이 상품평에서 얻은 /
from other users or customers.
다른 사용자들이나 고객들로부터의
This is more than double / 이것은 두 배 이상이다 /
those who say they hold distrust /
불신을 갖는다고 말한 사람들의 /
for reviews from other users or customers.
다른 사용자들이나 고객들로부터의 상품평에 대해
The smallest gap / 가장 적은 차이는 /
between the levels of trust and distrust /
신뢰와 불신 정도 사이의 /
among the four different types of information sources /
네 가지 다른 종류의 정보 출처 중에서 /
is shown in the companies or brands' graph.
회사나 상표에서 보인다
Fewer than one-fifth of adults say /
(미국) 성인의 1/5보다 적은 수치가 말한다 /
they trust information from television advertising, /
텔레비전 광고로부터의 정보를 신뢰한다고 /
outweighed by the share / 수치가 이를 능가했다 /
who distrust such information. 그런 정보를 불신하는 쪽의
Only 15% of adults say / they trust the information
(미국) 성인의 오직 15%만 말한다 / 그들이 정보를 신뢰한다고 /
provided by influencers, / 인플루언서에 의해 제공되는 /
while more than three times as many adults /
반면 이보다 세 배 이상 많은 수치의 미국 성인들이 /
say they distrust / the same source of information.
불신한다고 말한다 / 같은 정보 출처를

위 그래프는 2020년 미국 성인들을 대상으로 한 설문조사에 기초하여 네 가지 다른 종류의 정보 출처들에 대한 소비자들의 신뢰 정도를 보여준다. ① 미국 성인의 대략 절반이 다른 사용자들이나 고객들로부터의 상품평에서 얻은 정보를 신뢰한다고 말한다. ② 이것은 다른 사용자들이나 고객들로부터의 상품평에 대해 불신을 갖는다고 말한 미국 성인들의 두 배 이상이다. ③ 네 가지 다른 종류의 정보 출처 중에서 신뢰와 불신 정도 사이의 가장 적은 차이는 회사나 상표에서 보인다. ④ (미국) 성인의 1/5보다 적은 수치가 텔레비전 광고로부터의 정보를 신뢰한다고 말하는데, 그런 정보를 불신하는 쪽의 수치가 이를 능가했다. ⑤ (미국) 성인의 오직 15%만 인플루언서에 의해 제공되는 정보를 신뢰한다고 말하는데, 반면 이보다 세 배 이상 많은 수치의 미국 성인들이 같은 정보 출처를 불신한다고 말한다.

문제풀이

미국 성인의 23%가 텔레비전 광고로부터의 정보를 신뢰한다고 말하고, 이는 미국 성인의 1/5 이상이므로 ④ 'Fewer than one-fifth of adults say they trust information from television advertising, outweighed by the share who distrust such information.'가 도표의 내용과 일치하지 않는다.

어휘•어구

receive 받다
distrust 불신
outweigh ~보다 더 크다
influencer 영향력을 행사하는 사람, 인플루언서

정답률 84%

6. ⑤ 건강 관련 지출 GDP 점유율

직독/직해

The above graph shows /
위 그래프는 보여준다 /
health spending / as a share of GDP /
건강 관련 지출을 / GDP 점유율로 /
for selected OECD countries / in 2018.
선택된 OECD 국가들의 / 2018년
On average, / OECD countries were estimated /
평균적으로 / OECD 국가들은 추정되었다 /
to have spent 8.8 percent of their GDP / on health care.
GDP의 8.8%를 지출한 것으로 / 건강 관리에
Among the given countries above, /
위 국가 중에서 /
the US had the highest share, /
미국은 가장 높은 점유율을 보였다 /
with 16.9 percent, / 16.9%로 /
followed by Switzerland at 12.2 percent.
이어 스위스는 12.2%를 보였다
France spent more than 11 percent of its GDP, /
프랑스는 GDP의 11% 이상을 지출했다 /
while Turkey spent less than 5 percent of its GDP /
반면 터키는 GDP의 5% 이하를 지출했다 /
on health care. 건강 관리에
Belgium's health spending / as a share of GDP /
벨기에의 건강 관련 지출은 / GDP 점유율로서 /
sat between that of France and the UK.
프랑스와 영국의 그것 사이였다
There was a 3 percentage point difference /
3포인트 차이가 있었다 /
in the share of GDP / GDP의 점유율에는 /
spent on health care / between the UK and Greece.
건강 관리에 지출된 / 영국과 그리스 사이의

위 그래프는 선택된 OECD 국가들의 2018년 건강 관련 지출을 GDP 점유율로 보여준다. ① 평균적으로, OECD 국가들은 GDP의 8.8%를 건강 관리에 지출한 것으로 추정되었다. ② 위 국가 중에서 미국은 16.9%로 가장 높은 점유율을 보였고, 이어 스위스는 12.2%를 보였다. ③ 프랑스는 GDP의 11% 이상을 지출했던 반면, 터키는 GDP의 5% 이하를 건강 관리에 지출했다. ④ GDP 점유율로서 벨기에의 건강 관련 지출은 프랑스와 영국의 사이였다. ⑤ 영국과 그리스 사이의 건강 관리에 지출된 GDP의 점유율에는 3포인트 차이가 있었다.

문제풀이

영국이 건강 관리에 지출한 GDP 점유율은 9.8%이고, 그리스가 건강 관리에 지출된 GDP의 점유율은 7.8%이므로 두 국가 간에 2포인트 차이가 있다. 따라서 ⑤ 'There was a 3 percentage point difference in the share of GDP spent on health care between the UK and Greece.'가 도표의 내용과 일치하지 않는다.

어휘·어구

share 점유율
on average 평균적으로
estimate 추정하다

7. ③ 교육용 디지털 콘텐츠 사용을 위한 기기 비율

직독/직해

The above graph shows the percentage of students /
위 그래프는 학생들의 비율을 보여 준다 /
from kindergarten to 12th grade /
유치원에서 12학년까지의 /
who used devices / 기기를 사용한 /
to access digital educational content /
교육용 디지털 콘텐츠에 접근하기 위해 /
in 2016 and in 2019. 2016년과 2019년에
Laptops were the most used device /
노트북은 가장 많이 사용한 기기였다 /
for students to access digital content /
디지털 콘텐츠에 접근하기 위해 학생들이 /
in both years. 두 해 모두
Both in 2016 and in 2019, /
2016년과 2019년 모두 /
more than 6 out of 10 students /
10명 중 6명 이상의 학생들이 /
used tablets. 태블릿을 사용했다
More than half the students / used desktops /
절반이 넘는 학생들이 / 데스크톱을 사용했다 /
to access digital content / in 2016, /
디지털 콘텐츠에 접근하기 위해 / 2016년에는 /
and more than a third / used desktops /
그리고 1/3 이상의 학생들이 / 데스크톱을 사용했다 /
in 2019. 2019년에는
The percentage of smartphones in 2016 /
2016년 스마트폰의 비율은 /
was the same as that in 2019.
2019년 스마트폰의 비율과 같았다
E-readers ranked the lowest / in both years, /
전자책 단말기는 가장 낮은 순위를 차지했다 / 두 해 모두 /
with 11 percent in 2016 / and 5 percent in 2019.
2016년에는 11%였다 / 그리고 2019년에는 5%였다

위 그래프는 2016년과 2019년에 교육용 디지털 콘텐츠에 접근하기 위해 기기를 사용한 유치원에서 12학년까지의 학생들의 비율을 보여 준다. ① 노트북은 두 해 모두 디지털 콘텐츠에 접근하기 위해 학생들이 가장 많이 사용한 기기였다. ② 2016년과 2019년 모두 10명 중 6명 이상의 학생들이 태블릿을 사용했다. ③ 2016년에는 절반이 넘는 학생들이 디지털 콘텐츠에 접근하기 위해 데스크톱을 사용했고, 2019년에는 1/3 이상의 학생들이 데스크톱을 사용했다. ④ 2016년 스마트폰의 비율은 2019년 스마트폰의 비율과 같았다. ⑤ 전자책 단말기는 두 해 모두 가장 낮은 순위를 차지했는데, 2016년에는 11%였고 2019년에는 5%였다.

문제풀이

2016년에 디지털 콘텐츠에 접근하기 위해 데스크톱을 사용했던 학생들의 비율은 49%로 절반이 넘지 않는다. 따라서 ③ 'More than half the students used desktops to access digital content in 2016, and more than a third used desktops in 2019.'이 도표의 내용과 일치하지 않는다.

어휘·어구

kindergarten 유치원
device 기기, 장치
access 접근하다
educational 교육의
laptop 노트북 (컴퓨터)
e-reader 전자책 단말기
rank 순위를 차지하다

8. ⑤ 아이들의 스포츠 참여 평균 연령과 참여 기간

직독/직해

The above table shows / 위 표는 보여 준다 /
the average age of last regular participation of children /
마지막으로 정기적으로 참여한 아이들의 평균 연령을 /
in a sport / 스포츠에 /
and the average length of participation /
그리고 평균 참여 기간을 /
based on a 2019 survey.
2019년 조사를 기초로 하여
Among the eight sports above, /
위에 있는 여덟 개의 스포츠 중에서 /
soccer was the only sport / 축구는 유일한 스포츠였다 /
that children quit / 아이들이 중단한 /
at an average age of younger than 10.
평균 10세보다 어린 나이에
Children quit playing ice hockey and tennis /
아이들은 아이스하키와 테니스를 중단했다 /
at the same age on average, /
평균적으로 같은 연령에 /
but the average length of participation in tennis /
하지만 테니스에 참여한 평균 기간은 /
was shorter than that in ice hockey.
아이스하키에 참여한 평균 기간보다 짧았다
Basketball, field hockey, and golf /
농구, 필드하키 그리고 골프는 /
were sports which children quit playing /
아이들이 중단한 스포츠였다 /
on average before they turned 12, /
평균적으로 12세가 되기 전에 /
but golf had the shortest average participation length /
하지만 골프는 평균 참여 기간이 가장 짧았다 /
among the three sports. 이 세 스포츠 중에서
Skateboarding was a sport children quit /
스케이트보드는 아이들이 중단한 스포츠였다 /
at the average age of 12, / 평균 12세에 /
and the average length of participation /
그리고 그 평균 참여 기간은 /
was the same as golf. 골프와 같았다
Meanwhile, / 반면에 /
children quit participating in track and field /
아이들은 육상 경기 참여를 중단했다 /
at the average age of 13, / 평균 13세에 /
but the average length of participation /
하지만 평균 참여 기간은 /
was the shortest among the eight sports.
여덟 개의 스포츠 중에서 가장 짧았다

위 표는 2019년 조사를 기초로 하여 아이들이 마지막으로 스포츠에 정기적으로 참여한 평균 연령과 평균 참여 기간을 보여 준다. ① 위에 있는 여덟 개의 스포츠 중에서 축구는 아이들이 평균 10세보다 어린 나이에 중단한 유일한 스포츠였다. ② 아이들은 아이스하키와 테니스를 평균적으로 같은 연령에 중단했지만, 테니스에 참여한 평균 기간은 아이스하키에 참여한 평균 기간보다 짧았다. ③ 농구, 필드하키 그리고 골프는 아이들이 평균적으로 12세가 되기 전에 중단한 스포츠였지만, 골프는 이 세 스포츠 중에서 평균 참여 기간이 가장 짧았다. ④ 스케이트보드는 아이들이 평균 12세에 중단한 스포츠였고, 그 평균 참여 기간은 골프와 같았다. ⑤ 반면에, 아이들은 육상 경기 참여를 평균 13세에 중단했지만, 평균 참여 기간은 여덟 개의 스포츠 중에서 가장 짧았다.

문제풀이

평균 참여 기간은 여덟 개의 스포츠 중에서 가장 짧았던 스포츠는 테니스였으므로, ⑤ 'Meanwhile, children quit participating in track and field at the average age of 13, but the average length of participation was the shortest among the eight sports.'가 표의 내용과 일치하지 않는다.

어휘·어구

average 평균(의)
regular 규칙적인, 정기적인
participation 참여
length 길이
survey 조사
track and field 육상 경기

정답률 90%

9. ④ 실내 냉방을 위한 에너지 사용

직독/직해

The graph above shows the final energy consumption /
위 그래프는 최종 에너지 소비를 보여 준다 /
for indoor cooling by country / region in 2016.
2016년 실내 냉방을 위한 국가 / 지역별
The global final energy consumption for indoor cooling /
실내 냉방을 위한 전 세계의 최종 에너지 소비는 /
was over three times larger / in 2016 than in 1990.
3배 넘게 많았다 / 1990년보다 2016년에
It was the United States that had the largest final energy consumption, /
최종 에너지를 가장 많이 소비한 곳은 미국이었다 /
which amounted to 616 TWh.
그 양은 616 TWh에 달했다
The combined amount of the final energy consumption /
최종 에너지 소비의 양의 총합은 /
of the European Union, the Middle East, and Japan /
유럽 연합, 중동, 일본의 /
was less than the amount of China's final energy consumption.
중국의 최종 에너지 소비의 양보다 적었다
The difference in amount between India's and South Korea's final energy consumption /
인도와 한국의 최종 에너지 소비의 양의 차이는
was more than 60 TWh.
60 TWh보다 많았다
Indonesia' final energy consumption was the smallest /
인도네시아의 최종 에너지 소비는 가장 적었다 /
among the countries / regions above, /
위의 국가들 / 지역들 중에서 /
totaling 25 TWh.
총 25 TWh이었다

위 그래프는 2016년 실내 냉방을 위한 국가/지역별 최종 에너지 소비를 보여 준다. ① 2016년 실내 냉방을 위한 전 세계의 최종 에너지소비는 1990년의 최종 에너지 소비의 3배 넘게 많았다. ② 최종 에너지를 가장 많이 소비한 곳은 미국이었고, 그 양은 616 TWh에 달했다. ③ 유럽 연합, 중동, 일본의 최종 에너지 소비의 양의 총합은 중국의 최종 에너지 소비의 양보다 적었다. ④ 인도와 한국의 최종 에너지 소비의 양의 차이는 60 TWh보다 많았다. ⑤ 인도네시아의 최종 에너지 소비는 위의 국가들/지역들 중에서 가장 적었고, 총 25 TWh이었다.

문제풀이

한국의 최종 에너지 소비는 91 TWh이고 인도의 최종 에너지 소비는 41 TWh로 그 차이는 50 TWh이므로 도표와 일치하지 않는 것은 ④이다.

어휘·어구

consumption (전기 등의) 소비량
amount to (총계가) ~에 달하다
combined 합한, 결합된

10. ⑤ 인터넷 접속 장치들의 중요도 조사

직독/직해

The above graph shows / what devices British
위 도표는 보여준다 / 영국인들이 어떤 장치를
people considered the most important/
가장 중요하다고 간주했는지를 /
when connecting to the Internet in 2014 and 2016.
2014년과 2016년에 인터넷 접속을 할 때
More than a third of UK Internet users considered /
3분의 1이 넘는 영국 인터넷 사용자들은 생각했다 /
smartphones to be their most important device /
스마트폰이 가장 중요한 장치라고 /
for accessing the Internet / in 2016.
인터넷 접속을 위한 / 2016년에
In the same year, / 같은 해에 /
the smartphone overtook the laptop /
스마트폰이 랩탑을 추월하였다 /
as the most important device for Internet access.
인터넷 접속을 위해 가장 중요한 장치로서
In 2014, / 2014년에 /
UK Internet users were the least likely to select a tablet /
영국 인터넷 사용자들은 태블릿을 가장 적게 선택하는 경향이 있었다 /
as their most important device for Internet access.
인터넷 접속을 위한 가장 중요한 장치로
In contrast, / 대조적으로 /
they were the least likely to consider a desktop /
그들은 데스크탑을 가장 적게 선택하는 경향이 있었다 /
as their most important device /
그들의 가장 중용한 장치로서 /
for Internet access / in 2016.
인터넷 접속을 위한 / 2016년에
The proportion of UK Internet users /
영국 인터넷 사용자들의 비율은 /
who selected a desktop / 데스크탑을 선택한 /
as their most important device / 가장 중요한 장치로 /
for Internet access / increased by half /
인터넷 접속을 위한 / 절반만큼 증가하였다 /
from 2014 to 2016. 2014년으로부터 2016년까지

위 도표는 2014년과 2016년에 영국인들이 인터넷 접속을 할 때 어떤 장치들이 가장 중요하다고 생각했는지를 보여 준다. ① 2016년도에 3분의 1이 넘는 영국 인터넷 사용자들은 스마트폰을 가장 중요한 인터넷 접속 장치로 생각했다. ② 같은 해에, 스마트폰이 인터넷 접속을 위해 가장 중요한 장치로서 랩탑을 추월하였다. ③ 2014년에, 영국 인터넷 사용자들은 인터넷 접속을 위한 가장 중요한 장치로 태블릿을 가장 적게 선택하는 경향이 있었다. ④ 대조적으로, 2016년에는 인터넷 접속을 위한 가장 중요한 장치로 데스크탑을 가장 적게 선택하는 경향이 있었다. ⑤ 인터넷 접속을 위한 가장 중요한 장치로 데스크탑을 선택한 영국 인터넷 사용자들의 비율은 2016년도에 2014년도 비율의 절반만큼 증가하였다.

문제풀이

2014년도에 데스크탑을 인터넷 접속을 위한 가장 중요한 장치로 고려한 영국 인터넷 사용자의 비율은 20%이고 2016년도에는 12%로, 절반만큼 증가한 것이 아니라 반대로 감소하였으므로, 도표와 일치하지 않는 것은 ⑤이다.

어휘·어구

device 장치
consider 간주하다, 생각하다
access 접속, 접속하다
overtake 추월하다
be likely to do ~할 것 같다

본문 047쪽

문법 플러스 8. 가정법

1. took 2. would be 3. had taken
4. had been invented 5. Without
6. did not exist 7. Were it 8. took
9. saw 10. had turned

1 [해석]▶ 당신이 기차를 타면, 시간을 절약할 수 있을 텐데.
[해설]▶ 현재 사실과 반대되는 가정법 과거문장이다. 가정법 과거는 「If+주어+과거동사 ~ 주어+조동사 과거형+동사원형~」의 형태를 가진다. 그러므로 과거동사를 써야 한다.

2 [해석]▶만약 여러분이 큰 건물에서 사교 모임에 있고, 누군가 '지붕이 불타고 있어요'라고 말하는 것을 우연히 듣는다면, 여러분의 반응은 어떨까?
[해설]▶ if 조건절에 과거동사 were와 overheard가 나오고, what ~이하는 주절이다. 가정법 과거는 「If+주어+과거동사 ~, 주어+조동사 과거형+동사원형」의 형태를 취한다.

3 [해석]▶ 만약 그가 미리 조치를 취했더라면, 그런 불행을 피할 수 있었을 텐데.
[해설]▶ 가정법 과거완료는 과거 사실과 반대되는 것을 말할 때 사용한다. 가정법 과거완료는 「If+주어+had+과거분사 ~ 주어+조동사 과거형+have+과거분사~」의 형태를 취한다.

4 [해석]▶ 시계 바늘은 태양의 자연적인 움직임을 모방하기 위해 만들어졌다. 만약 시계가 남반구에서 발명되었더라면, '시계 방향'은 반대 방향이었을 것이라고 Fried는 생각한다.
[해설]▶ 과거 시점의 사실이나 행동이 현재 시점까지 영향을 미치는 경우 혼합가정법을 사용한다. 혼합가정법은 「If+주어+had+p.p.~ 주어+would+동사원형~」의 형태를 취한다. 과거 시점에 시계가 남반구에서 발명되었다면 현재 시점에 시계 방향이 반대로 움직일 거라는 의미이다.

5 [해석]▶ 사회적 유대의 형성과 유지가 없다면, 초기 인간들은 아마 그들의 물리적 환경에 대처하거나 적응할 수 없을지도 모른다.
[해설]▶ 조건절의 if를 대신하여 Without 이하의 전치사구가 쓰인 가정법 과거완료 구문이다.

6 [해석]▶ 너무 많은 회사가 마치 경쟁자들이 존재하지 않는 것처럼 자신들의 신제품을 광고한다.
[해설]▶ 「as if +가정법 과거」는 현재 사실과 반대되는 내용을 나타내며, 「as if +가정법 과거완료」는 과거 사실의 반대 내용을 나타낸다. 주절의 동사가 현재시제(advertise)이므로, 시제를 맞춰 「as if +가정법 과거」를 사용한다.

7 [해석]▶ 음악이 없다면, 우리 인생은 사막처럼 건조할 텐데.
[해설]▶ If it were not for ~ 라는 가정법 문장에서 If가 생략되면 「동사+주어」의 어순처럼 도치된다.

8 [해석]▶ 증가하고 있는 외국인의 수는 나라의 경제를 손상시키고 있다. 정부가 어떤 조치를 취해야 할 때이다.
[해설]▶ It is time that 다음에는 가정법 과거 시제가 와야 한다.

9 [해석]▶ 그녀는 지난주에 유명한 영화를 봤다고 말했다.
[해설]▶ 주장을 나타내는 동사(insist)에 이어지는 that절이 단순한 사실을 전달할 때는 「should+동사원형」을 쓰지 않고, 문장의 수와 시제에 맞추어 써야 한다.

10 해석▶ 만약 그날 화성을 향해 빛을 비추었다면, 186초 만에 화성에 도달했을 것이다.
[해설]▶ 가정법 과거완료는 과거사실의 반대를 나타낸다. 문장이 과거 사실의 반대를 가정하고 있으며 주절의 동사가 가정법 과거완료(would have reached)를 쓰고 있으므로, 조건절은 「If+주어+had+p.p.」를 써야 한다.

본문 048쪽

어휘 플러스 8. 파생어 (2)

1. memorial 2. objections
3. observations 4. produce
5. sensitive

1 [해석]▶ 예를 들어, 겨우 사람 손 크기의 이집트의 조각이 Leipzig의 전쟁 기념비를 구성하는 그 거대한 돌무더기보다 더 기념비적이다.

2 [해석]▶ 어떤 교수가 도덕적인 반대 때문에 사전에서 단어를 빼버린 편집자의 부정직에 대해 한 시간 동안 강의를 했다.

3 [해석]▶ 문제를 해결하기 위해서는 여러분이 어떻게 느끼는가 하는 것을 뛰어넘어야 하고 새로운 관찰로 이미 인지하고 있는 정보를 연결 시켜야 한다.

4 [해석]▶ Elffers는 그가 만든 먹을 수 있는 농산물 조각품들로 그 즐거움을 나누기를 바란다.

5 [해석]▶ 컴퓨터는 동일한 지역적인 혹은 환경적인 요소들을 관리하는 데 있어서 인간보다 민감하지도 못하며 정확하지도 않다.

09. 내용 일치 · 불일치

Day 09 본문 050쪽

1. ④ 2. ③ 3. ③ 4. ④ 5. ⑤
6. ③ 7. ⑤ 8. ④ 9. ③ 10. ⑤

정답률 90%

대표 기출 ③ Margaret Knight

직독/직해

Margaret Knight was an exceptionally prolific inventor /
Margaret Knight는 특출나게 다작한 발명가였다 /
in the late 19th century; /
19세기 후반에 /
journalists occasionally compared her to Thomas Edison /
기자들은 가끔 그녀를 Thomas Edison과 비교했다 /
by nicknaming her "a woman Edison."
그녀에게 '여자 Edison'이라는 별명을 지어 줌으로써
From a young age, / she built toys for her older brothers.
어린 나이부터 / 그녀는 오빠들을 위해 장난감을 만들었다
After her father died, / Knight's family moved to Manchester.
그녀의 아버지가 돌아가신 후 / Knight의 가족은 Manchester로 이사했다
Knight left school in 1850, at age 12, /
Knight는 1850년 12세의 나이에 학교를 그만두었다 /
to earn money for her family / at a nearby textile factory, /
가족을 위해 돈을 벌기 위해 / 가까이에 있는 직물 공장에서 /
where she witnessed / a fellow worker injured by faulty equipment.
그곳에서 그녀는 목격했다 / 동료 노동자가 결함 있는 장비에 의해 부상당하는 것을
That led her to create / her first invention, /
그것은 그녀가 만들도록 이끌었다 / 자신의 첫 번째 발명품을 /
a safety device for textile equipment, /
즉 직물 장비에 쓰이는 안전장치를 /
but she never earned money /
그러나 그녀는 결코 돈을 벌지는 못했다 /
from the invention. 그 발명품으로
She also invented a machine /
그녀는 또한 기계를 발명했다 /
that cut, folded and glued / 자르고, 접고, 붙이는 /
flat-bottomed paper bags / 밑이 평평한 종이 가방을 /
and was awarded her first patent in 1871 for it.
그리고 1871년에 그것으로 자신의 첫 특허를 받았다
It eliminated the need / for workers to assemble them /
그것은 필요를 없앴다 / 작업자들이 그것들을 조립할 /
slowly by hand. 천천히 손으로
Knight received 27 patents in her lifetime /
Knight는 자신의 일생 동안 27개의 특허를 받았다 /
and entered the National Inventors Hall of Fame in 2006.
그리고 2006년에 국립 발명가 명예의 전당에 입성했다 /

Margaret Knight는 19세기 후반에 특출나게 다작한 발명가였고, ① 기자들은 가끔 그녀에게 '여자 Edison'이라는 별명을 지어 주어 Thomas Edison과 비교했다. 어린 나이부터, 그녀는 오빠들을 위해 장난감을 만들었다. 그녀의 아버지가 돌아가신 후, Knight의 가족은 Manchester로 이사했다. ② Knight는 가족을 위해 가까이에 있는 직물 공장에서 돈을 벌기 위해 1850년, 12세의 나이에 학교를 그만두었는데, 그곳에서 그녀는 동료 노동자가 결함 있는 장비에 의해 부상당하는 것을 목격했다. ③ 그것은 그녀가 자신의 첫 번째 발명품, 즉 직물 장비에 쓰이는 안전장치를 만들도록 이끌었지만, 그녀는 결코 그 발명품으로 돈을 벌지는 못했다. ④ 그녀는 또한 밑이 평평한 종이 가방을 자르고, 접고, 붙이는 기계를 발명했고, 1871년에 그것으로 자신의 첫 특허를 받았다. 그것은 작업자들이 손으로 그것들을 천천히 조립할 필요를 없앴다. Knight는 자신의 일생 동안 27개의 특허를 받았고, ⑤ 2006년에 국립 발명가 명예의 전당에 입성했다.

문제풀이

'That led her to create her first invention, a safety device for textile equipment, but she never earned money from the invention.'에서 직물 장비에 쓰이는 안전장치를 만들도록 이끌었지만 결코 그 발명품으로 돈을 벌지는 못했다고 했으므로, ③은 글의 내용과 일치하지 않는다.

어휘·어구

exceptionally 유난히, 특별히
inventor 발명가
century 세기
journalist 기자
occasionally 가끔
compare 비교하다
nickname 별명을 붙이다
textile 직물
factory 공장
witness 목격하다
fellow 동료
injure 상처를 입히다
faulty 결함 있는
equipment 장비
safety 안전
device 장치
machine 기계
fold 접다
award 수여하다
eliminate 없애다, 제거하다
assemble 조립하다
receive 받다
lifetime 일생
Hall of Fame 명예의 전당

1. ④ Wilbur Smith

직독/직해

Wilbur Smith was a South African novelist /
Wilbur Smith는 남아프리카 소설가였다 /
specialising in historical fiction.
역사 소설을 전문으로 하는
Smith wanted to become a journalist, /
Smith는 언론인이 되고 싶었다 /
writing about social conditions in South Africa, /
남아프리카의 사회 환경에 관해 글을 쓰는 /
but his father was never supportive of his writing /
하지만 그의 아버지는 그가 글을 쓰는 것을 절대로 지지하지 않았다 /
and forced him to get a real job.
그리고 그가 실질적인 직업을 갖도록 강요했다
Smith studied further /
Smith는 더 공부했다 /
and became a tax accountant, /
그리고 세금 회계사가 되었다 /
but he finally turned back / to his love of writing.
하지만 그는 결국에는 돌아왔다 / 그가 사랑하는 글 쓰는 일로
He wrote his first novel, / *The Gods First Make Mad*, /
그는 첫 번째 소설을 썼다 / 'The Gods First Make Mad' /
and had received 20 rejections / by 1962.
그리고 20번의 거절을 당했다 / 1962년까지
In 1964, / Smith published another novel, /
1964년에 / Smith는 또 다른 소설을 출간했다 /
When the Lion Feeds, /
'When the Lion Feeds' /
and it went on to be successful, /
그리고 그것이 성공을 거두었다 /
selling around the world.
전 세계에 팔리면서
A famous actor and film producer /
한 유명한 배우이자 영화 제작자가 /
bought the film rights /
영화 판권을 샀다 /
for *When the Lion Feeds*, /
'When the Lion Feeds'에 대한 /
although no movie resulted.
비록 영화화되지는 않았지만
By the time of his death in 2021 /
2021년 죽기 전까지 /
he had published 49 novels, /
그는 49편의 소설을 출간했다 /
selling more than 140 million copies worldwide.
전 세계적으로 1억 4천만 부 이상을 판매했다

Wilbur Smith는 ① 역사 소설을 전문으로 하는 남아프리카 소설가였다. Smith는 남아프리카의 사회 환경에 관해 글을 쓰는 언론인이 되고 싶었지만, ② 그의 아버지는 그가 글을 쓰는 것을 절대로 지지하지 않았고 그가 실질적인 직업을 갖도록 강요했다. Smith는 더 공부하여 세금 회계사가 되었지만, 결국에는 그가 사랑하는 글 쓰는 일로 돌아왔다. ③ 그는 첫 번째 소설, 'The Gods First Make Mad'를 썼고 1962년까지 20번의 거절을 당했다. 1964년에 Smith는 또 다른 소설, 'When the Lion Feeds'를 출간했고, 그것이 전 세계에 팔리면서 성공을 거두었다. ④ 비록 영화화되지는 않았지만, 한 유명한 배우이자 영화 제작자가 'When the Lion Feeds'에 대한 영화 판권을 샀다. ⑤ 2021년 죽기 전까지 그는 49편의 소설을 출간했으며, 전 세계적으로 1억 4천만 부 이상을 판매했다.

문제풀이

'A famous actor and film producer bought the film rights for When the Lion Feeds, although no movie resulted.'에서 'When the Lion Feeds'가 영화화되지 않았다고 했으므로, ④는 글의 내용과 일치하지 않는다.

어휘·어구

novelist 소설가
specialise in ~을 전문으로 하다(= specialize in)
historical 역사적인
fiction 소설
journalist 언론인
condition 환경, 상황, 조건
accountant 회계사
receive 받다
rejection 거절
publish 출간하다
successful 성공적인
film right 영화 판권

2. ③ Claude Bolling

직독/직해

Pianist, composer, and big band leader, Claude Bolling, /
피아니스트, 작곡가, 그리고 빅 밴드 리더인 Claude Bolling은 /
was born on April 10, 1930, / in Cannes, France, /
1930년 4월 10일 태어났다 / 프랑스 칸에서 /
but spent most of his life / in Paris.
하지만 그의 삶의 대부분을 보냈다 / 파리에서
He began studying classical music / as a youth.

그는 클래식 음악을 공부하기 시작했다 / 젊었을 때

He was introduced to the world of jazz /
그는 재즈 세계를 소개받았다 /

by a schoolmate. 학교 친구를 통해

Later, / Bolling became interested in the music of Fats Waller, /
이후에 / Bolling은 Fats Waller의 음악에 관심을 갖게 되었다 /

one of the most excellent jazz musicians.
최고의 재즈 음악가들 중 한 명인

Bolling became famous / as a teenager /
그는 유명해졌다 / 10대 때 /

by winning the Best Piano Player prize /
Best Piano Player 상을 수상하면서 /

at an amateur contest in France.
프랑스의 아마추어 대회에서

He was also a successful film music composer, /
그는 또한 성공적인 영화 음악 작곡가였다 /

writing the music for more than one hundred films.
그리고 100편 이상의 영화 음악을 작곡했다

In 1975, / he collaborated with flutist Rampal /
1975년에 / 그는 플루트 연주자 Rampal과 협업했다 /

and published *Suite for Flute and Jazz Piano Trio*, /
그리고 'Suite for Flute and Jazz Piano Trio'를 발매했다 /

which he became most well-known for.
그것으로 그는 가장 잘 알려지게 되었다

He died in 2020, / leaving two sons, David and Alexandre.
그는 2020년에 사망했다 / 두 아들 David와 Alexandre를 남기고

피아니스트, 작곡가, 그리고 빅 밴드 리더인 Claude Bolling은 ① 1930년 4월 10일 프랑스 칸에서 태어났지만, 그의 삶의 대부분을 파리에서 보냈다. 그는 젊었을 때 클래식 음악을 공부하기 시작했다. ② 그는 학교 친구를 통해 재즈(재즈 세계)를 소개받았다. 이후에 Bolling은 최고의 재즈 음악가들 중 한 명인 Fats Waller의 음악에 관심을 갖게 되었다. ③ 그는 10대 때 프랑스의 아마추어 대회에서 Best Piano Player 상을 수상하면서 유명해졌다. ④ 그는 또한 성공적인 영화 음악 작곡가였고, 100편 이상의 영화 음악을 작곡했다. 1975년에, ⑤ 그는 플루트 연주자 Rampal과 협업했고, 'Suite for Flute and Jazz Piano Trio'를 발매했으며, 그것으로 그는 가장 잘 알려지게 되었다. 그는 두 아들 David와 Alexandre를 남기고 2020년에 사망했다.

문제풀이

'Bolling became famous as a teenager by winning the Best Piano Player prize at an amateur contest in France.'에서 Bolling은 10대 때 프랑스의 아마추어 대회에서 상을 수상했다고 했으므로, ③은 글의 내용과 일치하지 않는다.

어휘·어구

composer 작곡가
classical music 클래식 음악
introduce 소개하다
collaborate 협업하다
publish 발매하다

3. ③ Antonie van Leeuwenhoek

직독/직해

Antonie van Leeuwenhoek was a scientist /
Antonie van Leeuwenhoek은 과학자였다 /

well known for his cell research.
세포 연구로 잘 알려진

He was born in Delft, the Netherlands, /
그는 네덜란드 Delft에서 태어났다 /

on October 24, 1632. 1632년 10월 24일

At the age of 16, / he began to learn job skills /
16살에 / 그는 직업 기술을 배우기 시작했다 /

in Amsterdam. Amsterdam에서

At the age of 22, / Leeuwenhoek returned to Delft.
22살에 / Leeuwenhoek은 Delft로 돌아왔다

It wasn't easy / 쉽지 않았다 /

for Leeuwenhoek to become a scientist.
Leeuwenhoek이 과학자가 되기는

He knew only one language — Dutch — /
그는 오직 한 가지 언어, 즉 네덜란드어만을 알고 있었다 /

which was quite unusual / for scientists of his time.
그것은 상당히 드문 것이었다 / 그 당시 과학자들에게는

But his curiosity was endless, / and he worked hard.
하지만 그의 호기심은 끝이 없었다 / 그리고 그는 열심히 노력했다

He had an important skill.
그는 중요한 기술을 가지고 있었다

He knew / how to make things out of glass.
그는 알았다 / 유리로 물건을 만드는 법을

This skill came in handy / when he made lenses /
이 기술은 도움이 되었다 / 그가 렌즈를 만들 때 /

for his simple microscope.
자신의 간단한 현미경에 쓰일

He saw tiny veins / with blood flowing through them.
그는 미세한 혈관을 보았다 / (혈관을 통해) 피가 흐르고 있는

He also saw living bacteria / in pond water.
그는 또한 살아 있는 박테리아를 보았다 / 연못 물속에서

He paid close attention to / the things he saw /
그는 세심한 주의를 기울였다 / 자신이 본 것들에 /

and wrote down his observations.
그리고 관찰한 것을 기록했다

Since he couldn't draw well, / he hired an artist /
그는 그림을 잘 그릴 수 없었기 때문에 / 그는 화가를 고용했다 /

to draw pictures of / what he described.
그림으로 그리도록 / 자신이 설명하는 것을

Antonie van Leeuwenhoek은 ① 세포 연구로 잘 알려진 과학자였다. 그는 1632년 10월 24일 네덜란드 Delft에서 태어났다. 16살에 그는 Amsterdam에서 직업 기술을 배우기 시작했다. ② 22살에 Leeuwenhoek은 Delft로 돌아왔다. Leeuwenhoek이 과학자가 되기는 쉽지 않았다. ③ 그는 오직 한 가지 언어, 즉 네덜란드어만을 알고 있었는데, 그것은 그 당시 과학자들에게는 상당히 드문 것이었다. 하지만 그의 호기심은 끝이 없었고, 그는 열심히 노력했다. 그는 중요한 기술을 가지고 있었다. ④ 그는 유리로 물건을 만드는 법을 알았다. 이 기술은 그가 자신의 간단한 현미경에 쓰일 렌즈를 만들 때 도움이 되었다. 그는 피가 흐르고 있는 미세한 혈관을 보았다. 그는 또한 연못 물속에서 살아 있는 박테리아를 보았다. 그는 자신이 본 것들에 세심한 주의를 기울였고 관찰한 것을 기록했다. 그는 그림을 잘 그릴 수 없었기 때문에, ⑤ 화가를 고용하여 자신이 설명하는 것을 그림으로 그리게 했다.

문제풀이

'He knew only one language'에서 Leeuwenhoek은 한 가지 언어만 알고 있었다고 했으므로, ③은 글의 내용과 일치하지 않는다.

어휘·어구

known for ~으로 알려진
research 연구
language 언어
Dutch 네덜란드어
unusual 드문
curiosity 호기심
endless 끝없는
come in handy 도움이 되다
microscope 현미경
blood 피
flow 흐르다
bacteria 박테리아
pond 연못
pay attention to ~에 주의를 기울이다
observation 관찰
hire 고용하다
describe 설명하다

4. ④ Bessie Coleman

직독/직해

Bessie Coleman was born in Texas in 1892.
Bessie Coleman은 1892년에 텍사스에서 태어났다

When she was eleven, / she was told /
그녀가 11살이었을 때 / 그녀는 들었다

that the Wright brothers had flown their first plane.
Wright 형제가 그들의 첫 비행을 했다는 것을

Since that moment, / she dreamed about the day /
그때부터 / 그녀는 그 날을 꿈꿨다 /

she would soar through the sky.
자신이 하늘을 높이 날아오르는

At the age of 23, / Coleman moved to Chicago, /
23살 때 / Coleman은 시카고로 이사했다 /

where she worked at a restaurant /
그곳에서 그녀는 식당에서 일했다 /

to save money for flying lessons.
비행 수업을 위한 돈을 모으기 위해

However, / she had to travel to Paris /
그러나 / 그녀는 파리로 가야 했다 /

to take flying lessons /
비행 수업을 듣기 위해 /

because American flight schools at the time admitted neither women nor Black people.
그 당시 미국 비행 학교가 여성이나 흑인의 입학을 허가하지 않았기 때문에

In 1921, / she finally became the first Black woman /
1921년에 / 그녀는 마침내 최초의 흑인 여성이 되었다 /

to earn an international pilot's license.
국제 조종사 면허를 딴

She also studied flying acrobatics in Europe /
그녀는 또한 유럽에서 곡예 비행을 공부했다 /

and made her first appearance /
그리고 그녀의 첫 출현을 했다 /

in an airshow in New York in 1922.
1922년에 뉴욕의 에어쇼에

As a female pioneer of flight, /
여성 비행 개척자로서 /

she inspired the next generation /
그녀는 다음 세대에게 영감을 주었다 /

to pursue their dreams of flying.
그들의 비행의 꿈을 추구하도록

Bessie Coleman은 1892년에 텍사스에서 태어났다. 그녀가 11살이었을 때 그녀는 Wright 형제가 그들의 첫 비행을 했다는 것을 들었다. 그때부터 그녀는 자신이 하늘을 높이 날아오르는 그 날을 꿈꿨다. 23살 때 Coleman은 시카고로 이사했고 그곳에서 비행 수업을 위한 돈을 모으기 위해 식당에서 일했다. 그러나 그 당시 미국 비행 학교가 여성이나 흑인의 입학을 허가하지 않았기 때문에 그녀는 비행 수업을 듣기 위해 파리로 가야 했다. 1921년에 그녀는 마침내 국제 조종사 면허를 딴 최초의 흑인 여성이 되었다. 그녀는 또한 유럽에서 곡예 비행을 공부했고 1922년에 뉴욕의 에어쇼에 그녀의 첫 출현을 했다. 여성 비행 개척자로서 그녀는 다음 세대가 그들의 비행의 꿈을 추구하도록 영감을 주었다.

문제풀이

'She also studied flying acrobatics in Europe and made her first appearance in an airshow in New York in 1922.'에서 유럽에서 곡예 비행을 배웠고, 뉴욕의 에어쇼에 그녀의 첫 출현을 했다고 했으므로 ④는 글의 내용과 일치하지 않는다.

어휘·어구

soar 날아오르다
license 면허
acrobatics 곡예
inspire 영감을 주다
generation 세대

5. ⑤ Paul Laurence Dunbar

직독/직해

Paul Laurence Dunbar, / an African-American poet, /.
Paul Laurence Dunbar는 / 아프리카계 미국인 시인인 /
was born on June 27, 1872
1872년 6월 27일에 태어났다
By the age of fourteen, / Dunbar had poems published /
14세쯤이 되었을 때 / Dunbar는 시를 발표했다 /
in the *Dayton Herald*. 〈Dayton Herald〉에
While in high school / 고등학교에 다닐 때 /
he edited his high school newspaper.
그는 학교 신문을 편집했다
Despite being a fine student, /
훌륭한 학생이었음에도 불구하고 /
Dunbar was financially unable to attend college /
Dunbar는 재정상 대학에 갈 수 없었다 /
and took a job / as an elevator operator.
그리고 일자리를 얻었다 / 엘리베이터 운전자로
In 1893, / 1893년에 /
Dunbar published his first book, *Oak and Ivy*, /
Dunbar는 자신의 첫 번째 책인 〈Oak and Ivy〉를 출판했다 /
at his own expense. 자신의 비용으로
In 1895, / 1895년에 /
he published the second book, *Majors and Minors*, /
그는 두 번째 책인 〈Majors and Minors〉를 출판했다 /
which brought him national and international recognition. 이것은 그에게 국내외의 인정을 가져다주었다
The poems written in standard English /
표준 영어로 쓰인 시들은 /
were called "majors," / 'majors'라고 불렸다 /
and those in dialect / were termed "minors."
그리고 방언으로 쓰인 시들은 / 'minors'라고 불렸다
Although the "major" poems in standard English /
비록 표준 영어로 쓰인 'majors' 시들이
outnumber those written in dialect, /
방언으로 쓰인 시들보다 많지만 /
it was the dialect poems / 방언으로 쓰인 시들이었다 /
that brought Dunbar the most attention.
Dunbar에게 가장 큰 주목을 받게 해 준 것은

아프리카계 미국인 시인 Paul Laurence Dunbar는 1872년 6월 27일에 태어났다. ① 14세쯤이 되었을 때 Dunbar는 〈Dayton Herald〉에 시를 발표했다. ② 그는 고등학교에 다닐 때 학교 신문을 편집했다. ③ 훌륭한 학생이었음에도 불구하고 Dunbar는 재정상 대학에 갈 수 없었고 엘리베이터 운전자로 일자리를 얻었다. 1893년에 Dunbar는 자신의 첫 번째 책인 〈Oak and Ivy〉를 자신의 비용으로 출판했다. ④ 1895년에 그는 두 번째 책인 〈Majors and Minors〉를 출판했고, 이것은 그에게 국내외의 인정을 가져다주었다. 표준 영어로 쓰인 시들은 'majors'라고 불렸고, 방언으로 쓰인 시들은 'minors'라고 불렸다. ⑤ 비록 표준 영어로 쓰인 'majors' 시들이 방언으로 쓰인 시들보다 많지만, Dunbar에게 가장 큰 주목을 받게 해 준 것은 방언으로 쓰인 시들이었다.

문제풀이

'it was the dialect poems that brought Dunbar the most attention.'에서 Dunbar에게 가장 큰 주목을 받게 해 준 것은 방언으로 쓰인 시들이었다고 했으므로, ⑤는 글의 내용과 일치하지 않는다.

어휘·어구

publish 출판하다
financially 재정상
operator (기계의) 운전자
expense 비용
recognition 인정
standard 표준
dialect 방언
term 칭하다, 이름 짓다
outnumber ~보다 많다

6. ③ Lithops

Lithops are plants / Lithops는 식물이다 /
that are often called 'living stones' /
종종 '살아있는 돌'이라고 불리는 /
on account of their unique rock-like appearance.
독특한 바위 같은 겉모양 때문에
They are native to the deserts of South Africa /
이것은 원산지가 남아프리카 사막이다 /
but commonly sold in garden centers and nurseries.
하지만 식물원과 종묘원에서 흔히 팔린다
Lithops grow well / Lithops는 잘 자란다 /
in compacted, sandy soil with little water /
수분이 거의 없는 빡빡한 모래 토양에서 /
and extreme hot temperatures.
그리고 극도로 높은 온도에서
Lithops are small plants, /
Lithops는 작은 식물이다 /
rarely getting more than an inch /
1인치 이상 거의 자라지 않는다 /
above the soil surface / 토양의 표면 위로 /
and usually with only two leaves.
그리고 보통 단 두 장의 잎을 가지고 있다
The thick leaves resemble /
두꺼운 잎은 닮았다 /
the cleft in an animal's foot /
동물 발의 갈라진 틈과 /
or just a pair of grayish brown stones gathered together.
혹은 함께 모여 있는 한 쌍의 회갈색 빛을 띠는 돌과
The plants have no true stem /
이 식물은 실제 줄기는 없다 /
and much of the plant / is underground.
그리고 식물의 대부분이 / 땅속에 묻혀 있다.
Their appearance has / 겉모양은 가지고 있다 /
the effect of conserving moisture.
수분을 보존하는 효과를

① Lithops는 독특한 바위 같은 겉모양 때문에 종종 '살아있는 돌'이라고 불리는 식물이다. ② 이것은 원산지가 남아프리카 사막이지만, 식물원과 종묘원에서 흔히 팔린다. Lithops는 수분이 거의 없는 빡빡한 모래 토양과 극도로 높은 온도에서 잘 자란다. ③ Lithops는 작은 식물로, 토양의 표면 위로 1인치 이상 거의 자라지 않고 보통 단 두 장의 잎을 가지고 있다. 두꺼운 잎은 동물 발의 갈라진 틈이나 함께 모여 있는 한 쌍의 회갈색 빛을 띠는 돌과 닮았다. ④ 이 식물은 실제 줄기는 없고 식물의 대부분이 땅속에 묻혀 있다. ⑤ 겉모양은 수분을 보존하는 효과를 가지고 있다.

문제풀이

'rarely getting more than an inch above the soil surface'에서 토양의 표면 위로 1인치 이상 거의 자라지 않는다고 했으므로, ③은 글의 내용과 일치하지 않는다.

어휘·어구

on account of ~ 때문에
appearance 겉모습
native 토종의
garden center 화원
nursery 종묘원
compacted 꽉찬, 빡빡한
extreme 극도의
temperature 온도, 기온
surface 표면
grayish 회색빛의
conserve 보존하다
moisture 수분

정답률 91%

7. ⑤ Elizabeth Catlett

Elizabeth Catlett was born /
Elizabeth Catlett은 태어났다 /
in Washington, D.C. in 1915.
1915년 Washington, D.C.에서
As a granddaughter of slaves, /
노예의 손녀로서 /
Catlett heard the stories of slaves /
Catlett은 노예 이야기를 들었다 /
from her grandmother.
할머니로부터
After being disallowed entrance /
입학 거절을 당한 이후 /
from the Carnegie Institute of Technology /
Carnegie Institute of Technology로부터 /
because she was black, /
그녀가 흑인이라는 것 때문에 /
Catlett studied design and drawing /
Catlett은 디자인과 소묘를 공부했다 /
at Howard University. Howard 대학에서
She became one of the first three students /
그녀는 첫 세 명의 학생 중 한 명이 되었다 /
to earn a master's degree in fine arts /
순수 미술 석사 학위를 획득한 /
at the University of Iowa. Iowa 대학에서
Throughout her life, / she created art /
평생 / 그녀는 예술 작품을 창작했다 /
representing the voices of people /
사람들의 목소리를 대변하는 /
suffering from social injustice.
사회적 부당함으로 고통받는
She was recognized with many prizes and honors /
그녀는 많은 상과 표창으로 인정을 받았다 /
both in the United States and in Mexico.
미국과 멕시코 모두에서
She spent over fifty years / in Mexico, /
그녀는 50년 이상의 세월을 보냈다 / 멕시코에서 /
and she took Mexican citizenship / in 1962.
그리고 그녀는 멕시코 시민권을 받았다 / 1962년에
Catlett died in 2012 / at her home in Mexico.
Catlett은 생을 마쳤다 / 2012년에 멕시코에 있는 그녀의 집에서

Elizabeth Catlett은 1915년 Washington, D.C.에서 태어났다. 노예의 손녀로서 Catlett은 ① 할머니로부터 노예 이야기를 들었다. 흑인이라는 것 때문에 ② Carnegie Institute of Technology로부터 입학 거절을 당한 이후, Catlett은 Howard 대학에서 디자인과 소묘를 공부했다. ③ 그녀는 Iowa 대학에서 순수 미술 석사 학위를 획득한 첫 세 명의 학생 중 한 명이 되었다. 평생 그녀는 사회적 부당함으로 고통받는 사람들의 목소리를 대변하는 예술 작품을 창작했다. ④ 그녀는 미국과 멕시코 모두에서 많은 상과 표창으로 인정을 받았다. 그녀는 멕시코에서 50년 이상의 세월을 보냈고, ⑤ 1962년에 멕시코 시민권을 받았다. Catlett은 2012년에 멕시코에 있는 그녀의 집에서 생을 마쳤다.

문제풀이

'she took Mexican citizenship in 1962.'에서 1962년에 멕시코 시민권을 받았다고 했으므로, ⑤는 글의 내용과 일치하지 않는다.

어휘·어구

slave 노예
disallow 거절하다, 허가하지 않다
entrance 입학, 입장
master's degree 석사 학위
fine arts 순수 미술
throughout ~동안 죽
represent 대변하다, 나타내다
suffer from ~으로 고통받다
injustice 부당함, 부정
recognize 인정하다
honor 표창, 명예
citizenship 시민권

정답률 83%

8. ④ Sarah Breedlove

직독/직해

Born in 1867, / 1867년에 태어난 /
Sarah Breedlove was an American businesswoman / Sarah Breedlove는 미국인 여성 사업가였다 /
and social activist. 그리고 사회 운동가(였다)
Orphaned at the age of seven, / 7살에 고아가 된 /
her early life was marked by hardship. 그녀의 어린 시절은 고난으로 특징지어졌다
In 1888, / she moved to St. Louis, / 1888년에 / 그녀는 St. Louis로 이사했다 /
where she worked as a washerwoman / 그곳에서 그녀는 세탁부로 일했다 /
for more than a decade, / 10년 이상 동안 /
earning barely more than a dollar a day. 하루에 겨우 1달러가 넘는 돈을 벌면서
During this time, / long hours of backbreaking labor / 이 시기 동안 / 장시간의 고된 노동이 /
and a poor diet / caused her hair to fall out. 그리고 열악한 식사가 / 그녀의 머리카락을 빠지게 했다
She tried everything that was available / 그녀는 할 수 있는 모든 것을 시도했다 /
but had no success. 하지만 성공하지 못했다
After working as a maid for a chemist, / 한 화학자의 가정부로 일한 후 /
she invented a successful hair care product / 그녀는 성공적인 모발 관리 제품을 발명했다 /
and sold it across the country. 그리고 그것을 전국에 판매했다
Not only did she sell, / 그녀는 판매했을 뿐만 아니라 /
she also recruited and trained lots of women / 많은 여성을 모집하여 교육하기도 했다
as sales agents / for a share of the profits. 판매 대리인으로 / 수익금의 할당을 위해
In the process / 그 과정에서 /
she became America's first self-made female millionaire / 그녀는 미국 최초의 자수성가한 여성 백만장자가 되었다 /
and she gave Black women everywhere / 그리고 모든 곳의 흑인 여성들에게 주었다 /
an opportunity for financial independence. 재정적인 독립의 기회를

1867년에 태어난 Sarah Breedlove는 ① 미국인 여성 사업가이자 사회 운동가였다. 7살에 고아가 된 그녀의 어린 시절은 고난으로 특징지어졌다. ② 1888년에 그녀는 St. Louis로 이사했고, 그곳에서 그녀는 10년 이상 동안 세탁부로 일하면서 하루에 겨우 1달러가 넘는 돈을 벌었다. ③ 이 시기 동안 장시간의 고된 노동과 열악한 식사가 그녀의 머리카락을 빠지게 했다. 그녀는 할 수 있는 모든 것을 시도했지만 성공하지 못했다. ④ 한 화학자의 가정부로 일한 후 그녀는 성공적인 모발 관리 제품을 발명했고 그것을 전국에 판매했다. 그녀는 판매했을 뿐만 아니라, 수익금의 할당을 위해 많은 여성을 판매 대리인으로 모집하여 교육하기도 했다. 그 과정에서 그녀는 미국 최초의 자수성가한 여성 백만장자가 되었고 ⑤ 모든 곳의 흑인 여성들에게 재정적인 독립의 기회를 주었다.

문제풀이

'she invented a successful hair care product and sold it across the country'에서 성공적인 모발 관리 제품을 발명해서 전국에 판매했다고 했으므로, ④는 글의 내용과 일치하지 않는다.

어휘·어구

businesswoman 여성 사업가
social activist 사회 운동가
orphan 고아로 만들다
hardship 고난
barely 겨우
backbreaking 대단히 힘든
labor 노동
available 이용할 수 있는
chemist 화학자
successful 성공적인
recruit 모집하다
sales agent 판매원, 판매 대리인
profit 이익, 수익
millionaire 백만장자
financial 재정의, 재정적인
independence 독립

정답률 84%

9. ③ Jessie Redmon Fauset

직독/직해

Jessie Redmon Fauset was born in Snow Hill, New Jersey, in 1884. Jessie Redmon Fauset은 1884년 New Jersey의 Snow Hill에서 태어났다
She was the first black woman / 그녀는 최초의 흑인 여성이었다 /
to graduate from Cornell University. Cornell University를 졸업한
In addition to writing novels, poetry, short stories, and essays, / 소설, 시, 단편 소설, 수필을 쓰는 것 외에도 /
Fauset taught French in public schools in Washington, D.C. / Fauset은 Washington, D.C.의 공립학교에서 프랑스어를 가르쳤다 /
and worked as a journal editor. 그리고 저널 편집자로서 일했다
While working as an editor, / 편집자로 일하는 동안 /
she encouraged many well-known writers of the Harlem Renaissance. 그녀는 '흑인 예술 문화 부흥 운동'의 많은 유명한 작가들을 고무시켰다
Though she is more famous for being an editor than for being a fiction writer, / 비록 그녀는 소설가보다 편집자로서 더 유명하지만
many critics consider her novel *Plum Bun* Fauset's strongest work. 많은 비평가들은 그녀의 소설 Plum Bun을 Fauset의 가장 뛰어난 작품으로 간주한다
In it, she tells the story of a black girl / 그 속에서, 그녀는 한 흑인 소녀의 이야기를 한다 /
who could pass for white / 백인으로 여겨질 수 있는 /
but ultimately claims her racial identity and pride. 하지만 결국에는 자신의 인종적 정체성과 자부심을 주장한다
Fauset died of heart disease April 30, 1961, in Philadelphia. Fauset은 1961년 4월 30일에 Philadelphia에서 심장병으로 사망했다

Jessie Redmon Fauset은 1884년 New Jersey의 Snow Hill에서 태어났다. ① 그녀는 Cornell University를 졸업한 최초의 흑인 여성이었다. ② Fauset은 소설, 시, 단편 소설, 수필을 쓰는 것 외에도, Washington, D.C.의 공립학교에서 프랑스어를 가르쳤고, 저널 편집자로서 일했다. 편집자로 일하는 동안, 그녀는 Harlem Renaissance(흑인 예술 문화 부흥 운동)의 많은 유명한 작가들을 고무시켰다. ③ 비록 그녀는 소설가보다 편집자로서 더 유명하지만, 많은 비평가들은 그녀의 소설 'Plum Bun'을 Fauset의 가장 뛰어난 작품으로 간주한다. ④ 그 속에서, 그녀는 한 흑인 소녀의 이야기를 하는데, 그 소녀는 백인으로 여겨질 수 있지만 결국에는 자신의 인종적 정체성과 자부심을 주장한다. ⑤ Fauset은 1961년 4월 30일에 Philadelphia에서 심장병으로 사망했다.

문제풀이

'Though she is more famous for being an editor than for being a fiction writer, many critics consider her novel *Plum Bun* Fauset's strongest work.'에서 그녀가 소설가보다 편집자로서 더 유명하다고 했으므로 글의 내용과 일치하지 않는 것은 ③이다.

어휘·어구

graduate from ~를 졸업하다
in addition to ~에 더하여, ~이외에도
critic 비평가, 평론가
ultimately 결국에는
racial 인종의
identity 정체성

정답률 87%

10. ⑤ Sigrid Undset의 삶

Sigrid Undset was born on May 20, 1882, / Sigrid Undset은 1882년 5월 20일 태어났다 /
in Kalundborg, Denmark. 덴마크의 Kalundborg에서
She was the eldest of three daughters. 그녀는 세 자매 중 첫째 딸이었다
She moved to Norway / at the age of two. 그녀는 노르웨이로 이주하였다 / 2살에
Her early life was strongly influenced / 그녀의 어린 시절은 크게 영향을 받았다 /
by her father's historical knowledge. 그녀 아버지의 역사적 지식에 의해
At the age of sixteen, / she got a job / 16세의 나이에 / 그녀는 일자리를 얻었다 /
at an engineering company / to support her family. 기술회사에서 / 그녀의 가족을 부양하기 위해
She read a lot, / 그녀는 책을 많이 읽었다 /
acquiring a good knowledge of Nordic / 북유럽 문학에 관한 상당한 지식을 습득하였다 /
as well as foreign literature, / English in particular. 외국 문학뿐만 아니라 / 특히 영국 문학
She wrote thirty six books. 그녀는 36권의 책을 집필하였다
None of her books leaves the reader unconcerned. 독자의 관심을 끌지 못한 책은 없다.
She received the Nobel Prize for Literature / in 1928. 그녀는 노벨 문학상을 수상하였다 / 1928년에
One of her novels has been translated / 그녀의 소설 중 한 권은 번역되었다 /
into more than eighty languages. 80개 이상의 언어로
She escaped Norway / 그녀는 노르웨이를 떠났다 /
during the German occupation, / 독일 점령 기간 중 /
but she returned / after the end of World War Ⅱ. 그러나 그녀는 돌아왔다 / 2차 세계대전이 종료된 후

Sigrid Undset은 1882년 5월 20일 덴마크의 Kalundborg에서 태어났다. ① 그녀는 세 자매 중 첫째 딸이었다. 그녀는 2살에 노르웨이로 이주하였다. ② 그녀의 어린 시절은 아버지의 역사적 지식에 크게 영향을 받았다. ③ 그녀는 16세에 가족을 부양하기 위해 기술 회사에 취업을 하였다. 그녀는 책을 많이 읽었고, 외국 문학, 특히 영국 문학뿐만 아니라, 북유럽 문학에 관한 상당한 지식을 습득하였다. 그녀는 36권의 책을 집필하였다. 독자의 관심을 끌지 못한 책은 없다. ④ 1928년에 그녀는 노벨 문학상을 수상하였다. 그녀의 소설 중 한 권은 80개 이상의 언어로 번역되었다. ⑤ 그녀는 독일 점령 기간 중 노르웨이를 떠났으나, 2차 세계대전이 종료된 후 돌아왔다.

문제풀이

'She escaped Norway during the German occupation, but she returned after the end of World War Ⅱ.'로 보아 2차 세계 대전이 끝난 후 돌아왔다는 것을 알 수 있으므로, ⑤가 글의 내용과 일치하지 않는다.

어휘·어구

influence 영향을 미치다
acquire 획득하다, 습득하다
A as well as B B뿐만 아니라 A도 역시
unconcerned 무관심한
occupation 점령

본문 053쪽

문법 플러스 9. 부정사

1. continuing	2. to produce
3. to complete	4. to show
5. drink	6. to apply
7. to break	8. to be shocked
9. breathing	10. reporting

1 [해석]▶ 몇 분 후 차장이 기차 차량 앞쪽에서 돌아섰고, Einstein이 그의 좌석 밑에서 사라진 표를 계속해 찾고 있는 것을 보았다.
[해설]▶ 지각동사(see)의 목적어와 목적격보어가 능동 관계일 때 목적격보어는 동사원형 또는 현재분사를 사용한다.

2 [해석]▶ 학교의 기능이 지식인을 배출하는 것이라고 종종 믿어왔다.
[해설]▶ be동사 뒤에 to produce가 와서 that절 안에서 보어의 역할을 하고 있다. to produce 뒤에 목적어가 나오고 있으므로 to부정사의 능동태를 써야 한다.

3 [해석]▶ 지금 가능한 한 쉽게 구독 신청을 할 수 있도록 우리는 귀하가 작성할 회신용 카드를 보냈습니다.
[해설]▶ 의미상의 주어가 for you이므로 바로 뒤에는 to부정사가 나와야 한다.

4 [해석]▶ '당신이 먹는 것이 당신이다.' 그 구절은 흔히 여러분이 먹는 음식과 여러분의 신체 건강 사이의 관계를 보여주기 위해 사용된다.
[해설]▶ to show는 '~하기 위해'라는 의미로 to부정사의 부사적 용법(목적)으로 사용되었다. 「be used to+동사원형」은 '~하기 위해 사용되다'는 의미이다. 「be used to+동명사」는 '~하는 데 익숙하다'는 의미이다.

5 [해석]▶ 당신은 말을 물가로 데려갈 수는 있지만, 억지로 물을 먹일 수는 없다.
[해설]▶ 사역동사(make)의 목적어와 목적격보어가 능동 관계인 경우 목적격보어는 원형부정사가 사용된다.

6 [해석]▶ 그녀는 내가 그 직업에 지원하도록 용기를 주었다.
[해설]▶ 「encourage+목적어+목적격보어(to부정사)」와 같이 advise, allow, ask, cause, enable, encourage, expect, tell, want 등의 동사는 to부정사를 목적격보어로 쓴다.

7 [해석]▶ 인간들은 도덕성이 있고 동물들은 그렇지 않다는 믿음은 너무 오래된 가정이라 충분히 그것은 습관적 사고로 불릴 수 있고, 우리 모두가 알다시피 나쁜 습관은 고치기가 너무나 어렵다.
[해설]▶ to break는 앞에 있는 형용사 hard를 수식하는 부사적 용법의 to부정사로 쓰였다. 문맥상 '고치기가 어렵다'라는 의미가 되어야 하므로 to break가 적절하다.

8 [해석]▶ 아마 여러분은 너무 낮은 목표들을 세우고 그것들을 달성은 했으나 결국 자신이 원했던 것을 여전히 얻지 못한 것에 깜짝 놀라며 더욱 자주 실망했을 것이다.
[해설]▶ only to be shocked는 to부정사의 부사적 용법(결과)으로 쓰였다.

9 [해석]▶ 의사는 눈물을 흘리며 "유감이지만 Simba가 죽었어요."라고 말했다. 마침내, Simba는 숨 쉬는 것을 멈췄다.
[해설]▶ 「stop+동명사」는 '~을 멈추다'는 의미이고, 「stop+to부정사」는 '~하기 위해 멈추다'는 의미이다. 뒷 문장에서 의사가 Simba가 죽은 것을 말하고 있으므로, stop breathing(숨 쉬는 것을 멈추다)이 문맥상 적절하다.

10 해석▶ "오랜 친구를 잃어버린 느낌입니다. 심바의 탄생을 알려드린 때가 기억납니다."라고 한 의사가 말했다.
[해설]▶ 「remember+동명사」는 '(과거의)~한 것을 을 기억하다'의 의미이고, 「「remember+to부정사」는 '(미래에) ~해야 할 것을 기억하다'는 의미이다. 과거의 일을 기억한 것이므로 'remember reporting'이 문맥상 맞다.

본문 054쪽

어휘 플러스 9. 철자가 혼동되는 어휘 (3)

1. except	2. acquire
3. affect	4. altitude
5. approve	

1 [해석]▶ 그는 한 가지만 빼고는 여행에 필요한 모든 것을 가지고 있다.

2 [해석]▶ 우리는 모두 자신의 사회의 구성원으로서 우리가 획득하는 문화적 지식을 우리의 인식과 행동을 구성하는 데 사용한다.

3 [해석]▶ 예를 들어, 뉴턴은 질량이 힘을 발휘함으로써 서로에게 영향을 미친다고 생각했다. 반면에, 아인슈타인의 이론에서는 공간과 시간의 구부러짐을 통해 그 결과가 일어나며, 힘으로서의 중력의 개념이 없다.

4 [해석]▶ 극한의 고도로 인해 발생하는 치명적인 영향에 대한 그들의 지식은 제한적인 것이었으며 그들의 장비는 보잘 것 없었다.

5 [해석]▶ 당면한 위험이 없을 때는 간섭하지 말고 아이의 놀이를 인정해 주는 것이 대개 제일 좋다.

10. 안내문

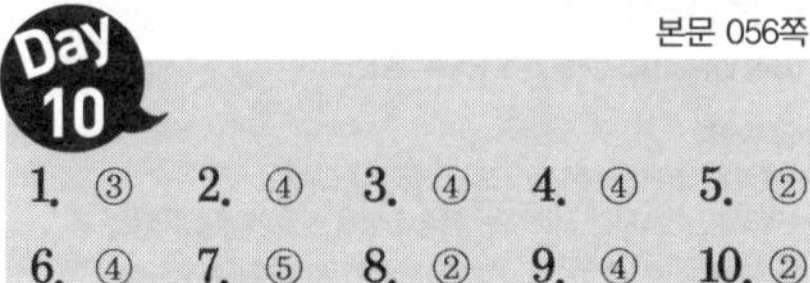

Day 10

본문 056쪽

1. ③	2. ④	3. ④	4. ④	5. ②
6. ④	7. ⑤	8. ②	9. ④	10. ②

정답률 93%

대표 기출 ⑤ E-Waste Recycling Day

전자 폐기물 재활용의 날

전자 폐기물 재활용의 날은 우리 시의 연례행사입니다.
휴대 전화, 태블릿, 그리고 노트북과 같이 재활용할 중고 전자 제품들을 가져오세요. 친환경적이 되세요!

▫ **언제**
– 2022년 12월 17일 토요일
– 오전 8시부터 오전 11시까지

▫ **어디서**
Lincoln 스포츠 센터

▫ **주의 사항**
• 허용되지 않는 품목들: 전구, 건전지, 전자레인지
• 기기 속 모든 개인 정보는 미리 삭제되어야 합니다.
• 이 행사는 무료이지만 지역 주민에게만 개방됩니다.

더 많은 정보를 위해 986-571-0204로 연락주세요.

문제풀이

'This event is free but open only to local residents.'에서 이 행사는 무료지만 지역 주민에게만 개방된다고 했으므로 ⑤ '주 지역에 상관없이 참가할 수 있다.'는 안내문의 내용과 일치하지 않는다.

어휘·어구

e-waste 전자 폐기물
recycle 재활용하다
annual 연례의
electronics 전자 기기
green 환경 친화적인
accepted 허용된
light bulb 전구
microwave 전자레인지
personal 개인의
device 기기
wipe out 완전히 파괴하다
in advance 미리
local 지역의
resident 주민
contact 연락하다

정답률 87%

1. ③ Undersea Walking Activity

해저 걷기 활동

해양 바닥에서 매력적인 수중 걷기를 즐기세요.
걸어 다니며 멋진 바다 생물을 직접 보세요!

▫ **연령 요건**
– 10세 이상

▫ **영업시간**
– 화요일부터 일요일까지
– 오전 9시부터 오후 4시까지

▫ **가격**
– $30 (보험료 포함)

▫ **가져와야 하는 것**
– 수영복과 수건

◎ **주의 사항**
– 숙련된 안전 요원이 활동 내내 여러분과 동행합니다.
– 특수 수중 헬멧 착용 시 여러분은 활동 중에 안경을 쓸 수 있습니다.
– 예약은 현장 혹은 www.seawalkwonder.com에서 온라인으로 할 수 있습니다.

문제풀이

'Experienced lifeguards accompany you throughout the activity.'에서 숙련된 안전 요원이 활동 내내 여러분과 동행한다고 했으므로, ③이 안내문의 내용과 일치한다.

어휘·어구

undersea 수중의
activity 활동
fascinating 매력적인
witness 눈 앞에서 보다, 목격하다
marine 해양의
requirement 필요 조건
operating hours 운영 시간
insurance 보험
include 포함하다
experienced 숙련된
lifeguard 안전 요원
accompany 동행하다
throughout 내내
reservation 예약
on-site 현장의

정답률 96%

2. ④ 2022 Springfield Park Yoga Class

2022 Springfield Park Yoga Class

Springfield Park에서의 인기 있는 요가 수업이 돌아옵니다!
공원 잔디밭에서 열리는 요가를 즐겨보세요. 만약 여러분이 공원에 오지 못한다면, 저희의 소셜미디어 플랫폼에서 온라인으로 저희와 함께하세요!

◈ **언제** : 9월, 토요일마다, 오후 2시부터 오후 3시까지
◈ **등록** : 매 수업이 시작하기 최소 두 시간 전까지,
여기에서 등록하세요.
◈ **주의 사항**
• 온라인 수업 대상: 여러분이 스트레칭을 할 만큼 충분한 공간을 가진 조용한 장소를 찾으세요.
• 공원에서의 수업 대상: 매트는 제공되지 않으니, 본인 것을 가져오세요!

※ 만약 날씨가 좋지 않으면 수업은 취소될 것입니다.

더 많은 정보를 위해, *여기를 클릭하세요.*

문제풀이

'For classes in the park: mats are not provided, so bring your own!'에서 매트는 제공되지 않으니, 본인 것을 가져오라고 했으므로, ④가 안내문의 내용과 일치하지 않는다.

어휘·어구

return 돌아오다
lawn 잔디
registration 등록
cancel 취소하다
unfavorable 좋지 않은

정답률 87%

3. ④ Kenner High School's Water Challenge

Kenner High School's Water Challenge

Kenner High School's Water Challenge는 수질 오염에 대한 대책을 제안하는 새로운 대회입니다. 수질 오염에 대처하기 위한 여러분의 아이디어를 공유해 주세요!

제출
• **어떻게**: 여러분의 제안서를 이메일로 admin@khswater.edu로 제출해 주세요.
• **언제**: 2022년 9월 5일부터 2022년 9월 23일까지

세부 사항
• 참가자들은 반드시 4인으로 구성된 팀으로 참가해야 하며 오직 한 팀에만 참여할 수 있습니다.
• 팀당 한 개의 제안서만 제출할 수 있습니다.
• 참가자들은 웹사이트에 제공된 제안서 양식을 사용해야 합니다.

상품
• 1등: 50달러 상품권
• 2등: 30달러 상품권
• 3등: 10달러 상품권

Challenge에 대해 더 알고 싶으면 www.khswater.edu를 방문해 주세요.

문제풀이

'Participants must use the proposal form provided on the website.'에서 웹사이트에 제공된 제안서 양식을 사용해야 한다고 했으므로, ④가 안내문의 내용과 일치한다.

어휘·어구

propose 제안하다
measure 대책, 조치
deal with 다루다, 대처하다
water pollution 수질 오염
proposal 제안서
limit 제한하다
gift certificate 상품권

정답률 95%

4. ④ Kids Taekwondo Program

Kids Taekwondo Program

이번 여름 방학에 태권도 프로그램을 즐기세요.

일정
• 날짜 : 8월 8일 – 8월 10일
• 시간 : 오전 9시 – 오전 11시

참가자
• 5세 이상 어린이 누구나

활동
• 자기방어 훈련
• 사교성 개발을 위한 팀빌딩 게임

참가비
• 1인당 $50 (간식 포함)

알림
• 가져올 것 : 물병, 수건
• 가져오지 말아야 할 것: 껌, 비싼 물건

문제풀이

'Participation Fee $50 per child (includes snacks)'에서 참가비 50달러에 간식이 포함된다고 했으므로, ④가 안내문의 내용과 일치하지 않는다.

어휘·어구

self-defense 자기방어
notice 알림, 공지

5. ② Moonlight Chocolate Factory Tour

Moonlight Chocolate Factory Tour

이 특별한 투어에 참여하여 우리의 가장 인기 있는 초콜릿 바를 즐길 기회를 가지세요.

운영 시간
- 월요일 – 금요일, 오후 2시 – 오후 5시

활동
- 초콜릿 제조 과정 견학
- 초콜릿 3종 (다크, 밀크 및 민트 초콜릿) 시식

알림
- 티켓 가격 : $30
- 마스크 착용은 필수입니다.
- 공장 내부에서 사진 촬영은 허용되지 않습니다.

문제풀이

'Watching our chocolate-making process'에서 초콜릿 제조 과정을 볼 수 있다고 했으므로, ②가 안내문의 내용과 일치한다.

어휘·어구

factory 공장
popular 인기 있는
operating hours 운영 시간
require 요구하다
allow 허용하다, 허락하다

6. ④ Rachel의 꽃 교실

Rachel의 꽃 교실

인생을 더 아름답게 만드세요!

수업 일정 (매주 월요일부터 금요일까지)

꽃꽂이	오전 11시 ~ 정오
플라워 박스 만들기	오후 1시 ~ 오후 2시

가격
- 각 수업 당 $50(꽃값과 다른 재료비 포함)
- 본인의 가위와 가방을 가져오세요.

다른 정보
- 온라인이나 전화로 수업 등록을 할 수 있습니다.
- 수업 당일 취소 시 환불 불가

연락하시려면, www.rfclass.com을 방문하시거나 03-221-2131로 전화주세요.

문제풀이

'You can sign up for classes either online or by phone.'에서 온라인이나 전화로 수업 등록을 할 수 있다고 했으므로, ④가 안내문의 내용과 일치하지 않는다.

어휘·어구

flower arrangement 꽃꽂이
material 재료
sign up for 등록하다
refund 환불
cancellation 취소
contact 연락하다

7. ⑤ 야간 궁궐 투어

야간 궁궐 투어

날짜: 4월 29일 금요일 – 5월 15일 일요일

시간

금요일	오후 7시 ~ 오후 8시 30분
토요일과 일요일	오후 6시 ~ 오후 7시 30분
	오후 8시 ~ 오후 9시 30분

티켓 예약:
- 1인당 15달러(8세 미만 어린이는 무료)
- 예약은 투어 시작 2시간 전까지 가능합니다.

프로그램 활동
- 투어 가이드와 단체 투어 (1시간)
- 전통 음식 시식과 음료 시음 (30분)

* 추가 비용 없이 전통 의상을 입어 볼 수 있습니다.
* 더 많은 정보를 원하시면, 저희 웹 사이트 www.palacenighttour.com에 방문하세요.

문제풀이

'You can try on traditional clothes with no extra charge.'에서 추가 비용 없이 전통 의상을 입어볼 수 있다고 했으므로, ⑤가 안내문의 내용과 일치한다.

어휘·어구

palace 궁궐
book 예약하다
traditional 전통적인
extra charge 추가 비용

8. ② 자연 사진 콘테스트 안내문

2021 Camptonville 자연 사진 콘테스트

이번이 매년 열리는 Camptonville 자연 사진 콘테스트의 네 번째 해입니다. 여러분은 자신의 가장 멋진 사진을 공유함으로써 Camptonville의 자연의 아름다움을 보여 줄 수 있습니다!

□ **제출**
- 최대 20장의 사진을 우리 웹 사이트 www.camptonvillephotocontest.org에 업로드하십시오.
- 마감 기한은 12월 1일입니다.

□ **상**
- 1위: $500 · 2위: $200 · 3위: $100
(수상자는 12월 31일에 우리 웹 사이트에 게시될 것입니다.)

□ **세부 사항**
- 모든 수상작은 시청에 전시될 것입니다.
- 더 많은 정보를 위해서 122-861-3971로 연락 주십시오.

문제풀이

'Upload a maximum of 20 photos onto our website www.camptonvillephotocontest.org.'에서 웹사이트에 사진을 올리라고 했으므로 안내문의 내용과 일치하지 않는 것은 ② '최대 20장의 사진을 이메일로 제출해야 한다.'이다.

어휘·어구

annual 매년의, 연례의
submission 제출
prize 상
detail 세부 사항
exhibit 전시하다

정답률 92%

9. ④ Willow Valley Hot Air Balloon Ride에 관한 안내문

Willow Valley 열기구 탑승

우리의 열기구를 타고 하늘에서 Willow Valley의 최고의 풍경을 즐겨보세요!

□ **정원:** 조종사 포함 8인까지

□ **시간 일정표**
- 봄 & 여름 (4월부터 9월까지): 오전 5시 – 오전 7시
- 가을 & 겨울 (10월부터 3월까지): 오전 6시 – 오전 8시
※ 비행 시간: 약 1시간

□ **요금:** 인당 $150 (보험은 포함되지 않음)

◎ **공지사항**
- 예약은 필수이며 온라인으로 이뤄져야 합니다.
- 여러분은 24시간 전까지는 전액 환불을 받을 수 있습니다.
- 더 많은 정보를 위해서 www.willowvalleyballoon.com을 방문해 주십시오.

문제풀이

'Reservations are required and must be made online.'에서 예약은 온라인으로 해야 한다고 했으므로 안내문의 내용과 일치하는 것은 ④ '예약은 온라인으로 해야 한다.'이다.

어휘·어구

air balloon 열기구
capacity 정원, 수용력
duration 지속 기간
insurance 보험
refund 환불
in advance 미리

10. ② Premier Reading Challenge

Premier Reading Challenge

이 행사는 대회는 아니고 오히려 학생들이 독서에 대한 사랑을 가지도록 영감을 주기 위한 도전 과제입니다.

- **참가자들**
  - 6학년부터 9학년까지의 학생들
- **날짜**
  - 6월 1일부터 12월 31일까지
- **도전 과제**
  - 6학년과 7학년 각각의 학생은 15권의 책을 읽어야 합니다.
  - 8학년과 9학년 각각의 학생은 20권의 책을 읽어야 합니다.
- **상품**
  - 모든 참가자에게 책갈피
  - 도전과제를 완수한 학생들에게 수료증
- **등록**
  - 오직 온라인으로만 — www.edu.prc.com

※ 더 많은 정보를 위해, 학교 도서관 사서를 만나거나 위에 있는 웹 사이트를 방문하세요.

문제풀이

'From June 1st to December 31s'에서 7개월간 진행되는 행사라고 했으므로, ②가 안내문의 내용과 일치하지 않는다.

어휘·어구

challenge 도전
competition 대회
inspire 영감을 주다
participant 참가자
bookmark 책갈피
certificate of achievement 수료증

본문 059쪽

문법 플러스 10. 동명사

1. Introducing 2. landing 3. creating
4. using 5. knowing 6. understanding
7. studying 8. to give 9. having
10. meeting

1 [해석]▶ 특히 새 범주가 예전의 것과 대조되지 않으면, 새로운 제품 범주를 도입하는 것은 어렵다.
[해설]▶ 동명사는 주어, 목적어, 보어 역할을 할 수 있다. introducing 이하는 주어 역할을 하는 동명사이며 동명사는 동사적 성질을 가지고 있으므로 뒤에 목적어 a new product category를 가져왔다. 특히 동명사 주어는 단수 취급을 하므로 유의한다.

2 [해석]▶ 그는 파리가 줄무늬에 앉기를 피하는 것처럼 보인다는 것을 알았다.
[해설]▶ avoid는 동명사만을 목적어로 가져오는 동사이다.

3 [해석]▶ 대화가 결과보다 변화의 과정에 초점을 둘 때, 그것은 지속 가능한 과정을 만들어내는 가치를 강화시킨다.
[해설]▶ 전치사(of) 뒤에 동사가 올 때는 동명사(creating) 형태를 사용한다. 단, but과 except 뒤에는 (to)부정사가 올 수 있다.

4 [해석]▶ 일단 누군가가 발견을 하면, 다른 사람들은 그들 자신의 연구에서 그 정보를 사용하기 전에 그것을 주의 깊게 검토한다.
[해설]▶ 전치사(before) 뒤에 동사가 올 때는 동명사(using) 형태를 사용한다.

5 [해석]▶ 아마도 그 사람은 당신이 어느 별을 보고 있는지를 정확하게 알기 어려울 것이다.
[해설]▶ 「have a hard time -ing」는 '하는 데 어려움을 겪다'의 뜻을 가진 동명사 관용 표현이다.

6 [해석]▶ 만약 이 관점이 옳다면, 우리는 문화적으로 친숙하지 않은 음악에 표현된 감정을 이해하는 데 분명 어려움이 있을 것이다.
[해설]▶ 「have difficulty in-ing」는 '하는 데 어려움을 겪다'의 뜻을 가진 동명사 관용 표현이다.

7 [해석]▶ 이 미스터리를 풀기 위해 야생 생물학자 Tim Cargo는 탄자니아에서 얼룩말을 연구하면 10년 이상을 보냈다.
[해설]▶ 「spend+시간-ing」는 '하는 데 시간을 쓰다'의 뜻을 갖는 동명사 관용 표현이다.

8 [해석]▶ 수의사가 와서 사자에게 약이 가득 담긴 고기를 주려고 했다.
[해설]▶ 「try+동명사」'하려고 노력하다', 「try+to부정사」는 '시험 삼아 해보다'는 의미이다. 문맥상 「try+동명사」가 맞다.

9 [해석]▶ 그녀는 피곤할 때면 커피를 마시지 않을 수 없다.
[해설]▶ can't help -ing는 '~하지 않을 수 없다, ~해야만 했다'는 의미이다.

10 해석▶ 나는 그녀를 만나기를 고대하고 있었다.
[해설]▶ look forward to -ing는 '~을 고대하다'는 의미이다.

본문 060쪽

어휘 플러스 10. 유의어 (3)

1. establish 2. exchange
3. evaluated 4. genuine
5. incredible

1 [해석]▶ 대학교를 졸업한 후 Rawlings는 저널리스트로 일하면서 동시에 소설가로 자리매김하려고 애썼다.

2 [해석]▶ 현대 세계에서는 거의 모든 나라가 다른 가치 있는 물건과 교환하기 위해 동전과 지폐를 사용한다.

3 [해석]▶ 이 시론(試論)은 순수성, 진실성, 우아함, 예의 바름의 기준에 따라 평가되었다. 그럼에도 이 기준은 너무도 모호해서 지원자들은 시험관의 문학적 선호를 인지하려고 애쓰는 것밖에 거의 도리가 없었다.

4 [해석]▶ 우리는 모든 젊은이들에게 그들의 성장 배경이 제아무리 형편없어도, 우리 사회에서 자신을 실현하고 건설적인 역할을 수행할 수 있는 진정한 기회를 그가 가지고 있음을 보여 주어야 한다.

5 [해석]▶ 우리의 괄목할 만한 성장률 때문에 확장되고 있는 회사에 소중한 공헌을 할 희망을 가지고 있는 패기만만한 프로그램 분석가를 계속해서 모집하게 되었습니다.

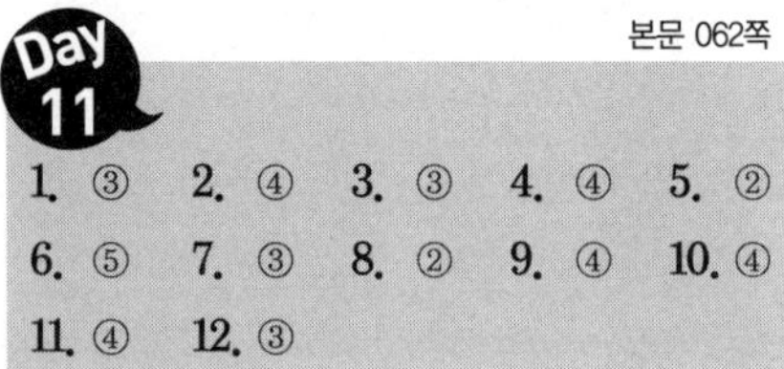

11. 어법 정확성 파악

Day 11 본문 062쪽

1. ③ 2. ④ 3. ③ 4. ④ 5. ②
6. ⑤ 7. ③ 8. ② 9. ④ 10. ④
11. ④ 12. ③

정답률 51%

대표 기출 ④ 인공 지능의 핵심적인 특징

직독/직해

You may have seen headlines in the news /
여러분은 뉴스에서 헤드라인들을 본 적이 있을 것이다 /
about some of the things / 몇 가지 일에 관한 /
machines powered by artificial intelligence /
인공 지능으로 구동되는 기계가 /
can do. 할 수 있는
However, / if you were to consider / all the tasks /
하지만 / 만약 여러분이 고려한다면 / 모든 작업을 /
that AI-powered machines could actually perform, /
AI로 구동되는 기계가 실제로 수행할 수 있는 /
it would be quite mind-blowing!
그것은 꽤 놀라울 것이다
One of the key features of artificial intelligence is /
인공 지능의 핵심 특징 중 하나는 ~이다 /
that it enables machines to learn new things, /
그것이 기계들이 새로운 것들을 학습할 수 있게 한다는 것(이다) /
rather than requiring programming /
프로그래밍을 필요로 하기보다는 /
specific to new tasks. 새로운 작업에 특화된
Therefore, / the core difference /
따라서 / 핵심적인 차이는 /
between computers of the future /
미래의 컴퓨터들과 /
and those of the past / is that future computers /
과거의 그것들 (사이의) / 미래의 컴퓨터가 ~이라는 점이다 /
will be able to learn and self-improve.
학습하고 스스로 개선할 수 있을 것(이라는 점이다)
In the near future, / 가까운 미래에 /
smart virtual assistants will know /
스마트 가상 비서는 알게 될 것이다 /
more about you / than your closest friends and family members do.
여러분에 대해 더 많이 / 여러분의 가장 가까운 친구와 가족이 아는 것보다
Can you imagine / how that might change our lives?
여러분은 상상할 수 있는가 / 그것이 우리의 삶을 어떻게 변화시킬지
These kinds of changes are exactly /
이런 종류의 변화는 정확히 ~이다 /
why it is so important /
왜 아주 중요한가에 대한 이유(이다) /
to recognize the implications /
영향을 인식하는 것이 /
that new technologies will have for our world.
새로운 기술들이 우리 세계에 미칠

여러분은 인공 지능으로 구동되는 기계가 할 수 있는 몇 가지 일에 관한 헤드라인들을 뉴스에서 본 적이 있을 것이다. 하지만, 만약 여러분이 AI로 구동되는 기계가 실제로 수행할 수 있는 모든 작업을 고려한다면, 그것은 꽤 놀라울 것이다! 인공 지능의 핵심 특징 중 하나는 그것이 새로운 작업에 특화된 프로그래밍을 필요로 하기보다는 기계들이 새로운 것들을 학습할 수 있게 한다는 것이다. 따라서, 미래의 컴퓨터들과 과거의 그것들 사이의 핵심적인 차이는 미래의 컴퓨터가 학습하고 스스로 개선할 수 있을 것이라는 점이다. 가까운 미래에, 스마트 가상 비서는 여러분에 대해 여러분의 가장 가까운 친구와 가족이 아는 것보다 더 많이 알게 될 것이다. 여러분은 그것이 우리의 삶을 어떻게 변화시킬지 상상할 수 있는가? 왜 이런 종류의 변화는 정확히 새로운 기술들이 우리 세계에 미칠 영향을 인식하는 것이 아주 중요한가에 대한 이유이다.

문제풀이

① [관계대명사]
that 뒤에 목적어가 없는 불완전한 문장이 왔고, 앞에 있는 선행사 all the tasks를 수식하는 관계대명사 절이므로 목적격 관계대명사 that은 적절하게 쓰였다.
② [문장의 동사]
문장의 주어인 One of the key features of artificial intelligence의 동사로 단수동사 is는 적절하게 쓰였다.
③ [대명사]
지시대명사 those는 의미상 computers라는 복수 명사를 대신 받아야 하므로 적절하게 쓰였다.
④ [대동사]
문장의 동사인 know를 대신하는 대동사가 와야 하므로 are를 do로 고쳐야 한다.
⑤ [가주어 진주어]
why가 이끄는 절의 주어 자리에 가주어 it이 왔고, to recognize 이하가 진주어로 왔으므로 적절하게 쓰였다.

어휘·어구

power 동력을 공급하다
artificial intelligence 인공 지능
consider 고려하다
perform 수행하다
mind-blowing 놀랄 만한
feature 특징
enable ~을 할 수 있게 하다
require 필요하다, 요구하다
specific 특화된
core 핵심
difference 차이
virtual 가상의
assistant 조수
imagine 상상하다
recognize 인식하다
implication 영향
technology 기술

정답률 71%

1. ③ 인간의 뇌 크기가 줄어든 이유

직독/직해

The human brain, / it turns out, /
인간의 뇌는 / 밝혀졌다 /
has shrunk in mass / by about 10 percent /
부피가 줄어들었다는 것이 / 약 10%만큼 /
since it peaked in size / 15,000-30,000 years ago.
크기가 정점에 도달한 이후로 / 15,000년에서 30,000년 전
One possible reason is /
한 가지 가능한 이유는 ~ 것이다 /
that many thousands of years ago /
수천 년 전에 /
humans lived in a world of dangerous predators /
인간은 위험한 포식자 세계에서 살았다는 (것이다) /
where they had to have their wits / about them /
그들의 기지를 발휘했어야 하는 / 그들에 대한 /
at all times / to avoid being killed.
항상 / 죽임을 당하는 것을 피하기 위해
Today, / we have effectively domesticated ourselves /
오늘날 / 우리는 우리 자신을 효율적으로 길들여 왔다 /
and many of the tasks of survival /
그리고 생존의 많은 과업이 /
— from avoiding immediate death /
즉각적인 죽음을 피하는 것부터 /
to building shelters to obtaining food — /
은신처를 짓고 음식을 얻어 내는 일까지 /
have been outsourced / to the wider society.
위탁되어 왔다 / 더 넓은 사회로
We are smaller than our ancestors too, /
우리는 우리의 조상보다 더 작기도 하다 /
and it is a characteristic of domestic animals /
그리고 가축의 한 특징이다 /
that they are generally smaller /
그것들이 일반적으로 더 작다는 것은 /
than their wild cousins. 그들의 야생 사촌보다
None of this may mean / we are dumber /
이것의 어떤 것도 의미하지는 않는다 / 우리가 더 어리석다는 것을 /
— brain size is not necessarily an indicator of human intelligence — /
뇌 크기가 반드시 인간 지능의 지표는 아니다 /
but it may mean / that our brains today /
하지만 그것은 의미할지도 모른다 / 오늘날 우리의 뇌가
are wired up differently, /
다르게 타고났다는 것을 /
and perhaps more efficiently, /
그리고 아마도 더 효율적으로 /
than those of our ancestors.
우리 조상들의 그것들보다

인간의 뇌는 15,000년에서 30,000년 전 크기가 정점에 도달한 이후로 부피가 약 10%만큼 줄어들었다는 것이 밝혀졌다. 한 가지 가능한 이유는 수천 년 전에 인간은 죽임을 당하는 것을 피하기 위해 항상 그들(위험한 포식자)에 대한 그들의 기지를 발휘했어야 하는 위험한 포식자 세계에서 살았다는 것이다. 오늘날, 우리는 우리 자신을 효율적으로 길들여 왔고 생존의 많은 과업이 — 즉각적인 죽음을 피하는 것부터 은신처를 짓고 음식을 얻어 내는 일까지 — 더 넓은 사회로 위탁되어 왔다. 우리는 우리의 조상보다 더 작기도 한데, 가축이 그들의 야생 사촌보다 일반적으로 더 작다는 것은 가축의 한 특징이다. 이것의 어떤 것도 우리가 더 어리석다는 것을 의미하지는 않지만 — 뇌 크기가 반드시 인간 지능의 지표는 아니다 — 그것은 오늘날 우리의 뇌가 다르게, 그리고 우리 조상들의 그것들보다 아마도 더 효율적으로 타고났다는 것을 의미할지도 모른다.

문제풀이

① [시제]
명백히 과거를 나타내는 부사구 '15,000–30,000 years ago'로 보아 since 절의 시제는 과거가 되어야 하므로 peaked는 적절하게 쓰였다.
② [관계부사]
where 뒤에 완전한 절이 왔고, 앞에 있는 선행사 'a world of dangerous predators'를 수식해야 하므로 관계부사 where는 적절하게 쓰였다.
③ [주어-동사의 수일치]
and 이후의 문장에서 주어는 'many of the tasks of survival'이므로 단수 동사 has를 복수 동사 have로 고쳐 써야 한다.
④ [접속사]
that 뒤에 완전한 절이 왔고, it이 가주어이므로 진주어를 이끌어 오는 접속사 that은 적절하게 쓰였다.
⑤ [지시대명사]
비교급 문장으로 brains를 받는 대명사 those는 적절하게 쓰였다.

어휘·어구

turn out 밝혀지다
shrink 줄어들다
mass 부피
possible 가능한
domesticate 길들이다
immediate 즉각적인
shelter 은신처
obtain 얻다
outsource 외부에 위탁하다

ancestor 조상
characteristic 특징
dumber 바보
necessarily 반드시
indicator 지표
intelligence 지능

2. ④ 첨단 생활방식으로 인한 천연 자원 사용의 증가

직독/직해

Despite all the high-tech devices /
모든 첨단 기기들에도 불구하고 /
that seem to deny the need for paper, /
종이의 필요성을 부정하는 것처럼 보이는 /
paper use in the United States /
미국에서 종이 사용은 /
has nearly doubled recently.
최근 거의 두 배로 증가했다
We now consume more paper / than ever: /
우리는 지금 더 많은 종이를 소비하고 있다 / 그 어느 때보다도
400 million tons globally / and growing.
전 세계적으로 4억 톤을 (소비하고 있다) / 그리고 증가하고 있다
Paper is not the only resource / that we are using more of.
종이가 유일한 자원은 아니다 / 우리가 더 많이 사용하고 있는
Technological advances often come with /
기술 발전은 흔히 수반한다 /
the promise of using fewer materials.
더 적은 재료의 사용 가능성을
However, the reality is / 하지만 현실은 ~이다 /
that they have historically caused /
그것들이 역사적으로 야기한다는 것 /
more materials use, / making us dependent on /
더 많은 재료 사용을 / 그래서 우리를 (~에) 의존하게 만든다 /
more natural resources. 더 많은 천연자원 사용에
The world now consumes / far more "stuff" / than it ever has.
세계는 이제 훨씬 더 많은 '것'을 소비한다 / 그 어느 때보다도
We use twenty-seven times more industrial minerals, /
우리는 27배 더 많은 산업 광물을 사용한다 /
such as gold, copper, and rare metals, /
금, 구리, 그리고 희귀 금속과 같은
than we did just over a century ago.
단지 1세기 이전에 사용했던 것보다
We also each individually use more resources.
우리는 또한 각자 더 많은 자원을 사용한다
Much of that / is due to our high-tech lifestyle.
그중 많은 부분이 / 우리의 첨단 생활방식 때문이다

종이의 필요성을 부정하는 것처럼 보이는 모든 첨단 기기들에도 불구하고, 미국에서 종이 사용은 최근 거의 두 배로 증가했다. 우리는 그 어느 때보다도 지금 더 많은 종이를 소비하고 있다. 전 세계적으로 4억 톤을 소비하고 있으며 증가하고 있다. 우리가 더 많이 사용하고 있는 유일한 자원은 종이만이 아니다. 기술 발전은 흔히 더 적은 재료의 사용 가능성을 수반한다. 하지만, 현실은 그것들이 역사적으로 더 많은 재료 사용을 야기하여 우리를 더 많은 천연자원 사용에 의존하게 만든다. 세계는 이제 그 어느 때보다도 훨씬 더 많은 '것'을 소비한다. 우리는 금, 구리, 그리고 희귀 금속과 같은 산업 광물을 단지 1세기 이전에 사용했던 것보다 27배 더 많이 사용한다. 우리는 또한 각자 더 많은 자원을 사용한다. 그중 많은 부분이 우리의 첨단 생활방식 때문이다.

문제풀이

① [문장의 동사]
문장 전체의 주어구는 paper use in the United States이므로 동사가 필요하다. 따라서 단수 주어에 맞게 단수 동사가 적절하게 쓰였다.
② [관계대명사]
뒤에 불완전한 문장(we are using more of)이 왔고, 앞에 the only resource라는 선행사가 왔으므로 목적격 관계대명사 that은 적절하게 쓰였다.
③ [동명사]
전치사 of의 목적어로 동명사 using은 적절하게 쓰였다.
④ [목적격 보어]
동사 make의 목적격 보어 자리에는 형용사가 와야 하므로 dependently를 dependent로 고쳐 써야 한다.
⑤ [대동사 do]
앞에 언급된 일반동사 use를 대신하는 동사가 필요하므로 대동사 did는 적절하게 쓰였다. than이 이끄는 절은 과거시제이므로 did가 쓰였다.

어휘·어구

despite ~에도 불구하고
device 기기
deny 부정하다
consume 소비하다
resource 자원
technological 기술적인
advance 발전, 진보
promise 가능성
material 재료
reality 현실
historically 역사적으로
natural resources 천연자원
industrial mineral 산업 광물
rare metal 희귀 금속
century 세기
individually 개별적으로, 개인적으로

3. ③ 인간은 유유상종의 경향이 있다

직독/직해

We usually get along best /
우리는 보통 가장 잘 지낸다 /
with people who we think are like us.
우리와 같다고 생각하는 사람들과
In fact, / we seek them out.
사실 / 우리는 그들을 찾아낸다
It's why / places like Little Italy, Chinatown, and Koreatown / exist.
그것이 이유이다 / 리틀 이탈리아, 차이나타운, 그리고 코리아타운과 같은 장소들이 / 존재하는
But I'm not just talking about /
하지만 나는 ~만을 말하는 것이 아니다 /
race, skin color, or religion.
인종, 피부색, 또는 종교
I'm talking about people / who share our values /
나는 사람들에 대해 말하는 것이다 / 우리의 가치관을 공유하는 /
and look at the world / the same way we do.
그리고 세상을 바라보는 / 우리와 같은 방식으로
As the saying goes, / 속담에서 말하듯이 /
birds of a feather flock together.
날개가 같은 새들이 함께 모인다
This is a very common human tendency /
이것은 매우 흔한 인간의 경향이다 /
that is rooted in / how our species developed.
뿌리박혀 있는 / 우리 종이 발전한 방식에
Imagine you are walking out in a forest.
여러분이 숲에 나가 걷는다고 상상해 보라
You would be conditioned to avoid /
여러분은 피하도록 조건화되어 있을 것이다 /
something unfamiliar or foreign /
친숙하지 않거나 낯선 것을 /
because there is a high likelihood /
가능성이 크기 때문에 /
that it would be interested in killing you.
그것이 여러분을 죽이는 데 관심이 있을
Similarities make us relate better / to other people /
유사점은 우리가 마음이 더 잘 통할 수 있도록 한다 / 다른 사람들과 /
because we think / they'll understand us /
왜냐하면 우리는 생각하기 때문이다 / 그들이 우리를 이해할 것으로 /
on a deeper level / than other people.
더 깊은 수준으로 / 다른 사람들보다

우리는 보통 우리와 같다고 생각하는 사람들과 가장 잘 지낸다. 사실, 우리는 그들을 찾아낸다. 그것이 리틀 이탈리아, 차이나타운, 그리고 코리아타운과 같은 장소들이 존재하는 이유이다. 하지만 나는 인종, 피부색, 또는 종교만을 말하는 것이 아니다. 나는 우리의 가치관을 공유하고 우리와 같은 방식으로 세상을 바라보는 사람들에 대해 말하는 것이다. 속담에서 말하듯이, 날개가 같은 새들이 함께 모인다. 이것은 우리 종이 발전한 방식에 뿌리박혀 있는 매우 흔한 인간의 경향이다. 여러분이 숲에 나가 걷는다고 상상해 보라. 친숙하지 않거나 낯선 것은 그런 것이 여러분을 죽이는 데 관심이 있을 가능성이 크기 때문에 여러분은 그런 것을 피하도록 조건화되어 있을 것이다. 유사점(을 갖고 있는 것)은 우리가 다른 사람들과 마음이 더 잘 통할 수 있도록 하는데, 그들이 우리를 다른 사람들보다 더 깊은 수준으로 이해할 것으로 생각하기 때문이다.

문제풀이

① [문장의 동사]
why가 이끄는 절의 주어구는 places like Little Italy, Chinatown, and Koreatown이므로 동사가 필요하다. 따라서 exist는 복수주어에 맞게 복수동사가 적절하게 쓰였다.
② [대동사 do]
앞에 언급된 일반동사 share, look을 대신하는 동사가 필요하므로 대동사 do는 적절하게 쓰였다.
③ [관계대명사]
뒤에 불완전한 문장(is rooted in how our species developed)이 왔고, 앞에 a very common human tendency라는 선행사가 왔으므로 what을 that으로 고쳐 써야 한다.
④ [대명사]
대명사 it은 앞에 언급된 something unfamiliar or foreign을 가리키기 때문에 적절하게 쓰였다.
⑤ [사역동사]
사역동사 make의 목적격보어로 동사원형인 relate는 적절하게 쓰였다.

어휘·어구

get along with ~와 잘 지내다
seek ~ out (특히 많은 노력을 기울여) ~을 찾아내다
exist 존재하다
religion 종교
value 가치관
saying 속담, 옛말
birds of a feather flock together 유유상종(類類相從)
common 흔한, 공동의
tendency 경향, 경향성
be rooted in ~에 뿌리박혀 있다
be conditioned to ~에 조건화되어 있다
unfamiliar 친숙하지 않은
likelihood 가능성
similarity 유사성
relate 마음이 통하다

4. ④ 식품 속 미네랄의 감소 원인

직독/직해

The reduction of minerals in our food / is the result /
우리의 식품 속 미네랄의 감소는 / 결과이다 /
of using pesticides and fertilizers /
살충제와 비료를 사용하는 것의 /
that kill off beneficial bacteria, earthworms, and

bugs /
이로운 박테리아, 지렁이 그리고 벌레를 죽이는 /
in the soil / that create many of the essential nutrients /
토양에 있는 / 많은 필수 영양소를 만들어 내는 /
in the first place / 우선적으로 /
and prevent the uptake of nutrients into the plant.
그리고 식물로의 영양소 흡수를 막는
Fertilizing crops with nitrogen and potassium /
농작물에 질소와 포타슘으로 비료를 주는 것은 /
has led to declines / 감소로 이어져 왔다 /
in magnesium, zinc, iron and iodine.
마그네슘, 아연, 철 그리고 아이오딘의
For example, / 예를 들어 /
there has been on average about a 30% decline /
평균적으로 약 30%의 감소가 있었다 /
in the magnesium content of wheat.
밀의 마그네슘 함량에서
This is partly due to potassium /
이는 부분적으로 포타슘 때문이다 /
being a blocker against magnesium absorption by plants.
식물에 의한 마그네슘 흡수에 방해물이 되는
Lower magnesium levels in soil also occur /
토양의 더 낮은 마그네슘 수치는 또한 나타난다 /
with acidic soils / 산성 토양에서 /
and around 70% of the farmland on earth is now acidic.
그리고 지구상에 있는 농지의 약 70%가 현재 산성이다
Thus, / the overall characteristics of soil determine the accumulation /
따라서 / 토양의 전반적인 특성은 축적을 결정한다 /
of minerals in plants.
식물 속 미네랄의
Indeed, / nowadays our soil is less healthy /
실제로 / 오늘날 우리의 토양은 덜 건강하다 /
and so are the plants grown on it.
그리고 그 위에서 길러진 식물도 그러하다

우리의 식품 속 미네랄의 감소는 우선적으로 많은 필수 영양소를 만들어 내는 토양에 있는 이로운 박테리아, 지렁이 그리고 벌레를 죽이고 식물로의 영양소 흡수를 막는 살충제와 비료를 사용하는 것의 결과이다. 농작물에 질소와 포타슘으로 비료를 주는 것은 마그네슘, 아연, 철 그리고 아이오딘의 감소로 이어져 왔다. 예를 들어 밀의 마그네슘 함량에서 평균적으로 약 30%의 감소가 있었다. 이는 부분적으로 포타슘이 식물에 의한 마그네슘 흡수에 방해물이 되기 때문이다. 토양의 더 낮은 마그네슘 수치는 산성 토양에서도 나타나는데 지구상에 있는 농지의 약 70%가 현재 산성이다. 따라서 토양의 전반적인 특성은 식물 속 미네랄의 축적을 결정한다. 실제로 오늘날 우리의 토양은 덜 건강하고 그 위에서 길러진 식물도 그러하다.

문제풀이

① [관계대명사 that]
that은 pesticides and fertilizers를 선행사로 하고, 동사 kill off의 주어로 쓰인 주격 관계대명사로 올바르게 사용되었다.

② [주어 동사의 수일치]
동사 has의 주어는 동명사 Fertilizing이고, 동명사는 단수 취급하므로 올바르게 사용되었다.

③ [동명사]
being은 전치사 due to의 목적어로 쓰였고, potassium은 동명사의 의미상의 주어로 쓰인 것으로 올바르게 사용되었다.

④ [정동사 vs 준동사]
and 뒤에 완전한 문장이 있으므로 그 앞의 문장도 역시 주어 동사를 갖춘 완전한 문장이 되어야 한다. 따라서 주어 Lower magnesium levels의 동사가 필요하므로 준동사 'occurring'을 정동사 'occur'로 고쳐야 한다.

⑤ [과거분사]
grown은 명사 the plants를 수식하는 분사로 식물이 길러지는 수동의 의미이므로 과거분사를 사용한 것은 올바른 용법이다.

어휘·어구

reduction 감소
beneficial 이로운
essential 필수적인
nutrient 영양소
in the first place 우선적으로
prevent 막다
nitrogen 질소
decline 감소하다
on average 평균적으로
content 함량
wheat 밀, 소맥
absorption 흡수
occur 나타나다
overall 전반적으로
characteristic 특성
determine 결정하다

정답률 

5. ② Say의 법칙

직독/직해

An economic theory of Say's Law holds /
경제이론인 Say의 법칙은 주장한다 /
that everything that's made / will get sold.
만들어진 모든 물품은 / 팔리기 마련이라고
The money from anything that's produced /
생산된 모든 물품으로부터 나오는 돈은 /
is used to buy something else.
다른 물품을 사는 데 사용된다
There can never be a situation / in which a firm finds /
상황은 절대 있을 수 없다 / 한 회사가 알게 되는 /
that it can't sell its goods / 물품을 팔 수 없어서 /
and so has to dismiss workers / 직원들을 해고해야 하는 /
and close its factories. 그리고 공장의 문을 닫아야 하는
Therefore, / 따라서 /
recessions and unemployment are impossible.
경기 후퇴와 실업은 불가능하다
Picture the level of spending / 지출의 정도를 상상해 보아라 /
like the level of water in a bath. 욕조 안의 물 높이로
Say's Law applies / Say의 법칙은 적용된다 /
because people use all their earnings /
사람들이 그들의 수입 전부를 사용하기 때문에 /
to buy things. 물품을 사는 데
But what happens / 하지만 무슨 일이 일어날까 /
if people don't spend all their money, /
만약 사람들이 그들의 돈을 전부 쓰지 않는다면 /
saving some of it instead?
대신 돈의 일부를 모으면서
Savings are a 'leakage' of spending /
저축은 지출의 '누수'이다 /
from the economy. 경제에서
You're probably imagining / 당신은 아마 상상하고 있을 것이다 /
the water level now falling, / 물 높이가 지금 낮아지고 있는 것을 /
so there's less spending / in the economy.
즉 지출이 적어지는 것을 / 경제에서
That would mean / firms producing less /
그것은 의미할 것이다 / 회사들이 더 적게 생산하는 것을 /
and dismissing some of their workers.
그리고 일부 직원들을 해고하는 것을

경제이론인 Say의 법칙은 만들어진 모든 물품은 팔리기 마련이라고 주장한다. 생산된 모든 물품으로부터 나오는 돈은 다른 물품을 사는 데 사용된다. 한 회사가 물품을 팔 수 없어서 직원들을 해고하고 공장의 문을 닫아야 하는 상황은 절대 있을 수 없다. 따라서 경기 후퇴와 실업은 불가능하다. 지출의 정도를 욕조 안의 물 높이로 상상해 보아라. Say의 법칙은 사람들이 그들의 수입 전부를 물품을 사는 데 사용하기 때문에 적용된다. 하지만 만약 사람들이 그들의 돈을 전부 사용하는 대신, 돈의 일부를 모은다면 무슨 일이 일어날까? 경제에서 저축은 지출의 '누수'이다. 당신은 아마 물 높이가 지금 낮아지고 있는 것, 즉 경제에서 지출이 적어지는 것을 상상하고 있을 것이다. 그것은 회사들이 더 적게 생산하고 일부 직원들을 해고하는 것을 의미할 것이다.

문제풀이

① [to부정사의 관용표현]
「be used to do」는 '~하는 데 사용되다'라는 표현으로 to 뒤에 동사원형 buy는 적절하게 쓰였다.

② [전치사+관계대명사]
which 뒤에 완전한 문장이 왔고, a situation을 선행사로 취해야 하므로 관계대명사 앞에 전치사 in을 써야 한다.

③ [접속사]
because 뒤에 주어(people)와 동사(use)로 이루어진 절이 왔으므로 이유의 접속사 because는 적절하게 쓰였다.

④ [지시대명사]
앞에 있는 명사 their money를 받는 지시대명사 it은 적절히게 쓰였다.

⑤ [동명사]
문장의 동사 mean의 목적어로 동명사 producing과 dismissing이 접속사 and로 병렬적으로 연결되었다. firms는 동명사의 의미상의 주어이다.

어휘·어구

situation 상황
dismiss 해고하다
unemployment 실업
apply 적용되다
leakage 누출, 누수

정답률 

6. ⑤ 진짜 미소와 가짜 미소의 구분법

직독/직해

There have been occasions /
경우들이 있었다 /
in which you have observed a smile /
당신이 미소를 관찰했던 /
and you could sense / it was not genuine.
그리고 당신이 느낄 수 있는 / 그것이 진짜가 아니라고
The most obvious way / 가장 명확한 방법은 /
of identifying a genuine smile from an insincere one /
진짜 미소와 거짓 미소를 알아보는 /
is that a fake smile primarily only affects /
가짜 미소는 주로 영향을 미친다는 것이다 /
the lower half of the face, /
얼굴의 절반 아래쪽 부분에만 /
mainly with the mouth alone. 주로 입에만
The eyes don't really get involved.
눈은 실제로 관련이 없다
Take the opportunity to look in the mirror /
거울을 볼 기회를 잡아라 /
and manufacture a smile / 그리고 미소를 지어봐라 /
using the lower half your face only.
당신의 얼굴의 절반 아랫부분만을 사용해서
When you do this, / 당신이 이렇게 할 때 /
judge how happy your face really looks /
당신의 얼굴이 실제로 얼마나 행복해 보이는지를 판단해 봐라
— is it genuine? 그것은 진짜인가
A genuine smile will impact /
진짜 미소는 영향을 줄 것이다 /
on the muscles and wrinkles around the eyes /
눈 주변의 근육과 주름에 /
and less noticeably, / 그리고 티가 덜 나게 /
the skin between the eyebrow and upper eyelid /
눈썹과 윗눈꺼풀 사이의 피부가 /
is lowered slightly / with true enjoyment.

살짝 내려온다 / 진정한 즐거움으로

The genuine smile can impact / on the entire face.
진짜 미소는 영향을 줄 수 있다 / 얼굴 전체에

당신이 미소를 관찰했는데 그것이 진짜가 아니라고 느낄 수 있는 경우들이 있었다. 진짜 미소와 거짓 미소를 알아보는 가장 명확한 방법은 가짜 미소는 주로 입에만, 얼굴의 절반 아래쪽 부분에만 주로 영향을 미친다는 것이다. 눈은 실제로 관련이 없다. 거울을 볼 기회를 잡아서 당신의 얼굴의 절반 아랫부분만을 사용해서 미소를 지어봐라. 당신이 이렇게 할 때, 당신의 얼굴이 실제로 얼마나 행복해 보이는지를 판단해 봐라. 그것은 진짜인가? 진짜 미소는 눈 주변의 근육과 주름에 영향을 줄 것이고, 티가 덜 나게 눈썹과 윗눈꺼풀 사이의 피부가 진정한 즐거움으로 살짝 내려온다. 진짜 미소는 얼굴 전체에 영향을 줄 수 있다.

문제풀이

① [전치사+관계대명사]
in which 뒤에 완전한 절이 왔고 앞에 있는 occasions를 선행사로 취해야 하므로 '전치사+관계대명사'인 in which는 적절하게 쓰였다.
② [대명사]
앞에 있는 a smile을 가리키는 대명사 one은 적절하게 쓰였다.
③ [현재분사]
명령문에서, 생략된 주어 you가 얼굴 절반 아랫부분을 사용하는 주체가 되므로, 능동의 의미를 갖는 현재분사 using은 적절하게 쓰였다.
④ [간접의문문]
동사 judge의 목적어 역할을 하고, 형용사 happy를 수식해야 하므로 의문부사 how는 적절하게 쓰였고, '주어+동사'의 간접의문문의 어순도 적절하다.
⑤ [주어와 동사의 수일치]
and 뒤 문장의 주어가 the skin between the eyebrow and upper eyelid이므로 단수동사 is로 고쳐야 한다.

어휘·어구

occasion 경우, 때
genuine 진짜의
obvious 명백한
identify 확인하다
insincere 거짓의
primarily 주로
affect ~에게 영향을 주다
involved 관련이 있는
manufacture 짓다, 제조하다
judge 판단하다
impact 영향을 주다
wrinkle 주름
noticeably 눈에 띄게
slightly 살짝, 약간
enjoyment 즐거움, 기쁨
entire 전체의

7. ③ 악기를 탐구하는 시간의 중요성

직독/직해

Although there is usually a correct way /
비록 올바른 방법이 대체로 있다고 해도 /

of holding and playing musical instruments, /
악기를 잡고 연주하는 /

the most important instruction to begin with /
먼저 가장 중요한 가르침은 /

is that they are not toys /
악기가 장난감이 아니라는 것이다 /

and that they must be looked after.
그리고 악기는 관리되어야 한다는 것(이다)

Allow children time /
아이들에게 시간을 주어라 /

to explore ways of handling and playing the instruments /
악기를 다루고 연주하는 방법을 탐구할 /

for themselves / before showing them.
직접 / 그것들을 알려 주기 전에

Finding different ways to produce sounds /
소리를 만들어 내는 여러 방법을 찾는 것은 /

is an important stage of musical exploration.
음악적 탐구의 중요한 단계이다

Correct playing comes from the desire /
정확한 연주는 욕구에서 나온다 /

to find the most appropriate sound quality /
가장 알맞은 음질을 찾으려는 /

and find the most comfortable playing position /
그리고 가장 편안한 연주 자세를 찾으려는 /

so that one can play with control / over time.
잘 다루면서 연주할 수 있도록 / 오랜 시간 동안

As instruments and music become more complex, /
악기와 음악이 더 복잡해짐에 따라 /

learning appropriate playing techniques /
알맞은 연주 기술을 익히는 것은 /

becomes increasingly relevant.
점점 더 유의미해진다

비록 악기를 잡고 연주하는 올바른 방법이 대체로 있다고 해도, 먼저 가장 중요한 가르침은 악기가 장난감이 아니라는 것과 악기는 관리되어야 한다는 것이다. 아이들에게 (악기를 직접 다루고 연주하는) 방법을 알려 주기 전에 악기를 직접 다루고 연주하는 방법을 탐구할 시간을 주어라. 소리를 만들어 내는 여러 방법을 찾는 것은 음악적 탐구의 중요한 단계이다. 정확한 연주는 가장 알맞은 음질을 찾고 오랜 시간 동안 잘 다루면서 연주할 수 있도록 가장 편안한 연주 자세를 찾으려는 욕구에서 나온다. 악기와 음악이 더 복잡해짐에 따라, 알맞은 연주 기술을 익히는 것은 점점 더 유의미해진다.

문제풀이

① [명사절 접속사 that]
동사 is의 보어 역할을 하는 명사절을 이끄는 접속사 that은 적절하게 쓰였다.
② [명령문]
문장의 형태가 명령문이므로 Allow는 적절하게 쓰였다.
③ [주어와 동사의 수일치]
동명사구인 Finding different ways to produce sounds가 문장의 주어이고, 동명사구는 단수 취급하므로 단수동사인 is로 바꿔 써야 한다.
④ [to부정사의 형용사적 용법]
앞에 있는 the desire를 수식하는 형용사적 용법의 to 부정사 to find는 적절하게 쓰였다.
⑤ [부사]
형용사 relevant를 수식하는 부사 increasingly는 적절하게 쓰였다.

어휘·어구

correct 옳은, 정확한
musical instrument 악기
instruction 가르침, 지도
to begin with 우선, 먼저
look after ~을 관리하다, ~을 돌보다
explore 탐구하다, 탐험하다
handle 다루다
produce 만들어 내다, 생산하다
stage 단계
desire 욕구, 욕망
appropriate 알맞은
quality 질, 품질
comfortable 편안한
position 자세
complex 복잡한
technique 기술
increasingly 점점
relevant 유의미한, 관련된

8. ② 동물의 냄새 인식은 그들의 생태에 달려있다

직독/직해

Each species of animals can detect /
각각의 동물 종들은 감지할 수 있다 /

a different range of odours.
서로 다른 범주의 냄새를

No species can detect all the molecules /
어떤 종도 모든 분자를 감지할 수는 없다 /

that are present in the environment /
환경에 존재하는 /

in which it lives / 그것이 살고 있는 /

— there are some things / that we cannot smell /
몇 가지 것들이 있다 / 우리는 냄새를 맡을 수 없는 /

but which some other animals can, / and vice versa.
하지만 몇몇 다른 동물들은 냄새를 맡을 수 있는 / 그 반대의 경우도 있다

There are also differences between individuals, /
개체들 간의 차이 역시 존재한다 /

relating to the ability to smell an odour, /
어떤 냄새를 맡을 수 있는 능력과 관련된 /

or how pleasant it seems.
혹은 그것이 얼마나 좋은 느낌을 주는지(와 관련된)

For example, / some people like the taste of coriander /
예를 들어 / 어떤 사람들은 고수의 맛을 좋아한다 /

— known as cilantro in the USA /
미국에서 고수(cilantro)라고 알려진 /

— while others find it soapy and unpleasant.
반면에 다른 사람들은 그것이 비누 맛이 나고 불쾌하다고 여긴다

This effect has an underlying genetic component /
이런 결과에는 내재된 유전적인 요소가 있다 /

due to differences in the genes /
유전자에서의 차이로 인하여 /

controlling our sense of smell.
우리의 후각을 조절하는

Ultimately, / 궁극적으로 /

the selection of scents detected by a given species, /
특정 종들에 의해 감지된 냄새들의 집합은 /

and how that odour is perceived, /
그리고 그 냄새가 어떻게 인식되는가는 /

will depend upon the animal's ecology.
그 동물의 생태에 달려 있을 것이다.

The response profile of each species /
각 종의 반응 도표는 /

will enable it to locate sources of smell /
그 종이 냄새의 원천을 찾게 해 줄 것이다 /

that are relevant to it / and to respond accordingly.
자신과 관련된 / 그리고 그에 따라 반응할 수 있게 (해 줄 것이다)

각각의 동물 종들은 서로 다른 범주의 냄새를 감지할 수 있다. 어떤 종도 그것이 살고 있는 환경에 존재하는 모든 분자를 감지할 수는 없는데, 우리는 냄새를 맡을 수 없지만 몇몇 다른 동물들은 냄새를 맡을 수 있는 몇 가지 것들이 있고, 그 반대의 경우도 있다. 어떤 냄새를 맡을 수 있는 능력이나 그것이 얼마나 좋은 느낌을 주는지와 관련된 개체들 간의 차이 역시 존재한다. 예를 들어, 어떤 사람들은 미국에서 고수(cilantro)라고 알려진 고수(coriander)의 맛을 좋아하는 반면, 다른 사람들은 그것이 비누 맛이 나고 불쾌하다고 여긴다. 이런 결과에는 우리의 후각을 조절하는 유전자에서의 차이로 인하여 내재된 유전적인 요소가 있다. 궁극적으로, 특정 종들에 의해 감지된 냄새들의 집합 그리고 그 냄새가 어떻게 인식되는가는 그 동물의 생태에 달려 있을 것이다. 각 종의 반응 도표는 그 종이 자신과 관련된 냄새의 원천을 찾고 그에 따라 반응할 수 있게 해 줄 것이다.

문제풀이

① [전치사+관계대명사]
which 뒤에 완전한 문장이 왔고, the environment를 선행사로 하는 「전치사+관계대명사」 in which는 적절하게 쓰였다.
② [형용사]
seems의 보어 역할을 하는 형용사가 필요하므로 pleasantly는 pleasant로 바꿔야 한다. 「it seems+

형용사」는 '~처럼 보이다'라는 의미이다.

③ [대명사]

it은 앞에 있는 the taste of coriander를 가리키는 대명사로 적절하게 쓰였다.

④ [분사]

controlling our sense of smell은 앞에 있는 the genes를 수식하는 역할을 하며, the genes와 controlling은 능동의 관계이다. 따라서 현재분사 controlling은 적절하게 쓰였다.

⑤ [to부정사]

enable은 목적격보어로 to부정사를 취하는 동사이므로 to locate는 적절하게 쓰였다. 「enable+목적어+to-v」는 '…가 ~을 가능하게 하다'라는 의미이다.

《 어휘·어구 》

detect 감지하다, 발견하다
range 범위, 범주
odour 냄새
molecule 분자
present 있는, 존재하는
vice versa 반대도 같음
individual 개체
underlying 근원적인
genetic component 유전 요소[성분]
ultimately 궁극적으로
scent 냄새
perceive 인지하다, 감지하다
ecology 생태
response profile 반응 도표
enable A to do A가 ~할 수 있게 하다
be relevant to ~와 관련이 있다
respond 반응하다
accordingly 그에 맞춰

9. ④ 음식 평가와 시각정보

직독/직해

Although it is obvious that part of our assessment of food is its visual appearance, /
비록 음식에 대한 우리 평가의 일부가 음식의 시각적 외관인 것은 분명하지만 /
it is perhaps surprising how visual input can override taste and smell.
어떻게 시각적인 입력 정보가 맛과 냄새에 우선할 수 있는가는 놀라울 것이다
People find it very difficult to correctly identify fruit-flavoured drinks /
사람들은 과일 맛이 나는 음료를 정확하게 식별하는 것이 매우 어렵다는 것을 알게 된다 /
if the colour is wrong, / 색깔이 잘못되어 있다면 /
for instance an orange drink that is coloured green.
만약 예를 들어 초록색 빛깔의 오렌지 음료와 같이
Perhaps even more striking is the experience of wine tasters.
포도주 맛을 감정하는 사람들의 경험은 훨씬 더 놀라울 것이다
One study of Bordeaux University students of wine and wine making /
포도주와 포도주 제조에 관해 공부하는 Bordeaux University 학생들을 대상으로 한 연구는 /
revealed that 다음을 보여주었다
they chose tasting notes appropriate for red wines, /
그들은 적포도주에 적합한 시음표를 선택했다 /
such as 'prune and chocolate', /
'자두와 초콜릿'과 같은 /
when they were given white wine coloured with a red dye.
그들이 붉은색 색소로 물들인 백포도주를 받았을 때
Experienced New Zealand wine experts /
숙련된 뉴질랜드 포도주 전문가들도 /
were similarly tricked into thinking that /
그와 비슷하게 속아서 다음과 같이 생각하게 되었다 /
the white wine Chardonnay was in fact a red wine, /
백포도주 Chardonnay가 실제로 적포도주라고 /
when it had been coloured with a red dye.
그것이 붉은색 색소로 물들였을 때

비록 음식에 대한 우리 평가의 일부가 음식의 시각적 외관인 것은 분명하지만, 어떻게 시각적인 입력 정보가 맛과 냄새에 우선할 수 있는가는 놀라울 것이다. 만약 예를 들어 초록색 빛깔의 오렌지 음료와 같이 색깔이 잘못되어 있다면, 사람들은 과일 맛이 나는 음료를 정확하게 식별하는 것이 매우 어렵다는 것을 알게 된다. 포도주 맛을 감정하는 사람들의 경험은 훨씬 더 놀라울 것이다. 포도주와 포도주 제조에 관해 공부하는 Bordeaux University 학생들을 대상으로 한 연구는 그들이 붉은색 색소로 물들인 백포도주를 받았을 때, '자두와 초콜릿'과 같은 적포도주에 적합한 시음표를 선택했다는 것을 보여주었다. 숙련된 뉴질랜드 포도주 전문가들도 마찬가지로 백포도주 Chardonnay를 붉은색 색소로 물들였을 때, 속아서 그것이 실제로 적포도주라고 생각하게 되었다.

문제풀이

① [의문사가 이끄는 명사절]

의문사 how가 이끄는 명사절이 형식상의 주어 it에 대해 내용상의 주어 역할을 하고 있으며 '의문사 + 주어 + 동사'의 어순으로 바르게 쓰였다.

② [5형식 동사]

불완전타동사 find의 목적격보어로서 형용사인 difficult가 바르게 쓰였다.

③ [주어와 동사의 수일치]

보어가 문두로 나가면서 주어와 동사가 도치된 문장이다. 주어 the experience of wine tasters에 대한 동사로서 단수형인 is는 바르게 쓰였다.

④ [수동태]

주어 they가 white wine을 주는 것이 아닌 받는 대상이므로 gave는 수동태인 were given으로 바꿔 써야 한다.

⑤ [명사절 접속사]

동명사 thinking의 목적어 역할을 하는 명사절을 이끄는 접속사 that이 바르게 쓰였다.

《 어휘·어구 》

obvious 명백한, 명확한
assessment 평가
appearance 외관, 겉보기
identify 인지하다, 확인하다
striking 인상적인, 현저한
reveal 드러내다, 알리다
dye 색소, 음료
be tricked into ~하도록 속임을 당하다

10. ④ 발달과정에 미치는 또래 집단의 강력한 영향

직독/직해

Positively or negatively, / our parents and families /
긍정적이든 부정적이든 / 우리의 부모와 가족은 우리에게 /
are powerful influences on us. 강력한 영향을 미친다
But even stronger, / especially when we're young, /
그러나 훨씬 강하다 / 특히 우리가 어렸을 때 /
are our friends. 우리의 친구들이
We often choose friends /
우리는 종종 친구들을 선택한다 /
as a way of expanding our sense of identity /
우리의 정체성을 확장하는 방법으로 /
beyond our families. 가족의 범위를 넘어서
As a result, / the pressure to conform /
그 결과 / 부합해야 한다는 압박감이 /
to the standards and expectations of friends and other social groups /
친구와 다른 사회 집단의 기준과 기대에 /
is likely to be intense. 거세질 가능성이 있다
Judith Rich Harris, / Judith Rich Harris는 /
who is a developmental psychologist, / argues /
발달 심리학자인 / 주장한다 /
that three main forces shape our development: /
세 가지 주요한 힘이 우리의 발달을 형성한다고 /
personal temperament, our parents, and our peers.
개인적인 기질, 우리의 부모, 우리의 또래들
The influence of peers, / she argues, /
또래들의 영향은 / 그녀는 주장한다 /
is much stronger / than that of parents.
훨씬 더 강하다 / 부모의 영향보다
"The world / that children share with their peers," /
세상은 / 아이들이 그들의 또래들과 공유하는 /
she says, / 그녀는 말한다 /
"is what shapes their behavior /
그들의 행동을 형성하는 것이다 /
and modifies the characteristics /
그리고 특성을 수정하는 것이다 /
they were born with, / 그들이 가지고 태어난 /
and hence determines / the sort of people /
따라서 결정한다 / 사람의 종류를 /
they will be / when they grow up."
그들이 될 / 그들이 성장했을 때

긍정적이든 부정적이든, 우리의 부모와 가족은 우리에게 강력한 영향을 미친다. 하지만 특히 우리가 어렸을 때, 훨씬 더 강한 영향을 주는 것은 우리의 친구들이다. 가족의 범위를 넘어서 우리의 정체성을 확장하는 방법으로 우리는 친구들을 선택한다. 그 결과, 친구와 다른 사회 집단의 기준과 기대에 부합해야 한다는 압박감이 거세질 가능성이 있다. 발달 심리학자 Judith Rich Harris는 우리의 발달을 형성하는 세 가지 주요한 힘은 개인적인 기질, 우리의 부모, 우리의 또래들이라고 주장한다. 또래들의 영향은 부모의 영향보다 훨씬 더 강하다고 그녀는 주장한다. "아이들이 그들의 또래들과 공유하는 세상은 그들의 행동을 형성하는 것이고, 그들이 가지고 태어난 특성을 수정하는 것이며, 따라서 그들이 자라서 어떤 사람이 될지를 결정하는 것이다."라고 그녀는 말한다.

문제풀이

① [비교급]

비교급은 강조부사 even의 수식을 받으므로, 비교급 stronger는 올바른 표현이다.

② [동명사]

동명사는 전치사 of의 목적어 역할을 하면서 our sense of identity를 목적어로 취할 수 있으므로, 동명사 expanding은 올바른 표현이다.

③ [주어와 동사의 수일치]

주어가 The pressure로 단수명사이므로, 단수동사 is는 올바른 표현이다.

④ [정동사 VS 준동사]

문장의 주어가 Judith Rich Harris이고 그 뒤에 관계사절(who is~)이 연결되어 주어와 동사가 멀어진 구조로, arguing을 정동사 argues로 고쳐야 한다.

⑤ [관계대명사]

The world를 선행사로 하고, 관계절 내에 타동사 share의 목적어가 비어있는 구조이므로, 관계대명사 that은 올바른 표현이다.

이렇게 풀자 어법상 틀린 부분을 찾는 문제는 밑줄 친 부분이 포함된 문장의 구조를 파악해야 한다.

① 비교급에 밑줄이 있는 경우에는 원급, 비교급, 최상급 등의 비교표현이 올바르게 쓰였는가를 확인해야 한다. 이 문장에서는 앞의 even이 비교급을 강조하는 표현이고 문맥상으로도 비교급을 사용해야 하므로 올바르게 사용되었다.
② -ing 형태에 밑줄이 있는 경우에는 우선은 정동사를 쓸 자리인지, 준동사를 써야 할 자리인지를 확인해야 한다. 전치사의 목적어 역할을 하며 명사구를 목적어로 취할 수 있는 것은 동명사이다.
③ 동사에 밑줄이 있는 경우에는 '수, 시제, 태'등을 확인해야 한다. 주어가 to부정사구의 수식을 받는 단수명사 The pressure이고, 'is'는 자동사로 수동태가 될 수 없으며, 문맥상 현재시제를 쓴 것이다.
④ -ing 형태에 밑줄이 있는 경우에는 정동사를 쓸 자리인지, 준동사를 써야 할 자리인지를 확인해야 한다. 밑줄

이 포함된 문장은 '주어 + 관계사절 + 동사 + that절'의 구조이므로, 동명사 arguing은 정동사인 argues로 바꿔 어야 한다.
⑤ that에 밑줄이 있는 경우에는 that의 용법이 올바르게 쓰였는가를 확인해야 한다. that은 절을 이끌 경우에는 '관계대명사절, 관계부사절, 명사절, 부사절'을 이끌 수 있다. 이 문장에서는 The world를 선행사로 하고, that이 이끄는 절 안에서 타동사 share의 목적어가 비어있는 구조이므로, that은 관계대명사로 쓰인 것이다.

《 어휘·어구 》

expand 확장하다
identity 정체성
beyond ~을 넘어서
pressure 압박감
conform 부합하다, 순응하다
intense 강렬한
peer 또래
behavior 행동
modify 수정하다
characteristic 특성
hence 그러므로

11. ④ 빛의 질의 중요성

직독/직해

Bad lighting can increase stress / on your eyes, /
나쁜 조명은 스트레스를 높일 수 있다 / 당신의 눈에 /
as can light that is too bright, /
너무 밝은 빛이 그럴 수 있는 것처럼 /
or light that shines directly into your eyes.
또는 당신의 눈에 직접적으로 비추는 빛이
Fluorescent lighting can also be tiring.
형광등도 역시 피로감을 줄 수 있다
What you may not appreciate is /
당신이 모를 수도 있는 것은 ~이다 /
that the quality of light may also be important.
빛의 질도 역시 중요할 수 있다는 것
Most people are happiest in bright sunshine— /
대부분의 사람은 밝은 햇빛 속에서 가장 행복하다 /
this may cause a release of chemicals in the body /
이것은 체내의 화학물질을 분비시킬 수도 있다 /
that bring a feeling of emotional well-being.
정서적인 행복감을 주는
Artificial light, which typically contains /
전형적으로 들어있는 인공조명이 /
only a few wavelengths of light, / 단지 몇 개의 빛 파장만 /
does not seem to have the same effect on mood /
분위기에 미치는 효과는 똑같지 않을 수 있다 /
that sunlight has. 햇빛이 미치는
Try experimenting / with working by a window /
실험해 보아라 / 창가에서 작업하거나 /
or using full spectrum bulbs / in your desk lamp.
또는 모든 파장이 있는 전구를 이용하여 / 책상 전등에 있는
You will probably find / 당신은 아마도 알게 될 것이다 /
that this improves the quality of your working environment.
이것이 당신의 작업 환경의 질을 향상시킨다는 것을

너무 밝은 빛이나, 눈에 직접적으로 비추는 빛처럼, 나쁜 조명은 당신의 눈에 스트레스를 높일 수 있다. 형광등도 역시 피로감을 줄 수 있다. 당신이 모를 수도 있는 것은 빛의 질도 역시 중요할 수 있다는 것이다. 대부분의 사람은 밝은 햇빛 속에서 가장 행복한데, 이것은 아마 정서적인 행복감을 주는 체내의 화학물질을 분비시킬 수도 있다. 전형적으로 단지 몇 개의 빛 파장만 들어있는 인공조명이 분위기에 미치는 효과는 햇빛이 미치는 효과와 똑같지 않을 수 있다. 창가에서 작업하거나 책상 전등에 있는 모든 파장이 있는 전구를 이용하여 실험해 보아라. 당신은 이것이 당신의 작업 환경의 질을 향상시킨다는 것을 아마도 알게 될 것이다.

문제풀이

① 동사 shines를 수식하는 부사로 directly가 온 것은 적절하다.
② 주어인 형광등이 '피로감을 주는' 것으로 능동의 의미이다. 따라서 현재분사 tiring이 온 것은 적절하다.
③ that은 뒤에 이어지는 절에서 주어 역할을 하며 선행사 chemicals를 수식하는 주격 관계대명사절을 이끌고 있으므로, 관계대명사 that이 온 것은 적절하다.
④ Artificial light가 주어이고, which typically contains only a few wavelengths of light는 Artificial light에 대해 부연 설명해 주는 계속적 용법의 관계대명사절이다. 따라서 단수 주어인 Artificial light에 맞춰 does로 고쳐야 한다.
⑤ 등위접속사 or에 의해 전치사 with의 목적어 역할을 하는 동명사 working과 병렬구조를 이루어야 하므로, 마찬가지로 using이 온 것은 적절하다.
따라서 정답은 ④이다.

이렇게 풀자_ 어법상 틀린 부분을 찾는 문제는 밑줄이 있는 부분의 형태와 문맥을 보고 어법에 맞게 쓰였는지 확인해야 한다.
① 부사는 동사의 앞이나 뒤에서 동사를 수식하거나 문장의 앞이나 뒤에서 문장 전체를 수식할 수 있다. 부사에 밑줄이 있는 경우는 보어처럼 부사가 아니라 형용사가 와야 하는 위치가 아닌지 살피도록 한다.
② 현재분사는 명사를 앞, 뒤에서 수식하거나, 문장의 보어 역할을 할 수 있다. 보어 역할을 할 경우 주어와의 의미 관계에 유의해야 하는데, 능동일 때는 현재분사가 수동일 때는 과거분사가 와야 한다.
③ 관계대명사에 밑줄이 있는 경우 선행사의 종류 및 격에 따라 적절하게 쓰였는지 살펴봐야 한다. 특히 선행사의 유무에 따라 선행사를 포함하고 있는 관계대명사 what이 들어가야 하는 것은 아닌지 주의 깊게 보도록 한다.
④ 동사에 밑줄이 그어진 경우는 주어, 동사의 수일치를 묻는 문제가 많다. 특히 관계대명사절 및 전치사구와 같은 수식어구 또는 삽입절이 주어와 동사 사이에 위치해 있는 경우, 주어가 무엇인지를 분명히 파악해야 한다.
⑤ 등위접속사 뒤에 위치한 -ing에 밑줄이 있는 경우는 병렬구조가 아닌지 확인해 본다.

《 어휘·어구 》

appreciate 인식하다
release 분비
chemical 화학 물질
emotional 감정의, 정서적인
artificial 인공의
typically 전형적으로, 보통
wavelength 파장
full spectrum 흰색을 구성하는 모든 종류의 가시 파장의
bulb 전구

정답률 35%

12. ③ 미세 플라스틱

직독/직해

Plastic is extremely slow to degrade /
플라스틱은 아주 느리게 분해된다 /
and tends to float, / 그리고 물에 떠다니는 경향이 있다 /
which allows it to travel in ocean currents /
이것이 그것을 해류를 따라 돌아다니게 해 준다 /
for thousands of miles. 수천 마일을
Most plastics break down into smaller and smaller pieces / 대부분의 플라스틱은 점점 더 작은 조각으로 분해된다 /
when exposed to ultraviolet (UV) light, /
자외선에 노출될 때 /
forming microplastics. 미세 플라스틱이 만들어진다
These microplastics are very difficult / to measure /
이러한 미세 플라스틱은 매우 어렵다 / 측정하기가
once they are small enough / to pass through the nets / typically used to collect them.
일단 그것들이 충분히 작아지면 / 그물망을 통과할 정도로 / 그것들을 수거하는 데 보통 사용되는
Their impacts on the marine environment and food webs / 해양 환경과 먹이 그물에 미치는 그것들의 영향은 /
are still poorly understood. 아직도 제대로 이해되지 않고 있다
These tiny particles are known to be eaten /
이렇게 작은 조각들은 먹힌다고 알려져 있다 /
by various animals / and to get into the food chain.
다양한 동물에게 / 먹이 사슬에 들어간다고 (알려져 있다)
Because most of the plastic particles in the ocean /
바닷속에 있는 대부분의 플라스틱 조각들은 /
are so small, / 너무 작다 /
there is no practical way / to clean up the ocean.
실질적인 방법은 없다 / 바다를 청소할
One would have to filter enormous amounts of water /
사람들은 막대한 양의 물을 여과해야 한다 /
to collect a relatively small amount of plastic.
비교적 적은 양의 플라스틱을 모으기 위해

플라스틱은 아주 느리게 분해되고 물에 떠다니는 경향이 있고, 이것이 플라스틱을 해류를 따라 수천 마일을 돌아다니게 해 준다. 대부분의 플라스틱은 자외선에 노출될 때 점점 더 작은 조각으로 분해되어 미세 플라스틱이 만들어진다. 이러한 미세 플라스틱은 일단 그것들을 수거하는 데 보통 사용되는 그물망을 통과할 정도로 충분히 작아지면 측정하기가 매우 어렵다. 미세 플라스틱이 해양 환경과 먹이 그물에 미치는 영향은 아직도 제대로 이해되지 않고 있다. 이렇게 작은 조각들은 다양한 동물에게 먹혀 먹이 사슬에 들어간다고 알려져 있다. 바닷속에 있는 대부분의 플라스틱 조각들은 너무 작아서 바다를 청소할 실질적인 방법은 없다. 비교적 적은 양의 플라스틱을 모으기 위해 막대한 양의 물을 여과해야 한다.

문제풀이

① 앞 문장 전체를 선행사로 하고 관계사절의 동사 allows의 주어 역할을 해야 하므로, 계속적 용법의 관계대명사 which가 온 것은 적절하다.
② 밑줄 친 -ing 앞에 컴마(,)가 있으므로 주절의 의미를 보충하는 분사구문이라는 것을 알 수 있는데, 문맥상 능동의 의미이므로 forming이 온 것은 적절하다.
③ collect의 목적어는 의미상 주어인 the nets를 가리키지 않고 the microplastics를 가리키므로, themselves를 them으로 바꿔 써야 한다.
④ most of the plastic particles가 주어이고 in the ocean은 주어를 수식하는 전치사구이므로, 복수 동사 are가 온 것은 적절하다.
⑤ relatively는 형용사 small을 수식하는 부사로 적절히 사용되었다.
따라서 정답은 ③이다.

이렇게 풀자_ 어법상 틀린 부분을 찾는 문제는 밑줄이 있는 부분의 형태와 문맥을 보고 어법에 맞게 쓰였는지 확인해야 한다. ①은 '관계대명사의 쓰임'을, ②는 '분사구문의 쓰임'을, ③은 '대명사의 역할'을, ④는 '주어-동사 일치'를, ⑤는 '부사의 역할'을 알아야 한다.

《 어휘·어구 》

extremely 극도로, 극히
float 떠가다
current 해류
break down 분해되다
expose 노출시키다
ultraviolet 자외선의
typically 보통, 대개
marine 해양의
particle 입자, 조각
practical 실질적인
filter 여과하다
relatively 비교적

본문 065쪽

문법 플러스 Ⅱ. 분사, 분사구문

1. dealing 2. designed 3. tiring
4. approaching 5. resulting
6. Being asked 7. dropping
8. trembling 9. crossed 10. serving

1 [해석]▶ 아버지는 무책임한 아이를 다루는 책임감 있는 사람이었다.
[해설]▶ 현재분사는 형용사와 같이 명사를 수식하는 역할을 할 수 있다. 무책임한 아이를 '다루는' 책임감 있는 사람이므로, 능동의 의미를 가지고 있는 현재분사 dealing이 나와 명사구 a responsible man을 수식해야 한다. 명사(man)와 현재분사(dealing) 사이에는 「관계대명사(who)+be동사(was)」가 생략되어 있다.

2 [해석]▶ 추측하는 대신에 과학자들은 그들의 생각이 사실인지 아니면 거짓인지 증명하도록 고안된 체계를 따른다.
[해설]▶ 과거분사는 형용사와 같이 명사를 수식하는 역할을 할 수 있다. a system이 '고안된' 대상이므로 과거분사인 designed가 나와야 한다. a system (which is) designed ~ 문장에서 「관계대명사+be동사」가 생략된 문장이다.

3 [해석]▶ 형광등도 역시 피로감을 줄 수 있다. 당신이 모를 수도 있는 것은 빛의 질도 역시 중요할 수 있다는 것이다.
[해설]▶ 분사는 주어의 상태를 설명하는 보어 역할을 할 수 있다. 문장 주어인 형광등이 '피로감을 주는' 것으로 능동의 의미이므로 주격보어 자리에는 현재분사가 tiring이 와야 한다.

4 [해석]▶ 만약에 당신이 가령 호모에렉투스처럼 정글을 돌아다니는 초기 인류라면, 당신은 동물이 다가오는 것을 볼지 모른다.
[해설]▶ 분사는 목적어의 상태를 설명하는 목적격보어의 역할을 할 수 있다. see는 지각동사로 목적어와 목적격보어가 능동 관계인 경우, 동사원형이나 현재분사를 취한다.

5 [해석]▶ 학생이 글을 다시 읽게 하는 질문을 던짐으로써 결국 동일한 글을 여러 번 읽게 함으로써 학생의 이해를 진전시키고 심화시키는 데 있어 교사는 적극적인 역할을 한다.
[해설]▶ 주절의 주어와 분사구문을 이끄는 주어가 능동 관계이면 현재분사가 이끄는 분사구문을 쓴다. resulting 이하는 결과를 의미하는 분사구문이다.

6 [해석]▶ 중국 식당 매니저에게 떠나도록 요청을 받고서, 그녀는 당황했다.
[해설]▶ 분사구문의 주어가 레스토랑 매니저에게 떠나도록 요청을 받은 것이므로 '수동분사구문'을 쓴다. When she was asked to leave~ 라는 부사절을 분사구문으로 바꾼 문장이다. (Being)을 생략한 채로 Asked ~로 주로 쓴다.

7 [해석]▶ 공책을 아래 떨어뜨린 후에 그녀는 Amy 옆 의자에 올라갔다.
[해설]▶ After she dropped ~라는 부사절을 분사구문으로 바꾼 문장이다. 분사구문은 문장의 의미를 명확히 보여주기 위해 접속사를 생략하지 않을 수 있다. 괄호 바로 뒤에 목적어가 있고, 분사구문의 주어와 주절의 주어가 능동 관계이므로 현재분사를 써야 한다.

8 [해석]▶ 그는 손을 떨며 관중을 바라보았다.
[해설]▶ 분사구문의 주어(His hands)와 주절의 주어(he)가 다를 때 분사구문의 주어를 분사 앞에 써 준다. 그의 손이 떠는 것이므로 능동의 현재분사를 써야 한다.

9 [해석]▶ 다리를 꼰 채로 그녀는 의자에 앉았다.
[해설]▶ 「with+목적어+분사」는 '…가 ~한 채로'의미이다. 목적어(her legs)와 분사(crossed)가 수동 관계이면 과거분사를 써야 한다.

10 해석▶ 오히려 비언어적 의사소통은 전달되고 있는 메시지 내용의 풍부함을 강화시키도록 도와주며, 보충으로서 기능해야 한다.
[해설]▶ serving이 이끄는 절은 부대상황을 나타내는 분사구문으로, 비언어적 의사소통이 메시지 내용의 풍부함을 강화시키도록 '도와주는' 것이므로 능동 형태인 serving을 써야 한다.

본문 066쪽

어휘 플러스 Ⅱ. 반의어 (3)

1. fertile 2. flexible
3. innocent 4. immoral
5. intolerable

1 [해석]▶ 포도나무의 뿌리가 땅 속으로 깊이 파고 들어가게 만들기 위해 우선 반드시 비옥한 땅은 아니더라도 배수 시설이 잘 된 비옥한 땅이 필요하다.

2 [해석]▶ 그 나뭇가지들은 복잡한 과정을 거쳐서 질겨지고 유연한 종이가 된다.

3 [해석]▶ 예를 들어, 미국의 법에 따르면 어떤 사람이 범죄로 고발되어도 그는 법정이 그 사람이 유죄라고 판정하기 전까지는 결백하다고 간주된다.

4 [해석]▶ 상처 입은 사람들은 그러한 행위를 심각한 결과를 수반하는 것으로, 그리고 용서할 수 없고 비도덕적인 진행 중에 있는 패턴의 일부로 바라보는 경향이 있다.

5 [해석]▶ 그들은 모두 불편해서 참을 수 없을 정도로 깨끗하고 잘 차려 입고 있었다.

12. 어휘 적절성 파악

Day 12 본문 068쪽

1. ⑤ 2. ② 3. ⑤ 4. ⑤ 5. ④
6. ③ 7. ③ 8. ③ 9. ② 10. ③

정답률 53%

대표 기출 ④ 식물의 성장은 옥신에 의해 조절됨

직독/직해

Plant growth is controlled /
식물의 성장은 조절된다 /
by a group of hormones called auxins /
옥신이라고 불리는 호르몬 그룹에 의해 /
found at the tips of stems and roots of plants.
식물의 줄기와 뿌리 끝에서 발견되는
Auxins produced at the tips of stems /
줄기 끝에서 생산된 옥신은 /
tend to accumulate / on the side of the stem /
축적되는 경향이 있다 / 줄기의 옆면에 /
that is in the shade.
그늘진 곳에 있는
Accordingly, / the auxins stimulate growth /
따라서 / 옥신은 성장을 자극한다 /
on the shaded side of the plant.
식물의 그늘진 면에서의
Therefore, / the shaded side grows faster /
그 결과 / 그늘진 면은 더 빨리 자란다 /
than the side facing the sunlight.
햇빛을 마주하는 면보다
This phenomenon causes the stem to bend /
이 현상은 줄기가 휘어지게 한다 /
and appear to be growing / towards the light.
그리고 성장하는 것처럼 보이게 한다 / 빛을 향하여
Auxins have the opposite effect / on the roots of plants.
옥신은 반대의 효과를 가진다 / 식물의 뿌리에서는
Auxins in the tips of roots / tend to limit growth.
뿌리 끝에 있는 옥신은 / 성장을 억제하는 경향이 있다
If a root is horizontal in the soil, /
만약 하나의 뿌리가 토양 속에서 수평이라면 /
the auxins will accumulate / on the lower side /
옥신은 축적될 것이다 / 아래쪽에 /
and interfere with its development.
그리고 그것(뿌리)의 발달을 방해할 것이다
Therefore, / the lower side of the root will grow slower / than the upper side.
그러므로 / 뿌리의 아래쪽은 더 느리게 자랄 것이다 / 위쪽보다
This will, in turn, cause the root to bend downwards, /
이는 결과적으로 뿌리가 아래로 휘어지게 할 것이다 /
with the tip of the root growing / in that direction.
뿌리의 끝부분이 자란 채 / 그 방향으로

식물의 성장은 식물의 줄기와 뿌리 끝에서 발견되는 옥신이라고 불리는 호르몬 그룹에 의해 조절된다. 줄기 끝에서 생산된 옥신은 그늘진 곳에 있는 줄기의 옆면에 축적되는 경향이 있다. 따라서, 옥신은 식물의 그늘진 면에서의 성장을 ① 자극한다. 그 결과 그늘진 면은 햇빛을 마주하는 면보다 더 빨리 자란다. 이 현상은 줄기가 휘어지게 하고 빛을 ② 향하여 성장하는 것처럼 보이게 한다. 옥신은 식물의 뿌리에서는 ③ 반대의 효과를 가진다. 뿌리 끝에 있는 옥신은 성장을 억제하는 경향이 있다. 만약 하나의 뿌리가 토양 속에서 수평이라면, 옥신은 아래쪽에 축적되어 그것의 발달을 방해할 것이다. 그러므로 뿌리의 아래쪽은 위쪽보다 ④ 더 빠르게 (→ 더 느리게) 자랄 것이다. 이는 결과적으로 뿌리의 끝부분이 그 방향으

로 자란 채 뿌리가 ⑤ 아래로 휘어지게 한다.

문제풀이

식물의 뿌리 끝에 있는 옥신은 성장을 억제하는 경향이 있다고 했으므로 뿌리의 아래쪽은 위쪽보다 성장이 느려야 한다는 흐름이 되어야 문맥상 자연스럽다. 따라서 ④ 'faster(더 빠르게)'를 'slower(더 느리게)'로 고쳐야 한다.

구조 다시보기

주제	식물의 성장은 옥신에 의해 조절됨
근거 1	줄기 끝에 있는 옥신은 식물의 그늘진 면에서의 성장을 자극함
부연	그늘진 면이 더 빨리 자라서 줄기가 휘어지게 하고 빛을 향해 성장하는 것처럼 보이게 함
근거 2	식물 뿌리에 있는 옥신은 성장을 억제하는 경향이 있음
부연	뿌리의 아래쪽이 위쪽보다 더 느리게 자라서 뿌리가 아래로 휘어지게 함

어휘·어구

growth 성장
control 조절하다
hormone 호르몬
auxin 옥신(식물에서 발견되는 호르몬)
stem 줄기
produce 생산하다
tend to-v ~하는 경향이 있다
accumulate 축적하다
accordingly 따라서
stimulate 자극하다
face 마주하다, 직면하다
sunlight 햇빛
phenomenon 현상
bend 구부러지다
appear ~처럼 보이다
towards ~을 향하여
opposite 반대의
effect 효과
limit 제한하다
horizontal 수평의
interfere 방해하다
development 발달
in turn 결과적으로
downwards 아래쪽으로
direction 방향

정답률 

1. ⑤ 허브의 위약 효과

직독/직해

It is widely believed / 널리 알려져 있다 /
that certain herbs somehow magically improve / 어떤 허브는 다소 마법처럼 향상시킨다고 /
the work of certain organs, / 특정 장기의 기능을 /
and "cure" specific diseases / as a result. 그리고 특정 질병을 '고친다'고 / 그 결과
Such statements are unscientific and groundless. 그런 진술은 비과학적이고 근거가 없다
Sometimes herbs appear to work, / 이따금 허브는 효과가 있는 것처럼 보인다 /
since they tend to increase / 그것들이 증가시키는 경향이 있기 때문에 /
your blood circulation / in an aggressive attempt / 혈액 순환을 / 적극적인 시도 속에서 /
by your body / to eliminate them / from your system. 당신 몸에 의한 / 그것들을 제거하려는 / 당신의 신체로부터
That can create a temporary feeling of a high, / 그것은 일시적으로 좋은 기분을 만들어 줄 수 있다 /
which makes it seem / 이는 보이게 만든다 /
as if your health condition has improved. 마치 당신의 건강 상태가 향상된 것처럼
Also, / herbs can have a placebo effect, / 또한 / 허브는 위약 효과를 가지고 있다 /
just like any other method, / 어떤 다른 방법과 마찬가지로 /
thus helping you feel better. 따라서 당신이 더 나아졌다고 느끼게 돕는다
Whatever the case, / it is your body / 어떤 경우든 / 바로 당신의 몸이다 /
that has the intelligence to regain health, / 건강을 되찾게 하는 지성을 가진 것은 /
and not the herbs. 허브가 아니라
How can herbs have the intelligence / 허브가 어떻게 지성을 가질 수 있겠는가 /
needed to direct your body / 당신의 몸을 인도하는 데 필요한 /
into getting healthier? 더 건강해지는 방향으로
That is impossible. 그것은 불가능하다
Try to imagine / 상상해 보라 /
how herbs might come into your body / 어떻게 허브가 당신의 몸 안으로 들어가는지를 /
and intelligently fix your problems. 그리고 영리하게 당신의 문제를 해결할 수 있는지를
If you try to do that, / you will see / 만약 당신이 그렇게 해 본다면 / 당신은 알게 될 것이다 /
how impossible it seems. 그것이 얼마나 불가능하게 보이는지
Otherwise, / it would mean / 그렇지 않다면 / 그것은 의미하는 것이 된다 /
that herbs are more intelligent / 허브가 더 지적이라는 것을 /
than the human body, / 인간의 몸보다 /
which is truly hard to believe. 이는 정말로 믿기 어렵다

어떤 허브는 다소 마법처럼 특정 장기의 기능을 향상시키고, 그 결과 특정 질병을 '고친다'고 널리 알려져 있다. 그런 진술은 비과학적이고 근거가 없다. 이따금 허브는 효과가 있는 것처럼 보이는데, 이는 당신의 신체로부터 그것들을 제거하려는 당신 몸의 적극적인 시도 속에서 그것들이 혈액 순환을 ① 증가시키는 경향이 있기 때문이다. 그것은 ② 일시적으로 좋은 기분을 만들어 줄 수 있는데, 이는 마치 당신의 건강 상태가 향상된 것처럼 보이게 만든다. 또한 허브는, 어떤 다른 방법과 마찬가지로, 위약 효과를 가지고 있어서 당신이 더 나아졌다고 느끼게 돕는다. 어떤 경우든, 건강을 ③ 되찾게 하는 지성을 가진 것은 허브가 아니라 바로 당신의 몸이다. 허브가 어떻게 당신의 몸을 더 건강해지는 방향으로 인도하는 데 필요한 지성을 가질 수 있겠는가? 그것은 불가능하다. 어떻게 허브가 당신의 몸 안으로 들어가서 영리하게 당신의 문제를 ④ 해결할 수 있는지를 상상해 보라. 만약 당신이 그렇게 해 본다면 당신은 그것이 얼마나 불가능하게 보이는지 알게 될 것이다. 그렇지 않다면, 그것은 허브가 인간의 몸보다 ⑤ 덜(→더) 지적이라는 것을 의미하는 것이 되는데, 이는 정말로 믿기 어렵다.

문제풀이

허브가 몸 안으로 들어가서 영리하게 문제를 해결할 수 있다고 생각한다면 결국 허브가 인간의 몸보다 더 지적이라는 것을 의미한다는 문맥이 되어야 자연스럽다. 따라서 ⑤ 'less(덜)'를 'more(더)'로 고쳐야 한다.

어휘·어구

somehow 다소
magically 마법처럼
improve 개선하다
organ 장기
cure 고치다, 치료하다
specific 특정한
disease 질병
statement 진술
groundless 근거 없는
blood circulation 혈액 순환
aggressive 적극적인
attempt 시도
eliminate 제거하다
temporary 일시적인
method 방법
regain 회복하다
direct 안내하다
impossible 불가능한

정답률 

2. ② 자신의 삶에 대한 통제력을 가져라

직독/직해

Do you sometimes feel like / you don't love your life? 당신은 가끔 ~처럼 느끼는가 / 당신의 삶을 사랑하지 않는다고
Like, / deep inside, / something is missing? 마치, 마음 깊은 곳에서 / 무언가가 빠진 것처럼
That's because we are living / someone else's life. 그건 바로 우리가 살고 있기 때문이다 / 다른 누군가의 삶을
We allow other people to influence / our choices. 우리는 다른 사람들이 영향을 주도록 허용한다 / 우리의 선택에
We are trying to meet their expectations. 우리는 그들의 기대감을 충족시키기 위해 애쓰고 있다
Social pressure is deceiving / — we are all impacted / 사회적 압력은 (우리를) 현혹시킨다 / 우리 모두는 영향을 받는다 /
without noticing it. 그것을 눈치채지도 못한 채
Before we realize / we are losing ownership of our lives, / 우리가 깨닫기도 전에 / 우리의 삶에 대한 소유권을 잃었다는 것을 /
we end up envying / how other people live. 우리는 결국 부러워하게 된다 / 다른 사람들이 어떻게 사는지를
Then, / we can only see the greener grass— / 그러면 / 우리는 더 푸른 잔디만 볼 수 있게 된다 /
ours is never good enough. 우리의 삶은 결코 만족할 만큼 충분히 좋지 않다
To regain that passion for the life / you want, / 삶에 대한 열정을 되찾기 위해서는 / 당신이 원하는 /
you must recover control of your choices. 당신은 당신의 선택에 대한 통제력을 회복해야 한다
No one but yourself / can choose how you live. 당신 자신을 제외한 그 누구도 / 당신이 어떻게 살지를 선택할 수 없다
But, how? 하지만 어떻게 해야 할까
The first step / to getting rid of expectations / 첫 단계는 / 기대감을 버리는 /
is to treat yourself kindly. 자신을 친절하게 대하는 것이다
You can't truly love other people / 당신은 다른 사람들을 진정으로 사랑할 수 없다 /
if you don't love yourself first. 만약 당신이 자신을 먼저 사랑하지 않으면
When we accept who we are, / there's no room / 우리가 우리를 있는 그대로 받아들일 때 / 여지는 남아있지 않다 /
for other's expectations. 다른 사람들의 기대감을 위한

당신은 가끔 당신의 삶을 사랑하지 않는다고 느끼는가? 마치, 마음 깊은 곳에서 무언가가 빠진 것처럼? 그건 바로 우리가 다른 누군가의 삶을 살고 있기 때문이다. 우리는 다른 사람들이 우리의 선택에 ① 영향을 주도록 허용한다. 우리는 그들의 기대감을 충족시키기 위해 애쓰고 있다. 사회적 압력은 (우리를) 현혹시킨다. 우리 모두는 그것을 눈치채지도 못한 채 영향을 받는다. 우리의 삶에 대한 소유권을 잃었다는 것을 깨닫기도 전에, 우리는 결국 다른 사람들이 어떻게 사는지를 ② 무시하게 된다(→부러워하게 된다). 그러면, 우리는 더 푸른 잔디(타인의 삶이 더 좋아 보이는 것)만 볼 수 있게 된다. 우리의 삶은 결코 만족할 만큼 충분히 좋지 않다. 당신이 원하는 삶에 대한 열정을 되찾기 위해서는 당신의 선택에 대한 통제력을 ③ 회복해야 한다. 당신 자신을 제외한 그 누구도 당신이 어떻게 살지를 선택할 수 없다. 하지만 어떻게 해야 할까? 기대감을 버리는 첫 단계는 자신을 ④ 친절하게 대하는 것이다. 만약 당신이 자신을 먼저 사랑하지 않으면 다른 사람들을 진정으로 사랑할 수 없다. 우리가 우리를 있는 그대로 받아들일 때, 다른 사람들의 ⑤ 기대감을 위한 여지는 남아있지 않다.

문제풀이

타인의 기대를 충족시키기 위해 자신의 삶을 살다 보면 자신의 삶에 대한 소유권을 잃어버리게 되고, 결국 타인의 삶을 부러워하며 자신의 삶에 만족하지 못하기 때문에 자신의 삶에 있어 선택에 대한 통제력을 회복해야 한다는 내용이다. 타인의 삶이 더 좋아 보이는 것만 본다는 것은 결국 타인이 어떻게 사는지를 보고 부러워한다는 문맥이 되어야 자연스러우므로, ② 'ignoring(무시하게 된다)'을 'envying(부러워하게 된다)' 등으로 고쳐야 한다.

어휘·어구

feel like ~처럼 느끼다
influence 영향을 미치다
meet 충족시키다
expectation 기대
social pressure 사회적 압력
deceiving 속이는, 현혹시키는
impact 영향을 주다
notice 눈치채다
ownership 소유권
end up v-ing 결국 ~하게 되다
regain 되찾다
passion 열정
recover 회복하다
get rid of ~을 없애다
treat 대하다, 다루다
accept 받아들이다
room 여지

정답률 45%

3. ⑤ 거절당하는 상황을 연습하라

직독/직해

Rejection is an everyday part of our lives, /
거절은 우리 삶의 일상적인 부분이다 /
yet most people can't handle it well.
하지만 대부분의 사람은 그것을 잘 감당하지 못한다
For many, / it's so painful /
많은 사람에게 / 거절이 너무 고통스러워서 /
that they'd rather not ask for something at all /
그들은 오히려 아예 무언가를 요청하지 않으려 한다 /
than ask and risk rejection.
요청하고 거절당할 위험을 감수하기보다는
Yet, / as the old saying goes, / if you don't ask, /
하지만 / 옛말처럼 / 만일 여러분이 요청하지 않으면 /
the answer is always no.
대답은 항상 '아니오'이다
Avoiding rejection negatively affects /
거절을 피하는 것은 부정적으로 영향을 미친다 /
many aspects of your life.
여러분의 삶의 많은 측면에
All of that happens / 이 모든 것은 일어난다 /
only because you're not tough enough to handle it.
단지 여러분이 그것을 감당할 만큼 강하지 않기 때문에
For this reason, / consider rejection therapy.
이런 이유로 / 거절 요법을 고려해 보라
Come up with a request or an activity /
요청이나 활동을 생각해 내라 /
that usually results in a rejection.
일반적으로 거절당할 만한
Working in sales / is one such example.
판매 분야에서 일하는 것이 / 그런 사례 중 하나이다
Asking for discounts at the stores / will also work.
매장에서 할인을 요청하는 것 / 또한 효과가 있을 것이다
By deliberately getting yourself rejected /
의도적으로 스스로를 거절당할 상황에 놓이게 함으로써 /
you'll grow a thicker skin /
여러분은 더 두꺼운 피부를 갖게 될 것이다 /
that will allow you to take on much more in life, /
인생에서 훨씬 더 많은 것을 떠맡을 수 있게 할 /
thus making you more successful /
그리하여 그것은 당신을 더 성공적으로 (~있게) 해 줄 것이다 /
at dealing with unfavorable circumstances.
호의적이지 않은 상황에 대처할 수 있게

거절은 우리 삶의 일상적인 부분이지만, 대부분의 사람은 그것을 잘 감당하지 못한다. 많은 사람에게 거절이 너무 고통스럽기 때문에, 그들은 요청하고 거절당할 ① 위험을 감수하기보다는 아예 무언가를 요청하지 않으려 한다. 하지만 옛말처럼, 만일 여러분이 요청하지 않으면 대답은 항상 '아니오'이다. 거절을 피하는 것은 여러분의 삶의 많은 측면에 ② 부정적으로 영향을 미친다. 이 모든 것은 여러분이 단지 거절을 감당할 만큼 ③ 강하지 않기 때문에 일어난다. 이런 이유로 거절 요법을 (시도하는 것을) 고려해 보라. 일반적으로 거절당할 만한 ④ 요청이나 활동을 생각해 내라. 판매 분야에서 일하는 것이 그런 사례 중 하나이다. 매장에서 할인을 요청하는 것 또한 효과가 있을 것이다. 의도적으로 스스로를 ⑤ 환영받을(→거절당할) 상황에 놓이게 함으로써 여러분은 더 둔감해지고, 인생에서 훨씬 더 많은 것을 떠맡을 수 있게 되며, 그리하여 그것은 호의적이지 않은 상황에 더 성공적으로 대처할 수 있게 해 줄 것이다.

문제풀이

거절당할 만큼 강하지 않기 때문에 대부분의 사람들이 거절을 감당하지 못한다는 내용으로, 의도적으로 스스로를 거절당하는 상황에 놓이게 해서 거절에 둔감해짐으로써 결국 미래의 거절 상황에 대처할 수 있게 해준다는 문맥이 되어야 자연스러우므로, ⑤ 'welcomed (환영받을)'를 'rejected(거절당할)' 등으로 고쳐야 한다.

구조 다시보기

도입	대부분의 사람은 거절을 잘 못함
이유	거절을 감당할 만큼 강하지 않기 때문임
주장	의도적으로 거절당할 상황에게 놓이게 함으로써 호의적이지 않은 상황에 더 성공적으로 대처할 수 있음

어휘·어구

rejection 거절
handle 감당하다
painful 고통스러운
risk 위험을 감수하다
negatively 부정적으로
affect 영향을 미치다
aspect 측면
tough 강한
consider 고려하다
therapy 요법
come up with 생각해내다
request 요청
deal with ~을 다루다
unfavorable 호의적이지 않은
circumstance 상황

정답률 25%

4. ⑤ 동물 종의 멸종을 막기 위한 동물원의 회복 프로그램

직독/직해

For species approaching extinction, /
멸종에 이르고 있는 종에게 /
zoos can act as a last chance for survival.
동물원은 생존을 위한 마지막 기회로 작용할 수 있다
Recovery programs are established /
회복 프로그램이 수립된다 /
to coordinate the efforts / 노력을 통합하기 위해 /
of field conservationists and wildlife authorities.
현장 환경 보호 활동가와 야생 동물 당국의
As populations of those species diminish /
그 종의 개체 수가 감소하면서 /
it is not unusual / 드물지 않다 /
for zoos to start captive breeding programs.
동물원이 포획 사육 프로그램을 시작하는 것은
Captive breeding acts to protect against extinction.
포획 사육은 멸종을 막기 위해 작용한다
In some cases / 어떤 경우에는 /
captive-bred individuals may be released /
포획 사육된 개체가 방생될 수도 있다 /
back into the wild, / supplementing wild populations.
다시 야생으로 / 야생 개체 수를 보충하면서
This is most successful in situations /
이것은 상황에서 가장 성공적이다 /
where individuals are at greatest threat /
개체가 가장 큰 위협에 놓여 있는 /
during a particular life stage.
특정한 생애 주기 동안에
For example, / turtle eggs may be removed /
예를 들어 / 거북이 알은 제거될 수도 있다 /
from high-risk locations / until after they hatch.
고위험 위치로부터 / 그것이 부화한 이후까지
This may increase the number of turtles /
이는 거북이 수를 증가시킬 수 있다 /
that survive to adulthood.
성체까지 생존하는
Crocodile programs have also been successful /
악어 프로그램 역시 성공적이었다 /
in protecting eggs and hatchlings, /
알과 부화한 유생을 보호하는 데 있어서 /
releasing hatchlings / 부화한 유생을 방생하면서 /
once they are better equipped /
일단 그들이 더 잘 갖추어지면 /
to protect themselves. 스스로를 보호하도록

멸종에 이르고 있는 종에게 동물원은 생존을 위한 마지막 기회로 작용할 수 있다. ① 회복 프로그램이 현장 환경 보호 활동가와 야생 동물 당국의 노력을 통합하기 위해 수립된다. 그 종의 개체 수가 ② 감소하면서 동물원이 포획 사육 프로그램을 시작하는 것은 드물지 않다. 포획 사육은 멸종을 막기 위해 작용한다. 어떤 경우에는 포획 사육된 개체가 다시 야생으로 방생되어 야생 개체 수를 보충할 수도 있다. 이는 개체가 ③ 특정한 생애 주기 동안에 가장 큰 위협에 놓여 있는 상황에서 가장 성공적이다. 예를 들어 거북이 알은 그것이 부화한 이후까지 고위험 위치로부터 제거될 수도 있다. 이는 성체까지 생존하는 거북이 수를 ④ 증가시킬 수 있다. 악어 프로그램 역시 알과 부화한 유생을 보호하는 데 있어서 성공적이었으며 일단 그것이 스스로를 보호하도록 더 잘 갖추어지면, 부화한 유생을 ⑤ 포획한다(→ 방생한다).

문제풀이

멸종 위기에 처한 동물들의 개체 수를 회복시키고자 동물원에서 포획 사육 프로그램을 사용한 후에 이렇게 포획 사육된 개체는 다시 야생으로 방생되어 야생 개체 수를 보충할 수도 있다는 내용의 글이다. 그 예로써 거북이와 악어 프로그램이 제시되었는데 악어 프로그램에서 알과 부화한 유생을 보호하는 데 있어서 성공하게 되고, 일단 그것이 스스로를 보호할 정도가 되면 포획하는 것이 아니라 방생하는 것이 글의 흐름에 적절하다. 따라서 ⑤ 'capturing(포획한다)'를 'releasing(방생한다)'로 바꿔 써야 한다.

이렇게 풀자 어휘 쓰임을 물어보는 문제는 글의 논리적 흐름 파악이 뒷받침되어야 한다. 이 글은 멸종 위기에 처한 동물들을 동물원에서 포획하여 사육한 후 야생에서 적용할 시기가 되면 다시 야생으로 돌려보내 준다는 내용의 글이고, 거북이와 악어의 예시를 들고 있다. 예시 앞의 'Captive breeding acts to protect against extinction. In some cases captive-bred individuals may be released back into the wild, supplementing wild populations.(포획 사육은 멸종을 막기 위해 작용한다. 어떤 경우에는 포획 사육된 개체가 다시 야생으로 방생되어 야생 개체 수를 보충할 수도 있다.)'에서 정답을 쉽게 유추할 수 있다.

어휘·어구

species 종, 종류
approach 접근하다, 이르다
recovery 회복
established 확립된
authority 당국
diminish 감소하다
release 방생하다
threat 위협
particular 특정한
remove 제거하다

정답률 54%

5. ④ 인간의 사회적 교류를 발전시키는 사냥

직독/직해

Hunting can explain / how humans developed /
사냥은 설명할 수 있다 / 인간이 어떻게 발전시켰는지를 /
reciprocal altruism and *social exchange*.
'상호 이타주의'와 '사회적인 교류'를
Humans seem to be unique among primates /
인간은 영장류 중에서 특별한 것 같다 /
in showing extensive reciprocal relationships /
광범위한 상호 관계를 보여준다는 점에서 /
that can last years, decades, or a lifetime.
몇 년, 수십 년, 혹은 평생 지속될 수 있는
Meat from a large game animal / 큰 사냥감 고기는 /
comes in quantities that exceed / 양을 초과한다 /
what a single hunter and his immediate family /
한 명의 사냥꾼과 그의 직계가족이 /
could possibly consume. 소비할 수 있을 만한
Furthermore, / hunting success is highly variable; /
게다가 / 사냥의 성공은 매우 가변적이다 /
a hunter who is successful one week /
한 주에는 성공한 사냥꾼이 /
might fail the next. 다음 주에는 실패할 수도 있다
These conditions encourage / 이런 조건들은 장려한다 /
food sharing from hunting. 사냥으로 인한 음식 공유를
The costs to a hunter of giving away meat /
사냥꾼이 고기를 나눠 주는 데 드는 비용은 /
he cannot eat immediately / 그가 당장 먹을 수 없는 /
are low / 적게 든다 /
because he cannot consume all the meat himself /
혼자서 고기를 전부 먹을 수 없기 때문에 /
and leftovers will soon spoil.
그리고 남은 고기는 곧 상하게 되기 때문에
The benefits can be large, however, /
그 혜택은 클 수 있다 / 하지만 /
when those who are given his food /
그 사람의 음식을 받은 사람들이 /
return the generous favor / 관대한 호의에 보답할 때 /
later on when he has failed to get food / for himself.
그 사람이 나중에 음식을 얻지 못했을 때 / 스스로
In essence, / hunters can store extra meat /
본질적으로 / 사냥꾼들은 여분의 고기를 저장할 수 있다 /
in the bodies of their friends and neighbors.
그들의 친구와 이웃의 몸에

사냥은 인간이 어떻게 '상호 이타주의'와 '사회적인 교류'를 발전시켰는지를 설명할 수 있다. 인간은 영장류 중에서 몇 년, 수십 년, 혹은 평생 지속될 수 있는 광범위한 상호 관계를 보여준다는 점에서 특별한 것 같다. 큰 사냥감 고기는 한 명의 사냥꾼과 그의 직계가족이 소비할 수 있을 만한 양을 ① 초과한다. 게다가, 사냥의 성공은 매우 ② 가변적이다. 한 주에는 성공한 사냥꾼이 다음 주에는 실패할 수도 있다. 이런 조건들은 사냥으로 인한 음식 공유를 ③ 장려한다. 사냥꾼이 당장 먹을 수 없는 고기를 나눠 주는 데 드는 비용은 혼자서 고기를 전부 먹을 수 없고 남은 고기는 곧 상하게 되기 때문에 ④ 많이(→ 적게) 든다. 하지만 그 사람이 나중에 스스로 음식을 얻지 못했을 때, 그 사람의 음식을 받은 사람들이 관대한 호의에 보답할 때 그 혜택은 클 수 있다. 본질적으로 사냥꾼들은 그들의 친구와 이웃의 몸에 여분의 고기를 저장할 수 있다.

문제풀이

한 명의 사냥꾼이 사냥감 고기를 소비하기에는 양이 많아서 다 소비할 수가 없고 남은 고기는 곧 상할 수 있기 때문에 남은 고기를 다른 사람들에게 나누어 주는 것이 비용 측면에서는 효율적이다. 따라서 문맥상 고기를 나눠 주는 데 드는 비용은 적게 든다는 것이 자연스러우므로 ④ 'high(높은)'를 'low(낮은)' 등으로 고쳐야 한다.

《 어휘·어구 》

extensive 광범위한
relationship 관계
exceed 초과하다
immediate family 직계가족
variable 가변적인
leftover 남은 음식
in essence 본질적으로

구조 다시보기

도입	사냥은 인간의 상호 이타주의와 사회적인 교류를 발전시킴
전개	사냥감 고기의 양과 사냥의 성공 가변성이 음식의 공유를 장려함
결론	사냥감 고기를 나누는 것은 결국 혜택을 주고받는 것임

정답률 36%

6. ③ 자연계의 복잡한 형태는 그것의 기능에 필수적이다

직독/직해

Detailed study over the past two or three decades /
지난 20년이나 30년 동안의 상세한 연구는 /
is showing / 보여주고 있다 /
that the complex forms of natural systems /
자연계의 복잡한 형태가 /
are essential to their functioning.
그것의 기능에 필수적이라는 것을
The attempt to straighten rivers /
강을 직선화하려는 시도는 /
and give them regular cross-sections /
그리고 규칙적인 횡단면으로 만들고자 하는 (시도는) /
is perhaps the most disastrous example /
아마도 가장 막심한 피해 사례일 수 있다 /
of this form-and-function relationship.
이런 형태-기능 관계의
The natural river / has a very irregular form: /
자연 하천은 / 매우 불규칙한 형태를 가지고 있다
it curves a lot, / spills across floodplains, /
그것은 많이 굽이친다 / 범람원을 가로질러 넘쳐흐른다 /
and leaks into wetlands, / giving it an ever-changing /
그리고 습지로 스며 들어간다 / 끊임없이 변화하게 만든다 /
and incredibly complex shoreline.
그리고 엄청나게 복잡한 강가를 (만든다)
This allows the river to accommodate /
이는 조절할 수 있게 한다 /
variations in water level and speed.
강의 수위와 속도 변화를
Pushing the river into tidy geometry /
강을 정돈된 기하학적 형태에 맞춰 넣는 것은 /
destroys functional capacity /
기능적인 수용 능력을 파괴한다 /
and results in disasters / 그리고 재난을 초래한다 /
like the Mississippi floods of 1927 and 1993 and, /
1927년과 1993년의 Mississippi강의 홍수와 같은
more recently, / 더 최근에는 /
the unnatural disaster of Hurricane Katrina.
허리케인 Katrina와 같은 비정상적인 재난을
A $50 billion plan / 500억 달러 계획은 /
to "let the river loose" in Louisiana /
Louisiana에서 "강을 자유롭게 흐르게 두어라."라는 /
recognizes that the controlled Mississippi is washing away /
통제된 Mississippi강이 유실시키고 있다는 것을 인정한 것이다 /
twenty-four square miles of that state annually.
매년 그 주의 24제곱마일을

지난 20년이나 30년 동안의 상세한 연구는 자연계의 복잡한 형태가 그것의 기능에 필수적이라는 것을 보여주고 있다. 강을 ① 직선화하고 규칙적인 횡단면으로 만들고자 하는 시도는 아마도 이런 형태-기능 관계의 가장 막심한 피해 사례일 수 있다. 자연 하천은 매우 ② 불규칙한 형태를 가지고 있다. 그것은 많이 굽이치고, 범람원을 가로질러 넘쳐흐르고, 습지로 스며 들어가서 끊임없이 변화하여, 엄청나게 복잡한 강가를 만든다. 이는 강의 수위와 속도 변화를 ③ 막을(→ 수용할) 수 있게 한다. 강을 정돈된 기하학적 형태에 맞춰 넣는 것은 기능적인 수용 능력을 ④ 파괴하고 1927년과 1993년의 Mississippi강의 홍수와, 더 최근에는, 허리케인 Katrina와 같은 비정상적인 재난을 초래한다. Louisiana에서 "강을 자유롭게 흐르게 두어라."라는 500억 달러 계획은 ⑤ 통제된 Mississippi강이 매년 그 주의 24제곱마일을 유실시키고 있다는 것을 인정한 것이다.

문제풀이

자연계의 복잡한 형태는 그것의 기능에 필수적이어서 인위적으로 강의 형태를 직선으로 변화시키는 것은 비정상적인 재난을 초래한다는 내용으로 보아, 자연 하천의 불규칙한 형태가 결국 강의 수위와 속도 변화를 수용할 수 있다는 문맥이 되어야 자연스럽다. 따라서 ③ 'prevent(막다)'를 'accommodate(수용하다)' 등으로 고쳐야 한다.

《 어휘·어구 》

essential 필수의
functioning 기능, 작용
attempt 시도
straighten 똑바르게 하다
regular 규칙적인
cross-section 횡단면
disastrous 재난의
relationship 관계
irregular 불규칙적인
spill 넘치다
floodplain 범람원
leak 새다
incredibly 엄청나게
shoreline 강가, 바닷가
variation 변화
tidy 잘 정돈된
recognize 인정하다
wash away ~을 유실되게 하다
square mile 제곱 마일

7. ③ 인공조명의 비용 하락

직독/직해

When the price of something fundamental drops greatly, /
기본적인 어떤 것의 가격이 크게 하락할 때 /
the whole world can change.
온 세상은 바뀔 수 있다
Consider light. 조명을 생각해 보자
Chances are you are reading this sentence /
아마 여러분은 이 문장을 읽고 있을 것이다 /
under some kind of artificial light.
어떤 종류의 인공조명 아래에서
Moreover, / you probably never thought /
게다가 / 아마도 여러분은 생각해 본 적이 없을 것이다 /
about whether using artificial light for reading /
독서를 위해 인공조명을 이용하는 것이 /
was worth it.
그럴 만한 가치가 있는지에 대해

Light is so cheap / that you use it without thinking.
조명은 너무 싸서 / 여러분은 생각 없이 그것을 이용한다
But in the early 1800s, / 그러나 1800년대 초반에는 /
it would have cost you four hundred times /
400배만큼의 비용이 들었을 것이다 /
what you are paying now /
여러분이 오늘날 지불하고 있는 것의 /
for the same amount of light.
같은 양의 조명에 대해
At that price, / you wouldnotice the cost /
그 가격이면 / 여러분은 비용을 의식할 것이다 /
and would think twice / before using artificial light /
그리고 다시 생각할 것이다 / 인공조명을 이용하기 전에 /
to read a book.
책을 읽기 위해
The drop in the price of light / lit up the world.
조명 가격의 하락은 / 세상을 밝혔다
Not only did it turn night into day, /
그것은 밤을 낮으로 바꾸었을 뿐만 아니라 /
but it allowed us to live and work /
우리가 살고 일할 수 있게 해 주었다 /
in big buildings / that natural light could not enter.
큰 건물에서 / 자연광이 들어올 수 없는
Nearly nothing we have today would be possible /
우리가 오늘날 누리는 것 중에 가능한 것은 거의 없을 것이다 /
if the cost of artificial light had not dropped /
인공조명의 비용이 하락하지 않았더라면 /
to almost nothing. 거의 공짜 수준으로

기본적인 어떤 것의 가격이 크게 하락할 때, 온 세상은 바뀔 수 있다. 조명을 생각해 보자. 아마 여러분은 어떤 종류의 인공조명 아래에서 이 문장을 읽고 있을 것이다. 게다가, 아마도 여러분은 독서를 위해 인공조명을 이용하는 것이 그럴 만한 가치가 있는지에 대해 생각해 본 적이 없을 것이다. 조명은 너무 ① 싸서 여러분은 생각 없이 그것을 이용한다. 그러나 1800년대 초반에는, 같은 양의 조명에 대해 여러분이 오늘날 지불하고 있는 것의 400배만큼의 비용이 들었을 것이다. 그 가격이면, 여러분은 비용을 ② 의식할 것이고 책을 읽기 위해 인공조명을 이용하기 전에 다시 생각할 것이다. 조명 가격의 ③ 증가(→하락)는 세상을 밝혔다. 그것은 밤을 낮으로 바꾸었을 뿐만 아니라, ④ 자연광이 들어올 수 없는 큰 건물에서 우리가 살고 일할 수 있게 해 주었다. 인공조명의 비용이 거의 공짜 수준으로 하락하지 않았더라면, 우리가 오늘날 누리는 것 중에 ⑤ 가능한 것은 거의 없을 것이다.

문제풀이

1800년대 초반에는 조명 가격이 지금의 400배만큼 비쌌기 때문에 인공조명을 사용하기가 쉽지 않았지만 인공조명 가격이 거의 공짜 수준으로 하락하면서 세상이 밝혀졌다는 문맥이 되어야 자연스럽다. 따라서 ③ 'increase(증가)'는 'drop(하락)'과 같은 낱말로 고쳐야 한다.

어휘·어구

fundamental 기본적인
drop 하락하다
consider 생각하다
chances are 아마 ~일 것이다
sentence 문장
artificial light 인공조명
probably 아마
worth 가치가 있는
cost ~의 비용이 들다; 비용
pay 지불하다
amount 양
notice 의식하다
increase 증가, 증가하다
light up (불을) 밝히다
turn A into B A를 B로 바꾸다
natural light 자연광
nearly 거의
possible 가능한

정답률 54%

8. ③ 사육으로 인한 뇌 크기 감소

직독/직해

Recent research suggests /
최근의 연구는 시사한다 /
that evolving humans' relationship with dogs /
진화하는 인간의 개와의 관계가 /
changed the structure of both species' brains.
두 종 모두의 뇌 구조를 바꾸었다는 것을
One of the various physical changes /
다양한 신체적인 변화 중 하나는 /
caused by domestication / 사육으로 인해 야기된 /
is a reduction in the size of the brain: /
뇌 크기의 감소이다 /
16 percent for horses, / 34 percent for pigs, /
말은 16% / 돼지는 34% /
and 10 to 30 percent for dogs.
그리고 개는 10%에서 30%까지 (감소했다)
This is because / 이것은 ~ 때문이다 /
once humans started to take care of these animals, /
일단 인간이 이 동물들을 돌보기 시작하면서 /
they no longer needed various brain functions /
그것들은 다양한 뇌 기능이 더는 필요하지 않았기 (때문이다) /
in order to survive. 생존하기 위해
Animals who were fed and protected by humans /
인간이 먹이를 주고 보호해 주는 동물들은 /
did not need many of the skills /
기술 중 많은 것이 필요하지 않았다 /
required by their wild ancestors /
그것들의 야생 조상들에 의해 요구된 /
and lost the parts of the brain /
그리고 뇌의 부분들을 잃어버렸다 /
related to those capacities. 그런 능력들과 관련된
A similar process occurred for humans, /
비슷한 과정이 인간에게 발생했는데 /
who seem to have been domesticated by wolves.
그들은 늑대에 의해 길들여진 것으로 보인다
About 10,000 years ago, / 약 만 년 전 /
when the role of dogs was firmly established /
개의 역할이 확실하게 정해졌을 때 /
in most human societies, /
대부분 인간 사회에서 /
the human brain also shrank / by about 10 percent.
인간의 뇌 또한 줄어들었다 / 10% 정도

최근의 연구는 진화하는 인간의 개와의 관계가 두 종 모두의 뇌 구조를 바꾸었다는 것을 시사한다. 사육으로 인해 야기된 다양한 (A) 신체적인 변화 중 하나는 뇌 크기의 감소인데, 말은 16%, 돼지는 34% 그리고 개는 10%에서 30%까지 감소했다. 이것은 일단 인간이 이 동물들을 돌보기 시작하면서 그것들은 생존하기 위해 다양한 뇌 기능이 더는 필요하지 않았기 때문이다. 인간이 먹이를 주고 보호해 주는 동물들은 그것들의 야생 조상들에 의해 요구된 기술 중 많은 것이 필요하지 않았고 그런 능력들과 관련된 뇌의 부분들을 (B) 잃어버렸다. 비슷한 과정이 인간에게 발생했는데, 그들은 늑대에 의해 길들여진 것으로 보인다. 약 만 년 전, 개의 역할이 대부분 인간 사회에서 확실하게 정해졌을 때, 인간의 뇌 또한 10% 정도 (C) 줄어들었다.

문제풀이

(A) 두 종 모두의 뇌 크기가 감소했다는 것은 '신체적인' 변화에 해당하므로 'physical'이 적절하다.
(B) 인간에 의해 사육당할 때 야생에서 살아남기 위해 필요한 기술 중 많은 것이 필요하지 않았다는 내용으로 보아 그런 능력과 관련된 뇌의 부분들을 '잃어버렸다'는 문맥이 되어야 자연스러우므로 'lost'가 적절하다.
(C) 비슷한 과정이 인간에게 발생했고, 개의 역할이 인간 사회에서 확실하게 정해졌을 때 인간의 뇌 또한 '줄어들었다'는 문맥이 되어야 자연스러우므로 'shrank'가 적절하다.

어휘·어구

evolving 진화하는
structure 구조
psychological 심리적인
domestication 사육, 길들이기
reduction 감소
function 기능
survive 생존하다
ancestor 조상
capacity 능력
occur 발생하다, 일어나다
establish 설립하다
expand 확대하다
shrink 줄어들다

정답률 60%

9. ② 유대를 위한 경쟁과 협력

직독/직해

Social connections are so essential for our survival and well-being /
사회적 관계는 우리의 생존과 웰빙을 위해 매우 필수적이어서
that we not only cooperate with others to build relationships, /
우리는 관계를 형성하기 위해 다른 사람과 협력할 뿐만 아니라
we also compete with others for friends.
친구를 얻기 위해 다른 사람과 경쟁하기도 한다.
And often we do both at the same time.
그리고 자주 우리는 동시에 둘 다를 한다
Take gossip. 가십을 생각해보자
Through gossip, / we bond with our friends, /
가십을 통해 / 우리는 유대를 친구들과 형성한다 /
sharing interesting details.
흥미로운 세부 사항을 공유하면서
But at the same time, / 그러나 동시에 /
we are creating potential enemies /
우리는 잠재적인 적을 만들어 낸다 /
in the targets of our gossip.
가십의 대상들 중에서
Or consider rival holiday parties /
또는 라이벌 관계의 휴일 파티를 생각해 보라 /
where people compete to see who will attend their party.
누가 '그들의' 파티에 참석할 것인지를 알아보기 위해 경쟁하는
We can even see this tension in social media /
우리는 심지어 소셜 미디어에서도 이러한 긴장감을 볼 수 있다 /
as people compete for the most friends and followers.
사람들이 가장 많은 친구들과 팔로워들을 얻기 위해 경쟁할 때
At the same time, / 동시에 /
competitive exclusion can also generate cooperation.
경쟁적 배제는 협력도 만들어 낼 수 있다
High school social clubs and country clubs use this formula to great effect:
고등학교 친목 동아리와 컨트리클럽은 이러한 공식을 사용하여 큰 효과를 발휘한다
It is through selective inclusion *and exclusion* /
선택적인 포함 '그리고 배제'를 통해서이다 /
that they produce loyalty and lasting social bonds.
그들이 충성과 지속적인 사회적 유대를 형성하는 것은

사회적 관계는 우리의 생존과 웰빙을 위해 매우 필수적이어서 우리는 관계를 형성하기 위해 다른 사람과 협력할 뿐만 아니라, 친구를 얻기 위해 다른 사람과 경쟁하기도 한다. 그리고 자주 우리는 동시에 둘 다를 한다. 가십을 생각해보자. 가십을 통해 우리는 친구들과 흥미로운 세부 사항을 공유하면서 유대를 형성한다. 그러나 동시에 우리는 가십의 대상들 중에서 잠재적인 적을 (A) 만들어 낸다. 또는 누가 '그들의' 파티에 참석할 것인지를 알아보기 위해 경쟁하는 라이벌 관계의 휴일 파티를 생각해 보라. 우리는 심지어 소셜 미디어에서도 사람들이 가장 많은 친구들과 팔로워들을 얻기 위해 경쟁할 때 이러한 (B) 긴장감을 볼 수 있다. 동시에 경쟁적 배제는 또한 협력도 (C) 만들어 낼 수 있다. 고등학교 친목 동아리와 컨트리클럽은 이러한 공식을 사용하여 큰 효과를 발휘한다. 그들이 충성과 지속적인 사회적 유대를 형성하는 것은 선택적인 포함 '그리고 배제'를 통해서이다.

문제풀이

(A) 가십을 통해 친구들과 유대를 형성하지만 동시에 가십의 대상자들 중에서 적을 만들어 낸다는 의미가 되어야 하므로, 빈칸에는 create(만들어 내다)의 현재분사형 creating이 적절하다. forgive는 '용서하다'라는 의미이다.
(B) 소셜 미디어에서 친구와 팔로워를 얻기 위한 경쟁에서도 누가 그들의 파티에 참여할지를 알아보기 위한 라이벌 관계의 휴일 파티에 있는 긴장감을 볼 수 있다는 의미가 되어야 하므로, 빈칸에는 tension(긴장감)이 적절하다. harmony는 '조화'라는 의미이다.
(C) 선택적 포함과 배제를 통해 충성과 유대를 만들어 내는 것의 예시가 이어지고 있으므로, 경쟁적 배제는 긴장감 외에 협력을 만들어 내기도 한다는 의미가 되어야 한다. 따라서 빈칸에는 generate(만들어 내다)가 적절하다. prevent는 '방지하다'라는 의미이다.

어휘·어구

cooperate 협력하다
compete 경쟁하다
bond 유대관계를 형성하다
potential 잠재적인
competitive 경쟁의, 경쟁적인
formula 공식, 식
inclusion 포함, 포함된 것
exclusion 배제, 배척
loyalty 충성, 충직
lasting 오래가는, 영원한

정답률 71%

10. ③ 에너지를 많이 소모하지만 효율적인 두뇌

직독/직해

The brain makes up just two percent of our body weight /
뇌는 몸무게의 2 퍼센트만을 차지한다 /
but uses 20 percent of our energy.
그러나 우리의 에너지의 20 퍼센트를 사용한다
In newborns, / it's no less than 65 percent.
신생아의 경우 / 그 비율은 65 퍼센트에 달한다
That's partly why babies sleep all the time /
그것은 부분적으로 아기들이 항상 잠을 자는 이유이다
— their growing brains exhaust them — /
뇌의 성장이 그들을 소진시킨다 /
and have a lot of body fat, /
그리고 많은 체지방을 보유하는 /
to use as an energy reserve / when needed.
에너지 비축량으로서 사용하기 위해서 / 필요할 때
Our muscles use even more of our energy, /
우리의 근육은 훨씬 더 많은 에너지를 사용한다 /
about a quarter of the total, /
전체의 약 4분의 1 정도로 /
but we have a lot of muscle.
그러나 우리는 많은 근육을 가지고 있다
Actually, / per unit of matter, /
실제로 / 물질 단위당 /
the brain uses by far more energy /
뇌는 훨씬 많은 에너지를 사용한다 /
than our other organs. 다른 기관보다
That means / 그것은 의미한다 /
that the brain is the most expensive of our organs.
우리 장기 중 뇌가 단연 가장 에너지 소모가 많다는 것을
But it is also marvelously efficient.
하지만 그것은 또한 놀랍도록 효율적이다
Our brains require /
우리의 뇌는 필요로 한다 /
only about four hundred calories of energy a day /
하루에 약 400 칼로리의 에너지만 /
— about the same / 거의 같다 /
as we get from a blueberry muffin.
우리가 블루베리 머핀에서 얻는 것과
Try running your laptop / for twenty-four hours /
노트북을 작동시켜 보아라 / 24시간동안 /
on a muffin / and see how far you get.
머핀으로 / 그리고 당신이 얼마나 멀리 가는지 보아라

뇌는 몸무게의 2 퍼센트만을 차지하지만 우리의 에너지의 20 퍼센트를 사용한다. 신생아의 경우, 그 비율은 65 퍼센트에 달한다. 그것은 부분적으로 아기들이 항상 잠을 자고 (뇌의 성장이 그들을 (A) 소진시키고), 체지방을 보유하는 이유인데, 필요할 때 보유한 에너지를 사용하기 위한 것이다. 근육은 전체의 약 4분의 1 정도로 훨씬 더 많은 에너지를 사용하기도 하지만, 많은 근육을 가지고 있기도 하다. 실제로, 물질 단위당, 뇌는 다른 기관보다 훨씬 (B) 많은 에너지를 사용한다. 그것은 우리 장기 중 뇌가 단연 가장 에너지 소모가 많다는 것을 의미한다. 하지만 그것은 또한 놀랍도록 (C) 효율적이다. 뇌는 하루에 약 400 칼로리의 에너지만 필요로 하는데, 블루베리 머핀에서 얻는 것과 거의 같다. 머핀으로 24시간 동안 노트북을 작동시켜서 얼마나 가는지 보라.

문제풀이

(A) 신생아의 경우 두뇌가 에너지의 65퍼센트를 사용한다고 했으므로, 성장하는 두뇌가 아기들을 소진시킨다고 해야한다. 따라서 'exhaust(소진시키다)'가 오는 것이 적절하다. warn은 '경고하다'의 뜻이다.
(B) 비록 근육이 훨씬 많은 에너지를 사용하지만, 그만큼 많은 근육을 가지고 있다고 말하고 있으며, 또한 우리 장기 중 뇌가 가장 에너지 소모가 많다고 언급하고 있으므로, 물질 단위 당 뇌는 다른 기관보다 훨씬 많은 에너지를 사용한다고 해야한다. 따라서 'more (많은)'가 오는 것이 적절하다.
(C) 뇌는 하루에 약 400칼로리의 에너지만 필요로 하는데, 그것은 블루베리 머핀에서 얻는 것과 거의 같다고 했으므로 뇌는 놀랍도록 효율적이라고 해야한다. 따라서 'efficient (효율적인)'가 오는 것이 적절하다. creative는 '창조적인'의 뜻이다.

어휘·어구

make up ~을 차지하다
newborn 신생아
no less than ~에 못지 않게
warn 경고하다
exhaust 소진시키다, 고갈시키다
reserve 보유량
quarter 4분의 1
per ~당
unit of matter 물질 단위
by far 훨씬, 더욱
marvelously 놀라울 정도로
creative 창조적인
efficient 효율적인

본문 071쪽

문법 플러스 12. 접속사

1. that 2. that 3. Once 4. Though
5. because 6. that 7. like 8. that
9. because of 10. In spite of

1 [해석]▶ 포도주 전문가들도 마찬가지로 백포도주 Chardonnay를 붉은색 색소로 물들였을 때, 속아서 그것이 실제로 적포도주라고 생각하게 되었다.
[해설]▶ thinking의 목적어 역할을 하는 명사절을 이끄는 접속사 that을 써야 한다.
2 [해석]▶ 19세기 이래로, 상점 주인들은 상품이 실제보다 더 싸다는 인상을 주기 위해 9로 끝나는 가격을 선택함으로써 이런 속임수를 이용해 왔다.
[해설]▶ 추상명사 impression과 동격을 이루는 내용이 나왔으므로 동격절을 이끄는 접속사 that이 필요하다.
3 [해석]▶ 일단 이상한 일이 일어나고 있다는 것을 깨닫자, 내 심장은 빠르게 뛰기 시작했다.
[해설]▶ '~하게 되자, …했다'라고 표현하려면, 조건의 의미를 갖는 부사절 접속사 once(일단 ~하자)를 사용하는 것이 적절하다.
4 [해석]▶ 비록 그녀는 소설가보다 편집자로서 더 유명하지만, 많은 비평가들은 그녀의 소설 'Plum Bun'을 Fauset의 가장 뛰어난 작품으로 간주한다.
[해설]▶ 부사절과 주절이 서로 반대되는 내용을 가지고 있으므로, 양보의 의미를 갖는 부사절 접속사 though를 쓰는 것이 적절하다.
5 [해석]▶ 우리가 정보와 관련된 맥락을 확인하는 것이 매우 중요한데, 우리가 그렇게 하지 않는다면 우리는 너무 성급하게 판단하고 반응할지도 모르기 때문이다.
[해설]▶ '왜냐하면 만약 우리가 그렇게 하지 않으면 ~할지도 모르기 때문에' 정보와 관련된 맥락을 확인하는 것이 매우 중요하다. 문맥상 이유를 나타내는 접속사 because가 필요하다.
6 [해석]▶ 오늘날 만들어진 제조 식품 중 다수가 너무 많은 화학 물질과 인공적인 재료를 함유하고 있어서 때로는 정확히 그 안에 무엇이 들어 있는지 알기가 어렵다.
[해설]▶ so... that ~ 구문은 '너무 … 해서 ~하다'는 의미이다.
7 [해석]▶ 식품 라벨은 책에서 발견되는 목차와 같다.
[해설]▶ like 이하는 are의 보어로 쓰였고, like는 전치사로서 '~와 같은'의 뜻이다.
8 [해석]▶ 아이스하키는 팀마다 선수 수가 다르다는 점에서 주요 스포츠 중에서는 이례적이다.
[해설]▶ 문맥상 'in that(~라는 점에서)'이 되어야 적절하다. 원칙적으로 that절은 전치사 뒤에는 나올 수 없지만, in that(~라는 점에서)과 except that(~라는 점을 제외하면)은 예외적으로 나올 수 있다.
9 [해석]▶ 우리는 철학이 우리로 하여금 발전시키도록 도와주는 정신적인 기술들 때문에 철학을 공부한다.
[해설]▶ 괄호 뒤에 뒤에 명사(구) the mental skill이 있으므로 because of를 써야 한다. skills (which) it helps~에서 「주어+동사」인 it helps는 명사 skill을 수식하는 목적격 관계절이다.
10 해석]▶ 그는 노력했지만 상을 받지 못했다.
[해설]▶ 전치사구 in spite of는 '~에도 불구하고'의 의미로서 바로 뒤에 명사(구)가 온다. 같은 표현으로는 despite가 있는데 despite 뒤에는 of를 덧붙여 쓰지 않는다.

본문 072쪽

어휘 플러스 12. 접두사

1. predict 2. proceed
3. supervised 4. exposed
5. disagreed

1 [해석]▶ 격정과 편견을 줄이고 이것들을 관찰과 추론으로 바꾸면 사건을 더 잘 이해하고 예측할 수 있다는 것을 그들은 알아냈다.
2 [해석]▶ 우리의 대금 청구서는 자동으로 순서대로 계속 발송되고, 종종 대금 청구서와 우편물 속에 있는 (독촉) 편지가 엇갈립니다.
3 [해석]▶ Steve는 4년 동안 회사의 창고 중 하나를 감독해 왔었다.
4 [해석]▶ 실험실에서 실시한 실험에서, 110 데시벨의 갑작스런 소음에 노출된 사람들은 문제를 해결하는 능력의 감소를 경험하였다.
5 [해석]▶ 당신이 개가 여러 번 외출하는 것이 중요하다고 말씀하셨기 때문에, 바로 그 이유 때문에 저는 개를 하루에 4번씩 산책시켰습니다. 당신도 생각나시겠지만, 저는 반대하면서도 개를 산책시켰습니다.

13. 빈칸 추론 (1) 어휘, 짧은 어구

Day 13

본문 074쪽

1. ② 2. ② 3. ⑤ 4. ① 5. ②
6. ② 7. ③ 8. ② 9. ① 10. ①
11. ⑤

대표 기출 ③ 자유를 제한하는 것이 자기 통제와 성과를 향상시킨다

직독/직해

To demonstrate how best to defeat /
가장 잘 고치는 방법을 설명하기 위해 /

the habit of delaying, / Dan Ariely, /
미루는 습관을 / Dan Ariely는 /

a professor of psychology and behavioral economics, /
심리학 교수이자 행동경제학 교수인 /

performed an experiment on students /
학생들을 대상으로 실험을 수행했다 /

in three of his classes at MIT.
MIT에서 자신의 수업 중 세 개에서

He assigned all classes three reports /
그는 모든 수업에 세 개의 보고서를 과제로 부여했다 /

over the course of the semester.
학기 과정 동안

The first class had to choose three due dates for themselves, /
첫 번째 수업의 학생들은 세 개의 마감일을 스스로 선택해야 했다 /

up to and including the last day of class.
종강일까지 포함해서

The second had no deadlines / — all three papers /
두 번째는 마감일이 없었고 / 보고서 세 개 모두 /

just had to be submitted / by the last day of class.
제출되기만 하면 되었다 / 종강일까지

In his third class, / 그의 세 번째 수업에서 /

he gave students three set deadlines /
그는 학생들에게 세 개의 정해진 마감일을 주었다 /

over the course of the semester.
학기 과정 동안

At the end of the semester, / he found /
학기 말에 / 그는 알아냈다 /

that students with set deadlines /
마감일이 정해진 학생들이 /

received the best grades, /
최고의 성적을 받았다는 것을 /

the students with no deadlines / had the worst, /
마감일이 없는 학생들은 / 최하의 성적을 받았다는 (것을) /

and those who could choose their own deadlines /
그리고 자신의 마감일을 선택할 수 있었던 학생들은 /

fell somewhere in the middle.
그 중간 어디쯤의 위치에 있었다는 (것을)

Ariely concludes / that restricting freedom /
Ariely는 결론짓는다 / 자유를 제한하는 것은 /

— whether by the professor / 교수에 의해서든 /

or by students who recognize /
아니면 인식한 학생들에 의해서든 /

their own tendencies to delay things /
일을 미루는 자신의 성향을 /

— improves self-control and performance.
자기 통제와 성과를 향상시킨다고

미루는 습관을 가장 잘 고치는 방법을 설명하기 위해, 심리학 교수이자 행동경제학 교수인 Dan Ariely는 MIT에서 자신의 수업 중 세 개에서 학생들을 대상으로 실험을 수행했다. 그는 학기 과정 동안 모든 수업에 세 개의 보고서를 과제로 부여했다. 첫 번째 수업의 학생들은 종강일까지 포함해서 세 개의 마감일을 스스로 선택해야 했다. 두 번째는 마감일이 없었고, 보고서 세 개 모두 종강일까지 제출되기만 하면 되었다. 그의 세 번째 수업에서, 그는 학기 과정 동안 학생들에게 세 개의 정해진 마감일을 주었다. 학기 말에, 그는 마감일이 정해진 학생들이 최고의 성적을 받았고, 마감일이 없는 학생들은 최하의 성적을 받았으며, 자신의 마감일을 선택할 수 있었던 학생들은 그 중간 어디쯤의 위치에 있었다는 것을 알아냈다. Ariely는, 교수에 의해서든 아니면 일을 미루는 자신의 성향을 인식한 학생들에 의해서든, 자유를 제한하는 것은 자기 통제와 성과를 향상시킨다고 결론짓는다.

① 보상을 제공하는 것
② 장애물을 제거하는 것
③ 자유를 제한하는 것
④ 과제를 늘리는 것
⑤ 경쟁을 장려하는 것

문제풀이

미루는 습관을 가장 잘 고치는 방법을 설명하기 위한 실험에서, 세 그룹의 학생들 중 마감일이 정해진 학생들이 최고의 성적을 받았다는 내용을 통해 빈칸에 ③ 'restricting freedom'이 들어가서 빈칸이 포함되는 문장이 'Ariely는, 교수에 의해서든 아니면 일을 미루는 자신의 성향을 인식한 학생들에 의해서든, 자유를 제한하는 것은 자기 통제와 성과를 향상시킨다고 결론짓는다.'가 되는 것이 가장 적절하다.

이렇게 풀자 실험에서 세 그룹의 학생들 중 마감일이 정해진 학생들이 최고의 성적을 받았고, 마감일을 스스로 정한 학생들이 중간 성적을, 마감일이 없었던 학생들은 최하의 성적을 받았다는 실험 결과를 통해 자유를 제한하고 마감일을 정해주는 것이 결국 자기 통제와 성과를 향상시킨다고 볼 수 있다. 이와 같은 본문 내용을 요약해 보면 빈칸에 들어갈 말을 올바르게 추론할 수 있다.

어휘·어구

demonstrate 설명하다, 증명하다
defeat 물리치다
delaying 지연, 미루기(v. delay)
professor 교수
psychology 심리학
behavioral economics 행동경제학
perform 수행하다
experiment 실험
assign 부여하다
semester 학기
due date 마감일
up to ~까지
deadline 마감일
submit 제출하다
receive 받다
conclude 결론짓다
recognize 인식하다
tendency 성향
improve 향상시키다
self-control 자기 통제
performance 성과
reward 보상
remove 제거하다
obstacle 장애물
restrict 제한하다
freedom 자유
assignment 과제
encourage 장려하다
competition 경쟁

1. ② 서로를 위해 일하게 함으로써 우리의 삶을 바꾸는 혁신

직독/직해

The best way / in which innovation changes our lives /
최고의 방법은 / 혁신이 우리의 삶을 바꾸는 /

is by enabling people to work for each other.
사람들이 서로를 위해 일할 수 있게 함으로써다

The main theme of human history is /
인류 역사의 주요 주제는 ~것이다 /

that we become steadily more specialized /
우리가 꾸준히 더 전문화되는 (것이다) /

in what we produce, / and steadily more diversified /
우리가 생산하는 것에서 / 그리고 꾸준히 더 다양화되는 (것이다) /

in what we consume: /
우리가 소비하는 것에서 /

we move away from unstable self-sufficiency /
즉, 우리는 불안정한 자급자족에서 옮겨간다는 것이다 /

to safer mutual interdependence.
더 안전한 서로 간의 상호 의존으로

By concentrating on serving other people's needs /
다른 사람들의 필요를 충족시키는 것에 집중함으로써 /

for forty hours a week / — which we call a job — /
일주일에 40시간 동안 / 즉 우리가 직업이라 부르는 것에 /

you can spend the other seventy-two hours /
여러분은 다른 72시간을 보낼 수 있다 /

(not counting fifty-six hours in bed) /
(잠자는 56시간은 계산에 넣지 않고) /

relying on the services / 서비스에 의지하면서 /

provided to you by other people.
다른 사람들에 의해 여러분에게 제공되는

Innovation has made it possible to work /
혁신은 일하는 것을 가능하게 했다 /

for a fraction of a second /
아주 짧은 시간 동안 /

in order to be able to afford /
여유를 가질 수 있기 위해 /

to turn on an electric lamp for an hour, /
한 시간 동안 전등을 켜는 /

providing the quantity of light /
빛의 양을 제공했다 /

that would have required a whole day's work /
하루 종일의 노동이 필요했었을 /

if you had to make it yourself /
만약 여러분이 그것을 스스로 만들어야 했다면 /

by collecting and refining / sesame oil or lamb fat /
모으고 정제함으로써 / 참기름이나 양의 지방을 /

to burn in a simple lamp, / as much of humanity did /
단순한 등을 켜기 위해 / 많은 인류가 했던 것처럼 /

in the not so distant past.
그렇게 멀지 않은 과거에

혁신이 우리의 삶을 바꾸는 최고의 방법은 사람들이 서로를 위해 일할 수 있게 함으로써다. 인류 역사의 주요 주제는 우리가 생산하는 데 꾸준히 더 전문화되고 소비하는 데 꾸준히 더 다양화되는 것이다. 즉, 우리는 불안정한 자급자족에서 더 안전한 서로 간의 상호 의존으로 옮겨간다는 것이다. 일주일에 40시간 동안 다른 사람들의 필요를 충족시키는 것, 즉 우리가 직업이라 부르는 것에 집중함으로써, 여러분은 다른 사람들에 의해 여러분에게 제공되는 서비스에 의지하면서 다른 72시간(잠자는 56시간은 계산에 넣지 않고)을 보낼 수 있다. 혁신은 전등을 한 시간 동안 켜는 여유를 가질 수 있기 위해 아주 짧은 시간 동안 일하는 것을 가능하게 했고, 그것은 만약 여러분이 그렇게 멀지 않은 과거에 많은 인류가 했던 것처럼 단순한 등을 켜기 위해 참기름이나 양의 지방을 모으고 정제함으로써 그것을 스스로 만들어야 했다면 하루 종일의 노동이 필요했었을 빛의 양을 제공했다.

① 옛날의 가치를 존중함
② 사람들이 서로를 위해 일할 수 있게 함
③ 창의적으로 생각할 기회를 제공함
④ 개인화된 서비스로 고객들을 만족시킴
⑤ 특이한 제품들을 소개하고 상품화함

문제풀이

우리는 직업을 통해 다른 사람에게 서비스를 제공하면서 나머지 시간 동안에는 다른 서비를 받을 수 있는데, 이는 혁신을 통해 가능하며 예전에는 하루 종일의 노동이 필요했을 일을 혁신을 통해 빨리 끝낼 수 있다는 내용이다. 따라서 빈칸에 ② 'enabling people to work for each other'가 들어

가서 빈칸이 포함되는 문장이 '혁신이 우리의 삶을 바꾸는 최고의 방법은 사람들이 서로를 위해 일할 수 있게 함으로써다.'가 되는 것이 가장 적절하다.

《 어휘·어구 》

innovation 혁신
enable ~을 할 수 있게 하다
main 주요한
theme 주제
steadily 꾸준히
specialized 전문화된
diversified 다양한
consume 소비하다
unstable 불안정한
self-sufficiency 자기 충족
mutual 상호의
interdependence 상호 의존
concentrate on ~에 집중하다
rely on ~에 의존하다
possible 가능한
afford ~할 여유가 있다
turn on ~을 켜다
electric lamp 전등
quantity 양
require 필요하다
collect 모이다
sesame oil 참기름
humanity 인류
distant 먼
respect 존중하다
value 가치
opportunity 기회
creatively 창의적으로
satisfy A with B B를 A로 만족시키다
personalized 개인화된
introduce 소개하다
commercialize 상품화하다
unusual 특이한

정답률 50%

2. ② 인간의 판단력을 빼앗는 로봇

직독/직해

We worry / that the robots are taking our jobs, /
우리는 걱정한다 / 로봇이 우리의 직업을 빼앗고 있다고 /
but just as common a problem is /
하지만 그만큼 흔한 문제는 ~이다 /
that the robots are taking our judgment.
로봇이 우리의 판단력을 빼앗고 있다는 것(이다)
In the large warehouses / 거대 창고에서 /
so common behind the scenes of today's economy, /
오늘날의 경제 배후에서 아주 흔한 /
human 'pickers' hurry around grabbing products /
인간 '집게'는 서둘러 상품을 집어낸다 /
off shelves / and moving them /
선반에서 / 그리고 그것들을 이동시킨다 /
to where they can be packed and dispatched.
포장되고 발송될 수 있는 곳으로
In their ears are headpieces: /
그들의 귀에는 헤드폰이 있다 /
the voice of 'Jennifer', / a piece of software, /
'Jennifer'의 목소리가 / 한 소프트웨어 프로그램인 /
tells them where to go / and what to do, /
그들에게 어디로 갈지를 말한다 / 그리고 무엇을 할지 /
controlling the smallest details of their movements.
그들의 움직임의 가장 작은 세부 사항들을 조종하면서
Jennifer breaks down instructions /
Jennifer는 지시 사항들을 쪼갠다 /
into tiny chunks, / to minimise error /
아주 작은 덩어리들로 / 실수를 최소화하기 위해 /
and maximise productivity / — for example, /
그리고 생산성을 최대화하기 위해 / 예를 들어 /
rather than picking eighteen copies of a book /
책 18권을 집어내기보다는 /
off a shelf, / 선반에서 /
the human worker would be politely instructed /
인간 작업자는 정중하게 지시받을 것이다 /
to pick five. 5권을 집어내라고
Then another five. 그러고 나서 또 다른 5권을
Then yet another five. 그러고 나서 다시 또 다른 5권을
Then another three. 그러고 나서 또 다른 3권을
Working in such conditions /
그런 조건에서 일하는 것은 /
reduces people to machines made of flesh.
사람을 살로 만들어진 기계로 격하시킨다
Rather than asking us to think or adapt, /
우리에게 생각하거나 적응하라고 요구하기보다 /
the Jennifer unit takes over the thought process /
Jennifer라는 장치는 사고 과정을 가져간다 /
and treats workers as an inexpensive source /
그리고 작업자들을 값싼 자원으로 취급한다 /
of some visual processing /
약간의 시각적인 처리 과정의 /
and a pair of opposable thumbs.
그리고 한 쌍의 마주 볼 수 있는 엄지손가락을 가진

우리는 로봇이 우리의 직업을 빼앗고 있다고 걱정하지만, 그만큼 흔한 문제는 로봇이 우리의 판단력을 빼앗고 있다는 것이다. 오늘날의 경제 배후에서 아주 흔한 거대 창고에서 인간 '집게'는 선반에서 서둘러 상품을 집어내고 포장되고 발송될 수 있는 곳으로 그것들을 이동시킨다. 그들의 귀에는 헤드폰이 있는데, 한 소프트웨어 프로그램인 'Jennifer'의 목소리가 그들의 움직임의 가장 작은 세부 사항들을 조종하면서 그들에게 어디로 갈지 그리고 무엇을 할지를 말한다. Jennifer는 실수를 최소화하고 생산성을 최대화하기 위해 지시 사항들을 아주 작은 덩어리들로 쪼갠다 — 예를 들어, 인간 작업자는 선반에서 책 18권을 집어내기보다는, 5권을 집어내라고 정중하게 지시받을 것이다. 그러고 나서 또 다른 5권을. 그러고 나서 다시 또 다른 5권을. 그러고 나서 또 다른 3권을. 그런 조건에서 일하는 것은 사람을 살로 만들어진 기계로 격하시킨다. 우리에게 생각하거나 적응하라고 요구하기보다, Jennifer라는 장치는 사고 과정을 가져가고 작업자들을 약간의 시각적인 처리 과정과 한 쌍의 마주 볼 수 있는 엄지손가락을 가진 값싼 자원으로 취급한다.

① 신뢰성　　② 판단력
③ 인내　　④ 사교성
⑤ 협동

문제풀이

로봇이 인간의 직업을 빼앗고 있다고 걱정하지만 진짜 문제는 바로 로봇이 인간이 하는 사고 과정을 가져가고 인간을 살로 만들어진 기계로 격하시켜 값싼 자원으로 취급한다는 내용의 글이다. 따라서 글의 빈칸에 ② 'judgment'가 들어가서 빈칸이 포함되는 문장이 '우리는 로봇이 우리의 직업을 빼앗고 있다고 걱정하지만, 그만큼 흔한 문제는 로봇이 우리의 판단력을 빼앗고 있다는 것이다.'가 되는 것이 가장 적절하다.

이렇게 풀자 글의 마지막 문장인 'Rather than asking us to think or adapt, the Jennifer unit takes over the thought process and treats workers as an inexpensive source of some visual processing and a pair of opposable thumbs.'를 통해 빈칸에 들어갈 말을 추론할 수 있다.

구조 다시보기

주제	로봇이 인간의 판단력을 빼앗고 있음
예시	소프트웨어 프로그램 'Jennifer'가 생산성을 최대화하기 위해 지시 사항을 분배해서 내림
부연	로봇이 인간의 사고 과정을 대신하여 인간을 살로 만들어진 기계로 격하시킴

《 어휘·어구 》

common 흔한
warehouse 창고
economy 경제
control 조종하다
detail 세부 사항
movement 움직임
break down 나누다, 분류하다, 쪼개다
instruction 지시 사항
minimise 최소화하다(= minimize)
maximise 최대화하다(= maximize)
productivity 생산성
politely 정중히
condition 조건
reduce 낮추다
flesh 살
adapt 적응하다
takes over 빼앗다
treat 취급하다, 대우하다
visual 시각의
processing 처리 과정
opposable 마주볼 수 있는
reliability 신뢰성
judgment 판단
endurance 인내
sociability 사교성
cooperation 협동

3. ⑤ 사람은 자신의 발달에 능동적인 기여자이다

직독/직해

The prevailing view / 지배적인 견해는 /
among developmental scientists /
발달 과학자들 사이에서 /
is that people are active contributors /
사람들이 능동적인 기여자라는 것이다 /
to their own development.
그들 자신의 발달에
People are influenced / 사람들은 영향을 받는다 /
by the physical and social contexts /
물리적인 환경과 사회적인 환경에 의해 /
in which they live, / but they also play a role /
그들이 사는 / 하지만 그들은 또한 역할을 한다 /
in influencing their development /
그들의 발달에 영향을 주는 데 /
by interacting with, and changing, / those contexts.
상호 작용하고, 그리고 변화시킴으로써 / 그 환경들과
Even infants influence / the world around them /
심지어 유아들도 영향을 준다 / 그들 주변의 세상에 /
and construct their own development /
그리고 그들 자신의 발달을 구성한다 /
through their interactions.
그들의 상호 작용을 통해
Consider an infant who smiles /
미소 짓는 유아를 생각해 보라 /
at each adult he sees; / he influences his world /
그가 바라보는 각각의 어른에게 / 그는 자신의 세상에 영향을 준다 /
because adults are likely to smile, /
어른들이 미소 지을 것이기 때문에 /
use "baby talk," / and play with him / in response.
'아기 말'을 사용할 것이기 (때문에) / 그리고 그와 함께 놀아줄 것이기 (때문에) / 반응하여
The infant brings adults into close contact, /
그 유아는 어른들을 친밀하게 연결시켜서 /
making one-on-one interactions /
일대일 상호 작용을 하게 만든다 /
and creating opportunities for learning.
그리고 학습의 기회를 만든다

By engaging the world around them, /
그들 주변 세상의 관심을 끎으로써 /
thinking, being curious, and interacting /
생각하고, 호기심을 가지고 상호 작용함으로써 /
with people, objects, and the world around them, /
그들 주변의 사람들, 사물들, 그리고 세상과 /
individuals of all ages are /
모든 연령대의 개인들은 ~이다 /
"manufacturers of their own development."
'그들 자신의 발달을 생산하는 사람'

발달 과학자들 사이에서 지배적인 견해는 사람들이 그들 자신의 발달에 능동적인 기여자라는 것이다. 사람들은 그들이 사는 물리적인 환경과 사회적인 환경에 의해 영향을 받지만, 그들은 또한 그 환경들과 상호 작용하고, 그리고 변화시킴으로써, 그들의 발달에 영향을 주는 역할을 한다. 심지어 유아들도 그들 주변의 세상에 영향을 주고 그들의 상호 작용을 통해 그들 자신의 발달을 구성한다. 그가 바라보는 각각의 어른에게 미소 짓는 유아를 생각해 보라. (그에) 반응하여, 어른들이 미소 짓고, "아기 말"을 사용하고, 그리고 그와 함께 놀아줄 것이기 때문에 그는 자신의 세상에 영향을 준다. 그 유아는 어른들을 친밀하게 연결시켜서 일대일 상호 작용을 하고 학습의 기회를 만든다. 그들 주변 세상의 관심을 끌고, 생각하고, 호기심을 가지고, 그리고 그들 주변의 사람들, 사물들, 그리고 세상과 상호 작용함으로써, 모든 연령대의 개인들은 '그들 자신의 발달을 생산하는 사람'이다.

① 그들 세대의 거울
② 사회적 갈등에 대한 방패
③ 그들 자신의 진로에 있어서 탐험가
④ 그들의 어린 시절 꿈의 추종자
⑤ 그들 자신의 발달을 생산하는 사람

문제풀이

사람들이 자신의 발달에 능동적인 기여자라 생각한다는 발달 과학자들의 견해에 대한 글이다. 사람은 주변 환경에 의해 영향을 받지만 환경과 상호 작용하고 변화시킴으로써 발달한다는 내용을 통해, 빈칸에 ⑤ 'manufacturers of their own development'가 들어가서 빈칸이 포함되는 문장이 '그들 주변 세상의 관심을 끌고, 생각하고, 호기심을 가지고, 그리고 그들 주변의 사람들, 사물들, 그리고 세상과 상호 작용함으로써, 모든 연령대의 개인들은 그들 자신의 발달을 생산하는 사람이다.'가 되는 것이 가장 적절하다.

어휘·어구

prevailing 지배적인
developmental 발달상의
active 능동적인
contributor 기여자
influence 영향을 주다
physical 물리적
context 환경, 상황
play a role in ~에서 역할을 하다
interact 상호 작용하다
construct 만들다
in response 반응하여, 대응하여
engage (관심을) 사로잡다
individual 개인
generation 세대
shield 방패
conflict 갈등
explorer 탐험가
career path 진로
follower 추종자
childhood 어린 시절
manufacturer 생산자

정답률 54%

4. ① 한계가 창의력을 증진시킬 수 있다

직독/직해

One of the big questions / faced this past year /
가장 큰 질문들 중 하나는 / 작년에 직면한 /
was how to keep innovation rolling /
어떻게 혁신을 지속할 것인가 하는 것이었다 /
when people were working entirely virtually.
사람들이 완전히 가상 공간에서 작업할 때
But experts say / 하지만 전문가들은 말한다 /
that digital work didn't have a negative effect /
디지털 작업이 부정적인 영향을 미치지 않았다고 /
on innovation and creativity.
혁신과 창의성에
Working within limits / pushes us to solve problems.
한계 내에서 일하는 것은 / 우리에게 문제를 해결하도록 독려한다
Overall, / virtual meeting platforms /
전반적으로 / 가상 미팅 플랫폼은 /
put more constraints / 더 많은 제약들을 가한다 /
on communication and collaboration /
의사소통과 협업에 /
than face-to-face settings. 대면 설정보다
For instance, / with the press of a button, /
예를 들어 / 버튼을 누르면 /
virtual meeting hosts can control /
가상 회의 진행자는 제어할 수 있다 /
the size of breakout groups /
소모임 그룹의 크기를 /
and enforce time constraints;
그리고 시간 제한을 강요할 수 있다
only one person can speak / at a time; /
오직 한 사람만이 말할 수 있다 / 한 번에 /
nonverbal signals, / 비언어적인 신호 /
particularly those below the shoulders, /
특히 어깨 아래의 신호는 /
are diminished; / 제한된다 /
"seating arrangements" are assigned by the platform, / not by individuals; /
'좌석 배치'는 플랫폼에 의해 할당된다 / 개인이 아닌
and visual access to others / may be limited /
그리고 다른 사람에 대한 시각적 접근은 / 제한될 수 있다 /
by the size of each participant's screen.
각 참가자의 화면 크기에 의해
Such restrictions are likely to stretch participants /
이런 제한점은 참가자들을 확장시켜서 /
beyond their usual ways of thinking, /
그들의 일반적인 사고방식 너머까지 /
boosting creativity. 창의력을 증진시킬 가능성이 있다

작년에 직면한 가장 큰 질문들 중 하나는 사람들이 완전히 가상 공간에서 작업할 때 어떻게 혁신을 지속할 것인가 하는 것이었다. 하지만 전문가들은 디지털 작업이 혁신과 창의성에 부정적인 영향을 미치지 않았다고 말한다. 한계 내에서 일하는 것은 우리에게 문제를 해결하도록 독려한다. 전반적으로, 가상 미팅 플랫폼은 대면 설정보다 의사소통과 협업에 더 많은 제약들을 가한다. 예를 들어, 버튼을 누르면, 가상 회의 진행자는 소모임 그룹의 크기를 제어할 수 있고, 시간 제한을 강요할 수 있다. 오직 한 번에 한 사람만이 말할 수 있다. 비언어적인 신호, 특히 어깨 아래의 신호는 제한된다. '좌석 배치'는 개인이 아닌 플랫폼에 의해 할당된다. 그리고 다른 사람에 대한 시각적 접근은 각 참가자의 화면 크기에 의해 제한될 수 있다. 이런 제한점은 참가자들을 그들의 일반적인 사고방식 너머까지 확장시켜서 창의력을 증진시킬 가능성이 있다.

① 제한점 ② 책임 ③ 기억 ④ 일치 ⑤ 전통

문제풀이

디지털 작업은 혁신과 창의성에 부정적인 역할을 미치지 않고, 한계 내에서 일하는 것은 오히려 우리가 문제를 해결할 수 있도록 독려한다는 내용의 글이다. 가상 회의는 여러 가지 제한 사항들이 있지만 이런 한계들로 인해 우리의 창의력이 증진될 수 있다는 내용이므로 글의 빈칸에 ① 'restrictions'가 들어가서 빈칸이 포함되는 문장이 '이런 제한점들은 참가자들을 그들의 일반적인 사고방식 너머까지 확장시켜서 창의력을 증진시킬 가능성이 있다.'가 되는 것이 가장 적절하다.

이렇게 풀자 'Working within limits pushes us to solve problems.'와 예로 들은 가상 회의 진행시 모임 그룹의 크기나 시간제한 등 여러 제한 사항들을 통해 빈칸에 들어갈 말을 추론할 수 있다.

구조 다시보기

도입	사람들은 가상 공간에서 작업 시 어떻게 혁신을 지속하는가
주제	한계 내에서 일하는 것이 문제 해결을 독려함
사례	가상 회의 시 그룹 크기 제어나 시간제한 등의 제약이 있음
결론	제한점들이 창의력을 증진시킬 가능성이 있음

어휘·어구

innovation 혁신
entirely 완전히
virtually 가상으로
expert 전문가
negative 부정적인
effect 영향
creativity 창의력
limit 한계
overall 대체로
constraint 제한
communication 의사소통
collaboration 협업
face-to-face 대면하는
breakout group 브레이크아웃 그룹(소그룹)
enforce 강요하다
nonverbal 비언어적인
signal 신호
particularly 특히
diminish 줄이다, 줄어들다
assign 할당하다, 배당하다
arrangement 배정, 배치
individual 개인
visual 시각의
access 접근
participant 참가자
stretch 늘이다
boost 증진시키다
restriction 제한점
responsibility 책임
coincidence 일치
tradition 전통

5. ② 수요 법칙이 적용되지 않는 기펜재

직독/직해

The law of demand is /
수요 법칙은 ~이다 /
that the demand for goods and services increases /
상품과 서비스에 대한 수요가 증가하는 것 /
as prices fall, / and the demand falls /
가격이 하락할수록 / 그리고 수요가 감소하는 것 /
as prices increase. 가격이 상승할수록
Giffen goods are special types of products /
'기펜재'는 특별한 유형의 상품이다 /
for which the traditional law of demand /
전통적인 수요 법칙이 /
does not apply. 적용되지 않는
Instead of switching to cheaper replacements, /
더 저렴한 대체품으로 바꾸는 대신 /
consumers demand more of giffen goods /
소비자들은 기펜재를 더 많이 수요한다 /
when the price increases / 가격이 상승할 때 /

and less of them / when the price decreases.
그리고 그것들을 덜 (수요한다) / 가격이 하락할 때

Taking an example, / rice in China is a giffen good /
예를 들어 / 중국에서 쌀은 기펜재이다 /

because people tend to purchase less of it / when the price falls.
사람들이 그것을 덜 구매하는 경향이 있기 때문에 / 가격이 하락할 때

The reason for this is, / when the price of rice falls, /
그 이유는 ~이다 / 쌀값이 하락하면 /

people have more money to spend / on other types of products /
사람들이 쓸 돈이 더 많아지기 때문이다 / 다른 종류의 상품에 /

such as meat and dairy / and, therefore, /
고기나 유제품 같은 / 그 결과 /

change their spending pattern.
자신들의 소비 패턴을 바꾸기 (때문이다)

On the other hand, / as rice prices increase, /
반면에 / 쌀값이 상승하면 /

people consume more rice.
사람들은 더 많은 쌀을 소비한다

수요 법칙은 가격이 하락할수록 상품과 서비스에 대한 수요가 증가하고, 가격이 상승할수록 수요가 감소하는 것이다. '기펜재'는 전통적인 수요 법칙이 적용되지 않는 특별한 유형의 상품이다. 더 저렴한 대체품으로 바꾸는 대신 소비자들은 가격이 상승할 때 기펜재를 더 많이, 가격이 하락할 때 그것들을 덜 수요한다. 예를 들어, 중국에서 쌀은 가격이 하락할 때 사람들이 덜 구매하는 경향이 있기 때문에 기펜재이다. 그 이유는, 쌀값이 하락하면, 사람들이 고기나 유제품 같은 다른 종류의 상품에 쓸 돈이 더 많아지고, 그 결과 자신들의 소비 패턴을 바꾸기 때문이다. 반면에, 쌀값이 상승하면, 사람들은 더 많은 쌀을 소비한다.

① 고기를 더 많이 주문한다
② 더 많은 쌀을 소비한다
③ 새로운 직업을 얻기 위해 노력한다
④ 그들의 저축을 늘린다
⑤ 해외 투자를 시작한다

문제풀이

수요 법칙이 적용되지 않는 특별한 유형의 상품인 기펜재에 관한 내용이다. 기펜재는 가격이 하락하면 수요가 줄고 가격이 상승할수록 수요가 늘어난다는 내용을 통해, 빈칸에 ② 'consume more rice'가 들어가서 빈칸이 포함되는 문장이 '반면에, 쌀값이 상승하면, 사람들은 더 많은 쌀을 소비한다.'가 되는 것이 가장 적절하다.

구조 다시보기

도입	수요 법칙의 정의 : 가격이 하락하면 수요가 늘고 가격이 상승하면 수요가 줄어듦
주제	기펜재는 수요 법칙이 적용되지 않음
부연	기펜제는 가격이 하락하면 수요가 줄고 가격이 상승하면 수요가 늘어남
사례	중국에서 쌀값이 상승할수록 더 많은 쌀이 소비됨

어휘·어구

law of demand 수요 법칙
giffen goods 기펜재
traditional 전통의
apply 적용하다
switch 바꾸다
replacement 대체품
purchase 구입하다
consume 소비하다
invest 투자하다
overseas 해외의

6. ② 실감나는 글을 쓰기 위해 세밀하게 표현하라

직독/직해

Generalization without specific examples /
구체적인 사례가 없는 일반화는 /

that humanize writing / 글을 인간미 있게 하는 /

is boring to the listener and to the reader.
듣는 사람과 읽는 사람에게 지루하다

Who wants to read platitudes / all day?
누가 상투적인 말을 읽고 싶겠는가 / 온종일

Who wants to hear the words /
누가 이런 말들을 듣고 싶겠는가 /

great, greater, best, smartest, finest, humanitarian, /
위대한, 더 위대한, 최고의, 제일 똑똑한, 가장 훌륭한, 인도주의적인 /

on and on and on / without specific examples?
계속해서 끊임없이 / 구체적인 사례 없이

Instead of using these 'nothing words,' /
이런 '공허한 말들'을 사용하는 대신에 /

leave them out completely /
그것들을 완전히 빼라 /

and just describe the particulars.
그리고 세부 사항들만을 서술하라

There is nothing worse /
더 끔찍한 것은 없다 /

than reading a scene in a novel /
소설에서의 장면을 읽는 것보다 /

in which a main character is described /
주인공을 묘사하는 /

up front as heroic or brave or tragic or funny, /
대놓고 영웅적이다, 용감하다, 비극적이다, 혹은 웃긴다고 /

while thereafter, / the writer quickly moves /
그런 다음에 / 작가가 빠르게 넘어가는 /

on to something else. 다른 것으로

That's no good, / no good at all.
그건 좋지 않고 / 전혀 좋지 않다

You have to use / less one word descriptions /
사용해야 한다 / 한 단어 묘사는 덜 /

and more detailed, engaging descriptions /
그리고 세밀하고 마음을 끄는 묘사를 더 많이 /

if you want to make something real.
만일 무언가를 실감 나는 것으로 만들고 싶다면

글을 인간미 있게 하는 구체적인 사례가 없는 일반화는 듣는 사람과 읽는 사람에게 지루하다. 누가 상투적인 말을 온종일 읽고 싶겠는가? 구체적인 사례 없이 위대한, 더 위대한, 최고의, 제일 똑똑한, 가장 훌륭한, 인도주의적인, 이런 말들을 누가 계속해서 끊임없이 듣고 싶겠는가? 이런 '공허한 말들'을 사용하는 대신에, 그것들을 완전히 빼고 세부 사항들만을 서술하라. 주인공을 대놓고 영웅적이다, 용감하다, 비극적이다, 혹은 웃긴다고 묘사하고, 그런 다음에 작가가 다른 것으로 빠르게 넘어가는 소설에서의 장면을 읽는 것보다 더 끔찍한 것은 없다. 그건 좋지 않고, 전혀 좋지 않다. 만일 무언가를 실감 나는 것으로 만들고 싶다면, 한 단어 묘사는 덜 사용하고, 세밀하고 마음을 끄는 묘사를 더 많이 사용해야 한다.

① 닮은 점들 **② 세부 사항들**
③ 공상들 ④ 지루한 것
⑤ 지혜

문제풀이

글을 흥미롭고 실감 나게 만들고 싶다면 일반적인 '공허한 말들'을 사용하는 대신 세밀하고 마음을 끄는 묘사를 많이 사용하라는 내용이므로, 글의 빈칸에 ② 'particulars'가 들어가서 빈칸이 포함되는 문장이 '이런 '공허한 말들'을 사용하는 대신에, 그것들을 완전히 빼고 세부 사항들만을 서술하라.'가 되는 것이 가장 적절하다.

이렇게 풀자 글의 마지막 문장인 'You have to use less one word descriptions and more detailed, engaging descriptions if you want to make something real.'을 통해 빈칸에 들어갈 말을 추론할 수 있다.

어휘·어구

generalization 일반화
specific 구체적인
humanize 인간미 있게 하다
finest 가장 훌륭한
humanitarian 인도주의적인
completely 완전히
describe 묘사하다 (n. description)
main character 주인공
up front 대놓고
heroic 대담한, 영웅적인
tragic 비극적인
thereafter 그 후
detailed 세밀한
similarity 유사성, 닮은 점
particular 자세한 사실, 세부 사항
fantasy 공상
boredom 지루한 것

7. ③ 대화는 지식을 공유하는 강력한 방법이다

직독/직해

Face-to-face interaction is a uniquely powerful /
대면 상호 작용은 유례없이 강력한 ~이다 /

— and sometimes the only — / 그리고 때로는 유일한 /

way to share many kinds of knowledge, /
많은 종류의 지식을 공유하는 방법(이다) /

from the simplest to the most complex.
가장 간단한 것부터 가장 복잡한 것까지

It is one of the best ways / 그것은 가장 좋은 방법 중 한 가지이다 /

to stimulate new thinking and ideas, too.
또한 새로운 생각과 아이디어를 자극하는

Most of us would have had difficulty learning /
우리 대부분이 ~을 배우는 데 어려움을 겪었을 것이다 /

how to tie a shoelace only from pictures, /
그림만으로 신발 끈 묶는 법을 /

or how to do arithmetic from a book.
혹은 책으로부터 계산하는 방법을 /

Psychologist Mihàly Csikszentmihàlyi found, /
심리학자 Mihàly Csikszentmihàlyi는 발견했다 /

while studying high achievers, /
높은 성취도를 보이는 사람들을 연구하면서 /

that a large number of Nobel Prize winners /
다수의 노벨상 수상자가 /

were the students of previous winners: /
이전 (노벨상) 수상자들의 학생들이라는 것을 /

they had access to / 그들은 ~에 접근할 수 있었다 /

the same literature as everyone else, /
다른 사람들과 똑같은 연구 문헌(에) /

but personal contact made /
하지만 개인적인 접촉이 만들었다 /

a crucial difference to their creativity.
그들의 창의성에 결정적인 차이를

Within organisations / this makes conversation /
조직 내에서 / 이것은 대화를 ~하게 만든다 /

both a crucial factor for highlevel professional skills /
고급 전문 기술을 위한 매우 중요한 요소로 /

and the most important way /
그리고 가장 중요한 방식으로 /

of sharing everyday information.
일상 정보를 공유하는

대면 상호 작용은 가장 간단한 것부터 가장 복잡한 것까지 많은 종류의 지식을 공유하는, 유례없이 강력한 — 때로는 유일한 — 방법이다. 그것은 또한 새로운 생각과 아이디어를 자극하는 가장 좋은 방법 중 한 가지이기도 하다. 우리 대부분이 그림만으로 신발 끈 묶는 법을 배웠거나, 책으로부터 계산하는 방법을 배웠다면 어려움을 겪었을 것이다. 심리학자 Mihàly Csikszentmihàlyi는 높은 성취도를 보이는 사람들을 연구하면서 다수의 노벨상 수상자가 이전 (노벨상) 수상자들의 학생들이라는 것을 발견했다. 그들은 다른 사람들과 똑같은 (연구) 문헌에 접근할 수 있었지만, 개인적인 접촉이 그들의 창의성에 결정적인 차이를 만들었다. 이로 인해 조직 내에서 대화는 고급 전문 기술을 위한 매우 중요한 요소이자 일상 정보를 공유하는 가장 중요한 방식이 된다.

① 천부적인 재능 ② 규칙적인 연습
③ 개인적인 접촉 ④ 복잡한 지식
⑤ 강력한 동기

문제풀이

대면 상호 작용은 많은 종류의 지식을 공유하는 가장 강력하고 유일한 방법이다. 이것은 다수의 노벨상 수상자들이 이전 노벨상 수상자들의 학생들인 경우가 많았다는 사실을 봐도 알 수 있는데 그들은 다른 사람들과 똑같은 문헌에 접근하더라도 스승들과의 대면 상호 작용을 통해 그들의 창의성에 결정적인 차이를 갖게 되었다. 따라서 빈칸에 ③ 'personal contact'가 들어가서 빈칸이 포함되는 문장이 '그들은 다른 사람들과 같은 (연구) 문헌에 접근할 수 있었지만, 개인적인 접촉이 그들의 창의성에 결정적인 차이를 만들었다.'가 되는 것이 가장 적절하다.

구조 다시보기

주제	대면 상호 작용은 지식을 공유하는 가장 강력하고 유일한 방법임
 근거	– 다수의 노벨 수상자는 이전 노벨 수상자들의 학생이었음 – 사용하는 문헌은 같더라도 개인 접촉이 창의성에 결정적인 차이를 만듦
부연	직장에서 대화는 고급 전문 기술을 위한 요소이자 일상 정보를 공유하는 중요한 방식임

어휘·어구

face-to-face 대면의
interaction 상호 작용
uniquely 유례 없이
simplest 가장 간단한
complex 복잡한
stimulate 자극하다
have difficulty -ing ~하는 데 어려움을 겪다
shoelace 신발 끈
psychologist 심리학자
previous 이전의
crucial 결정적인, 매우 중요한
creativity 창의성
factor 요소
professional 전문적인
natural talent 천부적인 재능
regular 규칙적인
personal 개인적인
contact 접촉
motivation 동기

정답률 65%

8. ② 사전 통보의 중요성

직독/직해

We don't send telegraphs to communicate anymore, /
우리는 통신하기 위해 더 이상 전보를 보내지 않는다 /
but it's a great metaphor /
그러나 그것은 훌륭한 비유이다 /
for giving advance notice.
사전 통보를 하는 것에 대한
Sometimes, / you must inform those close to you /
때때로 / 여러분은 자신에게 가까운 사람들에게 알려야 한다 /
of upcoming change / 다가오는 변화를 /
by conveying important information well in advance.
중요한 정보를 미리 잘 전달함으로써
There's a huge difference / between / saying, /
큰 차이가 있다 / 사이에는 / (~라고) 말하는 것 /
"From now on, / we will do things differently," /
지금부터 / 우리는 일을 다르게 할 겁니다 /
which doesn't give people enough time /
사람들에게 충분한 시간을 주지 않고 /
to understand and accept the change, /
그 변화를 이해하고 받아들일 /
and saying something like, / "Starting next month, /
그리고 (~와) 같이 어떤 말을 하는 것 (사이에는) / 다음 달부터 /
we're going to approach things differently."
우리는 일에 다르게 접근할 겁니다
Telegraphing empowers people to adapt.
전보를 보내는 것은 사람들이 적응할 수 있도록 해 준다
Telegraphing involves / 전보를 보내는 것은 포함한다 /
the art of seeing an upcoming event or circumstance /
다가오는 사건이나 상황을 보는 기술을 /
and giving others enough time /
그리고 다른 사람들에게 충분한 시간을 주는 /
to process and accept the change.
그 변화를 처리하고 받아들일
Telegraph anything / that will take people out of/
무엇이든 전보로 보내라 / 사람들을 벗어나게 할
what is familiar and comfortable to them.
그들에게 익숙하고 편안한 것에서
This will allow processing time /
이것은 처리 시간을 허용해 줄 것이다 /
for them to accept the circumstances /
그들이 그 상황을 받아들이는 /
and make the most of what's happening.
그리고 일어나고 있는 일을 최대한으로 활용할 수 있는

우리는 통신하기 위해 더 이상 전보를 보내지 않지만 그것은 사전 통보를 하는 것에 대한 훌륭한 비유이다. 때때로 여러분은 중요한 정보를 미리 잘 전달함으로써 다가오는 변화를 자신에게 가까운 사람들에게 알려야 한다. 사람들에게 그 변화를 이해하고 받아들일 충분한 시간을 주지 않는 "지금부터 우리는 일을 다르게 할 겁니다."라고 말하는 것과 "다음 달부터 우리는 일에 다르게 접근할 겁니다."와 같은 것을 말하는 것 사이에는 큰 차이가 있다. 전보를 보내는 것은 사람들이 적응할 수 있도록 해 준다. 전보를 보내는 것은 다가오는 사건이나 상황을 보고 다른 사람들에게 그 변화를 처리하고 받아들일 충분한 시간을 주는 기술을 포함한다. 사람들을 그들에게 익숙하고 편안한 것에서 벗어나게 할 무엇이든 전보로 보내라. 이것은 그들이 그 상황을 받아들이고 일어나고 있는 일을 최대한으로 활용할 수 있는 처리 시간을 허용해 줄 것이다.

① 단결시키다
② 적응시키다
③ 반대하다
④ 겨루다
⑤ 회복하다

문제풀이

사전 통보의 비유로 쓰인 전보 보내기가 사람들로 하여금 변화를 이해하고 받아들일 충분한 시간을 준다는 내용의 글이다. 따라서 빈칸에는 ② 'adapt'가 들어가서 빈칸이 포함된 문장이 '전보를 보내는 것은 사람들이 적응할 수 있도록 해 준다.'가 되는 것이 가장 적절하다.

이렇게 풀자 'give people enough time to understand and accept the change(사람들에게 그 변화를 이해하고 받아들일 충분한 시간을 준다)'와 'Telegraphing involves the art of seeing an upcoming event or circumstance and giving others enough time to process and accept the change.(전보를 보내는 것은 다가오는 사건이나 상황을 보고 다른 사람들에게 그 변화를 처리하고 받아들일 충분한 시간을 주는 기술을 포함한다.)'에서 'understand and accept', 'process and accept'와 같은 의미를 지닌 'adapt'가 빈칸에 들어가야 한다는 것을 쉽게 유추할 수 있다.

어휘·어구

metaphor 비유
advance 사전의
notice 공지, 안내문
convey 전달하다
from now on 지금부터
adapt 적응하다
involve 포함하다
process 과정
familiar 익숙한
comfortable 편안한

정답률 67%

9. ① 우리가 누구인지를 규정하는 기억

직독/직해

Not only does memory underlie our ability to think at all, /
기억이 어쨌든 (기억은) 사고하는 우리의 능력의 기반이 될 뿐만 아니라 /
it defines the content of our experiences /
그것은 우리의 경험의 내용을 규정한다 /
and how we preserve them / for years to come.
그리고 우리가 그것을 보존하는 방식을 / 다가올 수년간
Memory makes us who we are.
기억은 우리를 우리가 누구인지로 만들어 준다
If I were to suffer from heart failure /
비록 내가 심장 부전을 앓게 되어도 /
and depend upon an artificial heart, /
그리고 인공 심장에 의존한다 해도 /
I would be no less myself.
나는 역시 여느 때의 나일 것이다
If I lost an arm in an accident /
만약 내가 사고로 한 팔을 잃게 되어도 /
and had it replaced with an artificial arm, /
그리고 그것을 인공 팔로 교체한다 해도 /
I would still be essentially *me*.
나는 여전히 본질적으로 '나'일 것이다
As long as my mind and memories remain intact, /
나의 정신과 기억이 손상되지 않은 한 /
I will continue to be the same person, /
나는 계속 같은 사람일 것이다 /
no matter which part of my body (other than the brain) is replaced.
나의 신체의 (뇌를 제외한) 어떤 부분이 교체될지라도
On the other hand, / when someone suffers from advanced Alzheimer's disease /
반면 / 누군가 후기의 알츠하이머병을 앓게 될 때 /
and his memories fade, / people often say /
그리고 그의 기억이 흐려진다면 / 사람들은 종종 말한다 /
that he "is not himself anymore," /
그는 더 이상 여느 때의 그가 아니라고 /
or that it is as if the person "is no longer there," /
혹은 마치 그 사람이 '더 이상 그곳에 없는' 것 같다고 /
though his body remains unchanged.
비록 그의 신체는 변하지 않은 채로 남아 있음에도 불구하고

기억이 어쨌든 사고하는 우리의 능력의 기반이 될 뿐만 아니라 그것은 우리의 경험의 내용과 다가올 수년 간 우리가 그것을 보존하는 방식을 규정한다. 기억은 우리를 우리가 누구인지로 만들어 준다. 만약 내가 심장 부전을 앓고 인공 심장에 의존한다 해도 나는 역시 여느 때의 나일 것이다. 만약 내가 사고로 한 팔을 잃고 그것을 인공 팔로 교체한다 해도 나는 여전히 본질적으로 '나'일 것이다. 나의 정신과 기억이 손상되지 않은 한, 나의 신체의 (뇌를 제외한) 어떤 부분이 교체될지라도 나는 계속 같은 사람일 것이다. 반면 누군가 후기의 알츠하이머병을 앓고 그의 기억이 흐려진다면, 비록 그의 신체는 변하지 않은 채로 남아 있음에도 불구하고 사람들은 종종 그는 '더 이상 여느 때의 그가 아니라고' 혹은 마치 그 사람이 '더 이상 그곳에 없는' 것 같다고 말한다.

① 우리를 우리가 누구인지로 만들어 준다
② 우리의 신체와 관련이 있다
③ 우리가 기대하는 것을 반영한다
④ 우리가 다른 사람들을 이해하게 해 준다
⑤ 우리가 과거로부터 배울 수 있도록 도와준다

문제풀이

우리가 심장 질병이나 사고로 팔을 잃게 되어 인공 심장이나 인공 팔을 사용한다 할지라도 '나'는 여전히 '나'이지만, 기억은 우리 사고의 기반이고 우리 경험을 보존해 주는 것이므로 기억을 잃게 되면 '나'는 '나'가 될 수 없다는 내용의 글이다. 따라서 빈칸에는 ① 'makes us who we are'가 들어가서 빈칸을 포함한 문장이 '기억은 우리를 우리가 누구인지로 만들어 준다.'가 되는 것이 가장 적절하다.

구조 다시보기

 주제	기억은 경험의 내용과 그것을 보존하는 방식을 규정함

부연	기억이 우리를 우리가 누구인지로 만들어 줌
예시 1	신체의 일부가 바뀌어도 본질적으로 나는 바뀌지 않음
예시 2	기억을 잃게 되면 존재의 본질이 변함

어휘·어구

underlie 토대를 이루다
define 정의하다
preserve 보존하다
suffer from ~으로 고통받는
artificial 인공적인
replace 교체하다
as long as ~하는 한
on the other hand 반면에
fade 희미해지다

정답률 58%

10. ① 단순함이 기업에 비교우위를 준다

직독직해

Sometimes it is the simpler product /
때때로 더 단순한 제품이다 /
that gives a business a competitive advantage.
기업에게 비교우위를 주는 것은
Until recently, / bicycles had to have many gears, /
최근까지 / 자전거는 많은 기어를 가져야만 했다 /
often 15 or 20, / for them to be considered high-end.
보통 15개 혹은 20개의 / 최고급으로 여겨지기 위해
But fixed-gear bikes / with minimal features /
하지만 고정식 기어 자전거들은 / 최소한의 특징들을 가지고 있는 /
have become more popular, / as those who buy them /
점점 더 인기를 얻게 되었다 / 그것들을 사는 사람들이 /
are happy to pay more for much less.
훨씬 적은 것에 대해 기꺼이 더 지불함에 따라
The overall profitability of these bikes / is much higher /
이런 자전거들의 전반적인 수익성은 / 훨씬 더 크다 /
than the more complex ones / 더 복잡한 것들보다 /
because they do a single thing really well /
그것들이 한 가지를 정말 잘하기 때문이다 /
without the cost of added complexity.
추가되는 복잡성에 대한 비용 없이
Companies should be careful / of getting into a war /
기업들은 조심해야 한다 / 전쟁을 하는 것을 /
over adding more features / with their competitors, /
더 많은 특징들을 추가하는 / 그들의 경쟁 업체와 /
as this will increase cost / 이것이 비용을 증가시키기 때문이다 /
and almost certainly reduce profitability /
그리고 수익성을 거의 확실히 감소시킬 (것이기 때문이다)
because of competitive pressure on price.
가격에 대한 경쟁적인 압박 때문에

때때로 기업에게 비교우위를 주는 것은 더 단순한 제품이다. 최근까지, 자전거는 최고급으로 여겨지기 위해 보통 15개 혹은 20개의 많은 기어를 가져야만 했다. 하지만 최소한의 특징들을 가지고 있는, 고정식 기어 자전거들은 그것들을 사는 사람들이 훨씬 적은 것에 대해 기꺼이 더 지불함에 따라 점점 더 인기를 얻게 되었다. 이런 자전거들의 전반적인 수익성은 더 복잡한 것들보다 훨씬 더 큰데, 그것들이 추가되는 복잡성에 대한 비용 없이 한 가지를 정말 잘하기 때문이다. 기업들은 그들의 경쟁 업체와 더 많은 특징들을 추가하는 전쟁을 하는 것을 조심해야 하는데, 이것이 가격에 대한 경쟁적인 압박 때문에 비용을 증가시키고 수익성을 거의 확실히 감소시킬 것이기 때문이다.

① 더 단순한 제품
② 적정한 가격
③ 소비자 충성심
④ 맞춤형 디자인
⑤ 친환경적인 기술

문제풀이

많은 특징을 가지고 있는 제품보다는 추가 비용 없이 특별히 잘하는 한 가지 특징을 가지고 있는 제품이 기업에 수익성을 보장해준다는 내용이므로, 빈칸에 ① 'simpler product'가 들어가서, 빈칸이 포함되는 문장이 '때때로 기업에게 비교우위를 주는 것은 더 단순한 제품이다.'가 되는 것이 가장 적절하다.

이렇게 풀자 많은 기어를 가지고 있는 자전거보다는 최소한의 특징을 가지고 있는 고정식 기어 자전거가 더 인기가 있다는 내용을 통해 빈칸에 들어갈 말을 추론할 수 있다.

어휘·어구

competitive advantage 비교우위
consider 여기다
fixed-gear 고정식 기어의
minimal 최소의
feature 특징
overall 전반적인, 전체의
profitability 수익성
complexity 복잡성
competitor 경쟁자
pressure 압박, 압력
affordable (가격이) 알맞은
customized 개개인의 요구에 맞춘

구조 다시보기

주제	기업은 단순한 제품으로 비교우위를 얻을 수 있음
사례	최소한의 특징을 가진 고정식 기어 자전거가 인기를 얻음
부연	경쟁을 위해 특징을 추가하는 것은 비용을 증가시키고 수익을 감소시키므로 주의해야 함

정답률 67%

11. ⑤ 경제와 언어의 상관관계

직독직해

Many evolutionary biologists argue /
많은 진화 생물학자는 주장한다 /
that humans developed language /
인간이 언어를 발달시켰다고 /
for economic reasons. 경제적인 이유로
We needed to trade, / 우리는 거래해야 했다 /
and we needed to establish trust /
그리고 우리는 신뢰를 확립해야 했다 /
in order to trade. 거래하기 위해서
Language is very handy / 언어는 매우 편리하다 /
when you are trying to conduct business /
당신이 거래할 때 /
with someone. 누군가와
Two early humans could not only agree /
초기의 두 인간은 동의할 수 있었을 뿐만 아니라 /
to trade three wooden bowls /
3개의 나무로 만든 그릇을 거래하기로 /
for six bunches of bananas / 6다발의 바나나와 /
but establish rules as well.
규칙을 정할 수도 있었다
What wood was used / for the bowls?
무슨 나무가 사용되었나 / 그 그릇들을 만드는데
Where did you get the bananas?
어디에서 그 바나나를 얻었나
That business deal / 그 상업 거래는 /
would have been nearly impossible /
거의 불가능했을 것이다 /
using only gestures and confusing noises, /
단지 제스처와 혼란스러운 소음만을 사용해서는 /
and carrying it out / 그리고 그것을 실행하는 것이 /
according to terms agreed upon / 합의된 조항에 따라서 /
creates a bond of trust. 신뢰라는 결속을 만든다
Language allows us to be specific, /
언어는 우리가 구체적이게 해준다 /
and this is where conversation plays a key role.
그리고 이것이 대화가 중요한 역할을 하는 지점이다

많은 진화 생물학자는 인간이 경제적인 이유로 언어를 발달시켰다고 주장한다. 우리는 거래해야 했고, 거래하기 위해서 신뢰를 확립해야 했다. 언어는 당신이 누군가와 거래할 때 매우 편리하다. 초기의 두 인간은 3개의 나무로 만든 그릇을 6다발의 바나나와 거래하기로 동의할 수 있었을 뿐만 아니라 규칙을 정할 수도 있었다. 그 그릇들을 만드는데 무슨 나무가 사용되었나? 어디에서 그 바나나를 얻었나? 단지 제스처와 혼란스러운 소음만을 사용해서는 그 상업 거래는 거의 불가능했을 것이고, 합의된 조항에 따라서 그것을 실행하는 것이 신뢰라는 결속을 만든다. 언어는 우리가 구체적이게 해주고 이것이 대화가 중요한 역할을 하는 지점이다.

① 의사소통하기 위해 몸짓 언어를 사용했다고
② 누구에게 의존할지 본능적으로 알았다고
③ 자신의 욕구를 위해 종종 규칙을 바꿨다고
④ 자신의 생존을 위해 독립적으로 살았다고
⑤ 경제적인 이유로 언어를 발달시켰다고

문제풀이

인간은 거래를 위해 신뢰를 확립해야 했는데, 그를 위해서는 언어를 사용하는 것이 편리했다는 내용이다. 따라서 빈칸에 ⑤ 'developed language for economic reasons'가 들어가서, 빈칸이 포함되는 문장이 '많은 진화 생물학자는 인간이 경제적인 이유로 언어를 발달시켰다고 주장한다.'가 되는 것이 가장 적절하다.

어휘·어구

evolutionary 진화의
biologist 생물학자
establish 확립하다
handy 편리한
conduct business 거래하다, 사업을 하다
bunch 다발
confusing 혼란시키는
according to ~에 따라
terms 조항
bond 유대, 결속
communicate 의사소통하다
instinctively 본능적으로
depend on ~에 의존하다
independently 독립적으로
survival 생존
economic 경제적인

본문 077쪽

문법 플러스 13. 관계대명사

1. that 2. that 3. which 4. that
5. what 6. which 7. whatever
8. whom 9. which 10. what

1 [해석]▶ 대부분의 사람은 밝은 햇빛 속에서 가장 행복한데, 이것(밝은 햇빛)은 정서적인 행복감을 주는 체내의 화학물질을 분비시킬 수도 있다.
[해설]▶ 괄호의 관계사가 뒤에 이어지는 절에서 동사 bring의 주어 역할을 하며 선행사가 chemicals이므로 주격관계대명사 that이 와야 한다.

2 [해석]▶ 아이들이 그들의 또래들과 공유하는 세상은 그들의 행동을 형성하는 것이고, 그들이 가지고 태어난 특성을 수정하는 것이다.
[해설]▶ The world를 선행사로 하고, 관계절 내에 타동사 share의 목적어가 비어있는 구조이므로, 목적격 관계대명사 that이 와야 한다.

3 [해석]▶ 플라스틱은 아주 느리게 분해되고 물에 떠다니

는 경향이 있는데, 이것이 플라스틱을 해류를 따라 수천 마일을 돌아다니게 해 준다.
[해설]▶ 관계대명사 앞에 콤마가 나오므로 계속적 용법임을 알 수 있다. 또한 관계사 바로 뒤에 동사 allows가 나왔으므로, 주격관계대명사가 필요함을 알 수 있다. which는 앞 문장 전체를 선행사로 받는 주격관계대명사 계속적 용법으로 사용되었다.

4 [해석]▶ 기존 생각들은 과학자들이 그들이 설명할 수 없는 새로운 정보를 찾을 때 대체된다.
[해설]▶ 관계절 뒤에 타동사 explain의 목적어의 역할을 하며, 선행사인 new information을 수식하는 목적격 관계대명사가 와야 하므로 that이 맞다.

5 [해석]▶ 하지만, 이 새로운 그림 방식은 그것이 만들어지는 방식뿐만 아니라 보이는 것에 있어서도 대중들에게 도전적이었다는 것을 기억하는 것이 중요하다.
[해설]▶ 전치사 in의 목적어 역할을 해야 하고 뒤에 주어가 없이 동사가 나오면서 명사절을 이끌어야 하므로 선행사를 포함하는 관계대명사 what이 쓰여야 한다.

6 [해석]▶ 북반구에서, 그림자는 우리가 지금 시계 방향이라고 부르는 방향으로 회전한다.
[해설]▶ 위에 이어지는 절에서 5형식 동사 call의 목적어가 없으므로 목적격 관계대명사 which가 필요하다. 참고로, 관계부사 다음에는 완전한 절이 와야 한다.

7 [해석]▶ 감독은 자신이 관객으로 하여금 바라보기를 원하는 어떤 것이든 단지 카메라를 향하게 하면 된다.
[해설]▶ 전치사 at의 목적어로 쓰인 복합관계대명사 whatever(어떤 것이든)가 필요하다.

8 [해석]▶ 그는 우리가 대화를 나누고 있었던 그 작가다.
[해설]▶ 이 문장은 He is the author.와 We've been talking about him.이라는 두 문장을 관계사로 연결한 문장이다. 선행사가 사람 the author이고, 전치사 about의 목적격이 필요하므로 whom이 맞다.

9 [해석]▶ Sally는 얼음판에서 넘어졌다. 그리고 그것은 모두를 웃게 만들었다.
[해설]▶ 관계대명사 which가 앞 문장 전체를 선행사로 한 계속적 용법으로 사용되었다.

10 해석▶ 그는 자신 안에 있는 모든 것을 단지 끄집어내, 우리에게 풍부한 음악의 보물을 가져다 주었다.
[해설]▶ 괄호 앞에 선행사가 없는 것을 주의한다. 관계대명사 what(= the thing that / that which)은 선행사와 관계사의 역할을 겸하고 있다.

본문 078쪽

어휘 플러스 13. 철자가 혼동되는 어휘 (4)

1. consumed
2. contribute
3. consistent
4. concentrating
5. highly

1 [해석]▶ 제3세계의 목재 소비 중 9/10는 요리와 난방에 쓰인다.

2 [해석]▶ 화가, 작가, 음악가, 이 모든 예술가들은 모든 사람들의 보다 나은 삶을 위해 기여하고 있는 것이다.

3 [해석]▶ 또 다른 일관된 연구 결과는 어떤 외적인 보상을 얻기 위해 명시적으로 어떤 학습 활동을 할 때 사람들은 그 보상을 보장해 주는 가장 덜 힘든 방식을 추구함으로써 반응한다는 것이다.

4 [해석]▶ 이 구멍은 바람이 약한 날에는 바람을 모으고, 바람이 강하게 불 때는 그것이 통과해가도록 함으로써 바람의 속도에 상관없이 연을 빨리 날게 하도록 도와준다.

5 [해석]▶ 보통의 소비자들은 아주 귀중하게 여겨지는 원작들의 복사본을 소유할 수 있다

14. 빈칸 추론 (2) 긴 어구, 문장

Day 14

본문 080쪽

1. ③ 2. ① 3. ⑤ 4. ③ 5. ②
6. ① 7. ① 8. ② 9. ④ 10. ①

정답률 61%

대표 기출 ③ 유혹으로부터 스스로를 차단함으로써 습관을 깰 수 있다

직독/직해

If you've ever made a poor choice, /
여러분이 좋지 못한 선택을 한 적이 있다면 /

you might be interested in learning /
여러분은 배우는 데 관심이 있을지도 모른다 /

how to break that habit. 그 습관을 깨는 방법을

One great way / to trick your brain into doing so /
한 가지 좋은 방법은 / 그렇게 하도록 여러분의 뇌를 속이는 /

is to sign a "Ulysses Contract."
'Ulysses 계약'에 서명하는 것이다

The name of this life tip / 이런 인생 조언의 이름은 /

comes from the Greek myth about Ulysses, /
Ulysses에 관한 그리스 신화에서 유래된다 /

a captain whose ship sailed past /
그 선장은 자신의 배로 항해해서 지나갔다 /

the island of the Sirens, / 사이렌의 섬을 /

a tribe of dangerous women /
위험한 여성 부족인 /

who lured victims to their death /
희생자들을 죽음으로 유혹한 /

with their irresistible songs.
저항할 수 없는 노래들로

Knowing that he would otherwise be unable to resist, /
그는 그렇게 하지 않으면 저항할 수 없다는 것을 알고 /

Ulysses instructed his crew /
Ulysses는 자신의 선원들에게 지시했다 /

to stuff their ears with cotton /
그들의 귀를 솜으로 막으라고 /

and tie him to the ship's mast /
그리고 그를 배의 돛대에 묶으라고 /

to prevent him from turning their ship /
자신이 배를 돌리는 것을 막기 위해 /

towards the Sirens. 사이렌으로

It worked for him / and you can do the same thing /
그것은 그에게 효과가 있었다 / 그리고 여러분은 같은 일을 할 수 있다 /

by locking yourself / out of your temptations.
스스로를 차단함으로써 / 여러분의 유혹으로부터

For example, / if you want to stay off your cellphone /
예를 들어 / 여러분의 휴대 전화를 멀리하고 싶다면 /

and concentrate on your work, /
그리고 여러분의 일에 집중하고 싶다면 /

delete the apps / that distract you /
앱들을 삭제해라 / 여러분의 주의를 산만하게 하는 /

or ask a friend to change your password!
혹은 여러분의 비밀번호를 바꿔달라고 친구에게 요청하라

여러분이 좋지 못한 선택을 한 적이 있다면, 여러분은 그 습관을 깨는 방법을 배우는 데 관심이 있을지도 모른다. 그렇게 하도록 여러분의 뇌를 속이는 한 가지 좋은 방법은 'Ulysses 계약'에 서명하는 것이다. 이런 인생 조언의 이름은 저항할 수 없는 노래들로 희생자들을 죽음으로 유혹한 위험한 여성 부족인 사이렌의 섬을 자신의 배로 항해해서 지나갔던 선장 Ulysses에 관한 그리스 신화에서 유래된다. 그는 그렇게 하지 않으면 저항할 수 없다는 것을 알고 Ulysses는 자신이 배를 사이렌으로 돌리는 것을 막기 위해 자신의 선원들에게 그들의 귀를 솜으로 막고 그를 배의 돛대에 묶으라고 지시했다. 그것은 그에게 효과가 있었고 여러분은 여러분의 유혹으로부터 스스로를 차단함으로써 같은 일을 할 수 있다. 예를 들어, 여러분의 휴대전화를 멀리하고 여러분의 일에 집중하고 싶다면, 여러분의 주의를 산만하게 하는 앱들을 삭제하거나 친구에게 여러분의 비밀번호를 바꿔달라고 요청하라!

① 모든 것을 건다는 마음가짐에서 벗어남
② 여러분이 변하기를 원하는 이유를 찾음
③ 여러분의 유혹으로부터 스스로를 차단함
④ 계획을 세우고 과정을 뒤쫓음
⑤ 한 번에 한 가지 안 좋은 습관을 깨는 데 집중함

문제풀이

안 좋은 습관을 깨는 방법으로 Ulysses 계약에 서명하는 것을 제시하고 있는데, 선장 Ulysses가 저항할 수 없는 유혹에서 벗어나기 위해 선원들에게 자신을 배의 돛대에 묶으라고 지시했다는 내용이다. 따라서 빈칸에 ③ 'locking yourself out of your temptations'이 들어가서 빈칸이 포함되는 문장이 '그것은 그에게 효과가 있었고 여러분은 여러분의 유혹으로부터 스스로를 차단함으로써 같은 일을 할 수 있다.'가 되는 것이 가장 적절하다.

이렇게 풀자 글의 마지막 부분에 제시된 사례, 휴대전화를 멀리하고 일에 집중하고 싶으면 주의를 산만하게 하는 앱들을 삭제하거나 친구에게 비밀번호를 바꿔달라고 요청하라는 내용을 통해 빈칸에 들어갈 말을 추론할 수 있다.

어휘·어구

trick 속이다
contract 계약
captain 선장
tribe 부족
dangerous 위험한
victim 희생자
irresistible 저항할 수 없는
resist 저항하다
instruct 지시하다
tie 묶다
prevent... from ~ing …가 ~하는 것을 막다
delete 삭제하다
distract 주의를 산만하게 하다
password 비밀번호
let go of ~을 놓다
all-or-nothing 모든 것을 건
mindset 마음가짐
reason 이유
temptation 유혹
track 뒤쫓다
progress 과정, 진보

정답률 55%

1. ③ 집은 실내 환경에 적응된 종들을 수용하고 새로운 방향으로 진화를 유도함

직독/직해

Our homes aren't just ecosystems, /
우리의 집들은 단순한 생태계가 아니라 /

they're unique ones, / hosting species /
독특한 곳이며 / 종(種)들을 수용하고 /

that are adapted to indoor environments /
실내 환경에 적응된 /

and pushing evolution / in new directions.
진화를 밀어붙인다 / 새로운 방향으로

Indoor microbes, insects, and rats / have all evolved /
실내 미생물, 곤충, 그리고 쥐들은 / 모두 진화시켜왔다 /

the ability to survive / our chemical attacks, /
살아남을 수 있는 능력을 / 우리의 화학적 공격에서 /

developing resistance / 내성을 키우면서 /

to antibacterials, insecticides, and poisons.
항균제, 살충제, 그리고 독에 대한

German cockroaches are known /
독일 바퀴벌레는 ~로 알려져 있다 /

to have developed a distaste for glucose, /
포도당에 대한 혐오감을 발달시켜 온 것(으로) /

which is commonly used as bait / in roach traps.
미끼로 흔히 사용되는 / 바퀴벌레 덫에서

Some indoor insects, / 일부 실내 곤충들은 /

which have fewer opportunities to feed /
그것들은 먹이를 잡아먹을 기회가 더 적었는데 /

than their outdoor counterparts, /
야외(에 사는) 상대방에 비해 /

seem to have developed / 발달시켜 온 것으로 보인다 /

the ability to survive / when food is limited.
생존할 능력을 / 먹이가 제한적일 때

Dunn and other ecologists have suggested /
Dunn과 다른 생태학자들은 말해 왔다 /

that as the planet becomes more developed and more urban, /
지구가 점점 더 발전되고 더 도시화되면서 /

more species will evolve the traits /
더 많은 종들이 특성을 진화시킬 것이라고 /

they need to thrive indoors.
그들이 실내에서 번성하기 위해 필요한

Over a long enough time period, /
충분히 긴 시간에 걸쳐 /

indoor living could drive our evolution, too.
실내 생활은 또한 우리의 진화를 이끌 수 있었다

Perhaps my indoorsy self / represents the future of humanity.
아마도 실내 생활을 좋아하는 내 모습은 / 인류의 미래를 대변할 것이다

우리의 집들은 단순한 생태계가 아니라 독특한 곳이며, 실내 환경에 적응된 종(種)들을 수용하고 새로운 방향으로 진화를 밀어붙인다. 실내 미생물, 곤충, 그리고 쥐들은 모두 항균제, 살충제, 그리고 독에 대한 내성을 키우면서 우리의 화학적 공격에서 살아남을 수 있는 능력을 진화시켜왔다. 독일 바퀴벌레는 바퀴벌레 덫에서 미끼로 흔히 사용되는 포도당에 대한 혐오감을 발달시켜 온 것으로 알려져 있다. 야외(에 사는) 상대방에 비해 먹이를 잡아먹을 기회가 더 적은 일부 실내 곤충들은 먹이가 제한적일 때 생존할 능력을 발달시켜 온 것으로 보인다. Dunn과 다른 생태학자들은 지구가 점점 더 발전되고 더 도시화되면서, 더 많은 종들이 실내에서 번성하기 위해 그들이 필요한 특성들을 진화시킬 것이라고 말해 왔다. 충분히 긴 시간에 걸쳐, 실내 생활은 또한 우리의 진화를 이끌 수 있었다. 아마도 실내 생활을 좋아하는 내 모습은 인류의 미래를 대변할 것이다.

① 스스로를 보호하기 위해 화학 물질을 생성할
② 파괴된 서식지로 멸종될
③ 실내에서 번성하기 위해 그들이 필요한 특성들을 진화시킬
④ 그들의 먹이를 찾기 위해 외부 유기체와 경쟁할
⑤ 야생 생물과 인간 사이의 경계를 허물

문제풀이

우리의 집들은 단순한 생태계가 아니라 실내 환경에 적응된 종(種)들을 수용하고 새로운 방향으로 진화를 유도해서, 실내 미생물, 곤충, 쥐들은 각종 화학물질에서 살아남을 수 있는 능력을 진화시켰다는 내용이므로, 빈칸에 ③ 'evolve the traits they need to thrive indoors'가 들어가서 빈칸이 포함되는 문장이 'Dunn과 다른 생태학자들은 지구가 점점 더 발전되고 더 도시화되면서, 더 많은 종들이 실내에서 번성하기 위해 그들이 필요한 특성들을 진화시킬 것이라고 말해 왔다.'가 되는 것이 가장 적절하다.

구조 다시보기

주제	우리의 집은 실내 환경에 적응된 종들을 수용하고 새로운 방향으로 진화를 유도함
부연1	실내 미생물, 곤충, 쥐들은 각종 화학 물질에 내성을 키워 살아남는 능력을 진화시켰음
부연2	독일 바퀴벌레는 미끼로 사용되는 포도당에 대한 혐오감을 발달시켜 옴
부연3	일부 실내 곤충들은 먹이가 제한적일 때 생존할 능력을 발달시켜옴

결론	지구가 더 발전함에 따라 더 많은 종(種)들이 실내에서 번성하기 위해 필요한 특성을 진화시킬 것임

《 어휘·어구 》

ecosystem 생태계
unique 독특한
adapt 적응시키다
environment 환경
evolution 진화
direction 방향
microbe 미생물
ability 능력
survive 생존하다
chemical 화학의
attack 공격; 공격하다
develop 발달시키다
resistance 저항
antibacterial 항균의
insecticide 살충제
poison 독
cockroach 바퀴벌레
distaste 혐오
roach 바퀴벌레
counterpart 상대
limit 제한하다
ecologist 생태학자
urban 도시의
period 시간, 기간
represent 대변하다
trait 특성
thrive 번성하다
protect 보호하다
extinct 멸종한
destroy 파괴하다
habitat 서식지
compete 경쟁하다
organism 유기체
boundary 경계

정답률 52%

2. ① 신선함의 요구는 환경적인 대가를 치르게 한다

직독/직해

The demand for freshness /
신선함에 대한 요구는 /
can have hidden environmental costs.
숨겨진 환경적인 대가를 지니고 있을 수 있다
While freshness is now being used as a term /
신선함이 현재 하나의 용어로 사용되고 있는 반면 /
in food marketing / as part of a return to nature, /
식품 마케팅에서 / 자연으로의 회귀의 일부로써 /
the demand for year-round supplies of fresh produce /
신선한 식품의 연중 공급에 대한 요구는 /
such as soft fruit and exotic vegetables /
부드러운 과일이나 외국산 채소 같은 /
has led to the widespread use of hot houses /
광범위한 온실 사용으로 이어져 왔다 /
in cold climates / 추운 기후에서의 /
and increasing reliance on total quality control /
총체적인 품질 관리에 대한 의존성 증가로 (이어져 왔다) /
— management by temperature control, /
즉 온도 조절에 의한 관리 /
use of pesticides / and computer/satellite-based logistics.
살충제 사용 / 그리고 컴퓨터/위성 기반 물류에 대한 의존성 증가로 (이어져 왔다)
The demand for freshness /
신선함에 대한 요구는 /
has also contributed to concerns /
또한 우려의 원인이 되어 왔다 /
about food wastage. 식량 낭비에 대한
Use of 'best before', / 'sell by' / and 'eat by' labels /
'유통 기한'의 사용 / '판매 시한'/ 그리고 '섭취 시한' 라벨 (사용은) /
has legally allowed institutional waste.
제도적인 폐기물 (생산)을 법적으로 허용해 왔다
Campaigners have exposed the scandal /
운동가들은 추문을 폭로해 왔다 /
of over-production and waste.
과잉 생산과 폐기물에 대한
Tristram Stuart, / Tristram Stuart는 /
one of the global band of anti-waste campaigners, /
폐기물 반대 세계 연대 소속 운동가 중 한 명인 /
argues that, / with freshly made sandwiches, /
~를 주장한다 / 신선하게 만들어진 샌드위치와 함께 /
overordering is standard practice /
초과 주문이 일반적인 행태이며 /
across the retail sector /
소매 산업 분야 전반에서 이루어지는 /
to avoid the appearance of empty shelf space, /
판매대가 비어 보이는 것을 막기 위한 /
leading to high volumes of waste /
이것은 엄청난 양의 폐기물로 이어진다고 /
when supply regularly exceeds demand.
공급이 정기적으로 수요를 초과하면

신선함에 대한 요구는 숨겨진 환경적인 대가를 지니고 있을 수 있다. 자연으로의 회귀의 일부로써 신선함이 현재 식품 마케팅에서 하나의 용어로 사용되고 있는 반면, 부드러운 과일이나 외국산 채소 같은 신선한 식품의 연중 공급에 대한 요구는 추운 기후에서의 광범위한 온실 사용과 총체적인 품질 관리, 즉 온도 조절에 의한 관리, 살충제 사용, 그리고 컴퓨터/위성 기반 물류에 대한 의존성 증가로 이어져 왔다. 신선함에 대한 요구는 또한 식량 낭비에 대한 우려의 원인이 되어 왔다. '유통 기한', '판매 시한', 그리고 '섭취 시한' 라벨 사용은 제도적인 폐기물 (생산)을 법적으로 허용해 왔다. 운동가들은 과잉 생산과 폐기물에 대한 추문을 폭로해 왔다. 폐기물 반대 세계 연대 소속 운동가 중 한 명인 Tristram Stuart는 신선하게 만들어진 샌드위치와 함께, 판매대가 비어 보이는 것을 막기 위한 초과 주문이 소매 산업 분야 전반에서 이루어지는 일반적인 행태이며, 이것은 공급이 정기적으로 수요를 초과하면 엄청난 양의 폐기물로 이어진다고 주장한다.

① **숨겨진 환경적인 대가를 지니고 있을**
② 세계적인 기아 문제를 악화시킬
③ 기술적 진보를 일으킬
④ 음식의 영양과 질을 향상시킬
⑤ 지역 사회의 식단을 다양화할

문제풀이

신선한 식품에 대한 지나친 요구는 광범위한 온실 사용과 총체적인 품질 관리에 의존하게 만들고 식량 낭비를 유발할 수 있다는 내용의 글이다. 따라서 빈칸에 ① 'have hidden environmental costs'가 들어가서 빈칸이 포함되는 문장이 '신선함에 대한 요구는 숨겨진 환경적인 대가를 지니고 있을 수 있다.'가 되는 것이 가장 적절하다.

이렇게 풀자 'the widespread use of hot houses', 'increasing reliance on total quality control', 'concerns about food wastage', 'the scandal of over-production and waste', 'high volumes of waste'를 통해 신선함에 대한 지나친 요구는 환경에 부정적인 영향을 미칠 수 있다는 것을 추론할 수 있다.

《 어휘·어구 》

demand 요구
freshness 신선함
term 용어
return 회귀
year-round 연중 계속되는
supply 공급
exotic 외국산의
widespread 광범위한
hot house 온실
climate 기후
reliance 의존성
management 관리
temperature control 온도 조절
satellite 위성
contribute to ~에 기여하다
concern 우려, 걱정
wastage 낭비
best before 유통 기한
sell by 판매 시한
legally 법적으로
institutional 제도적인
expose 폭로하다, 노출하다
scandal 추문
over-production 과잉 생산
standard 일반적인
practice 관행
retail sector 소매 산업 분야
appearance 모습
volume 양
regularly 정기적으로
exceed 초과하다
hidden 숨겨진
environmental 환경적인
worsen 악화시키다
bring about ~을 초래하다, 일으키다
technological 기술적인
advance 진보, 발전
nutrition 영양
diversify 다양화하다
local community 지역 사회

정답률 55%

3. ⑤ 사람은 두 개의 정보를 동시에 처리할 수 없다

직독/직해

In the studies of Colin Cherry /
Colin Cherry의 연구에서 /
at the Massachusetts Institute for Technology /
매사추세츠 공과 대학의 /
back in the 1950s, / 1950년 당시 /
his participants listened to voices / in one ear /
그의 참가자들은 목소리를 들었다 / 한쪽 귀로 /
at a time / and then through both ears /
한 번은 / 그리고 나서 양쪽 귀로 /
in an effort to determine /
판단하기 위해 /
whether we can listen to two people talk /
우리가 두 사람이 이야기하는 것을 들을 수 있는지 /
at the same time.
동시에
One ear always contained a message /
한쪽 귀로는 메시지를 계속 포함하였다(들려주었다) /
that the listener had to repeat back /
듣는 사람이 다시 반복해야 하는 /
(called "shadowing") / ('shadowing'이라 불리는) /
while the other ear included / people speaking.
다른 한쪽 귀로는 포함하였다(들려주었다) / 사람들이 말하는 것을
The trick was to see / 속임수는 알아보기 위한 것이었다 /
if you could totally focus on the main message /
사람들이 주된 메시지에 완전히 집중할 수 있는지를 /
and also hear someone talking / in your other ear.
그리고 누군가가 말하는 것 또한 들을 수 있는지를 / 다른 귀로는
Cleverly, / Cherry found it was impossible /
영리하게도 / Cherry는 불가능하다는 것을 발견했다 /
for his participants to know /
참가자들이 아는 것이 /
whether the message in the other ear /

다른 한쪽 귀로 들리는 메시지가 /

was spoken by a man or woman, /
남자가 말한 것인지 아니면 여자가 말한 것인지 /

in English or another language, /
영어인지 다른 외국어인지 /

or was even comprised of real words at all!
혹은 심지어 실제 단어로 구성된 것인지조차

In other words, / people could not process /
다시 말해 / 사람들은 처리할 수 없었다 /

two pieces of information / at the same time.
두 개의 정보를 / 동시에

1950년 당시 매사추세츠 공과 대학의 Colin Cherry의 연구에서, 우리가 두 사람이 이야기하는 것을 동시에 들을 수 있는지 판단하기 위해 참가자들은 한 번은 한쪽 귀로 목소리를 듣고, 그러고 나서 양쪽 귀로 들었다. 한쪽 귀로는 듣는 사람이 다시 반복해야 하는('shadowing'이라 불리는) 메시지를 계속 들려주었고 다른 한쪽 귀로는 사람들이 말하는 것을 들려주었다. 속임수는 사람들이 주된 메시지에 완전히 집중할 수 있으면서 다른 귀로는 누군가가 말하는 것 또한 들을 수 있는지를 알아보기 위한 것이었다. 영리하게도, Cherry는 참가자들이 다른 한쪽 귀로 들리는 메시지가 남자가 말한 것인지 아니면 여자가 말한 것인지, 영어인지 다른 외국어인지, 혹은 심지어 실제 단어로 구성된 것인지조차 아는 것이 불가능하다는 것을 발견했다! 다시 말해, 사람들은 두 개의 정보를 동시에 처리할 수 없었다.

① 그 순간 그들이 무엇을 해야 하는지 결정할
② 너무 많은 단어가 있는 메시지를 기억할
③ 어떤 정보가 더 정확한지 분석할
④ 다른 사람 말을 들으면서 자신의 생각을 말할
⑤ 두 개의 정보를 동시에 처리할

문제풀이

참가자들은 한쪽 귀로 주된 메시지를 들으면서 다른 한쪽으로 다른 메시지를 들으면 다른 메시지가 어떤 내용인지 전혀 알 수 없었다는 연구 결과로 보아, 빈칸에 ⑤ 'process two pieces of information at the same time'이 들어가서 빈칸이 포함되는 문장이 '다시 말해, 사람들은 두 개의 정보를 동시에 처리할 수 없었다.'가 되는 것이 가장 적절하다.

구조 다시보기

실험 명제	우리는 두 사람이 이야기하는 것을 동시에 들을 수 있나?
실험 과정	한쪽 귀로는 shadowing 메시지를, 다른 한쪽으로는 사람들이 말하는 것을 들려줌
실험 결과	사람들은 듣고 있는 두 개의 정보를 동시에 처리할 수 없음

어휘·어구

at the same time 동시에
contain 담고 있다
include 포함하다
trick 속임수
comprise 구성하다
analyze 분석하다
accurate 정확한
process 처리하다

정답률 47%

4. ③ 선천적 성질보다는 후천적 환경의 영향이 크다

직독/직해

In a study at Princeton University in 1992, /
1992년 프린스턴 대학의 한 연구에서 /

research scientists looked at /
연구 과학자들은 ~을 관찰했다 /

two different groups of mice.
다른 두 개의 쥐 집단을

One group was made intellectually superior /
한 집단은 지적으로 우월하도록 만들어졌다 /

by modifying the gene /
유전자를 변형함으로써 /

for the glutamate receptor.
글루타민산염 수용체에 대한

Glutamate is a brain chemical /
글루타민산염은 뇌 화학 물질이다 /

that is necessary in learning.
학습에 필수적인

The other group was genetically manipulated /
다른 집단은 유전적으로 조작되었다 /

to be intellectually inferior, /
지적으로 열등하도록 /

also done by modifying the gene /
역시 유전자를 변형함으로써 /

for the glutamate receptor.
글루타민산염 수용체에 대한

The smart mice were then raised /
그 후 똑똑한 쥐들은 길러졌다 /

in standard cages, /
표준 우리에서 /

while the inferior mice were raised / in large cages /
반면 열등한 쥐들은 길러졌다 / 큰 우리에서 /

with toys and exercise wheels /
장난감과 운동용 쳇바퀴가 있는 /

and with lots of social interaction.
그리고 사회적인 상호작용이 많은

At the end of the study, / 연구가 끝날 즘 /

although the intellectually inferior mice /
비록 지적으로 열등한 쥐들은 /

were genetically handicapped, /
유전적으로 장애가 있었지만 /

they were able to perform /
그들은 수행할 수 있었다 /

just as well as their genetic superiors.
그들의 유전적인 우월군들만큼 잘

This was a real triumph for nurture / over nature.
이것은 양육의 진정한 승리였다 / 천성에 대한

Genes are turned on or off /
유전자는 작동하거나 멈춘다 /

based on what is around you.
여러분 주변에 있는 것에 따라

1992년 프린스턴 대학의 한 연구에서, 연구 과학자들은 다른 두 개의 쥐 집단을 관찰했다. 한 집단은 글루타민산염 수용체에 대한 유전자를 변형함으로써 지적으로 우월하도록 만들어졌다. 글루타민산염은 학습에 필수적인 뇌 화학 물질이다. 다른 집단도 역시 글루타민산염 수용체에 대한 유전자를 변형함으로써, 지적으로 열등하도록 유전적으로 조작되었다. 그 후 똑똑한 쥐들은 표준 우리에서 길러진 반면 열등한 쥐들은 장난감과 운동용 쳇바퀴가 있고 사회적인 상호 작용이 많은 큰 우리에서 길러졌다. 연구가 끝날 즘, 비록 지적으로 열등한 쥐들은 유전적으로 장애가 있었지만, 그들은 그들의 유전적인 우월군들만큼 잘 수행할 수 있었다. 이것은 천성(선천적 성질)에 대한 양육(후천적 환경)의 진정한 승리였다. 유전자는 여러분 주변에 있는 것에 따라 작동하거나 멈춘다.

① 생존을 위해 스스로
② 사회적 상호 작용 없이
③ 여러분 주변에 있는 것에 따라
④ 유전적 우월성에 따라
⑤ 우리 스스로를 즐겁게 하기 위해

문제풀이

글루타민산염 수용체에 대한 유전자를 변형함으로써 지적으로 우월한 쥐 집단과 지적으로 열등한 쥐 집단 간의 비교 실험에서 우월한 쥐는 표준 우리에서 길러지고, 열등한 쥐는 상호 작용이 많은 큰 우리에서 길러졌을 때, 그 결과는 지적으로 열등하더라도 환경이 받쳐주면 지적으로 우월한 쥐만큼 잘 수행할 수 있다는 내용이다. 결국 선천적 성질보다는 후천적 환경의 영향이 더 크다는 내용으로 보아 빈칸에 ③ 'based on what is around you'가 들어가서 빈칸이 포함되는 문장이 '유전자는 여러분 주변에 있는 것에 따라 작동하거나 멈춘다.'가 되는 것이 가장 적절하다.

어휘·어구

intellectually 지적으로
superior 우월한; 상급자
modify 변형하다, 수정하다
gene 유전자
receptor 수용체, 수용기
chemical 화학 제품
necessary 필수적인, 필요한
genetically 유전적으로
inferior 열등한
standard 표준의
social interaction 사회적 상호 작용
handicapped 장애가 있는
perform 수행하다
triumph 승리
nurture 양육
survival 생존
free from ~이 없는
superiority 우월성
entertain 즐겁게 하다

정답률 48%

5. ② 기후 변화에 대응하는 데 실패한 이유

직독/직해

Researchers are working on a project /
연구원들은 프로젝트를 진행하고 있다 /

that asks coastal towns / 해안가 마을들에게 묻는 /

how they are preparing for / rising sea levels.
그들이 어떻게 대비하고 있는지를 / 해수면 상승에

Some towns have risk assessments; /
어떤 마을들은 위험 평가를 하고 /

some towns even have a plan.
어떤 마을들은 심지어 계획을 가지고 있다

But it's a rare town / 하지만 마을은 드물다 /

that is actually carrying out a plan.
실제로 계획을 실행하고 있는

One reason we've failed / to act on climate change /
우리가 실패해온 한 가지 이유는 / 기후 변화에 대응하는 데 /

is the common belief / 일반적인 믿음 때문이다 /

that it is far away in time and space.
그것이 시공간적으로 멀리 떨어져 있다는

For decades, / climate change was a prediction /
수십 년 동안 / 기후 변화는 예측이었다 /

about the future, / 미래에 대한 /

so scientists talked about it / in the future tense.
그래서 과학자들은 그것에 대해 이야기했다 / 미래 시제로

This became a habit / — so that even today many scientists still use the future tense, /
이것이 습관이 되었다 / 따라서 심지어 오늘날에도 많은 과학자들이 여전히 미래 시제를 사용하고 있다 /

even though we know /
비록 우리가 알고 있음에도 불구하고 /

that a climate crisis is ongoing.
기후 위기가 진행 중이라는 사실을

Scientists also often focus on regions /
과학자들은 또한 지역에 초점을 맞추고 있다 /

most affected by the crisis, /
위기에 의해 영향을 가장 많이 받는 /

such as Bangladesh or the West Antarctic Ice Sheet, /
자주 방글라데시나 서남극 빙상처럼 /

which for most Americans are physically remote.
그 지역은 대부분의 미국인들에게는 물리적으로 멀리 떨어져 있다

연구원들은 해안가 마을들이 어떻게 해수면 상승에 대비하고 있는지를 묻는 프로젝트를 진행하고 있다. 어떤 마을들은 위험 평가를 하고, 어떤 마을들은 심지어 계획을 가지고 있다. 하지만 실제로 계획을 실행하고 있는 마을은 드물다. 우리가 기후 변화에 대응하는 데 실패해온 한 가지 이유는 그것이 시공간적으로 멀리 떨어져 있다는 일반적인 믿음 때문이다. 수십 년 동안, 기후 변화는 미래에 대한 예측이었고, 그래서 과학자들은 미래 시제로 기후 변화에 대해 이야기했다. 이것이 습관이 되어 비록 우리가 기후 위기가 진행 중이라는 사실을 알고 있음에도 불구하고 따라서 심지어 오늘날에도 많은 과학자들이 여전히 미래 시제를 사용하고 있다.

과학자들은 또한 자주 방글라데시나 서남극 빙상처럼 위기에 의해 영향을 가장 많이 받는 지역에 초점을 맞추고 있으며, 그 지역은 대부분의 미국인들에게는 물리적으로 멀리 떨어져 있다.

① 그것이 과학과 관련이 없다
② 그것이 시공간적으로 멀리 떨어져 있다
③ 에너지 효율성이 가장 중요하다
④ 신중한 계획이 문제를 해결할 수 있다
⑤ 그것이 발생하는 걸 막는 데 너무 늦었다

문제풀이

이 글은 우리가 기후 변화에 실패해온 이유를 시공간적인 측면에서 기술하고 있다. 빈칸 뒷부분에서 수십 년 동안, 기후 변화는 미래에 대한 예측이었고, 현재 기후 위기가 진행 중임에도 불구하고 많은 과학자들조차 미래의 일이라고 생각한다며 시간적 측면의 관점을 제시한다. 또한 기후 변화는 위기에 의해 가장 영향을 많이 받는 지역에 초점을 맞추고 있지만 물리적으로 멀리 떨어져 있는 곳으로 본다는 공간적 측면의 관점을 제시하고 있다. 따라서 빈칸에 ② 'it is far away in time and space'가 들어가서 빈칸이 포함되는 문장이 '우리가 기후 변화에 대응하는 데 실패해온 한 가지 이유는 그것이 시공간적으로 멀리 떨어져 있다는 일반적인 믿음 때문이다.'가 되는 것이 가장 적절하다.

어휘·어구

coastal 해안의
assessment 평가
carry out 실행하다, 수행하다
common 일반적인
prediction 예측
tense 시제
crisis 위기
ongoing 진행하는
region 지역
affect ~에게 영향을 주다
West Antarctic Ice Sheet 서남극 빙상
physically 물리적으로
remote 먼, 멀리 떨어진
be related to ~와 관계가 있다
efficiency 효율성
matter 중요하다
prevent A from v-ing A가 ~하는 것을 막다

정답률 63%

6. ① 자막의 부재가 등장인물의 감정을 잘 느끼게 한다

직독/직해

Most times a foreign language is spoken in film, / 영화에서 외국어가 사용되는 대부분의 경우 /
subtitles are used to translate / 자막은 (~를) 통역하려고 사용된다 /
the dialogue for the viewer. 관객을 위해 대화를
However, / there are occasions / 하지만 / 경우들이 있다 /
when foreign dialogue is left unsubtitled / 외국어 대화가 자막 없이 처리되는 /
(and thus incomprehensible to most of the target audience). 그래서 대부분의 주요 대상 관객이 이해하지 못하게
This is often done / if the movie is seen mainly / 흔히 이렇게 처리된다 / 영화가 주로 보이는 경우에는 /
from the viewpoint of a particular character / 특정한 등장인물의 관점에서 /
who does not speak the language. 그 언어를 할 줄 모르는
Such absence of subtitles / 그러한 자막의 부재는 /
allows the audience to feel / 관객이 느끼게 한다 /
a similar sense of incomprehension and alienation / 비슷한 몰이해와 소외감을 /
that the character feels. 등장인물이 느끼는 것과
An example of this is seen / 이것의 한 예는 보인다 /
in *Not Without My Daughter*. 〈Not Without My Daughter〉에서
The Persian language dialogue / 페르시아어 대화에는 /
spoken by the Iranian characters / is not subtitled / 이란인 등장인물들이 하는 / 자막이 없다 /
because the main character Betty Mahmoody / 왜냐하면 주인공 Betty Mahmoody가 /
does not speak Persian / 페르시아어를 하지 못하기 때문에 /
and the audience is seeing / 그리고 관객은 보고 있게 된다 /
the film from her viewpoint. 그녀의 시각에서 영화를

영화에서 외국어가 사용되는 대부분의 경우, 자막은 관객을 위해 대화를 통역하려고 사용된다. 하지만 외국어 대화가 자막 없이 (그래서 대부분의 주요 대상 관객이 이해하지 못하게) 처리되는 경우들이 있다. 영화가 그 언어를 할 줄 모르는 특정한 등장인물의 관점에서 주로 보이는 경우에는 흔히 이렇게 처리된다. 그러한 자막의 부재는 관객이 등장인물이 느끼는 것과 비슷한 몰이해와 소외감을 느끼게 한다. 이것의 한 예는 〈Not Without My Daughter〉에서 보인다. 주인공 Betty Mahmoody가 페르시아어를 하지 못하기 때문에 이란인 등장인물들이 하는 페르시아어 대화에는 자막이 없고, 관객은 그녀의 시각에서 영화를 보고 있게 된다.

① 그녀의 시각에서 영화를 보고
② 그녀의 언어 능력에 의해 감명받고
③ 그녀의 아름다운 목소리에 매료되고
④ 열띤 논의에 참여하고
⑤ 영화에서 사용된 언어를 배우고

문제풀이

영화에서 외국어가 사용될 경우 관객의 이해를 위해 자막이 사용되지만, 외국어를 할 줄 모르는 등장인물의 관점에서 관객이 등장인물과 비슷한 감정을 갖게 하기 위해 자막 없이 처리되는 영화들이 있다는 내용이다. 따라서 빈칸에 ① 'seeing the film from her viewpoint'가 들어가서 빈칸이 포함되는 문장이 '주인공 Betty Mahmoody가 페르시아어를 하지 못하기 때문에 이란인 등장인물들이 하는 페르시아어 대화에는 자막이 없고, 관객은 그녀의 시각에서 영화를 보고 있게 된다.'가 되는 것이 가장 적절하다.

어휘·어구

foreign 외국의
translate 통역하다
dialogue 대화
viewer 관객
occasion 경우
target audience 주요 대상 관객
mainly 주로
viewpoint 관점, 시각
particular 특정한
absence 부재
impress ~에게 감명을 주다
attract to ~로 끌다
participate in ~에 참여하다
heated debate 열띤 논의

정답률 21%

7. ① 홈 이점은 실제로 부담이 된다

직독/직해

One dynamic that can change dramatically / 극적으로 바뀔 수 있는 한 가지 역학은 /
in sport / 스포츠에서 /
is the concept of the home-field advantage, / 홈 이점이라는 개념이다 /
in which perceived demands and resources / 여기에서는 인식된 부담과 자원이 /
seem to play a role. 역할을 하는 것처럼 보인다
Under normal circumstances, / 일반적인 상황에서 /
the home ground would appear to provide / 홈그라운드는 제공하는 것처럼 보인다 /
greater perceived resources / 인식된 자원을 더 많이 /
(fans, home field, and so on). 팬, 홈경기장 등(과 같은)
However, / researchers Roy Baumeister and Andrew Steinhilber / 하지만, / 연구원 Roy Baumeister와 Andrew Steinhilber는 /
were among the first to point out / 처음으로 지적한 사람 중 한 명이었다 /
that these competitive factors can change; / 이런 경쟁력이 있는 요소들이 바뀔 수도 있다고 /
for example, / 예를 들어 /
the success percentage for home teams / 홈 팀들의 성공률은 /
in the final games of a playoff / or World Series / 우승 결정전이나 / (미국 프로 야구) 선수권의 마지막 경기에서 /
seems to drop. 떨어지는 것처럼 보인다
Fans can become part of the perceived demands / 팬들은 인식된 부담의 일부가 될 수 있다 /
rather than resources / 자원보다는 /
under those circumstances. 이런 상황에서
This change in perception / can also explain / 이런 인식의 변화는 / 또한 설명할 수 있다 /
why a team that's struggling / 왜 고전하는 팀이 /
at the start of the year / 연초에 /
will often welcome a road trip / 길을 떠나는 것을 흔히 반기는지 /
to reduce perceived demands and pressures. 인식된 부담과 압박을 줄이기 위해

스포츠에서 극적으로 바뀔 수 있는 한 가지 역학은 홈 이점이라는 개념으로, 여기에서는 인식된 부담과 자원이 역할을 하는 것처럼 보인다. 일반적인 상황에서, 홈그라운드는 인식된 자원(팬, 홈경기장 등)을 더 많이 제공하는 것처럼 보인다. 하지만, 연구원 Roy Baumeister와 Andrew Steinhilber는 이런 경쟁력이 있는 요소들이 바뀔 수도 있다고 처음으로 지적한 사람 중 한 명이었다. 예를 들어, 우승 결정전이나 (미국 프로 야구) 선수권의 마지막 경기에서 홈 팀들의 성공률은 떨어지는 것처럼 보인다. 이런 상황에서 팬들은 자원보다는 인식된 부담의 일부가 될 수 있다. 이런 인식의 변화는 왜 연초에 고전하는 팀이 인식된 부담과 압박을 줄이기 위해 길을 떠나는 것(원정 경기를 가는 것)을 흔히 반기는지 또한 설명할 수 있다.

① 길을 떠나는 것을 흔히 반기는지
② 국제 경기를 피하는지
③ 티켓 판매 증진에 집중하는지
④ 친환경 경기장을 갖기를 원하는지
⑤ 다가올 경기를 광고하기 위해 애쓰는지

문제풀이

스포츠에서 홈그라운드가 이점이 있는 것처럼 보이지만 실제로는 홈 이점이 좋은 자원이라기보다는 인식된 부담의 일부가 될 수 있어서 홈 팀들의 성공률이 떨어지는 것처럼 보인다는 내용이다. 따라서 빈칸에 ① 'often welcome a road trip'이 들어가서 빈칸이 포함되는 문장이 '이런 인식의 변화는 왜 연초에 고전하는 팀이 인식된 부담과 압박을 줄이기 위해 길을 떠나는 것(원정 경기를 가는 것)을 흔히 반기는지 또한 설명할 수 있다.'가 되는 것이 가장 적절하다.

어휘·어구

dynamic 역학
dramatically 극적으로
concept 개념
home-field advantage 홈 이점

demand 부담, 요구
resource 자원
play a role 역할을 하다
normal 보통의, 평범한
circumstance 상황
provide 제공하다
researcher 연구원
point out 지적하다
competitive 경쟁력이 있는
struggling 고전하는
reduce 줄이다
pressure 압박
international 국제적인
match 경기
stadium 경기장
advertise 광고하다
upcoming 다가오는

8. ② 언어를 익히게 만드는 아기들의 소리 패턴 기억

직독/직해

Over time, / babies construct expectations /
시간이 지나면서 / 아기는 기대를 형성한다 /
about what sounds they will hear when.
자신이 어떤 소리를 언제 들을지에 대한
They hold in memory the sound patterns /
그들은 소리 패턴을 기억한다 /
that occur on a regular basis.
규칙적으로 발생하는
They make hypotheses like, /
그들은 다음과 같은 가설을 세운다 /
"If I hear *this* sound first, /
내가 '이' 소리를 먼저 들으면 /
it probably will be followed by *that* sound."
그것에 아마도 '저' 소리가 따라올 것이다'
Scientists conclude / that much of babies' skill /
과학자들은 결론짓는다 / 아기의 기술의 상당 부분이 /
in learning language / is due to their ability /
언어를 배우는 / 능력 때문이라고 /
to calculate statistics.
통계를 계산하는
For babies, / this means /
아기에게 있어 / 이것은 의미한다 /
that they appear to pay close attention to the patterns /
그들이 패턴에 세심한 주의를 기울이는 것처럼 보인다는 것을 /
that repeat in language.
언어에서 반복되는
They remember, / in a systematic way, /
그들은 기억한다 / 체계적인 방식으로 /
how often sounds occur, / in what order, /
소리가 얼마나 자주 발생하는지 / 어떤 순서로 /
with what intervals, / and with what changes of pitch.
어떤 간격으로 / 그리고 어떤 음조의 변화를 가지고
This memory store allows them to track, /
이 기억 저장소는 그들이 추적하는 것을 허용해 준다 /
within the neural circuits of their brains, /
자신의 뇌의 신경 회로 내에서 /
the frequency of sound patterns /
소리 패턴의 빈도를 /
and to use this knowledge /
그리고 이 지식을 사용하도록 /
to make predictions about the meaning /
의미에 대한 예측을 하기 위해 /
in patterns of sounds. 소리 패턴의

시간이 지나면서 아기는 자신이 어떤 소리를 언제 들을지에 대한 기대를 형성한다. 그들은 규칙적으로 발생하는 소리 패턴을 기억한다. 그들은 '내가 '이' 소리를 먼저 들으면 그것에 아마도 '저' 소리가 따라올 것이다'와 같은 가설을 세운다. 과학자들은 언어를 배우는 아기의 기술의 상당 부분이 그들의 통계를 계산하는 능력 때문이라고 결론짓는다. 아기에게 있어 이것은 그들이 언어에서 반복되는 패턴에 세심한 주의를 기울이는 것처럼 보인다는 것을 의미한다. 그들은 소리가 얼마나 자주, 어떤 순서로, 어떤 간격으로 그리고 어떤 음조의 변화를 가지고 발생하는지를 체계적인 방식으로 기억한다. 이 기억 저장소는 그들이 자신의 뇌의 신경 회로 내에서 소리 패턴의 빈도를 추적하고, 소리 패턴의 의미에 대한 예측을 하기 위해 이 지식을 사용하도록 해 준다.

① 사회적 압력의 결여
② 통계를 계산하는 능력
③ 다른 사람들과 교류하고자 하는 소망
④ 단순한 소리에 대한 선호
⑤ 간병인의 흉내를 내는 경향

문제풀이

아기들은 규칙적으로 발생하는 소리의 패턴을 기억하며, 이 기억을 바탕으로 소리를 예측한다는 내용의 글이다. 아기들은 소리의 빈도, 순서, 간격, 그리고 음조의 변화를 체계적인 방식으로 기억하여 이 소리 패턴의 빈도를 추적하고, 그 의미를 예측하기 위해 이 지식을 사용하는데 과학자들은 아기들이 언어를 배우는 기술이 바로 이러한 능력 때문이라고 결론짓는다고 하였으므로, 빈칸에는 체계적인 방식으로 소리 패턴을 기억하여 그것을 활용한다는 의미를 갖는 말이 들어가야 한다. 따라서 빈칸에는 ② 'ability to calculate statistics'가 들어가서 빈칸을 포함한 문장이 '과학자들은 언어를 배우는 아기의 기술의 상당 부분이 그들의 통계를 계산하는 능력 때문이라고 결론짓는다.'가 되어야 한다.

이렇게 풀자 빈칸에 들어갈 말이 빈칸 이외의 문장에 직접적으로 드러나 있지 않은 경우에는 선택지의 오답을 소거하는 방식으로 풀 수 있다. 선택지 중 ① '사회적 압력의 결여', ③ '다른 사람들과 교류하고자 하는 소망', ⑤ '간병인의 흉내를 내는 경향'의 내용은 본문에 전혀 언급되지 않았고, ④ '단순한 소리에 대한 선호'역시 본문의 내용과는 거리가 먼 선택지이다.

어휘·어구

construct 구성하다
expectation 기대
basis 토대, 기초
conclude 결론을 내리다
statistic 통계
attention 주의
interval 간격
pitch 음조
track 추적하다
frequency 빈도
neural circuits 신경 회로
prediction 예측

9. ④ 심해 생물이 생물 발광을 활용하는 이유

직독/직해

Some deep-sea organisms are known /
일부 심해 생물은 알려져 있다 /
to use bioluminescence as a lure, /
가짜 미끼로써 생물 발광을 활용한다고 /
to attract prey / with a little glow /
먹이를 유혹하기 위해 / 작은 빛으로 /
imitating the movements of their favorite fish, /
그들이 좋아하는 물고기의 움직임을 모방하는 /
or like fireflies, / as a sexual attractant to find mates.
혹은 반딧불이처럼 / 짝을 찾기 위해 성적 유인 물질로써
While there are many possible evolutionary theories /
많은 가능한 진화 이론이 있지만 /
for the survival value of bioluminescence, /
생물 발광의 생존가에 대한 /
one of the most fascinating /
가장 흥미로운 것 중 하나는 /
is to create a cloak of invisibility.
보이지 않는 망토를 만드는 것이다
The color of almost all bioluminescent molecules /
거의 모든 생물 발광 분자의 색깔은 /
is blue-green, / the same color as the ocean above.
청록색이다 / 바다 위층과 같은 색인
By self-glowing blue-green, /
청록색으로 자체 발광함으로써 /
the creatures no longer cast a shadow /
생물은 더 이상 그림자를 드리우지 않는다 /
or create a silhouette, / 혹은 실루엣을 만들어 내지 않는다 /
especially when viewed from below /
특히 아래에서 보여질 때 /
against the brighter waters above.
위쪽의 더 밝은 물을 배경으로
Rather, / by glowing themselves, /
오히려 / 자신을 빛냄으로써 /
they can blend into the sparkles, reflections, /
그들은 반짝임, 반사에 섞일 수 있다 /
and scattered blue-green glow /
그리고 분산된 청록색 빛에 /
of sunlight or moonlight. 햇빛 혹은 달빛의
Thus, / they are most likely making their own light /
따라서 / 그들은 자신만의 빛을 분명 만들어 내고 있을 것이다 /
not to see, / but to be un-seen.
보기 위해서가 아니라 / 보이지 않기 위해서

일부 심해 생물은 그들이 좋아하는 물고기의 움직임을 모방하는 작은 빛으로 먹이를 유혹하기 위해 가짜 미끼로써, 혹은 반딧불이처럼 짝을 찾기 위해 성적 유인 물질로써 생물 발광을 활용한다고 알려져 있다. 생물 발광의 생존가에 대한 많은 가능한 진화 이론이 있지만 가장 흥미로운 것 중 하나는 보이지 않는 망토를 만드는 것이다. 거의 모든 생물 발광 분자의 색깔은 바다 위층과 같은 색인 청록색이다. 청록색으로 자체 발광함으로써 생물은 특히 위쪽의 더 밝은 물을 배경으로 아래에서 보여질 때 더 이상 그림자를 드리우거나 실루엣을 만들어 내지 않는다. 오히려 자신을 빛냄으로써 그들은 햇빛 혹은 달빛의 반짝임, 반사 그리고 분산된 청록색 빛에 섞일 수 있다. 따라서 그들은 보기 위해서가 아니라 보이지 않기 위해서 자신만의 빛을 분명 만들어 내고 있을 것이다.

① 구조 신호를 보내다
② 근처의 적들을 위협하다
③ 숨은 먹잇감의 베일을 벗기다
④ 보이지 않는 망토를 만든다
⑤ 항법 장치 역할을 하다

문제풀이

심해 생물이 생물 발광을 활용하는 것은 먹이를 유인하거나 짝을 찾기 위해서라고 알려져 있지만, 흥미로운 사실은 생물 발광의 색이 바다 위층과 같은 색인 청록색이어서 햇빛 혹은 달빛의 반짝임, 반사 그리고 분산된 청록색 빛에 섞이게 되어 다른 생명체가 보지 못하게 만든다는 내용의 글이다. 따라서 빈칸에는 ④ 'create a cloak of invisibility'가 들어가 빈칸을 포함한 문장이 '생물 발광의 생존가에 대한 많은 가능한 진화 이론이 있지만 가장 흥미로운 것 중 하나는 보이지 않는 망토를 만드는 것이다.'가 되는 것이 가장 적절하다.

이렇게 풀자 결론을 도출하는 연결사 'Thus' 다음의 내용 'they are most likely making their own light not to see, but to be un-seen.(그들은 보기 위해서가 아니라 보이지 않기 위해서 자신만의 빛을 분명 만들어 내고 있을 것이다.)'에서 쉽게 빈칸에 들어갈 내용을 유추할 수 있다.

어휘·어구

organism 생물
attract 매혹하다
prey 먹이

glow 빛나다
mate 짝, 친구
evolutionary 진화론적인
fascinating 흥미로운
creature 생물
blend 혼합
reflection 반사
scattered 여기저기 흩어진

정답률 42%

10. ① 인간은 실수로부터 얻은 이익을 공유해서 영리하다

직독/직해

One big difference between science and stage magic is / 과학과 무대 마술 간의 한 가지 큰 차이는 ~이다 /
that while magicians hide their mistakes from the audience, / 마술사들이 그들의 실수를 관중에게 숨기는 반면 /
in science / you make your mistakes in public. 과학에서는 / 공공연히 실수를 한다는 것이다
You show them off / 당신은 그것들을 드러내 보여준다 /
so that everybody can learn from them. 모두가 실수로부터 배울 수 있도록
This way, / 이런 식으로 /
you get the advantage of everybody else's experience, / 당신은 다른 모든 사람의 경험이라는 이익을 얻는다 /
and not just your own idiosyncratic path / 그리고 단지 당신 자신만의 특유한 길뿐만 아니라 /
through the space of mistakes. 실수라는 영역을 거쳐 온
This, by the way, / is another reason / 한편, 이것은 / 또 다른 이유이다 /
why we humans are so much smarter / 우리 인간이 훨씬 더 영리한지에 관한 /
than every other species. 모든 다른 종보다
It is not that our brains are bigger or more powerful, / 그것은 우리의 뇌가 더 크거나 더 강력해서가 아니다 /
or even that we have the ability / 혹은 심지어 우리가 능력을 갖춰서가 아니다 /
to reflect on our own past errors, / 우리 자신의 과거 실수를 반추하는 /
but that we share the benefits / 우리가 이익들을 나눠서이다 /
that our individual brains have earned / 우리 개개인의 뇌가 얻어낸 /
from their individual histories of trial and error. 그들 개개인들의 시행착오의 역사로부터

과학과 무대 마술 간의 한 가지 큰 차이는 마술사들이 그들의 실수를 관중에게 숨기는 반면, 과학에서는 공공연히 실수를 한다는 것이다. 당신은 모두가 실수로부터 배울 수 있도록 실수를 드러내 보여준다. 이런 식으로, 당신은 단지 실수라는 영역을 거쳐 온 당신 자신만의 특유한 길(에서 얻은 이익)뿐만 아니라, 다른 모든 사람의 경험이라는 이익을 얻는다. 한편, 이것은 우리 인간이 모든 다른 종보다 훨씬 더 영리한지에 관한 또 다른 이유이다. 그것은 우리의 뇌가 더 크거나 더 강력해서, 혹은 심지어 우리가 우리 자신의 과거 실수를 반추하는 능력을 갖춰서가 아니라, 우리 개개인의 뇌가 그들 개개인들의 시행착오의 역사로부터 얻어낸 이익들을 나눠서이다.

① **이익들을 나눠서이다**
② 통찰력을 간과해서이다
③ 창의적인 기술들을 개발해서이다
④ 업적을 과장해서이다
⑤ 지식을 과소평가해서이다

문제풀이

인간은 자신의 실수뿐만 아니라 다른 모든 사람의 시행착오로부터 배우기 때문에 다른 종보다 더 영리하다는 내용이다. 따라서 빈칸에 ① 'share the benefits'가 들어가서, 빈칸이 포함되는 문장이 '그것은 우리의 뇌가 더 크거나 더 강력해서, 혹은 심지어 우리가 우리 자신의 과거 실수를 반추하는 능력을 갖춰서가 아니라, 우리 개개인들의 뇌가 그들 개개인의 시행착오의 역사로부터 얻어낸 이익들을 나눠서이다.'가 되는 것이 가장 적절하다.

《어휘·어구》

difference 차이
audience 관중
in public 공공연히
advantage 이점
species 종
reflect on ~을 되돌아보다
individual 개개인의, 개별의
trial and error 시행착오
benefit 이익
overlook 간과하다
insight 통찰력
exaggerate 과장하다
achievement 업적
underestimate 과소평가하다
knowledge 지식

본문 083쪽

문법 플러스 14. 관계부사

1. where 2. when 3. why 4. the way
5. in which 6. where 7. whenever
8. However 9. where 10. wherever

1 [해석]▶ 물이 맑고 충분한 빛이 있는 수면 근처에서는 아마추어 사진작가가 저렴한 수중 카메라로 멋진 사진을 찍을 가능성이 아주 높다.
[해설]▶ 관계사가 관계절 내에서 부사구의 역할을 하며, 관계사 앞에 장소를 나타내는 선행사(the surface)가 왔으므로 관계부사 where가 와야 한다.

2 [해석]▶ 그녀가 가장 덜 바쁜 날은 화요일이다.
[해설]▶ 괄호 앞의 선행사가 시간(the day)을 나타내므로 관계부사는 when이 알맞다.

3 [해석]▶ 그 모임에 참석하지 않은 이유를 내게 말해줘.
[해설]▶ 괄호 앞의 선행사가 이유(the reason)를 나타내므로 관계부사는 why가 알맞다.

4 [해석]▶ 문화와 성별은 사람들이 인식하고, 해석하고, 갈등에 반응하는 방식에 영향을 미칠 수도 있다.
[해설]▶ the way 뒤에 how가 생략되어 있다. 관계부사 how는 선행사 the way와 함께 쓸 수 없다.

5 [해석]▶ 여러분이 운동하고 있을 기온과 환경 조건에 적절한 의류를 선택하라.
[해설]▶ 괄호 뒤에 문장 성분을 모두 갖춘 완전한 문장이 왔으므로, 관계부사 역할을 하는 in which가 오는 것이 적절하다.

6 [해석]▶ 그녀는 동물원에 갔는데 그곳에서 핸드폰을 잃어버렸다.
[해설]▶ 관계부사의 계속적 용법이다. 선행사가 장소를 나타내는 the zoo이고 괄호 이하 부분이 완전한 문장이므로, 관계부사는 where가 와야 한다

7 [해석]▶ 그녀는 일이 잘못될 때마다 항상 나를 비난한다.
[해설]▶ 복합관계부사 whenever는 '~할 때마다(= at any time when)'의 의미를 가지고 있다.

8 [해석]▶ 아무리 누추해도 집과 같은 곳은 없다.
[해설]▶ 「however+형용사+주어+동사」는 '아무리 ~할지라도'의 의미이며 양보적 의미가 있다.

9 [해석]▶ 이곳은 그녀가 캠핑 가는 것을 매우 좋아하는 장소이다.
[해설]▶ 괄호 앞에 장소를 나타내는 선행사 the place가 있고, 괄호 뒤 부분이 완전한 문장이므로 관계부사 where가 와야 한다. 복합관계부사는 선행사를 포함하고 있으므로 부적절하다.

10 해석▶ 대통령은 어디를 가든지 경호를 받게 된다.
[해설]▶ 문맥상 '어디를 가든지'라는 의미가 와야 하므로 복합관계부사 wherever가 적절하다.

본문 084쪽

어휘 플러스 14. 유의어 (4)

1. observe 2. overcome
3. pollute 4. predict
5. proves

1 [해석]▶ 올해 8월 27일에는 많은 사람들이 지구와 화성이 가까워지는 현상을 관찰하기 위해 야외로 나갔다.

2 [해석]▶ 이 문제를 극복하는 유일한 방법은 타인들과 더 연결되는 것이고, 이 연결은 두려움과 고립을 줄일 것이다.

3 [해석]▶ 기술이 공기를 오염시키는 자동차를 생산했다면 그것은 공학자들이 설계할 때 오염이 고려해야 했던 문제로서 인식되지 않았기 때문이다.

4 [해석]▶ 심리학 연구자들은 인간의 행동을 설명하는 데 도움을 주고 예측할 수 있는 연구를 수행하기 위해 과학적인 방법을 따른다.

5 [해석]▶ 그러나 최근에는 우리 마음이 병과 치료에 영향을 미친다는 것을 증명하는 많은 연구가 있다.

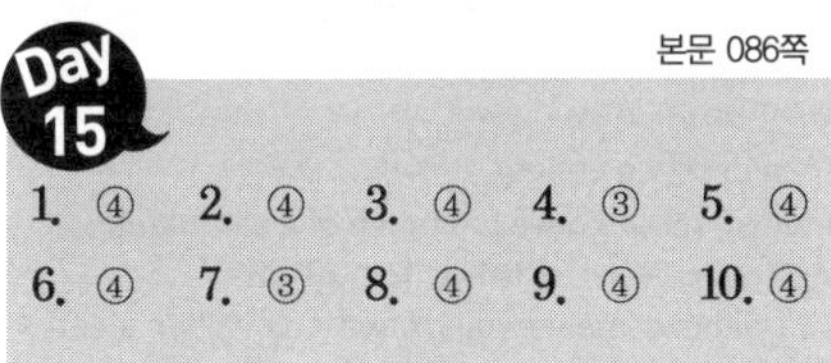

15. 흐름에 무관한 문장 찾기

Day 15 본문 086쪽

1. ④ 2. ④ 3. ④ 4. ③ 5. ④
6. ④ 7. ③ 8. ④ 9. ④ 10. ④

정답률 71%

대표 기출 ④ 시 쓰기의 신체적 이점과 정신적 이점

직독/직해

Developing a personal engagement with poetry /
시와의 개인적 관계를 발전시키는 것은 /
brings a number of benefits /
많은 이점을 가져다준다 /
to you as an individual, / 한 개인으로서의 여러분에게 /
in both a personal and a professional capacity.
개인적인 능력과 전문적인 능력 모두에서
Writing poetry has been shown /
시를 쓰는 것은 ~한 것으로 보여 왔다 /
to have physical and mental benefits, /
신체적 이점과 정신적 이점을 지닌 (것으로) /
with expressive writing found /
표현적 글쓰기가 ~한 것으로 밝혀지면서 /
to improve immune system and lung function, /
면역 체계와 폐 기능을 향상시키는 것(으로) /
diminish psychological distress, /
심리적 고통을 줄이는 (것으로) /
and enhance relationships.
그리고 관계를 증진시키는 (것으로)
Poetry has long been used /
시는 오랫동안 사용되어 왔다 /
to aid different mental health needs, /
여러 정신 건강에 필요한 것들을 지원하기 위해 /
develop empathy, / and reconsider our relationship /
공감 능력을 개발(하기 위해) / 그리고 우리의 관계를 재고하기 위해 /
with both natural and built environments.
자연적인 환경과 만들어진 환경 둘 다와의
Poetry is also an incredibly effective way /
시는 또한 믿을 수 없을 정도로 효과적인 방법이고 /
of actively targeting the cognitive development period, /
적극적으로 인지 발달 시기를 겨냥하는 /
improving your productivity and scientific creativity in the process.
그 과정에서 여러분의 생산성과 과학적인 창의력을 향상시킨 /
Poetry is considered / 시는 여겨진다 /
to be an easy and useful means /
쉽고 유용한 수단으로 /
of expressing emotions, / 감정을 표현하는 /
but you fall into frustration /
하지만 여러분은 좌절감에 빠진다 /
when you realize its complexity.
여러분이 그것의 복잡성을 깨달았을 때
In short, / poetry has a lot to offer, /
간단히 말해서 / 시는 제공할 많은 것을 가지고 있다 /
if you give it the opportunity / to do so.
여러분이 시에게 기회를 준다면 / 그렇게 할

시와의 개인적 관계를 발전시키는 것은 개인적인 능력과 전문적인 능력 모두에서 한 개인으로서의 여러분에게 많은 이점을 가져다준다. 표현적 글쓰기가 면역 체계와 폐 기능을 향상시키고, 심리적 고통을 줄이며 관계를 증진시키는 것으로 밝혀지면서, 시를 쓰는 것은 신체적 이점과 정신적 이점을 지닌 것으로 보여 왔다. 시는 여러 정신 건강에 필요한 것들을 지원하고, 공감 능력을 개발하고, 자연적인 환경과 만들어진 환경 둘 다와의 관계를 재고하기 위해 오랫동안 사용되어 왔다. 시는 또한 인지 발달 시기를 적극적으로 겨냥하는 믿을 수 없을 정도로 효과적인 방법이고, 그 과정에서 여러분의 생산성과 과학적인 창의력을 향상시킨다. (시는 감정을 표현하는 쉽고 유용한 수단으로 여겨지지만, 그것의 복잡성을 깨달았을 때 여러분은 좌절감에 빠진다.) 간단히 말해서, 여러분이 시에게 그렇게 할 기회를 준다면, 시는 제공할 많은 것을 가지고 있다.

문제풀이

시 쓰기의 신체적 이점과 정신적 이점에 대해 설명한 글이다. 하지만 ④는 시를 쓸 때 그것의 복잡성을 깨닫게 되면 좌절감에 빠지게 된다는 부정적인 측면에 대한 내용이므로 글의 전체 흐름에서 벗어난다.

구조 다시보기

주제	시 쓰기는 신체적 이점과 정신적 이점이 있음
근거 1	면역 체계와 폐 기능을 향상시키고 심리적 고통을 줄이며 관계를 증진시킴
근거 2	인지 발달에 효과적이고, 생산성과 과학적 창의력을 향상시킴

어휘·어구

personal 개인적인
engage with ~와 관계를 유지하다
poetry 시
benefit 이점
individual 개인
personal 개인적인
professional 직업의
capacity 능력
physical 신체적인
mental 정신적인
expressive 표현하는
improve 향상시키다
immune system 면역 체계
lung function 폐 기능
diminish 줄이다
psychological 심리적인
distress 고통
enhance 높이다
relationship 관계
aid 돕다
empathy 공감
reconsider 재고하다
natural 자연의
environment 환경
incredibly 믿을 수 없을 정도로
effective 효과적인
actively 적극적으로
target 겨냥하다
development 발달
period 시기
productivity 생산성
creativity 창의성
process 과정
means 수단
express 표현하다
emotion 감정
frustration 좌절
realize 깨닫다
complexity 복잡성

정답률 52%

1. ④ ICTs의 빠른 진화의 장점

직독/직해

The fast-paced evolution / 빠른 속도의 진화는 /
of Information and Communication Technologies (ICTs) /
정보와 의사소통 기술(ICTs)의 /
has radically transformed /
급격하게 변화시켜 왔다 /
the dynamics and business models /
역동성과 비즈니스 모델을 /
of the tourism and hospitality industry.
관광업과 서비스업의
This leads to new levels/forms of competitiveness /
이것은 새로운 수준/형태의 경쟁으로 이어진다 /
among service providers / 서비스 제공자 간의 /
and transforms the customer experience /
그리고 고객 경험을 변화시킨다 /
through new services. 새로운 서비스를 통해
Creating unique experiences /
독특한 경험을 만드는 것 /
and providing convenient services to customers /
그리고 고객에게 편리한 서비스를 제공하는 것은 /
leads to satisfaction / 만족감으로 이어진다 /
and, eventually, customer loyalty /
그리고 결국에는, 고객 충성도(로 이어진다) /
to the service provider or brand (i.e., hotels).
서비스 제공자나 브랜드(즉, 호텔)에 대한
In particular, / the most recent *technological* boost /
특히 / 가장 최근의 기술적 향상은 /
received by the tourism sector /
관광업 분야에서 받아들여진 /
is represented by mobile applications.
모바일 애플리케이션에 의해 대표된다
Increasing competitiveness among service providers /
서비스 제공자 간의 경쟁을 증가시키는 것이 /
does not necessarily mean /
반드시 의미하지는 않는다 /
promoting quality of customer services.
고객 서비스의 질을 증진시키는 것을
Indeed, / empowering tourists with mobile access to services /
사실 / 관광객에게 서비스에 대한 모바일 접근 권한을 주는 것은 /
such as hotel reservations, airline ticketing, /
호텔 예약, 항공권 발권과 같은 /
and recommendations for local attractions /
그리고 지역 관광지를 추천하는 것과 같은 /
generates strong interest and considerable profits.
강한 흥미와 상당한 수익을 만들어 낸다

정보와 의사소통 기술(ICTs)의 빠른 속도의 진화는 관광업과 서비스업의 역동성과 비즈니스 모델을 급격하게 변화시켜 왔다. ① 이것은 서비스 제공자 간의 새로운 수준/형태의 경쟁으로 이어지고, 새로운 서비스를 통해 고객 경험을 변화시킨다. ② 독특한 경험을 만드는 것과 고객에게 편리한 서비스를 제공하는 것은 만족감과 결국에는, 서비스 제공자나 브랜드(즉, 호텔)에 대한 고객 충성도로 이어진다. ③ 특히, 관광업 분야에서 받아들여진 가장 최근의 기술적 향상은 모바일 애플리케이션에 의해 대표된다. ④ (서비스 제공자 간의 경쟁을 증가시키는 것이 반드시 고객 서비스의 질을 증진시키는 것을 의미하지는 않는다.) ⑤ 사실, 관광객에게 호텔 예약, 항공권 발권, 그리고 지역 관광지를 추천하는 것과 같은 서비스에 대한 모바일 접근 권한을 주는 것은 강한 흥미와 상당한 수익을 만들어 낸다.

문제풀이

정보와 의사소통 기술이 빠르게 진화하면서 서비스 제공자끼리는 경쟁을 하고 고객은 편리한 서비스를 이용하게 되어 만족감을 얻어 결국 충성 고객이 된다는 내용이다. 하지만 ④는 서비스 제공자 간의 경쟁이 증가하는 것이 반드시 고객 서비스의 질을 증진시키는 것을 의미하지 않는다는 내용이므로 글의 전체 흐름에서 벗어난다.

어휘·어구

fast-paced 빠른 속도의
evolution 진화

radically 급격하게
transform 변화시키다
dynamics 역동성
competitiveness 경쟁
unique 독특한
convenient 편리한
satisfaction 만족
eventually 결국
customer loyalty 고객 충성도
in particular 특히
boost 향상, 증가
sector 분야
represent 대표하다
mobile application 모바일 애플리케이션(모바일 응용 소프트웨어)
promote 증진하다, 촉진하다
empower 권한을 주다
access 접근
reservation 예약
recommendation 추천
attraction 관광지
generate 만들어 내다, 발생시키다
considerable 상당한
profit 수익

정답률 70%

2. ④ 패션이 우리의 삶에서 하는 역할

직독/직해

According to Marguerite La Caze, /
Marguerite La Caze에 따르면 /
fashion contributes to our lives /
패션은 우리의 삶에 기여한다 /
and provides a medium / for us to develop and exhibit important social virtues.
그리고 수단을 제공한다 / 우리가 중요한 사회적 가치를 개발하고 나타내는
Fashion may be beautiful, innovative, and useful; /
패션은 아름다울 수 있고, 혁신적일 수 있으며, 유용할 수 있다 /
we can display creativity and good taste /
우리는 창의성과 좋은 취향을 드러낼 수 있다 /
in our fashion choices.
우리의 패션을 선택하는 데 있어
And in dressing with taste and care, /
그리고 취향과 관심에 따라 옷을 입을 때 /
we represent both self-respect and a concern /
우리는 자아 존중과 관심 모두를 보여 준다 /
for the pleasure of others.
타인의 즐거움에 대한
There is no doubt / that fashion can be a source of interest and pleasure /
의심할 여지가 없다 / 패션은 흥미와 즐거움의 원천이 될 수 있다는 데 /
which links us to each other.
우리와 타인을 연결하는
Although the fashion industry developed /
비록 패션 산업은 발달했지만 /
first in Europe and America, /
유럽과 미국에서 처음 /
today it is an international and highly globalized industry.
오늘날에는 국제적이고 매우 세계화된 산업이 되었다
That is, / fashion provides a sociable aspect /
다시 말해 / 패션은 친교적인 측면을 제공한다 /
along with opportunities /
기회와 함께 /
to imagine oneself differently— /
자신을 다르게 상상하는 /
to try on different identities.
즉, 다른 정체성을 시도하는

Marguerite La Caze에 따르면, 패션은 우리의 삶에 기여하고 우리가 중요한 사회적 가치를 개발하고 나타내는 수단을 제공한다. ① 패션은 아름다울 수 있고, 혁신적일 수 있으며, 유용할 수 있다. 우리는 패션을 선택하는 데 있어 창의성과 좋은 취향을 드러낼 수 있다. ② 그리고 취향과 관심에 따라 옷을 입을 때, 우리는 자아 존중과 타인의 즐거움에 대한 관심 모두를 보여 준다. ③ 의심할 여지없이, 패션은 우리와 타인을 연결하는 흥미와 즐거움의 원천이 될 수 있다. ④ (비록 패션 산업은 유럽과 미국에서 처음 발달했지만, 오늘날에는 국제적이고 매우 세계화된 산업이 되었다.) ⑤ 다시 말해, 패션은 자신을 다르게 상상하는, 즉, 다른 정체성을 시도하는 기회와 함께 친교적인 측면을 제공한다.

문제풀이

패션이 우리의 삶에서 하는 역할에 대한 내용이다. 하지만 ④는 처음에 패션 산업은 유럽과 미국에서 발달했지만 오늘날에는 세계화된 산업이 되었다는 내용이므로 글의 전체 흐름에서 벗어난다.

어휘·어구

contribute to ~에 기여하다
medium 수단
exhibit 보여주다, 전시하다
innovative 혁신적인
useful 유용한
taste 취향
care 관심
represent 표현하다, 나타내다
self-respect 자아 존중, 자존심
concern 관심
pleasure 즐거움, 기쁨
link 연결하다
industry 산업
international 국제적인
globalized 세계화된
sociable 친교적인
aspect 측면
along with ~와 함께
opportunity 기회
identity 정체성

정답률 62%

3. ④ 음료에 있는 가벼운 자극제는 섭취에 주의해야 한다

직독/직해

Who hasn't used a cup of coffee /
커피 한 잔을 이용해 보지 않은 사람이 있을까 /
to help themselves stay awake /
깨어 있는 것을 돕기 위해 /
while studying? 공부하는 동안
Mild stimulants commonly found /
흔히 발견되는 가벼운 자극제는 /
in tea, coffee, or sodas / 차, 커피 혹은 탄산음료에서 /
possibly make you more attentive /
여러분을 더 주의 깊게 만든다 /
and, thus, better able to remember.
그래서 더 잘 기억할 수 있게 (한다)
However, / you should know /
하지만 / 여러분은 알아야 한다 /
that stimulants are as likely to have negative effects / on memory /
자극제가 부정적인 영향을 미칠 수 있다는 것을 / 기억에 /
as they are to be beneficial.
이로울 수 있는 만큼
Even if they could improve performance /
비록 그것이 수행을 향상할 수 있다 할지라도 /
at some level, / 특정 수준에서 /
the ideal doses are currently unknown.
이상적인 복용량은 현재 알려지지 않았다
If you are wide awake and well-rested, /
만약 여러분이 완전히 깨어 있고 잘 쉬었다면 /
mild stimulation from caffeine /
카페인으로부터의 가벼운 자극은 /
can do little / 거의 영향을 주지 못할 수 있다 /
to further improve your memory performance.
여러분의 기억력을 더욱 향상하는 데
In contrast, / many studies have shown /
반면에 / 많은 연구에서 밝혀졌다 /
that drinking tea is healthier /
차를 마시는 것이 건강에 더 좋다는 것이 /
than drinking coffee. 커피를 마시는 것보다
Indeed, / if you have too much of a stimulant, /
실제로 / 여러분이 자극제를 너무 많이 섭취하면 /
you will become nervous, / find it difficult to sleep, /
신경이 과민해지고 / 잠을 자는 것이 어렵다는 것을 알게 되고 /
and your memory performance will suffer.
기억력도 저하될 것이다

공부하는 동안 깨어 있는 것을 돕기 위해 커피 한 잔을 이용해 보지 않은 사람이 있을까? 차, 커피 혹은 탄산음료에서 흔히 발견되는 가벼운 자극제는 여러분을 더 주의 깊게 만들어서 더 잘 기억할 수 있게 한다. ① 하지만, 자극제가 기억에 이로울 수 있는 만큼 부정적인 영향을 미칠 수 있다는 것을 여러분은 알아야 한다. ② 비록 그것이 특정 수준에서 수행을 향상할 수 있다 할지라도, (자극제의) 이상적인 복용량은 현재 알려지지 않았다. ③ 만약 여러분이 완전히 깨어 있고 잘 쉬었다면, 카페인으로부터의 가벼운 자극은 여러분의 기억력을 더욱 향상하는 데 거의 영향을 주지 못할 수 있다. ④ (반면에, 많은 연구에서 커피를 마시는 것보다 차를 마시는 것이 건강에 더 좋다는 것이 밝혀졌다.) ⑤ 실제로 여러분이 자극제를 너무 많이 섭취하면, 신경이 과민해지고, 잠을 자는 것이 어렵다는 것을 알게 되고, 기억력도 저하될 것이다.

문제풀이

커피나 탄산음료 등에서 발견되는 가벼운 자극제는 이점과 단점이 있기 때문에 주의해서 복용해야 한다는 내용이다. 하지만 ④는 커피보다는 차를 마시는 것이 건강에 더 좋다는 내용이므로 글의 전체 흐름에서 벗어난다.

구조 다시보기

도입	음료에서 발견되는 가벼운 자극제는 이점이 있음
주제	자극제는 이로운 만큼 부정적인 영향을 미칠 수도 있음
근거	– 신체 상태가 좋은 경우 자극제는 기억력 향상에 영향을 주지 않음 – 지나친 섭취는 신경과민, 수면 장애, 기억력 저하를 일으킴

어휘·어구

mild 가벼운
soda 탄산음료
attentive 주의 깊은
negative 부정적인
memory 기억력
beneficial 이로운
improve 향상하다
performance 수행
ideal 이상적인
currently 현재
unknown 알려지지 않은
well-rested 잘 쉰
further 더욱
in contrast 반면에
indeed 실제로

정답률 66%

4. ③ 세상을 왜곡되게 믿게 만드는 검색 알고리즘

직독/직해

Internet activist Eli Pariser noticed /
인터넷 활동가인 Eli Pariser는 주목했다 /

how online search algorithms encourage /
어떻게 온라인 검색 알고리즘이 조장하는지 /
our human tendency to grab hold of everything /
우리의 인간 경향성이 모든 것을 움켜쥐도록 /
that confirms the beliefs /
신념이 옳음을 확인해 주는 /
we already hold, / while quietly ignoring information /
우리가 이미 갖고 있는 / 반면에 정보를 조용히 무시하는지 /
that doesn't match those beliefs.
그러한 신념과 맞지 않는
We set up a so-called "filter-bubble" around ourselves, /
우리는 자신의 주변에 소위 '필터 버블'을 설치한다 /
where we are constantly exposed /
그곳에서 우리는 끊임없이 노출된다 /
only to that material / that we agree with.
그 자료에만 / 우리가 동의하는
We are never challenged, /
우리는 결코 이의를 제기 받지 않으며 /
never giving ourselves the opportunity /
우리 자신에게 기회를 주지 않는다 /
to acknowledge the existence of diversity and difference.
다양성과 차이의 존재를 인정할 (기회를)
Creating a difference / that others don't have /
차이를 만들어내는 것이 / 다른 사람이 갖지 못한 /
is a way to succeed in your field, /
자신의 분야에서 성공하는 방법이며 /
leading to the creation of innovations.
혁신의 창조를 이끈다
In the best case, / we become naive and sheltered, /
최상의 경우 / 우리는 세상을 모르고 보호 받는다 /
and in the worst, /
그리고 최악의 경우 /
we become radicalized with extreme views, /
우리는 극단적인 시각으로 과격화되며 /
unable to imagine life / 삶을 상상할 수 없게 된다 /
outside our particular bubble.
우리의 특정 버블 밖의
The results are disastrous: /
그 결과는 참담하여 /
intellectual isolation and the real distortion /
지적 고립과 진정한 왜곡(이 있다) /
that comes with / believing / that the little world /
따라오는 / 믿게 되어 / 작은 세계가 /
we create for ourselves / is *the* world.
우리가 스스로 만드는 / '전' 세계라고

인터넷 활동가인 Eli Pariser는 온라인 검색 알고리즘이 우리가 이미 갖고 있는 신념이 옳음을 확인해 주는 모든 것을 움켜쥐고, 반면에 그러한 신념과 맞지 않는 정보는 조용히 무시하는 우리의 인간 경향성을 어떻게 조장하는지에 주목했다. ① 우리는 자신의 주변에 소위 '필터 버블'을 설치하는데 그곳에서 우리는 자신이 동의하는 그 자료에만 끊임없이 노출된다. ② 우리는 결코 이의를 제기 받지 않으며 스스로에게 다양성과 차이의 존재를 인정할 기회를 주지 않는다. (다른 사람이 갖지 못한 차이를 만들어 내는 것이 자신의 분야에서 성공하는 방법이며 혁신의 창조를 이끈다.) ④ 최상의 경우 우리는 세상을 모르고 보호 받으며, 최악의 경우 우리는 극단적인 시각으로 과격화되며 우리의 특정 버블 밖의 삶을 상상할 수 없게 된다. ⑤ 그 결과는 참담하여, 예를 들면 지적 고립과 우리가 스스로 만드는 작은 세계가 '전' 세계라고 믿게 되어 따라오는 진정한 왜곡이 있다.

문제풀이

이 글은 검색 알고리즘은 우리가 우리의 신념과 일치하는 정보만을 찾고, 그렇지 않은 정보는 무시하는 경향을 갖게 하여, 우리가 동의하는 자료에만 노출되는 '필터 버블'을 설치하게 되는데 이는 다양성과 차이의 존재를 인정하지 않고 스스로 만든 세계에만 갇히게 된다는 내용의 글이다. 하지만 ③은 다른 사람과 다른 차이를 만들어 내는 것이 성공의 방법이라는 내용이므로 글의 전체 흐름에서 벗어난다.

어휘·어구

tendency 경향
grab 움켜잡다
confirm 확인하다
set up 설치하다
constantly 지속적으로
expose A to B A를 B에 노출시키다
material 물질
acknowledge 인정하다
diversity 다양성
shelter 보호
extreme 극단적인
disastrous 비참한
intellectual 지적인
isolation 고립

정답률 70%

5. ④ Zeigarnik 효과

직독/직해

The Zeigarnik effect is commonly referred to /
Zeigarnik 효과는 일반적으로 일컫는다 /
as the tendency of the subconscious mind /
잠재적인 마음의 경향을 /
to remind you of a task / 당신에게 과업을 상기시켜주는 /
that is incomplete / until that task is complete.
끝나지 않은 / 그 과업이 끝날 때까지
Bluma Zeigarnik was a Lithuanian psychologist /
Bluma Zeigarnik는 리투아니아 심리학자이다 /
who wrote in the 1920s / 1920년대에 쓴 /
about the effects of leaving tasks incomplete.
과업을 완성하지 못한 채로 남겨두는 것의 효과에 관해
She noticed the effect / while watching waiters serve /
그녀는 그 효과를 알아차렸다 / 웨이터들이 서빙하는 것을 보면서 /
in a restaurant. 한 식당에서
The waiters would remember an order, /
그 웨이터들은 주문을 기억했다 /
however complicated, / 아무리 복잡하더라도 /
until the order was complete, / 그 주문이 끝날 때까지 /
but they would later find / 하지만 그들은 나중에는 알았다 /
it difficult to remember the order.
그 주문을 기억하는 것이 어렵다는 것을
Zeigarnik did further studies /
Zeigarnik는 더 깊은 연구를 했다 /
giving both adults and children puzzles to complete /
어른들과 아이들 모두에게 완성할 퍼즐을 주고 /
then interrupting them / during some of the tasks.
그러고 나서 그들을 방해하는 / 그 과업들 중 몇몇을 하는 도중에
They developed cooperation skills /
그들은 협동 기술을 발달시켰다 /
after finishing tasks / 과업들을 끝낸 후
by putting the puzzles together.
퍼즐을 같이 맞춤으로써
The results showed / 그 결과들은 보여주었다 /
that both adults and children remembered /
어른들과 아이들 모두 기억했다는 것을 /
the tasks that hadn't been completed /
완성되지 못한 과업들을 /
because of the interruptions / 방해 때문에 /
better than the ones that had been completed.
완성된 것들보다 더 잘

Zeigarnik 효과는 일반적으로 당신에게 그 과업이 끝날 때까지 끝나지 않은 과업을 상기시켜주는 잠재적인 마음의 경향을 일컫는다. Bluma Zeigarnik는 1920년대에 과업을 완성하지 못한 채로 남겨두는 것의 효과에 관해 쓴 리투아니아 심리학자이다. ① 그녀는 한 식당에서 웨이터들이 서빙하는 것을 보면서 그 효과를 알아차렸다. ② 그 웨이터들은 아무리 복잡하더라도 그 주문이 끝날 때까지 주문을 기억했는데, 그들은 나중에는 그 주문을 기억하는 것이 어렵다는 것을 알았다. ③ Zeigarnik는 어른들과 아이들 모두에게 완성할 퍼즐을 주고 그 과업들 중 몇몇을 하는 도중에 그들을 방해하는 더 깊은 연구를 했다. ④ (그들은 퍼즐을 같이 맞춤으로써 과업들을 끝낸 후 협동 기술을 발달시켰다.) ⑤ 그 결과들은 어른들과 아이들 모두 방해 때문에 완성되지 못한 과업들을 완성된 것들보다 더 잘 기억했다는 것을 보여주었다.

문제풀이

Zeigarnik 효과에 대한 글로, 일반적으로 사람들은 완성되지 않은 과업을 완성된 과업보다 더 잘 기억한다는 내용이다. 하지만 ④는 과업을 끝낸 후 협동 기술이 발달했다는 내용이므로 글의 전체 흐름에서 벗어난다.

어휘·어구

refer to A as B A를 B라고 일컫다
tendency 경향
subconscious 잠재의식의
incomplete 미완성의
psychologist 심리학자
complicated 복잡한
interrupt 방해하다
cooperation 협동

정답률 62%

6. ④ 도시의 회복력

직독/직해

Health and the spread of disease /
건강과 질병 확산은 /
are very closely linked to /
~에 매우 밀접하게 연관되어 있다 /
how we live / and how our cities operate.
우리가 어떻게 사는지와 / 그리고 우리의 도시가 어떻게 작동하는냐와
The good news / 좋은 소식은 /
is that cities are incredibly resilient.
도시가 믿을 수 없을 정도로 회복력이 있다는 것이다
Many cities have experienced epidemics / in the past /
많은 도시는 전염병을 경험했다 / 과거에 /
and have not only survived, / but advanced.
그리고 살아남았을 뿐만 아니라 / 발전했다
The nineteenth and early-twentieth centuries /
19세기와 20세기 초는 /
saw destructive outbreaks /
파괴적인 창궐을 목격했다 /
of cholera, typhoid, and influenza /
콜레라, 장티푸스, 그리고 독감의 /
in European cities. 유럽 도시들에서
Doctors such as Jon Snow, from England, /
영국 출신의 Jon Snow와 같은 의사들은 /
and Rudolf Virchow, of Germany, /
그리고 독일의 Rudolf Virchow와 (같은) /
saw the connection / 연관성을 알게 되었다 /
between poor living conditions, overcrowding, sanitation, and disease.
열악한 생활 상태, 인구 과밀, 위생, 그리고 질병 간의
A recognition of this connection /
이 연관성에 대한 인식은 /
led to the replanning and rebuilding of cities /
도시 재계획과 재건축으로 이어졌다 /
to stop the spread of epidemics.
전염병의 확산을 막기 위한
In spite of reconstruction efforts, /
재건 노력에도 불구하고 /
cities declined in many areas /
도시는 많은 지역에서 쇠퇴했다 /
and many people started to leave.
그리고 많은 사람이 떠나기 시작했다
In the mid-nineteenth century, /
19세기 중반에 /
London's pioneering sewer system, /
런던의 선구적인 하수 처리 시스템은 /
which still serves it today, /
오늘날까지도 여전히 사용되고 있는 /
was built as a result of understanding /
이해의 결과로 만들어졌다 /

the importance of clean water /
깨끗한 물의 중요성에 관한 /
in stopping the spread of cholera.
콜레라의 확산을 막는 데 있어

건강과 질병 확산은 우리가 어떻게 살고 우리의 도시가 어떻게 작동하느냐와 매우 밀접하게 연관되어 있다. 좋은 소식은 도시가 믿을 수 없을 정도로 회복력이 있다는 것이다. 많은 도시는 과거에 전염병을 경험했고 살아남았을 뿐만 아니라 발전했다. ① 19세기와 20세기 초 유럽 도시들은 콜레라, 장티푸스, 그리고 독감의 파괴적인 창궐을 목격했다. ② 영국 출신의 Jon Snow와 독일의 Rudolf Virchow와 같은 의사들은 열악한 생활 상태, 인구 과밀, 위생, 그리고 질병 간의 연관성을 알게 되었다. ③ 이 연관성에 대한 인식은 전염병의 확산을 막기 위한 도시 재계획과 재건축으로 이어졌다. ④ (재건 노력에도 불구하고, 도시는 많은 지역에서 쇠퇴했고, 많은 사람이 떠나기 시작했다.) ⑤ 19세기 중반에, 오늘날까지도 여전히 사용되고 있는 런던의 선구적인 하수 처리 시스템은 콜레라의 확산을 막는 데 있어 깨끗한 물의 중요성에 관한 이해의 결과로 만들어졌다.

문제풀이

많은 도시가 과거에 전염병을 경험했고, 전염병의 확산을 막기 위해 재건축되었다는 내용의 글이다. 하지만 ④는 재건 노력에도 불구하고 도시는 많은 지역에서 쇠퇴해서 많은 사람이 떠나기 시작했다는 내용이므로, 글의 전체 흐름에서 벗어난다.

어휘·어구

- **operate** 작동하다
- **incredibly** 믿을 수 없을 정도로
- **epidemic** 유행병, 전염병
- **advance** 발전하다
- **destructive** 파괴적인
- **outbreak** 발발, 창궐
- **typhoid** 장티푸스
- **influenza** 독감
- **connection** 연관
- **overcrowding** 과밀
- **sanitation** 위생
- **recognition** 인식, 인지
- **reconstruction** 재건
- **decline** 쇠퇴하다
- **pioneering** 선구적인, 개척의

7. ③ 변화된 뮤지션들의 입지

직독/직해

Today's music business / 오늘날의 음악 사업은 /
has allowed musicians to take matters /
뮤지션들이 일을 가져올 수 있게 해 주었다 /
into their own hands. 자기 자신의 손으로
Gone are the days / 시대는 지났다 /
of musicians waiting for a gatekeeper /
뮤지션들이 문지기가 ~해주기를 기다리는 /
(someone who holds power / 권력을 쥐고 사람 /
and prevents you from being let in) /
그리고 당신이 들어가는 것을 막는 (사람) /
at a label or TV show / 음반사나 TV 프로그램의 /
to say they are worthy of the spotlight.
그들이 주목받을 만하다고 말해주기를
In today's music business, / 오늘날의 음악 사업에서는 /
you don't need to ask for permission /
여러분은 허락을 요청할 필요가 없다 /
to build a fanbase / and you no longer need to pay /
팬층을 만들기 위해서 / 그리고 여러분은 더 이상 지불할 필요도 없다 /
thousands of dollars to a company / to do it.
수천 달러를 회사에 / 그것을 하려고
There are rising concerns /
우려가 증가하고 있다 /
over the marketing of child musicians /
어린 뮤지션들을 마케팅하는 데에 대한 /
using TV auditions. TV 오디션을 이용해서
Every day, / musicians are getting their music out /
매일 / 뮤지션들은 자신들의 음악을 내놓고 있다 /
to thousands of listeners / without any outside help.
수천 명의 청취자에게 / 어떤 외부의 도움 없이도
They simply deliver it / to the fans directly, /
그들은 간단히 그것을 전달한다 / 팬들에게 직접 /
without asking for permission or outside help /
허락이나 외부의 도움을 요청하지 않고 /
to receive exposure / 노출을 얻기 위해 /
or connect with thousands of listeners.
혹은 수천 명의 청취자와 관계를 형성하기 위해

오늘날의 음악 사업은 뮤지션들이 스스로 일을 처리할 수 있게 해 주었다. ① 뮤지션들이 음반사나 TV 프로그램의 문지기(권력을 쥐고 사람들이 들어가는 것을 막는 사람)가 그들[뮤지션들]이 주목받을 만하다고 말해주기를 기다리던 시대는 지났다. ② 오늘날의 음악 사업에서는 팬층을 만들기 위해서 허락을 요청할 필요가 없고, 그것을 하려고 더 이상 회사에 수천 달러를 지불할 필요도 없다. ③ (TV 오디션을 이용해서 어린 뮤지션들을 마케팅하는 데에 대한 우려가 증가하고 있다.) ④ 매일 뮤지션들은 어떤 외부의 도움 없이도 수천 명이 청취자에게 자신들의 음악을 내놓고 있다. ⑤ 그들은 노출을 얻거나 수천 명의 청취자와 관계를 형성하기 위해 허락이나 외부의 도움을 요청하지 않고, 간단히 자신들의 음악을 팬들에게 직접 전달한다.

문제풀이

오늘날의 음악 산업은 뮤지션들이 스스로 일을 처리할 수 있게 해주었기 때문에 뮤지션들은 어떤 외부의 도움 없이도 팬층을 만들 수 있다는 내용이다. 하지만 ③은 TV 오디션을 이용해서 어린 뮤지션들을 마케팅하는 데 우려가 증가하고 있다는 내용이므로 글의 전체 흐름에서 벗어난다.

어휘·어구

- **business** 사업
- **gatekeeper** 문지기, 정보 관리[통제]자
- **prevent** 막다
- **let in** ~을 들여 보내다
- **label** 음반사
- **spotlight** 주목
- **ask for** ~을 요청하다
- **permission** 허락, 허가
- **fanbase** 팬층
- **concern** 우려, 염려
- **directly** 직접, 곧장
- **receive** 받다
- **exposure** 노출, 매스컴 출연
- **connect with** ~와 연결하다

정답률 66%

8. ④ 바넘 효과

직독/직해

The Barnum Effect is the phenomenon /
바넘 효과는 현상이다 /
where someone reads or hears something very general /
누군가가 매우 일반적인 것을 읽거나 듣는 /
but believes that it applies to them.
하지만 그것이 자신에게 적용된다고 믿는
These statements appear to be very personal /
이런 진술들은 매우 개인적인 것처럼 보인다 /
on the surface / 표면적으로는 /
but in fact, / they are true for many.
하지만 실제로는 / 그것들은 많은 사람에게 적용된다
Human psychology allows us to want to believe /
인간 심리는 우리가 믿고 싶어 하게 한다 /
things that we can identify /
우리가 동일시할 수 있는 것들을 /
with on a personal level / 개인적 차원에서 /
and even seek information /
그리고 심지어 정보를 찾고 (싶게 한다) /
where it doesn't necessarily exist, /
그것이 반드시 존재하지는 않는 경우에도 /
filling in the blanks with our imagination /
우리의 상상으로 공백들을 채우면서 /
for the rest. 나머지에 대해서는
This is the principle / that horoscopes rely on, /
이것은 원리이다 / 별자리 운세가 의존하는 /
offering data that appears to be personal /
개인적인 것처럼 보이는 정보를 제공하는 /
but probably makes sense to countless people.
하지만 수많은 사람에게 대개 들어맞는
Reading daily horoscopes in the morning /
매일 아침 별자리 운세를 읽는 것은 /
is beneficial / 유익하다 /
as they provide predictions /
그것들이 예측을 제공하기 때문에 /
about the rest of the day. 남은 하루에 대한
Since the people reading them / 그것들을 읽는 사람들이 /
want to believe the information so badly, /
그 정보를 너무나도 믿고 싶어 하므로 /
they will search for meaning / 그들은 의미를 찾을 것이다 /
in their lives that make it true. 그것을 사실로 만드는 삶에서

바넘 효과는 누군가가 매우 일반적인 것을 읽거나 듣지만, 그것이 자신에게 적용된다고 믿는 현상이다. ① 이런 진술들은 표면적으로는 매우 개인적인 것처럼 보이지만, 실제로는 많은 사람에게 적용된다. ② 인간 심리는 우리가 개인적 차원에서 동일시할 수 있는 것들을 믿고, 나머지에 대해서는 우리의 상상으로 공백들을 채우면서 그것(정보)이 반드시 존재하지는 않는 경우에도 심지어 정보를 찾고 싶어 하게 한다. ③ 이것은 개인적인 것처럼 보이지만 수많은 사람에게 대개 들어맞는 정보를 제공하는 별자리 운세가 의존하는 원리이다. ④ (매일 아침 별자리 운세를 읽는 것은 그것들이 남은 하루에 대한 예측을 제공하기 때문에 유익하다.) ⑤ 그것들을 읽는 사람들이 그 정보를 너무나도 믿고 싶어 하므로, 그들은 그것을 사실로 만드는 삶에서 의미를 찾을 것이다.

문제풀이

매우 일반적인 사실들이 자신에게 적용된다고 믿는 현상인 바넘 효과에 관한 글로, 별자리 운세에 의존하는 원리를 사례로 들고 있다. 하지만 ④는 매일 아침 별자리 운세를 읽는 것의 유익성에 관한 내용이므로 글의 전체 흐름에서 벗어난다.

어휘·어구

- **phenomenon** 현상
- **apply to** ~에 적용되다
- **statement** 진술
- **personal** 개인적인
- **psychology** 심리, 심리학
- **identify** 동일시하다
- **seek** 찾다, 추구하다
- **principle** 원리, 원칙
- **rely on** ~에 의존하다
- **countless** 셀 수 없이 많은
- **beneficial** 유익한
- **prediction** 예언, 예측

정답률 63%

9. ④ 훨씬 더 큰 에너지의 원천

직독/직해

In a single week, / 단 한 주 만에 /
the sun delivers more energy to our planet /
태양은 더 많은 에너지를 지구에 전달한다 /
than humanity has used through the burning of coal, oil, and natural gas /
인간이 석탄, 석유, 그리고 천연가스의 연소를 통해 사용해 온 것보다 /
through *all of human history*.

'모든 인간의 역사' 에 걸쳐

And the sun will keep shining on our planet for billions of years.
그리고 태양은 수십억 년 동안, 계속하여 지구를 비출 것이다

Our challenge isn't that we're running out of energy.
우리의 당면 과제는 우리의 에너지가 고갈되고 있다는 것이 아니다

It's that we have been focused on the wrong source — /
그것은 우리가 잘못된 원천에 집중하고 있다는 것이다

the small, finite one that we're using up.
우리가 고갈시키고 있는 양이 적고 한정적인 것

Indeed, all the coal, natural gas, and oil we use today /
사실, 우리가 오늘날 사용하고 있는 모든 석탄, 천연가스, 그리고 석유는 /

is just solar energy from millions of years ago, /
수백 만 년 전에 온 태양에너지일 뿐이다 /

a very tiny part of which was preserved deep underground.
그것의 극히 일부분만이 지하 깊은 곳에 보존되어 있었다

Our efforts to develop technologies /
기술을 개발하기 위한 우리의 노력은 /

that use fossil fuels /
화석 연료를 사용하는 /

have shown meaningful results.
의미 있는 결과를 거둬왔다

Our challenge, and our opportunity, /
우리의 기회이자 당면 과제는 /

is to learn to efficiently and cheaply use the *much more abundant* source /
'훨씬 더 풍부한' 원천을 효율적으로 그리고 저비용으로 사용하는 것을 배우는 것이다 /

that is the new energy striking our planet each day from the sun.
태양으로부터 매일 지구에 도달하는 새로운 에너지인

단 한 주 만에, 태양은 '모든 인간의 역사' 에 걸쳐 인간이 석탄, 석유, 그리고 천연가스의 연소를 통해 사용해 온 것보다 더 많은 에너지를 지구에 전달한다. 그리고 태양은 수십억 년 동안, 계속하여 지구를 비출 것이다. ① 우리의 당면 과제는 우리의 에너지가 고갈되고 있다는 것이 아니다. ② 그것은 우리가 잘못된 원천 — 우리가 고갈시키고 있는 (양이) 적고 한정적인 것 — 에 집중하고 있다는 것이다. ③ 사실, 우리가 오늘날 사용하고 있는 모든 석탄, 천연가스, 그리고 석유는 수백 만 년 전에 온 태양에너지일 뿐이며, 그것의 극히 일부분만이 지하 깊은 곳에 보존되어 있었다. ④ 화석 연료를 사용하는 기술을 개발하기 위한 우리의 노력은 의미 있는 결과를 거둬왔다. ⑤ 우리의 기회이자 당면 과제는 태양으로부터 매일 지구에 도달하는 새로운 에너지인 '훨씬 더 풍부한' 원천을 효율적으로 그리고 저비용으로 사용하는 것을 배우는 것이다.

문제풀이

우리는 양이 적고 한정된 자원에 집중할 것이 아니라 훨씬 더 풍부한 원천인 태양에너지를 효율적으로 그리고 저비용으로 사용하는 것을 배워야 한다는 내용의 글인데, 화석 연료를 사용하는 기술 개발의 노력이 의미 있는 결과를 거둬왔다는 내용의 ④는 흐름과 상반된다.

이렇게 풀자 각 문장의 연결이 어색하지 않은지, 갑자기 내용이 전환되거나 단절되지 않는지 살피며 읽어야 한다. 한편 전체 흐름과 무관한 문장에서도 글의 소재와 동일한 화제가 쓰이는 것에 유의해야 한다. 여기서는 정답 문장에서 fossil fuels라는 단어로 혼동을 유도하고 있지만, 오히려 전체 흐름과 상반된 내용이다.

어휘·어구

deliver 전달하다
humanity 인류, 인류애
run out of ~이 고갈되다
finite 한정적인
use up ~을 다 써버리다
preserve 보존하다
fossil fuel 화석 연료
abundant 풍부한

정답률 61%

10. ④ 정보 공개에 대한 문화 차이

직독/직해

Given the widespread use of emoticons /
이모티콘이 널리 사용되고 있다는 점을 고려할 때 /

in electronic communication, / 전자 통신에서 /

an important question / is whether they help /
중요한 문제는 / 그들이 도움을 주는가의 여부이다 /

Internet users to understand emotions /
인터넷 사용자들이 감정을 이해하는데 /

in online communication.
온라인상의 의사소통에서

Emoticons, / particularly character-based ones, /
이모티콘은 / 특히 문자에 기반한 것들은 /

are much more ambiguous /
훨씬 더 모호하다 /

relative to face-to-face cues /
면대면을 통한 단서에 비해 /

and may end up being interpreted very differently /
그리고 결국 매우 다르게 해석될 수 있다 /

by different users. 다른 사용자들에 의해

Nonetheless, / research indicates /
그럼에도 불구하고 / 연구는 보여준다 /

that they are useful tools /
그것들이 유용한 도구라는 것을 /

in online text-based communication.
온라인상의 텍스트 기반 의사소통에서

One study of 137 instant messaging users revealed /
137명의 인스턴트 메시지 사용자들을 대상으로 한 연구는 밝혀냈다 /

that emoticons allowed / 이모티콘이 허락했다는 것을 /

users to correctly understand /
사용자들이 정확하게 이해하는 것을 /

the level and direction of emotion, attitude, and attention expression /
감정, 태도, 주의력 표현의 정도와 방향을 /

and that emoticons were a definite advantage /
그리고 이모티콘이 확실한 장점이라는 것을 /

in non-verbal communication.
비언어적 의사소통에서

In fact, / there have been few studies /
사실 / 연구는 거의 없었다 /

on the relationships / 관계에 관한 /

between verbal and non-verbal communication.
언어적 의사소통과 비언어적 의사소통 간의

Similarly, / another study showed /
마찬가지로 / 또 다른 연구는 보여주었다 /

that emoticons were useful /
이모티콘이 유용하다는 것을 /

in strengthening the intensity of a verbal message, /
언어적 메시지의 강도를 강화하는 데 /

as well as in the expression of sarcasm.
풍자의 표현에서뿐만 아니라

전자 통신에서 이모티콘이 널리 사용되고 있다는 점을 고려할 때, 중요한 문제는 인터넷 사용자들이 온라인상의 의사소통에서 감정을 이해하는데 그것들이 도움을 주는가의 여부이다. ① 이모티콘, 특히 문자에 기반한 것들은, 면대면을 통한 단서에 비해 훨씬 더 모호하며, 결국 다른 사용자들에 의해 매우 다르게 해석될 수 있다. ② 그럼에도 불구하고, 연구는 그것들이 온라인상의 텍스트 기반 의사소통에서 유용한 도구라는 것을 보여준다. ③ 137명의 인스턴트 메시지(실시간 텍스트 통신) 사용자들을 대상으로 한 연구는 이모티콘이 사용자들로 하여금 감정, 태도, 주의력 표현의 정도와 방향을 정확하게 이해할 수 있게 해주고 이모티콘이 비언어적 의사소통에서 확실한 장점이라는 것을 밝혀냈다. ④ (사실, 언어적 의사소통과 비언어적 의사소통 간의 관계에 관한 연구는 거의 없었다.) ⑤ 마찬가지로, 또 다른 연구는 이모티콘이 풍자의 표현에서뿐만 아니라, 언어적 메시지의 강도를 강화하는 데 유용하다는 것을 보여주었다.

문제풀이

이모티콘, 특히 문자기반 이모티콘이 대면 단서들에 비해 애매모호해서 사용자에 따라 다르게 해석될 수 있지만, 그럼에도 불구하고 이모티콘이 온라인 의사소통에서 감정을 이해하는데 도움을 준다는 내용의 글이다. 하지만 ④는 '언어적 의사소통과 비언어적 의사소통의 관계에 관한 연구는 거의 없었다'는 의미로 글의 전체 흐름과 관계가 없다.

이렇게 풀자 흐름과 관계없는 문장을 찾는 문제에서는 대개 첫 문장이 주제문이거나 주제와 관련된 문제를 제기하는 문장이다. 첫 문장에서 핵심 키워드를 파악하고, 이어진 각각의 문장의 주어나, 연결사를 중심으로 글의 흐름을 따라가면 답을 쉽게 찾을 수 있다. 첫 문장에서 'emoticons'이 핵심 키워드라는 것을 알 수 있고, ①의 주어 'Emoticons'이고, ②의 연결사 'Nontheless' 뒤의 문장에서 'reseach indicates that they ~'의 'they'가 가리키는 것이 'emoticons'이며, ③의 'One study of 137 ~'와 ⑤의 Similarly 뒤의 'another study'는 ②의 'research'에 대한 구체적 내용이라는 것을 알 수 있다. 따라서 ④가 글의 흐름과 무관한 문장이라는 것을 쉽게 파악할 수 있다.

구조 다시보기

문제 제기	온라인 소통에서 이모티콘이 감정을 이해하는데 도움이 될까?
일반적 통념	이모티콘은 애매해서 사용자마다 다르게 받아들일 수 있음
반전(주제)	연구에 따르면 이모티콘은 온라인 소통에서 유용한 도구임
이유	사용자의 감정, 태도, 관심이 어떤지를 정확하게 나타냄
연구 결과	풍자에 유용하고 전달하는 말의 강도를 높여 줌

어휘·어구

given ~을 고려할 때
widespread 광범위한, 널리 퍼진
electronic 전자의
communication (의사) 소통
character 문자, 글자
cue 단서
face-to-face 대면하는, 마주보는
end up -ing 결국 ~이 되다
interpret 해석하다, 설명하다
indicate 나타내다, 보여주다
correctly 바르게, 정확하게
reveal 밝히다, 드러내다
direction 방향
attitude 태도
attention 관심
definite 확실한
non-verbal 비언어의
strengthen 강화시키다
intensity 강도
verbal 언어의

본문 089쪽

문법 플러스 15. 병렬 구조

1. generous 2. bitterly 3. snapped
4. use 5. socialize 6. act 7. grab
8. destroyed 9. to finish 10. that

1 [해석]▶ 그 노인은 매우 친절하고 관대하다.
[해설]▶ be동사의 보어인 형용사 kind와 generous가 등위접속사 and로 연결된 병렬 구조를 이루고 있다.

2 [해석]▶ 그는 그 전쟁에 대해 화내며 신랄하게 말했다.
[해설]▶ 부사 angrily가 동사 spoke를 수식하고 있다. 등위접속사 뒤에 나오는 괄호 부분도 같은 모양을 이루며 병렬 구조를 이루려면 부사 bitterly가 와야 한다.

3 [해석]▶ Sally는 손을 든 다음 손가락을 딱딱 부러뜨렸다.
[해설]▶ 등위접속사 and가 동사 raised와 snapped를 연결

하는 병렬 구조를 이루고 있다.

4 [해석]▶ 창가에서 작업하거나 책상 전등에 있는 모든 파장이 있는 전구를 이용하여 실험해 보아라.
[해설]▶ 등위접속사 or에 의해 전치사 with의 목적어 역할을 하는 동명사 working과 병렬 구조를 이루어야 하므로 using이 와야 적절하다.

5 [해석]▶ 매일 학교가 끝날 때, 수십 명의 학생이 숙제하기 위해, 도서관의 컴퓨터를 이용하기 위해, 혹은 안전한 장소에서 교제하기 위해 도서관에 옵니다.
[해설]▶ to do와 (to) use와 (to) socialize가 등위접속사 or로 병렬로 연결되어 있다. to부정사의 부사적 용법(목적)으로 쓰였다.

6 [해석]▶ 하지만, 오늘날 디지털 시대의 도구들은 우리에게 새로운 방식으로 정보를 공유하고 실행하는 방법을 제공하고 있다.
[해설]▶ to easily get, (to) share and (to) act가 병렬 구조를 이루며 명사 way를 수식하고 있다.

7 [해석]▶ 갑자기, 나는 계단 사이로부터 손 하나가 뻗어 나와 내 발목을 잡는 것을 보았다.
[해설]▶ Suddenly, I saw a hand reach out from between the steps and **(I saw a hand)** grab my ankles.와 같이 접속사 and가 병렬 구조를 이루고 있는 문장이다. reach와 grab이 지각동사 saw의 목적격보어로 사용되었다.

8 [해석]▶ 비록 에너지는 형체가 변할 수는 있지만, 창조되거나 파괴될 수는 없다.
[해설]▶ neither A and B에서 A, B는 형태와 기능이 같아야 하므로 「조동사(can)+be+과거분사」에서 과거분사가 와야 한다.

9 [해석]▶ 올바르게 하는 것은 빨리 마치는 것보다 더 중요하다.
[해설]▶ 비교 구문에서 비교 대상은 같은 형태를 취해야 한다. 그래서 주어가 to부정사이므로 be more ~ than 뒤에 나오는 괄호 부분에도 to부정사가 나와야 한다.

10 해석▶ 도쿄의 인구는 서울의 인구보다 더 많다.
[해설] 명사의 반복을 피하기 위해 「the+명사(population)」 대신 that을 쓴다. 단, 명사가 복수일 경우에는 those를 쓴다. 단수 집합명사 population이 왔으므로 that을 써야 한다.

본문 090쪽

어휘 플러스 15. 반의어 (4)

1. illegally 2. mental
3. separates 4. optimistic
5. positive

1 [해석]▶ 우리는 게임을 불법적으로 다운받아서는 안 된다.

2 [해석]▶ 그 파장은 관찰자의 눈에 들어올 때 연쇄적인 신경 화학적 현상을 유발시키며, 그 현상이 끝날 때 우리가 색깔이라 부르는 내적인 정신적 이미지를 만들어낸다.

3 [해석]▶ 이것은 사람을 다른 동물로부터 구별 짓게 할 뿐 아니라, 사람들을 동물 수준으로 끌어내린다.

4 [해석]▶ 학생들의 태도가 더 낙관적이 되면서 수학에 대한 그들의 자신감도 늘었다.

5 [해석]▶ 사회 과학에 있어서 많은 경우, 증거는 특정 이론을 증명해 보이기 위해서만, 즉 그 이론을 뒷받침하는 긍정적인 사례들을 찾기 위해서만 활용된다.

16. 문단 내 글의 순서 파악

Day 16 본문 092쪽

1. ⑤ 2. ② 3. ⑤ 4. ③ 5. ⑤
6. ③ 7. ② 8. ③ 9. ⑤ 10. ④
11. ③ 12. ④

정답률 67%

대표 기출 ③ 로봇에 의해 위협받고 있는 일사리들

직독/직해

Things are changing. 상황이 변화하고 있다
It has been reported / 보도되어 왔다 /
that 42 percent of jobs in Canada / are at risk, /
캐나다의 일자리 중 42%가 / 위기에 처해 있다고 /
and 62 percent of jobs in America /
그리고 미국의 일자리 중 62%가 /
will be in danger / due to advances in automation.
위기에 처할 (것이라고) / 자동화의 발전으로 인해
(B) You might say / 여러분은 말할지 모른다 /
that the numbers seem a bit unrealistic, /
그 숫자들이 약간 비현실적으로 보인다고 /
but the threat is real. 그 위협은 현실이다
One fast food franchise / has a robot /
한 패스트푸드 체인점은 / 로봇을 가지고 있다 /
that can flip a burger / in ten seconds.
버거 하나를 뒤집을 수 있는 / 10초 안에
It is just a simple task / 그것은 단지 단순한 일이다 /
but the robot could replace an entire crew.
하지만 그 로봇은 전체 직원을 대체할 수도 있다
(C) Highly skilled jobs are also at risk.
고도로 숙련된 직업들이 또한 위기에 처해 있다
A supercomputer, / for instance, /
슈퍼컴퓨터는 / 예를 들어, /
can suggest available treatments /
이용 가능한 치료법을 제안할 수 있다 /
for specific illnesses / in an automated way, /
특정 질병들에 관해 / 자동화된 방식으로 /
drawing on the body of medical research and data /
방대한 양의 의학 연구와 데이터를 이용하여 /
on diseases. 질병에 대한
(A) However, / what's difficult to automate /
하지만 / 자동화하기 어려운 것은 /
is the ability / to creatively solve problems.
능력이다 / 창의적으로 문제들을 해결하는
Whereas workers in "doing" roles /
'(기계적인 일을) 하는' 역할의 노동자들은 ~인 반면 /
can be replaced by robots, /
로봇들에 의해 대체될 수 있는 (반면) /
the role of creatively solving problems /
창의적으로 문제를 해결하는 역할은 /
is more dependent on / an irreplaceable individual.
더 의존한다 / 대체 불가능한 개인에

상황이 변화하고 있다. 캐나다의 일자리 중 42%가 위기에 처해 있고, 미국의 일자리 중 62%가 자동화의 발전으로 인해 위기에 처할 것이라고 보도되어 왔다.
(B) 여러분은 그 숫자들이 약간 비현실적으로 보인다고 말할지 모르지만, 그 위협은 현실이다. 한 패스트푸드 체인점은 10초 안에 버거 하나를 뒤집을 수 있는 로봇을 가지고 있다. 그것은 단지 단순한 일이지만 그 로봇은 전체 직원을 대체할 수도 있다.
(C) 고도로 숙련된 직업들 또한 위기에 처해 있다. 예를 들어, 슈퍼컴퓨터는 질병에 대한 방대한 양의 의학 연구와 데이터를 이용하여 자동화된 방식으로 특정 질병들에 관해 이용 가능한 치료법을 제안할 수 있다.
(A) 하지만, 자동화하기 어려운 것은 창의적으로 문제들을 해결하는 능력이다. '(기계적인 일을) 하는' 역할의 노동자들은 로봇들에 의해 대체될 수 있는 반면, 창의적으로 문제를 해결하는 역할은 대체 불가능한 개인에 더 의존한다.

문제풀이

캐나다와 미국의 일자리들이 자동화의 발전으로 인해 위기에 처할 것이라는 내용의 주어진 글 다음에, 그에 대한 구체적인 사례로 10초 안에 버거 하나를 뒤집을 수 있는 로봇을 가지고 있는 한 패스트푸드 체인점을 소개한 (B)가 오고, 고도로 숙련된 직업들 또한 위기에 처해 있다고 하면서 그에 대한 사례로 슈퍼컴퓨터를 언급한 (C)가 온 뒤, 마지막으로 자동화하기 어려운 것은 창의적으로 문제를 해결하는 능력이고, 창의적 문제 해결 역할은 대체 불가능한 개인에 더 의존한다는 내용의 (A)가 오는 것이 가장 적절하다.

이렇게 풀자 (B)의 'the numbers'는 주어진 문장에서 언급된 42%와 62%를 가리키므로 주어진 문장 다음에 (B)가 오고, (C)의 첫 문장 'Highly skilled jobs are also at risk.'의 'also'로 보아 앞에도 위기 상황을 설명한 내용이 나와야 하므로 (C)는 (B) 다음에 와야 하며, (A)의 'However'로 보아 앞에 제시된 내용과 상반된 내용이 서술됨을 알 수 있으므로 (C) 다음에 (A)가 와야 한다.

구조 다시보기

도입	자동화의 발전으로 일자리가 위기에 처할 것임
사례 1	패스트푸드 체인점에서 단순한 일을 하는 로봇이 전체 직원을 대체할 수 있음
사례 2	고도로 숙련된 직업 또한 슈퍼컴퓨터에 의해 위기에 처해 있음
반전	창의적으로 문제를 해결하는 역할은 대체 불가능한 개인에 더 의존함

어휘·어구

report 보도하다
at risk 위험에 처한(= in danger)
due to ~ 때문에
advance 발전
automation 자동화
automate 자동화하다
ability 능력
solve 해결하다
problem 문제
whereas ~임에 반하여
replace 대체하다
role 역할
dependent 의존하는
irreplaceable 대체할 수 없는
unrealistic 비현실적인
threat 위협
franchise 프랜차이즈
flip 뒤집다
task 일
entire 전체의
crew 동료, 직원
skilled 숙련된
available 이용할 수 있는
treatment 치료법
specific 특정한
illness 질병
automated 자동화된
draw on ~을 이용하다
body 많은 양
medical 의학의
disease 질병

1. ⑤ 너도 밤나무 뿌리의 역할

직독/직해

Each beech tree grows / in a particular location /
각각의 너도 밤나무는 자란다 / 특정한 장소에서 /
and soil conditions can vary greatly /
그리고 토양 조건들은 크게 달라질 수 있다 /
in just a few yards. 단 몇 야드 안에서도
The soil can have a great deal of water /
토양은 다량의 물을 가질 수 있다 /
or almost no water. 혹은 거의 물이 없을 (수도 있다)
It can be full of nutrients or not.
그것은 영양분이 가득할 수도 있고 아닐 수도 있다
(C) Accordingly, / each tree grows /
이에 따라 / 각 나무는 자란다 /
quickly or more slowly /
빠르게 혹은 더 느리게 /
and produces more or less sugar, /
그리고 더 많은 혹은 더 적은 당분을 생산한다 /
and thus you would expect /
그래서 여러분은 기대할 것이다 /
every tree to be photosynthesizing /
모든 나무가 광합성을 할 것이라고 /
at a different rate. 다른 정도로
(B) However, the rate is the same.
하지만 그 정도는 동일하다
Whether they are thick or thin, /
그들이 굵든 아니면 가늘든 간에 /
all the trees of the same species / are using light /
같은 종의 모든 나무는 / 빛을 사용한다 /
to produce the same amount of sugar / per leaf.
같은 양의 당을 생산하기 위해 / 이파리당
Some trees have plenty of sugar /
어떤 나무들은 충분한 당을 지니고 있다 /
and some have less, / but the trees equalize /
그리고 어떤 것들은 더 적게 지니고 있다 / 하지만 나무들은 균등하게 한다 /
this difference between them /
그들 사이의 이 차이를 /
by transferring sugar. 당을 전달함으로써
(A) This is taking place underground /
이것은 지하에서 일어나고 있다 /
through the roots. 뿌리들을 통해
Whoever has an abundance of sugar /
풍부한 당을 가진 나무가 누구든 간에 /
hands some over; / 일부를 건네주고 /
whoever is running short / gets help.
부족해지는 나무는 누구든 간에 / 도움을 받는다
Their network acts as a system / to make sure /
그들의 연결망은 시스템 역할을 한다 / 확실히 하기 위한 /
that no trees fall too far behind.
어떤 나무도 너무 뒤처지지 않는 것을

각각의 너도 밤나무는 특정한 장소에서 자라고 토양 조건들은 단 몇 야드 안에서도 크게 달라질 수 있다. 토양은 다량의 물을 가지거나 거의 물이 없을 수도 있다. 그것은 영양분이 가득할 수도 아닐 수도 있다.
(C) 이에 따라, 각 나무는 빠르게 혹은 더 느리게 자라고, 더 많은 혹은 더 적은 당분을 생산하는데, 그래서 여러분은 모든 나무가 다른 정도로 광합성을 할 것이라고 기대할 것이다.
(B) 하지만, 그 정도는 동일하다. 그들이 굵든 아니면 가늘든 간에, 같은 종의 모든 나무는 빛을 사용하여 이파리당 같은 양의 당을 생산한다. 어떤 나무들은 충분한 당을 지니고 어떤 것들은 더 적게 지니지만, 나무들은 당을 전달함으로써 그들 사이의 이 차이를 균등하게 한다.
(A) 이것은 뿌리들을 통해 지하에서 일어나고 있다. 풍부한 당을 가진 나무가 누구든 간에 일부를 건네주고, 부족해지는 나무는 누구든 간에 도움을 받는다. 그들의 연결망은 어떤 나무도 너무 뒤처지지 않는 것을 확실히 하기 위한 시스템 역할을 한다.

문제풀이

각각의 너도 밤나무는 특정한 장소에서 자라는데 토양 조건들이 몇 야드 안에서도 크게 달라질 수 있다는 내용의 주어진 글 다음에, 토양 조건에 따라 성장 속도, 당분 생산량, 광합성 정도가 다르다고 기대할 것이라는 내용의 (C)가 오고, 기대와 달리 정도가 동일한데, 이는 나무들이 당을 전달함으로써 차이를 균등하게 만들기 때문이라는 내용의 (B)가 온 뒤, 마지막으로 이는 뿌리를 통해 지하에서 일어나고 있고, 뿌리라는 연결망이 어떤 나무도 뒤처지지 않게 하는 시스템 역할을 한다는 내용의 (A)가 오는 것이 가장 적절하다.

이렇게 풀자 (C)의 'Accordingly'는 주어진 문장에서 언급된 '서로 다른 토양 조건들에 따라서'를 받으므로 주어진 문장 뒤에 (C)가 오고, (B)의 'However'로 보아 (C)의 뒷부분에서 언급된 기대와는 다른 내용이 언급되고 있으므로 (C) 뒤에 (B)가 와야 하며, (A)의 'This'는 (B)에서 언급된 너도 밤나무가 서로 당을 전달함으로써 당의 차이를 균등하게 한다는 내용을 받으므로 (B) 뒤에 (A)가 와야 함을 알 수 있다.

어휘·어구

particular 특정한
location 장소, 위치
condition 조건
vary 다양하다
yard 야드
be full of ~로 가득차다
nutrient 영양소
take place 일어나다, 발생하다
underground 지하의
whoever ~하는 누구든지
abundance 풍부, 많음
sugar 당
hand over 넘겨주다
run short 부족하다
network 연결망
fall behind 뒤처지다, 낙오하다
rate 정도, 비율
species 종
per ~당
plenty of 많은
equalize 동등하게 하다
difference 차이
transfer 옮기다
accordingly 그에 맞춰
expect 기대하다

2. ② 굶주림에 대한 원인

직독/직해

With nearly a billion hungry people / in the world, /
거의 10억 명의 굶주린 사람들이 있는데 / 전 세계에 /
there is obviously no single cause.
분명 원인이 단 하나만 있는 것은 아니다
(B) However, / far and away the biggest cause is poverty.
하지만 / 가장 큰 원인은 단연 빈곤이다
Seventy-nine percent of the world's hungry live in nations /
세계의 굶주린 사람들의 79%가 국가에 산다 /
that are net exporters of food.
식량 순 수출을 하는
How can this be? 어떻게 이럴 수가 있을까
(A) The reason people are hungry /
사람들이 굶주리는 이유는 /
in those countries / 그런 국가에서 /
is that the products produced there / can be sold /
그곳에서 생산된 산물들이 / 팔릴 수 있다는 (것이다) /
on the world market / for more than /
세계 시장에서 / ~보다 더 비싸게 /
the local citizens can afford to pay for them.
현지 시민들이 그것들에 지불할 수 있는 것(보다)
In the modern age / you do not starve /
현대에는 / 여러분은 굶주리는 것이 아니다 /
because you have no food, / you starve /
식량이 없어서 / 여러분은 굶주리는 것이다 /
because you have no money.
돈이 없어서
(C) So the problem really is that food is, /
그래서 문제는 실로 식량이 ~라는 것이다 /
in the grand scheme of things, / too expensive /
거대한 체계로 볼 때 / 너무 비싸다 /
and many people are too poor to buy it.
그리고 많은 사람이 너무 가난해서 그것을 구매할 수 없다
The answer will be in continuing /
해답은 지속하는 데 있을 것이다 /
the trend of lowering the cost of food.
식량의 가격을 낮추는 추세를

전 세계에 거의 10억 명의 굶주린 사람들이 있는데, (이에 대해) 분명 원인이 단 하나만 있는 것은 아니다.
(B) 하지만, 가장 큰 원인은 단연 빈곤이다. 세계의 굶주린 사람들의 79%가 식량 순 수출국에 산다. 어떻게 이럴 수가 있을까?
(A) 그런 국가에서 사람들이 굶주리는 이유는 그곳에서 생산된 산물들이 현지 시민들이 그것들에 지불할 수 있는 것보다 더 비싸게 세계 시장에서 팔릴 수 있기 때문이다. 현대에는 여러분이 식량이 없어서 굶주리는 것이 아니라, 돈이 없어서 굶주리는 것이다.
(C) 그래서 문제는 실로 식량이 거대한 체계로 볼 때, 너무 비싸고 많은 사람이 너무 가난해서 그것을 구매할 수 없다는 것이다. 해답은 식량의 가격을 낮추는 추세를 지속하는 데 있을 것이다.

문제풀이

전 세계에 거의 10억 명의 굶주린 사람들이 있는데, 이에 대한 원인이 하나는 아니라는 주어진 글 다음에, 가장 큰 원인은 빈곤인데, 세계의 굶주린 사람들의 79%가 식량 순 수출국에 사는 데 어떻게 이럴 수 있을까라며 반문을 하는 (B)가 오고, 그에 대한 이유를 설명하는 (A)가 온 뒤, 마지막으로 이런 상황에 대한 해답을 제시하는 (C)가 오는 것이 가장 적절하다.

이렇게 풀자 (B)의 마지막 부분에 언급된 'How can this be?'에 대한 답을 (A)에서 서술하고 있기 때문에 (B) 다음에 (A)가 오고, (A)에서 언급된 굶주림의 이유에 대한 해결책을 (C)에서 제시하고 있기 때문에 (A) 다음에 (C)가 와야 한다.

어휘·어구

billion 10억
obviously 분명히
single 단 하나의
cause 원인
modern 현대의
starve 굶주리다
far and away 단연, 훨씬
poverty 가난

구조 다시보기

도입	사람들이 굶주리는 이유가 단 하나만 있는 것은 아님
주제	굶주림의 가장 큰 원인은 빈곤인데, 굶주린 사람들의 대부분이 식량 순 수출국에 거주함
부연	현지인들은 생산된 산물을 비싼 가격 때문에 돈이 없어서 살 수가 없음
결론	식량의 가격을 낮추는 추세를 유지해서 굶주림의 문제를 해결해야 함

3. ⑤ 일 처리에 적합한 시간대가 있다

직독/직해

Most people have a perfect time of day /

대부분의 사람들은 하루 중 완벽한 시간을 갖는다 /
when they feel / they are at their best, /
그들이 느끼는 / 그들이 자신의 최고 상태에 있다고 /
whether in the morning, evening, or afternoon.
아침이든 저녁이든 아니면 오후든 간에
(C) Some of us are night owls, / some early birds, /
우리 중 몇몇은 밤 올빼미이다 / 몇몇은 일찍 일어나는 새이다 /
and others in between / may feel most active /
그리고 그 사이에 있는 누군가는 / 가장 활력을 느낄 수 있다 /
during the afternoon hours. 오후 시간 동안
If you are able to organize your day /
만약 여러분이 하루를 계획할 수 있다면 /
and divide your work, / make it a point to deal with /
그리고 업무를 분배할 (수 있다면) / 반드시 처리해라 /
tasks that demand attention /
집중을 요구하는 과업을 /
at your best time of the day.
하루 중 여러분의 최적의 시간에
(B) However, / if the task you face /
그러나 / 만약 여러분이 직면한 과업이 /
demands creativity and novel ideas, /
창의성과 새로운 아이디어를 요구한다면 /
it's best to tackle it / at your "worst" time of day!
그것을 다루는 것이 최선이다 / 하루 중 여러분의 '최악의' 시간에
So if you are an early bird, /
그래서 만약 여러분이 일찍 일어나는 새라면 /
make sure to attack your creative task /
반드시 여러분의 창의적인 작업에 착수해라 /
in the evening, / and vice versa / for night owls.
저녁에 / 그리고 반대로 해라 / 밤 올빼미라면
(A) When your mind and body are less alert /
여러분의 정신과 신체가 주의력이 덜할 때 /
than at your "peak" hours, /
여러분의 '정점의' 시간보다 /
the muse of creativity awakens /
창의성의 영감이 깨어난다 /
and is allowed to roam more freely.
그리고 더 자유롭게 거니는 것이 허용된다
In other words, / 다시 말해 /
when your mental machinery is loose /
여러분의 정신 기제가 느슨할 때 /
rather than standing at attention, /
주의력 있게 기립해 있을 때보다 /
the creativity flows.
창의성이 샘솟는다

대부분의 사람들은 아침이든 저녁이든 아니면 오후든 간에, 하루 중 그들이 자신의 최고 상태에 있다고 느끼는 완벽한 시간을 갖는다.
(C) 우리 중 몇몇은 밤 올빼미이고, 몇몇은 일찍 일어나는 새이며, 그 사이에 있는 누군가는 오후 시간 동안 가장 활력을 느낄 수 있다. 만약 여러분이 하루를 계획하고 업무를 분배할 수 있다면, 반드시 집중을 요구하는 과업을 하루 중 여러분의 최적의 시간에 처리해라.
(B) 그러나 만약 여러분이 직면한 과업이 창의성과 새로운 아이디어를 요구한다면, 하루 중 여러분의 '최악의' 시간에 그것을 다루는 것이 최선이다! 그래서 만약 여러분이 일찍 일어나는 새라면, 반드시 저녁에 창의적인 작업에 착수하고, 밤 올빼미라면 반대로 해라.
(A) 여러분의 정신과 신체가 여러분의 '정점의' 시간보다 주의력이 덜할 때, 창의성의 영감이 깨어나 더 자유롭게 거니는 것이 허용된다. 다시 말해, 여러분의 정신 기제가 주의력 있게 기립해 있을 때보다 느슨할 때 창의성이 샘솟는다.

문제풀이

대부분의 사람들은 하루 중 자신의 최고 상태에 있다고 느끼는 완벽한 시간을 갖는다는 주어진 글 다음에, 이에 대한 부연 설명과 함께 집중을 요구하는 과업은 최적의 시간에 처리하라고 말하는 (C)가 오고, 이에 반해 창의성이 요구되는 작업은 하루 중 최악의 시간에 처리하라는 내용의 (B)가 온 뒤, 이에 대해 부연 설명을 하는 (A)가 마지막에 오는 것이 가장 적절하다.

이렇게 풀자 (B)의 'However'로 보아 앞 문장과는 반대의 내용이 서술됨을 알 수 있으므로 (B)는 (C) 다음에 오고, (A)는 (B)의 내용에 대한 부연 설명이므로 (B) 다음에 (A)가 와야 함을 알 수 있다.

어휘·어구

alert 정신이 초롱초롱한, 기민한
muse 영감, 시상
creativity 창의성
awaken 깨우다, 일으키다
mental machinery 정신 기제
loose 느슨한
attention 주의력
tackle 다루다, 해결하다
attack 착수하다, 달려들다
vice versa 반대로
active 활동적인
organize 준비하다, 정리하다
divide 나누다
deal with 처리하다, 다루다

4. ③ 선생님의 손에 감사하는 Douglas

직독/직해

Mrs. Klein told her first graders /
Klein 선생님은 1학년 학생들에게 말했다 /
to draw a picture of / ~의 그림을 그리라고 /
something to be thankful for.
감사히 여기는 것(의)
She thought / that most of the class would draw /
그녀는 생각했다 / 반 아이들 대부분이 그릴 것이라고 /
turkeys or Thanksgiving tables.
칠면조나 추수감사절 식탁을
But Douglas drew something different.
하지만 Douglas는 색다른 것을 그렸다
(B) Douglas was a boy / Douglas는 소년이었다 /
who usually spent time alone /
주로 혼자 시간을 보냈던 /
and stayed around her / 그리고 그녀 주변에 머물렀던 /
while his classmates went outside together /
그의 반 친구들이 함께 밖에 나가 있는 동안 /
during break time. 쉬는 시간에
What the boy drew / was a hand.
그 소년이 그린 것은 / 손이었다.
But whose hand? 그런데 누구의 손일까
His image immediately attracted /
그의 그림은 즉시 끌었다 /
the other students' interest.
다른 학생들의 관심을
(C) So, / everyone rushed to talk /
그래서 / 모두 앞다투어 말하려 했다 /
about whose hand it was.
그것이 누구의 손인지에 관해
"It must be the hand of God / that brings us food," /
그것은 신의 손이 틀림없어 / 우리에게 음식을 가져다주는 /
said one student. 한 학생이 말했다
"A farmer's," / said a second student, /
농부의 손이야 / 두 번째 학생이 말했다 /
"because they raise the turkeys."
왜냐하면 그들은 칠면조를 기르거든
"It looks more like a police officer's," /
경찰관의 손과 더 비슷해 보여 /
added another, / "they protect us."
또 다른 학생이 덧붙였다 / 그들은 우리를 보호해 줘
(A) The class was so responsive /
반 아이들이 너무나 호응적이어서 /
that Mrs. Klein had almost forgotten /
Klein 선생님은 하마터면 잊어버릴 뻔했다 /
about Douglas.
Douglas에 대해
After she had the others at work on another project, /
그녀는 다른 아이들에게 또 다른 과제를 하도록 지도한 후 /
she asked Douglas / whose hand it was.
그녀는 Douglas에게 물었다 / 그 손이 누구의 것인지
He answered softly, /
그는 조용히 대답했다 /
"It's yours. / Thank you, Mrs. Klein."
그건 선생님 손이에요. / 고마워요, Klein 선생님

Klein 선생님은 1학년 학생들에게 감사히 여기는 것을 그리라고 말했다. 그녀는 반 아이들 대부분이 칠면조나 추수감사절 식탁을 그릴 것이라고 생각했다. 하지만 Douglas는 색다른 것을 그렸다.
(B) 그의 반 친구들이 쉬는 시간에 함께 밖에 나가 있는 동안, 주로 Douglas는 혼자 시간을 보내고 그녀 주변에 머무르던 소년이었다. 그 소년이 그린 것은 손이었다. 그런데 누구의 손일까? 그의 그림은 즉시 다른 학생들의 관심을 끌었다.
(C) 그래서, 모두 그것이 누구의 손인지에 관해 앞다투어 말하려 했다. "그것은 우리에게 음식을 가져다주는 신의 손이 틀림없어."라고 한 학생이 말했다. "농부의 손이야, 왜냐하면 그들은 칠면조를 기르거든."이라고 두 번째 학생이 말했다. "경찰관의 손과 더 비슷해 보여, 그들은 우리를 보호해 줘."라고 또 다른 학생이 덧붙였다.
(A) 반 아이들이 너무나 호응적이어서 Klein 선생님은 Douglas에 대해 하마터면 잊어버릴 뻔했다. 그녀는 다른 아이들에게 또 다른 과제를 하도록 지도한 후, Douglas에게 그 손이 누구의 것인지 물었다. "그건 선생님 손이에요, 고마워요, Klein 선생님."이라고 그는 조용히 대답했다.

문제풀이

Klein 선생님이 학생들에게 감사히 생각하는 것을 그리라고 했는데 예상과 달리 Douglas는 색다른 것을 그렸다는 주어진 글 다음에, 그가 그린 손 그림이 다른 학생들의 관심을 끌었다는 내용의 (B)가 오고, 그 손이 누구의 손인지에 대해 학생들의 의견을 말하는 내용의 (C)가 온 뒤, 마지막으로 선생님의 손을 그렸다면서 선생님에게 감사를 표현하는 내용의 (A)가 마지막에 오는 것이 가장 적절하다.

어휘·어구

responsive 호응하는
classmate 반 친구
break time 쉬는 시간
immediately 즉시
attract (관심 등을) 끌다
interest 흥미
protect 보호하다

5. ⑤ 흡혈귀가 존재할 수 없다는 증거

직독/직해

According to legend, /
전설에 따르면 /
once a vampire bites a person, /
일단 흡혈귀가 사람을 물면 /
that person turns into a vampire /
그 사람은 흡혈귀로 변한다 /
who seeks the blood of others.
다른 사람의 피를 갈구하는
A researcher came up with some simple math, /
한 연구자가 간단한 계산법을 생각해냈다 /
which proves /
이 간단한 계산법은 증명한다 /
that these highly popular creatures can't exist.
이 잘 알려진 존재가 실존할 수 없다는 것을
(C) University of Central Florida physics professor Costas Efthimiou's work /
University of Central Florida의 물리학과 교수 Costas Efthimiou의 연구가
breaks down the myth.
그 미신을 무너뜨렸다
Suppose that on January 1st, 1600, /
우선 1600년 1월 1일에 ~라고 가정해 보자 /
the human population was just over five hundred million.
인구가 5억 명이 조금 넘는다고

(B) If the first vampire came into existence that day /
그날 최초의 흡혈귀가 생겨나서 /
and bit one person a month, /
한 달에 한 사람을 물었다면, /
there would have been two vampires by February 1st, 1600.
1600년 2월 1일까지 흡혈귀가 둘 있었을 것이다.
A month later there would have been four, /
한 달 뒤면 넷,
the next month eight, / then sixteen, and so on.
그 다음 달은 여덟, / 그리고 열여섯 등등으로 계속 늘어나는 것이다
(A) In just two-and-a-half years, /
불과 2년 반 만에, /
the original human population would all have become vampires with no humans left.
원래의 인구는 모두 흡혈귀가 되어 더 이상 남아있지 않았을 것이다
But look around you.
하지만 주위를 둘러보아라
Have vampires taken over the world?
흡혈귀가 세상을 정복하였는가
No, because there's no such thing.
아니다, 왜냐하면 흡혈귀는 존재하지 않으니까

전설에 따르면, 일단 흡혈귀가 사람을 물면 그 사람은 다른 사람의 피를 갈구하는 흡혈귀로 변한다. 한 연구자가 이 잘 알려진 존재가 실존할 수 없다는 것을 증명하는 간단한 계산법을 생각해냈다.
(C) University of Central Florida의 물리학과 교수 Costas Efthimiou의 연구가 그 미신을 무너뜨렸다. 우선, 1600년 1월 1일에 인구가 5억 명이 조금 넘는다고 가정해 보자.
(B) 그날 최초의 흡혈귀가 생겨나서 한 달에 한 사람을 물었다면, 1600년 2월 1일까지 흡혈귀가 둘 있었을 것이다. 한 달 뒤면 넷, 그 다음 달은 여덟, 그리고 열여섯 등등으로 계속 늘어나는 것이다.
(A) 불과 2년 반 만에, 원래의 인구는 모두 흡혈귀가 되어 더 이상 남아있지 않았을 것이다. 하지만 주위를 둘러보아라. 흡혈귀가 세상을 정복하였는가? 아니다. 왜냐하면 흡혈귀는 존재하지 않으니까.

문제풀이

흡혈귀가 사람을 물면 그 사람은 흡혈귀로 변한다는 전설이 있지만 한 연구자가 실제로 흡혈귀는 존재할 수 없다는 것을 증명하는 간단한 계산법을 생각해냈다는 주어진 글 다음에, 연구자와 계산법을 소개하는 (C)가 오고, 계산법을 부연 설명하는 (B)가 온 뒤, 계산법의 결론을 내리는 (A)가 마지막에 오는 것이 가장 적절하다.

이렇게 풀자 주어진 문장에서 언급된 연구자가 개발한 간단한 계산법을 바로 (C)에서 소개하고 있으므로 주어진 문장 다음에 (C)가 오고, (B)의 'that day'는 (C)에서 언급된 'January 1st, 1600'을 가리키므로 (B)는 (C) 다음에 와야 함을 알 수 있다.

어휘·어구

legend 전설
turn into ~으로 변하다
come up with ~을 찾아내다
prove 증명하다
creature 존재
exist 존재하다
original 원래의
population 인구
take over 점령하다, 꿰차다
come into existence 생기다, 나타나다
break down 부수다, 깨뜨리다
myth 사회적 통념, 미신
suppose 가정하다

정답률 61%

6. ③ 사람들의 필요를 충족시킨 시골 건축업자들의 단순한 방식

직독/직해

Toward the end of the 19th century, /
19세기 말이 되면서 /
a new architectural attitude emerged.
새로운 건축학적 사고방식이 나타났다
Industrial architecture, / the argument went, /
산업 건축은 / 그 주장에 따르면 /
was ugly and inhuman; / 추하고 비인간적이었다 /
past styles had more to do with pretension /
과거의 스타일은 허세와 더 관련이 있었다 /
than what people needed / in their homes.
사람들이 필요했던 것보다는 / 자신들의 집에서
(B) Instead of these approaches, /
이런 접근 대신에 /
why not look at the way /
방식을 살펴보는 것은 어떠한가 /
ordinary country builders worked / in the past?
평범한 시골 건축업자들이 일했던 / 과거에
They developed their craft skills / over generations, /
그들은 자신들의 공예 기술을 발전시켰다 / 세대를 거쳐 /
demonstrating mastery of both tools and materials.
도구와 재료 둘 다에 숙달한 기술을 보이면서
(C) Those materials were local, /
그 재료들은 지역적이다 /
and used with simplicity — /
그리고 단순하게 사용되었다 /
houses built this way / had plain wooden floors /
이런 방식으로 지어진 집들은 / 평범한 나무 바닥을 가지고 있다 /
and whitewashed walls inside.
그리고 실내가 회반죽을 바른 벽을 (가지고 있다)
(A) But they supplied people's needs perfectly /
하지만 그것들은 사람들의 필요를 완벽하게 충족시켰다 /
and, at their best, / had a beauty /
그리고 가장 잘 된 경우에는 / 아름다움을 갖추고 있었다 /
that came from the craftsman's skill /
장인의 솜씨에서 비롯된 /
and the rootedness of the house in its locality.
그리고 그 집의 지역에 뿌리내림에서

19세기 말이 되면서, 새로운 건축학적 사고방식이 나타났다. 그 주장에 따르면, 산업 건축은 추하고 비인간적이었다. 과거의 스타일은 사람들이 자신들의 집에서 필요했던 것보다는 허세와 더 관련이 있었다.
(B) 이런 접근 대신에, 평범한 시골 건축업자들이 과거에 일했던 방식을 살펴보는 것은 어떠한가? 그들은 도구와 재료 둘 다에 숙달한 기술을 보이면서 세대를 거쳐 공예 기술을 발전시켰다.
(C) 그 재료들은 지역적이고, 단순하게 사용되었는데, 이런 방식으로 지어진 집들은 실내가 평범한 나무 바닥과 회반죽을 바른 벽으로 되어 있었다.
(A) 하지만 그것들은 사람들의 필요를 완벽하게 충족시켰고, 가장 잘 된 경우에는, 장인의 솜씨와 그 집의 지역에 뿌리내림에서 비롯된 아름다움을 갖추고 있었다.

문제풀이

19세기 말에 등장한 새로운 건축학적 사고방식에 따르면 산업 건축은 추하고 비인간적이었다는 주어진 글 다음에, 그런 접근 대신 평범한 시골 건축업자들의 과거 작업 방식을 살펴보자고 하면서 작업 방식을 설명하는 (B)가 이어지고, 작업 방식의 특징에 대해 추가 설명을 하는 (C)가 이어진 다음, 그 작업 방식은 사람들의 필요를 완벽하게 충족시키면서 아름다움까지 갖추고 있다는 내용의 (A)가 마지막에 오는 것이 가장 적절하다.

이렇게 풀자 (C)의 'Those materials'는 (B)의 뒤에서 언급된 재료들을 가리키므로 (B) 다음에 (C)가 와야 하고, (A)의 'But'으로 보아 앞 문장과는 대조적인 내용이 언급되어야 하므로, (C)에서 언급된 단순한 재료들로 실내가 평범함에도 불구하고 사람들의 필요를 완벽하게 충족시켰다는 내용으로 연결이 되는 게 자연스러우므로 (C) 다음에 (A)가 와야 한다.

어휘·어구

century 세기
architectural 건축학의
attitude 사고방식
emerge 나타나다
industrial 산업의
argument 주장
inhuman 비인간적인
craftsman 장인
rootedness 뿌리내림
locality 지역
approach 접근
ordinary 평범한
generation 세대
demonstrate 보여 주다
mastery 숙달한 기술
material 재료
simplicity 단순함
plain 평범한
whitewashed 회반죽을 바른

정답률 61%

7. ② 좋은 음악과 연주 그리고 나쁜 음악과 연주가 있다

직독/직해

Robert Schumann once said, /
Robert Schumann은 말한 적이 있다 /
"The laws of morals are those of art."
도덕의 법칙은 예술의 법칙이다
What the great man is saying here /
이 위인이 여기서 말하고 있는 것은 /
is that there is good music /
좋은 음악이 있다는 것이다 /
and bad music. 그리고 나쁜 음악이
(B) The greatest music, / 가장 위대한 음악은 /
even if it's tragic in nature, /
심지어 그것이 사실상 비극적일지라도 /
takes us to a world higher / than ours; /
우리를 더 높은 세상으로 데려 간다 / 우리의 세상보다 /
somehow the beauty uplifts us.
그래서 어떻게든지 아름다움은 우리를 향상시킨다
Bad music, / on the other hand, / degrades us.
나쁜 음악은 / 반면에 / 우리를 격하시킨다
(A) It's the same with performances: /
연주도 마찬가지이다 /
a bad performance / 나쁜 연주가 /
isn't necessarily the result of incompetence.
반드시 무능의 결과는 아니다
Some of the worst performances occur /
최악의 연주 중 일부는 발생한다 /
when the performers, / 연주자들이 /
no matter how accomplished, /
아무리 숙달되었더라도 /
are thinking more of themselves /
자기 자신을 더 생각하고 있을 때이다 /
than of the music they're playing.
자신들이 연주하고 있는 곡보다
(C) These doubtful characters /
이 미덥지 못한 사람들은 /
aren't really listening to / 정말로 듣고 있는 것이 아니다 /
what the composer is saying — /
작곡가가 말하는 것을 /
they're just showing off, /
그들은 단지 뽐내고 있을 뿐이다 /
hoping that they'll have a great 'success' /
큰 '성공'을 거두기를 바라면서 /
with the public. 대중적으로
The performer's basic task / is to try to understand /
연주자의 기본 임무는 / 이해하려고 노력하는 것이다 /
the meaning of the music, /
음악의 의미를 /
and then to communicate it honestly to others.
그러고 나서 그것을 다른 사람들에게 정직하게 전달하는 것이다

Robert Schumann은 "도덕의 법칙은 예술의 법칙이다."라고 말한 적이 있다. 이 위인이 여기서 말하고 있는 것은 좋은 음악과 나쁜 음악이 있다는 것이다.

(B) 가장 위대한 음악은 심지어 그것이 사실상 비극적일지라도 우리를 우리의 세상보다 더 높은 세상으로 데려간다. 그래서 어떻게든지 아름다움은 우리를 향상시킨다. 반면에 나쁜 음악은 우리를 격하시킨다.
(A) 연주도 마찬가지이다. 나쁜 연주가 반드시 무능의 결과는 아니다. 최악의 연주 중 일부는 연주자들이 아무리 숙달되었더라도 자신들이 연주하고 있는 곡보다 자기 자신을 더 생각하고 있을 때 발생한다.
(C) 이 미덥지 못한 사람들은 작곡가가 말하는 것을 정말로 듣고 있는 것이 아니다. 그들은 대중적으로 큰 '성공'을 거두기를 바라면서 단지 뽐내고 있을 뿐이다. 연주자의 기본 임무는 음악의 의미를 이해하려고 노력하고, 그러고 나서 그것을 다른 사람들에게 정직하게 전달하는 것이다.

문제풀이

Robert Schumann이 좋은 음악과 나쁜 음악이 있다고 말했다는 주어진 글 다음에, 위대한 음악은 우리를 향상시키지만 나쁜 음악은 우리를 격하시킨다는 내용의 (B)가 이어지고, 연주도 마찬가지이며 최악의 연주는 연주자들이 곡보다 자신을 더 생각하고 있을 때 발생한다는 내용의 (A)가 온 뒤, 최악의 연주자들에 대해 부연 설명을 하면서 연주자의 기본 임무에 대해 설명하는 (C)가 마지막에 오는 것이 가장 적절하다.

구조 다시보기

도입	좋은 음악과 나쁜 음악이 있음
부연	좋은 음악은 우리를 향상시키는 반면 나쁜 음악은 우리를 격하시킴
전환	연주도 마찬가지이며 최악의 연주는 연주자들이 음악보다 자신을 더 생각할 때 발생함
부연	최악의 연주자들은 작곡가의 의도를 듣지 않고 본인들을 뽐내고 있을 뿐임
결론	연주자의 기본 임무는 음악의 의미를 이해하고 그것을 사람들에게 정직하게 전달하는 것임

어휘·어구

moral 도덕의
performance 연주
necessarily 반드시
occur 일어나다, 발생하다
no matter how ~하더라도
accomplished 숙달된
tragic 비극적인
in nature 사실상
somehow 어떻게든지
uplift 향상하다
on the other hand 반면에
doubtful 미덥지 못한
character 사람, 등장인물
composer 작곡가
show off 뽐내다
communicate 전달하다
honestly 정직하게

정답률 44%

8. ③ 전자 상거래의 팽창

직독직해

Roughly twenty years ago, / 대략 20년 전 /
brick-and-mortar stores began to give way / 오프라인 거래 상점이 바뀌기 시작했다 /
to electronic commerce. 전자 상거래로
For good or bad, / 좋든 나쁘든 간에 /
the shift fundamentally changed consumers' perception / 그 변화는 소비자의 인식을 근본적으로 바꾸었다 /
of the shopping experience. 쇼핑 경험에 대한
(B) Nowhere was the shift more obvious / 그 변화가 더 분명한 곳은 없었는데 /
than with book sales, / 책 판매보다 /
which is how online bookstores got their start. 그것이 온라인 서점이 시작된 방식이다
Physical bookstores simply could not stock / 물리적인 서점은 구비할 수 없었다 /
as many titles as a virtual bookstore could. (온라인) 가상 서점이 할 수 있는 만큼 많은 서적을
There is only so much space available on a shelf. 책꽂이 위의 활용 가능한 공간은 딱 그 정도밖에 없다
(C) In addition to greater variety, / 더 많은 다양성뿐만 아니라 /
online bookstores were also able to offer aggressive discounts / 온라인 서점은 공격적인 할인을 또한 제공할 수 있었다 /
thanks to their lower operating costs. 그들의 더 낮은 운영비 덕분에
The combination of lower prices and greater selection / 더 낮은 가격과 더 많은 선택의 결합은 /
led to the slow, steady rise of online bookstores. 온라인 서점의 느리지만 꾸준한 상승으로 이어졌다
(A) Before long, / the e-commerce book market naturally expanded / 머지않아 / 전자 상거래 책 시장은 자연스럽게 확장되었다
to include additional categories, / 추가적인 항목을 포함하도록 /
like CDs and DVDs. CD와 DVD 같은
E-commerce soon snowballed / 전자 상거래는 곧 눈덩이처럼 불어났다 /
into the enormous industry / it is today, / 거대 산업으로 / 오늘날의 /
where you can buy everything / 그곳에서 모든 것을 살 수 있다 /
from toilet paper to cars / online. 여러분은 화장실 휴지에서 자동차까지 / 온라인으로

대략 20년 전 오프라인 거래 상점이 전자 상거래로 바뀌기 시작했다. 좋든 나쁘든 간에 그 변화는 쇼핑 경험에 대한 소비자의 인식을 근본적으로 바꾸었다.
(B) 그 변화가 책 판매보다 더 분명한 곳은 없었는데 그것이 온라인 서점이 시작된 방식이다. 물리적인 서점은 가상 서점이 할 수 있는 만큼 많은 서적을 구비할 수 없었다. 책꽂이 위의 활용 가능한 공간은 딱 그 정도밖에 없다.
(C) 더 많은 다양성뿐만 아니라 온라인 서점은 그들의 더 낮은 운영비 덕분에 공격적인 할인을 또한 제공할 수 있었다. 더 낮은 가격과 더 많은 선택의 결합은 온라인 서점의 느리지만 꾸준한 상승으로 이어졌다.
(A) 머지않아 전자 상거래 책 시장은 CD와 DVD 같은 추가적인 항목을 포함하도록 자연스럽게 확장되었다. 전자 상거래는 곧 오늘날의 거대 산업으로 눈덩이처럼 불어났고 그곳에서 여러분은 화장실 휴지에서 자동차까지 모든 것을 온라인으로 살 수 있다.

문제풀이

대략 20년 전에 오프라인 상점이 전자 상거래로 바뀌게 되었고 그 변화가 소비자 인식을 바꾸었다는 주어진 글 다음에 (B) 그 변화가 가장 분명한 곳이 온라인 서점으로 온라인 서점은 물리적 서점에 비해 많은 서적을 구비할 수 있게 되었다는 내용이 이어지고 (C) 온라인 서점은 많은 책들을 구비함으로써 (소비자에게) 더 많은 다양성과 선택을 제공하고 더 낮은 운영비 덕분에 더 낮은 가격을 제공하게 되어, 느리지만 꾸준한 상승으로 이어졌다는 내용으로 이어지고 (A) 꾸준한 상승으로 전자 상거래 책 시장은 CD와 DVD로 확장하게 되었고, 결국 전자 상거래는 오늘날 거대 산업으로 팽창했다는 내용이 마지막으로 이어지는 것이 글의 순서로 가장 적절하다.

어휘·어구

roughly 대략
commerce 상업
perception 인식
obvious 분명한
physical 물리적인
virtual 실질상의
offer 제공하다
aggressive 공격적인
operating 운영상의
combination 결합
selection 선택
steady 꾸준한
before long 머지않아
expand 확장하다
enormous 엄청난

정답률 45%

9. ⑤ 문학 작품의 표현 방식과 이해

직독직해

Literary works, / by their nature, / 문학 작품들은 / 그 본질상 /
suggest rather than explain; / 설명하기보다는 암시한다 /
they imply rather than state their claims boldly and directly. 그들은 그들의 주장을 뚜렷하고 직접적으로 진술하기보다는 함축한다
(C) This broad generalization, / however, / 이 넓은 일반화는 / 그러나 /
does not mean / 의미하지는 않는다 /
that works of literature do not include direct statements. 문학 작품들이 직접적인 진술을 포함하지 않는다는 것을
Depending on when they were written and by whom, / 그들이 언제 그리고 누구에 의해 쓰였는지에 따라 /
literary works may contain large amounts of direct telling / 문학 작품들은 많은 양의 직접적 말하기를 포함할 수도 있다 /
and lesser amounts of suggestion and implication. 그리고 더 적은 양의 암시와 함축을 (포함할 수도 있다)
(B) But whatever the proportion of a work's showing to telling, / 하지만 작품의 말하기 대(對) 보여 주기의 비율이 어떻든지 간에 /
there is always something / for readers to interpret. 항상 무언가가 존재한다 / 독자가 해석해야 하는
Thus we ask the question / 그러므로 우리는 질문을 한다 /
"What does the text suggest?" / 그 텍스트가 무엇을 암시하는가 /
as a way / to approach literary interpretation, / 방법이자 / 문학적 해석에 접근하는 /
as a way / to begin thinking about a text's implications. 방법으로써 / 텍스트의 함축에 대해 생각하는 것을 시작하는
(A) What a text implies / 텍스트가 무엇을 함축하는지는 /
is often of great interest to us. 종종 우리에게 매우 흥미롭다
And our work of figuring out a text's implications / 그리고 텍스트의 함축을 알아내는 우리의 작업은 /
tests our analytical powers. 우리의 분석적 능력을 시험한다
In considering what a text suggests, / 텍스트가 무엇을 암시하는지를 고려하는 과정에서 /
we gain practice / in making sense of texts. 우리는 기량을 얻게 된다 / 텍스트를 이해하는

문학 작품들은 그 본질상 설명하기보다는 암시하는데, 그들은 그들의 주장을 뚜렷하고 직접적으로 진술하기보다는 함축한다.
(C) 그러나 이 넓은 일반화는 문학 작품들이 직접적인 진술을 포함하지 않는다는 것을 의미하지는 않는다. 그들이 언제 그리고 누구에 의해 쓰였는지에 따라 문학 작품들은 많은 양의 직접적 말하기와 더 적은 양의 암시와 함축을 포함할 수도 있다.
(B) 하지만 작품의 말하기 대(對) 보여 주기의 비율이 어떻든지 간에 독자가 해석해야 하는 무언가가 항상 존재한다. 그러므로 우리는 문학적 해석에 접근하는 방법이자 텍스트의 함축에 대해 생각하는 것을 시작하는 방법으로써, "그 텍스트가 무엇을 암시하는가?"라는 질문을 한다.

(A) 텍스트가 무엇을 함축하는지는 종종 우리에게 매우 흥미롭다. 그리고 텍스트의 함축을 알아내는 우리의 작업은 우리의 분석적 능력을 시험한다. 텍스트가 무엇을 암시하는지를 고려하는 과정에서 우리는 텍스트를 이해하는 기량을 얻게 된다.

문제풀이

문학 작품들은 설명하거나 주장을 직접적으로 진술하는 대신에 암시하거나 함축한다는 내용의 주어진 글 다음에 'But'으로 시작하여 이런 일반화가 문학 작품들이 직접적인 진술을 포함하지 않는다는 것을 의미하지는 않는다는 (C)가 이어지고, (C)의 마지막 부분에서 언급한 직접적 말하기의 양과 암시와 함축의 양을 말하기 대(對) 보여 주기의 비율로 언급한 (B)가 이어진 다음, '텍스트가 무엇을 암시하는가?'라는 질문을 통해 문학적 해석에 접근한다는 (B)의 마지막 부분에 이어서, 텍스트가 무엇을 암시하는지를 알아내는 작업을 통해 텍스트를 이해하는 기량을 얻게 된다는 내용의 (A)가 마지막으로 이어지는 것이 글의 순서로 가장 적절하다.

이렇게 풀자 글의 순서를 묻는 문제에서는 '지칭어, 반복어구, 연결사' 등을 살펴보아야 한다. 이 글에서는 (B)의 But, the proportion (C)의 This broad generalization, however 등이 단서가 될 수 있다.

어휘·어구

literary 문학의
imply 암시하다
claim 주장
generalization 일반화
work of literature 문학 작품
statement 진술
contain 포함하다
suggestion 암시
proportion 비율
interpret 해석하다
interpretation 해석
figure out ~을 알아내다
analytical 분석적인
make sense of ~을 이해하다

정답률 39%

10. ④ 간단한 요청에 응한 사람이 더 큰 요청에 호의적이다

In a study, / 한 연구에서 /
a researcher pretending to be a volunteer / 자원봉사자로 가장한 연구원이 /
surveyed a California neighborhood, / 한 캘리포니아 동네에서 설문조사를 했다 /
asking residents if they would allow / 주민들에게 허락할지를 물으면서 /
a large sign reading "Drive Carefully" to be displayed / '운전 조심'이라 쓰인 큰 표지판을 세워 두는 것을 /
on their front lawns. 그들의 앞마당에
(C) To help them understand / 그들의 이해를 돕기 위해서 /
what it would look like, / 그것이 어떻게 보일지에 대한 /
the volunteer showed his participants / 그 자원봉사자는 참여자들에게 보여주었다 /
a picture of the large sign / 큰 표지판 사진을 /
blocking the view of a beautiful house. 아름다운 집의 전망을 막는
Naturally, / most people refused, / 당연히 / 대부분의 사람들은 거절했다 /
but in one particular group, / 하지만 한 특정 그룹에서 /
an incredible 76 percent actually approved. 놀랍게도 76%가 실제로 승낙했다
(A) The reason that they agreed / was this: / 그들이 동의한 이유는 / 이것이었다 /
two weeks earlier, / 2주 전에 /
these residents had been asked / 이 주민들은 요청받은 적이 있었다 /
by another volunteer / 또 다른 자원봉사자로부터 /
to make a small commitment / to display a tiny sign / 작은 약속을 하도록 / 아주 작은 표지판을 붙인다는 /
that read "Be a Safe Driver" / in their windows. '안전운전자가 되세요'라고 쓰인 / 그들의 창문에
(B) Since it was such a small and simple request, / 그것이 아주 작고 간단한 요청이었기 때문에 /
nearly all of them agreed. 거의 그들 모두가 동의했다
The astonishing result was / 놀라운 결과는 ~이었다 /
that the initial small commitment / 처음의 작은 약속이 /
deeply influenced their willingness to accept / 기꺼이 받아들이는 데 깊은 영향을 끼쳤다는 것(이었다) /
the much larger request / 훨씬 더 큰 요청을 /
two weeks later. 2주 후에

한 연구에서, 자원봉사자로 가장한 연구원이 한 캘리포니아 동네에서 주민들에게 그들의 앞마당에 '운전 조심'이라 쓰인 큰 표지판을 세워 두는 것을 허락할지를 물으면서 설문조사를 했다.
(C) 그것이 어떻게 보일지에 대한 그들의 이해를 돕기 위해서, 그 자원봉사자는 참여자들에게 아름다운 집의 전망을 막는 큰 표지판 사진을 보여주었다. 당연히 대부분의 사람들은 거절했지만, 한 특정 그룹에서, 놀랍게도 76%가 실제로 승낙했다.
(A) 그들이 동의한 이유는 이것이었다. 2주 전에, 이 주민들은 또 다른 자원봉사자로부터 '안전운전자가 되세요'라고 쓰인 아주 작은 표지판을 그들의 창문에 붙인다는 작은 약속을 하도록 요청받은 적이 있었다.
(B) 그것이 아주 작고 간단한 요청이었기 때문에, 거의 그들 모두가 동의했다. 놀라운 결과는, 처음의 작은 약속이 그들이 2주 후의 훨씬 더 큰 요청을 기꺼이 받아들이는 데 깊은 영향을 끼쳤다는 것이었다.

문제풀이

한 연구원이 캘리포니아 동네에서 주민들에게 그들의 앞마당에 '운전 조심'이라는 큰 표지판을 세워두는 것을 허락할지에 대한 설문조사를 했다는 내용의 주어진 글 다음에, 설문조사의 결과를 언급하는 (C)가 이어지고, 결과에 대한 이유를 설명하는 (A)가 이어진 다음, 이유에 대해 부연설명을 하는 (B)가 마지막에 오는 것이 가장 적절하다.

어휘·어구

survey 설문조사하다
neighborhood 동네, 이웃
display 전시하다
commitment 약속
request 요청
astonishing 놀랄 만한
initial 처음의
influence 영향을 미치다
willingness 기꺼이 하는 마음
accept 받아들이다
refuse 거절하다
particular 특별한
incredible 믿을 수 없는
approve 찬성하다

11. ③ 화학 방정식

If you had to write a math equation, / 만약 여러분이 수학 등식을 써야 한다면 /
you probably wouldn't write, / 여러분은 아마도 쓰지 않을 것이다 /
"Twenty-eight plus fourteen equals forty-two." 28 더하기 14는 42와 같다
It would take too long to write / 그것은 쓰는 데 너무 오래 걸릴 것이다 /
and it would be hard to read quickly. 그리고 그것은 빨리 읽기 어려울 것이다
(B) You would write, / "28+14=42." 여러분은 쓸 것이다 / 28+14=42
Chemistry is the same way. 화학도 마찬가지이다
Chemists have to write chemical equations / 화학자들은 화학 방정식을 써야 한다 /
all the time, / 항상 /
and it would take too long to write and read / 그것은 쓰고 읽는 데 너무 오래 걸릴 것이다 /
if they had to spell everything out. 그들이 모든 것을 상세히 다 써야 한다면
(C) So chemists use symbols, / 그래서 화학자들은 기호를 사용한다 /
just like we do in math. 우리가 수학에서 하는 것처럼
A chemical formula lists all the elements / 화학식은 모든 원소를 나열한다 /
that form each molecule / 각 분자를 구성하는 /
and uses a small number / 그리고 작은 숫자를 사용한다 /
to the bottom right of an element's symbol / 원소 기호의 오른쪽 아래에 /
to stand for the number of atoms of that element. 그 원소의 원자 수를 나타내기 위해서
(A) For example, / 예를 들어 /
the chemical formula for water / is H_2O. 물의 화학식은 / H_2O이다
That tells us / that a water molecule is made up of / 그것은 우리에게 말해 준다 / 하나의 물 분자는 이루어져 있다는 것을 /
two hydrogen ("H" and "2") atoms / 두 개의 수소 원자('H'와 '2')로 /
and one oxygen ("O") atom. 그리고 하나의 산소 원자('O')로

만약 여러분이 수학 등식을 써야 한다면, 여러분은 아마도 '28 더하기 14는 42와 같다.'라고 쓰지 않을 것이다. 그것은 쓰는 데 너무 오래 걸리고 빨리 읽기 어려울 것이다.
(B) 여러분은 '28+14=42'라고 쓸 것이다. 화학도 마찬가지이다. 화학자들은 항상 화학 방정식을 써야 하고, 그들이 모든 것을 상세히 다 써야 한다면 쓰고 읽는 데 너무 오래 걸릴 것이다.
(C) 그래서 화학자들은 우리가 수학에서 하는 것처럼 기호를 사용한다. 화학식은 각 분자를 구성하는 모든 원소를 나열하고 그 원소의 원자 수를 나타내기 위해서 원소 기호의 오른쪽 아래에 작은 숫자를 사용한다.
(A) 예를 들어, 물의 화학식은 H_2O이다. 그것은 우리에게 하나의 물 분자는 두 개의 수소 원자('H'와 '2')와 하나의 산소 원자('O')로 이루어져 있다는 것을 말해 준다.

문제풀이

수학 등식을 글씨로 풀어쓰면 쓰는 데 오래 걸리고 빨리 읽기 어려울 것이라는 주어진 글 다음에, 수학에서 등식을 숫자와 수학 기호로 나타내듯이 화학도 마찬가지 이유로 화학 방정식을 쓴다는 내용의 (B)가 오고, 화학식의 특징을 구체적으로 설명하는 (C)가 온 뒤, 화학식의 특징을 잘 보여주는 사례로 물의 화학식을 예로 든 (A)가 마지막에 오는 것이 가장 적절하다.

구조 다시보기

도입	읽고 쓰기 쉽게 수학 등식을 씀
주제	화학도 읽고 쓰기 쉽게 화학 방정식을 씀
부연	화학식은 원소 기호의 오른쪽 아래에 작은 숫자를 사용함
예시	물의 화학식은 H_2O임

《 어휘·어구 》

equation 등식, 방정식
probably 아마
equal ~과 같다
be made up of ~으로 이루어지다
hydrogen 수소
atom 원자
oxygen 산소
chemistry 화학
chemist 화학자
all the time 항상
spell ~ out ~을 상세히 다 쓰다
symbol 기호
list 나열하다, 열거하다
element 원소, 요소
form 구성하다, 형성하다
bottom 아래(의)
stand for ~을 나타내다, ~을 대표하다

정답률 59%

12. ④ 독립 변인과 종속 변인 간의 인과 관계

Even though two variables seem to be related, /
비록 두 변인이 관련이 있는 것처럼 보일지라도 /
there may not be a causal relationship.
인과 관계가 없을 수도 있다
(C) In fact, / the two variables may merely seem to be associated with each other /
실제로 / 그 두 변인은 단지 서로 관련이 있는 것처럼 보일 수도 있다 /
due to the effect of some third variable.
어떤 제3 변인의 영향 때문에
Sociologists call such misleading relationships spurious.
사회학자들은 그런 오해의 소지가 있는 관계를 허위라 부른다
A classic example is the apparent association /
전형적인 예는 명백한 연관성이다 /
between children's shoe size and reading ability.
아이들의 신발 크기와 읽기 능력 간의
It seems that / as shoe size increases, /
~처럼 보인다 / 신발 크기가 커질수록 /
reading ability improves. 읽기 능력이 향상되는
(A) Does this mean / 이것이 의미하는가 /
that the size of one's feet (independent variable) /
발 크기(독립 변인)가 /
causes an improvement / 향상을 유발한다는 것을 /
in reading skills (dependent variable)?
읽기 능력(종속 변인)의
Certainly not. 물론 아니다
This false relationship is caused /
이런 허위 관계는 발생한다 /
by a third factor, age, / 제3 변인인 연령에 의해 /
that is related to shoe size /
신발 크기와도 관련이 있는 /
as well as reading ability. 읽기 능력뿐만 아니라
(B) Hence, / 따라서 /
when researchers attempt to make causal claims /
연구자들이 인과 관계를 주장하려고 할 때 /
about the relationship between an independent and a dependent variable, /
독립 변인과 종속 변인 간의 관계에 대한 /
they must control for — or rule out — /
그들은 통제하거나 배제해야 한다 /
other variables that may be creating a spurious relationship.
허위 관계를 만들어 낼지도 모르는 다른 변인들을

비록 두 변인이 관련이 있는 것처럼 보일지라도 인과 관계가 없을 수도 있다.
(C) 실제로, 그 두 변인은 어떤 제3 변인의 영향 때문에 단지 서로 관련이 있는 것처럼 보일 수도 있다. 사회학자들은 그런 오해의 소지가 있는 관계를 허위라 부른다. 전형적인 예는 아이들의 신발 크기와 읽기 능력 간의 명백한 연관성이다. 신발 크기가 커질수록, 읽기 능력이 향상되는 것처럼 보인다.
(A) 이것이 발 크기(독립 변인)가 읽기 능력(종속 변인)의 향상을 유발한다는 것을 의미하는가? 물론 아니다. 이런 허위 관계는 읽기 능력뿐만 아니라 신발 크기와도 관련이 있는 제3 변인인 연령에 의해 발생한다.
(B) 따라서, 연구자들이 독립 변인과 종속 변인 간의 관계에 대한 인과 관계를 주장하려고 할 때 그들은 허위 관계를 만들어 낼지도 모르는 다른 변인들을 통제하거나 배제해야 한다.

문제풀이

두 변인이 관련이 있는 것처럼 보일지라도 인과 관계가 없을 수도 있다는 주어진 글 다음에, 실제로 어떤 제3 변인의 영향 때문에 서로 관련이 있는 것처럼 보일 수도 있다는 내용의 (C)가 오고, (C)의 뒷부분에서 신발 크기와 읽기 능력 간의 연관성에 대해 구체적으로 설명하는 (A)가 온 뒤, 마지막으로 독립 변인과 종속 변인 간의 인과 관계를 주장할 때에는 다른 변인들을 통제하거나 배제해야 한다는 내용의 (B)가 오는 것이 글의 순서로 가장 적절하다.

《 어휘·어구 》

variable 변수
causal 인과 관계의
independent variable 독립 변수
dependent variable 종속 변수
factor 요인
rule out ~을 배제하다
be associated with ~와 관련되다
sociologist 사회학자
misleading 오해하기 쉬운
apparent 분명한, 명백한
association 연관(성)
improve 향상시키다

본문 097쪽

문법 플러스 16. 명사, 대명사

1. they 2. its 3. this 4. that 5. are
6. the other 7. yourself 8. themselves
9. each other 10. some books of hers

1 [해석]▶ 복권을 구입하는 많은 사람들은 자신이 뽑은 숫자가 자신들에 의해서 선택되었기 때문에 '더 좋은' 번호라고 확신한다.
[해설]▶ 주절의 주어로 쓰인 the numbers를 가리키므로 대명사 they가 와야 한다.

2 [해석]▶ 성능이 좋은 회전 전등이 우리의 길과 주변의 생물을 쉽게 비추어 줄 것이고, 바닷속 모습을 진정한 색채 그대로 보여줄 것이다.
[해설]▶ marine life의 진정한 색채를 보여주는 것이므로 단수 소유격을 써야 한다.

3 [해석]▶ 그는 차가운 우유를 좀 마셨는데, 이것이 그의 갈증을 해소해 주었다.
[해설]▶ 지시대명사 this는 앞에 언급된 어구나 내용(He drank some cold milk.)을 받을 수 있다.

4 [해석]▶ 베트남의 기후는 한국의 기후보다 더 덥다.
[해설]▶ 앞에 나온 단수명사(The climate)의 반복을 피하기 위해 지시대명사 that을 사용한다. 복수인 경우에는 those를 사용해야 한다.

5 [해석]▶ 누나들은 둘 다 뉴욕에 있다.
[해설]▶ 부정대명사 both는 복수동사를 가져온다.

6 [해석]▶ 식탁에 사과 두 개가 있는데, 하나는 네 것이고, 다른 하나는 내 거야.
[해설]▶ 둘 중 하나는 one..., 다른 하나는 the other 표현을 사용한다.

7 [해석]▶ 무엇인가를 해보려고 노력했다가 실패하면, 왜 하려고 했던 일을 실패했는지 자신에게 물어봐야 한다.
[해설]▶ 주어와 목적어가 일치하는 경우 재귀대명사를 사용한다. 주어 you의 재귀대명사는 yourself이다.

8 [해석]▶ 이러한 미세플라스틱은 일단 그것들을 수거하는 데 보통 사용되는 그물망을 통과할 정도로 충분히 작아지면 측정하기가 매우 어렵다.
[해설]▶ collect의 목적어는 의미상의 주어인 the nets가 아니라 the microplastics(= they)이므로, 재귀대명사 themselves가 와야 한다.

9 [해석]▶ 두 선수는 그 실수에 대해 서로를 비난했다. 즉 한 사람이 다른 한 사람을 비난했다.
[해설]▶ themselves가 목적어가 되면 자책했다는 의미가 된다. 뒤에 이어지는 한 사람이 다른 사람을 비난했다는 말과 어울리지 않는다. 서로를 비난했다는 의미가 흐름에 어울리므로 each other가 적절하다.

10 해석▶ 그녀는 나에게 그녀의 책 몇 권을 주었다.
[해설]▶ 한정어(some)가 명사(books) 앞에 올 때는 소유격(her)이 명사 앞에 오지 못하고, 「한정어+명사+of+소유대명사(hers)」의 형태로 쓴다.

본문 098쪽

어휘 플러스 16. 접미사

1. notice 2. employers
3. passionate 4. attractive
5. fascinated

1 [해석]▶ 최근 산불로 야기된 심각한 연기 때문에 교육부는 모든 학교는 추가 통지가 있을 때까지 휴교한다고 발표했습니다.

2 [해석]▶ 쾌적한 근로 환경을 유지하기 위해서, 고용주들은 늦게 출근하거나 다른 사람들을 방해하는 것과 같은 행동을 허용할 수가 없다.

3 [해석]▶ 콘서트가 끝났을 때, 그녀는 그의 열정적인 연주에 갈채를 보냈고 오랫동안 박수를 쳤다.

4 [해석]▶ 아트 디자이너들은 드레스가 가장 매력적으로 보이는 분위기와 환경으로 모델의 드레스를 그려야만 한다.

5 [해석]▶ 그들은 이 야생 식물의 아름다움에 매료되었고, 이 식물들이 직면한 비극적인 현실을 발견하고 나서 이것들을 보호해야 한다는 동기를 갖게 되었다.

17. 주어진 문장의 위치 파악

Day 17 본문 100쪽

1. ⑤ 2. ③ 3. ④ 4. ⑤ 5. ④
6. ⑤ 7. ④ 8. ② 9. ④ 10. ⑤
11. ③ 12. ②

정답률 60%

대표 기출 ③ 파장으로 이동하는 소리

직독/직해

Sound and light / travel in waves.
소리와 빛은 / 파장으로 이동한다

An analogy often given for sound /
소리 현상에 대해 자주 언급되는 한 비유는 /

is that of throwing a small stone /
작은 돌멩이를 던지는 것이다 /

onto the surface of a still pond.
고요한 연못 표면에

Waves radiate outwards / from the point of impact, /
파장이 바깥으로 퍼져나간다 / 충격 지점으로부터 /

just as sound waves radiate /
음파가 사방으로 퍼지는 것처럼 /

from the sound source. 음원으로부터

This is due to a disturbance / in the air around us.
이것은 교란 작용 때문이다 / 우리 주변 공기 중의

If you bang two sticks together, /
만약에 당신이 두 개의 막대기를 함께 꽝 친다면 /

you will get a sound. 소리를 듣게 될 것이다

As the sticks approach each other, /
막대기들이 서로 가까워질 때 /

the air immediately in front of them is compressed /
그것들 바로 앞에 있는 공기가 압축된다 /

and energy builds up. 그리고 에너지가 축적된다

When the point of impact occurs, /
충돌점이 발생하면 /

this energy is released /
이 에너지는 퍼져나간다 /

as sound waves. 음파로

If you try the same experiment /
당신이 같은 실험을 해보면 /

with two heavy stones, / 두 개의 무거운 돌을 가지고 /

exactly the same thing occurs, /
똑같은 일이 발생한다 /

but you get a different sound /
하지만 당신은 다른 소리를 듣게 된다 /

due to the density and surface of the stones, /
돌의 밀도와 표면 때문에 /

and as they have likely displaced more air, /
그리고 그 돌이 아마 더 많은 공기를 바꿔 놓았기 때문에 /

a louder sound. 더 큰 소리를 (듣게 된다)

And so, / a physical disturbance /
따라서 / 물리적 교란 작용이 /

in the atmosphere around us /
우리 주변의 대기 중에서 일어나는 /

will produce a sound. 소리를 만든다

소리와 빛은 파장으로 이동한다. 소리 현상에 대해 자주 언급되는 한 비유는 작은 돌멩이를 고요한 연못 표면에 던지는 것이다. 음파가 음원으로부터 사방으로 퍼지는 것처럼 파장이 충격 지점으로부터 바깥으로 퍼져나간다. (①) 이것은 우리 주변 공기 중의 교란 작용 때문이다. (②) 만약에 당신이 두 개의 막대기를 함께 꽝 친다면, 소리를 듣게 될 것이다. (③) 막대기들이 서로 가까워질 때, 그것들 바로 앞에 있는 공기가 압축되고 에너지가 축적된다. 충돌점이 발생하면 이 에너지는 음파로 퍼져나간다. (④) 당신이 두 개의 무거운 돌을 가지고 같은 실험을 해보면 똑같은 일이 발생하지만, 돌의 밀도와 표면 때문에 당신은 다른 소리를 듣게 되고, 그 돌이 아마 더 많은 공기를 바꿔 놓았기 때문에 당신은 더 큰 소리를 듣게 된다. (⑤) 따라서 우리 주변의 대기 중에서 일어나는 물리적 교란 작용이 소리를 만든다.

문제풀이

주어진 문장은 막대기들이 서로 가까워질 때 막대기 바로 앞에 있는 공기가 압축되고 에너지가 축적된다는 내용으로, ③ 앞에서 두 개의 막대기를 칠 경우 소리를 듣게 된다는 내용이 나오고, ③ 뒤에서 주어진 문장의 현상이 발생한 경우에 대한 결과를 설명하고 있으므로, 주어진 문장은 ③에 들어가야 글의 흐름이 자연스럽다.

구조 다시보기

도입	소리와 빛은 파장으로 이동함
주제	음파는 주변 공기 중의 교란 작용 때문에 충격 지점으로부터 퍼져나감
예시	두 개의 막대기가 충돌하면 에너지가 음파로 퍼져나감
주제 재진술	주변 대기 중에서 일어나는 물리적 교란 작용이 소리를 만듦

어휘·어구

immediately 바로 가까이에
compress 압축하다
disturbance 방해, 교란
bang 꽝하고 치다
impact 충돌
occur 발생하다
release 방출하다
density 밀도
displace 바꾸다
atmosphere 공기

정답률 50%

1. ⑤ 언어는 서로 협력하는 우리의 능력에 기여한다

직독/직해

Should we use language / to understand mind /
우리는 언어를 사용해야 하는가 / 사고를 이해하기 위해 /

or mind / to understand language?
아니면 사고를 (사용해야 하는가) / 언어를 이해하기 위해

Analytic philosophy historically assumes /
분석 철학은 역사적으로 가정한다 /

that language is basic / 언어가 기본이라는 것을 /

and that mind would make sense /
그리고 사고가 이치에 맞을 것이라고 /

if proper use of language was appreciated.
적절한 언어의 사용이 제대로 인식된다면

Modern cognitive science, however, / rightly judges /
하지만 현대 인지 과학은 / 당연히 판단한다 /

that language is just one aspect /
언어가 ~의 한 측면일 뿐이라고 /

of mind of great importance /
매우 중요한 사고의 /

in human beings / but not fundamental /
인간에게 / 그러나 근본적이지는 않다고 /

to all kinds of thinking. 모든 종류의 사고에

Countless species of animals /
수많은 종의 동물들이 /

manage to navigate the world, / solve problems, /
세계를 항해하고 / 문제를 해결하고 /

and learn without using language, /
그리고 언어를 사용하지 않고 학습해낸다 /

through brain mechanisms /
두뇌의 메커니즘을 통해 /

that are largely preserved / in the minds of humans.
대체로 보존된 / 인간의 사고 속에

There is no reason to assume /
가정할 이유는 없다 /

that language is fundamental / to mental operations.
언어가 기본이라고 / 정신 작용의

Nevertheless, / language is enormously important /
그럼에도 불구하고 / 언어는 굉장히 중요하다 /

in human life / and contributes largely to our ability /
인간의 삶에서 / 그리고 우리의 능력에 상당히 기여한다 /

to cooperate with each other / 서로 협력하는 /

in dealing with the world. 세계를 다루는 데 있어

Our species *homo sapiens* /
우리 종족, '호모 사피엔스'는 /

has been astonishingly successful, /
놀라울 정도의 성공을 거두어 왔는데 /

which depended in part on language, /
이것은 언어에 부분적으로 의존했다 /

first as an effective contributor /
처음에는 효과적인 기여 요소로서 /

to collaborative problem solving / and much later, /
협력적인 문제 해결에 / 그리고 훨씬 나중에는 /

as collective memory / through written records.
집단 기억으로서의 / 글로 쓰인 기록을 통한

우리는 사고를 이해하기 위해 언어를 사용해야 하는가 아니면 언어를 이해하기 위해 사고를 사용해야 하는가? (①) 분석 철학은 언어가 기본이고, 적절한 언어의 사용이 제대로 인식된다면 그 사고가 이치에 맞을 것이라고 역사적으로 가정한다. (②) 하지만 현대 인지 과학은 언어가 인간에게 매우 중요한 사고의 한 측면일 뿐 모든 종류의 사고에 근본적이지는 않다고 당연히 판단한다. (③) 수많은 종의 동물들이 인간의 사고 속에 대체로 보존된 두뇌의 메커니즘을 통해 언어를 사용하지 않고 세계를 항해하고, 문제를 해결하고, 학습해낸다. (④) 언어가 정신 작용의 기본이라고 가정할 이유는 없다. (⑤) 그럼에도 불구하고, 언어는 인간의 삶에서 굉장히 중요하고 세계를 다루는 데 있어 서로 협력하는 우리의 능력에 상당히 기여한다. 우리 종족, '호모 사피엔스'는 놀라울 정도의 성공을 거두어 왔는데, 이것은 처음에는 협력적인 문제 해결에 효과적인 기여 요소로서, 그리고 훨씬 나중에는 글로 쓰인 기록을 통한 집단 기억으로서의 언어에 부분적으로 의존했다.

문제풀이

현대 인지 과학은 언어가 인간에게 매우 중요한 사고의 한 측면일 뿐이지 모든 종류의 사고에 근본적이지 않다고 판단하지만, 언어는 협력적인 문제 해결에 효과적인 기여 요소로써 언어를 통해 우리는 놀라운 성공을 거두어 왔다는 내용이다. 주어진 문장은 언어는 인간의 삶에서 굉장히 중요하고 세계를 다루는 데 있어 서로 협력하는 우리의 능력에 상당히 기여한다는 내용으로, ⑤ 뒤에서 우리 종족이 성공할 수 있었던 이유는 언어가 협력적인 문제 해결에 효과적으로 기여했다는 내용이 서술된 것으로 보아 주어진 문장은 ⑤에 들어가야 흐름이 자연스럽다.

어휘·어구

nevertheless 그럼에도 불구하고
language 언어
enormously 엄청나게, 대단히
contribute 기여하다
cooperate 협력하다
deal with ~을 다루다
analytic 분석의
philosophy 철학
assume 가정하다
make sense 이치에 맞다
proper 적당한
cognitive 인지의
judge 판단하다
aspect 측면
importance 중요성
fundamental 근본적인
countless 수많은
manage to 해내다

navigate 항해하다
mechanism 메커니즘
preserve 보존하다, 유지하다
operation 작용
astonishingly 놀라울 정도로
depend 의존하다
effective 효과적인
contributor 기여 요인
collaborative 협력적인

정답률 55%

2. ③ 다른 화학적 성질과 온도를 가진 물의 특징

직독/직해

Take two glasses of water.
물 두 잔을 가져와라

Put a little bit of orange juice / into one /
약간의 오렌지주스를 넣어라 / 하나의 잔에는 /

and a little bit of lemon juice / into the other.
그리고 약간의 레몬주스를 넣어라 / 다른 잔에는

What you have / 여러분이 가지고 있는 것은 /

are essentially two glasses of water /
본질적으로 물 두 잔이다 /

but with a completely different chemical makeup.
하지만 완전히 다른 화학적인 성질을 지닌 (것들이다)

If we take the glass / containing orange juice /
만약 우리가 잔을 가져온다면 / 오렌지주스가 든 /

and heat it, / 그리고 그것을 가열하면 /

we will still have two different glasses of water /
우리는 여전히 서로 다른 물잔을 가지고 있을 것이다 /

with different chemical makeups, /
다른 화학적인 성질을 지닌 두 개의 /

but now they will also have different temperatures.
하지만 이제 그것들은 또한 다른 온도를 가질 것이다

If we could magically remove the glasses, /
만약 우리가 마법처럼 그 유리잔들을 없앨 수 있다면 /

we would find / 우리는 알게 될 것이다 /

the two water bodies would not mix well.
두 액체가 잘 섞이지 않는다는 것을

Perhaps they would mix a little / where they met; /
어쩌면 그것들은 조금 섞일 것이다 / 그것들이 만났던 곳에서 /

however, / they would remain separate /
하지만 / 그것들은 분리된 상태로 남아 있을 것이다 /

because of their different chemical makeups and temperatures.
그것들의 다른 화학적인 성질과 온도 때문에

The warmer water would float /
더 따뜻한 물은 떠 있을 것이다 /

on the surface of the cold water /
찬물의 표면에 /

because of its lighter weight.
그것의 더 가벼운 무게 때문에

In the ocean / we have bodies of water /
바다에서 / 우리는 액체들을 가지고 있다 /

that differ in temperature and salt content; /
온도와 염분에서 다른 /

for this reason, / they do not mix.
이런 이유로 / 그것들은 섞이지 않는다

물 두 잔을 가져와라. 하나의 잔에는 약간의 오렌지주스를 넣고 다른 잔에는 약간의 레몬주스를 넣어라. (①) 여러분이 가지고 있는 것은 본질적으로 물 두 잔이지만 완전히 다른 화학적인 성질을 지닌 것들이다. (②) 만약 우리가 오렌지주스가 든 잔을 가져와서 그것을 가열하면, 우리는 여전히 다른 화학적인 성질을 지닌 두 개의 다른 물잔을 가지고 있을 것이지만, 이제 그것들은 또한 다른 온도를 가질 것이다. (③) 만약 우리가 마법처럼 그 유리잔들을 없앨 수 있다면, 우리는 두 액체가 잘 섞이지 않는다는 것을 알게 될 것이다. 어쩌면 그것들은 그것들이 만났던 곳에서 조금 섞일 것이다. 하지만, 그것들의 다른 화학적인 성질과 온도 때문에 그것들은 분리된 상태로 남아 있을 것이다. (④) 더 따뜻한 물은 그것의 더 가벼운 무게 때문에 찬물의 표면에 떠 있을 것이다. (⑤) 바다에서 우리는 온도와 염분에서 다른 액체들을 가지고 있다. 이런 이유로, 그것들은 섞이지 않는다.

문제풀이

주어진 문장에서 언급된 'the glasses'는 ③ 앞 문장들에서 언급된 열을 가한 오렌지주스와 약간의 레몬주스를 가리키고, ③ 뒤에서 그것들이 만났던 곳에서 조금 섞일 것이라는 내용으로 보아 주어진 문장은 ③에 와야 글의 내용이 자연스럽게 연결된다. 따라서 주어진 문장은 ③에 들어가는 것이 가장 적절하다.

어휘·어구

magically 마법적으로
essentially 본질적으로
completely 완전히
chemical 화학적인
makeup 성질
contain 포함하다
temperature 온도
separate 분리하다
float 뜨다
surface 표면
weight 무게
salt content 염분

정답률 51%

3. ④ 텔레비전 시청은 사회적 관계에 부정적인 영향을 끼칠 수 있다

직독/직해

Television is the number one leisure activity /
텔레비전은 제1의 여가 활동이다 /

in the United States and Europe, /
미국과 유럽에서 /

consuming more than half of our free time.
우리의 여가 시간 중 절반 이상을 소비한다

We generally think of television /
우리는 일반적으로 텔레비전을 ~로 생각한다 /

as a way to relax, tune out, /
휴식하고, 관심을 끄는 하나의 방법으로 /

and escape from our troubles / for a bit each day.
그리고 우리의 문제들로부터 탈출하는 (하나의 방법으로) / 매일 잠시나마

While this is true, / there is increasing evidence /
이는 사실이긴 하지만 / 증거가 늘어나고 있다 /

that we are more motivated to tune in to /
우리는 ~을 보려는 동기가 더 부여된다는 (증거가) /

our favorite shows and characters /
우리가 좋아하는 쇼들과 등장인물들을 /

when we are feeling lonely /
우리가 외롭다고 느끼고 있을 때 /

or have a greater need for social connection.
혹은 사회적 관계를 위한 더 큰 욕구를 가질 때

Television watching does satisfy /
텔레비전을 보는 것이 정말로 만족시킨다 /

these social needs / to some extent, /
이런 사회적인 욕구를 / 어느 정도까지는 /

at least in the short run. 적어도 단기적으로는

Unfortunately, / 불행히도 /

it is also likely to "crowd out" other activities /
그것은 또한 다른 활동들을 '몰아내기' 쉽다 /

that produce more sustainable social contributions /
더 지속적인 사회적 기여를 만드는 /

to our social well-being. 우리의 사회적 행복을 위한

The more television we watch, /
우리가 텔레비전을 더 많이 볼수록 /

the less likely we are to volunteer our time /
우리는 우리의 시간을 기꺼이 할애하는 걸 덜 하기 쉽다 /

or to spend time with people /
혹은 사람들과 함께 시간을 (덜 보내기 쉽다) /

in our social networks. 사회적 관계망 속에서

In other words, / 다시 말해 /

the more time we make for *Friends*, /
우리가 (시트콤) 'Friends'를 위해 더 많은 시간을 낼수록 /

the less time we have for friends / in real life.
친구들을 위해서는 시간을 덜 갖게 된다 / 실제

텔레비전은 미국과 유럽에서 제1의 여가 활동이고, 우리의 여가 시간 중 절반 이상을 소비한다. (①) 우리는 일반적으로 텔레비전을 휴식하고, 관심을 끄고, 매일 잠시나마 우리의 문제들로부터 탈출하는 하나의 방법으로 생각한다. (②) 이는 사실이긴 하지만, 우리가 외롭다고 느끼고 있거나 사회적 관계를 위한 더 큰 욕구를 가질 때, 우리가 좋아하는 쇼들과 등장인물들을 보려는 동기가 더 부여된다는 증거가 늘어나고 있다. (③) 적어도 단기적으로는, 텔레비전을 보는 것이 이런 사회적인 욕구를 어느 정도까지는 정말로 만족시킨다. (④) 불행히도, 그것은 또한 우리의 사회적 행복을 위한 더 지속적인 사회적 기여를 만드는 다른 활동들을 '몰아내기' 쉽다. 우리가 텔레비전을 더 많이 볼수록, 우리는 사회적 관계망 속에서 우리의 시간을 기꺼이 할애하거나 사람들과 함께 시간을 덜 보내기 쉽다. (⑤) 다시 말해, 우리가 (TV 시트콤) 'Friends'를 위해 더 많은 시간을 낼수록, 실제 친구들을 위해서는 시간을 덜 갖게 된다.

문제풀이

주어진 문장의 'Unfortunately'로 보아, 앞 문장과는 반대의 내용이 전개될 것임을 알 수 있고, ④ 앞에서는 텔레비전 보는 것의 장점이 언급되었고, ④ 뒤에서는 텔레비전 보는 것의 문제점이 언급되었으므로, 주어진 문장은 ④에 들어가야 글의 흐름이 자연스럽다.

어휘·어구

crowd out 밀어내다
sustainable 지속 가능한
contribution 기여
well-being 행복
consume 소비하다
relax 휴식하다
tune out 그만두다
escape 탈출하다
trouble 문제
evidence 증거
motivate 동기를 부여하다
tune in to (TV 프로그램을) 시청하다, 채널을 ~에 맞추다
character 등장인물
connection 연결
satisfy 만족시키다
to some extent 어느 정도는
volunteer 자진하여 제공하다

구조 다시보기

도입	텔레비전은 제1의 여가 활동임
부연	텔레비전 시청은 휴식을 위한 하나의 방법이면서 사회적인 욕구를 어느 정도 만족시킬 수 있음
반전	텔레비전 시청은 우리의 사회적 행복을 위한 활동들을 몰아냄
부연	텔레비전 시청을 더 많이 할수록 사람들과 사회적 교류를 할 시간이 줄어듦

정답률 46%

4. ⑤ 정량적인 측정을 하는 온도계가 필요하다

직독/직해

We often associate the concept of temperature /
우리는 종종 온도 개념을 ~와 연관 짓는다 /

with how hot or cold an object feels /
물건이 얼마나 뜨겁거나 차갑게 느껴지는지 /

when we touch it. 우리가 그것을 만질 때

In this way, / our senses provide us /
이런 식으로 / 우리의 감각은 우리에게 제공한다 /

with a qualitative indication of temperature.
온도의 정성적인 지표를

Our senses, however, are unreliable /
그러나 우리의 감각은 신뢰할 수 없다 /
and often mislead us. 그리고 종종 우리를 잘못 인도한다
For example, / if you stand in bare feet /
예를 들어 / 여러분이 맨발로 서 있다면 /
with one foot on carpet / 한쪽 발은 카펫 위에 /
and the other on a tile floor, /
그리고 다른 한쪽 발은 타일 바닥 위에 /
the tile feels colder / than the carpet /
타일이 더 차갑게 느껴질 것이다 / 카펫보다 /
even though both are at the same temperature.
둘 다 같은 온도임에도 불구하고
The two objects feel different /
그 두 물체는 다르게 느껴진다 /
because tile transfers energy by heat /
타일이 에너지를 열의 형태로 전달하기 때문에 /
at a higher rate / than carpet does.
더 높은 비율로 / 카펫이 전달하는 것보다
Your skin "measures" / 여러분의 피부는 '측정한다' /
the rate of energy transfer by heat /
열에너지 전도율을 /
rather than the actual temperature.
실제 온도보다는
What we need is / 우리가 필요한 것은 ~이다 /
a reliable and reproducible method /
신뢰할 수 있고 재현 가능한 수단(이다) /
for measuring the relative hotness or coldness of objects /
물체의 상대적인 뜨거움이나 차가움을 측정하기 위한 /
rather than the rate of energy transfer.
에너지 전도율보다는
Scientists have developed / 과학자들은 개발해 왔다 /
a variety of thermometers / 다양한 온도계를 /
for making such quantitative measurements.
그런 정량적인 측정을 하기 위해

우리는 종종 온도 개념을 우리가 물건을 만질 때 그것이 얼마나 뜨겁거나 차갑게 느껴지는지와 연관 짓는다. 이런 식으로, 우리의 감각은 우리에게 온도의 정성적인 지표를 제공한다. (①) 그러나, 우리의 감각은 신뢰할 수 없고 종종 우리를 잘못 인도한다. (②) 예를 들어, 여러분이 한쪽 발은 카펫 위에, 다른 한쪽 발은 타일 바닥 위에 맨발로 서 있다면, 둘 다 같은 온도임에도 불구하고 카펫보다 타일이 더 차갑게 느껴질 것이다. (③) 타일이 카펫이 전달하는 것보다 더 높은 비율로 에너지를 열의 형태로 전달하기 때문에 그 두 물체는 다르게 느껴진다. (④) 여러분의 피부는 실제 온도보다는 열에너지 전도율을 '측정한다'. (⑤) 우리가 필요한 것은 에너지 전도율보다는 물체의 상대적인 뜨거움이나 차가움을 측정하기 위한 신뢰할 수 있고 재현 가능한 수단이다. 과학자들은 그런 정량적인 측정을 하기 위해 다양한 온도계를 개발해 왔다.

문제풀이

우리의 피부는 실제 온도보다는 열에너지 전도율을 측정하기 때문에 우리에게 필요한 것은 물체의 상대적인 뜨거움이나 차가움을 측정할 수 있는 수단이 필요한데, 이를 위해 과학자들이 그런 정량적인 측정을 할 수 있는 다양한 온도계를 개발해 왔다는 흐름이 되어야 자연스럽다. 따라서 주어진 문장은 ⑤에 들어가는 것이 가장 적절하다.

《 어휘 · 어구 》

reliable 신뢰성 있는
reproducible 재현 가능한
method 방법
measuring 측정(= measurement)
relative 상대적인
energy transfer 에너지 전달[전도]
associate A with B A를 B와 연관짓다
concept 개념
temperature 온도
qualitative 정성적인
indication 지표
mislead 잘못 인도하다
bare 벌거벗은
actual 실제의
quantitative 정량적인

정답률 77%

5. ④ 마찰(력)의 특징과 역할

직독/직해

Friction is a force / between two surfaces that are sliding, /
마찰력은 힘이다 / 미끄러지는 두 표면 사이에 작용하는 /
or trying to slide, / across each other.
혹은 미끄러지려고 하는 / 서로 엇갈리게
For example, / when you try to push a book /
예를 들어 / 당신이 책을 밀려고 할 때 /
along the floor, / friction makes this difficult.
바닥을 따라 / 마찰이 이를 어렵게 만든다
Friction always works in the direction /
마찰은 항상 그 방향으로 작용한다 /
opposite to the direction /
방향과 반대되는 /
in which the object is moving, / or trying to move.
물체가 움직이는 / 혹은 움직이려고 하는
So, / friction always slows a moving object down.
그래서 / 마찰은 항상 움직이는 물체를 느리게 만든다
The amount of friction / depends on the surface materials.
마찰의 양은 / 표면 물질에 따라 달라진다
The rougher the surface is, / the more friction is produced.
표면이 거칠수록 / 더 많은 마찰력이 발생한다
Friction also produces heat.
마찰은 또한 열을 발생시킨다
For example, / if you rub your hands together quickly, /
예를 들어 / 당신이 손을 빠르게 비비면 /
they will get warmer.
손이 더 따뜻해질 것이다
Friction can be a useful force /
마찰력은 유용한 힘으로 작용할 수 있다 /
because it prevents our shoes slipping /
그것이 신발이 미끄러지는 것을 방지하기 때문에 /
on the floor / when we walk /
바닥에서 / 우리가 걸을 때 /
and stops car tires skidding /
그리고 자동차 타이어가 미끄러지는 것을 막아주므로 /
on the road. 도로에서
When you walk, / friction is caused /
당신이 걸을 때 / 마찰은 발생한다 /
between the tread on your shoes and the ground, /
당신의 신발 접지면과 바닥 사이에 /
acting to grip the ground / and prevent sliding.
이 마찰은 땅을 붙잡는 역할을 한다. /그리고 미끄러지는 것을 방지하는 (역할을 한다)

마찰력은 서로 엇갈리게 미끄러지거나 미끄러지려고 하는 두 표면 사이에 작용하는 힘이다. 예를 들어, 당신이 바닥을 따라 책을 밀려고 할 때, 마찰이 이를 어렵게 만든다. 마찰은 항상 물체가 움직이거나 움직이려고 하는 방향과 반대 방향으로 작용한다. 그래서 마찰은 항상 움직이는 물체를 느리게 만든다. (①) 마찰의 양은 표면 물질에 따라 달라진다. (②) 표면이 거칠수록 더 많은 마찰력이 발생한다. (③) 마찰은 또한 열을 발생시킨다. (④) 예를 들어, 당신이 손을 빠르게 비비면, 손이 더 따뜻해질 것이다. 마찰력은 우리가 걸을 때 신발이 바닥에서 미끄러지는 것을 방지하고 자동차 타이어가 도로에서 미끄러지는 것을 막아주므로 유용한 힘으로 작용할 수 있다. (⑤) 당신이 걸을 때, 마찰은 당신의 신발 접지면과 바닥 사이에 발생하며, 이 마찰은 땅을 붙잡아 미끄러지는 것을 방지하는 역할을 한다.

문제풀이

주어진 문장의 'For example'로 보아 앞 문장에 대한 예시가 제시될 것임을 알 수 있고, ④ 앞에서 마찰이 열을 발생시킨다는 내용이 언급되었고, 주어진 문장이 바로 마찰이 열을 발생시키는 예시이므로 주어진 문장은 ④에 들어가야 글의 흐름이 자연스럽다.

구조 다시보기

주제	마찰력은 미끄러지려 하는 두 표면 사이에 작용하는 힘
부연 1	마찰력은 물체가 움직이려는 방향과 반대로 작용해서 물체의 움직임을 느리게 만듦
부연 2	마찰의 양은 표면 물질에 따라 달라짐
부연 3	마찰은 열을 발생시킴
결론	마찰은 미끄러지는 것을 막아서 유용한 힘으로 작용할 수 있음

《 어휘 · 어구 》

rub 비비다
friction 마찰(력)
surface 표면
slide 미끄러지다
direction 방향
opposite 반대편의
depend on ~에 달렸다
material 물질
produce 발생시키다
useful 유용한
grip 붙잡다

6. ⑤ 다른 감각을 통해 세상을 이해하는 시각 장애인

직독/직해

Humans born without sight /
선천적으로 시각 장애를 가진 사람들은 /
are not able to collect visual experiences, /
시각적 경험을 수집할 수 없다 /
so they understand the world /
그래서 그들은 세상을 이해한다 /
entirely through their other senses.
전적으로 다른 감각을 통해
As a result, / people with blindness at birth /
그 결과 / 선천적으로 시각 장애를 가진 사람들은 /
develop an amazing ability /
놀라운 능력을 개발한다 /
to understand the world / through the collection of experiences and memories /
세상을 이해하는 / 경험과 기억의 수집을 통해 /
that come from these non-visual senses.
이런 비시각적 감각에서 오는
The dreams of a person / who has been without sight since birth /
사람이 꾸는 꿈은 / 선천적으로 시각 장애를 가진 /
can be just as vivid and imaginative /
생생하고 상상력이 풍부할 수 있다 /
as those of someone with normal vision.
정상적인 시력을 가진 사람의 꿈처럼
They are unique, however, /
그러나 그들은 특별하다 /
because their dreams are constructed /
왜냐하면 그들의 꿈은 구성되기 때문에 /
from the non-visual experiences and memories /
비시각적 경험과 기억으로부터 /
they have collected. 그들이 수집해온
A person with normal vision /
정상적인 시력을 가진 사람들은 /
will dream about a familiar friend /
친숙한 친구에 대해 꿈을 꿀 것이다 /
using visual memories of shape, lighting, and colour.
형태, 빛 그리고 색의 시각적 기억을 사용하여
But, / a blind person will associate the same friend /
하지만 / 시각 장애인은 그 친구를 연상할 것이다 /
with a unique combination of experiences /
독특한 경험의 조합으로 /

from their non-visual senses /
비시각적 감각에서 나온 /

that act to represent that friend.
그 친구를 구현하는 데 작용하는

In other words, / people blind at birth /
다시 말해 / 선천적 시각장애인들은 /

have similar overall dreaming experiences /
전반적으로 비슷한 꿈을 경험한다 /

even though they do not dream in pictures.
비록 그들이 시각적인 꿈을 꾸지는 않지만

선천적으로 시각 장애를 가진 사람들은 시각적 경험을 수집할 수 없어서, 그들은 세상을 전적으로 다른 감각을 통해 이해한다. (①) 그 결과, 선천적으로 시각 장애를 가진 사람들은 이런 비시각적 감각에서 오는 경험과 기억의 수집을 통해 세상을 이해하는 놀라운 능력을 개발한다. (②) 선천적으로 시각 장애를 가진 사람이 꾸는 꿈은 정상적인 시력을 가진 사람의 꿈처럼 생생하고 상상력이 풍부할 수 있다. (③) 그러나 그들의 꿈은 그들이 수집해온 비시각적 경험과 기억으로부터 구성되기 때문에 그들은 특별하다. 정상적인 시력을 가진 사람들은 형태, 빛 그리고 색의 시각적 기억을 사용하여 친숙한 친구에 대해 꿈을 꿀 것이다. (⑤) 하지만, 시각 장애인은 그 친구를 구현하는 데 작용하는 비시각적 감각에서 나온 독특한 경험의 조합으로 그 친구를 연상할 것이다. 다시 말해, 선천적 시각장애인들은 비록 시각적인 꿈을 꾸지는 않지만, 전반적으로 비슷한 꿈을 경험한다.

문제풀이

주어진 문장의 'But'으로 보아 앞 문장과는 상반되는 내용이 제시될 것임을 알 수 있고, ⑤ 뒤의 'In other words'로 보아 앞 문장에 대한 부연 내용이 제시될 것임을 알 수 있다. 또한 ⑤ 앞뒤 문장 간에 단절이 있으므로 주어진 문장은 ⑤에 들어가는 것이 가장 적절하다.

《어휘·어구》

associate 연결 짓다, 연상하다
unique 독특한, 특별한
combination 조합, 결합
experience 경험
non-visual 비시각적
represent 묘사하다
sight 시각
entirely 완전히
blindness 맹인
ability 능력
vivid 생생한
imaginative 상상의
normal 정상의
vision 시력
construct 구성하다
familiar 친밀한
similar 비슷한
overall 전반적으로

정답률 56%

7. ④ 생태계에서 생물종이 다양할 경우의 이점

직독/직해

When an ecosystem is biodiverse, /
생태계에 생물종이 다양할 때 /

wildlife have more opportunities /
야생 생물은 더 많은 기회를 얻는다 /

to obtain food and shelter.
먹이와 서식지를 얻을

Different species react and respond to /
다양한 종들은 작용하고 반응한다 /

changes in their environment differently.
그들의 환경 변화에 다르게

For example, / imagine a forest /
예를 들어 / 숲을 상상해봐라 /

with only one type of plant in it, /
그 안에 단 한 종류의 식물만 있는 /

which is the only source of food and habitat /
그 식물은 유일한 먹이원이자 서식지이다 /

for the entire forest food web.
숲의 먹이 그물 전체의

Now, / there is a sudden dry season /
이제 / 갑작스러운 건기가 있다 /

and this plant dies. 그리고 이 식물이 죽는다

Plant-eating animals completely lose /
초식 동물들은 완전히 잃는다 /

their food source / and die out, /
그들의 먹이원을 / 그리고 죽는다 /

and so do the animals / that prey upon them.
그리고 동물들도 그렇게 된다 / 그들을 먹이로 삼는

But, / when there is biodiversity, /
하지만 / 종 다양성이 있을 때 /

the effects of a sudden change /
갑작스러운 변화의 영향은 /

are not so dramatic.
그렇게 극적이지 않다

Different species of plants /
다양한 종의 식물들이 /

respond to the drought differently, /
가뭄에 다르게 반응한다 /

and many can survive a dry season.
그리고 많은 식물이 건기에 살아남을 수 있다

Many animals have a variety of food sources /
많은 동물은 다양한 먹이원을 가지고 있다 /

and don't just rely on one plant; /
그리고 단지 한 식물에만 의존하지는 않는다 /

now our forest ecosystem /
그래서 이제 우리의 숲 생태계는 /

is no longer at the death!
더 이상 종말에 처해 있지 않다!

생태계에 생물종이 다양할 때, 야생 생물은 먹이와 서식지를 얻을 더 많은 기회를 얻는다. 다양한 종들은 그들의 환경 변화에 다르게 작용하고 반응한다. (①) 예를 들어, 단 한 종류의 식물만 있는 숲을 상상해 보면, 그 식물은 숲의 먹이 그물 전체의 유일한 먹이원이자 서식지이다. (②) 이제, 갑작스러운 건기가 오고 이 식물이 죽는다. (③) 초식 동물들은 그들의 먹이원을 완전히 잃고 죽게 되며, 그들을 먹이로 삼는 동물들도 그렇게 된다. (④) 하지만 종 다양성이 있을 때, 갑작스러운 변화의 영향은 그렇게 극적이지 않다. 다양한 종의 식물들이 가뭄에 다르게 반응하고, 많은 식물이 건기에 살아남을 수 있다. (⑤) 많은 동물은 다양한 먹이원을 가지고 있고, 단지 한 식물에만 의존하지는 않는다. 그래서 이제 우리의 숲 생태계는 더 이상 종말에 처해 있지 않다!

문제풀이

주어진 문장의 'But'으로 보아 앞 문장과는 상반된 내용이 서술될 것임을 알 수 있고, ④ 앞에서는 한 종류의 식물만 있는 숲에서는 그 식물이 사라지면 초식 동물과 그들을 먹는 다른 동물들이 죽게 된다는 내용이, ④ 뒤에서는 다양한 종의 식물들이 건기에 살아남을 수 있다는 내용이 언급되면서 두 문장 간에 단절이 있다. 따라서 주어진 문장은 ④에 들어가야 글의 흐름이 자연스럽다.

《어휘·어구》

effect 영향
sudden 갑작스러운
dramatic 극적인
ecosystem 생태계
wildlife 야생 생물
opportunity 기회
obtain 얻다
shelter 서식지
species 종
react 작용하다
respond 반응하다
environment 환경
completely 완전히
prey upon ~을 잡아먹다
drought 가뭄
survive 살아남다
a variety of 다양한
rely on 의존하다
at the death 종말에 처한

정답률 38%

8. ② 우리는 많은 방식으로 밤하늘과 연결되어 있다

직독/직해

We are connected to the night sky / in many ways.
우리는 밤하늘과 연결되어 있다 / 많은 방식으로

It has always inspired / 그것은 항상 영감을 주었다 /

people to wonder and to imagine.
사람들이 궁금해 하고 상상하도록

Since the dawn of civilization, /
문명의 시작부터 /

our ancestors created myths /
우리 조상들은 신화를 만들었다 /

and told legendary stories / about the night sky.
그리고 전설적인 이야기를 했다 / 밤하늘에 관한

Elements of those narratives became embedded /
그런 이야기들의 요소들은 깊이 새겨졌다 /

in the social and cultural identities /
사회적 그리고 문화적 정체성에 /

of many generations. 여러 세대의

On a practical level, / 실용적인 수준에서 /

the night sky helped past generations /
밤하늘은 과거 세대들을 도왔다 /

to keep track of time / and create calendars — /
시간을 기록하게 (도왔다) / 그리고 달력을 만들게 (도왔다) /

essential to developing societies /
이는 사회를 발전시키는 데 필수적이었다 /

as aids to farming and seasonal gathering.
농업과 계절에 따른 수확의 보조 도구로서

For many centuries, / 수 세기 동안 /

it also provided a useful navigation tool, /
그것은 또한 유용한 항해 도구를 제공했다 /

vital for commerce / and for exploring new worlds.
무역에 필수적인 / 그리고 새로운 세계를 탐험하는 데 (필수적인)

Even in modern times, /
심지어 현대에도 /

many people in remote areas of the planet /
지구의 외딴 지역에 있는 많은 사람이 /

observe the night sky / 밤하늘을 관찰한다 /

for such practical purposes.
그런 실용적인 목적을 위해

우리는 많은 방식으로 밤하늘과 연결되어 있다. (①) 그것은 항상 사람들이 궁금해 하고 상상하도록 영감을 주었다. (②) 문명의 시작부터, 우리 조상들은 밤하늘에 관한 신화를 만들었고 전설적인 이야기를 했다. 그런 이야기들의 요소들은 여러 세대의 사회적 그리고 문화적 정체성에 깊이 새겨졌다. (③) 실용적인 수준에서, 밤하늘은 과거 세대들이 시간을 기록하고 달력을 만드는 것을 도왔고, 이는 농업과 계절에 따른 수확의 보조 도구로서 사회를 발전시키는 데 필수적이었다. (④) 수 세기 동안, 그것은 또한 무역과 새로운 세계를 탐험하는 데 필수적인 유용한 항해 도구를 제공했다. (⑤) 심지어 현대에도, 지구의 외딴 지역에 있는 많은 사람이 그런 실용적인 목적을 위해 밤하늘을 관찰한다.

문제풀이

② 다음 문장에서 언급된 'those narratives'는 주어진 문장에서 언급된 밤하늘에 관한 신화와 전설적인 이야기를 가리키므로 주어진 문장은 ②에 들어가는 것이 가장 적절하다.

이렇게 풀자 ② 앞의 문장은 밤하늘이 항상 사람들을 궁금하게 하고 상상하도록 영감을 주었다는 내용이 나오고, ② 뒤에서는 그런 이야기들의 요소들이 여러 세대의 사회적·문화적 정체성에 깊이 새겨졌다는 내용이 나오므로 두 문장 사이에 단절이 있다. 또한 ② 다음 문장에서 언급된 'those narratives'가 가리키는 내용이 주어진 문장에 있으므로 주어진 문장은 ②에 들어가야 한다.

《어휘·어구》

dawn 시작, 새벽
civilization 문명
ancestor 선조
myth 신화
legendary 전설의
inspire 영감을 주다
wonder 궁금하다
element 요소
narrative 서술, 묘사
identity 정체성
generation 세대
practical 실용적인
keep track of ~을 기록하다
calendar 달력
essential 필수적인
aid 보조 도구
seasonal 계절에 따른
gathering 수확
provide 제공하다
useful 유용한
navigation 항해
explore 탐험하다
remote 외딴
planet 지구
observe 관찰하다
purpose 목적

정답률 62%

9. ④ 영양 보충제의 한계

직독/직해

According to top nutrition experts, /
최고의 영양 전문가들에 의하면 /
most nutrients are better absorbed and used /
대부분의 영양소가 더 잘 흡수되고 사용된다 /
by the body / when consumed from a whole food /
신체에 의해 / 자연식품으로부터 섭취되었을 때 /
instead of a supplement.
보충제 대신에
However, / many people feel the need /
그러나 / 많은 사람들이 필요성을 느낀다 /
to take pills, powders, and supplements /
알약, 분말 그리고 보충제를 섭취할 /
in an attempt to obtain nutrients /
영양소를 얻기 위한 시도로 /
and fill the gaps in their diets.
그리고 자신의 식단에 있어 부족한 부분을 채우기 위한 (시도로)
We hope / these will give us more energy, /
우리는 바란다 / 이것들이 우리에게 더 많은 에너지를 주기를 /
prevent us from catching a cold / in the winter, /
감기에 걸리는 것을 막아 주기를 / 겨울에 /
or improve our skin and hair.
혹은 우리의 피부와 모발을 개선해 주기를
But in reality, / 그러나 실제로는 /
the large majority of supplements are artificial /
대다수의 보충제가 인위적이다 /
and may not even be completely absorbed /
그리고 완전히 흡수조차 되지 않을 수도 있다 /
by your body. 여러분의 신체에 의해
Worse, / 심하게는 /
some are contaminated with other substances /
어떤 것들은 다른 물질로 오염되어 있다 /
and contain ingredients / not listed on the label.
그리고 성분을 포함한다 / 라벨에 실려 있지 않은
For example, / 예를 들어 /
a recent investigative report found heavy metals /
최근 한 조사 보고는 중금속을 발견했다 /
in 40 percent of 134 brands of protein powders /
단백질 분말 134개 브랜드 중 40퍼센트에서 /
on the market. 시장에 있는
With little control and regulation, /
단속과 규제가 거의 없다면 /
taking supplements is a gamble and often costly.
보충제를 섭취하는 것은 도박이며 종종 대가가 크다

최고의 영양 전문가들에 의하면 많은 영양소가 보충제 대신에 자연식품으로부터 섭취되었을 때 신체에 의해 더 잘 흡수되고 사용된다. (①) 그러나 많은 사람들이 영양소를 얻고 자신의 식단에 있어 부족한 부분을 채우기 위한 시도로 알약, 분말 그리고 보충제를 섭취할 필요성을 느낀다. (②) 우리는 이것들이 우리에게 더 많은 에너지를 주고, 우리가 겨울에 감기에 걸리는것을 막아 주거나 혹은 우리의 피부와 모발을 개선해 주기를 바란다. (③) 그러나 실제로는 대다수의 보충제가 인위적이고 여러분의 신체에 의해 완전히 흡수조차 되지 않을 수도 있다. (④) 심하게는 어떤 것들은 다른 물질로 오염되어 있으며 라벨에 실려 있지 않은 성분을 포함한다. 예를 들어 최근 한 조사 보고는 시장에 있는 단백질 분말 134개 브랜드 중 40퍼센트에서 중금속을 발견했다. (⑤) 단속과 규제가 거의 없다면 보충제를 섭취하는 것은 도박이며 종종 대가가 크다.

문제풀이

주어진 문장은 어떤 것들은 다른 물질로 오염되어 있고 라벨에 실려 있지 않은 성분을 포함한다는 내용으로, 처음에 나온 'Worse'로 보아 그 앞에 부정적인 내용이 나와야 한다는 것을 알 수 있고, ④ 다음의 'heavy metals(중금속)'이 주어진 문장에서 언급한 오염물질의 예가 된다는 것을 알 수 있다. 따라서 주어진 문장은 ④에 들어가는 것이 가장 적절하다.

구조 다시보기

주제	영양소는 보충제 대신에 자연식품으로부터 섭취되어야 함
반전 1	많은 사람들이 영양소를 얻고, 부족한 식단을 보충하기 위해 보충제 섭취의 필요성을 느낌
반전 2	보충제는 인위적이고 오염될 수 있음
결론	단속과 규제가 없으면 보충제 섭취가 위험할 수 있음

《어휘·어구》

nutrition 영양
absorb 흡수하다
pill 알약
attempt 시도
obtain 얻다
improve 개선시키다
in reality 실제로
majority 대다수
completely 완전히
substance 물질
ingredient 성분
protein 단백질
regulation 규제
costly 대가가 큰

정답률 36%

10. ⑤ 운동 에너지와 위치 에너지

직독/직해

In general, / kinetic energy is the energy /
일반적으로 / 운동 에너지는 에너지이다 /
associated with motion, /
운동과 관련 있는 /
while potential energy represents the energy /
반면에 위치 에너지는 에너지를 나타낸다 /
which is "stored" / in a physical system.
'저장되는' / 물리계에
Moreover, / the total energy is always conserved.
게다가 / 총에너지는 항상 보존된다
But while the total energy remains unchanged, /
그러나 총에너지가 변하지 않는 채로 있는 반면 /
the kinetic and potential parts of the total energy can change / all the time.
총에너지의 운동과 위치 에너지 비율은 변할 수 있다 / 항상
Imagine, / for example, /
상상해 보자 / 예를 들어 /
a pendulum which swings back and forth.
앞뒤로 흔들리는 추를
When it swings, / it sweeps out an arc /
그것이 흔들릴 때 / 그것은 호 모양으로 쓸어내리듯 움직인다 /
and then slows down / as it comes closer /
그리고 나서 속도가 줄어든다 / 그것이 가까워지면서 /
to its highest point, / 그 최고점에 /
where the pendulum does not move at all.
이 지점에서 추는 더 이상 움직이지 않는다
So at this point, / the energy is completely given /
그래서 이 지점에서 / 에너지는 완전히 주어지게 된다 /
in terms of potential energy.
위치 에너지로
But after this brief moment of rest, /
하지만 이 짧은 순간의 멈춤 이후에 /
the pendulum swings back again /
그 추는 다시 뒤로 흔들리게 된다 /
and therefore part of the total energy is then given /
따라서 총에너지의 일부가 그때 주어지게 된다 /
in the form of kinetic energy.
운동 에너지의 형태로
So as the pendulum swings, /
그래서 그 추가 흔들리면서 /
kinetic and potential energy constantly change into each other.
운동과 위치 에너지는 끊임없이 서로 바뀐다

일반적으로 운동 에너지는 운동과 관련 있는 에너지이며 반면에 위치 에너지는 물리계에 '저장되는' 에너지를 나타낸다. 게다가 총에너지는 항상 보존된다. (①) 그러나 총에너지가 변하지 않는 채로 있는 반면 총에너지의 운동과 위치 에너지 비율은 항상 변할 수 있다. (②) 예를 들어 앞뒤로 흔들리는 추를 상상해 보자. (③) 그것이 흔들릴 때 호 모양으로 쓸어내리듯 움직이다가 그리고 나서 그것이 그 최고점에 가까워지면서 속도가 줄어드는데, 이 지점에서 추는 더 이상 움직이지 않는다. (④) 그래서 이 지점에서 에너지는 완전히 위치 에너지로 주어지게 된다. (⑤) 하지만 이 짧은 순간의 멈춤 이후에 그 추는 다시 뒤로 흔들리게 되며 따라서 총에너지의 일부가 그때 운동 에너지의 형태로 주어지게 된다. 그래서 그 추가 흔들리면서 운동과 위치 에너지는 끊임없이 서로 바뀐다.

문제풀이

이 글은 총에너지는 변하지 않지만, 위치 에너지와 운동 에너지는 끊임없이 서로 바뀐다는 내용의 글이다. 주어진 문장의 'this brief moment of rest(이 짧은 순간의 멈춤)'가 의미하는 것은 흔들리는 추가 최고점에 도달했을 때 더 이상 움직이지 않는 순간을 의미하는데, ④ 다음의 'at this point(이 지점에서)'도 역시 추가 움직이지 않는 순간을 의미한다. ④의 이 지점에서 에너지는 완전히 위치 에너지로 주어지게 된다는 내용이 있는 것으로 보아, 주어진 문장의 추가 다시 흔들릴 때는 총에너지의 일부가 운동 에너지의 형태로 주어지게 된다는 내용이 ⑤에 와야 한다는 것을 알 수 있다. 따라서 주어진 문장이 들어갈 가장 적절한 곳은 ⑤이다.

《어휘·어구》

In general 일반적으로
kinetic energy 운동 에너지
associate 관련 있다
potential energy 위치 에너지
represent 나타내다
conserve 보존하다
swing 흔들리다

sweep 쓸어내리다
slow down 느리게 하다
in terms of ~의 면에서

정답률 69%

11. ③ 카페인의 각성 효과에 관한 연구

직독/직해

Studies have consistently shown /
연구는 일관적으로 보여주었다 /
caffeine to be effective / 카페인이 효과적이라는 것을 /
when used together with a pain reliever /
진통제와 함께 사용할 때 /
to treat headaches. 두통을 치료하기 위해
The positive correlation / 양의 상관관계 /
between caffeine intake and staying alert throughout the day /
카페인 섭취와 온종일 각성된 상태로 있는 것 사이에는 /
has also been well established. 또한 잘 확립되어 있다
As little as 60 mg / 60mg만큼의 적은 양으로도 /
(the amount typically in one cup of tea) /
일반적으로 차 한 잔에 들어 있는 양 /
can lead to a faster reaction time.
반응 시간이 더 빨라질 수 있다
However, / using caffeine /
하지만 / 카페인을 사용하는 것은 /
to improve alertness and mental performance /
각성과 정신적 수행능력을 향상시키기 위해 /
doesn't replace getting a good night's sleep.
숙면을 취하는 것을 대체하지 못한다
One study from 2018 showed / 2018년 한 연구는 보여주었다 /
that coffee improved reaction times /
커피가 반응 시간은 개선했다 /
in those with or without poor sleep, /
수면이 부족한 사람들이나 부족하지 않은 사람들에게나 /
but caffeine seemed to increase errors /
그러나 카페인은 오류를 증가시키는 것 같다는 것을 /
in the group with little sleep. 수면이 부족한 집단 내에서는
Additionally, / this study showed /
게다가 / 이 연구는 보여주었다 /
that even with caffeine, / 심지어 카페인을 섭취해도 /
the group with little sleep / did not score as well as /
수면이 부족한 그룹은 / 점수를 잘 받지 못했다는 것을 /
those with adequate sleep.
적절한 수면을 취한 집단만큼
It suggests / that caffeine does not fully make up for /
그것은 보여준다 / 카페인이 충분히 보충하지 못한다는 것을 /
inadequate sleep. 불충분한 수면을

연구는 카페인이 두통을 치료하기 위해 진통제와 함께 사용할 때 효과적이라는 것을 일관적으로 보여주었다. (①) 카페인 섭취와 온종일 각성된 상태로 있는 것 사이에는 양의 상관관계 또한 잘 확립되어 있다. (②) 60mg (일반적으로 차 한 잔에 들어 있는 양)만큼의 적은 양으로도 반응 시간이 더 빨라질 수 있다. (③) 하지만, 각성과 정신적 수행능력을 향상시키기 위해 카페인을 사용하는 것은 숙면을 취하는 것을 대체하지 못한다. 2018년 한 연구는 커피가 수면이 부족한 사람들에게나 부족하지 않은 사람들에게나 반응 시간은 개선했지만, 카페인은 수면이 부족한 집단 내에서는 오류를 증가시키는 것 같다는 것을 보여주었다. (④) 게다가, 이 연구는 심지어 카페인을 섭취해도, 수면이 부족한 그룹은 적절한 수면을 취한 집단만큼 점수를 잘 받지 못했다는 것을 보여주었다. (⑤) 그것은 카페인이 불충분한 수면을 충분히 보충하지 못한다는 것을 보여준다.

문제풀이

두통 치료 시에 카페인이 진통제와 함께 사용될 때 효과적이고 카페인 섭취가 각성 상태를 유지할 수 있지만, 수면을 대체할 수 있는 대안은 될 수 없다는 내용이다. ③ 앞에서는 카페인 섭취의 효과에 관해 설명하고 있고 ③ 뒤에서는 수면 부족 집단에서 카페인은 오류를 증가시키는 등 효과가 없다는 것을 설명하고 있다. 따라서 주어진 문장은 ③에 들어가야 글의 흐름이 자연스럽다.

《어휘·어구》

alertness 각성도
mental 정신의
performance 성과, 수행능력
replace 대체하다
consistently 일관적으로
effective 효과적인
pain reliever 진통제
correlation 상관관계
intake 섭취
establish 확립하다
typically 보통, 일반적으로
reaction 반응
additionally 게다가
adequate 적당한
make up for ~을 보충하다

정답률 57%

12. ② 성공을 보상하는 방법

직독/직해

Rewarding business success / 사업 성공을 보상하는 것은 /
doesn't always have to be done /
항상 이루어져야 하는 것은 아니다 /
in a material way. 물질적인 방식으로
A software company I once worked for /
내가 한때 일했던 한 소프트웨어 회사는 /
had a great way / 멋진 방법을 가지고 있었다 /
of recognizing sales success. 판매 성공을 인정해주는
The sales director kept an air horn /
판매부서 관리자는 경적을 두었다 /
outside his office / 그의 사무실 밖에 /
and would come out and blow the horn /
그리고 나와서 경적을 불곤 했다 /
every time a salesperson settled a deal.
영업직원이 거래를 성사할 때마다
The noise, of course, / 물론, 그 소리는 /
interrupted anything and everything /
어떤 것이라도, 그리고 모든 것을 방해했다 /
happening in the office / 사무실에서 일어나는 /
because it was unbelievably loud.
믿을 수 없을 정도로 시끄러웠기 때문에
However, / 하지만 /
it had an amazingly positive impact / on everyone.
그것은 놀랄 만큼 긍정적인 영향을 주었다 / 모두에게
Sometimes rewarding success /
이따금, 성공을 보상하는 것은 /
can be as easy as that, / 그처럼 쉬울 수 있다 /
especially when peer recognition is important.
특히 동료의 인정이 중요할 때
You should have seen the way / 당신은 그 방식을 봤어야 했다 /
the rest of the sales team / 그 판매부서의 나머지 사람들이 /
wanted the air horn blown / for them.
경적이 불어지기를 바라는 / 그들을 위해

사업 성공을 보상하는 것은 항상 물질적인 방식으로 이루어져야 하는 것은 아니다. (①) 내가 한때 일했던 한 소프트웨어 회사는 판매 성공을 인정해주는 멋진 방법을 가지고 있었다. (②) 판매부서 관리자는 그의 사무실 밖에 경적을 두었고 영업직원이 거래를 성사할 때마다 나와서 경적을 불곤 했다. 물론, 그 소리는 믿을 수 없을 정도로 시끄러웠기 때문에 사무실에서 일어나는 어떤 것이라도, 그리고 모든 것을 방해했다. (③) 하지만 그것은 모두에게 놀랄 만큼 긍정적인 영향을 주었다. (④) 이따금, 성공을 보상하는 것은 그처럼 쉬울 수 있는데, 특히 동료의 인정이 중요할 때 그렇다. (⑤) 당신은 그 판매부서의 나머지 사람들이 그들을 위해 경적이 불어지기를 바라는 그 방식을 봤어야 했다.

문제풀이

성공을 보상하는 방법이 항상 물질적인 방식으로 이루어져야 하는 것은 아니라는 내용으로, 필자가 일했던 회사에서 판매 성공을 인정해주는 방법을 구체적으로 설명하고 있는 글이다. 주어진 문장은 판매부서 관리자가 영업직원이 거래를 성사할 때마다 경적을 불곤 했다는 내용으로, ② 앞에서는 판매 성공을 인정해주는 멋진 방법이 있다고 언급했고, ② 뒤에서 그 소리가 너무 시끄러워서 모든 것을 방해했다는 내용이 나오므로 주어진 문장은 ②에 들어가는 것이 가장 적절하다.

이렇게 풀자 주어진 문장은 ② 앞에서 언급된 판매 성공을 인정해주는 멋진 방법에 대한 구체적인 설명이므로 주어진 문장은 ② 다음에 와야 한다.

《어휘·어구》

reward 보상하다
material 물질적인
recognize 인정하다
interrupt 방해하다
unbelievably 믿을 수 없을 정도로
impact 영향
peer 동료

본문 103쪽

문법 플러스 17. 형용사, 부사

1. alive 2. directly 3. relatively
4. neat 5. high 6. highly 7. Most
8. almost 9. late 10. bring it back

1 [해석]▶ 나는 살아 있는 새 한 마리를 잡았다.
[해설]▶ live는 동사로 '살다'의 의미이며 형용사로 '살아 있는, 생방송의'라는 뜻이 있다. 형용사 live는 주로 명사 앞에 나와서 명사를 수식한다. 형용사 alive는 주로 명사 뒤에서 서술 용법으로 사용된다. 이 문장은 I caught a bird (which was) alive.에서 「관계대명사+be동사」가 생략되어 있는 문장이다. 관계절 안에서 alive가 be동사 was 뒤에 나와 서술 용법으로 사용되었다.

2 [해석]▶ 너무 밝은 빛이나, 눈에 직접적으로 비추는 빛처럼, 나쁜 조명은 당신의 눈에 스트레스를 높일 수 있다.
[해설]▶ 부사는 형용사, 동사, 부사를 수식한다. 이 문장은 동사 shines를 수식하는 품사가 와야 하므로 부사 directly가 오는 것이 맞다.

3 [해석]▶ 상대적으로 적은 양의 플라스틱을 모으기 위해 막대한 양의 물을 여과해야 한다.
[해설]▶ 형용사 small을 수식하려면 부사(relatively)가 나와야 한다.

4 [해석]▶ 우리가 자라면서, 어머니께서는 우리의 방을 깨끗하게 치우는 것으로 우리의 본분을 다하게 했다.
[해설]▶ 「keep+목적어+목적격보어」의 구문으로 보어가 될 수 있는 형용사가 나와야 한다.

5 [해석]▶ 연이 하늘 높이 날았다.
[해설]▶ 부사 high는 '높이', 부사 highly는 '매우'의 의미이다.

6 [해석]▶ 그녀는 새로운 곳에 있다는 기대감이 가득했으며 매우 기분이 좋았다.
[해설]▶ 부사 high는 '높이', 부사 highly는 '매우'의 의미이다. 여기서는 문맥상 '매우'가 적절하다.

7 [해석]▶ 대부분의 사람들이 그에 대해 걱정하기 시작했다.
[해설]▶ 괄호 뒤에 명사가 나오므로 형용사 'most(대부분)'가 나와야 맞다.

8 [해석]▶ 많은 사람들은 그 비결이 거의 매 식사마다 나

오는 전통 한국 음식인 김치에 있다고 생각한다.
[해설]▶ almost(거의 대부분)는 부사로 쓰인다. almost 뒤에는 종종 all, every, any 등이 온다. almost every meal '거의 대부분의 식사'라는 의미이다.

9 [해석]▶ Sam은 오늘 아침에 늦게 일어났다. 그래서 학교에 지각했다.
[해설]▶ 부사 late는 '늦게', lately는 '최근에'라는 의미이다.

10 해석▶ 그녀는 그것을 다음 때까지 돌려주기로 약속했다.
[해설]▶ 동사와 부사가 결합된 동사구에서 목적어가 대명사일 경우에는 「동사+대명사+부사」의 어순이 되어야 한다.

본문 104쪽

어휘 플러스 17. 철자가 혼동되는 어휘 (5)

1. alternative 2. inhibits
3. neutral 4. status
5. stale

1 [해석]▶ 태양 에너지가 예측 가능한 미래에 우리를 위한 실용적인 대체 에너지원이 될 수 있다.

2 [해석]▶ 그것들의 물리적 배치는 어떤 사용을 권장하고 다른 사용을 억제한다. 우리는 특별히 초대받지 않는다면 극장의 무대 뒤로 가지 않는다.

3 [해석]▶ 몇몇 대학들은 그 시대의 중요한 쟁점에 대해서 대학은 중립적이고 문제에 개입하지 말아야 한다는 이유 등으로 그들의 침묵을 정당화하고 있다.

4 [해석]▶ 교복은 개인적 취향과 아이들 부모의 재정 상태를 감추도록 도와준다.

5 [해석]▶ 그러나 그러한 정신적 예행연습이 주의력을 빼앗아 다른 곳에 집중하려는 온갖 시도를 방해하는 진부한 일상에 사로잡힐 때, 그것은 파멸적인 인지적 정지 상태가 된다.

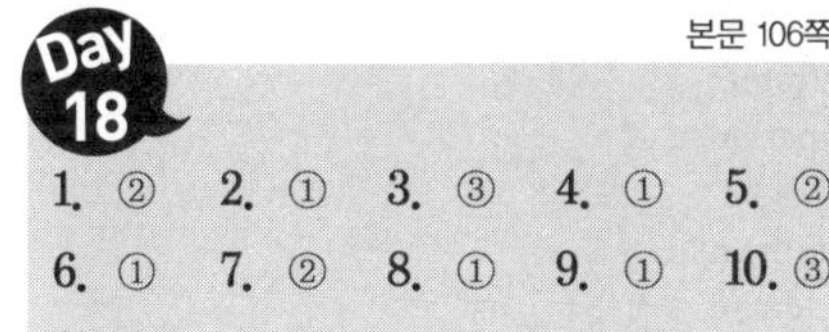

18. 문단 요약

Day 18 본문 106쪽

1. ② 2. ① 3. ③ 4. ① 5. ②
6. ① 7. ② 8. ① 9. ① 10. ③
11. ①

정답률 67%

대표 기출 ① 작은 노트가 사람들의 행동을 변화시킴

직독/직해

A woman named Rhonda / Rhonda라는 이름의 여자는 /
who attended the University of California at Berkeley /
Berkeley에 있는 California 대학에 다니던 /
had a problem. 한 가지 문제 상황이 있었다
She was living near campus /
그녀는 캠퍼스 근처에 살고 있었는데 /
with several other people /
여러 사람과 함께 /
— none of whom knew one another.
그들 중 아무도 서로를 알지 못했다
When the cleaning people came each weekend, /
청소부가 주말마다 왔을 때 /
they left several rolls of toilet paper /
그들은 몇 개의 두루마리 화장지를 두고 갔다 /
in each of the two bathrooms.
화장실 두 칸에 각각
However, by Monday / 하지만 월요일 즈음 /
all the toilet paper would be gone.
모든 화장지가 없어지곤 했다
It was a classic tragedy-of-the-commons situation: /
그것은 전형적인 공유지의 비극 상황이었다 /
because some people took more toilet paper /
일부 사람들이 더 많은 휴지를 가져갔기 때문에 /
than their fair share, / 자신들이 사용할 수 있는 몫보다 /
the public resource was destroyed /
공공재가 파괴되었다 /
for everyone else. 그 외 모두를 위한
After reading a research paper about behavior change, /
행동 변화에 관한 한 연구 논문을 읽고 나서 /
Rhonda put a note in one of the bathrooms /
Rhonda는 쪽지를 화장실 한곳에 두었다 /
asking people not to remove the toilet paper, /
사람들에게 화장실 화장지를 가져가지 말라는 /
as it was a shared item.
그것은 공유재이기 때문에
To her great satisfaction, / one roll reappeared /
아주 만족스럽게도 / 화장지 한 개가 다시 나타났다 /
in a few hours, / and another the next day.
몇 시간 후에 / 그리고 그다음 날에는 또 하나가 다시 나타났다
In the other note-free bathroom, / however, /
쪽지가 없는 화장실에서는 / 그러나 /
there was no toilet paper / 화장지가 없었다 /
until the following weekend, / 그다음 주말까지 /
when the cleaning people returned.
청소부가 돌아오는
➡ A small reminder brought about a change /
하나의 작은 상기시키는 메모가 변화를 가져왔다 /
in the behavior of the people /
사람들의 행동에 /
who had taken more of the shared goods /
더 많은 공유재를 가져갔던 /
than they needed. 그들이 필요한 것보다

Berkeley에 있는 California 대학에 다니던 Rhonda라는 이름의 여자는 한 가지 문제 상황이 있었다. 그녀는 여러 사람과 함께 캠퍼스 근처에 살고 있었는데, 그들 중 아무도 서로를 알지 못했다. 청소부가 주말마다 왔을 때 그들은 화장실 두 칸에 각각 몇 개의 두루마리 화장지를 두고 갔다. 하지만 월요일 즈음 모든 화장지가 없어지곤 했다. 그것은 전형적인 공유지의 비극 상황이었다. 일부 사람들이 자신들이 사용할 수 있는 몫보다 더 많은 휴지를 가져갔기 때문에 그 외 모두를 위한 공공재가 파괴되었다. 행동 변화에 관한 한 연구 논문을 읽고 나서, Rhonda는 화장실 화장지는 공유재이기 때문에 사람들에게 그것을 가져가지 말라는 쪽지를 화장실 한곳에 두었다. 아주 만족스럽게도, 몇 시간 후에 화장지 한 개가 다시 나타났고, 그다음 날에는 또 하나가 다시 나타났다. 그러나 쪽지가 없는 화장실에서는 청소부가 돌아오는 그다음 주말까지 화장지가 없었다.
➡ 하나의 작은 (A) 상기물은 그들이 필요한 것보다 더 많은 (B) 공유재를 가져갔던 사람들의 행동에 변화를 가져왔다.

① **상기시키는 메모 …… 공유된**
② 상기시키는 메모 …… 재활용된
③ 실수 …… 저장된
④ 실수 …… 빌린
⑤ 운 …… 제한된

문제풀이

공유지에 놓인 공공재가 파괴되는 상황을 겪은 Rhonda가 행동 변화에 관한 연구 논문을 읽고 한 쪽의 화장실에만 공유재인 화장지를 가져가지 말라는 쪽지를 두었더니 사라졌던 화장지가 다시 나타났다는 내용을 통해 요약문의 빈칸 (A)에는 'reminder(상기시키는 메모)'가, (B)에는 'shared(공유된)'가 가장 적절하다.

어휘·어구

tragedy-of-the-commons 공유지의 비극
situation 상황
public resource 공공자원
remove 제거하다
satisfaction 만족
reappear 다시 나타나다
note-free 쪽지가 없는
reminder 상기시키는 것
fortune 운, 행운
limited 제한된

정답률 63%

1. ② 삶의 의미를 찾는 강력한 도구인 성찰적 일기 쓰기

직독/직해

One of the most powerful tools /
가장 강력한 도구 중 하나는 /
to find meaning in our lives / is reflective journaling /
우리의 삶에서 의미를 찾는 / 성찰적 일기 쓰기이다 /
— thinking back on and writing about /
즉 돌아보고 그것에 대해 쓰는 것(이다) /
what has happened to us. 우리에게 일어났던 일을
In the 1990s, / Stanford University researchers /
1990년대에 / Stanford University 연구자들이 /
asked undergraduate students / on spring break /
학부생들에게 요청했다 / 봄방학에 /
to journal / 쓰도록 /
about their most important personal values /
그들의 가장 중요한 개인적인 가치에 대해 /
and their daily activities; / 그들의 하루 활동들에 대해 /
others were asked to write /
반면, 다른 사람들은 쓰도록 요청받았다 /
about only the good things / that happened to them /
좋은 일들에 대해서만 / 그들에게 일어났던 /
in the day. 그날
Three weeks later, / 3주 후에 /
the students who had written about their values /
자신의 가치에 관해 썼던 학생들은 /

were happier, healthier, / and more confident /
더 행복하고, 더 건강했다 / 그리고 더 자신 있었다 /
about their ability to handle stress /
스트레스를 다루는 자신의 능력에 대해 /
than the ones / who had only focused on the good stuff.
학생들보다 / 좋은 것에만 초점을 맞췄던
By reflecting / on how their daily activities supported their values, /
성찰함으로써 / 어떻게 그들 하루의 활동들이 그들의 가치를 뒷받침하는지에 관해 /
students had gained a new perspective /
학생들은 새로운 관점을 얻었다 /
on those activities and choices.
그 활동들과 선택들에 대해
Little stresses and hassles /
작은 스트레스와 귀찮은 일들은 /
were now demonstrations /of their values in action.
이제 보여주는 것이었다 / 행동에서 그들의 가치를
Suddenly, / their lives were full of /
갑자기 / 그들의 삶은 ~로 가득 찼다 /
meaningful activities. 의미 있는 활동으로
And all they had to do / was reflect and write about it /
그리고 그들이 했어야 할 모든 일은 / 그것에 대해 돌아보고 쓰는 것이었다 /
— positively reframing their experiences /
그들의 경험을 긍정적으로 재구성하면서 /
with their personal values. 개인적인 가치로
→ Journaling about daily activities /
일상 활동에 대해 일기를 쓰는 것은 /
based on what we believe to be worthwhile /
우리가 가치 있다고 믿는 것에 근거하여 /
can make us feel / that our life is meaningful /
우리가 느끼게 만들 수 있다 / 우리의 삶이 의미 있다는 것을 /
by rethinking our experiences / in a new way.
우리의 경험들을 다시 생각함으로써 / 새로운 방식으로

우리의 삶에서 의미를 찾는 가장 강력한 도구 중 하나는 성찰적 일기 쓰기, 즉 우리에게 일어났던 일을 돌아보고 그것에 대해 쓰는 것이다. 1990년대에 Stanford University 연구자들이 봄방학에 학부생들에게 그들의 가장 중요한 개인적인 가치와 그들의 하루 활동들에 대해 쓰도록 요청했다. 반면, 다른 사람들은 그날 그들에게 일어났던 좋은 일들만 쓰도록 요청받았다. 3주 후에, 자신의 가치에 관해 썼던 학생들은 좋은 것에만 초점을 맞췄던 학생들보다 더 행복하고, 더 건강하고, 스트레스를 다루는 자신의 능력에 대해 더 자신 있었다. 어떻게 그들 하루의 활동들이 그들의 가치를 뒷받침하는지에 관해 성찰함으로써, 학생들은 그 활동들과 선택들에 대해 새로운 관점을 얻었다. 작은 스트레스와 귀찮은 일들은 이제 행동에서 그들의 가치를 보여주는 것이었다. 갑자기, 그들의 삶은 의미 있는 활동으로 가득 찼다. 그리고 그들이 했어야 할 모든 일은 그들의 경험을 개인적인 가치로 긍정적으로 재구성하면서 그것에 대해 돌아보고 쓰는 것이었다.
→ 우리가 (A) 가치 있다고 믿는 것에 근거하여 일상 활동에 대해 일기를 쓰는 것은 새로운 방식으로 우리의 경험들을 (B) 다시 생각함으로써 우리가 자신의 삶이 의미 있다는 것을 느끼게 만들 수 있다.

	(A)	(B)		(A)	(B)
①	사실적인	… 다시 생각함	②	**가치 있는**	**… 다시 생각함**
③	구식의	… 일반화함	④	객관적인	… 일반화함
⑤	힘든	… 묘사함			

문제풀이

어떻게 하루 활동이 그들의 가치를 뒷받침하는지에 관해 성찰적 일기를 썼던 학생들이 단지 좋은 것에만 초점을 맞춰 일기를 썼던 학생들보다 더 행복하고, 더 건강하고, 스트레스를 다루는 능력에 있어 더 자신 있었다는 실험 결과를 통해, 요약문의 빈칸 (A)에는 'worthwhile(가치 있는)'이, (B)에는 'rethinking(다시 생각함)'이 가장 적절함을 알 수 있다.

어휘·어구

reflective 사색적인
happen 일어나다
undergraduate student 학부생, 대학생
value 가치
activity 활동
confident 자신감 있는
handle 다루다
reflect 깊이 생각하다
support 뒷받침하다
perspective 관점
demonstration 증명
action 행동
meaningful 의미 있는
positively 긍정적으로
reframe 다시 구성하다
experience 경험
factual 사실적인
worthwhile 가치 있는
outdated 구식의
generalize 일반화하다
objective 객관적인
demanding 힘든
describe 묘사하다, 설명하다

정답률 46%

2. ① 기부할 이유를 단독으로 제시하는 것이 효과적이다

직독/직해

My colleagues and I ran an experiment /
동료들과 나는 한 연구를 진행했다 /
testing two different messages /
두 개의 다른 메시지들을 실험하는 /
meant to convince thousands of resistant alumni /
수천 명의 저항하는 졸업생을 납득시키는 것을 의도한 /
to make a donation. 기부하도록
One message emphasized / 하나의 메시지는 강조했다 /
the opportunity to do good: / 좋은 일을 할 기회를 /
donating would benefit / students, faculty, and staff.
기부하는 것은 이익을 줄 것이다 / 학생들, 교직원, 그리고 직원들에게
The other emphasized / the opportunity to feel good: /
다른 하나는 강조했다 / 좋은 기분을 느끼는 기회를 /
donors would enjoy / the warm glow of giving.
기부자들은 즐길 것이다 / 기부의 따뜻한 온기를
The two messages were equally effective: /
그 두 메시지들은 똑같이 효과적이었다 /
in both cases, / 6.5 percent of the unwilling alumni /
두 경우 모두에서 / 6.5%의 마음 내키지 않은 졸업생이 /
ended up donating. 결국에는 기부했다
Then we combined them, /
그러고 나서 우리는 그것들을 결합했다 /
because two reasons are better than one.
왜냐하면 두 개의 이유가 한 개보다 더 낫기 때문이다
Except they weren't. 하지만 그렇지 않았다
When we put the two reasons together, /
우리가 그 두 이유들을 합쳤을 때 /
the giving rate dropped / below 3 percent.
기부율은 떨어졌다 / 3% 아래로
Each reason alone / 각각의 이유가 단독으로는 /
was more than twice as effective as the two combined.
그 두 개가 합쳐진 것보다 두 배 이상 더 효과적이었다
The audience was already skeptical.
청중은 이미 회의적이었다
When we gave them different kinds of reasons to donate, /
우리가 그들에게 기부할 서로 다른 종류의 이유를 주었을 때 /
we triggered their awareness /
우리는 그들의 인식을 유발했다 /
that someone was trying to persuade them /
누군가가 그들을 설득하려고 하는 중이라는 /
— and they shielded themselves / against it.
그리고 그들은 스스로를 보호했다 / 그것에 맞서
→ In the experiment mentioned above, /
위에서 언급된 실험에서 /
when the two different reasons to donate /
기부할 두 개의 서로 다른 이유들이 /
were given simultaneously, /
동시에 주어졌을 때 /
the audience was less likely to be convinced /
청자는 납득될 가능성이 더 작았다 /
because they could recognize /
알아차릴 수 있었기 때문에 /
the intention to persuade them.
자신을 설득시키려는 의도를

동료들과 나는 수천 명의 저항하는 졸업생이 기부하도록 납득시키는 것을 의도한 두 개의 다른 메시지들을 실험하는 한 연구를 진행했다. 하나의 메시지는 좋은 일을 할 기회를 강조했다. 기부하는 것은 학생들, 교직원, 그리고 직원들에게 이익을 줄 것이다. 다른 하나는 좋은 기분을 느끼는 기회를 강조했다. 기부자들은 기부의 따뜻한 온기를 즐길 것이다. 그 두 메시지들은 똑같이 효과적이었다. 두 경우 모두에서, 6.5%의 마음 내키지 않은 졸업생이 결국에는 기부했다. 그러고 나서 우리는 그것들을 결합했는데, 왜냐하면 두 개의 이유가 한 개보다 더 낫기 때문이다. 하지만 그렇지 않았다. 우리가 그 두 이유들을 합쳤을 때, 기부율은 3% 아래로 떨어졌다. 각각의 이유가 단독으로는 그 두 개가 합쳐진 것보다 두 배 이상 더 효과적이었다. 청중은 이미 회의적이었다. 우리가 그들에게 기부할 서로 다른 종류의 이유를 주었을 때, 우리는 누군가가 그들을 설득하려고 하는 중이라는 그들의 인식을 유발했고 — 그리고 그들은 그것에 맞서 스스로를 보호했다.
→ 위에서 언급된 실험에서, 기부할 두 개의 서로 다른 이유들이 (A) 동시에 주어졌을 때, 청자는 자신을 설득시키려는 의도를 알아차릴 수 있었기 때문에 (B) 납득될 가능성이 더 작았다.

	(A)		(B)
①	**동시에**	……	**납득될**
②	개별적으로	……	당황한
③	자주	……	짜증난
④	개별적으로	……	만족한
⑤	동시에	……	화가난

문제풀이

졸업생들에게 기부하도록 설득하기 위해 각각의 이유를 개별적으로 제시했을 경우가 이유를 합쳐서 제시했을 때 보다 효과적이었다는 실험 결과로 보아, 요약문의 빈칸 (A)에는 'simultaneously(동시에)'가, (B)에는 'convinced(납득될)'가 가장 적절하다.

어휘·어구

colleague 동료
experiment 실험
convince 납득시키다
resistant 저항하는
donation 기부
emphasize 강조하다
opportunity 기회
donor 기부자
glow 온기, 만족감
equally 동등하게
effective 효과적인
unwilling 내키지 않는
ended up v-ing 결국 ~하게 되다
combine 결합시키다
trigger 유발하다
awareness 인식
persuade 설득하다
shield 보호하다
mentioned 언급된
recognize 알아차리다
simultaneously 동시에
convinced 납득될
separately 개별적으로
confused 당황한
frequently 자주
annoyed 짜증 난
offended 화가 난

정답률 68%

3. ③ 청소년들의 학문적 성공의 요인

직독/직해

According to a study of Swedish adolescents, /
스웨덴 청소년들에 대한 연구에 따르면 /

an important factor of adolescents' academic success /
청소년들의 학문적 성공의 중요한 요인은 /

is how they respond to challenges.
그들이 어려움에 반응하는 방식이다

The study reports / that when facing difficulties, /
그 연구는 보고한다 / 어려움을 직면했을 때 /

adolescents exposed to an authoritative parenting style /
권위가 있는 양육 방식에 노출된 청소년들은 /

are less likely to be passive, helpless, /
덜 수동적이고, 덜 무기력하다고 /

and afraid to fail. 그리고 실패를 덜 두려워한다고

Another study of nine high schools /
9개 고등학교에서 진행된 또 다른 연구는 /

in Wisconsin and northern California /
Wisconsin과 northern California에 있는 /

indicates / that children of authoritative parents /
밝히고 있다 / 권위가 있는 부모들의 아이들이 /

do well in school, /
학습을 잘 한다고 /

because these parents put a lot of effort /
그 이유는 이런 부모들이 많은 노력을 기울이기 때문이었다 /

into getting involved in their children's school activities.
아이들의 학교 활동에 관여하는 데 있어

That is, / authoritative parents are significantly more likely to help /
즉 / 권위가 있는 부모들은 도와줄 가능성이 훨씬 더 크다 /

their children with homework, / to attend school programs, /
아이들의 숙제를 (도와줄) / 학교 프로그램에 참여할 /

to watch their children in sports, / and to help students select courses.
스포츠에 참여하는 아이들을 지켜볼 / 그리고 아이들의 과목 선택을 도와줄

Moreover, / these parents are more aware of /
게다가 / 이런 부모들은 ~에 대해 더 잘 인지한다 /

what their children do /
그들의 아이들이 학교에서 하고 있는 일 /

and how they perform in school.
그리고 그들이 학교에서 수행하는 방식(에 대해)

Finally, / authoritative parents praise /
마지막으로 / 권위가 있는 부모들은 칭찬한다 /

academic excellence and the importance of working hard /
학문적 탁월함과 근면함의 중요성을 /

more than other parents do.
다른 부모들보다 더 많이

→ The studies above show /
위 연구는 보여준다 /

that the children of authoritative parents /
권위가 있는 부모의 아이들이 /

often succeed academically, /
종종 학업 성취가 좋다는 것을 /

since they are more willing to deal with their difficulties /
그들이(아이들이) 어려움에 더 기꺼이 대처하려 하기 때문에 /

and are affected by their parents' active involvement.
그리고 부모들의 적극적인 관여에 의해 영향을 받기 때문에

스웨덴 청소년들에 대한 연구에 따르면, 청소년들의 학문적 성공의 중요한 요인은 그들이 어려움에 반응하는 방식이다. 그 연구는, 어려움을 직면했을 때, 권위가 있는 양육 방식에 노출된 청소년들은 덜 수동적이고, 덜 무기력하며, 실패를 덜 두려워한다고 보고하고 있다. Wisconsin과 northern California에 있는 9개 고등학교에서 진행된 또 다른 연구는 권위가 있는 부모들의 아이들이 학습을 잘 하는데, 그 이유는 이런 부모들이 아이들의 학교 활동에 관여하는 데 있어 많은 노력을 기울이기 때문이라고 밝히고 있다. 즉, 권위가 있는 부모들은 아이들의 숙제를 도와주고, 학교 프로그램에 참여하며, 스포츠에 참여하는 아이들을 지켜보고, 아이들의 과목 선택을 도와줄 가능성이 훨씬 더 크다. 게다가, 이런 부모들은 그들의 아이들이 학교에서 하고 있는 일과 수행하는 방식에 대해 더 잘 인지한다. 마지막으로, 권위가 있는 부모들은 다른 부모들보다 학문적 탁월함과 근면함의 중요성을 더 많이 칭찬한다.

→ 위 연구는 권위가 있는 부모의 아이들이 어려움에 더 (A) 기꺼이 대처하려 하며, 그 부모들의 (B) 적극적인 관여에 의해 영향을 받기 때문에 종종 학업 성취가 좋다는 것을 보여준다.

	(A)		(B)
①	할 것 같은	······	무작위의
②	기꺼이	······	최소의
③	**기꺼이**	**······**	**적극적인**
④	주저하는	······	원치 않는
⑤	주저하는	······	변함없는

문제풀이

이 글은 권위가 있는 부모의 자녀들은 덜 수동적이고 덜 무기력하며 실패를 덜 두려워해서 학습을 잘하는데, 이는 부모가 자녀들의 학교 활동에 관여하는 데 많은 노력을 기울이고, 자녀들이 학교에서 하는 일을 더 잘 인지하며, 자녀들에게 학문적 탁월함과 근면함의 중요성을 더 많이 칭찬하기 때문이라는 내용의 글이다. 따라서 요약문의 빈칸 (A)에는 'willing(기꺼이)'이, (B)에는 'active(적극적인)'가 가장 적절하다.

어휘·어구

adolescent 청소년
respond 반응하다
challenge 어려움, 도전
expose 노출하다
authoritative 권위가 있는
passive 수동적인
helpless 무기력한
indicate 나타내다
significantly 상당히
select 선택하다
be aware of ~을 인지하다, 알다
perform 수행하다
excellence 탁월함
involvement 관여, 개입
random 무작위의
minimal 최소의
hesitant 주저하는
constant 변함없는

정답률 57%

4. ① 망가니즈를 이용하는 common blackberry의 능력

직독/직해

The common blackberry (*Rubus allegheniensis*) has /
common blackberry(Rubus allegheniensis)는 가지고 있다 /

an amazing ability to move manganese /
망가니즈를 옮기는 놀라운 능력을 /

from one layer of soil to another /
토양의 한 층에서 다른 층으로 /

using its roots. 뿌리를 이용하여

This may seem like a funny talent /
이것은 기이한 재능처럼 보일 수도 있다 /

for a plant to have, / but it all becomes clear /
식물이 가지기에는 / 그러나 그것은 전부 명확해진다 /

when you realize the effect /
여러분이 영향을 깨닫고 나면 /

it has on nearby plants. 그것이 근처의 식물들에 미치는

Manganese can be very harmful to plants, /
망가니즈는 식물들에게 매우 해로울 수 있다 /

especially at high concentrations.
특히 고농도일 때 그렇다

Common blackberry is unaffected /
common blackberry는 영향을 받지 않는다 /

by damaging effects of this metal /
이 금속 원소의 해로운 효과에 의해 /

and has evolved two different ways /
그리고 다른 두 가지 방법을 발달시켰다 /

of using manganese to its advantage.
망가니즈를 자신에게 유리하게 사용하는

First, / it redistributes manganese /
첫 번째로 / 그것은 망가니즈를 재분배한다 /

from deeper soil layers to shallow soil layers /
깊은 토양층으로부터 얕은 토양층으로 /

using its roots as a small pipe.
그것의 뿌리를 작은 관으로 사용하여

Second, / it absorbs manganese / as it grows, /
두 번째로 / 그것은 망가니즈를 흡수한다 / 성장하면서 /

concentrating the metal in its leaves.
그 금속 원소를 잎에 농축한다

When the leaves drop and decay, /
잎이 떨어지고 부패할 때 /

their concentrated manganese deposits /
그것의 농축된 망가니즈 축적물은 /

further poison the soil around the plant.
그 식물 주변의 토양을 독성 물질로 더욱 오염시킨다

For plants / that are not immune to /
식물들에게 / 면역이 없는 /

the toxic effects of manganese, /
망가니즈의 유독한 영향에 /

this is very bad news. 이것은 매우 나쁜 소식이다

Essentially, / 본질적으로 /

the common blackberry eliminates competition /
common blackberry는 경쟁자를 제거한다 /

by poisoning its neighbors / with heavy metals.
그것의 이웃을 중독시킴으로써 / 중금속으로

→ The common blackberry has an ability to increase /
common blackberry는 증가시키는 능력을 가지고 있다 /

the amount of manganese /
망가니즈의 양을 /

in the surrounding upper soil, /
주변의 위쪽 토양에 있는 /

which makes the nearby soil quite deadly /
그것은 근처의 토양을 치명적이게 만든다 /

for other plants. 다른 식물에게

---

common blackberry(*Rubus allegheniensis*)는 뿌리를 이용하여 토양의 한 층에서 다른 층으로 망가니즈를 옮기는 놀라운 능력을 가지고 있다. 이것은 식물이 가지기에는 기이한 재능처럼 보일 수도 있지만, 그것이 근처의 식물들에 미치는 영향을 깨닫고 나면 전부 명확해진다. 망가니즈는 식물들에 매우 해로울 수 있고, 특히 고농도일 때 그렇다. common blackberry는 이 금속 원소의 해로운 효과에 의해 영향을 받지 않으며, 망가니즈를 자신에게 유리하게 사용하는 다른 두 가지 방법을 발달시켰다. 첫 번째로, 그것은 뿌리를 작은 관으로 사용하여 망가니즈를 깊은 토양층으로부터 얕은 토양층으로 재분배한다. 두 번째로, 그것은 성장하면서 망가니즈를 흡수하여 그 금속 원소를 잎에 농축한다. 잎이 떨어지고 부패할 때, 그것의 농축된 망가니즈 축적물은 그 식물 주변의 토양을 독성 물질로 더욱 오염시킨다. 망가니즈의 유독한 영향에 면역이 없는 식물들에게 이것은 매우 나쁜 소식이다. 본질적으로, common blackberry는 중금속으로 그것의 이웃을 중독시킴으로써 경쟁자를 제거한다.

→ common blackberry는 주변의 위쪽 토양에 있는 망가니즈의 양을 (A) 증가시키는 능력이 있는데, 그것은 근처의 토양이 다른 식물에게 (B) 치명적이게 만든다.

	(A)		(B)
①	**증가시키는**	**······**	**치명적이게**
②	증가시키는	······	유리하게
③	나타내는	······	영양가 있는
④	줄이는	······	건조하게
⑤	줄이는	······	따뜻하게

문제풀이

common blackberry는 식물들에게 매우 해로운 망가니즈를 자신의 뿌리를 이용하여 옮기는 능력이 있고, 망가니즈를 자신에게 유리하게 사용하는 방법을 발달시켰다는 내용의 글이다. 망가니즈를 깊은 토양층으로부터 얕은 토양층으로 재분배하고, 성장하면서 망가니즈를 흡수해서 잎에 농축한 뒤, 잎이 떨어지고 부패하면 농축된 망가니즈 축적물이 주변 토양을 오염시켜서 경쟁자를 제거한다는 내용을 통해, 요약문의 빈칸 (A)에는 'increase(증가시키다)'가, (B)에는 'deadly(치명적이게)'가 가장 적절하다.

《 어휘·어구 》

layer 층
funny 기이한
talent 재능
realize 깨닫다
effect 영향
nearby 근처
harmful 해로운
especially 특히
concentration 농도
unaffected 영향을 받지 않는
damaging 해로운
evolve 발달시키다
advantage 장점, 이점
redistribute 재분배하다
shallow 얕은
absorb 흡수하다
decay 썩다
poison (독성 물질로) 오염시키다, 중독시키다
immune 면역이 있는
toxic 유독한
essentially 본질적으로
eliminate 제거하다
competition 경쟁자
neighbor 이웃
surrounding 주변의
advantageous 유리한
indicate 가리키다, 나타내다
nutritious 영양분이 있는, 영양의
reduce 줄이다

정답률 53%

5. ② 과학적 불확실성에 대한 미디어의 지나친 단순화

직독/직해

There is often a lot of uncertainty /
종종 많은 불확실성이 존재한다 /
in the realm of science, / 과학의 영역에는 /
which the general public finds uncomfortable.
일반 대중은 그것을 불편하다고 느낀다
They don't want "informed guesses," /
그들은 '정보에 근거한 추측'을 원하지 않고 /
they want certainties / that make their lives easier, /
그들은 확실성을 원하는데 / 자신의 삶을 더 편하게 만들어 주는 /
and science is often unequipped /
그런데 과학이 종종 갖춰져 있지 않다 /
to meet these demands. 이러한 요구를 만족시키도록
In particular, / 특히 /
the human body is fantastically complex, /
인간의 신체는 굉장히 복잡하다 /
and some scientific answers can never be provided /
그리고 어떤 과학적인 답변은 절대 제공될 수 없다 /
in black-or-white terms. 흑백 양자택일의 말로는
All this is why the media tends to oversimplify scientific research /
이 모든 것이 미디어가 과학적 연구를 지나치게 단순화하는 경향이 있는 이유이다 /
when presenting it to the public.
그것을 대중에게 제시할 때
In their eyes, / 그들의 눈에는 /
they're just "giving people what they want" /
그들은 단지 '사람들에게 그들이 원하는 것을 제공하고' 있는 것이다 /
as opposed to offering more accurate but complex information /
더 정확하지만 복잡한 정보를 제공하는 것과는 반대로 /
that very few people will read or understand.
극소수의 사람들만이 읽거나 이해할
A perfect example of this /
이것의 완벽한 하나의 예시는 /
is how people want definitive answers /
사람들이 확정적인 답변을 원하는 방식이다 /
as to which foods are "good" and "bad."
어떤 음식이 '좋은'지 그리고 '나쁜'지에 관해
Scientifically speaking, / 과학적으로 말하자면 /
there are no "good" and "bad" foods; /
'좋고', '나쁜' 음식은 없다 /
rather, / food quality exists on a continuum, /
오히려 / 음식의 질은 연속체상에 존재한다 /
meaning / that some foods are better than others /
의미한다 / 어떤 음식들이 다른 것들보다 '더 낫다'는 것을 /
when it comes to general health and well-being.
일반 건강과 웰빙 면에서
→ With regard to general health, /
일반 건강과 관련하여 /
science, / by its nature, /
과학은 / 본질적으로 /
does not satisfy the public's demands / for certainty, /
대중의 요구를 만족시키지 않는다 / 확실성에 대한 /
which leads to the media giving less complicated answers / to the public.
이것은 미디어가 덜 복잡한 답변을 제공하도록 이끈다 / 대중에게

과학의 영역에는 종종 많은 불확실성이 존재하며 일반 대중은 그것을 불편하다고 느낀다. 그들은 '정보에 근거한 추측'을 원하지 않으며 그들은 자신의 삶을 더 편하게 만들어 주는 확실성을 원하는데, 과학이 종종 이러한 요구를 만족시키도록 갖춰져 있지 않다. 특히 인간의 신체는 굉장히 복잡하며 어떤 과학적인 답변은 흑백 양자택일의 말로는 절대 제공될 수 없다. 이 모든 것이 미디어가 과학적 연구를 대중에게 제시할 때 그것을 지나치게 단순화하는 경향이 있는 이유이다. 그들의 눈에는 극소수의 사람들만이 읽거나 이해할 더 정확하지만 복잡한 정보를 제공하는 것과는 반대로 그들은 단지 '사람들에게 그들이 원하는 것을 제공하고' 있는 것이다. 이것의 완벽한 하나의 예시는 어떤 음식이 '좋은'지 그리고 '나쁜'지에 관해 사람들이 확정적인 답변을 원하는 방식이다. 과학적으로 말하자면 '좋고', '나쁜' 음식은 없으며, 오히려 음식의 질은 연속체상에 존재하는데 이는 어떤 음식들이 다른 것들보다 일반 건강과 웰빙면에서 '더 낫다'는 것을 의미한다.
→ 일반 건강과 관련하여 과학이 본질적으로 확실성에 대한 대중의 요구를 (A) 만족시키지 않으며, 이것은 미디어가 대중에게 덜 (B) 복잡한 답변을 제공하도록 이끈다.

	(A)		(B)
①	만족시키다	……	단순한
②	**만족시키다**	……	**복잡한**
③	무시하다	……	어려운
④	무시하다	……	단순한
⑤	거부하다	……	복잡한

문제풀이

'과학의 영역에는 일반 대중이 불편하게 여기는 불확실성이 존재하고, 특히 건강에 관련해서는 과학적인 답변이 대중의 요구를 만족시키지 못하고, 이것이 미디어가 과학적 연구를 대중에게 제시할 때 지나치게 단순화하는 경향이 있는 이유다.'라는 요지의 글이다. 따라서 요약문의 (A)에는 'science is often unequipped to meet these demands(과학이 종종 이러한 요구를 만족시키도록 갖춰져 있지 않다.)'에서 'meet(만족시키다)'와 같은 의미를 갖는 'satisfy(만족시키다)'가, (B)에는 'All this is why media tends to oversimplify scientific research when presenting it to the public.(이 모든 것이 미디어가 과학적 연구를 대중에게 제시할 때 그것을 지나치게 단순화하는 경향이 있는 이유이다.)'에서 'oversimplified(지나치게 단순한)'와 반대의 의미가 있는 'complicated(복잡한)'가 가장 적절하다.

《 어휘·어구 》

uncertainty 불확실성
uncomfortable 불편한
demand 요구하다
in particular 특히
complex 복잡한
terms 조건, 관점
oppose 대립하다
offering 제공
accurate 정확한

정답률 41%

6. ① 의견 불일치가 학습의 흥미를 높인다

직독/직해

Nancy Lowry and David Johnson conducted an experiment /
Nancy Lowry와 David Johnson은 실험을 했다 /
to study a teaching environment / 교수 환경을 연구하기 위해 /
where fifth and sixth graders / 5학년과 6학년 학생들이 /
were assigned to interact on a topic.
한 주제에 대해 상호작용을 하게 하는
With one group, / the discussion was led /
한 그룹에서는 / 토론이 유도되었다 /
in a way that built an agreement. 합의를 도출하는 방식으로
With the second group, / 두 번째 그룹에서는 /
the discussion was designed to produce /
토론이 만들도록 설계되었다 /
disagreements about the right answer.
옳은 정답에 대해 불일치를
Students who easily reached an agreement /
쉽게 합의에 도달한 학생들은 /
were less interested in the topic, / 주제에 흥미를 덜 느꼈다 /
studied less, / and were less likely to visit the library /
더 적게 공부했다 / 그리고 도서관에 가는 경향이 더 적었다 /
to get additional information. 추가적인 정보를 얻기 위해
The most noticeable difference, / though, /
가장 눈에 띄는 차이는 / 하지만 /
was revealed / when teachers showed a special film /
나타났다 / 교사가 특별한 영화를 보여주었을 때 /
about the discussion topic / — during lunch time!
토론 주제와 관련된 / 점심시간 동안
Only 18 percent of the agreement group /
동의한 그룹의 18%만이 /
missed lunch time / 점심시간을 놓쳤다 /
to see the film, / 영화를 보기 위해 /
but 45 percent of the students from the disagreement group /
하지만 동의하지 않은 그룹 학생들의 45%는 /
stayed for the film. 그 영화를 보기 위해 남았다
The thirst to fill a knowledge gap / — to find out /
지식 차이를 채우려는 열망은 / 알기 위해 /
who was right within the group /
그룹 내에서 누가 옳았는지 /
— can be more powerful / 더 강할 수 있다 /
than the thirst for slides and jungle gyms.
미끄럼틀과 정글짐을 향한 열망보다
➡ According to the experiment above, /
위의 실험에 따르면 /
students' interest in a topic increases /
주제에 대한 학생들의 흥미는 증가한다 /
when they are encouraged to differ.
학생들이 (의견을) 달리하도록 장려될 때

Nancy Lowry와 David Johnson은 교수 환경을 연구하기 위해 5학년과 6학년 학생들이 한 주제에 대해 상호작용을 하게 하는 실험을 했다. 한 그룹에서는 토론이 합의를 도출하는 방식으로 유도되었다. 두 번째 그룹에서는 토론이 옳은 정답에 대해 불일치를 낳도록 설계되었다. 쉽게 합의에 도달한 학생들은 주제에 흥미를 덜 느끼고 더 적게 공부했으며, 추가적인 정보를 얻기 위해 도서관에 가는 경향이 더 적었다. 하지만 가장 눈에 띄는 차이는 교사가 점심시간 동안 토론 주제와 관련된 특별한 영화를 보여주었을 때 나타났다. 동의한 그룹의 18%만이 영화를 보기 위해 점심시간을 놓쳤으나, 동의하지 않은 그룹 학생들의 45%는 그 영화를 보기 위해 남았다. 그룹 내에서 누가 옳았는지 알기 위해 지식 차이를 채우려는 열망은 미끄럼틀과 정글짐을 향한 열망보다 더 강할 수 있다.
➡ 위의 실험에 따르면, 주제에 대한 학생들의 흥미는 학생들이 (B) (의견을) 달리하도록 장려될 때 (A) 증가한다.

① 증가한다 …… 달리하도록
② 증가한다 …… 인정하도록
③ 증가한다 …… 협력하도록
④ 감소한다 …… 참여하도록
⑤ 감소한다 …… 논쟁하도록

문제풀이

토론의 합의를 쉽게 도출한 그룹보다 토론에서 불일치가 많았던 그룹의 학생들이 누가 옳았는지를 알기 위해 지식 차이를 채우려는 열망이 강하다는 실험 결과를 보아, 요약문의 빈칸 (A)에는 'increases(증가한다)'가, (B)에는 'differ(다르다)'가 가장 적절하다.

《 어휘·어구 》

conduct an experiment 실험을 하다
environment 환경
assign 부여하다
interact 상호 작용하다
discussion 토론
disagreement 불일치
additional 추가적인
noticeable 눈에 띄는
thirst 열망, 갈망
encourage 장려하다
cooperate 협동하다
argue 논쟁하다

7. ② 휴대전화의 존재 여부에 따른 공감 수준의 차이

직독/직해

In one study, / 한 연구에서 /
researchers asked pairs of strangers / 연구자들은 서로 모르는 사람들끼리 짝을 이루어 /
to sit down in a room / and chat. 한 방에 앉아 있게 했다 / 그리고 이야기하게 했다
In half of the rooms, / a cell phone was placed / 절반의 방에는 / 휴대전화가 놓여 있었다 /
on a nearby table; / 근처 탁자 위에 /
in the other half, / no phone was present. 나머지 절반에는 / 휴대전화가 없었다
After the conversations had ended, / 대화가 끝난 후 /
the researchers asked the participants / 연구자들은 참가자들에게 물었다 /
what they thought of each other. 그들이 서로 어떻게 생각하는지를
Here's what they learned: 여기에 그들이 알게 된 것이 있다 /
when a cell phone was present in the room, / 방에 휴대전화가 있을 때 /
the participants reported / 참가자들은 말했다 /
the quality of their relationship was worse / 자신들의 관계의 질이 더 나빴다고 /
than those who'd talked / 대화했던 참가자들에 비해 /
in a cell phone-free room. 휴대전화가 없는 방에서
The pairs who talked / 대화한 짝들은 /
in the rooms with cell phones / 휴대전화가 있는 방에서 /
thought their partners showed less empathy. 자신의 상대가 공감을 덜 보여 주었다고 생각했다
Think of all the times / you've sat down / 모든 순간을 생각해 보라 / 당신이 자리에 앉아 있던 /
to have lunch with a friend / 친구와 함께 점심을 먹기 위해 /
and set your phone on the table. 그리고 탁자 위에 휴대전화를 놓았던
You might have felt good about yourself / 여러분은 스스로 잘했다고 느꼈을지 모른다 /
because you didn't pick it up / 여러분이 휴대전화를 집어 들지 않았으므로 /
to check your messages, / 메시지를 확인하기 위해 /
but your unchecked messages / 그러나 여러분의 확인되지 않은 메시지는 /
were still hurting your connection / 여전히 관계를 상하게 하고 있었다 /
with the person sitting across from you. 맞은편에 앉아 있는 사람과의
➡ The presence of a cell phone/ 휴대전화의 존재는 /
weakensthe connection / 관계를 약화시킨다 /
between people involved in conversations, / 대화에 참여하는 사람들 간의 /
even when the phone is being ignored. 심지어 휴대전화가 무시되고 있을 때조차

한 연구에서, 연구자들은 서로 모르는 사람들끼리 짝을 이루어 한 방에 앉아서 이야기하게 했다. 절반의 방에는 근처 탁자 위에 휴대전화가 놓여 있었고, 나머지 절반에는 휴대전화가 없었다. 대화가 끝난 후, 연구자들은 참가자들에게 그들이 서로 어떻게 생각하는지를 물었다. 여기에 그들이 알게 된 것이 있다. 휴대전화가 없는 방에서 대화했던 참가자들에 비해 방에 휴대전화가 있을 때 참가자들은 자신들의 관계의 질이 더 나빴다고 말했다. 휴대전화가 있는 방에서 대화한 짝들은 자신의 상대가 공감을 덜 보여 주었다고 생각했다. 친구와 점심을 먹기 위해 자리에 앉아 탁자 위에 휴대전화를 놓았던 모든 순간을 생각해 보라. 메시지를 확인하기 위해 휴대전화를 집어 들지 않았으므로 스스로 잘했다고 느꼈을지 모르지만, 확인되지 않은 여러분의 메시지는 여전히 맞은편에 앉아 있는 사람과의 관계를 상하게 하고 있었다.
➡ 휴대전화의 존재는 심지어 휴대전화가 (B) 무시되고 있을 때조차 대화에 참여하는 사람들 간의 관계를 (A) 약화시킨다.

	(A)		(B)
①	약화시킨다	……	응답받고
②	**약화시킨다**	……	**무시되고**
③	새롭게 한다	……	응답받고
④	유지한다	……	무시되고
⑤	유지한다	……	갱신되고

문제풀이

휴대전화가 있는 방과 없는 방에서 낯선 사람들끼리 대화를 한 후 서로 느끼는 공감 정도에 대한 실험 글로, 휴대전화가 있는 경우 상대방이 자신에 대해 공감을 덜 보여주었다고 생각했다는 결과를 통해 요약문의 빈칸 (A)에는 'weakens(약화시키다)'가, (B)에는 'ignored(무시하다)'가 가장 적절하다.

《 어휘·어구 》

pair 짝
stranger 모르는 사람, 낯선 사람
chat 이야기하다
place 놓다, 두다
nearby 근처의
present 있는, 존재하는
conversation 대화
participant 참가자
report 말하다, 전하다
quality 질
relationship 관계
partner 상대
connection 관계, 연결
presence 존재
involved 관련된
weaken 약화시키다
ignore 무시하다
renew 새롭게 하다
maintain 유지하다
update 갱신하다

8. ① 내집단과 동일시하려는 경향

직독/직해

In their study in 2007 / 2007년 그들의 연구에서 /
Katherine Kinzler and her colleagues at Harvard showed / Katherine Kinzler와 그녀의 하버드 동료들은 보여 주었다 /
that our tendency to identify with an in-group / 내(內)집단과 동일시하려는 우리의 경향이 /
to a large degree / 상당 부분 /
begins in infancy / and may be innate. 유아기에 시작되다는 (것을) / 그리고 선천적일지 수도 있다는 (것을)
Kinzler and her team took a bunch of five-month-olds / Kinzler와 그녀의 팀은 5개월 된 아기들을 골랐다 /
whose families only spoke English / 가족들이 오직 영어만 말하는 /
and showed the babies two videos. 그리고 그 아이들에게 두 개의 영상을 보여 주었다
In one video, / a woman was speaking English. 한 영상에서는 / 한 여성이 영어를 말하고 있었다
In the other, / a woman was speaking Spanish. 다른 영상에서는 / 한 여성이 스페인어를 말하고 있었다
Then they were shown a screen / 그러고 나서 그들에게 화면을 보여 주었다 /
with both women side by side, / 나란히 있는 두 여성이 있는 /
not speaking. 모두 말없이
In infant psychology research, / 유아 심리학 연구에서 /
the standard measure for affinity or interest / 애착이나 관심의 표준 척도는 /
is attention / — babies will apparently stare longer / 주목인데 / 아기들은 분명히 더 오래 쳐다볼 것이다 /
at the things they like more. 그들이 더 좋아하는 것들을
In Kinzler's study, / Kinzler의 연구에서 /
the babies stared at the English speakers longer. 아기들은 영어 사용자들을 더 오래 쳐다보았다.
In other studies, / researchers have found / 다른 연구들에서 / 연구자들은 발견했다 /
that infants are more likely to take / 유아들이 받을 가능성이 더 높다는 것을 /
a toy offered by someone / 어떤 사람이 제공하는 장난감을 /
who speaks the same language as them. 자신들과 같은 언어를 사용하는
Psychologists routinely cite these and other experiments / 심리학자들은 이것들과 다른 실험들을 반복해서 인용한다 /
as evidence of our built-in evolutionary preference / 우리의 내재된 진화론적인 선호에 대한 증거로 /
for "our own kind." '우리와 같은 종류'에 관한
➡ Infants' more favorable responses / 유아들의 더 호의적인 반응은 /
to those who use a familiar language / 친숙한 언어를 사용하는 사람들에 대한 /
show that there can be a(n) inborn tendency / 선천적인 경향이 있을 수 있음을 보여 준다 /
to prefer in-group members. 내집단 구성원들을 선호하는

2007년 그들의 연구에서 Katherine Kinzler와 그녀의 하버드 동료들은 내(內)집단과 동일시하려는 우리의 경향이 상당 부분 유아기에 시작되고 선천적일지 수도 있다는 것을 보여 주었다. Kinzler와 그녀의 팀은 가족들이 오직 영어만 말하는 한 무리의 5개월 된 아기들을 골라 그들에게 두 개의 영상을 보여 주었다. 한 영상에서는, 한 여성이 영어를 말하고 있었다. 다른 영상에서는, 한 여성이 스페인어를 말하고 있었다. 그러고 나서 그들에게 두 여성 모두 말없이 나란히 있는 화면을 보여 주었다. 유아 심리학 연구에서 애착이나 관심의 표준 척도는 주목인데, 아기들은 분명히 그들이 더 좋아하는 것들을 더 오래 쳐다볼 것이다. Kinzler의 연구에서 아기들은 영어 사용자들을 더 오래 쳐다보았다. 다른 연구들에서 연구자들은 유아들이 자신들과 같은 언어를 사용하는 사람이 제공하는 장난감을 받을 가능성이 더 높다는 것을 발견했다. 심리학자들은 '우리와 같

은 종류'에 관한 우리의 내재된 진화론적인 선호에 대한 증거로 이것들과 다른 실험들을 반복해서 인용한다.

➡ (A) 친숙한 언어를 사용하는 사람들에 대한 유아들의 더 호의적인 반응은 내집단 구성원들을 선호하는 (B) 선천적인 경향이 있을 수 있음을 보여 준다.

① 친숙한 …… 선천적인
② 친숙한 …… 후천적인
③ 외국의 …… 문화적인
④ 외국의 …… 학습된
⑤ 공식적인 …… 타고난

문제풀이

내(內)집단과 동일시하려는 우리의 경향이 상당 부분 유아기에 시작되고 선천적일 수 있다는 내용의 글이다. 오직 영어만 말하는 아기들은 영어 사용자들을 더 오래 쳐다보았고, 자신들과 같은 언어를 사용하는 사람이 제공하는 장난감을 받을 가능성이 더 높다는 것을 발견했다는 실험 결과를 통해 요약문의 (A)에는 'familiar(친숙한)'가, (B)에는 'inborn(선천적인)'이 들어가는 것이 가장 적절하다.

어휘·어구

colleague 동료
tendency 경향
identify 동일시하다
to a degree 어느 정도
infancy 유아기
innate 타고난
side by side 나란히
psychology 심리학
standard 표준의
measure 척도, 기준
attention 주의, 집중
apparently 명백히
routinely 일상적으로, 언제나
cite 인용하다
evidence 증거
evolutionary 진화의, 발달의
preference 선호
favorable 호의적인
response 반응
familiar 친숙한
inborn 선척적인
acquired 후천적인
innate 타고난

정답률 67%

9. ① 음악과 감정의 연관성

One way that music could express emotion /
음악이 감정을 표현할 수 있는 한 방법은 /
is simply through a learned association.
단지 학습된 연관을 통해서이다
Perhaps there is nothing naturally sad about a piece of music /
악곡에 대해 본질적으로 슬픈 무언가가 있는 것은 아닐 것이다 /
in a minor key, or played slowly with low notes.
단조나 낮은 음으로 느리게 연주되는
Maybe we have just come to hear certain kinds of music as sad /
우리는 어떤 종류의 음악을 슬프다고 듣게 되는 것 같다 /
because we have learned to associate them in our culture with sad events like funerals.
우리가 우리의 문화 속에서 그것들을 장례식과 같은 슬픈 일과 연관시키는 것을 학습해 왔기 때문에
If this view is correct, /
만약 이 관점이 옳다면 /
we should have difficulty interpreting the emotions /
우리는 감정을 이해하는 데 분명 어려움이 있을 것이다 /
expressed in culturally unfamiliar music.
문화적으로 친숙하지 않은 음악에 표현되는
Totally opposed to this view is the position /
이 관점과 완전히 반대되는 입장이 있다 /
that the link between music and emotion is one of resemblance.
음악과 감정 사이의 연결고리는 유사함이라는 것이다
For example, /
예컨대 /
when we feel sad / 슬프다고 느낄 때 /
we move slowly and speak slowly and in a low-pitched voice.
우리는 느리게 움직이고 낮은 음의 목소리로 느리게 말한다
Thus when we hear slow, low music, /
따라서 우리가 느리고 낮은 음의 음악을 들을 때 /
we hear it as sad.
우리는 그것을 슬프게 듣는다
If this view is correct, /
만약 이 관점이 옳다면
we should have little difficulty understanding the emotion /
우리는 감정을 이해하는데 분명 어려움이 거의 없을 것이다 /
expressed in culturally unfamiliar music.
문화적으로 친숙하지 않은 음악에 표현되는
➡ It is believed that /
다음과 같이 믿어진다 /
emotion expressed in music can be understood /
음악에 표현된 감정은 이해될 수 있다 /
through a culturally learned association /
문화적으로 학습된 연관을 통해서 /
or it can be understood /
또는 그것은 이해될 수 있다 /
due to the similarity between music and emotion.
음악과 감정 사이의 유사성 때문에

음악이 감정을 표현할 수 있는 한 방법은 단지 학습된 연관을 통해서이다. 단조나 낮은 음으로 느리게 연주된 악곡에 대해 본질적으로 슬픈 무언가가 있는 것은 아닐 것이다. 우리는 어떤 종류의 음악을 슬프다고 듣게 되는데 우리가 우리의 문화 속에서 그것들을 장례식과 같은 슬픈 일과 연관시키는 것을 학습해 왔기 때문일 것이다. 만약 이 관점이 옳다면, 우리는 문화적으로 친숙하지 않은 음악에 표현된 감정을 이해하는데 분명 어려움이 있을 것이다. 이 관점과 완전히 반대되는 입장은 음악과 감정 사이의 연결고리는 유사함이라는 것이다. 예컨대, 슬프다고 느낄 때 우리는 느리게 움직이고 낮은 음의 목소리로 느리게 말한다. 따라서 우리가 느리고 낮은 음의 음악을 들을 때, 우리는 그것을 슬프게 듣는다. 만약 이 관점이 옳다면, 우리는 문화적으로 친숙하지 않은 음악에 표현된 감정을 이해하는데 분명 어려움이 거의 없을 것이다.

➡ 음악에 표현된 감정은 (A) 문화적으로 학습된 연관을 통해서 이해될 수 있다고 믿어지거나, 혹은 음악과 감정 사이의 (B) 유사성 때문에 이해될 수 있다고 믿어진다.

① 문화적으로 — 유사성
② 문화적으로 — 균형
③ 사회적으로 — 차이
④ 바르지 않게 — 관련
⑤ 바르지 않게 — 대조

문제풀이

음악이 감정을 표현할 수 있는 두 가지 관점에 관한 글이다. 한 방법은 문화 속에서 학습된 음악과 감정의 연관을 통해서이고 그와 대조되는 관점은 음악과 감정 사이에 유사함이라는 연결고리가 있다는 것이다. 따라서 빈칸 (A)에는 'culturally(문화적으로)'가, (B)에는 'similarity(유사성)'이 들어가는 것이 적절하다. 따라서 정답은 ①이다.

어휘·어구

association 관련, 연관
minor key 단조
associate A with B A와 B를 연결 지어 생각하다
funeral 장례식
have difficulty -ing ~하는 데 어려움을 겪다
opposed 반대의, 대립된
resemblance 유사성, 닮음

정답률 73%

10. ③ 긍정적 이미지를 만들어 주는 좋은 코치

직독/직해

Have you noticed / that some coaches get the most out of their athletes / while others don't?
당신은 알아챘는가 / 어떤 코치들은 선수들에게서 최상의 결과를 이끌어낸다는 것을 / 반면 다른 코치들은 그렇지 않다는 것을
A poor coach will tell you / what you did wrong /
서투른 코치는 당신에게 말할 것이다 / 당신이 무엇을 잘못했는지 /
and then tell you not to do it again: /
그러고 나서 당신에게 다시 그러지 말라고 말할 것이다 /
"Don't drop the ball!"
공을 떨어뜨리지 마라
What happens next? /
그다음엔 무슨 일이 일어날까 /
The images you see in your head /
당신이 머릿속에서 보게 되는 이미지는 /
are images of you dropping the ball!
당신이 공을 떨어뜨리는 이미지이다
Naturally, / your mind recreates /
당연히 / 당신의 마음은 재현한다 /
what it just "saw" / based on what it's been told.
방금 "본" 것을 / 그것이 들은 것을 바탕으로
Not surprisingly, / you walk on the court /
놀랄 것도 없이 / 당신은 코트로 걸어간다 /
and drop the ball.
그리고 공을 떨어뜨린다
What does the good coach do?
좋은 코치는 무엇을 하는가
He or she points out / what could be improved, /
그 또는 그녀는 지적한다 / 개선될 수 있는 것을 /
but will then tell you /
그러나 그 후에 나서 당신에게 말할 것이다 /
how you could or should perform: /
어떻게 할 수 있는지 또는 어떻게 해야 하는지 /
"I know you'll catch the ball perfectly this time."
이번에는 네가 공을 완벽하게 잡을 거라는 걸 알아
Sure enough, / the next image in your mind /
아니나 다를까 / 다음으로 당신의 마음속에 떠오르는 이미지는 /
is you catching the ball and scoring a goal.
당신이 공을 '잡고' '득점하는' 것이다
Once again, / 다시 한번 /
your mind makes your last thoughts part of reality /
당신의 마음은 당신의 마지막 생각을 현실의 일부로 만든다 /
— but this time, / that "reality" is positive, not negative.
그러나 이번에는 / 그 "현실"이 부정적이지 않고, 긍정적이다
➡ Unlike ineffective coaches, /
유능하지 않은 코치와 달리 /
who focus on players' mistakes, /
선수의 실수에 초점을 맞추는 /
effective coaches help players improve /
유능한 코치는 선수들이 향상되도록 돕는다
by encouraging them to picture successful plays.
성공적인 경기를 상상하도록 격려함으로써

어떤 코치들은 선수들에게서 최상의 결과를 이끌어내는 반면, 다른 코치들은 그렇지 않다는 것을 알아챘는가? 서투른 코치는 당신이 무엇을 잘못했는지 알려 주고 나서, 다시는 그러지 말라고 말할 것이다: "공을 떨어뜨리지 마라!" 그다음엔 무슨 일이 일어날까? 당신이 머릿속에서 보게 되는 이미지는 당신이 공을 떨어뜨리는 이미지이다! 당연히, 당신의 마음은 그것이 들은 것을 바탕으로 방금 "본" 것을 재현한다. 놀랄 것도 없이, 당신은 코트에 걸어가서 공을 떨어뜨린다. 좋은 코치는 무엇을 하는가? 그 사람은 개선될 수 있는 것을 지적하지만, 그 후에 어떻게 할 수 있는지 또는 어떻게 해야 하는지에 대해 말할 것이다: "이번에는 네가 공을 완벽하게 잡을 거라는 걸 알아." 아니나 다를까, 다음으로 당신의 마음속에 떠오르는 이미지는 당신이 공을 '잡고' '득점하는' 것이다. 다시 한번, 당신의 마음은 당신의 마지막 생각을 현실의 일부로 만들지만, 이번에는, 그 "현실"이 부정적이지 않고, 긍정적이다.

➡ 선수의 (A) 실수에 초점을 맞추는 유능하지 않은 코치와 달리, 유능한 코치는 선수들이 성공적인 경기를 (B) 상상하도록 격려함으로써 그들이 향상되도록 돕는다.

① 점수 …… 완성하다
② 점수 …… 기억하다
③ 실수 …… 상상하다
④ 실수 …… 무시하다
⑤ 장점 …… 성취하다

문제풀이

서투른 코치는 공을 떨어뜨리지 말라고 말하고, 이 말을 들은 선수는 머릿속에 공이 떨어지는 모습만 남게 되어 같은 실수를 되풀이 하게 되지만, 유능한 코치는 공을 완벽하게 잡고 득점할 수 있을 것이라는 말을 하여 선수의 머릿속에 긍정적인 이미지를 심어준다는 내용의 글이다. 따라서 요약문의 빈칸 (A)는 'mistakes(실수)'가 (B)에는 'picture(상상하다)'가 오는 것이 적절하다.

○ 이렇게 풀자 요약문과 선택지를 먼저 읽어봄으로써 글의 주제를 추론해 보고, 글을 읽으면서 파악한 요지를 바탕으로 요약문의 빈칸에 들어갈 말로 가장 적절한 단어를 선택지에서 고르면 된다. 유능하지 않은 코치가 초점을 맞추는 것이 무엇인지, 유능한 코치가 선수들에게 성공적인 경기를 하기 위해 무엇을 격려하는지에 유의하면서 글을 읽어야 한다. 'A poor coach will tell you what you did wrong and then tell you not to do it again: "Don't drop the ball!"(서투른 코치는 당신이 무엇을 잘못했는지 알려 주고 나서 다시는 그러지 말라고 말할 것이다: "공을 떨어뜨리지 마라!")'에서 'what you did wrong'에 해당하는 말이 요약문의 빈칸 (A)에 적절하다는 것을 알 수 있고, 'He or she points out what could be improved, but will then tell you how you could or should perform: "I know you'll catch the ball perfectly this time."(그 사람은 개선될 수 있는 것을 지적하지만, 그 후에 어떻게 할 수 있는지 또는 어떻게 해야 하는지에 대해 말할 것이다: "이번에는 네가 공을 완벽하게 잡을 거라는 걸 알아.")'에서 요약문의 빈칸 (B)에 들어갈 말이 '긍정적인 이미지를 상상하도록 한다'의 의미가 될 수 있는 'picture(상상하다)'가 적절하다는 것을 알 수 있다.

《 어휘·어구 》

notice 알아채다
athlete (운동) 선수
naturally 당연히
point out ~을 지적하다
improve 개선시키다, 향상시키다
perform 수행하다
positive 긍정적인
negative 부정적인
ineffective 무능한, 효과없는
encourage 격려하다
complete 완성하다
picture 상상하다
ignore 무시하다
strength 장점
achieve 성취하다, 달성하다

11. ① 운전 중에 비협조적인 이유

직독/직해

While there are many evolutionary or cultural
진화적이거나 문화적인 많은 이유가 있지만
reasons / for cooperation, /
/ 협동에 대한 /
the eyes are one of the most important means of
눈은 가장 중요한 협동 수단 중 하나이다
cooperation, / and eye contact may be the most
/ 그리고 시선의 마주침은 가장 강력한 인간의 힘일지도 모른다
powerful human force / we lose in traffic.
/ 우리가 차량 운행 중에 잃는
It is, arguably, the reason / why humans, normally
이것이 거의 틀림없이 그 이유이다 / 왜 보통은 꽤 협조적인 종인 인간이
a quite cooperative species, / can become so
/ 그렇게 비협조적이 될 수 있는지
noncooperative / on the road.
/ 도로에서
Most of the time we are moving too fast — /
대부분의 시간에 우리가 너무 빨리 움직이고 있다 /
we begin to lose the ability / to keep eye contact
우리는 능력을 잃기 시작한다 / 시속 20마일 정도에서 시선을
around 20 miles per hour — / or it is not safe to
마주치는 / 또는 보는 것이 안전하지 않다
look.
Maybe our view is blocked.
어쩌면 우리의 시야가 차단되어 있을 수도 있다
Often other drivers are wearing sunglasses, /
흔히 다른 운전자들이 선글라스를 끼고 있다 /
or their car may have tinted windows.
또는 그들의 차는 색이 옅게 들어간 창문이 있을 지도 모른다
(And do you really want to make eye contact /
그리고 당신은 정말로 시선을 마주치고 싶은가? /
with those drivers?) 그러한 운전자들과
Sometimes we make eye contact / through the
때로는 우리는 시선을 마주친다 / 백미러를 통해 /
rearview mirror, /
but it feels weak, not quite believable at first, /
하지만 그것은 약하게, 처음에는 그다지 신뢰할 수 없게 느껴진다 /
as it is not "face-to-face."
그것은 '얼굴을 마주하는' 것이 아니기 때문에

협동을 하는 진화적이거나 문화적인 많은 이유가 있지만, 눈은 가장 중요한 협동 수단 중 하나이고, 시선의 마주침은 우리가 차량 운행 중에 잃는 가장 강력한 인간의 힘일지도 모른다. 그것은 보통은 꽤 협조적인 종인 인간이 도로에서 그렇게 비협조적이 될 수 있는 이유라고 주장할 수 있다. 대부분의 시간에 우리가 너무 빨리 움직이고 있어서, 우리는 시속 20마일 정도에서 시선을 마주치는 능력을 잃기 시작하거나, 혹은 (서로를) 보는 것이 안전하지 않다. 어쩌면 우리의 시야가 차단되어 있을지도 모른다. 흔히 다른 운전자들이 선글라스를 끼고 있거나 그들의 차는 색이 옅게 들어간 창문이 있을 수 있다. (그리고 당신은 정말로 그러한 운전자들과 시선을 마주치고 싶은가?) 때로는 우리는 백미러를 통해 시선을 마주치지만, '얼굴을 마주하고 있는 것'이 아니기 때문에 약하게, 처음에는 그다지 신뢰할 수 없게 느껴진다.
➡ 운전하는 동안, 사람들은 (A) 비협조적이 되는데, 왜냐하면 그들이 (B) 거의 시선을 마주치지 않기 때문이다.

① 비협조적인 — 거의 없는
② 주의하는 — 직접적인
③ 자신이 있는 — 정기적인
④ 비협조적인 — 직접적인
⑤ 주의하는 — 거의 없는

문제풀이

눈은 협동을 하는 매우 중요한 수단인데 우리는 운전을 하는 중에 여러 가지 이유로 다른 운전자와 눈을 마주치지 않기 때문에, 운전 중에는 비협조적이 된다고 했다. 따라서 빈칸 (A)에는 'uncooperative(비협조적인)'가, (B)에는 'little(거의 없는)'이 들어가는 것이 적절하다. 따라서 정답은 ①이다.

《 어휘·어구 》

evolutionary 진화적인
cooperation 협동, 협력
means 수단
eye contact 눈맞춤, 시선을 마주침
force 힘
traffic (차량) 운행, 교통
arguably 이론의 여지는 있지만, 거의 틀림없이
normally 보통은
cooperative 협동의, 협조적인
noncooperative 비협조적인
block 막다, 차단하다
rearview mirror 백미러
uncooperative 비협조적인
regular 정기적인, 규칙적인

본문 111쪽

문법 플러스 18. 비교 구문

1. expensive 2. much 3. than
4. large 5. more 6. boys 7. as
8. brave 9. higher 10. much

1 [해석]▶ 이 핸드폰은 네 것만큼 비싸지 않다.
[해설]▶ as ~ as 형태의 원급 비교 구문이다. as ~ as 사이에는 형용사나 부사의 원급이 와야 한다.

2 [해석]▶ 우리는 가능한 한 많은 정보를 모아서 가능한 한 많은 시간을 심사숙고하는 데 시간을 보내면 우리가 늘 더 나을 거라고 믿는다.
[해설]▶ as ~ as 형태의 원급 비교 구문으로서 as ~ as 사이에는 형용사나 부사의 원급이 와야 한다. 이 문장은 time을 수식하는 형용사 much가 와야 한다.

3 [해석]▶ 이 연구는 스토리텔러들에 의해서 제시된 자료가 전통적인 방법을 통해서 얻은 자료보다 훨씬 더 많은 흥미와 개인적인 영향을 지닌다는 것을 보여준다.
[해설]▶ more ~ than 형태의 비교급 비교 구문이다.

4 [해석]▶ 이 방은 저 방보다 거의 두 배다 더 크다.
[해설]▶ 「배수+as 원급 as ~」는 '~보다 몇 배 …하게'의 의미이다.

5 [해석]▶ 오래된 신발이 종종 새 신발보다 더 편안하다.
[해설]▶ more comfortable than~은 '~보다 더 편안한'의 미이다. 문맥상 more가 적절하다.

6 [해석]▶ 그는 자기 반의 모든 학생들보다 더 영리하다.
[해설]▶ 「주어+비교급+than+all the other+복수명사」는 최상급의 의미를 가지고 있다.

7 [해석]▶ 그녀는 학자라기보다는 언론가이다.
[해설]▶ not so much A as B는 'A라기 보다는 차라리 B'라는 의미이다.

8 [해석]▶ Lee 장군은 살아 있었던 장군 중에 가장 용감한 군인이었다.
[해설]▶ as 원급 as ever 동사는 '(지금까지) ~중에서 가장 …한'이라는 최상급 표현이다.

9 [해석]▶ 그러나 기대감이 더 높아질수록 만족하기는 더 어렵다.
[해설]▶ 「the+비교급..., the+비교급~」은 '…하면 할수록, 더 ~하다'의 의미이다.

10 해석▶ 과학적 지식으로 무장해서, 사람들은 우리가 사는 방식을 변화시키는 도구와 기기를 만들고, 그것은 우리의 삶을 훨씬 더 쉽고 나아지게 만든다.
[해설]▶ 비교급을 강조하려면 부사 much, even, still, far, a lot 등을 쓴다. very는 원급의 형용사나 부사를 수식하기 위해 사용한다.

본문 112쪽

어휘 플러스 18. 유의어 (5)

1. relieve 2. request
3. remove 4. sufficient
5. support

1 [해석]▶ 웃음은 스트레스 반응과 관련된 호르몬을 줄여줍니다. 이처럼, 웃음은 스트레스, 우울증, 불안감, 그리고 분노를 경감시키는 데 도움을 줍니다.

2 [해석]▶ 불행히도, 지금 우리의 일로 인해 우리 둘 다 대부분의 주마다 여행을 하고 있으며, 그래서 일간 신문을

계속 구독할 수가 없습니다. 그래서 우리는 귀사가 우리 집에 배달을 중단할 것을 요청합니다.

3 [해석]▶ 그것들은 삶아지고, 끓여지고 그러고 나서 여러 번 씻겨 지면서 불순물들이 제거되게 된다.

4 [해석]▶ 그러나 여러분이 결정을 할 때, 직감을 따르는 것은 필요하지만 충분한 것은 아니다. 결정을 내리는 지침으로 여러분의 직감을 사용하는 법을 배우는 것은 노력을 필요로 한다.

5 [해석]▶ 할머니는 학교에 다니고 싶어 했지만, 혹독한 이주민의 삶이 그녀로 하여금 가족을 부양하도록 내몰았다.

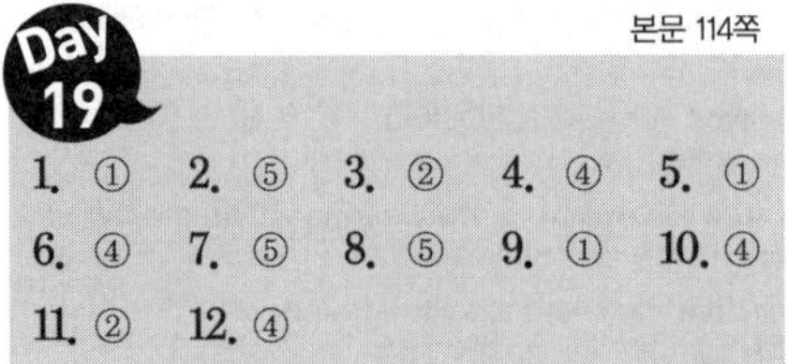

19. 장문의 이해 (1)

Day 19

본문 114쪽

1. ① 2. ⑤ 3. ② 4. ④ 5. ①
6. ④ 7. ⑤ 8. ⑤ 9. ① 10. ④
11. ② 12. ④

대표 기출 | 점진적인 노력으로 사회적 불안감을 극복하라

직독/직해

If you were afraid of standing on balconies, /
만약 당신이 발코니에 서 있는 것을 두려워한다면 /
you would start on some lower floors /
당신은 더 낮은 층에서 시작할 것이다 /
and slowly work your way up to higher ones.
그리고 천천히 더 높은 층으로 올라갈 (것이다)
It would be easy / 쉬울 것이다 /
to face a fear of standing on high balconies /
높은 발코니에 서 있는 두려움을 직면하는 것은 /
in a way that's totally controlled.
완전히 통제된 방식으로
Socializing is trickier.
사람을 사귄다는 것은 더 까다롭다
People aren't like inanimate features of a building /
사람들은 건물과 같은 무생물이 아니다 /
that you just have to be around to get used to.
주변에 있어서 익숙해지는
You have to interact with them, /
당신은 그들과 상호 작용해야 한다 /
and their responses can be unpredictable.
그리고 그들의 반응을 예측하기가 힘들 수 있다
Your feelings toward them / are more complex too.
그들을 향한 당신의 느낌은 / 역시 더 복잡하다
Most people's self-esteem /
대부분 사람의 자존감은 /
isn't going to be affected that much /
그렇게 많이 영향을 받지 않을 것이다 /
if they don't like balconies, /
그들이 발코니를 좋아하지 않는다고 해도
but your confidence can suffer /
하지만 당신의 자신감은 상처받을 수 있다. /
if you can't socialize effectively.
당신이 효과적으로 사람들을 사귈 수 없다면
It's also harder / to design a tidy way /
또한 더 어렵다 / 깔끔한 방법을 설계하는 것은 /
to gradually face many social fears.
많은 사교적 두려움을 점차적으로 마주할
The social situations / 사교적 상황이 /
you need to expose yourself to /
자신을 드러낼 필요가 있는 /
may not be available / when you want them, /
이용 가능하지 않을 수 있다 / 당신이 그것들을 원할 때 /
or they may not go well enough / for you to sense /
또는 그것들은 충분히 잘 진행되지 않을 수도 있다 / 당신이 감지할 만큼 /
that things are under control.
상황이 통제 가능하다고
The progression from one step to the next /
한 단계에서 다음 단계로의 진행은 /
may not be clear, / 분명하지 않을 수 있다 /
creating unavoidable large increases in difficulty /
피할 수 없이 큰 어려움이 늘어나게 된다 /
from one to the next.
한 단계에서 다음 단계로 진행할 때
People around you / aren't robots /
당신의 주변 사람들은 / 로봇이 아니다 /
that you can endlessly experiment /
끊임없이 실험할 수 있는 /
with for your own purposes.
당신 자신의 목적을 가지고
This is not to say / 이것은 말하는 것은 아니다 /
that facing your fears is pointless /
당신의 두려움을 직면하는 것이 의미가 없다고 /
when socializing. 사람을 사귈 때
The principles of gradual exposure /
점진적인 노출의 원칙은 /
are still very useful. 여전히 매우 유용하다
The process of applying them / is just messier, /
그것들을 적용하는 과정은 / 더 복잡하다 /
and knowing that before you start / is helpful.
그리고 당신이 시작하기 전에 그것을 아는 것은 / 도움이 된다

만약 당신이 발코니에 서 있는 것을 두려워한다면, 당신은 더 낮은 층에서 시작해서 천천히 더 높은 층으로 올라갈 것이다. 완전히 통제된 방식으로 높은 발코니에 서 있는 두려움을 직면하는 것은 쉬울 것이다. 사람을 사귄다는 것은 (a) 더 까다롭다. 사람들은 주변에 있어서 익숙해지는 건물과 같은 무생물이 아니다. 당신은 그들과 상호 작용해야 하고 그들의 반응을 예측하기가 힘들 수 있다. 그들을 향한 당신의 느낌 역시 더 복잡하다. 대부분 사람의 자존감은 그들이 발코니를 좋아하지 않는다고 해도 그렇게 많이 영향을 받지 않을 것이지만, 당신이 효과적으로 사람들을 사귈 수 없다면 당신의 자신감은 (b) 상처받을 수 있다.
많은 사교적 두려움을 점차적으로 마주할 깔끔한 방법을 설계하는 것 또한 더 어렵다. 자신을 드러낼 필요가 있는 사교적 상황이 당신이 원할 때 (c) 이용 가능하지 않을 수 있고, 또는 그것들은 상황이 통제 가능하다고 감지할 만큼 잘 진행되지 않을 수도 있다. 한 단계에서 다음 단계로의 진행은 분명하지 않을 수 있고, 한 단계에서 다음 단계로 진행할 때 피할 수 없이 큰 어려움이 (d) 줄어들게(→ 늘어나게) 된다. 당신의 주변 사람들은 당신 자신의 목적을 위해 끊임없이 실험할 수 있는 로봇이 아니다. 이것은 사람을 사귈 때 당신의 두려움을 직면하는 것이 의미가 없다고 말하는 것은 아니다. 점진적인 노출의 원칙은 여전히 매우 (e) 유용하다. 그것들을 적용하는 과정은 더 복잡하지만, 당신이 시작하기 전에 그것을 아는 것은 도움이 된다.

어휘·어구

socialize 교제하다
tricky 까다로운
inanimate 무생물의
get used to ~에 익숙해지다
response 반응
unpredictable 예측할 수 없는
self-esteem 자부심, 자존감
confidence 자신감
expose 노출시키다
progression 진행
unavoidable 피할 수 없는
endlessly 끝없이
pointless 무의미한
principle 원리, 원칙
messy 복잡한, 엉망진창인
relaxation 휴식
get over ~에서 회복하다
fear of heights 고소 공포증
overcome 극복하다

정답률 44%

41. ⑤

① 자존감을 향상시키는 법
② 당신이 두려워하는 사람과의 사교: 좋은가 나쁜가?
③ 휴식은 사회적 두려움을 극복하게 이끌 수 있다
④ 사회적인 노출은 고소 공포증과 관련 있는가?
⑤ 사회적 불안감을 극복하는 것은 어렵다: 점차 노력하라

문제풀이

사람들과 사교하는 것은 까다로운 일이고, 많은 사교적 두려움을 점차적으로 마주할 수 있는 방법을 설계하는 것 또한 어렵지만 점진적인 노출을 하면서 두려움을 극복하도록 하는 것이 유용하다는 내용이므로, 글의 제목으로 ⑤ 'Overcoming

Social Anxiety Is Difficult; Try Gradually(사회적 불안감을 극복하는 것은 어렵다: 점차 노력하라)'가 가장 적절하다.

42. ④

문제풀이

사교적 상황에서 상황 통제가 감지될 만큼 잘 진행되지 않고 다음 단계로의 진행이 분명하지 않을 경우 어려움이 늘어가게 된다는 문맥이 되어야 자연스러우므로, (d) 'decreases(줄어들다)'를 'increases(늘어나다)'로 바꿔야 한다.

1~2 시각을 위해 함께 작동하는 눈과 두뇌

직독/직해

Mike May lost his sight at the age of three.
Mike May는 세 살 때 자신의 시력을 잃었다

Because he had spent the majority of his life /
그는 자신의 인생 대부분을 보냈기 때문에 /

adapting to being blind / 보이지 않는 것에 적응하는 데 /

— and even cultivating a skiing career / in this state /
그리고 심지어 스키 경력을 쌓는 데도 / 이 상태에서 /

— his other senses compensated /
그의 다른 감각들은 보충되었다 /

by growing stronger.
더 강해지는 것을 통해

However, / when his sight was restored through a surgery in his forties, /
하지만 / 수술을 통해 40대에 그의 시력이 회복되었을 때 /

his entire perception of reality / was disrupted.
그의 현실에 대한 전반적 인식은 / 방해받았다

Instead of being thrilled / that he could see now, /
감격하는 대신에 / 이제 볼 수 있다는 것에 /

as he'd expected, / his brain was so overloaded /
그가 예상했던 것처럼 / 자신의 뇌가 너무 과부하가 걸려 /

with new visual stimuli / 새로운 시각적인 자극으로 /

that the world became / 세상은 ~이 되었다 /

a frightening and overwhelming place.
두렵고 압도적인 장소가

After he'd learned to know his family /
자신의 가족을 아는 것을 배운 후에 /

through touch and smell, /
만지는 것과 냄새를 통해 /

he found / that he couldn't recognize his children /
그는 알게 되었다 / 그가 자신의 아이들을 알아볼 수 없다는 것을 /

with his eyes, / and this left him puzzled.
자신의 눈으로 / 그리고 이것은 그를 혼란스러운 상태로 남겨 두었다

Skiing also became a lot harder /
스키 또한 훨씬 더 어려워졌다 /

as he struggled to adapt / to the visual stimulation.
그가 적응하려고 힘쓰면서 / 시각적인 자극에

This confusion occurred / 이 혼란은 일어났다 /

because his brain hadn't yet learned to see.
그의 뇌가 보는 것을 아직 배우지 못했기 때문에

Though we often tend to assume /
비록 우리는 종종 가정하는 경향이 있지만 /

our eyes function / as video cameras /
우리의 눈이 기능한다고 / 비디오 카메라로서 /

which relay information to our brain, /
우리의 뇌에 정보를 전달하는 /

advances in neuroscientific research /
신경 과학 연구의 발전은 /

have proven / that this is actually not the case.
증명했다 / 이것이 실제로는 그렇지 않다는 것을

Instead, / sight is a collaborative effort /
대신 / 시각은 협력적인 노력이다 /

between our eyes and our brains, /
우리의 눈과 뇌 사이의 /

and the way we process visual reality /
그리고 우리가 시각적인 현실을 처리하는 방법은 /

depends on the way / these two communicate.
방식에 달려 있다 / 이 두 가지가 소통하는

If communication between our eyes and our brains is disturbed, /
만약 우리의 눈과 뇌 사이의 의사소통이 방해된다면 /

our perception of reality is altered accordingly.
현실에 대한 우리의 인식은 그에 따라 바뀐다

And because other areas of May's brain had adapted to process information/
그리고 May의 뇌의 다른 부분들은 정보를 처리하는 것에 적응했었기 때문에 /

primarily through his other senses, /
주로 그의 다른 감각을 통해

the process of learning / how to see /
배우는 과정은 / 보는 방법을 /

was harder / than he'd anticipated.
더 어려웠다 / 그가 예상했던 것보다

Mike May는 세 살 때 자신의 시력을 잃었다. 그는 자신의 인생 대부분을 보이지 않는 것에 적응하는 데, 그리고 심지어 이 상태에서 스키 경력을 쌓는 데도 보냈기 때문에, 그의 다른 감각들은 (a) 더 강해지는 것을 통해 보충되었다. 하지만 40대에 수술을 통해 그의 시력이 회복되었을 때, 그의 현실에 대한 전반적 인식은 (b) 방해받았다. 그가 예상했던 것처럼 이제 볼 수 있다는 것에 감격하는 대신에, 자신의 뇌가 새로운 시각적인 자극으로 너무 과부하가 걸려 세상은 두렵고 압도적인 장소가 되었다. 만지는 것과 냄새를 통해 자신의 가족을 아는 것을 배운 후에, 그는 자신의 눈으로 자신의 아이들을 알아볼 수 없다는 것을 알게 되었고, 이것은 그를 혼란스러운 상태로 남겨 두었다. 스키 또한 그가 시각적인 자극에 적응하려고 힘쓰면서 훨씬 더 어려워졌다. 이 (c) 혼란은 그의 뇌가 아직 보는 것을 배우지 못했기 때문에 일어났다. 비록 우리는 종종 우리의 눈이 우리의 뇌에 정보를 전달하는 비디오 카메라로서 기능한다고 가정하는 경향이 있지만, 신경 과학 연구의 발전은 이것이 실제로는 그렇지 않다는 것을 증명했다. 대신, 시각은 우리의 눈과 뇌 사이의 협력적인 노력이며, 우리가 (d) 시각적인 현실을 처리하는 방법은 이 두 가지가 소통하는 방식에 달려 있다. 만약 우리의 눈과 뇌 사이의 의사소통이 방해된다면, 현실에 대한 우리의 인식은 그에 따라 바뀐다. 그리고 May의 뇌의 다른 부분들은 주로 그의 다른 감각을 통해 정보를 처리하는 것에 적응했었기 때문에, 보는 방법을 배우는 과정은 그가 예상했던 것보다 (e) 더 쉬웠다(→ 더 어려웠다).

어휘·어구

sight 시력
majority 대부분
adapt 적응하다
cultivate 구축하다, 쌓다
career 경력
state 상태
compensate 보상하다
restore 회복하다
surgery 수술
entire 전체의
perception 인식
reality 현실
disrupt 방해하다
overloaded 과부화된
visual 시각적인
stimulus 자극(*pl.* stimuli)
overwhelming 압도적인
recognize 알아보다
puzzled 어리둥절해하는
struggle 애쓰다
stimulation 자극
confusion 혼란
occur 발생하다
assume 가정하다
function 기능
relay 전달하다
advance 발전, 진보
neuroscientific 신경 과학의
prove 증명하다, 입증하다
collaborative 협력적인
effort 노력
process 과정
communicate 의사소통하다
disturb 방해하다
alter 바꾸다, 변경하다
accordingly 그에 맞춰
primarily 주로
anticipate 예상하다
sight 시각
visualization 시각화
useful 유용한
tool 도구
collaboration 협력

1. ①

① 시각을 위해 함께 작동하는 눈과 두뇌
② 시각화: 배움을 위한 유용한 도구
③ 시각과 소리의 협력
④ 새로운 시각적인 자극을 무시하는 방법
⑤ 당신은 당신이 믿는 것을 본다

문제풀이

인생의 대부분을 보이지 않는 것에 적응하며 살다가 수술을 통해 시력을 회복한 뒤, 뇌가 새로운 시각적인 자극으로 과부화가 걸려 오히려 눈과 뇌 사이의 의사소통이 방해되었는 내용과 시각은 우리의 눈과 뇌 사이의 협력적인 노력이라는 내용으로 보아 글의 제목으로 ① 'Eyes and Brain Working Together for Sight(시각을 위해 함께 작동하는 눈과 두뇌)'가 가장 적절하다.

2. ⑤

문제풀이

시력을 잃은 상태에서 뇌의 다른 부분들은 주로 다른 감각을 통해 정보를 처리하는 것에 적응했었기 때문에, 새로운 시각적인 자극에 적응하는 게 힘들었을 것임을 추론할 수 있다. 따라서 보는 방법을 배우는 과정은 그가 예상했던 것보다 (e) 'easier(더 쉬웠다)'를 'harder(더 어려웠다)' 등으로 바꿔야 한다.

3~4 곤충에 대한 당신의 인식을 바꿔라

직독/직해

In a society / that rejects the consumption of insects /
사회에서는 / 곤충 섭취를 거부하는 /

there are some individuals / 몇몇 개인들이 있다 /

who overcome this rejection, /
이런 거부를 극복한 /

but most will continue with this attitude.
하지만 대부분은 이런 태도를 지속할 것이다

It may be very difficult / 매우 어려울지도 모른다 /

to convince an entire society /
전체 사회에 납득시키는 것은 /

that insects are totally suitable for consumption.
곤충이 섭취에 완전히 적합하다는 것을

However, / there are examples /
하지만 / 사례들이 있다 /

in which this reversal of attitudes /
이런 태도의 역전이 /

about certain foods / 특정 음식에 대한 /

has happened to an entire society.
전체 사회에 발생해 온

Several examples in the past 120 years /
지난 120년간 몇몇 사례는 /

from European-American society are: /
유럽아메리카 사회로부터의 ~이 있다 /

considering lobster a luxury food /
랍스터(바닷가재)를 고급진 음식으로 여기는 것 /

instead of a food for servants and prisoners; /
하인과 죄수용 음식 대신에 /

considering sushi a safe and delicious food; /
초밥을 안전하고 맛있는 음식으로 여기는 것 /

and considering pizza not just a food /
그리고 피자를 단지 음식으로 여기지 않는 것이다 /

for the rural poor of Sicily.
시칠리아 시골의 가난한 사람용

In Latin American countries, /
라틴 아메리카 국가들에서는 /

where insects are already consumed, /
그곳은 곤충이 이미 섭취되는데 /

a portion of the population / 인구의 일부는 /

hates their consumption / 그것들의 섭취를 싫어한다 /

and associates it with poverty.
그리고 그것을 빈곤과 연관 짓는다

There are also examples of people /
사람들의 사례들 또한 있다 /

who have had the habit of consuming them /
그것을(곤충을) 섭취하는 습관이 있었던 /

and discarded that habit / due to shame, /
그리고 그 습관을 버린 / 수치심 때문에

and because they do not want to be categorized /
그리고 그들은 분류되고 싶지 않았기 때문에 /

as poor or uncivilized.
가난하거나 미개하다고

According to Esther Katz, an anthropologist, /
인류학자인 Esther Katz에 따르면 /

if the consumption of insects /
만약 곤충 섭취가 /

as a food luxury / is to be promoted, /
음식 호사로서 / 장려된다면 /

there would be more chances /
가능성이 더 많을 것이다 /

that some individuals who do not present this habit /
이 습관을 보이지 않은 몇몇 개인들이 /

overcome ideas under which they were educated.
그들이 교육받았던 생각을 극복할

And this could also help to revalue /
그리고 이것은 또한 재평가하는 데에도 도움을 줄 수 있다 /

the consumption of insects /
곤충의 섭취를 /

by those people who already eat them.
이미 그것을 먹고 있는 그 사람들에 의한

곤충 섭취를 거부하는 사회에서는 이런 거부를 극복한 몇몇 개인들이 있지만, 대부분은 이런 태도를 지속할 것이다. 곤충이 섭취에 완전히 적합하다는 것을 전체 사회에 납득시키는 것은 매우 (a) 어려울지도 모른다. 하지만, 특정 음식에 대한 이런 태도의 (b) 역전이 전체 사회에 발생해 온 사례들이 있다. 지난 120년간 유럽아메리카 사회로부터의 몇몇 사례는 랍스터(바닷가재)를 하인과 죄수용 음식 대신에 고급진 음식으로 여기는 것, 초밥을 안전하고 맛있는 음식으로 여기는 것, 그리고 피자를 단지 시칠리아 시골의 가난한 사람용 음식으로 여기지 않는 것이다. 곤충이 이미 섭취되는 라틴 아메리카 국가들에서는 인구의 일부는 그것들의 섭취를 싫어하고 그것을 빈곤과 (c) 연관 짓는다. 그것을 섭취하는 습관이 있어왔으나 수치심 때문에 그리고 그들은 가난하거나 미개하다고 분류되고 싶지 않았기 때문에 그 습관을 (d) 장려한(→ 버린) 사람들의 사례들 또한 있다. 인류학자인 Esther Katz에 따르면, 만약 음식 호사로서의 곤충 섭취가 장려된다면, 이 습관을 보이지 않은 몇몇 개인들이 그들이 교육받았던 생각을 극복할 가능성이 더 많을 것이다. 그리고 이것은 또한 이미 그것을 먹고 있는 그 사람들에 의한 곤충의 섭취를 (e) 재평가하는 데에도 도움을 줄 수 있다.

《어휘·어구》

consumption 섭취, 소비
insect 곤충
overcome 극복하다
continue 계속되다
convince 납득시키다
entire 전체의
suitable 적합한
reversal 역전
portion 일부
population 인구
associate 연관 짓다
poverty 빈곤, 가난
encourage 장려하다
shame 수치심
categorize 분류하다
uncivilized 미개한
anthropologist 인류학자
promote 장려하다
present 보여주다
revalue 재평가하다
variety 다양
edible 식용의
perspective 관점, 시각
shortage 부족
uniqueness 독창성

정답률 61%

3. ②

① 식탁 위가 더 다양할수록 당신은 더 건강해진다
② 식용인가 아닌가? 곤충에 대한 당신의 시각을 바꿔라
③ 곤충: 세계 음식 부족을 해결할 열쇠
④ 음식 문화에서 독창성이 사라지게 하지 마라
⑤ 음식으로 다양한 문화를 경험하는 것

문제풀이

곤충 섭취를 전체 사회에 납득시키는 것은 어려울 수 있지만 곤충 섭취가 장려된다면 사람들이 곤충 섭취를 재평가할 것이라는 내용의 글이다. 따라서 글의 제목으로 ② 'Edible or Not? Change Your Perspectives on Insects(식용인가 아닌가? 곤충에 대한 당신의 인식을 바꿔라)'가 가장 적절하다.

정답률 59%

4. ④

문제풀이

곤충을 섭취하는 습관이 있었지만 수치심과 가난하거나 미개하다고 분류되고 싶지 않아서 곤충을 섭취하는 습관을 버린 사람들이 있었다는 문맥이 되어야 자연스럽다. 따라서 (d) 'encouraged(장려했다)'를 'discarded(버렸다)' 등으로 바꿔야 한다.

5~6 심장을 위한 최고의 취침 시간

직독/직해

U.K. researchers say / 영국 연구원들은 말한다 /

a bedtime of between 10 p.m. and 11 p.m. / is best.
밤 10시~11시 사이의 취침 시간이 / 가장 좋다고

They say / 그들은 말한다 /

people who go to sleep between these times /
이 시간대 사이에 잠자는 사람들이 /

have a lower risk of heart disease.
더 낮은 심장 질환의 위험성을 가지고 있다고

Six years ago, / the researchers collected /
6년 전 / 연구원들은 수집했다 /

data on the sleep patterns of 80,000 volunteers.
8만 명의 자원자들의 수면 데이터를

The volunteers had to wear a special watch /
자원자들은 특수 시계를 착용해야만 했다 /

for seven days / so the researchers could collect /
7일 동안 / 그래서 연구원들은 수집할 수 있었다 /

data on their sleeping and waking times.
그들의 수면과 기상 시간에 대한 데이터를

The scientists then monitored /
그러고 나서 연구원들은 관찰했다 /

the health of the volunteers.
자원자들의 건강을

Around 3,000 volunteers later /
약 3천 명의 자원자들이 이후에 /

showed heart problems. 심장 문제를 보였다

They went to bed earlier or later /
그들은 더 이르거나 더 늦은 시간에 잠자리에 들었다 /

than the ideal 10 p.m.to 11 p.m. timeframe.
밤 10시~11시 사이의 이상적인 시간대보다

One of the authors of the study, Dr. David Plans, /
그 연구 저자 중 한 명인, Dr. David Plans는 /

commented on his research /
그의 연구에 대해 언급했다 /

and the effects of bedtimes on the health of our heart.
그리고 우리의 심장 건강에 취침 시간이 끼치는 영향에 대해

He said / the study could not give a certain cause /
그는 말했다 / 연구가 특정한 원인을 제시할 수는 없다고 /

for their results, / 그들의 결과에 /

but it suggests / that early or late bedtimes /
그러나 그것은 제시한다 / 이르거나 늦은 취침 시간이 /

may be more likely to disrupt the body clock, /
체내 시계를 혼란케 할 가능성이 더 높을 수 있다 /

with negative consequences for cardiovascular health.
심장 혈관 건강에 부정적인 결과와 함께

He said / that it was important /
그는 말했다 / 중요하다고 /

for our body to wake up to the morning light, /
우리 몸이 아침 빛에 맞추어 일어나는 것이 /

and that the worst time to go to bed /
그리고 잠자리에 드는 가장 나쁜 시간은 /

was after midnight / because it may reduce /
자정 이후였다 / 그것은 낮출 수도 있기 때문이다 /

the likelihood of seeing morning light /
아침 빛을 볼 가능성을 /

which resets the body clock. 체내 시계를 재설정하는

He added / that we risk cardiovascular disease /
그는 덧붙였다 / 우리가 심장 혈관 질환의 위험을 안게 된다고 /

if our body clock is not reset properly.
만약 우리의 체내 시계가 적절하게 재설정되지 않으면

영국 연구원들은 밤 10시~11시 사이의 취침 시간이 가장 좋다고 말한다. 그들은 이 시간대 사이에 잠자는 사람들이 (a) 더 낮은 심장 질환의 위험성을 가지고 있다고 말한다. 6년 전, 연구원들은 8만 명의 자원자들의 수면 패턴 데이터를 수집했다. 자원자들은 7일 동안 특수 시계를 착용해야만 했고, 그래서 연구원들은 그들의 수면과 기상 시간에 대한 데이터를 수집할 수 있었다. 그러고 나서 연구원들은 자원자들의 건강을 관찰했다. 약 3천 명의 자원자들이 이후에 심장 문제를 보였다. 그들은 밤 10시~11시 사이의 (b) 이상적인 시간대보다 더 이르거나 더 늦은 시간에 잠자리에 들었다.
그 연구 저자 중 한 명인, Dr. David Plans는 그의 연구와 우리의 심장 건강에 취침 시간이 끼치는 (c) 영향에 대해 언급했다. 그는 연구가 그들의 결과에 특정한 원인을 제시할 수는 없지만, 이르거나 늦은 취침 시간이 심장 혈관 건강에 (d) 긍정적인(→ 부정적인) 결과와 함께 체내 시계를 혼란케 할 가능성이 더 높을 수 있다고 연구가 제시한다고 말했다. 그는 우리 몸이 아침 빛에 맞추어 일어나는 것이 중요하고, 잠자리에 드는 가장 나쁜 시간이 자정 이후인데 그것은 체내 시계를 재설정하는 아침 빛을 볼 가능성을 (e) 낮출 수도 있기 때문이다. 그는 만약 우리의 체내 시계가 적절하게 재설정되지 않으면, 우리가 심장 혈관 질환의 위험을 안게 된다고 덧붙였다.

《어휘·어구》

heart disease 심장 질환
volunteer 자원자
monitor 추적 관찰하다
timeframe 기간
comment 언급하다
positive 긍정적인

consequence 결과
reduce 줄이다
likelihood 가능성
reset 재설정하다
properly 적절히
sound sleep 숙면
reflect 반영하다
personality 성격
regular 규칙적인

정답률 

5. ①

① 당신의 심장을 위한 최고의 취침 시간
② 늦은 취침 시간은 나이의 문제이다
③ 숙면을 위해: 불을 꺼라
④ 수면 패턴이 성격을 반영한다
⑤ 규칙적인 운동: 양질의 수면을 위한 기적

문제풀이

밤 10시~11시 사이의 취침 시간 심장 건강을 위해 가장 좋은 시간대라는 내용의 글이다. 따라서 글의 제목으로 ① 'The Best Bedtime for Your Heart(당신의 심장을 위한 최고의 취침 시간)'가 가장 적절하다.

정답률 

6. ④

문제풀이

심장 건강을 위해 가장 이상적인 취침 시간은 밤 10시~11시 사이이고, 이 시간대보다 더 이르거나 더 늦게 취침을 하는 경우 심장 문제가 생겼다는 연구 결과를 통해 이르거나 늦은 취침 시간은 심장 혈관 건강에 부정적인 결과를 가져올 수 있다는 내용이 되어야 자연스럽다. 따라서 (d) 'positive(긍정적인)'를 'negative(부정적인)'로 바꿔야 한다.

7~8 불행으로부터 자신을 구하기 위해 타인을 이해하라

직독/직해

The longest journey we will make /
우리가 갈 가장 긴 여정은

is the eighteen inches / 18인치이다 /

between our head and heart.
우리의 머리에서 가슴까지의

If we take this journey, / it can shorten our misery /
만약 우리가 이 여행을 한다면 / 그것은 우리의 비참함을 줄일 수 있다 /

in the world. 세상에서

Impatience, judgment, frustration, and anger /
조급함, 비난, 좌절, 그리고 분노가 /

reside in our heads. 우리의 머릿속에 있다

When we live in that place too long, /
우리가 그 장소에서 너무 오래 살면 /

it makes us unhappy. 그것은 우리를 불행하게 만든다.

But when we take the journey /
하지만 우리가 여행을 하면 /

from our heads to our hearts, /
머리부터 가슴까지 /

something shifts inside.
내면에서 무엇인가가 바뀐다

What if we were able to love /
우리가 사랑할 수 있다면 어떻게 될까 /

everything that gets in our way?
우리를 가로막는 모든 것을

What if we tried loving /
만일 우리가 사랑하려고 노력한다면 어떨까 /

the shopper who unknowingly steps / in front of us in line, /
무심코 들어온 그 쇼핑객을 / 줄을 서 있는 우리 앞에 /

the driver who cuts us off / in traffic, /
우리 앞에 끼어든 그 운전자를 / 차량 흐름에서 /

the swimmer who splashes us with water /
우리에게 물을 튀게 한 수영하는 그 사람을 /

during a belly dive, / 배 쪽으로 다이빙하면서 /

or the reader who pens /
혹은 ~을 쓴 그 독자를 /

a bad online review of our writing?
우리의 글에 대해 좋지 않은 온라인 후기를

Every person who makes us miserable /
우리를 비참하게 만드는 모든 사람은 /

is like us — / a human being, /
우리와 같다 / 인간 /

most likely doing the best they can, /
그들은 아마도 최선을 다하고 있으며 /

deeply loved by their parents, / a child, or a friend.
부모로부터 깊이 사랑받는 / 자녀 혹은 친구(일 것이다)

And how many times have we unknowingly stepped /
그리고 우리는 몇 번이나 무심코 들어갔을까 /

in front of someone in line?
줄을 서 있는 누군가의 앞에

Cut someone off in traffic?
차량 흐름에서 누군가에게 끼어든 적은

Splashed someone in a pool?
수영장에서 누군가에게 물을 튀게 한 적은

Or made a negative statement /
혹은 부정적인 진술을 한 적은 /

about something we've read? 우리가 읽은 것에 대해

It helps to remember / that a piece of us resides /
기억하는 것은 도움이 된다 / 우리의 일부가 있다는 것을 /

in every person we meet. 우리가 만나는 모든 사람 속에

우리가 갈 가장 긴 여정은 우리의 머리에서 가슴까지의 18인치이다. 만약 우리가 이 여행을 한다면, 그것은 세상에서 우리의 비참함을 줄일 수 있다. 조급함, 비난, 좌절, 그리고 분노가 우리의 머릿속에 있다. 우리가 그 장소에서 너무 오래 살면, 그것은 우리를 불행하게 만든다. 하지만 우리가 머리부터 가슴까지 여행을 하면, 내면에서 무엇인가가 바뀐다. 우리를 가로막는 모든 것을 우리가 사랑할 수 있다면 어떻게 될까? 만일 줄을 서 있는 우리 앞에 무심코 들어온 그 쇼핑객을, 차량 흐름에서 우리 앞에 끼어든 그 운전자를, 배 쪽으로 다이빙하면서 우리에게 물을 튀게 한 수영하는 그 사람을, 우리의 글에 대해 좋지 않은 온라인 후기를 쓴 그 독자를 우리가 사랑하려고 노력한다면 어떨까? 우리를 비참하게 만드는 모든 사람은 우리와 같다. 그들은 아마도 최선을 다하고 있으며, 부모로부터 깊이 사랑받는 인간, 자녀 혹은 친구일 것이다. 그리고 우리는 몇 번이나 무심코 줄을 서 있는 누군가의 앞에 들어갔을까? 차량 흐름에서 누군가에게 끼어든 적은? 수영장에서 누군가에게 물을 튀게 한 적은? 혹은 우리가 읽은 것에 대해 부정적인 진술을 한 적은 몇 번이었을까? 우리가 만나는 모든 사람 속에 우리의 일부가 있다는 것을 부정하는(→기억하는) 것은 도움이 된다.

《 어휘·어구 》

journey 여정, 여행
shorten 줄이다
misery 비참함
impatience 조급함
judgment 비난
frustration 좌절
anger 분노
shift 바뀌다
unknowingly 무심코
cut off 끼어들다
in traffic 차량 흐름에서
splash (액체류를) 튀기다
pen (글을) 쓰다
review 후기
miserable 비참한
human being 인간
child 자녀
negative 부정적인
statement 진술
deny 부정하다
forgive 용서하다
kindness 친절
healer 치료자
celebrate 축하하다
moment 순간
unhappiness 불행

정답률 

7. ⑤

① 왜 다른 사람을 용서하는 게 그렇게 어려운가?
② 심지어 친절한 행위도 누군가를 다치게 할 수 있다
③ 시간은 상처받은 마음을 위한 최고의 치유자이다
④ 여러분의 일상에서 행복한 순간들을 축하하라
⑤ 불행으로부터 여러분을 구하기 위해 다른 사람을 이해하라

문제풀이

우리를 비참하게 만드는 모든 사람은 결국 우리와 같은 인간, 자녀, 친구이므로 우리를 가로막는 모든 사람을 우리가 사랑해야 하고, 모든 사람 속에 우리의 일부가 있다는 내용이다. 따라서 글의 제목으로 ⑤ 'Understand Others to Save Yourself from Unhappiness(불행으로부터 여러분을 구하기 위해 다른 사람을 이해하라)'가 가장 적절하다.

정답률 

8. ⑤

문제풀이

우리를 비참하게 만드는 모든 사람은 우리와 같다고 한 것으로 보아 우리가 만나는 모든 사람 속에 우리의 일부가 있다는 것을 기억하는 것이 도움이 된다는 내용이 되어야 자연스럽다 따라서 (e) 'deny(부정하다)'를 'remember(기억하다)' 등으로 바꿔야 한다.

9~10 유전자가 아니라 우리 손에 달려있는 건강

직독/직해

Since the turn of the twentieth century /
20세기로 전환된 이래로 /

we've believed in genetic causes of diagnoses /
우리는 진단의 유전적인 원인을 믿어 왔다 /

—a theory called genetic determinism.
즉 유전자 결정론이라 불리는 이론을

Under this model, / 이 모델 하에서 /

our genes (and subsequent health) are determined at birth.
우리의 유전자는 (그리고 차후의 건강은) 태어날 때 결정된다

We are "destined" / to inherit certain diseases /
우리는 운명이다 / 특정 질병을 물려받을 /

based on the misfortune of our DNA.
자신의 DNA의 불행을 바탕으로

Genetic determinism doesn't consider the role /
유전자 결정론은 역할을 고려하지 않는다 /

of family backgrounds, traumas, habits, or /
가정 환경, 정신적 충격, 습관 /

anything else within the environment.
또는 환경 내의 다른 어떤 것의 (역할을)

In this dynamic / we are not active participants /
이 역학 관계에서 / 우리는 능동적인 참여자가 아니다 /

in our own health and wellness.
우리 자신의 건강과 안녕에 있어
Why would we be?
우리는 왜 이러할까
If something is predetermined, / it's not necessary /
만약 무언가가 미리 결정되어 있다면 / 필요하지 않다 /
to look at anything beyond our DNA.
우리의 DNA를 넘어서 어떤 것을 보는 것이
But the more science has learned / about the body /
하지만 과학이 더 많이 알게 될수록 / 신체에 관하여 /
and its interaction with the environment around it /
그리고 그것의 그 주변 환경과의 상호 작용에 관하여 /
(in its various forms, / 다양한 형태로 /
from our nutrition to our relationships to our racially oppressive systems), /
우리의 영양에서부터 우리의 관계 그리고 우리의 인종적으로 억압적인 시스템에 이르기까지의
the more complicated the story becomes.
그 이야기는 더욱 복잡해진다
We are not merely expressions of coding /
우리는 단지 (유전) 암호화의 표현이 아니라 /
but products of a remarkable variety of interactions /
놀랍도록 다양한 상호 작용의 산물이다 /
that are both within and outside of our control.
우리의 통제 내부와 외부 모두에 있는
Once we see beyond the narrative /
일단 우리가 이야기를 넘어서 보게 된다면 /
that genetics are destiny, /
유전자가 운명이라는 /
we can take ownership of our health.
우리는 자신의 건강에 대한 소유권을 가질 수 있다
This allows us to see /
이것은 우리에게 알 수 있게 해주었다 /
how "choiceless" we once were /
자신이 한때 얼마나 '선택권이 없는' 상태였는지 /
and empowers us with the ability /
그리고 우리에게 능력을 부여한다 /
to create real and lasting change.
실제적이고 지속적인 변화를 만들어 낼 수 있는

20세기로 전환된 이래로 우리는 진단의 유전적인 원인, 즉 유전자 결정론이라 불리는 이론을 믿어 왔다. 이 모델 하에서 우리의 유전자는 (그리고 차후의 건강은) 태어날 때 결정된다. 우리는 자신의 DNA의 불행을 바탕으로 특정 질병을 물려받을 '운명'이다. 유전자 결정론은 가정 환경, 정신적 충격, 습관 또는 환경 내의 다른 어떤 것의 역할을 (a) 고려하지 않는다. 이 역학 관계에서 우리는 우리 자신의 건강과 안녕에 있어 (b) 능동적인 참여자가 아니다. 우리는 왜 이러할까? 만약 무언가가 미리 결정되어 있다면 우리의 DNA를 넘어서 어떤 것을 보는 것이 (c) 필요하지 않다. 하지만 과학이 신체와 그것의 그 주변 환경 (우리의 영양에서부터 우리의 인종적으로 억압적인 시스템에 대한 관계에 이르기까지의 다양한 형태로)과의 상호 작용에 대해 더 많이 알게 될수록, 그 이야기는 더욱 (d) 단순해진다(→ 복잡해진다). 우리는 단지 (유전)암호화의 표현이 아니라 우리의 통제 내부와 외부 모두에 있는 놀랍도록 다양한 상호 작용의 산물이다. 일단 우리가 유전자가 (e) 운명이라는 이야기를 넘어서 보게 된다면 우리는 자신의 건강에 대한 소유권을 가질 수 있다. 이것은 우리에게 자신이 한때 얼마나 '선택권이 없는' 상태였는지 알 수 있게 해 주며 우리에게 실제적이고 지속적인 변화를 만들어 낼 수 있는 능력을 부여한다.

《어휘·어구》

inherit 물려받다
based on ~에 근거하여
misfortune 불행
participant 참여자
interaction 상호 작용
expression 표현, 표정
remarkable 놀랄 만한
narrative 이야기
ownership 소유권

정답률 55%

9. ①

① 건강은 유전자뿐만 아니라 우리 손에 달려 있다
② 유전학: 인간의 건강 증진을 위한 해결책
③ 어떻게 DNA가 생물학에서 환경을 지배했을까?
④ 건강에 대해 절대 자신감을 갖지 마라, 하지만 계속해서 확인하라!
⑤ 과학 혁신이 사회적 상호작용에 영향을 미치는 이유

문제풀이

이 글은 우리 인간의 건강이 단순히 유전자에 의해서만 결정되는 것이 아니라, 우리가 통제할 수 있는 외부적 환경에 의해서도 결정될 수 있으므로, 유전적 결정론을 넘어선 시각을 갖고, 자신의 건강에 대한 소유권을 주장하여 실제적이고 지속적인 변화를 만들어 내야 한다는 내용의 글이므로 글의 제목으로 가장 적절한 것은 ① 'Health Is in Our Hands, Not Only in Our Genes(건강은 유전자뿐만 아니라 우리 손에 달려 있다.)'이다.

10. ④

문제풀이

과학이 신체와 그것의 주변 환경과의 상호 작용에 대해 더 많이 알게 될수록 그 이야기는 유전자 만에 의해서 결정되는 것보다는 더욱 복잡해진다고 해야 하므로 (d) 'simplistic(단순한)'을 'complicated(복잡한)' 등의 단어로 고쳐야 한다.

11~12 회사는 고객의 불만을 받아들여야 한다

직독/직해

The market's way of telling a firm / about its failures /
회사에게 말해주는 시장의 방식은 / 실패에 대해 /
is harsh and brief. 가혹하면서 간단하다
Not only are complaints less expensive to handle /
불평은 다루기에 비용이 덜 들뿐만 아니라 /
but they also can cause the seller to improve.
판매자가 향상하게 만들 수도 있다
The seller may learn something / as well.
판매자는 교훈을 얻을지도 모른다 / 또한
I remember a cosmetics company /
나는 한 화장품 회사를 기억한다 /
that received complaints / 불평을 받은 /
about sticky sunblock lotion. 끈적거리는 선크림 로션에 대한
At the time, / 그 당시에 /
all such lotions were more or less sticky, /
그런 로션은 모두 다소 끈적거렸다 /
so the risk of having customers buy products /
그래서 고객들이 제품을 사게 하는 위험은 /
from a rival company / 경쟁사의 /
was not great. 크지 않았다
But this was also an opportunity.
하지만 이것은 또한 기회였다
The company managed to develop a product /
그 회사는 제품을 개발해냈다 /
that was not sticky / 끈적거리지 않는 /
and captured 20 percent of the market /
그리고 시장의 20%를 점유했다 /
in its first year. 첫해에
Another company had the opposite problem.
또 다른 회사는 반대의 문제를 가졌다
Its products were not sticky enough.
그 회사의 상품은 충분히 끈적거리지 않았다
The company was a Royal Post Office /
그 회사는 Royal Post Office였다 /
in Europe / 유럽에 있는 /
and the product was a stamp.
그리고 상품은 우표였다
The problem was / 문제는 ~이었다 /
that the stamp didn't stick to the envelope.
우표가 편지 봉투에 붙지 않았다는 것
Management contacted the stamp producer /
경영진은 우표 제작자에게 연락했다 /
who made it clear / 그는 명확히 밝혔다 /
that if people just moistened the stamps properly, /
만약 사람들이 우표를 적절히 적시기만 한다면 /
they would stick to any piece of paper.
우표가 어떤 종이에도 달라붙을 것이라는 점을
What to do? 어떻게 할까
Management didn't take long / 경영진이 오래 걸리지 않았다 /
to come to the conclusion / 결론에 도달하는 데에는 /
that it would be more costly / 비용이 덜 들 것이라는 /
to try to educate its customers /
고객에게 교육하려고 시도하는 것에 /
to wet each stamp / rather than to add more glue.
각각의 우표를 적시도록 / 더 많은 풀을 첨가하는 것보다는
The stamp producer was told / to add more glue /
우표 제작자는 지시받았다 / 더 많은 풀을 첨가하라고 /
and the problem didn't occur again.
그리고 그 문제는 더 이상 일어나지 않았다
Since it is better for the firm /
회사에게는 더 나은 일이기 때문에 /
to have buyers complain 구매자가 불평하게 하는 것이 /
rather than go elsewhere, / 다른 곳으로 가게 하는 것보다는 /
it is important to make it easier /
더 쉽게 만드는 것이 중요하다 /
for dissatisfied customers to complain.
불만족한 고객들이 불평하는 것을

회사에게 실패에 대해 말해주는 시장의 방식은 가혹하면서 간단하다. 불평은 다루기에 비용이 덜 들뿐만 아니라 판매자가 (a) 향상하게 만들 수도 있다. 판매자는 또한 교훈을 얻을지도 모른다. 나는 끈적거리는 선크림 로션에 대한 불평을 받은 한 화장품 회사를 기억한다. 그 당시에, 그런 로션은 모두 다소 끈적거렸고, 그래서 고객들이 경쟁사의 제품을 사게 하는 위험은 (b) 크지 않았다. 하지만 이것은 또한 기회였다. 그 회사는 끈적거리지 않는 제품을 개발해냈고, 첫해에 시장의 20%를 점유했다. 또 다른 회사는 (c) 반대의 문제를 가졌다. 그 회사의 상품은 충분히 끈적거리지 않았다. 그 회사는 유럽에 있는 Royal Post Office였고 상품은 우표였다. 문제는 우표가 편지 봉투에 붙지 않았다는 것이었다. 경영진은 우표 제작자에게 연락했는데, 그는 만약 사람들이 우표를 적절히 적시기만 한다면, 우표가 어떤 종이에도 달라붙을 것이라는 점을 명확히 밝혔다. 어떻게 할까? (우표에) 더 많은 풀을 첨가하는 것보다는 고객에게 각각의 우표를 적시도록 교육하려고 시도하는 것에 비용이 (d) 덜(→ 더) 들 것이라는 결론에 경영진이 도달하는 데에는 오래 걸리지 않았다. 우표 제작자는 더 많은 풀을 첨가하라고 지시받았고, 그 문제는 더 이상 일어나지 않았다.
구매자가 다른 곳으로 가게 하는 것보다는 불평하게 하는 것이 회사에게는 더 나은 일이기 때문에, 불만족한 고객들이 불평하는 것을 (e) 더 쉽게 만드는 것이 중요하다.

《어휘·어구》

harsh 가혹한
brief 간단한
complaint 불평
handle 다루다
cosmetics 화장품
sticky 끈적끈적한
manage 해내다
capture 점유하다, 차지하다
opposite 반대의
stick 붙이다
management 경영진
contact 연락하다
moisten 적시다
properly 적절히
come to the conclusion 결론에 도달하다
dissatisfied 불만스런
matter 중요하다
necessarily 반드시
unsolved 해결되지 않은
enemy 적

정답률 61%

11. ②

① 고객들에게 가장 중요한 디자인
② 불평: 왜 회사는 그것들을 환영해야 하는가
③ 저렴한 가격이 반드시 낮은 품질을 의미하지는 않는다
④ 다소 끈적이는: 해결되지 않은 문제
⑤ 경쟁자를 적이 아닌 친구처럼 대하라

문제풀이

화장품 회사와 우표 제작 회사가 소비자들의 불평을 받아들여 제품의 품질을 개선한 사례들로 보아, 글의 제목으로 ② 'Complaints: Why Firms Should Welcome Them(불평: 왜 회사는 그것들을 환영해야 하는가)'이 가장 적절하다.

정답률 44%

12. ④

문제풀이

접착력이 없는 우표에 대한 해결책으로 우표 제작자에게 더 많은 풀을 첨가하라고 지시했다는 것으로 보아, 고객에게 우표를 적시도록 교육하려는 시도가 비용이 더 들 것이라 판단했을 것이므로 (d) 'less(덜)'를 'more(더)'로 바꿔야 한다.

본문 118쪽

문법 플러스 19. 어순에 주의해야 할 구문

1. they had 2. if 3. how much the interactions 4. such 5. strong enough 6. If[whether] I could help him with his science project 7. what I wanted 8. if[whether] I enjoyed my trip 9. why the ski is blue 10. what major he was going into

1 [해석]▶ 나는 직원에게 컴퓨터에 관한 책이 어느 곳에 있는지 물었다.
[해설]▶ 직접의문문 Where did you have books about computers?가 동사 ask의 직접목적어로 들어가면 간접의문문 「의문사+주어+동사」의 어순을 취한다.
2 [해석]▶ 저는 당신이 야구 선수가 된 것을 후회한 적이 있는지 궁금합니다.
[해설]▶ 의문문이 동사의 목적어로 사용될 때 의문사가 없는 의문문의 경우, 접속사 if나 whether를 앞에 쓰고 「주어+동사」의 어순을 취한다.
3 [해석]▶ 이러한 단순한 행동의 직접적인 결과로서 당신은 당신의 인생에서 그 사람들과의 상호 작용이 얼마나 많이 개선될 것인지를 보게 될 것이다.
[해설]▶ 의문부사 how가 형용사나 부사를 수식하는 경우, 「how+형용사/부사+주어+동사」의 어순을 갖는다.
4 [해석]▶ 그들은 작은 사고에도 그처럼 소란을 피웠다.
[해설]▶ 「such+관사+명사」의 구조를 취한다.
5 [해석]▶ 그 로프는 네 몸무게를 유지해 줄 정도로 강하다.
[해설]▶ 형용사가 enough 앞에 나오는 것에 유의한다.
6 [해석]▶ 피터는 과학 프로젝트를 도와줄 수 있냐고 물었다.
[해설]▶ 의문사가 없는 직접의문문이 다른 문장의 일부로 들어가는 경우, 접속사 if 또는 whether를 넣고 다음에 주어, 동사 순서로 쓴다.
7 [해석]▶ 샐리가 내게 무엇을 원하는지 물었다.
[해설]▶ 의문사가 있는 직접의문문이 다른 문장의 일부로 들어가는 경우, 의문사(what)를 넣고 다음에 주어, 동사 순서로 쓴다.
8 [해석]▶ 벤이 내게 여행을 즐겼냐고 물었다.
[해설]▶ 의문사가 없는 직접의문문이 문장의 일부로 들어가는 경우, 접속사 if 또는 whether를 넣고 다음에 주어, 동사 순서로 쓴다.
9 [해석]▶ 아들은 종종 내게 왜 하늘이 파란색이냐고 물었다.
[해설]▶ 의문사가 있는 직접의문문이 다른 문장의 일부로 들어가는 경우, 의문사(why)를 넣고 다음에 주어, 동사 순서로 쓴다.
10 해석▶ 사라는 그에게 무슨 과에 진학할 거냐고 물었다.
[해설]▶ 의문사(what)가 뒤에 있는 명사를 수식하는 의문형용사로 사용되었다. 이와 같은 직접의문문을 문장의 다른 일부로 넣는 경우, 의문사 바로 뒤에 명사를 붙이고 다음에 주어, 동사 순서로 쓴다.

본문 119쪽

어휘 플러스 19. 반의어 (5)

B. 1. rejected 2. rigid 3. surpluses 4. verbal 5. vulnerable

1 [해석]▶ Sam은 그 아이디어를 터무니없다고 받아들이지 않았다.
2 [해석]▶ 논쟁은 때때로 엄격한 집안에서는 무례한 행동으로 간주된다.
3 [해석]▶ 체액을 제공하는 기증자(박쥐)는 일반적으로 자기에게서 남는 것을 함께 나누고, 그렇게 해서 아사에 처한, 먹이를 찾는데 성공하지 못한 약탈자(박쥐)들을 구한다고 Wilkinson은 밝혀냈다.

4 [해석]▶ 누군가 당신에게 전화를 한다. 분명히 당신이 그녀의 목소리를 인지할 것이라고 가정하고, 그녀는 당신이 그녀를 식별하는데 도움을 줄 말의 내용을 전혀 제공하지 않는다.
5 [해석]▶ 안전벨트 법률 제정의 주요 효과는 차량 안에서 이미 가장 잘 보호받고 있는 사람들로부터 가장 취약한 사람들, 즉, 차 밖에 있는 보행자들과 자전거를 타는 사람들로 위험에 대한 부담이 옮겨가는 것이었다.

본문 119쪽

D. 1. appreciate 2. invaluable 3. favorable 4. progressive 5. weaken

1 [해석]▶ 미국은 문화의 도가니이기 때문에 모든 미국인은 서로에 대해 알 필요가 있고 다양한 인종 집단이 기여한 공적을 높이 평가할 필요가 있다.
2 [해석]▶ 귀하는 1979년에 우편실에서 시작한 이래로 이 회사에 대한 귀하의 공헌이 아주 귀중했습니다.
3 [해석]▶ 연구에 따르면 우리는 재능, 상냥함, 정직 그리고 지성과 같은 좋은 특성들을 잘생긴 사람들에게 무의식적으로 부여한다는 것이 밝혀졌다.
4 [해석]▶ RPC는 1996년에 설립된 것으로 스스로를 사회의 변화를 위해 싸우는 진보 단체로 묘사한다.
5 [해석]▶ 외국 수입품에 대한 과도한 의존은 위기시 국가의 자기 방어 능력을 약화시킬 수도 있다.

20. 장문의 이해 (2)

Day 20

본문 122쪽

1. ④	2. ③	3. ③	4. ④	5. ②
6. ④	7. ②	8. ④	9. ⑤	10. ③
11. ②	12. ⑤			

대표 기출 Marie의 공감과 따뜻함

직독/직해

[A] On my daughter Marie's 8th birthday, /
나의 딸 Marie의 8번째 생일에 /
she received a bunch of presents /
그녀는 많은 선물을 받았다 /
from her friends at school. 학교에서 친구들로부터
That evening, / 그날 저녁 /
with her favorite present, a teddy bear, /
그녀가 가장 좋아하는 선물인 테디 베어를 /
in her arms, / we went to a restaurant /
팔에 안고 / 우리는 식당에 갔다 /
to celebrate her birthday.
그녀의 생일을 축하하기 위해
Our server, / a friendly woman, /
우리의 종업원은 / 다정한 여성인 /
noticed my daughter holding the teddy bear /
나의 딸이 테디 베어를 안고 있는 것을 알아차렸다 /
and said, / "My daughter loves teddy bears, too."
그리고 말했다 / "제 딸도 테디 베어를 좋아해요."
Then, / we started chatting about her family.
그러고 나서 / 우리는 그녀의 가족에 대해 담소를 나누기 시작했다
[D] The server mentioned / during the conversation /
그 종업원은 말했다 / 대화 중에 /
that her daughter was in the hospital /
자신의 딸이 병원에 있다고 /
with a broken leg. 다리가 부러져서
She also said / that Marie looked about the same age as her daughter.
그녀는 또한 말했다 / Marie가 자신의 딸과 또래처럼 보인다고 /
She was so kind and attentive all evening, /
그녀는 저녁 내내 매우 친절했고 세심했다 /
and even gave Marie cookies for free.
그리고 심지어 Marie에게 쿠키를 무료로 주었다
After we finished our meal, / we paid the bill /
우리가 식사를 마친 후 / 우리는 요금을 지불했다 /
and began to walk to our car /
그리고 우리 차로 걸어가기 시작했다 /
when unexpectedly Marie asked me to wait /
그때 갑자기 Marie가 나에게 기다려 달라고 부탁했다 /
and ran back into the restaurant.
그리고 식당으로 다시 뛰어 들어갔다
[B] When Marie came back out, / I asked her /
Marie가 돌아왔을 때 / 나는 그녀에게 물었다 /
what she had been doing.
무엇을 하고 있었느냐고
She said / that she gave her teddy bear to our server /
그녀는 말했다 / 그녀가 자신의 테디 베어를 종업원에게 주었다고 /
so that she could give it to her daughter.
그녀가 그것을 자신의 딸에게 줄 수 있게 하기 위해 /
I was surprised at her sudden action /
나는 그녀의 갑작스러운 행동에 놀랐다 /
because I could see / 나는 알 수 있었기 때문에 /
how much she loved that bear already.
그녀가 이미 그 테디 베어를 얼마나 좋아하는지

She must have seen the look on my face, /
그녀는 내 얼굴 표정을 본 것이 분명했다 /
because she said, /
왜냐하면 그녀가 말했기 때문에 /
"I can't imagine / being stuck in a hospital bed. /
"저는 상상할 수가 없어요 / 병원 침대에 갇혀 있는 것을 /
I just want her to get better soon."
전 단지 그녀가 빨리 낫기를 바랄 뿐이에요."
(C) I felt moved by Marie's words /
나는 Marie의 말에 감동받았다 /
as we walked toward the car.
우리가 차를 향해 걸어갈 때
Then, / our server ran out to our car /
그때 / 우리의 종업원이 우리 차로 달려 나왔다 /
and thanked Marie for her generosity.
그리고 Marie의 관대함에 고마워했다
The server said / that she had never had anyone /
종업원은 말했다 / 그녀가 어떤 사람도 결코 가진 적이 없었다고 /
doing anything like that / for her family before.
그런 일을 해 준 / 이전에 자신의 가족을 위해
Later, / Marie said / it was her best birthday ever.
나중에 / Marie는 말했다 / 그날이 그녀의 최고의 생일이었다고
I was so proud of her empathy and warmth, /
나는 그녀의 공감과 따뜻함이 너무 자랑스러웠다 /
and this was an unforgettable experience /
그리고 이것은 잊을 수 없는 경험이었다 /
for our family. 우리 가족에게

(A) 나의 딸 Marie의 8번째 생일에, 그녀는 학교에서 친구들로부터 많은 선물을 받았다. 그날 저녁, 그녀가 가장 좋아하는 선물인 테디 베어를 팔에 안고 우리는 그녀의 생일을 축하하기 위해 식당에 갔다. 다정한 여성인 우리의 종업원은 나의 딸이 테디 베어를 안고 있는 것을 알아차렸고, "제 딸도 테디 베어를 좋아해요."라고 말했다. 그리고 나서, 우리는 (a) 그녀의 가족에 대해 담소를 나누기 시작했다.
(D) 그 종업원은 대화 중에 자신의 딸이 다리가 부러져서 병원에 있다고 말했다. (e) 그녀는 또한 Marie가 자신의 딸과 또래처럼 보인다고 말했다. 그녀는 저녁 내내 매우 친절했고 세심했으며, 심지어 Marie에게 쿠키를 무료로 주었다. 우리가 식사를 마친 후, 요금을 지불하고 우리 차로 걸어가기 시작했는데, 그때 갑자기 Marie가 나에게 기다려 달라고 부탁하고 식당으로 다시 뛰어 들어갔다.
(B) Marie가 돌아왔을 때, 나는 그녀에게 무엇을 하고 있었느냐고 물었다. 그녀는 자신의 테디 베어를 우리의 종업원에게 주어 그녀가 (b) 자신의 딸에게 그것을 줄 수 있게 했다고 말했다. 나는 그녀가 이미 그 테디 베어를 얼마나 좋아하는지 알 수 있었기 때문에 그녀의 갑작스러운 행동에 놀랐다. (c) 그녀는 내 얼굴 표정을 분명히 봤을 것인데, 왜냐하면 그녀가 "저는 병원 침대에 갇혀 있는 것을 상상할 수가 없어요. 전 단지 그녀가 빨리 낫기를 바랄 뿐이에요."라고 말했기 때문이다.
(C) 우리가 차를 향해 걸어갈 때 나는 Marie의 말에 감동받았다. 그때 우리의 종업원이 우리 차로 달려 나와 Marie의 관대함에 고마워했다. 종업원은 (d) 그녀가 이전에 자신의 가족을 위해 그런 일을 해 준 어떤 사람도 결코 가진 적이 없었다고 말했다. 나중에 Marie는 그날이 그녀의 최고의 생일이었다고 말했다. 나는 그녀의 공감과 따뜻함이 너무 자랑스러웠고, 이것은 우리 가족에게 잊을 수 없는 경험이었다.

어휘·어구

receive 받다
celebrate 축하하다
notice 알아차리다
chat 담소를 나누다, 잡담하다
sudden 갑작스러운
action 행동
imagine 상상하다
be stuck in ~에 갇히다
server 종업원
generosity 관대함
empathy 공감
warmth 따뜻함
unforgettable 잊을 수 없는
experience 경험
mention 말하다, 언급하다
conversation 대화
attentive 세심한
unexpectedly 갑자기, 예상외로

정답률 82%

43. ④

문제풀이

딸이 가장 좋아하는 선물인 테디 베어를 안고 딸의 생일을 축하하기 위해 식당에 갔다가 다정한 종업원을 만나 테디 베어를 좋아하는 자신의 딸에 대해 말하는 종업원과 담소를 나누기 시작했다는 주어진 글 (A) 다음에, 종업원의 딸이 Marie와 같은 또래인데 지금은 다리가 부러져서 병원에 있다고 말하고 난 후 종업원으로부터 저녁 내내 만족스러운 서비스를 받고 나서 차로 걸어가는 중에 Marie가 식당으로 다시 뛰어 들어갔다는 내용의 (D)가 오고, 자신의 테디 베어를 종업원에게 주고, 종업원의 딸이 빨리 낫기를 바란다고 말하는 내용의 (B)가 온 뒤, Marie의 말에 감동을 받고, Marie 자신도 그날이 그녀의 최고 생일이었다고 말하는 것을 보고 딸을 자랑스러워했다는 내용의 (C)가 마지막에 오는 것이 글의 순서로 가장 적절하다.

정답률 71%

44. ③

문제풀이

병원 침대에 갇혀 있는 것을 상상할 수 없다고 하면서 그녀가 빨리 낫기를 바란다는 내용으로 보아 (c)는 Marie를 가리키고, 나머지는 모두 종업원을 가리킨다.

정답률 77%

45. ④

문제풀이

(D)의 'The server mentioned during the conversation that her daughter was in the hospital with a broken leg.'에서 종업원은 자신의 딸이 다리가 부러져서 병원에 있다고 했으므로, ④가 윗글에 관한 내용으로 적절하지 않다.

1~3 손자를 위해 최고의 학교를 찾은 할아버지

직독/직해

(A) A boy had a place / at the best school in town.
한 소년이 한 자리를 얻었다 / 마을에 있는 가장 좋은 학교에
In the morning, / 아침에 /
his granddad took him to the school.
그의 할아버지는 그를 학교에 데리고 갔다
When he went onto the playground /
그가 운동장으로 갔을 때 /
with his grandson, / 그의 손자와 함께 /
the children surrounded them.
아이들이 그들을 둘러쌌다
"What a funny old man," / one boy smirked.
"진짜 우스꽝스러운 할아버지다." / 한 소년이 히죽히죽 웃었다
A girl with brown hair / pointed at the pair /
갈색 머리의 한 소녀가 / 그 둘을 향해 손가락질했다 /
and jumped up and down.
그리고 위아래로 뛰었다
Suddenly, / the bell rang /
갑자기 / 종이 울렸다 /
and the children ran off / to their first lesson.
그리고 아이들이 급히 뛰어갔다 / 그들의 첫 수업에
(D) The old man took his grandson firmly by the hand, /
노인은 손자의 손을 꽉 잡았다 /
and led him out of the school gate.
그리고 그를 교문 밖으로 데리고 나갔다
"Brilliant, / I don't have to go to school!" /
"굉장한걸 / 나 학교에 가지 않아도 되네!" /
the boy exclaimed.
라고 소년이 소리쳤다
"You do, / but not this one," / his granddad replied.
"가긴 가야지 / 하지만 이 학교는 아니야." / 그의 할아버지가 대답했다
"I'll find you a school myself."
"내가 직접 네게 학교를 찾아주마."
Granddad took his grandson back /
할아버지는 손자를 데리고 돌아갔다 /
to his own house, / 자신의 집으로 /
asked grandma to look after him, /
할머니에게 그를 돌봐달라고 했다 /
and went off to look for a teacher himself.
그리고 그 자신이 선생님을 찾아 나섰다.
Every time he spotted a school, /
학교를 발견할 때마다 /
the old man went onto the playground, /
노인은 운동장으로 갔다 /
and waited for the children to come out /
그리고 아이들이 나오기를 기다렸다 /
at break time. 쉬는 시간에
(B) In some schools / 몇몇 학교에서는 /
the children completely ignored the old man /
아이들이 노인을 완전히 무시했다 /
and in others, / they made fun of him.
그리고 다른 학교들에서는 / 아이들이 그를 놀렸다
When this happened, / he would turn sadly /
이런 일이 일어났을 때 / 그는 슬프게 돌아서곤 했다 /
and go home. 그리고 집으로 가곤했다
Finally, / he went onto the tiny playground /
마침내 / 그는 아주 작은 운동장으로 갔다 /
of a very small school, / 매우 작은 한 학교의 /
and leant against the fence, / exhausted.
그리고 울타리에 기댔다 / 지쳐서
The bell rang, / and the crowd of children /
종이 울렸다 / 그리고 아이들의 무리가 /
ran out onto the playground.
운동장으로 달려 나왔다
"Sir, are you all right? /
"할아버지, 괜찮으세요? /
Shall I bring you a glass of water?" / a voice said.
물 한 잔 가져다드릴까요?" / 누군가가 말했다
"We've got a bench in the playground /
"우리 운동장에 벤치가 있어요 /
— come and sit down," / another voice said.
오셔서 앉으세요." / 또 다른 누군가가 말했다
Soon a young teacher / 곧 한 젊은 선생님이 /
came out onto the playground.
운동장으로 나왔다
(C) The old man greeted him / and said: /
노인은 그에게 인사했다 / 그리고 말했다 /
"Finally, / I've found my grandson /
"마침내 / 제가 제 손자에게 찾아주었네요 /
the best school in town."
마을 최고의 학교를."
"You're mistaken, sir. / Our school is not the best /
"잘못 아신 겁니다, 어르신. / 우리 학교는 최고가 아니에요 /
— it's small and cramped."
작고 비좁은걸요."
The old man didn't argue / with the teacher.
노인은 논쟁을 벌이지 않았다 / 선생님과
Instead, / he made arrangements /
대신에 / 그는 준비해 주었다 /
for his grandson to join the school, /
손자가 그 학교에 다닐 수 있도록 /

and then the old man left.
그리고 그런 다음에 노인은 떠났다
That evening, / the boy's mom said to him: /
그날 저녁 / 소년의 어머니는 그에게 말했다 /
"Dad, / you can't even read. / How do you know /
"아버지 / 글을 읽을 줄도 모르시잖아요. / 어떻게 아세요 /
you've found the best teacher of all?" /
최고의 선생님을 찾았다는 것을?"
"Judge a teacher by his pupils," /
"선생님은 그 제자를 보고 판단해야 해." /
the old man replied. 노인이 대답했다

(A) 한 소년이 마을에 있는 가장 좋은 학교에 한 자리를 얻었다. 아침에 그의 할아버지는 그를 학교에 데리고 갔다. (a) 그가 그의 손자와 함께 운동장으로 갔을 때, 아이들이 그들을 둘러쌌다. "진짜 우스꽝스러운 할아버지다."라며 한 소년이 히죽히죽 웃었다. 갈색 머리의 한 소녀가 그 둘(노인과 소년)을 향해 손가락질하며 위아래로 뛰었다. 갑자기 종이 울렸고, 아이들이 그들의 첫 수업에 급히 뛰어갔다.
(D) 노인은 손자의 손을 꽉 잡고, 그를 교문 밖으로 데리고 나갔다. "굉장한걸, 나 학교에 가지 않아도 되네!"라고 소년이 소리쳤다. "가긴 가야지, 하지만 이 학교는 아니야."라고 그의 할아버지가 대답했다. "내가 직접 네게 학교를 찾아주마." 할아버지는 손자를 자신의 집으로 데리고 돌아가 할머니에게 그를 돌봐달라고 하고 나서, (e) 그 자신이 선생님을 찾아 나섰다. 학교를 발견할 때마다, 노인은 운동장으로 가서 아이들이 쉬는 시간에 나오기를 기다렸다.
(B) 몇몇 학교에서는 아이들이 노인을 완전히 무시했고, 다른 학교들에서는 아이들이 (b) 그를 놀렸다. 이런 일이 일어났을 때, 그는 슬프게 돌아서서 집으로 가곤 했다. 마침내, 그는 매우 작은 한 학교의 아주 작은 운동장으로 갔고, 지쳐서 울타리에 기댔다. 종이 울렸고, 아이들의 무리가 운동장으로 달려 나왔다. "할아버지, 괜찮으세요? 물 한 잔 가져다드릴까요?" 누군가가 말했다. "우리 운동장에 벤치가 있어요 — 오셔서 앉으세요." 또 다른 누군가가 말했다. 곧 한 젊은 선생님이 운동장으로 나왔다.
(C) 노인은 (c) 그에게 인사하고 이렇게 말했다. "마침내, 제가 제 손자에게 마을 최고의 학교를 찾아주었네요." "잘못 아신 겁니다, 어르신. 우리 학교는 최고가 아니에요 — 작고 비좁은걸요." 노인은 선생님과 논쟁을 벌이지 않았다. 대신에, 그는 손자가 그 학교에 다닐 수 있도록 준비해 주고, 그런 다음에 노인은 떠났다. 그날 저녁, 소년의 어머니는 (d) 그에게 말했다. "아버지, 글을 읽을 줄도 모르시잖아요. 최고의 선생님을 찾았다는 것을 어떻게 아세요?" "선생님은 그 제자를 보고 판단해야 해."라고 노인이 대답했다.

어휘·어구

surround 둘러싸다
run off 급히 뛰어가다
completely 완전히
make fun of ~을 놀리다
lean 기대다
exhaust 지치다
argue 논쟁하다
make an arrangement for ~의 준비를 하다
firmly 강하게
brilliant 굉장한, 멋진
exclaim 외치다
spot 찾다, 발견하다

정답률 72%

1. ④

문제풀이

할아버지가 마을에서 가장 좋은 학교로 손자와 함께 갔는데 그들을 보고 나서 학교 학생들이 놀렸다는 내용의 주어진 글 다음에, 할아버지가 손자를 바로 데리고 나와 자신이 직접 손자를 위해 가장 좋은 학교를 찾아다니는 상황의 (D)가 오고, 지쳐서 아주 작은 학교의 울타리에 기댔는데 학생들이 할아버지를 위해 친절을 베푸는 상황이 묘사된 (B)가 온 뒤, 손자를 그 학교에 보내기로 결정했다는 내용의 (C)가 마지막에 오는 것이 글의 순서로 가장 적절하다.

정답률 71%

2. ③

문제풀이

노인이 인사를 했다는 것과 자신의 학교는 최고의 학교가 아니라는 말을 하는 상황으로 보아, (c)는 작은 학교의 선생님을 가리키고, 나머지는 모두 할아버지를 가리킨다.

정답률 74%

3. ③

문제풀이

(C)의 'The old man didn't argue with the teacher.'에서 노인은 선생님과 논쟁을 벌이지 않았다고 했으므로, ③이 윗글에 관한 내용으로 적절하지 않다.

4~6 농부의 소중한 시계를 찾아준 어린 소년

직독/직해

(A) Once, / a farmer lost his precious watch /
어느 날, / 한 농부가 그의 귀중한 시계를 잃어버렸다 /
while working in his barn.
헛간에서 일하는 동안
It may have appeared to be an ordinary watch /
그것은 평범한 시계로 보일 수도 있었다 /
to others, / 다른 사람들에게는 /
but it brought a lot of happy childhood memories /
하지만 그것은 어린 시절의 많은 행복한 기억을 불러왔다 /
to him. 그에게
It was one of the most important things / to him.
그것은 가장 중요한 것들 중 하나였다 / 그에게
After searching for it / for a long time, /
그것을 찾아본 뒤 / 오랜 시간 동안 /
the old farmer became exhausted.
그 나이 든 농부는 지쳤다
(D) However, / the tired farmer did not want to give up /
하지만 / 지친 농부는 포기하고 싶지 않았다 /
on the search for his watch / 그의 시계를 찾는 것을 /
and asked a group of children /
그리고 한 무리의 아이들에게 요청했다 /
playing outside / to help him.
밖에서 놀던 / 그를 도와 달라고
He promised an attractive reward /
그는 매력적인 보상을 약속했다 /
for the person who could find it.
그것을 찾을 수 있는 사람에게
After hearing about the reward, /
보상에 대해 듣고 난 후 /
the children hurried inside the barn /
아이들은 헛간 안으로 서둘러 들어갔다 /
and went through and round the entire pile of hay /
그리고 전체 건초 더미 사이와 주변으로 걸어갔다 /
looking for the watch. 시계를 찾으러
After a long time searching for it, /
시계를 찾느라 오랜 시간을 보낸 후 /
some of the children got tired / and gave up.
아이들 중 일부는 지쳤다 / 그리고 포기했다
(B) The number of children looking for the watch /
시계를 찾는 아이들의 수가 /
slowly decreased / 천천히 줄어들었다 /
and only a few tired children / were left.
그리고 오직 지친 아이들 몇 명만이 / 남았다
The farmer gave up / all hope of finding it /
농부는 포기했다 / 시계를 찾을 거라는 모든 희망을 /
and called off the search.
그리고 찾는 것을 멈추었다

Just when the farmer was closing the barn door, /
농부가 막 헛간 문을 닫고 있었을 때 /
a little boy came up to him / and asked the farmer /
한 어린 소년이 그에게 다가왔다 / 그리고 농부에게 요청했다 /
to give him another chance.
자신에게 또 한 번의 기회를 달라고
The farmer did not want to lose out /
농부는 놓치고 싶지 않았다 /
on any chance of finding the watch /
시계를 찾을 어떤 가능성도 /
so let him in the barn.
그래서 그를 헛간 안으로 들어오게 해주었다
(C) After a little while / the boy came out /
잠시 후 / 소년이 나왔다 /
with the farmer's watch in his hand.
한 손에 농부의 시계를 들고
He was happily surprised /
그는 행복에 겨워 놀랐다 /
and asked how he had succeeded /
그리고 소년이 어떻게 성공했는지를 물었다 /
to find the watch / while everyone else had failed.
시계를 찾는 데 / 다른 모두가 실패했던 반면
He replied / "I just sat there /
그는 답했다 / "저는 그냥 거기에 앉아있었어요 /
and tried listening for the sound of the watch. /
그리고 시계 소리를 들으려고 했어요 /
In silence, / it was much easier / to hear it /
침묵 속에서 / 훨씬 쉬웠어요 / 그것을 듣는 것이 /
and follow the direction of the sound."
그리고 소리의 방향을 따라가는 것이
He was delighted to get his watch back /
그는 자신의 시계를 되찾아서 기뻤다 /
and rewarded the little boy / as promised.
그리고 그 어린 소년에게 보상해 주었다 / 약속했던 대로

(A) 어느 날, 한 농부가 헛간에서 일하는 동안 그의 귀중한 시계를 잃어버렸다. 그것은 다른 사람들에게는 평범한 시계로 보일 수도 있었지만, 그것은 그에게 어린 시절의 많은 행복한 기억을 불러왔다. 그것은 (a) 그에게 가장 중요한 것들 중 하나였다. 오랜 시간 동안 그것을 찾아본 뒤 그 나이 든 농부는 지쳤다.
(D) 하지만 지친 농부는 그의 시계를 찾는 것을 포기하고 싶지 않아서 밖에서 놀던 한 무리의 아이들에게 도와 달라고 요청했다. 그는 그것을 찾을 수 있는 사람에게 매력적인 보상을 약속했다. 보상에 대해 듣고 난 후, 아이들은 헛간 안으로 서둘러 들어갔고 시계를 찾으러 전체 건초 더미 사이와 주변으로 걸어갔다. 시계를 찾느라 오랜 시간을 보낸 후, 아이들 중 일부는 지쳐서 포기했다.
(B) 시계를 찾는 아이들의 수가 천천히 줄어들었고 지친 아이들 몇 명만이 남았다. 농부는 시계를 찾을 거라는 모든 희망을 포기하고 찾는 것을 멈추었다. 농부가 막 헛간 문을 닫고 있었을 때, 한 어린 소년이 그에게 다가와서 자신에게 또 한 번의 기회를 달라고 요청했다. 농부는 시계를 찾을 어떤 가능성도 놓치고 싶지 않아서 (b) 그를 헛간 안으로 들어오게 해주었다.
(C) 잠시 후 소년이 한 손에 농부의 시계를 들고 나왔다. (c) 그는 행복에 겨워 놀랐고 다른 모두가 실패했던 반면 소년이 어떻게 시계를 찾는 데 성공했는지를 물었다. 그는 "저는 그냥 거기에 앉아서 시계 소리를 들으려고 했어요. 침묵 속에서, 그것을 듣고 소리의 방향을 따라가는 것이 훨씬 쉬웠어요."라고 답했다. (d) 그는 자신의 시계를 되찾아서 기뻤고 약속했던 대로 그 어린 소년에게 보상해 주었다.

어휘·어구

precious 귀중한
appear ~처럼 보이다
ordinary 평범한
childhood 어린 시절, 유년 시절
exhausted 기진맥진한
decrease 줄다
call off 멈추다, 중지하다
succeed 성공하다
silence 침묵
direction 방향
delighted 기쁜
reward 보상(하다)
attractive 매력적인
hay 건초(마른 풀)

정답률 81%

4. ④

문제풀이

한 농부가 헛간에서 자신의 귀중한 시계를 잃어버려 오랜 시간 찾아본 뒤 지쳤다는 내용의 주어진 글 (A) 다음에 농부가 밖에서 놀던 아이들에게 시계를 찾으면 보상을 해주겠다는 약속을 하고 아이들이 헛간에 들어와서 시계를 찾았지만 아이들 중 일부는 지쳐서 포기했다는 내용의 (D)가 온 뒤, 아이들이 점점 시계를 찾는 데 지쳐서 농부가 모든 희망을 포기하고 멈추려는 순간 한 어린 소년이 다가와서 찾을 기회를 다시 달라고 요청했다는 내용의 (B)가 오고, 결국 소년이 농부의 시계를 찾게 되고 어떻게 찾게 되었는지에 대해 설명하고 난 뒤, 농부가 약속대로 보상을 해주었다는 내용의 (C)가 마지막에 오는 것이 글의 순서로 가장 적절하다.

5. ②

문제풀이

농부가 시계를 찾을 어떤 가능성도 놓치고 싶지 않아서 헛간 안으로 들어오게 해주었다는 것으로 보아 (b)는 어린 소년을 가리키고, 나머지는 모두 농부를 가리킨다.

6. ④

문제풀이

(D)의 'After hearing about the reward, the children hurried inside the barn and went through and round the entire pile of hay looking for the watch.'에서 아이들이 시계를 찾기 위해 헛간 안으로 들어갔다고 했으므로, ④가 윗글에 관한 내용으로 적절하지 않다.

7~9 긍정적인 마음가짐

직독/직해

(A) One day a young man was walking along a road /
어느 날 한 젊은이가 길을 따라 걷고 있었다 /
on his journey from one village to another.
한 마을에서 다른 마을로 여행하면서
As he walked / he noticed a monk /
그는 걷다가 / 한 수도승을 보았다 /
working in the fields. 들판에서 일하는
The young man turned to the monk / and said, /
그 젊은이는 그 수도승을 향해 돌아봤다 / 그리고 말했다 /
"Excuse me. / Do you mind if I ask you a question?"
실례합니다 / 제가 수도승께 질문을 하나 드려도 되겠습니까
"Not at all," / replied the monk.
물론입니다 / 그 수도승은 대답했다
(C) "I am traveling / from the village in the mountains /
저는 가고 있습니다 / 산속 마을에서 /
to the village in the valley / and I was wondering /
골짜기 마을로 / 그리고 궁금합니다 /
if you knew / what it is like in the village in the valley."
수도승께서 아시는지 / 골짜기 마을은 어떤지 /
"Tell me," / said the monk, /
저에게 말해 보십시오 / 수도승은 말했다 /
"what was your experience of the village in the mountains?"
산속 마을에서의 경험은 어땠습니까
"Terrible," / replied the young man.
끔찍했습니다 / 그 젊은이는 대답했다
"I am glad / to be away from there.
저는 기쁩니다 / 그곳에서 벗어나게 되어
I found the people most unwelcoming.
그곳 사람들이 정말로 불친절하다고 생각했습니다
So tell me, / what can I expect /
그러니 저에게 말씀해 주십시오 / 제가 무엇을 기대할 수 있을까요 /
in the village in the valley?" 골짜기 마을에서
"I am sorry to tell you," / said the monk, /
말씀드리기에 유감입니다 / 수도승이 말했다 /
"but I think / 하지만 저는 생각합니다 /
your experience will be much the same there."
선생님의 경험은 거기에서도 거의 같을 것이라고
The young man lowered his head helplessly /
그 젊은이는 힘없이 고개를 숙였다 /
and walked on. 그리고 계속 걸어갔다
(B) A while later / 잠시 후에 /
a middle-aged man journeyed down the same road /
한 중년 남자가 같은 길을 걸어왔다 /
and came upon the monk.
그리고 그 수도승을 만났다
"I am going to the village in the valley," /
저는 골짜기 마을로 가고 있습니다 /
said the man. 그 남자는 말했다
"Do you know what it is like?"
그곳이 어떤지 아십니까
"I do," replied the monk, /
알고 있습니다 / 그 수도승은 대답했다 /
"but first tell me about the village /
하지만 저에게 먼저 마을에 관해 말해 주십시오 /
where you came from." 선생님께서 떠나오신
"I've come from the village in the mountains," /
저는 산속 마을에서 왔습니다 /
said the man. 그 남자는 말했다
"It was a wonderful experience. /
그것은 멋진 경험이었습니다 /
I felt as though I was a member of the family /
저는 마치 가족의 일원인 것처럼 느꼈습니다 /
in the village." 그 마을의
(D) "Why did you feel like that?" / asked the monk.
선생님께서는 왜 그렇게 느끼셨습니까 / 그 수도승은 물었다
"The elders gave me much advice, /
어르신들은 저에게 많은 조언을 해 주셨습니다. /
and people were kind and generous./
그리고 사람들은 친절하고 너그러웠습니다 /
I am sad / to have left there. /
저는 슬픕니다 / 그곳을 떠나서 /
And what is the village in the valley like?" /
그런데 골짜기의 마을은 어떻습니까 /
he asked again. 그는 다시 물었다
"I think / you will find it much the same," /
저는 생각합니다 / 그곳이 거의 같다고 생각하실 거로 /
replied the monk. 수도승은 대답했다
"I'm glad to hear that," /
그 말씀을 들으니 기쁩니다 /
the middle-aged man said smiling /
그 중년 남자는 미소를 지으며 말했다 /
and journeyed on. 그리고 여행을 계속했다

(A) 어느 날 한 젊은이가 한 마을에서 다른 마을로 여행하면서 길을 따라 걷고 있었다. 그는 걷다가 들판에서 일하는 한 수도승을 보았다. 그 젊은이는 그 수도승을 향해 돌아보며 "실례합니다. 제가 수도승께 질문을 하나 드려도 되겠습니까?"라고 말했다. "물론입니다."라고 그 수도승은 대답했다.

(C) "저는 산속 마을에서 골짜기 마을로 가고 있는데 수도승께서 골짜기 마을은 어떤지 아시는지 궁금합니다." 수도승은 "저에게 말해 보십시오. 산속 마을에서의 경험은 어땠습니까?"라고 말했다. "끔찍했습니다."라고 그 젊은이는 대답했다. "저는 그곳에서 벗어나게 되어 기쁩니다. 그곳 사람들이 정말로 불친절하다고 생각했습니다. 그러니 저에게 말씀해 주십시오. 제가 골짜기 마을에서 무엇을 기대할 수 있을까요?" "말씀드리기에 유감이지만, 제 생각에 선생님의 경험은 거기에서도 거의 같을 것 같습니다."라고 수도승이 말했다. 그 젊은이는 힘없이 고개를 숙이고 계속 걸어갔다.

(B) 잠시 후에 한 중년 남자가 같은 길을 걸어와서 그 수도승을 만났다. 그 남자는 "저는 골짜기 마을로 가고 있습니다. 그곳이 어떤지 아십니까?"라고 말했다. "알고 있습니다만, 먼저 저에게 선생님께서 떠나오신 마을에 관해 말해 주십시오."라고 그 수도승은 대답했다. 그 남자는 "저는 산속 마을에서 왔습니다. 그것은 멋진 경험이었습니다. 저는 마치 그 마을의 가족의 일원인 것처럼 느꼈습니다."라고 말했다.

(D) 그 수도승은 "선생님께서는 왜 그렇게 느끼셨습니까?"라고 물었다. "어르신들은 저에게 많은 조언을 해 주셨고, 사람들은 친절하고 너그러웠습니다. 저는 그곳을 떠나서 슬픕니다. 그런데 골짜기의 마을은 어떻습니까?"라고 그는 다시 물었다. "저는 선생님은 그곳이 (산속 마을과) 거의 같다고 생각하실 거로 생각합니다."라고 수도승은 대답했다. "그 말씀을 들으니 기쁩니다."라고 그 중년 남자는 미소를 지으며 말하고서 여행을 계속했다.

어휘·어구

journey 여행
field 들판
reply 대답하다
middle-aged 중년의
come upon ~을 만나다
valley 골짜기
experience 경험
unwelcoming 불친절한
helplessly 힘없이
generous 너그러운

7. ②

문제풀이

한 젊은이가 여행하다가 수도승을 보고 질문을 해도 되냐고 묻는 상황의 주어진 글 (A) 다음에, 골짜기 마을이 어떤지를 묻는 젊은이에게 수도승이 산속 마을의 경험을 묻고, 젊은이가 끔찍한 경험이었다고 대답하자 골짜기 마을에서도 끔찍할 것이라 대답하는 상황의 (C)가 온 뒤, 한 중년 남자가 수도승에게 같은 질문을 하자 수도승이 떠나온 마을이 어땠냐고 묻고, 중년 남자가 멋진 경험이었다고 대답하는 상황의 (B)가 오고, 수도승이 중년 남자에게 멋진 경험이라 생각한 이유를 물은 뒤 골짜기 마을에서도 같은 경험을 할 거라는 대답을 하자 이 대답을 듣고 중년 남자는 행복해하며 여행을 계속했다는 내용의 (D)가 마지막에 오는 것이 글의 순서로 가장 적절하다.

8. ④

문제풀이

산속 마을에서의 경험이 끔찍했다고 하면서 골짜기 마을에서 무엇을 기대할 수 있을지를 묻는 것으로 보아 (d)는 젊은이를 가리키고, 나머지는 모두 수도승을 가리킨다.

9. ⑤

문제풀이

(D)의 'I am sad to have left there.'에서 산속 마을을 떠나서 슬프다고 했으므로, ⑤가 윗글에 관한 내용으로 적절하지 않다.

10~12 사려 깊은 왕자

직독/직해

(A) One day / a poor man brought a bunch of grapes /
어느 날 / 한 가난한 남자가 한 송이의 포도를 가져왔다 /
to a prince / as a gift.
왕자에게 / 선물로
He was very excited / 그는 매우 흥분했다 /
to be able to bring a gift for him /
그를 위한 선물을 가져올 수 있어서 /
because he was too poor to afford more.
그가 너무 가난해서 그 이상의 여유가 없었기 때문에
He placed the grapes / beside the prince / and said, /
그는 포도를 놓았다 / 그 왕자의 옆에 / 그리고 말했다 /
"Oh, Prince, please accept this small gift from me."
오, 왕자님, 저의 이 작은 선물을 부디 받아주세요
His face beamed with happiness /
그의 얼굴은 행복으로 빛났다 /
as he offered his small gift.
그가 자신의 작은 선물을 바치면서
(C) The prince thanked him politely.
그 왕자는 그에게 정중하게 감사를 표했다
As the man looked at him expectantly, /
그 남자가 기대에 부풀어 그를 바라보았을 때 /
the prince ate one grape.
그 왕자는 포도 한 알을 먹었다
Then he ate another one.
그러고 나서 그는 또 다른 하나를 먹었다
Slowly the prince finished the whole bunch of grapes by himself.
천천히 그 왕자는 혼자서 포도 한 송이 전부를 다 먹었다
He did not offer grapes / to anyone near him.
그는 포도를 권하지 않았다 / 자신의 곁에 있는 어떤 이에게도
The man / who brought those grapes to him /
그 남자는 / 그 포도를 그에게 가져온 /
was very pleased and left.
매우 기뻐하고 떠났다
The close friends of the prince /
그 왕자의 가까운 친구들은 /
who were around him / were very surprised.
그의 주변에 있던 / 매우 놀랐다
(D) Usually / the prince shared /
평소에 / 그 왕자는 나눴다 /
whatever he had / with others.
자신이 가지고 있는 어떤 것이든 / 다른 사람들과
He would offer them / whatever he was given /
그는 권하곤 했다 / 자신이 받은 것은 무엇이든지 /
and they would eat it together.
그리고 그들은 그것을 함께 먹곤 했다
This time was different.
이번에는 달랐다
Without offering it to anyone, /
아무에게도 그것을 권하지 않고 /
he finished the bunch of grapes by himself.
그는 포도 한 송이를 혼자 다 먹었다
One of the friends asked, /
그 친구들 중 한 명이 물었다 /
"Prince! How come you ate all the grapes /
왕자님! 어찌하여 포도를 다 드셨습니까 /
by yourself / and did not offer them /
혼자서 / 그리고 그것을 권하지 않으셨나요 /
to any one of us?" 우리 중 그 누구에게도
He smiled and said / 그는 웃으며 말했다 /
that he ate all the grapes by himself /
그가 혼자서 모든 포도를 다 먹었다고 /
because the grapes were too sour.
그 포도가 너무 시어서
(B) If the prince had offered the grapes to them, /
만약 그 왕자가 그들에게 그 포도를 권했다면 /
they might have made funny faces /
그들은 우스꽝스러운 표정을 지었을 것이다 /
and shown their distaste for the grapes.
그리고 포도에 대한 불쾌감을 드러냈을 것이다
That would have hurt the feelings of that poor man.
그것은 그 가난한 남자의 감정을 상하게 했을 것이다
He thought to himself / that it would be better /
그는 속으로 생각했다 / 더 낫다고 /
to eat all of them cheerfully / and please him.
모든 포도를 기분 좋게 먹는 것이 / 그리고 그를 기쁘게 하는 것이
He did not want to hurt the feelings of that poor man.
그는 그 가난한 남자의 감정을 상하게 하고 싶지 않았다
Everyone around him was moved by his thoughtfulness.
그의 주위의 모든 사람들은 그의 사려 깊음에 감동 받았다

(A) 어느 날 한 가난한 남자가 한 송이의 포도를 왕자에게 선물로 가져왔다. 그는 너무 가난해서 그 이상의 여유가 없었기 때문에 (a) 그를 위한 선물을 가져올 수 있어서 매우 흥분했다. 그는 그 왕자의 옆에 포도를 놓고 "오, 왕자님, 저의 이 작은 선물을 부디 받아주세요."라고 말했다. 그의 얼굴은 그가 자신의 작은 선물을 바치면서 행복으로 빛났다.
(C) 그 왕자는 그에게 정중하게 감사를 표했다. 그 남자가 기대에 부풀어 그를 바라보았을 때 그 왕자는 포도 한 알을 먹었다. 그러고 나서 (c) 그는 또 다른 하나를 먹었다. 천천히 그 왕자는 혼자서 포도 한 송이 전부를 다 먹었다. 그는 자신의 곁에 있는 어떤 이에게도 포도를 권하지 않았다. 그 포도를 (d) 그에게 가져온 남자는 매우 기뻐하고 떠났다. 그 왕자의 주변에 있던 그의 가까운 친구들은 매우 놀랐다.
(D) 평소에 그 왕자는 자신이 가지고 있는 어떤 것이든 다른 사람들과 나눴다. 그는 그들에게 자신이 받은 것은 무엇이든지 권하고 그들은 그것을 함께 먹곤 했다. 이번에는 달랐다. 아무에게도 그것을 권하지 않고 (e) 그는 포도 한 송이를 혼자 다 먹었다. 그 친구들 중 한 명이 "왕자님! 어찌하여 혼자서 포도를 다 드시고 우리 중 그 누구에게도 그것을 권하지 않으셨나요?"라고 물었다. 그는 웃으며 그 포도가 너무 시어서 혼자서 모든 포도를 다 먹었다고 말했다.
(B) 만약 그 왕자가 그들에게 그 포도를 권했다면 그들은 우스꽝스러운 표정을 지으며 포도에 대한 불쾌감을 드러냈을 것이다. 그것은 그 가난한 남자의 감정을 상하게 했을 것이다. 그는 모든 포도를 기분 좋게 먹고 (b) 그를 기쁘게 하는 것이 더 낫다고 속으로 생각했다. 그는 그 가난한 남자의 감정을 상하게 하고 싶지 않았다. 그의 주위의 모든 사람들은 그의 사려 깊음에 감동 받았다.

어휘·어구

bunch 무리, 다발
afford ~할 여유가 있다
beam 빛나다
politely 정중하게
expectantly 기대하여
the whole 전체, 전부
pleased 기쁜
share ~ with ... ~을 …와 나누다
sour 신맛이 나는
distaste 싫어하는
cheerfully 쾌활하게, 명랑하게
thoughtfulness 사려 깊은

정답률 

10. ③

문제풀이
한 가난한 남자가 한 송이의 포도를 왕자에게 선물로 바치는 내용의 주어진 글 (A) 다음에 왕자가 그 남자에게 감사하며 혼자서 포도 한 송이를 다 먹자, 주변에 있던 왕자의 가까운 친구들이 매우 놀랐다는 내용의 (C)가 이어지고, 평소에 왕자는 자신이 가진 것을 다른 사람들과 나눴지만 이번에는 포도 한 송이를 다 먹었는데 그 이유가 포도가 시었기 때문이라는 내용의 (D)가 이어진 다음, 만일 왕자가 다른 사람들에게 포도를 권했다면 그들이 신 포도에 대한 불쾌감을 드러내어 그 가난한 남자의 감정을 상하게 할까 봐 혼자 포도 한 송이를 다 먹었다는 왕자의 사려 깊음이 언급된 (B)가 마지막으로 이어지는 것이 글의 순서로 가장 적절하다.

정답률 

11. ②

문제풀이
(b)는 가난한 남자를 가리키고, 나머지는 모두 왕자를 가리킨다.

정답률 

12. ⑤

문제풀이
(D)의 'Without offering it to anyone, he finished the bunch of grapes by himself.(아무에게도 그것을 권하지 않고 그는 포도 한 송이를 혼자 다 먹었다.)로 보아 왕자에 관한 내용으로 일치하지 않는 것은 ⑤이다.

본문 127쪽

문법 플러스 20. 강조와 도치

1. that 2. do 3. comes the last train 4. was her astonishment 5. does the teacher 6. neither 7. did I 8. did she 9. did I realize 10. does ths flower

1 [해석]▶ 지진이 발생한 것은 정확히 9시였다.
[해설]▶ It was ~ that 강조 구문이다. 강조 대상이 시간인 경우, that 대신에 when으로 바꿀 수 있다. 또한 강조 대상이 장소인 경우, that 대신에 where로 바꿀 수 있다.

2 [해석]▶ 너는 정말로 창백해 보여.
[해설]▶ 동사를 강조하려면 do / does / did를 넣는다. 주어가 2인칭이므로, do가 맞다.

3 [해석]▶ 막차 기차가 온다.
[해설]▶ 부사(구) here를 강조하기 위해 문두로 둔 경우, 「동사+주어」 어순으로 바뀐다.

4 [해석]▶ 그녀는 너무 놀라서 말을 하지 못했다.
[해설]▶ 보어(so great)를 강조하기 위해 문두로 둔 경우, 「동사+주어」 어순으로 바뀐다.

5 [해석]▶ 오로지 그 상황을 이해하고 난 후에야, 선생님은 말씀을 하셨다.
[해설]▶ only와 결합된 어구를 강조하기 위해 문두로 둔 경우, 「동사+주어」 어순으로 바뀐다.

6 [해석]▶ 그는 영어를 말하지 못하는데, 나도 그렇다.
[해설]▶ 「neither+동사+주어」는 앞 문장에 대해 부정 동의 표현이다.

7 [해석]▶ Sally가 미생물학을 수강 신청하자, 나도 그랬다.
[해설]▶ 「So+동사+주어」는 앞 사실에 대해 '주어도 그렇다'는 의미이다.

8 [해석]▶ 그녀는 그 상황을 거의 이해하지 못했다.
[해설]▶ 부정어(little)를 강조하기 위해 문두로 둔 경우, 「동사+주어」 또는 「조동사+주어+동사」의 어순으로 바뀐다.

9 [해석]▶ 그때가 되어서야, 나는 바다에서 발생한 사고의 끔찍함을 인식했다.
[해설]▶ 부정어(Not until then)를 강조하기 위해 문두로 둔 경우, 「동사+주어」 또는 「조동사+주어+동사」의 어순으로 바뀐다.

10 해석▶ 이 꽃은 보기에 예쁠 뿐만 아니라 얼마나 많은 스모그가 그 도시의 공기 중에 있는지를 알려 주는 데 사용된다.
[해설]▶ 부정어(Not only)가 문두에 오는 경우 주어와 동사가 도치된다. 「동사+주어」 또는 「조동사+주어+동사」의 어순으로 써야 한다.

본문 128쪽

어휘 플러스+ 20. 다의어

1. features 2. issues
3. present 4. term
5. accounted

1 [해석]▶ 가벼운 안개가 보다 낮은 곳에 있는 풍경의 지형을 부분적으로 감추면서 대지를 따라 깔려 있었지만, 그 위에는 보다 큰 나무들이 맑은 하늘을 배경으로 윤곽이 뚜렷한 무리를 이루어 드러나 있었다.

2 [해석]▶ RPC 단체는 또한 공정 주택 거래와 양성 평등과 환경 정의와 같은 이슈를 위해 노력하고 있다.

3 [해석]▶ 과거와 현재는 우리의 수단이고, 단지 미래만이 우리의 목적이다.

4 [해석]▶ 완곡어법이라는 말은 '좋은 단어들로 말하다'를 의미하는 그리스 단어에서 비롯되었으며, 무언가를 말하는 더 듣기 좋고 불쾌감이 덜한 방식으로 직설적이거나 보다 직접적인 방식을 대체하는 것과 관련되어 있다.

5 [해석]▶ 석탄과 토탄을 제외하고, 수력은 1971년과 2007년 모두에서 전체 전력 생산의 20퍼센트 이상을 차지한 유일한 에너지원이었다.

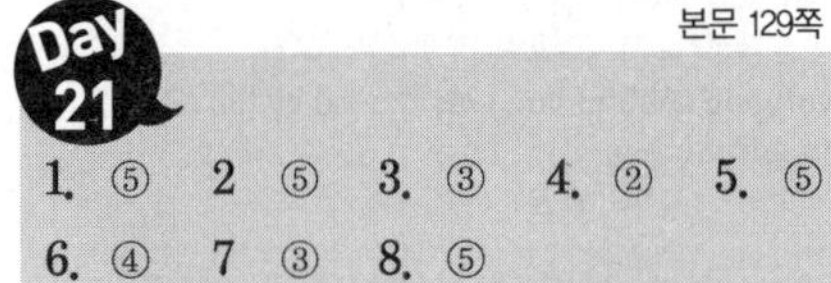

미니 고난도 Test 1회

본문 129쪽

Day 21

1. ⑤ 2 ⑤ 3. ③ 4. ② 5. ⑤
6. ④ 7 ③ 8. ⑤

정답률 44%

1. ⑤ 인성 함양에 있어 양날의 검이 되는 승리

직독/직해

Research has confirmed /
연구는 확인했다 /
that athletes are less likely to participate in unacceptable behavior /
운동선수는 받아들여지지 않는 행동을 덜 할 것이라고 /
than are non-athletes.
선수가 아닌 사람들보다
However, / 하지만 /
moral reasoning and good sporting behavior /
도덕적 분별력과 바람직한 스포츠 행위가 /
seem to decline / 감소하는 것 같다 /
as athletes progress to higher competitive levels, /
운동선수가 더 높은 경쟁적 수준까지 올라감에 따라 /
in part because of the increased emphasis on winning.
부분적으로 승리에 대한 강조가 커지기 때문에
Thus winning can be a double-edged sword /
따라서 승리는 양날의 검이 될 수 있다 /
in teaching character development.
인성 함양을 가르치는 데 있어
Some athletes may want to win so much /
어떤 선수는 너무나도 이기고 싶어서 /
that they lie, cheat, and break team rules.
거짓말하고 속이고 팀 규칙을 위반한다
They may develop undesirable character traits /
그들은 바람직하지 못한 인격 특성을 계발할지 모른다 /
that can enhance their ability /
자신의 능력을 강화할 수 있는 /
to win in the short term. 단시간에 이기고자
However, / 하지만 /
when athletes resist the temptation to win /
선수가 이기고자 하는 유혹에 저항할 때 /
in a dishonest way, / 부정한 방법으로 /
they can develop positive character traits /
그들은 긍정적인 인격 특성을 계발할 수 있다 /
that last a lifetime. 일생동안 지속되는
Character is a learned behavior, /
인성은 학습되는 행동이다 /
and a sense of fair play develops /
그리고 페어 플레이 정신이 발달한다
only if coaches plan to teach /
오직 코치가 가르치고자 계획할 때만 /
those lessons systematically.
그런 교훈을 체계적으로

운동선수는 선수가 아닌 사람들보다 받아들여지지 않는 행동을 덜 할 것이라고 연구는 확인했다. 하지만 부분적으로 승리에 대한 강조가 커지기 때문에 운동선수가 더 높은 경쟁적 수준까지 올라감에 따라 도덕적 분별력과 바람직한 스포츠 행위가 감소하는 것 같다. 따라서 승리는 인성 함양을 가르치는 데 있어 양날의 검이 될 수 있다. 어떤 선수는 너무나도 이기고 싶어서 거짓말하고 속이고 팀 규칙을 위반한다. 그들은 단시간에 이기고자 자신의 능력을 강화할 수 있는 바람직하지 못한 인격 특성을 계발할지 모른다. 하지만 선수가 부정한 방법으로 이기고자 하는 유혹에 저항할 때 그들은 일생동안 지속되는 긍정적인 인격 특성을 계발할 수 있다. 인성은 학습되는 행동이고, 코치가 그런 교훈을 체계적으로 가르치고자 계획할 때만 페어 플레이 정신이 발달한다.

① 식은 죽 먹기
② 일방통행
③ 손 안에 든 새
④ 물 밖에 나온 물고기
⑤ 양날의 검

문제풀이

운동선수의 승리를 위한 욕구가 인성 함양을 기르는 데 있어 해가 된다는 내용이므로, 빈칸에 ⑤ 'a double-edged sword'가 들어가서, 빈칸이 포함되는 문장이 '따라서 승리는 인성 함양을 가르치는 데 있어 양날의 검이 될 수 있다.'가 되는 것이 가장 적절하다.

구조 다시보기

도입	운동선수는 일반인들보다 용인되지 않는 행동을 덜 함
반론	승리에 대한 욕구가 커질수록 인성 함양을 가르치는 데 있어 해가 됨
결론	부정한 방법으로 승리를 하고자 하는 유혹에 저항해야 긍정적인 인성 계발이 가능함

《어휘·어구》

confirm 확인하다
participate in ~에 참여하다
unacceptable 받아들이기 어려운
moral reasoning 도덕적 추론[분별]
decline 감소하다
competitive 경쟁적인
emphasis 강조
resist 저항하다
character 인격, 성격
undesirable 바람직하지 않은
enhance 강화하다, 향상하다
temptation 유혹
systematically 체계적으로
double-edged sword 양날의 검

정답률 36%

2. ⑤ 실질적인 자유

직독/직해

It is important to distinguish / 구별하는 것은 중요하다 /
between being legally allowed to do something, /
무언가를 할 수 있도록 법적으로 허용되는 것과 /
and actually being able to go and do it.
실제로 그것을 해 버릴 수 있는 것을
A law could be passed / allowing everyone, /
법이 통과될 수도 있다 / 모든 사람에게 허용하는 /
if they so wish, / 그들이 원한다면 /
to run a mile in two minutes.
2분 안에 1마일을 달릴 수 있게
That would not, / however, /
그렇게 하는 것이 ~하지 않을 것이다 / 하지만 /
increase their effective freedom, /
그들의 '실질적인' 자유를 증가시키지는 (않을 것이다) /
because, although allowed to do so, /
왜냐하면 그렇게 하는 것이 허용될지라도 /
they are physically incapable of it.
물리적으로 그렇게 할 수 없기 때문에
Having a minimum of restrictions /
최소한의 제약을 두는 것은 /
and a maximum of possibilities /
그리고 최대한의 가능성을 (두는 것은) /
is fine. 괜찮다

But in the real world / 그러나 현실 세계에서 /
most people will never have the opportunity /
대부분 사람에게는 기회가 없을 것이다 /
either to become all / 모든 것이 되든지 /
that they are allowed to become, /
자신이 되도록 허용된 /
or to need to be restrained from doing everything /
모든 것을 하는 것을 저지당해야 할 /
that is possible for them to do.
그들이 할 수 있는 가능성이 있는
Their effective freedom / 그들의 실질적인 자유는 /
depends on actually having the means and ability /
할 수 있는 수단과 능력을 갖추고 있는가에 달려 있다 /
to do what they choose. 사실 그들이 선택하는 것을

무언가를 할 수 있도록 법적으로 허용되는 것과, 실제로 그것을 해 버릴 수 있는 것을 구별하는 것은 중요하다. 왜냐하면, 모든 사람이 2분 안에 1마일을 달릴 수 있게 허용하는 법이 통과될 수도 있다. 하지만 그렇게 하는 것이 허용될지라도 물리적으로 그렇게 할 수 없기 때문에, 그것이 그들의 '실질적인' 자유를 증가시키지는 않을 것이다. 최소한의 제약과 최대한의 가능성을 두는 것은 괜찮다. 그러나 현실 세계에서, 대부분 사람에게는 자신이 되도록 허용된 모든 것이 될 기회가 없거나, 그들이 할 수 있는 모든 것을 하는 것을 저지당해야 할 기회가 없을 것이다. 그들의 실질적인 자유는 사실 그들이 선택하는 것을 할 수 있는 수단과 능력을 갖추고 있는가에 달려 있다.

① 다른 사람의 자유 권리를 존중하는가
② 도움이 필요한 사람을 보호하고 돕는가
③ 사회적으로 용인된 행동이 무엇인가를 배우는가
④ 그들이 다른 사람들에게서 얼마나 기대할 수 있는지를 결정하는가
⑤ 그들이 선택하는 것을 할 수 있는 수단과 능력을 갖추고 있는가

문제풀이

법적으로 허용되는 것과 실제로 할 수 있는 것을 구별하는 것이 중요하며, 법적 허용이 실질적인 자유를 증가시키지는 않기 때문에 최소한의 제약과 최대한의 가능성을 두는 것이 좋다는 내용이다. 따라서 빈칸에 ⑤ 'having the means and ability to do what they choose'가 들어가서 빈칸이 포함되는 문장이 '그들의 실질적인 자유는 사실 그들이 선택하는 것을 할 수 있는 수단과 능력을 갖추고 있는가에 달려 있다.'가 되는 것이 가장 적절하다.

구조 다시보기

도입	법적 허용과 실제 이행의 구별이 중요함
부연	법적 허용이 실질적 자유를 증가시키지 않을 수 있음
전개	최소한의 제약과 최대한의 가능성을 주는 것이 좋음
결론	실질적인 자유는 스스로 선택할 수 있는 수단과 능력을 갖추고 있어야 함

《 어휘·어구 》

distinguish 구별하다
legally 법적으로
allow 허용하다
actually 실제로, 사실
effective 실질적인, 효과적인
freedom 자유
physically 물리적으로
incapable 할 수 없는
minimum 최소한
maximum 최대한
possibility 가능성
opportunity 가능성, 기회
freedom 자유
depend on ~에 달려 있다, ~에 의존하다
respect 존중하다
right 권리
protect 보호하다
the needy 빈곤한 사람들
acceptable 받아들일 수 있는
determine 결정하다
means 수단
ability 능력

정답률 

3. ③ 다른 사람에게 기울이는 관심의 한계

직독/직해

Paying attention to some people and not others /
일부 사람들에게 주의를 기울이고 다른 사람들에게 그렇지 않는 것이 /
doesn't mean / you're being dismissive or
의미하는 것은 아니다 / 여러분이 남을 무시하거나 거만하다는 것을
arrogant.
It just reflects a hard fact:
그것은 단지 명백한 사실을 나타낼 뿐이다
there are limits on the number of people /
사람의 수에 한계가 있다 /
we can possibly pay attention to /
우리가 아마 주의를 기울이거나 /
or develop a relationship with.
관계를 발전시킬 수 있는
Some scientists even believe /
일부 과학자들은 심지어 믿기도 한다
that the number of people / 사람의 수가 /
with whom we can continue stable social
우리가 안정된 사회적 관계를 지속할 수 있는
relationships / might be limited naturally /
/ 자연스럽게 제한되는지도 모른다 /
by our brains.
우리의 뇌에 의해
The more people you know of different
여러분이 다른 배경의 사람들을 더 많이 알수록
backgrounds, / the more colorful your life
/ 여러분의 삶은 그만큼 더 다채로워진다
becomes.
Professor Robin Dunbar has explained /
Robin Dunbar 교수는 설명해 왔다 /
that our minds are only really capable of forming
우리의 마음은 오로지 정말로 의미 있는 관계를 형성할 수 있을 뿐이라고
meaningful relationships / with a maximum of
/ 최대 약 150명의 사람과
about a hundred and fifty people.
Whether that's true or not, / it's safe / to assume /
그것이 사실이든 아니든 간에 / 안전하다 / 가정하는 것이
that we can't be real friends with everyone.
우리가 모두와 진정한 친구가 될 수는 없다고

일부 사람들에게 주의를 기울이고 다른 사람들에게 그렇게 하지 않는 것이 여러분이 남을 무시하고 있다거나 거만하게 굴고 있다는 것을 의미하지는 않는다. ① 그것은 단지 명백한 사실을 나타낼 뿐인데, 우리가 아마 주의를 기울이거나 관계를 발전시킬 수 있는 사람의 수에 한계가 있다는 것이다. ② 일부 과학자는 우리가 안정된 사회적 관계를 지속할 수 있는 사람의 수가 우리의 뇌에 의해 자연스럽게 제한되는 것일지도 모른다고까지 심지어 믿는다. ③ (여러분이 다른 배경의 사람들을 더 많이 알수록, 여러분의 삶은 더 다채로워진다.) ④ Robin Dunbar 교수는 우리의 마음은 오로지 정말로 최대 약 150명의 사람과 의미 있는 관계를 형성할 수 있을 뿐이라고 설명했다. ⑤ 그것이 사실이든 아니든 간에, 우리가 모든 사람과 진정한 친구가 될 수는 없다고 가정하는 것이 안전하다.

문제풀이

우리가 주의를 기울일 수 있는 사람의 범위에 한계가 있기 때문에 의미 있는 관계를 형성할 수 있는 사람의 수가 제한되어 있다는 내용의 글인데, 배경이 다른 사람들을 많이 알수록 삶이 더 다채로워진다고 한 ③은 글의 전체 흐름에서 벗어나 있다.

이렇게 풀자 각 문장의 연결이 어색하지 않은지, 갑자기 내용이 전환되거나 단절되지 않는지 살피며 읽어야 한다. 글의 흐름과 무관한 문장에서도 글의 소재는 동일하게 쓰이는 것에 유의해야 한다. 여기서는 정답 문장에서 people이라는 단어로 혼동을 유도하고 있지만 그 내용은 전체 흐름과 상반되어 있다.

《 어휘·어구 》

pay attention to ~에 주의를 기울이다
reflect 나타내다, 반영하다
hard fact 명백한 사실
stable 안정된
social relationship 사회적 관계
be capable of ~을 할 수 있다
form 형성하다
meaningful 의미 있는
assume 가정하다

정답률 39%

4. ② 민족 관계에 의해 영향을 받는 사람들의 건강

직독/직해

Many studies have shown / that people's health and
많은 연구는 보여주었다 / 사람들의 건강과 주관적인 웰빙은
subjective well-being / are affected by ethnic relations.
/ 민족 관계에 의해 영향을 받는다는 것을
Members of minority groups in general /
소수 집단의 구성원들이 일반적으로 /
have poorer health outcomes / than the majority group.
더 안 좋은 건강 결과를 갖고 있다 / 다수 집단보다
(B) But that difference remains / even when obvious
하지만 그런 차이가 남아 있다 / 심지어 명백한 요소들이 ~할 때
factors, / such as social class and access to medical
/ 사회 계층과 의료 서비스에 대한 접근성 같은
services / are controlled for.
/ 통제될 (때조차도)
This suggests / 이것은 보여준다 /
that dominance relations have their own effect on
우열 관계가 사람들의 건강에 그 자체의 영향을 미친다는 것을
people's health.
How could that be the case? 그것이 어떻게 그럴 수 있을까
(A) One possible answer is stress.
하나의 가능한 답은 스트레스이다
From multiple physiological studies, / we know /
다수의 생리학 연구를 통해 / 우리는 안다 /
that encounters with members of other ethnic-racial
다른 민족적-인종적 범주의 구성원들과 마주치는 것이
categories, / even in the relatively safe environment of
/ 심지어 비교적 안전한 실험실 환경에서조차도
laboratories, / trigger stress responses.
/ 스트레스 반응을 유발한다는 (것을)
(C) Minority individuals have many encounters /
소수 집단의 개인들은 마주치는 일이 많고 /
with majority individuals, / 다수 집단의 개인들과 /
each of which / may trigger such responses.
각각의 마주침은 / 그런 반응을 유발할지도 모른다
However minimal these effects may be, /
이런 영향이 아무리 작을지라도 /
their frequency may increase total stress, /
그것의 빈번한 발생이 총체적인 스트레스를 증가시킬지도 모르며 /
which would account for / 이는 설명할 것이다 /
part of the health disadvantage of minority individuals.
소수 집단 개인들의 건강상 불이익의 일부를

많은 연구는 사람들의 건강과 주관적인 웰빙은 민족 관계에 의해 영향을 받는다는 것을 보여주었다. 소수 집단의 구성원들이 일반적으로 다수 집단보다 더 안 좋은 건강 결과를 갖고 있다.
(B) 하지만 사회 계층과 의료 서비스에 대한 접근성 같은 명백한 요소들이 통제될 때조차도 그런 차이가 남아 있다. 이것은 우열 관계가 사람들의 건강에 그 자체의 영향을 미친다는 것을 보여준다. 그것이 어떻게 그럴 수 있을까?
(A) 하나의 가능한 답은 스트레스이다. 다수의 생리학 연구를 통해, 우리는 심지어 비교적 안전한 실험실 환경에서조차도 다른 민족적-인종적 범주의 구성원들과 마주치는 것이 스트레스 반응을 유발한다는 것을 안다.

(C) 소수 집단의 개인들은 다수 집단의 개인들과 마주치는 일이 많고, 각각의 마주침은 그런 반응을 유발할지도 모른다. 이런 영향이 아무리 작을지라도 그것의 빈번한 발생이 총체적인 스트레스를 증가시킬지도 모르며, 이는 소수 집단 개인들의 건강상 불이익의 일부를 설명할 것이다.

문제풀이

사람들의 건강과 주관적인 웰빙은 민족 관계에 의해 영향을 받고, 소수 집단의 구성원들이 일반적으로 다수 집단보다 건강이 안 좋다는 내용의 주어진 글 다음에, 다른 요소들을 통제해도 그런 차이가 남아 결국 우열 관계가 사람들의 건강에 영향을 미친다는 내용의 (B)가 오고, (B)의 내용에 대한 근거를 설명하는 (A)가 온 뒤, 마지막으로 (A)에서 언급한 스트레스 반응을 유발하는 것에 대해 부연 설명을 하는 (C)가 오는 것이 가장 적절하다.

어휘·어구

subjective 주관적인
ethnic 민족의
minority 소수
outcome 결과
majority 다수
multiple 많은, 다수의
physiological 생리학의
encounter 접하다, 마주치다; 만남
relatively 비교적
response 반응
remain 남아 있다
obvious 명백한, 분명한
access 접근
dominance relation 우위 관계
minimal 아주 적은, 최소의
frequency 빈도, 잦음
disadvantage 약점, 불리한 점

정답률 43%

5. ⑤ 첫인상의 중요성

직독/직해

You've probably heard the expression, /
여러분은 아마도 표현을 들어본 적이 있을 것이다 /
"first impressions matter a lot". 첫인상이 매우 중요하다
Life really doesn't give many people a second chance /
삶은 실제로 많은 사람에게 두 번째 기회를 주지 않는다 /
to make a good first impression. 좋은 첫인상을 만들
It has been determined / that it takes only a few
밝혀져 왔다 / 단지 몇 초 밖에 걸리지 않는다는 것이
seconds / for anyone to assess another individual.
/ 누군가가 또 다른 개인을 평가하는 데
This is very noticeable in recruitment processes, /
이것은 채용 과정에서 매우 두드러지는데 /
where top recruiters can predict / the direction of
최고의 모집자는 예측할 수 있다 / 자신의 최종 결정의 방향을
their eventual decision / on any candidate /
/ 지원자에 대한 /
within a few seconds of introducing themselves.
(지원자가) 자신을 소개하는 몇 초 안에
So, / a candidate's CV may 'speak' knowledge and
그래서 / 후보자의 이력서가 지식과 능력을 '진술'할지도 모르지만
competence, / but their appearance and introduction /
/ 그들의 외모와 소개는 /
may tell of a lack of coordination, fear, and poor
신체 조정 능력의 부족, 불안과 서투른 대인 관계 기술을 알려줄지도 모른다
interpersonal skills.
In this way, / quick judgements are not only relevant
이런 식으로 / 빠른 판단들이 단지 채용 문제에만 관련된 것은 아니고
in employment matters; / they are equally applicable /
/ 이것들은 똑같이 적용된다 /
in love and relationship matters too.
또한 사랑과 관계 문제에도
On a date with a wonderful somebody /
멋진 누군가와의 데이트에서 /
who you've painstakingly tracked down for months, /
여러분이 몇 달 동안 공들여 찾아낸 /
subtle things like bad breath or wrinkled clothes /
입 냄새나 구겨진 옷과 같은 미묘한 것들이 /
may spoil your noble efforts.
여러분의 숭고한 노력을 망칠 수도 있다

여러분은 아마도 '첫인상이 매우 중요하다'라는 표현을 들어본 적이 있을 것이다. (①) 삶은 실제로 많은 사람에게 좋은 첫인상을 만들 두 번째 기회를 주지 않는다. (②) 누군가가 또 다른 개인을 평가하는 데 단지 몇 초 밖에 걸리지 않는다는 것이 밝혀져 왔다. (③) 이것은 채용 과정에서 매우 두드러지는데, 채용 과정에서 최고의 모집자는 (지원자가) 자신을 소개하는 몇 초 안에 지원자에 대한 자신의 최종 결정의 방향을 예측할 수 있다. (④) 그래서 후보자의 이력서가 지식과 능력을 '진술'할지도 모르지만, 그들의 외모와 소개는 신체 조정 능력의 부족, 불안, 그리고 서투른 대인 관계 기술을 알려줄지도 모른다. (⑤) 이런 식으로 빠른 판단들이 단지 채용 문제에만 관련된 것은 아니고, 이것들은 또한 사랑과 관계 문제에도 똑같이 적용된다. 여러분이 몇 달 동안 공들여 찾아낸 멋진 누군가와의 데이트에서, 입 냄새나 구겨진 옷과 같은 미묘한 것들이 여러분의 숭고한 노력을 망칠 수도 있다.

문제풀이

주어진 문장은 빠른 판단들이 채용 문제뿐만 아니라 사랑과 관계 문제에도 똑같이 적용된다는 내용으로, ⑤ 뒤 문장에서 주어진 문장에 대한 구체적인 사례가 제시되었으므로 주어진 문장은 ⑤에 들어가는 것이 가장 적절하다.

이렇게 풀자 _ 첫 인상으로 다른 사람을 평가하는 데 시간이 별로 걸리지 않고 이런 빠른 판단은 채용 문제와 사랑, 관계 문제에도 적용된다는 것이 중심 내용이다.

어휘·어구

relevant 관련 있는
employment 채용, 고용
equally 동등하게
applicable 해당되는, 적용되는
first impression 첫인상
assess 평가하다
noticeable 뚜렷한, 현저한
recruitment process 채용 과정
predict 예측하다, 예견하다
eventual 최종적인
candidate 후보자, 지원자
competence 능숙함
appearance 외모
coordination 신체 조정력
interpersonal skill 대인 기술
painstakingly 힘들여, 공들여
subtle 미묘한, 감지하기 힘든
noble 숭고한, 고귀한

정답률 53%

6. ④ 할인의 상대적인 가치

직독/직해

The perception of the same amount of discount on
상품의 동일한 할인액에 대한 인식은
a product / depends on its relation to the initial price.
/ 그것의 최초 가격과의 관계에 달려있다
In one study, / respondents were presented with a
한 연구에서 / 응답자들은 어떤 구매 상황을 제시받았다
purchase situation.
The persons put in the situation / 상황에 있는 사람들이 /
of buying a calculator that cost $15 /
가격이 15달러인 계산기를 사는 /
found out from the vendor / that the same product
판매자로부터 알게 되었다 / 같은 제품을 살 수 있다는 것을
was available / in a different store 20 minutes away /
/ 20분 떨어진 다른 상점에서 /
and at a promotional price of $10.
10달러의 판촉 행사 가격에
In this case, / 68% of respondents decided to make
이 경우에 / 응답자의 68%가 그 가게까지 가기로 결심했다
their way down to the store / in order to save $5.
/ 5달러를 절약하기 위해서
In the second condition, / which involved buying a
두 번째 상황에서 / 이는 125달러짜리 재킷을 구매하는 것을 포함했는데
jacket for $125, / the respondents were also told /
/ 응답자들은 또한 들었다 /
that the same product was available /
같은 제품을 살 수 있다고 /
in a store 20 minutes away / and cost $120 there.
20분 떨어진 상점에서 / 그리고 그곳에서는 가격이 120달러라고
This time, / only 29% of the persons said /
이번에는 / 단지 사람들의 29%만이 말했다 /
that they would get the cheaper jacket.
그들이 더 저렴한 재킷을 살 것이라고
In both cases, / the product was $5 cheaper, /
두 경우 모두에서 / 제품은 5달러 더 저렴했지만 /
but in the first case, / 첫 번째 경우에는 /
the amount was 1/3 of the price, /
그 액수가 가격의 1/3이었고 /
and in the second, / it was 1/25 of the price.
두 번째 경우에는 / 액수가 가격의 1/25이었다
What differed in both of these situations /
이 두 상황 모두에서 차이가 있었던 것은 /
was the price context of the purchase.
구매의 가격 맥락이었다
When the same amount of discount is given /
같은 할인액이 주어질 때 /
in a purchasing situation, / 구매 상황에서 /
the relative value of the discount /
그 할인의 상대적인 가치가 /
affects how people perceive its value.
사람들이 그 가치를 어떻게 인식하는지에 영향을 미친다

상품의 동일한 할인액에 대한 인식은 그것의 최초 가격과의 관계에 달려 있다. 한 연구에서, 응답자들은 어떤 구매 상황을 제시받았다. 가격이 15달러인 계산기를 사는 상황에 있는 사람들이 같은 제품을 20분 떨어진 다른 상점에서 10달러의 판촉 행사 가격에 살 수 있다는 것을 판매자로부터 알게 되었다. 이 경우에, 응답자의 68%가 5달러를 절약하기 위해서 그 가게까지 가기로 결심했다. 두 번째 상황에서, 이는 125달러짜리 재킷을 구매하는 것을 포함했는데, 응답자들은 또한 같은 제품을 20분 떨어진 상점에서 살 수 있고 그곳에서는 가격이 120달러라고 들었다. 이번에는, 단지 사람들의 29%만이 더 저렴한 재킷을 살 것이라고 말했다. 두 경우 모두에서 제품은 5달러 더 저렴했지만, 첫 번째 경우에는 그 액수가 가격의 1/3이었고, 두 번째 경우에는 액수가 가격의 1/25이었다. 이 두 상황 모두에서 차이가 있었던 것은 구매의 가격 맥락이었다.
➡ 구매 상황에서 같은 할인액이 주어질 때, 그 할인의 (A) 상대적인 가치가 사람들이 그 가치를 어떻게 (B) 인식하는지에 영향을 미친다.

① 절대적인 …… 조정하는지
② 절대적인 …… 표현하는지
③ 동일한 …… 만들어내는지
④ **상대적인 …… 인식하는지**
⑤ 상대적인 …… 알리는지

문제풀이

두 개의 구매 상황에서 같은 할인액이 주어졌지만, 첫 번째 경우에는 그 액수가 가격의 1/3이었고 두 번째 경우에는 액수가 가격의 1/25이었기 때문에 첫 번째 경우에 더 많은 사람이 구매했다는 실험 결과를 통해 할인의 상대적인 가치로 사람들이 그 가치를 인식한다는 것을 알 수 있다. 따라서 요약문의 빈칸 (A)에는 'relative(상대적인)'가, (B)에는 'perceive(인식하다)'가 가장 적절하다.

어휘·어구

perception 인식
initial 처음의, 초기의
respondent 응답자
calculator 계산기
vendor 판매자

promotional price 판촉 행사 가격
amount 양, 금액
context 맥락

7~8 우리의 유전자에 근원을 두고 있는 과식

직독/직해

A quick look at history shows /
역사를 빠르게 살펴보면 보인다 /
that humans have not always had the abundance
인간은 음식의 풍부함을 항상 가졌던 것은 아니다
of food / that is enjoyed throughout most of the
/ 오늘날 대부분 발전된 세상에서 즐기는
developed world today.
In fact, / there have been numerous times in history /
실제로 / 역사적으로 수많은 시기가 있었다 /
when food has been rather scarce. 음식이 꽤 부족했던
As a result, / people used to eat more /
그 결과 / 사람들은 더 많이 먹곤 했다 /
when food was available / since the availability of
음식이 있을 때 / 다음 식사의 가능성이 확실하지 않았기 때문에
the next meal was questionable.
Overeating in those times / was essential to ensure
그 시기의 과식이란 / 생존을 보장하는 데 필수였고
survival, / and humans received satisfaction from
/ 인간은 더 많이 먹는 것으로부터 만족을 얻었다
eating more / than was needed for immediate purposes.
/ 당장의 목적에 필요한 것보다
On top of that, / the highest pleasure was derived
더욱이 / 가장 큰 기쁨은 먹는 것으로부터 얻어졌고
from eating / the most calorie-dense foods, /
/ 가장 칼로리가 높은 음식을 /
resulting in a longer lasting energy reserve.
이는 더 오래 지속되는 에너지 비축을 초래했다
Even though there are parts of the world /
비록 세계의 일부 지역들이 있지만 /
where, unfortunately, food is still scarce, /
불행하게도 음식이 여전히 부족한 /
most of the world's population today /
오늘날 세계 인구의 대부분은 /
has plenty of food available to survive and thrive.
생존과 번영을 위해 이용 가능한 많은 음식을 가지고 있다
However, this abundance is new, / and your body
하지만 이런 풍요로움은 새로운 것이고 / 당신의 몸은 따라잡지 못해서
has not caught up, / still naturally rewarding you /
/ 여전히 자연스럽게 보상한다 /
for eating more than you need /
당신이 필요한 것보다 더 많이 먹는 것에 대해 /
and for eating the most calorie-dense foods.
그리고 가장 칼로리가 높은 음식을 먹는 것에 대해
These are innate habits / and not simple addictions.
이것들은 타고난 습관이지 / 단순한 중독은 아니다
They are self-preserving mechanisms / initiated by
그것들은 자기 보호 기제이고 / 당신의 몸에서 시작된
your body, / ensuring your future survival, /
/ 당신의 미래 생존을 보장해 주지만 /
but they are irrelevant now. 그것들은 이제 관련이 없다
Therefore, / it is your responsibility to communicate
따라서 / 당신의 몸과 대화하는 것은 당신의 책임이다
with your body / regarding the new environment of
/ 음식이 풍부한 새로운 환경과 관련하여
food abundance / and the need to change the inborn
/ 그리고 타고난 과식 습관을 변화시킬 필요와 (관련하여)
habit of overeating.

역사를 빠르게 살펴보면 인간은 오늘날 대부분 발전된 세상에서 즐기는 음식의 풍부함을 항상 가졌던 것은 아니다. 실제로, 역사적으로 음식이 꽤 부족했던 수많은 시기가 있었다. 그 결과, 사람들은 다음 식사의 가능성이 (a) 확실하지 않았기 때문에 음식이 있을 때 더 많이 먹곤 했다. 그 시기의 과식이란 생존을 보장하는 데 필수였고, 인간은 당장의 목적에 필요한 것보다 더 많이 먹는 것으로부터 만족을 얻었다. 더욱이, 가장 큰 기쁨은 가장 칼로리가 높은 음식을 먹는 것으로부터 얻어졌고, 이는 (b) 더 오래 지속되는 에너지 비축을 초래했다.
비록 불행하게도 음식이 여전히 부족한 세계의 일부 지역들이 있지만, 오늘날 세계 인구의 대부분은 생존과 번영을 위해 이용 가능한 많은 음식을 가지고 있다. 하지만 이런 풍요로움은 새로운 것이고, 당신의 몸은 따라잡지 못해서, 당신은 당신이 필요한 것보다 더 많이 먹고 당신이 가장 칼로리가 높은 음식을 먹는 것에 대해 (몸이) 여전히 자연스럽게 (c) 보상한다. 이것들은 타고난 습관이지 단순한 중독은 아니다. 그것들은 당신의 몸에서 시작된 자기 보호 기제이고, 당신의 미래 생존을 보장해 주지만, 그것들은 이제 (d) 관련이 없다. 따라서 음식이 풍부한 새로운 환경과 타고난 과식 습관을 (e) 강화시킬(→ 변화시킬) 필요와 관련하여 당신의 몸과 대화하는 것은 당신의 책임이다.

《 어휘·어구 》

abundance 풍부
throughout ~동안 죽, 내내
numerous 많은
scarce 부족한
availability 가능성
questionable 의문의 여지가 있는, 의심스러운
overeat 과식하다
essential 필수적인
survival 생존
pleasure 기쁨
reserve 비축
population 인구
addiction 중독
initiate 시작하다
irrelevant 무관한, 상관없는
responsibility 책임

7. ③

① 맛있는 음식과 건강한 음식 중 무엇이 더 나은가?
② 좀더 균형 잡힌 식단을 위한 간단한 단계
③ 과식: 우리의 유전자에 근원을 두고 있다
④ 칼로리가 높은 음식이 우리의 몸을 망치는 방법
⑤ 우리의 식습관은 우리의 성격을 보여준다

문제풀이

음식이 부족했던 과거에는 과식이란 생존을 보장하는 데 필수였지만, 오늘날에는 생존과 번영을 위해 이용 가능한 많은 음식이 있음에도 불구하고 우리의 몸은 여전히 칼로리가 높은 음식을 먹는 것에 대해 보상을 하고 이는 결국 타고난 습관이라는 내용이다. 따라서 글의 제목으로 ③ 'Overeating: It's Rooted in Our Genes(과식: 우리의 유전자에 근원을 두고 있다)'가 가장 적절하다.

정답률 42%

8. ⑤

문제풀이

과식은 타고난 습관이기 때문에 음식이 풍부한 환경과 타고난 과식 습관을 변화시키기 위해서 당신의 몸과 대화하는 것은 결국 당신의 책임이라는 문맥이 되어야 자연스러우므로, (e) 'strengthen(강화시키다)'은 문맥상 어색함을 알 수 있다.

미니 고난도 Test 2회

Day 22 본문 131쪽

1. ③ 2. ③ 3. ③ 4. ② 5. ②
6. ④ 7. ④ 8. ③

정답률 47%

1. ③ 뉴스 보도가 문제 인식에 끼치는 영향

직독/직해

As the tenth anniversary of the terrorist attacks of September 11, 2001, approached, /
2001년 9월 11일 테러리스트 공격의 10 주년 추모일이 다가오면서 /
9/11-related media stories /
9/11 관련 언론 기사의 양이 /
peaked in the days immediately surrounding the anniversary date /
추모일 바로 전후로 최고조까지 올라갔다 /
and then dropped off rapidly in the weeks thereafter.
그 후 몇 주 동안 급격히 떨어졌다
Surveys conducted during those times /
그 시기 동안 실시된 조사는 /
asked citizens to choose two "especially important" events /
시민들에게 '특히 중요한' 두 가지 사건을 선택하도록 요청했다 /
from the past seventy years.
지난 70년 동안 있었던
Two weeks prior to the anniversary, /
추모일 2주 전 /
before the media blitz began, /
미디어 대선전이 시작되기 전인 /
about 30 percent of respondents named 9/11.
응답자의 약 30퍼센트가 9/11을 언급했다
But as the anniversary drew closer, /
그러나 추모일이 더 가까워지면서 /
and the media treatment intensified, /
그리고 미디어 보도가 증가함에 따라 /
survey respondents started identifying 9/11 in increasing numbers — /
점점 더 많은 수의 응답자들이 9/11을 선택하기 시작했다 /
to a high of 65 percent.
최고 65퍼센트까지 올랐다
Two weeks later, though, /
그러나 2주 후에 /
after reportage had decreased to earlier levels, /
보도가 이전 수준으로 줄어든 후 /
once again only about 30 percent of the participants /
다시 한 번 참가자의 약 30퍼센트만이 /
placed it among their two especially important events of the past seventy years.
그것을 지난 70년 동안의 특히 중요한 두 가지 사건으로 선택했다
Clearly, the amount of news coverage can make a big difference /
명백하게, 뉴스 보도의 양은 큰 차이를 만들 수 있다 /
in the *perceived* significance of an issue among observers /
관찰자들 사이에서 문제의 중요성을 '인식하는' 데 있어 /
as they are exposed to the coverage.
그들이 그 보도에 노출될 때

2001년 9월 11일 테러리스트 공격의 10 주년 추모일이 다가오면서, 9/11 관련 언론 기사의 양이 추모일 바로 전후로 최고조까지 올라갔고,

그 후 몇 주 동안 급격히 줄어들었다. 그 시기 동안 실시된 조사는 시민들에게 지난 70년 동안 있었던 '특히 중요한' 두 가지 사건을 선택하도록 요청했다. 미디어 대선전이 시작되기 전인 추모일 2주 전, 응답자의 약 30퍼센트가 9/11을 언급했다. 그러나 추모일이 더 가까워지고, 미디어 보도가 증가함에 따라, 더 많은 응답자들이 9/11을 선택하기 시작했고, 그 수가 65퍼센트까지 올랐다. 그러나 보도가 2주 후에 이전 수준으로 줄어들자, 다시 한 번 참가자의 약 30퍼센트만이 그것을 지난 70년 동안의 특히 중요한 두 가지 사건으로 선택했다. 명백하게, 뉴스 보도의 양은 그들이 그 보도에 노출될 때 관찰자들 사이에서 문제의 중요성을 '인식하는' 데 있어 큰 차이를 만들 수 있다.

① 정확성
② 어조
③ 양
④ 원천
⑤ 유형

문제풀이

9/11 관련 언론 기사의 수가 증가했다가 줄어드는 것과 동일하게 시민들이 9/11 테러리스트 공격을 중요한 사건으로 인식하는 정도가 변화했다는 사실을 제시했다. 따라서 빈칸에는 ③ 'amount'가 들어가서 빈칸을 포함한 문장이 '명백하게, 뉴스 보도의 양은 그들이 그 보도에 노출될 때 관찰자들 사이에서 문제의 중요성을 '인식하는' 데 있어 큰 차이를 만들 수 있다.'가 되는 것이 가장 적절하다.

구조 다시보기

예시	• 9/11 테러리스트 공격 10주년 추모일 전후로 관련 언론 기사의 양이 올라갔다가 내려감 • 언론 기사의 양의 증가와 하락과 동일하게 9/11 테러리스트 공격을 중요한 사건으로 여기는 시민들의 수도 증가했다가 하락함
요지	뉴스 보도의 양이 관찰자들의 문제의 중요성 인식에 큰 차이를 만듦

어휘·어구

approach ~에 접근하다
respondent 응답자
draw closer 가까워져 오다
intensify 증가하다
perceived 감지된, 인식된
significance 중요성
observer 관찰자, 관측자

정답률 35%

2. ③ 성장의 상한치 설정

직독/직해

Back in 1996, / 1996년에 /
an American airline was faced with an interesting problem.
한 미국 항공사는 흥미로운 문제에 직면했다
At a time when most other airlines were losing money /
대부분의 다른 항공사들이 손해를 보던 시기에 /
or going under, / 혹은 파산하던 (시기에) /
over 100 cities were begging the company /
100개 이상의 도시가 그 회사에 부탁하고 있었다 /
to service their locations.
그들의 지역에 취항할 것을
However, / that's not the interesting part.
하지만 / 그것이 흥미로운 부분은 아니다
What's interesting / is that the company turned down /
흥미로운 것은 / 회사가 거절했다는 것이다 /
over 95 percent of those offers /
그 제안 중 95% 이상을 /
and began serving only four new locations.
그리고 오직 네 개의 새로운 지역만 취항을 시작했다(는 것이다)
It turned down tremendous growth /
그것은 엄청난 성장을 거절했다 /
because company leadership had set /
회사 수뇌부가 설정했기 때문에 /
an upper limit for growth. 성장의 상한치를
Sure, / its executives wanted to grow each year, /
물론 / 그 회사의 경영진들은 매년 성장하기를 원했다 /
but they didn't want to grow too much.
하지만 그들은 너무 많이 성장하는 것을 원하지 않았다
Unlike other famous companies, /
다른 유명 회사들과는 달리 /
they wanted to set their own pace, /
그들은 자신만의 속도를 정하기를 원했다 /
one that could be sustained / in the long term.
지속될 수 있는 것을 / 장기간
By doing this, / 이렇게 함으로써 /
they established a safety margin for growth /
그들은 성장의 안전 한계를 설정했다 /
that helped them continue to thrive /
그들이 계속해서 번창하는 데 도움이 되었던 /
at a time when the other airlines were flailing.
다른 항공사들이 마구 흔들릴 때

1996년에 한 미국 항공사는 흥미로운 문제에 직면했다. 대부분의 다른 항공사들이 손해를 보거나 파산하던 시기에, 100개 이상의 도시가 그 회사에 그들의 지역에 취항할 것을 부탁하고 있었다. 하지만, 그것이 흥미로운 부분은 아니다. 흥미로운 것은 회사는 그 제안 중 95% 이상을 거절했고, 오직 네 개의 새로운 지역만 취항을 시작했다는 것이다. 그것은 엄청난 성장을 거절했는데, 회사 수뇌부가 성장의 상한선을 설정했기 때문이었다. 물론, 그 회사의 경영진들은 매년 성장하기를 원했지만, 그들은 너무 많이 성장하는 것을 원하지 않았다. 다른 유명 회사들과는 달리, 그들은 장기간 지속될 수 있는 것, 즉 자신만의 속도를 정하기를 원했다. 이렇게 함으로써 그들은 다른 항공사들이 마구 흔들릴 때 그들이 계속해서 번창하는 데 도움이 되었던 성장의 안전 여유를 설정했다.

① 심각한 재정적 위기에 직면하고 있었기
② 마케팅에서 구체적인 장기 계획이 없었기
③ 회사 수뇌부가 성장의 상한선을 설정했기
④ 회사 수뇌부가 경쟁하는 항공사들의 미래를 걱정했기
⑤ 회사가 이익보다 의무를 더 많이 강조했기

문제풀이

한 미국 항공사가 각 도시의 제안을 95% 이상 거절하고, 너무 많이 성장하는 것보다는 자신만의 속도를 정해 성장이 장기간 지속될 수 있게 함으로써 성장의 안전 한계를 설정했다는 내용으로 보아, 빈칸에 ③ 'company leadership had set an upper limit for growth'가 들어가서 빈칸이 포함되는 문장이 '그것은 엄청난 성장을 거절했는데, 회사 수뇌부가 성장의 상한선을 설정했기 때문이었다.'가 되는 것이 가장 적절하다.

구조 다시보기

도입	미국 항공사는 도시의 제안 중 95%를 거절함
전개	회사 수뇌부가 성장의 상한선을 설정함
결과	성장의 안전 한계를 설정함으로써 위기 상황에서도 계속해서 번창할 수 있음

어휘·어구

face 직면하다
go under 도산하다
location 위치, 장소
turn down ~을 거절하다
tremendous 많은, 엄청난
executive 임원, 경영자
sustain 유지하다, 지속하다
in the long term 장기적으로
establish 설립하다, 세우다
thrive 번창하다, 번영하다
financial 재정적인
leadership 수뇌부, 지도부
upper limit 상한선
competing 경쟁하는
emphasize 강조하다
moral duty 도덕적 의무

정답률 68%

3. ③ 야구 훈련에 필요한 근력 운동

직독/직해

Training and conditioning for baseball /
야구를 위한 훈련과 몸만들기는 /
focuses on developing / 신장하는 데 초점을 둔다 /
strength, power, speed, quickness and flexibility.
체력, 힘, 속도, 신속함과 유연성을
Before the 1980s, / strength training was not an
1980년대 이전에 / 근력 운동은 중요한 부분이 아니었다
important part / of conditioning for a baseball player.
/ 야구 선수를 위한 몸만들기의
People viewed baseball as a game of skill and
사람들은 야구를 기술과 테크닉의 경기로 보았다
technique / rather than strength, /
/ 근력보다는 /
and most managers and coaches /
그리고 대부분의 감독과 코치는 /
saw strength training as something for bodybuilders, /
근력 운동을 보디빌더를 위한 것으로 여겼다 /
not baseball players. 야구 선수가 아닌
Unlike more isolated bodybuilding exercises, /
더 분리된 보디빌딩 운동과 달리 /
athletic exercises train / 운동선수용 운동은 훈련시킨다 /
as many muscle groups and functions as possible /
가능한 많은 근육군과 기능을 /
at the same time. 동시에
They feared / that weight lifting and building large
그들은 두려워했다 / 무게를 들어 올리는 것과 큰 근육을 키우는 것이
muscles / would cause players to lose flexibility /
/ 선수들로 하여금 유연성을 잃도록 유발하고 /
and interfere with quickness and proper technique.
신속함과 적절한 기술을 방해할 것을
Today, though, experts understand / the importance
하지만 오늘날 전문가들은 이해한다 / 근력 운동의 중요성을
of strength training / and have made it part of the
/ 그리고 그것을 경기의 일부로 만들어 왔다
game.

야구를 위한 훈련과 몸만들기는 체력, 힘, 속도, 신속함과 유연성을 신장하는 데 초점을 둔다. ① 1980년대 이전에 근력 운동은 야구 선수를 위한 몸만들기의 중요한 부분이 아니었다. ② 사람들은 야구를 근력보다는 기술과 테크닉의 경기로 보았고, 대부분의 감독과 코치는 근력 운동을 야구 선수가 아닌 보디빌더를 위한 것으로 여겼다. ③ (더 분리된 보디빌딩 운동과 달리 운동선수용 운동은 가능한 많은 근육군과 기능을 동시에 훈련시킨다.) ④ 그들은 무게를 들어 올리는 것과 큰 근육을 키우는 것이 선수들로 하여금 유연성을 잃도록 유발하고 신속함과 적절한 기술을 방해할 것을 두려워했다. ⑤ 하지만 오늘날 전문가들은 근력 운동의 중요성을 이해하고 그것을 경기의 일부로 만들어 왔다.

문제풀이

이 글은 근력 운동은 1980년대 이전에는 야구 선수의 훈련에 있어 중요한 것이 아니었지만 오늘날에는 근력 운동의 중요성이 강조되었다는 내용이다. 하지만 ③은 운동선수용 운동이 가능한 많은 근육군과 기능을 동시에 훈련시킨다는 내용이므로 글의 전체 흐름에서 벗어난다.

이렇게 풀자_ 이전에는 근력 운동이 보디빌더를 위한 것으로 여겨졌지만 오늘날에는 근력 운동의 중요성을 이해하고 경기의 일부로 만들었다는 것이 글의 중심 내용이다. 운동선수용 운동의 특징을 설명하고 있는 ③은 글의 흐름상 어울리지 않는다.

어휘·어구

conditioning 훈련, 길들이기
flexibility 유연성
strength training 근력 운동
isolated 분리된, 고립된
athletic 운동의
interfere 간섭하다, 방해하다
quickness 신속함
proper 적당한, 적절한

4. ② 스포츠에서 사용되는 공의 특징

직독/직해

Almost all major sporting activities /
거의 모든 주요 스포츠 활동은 /
are played with a ball. 공을 갖고 행해진다
(B) The rules of the game / always include rules /
경기 규칙들은 / 규칙들을 항상 포함한다 /
about the type of ball / that is allowed, /
공의 유형에 관한 / 허용되는 /
starting with the size and weight of the ball.
공의 크기와 무게부터 시작해서
The ball must also have / a certain stiffness.
공은 또한 갖추어야 한다 / 특정 정도의 단단함을
(A) A ball might have / 공은 갖출 수 있다 /
the correct size and weight /
적절한 크기와 무게를 /
but if it is made as a hollow ball of steel /
그러나 만약 속이 빈 강철 공으로 만들어지면 /
it will be too stiff /
그것은 너무 단단할 것이다 /
and if it is made from light foam rubber /
그리고 가벼운 발포 고무로 만들어지면 /
with a heavy center / 무거운 중심부를 가진 /
it will be too soft. 그 공은 너무 물렁물렁할 것이다
(C) Similarly, / along with stiffness, /
마찬가지로 / 단단함과 더불어 /
a ball needs to bounce properly.
공은 적절히 튈 필요가 있다
A solid rubber ball would be too bouncy /
순전히 고무로 된 공은 지나치게 잘 튈 것이다 /
for most sports, / 대부분의 스포츠에 /
and a solid ball made of clay /
그리고 순전히 점토로 만든 공은 /
would not bounce at all.
전혀 튀지 않을 것이다

거의 모든 주요 스포츠 활동은 공을 갖고 행해진다.
(B) 경기 규칙들은 공의 크기와 무게부터 시작해서 허용되는 공의 유형에 관한 규칙들을 항상 포함한다. 공은 또한 특정 정도의 단단함을 갖추어야 한다.
(A) 공은 적절한 크기와 무게를 갖출 수 있지만, 만약 속이 빈 강철 공으로 만들어지면 그것은 너무 단단할 것이고, 무거운 중심부를 가진 가벼운 발포 고무로 만들어지면 그 공은 너무 물렁물렁할 것이다.
(C) 마찬가지로, 단단함과 더불어 공은 적절히 튈 필요가 있다. 순전히 고무로 된 공은 대부분의 스포츠에 지나치게 잘 튈 것이고, 순전히 점토로 만든 공은 전혀 튀지 않을 것이다.

문제풀이

주요 스포츠 활동에서 공이 쓰인다는 주어진 글 다음에, 공의 크기, 무게, 유형, 단단함 등에 관한 규칙들이 있다는 내용의 (B)가 오고, 공의 단단함에 대해 구체적으로 설명하는 (A)가 온 뒤, 마지막으로 공의 탄성에 대해 언급하는 (C)가 오는 것이 가장 적절하다.

이렇게 풀자 (B)의 뒷부분에서 언급된 공의 단단함에 대해 구체적으로 설명하는 (A)가 (B) 뒤에 와야 하고, (C)의 'Similarly, along with stiffness(마찬가지로, 단단함과 더불어)'로 보아 (C)는 앞 문단과 비슷한 내용이 언급될 것임을 알 수 있다. 따라서 (C)는 (A) 뒤에 오는 것이 적절하다.

어휘·어구

major 주요한
correct 적절한, 올바른
weight 무게
hollow 속이 빈
steel 강철
stiff 딱딱한
light 가벼운
include 포함하다
certain 특정한, 어떤
similarly 비슷하게
along with ~와 더불어
bounce 튀다
properly 적절히
solid 순수한(다른 물질이 섞이지 않은), 고체의
rubber 고무
bouncy 잘 튀는
clay 점토

5. ② 작은 성공은 장기적으로 의미가 있다

직독/직해

It is so easy to overestimate /
과대평가하기는 매우 쉽다 /
the importance of one defining moment /
결정적인 한순간의 중요성을 /
and underestimate the value /
그리고 가치를 과소평가하기는 /
of making small improvements / on a daily basis.
작은 발전을 이루는 것의 / 매일
Too often, / we convince ourselves /
너무나 자주 / 우리는 굳게 믿는다 /
that massive success requires massive action.
거대한 성공에는 거대한 행동이 필요하다고
Whether it is losing weight, /
체중을 줄이는 것이든 /
winning a championship, /
결승전에서 이기는 것이든 /
or achieving any other goal, /
혹은 어떤 다른 목표를 달성하는 것이든 간에 /
we put pressure on ourselves /
우리는 우리 스스로에게 압력을 가한다 /
to make some earthshaking improvement /
지축을 흔들 정도의 발전을 이루도록 /
that everyone will talk about.
모두가 이야기하게 될
Meanwhile, / improving by 1 percent /
한편 / 1% 발전은 /
isn't particularly notable, /
특별히 눈에 띄지는 않는다 /
but it can be far more meaningful / in the long run.
하지만 그것은 훨씬 더 의미가 있을 수 있다 / 장기적으로는
The difference this tiny improvement can make /
이 작은 발전이 이룰 수 있는 변화는 /
over time / is surprising.
시간이 지남에 따라 / 놀랍다
Here's how the math works out: /
다음과 같이 계산이 이루어진다 /
if you can get 1 percent better /
만약 여러분이 1%씩 더 나아질 수 있다면 /
each day for one year, / 1년 동안 매일 /
you'll end up thirty-seven times better /
여러분은 결국 37배 더 나아질 것이다 /
by the time you're done. 끝마칠 때 즈음에
Conversely, / if you get 1 percent worse /
역으로 / 만약 여러분이 1%씩 나빠진다면 /
each day for one year, / 1년 동안 매일 /
you'll decline nearly down to zero.
여러분은 거의 0까지 떨어질 것이다
What starts as a small win or a minor failure /
작은 승리나 사소한 패배로 시작한 것은 /
adds up to something much more.
쌓여서 훨씬 더 큰 무언가가 된다

결정적인 한순간의 중요성을 과대평가하고 매일 작은 발전을 이루는 것의 가치를 과소평가하기는 매우 쉽다. 너무나 자주 우리는 거대한 성공에는 거대한 행동이 필요하다고 굳게 믿는다. (①) 체중을 줄이는 것이든, 결승전에서 이기는 것이든, 혹은 어떤 다른 목표를 달성하는 것이든 간에, 우리는 모두가 이야기하게 될 지축을 흔들 정도의 발전을 이루도록 우리 스스로에게 압력을 가한다. (②) 한편, 1% 발전은 특별히 눈에 띄지는 않지만, 장기적으로는 훨씬 더 의미가 있을 수 있다. 시간이 지남에 따라 이 작은 발전이 이룰 수 있는 변화는 놀랍다. (③) 다음과 같이 계산이 이루어지는데, 만약 여러분이 1년 동안 매일 1%씩 더 나아질 수 있다면, 끝마칠 때 즈음에 여러분은 결국 37배 더 나아질 것이다. (④) 역으로, 만약 여러분이 1년 동안 매일 1%씩 나빠진다면 여러분은 거의 0까지 떨어질 것이다. (⑤) 작은 승리나 사소한 패배로 시작한 것은 쌓여서 훨씬 더 큰 무언가가 된다.

문제풀이

주어진 문장은 1% 발전은 눈에 띄지는 않지만 장기적으로 훨씬 더 의미가 있을 수 있다는 내용이다. ② 뒤에 언급된 'this tiny improvement'는 주어진 문장의 'improving by 1 percent'를 가리키고, ② 앞문장과 뒷문장 간의 흐름이 단절되었기 때문에 주어진 문장은 ②에 들어가야 글의 흐름이 자연스럽다.

어휘·어구

meanwhile 한편
improve 발전하다
particularly 특별히
notable 눈에 띄는
meaningful 의미 있는
in the long run 장기적으로
overestimate 과대평가하다
defining 결정적인, 정의하는
moment 순간
underestimate 과소평가하다
value 가치
on a daily basis 매일
convince 굳게 믿게 하다, 확신시키다
massive 거대한
success 성공
require 필요로 하다
action 행동, 조치
lose weight 체중을 줄이다
win a championship 결승전에서 이기다
achieve 달성하다, 성취하다
pressure 압력
earthshaking 지축을 흔드는
tiny 작은, 사소한
end up 결국 ~하게 되다
conversely 역으로
decline 떨어지다, 하락하다
nearly 거의
minor 사소한
failure 패배

6~8 스승과 두 제자의 일화

직독/직해

(A) Two students met their teacher / at the start of
두 명의 제자는 그들의 스승을 만났다 / 숲을 가로지르는 길의 출발선에서
a track through a forest.
He gave them instructions to follow / the path to
스승은 그들에게 따라가라고 지시했다 / 그 길 끝까지
its end, / in preparation for a test later in the week.
/ 그 주의 후반에 있을 테스트를 위한 준비로
The path split into two: / one was clear and smooth, /
길은 두 갈래로 갈라졌는데 / 하나는 막힌 것이 없고 평탄했지만 /
the other had fallen logs / and other obstacles in
다른 하나는 쓰러진 통나무들이 있었고 / 다른 장애물들이 길을 막고 있었다
the way.
One student chose to avoid the obstacles, / taking
한 제자는 그 장애물들을 피하기로 결정하고 / 끝까지 더 쉬운 길을 갔다
the easier path to the end.
He felt clever / as he ran without stopping.
그는 똑똑하다고 느꼈다 / 쉬지 않고 달려가면서

(D) The second student chose to tackle the obstacles, /
두 번째 제자는 장애물들에 덤벼들기로 결정했다 /
battling through every challenge / in his path.
모든 어려움을 통과해 싸우면서 / 그의 길에 있는
The student who chose the easy path / finished first /
쉬운 길을 선택했던 제자가 / 먼저 마쳤고 /
and felt proud of himself. 자신을 자랑스럽게 느꼈다
"I'm glad / I chose to avoid the rocks and logs.
난 기뻐 / 내가 바위와 통나무들을 피하기로 선택해서
They were only there / to slow me down," /
그것들은 그곳에 있었을 뿐이야 / 내 속도를 늦추기 위해 /
he thought to himself. 그는 마음속으로 생각했다
The second student arrived at the finish / feeling
두 번째 제자는 (그 길의) 끝에 도착했다 / 피곤함을 느끼고
tired / and regretting the path / he had chosen.
/ 길을 후회하면서 / 그가 선택했던
The teacher smiled at them both.
스승은 그들 둘 다를 보며 미소 지었다
(B) He requested / that they join him at a specific
그는 요청했다 / 그들에게 특정 장소에서 그와 만나자고
location / in three days.
/ 사흘 후에
When they arrived, / they could see a ravine /
그들이 도착했을 때 / 그들은 계곡을 볼 수 있었다 /
that was a few meters wide. 몇 미터 너비의
The students looked at their teacher / and he said
제자들은 그들의 스승을 보았고 / 스승은 딱 한 마디 말했다
just one word.
"Jump!" 뛰어라
The first student looked at the distance / and his
첫 번째 제자는 그 거리를 보고 / 가슴이 내려앉았다
heart sank.
The teacher looked at him. 스승이 그를 보았다
"What's wrong? / This is the leap to greatness. /
뭐가 문제인가 / 이건 위대함을 위한 도약이다 /
Everything that you've done until now / should have
네가 지금까지 해 온 모든 것이 / 널 준비시켰을 것이다
prepared you / for this moment."
/ 이 순간을 위해
(C) The student shrugged his shoulders / and walked
그 제자는 그의 어깨를 으쓱하고는 / 떠나버렸다
away, / knowing he hadn't prepared adequately for
/ 자신이 위대함을 위해 적절한 준비가 되어있지 않았다는 것을 알고
greatness.
The second student looked at the teacher / and smiled.
두 번째 제자는 스승을 보고 / 미소 지었다
He knew now / that the obstacles that had been
그는 이제 알았다 / 그의 길에 놓여있던 장애물들이
placed in his path / were part of his preparation.
/ 그의 준비의 일부였다는 것을
By choosing to overcome challenges, / not avoid
어려움들을 극복하는 것을 선택함으로써 / 그것들을 피하는 것이 아니라
them, / he was ready to make the leap.
/ 그는 도약할 준비가 되었다
He ran as fast as he could / and launched himself
그는 가능한 한 빨리 달렸고 / 자신을 공중으로 내던졌다
into the air.
He made it across! 그는 건넜다

(A) 두 명의 제자는 숲을 가로지르는 길의 출발선에서 그들의 스승을 만났다. 스승은 그들에게 그 주의 후반에 있을 테스트를 위한 준비로, 그 길 끝까지 따라가라고 지시했다. 길은 두 갈래로 갈라졌는데, 하나는 막힌 것이 없고 평탄했지만, 다른 하나는 쓰러진 통나무들과 다른 장애물들이 길을 막고 있었다. 한 제자는 그 장애물들을 피하기로 결정하고, 끝까지 더 쉬운 길을 갔다. (a) 그는 쉬지 않고 달려가면서 자신이 똑똑하다고 느꼈다.
(D) 두 번째 제자는 그의 길에 있는 모든 어려움을 통과해 싸우면서 장애물들에 덤벼들기로 결정했다. 쉬운 길을 선택했던 제자가 먼저 마쳤고 자신을 자랑스럽게 느꼈다. '난 내가 바위와 통나무들을 피하기로 선택해서 기뻐. 그것들은 내 속도를 늦추기 위해 그곳에 있었을 뿐이야.'라고 (e) 그는 마음속으로 생각했다. 두 번째 제자는 피곤함을 느끼고 그가 선택했던 길을 후회하면서 (그 길의) 끝에 도착했다. 스승은 그들 둘 다를 보며 미소 지었다.
(B) 그는 그들에게 사흘 후 특정 장소에서 그와 만나자고 요청했다. 그들이 도착했을 때, 그들은 몇 미터 너비의 계곡을 볼 수 있었다. 제자들은 그들의 스승을 보았고, 스승은 딱 한 마디 말했다. "뛰어라!" 첫 번째 제자는 그 거리를 보고 가슴이 내려앉았다. 스승이 (b) 그를 보았다. "뭐가 문제인가? 이건 위대함을 위한 도약이다. 네가 지금까지 해 온 모든 것이 이 순간을 위해 널 준비시켰을 것이다."
(C) 그 제자는 (c) 그의 어깨를 으쓱하고는 자신이 위대함을 위해 적절한 준비가 되어있지 않았다는 것을 알고 떠나 버렸다. 두 번째 제자는 스승을 보고 미소 지었다. 그는 이제 그의 길에 놓여있던 장애물들이 그의 준비의 일부였다는 것을 알았다. 그는 어려움들을 피하는 것이 아니라, 극복하는 것을 선택함으로써 도약할 준비가 되었다. (d) 그는 가능한 한 빨리 달렸고 자신을 공중으로 내던졌다. 그는 건넜다!

어휘·어구

instruction 지시
preparation 준비
split 나누다
location 위치, 장소
distance 거리
greatness 위대함
shrug 으쓱하다
adequately 충분히, 적절히
overcome 극복하다
leap 뛰기, 도약
launch 내던지다; 발사하다

정답률 59%

6. ④

문제풀이

한 스승이 두 명의 제자에게 길을 제시하면서 그 길 끝까지 따라가라고 지시한 후, 한 제자는 더 쉬운 길을 택해서 자신이 똑똑하다고 느꼈다는 내용의 주어진 글 다음에, 두 번째 제자는 어려운 길을 택한 후 자신이 한 선택을 후회하면서도 힘들게 모든 어려움을 통과해 길의 끝에 도착했다는 내용의 (D)가 오고, 스승이 사흘 후 특정 장소에서 만나 몇 미터 너비의 계곡으로 뛰라는 지시를 내리는 상황의 (B)가 온 뒤, 마지막으로 어려운 길을 택했던 제자가 결국 스승의 지시대로 자신을 공중으로 내던진 상황의 (C)가 오는 것이 가장 적절하다.

이렇게 풀자_ 단락별로 주요 사건이 일어나는 시간과 그 배경이 되는 공간을 염두에 두면서 글 전체의 흐름을 파악해야 한다. 연결사나 지시어, 대명사 등이 중요한 단서가 되므로 각 단락의 첫 문장과 마지막 문장에 나오는 이런 표현들에 주목한다. 이 글은 한 스승이 두 명의 제자에게 과업을 주고, 쉬운 과업을 택한 제자와 어려운 과업을 택해 끝까지 과업을 완수해낸 제자의 일화를 묘사하고 있다.

정답률 57%

7. ④

문제풀이

가능한 한 빨리 달렸고 자신을 공중으로 내던졌다는 것으로 보아 (d)는 두 번째 제자를 가리키고, 나머지는 모두 첫 번째 제자를 가리킨다.

8. ③

문제풀이

(C)의 'The student shrugged his shoulders and walked away, knowing he hadn't prepared adequately for greatness.'에서 첫 번째 제자는 위대함을 위해 적절한 준비가 되어있지 않았다는 것을 알고 떠나버렸다고 했으므로, ③이 글의 내용으로 적절하지 않다.

미니 고난도 Test 3회

Day 23

본문 133쪽

1. ② 2. ① 3. ④ 4. ③ 5. ③
6. ① 7. ② 8. ④

1. ② 결과를 평가할 때 치우침에 주의할 것

직독/직해

When reading another scientist's findings, /
다른 과학자의 실험 결과물을 읽을 때 /
think critically about the experiment.
그 실험에 대해 비판적으로 생각하라
Ask yourself: / Were observations recorded /
당신 자신에게 물어라 / 관찰들이 기록되었는지 /
during or after the experiment?
실험 도중에 혹은 후에
Do the conclusions make sense?
결론이 타당한가
Can the results be repeated?
그 결과들은 반복될 수 있는가
Are the sources of information reliable?
정보의 출처는 신뢰할만 한가
You should also ask / if the scientist or group /
당신은 또한 물어야 한다 / 그 과학자나 그룹이 /
conducting the experiment / was unbiased.
실험을 수행한 / 한쪽으로 치우치지 않았는지
Being unbiased means /
한쪽으로 치우치지 않음은 의미한다 /
that you have no special interest /
당신이 특별한 이익을 얻지 않는다는 것을 /
in the outcome of the experiment.
실험의 결과로
For example, / 예를 들어 /
if a drug company pays for an experiment to test /
만약 한 제약회사가 시험하기 위한 실험의 비용을 지불한다면 /
how well one of its new products works, /
그것의 새로운 제품 중 하나가 얼마나 잘 작용하는지 /
there is a special interest involved: /
특별한 이익이 관련된 것이다 /
The drug company profits /
그 제약회사는 이익을 본다 /
if the experiment shows /
만일 그 실험이 보여준다면 /
that its product is effective.
그 제품이 효과가 있다는 것을
Therefore, / the experimenters aren't objective.
그러므로 / 그 실험자들은 객관적이지 않다
They might ensure / the conclusion is positive /
그들은 보장할지도 모른다 / 그 결론이 긍정적이라는 것을 /
and benefits the drug company.
그리고 제약회사에 이익을 준다는 것을
When assessing results, / think about any biases /
결과들을 평가할 때 / 어떤 치우침에 대해 생각하라 /
that may be present!
있을지도 모르는

다른 과학자의 실험 결과물을 읽을 때, 그 실험에 대해 비판적으로 생각하라. 당신 자신에게 물어라. 관찰들이 실험 도중에 혹은 후에 기록되었나? 결론이 타당한가? 그 결과들은 반복될 수 있는가? 정보의 출처는 신뢰할만 한가? 당신은 실험을 수행한 그 과학자나 그룹이 한쪽으로 치우치지 않았는지 역시 물어야 한다. 한쪽으로 치우치지 않음은 당신이 실험의 결과로 특별한 이익을 얻지 않는다는 것을 의미한다. 예를 들면, 만약

한 제약회사가 그 회사의 새로운 제품 중 하나가 얼마나 잘 작용하는지 시험해보기 위한 실험 비용을 지불한다면, 특별한 이익이 관련된 것이다: 만약 실험이 그 제품이 효과 있음을 보여준다면, 그 제약회사는 이익을 본다. 따라서, 그 실험자들은 객관적이지 않다. 그들은 결론이 제약 회사에 우호적이고 이익을 주도록 보장할지도 모른다. 결과들을 평가할 때, 있을지도 모르는 어떤 치우침에 대해 생각하라!

① 창의적인
② 객관적인
③ 신뢰할 수 없는
④ 믿을 수 없는
⑤ 결단력 있는

문제풀이

다른 과학자들의 실험결과를 읽을 때는 여러 질문을 통해 편향성을 가지지 않도록 비판적으로 생각해야 하며, 또한 편향되지 않다는 것은 실험의 결과에 어떤 특별한 이익이 없다는 것을 의미하고, 만일 실험 비용을 부담한 제약회사의 제품이 효과가 있다는 것을 보여준다면, 그 실험은 객관적이지 못하다는 내용의 글이다. 따라서 빈칸에는 ② 'objective'가 들어가서, 빈칸을 포함한 문장이 '따라서, 그 실험자들은 객관적이지 않다.'가 돼야 한다.

구조 다시보기

주제	과학 연구 결과를 읽을 때는 비판적 시각을 가져야 함
부연	비판적 시각을 갖기 위한 다양한 질문
예시	비용을 지불한 제약회사의 실험결과는 객관성이 결여됨
주제 재진술	연구의 결과물을 평가할 때는 어떤 편견이 있는지 생각할 것

어휘·어구

findings 발견, 결과
critically 비판적으로
observation 관찰
experiment 실험
reliable 신뢰할 만한
conduct 수행하다
unbiased 치우치지 않은
outcome 결과
interest 이익, 이해관계
involved 관련된
assess 평가하다
bias 편견, 치우침
untrustworthy 신뢰할 수 없는
decisive 결단력 있는

2. ① 아기들이 흔드는 동작을 좋아하는 이유

직독/직해

We're often told that newborns and infants are comforted by rocking /
우리는 신생아와 유아가 흔들림에 의해 편안해진다는 말을 자주 듣는다 /
because this motion is similar to what they experienced in the womb, /
이런 움직임이 자궁 안에서 그들이 경험했던 것과 유사하기 때문에 /
and that they must take comfort in this familiar feeling.
그래서 그들이 이런 친숙한 느낌에서 편안해지는 것이 틀림없다고
This may be true; 이것은 사실일 수 있다
however, to date there are no convincing data /
하지만 현재까지 설득력 있는 데이터는 없다 /
that demonstrate a significant relationship /
상당한 관계가 있음을 입증하는 /
between the amount of time a mother moves during pregnancy /
임신기간 동안 엄마가 움직이는 시간의 양과 /
and her newborn's response to rocking.
흔들림에 대한 신생아의 반응 사이에
Just as likely is the idea /
다음의 생각도 그만큼 가능할 법하다 /
that newborns come to associate gentle rocking with being fed.
신생아가 부드러운 흔들림을 젖을 먹는 것과 연관시키게 된다는
Parents understand that rocking quiets a newborn, /
부모는 흔들어 주는 것이 신생아를 달래 준다는 것을 이해하고 있다 /
and they very often provide gentle, repetitive movement during feeding.
그래서 그들은 젖을 주는 동안 부드럽고, 반복적인 움직임을 매우 자주 제공한다
Since the appearance of food is a primary reinforcer, /
음식의 등장은 일차 강화물이기 때문에 /
newborns may acquire a fondness for motion /
신생아는 움직임을 좋아하게 되는 것일 수 있다 /
because they have been conditioned /
그들이 조건화되어 왔기 때문이다 /
through a process of associative learning.
연관 학습의 과정을 통해

신생아와 유아가 흔들림에 의해 편안해지는데, 이것은 이런 움직임이 자궁 안에서 그들이 경험했던 것과 유사하기 때문이고, 그들이 이런 친숙한 느낌에서 편안해지는 것이 틀림없다는 말을 자주 듣는다. 이것은 사실일 수 있지만, 현재까지 임신기간 동안 엄마가 움직이는 시간의 양과 흔들림에 대한 신생아의 반응 사이에 상당한 관계가 있음을 입증하는 설득력 있는 데이터는 없다. 신생아가 부드러운 흔들림을 젖을 먹는 것과 연관시키게 된다는 생각도 그만큼 가능할 법하다. 부모는 흔들어 주는 것이 신생아를 달래 준다는 것을 알고 있어서, 그들은 젖을 주는 동안 부드럽고, 반복적인 움직임을 매우 자주 제공한다. 음식의 등장은 일차 강화물이기 때문에, 신생아는 움직임을 좋아하게 되고, 그 이유는 그들이 연관 학습의 과정을 통해 조건화되어 왔기 때문이다.

① 움직임을 좋아하게 되고
② 지속적으로 젖을 주기를 원하고
③ 심하게 흔드는 것을 싫어하고
④ 음식의 맛을 기억하고
⑤ 자신의 엄마와 유대관계를 형성하고

문제풀이

아기들이 흔들림에 의해 편안해지는 이유는 그들이 자궁에서 경험한 것과 친숙해서라는 말은 가능성은 있지만 입증되지 않았고, 그만큼 가능성 있는 또 하나의 이야기는 부모가 부드럽게 흔들면서 아기에서 젖을 주기 때문에 아기가 부드럽게 흔드는 것을 좋아하게 되었을 것이라는 것이다. 따라서 빈칸에는 ① 'acquire a fondness for motion'이 들어가서 빈칸을 포함한 문장이 '음식의 등장은 일차 강화물이기 때문에, 신생아는 움직임을 좋아하게 되고, 그 이유는 그들이 연관 학습의 과정을 통해 조건화되어 왔기 때문이다.'가 되는 것이 가장 적절하다.

이렇게 풀자 빈칸 추론 유형에서 빈칸이 마지막 부분에 있는 경우는 글의 핵심을 묻는 경우인데, 이 글은 아기들이 부드럽게 흔들어주는 동작을 좋아하는 이유는 그 동작 이후에 젖을 주기 때문일 수 있다는 내용의 글이다. 'Just as likely is the idea that newborns come to associate gentle rocking with being fed.(신생아가 부드러운 흔들림을 젖을 먹는 것과 연관시키게 된다는 생각도 그만큼 가능할 법하다.)'에서 빈칸에 들어갈 말을 유추할 수 있다.

어휘·어구

rock 흔들리다
to date 지금까지, 현재까지
convincing 설득력 있는
demonstrate 분명히 보여주다, 입증하다
significant 상당한
associate 연관시키다
repetitive 반복적인
primary 제1의, 주요한
associative 연상의, 연상 작용의
acquire 배우다, 얻다
fondness 좋아함, 애정
consistent 일관된, 변함없는
bond 유대, 결속

3. ④ 쇼핑을 용이하게 만드는 상점 내 중앙 통로

직독/직해

Wouldn't it be nice / if you could take your customers
좋지 않을까 / 여러분이 고객들의 손을 잡을 수 있다면
by the hand / and guide each one through your store /
/ 그리고 여러분의 상점 내 여기저기로 각 고객을 안내할 수 있다면 /
while pointing out all the great products /
모든 훌륭한 제품을 가리키면서 /
you would like them to consider buying?
여러분이 그들에게 구매를 고려하게 하고 싶은
Most people, however, / 하지만 대부분 사람은 /
would not particularly enjoy having a stranger
특히 낯선 사람이 그들의 손을 잡는 것을 즐기지는 않을 것이다
grab their hand / and drag them through a store.
/ 그리고 그들을 상점 내 여기저기로 끌고 다니게 하는 것을
Rather, / let the store do it for you.
오히려 / 여러분을 위해 상점이 그것을 하게 하라
Have a central path / that leads shoppers through
중앙 통로를 만들어라 / 고객들을 상점 내 여기저기로 이끄는
the store / and lets them look at /
/ 그리고 그들이 볼 수 있게 하라 /
many different departments or product areas.
많은 다양한 매장이나 상품이 있는 곳을
You can use / this effect of music on shopping behavior /
여러분은 활용할 수 있다 / 소비 행동에 대한 음악의 이런 효과를 /
by playing it in the store. 상점에서 음악을 트는 것으로
This path leads / your customers from the entrance /
이 길은 이어진다 / 입구에서부터 여러분의 고객들을 /
through the store / 상점 내 여기저기를 /
on the route you want them to take all the way /
그들이 걸었으면 하고 여러분이 바라는 경로로 /
to the checkout. 계산대까지

여러분이 고객들의 손을 잡고 그들에게 구매를 고려하게 하고 싶은 모든 훌륭한 제품을 가리키면서 여러분의 상점 내 여기저기로 각 고객을 안내할 수 있다면 좋지 않을까? ① 하지만 대부분 사람은 특히 낯선 사람이 그들의 손을 잡고 상점 내 여기저기로 끌고 다니게 하는 것을 즐기지는 않을 것이다. ② 오히려, 여러분을 위해 상점이 그것을 하게 하라. ③ 고객들을 상점 내 여기저기로 이끄는 중앙 통로를 만들어서 그들이 많은 다양한 매장이나 상품이 있는 곳을 볼 수 있게 하라. ④ (여러분은 상점에서 음악을 트는 것으로 소비 행동에 대한 음악의 이런 효과를 활용할 수 있다.) ⑤ 이 길은 여러분의 고객들을 그들이 걸었으면 하고 여러분이 바라는 경로로 상점 내 여기저기를 통해 입구에서부터 계산대까지 이어진다.

문제풀이

이 글은 고객들을 상점 내 여기저기로 이끄는 중앙 통로를 만들어 그들이 다양한 매장이나 상품이 있는 곳을 볼 수 있게 하라는 내용이다. 하지만 ④는 상점에서 음악을 트는 것이 소비 행동에 대한 음악의 효과를 활용한다는 내용이므로 나머지 글의 흐름과 관계가 없다.

이렇게 풀자_ 갑자기 내용이 전환되거나, 앞뒤 문맥과 연결되지 않는 내용은 아닌지를 살피며 꼼꼼히 글을 읽어야 한다. 상점 내 고객들이 다양한 상품을 쇼핑할 수 있게 중앙 통로를 만들라는 내용 흐름 속에 상점에서의 음악이 소비 행동에 미치는 영향을 언급하는 내용은 부자연스럽다.

어휘·어구

drag 끌다
central 중앙의
behavior 행동
entrance 입구

route 경로
checkout 계산대

정답률 39%

4. ③ 현실적인 낙관주의자와 비현실적인 낙관주의자

직독/직해

To be successful, / you need to understand the vital
성공하기 위해 / 당신은 중요한 차이를 이해해야 한다
difference / between believing you will succeed, /
/ 당신이 성공할 것이라고 믿는 것과 /
and believing you will succeed easily.
당신이 쉽게 성공할 것이라고 믿는 것 사이의
(B) Put another way, / it's the difference /
다시 말해 / 그것은 차이이다 /
between being a realistic optimist, / and an unrealistic optimist
현실적인 낙관주의자가 되는 것과 / 비현실적인 낙관주의자가 되는 것 간의
Realistic optimists believe / they will succeed, /
현실적인 낙관주의자들은 믿을 뿐만 아니라 / 그들이 성공할 것이라고 /
but also believe they have to make success happen /
또한 그들이 성공이 일어나게 만들어야 한다고 믿는다 /
— through things like careful planning / and choosing the right strategies.
신중한 계획과 같은 것들을 통해 / 그리고 올바른 전략을 선택하는 것
(C) They recognize the need for giving serious thought /
그들은 심각하게 고려할 필요가 있다는 것을 인식한다 /
to how they will deal with obstacles.
어떻게 그들이 장애물들을 다룰지에 관해
This preparation only increases their confidence /
이런 준비만이 그들의 자신감을 높여 준다 /
in their own ability / to get things done.
그들 자신의 능력에 대한 / 일이 수행될 수 있게 하는
(A) Unrealistic optimists, / on the other hand, /
비현실적인 낙관주의자들은 / 반면에 /
believe that success will happen to them /
성공이 그들에게 일어날 것을 믿는다 /
— that the universe will reward them / for all their positive thinking, / or that somehow they will be
우주가 그들에게 보상할 것이라고 / 자신의 모든 긍정적인 사고에 대해
/ 혹은 어떤 식으로든 그들이 하룻밤 사이에 변할 것이라고 (믿는다)
transformed overnight / into the kind of person /
/ 그런 종류의 사람으로 /
for whom obstacles don't exist anymore.
장애물이 더 이상 존재하지 않는

성공하기 위해, 당신은 당신이 성공할 것이라고 믿는 것과 쉽게 성공할 것이라고 믿는 것 사이의 중요한 차이를 이해해야 한다.
(B) 다시 말해, 그것은 현실적인 낙관주의자가 되는 것과 비현실적인 낙관주의자가 되는 것 간의 차이이다. 현실적인 낙관주의자들은 그들이 성공할 것이라고 믿을 뿐만 아니라, 그들이 신중한 계획과 올바른 전략을 선택하는 것과 같은 것들을 통해 성공이 일어나게 만들어야 한다고 믿는다.
(C) 그들은 어떻게 그들이 장애물들을 다룰지에 관해 심각하게 고려할 필요가 있다는 것을 인식한다. 이런 준비만이 일이 수행될 수 있게 하는 그들 자신의 능력에 대한 자신감을 높여 준다.
(A) 반면에, 비현실적인 낙관주의자들은 성공이 그들에게 일어날 것, 즉 우주가 그들에게 자신의 모든 긍정적인 사고에 대해 보상할 것이라고, 혹은 어떤 식으로든 그들이 하룻밤 사이에 장애물이 더 이상 존재하지 않는 그런 종류의 사람으로 변할 것이라고 믿는다.

문제풀이

주어진 글은 성공하기 위해 당신이 성공할 것이라고 믿는 것과 쉽게 성공할 것이라고 믿는 것 사이의 중요한 차이를 이해해야 한다는 내용으로, 주어진 글에 대해 재진술하며 현실적인 낙관주의자들에 대해 언급하는 (B)가 주어진 글 뒤에 오고, (B)에서 언급된 현실적인 낙관주의자들에 대해 부연 설명하는 (C)가 온 뒤, 현실적인 낙관주의자들과는 다른 비현실적인 낙관주의자들에 대해 설명하는 (A)가 마지막에 오는 것이 자연스럽다.

이렇게 풀자_ (B)의 'Put another way(다시 말해)'로 보아 (B)는 앞글에 대한 재진술임을 알 수 있고, (C)의 'They'는 (B)에서 언급된 현실적인 낙관주의자들을 가리키므로 (C)는 (B) 뒤에 와야 하며, (A)의 'on the other hand(반면에)'로 보아 (A)는 앞글과는 상반되는 내용이 제시될 것임을 알 수 있으므로 (C) 뒤에 (A)가 와야 한다.

어휘·어구

difference 차이
unrealistic 비현실적인
optimist 낙관주의자
obstacle 장애물
put another way 다시 말해서
strategy 전략, 계획
deal with ~을 다루다
preparation 준비

정답률 43%

5. ③ 뇌가 생체 시계 재설정 목적으로 사용할 수 있는 요소

직독/직해

Daylight isn't the only signal / that the brain can use /
햇빛은 유일한 신호는 아니다 / 뇌가 사용할 수 있는 /
for the purpose of biological clock resetting, /
생체 시계 재설정을 목적으로 /
though it is the principal and preferential signal, /
비록 그것이 중요하고 우선되는 신호지만 /
when present. (햇빛이) 있을 때는
So long as they are reliably repeating, /
확실하게 반복되는 한 /
the brain can also use other external cues, /
뇌는 다른 외부적인 신호들을 사용할 수도 있다 /
such as food, exercise, and even regularly timed social interaction.
음식, 운동 그리고 심지어는 정기적인 사회적 상호 작용과 같은
All of these events / 이 모든 경우는 /
have the ability to reset the biological clock, /
생체 시계를 재설정하는 능력을 가지고 있다 /
allowing it to strike a precise twenty-four-hour note.
정확한 24시간 음을 치게 하는
It is the reason / 그것이 이유이다 /
that individuals with certain forms of blindness /
어떤 유형의 시력 상실을 가진 개인도 /
do not entirely lose their circadian rhythm.
24시간 주기의 리듬을 완전히 잃지 않는
Despite not receiving light cues /
빛 신호를 받지 않음에도 불구하고 /
due to their blindness, /
그들의 시력 상실 때문에 /
other phenomena act as their resetting triggers.
다른 현상들이 재설정의 유인 역할을 한다
Any signal / 어떤 신호든지 /
that the brain uses for the purpose of clock resetting /
뇌가 시계 재설정을 목적으로 이용하는 /
is termed a zeitgeber, / 자연 시계라 불린다 /
from the German "time giver" or "synchronizer."
'시간 제공자'나 '동기화 장치'라는 독일어에서 유래한
Thus, / 따라서 /
while light is the most reliable and thus the primary zeitgeber, /
빛이 가장 신뢰할 수 있어서 주된 자연 시계인 반면 /
there are many factors / that can be used /
많은 요인이 있다 / 사용될 수 있는 /
in addition to, or in the absence of, daylight.
햇빛과 함께 혹은 햇빛이 없을 때

비록 (햇빛이) 있을 때는 그것이 중요하고 우선되는 신호지만, 햇빛은 뇌가 생체 시계 재설정을 목적으로 사용할 수 있는 유일한 신호는 아니다. (①) 확실하게 반복되는 한, 뇌는 음식, 운동 그리고 심지어는 정기적인 사회적 상호 작용과 같은 다른 외부적인 신호들을 사용할 수도 있다. (②) 이 모든 경우는 생체 시계를 재설정하는 능력이 있어서 정확한 24시간 음을 치게 한다. (③) 그것이 어떤 유형의 시력 상실을 가진 개인도 24시간 주기의 리듬을 완전히 잃지 않는 이유이다. 그들의 시력 상실 때문에 빛 신호를 받지 않음에도 불구하고, 다른 현상들이 재설정의 유인 역할을 한다. (④) 뇌가 시계 재설정을 목적으로 이용하는 어떤 신호든지 '시간 제공자'나 '동기화 장치'라는 독일어에서 유래한 자연 시계라 불린다. (⑤) 따라서, 빛이 가장 신뢰할 수 있어서 주된 자연 시계인 반면, 햇빛과 함께 혹은 햇빛이 없을 때 사용될 수 있는 많은 요인이 있다.

문제풀이

주어진 문장의 'It'은 생체 시계를 재설정하는 능력을 가리키고, 생체 시계를 재설정하는 능력으로 인해 시력을 상실한 사람도 24시간 주기의 리듬을 완전히 잃지 않는다는 흐름이 되어야 자연스럽다. 따라서 주어진 문장은 ③에 들어가는 것이 가장 적절하다.

이렇게 풀자 주어진 문장의 'It'이 가리키는 내용과 ③ 뒤의 'their blindness'에서 their가 누구를 가리키는지를 파악하면 주어진 문장의 위치를 찾을 수 있다.

구조 다시보기

도입	햇빛은 뇌가 생체 시계 재설정을 목적으로 사용할 수 있는 유일한 신호는 아님
전개	다른 외부적인 신호들을 사용해서 생체 시계를 재설정하는 능력이 있음
결과	빛이 가장 신뢰할 수 있는 자연 시계이지만 빛이 없어도 사용할 수 있는 많은 요인이 있음

어휘·어구

blindness 실명
signal 신호
biological clock 생체 시계
principal 주요한
preferential 우선의, 특혜의
reliably 확실히, 믿을 수 있게
external 외부의
cue 신호
interaction 상호 작용
strike 치다
precise 정확한, 정밀한
receive 받다
phenomenon 현상(pl. phenomena)
trigger 유인
zeitgeber 자연 시계(생물 시계의 움직임에 영향을 주는 빛 · 어둠 · 기온 등의 요소)
synchronizer 동기화 장치
reliable 믿을 만한
in the absence of ~이 없어서

정답률 42%

6. ① 연령별로 또래들의 존재가 게임 활동에 미치는 영향

직독/직해

In a study, / psychologist Laurence Steinberg of
한 연구에서 / Temple 대학교의 심리학자인 Laurence Steinberg와
Temple University / and his co-author, psychologist
/ 그의 공동 저자인 심리학자 Margo Gardner는
Margo Gardner / divided 306 people into three age groups: /
/ 306명의 사람들을 세 연령 집단으로 나누었다
young adolescents, with a mean age of 14; /
/ 평균 나이 14세인 어린 청소년 /
older adolescents, with a mean age of 19; /
평균 나이 19세인 나이가 더 많은 청소년 /
and adults, aged 24 and older.
그리고 나이가 24세 이상인 성인으로
Subjects played a computerized driving game /
피실험자들은 컴퓨터 운전 게임을 했다 /
in which the player must avoid crashing /
게임 참가자가 충돌하는 것을 피해야 하는 /
into a wall that appears, without warning, /
경고 없이 나타나는 벽에 /

on the roadway. 도로에
Steinberg and Gardner / randomly assigned some
Steinberg와 Gardner는 / 무작위로 몇몇 참가자들을 게임을 하게 했다 /
participants to play /
alone or with two same-age peers looking on.
혼자 게임 하거나 혹은 두 명의 같은 나이 또래들이 지켜보는 가운데
Older adolescents scored about 50 percent higher /
나이가 더 많은 청소년들은 약 50% 더 높은 점수를 기록했고 /
on an index of risky driving / when their peers were
위험 운전 지수에서 / 그들의 또래들이 방에 있을 때
in the room / — and the driving of early adolescents /
/ 그리고 어린 청소년들의 운전은 /
was fully twice as reckless / when other young teens
무려 두 배 더 무모했다 / 다른 어린 십 대들이 주변에 있을 때
were around.
In contrast, / adults behaved in similar ways /
대조적으로 / 성인들은 유사한 방식으로 행동했다 /
regardless of whether they were on their own or
그들이 혼자 있든 다른 사람에 의해 관찰되든지에 상관없이
observed by others.
The presence of peers / 또래들의 존재는 /
makes adolescents, but not adults, / more likely to
성인들은 아니지만 청소년들이 / 더 위험을 감수하게 만든다
take risks.

한 연구에서, Temple 대학교의 심리학자인 Laurence Steinberg와 그의 공동 저자인 심리학자 Margo Gardner는 306명의 사람들을 세 연령 집단 즉, 평균 나이 14세인 어린 청소년, 평균 나이 19세인 나이가 더 많은 청소년, 그리고 나이가 24세 이상인 성인으로 나누었다. 피실험자들은 게임 참가자가 도로에 경고 없이 나타나는 벽에 충돌하는 것을 피해야 하는 컴퓨터 운전 게임을 했다. Steinberg와 Gardner는 무작위로 몇몇 참가자들을 혼자 게임 하거나 혹은 두 명의 같은 나이 또래들이 지켜보는 가운데 게임을 하게 했다. 나이가 더 많은 청소년들은 그들의 또래들이 방에 있을 때 위험 운전 지수에서 약 50% 더 높은 점수를 기록했고, 어린 청소년들의 운전은 다른 어린 십 대들이 주변에 있을 때 무려 두 배 더 무모했다. 대조적으로, 성인들은 그들이 혼자 있든 다른 사람에 의해 관찰되든지에 상관없이 유사한 방식으로 행동했다.
➡ 또래들의 (A) 존재는, 성인들은 아니지만 청소년들이 더 (B) 위험을 감수하게 만든다.

① **존재 ········ 위험을 감수하게**
② 존재 ········ 조심스럽게 행동하게
③ 무관심 ········ 잘 하지 못하게
④ 부재 ········ 모험을 즐기게
⑤ 부재 ········ 독립적으로 행동하게

문제풀이

청소년들은 또래들이 지켜보는 가운데 컴퓨터 운전 게임을 할 경우 위험 운전 지수에서 더 높은 점수를 기록하고 더 무모했던 반면, 성인들은 그들이 혼자 있든 다른 사람에 의해 관찰되든 상관없이 유사한 방식으로 행동했다는 내용으로 보아, 요약문의 빈칸 (A)에는 'presence(존재)'가, (B)에는 'take risks(위험을 감수하다)'가 가장 적절하다.

이렇게 풀자_ 세 연령 집단의 피실험자들이 또래가 있을 경우 컴퓨터 운전 게임에서 어떻게 행동했는지에 관한 내용을 통해 요약문의 빈칸에 들어갈 말을 추론할 수 있다.

어휘·어구

co-author 공동 저자
divide 나누다
adolescent 청소년
mean 평균의
subject 연구 대상, 피실험자
computerized 컴퓨터화된
randomly 무작위로
assign 배정하다
index 지수
regardless of ~에 상관없이

7~8 잘못된 정보를 줄 수 있는 광고 속의 통계 자료

직독/직해

Many advertisements cite statistical surveys.
많은 광고가 통계 조사를 인용한다
But we should be cautious / because we usually do
하지만 우리는 신중해야 한다 / 우리는 대개 모르기 때문에
not know / how these surveys are conducted.
/ 이런 조사들이 어떻게 실시되는지를
For example, a toothpaste manufacturer /
예를 들어, 어떤 치약 제조 업체가 /
once had a poster that said, /
예전에 적혀 있는 포스터를 올렸다 /
"More than 80% of dentists / recommend *Smiley Toothpaste*."
80%보다 많은 치과의사들이 / 'Smiley Toothpaste'를 추천한다
This seems to say / 이것은 말하는 것 같다 /
that most dentists prefer *Smiley Toothpaste* /
대부분의 치과의사들이 'Smiley Toothpaste'를 선호한다고 /
to other brands. 다른 브랜드보다
But it turns out / 그러나 드러났다 /
that the survey questions allowed the dentists /
그 조사 항목이 치과의사들에게 ~하도록 했다 /
to recommend more than one brand, /
한 가지가 넘는 브랜드를 추천할 수 있게 /
and in fact another competitor's brand was recommended /
그리고 실제로 또 다른 경쟁업체의 브랜드도 추천되었다는 것이 /
just as often as *Smiley Toothpaste*!
'Smiley Toothpaste'만큼 많이
No wonder the UK Advertising Standards Authority
2007년에 영국 Advertising Standards Authority가 판결을 내렸던 것은 당연했다 /
ruled in 2007 / that the poster was misleading /
/ 그 포스터가 잘못된 정보를 주는 것으로 /
and it could no longer be displayed.
그리고 그것이 더 이상 게시될 수 없었음은
A similar case concerns a well-known cosmetics
유명 화장품 회사의 경우도 유사하다
firm / marketing a cream /
/ 크림을 판매하는 /
that is supposed to rapidly reduce wrinkles.
주름을 빠른 속도로 줄여 준다고 한
But the only evidence provided is /
하지만 주어진 유일한 증거라고는 ~것뿐이다 /
that "76% of 50 women agreed."
50명의 여성 중 76%가 동의했다
But what this means is / 그러나 이것이 의미하는 것은 ~이다 /
that the evidence is based on just the personal
그 증거가 개인적 의견에 근거한다는 것 /
opinions / from a small sample /
/ 소수의 표본에서 얻은 /
with no objective measurement of their skin's condition.
그들의 피부 상태에 대한 객관적인 측정 없는
Furthermore, we are not told /
그뿐만 아니라, 우리는 듣지 못한다 /
how these women were selected.
이 여성들이 어떻게 선별되었는지
Without such information, / 그러한 정보 없이 /
the "evidence" provided is pretty much useful.
주어진 "증거"는 매우 유용하다
Unfortunately, such advertisements are quite typical, /
유감스럽게도, 그러한 광고들은 아주 전형적이다 /
and as consumers / we just have to use our own
그리고 소비자로서 / 우리는 스스로 판단해야만 하며 /
judgment / and avoid taking advertising claims too
/ 그리고 광고의 주장을 너무 진지하게 받아들이는 것을 피해야 한다
seriously.

많은 광고가 통계 조사를 인용한다. 하지만 우리는 대개 이런 조사들이 어떻게 실시되는지를 모르기 때문에 (a) 신중해야 한다. 예를 들어, 어떤 치약 제조 업체가 예전에 "80%보다 많은 치과의사들이 'Smiley Toothpaste'를 추천한다."라고 적혀 있는 포스터를 올렸다. 이것은 대부분의 치과의사들이 다른 브랜드보다 'Smiley Toothpaste'를 (b) 선호한다고 말하는 것 같다. 그러나 그 조사 항목이 치과의사들에게 한 가지가 넘는 브랜드를 추천할 수 있게 했다는 것과 실제로 또 다른 경쟁업체의 브랜드도 'Smiley Toothpaste'만큼 많이 추천되었다는 것이 드러났다! 2007년에 영국 Advertising Standards Authority는 그 포스터가 (c) 잘못된 정보를 주는 것으로 판결을 내렸고 그것이 더 이상 게시될 수 없었음은 당연했다. 주름을 빠른 속도로 줄여 준다고 한 크림을 판매하는 유명 화장품 회사의 경우도 유사하다. 하지만 주어진 유일한 증거라고는 "50명의 여성 중 76%가 동의했다."라는 것뿐이다. 그러나 이것이 의미하는 것은 그 증거가 피부 상태에 대한 객관적인 측정 없는 소수의 표본에서 얻은 개인적 의견에 근거한다는 것이다. 그뿐만 아니라, 우리는 이 여성들이 어떻게 선별되었는지 듣지 못한다. 그러한 정보 없이, 주어진 "증거"는 매우 (d) 유용하다. 유감스럽게도, 그러한 광고들은 아주 전형적이고, 소비자로서 우리는 스스로 판단해야만 하며 광고의 주장을 너무 진지하게 받아들이는 것을 (e) 피해야 한다.

구조 다시보기

도입	통계 조사를 인용한 광고는 조사가 실시된 방법을 알 수 없으므로 신중하게 받아들여야 함
예시 1	어떤 치약 제조 업체의 치과의사 추천과 관련된 통계 수치가 잘못된 정보를 주는 것으로 판결이 남
예시 2	크림 판매를 위해 유명 화장품 회사가 인용한 통계 수치도 객관적인 측정이 아니었음
결론	소비자로서 우리 스스로 판단하고 광고의 주장을 진지하게 받아들이지 말아야 함

어휘·어구

advertisement 광고
cite 인용하다
statistical 통계적인, 통계학상의
survey 조사
cautious 신중한
conduct 실시하다
manufacturer 제조사
turn out 나타나다
competitor 경쟁자, 경쟁사
rule 결정[판결]을 내리다
misleading 잘못된 정보를 주는
concern 관한 것이다
cosmetics 화장품
firm 회사
rapidly 빨리, 급속히
wrinkle 주름
evidence 증거
objective 객관적인
be based on ~에 근거하다
typical 전형적인
consumer 소비자
judgment 판단
claim 주장, 요구

정답률 60%

7. ②

① 광고와 경제 사이의 연결
② 광고 속의 통계 자료는 믿을 만 한가?
③ 광고 속의 통계 자료는 객관적이다!
④ 공익 광고의 밝은 측면
⑤ 품질과 가격 중 어느 것이 더 중요한가?

문제풀이

치약과 화장품 광고를 예로 들며 광고에 인용된 통계 자료가 잘못된 정보를 줄 수 있다고 하면서 광고가 믿을 만한 것인지는 소비자가 스스로 판단해야 하고 광고를 너무 진지하게 받아들이지는 않아야 한다는 이야기를 하고 있는 글이다. 이러한 글의 내용을 가장 잘 나타낸 제목으로는 ② 'Are Statistical Data in Advertisements Reliable? (광고 속의 통계 자료는 믿을 만 한가?)'이 적절하다.

이렇게 풀자_ 글의 주제를 정확하게 파악하여 주제를 대표하는 포괄적이고 상징적인 제목을 골라야 한다. 'No wonder the UK Advertising Standards Authority ruled in 2007 that the poster was misleading and it could no longer be displayed.(2007년에 영국 Advertising Standards Authority는 그 포스터가 잘못된 정보를 주는 것으로 판결을 내렸고 그것이 더 이상 게시될 수 없었음

은 당연했다.)'와 'Unfortunately, such advertisements are quite typical, and as consumers we just have to use our own judgment and avoid taking advertising claims too seriously.(유감스럽게도, 그러한 광고들은 아주 전형적이고, 소비자인 우리는 스스로 판단해야 하며 광고의 주장을 너무 진지하게 받아들이는 것을 피해야 한다.)'에 이 글의 주제가 가장 잘 드러나 있다.

정답률 46%

8. ④

문제풀이

크림에 대한 조사 증거가 피부 상태에 대한 객관적인 측정 없는 소수의 표본에서 얻은 개인적인 의견이라는 점과 조사 대상의 선별 방식이 밝혀지지 않았다는 점을 볼 때, 그 증거는 쓸모가 없는 것임을 알 수 있다. 따라서 (d) 'useful(유용한)'을 'useless(쓸모가 없는)'로 바꿔야 한다.

이렇게 풀자_ 먼저 글의 주제와 흐름을 파악한 뒤 밑줄 친 어휘가 포함된 문장 전후 문맥을 파악해서 적절하게 쓰였는지를 판단하면 된다. 'But what this means is that the evidence is based on just the personal opinions from a small sample with no objective measurement of their skin's condition.(그러나 이것이 의미하는 것은 그 증거가 피부 상태에 대한 객관적인 측정 없는 소수의 표본에서 얻은 개인적 의견에 근거한다는 것이다.)'과 'Furthermore, we are not told how these women were selected.(그뿐만 아니라, 우리는 이 여성들이 어떻게 선별되었는지 알 수 없다.)'를 통해 그 증거의 특징을 파악하면 (d) useful(유용한)이 적절하지 않다는 것을 알 수 있다.

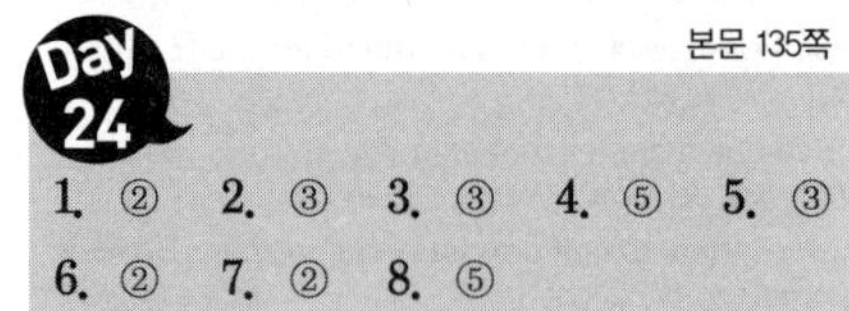

미니 고난도 Test 4회

Day 24

본문 135쪽

1. ② 2. ③ 3. ③ 4. ⑤ 5. ③
6. ② 7. ② 8. ⑤

정답률 36%

1. ② 역할은 상호 작용과 행동을 규제한다

직독/직해

People engage in typical patterns of interaction /
사람들은 전형적인 양식의 상호 작용에 참여한다 /
based on the relationship / 관계에 근거해서 /
between their roles and the roles of others.
자신의 역할과 다른 사람의 역할 사이의
Employers are expected to interact with employees /
고용주들은 직원들과 상호 작용하도록 기대된다 /
in a certain way, / 특정한 방식으로 /
as are doctors with patients. 의사들이 환자들과 그런 것처럼
In each case, / actions are restricted by the role
각각의 경우에서 / 행동은 역할 책임과 의무에 의해 제한된다 /
responsibilities and obligations /
associated with individuals' positions within society.
사회 내의 개인의 지위와 관련된
For instance, / parents and children are linked /
예를 들어 / 부모와 자식은 연결된다 /
by certain rights, privileges, and obligations.
특정한 권리, 특권, 그리고 의무에 의해
Parents are responsible for providing /
부모는 제공할 책임이 있다 /
their children with the basic necessities of life /
자기 자녀에게 기본적인 생필품을 /
— food, clothing, shelter, and so forth. 의식주 등
These expectations are so powerful / that not
이런 기대가 너무 강해서 / 그것들을 충족시키지 못하는 것은
meeting them / may make the parents vulnerable /
/ 부모를 비난받기 쉽게 할 수도 있다 /
to charges of negligence or abuse. 태만이나 학대 혐의로
Children, in turn, are expected to do / as their
이번에는 아이들이 행동하도록 기대된다 / 자신의 부모가 말하는 대로
parents say.
Thus, / interactions within a relationship /
따라서 / 관계 내의 상호 작용은 /
are functions not only of the individual personalities of
관련된 사람들 개개인 성격의 작용일 뿐만 아니라
the people involved / but also of the role requirements /
/ 역할 요구의 (작용이다) /
associated with the statuses they have.
그들이 지닌 지위와 관련된

사람들은 자신의 역할과 다른 사람의 역할 사이의 관계에 근거해서 전형적인 양식의 상호 작용에 참여한다. 의사들이 환자들과 그런 것처럼 고용주들은 직원들과 특정한 방식으로 상호 작용하도록 기대된다. 각각의 경우에서, 행동은 사회 내의 개인의 지위와 관련된 역할 책임과 의무에 의해 제한된다. 예를 들어 부모와 자식은 특정한 권리, 특권, 그리고 의무에 의해 연결된다. 부모는 자기 자녀에게 의식주 등 기본적인 생필품을 제공할 책임이 있다. 이런 기대가 너무 강해서 그것들을 충족시키지 못하는 것은 부모를 태만이나 학대 혐의로 비난받기 쉽게 할 수도 있다. 이번에는 아이들이 자신의 부모가 말하는 대로 행동하도록 기대된다. 따라서 관계 내의 상호 작용은 관련된 사람들 개개인 성격의 작용일 뿐만 아니라 그들이 지닌 지위와 관련된 역할 요구의 작용이다.

① 직업 ② 지위 ③ 능력
④ 동기 ⑤ 관점

문제풀이

사람들은 개인들의 역할에 근거해서 상호 작용하고 행동에도 제약을 받는다는 내용의 글로, 행동은 사회에서 개인의 지위와 관련된 역할 책임과 의무에 의해 제한된다는 것으로 보아 빈칸에 ② 'statuses'가 들어가서 빈칸이 포함되는 문장이 '따라서 관계 내의 상호 작용은 관련된 사람들 개개인 성격의 작용일 뿐만 아니라 그들이 지닌 지위와 관련된 역할 요구의 작용이다.'가 되는 것이 가장 적절하다.

구조 다시보기

도입	사람들은 역할에 근거해서 상호 작용에 참여함
부연	행동은 개인의 지위와 관련된 역할 책임과 의무에 의해 제한됨
예시	부모와 자식 간의 책임과 의무
결론	상호 작용은 개개인 성격의 작용일 뿐만 아니라 지위와 관련된 역할 요구의 작용임

어휘·어구

engage in ~에 참여하다
typical 전형적인
interaction 상호 작용
restrict 제한하다
responsibility 책임
obligation 의무
associated with ~와 관련된
privilege 특권
responsible 책임이 있는
necessity 필수품
so forth ~등등
expectation 기대
abuse 학대

정답률 34%

2. ③ 차이점에 집중하는 것은 중요한 유사점을 놓치게 한다

직독/직해

Focusing on the differences among societies /
사회들 간의 차이점에 집중하는 것은 /
conceals a deeper reality: / 더 깊은 실체를 숨긴다
their similarities are greater and more profound /
즉 그것들의 유사점은 더 크고 더 심오하다 /
than their dissimilarities. 그것들의 차이점보다
Imagine studying two hills / while standing on a
두 개의 언덕을 유심히 본다고 상상해 보라 / 만 피트 높이의 고원에 서서
ten-thousand-foot-high plateau.
Seen from your perspective, / 여러분의 관점에서 보면 /
one hill appears to be three hundred feet high, /
한 언덕은 300피트 높이인 것처럼 보이고 /
and the other appears to be nine hundred feet.
다른 언덕은 900피트 높이인 것처럼 보인다
This difference may seem large, / 이 차이가 커 보일 수 있고 /
and you might focus your attention /
여러분은 자신의 관심을 집중시킬지도 모른다 /
on what local forces, such as erosion, /
침식과 같은 어떤 국부적인 힘이 /
account for the difference in size.
크기의 차이를 설명하는지에
But this narrow perspective misses / the opportunity
하지만 이 좁은 관점은 놓친다 / 다른 관점을 연구할 기회를
to study the other, / more significant geological forces /
/ 더 상당한 지질학적인 힘을 /

that created what are actually two very similar
사실상 매우 비슷한 두 개의 산인 것을 만들어 낸
mountains, / one 10,300 feet high / and the other
/ 하나는 10,300피트 높이이고 / 다른 하나는 10,900피트 높이인
10,900 feet.
And when it comes to human societies, /
그리고 인간 사회에 관한 한 /
people have been standing on a ten-thousand-foot
사람들은 만 피트의 고원에 서서
plateau, / letting the differences among societies /
/ 사회들 간의 차이점이 /
mask the more overwhelming similarities.
더 압도적인 유사점을 가리게 두고 있다

사회들 간의 차이점에 집중하는 것은 더 깊은 실체를 숨긴다. 즉 그것들의 유사점은 차이점보다 더 크고 더 심오하다. 만 피트 높이의 고원에 서서 두 개의 언덕을 유심히 본다고 상상해 보라. 여러분의 관점에서 보면, 한 언덕이 300피트 높이인 것처럼 보이고 다른 언덕이 900피트 높이인 것처럼 보인다. 이 차이가 커 보일 수 있고 여러분은 자신의 관심을 침식과 같은 어떤 국부적인 힘이 크기의 차이를 설명하는지에 집중시킬지도 모른다. 하지만 이 좁은 관점은 다른 관점, 즉 하나는 10,300피트 높이이고 다른 하나는 10,900피트 높이인 사실상 매우 비슷한 두 개의 산인 것을 만들어 낸 더 상당한 지질학적인 힘을 연구할 기회를 놓친다. 인간 사회에 관한 한, 사람들은 만 피트의 고원에 서서 사회들 간의 차이점이 더 압도적인 유사점을 가리게 두고 있다.

① 각 사회의 독특함을 증명하게
② 다른 문화 간의 이해를 방해하게
③ 더 압도적인 유사점을 가리게
④ 다양성이 무엇인지에 관한 그들의 인식을 변하게
⑤ 그들이 자신의 정신적인 틀에서 벗어나도록 격려하게

문제풀이

이 글은 차이점에 집중하는 것은 좁은 관점으로써 유사점에서 알 수 있는 중요한 것들을 놓치게 한다는 내용이다. 만 피트의 고원에 서서 두 개의 언덕을 보는 것은 사람들이 좁은 관점을 가지고 높이의 차이점에 집중함으로써 사실상 높이가 매우 비슷한 두 개의 산이 지닌 지질학적인 힘을 연구할 기회를 놓치게 된다는 내용을 통해 빈칸에 ③ 'mask the more overwhelming similarities'가 들어가서 빈칸이 포함되는 문장이 '인간 사회에 관한 한, 사람들은 만 피트의 고원에 서서 사회들 간의 차이점이 더 압도적인 유사점을 가리게 두고 있다.'가 되는 것이 가장 적절하다.

이렇게 풀자_ 유사점은 차이점보다 더 크고 더 심오하지만 사람들은 차이점에 집중하느라 유사점에서 알 수 있는 중요한 것들을 놓친다는 내용을 통해 빈칸에 들어갈 말을 추론할 수 있다.

어휘·어구

conceal 감추다, 숨기다
reality 실체, 현실
similarity 유사성
profound 심오한, 깊은
plateau 고원
account for 설명하다
significant 중요한, 의미 있는
geological 지질학적인

정답률 51%

3. ③ 자연의 권리

직독/직해

Water is the ultimate commons.
물은 궁극적인 공유 자원이다
Once, / watercourses seemed boundless /
한때 / 강은 무한한 것처럼 보였고 /
and the idea of protecting water /
물을 보호한다는 발상은 /
was considered silly. 어리석게 여겨졌다
But rules change. 그러나 규칙은 변한다
Time and again, / 반복적으로 /
communities have studied water systems /
사회는 수계(水系)를 연구해 왔고 /
and redefined wise use. 현명한 사용을 재정의해 왔다
Now / Ecuador has become the first nation /
현재 / 에콰도르는 첫 번째 국가가 되었다 /
on Earth / 지구상 /
to put the rights of nature / in its constitution.
자연의 권리를 포함시킨 / 헌법에
This move has proclaimed /
이러한 움직임은 주장한다 /
that rivers and forests are not simply property /
강과 숲이 단순히 재산이 아니라 /
but maintain their own right / to flourish.
그들 스스로가 권리를 가진다고 / 번영할
Developing a water-based transportation system /
수로 기반 교통 체제를 발달시키는 것은 /
will modernize Ecuador's transportation
에콰도르의 교통 기반 시설을 현대화시킬 것이다
infrastructure.
According to the constitution, / 이 헌법에 따라 /
a citizen might file suit /
시민은 소송을 제기할 수도 있다 /
on behalf of an injured watershed, /
훼손된 (강) 유역을 대표해서 /
recognizing / that its health is crucial to the
인식하며 / 강의 건강은 공공의 선에 필수적임을
common good.
More countries are acknowledging nature's rights /
더 많은 나라들이 자연의 권리를 인정하고 있으며 /
and are expected / to follow Ecuador's lead.
기대된다 / 에콰도르의 주도를 따를 것으로

물은 궁극적인 공유 자원이다. 한때, 강은 끝없는 것처럼 보였고 물을 보호한다는 발상은 어리석게 여겨졌다. 그러나 규칙은 변한다. 사회는 반복적으로 수계(水系)를 연구해 왔고 현명한 사용을 재정의해 왔다. ① 현재 에콰도르는 자연의 권리를 헌법에 포함시킨 지구상 첫 번째 국가가 되었다. ② 이러한 움직임은 강과 숲이 단순히 재산이 아니라 그들 스스로가 번영할 권리를 가진다고 주장한다. ③ (수로 기반 교통 체제를 발달시키는 것은 에콰도르의 교통 기반 시설을 현대화시킬 것이다.) ④ 이 헌법에 따라 시민은 강의 건강은 공공의 선에 필수적임을 인식하며, 훼손된 (강) 유역을 대표해서 소송을 제기할 수도 있다. ⑤ 더 많은 나라들이 자연의 권리를 인정하고 있으며 에콰도르의 주도를 따를 것으로 기대된다.

문제풀이

자연의 권리를 헌법에 포함시킨 에콰도르의 선례를 들어, 더 많은 나라들이 자연의 권리를 인정하고 있음을 설명하고 있다. 그러나 ③ 'Developing a water-based transportation system will modernize Ecuador's transportation infrastructure.'은 주로 기반 교통 체제의 발달에 관한 내용으로 나머지 글의 흐름과 관계가 없다.

이렇게 풀자_ 각 문장을 읽으면서 연결이 어색하지 않은지, 갑자기 내용이 전환되거나 단절되지 않는지를 꼼꼼히 살피며 글을 읽도록 한다. 여기서는 자연의 권리를 포함시킨 에콰도르의 헌법(constitution)에 대한 내용 뒤에 에콰도르의 교통 체제(transportation system)에 대한 내용이 연결되어 흐름이 어색함을 알 수 있다.

어휘·어구

ultimate 궁극적인, 최후의
watercourse 강, 물줄기
boundless 끝이 없는, 한이 없는
time and again 몇 번이고, 되풀이하여
redefine 재정의하다
constitution 헌법
proclaim 주장하다, 선언하다
property 재산, 소유물
flourish 번영하다, 번창하다
transportation system 교통 체제, 수송 체계
infrastructure 사회[공공] 기반 시설
file suit 소송을 제기하다
on behalf of ~을 대표하여, ~을 대신하여
crucial 결정적인, 중대한
acknowledge 인정하다

정답률 41%

4. ⑤ 망막에 형성되는 반사된 이미지

직독/직해

Mirrors and other smooth, shiny surfaces reflect light.
거울과 부드럽고, 광택이 나는 다른 표면들은 빛을 반사한다
We see reflections from such surfaces /
우리는 그런 표면들로부터 반사된 것을 본다 /
because the rays of light form an image /
광선이 이미지를 형성하기 때문에 /
on the retina of our eyes.
우리 눈의 망막에
(C) Such images are always reversed.
그런 이미지들은 항상 거꾸로 되어있다
Look at yourself in a mirror, /
거울에 비친 여러분의 모습을 봐라 /
wink your right eye /
오른쪽 눈을 깜박여라 /
and your left eye seems to wink back at you.
그러면 왼쪽 눈이 여러분에게 눈을 깜박이는 것처럼 보인다
You can use a mirror to send a coded message to a friend.
여러분은 거울을 사용하여 친구에게 암호로 된 메시지를 보낼 수 있다
(B) Stand a mirror upright on the table, /
거울을 탁자 위에 수직으로 세워라 /
so that a piece of paper on the table can be clearly seen in the mirror.
탁자 위에 놓인 한 장의 종이가 거울 속에 명확하게 보일 수 있도록
Now write a message /
이제 메시지를 적어라 /
that looks right when you look in the mirror.
거울을 볼 때 정상적으로 보이는
(A) Keep your eyes on the reflected image /
눈은 반사되는 이미지를 계속 보아라 /
while you are writing and not on your paper.
쓰는 동안 종이가 아니라
After a little practice, /
조금 연습을 하고나면 /
it will be easier to write "backwards."
'거꾸로' 쓰는 것이 좀 더 쉬울 것이다
When your friend receives such a message /
여러분의 친구가 그런 메시지를 받으면 /
he will be able to read it /
그는 그것을 읽을 수 있을 것이다 /
by holding the paper up to a mirror.
그 종이를 거울에 비춰 봄으로써

거울과 부드럽고, 광택이 나는 다른 표면들은 빛을 반사한다. 광선이 우리 눈의 망막에 이미지를 형성하기 때문에 우리는 그런 표면들로부터 반사된 것을 본다.
(C) 그런 이미지들은 항상 거꾸로 되어있다. 거울에 비친 여러분의 모습을 보며 오른쪽 눈을 깜박여 보아라. 그러면 왼쪽 눈이 여러분에게 눈을 깜박이는 것처럼 보일 것이다. 여러분은 거울을 사용하여 친구에게 암호로 된 메시지를 보낼 수 있다.
(B) 탁자 위에 놓인 한 장의 종이가 거울 속에 명확하게 보일 수 있도록 거울을 탁자 위에 수직으로 세워라. 이제 거울을 볼 때 정상적으로 보이는 메시지를 적어라.
(A) 쓰는 동안 종이가 아니라 반사되는 이미지를 계속 보아라. 조금 연습을 하고나면, '거꾸로' 쓰는 것이 더 쉬울 것이다. 여러분의 친구가 그런 메시지를 받으면, 그는 그 종이를 거울에 비춰 봄으로써 그것을 읽을 수 있을 것이다.

문제풀이

광택이 나는 표면들이 빛을 반사하고 광선이 우리 눈의 망막에 이미지를 형성해 우리가 그런 표면들로부터 반사된 것을 본다는 내용의 주어진 글 다음에, 그런 이미지는 거꾸로 되어 있으며 거울을

사용해 암호 메시지를 보낼 수 있다는 내용의 (C)가 오고, 거울을 탁자에 바로 세우고 거울로 볼 때 정상적으로 보이는 메시지를 적으라는 내용의 (B)가 온 후, 친구는 그 메시지를 거울에 비춰 봄으로써 그것을 읽을 수 있다는 내용의 (A)가 오는 것이 적절하다.

어휘·어구

reflect 반사하다
ray 광선
backwards 거꾸로, 뒤로 (=backward)
upright 수직으로
reversed 거꾸로 된
coded 암호로 적힌, 코드화된

5. ③ 침팬지의 호혜주의

직독/직해

Reciprocity can be explored in captivity /
호혜주의는 포획 상황에서 탐구될 수 있다 /
by handing one chimpanzee a large amount of food, /
침팬지 한 마리에게 많은 양의 먹이를 건네줌으로써 /
such as a watermelon or leafy branch, /
수박이나 잎이 많은 가지처럼 /
and then observing what follows.
그리고 뒤이어 일어나는 것을 관찰함으로써
The owner will be center stage, /
먹이 소유자가 중심에 있게 된다/
with a group of others around him or her, /
다른 침팬지들에 둘러싸여 /
soon to be followed by newly formed groups /
새로이 형성된 무리들이 곧 뒤따르게 된다 /
around those who obtained a sizable share, /
꽤 큰 몫을 얻은 침팬지들 주변으로 /
until all food has been distributed.
모든 먹이가 다 분배될 때까지
Beggars may complain and cry, /
구걸하는 침팬지들은 불평하고 울부짖을 수도 있다 /
but aggressive conflicts are rare.
하지만 호전적인 충돌은 드물다
The few times that they do occur, /
간혹 그러한 일이 일어날 때 /
it is the possessor who tries to make someone leave the circle.
누군가를 무리에서 떠나게 하려는 것은 먹이 소유자다
She will hit them over their head with her branch /
먹이 소유자는 그들의 머리를 나뭇가지로 때린다 /
or bark at them in a high-pitched voice /
또는 그들에게 고음으로 울부짖는다 /
until they leave her alone.
그들이 자신을 귀찮게 하지 않을 때까지
Whatever their rank, /
그들의 서열을 막론하고 /
possessors control the food flow.
먹이 소유자가 먹이의 흐름을 제어한다
Once chimpanzees enter reciprocity mode, /
침팬지들이 호혜주의 상태에 접어들게 되면/
their social rank no longer matters.
사회적 서열은 더 이상 중요한 것이 아니다

호혜주의는 포획된 상황에서 침팬지 한 마리에게 수박이나 잎이 많은 가지처럼 많은 양의 먹이를 건네주고 뒤이어 일어나는 것을 관찰함으로써 탐구될 수 있다. (①) 먹이 소유자가 다른 침팬지들에 둘러싸여 중심에 있게 되고, 모든 먹이가 다 분배될 때까지 꽤 큰 몫을 얻은 침팬지들 주변으로 새로이 형성된 무리들이 곧 뒤따르게 된다. (②) 먹이를 구걸하는 침팬지들은 불평하고 울부짖을 수도 있지만 호전적인 충돌은 드물다. (③) 간혹 그러한 일이 일어날 때, 누군가를 무리에서 떠나게 하려는 것은 먹이 소유자다. 먹이 소유자는 그들이 자신을 귀찮게 하지 않을 때까지 그들의 머리를 나뭇가지로 때리거나 그들에게 고음으로 울부짖는다. (④) 그들의 서열이 무엇이든 간에, 먹이 소유자가 먹이의 흐름을 제어한다. (⑤) 침팬지들이 호혜주의 상태에 접어들게 되면, 사회적 서열은 더 이상 중요한 것이 아니다.

문제풀이

간혹 그런 일들이 발생할 때 누군가 그 무리를 떠나게 하려는 자는 먹이 소유자라는 내용의 주어진 문장은, 호전적인 충돌은 드물다는 내용 다음인 ③에 들어가는 것이 적절하다. 또한 그 호전적인 갈등의 상황을 구체적으로 묘사한 ③ 다음의 문장이 주어진 문장 다음에 이어지는 것이 자연스러운 흐름이다.

구조 다시보기

도입	침팬지 한 마리에게 많은 먹이를 주고 관찰함으로써 호혜주의를 탐구할 수 있음
전개	• 먹이 소유자 중심으로 무리가 형성되어 먹이 분배가 이뤄짐 • 드물게 발생하는 충돌의 상황에서 누군가 무리에서 떠나게 하려는 것은 먹이 소유자임
결론	호혜주의 상태에서는 사회적 서열은 중요하지 않음

어휘·어구

captivity 사로잡힘, 속박
observe 관찰하다
obtain 얻다, 획득하다
sizable 꽤 큰
share 몫, 지분
distribute 분배하다, 배급하다
aggressive 공격적인, 호전적인
conflict 충돌, 다툼
rare 드문, 진기한
rank 지위, 계급

6~8 아버지의 연설문에 감동한 아들

직독/직해

(A) When I was 17, / I discovered a wonderful thing.
17살 때 / 나는 놀라운 물건을 발견했다
My father and I were sitting / on the floor of his study.
아버지와 나는 앉아 있었다 / 아버지의 서재 바닥에
We were organizing his old papers.
우리는 아버지의 오래된 서류들을 정리하고 있었다
Across the carpet / I saw a fat paper clip.
카펫 너머로 / 나는 두꺼운 종이 클립을 보았다
Its rust dusted / 그것의 녹이 더럽혔다 /
the cover sheet of a report of some kind.
어떤 종류의 보고서 표지 겉장을
I picked it up. 나는 그것을 집어 들었다
I started to read. 나는 읽기 시작했다
Then I started to cry. 그러고 나서 나는 울기 시작했다.
(C) It was a speech / he had written in 1920, /
그것은 연설문이었다 / 그가 1920년에 썼던 /
in Tennessee. Tennessee 주에서
Then only 17 himself and graduating from high school, /
그 당시 아버지는 단지 17살에 고등학교를 졸업했을 뿐인데 /
he had called for equality / for African Americans.
그는 평등을 요구하였다 / 아프리카계 미국인들을 위한
I marvelled, / proud of him, /
나는 놀라워했다 / 아버지를 자랑스러워하면서 /
and wondered how, /
그리고 어떻게 ~했는지 궁금했다 /
in 1920, / so young, so white, / and in the deep South, /
1920년에 / 그렇게 어리고 백인이었던 / 그리고 최남부 지역에서 /
where the law still separated black from white, /
법으로 백인과 흑인을 여전히 분리하던 /
he had had the courage to deliver it.
그가 그 연설을 할 용기를 가지고 있었는지
I asked him about it.
나는 그에게 그것에 관해 물어봤다
(B) "Daddy," I said, / handing him the pages, /
"아빠" 나는 말했다 / 그에게 서류를 건네 드리며 /
"this speech / — how did you ever get permission /
이 연설 / 어떻게 허락을 받으셨나요 /
to give it? / 이것을 하도록 /
And weren't you scared?" / "Well, honey," / he said, /
두렵지 않으셨나요 / 얘야 / 그가 말했다
"I didn't ask for permission. / I just asked myself, /
나는 허락을 구하지 않았단다 / 난 단지 내 스스로에게 물어보았지 /
'What is the most important challenge /
가장 중요한 도전 과제는 무엇인가 /
facing my generation?' / 우리 세대가 직면하고 있는
I knew immediately. / Then I asked myself, /
난 즉시 알았어 / 그러고 나서 나는 스스로에게 물었단다 /
'And if I weren't afraid, / what would I say about it /
내가 두려워하지 않는다면 / 이것에 대해 무엇을 말할까? /
in this speech?'" 이 연설에서
(D) "I wrote it. / And I delivered it. /
"난 글을 썼어 / 그리고 그것을 연설을 했지 /
About half way through / I looked out to see /
반쯤 연설을 계속 했을 때 / 나는 바라보았어 /
the entire audience of teachers, students, and parents stand up /
교사, 학생, 그리고 학부모로 이루어진 전체 청중이 일어나더니 /
— and walk out. / Left alone on the stage, /
나가 버리는 것을 / 무대에 홀로 남겨진 채 /
I thought to myself, /
나는 마음속으로 생각했어 /
'Well, I guess I need to be sure to do /
그래, 나는 확실히 해내야 할 것 같아 /
only two things with my life: /
내 인생에서 딱 두 가지만 /
keep thinking for myself, / and not get killed.'"
계속 스스로 생각하는 것과 / 그리고 죽임을 당하지 않는 것
He handed the speech back to me, / and smiled. /
아버지는 연설문을 나에게 돌려주셨다 / 그리고 미소 지으셨다 /
"You seem to have done both," / I said.
당신은 그 두 가지 모두를 해내신 것처럼 보이네요 / 나는 말했다

17살 때 나는 놀라운 물건을 발견했다. 아버지와 나는 아버지의 서재 바닥에 앉아 있었다. 우리는 아버지의 오래된 서류들을 정리하고 있었다. 나는 카펫 너머에 있는 두꺼운 종이 클립을 보았다. 그것의 녹이 어떤 종류의 보고서 표지 겉장을 더럽혔다. 나는 그것을 집어 들었다. 나는 읽기 시작했다. 그러고 나서 나는 울기 시작했다.
(C) 그것은 1920년에 Tennessee 주에서 아버지가 썼던 연설문이었다. 그 당시 아버지는 단지 17살에 고등학교를 졸업했을 뿐인데, 아프리카계 미국인들을 위한 평등을 요구하였다. 아버지를 자랑스러워하면서 (b) 나는 놀라워했고, 1920년에 법으로 백인과 흑인을 여전히 분리하던 최남부 지역에서 그렇게 어리고 백인이었던 (c) 그가 어떻게 그 연설을 할 용기를 가지고 있었는지 궁금했다. 나는 그에게 그것에 관해 물어봤다.
(B) 그에게 서류를 건네 드리며 "아빠, 이 연설, 어떻게 이것을 하도록 허락을 받으셨나요? 두렵지 않으셨나요?"라고 말했다. "얘야" 그가 말했다. "나는 허락을 구하지 않았단다. 난 단지 '우리 세대가 직면하고 있는 가장 중요한 도전 과제는 무엇인가?'라고 내 스스로에게 물어보았지. 난 즉시 알았어. 그 뒤 ' 내가 두려워하지 않는다면, 이 연설에서 이것에 대해 무엇을 말할까?'라고 (a) 나는 스스로에게 물었단다."
(D) "난 글을 썼어. 그리고 그것을 연설을 했지. 반쯤 연설을 계속했을 때 교사, 학생, 그리고 학부모로 이루어진 전체 청중이 일어나더니 나가 버리는 것을 바라보았어. 무대에 홀로 남겨진 채 '그래, 내 인생에서 딱 두 가지만 확실히 해내야 할 것 같아. 계속 스스로 생각하는 것과 죽임을 당하지 않는 것.'이라고 (d) 나는 마음속으로 생각했어." 아버지는 연설문을 나에게 돌려주며 미소 지으셨다. "(e) 당신은 그 두 가지 모두를 해내신 것처럼 보이네요"라고 나는 말했다.

어휘·어구

organize 정리하다
rust 녹슬다
permission 허가
challenge 도전
generation 세대
equality 평등
marvel 경이로워하다, 경탄하다
separate 분리하다
courage 용기

6. ②

문제풀이

17살 때 아버지의 오래된 서류 중 하나를 발견하고 읽으면서 울기 시작했다는 주어진 글 (A) 다음에, 아버지가 17살 당시에 썼던 아프리카계 미국인들을 위한 평등을 요구했던 연설문이라 사실을 알고 연설할 용기를 어떻게 가지게 되었는지를 묻는 상황의 (C)가 오고, 아버지가 연설문을 썼던 배경에 관해 설명하는 (B)가 온 뒤, 그에 대한 추가 설명을 듣고 아버지에게 연설문을 돌려주며 아버지를 자랑스러워하는 내용의 (D)가 마지막에 오는 것이 글의 순서로 가장 적절하다.

7. ②

문제풀이

아버지를 자랑스러워하면서 놀라워했다고 한 것으로 보아 (b)는 필자를 가리키고, 나머지는 모두 필자의 아버지를 가리킨다.

정답률 72%

8. ⑤

문제풀이

(D)의 'I looked out to see the entire audience of teachers, students, and parents stand up — and walk out'에서 교사, 학생, 그리고 학부모로 이루어진 전체 청중이 일어나더니 나가 버리는 것을 바라보았다고 했으므로, ⑤가 윗글에 관한 내용으로 적절하지 않다.

수능 필수 영숙어 1

S I M U L

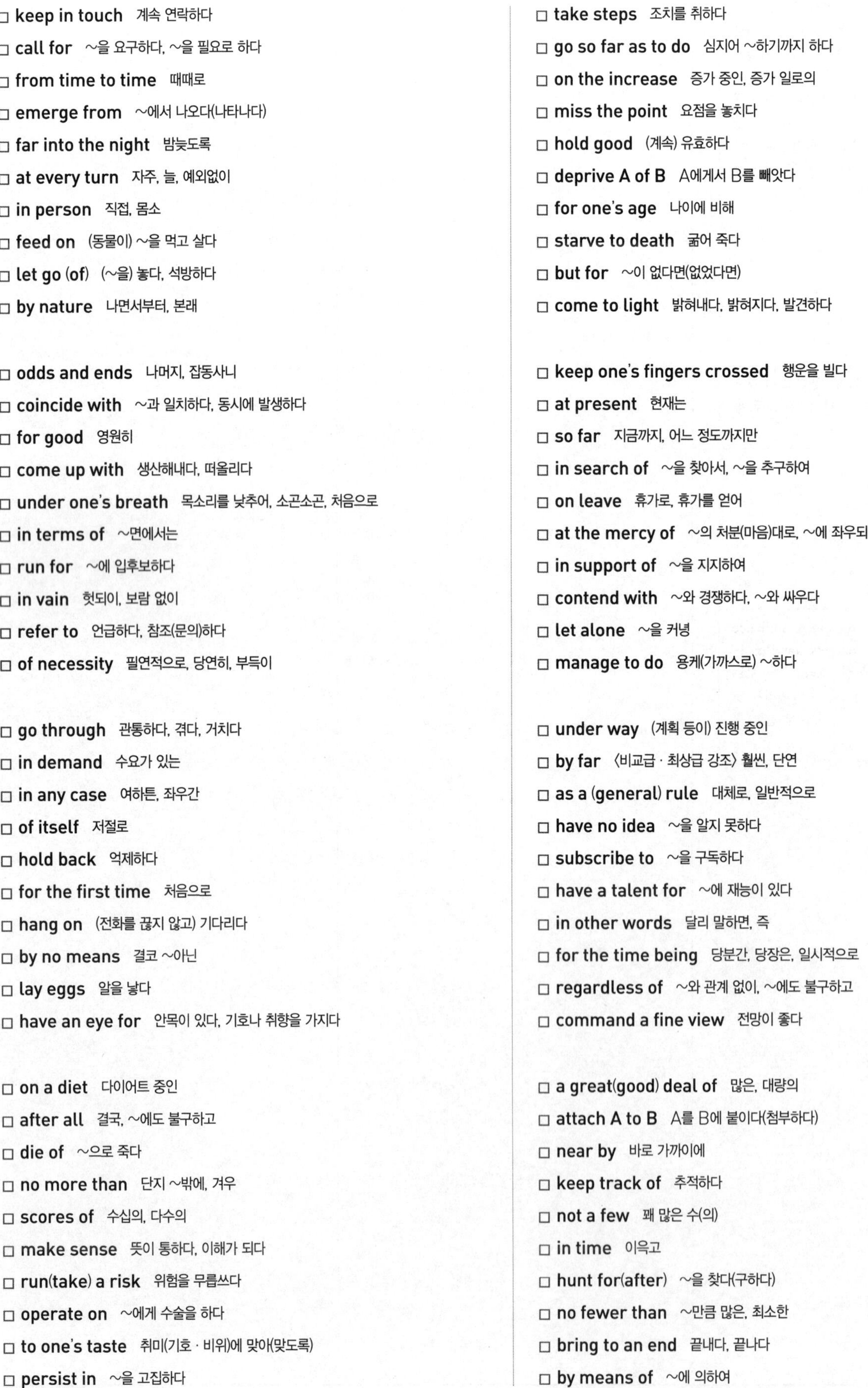

□ keep in touch 계속 연락하다
□ call for ~을 요구하다, ~을 필요로 하다
□ from time to time 때때로
□ emerge from ~에서 나오다(나타나다)
□ far into the night 밤늦도록
□ at every turn 자주, 늘, 예외없이
□ in person 직접, 몸소
□ feed on (동물이) ~을 먹고 살다
□ let go (of) (~을) 놓다, 석방하다
□ by nature 나면서부터, 본래

□ odds and ends 나머지, 잡동사니
□ coincide with ~과 일치하다, 동시에 발생하다
□ for good 영원히
□ come up with 생산해내다, 떠올리다
□ under one's breath 목소리를 낮추어, 소곤소곤, 처음으로
□ in terms of ~면에서는
□ run for ~에 입후보하다
□ in vain 헛되이, 보람 없이
□ refer to 언급하다, 참조(문의)하다
□ of necessity 필연적으로, 당연히, 부득이

□ go through 관통하다, 겪다, 거치다
□ in demand 수요가 있는
□ in any case 여하튼, 좌우간
□ of itself 저절로
□ hold back 억제하다
□ for the first time 처음으로
□ hang on (전화를 끊지 않고) 기다리다
□ by no means 결코 ~아닌
□ lay eggs 알을 낳다
□ have an eye for 안목이 있다, 기호나 취향을 가지다

□ on a diet 다이어트 중인
□ after all 결국, ~에도 불구하고
□ die of ~으로 죽다
□ no more than 단지 ~밖에, 겨우
□ scores of 수십의, 다수의
□ make sense 뜻이 통하다, 이해가 되다
□ run(take) a risk 위험을 무릅쓰다
□ operate on ~에게 수술을 하다
□ to one's taste 취미(기호 · 비위)에 맞아(맞도록)
□ persist in ~을 고집하다

□ take steps 조치를 취하다
□ go so far as to do 심지어 ~하기까지 하다
□ on the increase 증가 중인, 증가 일로의
□ miss the point 요점을 놓치다
□ hold good (계속) 유효하다
□ deprive A of B A에게서 B를 빼앗다
□ for one's age 나이에 비해
□ starve to death 굶어 죽다
□ but for ~이 없다면(없었다면)
□ come to light 밝혀내다, 밝혀지다, 발견하다

□ keep one's fingers crossed 행운을 빌다
□ at present 현재는
□ so far 지금까지, 어느 정도까지만
□ in search of ~을 찾아서, ~을 추구하여
□ on leave 휴가로, 휴가를 얻어
□ at the mercy of ~의 처분(마음)대로, ~에 좌우되어
□ in support of ~을 지지하여
□ contend with ~와 경쟁하다, ~와 싸우다
□ let alone ~을 커녕
□ manage to do 용케(가까스로) ~하다

□ under way (계획 등이) 진행 중인
□ by far 〈비교급 · 최상급 강조〉 훨씬, 단연
□ as a (general) rule 대체로, 일반적으로
□ have no idea ~을 알지 못하다
□ subscribe to ~을 구독하다
□ have a talent for ~에 재능이 있다
□ in other words 달리 말하면, 즉
□ for the time being 당분간, 당장은, 일시적으로
□ regardless of ~와 관계 없이, ~에도 불구하고
□ command a fine view 전망이 좋다

□ a great(good) deal of 많은, 대량의
□ attach A to B A를 B에 붙이다(첨부하다)
□ near by 바로 가까이에
□ keep track of 추적하다
□ not a few 꽤 많은 수(의)
□ in time 이윽고
□ hunt for(after) ~을 찾다(구하다)
□ no fewer than ~만큼 많은, 최소한
□ bring to an end 끝내다, 끝나다
□ by means of ~에 의하여

수능 필수 영숙어 2

- □ the other way round 반대로, 거꾸로
- □ stand out 두드러지다, 탁월(걸출)하다
- □ fall ill(sick) 병이 나다
- □ be fed up with ~에 진저리가 나다
- □ long for ~을 갈망(열망)하다
- □ eat one's words 앞서 한 말을 취소하다
- □ come of age 성년에 이르다
- □ beware of 주의(조심)하다
- □ in general 대개(대체로), 일반적으로
- □ none other than 다름 아닌 바로 ~인

- □ give way to ~에 양보하다, ~에 굴복하다
- □ on end 세로로, 똑바로; 계속
- □ apologize (to A) for B (A에게) B에 대해 사과(변명)하다
- □ go into details 상세하게 말하다(논하다)
- □ form the habit of ~ing ~하는 습관을 들이다(붙이다)
- □ in a row 연속하여
- □ give ~ a ride(lift) ~을 차에 태워 주다
- □ be in charge of ~을 떠맡다, 담당하다, 책임지다
- □ in turn 차례차례, 결국
- □ single out 선발하다, 지목하다

- □ carry out 수행하다, 성취하다
- □ with all one's might 전력을 다하여, 힘껏
- □ every inch 완전히
- □ get along with ~와 잘 지내다
- □ at first 처음에는, 원래는
- □ lie on one's back 반듯이(등을 대고) 눕다
- □ by degrees 서서히, 조금씩, 점차로
- □ at odds with ~와 의견이 일치하지 않는
- □ cope with ~에 대처하다, 겨루다
- □ in consequence of ~의 결과, ~때문에

- □ far from 결코 ~아닌, ~하기는 커녕
- □ for a change 뭔가 색다르게, 기분 전환으로
- □ dwell on(upon) ~을 깊이 생각하다
- □ comply with ~에 따르다(응하다)
- □ go dutch (비용을) 각자 내다
- □ near at hand 가까이에, 머지않아
- □ in part 일부분, 부분적으로, 어느 정도
- □ for some reason or other 무슨(어찌된) 이유에선지
- □ happen to do 우연히(어쩌다가, 마침) ~하다
- □ go astray 길을 잘못 들다, 길을 잃다

- □ contribute A to B A를 B에 기부하다, B에 기여(공헌)하다
- □ figure out 계산하다, 이해하다
- □ engage in ~에 종사하다
- □ set ~ free ~을 석방하다(자유롭게 하다)
- □ out of breath 숨이 차서, 헐떡이며
- □ keep a diary 일기를 쓰다
- □ cut off 잘라내다, 중단(단절)하다
- □ for the present 당분간, 지금은
- □ bring ~ to light 밝히다, 폭로하다
- □ reflect on ~을 반성(숙고)하다

- □ by way of ~을 경유하여(지나서), ~의 수단(방법)으로
- □ in pursuit of ~을 추구하여
- □ make progress (in) 진보(전진 · 향상)하다
- □ under no circumstances 결코 ~ 않다, 무슨 일이 있어도 ~ 않다
- □ work out 운동하다, (일이) 잘 진행되다, 해결하다
- □ have one's own way 제멋대로 하다
- □ in the light of ~을 고려하여
- □ in honor of ~에 경의를 표하여, ~을 기념하여
- □ on the face of it 겉보기에는, 표면상
- □ hasten to do 서둘러 ~하다

- □ just in case 만일의 경우에
- □ upside down 거꾸로, 뒤집어서, 뒤죽박죽, 엉망으로
- □ approve of ~을 승인하다, ~을 찬성하다
- □ take place 일어나다, 행해지다, 개최되다
- □ once (and) for all 단 한 번만, 이번만
- □ indulge in ~에 빠지다, ~을 마음껏 즐기다
- □ as well ~ 역시, 게다가
- □ count for little(nothing) 거의(전혀) 가치가 없다
- □ be to blame (for) (~에 대해) 책임이 있다
- □ in a way 어떤 관점(면)에서는

- □ at (the) bottom 내심(속마음)은, 실은, 근본은
- □ at any rate 여하튼, 적어도
- □ more or less 다소간, 어느 정도, 대략
- □ close to ~의 가까이에, 약, 대체로
- □ in effect 사실상, 실제로는
- □ as yet 지금까지는, 지금으로서는, 아직
- □ clear A of B A에서 B를 (깨끗이) 없애다(치우다)
- □ in all 전부, 모두 합쳐
- □ cure A of B A에게서 B를 낫게 하다(치유하다)
- □ leave ~ behind ~을 남기고 가다(오다)

시험 직전까지 꼭 챙겨 봐야 할 영어 오답 Note

틀린 문제를 붙이고 틀린 이유, 몰랐던 단어, 숙어와 문장을 정리하여 나만의 오답노트를 작성해보세요.
꾸준히 작성한 오답노트를 유형별로 분류해보면 자신이 자주 틀리는 유형이 무엇인지, 어떤 실수가 반복되는지 알 수 있어, 자신의 약점을 파악하고 고쳐나가는 데 큰 도움이 됩니다.

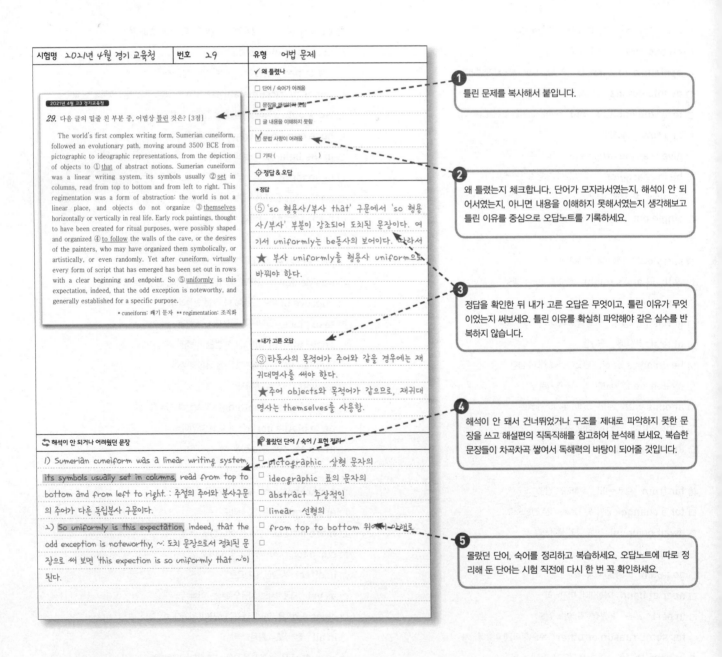

시험명 2021년 4월 경기 교육청	번호 29	유형 어법 문제

2021년 4월 고3 경기교육청

29. 다음 글의 밑줄 친 부분 중, 어법상 <u>틀린</u> 것은? [3점]

The world's first complex writing form, Sumerian cuneiform, followed an evolutionary path, moving around 3500 BCE from pictographic to ideographic representations, from the depiction of objects to ① <u>that</u> of abstract notions. Sumerian cuneiform was a linear writing system, its symbols usually ② <u>set</u> in columns, read from top to bottom and from left to right. This regimentation was a form of abstraction: the world is not a linear place, and objects do not organize ③ <u>themselves</u> horizontally or vertically in real life. Early rock paintings, thought to have been created for ritual purposes, were possibly shaped and organized ④ <u>to follow</u> the walls of the cave, or the desires of the painters, who may have organized them symbolically, or artistically, or even randomly. Yet after cuneiform, virtually every form of script that has emerged has been set out in rows with a clear beginning and endpoint. So ⑤ <u>uniformly</u> is this expectation, indeed, that the odd exception is noteworthy, and generally established for a specific purpose.

* cuneiform: 쐐기 문자 ** regimentation: 조직화

✓ 왜 틀렸나

- ☐ 단어 / 숙어가 어려움
- ☐ 문장을 해석하지 못함
- ☐ 글 내용을 이해하지 못함
- ☑ 문법 사항이 어려움
- ☐ 기타 (　　　)

정답 & 오답

*정답

⑤ 'so 형용사/부사 that' 구문에서 'so 형용사/부사' 부분이 강조되어 도치된 문장이다. 여기서 uniformly는 be동사의 보어이다. 따라서 ★ 부사 uniformly를 형용사 uniform으로 바꿔야 한다.

*내가 고른 오답

③ 타동사의 목적어가 주어와 같을 경우에는 재귀대명사를 써야 한다.
★주어 objects와 목적어가 같으므로, 재귀대명사는 themselves를 사용함.

해석이 안 되거나 어려웠던 문장

1) Sumerian cuneiform was a linear writing system, its symbols usually set in columns, read from top to bottom and from left to right. : 주절의 주어와 분사구문의 주어가 다른 독립분사 구문이다.

2) So uniformly is this expectation, indeed, that the odd exception is noteworthy, ~: 도치 문장으로서 정치된 문장으로 써 보면 'this expection is so uniformly that ~'이 된다.

몰랐던 단어 / 숙어 / 표현 정리

- ☐ pictographic 상형 문자의
- ☐ ideographic 표의 문자의
- ☐ abstract 추상적인
- ☐ linear 선형의
- ☐ from top to bottom 위에서 아래로
- ☐

❶ 틀린 문제를 복사해서 붙입니다.

❷ 왜 틀렸는지 체크합니다. 단어가 모자라서였는지, 해석이 안 되어서였는지, 아니면 내용을 이해하지 못해서였는지 생각해보고 틀린 이유를 중심으로 오답노트를 기록하세요.

❸ 정답을 확인한 뒤 내가 고른 오답은 무엇이고, 틀린 이유가 무엇이었는지 써보세요. 틀린 이유를 확실히 파악해야 같은 실수를 반복하지 않습니다.

❹ 해석이 안 돼서 건너뛰었거나 구조를 제대로 파악하지 못한 문장을 쓰고 해설편의 직독직해를 참고하여 분석해 보세요. 복습한 문장들이 차곡차곡 쌓여서 독해력의 바탕이 되어줄 것입니다.

❺ 몰랐던 단어, 숙어를 정리하고 복습하세요. 오답노트에 따로 정리해 둔 단어는 시험 직전에 다시 한 번 꼭 확인하세요.

뒷면에 있는 오답노트 양식을 가위로 잘라내 복사하거나, PDF 파일을 프린트하여 사용하세요.
골드교육 홈페이지(www.goldedu.co.kr)에서 오답노트의 PDF 파일을 무료로 다운받을 수 있습니다.